Financial
Analysis and Planning

THEORY AND APPLICATION

A BOOK OF READINGS

Financial
Analysis and Planning
THEORY AND APPLICATION
A BOOK OF READINGS

Cheng F. Lee
University of Illinois at
Urbana-Champaign

ADDISON-WESLEY PUBLISHING COMPANY
Reading, Massachusetts • Menlo Park, California
London • Amsterdam • Don Mills, Ontario • Sydney

ISBN 0-201-04449-8
ABCDEFGHIJ-HA-898765432

To
My wonderful wife Schwinne Chwen
and our two fantastic children
John C.
Alice C.

Permissions and Acknowledgements

We would like to thank the authors and publishers who allowed us to reprint the articles appearing in this work. The necessary permissions are in the order the articles appear.

1. *Financial Management*, (Spring 1981).
   Reprinted by permission of the publisher and authors.

2. *Journal of Accounting Research*, (Autumn 1969).
   Reprinted by permission of the publisher and author.

3. *Journal of Financial and Quantitative Analysis*, Vol. 16 (1981).
   Reprinted by permission of the publisher and authors.

4. *Journal of Finance*, Vol. 23 (1968) 1.
   Reprinted by permission of the publisher and author.

5. *Journal of Finance*, Vol. 32 (1977).
   Reprinted by permission of the publisher and author.

6. *Journal of Financial Economics*, Vol. 3 (1976).
   Reprinted by permission of the publisher and authors.

7. *Journal of Finance*, Vol. 34 (1979).
   Reprinted by permission of the publisher and authors.

8. *Journal of Finance*, Vol. 28 (1973).
   Reprinted by permission of the publisher and authors.

9. *Financial Management*, (Summer 1981).
   Reprinted by permission of the publisher and authors.

10. *Financial Management*, (1979).
    Reprinted by permission of the publisher and authors.

11. *Bell Journal of Economics*, (Spring 1976).
    Reprinted by permission of the publisher and author.

12. *Journal of Financial and Quantitative Analysis,* Vol. 13 (1978).
    Reprinted by permission of the publisher and authors.

13. *Financial Management*, (Autumn 1979).
    Reprinted by permission of the publisher and author.

14. *Journal of Finance*, Vol. 29 (1974).
    Reprinted by permission of the publisher and author.

15. *Journal of Finance*, Vol. 33 (1978).
    Reprinted by permission of the publisher and author.

16. *Financial Management*, (Winter 1974).
    Reprinted by permission of the publisher and author.

17. *Journal of Finance*, Vol. 32 (1977).
    Reprinted by permission of the publisher and authors.

18. *Management Science*, Vol. 15 (1969).
    Reprinted by permission of the publisher and author.

19. *Financial Management*, (Winter 1975).
    Reprinted by permission of the publisher and author.

20. *Journal of Finance*, Vol. 30 (1975).
    Reprinted by permission of the publisher and authors.

21. *Journal of Finance*, Vol. 34 (1979).
    Reprinted by permission of the publisher and author.

22. *Journal of Finance*, Vol. 29 (1974).
    Reprinted by permission of the publisher and author.

23. *Financial Management*, (Spring 1978).
    Reprinted by permission of the publisher and author.

24. *Journal of Finance*, Vol. 26 (1971).
    Reprinted by permission of the publisher and authors.

25. *Journal of Finance*, Vol. 31 (1976).
    Reprinted by permission of the publisher and authors.

26. *Journal of Business*, Vol. 34 (1961).
    Reprinted by permission of the publisher and authors.

27. *Journal of Portfolio Management*, Vol. 2 (1976).
    Reprinted by permission of the publisher and authors.

28. *Journal of Risk and Insurance*, (March 1980).
    Reprinted by permission of the publisher and authors.

29. *Journal of Finance*, Vol. 31 (1976).
    Reprinted by permission of the publisher and author.

30. *Financial Executive*, (February 1981).
    Reprinted by permission of the publisher and author.

31. *Journal of Banking and Finance*, Vol. 1 (1977).
    Reprinted by permission of the publisher and author.

32. *Financial Management*, (Winter 1974).
    Reprinted by permission of the publisher and authors.

33. *Accounting Review*, (October 1969).
    Reprinted by permission of the publisher and authors.

34. *Journal of Financial and Quantitative Analysis*, Vol. 8 (1973).
    Reprinted by permission of the publisher and author.

35. *Financial Management*, (Spring 1974).
    Reprinted by permission of the publisher and authors.

36. Working Paper, University of Illinois at Urbana-Champaign (1981).
    Reprinted by permission of the authors.

37. *Financial Management*, (Autumn 1980).
    Reprinted by permission of the publisher and authors.

38. *Data Resource U.S. Review*, (February 1981).
    Reprinted by permission of the publisher and author.

39. *Journal of Financial and Quantitative Analysis*, Vol. 8 (1973).
    Reprinted by permission of the publisher and authors.

40. *Analytical Methods in Financial Planning*, (Fourth Edition), (1980).
    The Chase Manhattan Bank.
    Reprinted by permission of the publisher and author.

41. *Journal of Finance*, Vol. 29 (1974).
    Reprinted by permission of the publisher and author.

42. *Journal of Finance*, Vol. 25 (1970).
    Reprinted by permission of the publisher and author.

43. *Journal of Finance*, Vol. 26 (1971).
    Reprinted by permission of the publisher and authors.

44. *Financial Management*, (Spring 1978).
    Reprinted by permission of the publisher and authors.

45. *Financial Management*, (1981).
    Reprinted by permission of the publisher and author.

46. *Quarterly Journal of Economics and Business*, Vol. 21 (1981).
   Reprinted by permission of the publisher and author.

47. *Sloan Management Review*, (Spring 1974).
   Reprinted by permission of the publisher and author.

48. *Financial Analysts Journal*, (1978).
   Reprinted by permission of the publisher and authors.

Preface

A. Organization and Suggestions

Based upon my teaching and research experience on the subject of financial analysis and planning, this introduction will review, discuss, and integrate both theoretical and practical corporate analysis and planning literature. In this readings book, financial analysis and planning is classified into ten topics:

1. accounting information and financial management;
2. valuation theory and capital structure (M&M, CAPM, and option theory);
3. cost of capital determination and estimation;
4. the capital budgeting decision;
5. the financing decision;
6. dividend policy;
7. merger: theory and evidence;
8. working capital management;
9. financial planning and forecasting;
10. an overview of finance theory and practice.

The principles used to select the papers and classify them into ten topics are: (1) to integrate theory with practice; and (2) to strike a balance between the overview and detailed understanding. There are two kinds of literature in each topic, i.e., primary and supporting literature. The primary literature, those articles included in this book, are required reading for every student. The supporting literature, suggested at the end of every section, are optional reading. There are 48 primary and 80 supporting articles as listed in the end of each part. The 48 primary articles can be covered in a one-semester second financial management course. For a quarter course, the primary articles preceded by an asterisk (*) can be omitted. The supporting papers will be helpful to all graduate finance students for further reference.

Prerequisites to understand this book include one term of accounting; one term of economics; one term of quantitative methods (or statistics); and one term of financial management. Before reading the papers, the student should read the introduction to each part to obtain an overall picture of the topic.

A useful homework assignment is to ask for a short paper that extends the topic introduction into a more detailed review and critique. For each short paper, students are advised to understand the interrelationship between theory and practice, and the real world application potential of the concepts, methods, and theories which are discussed. These short papers can then be integrated into a theoretical and methodological portion of a financial analysis and planning term paper. For the empirical portion of the paper, students can use (1) an individual firm's accounting, stock price, bond price, and option data and (2) economic indicator data to do some financial analysis and planning case studies. One of the planning models discussed in Parts 8 and 9 could be used to do empirical analysis of a firm's investment, financing, and dividend policies.

The papers included in each topic generally discuss other topics as well. Therefore, it is useful for students to identify the primary and secondary material in studying each paper. The interrelated nature of most of the papers included in this readings book will help students visualize the integrated picture of financial analysis and planning.

From my personal teaching experience at the University of Georgia, State University of New York at Buffalo, and the University of Illinois at Urbana-Champaign, I have found that the reading lists presented in this book can be used in a second undergraduate financial management course and a second MBA financial management course by itself or in combination with a text, such as:

1. Haley and Schall, *Theory of Financial Decisions*, McGraw-Hill, New York (1979).
2. Copeland and Weston, *Financial Theory and Corporate Policy*, Addison-Wesley, Reading, Mass. (1979).
3. Van Horne, *Financial Management and Policy*, Prentice Hall, Englewood Cliffs, NJ (1980).
4. Brealey and Myers, *Principles of Corporate Finance*, McGraw Hill, New York (1981).
5. Weston and Brigham, *Managerial Finance*, Dryden Press, Hinsdale, Ill. (1981).
6. Brigham, *Financial Management—Theory and Practice*, Dryden Press, Hinsdale, Ill. (1979).

In addition, I believe that this readings book can be used as a reference in the first graduate financial management courses as well as by corporate financial managers in conducting their financial analysis and planning.

B.   Acknowledgements

Authors and publishers of the articles are the main contributors to this readings book. Two reviewers, Joseph E. Finnerty and Timothy J. Nantell, were most helpful in providing suggestions in determining the final article selection and presentation. Another reviewer's (Charles Martin) suggestions were also extremely helpful. I am also indebted to the following individuals: Andrew H. Chen, James A. Gentry, Charles M. Linke, Kenton J. Zumwalt, and Joan C. Junkus. In addition, I am also indebted to the finance editor at Addison-Wesley, Bill Hamilton, who kept the project moving. Finally, I am grateful for the support of my wonderful wife, Schwinne Chwen and my two fantastic children, John and Alice.

There are undoubtedly some errors in the finished product, both typographical and conceptual, as well as differences of opinion on article selection. I would like to invite the readers to send suggestions, comments, criticisms, and corrections to the author at the Department of Finance, University of Illinois at Urbana-Champaign, Champaign, Illinois 61820.

C.F. Lee

Table of Contents

Part I

Accounting Information
and Financial Management

Introduction

Accounting information has been used extensively in the analysis of such issues as the prediction of firm failure, bond ratings, stock rates of return, in merger study, and in beta forecasting. The four papers included in Part I present a general overview of the topic as well as specific examples of the application of accounting information to problems in financial management.

First, Chen and Shimerda's (1981) paper carefully synthesizes the empircal results of previous studies of accounting ratios and their uses in financial management and investment analysis, and uses up-dated financial data to re-examine these results. To summarize the main points of their empirical analysis, they conclude that the seven most basic financial factors are: financial leverage; capital turnover; return on investment; inventory turnover; receivables turnover; short-term liquidity; and cash position.

Two of the papers in this section concern the specification of models using accounting information, first, to examine the change over time in firm financial ratios and the adjustment process involved, and secondly to incorporate various financial ratios as explanatory variables in predicting security returns. Two alternative linear models can be used to incorporate financial ratio information into financial management decisions and investment analysis: linear regression and linear discriminant analysis. Linear regression is used by both Lev (1969) and Lee and Zumwalt (LZ) (1981). Lev uses both a linear and a log-linear regression specification to forecast vital financial ratios and determine the speed of adjustment of these ratios. In performing this analysis, Lev uses historical industry-wide averages. Lev's empirical results are consistent with the idea that firms do adjust their ratios to an industry norm.

LZ's paper incorporates several important financial ratios into a single index market model and uses them to construct a multi-index security rate of return generating process model. To perform their empirical study, rates of return for the jth firm in this multi-index model are linearly related to market rates of return, dividend policy variables, financing policy variables, and a profitability measures variable. To investigate the associations between alternative accounting profitability measures and security returns, six profitability measures were used: sales/total assets; EBIT/total assets; net income/total assets; net income/common equity; EBDT/sales; and net income/sales. LZ's study concludes that accounting profitability information is an important source of extra-market information in asset pricing, and the EBIT/total assets and net income/common equity provide the most consistent empirical results. It should be noted that the seemingly uncorrelated regression (SUR) technique used to improve the efficiency of estimates is relatively complicated; however, it is not necessary to follow the exact derivation procedure in order to understand the essence of the paper.

Finally, Altman's paper (1968) uses a linear discrimination function and financial ratios to estimate financial "Z scores" and to predict the probability of bankruptcy for a firm. Altman's well-known results can be summarized in the linear discriminant function:

Z score = f (net working capital/total assets; retained earnings/
total assets; EBIT/total assets; market value of common
and preferred stock/book value of debt; and sales/
total assets).

The larger the Z score, the less the probability of bankruptcy.

This method has many uses, and has been extended to credit analysis, financial distress analysis of the banking industry, and the insurance industry.

Accounting information from the balance sheet, income statement, retained earnings statement and the sources and uses of funds statement are most useful for analyzing a firm's long-term as well as short-term financial position. The issues related to short-term and long-term financial analysis and planning will be explored in Parts VIII and IX, respectively. The four papers in Part I serve to demonstrate how basic accounting information can be incorporated with some basic financial concepts and statistical methods to perform useful financial management analysis. The reader is encouraged to explore these issues further. Some other useful reading papers on the topic of accounting information and its uses in finance are listed at the end of this section.

An Empirical Analysis of Useful Financial Ratios

Kung H. Chen and Thomas A. Shimerda

Kung H. Chen is Associate Professor of Accounting at the University of Nebraska–Lincoln, and Thomas A. Shimerda is Assistant Professor of Accounting at Creighton University.

■ Financial ratios have played an important part in evaluating the performance and financial condition of an entity. Over the years, empirical studies have repeatedly demonstrated the usefulness of financial ratios. For example, financially-distressed firms can be separated from the non-failed firms in the year before the declaration of bankruptcy at an accuracy rate of better than 90% by examining financial ratios [1]. In determining bond ratings, when financial ratios were the only variables used, the resulting ratings were virtually identical with institutional ratings [21].

There is one recurring question with the use of financial ratios: which ratios, among the hundreds that can be computed easily from the available financial data, should be analyzed to obtain the information for the task at hand? We hope here to help resolve the problem of ratio selection by examining ratios found useful in recent empirical studies, reconciling the differences in the ones found useful in these studies, and categorizing them by seven factors suggested in the literature.

There are many useful ratios reported in the literature. Discrimination is needed to identify a limited set of financial ratios. Naturally, different researchers often include different ratios. Consequently, results on the usefulness of specific ratios vary. Exhibit 1 summarizes a number of such studies and the ratios they employed. The 26 studies analyze more than 100 financial items, of which 65 are accounting ratios. Forty-one of these are considered useful and/or are used in the final analysis by one or more of the researchers. Given such a heterogeneous set of useful financial ratios, the decision-maker has to be at a loss in selecting which ratios to use for the task at hand. Conceivably, 41 ratios cannot all be significant or equally important in a multi-ratio model. The decision-maker may hesitate to omit a ratio if it has been found useful in one or more of the empirical studies.

Yet, it is impossible to include most of the useful ratios found in the literature. Which ratios, then, should be deleted, and which should be included? Should the results from only one study, the results from a combination of studies, or the results from all the studies be used? If only one study is to be used, which one should it be?

Exhibit 1. Financial Ratios Incorporated in Predictive Studies

Ratio	FIRM FAILURE 1966 Tamari	1966 Beaver	1968 Altman	1972 Deakin	1972 Edmister	1974 Blum	1975 Libby	1975 Elam	BOND RATINGS 1966 Horrigan	1969 Pogue & Soldofsky	1970 West	1973 Pinches & Mingo	MARKET RETURN 1971 Martin	1973 O'Connor	MERGERS 1973 Stevens	BETA 1973 Breen & Lerner	Sub-total Found Useful*	Total Mentioned	PRIOR TO 1965 1932 Fitzpatrick	1935 Winakor & Smith	1942 Merwin	1945 Chudson	1958 Hickman	1958 Saulnier	1961 Moore & Atkinson	1962 Jackendoff	1962 Wojenlower	1963 Jen	Subtotal	Total Found Useful
NI/CE						*																							1	1
Non OI BT/S(7)												X																	1	1
EPS							X																							
Int/C+MS											X	X																		
LTB/TA								X																						
LTD/CA																														
OI/TD								X																					1	1
NI/EBT											X																		1	1
Cap Exp/S(6)																													1	1
NW/LTD						X	X			X																			3	1
OI/Int						X	X		X	X																			1 2	2
EBT/NW					X																								1 1	1
EBT/TA					X	X																							1 1	1
NW+LTD/FA					X																								1 1	1
CA/TD					X																								1 1	1
Inv/WC					X																								1 1	1
S/CL			X																										1 1	1
CGS/Inv			X								X																		2 1	2
NI+Int/TA			X																										1	1
EBT/S			X	X	X						X	X																	3 1	3
GP/S			X																										1	1
S/FA			X		X		X	X																					4 2	4
Def.Inter(5)		X																											1 1	1
C Inter(4)		X																											1	1
S/QA		X	X	*		X X						X						1 1										5 5	
S/C+MS		X X	X	*		X X												1 3 5										5	
QA/TA		X X	X	*		X X												1 3									1 1	1 1
NI/TD		X																2 1										
NI+DDA/NW(1)		X X				*											3 6									1 3 2	1
CL/TA		X X	X			*											2 1									1 1	
C+MS/CL		X X	X	*		X X											1 4 6									2 1	
LTD/FA	X	X															1 4									1	
S/AR	X X				X												1 4									1	
NW/TA								X									1 3			X						1 1	
NW/FA			X		X					X							1 3		X							1	
NI+DDA/#Shs(1)											*		*																1	
NI/NW		X		*		X			X *	X		X						3 1	X						X			2 1 1 5 1 1	
CL/Inv										*																			
Div Ratio								X X	X		*							3 2									1 1	
NI+Int/Int		X X						*		*								5 2 4									1 1 1	
LTD/TA		X X					*	*		*		X						4 5									1 1 1	
OI/S						*		*	* *		*						4 2									3 4 1	1
NI/S		X X				*		X X		X		X					2 6 4			X			X			2 1	2
NI+DDA/TA(1)		X				*											2 2 1									1 1	
NI+DDA/S(1)		X				*											3 2									1 3 1	
C+MS/TA		X X	*			*									X		2 2									1 1 1	
CA/TA		X	*		*												2 3									1 3 1	
Quick Flow(3)			*														1 1									1	
QA/Inv			*														1 1									1	
Inv/S	* X X	X		*		X	X									2 1									1 2 1	
CL/NW			*														1 1									1 1	
NW/S		X		*		X		X		X							2 1									1 5 1	
NI+DDA/CL(1)		X		*		*											1 1									1 1	
WC/S	* X X	X		*		X X			X							1 2 5									1 2	
CA/S		X X				X X			X							1 3 1									1 3 1	
RE/TA		*																											
S/TA		X *		X		X X		X *								1 3									1 1 1	
EBIT/TA		X *				X X		X *								1 3										
No Cr.Inter(2)		*																											
CA/CL	* * X X	X X		* *		* *											5 4						X	X	X X	1 5 6	
WC/TA	* * X *	X X		* X	X X X										X X	X	3 4			X			X	X	X X X	1 5	
TD/TA	* X X *	X X X	X X X X X					X X						X	X	7 7				X		X	X	X X X	1 5 6	
NI+DDA/TD(1)		X *	X X	X X X X X				*								6 3									1 3	
QA/CL		X X	* * X	X X X X X		X		X								6 7									1 5	
NI/TA	* * X	X * X	* X X X X			*		*			X			X X	6 7					X				1 1	
NW/TL	* X X	X *	X					*		X	*						7 10									1 2	

*Ratio found useful in study: (X) Ratio mentioned in study: (1) Net Income plus Depreciation, Depletion, Amortization; (2) No Credit Interval = Quick Assets minus CL/Operating Expense minus Depreciation, Depletion, Amortization; (3) Quick Flow = C+MS+AR+(Annual Sales divided by 12); [(CGS−Depreciation+Selling and Administration+Interest) divided by 12]; (4) Cash Interval = C+MS/Operating Expense minus Depreciation, Depletion, Amortization; (5) Defensive Interval = QA/Operating Expense Minus Depreciation, Depletion, Amortization; (6) Capital Expenditure/Sales; (7) Non-operating Income before Taxes/Sales.

Most of the studies reported high predictive powers for their ratios. This would seem to suggest that good results can be attained by using the useful ratios from any study. The researcher can afford the luxury of studying a selected group of firms whose fates are known and then searching for the set of financial ratios that has the highest predictive power for the known results. Those whose business it is to make predictions, though, cannot afford such a procedure. Without further testing and re-examination of the findings, the result from any one study is applicable only to firms with the same characteristics as those included in that study.

Ideally, the financial ratios analyzed should be selected on some theoretical basis, coupled with demonstrated empirical evidence of their usefulness. An acceptable theoretical foundation for the selection of ratios for decision-making has yet to be found, and the scattered heterogeneous empirical evidence in published studies does not identify a complete set of useful ratios. Although in this paper an approach to obtain an efficient set of financial ratios will be presented, we do not present an absolute model for selecting specific ratios. The result will suggest, however, that a useful set of ratios can be developed from seven basic financial factors.

Overlapping of Ratios

Many of the ratios included in the studies are highly correlated with one other. Jackendoff [14] demonstrates this overlapping:

> Another type of redundancy arises from the use of ratios which are easily derived from one another, although the components are not identical as is true in inversions. . . . One of the most obvious sets of such related ratios includes:
> 1. Worth to total debt (or its inverse, total debt to worth).
> 2. Worth to total assets.
> 3. Total debt to total assets.
> These are simply variants of the equation:

Total Assets = Total Debt + Net Worth
[14, p. 7].

In spite of his extensive study, such overlapping can still be found in most of the recent studies. For example, the 56 items used in the computation of the 28 ratios included in the Elam study [9] are derived from only 18 different pieces of financial data, and the 28 items for Deakin's ratios [7] consist of only 10 separate pieces of data. The elimination of such overlapping would aid in the development of a useful set of financial ratios.

Uses of Principal Component Analysis

Not all overlapping ratios, however, can be eliminated by visual inspection. A statistical tool designed to summarize such inter-relationships is principal component analysis. One of the functions performed by principal component analysis is to group variables into a few factors that retain a maximum of information contained in the original variable set. This tool is a useful first step for subsequent analyses. The use of principal component analysis, along with other statistical methods, produces a more powerful and basic analysis [11, p. 319].

Five of the recent studies have employed principal component analysis. The results of these analyses are summarized in Exhibit 2. In each study, the number of variables was significantly reduced from the original set of variables, yet the reduced set of ratios still accounted for the majority of the variance accounted for by the original set of financial ratios. Pinches and Mingo [21] reduced their data set for bond ratings from 35 to 7 variables (an 80% reduction) and still accounted for 63% of the variation in the original data matrix. Stevens [27] reduced 20 variables to 6 (a 70% reduction) and accounted for 82% of the total variance. Libby [16] reduced his 14–ratio set to 5 ratios (a 64% reduction) with very little loss in the predictive ability of the model.

The attempt by Pinches, Mingo, and Caruthers [22;

Exhibit 2. Data Reduction in Factor–Analyzed Financial Ratio Space

Study	Variable Space	Factor Space	% Reduction In Space	% Variation Still Explained
Pinches and Mingo (1973)	35	7	80	63
Pinches, Mingo, and Caruthers (1973)	48	7	85	91, 92, 87, 92
Stevens (1973)	20	6	70	82
Libby (1975)	14	5	64	Not Reported
Pinches, Eubank, Mingo, and Caruthers (1975)	48	7	85	92

6

hereafter, PMC] to develop an empirically based classification of financial ratios resulted in seven classifications of ratios across industries. These seven patterns occurred in each year examined, accounting for a consistently high amount of the variance contained in the original data matrix. The composition of these classifications remained relatively stable over the 19-year period studied. A subsequent study by Pinches, Eubank, Mingo, and Caruthers [23; hereafter, PEMC] showed the short-term stability of these factors. They also demonstrated that a hierarchical classification of empirical financial ratios can be constructed.

Diversity of Factors

The PMC and PEMC studies suggest the existence of common ratio classifications and offer an empirical basis for grouping financial ratios. According to their findings, financial ratios can be represented by seven factors — Return on Investment, Financial Leverage, Capital Turnover, Short-Term Liquidity, Cash Position, Inventory Turnover, and Receivables Turnover. A slightly different set of factors is found in an earlier study by Pinches and Mingo [21]. The studies by Stevens and Libby mentioned above also attempt to derive a reduced set of financial ratios to represent the original set of financial ratios, using different sets of factors from those in the PMC and PEMC studies; these can be seen in Exhibit 3. A total of 12 factors is suggested in these studies, with each study seemingly proposing a different set of factors to represent the variable space portrayed by the financial ratios. For example, of the four factors found in Stevens's study only one is included in the PMC and PEMC factors. Similarly, only one of the five factors suggested by Libby is found among the factors in the PMC and PEMC studies.

It seems that the results from principal component analyses are as diverse as the financial ratios themselves. Different sets of factors can be found in different studies with very little commonality among any of them. Using such results as a guide for the selection of financial ratios is hardly a viable solution, if not actually a waste of time. Inevitably, before the results from principal component analysis can be applied to studies on financial ratios, a satisfactory answer to the question of what are the common factors representing the financial ratios must be formulated. A detailed analysis of the five studies reveals that some of the twelve factors vary in name only. They can be described according to the seven common factors suggested in Exhibit 4.

A Reconciliation of Factors

To a great extent, the diversity of factors reported in the literature can be attributed to the difference in variables included in the principal component analyses, as indicated in the following detailed analysis.

Profitability and Return on Investment

Stevens [27] found five ratios — earnings before interest and taxes (EBIT)/total assets, EBIT/sales, earnings before taxes (EBT)/sales, net income/net worth, and net income/total assets — with high loadings[1] on his profitability factor. Each of these ratios also had a high loading on the return on investment factor in the PMC and PEMC studies. The net income/total assets ratio was the most representative ratio among the ratios in Libby's [16] profitability factor. The profitability factor found by both Stevens and Libby was the same as the return on investment factor in the PMC and PEMC studies.

Activity, Receivable Turnover, and Capital Turnover

A slightly more confusing picture is found in the activity factor of the Stevens [27] study. Two ratios have high loadings on this factor — sales/quick assets (S/QA) has a loading of 0.794, and sales/total assets (S/TA) has a loading of 0.85. The S/QA ratio in the PMC and PEMC studies has a high factor loading on the receivables turnover factor, while the S/TA ratio has a high loading on the capital turnover factor. Such diverse results can be explained by differences in the original variables included in the principal component analysis in these studies.

Principal component analysis is variable-sensitive: different factors may be obtained if different sets of variables are fed into the principal component analysis. Substantially more ratios are included in the PMC and PEMC studies than in the Stevens study [27]. Among the ratios included in the PMC and PEMC studies are five ratios relating to receivable turnover, including the S/QA ratio. But Stevens includes only one of the five ratios in his analysis. Because the variances of these 5 ratios are similar, and 5 of a total of 48 ratios in a 7-factor result will cer-

---

[1]A factor loading represents the extent to which the variable is related to the factor and is commonly thought of as the correlation between the variable and the factor. For a more detailed discussion on the meaning of factor loadings, see William D. Wells and J. N. Sheth, "Factor Analysis in Marketing Research" [29].

Exhibit 3. Factors Found in Five Empirical Analyses of Financial Ratios

Factors	Pinches and Mingo (1973)	Pinches, Mingo, and Caruthers (1973)	Stevens**	Libby (1975)	Pinches, Eubank, Mingo, and Caruthers (1975)
Asset Balance				X	
Activity			X	X	
Profitability			X	X	
Liquidity			X	X	
Cash Position		X		X	X
Short–Term Liquidity		X			X
Receivables Turnover		X			X
Inventory Turnover		X			X
Return on Investment	X	X			X
Short–Term Capital Intensiveness	X	X*			X*
Long–Term Capital Intensiveness	X	X*			X*
Financial Leverage	X	X			X

*These studies had one factor, capital turnover, which included the ratios from the above two factors.
**Seven factors were found in the Pinches and Mingo study. Variables in three of the factors — size, debt and debt coverage stability, and earnings stability — were not ratio measures. Thus they were excluded. For the same reason, two factors found in the Stevens study — dividend policy and price earnings — were excluded.

Exhibit 4. A Reconciliation of Factors Depicting Financial Ratios

Study	Financial Leverage	Capital Turnover	Return on Investment	Seven Basic Factors Inventory Turnover	Receivables Turnover	S-T Liquidity	Cash Position
PMC	X	X	X	X	X	X	X
PEMC	X	X	X	X	X	X	X
Stevens	X	Liquidity	Profitability		Activity		
Libby		Asset Balance	Profitability	Activity		Liquidity	X

tainly account for a significant portion of the total variance defined by the 48 ratios, the S/QA ratio forms a separate factor with other similar ratios in the PMC and PEMC studies.

On the other hand, the S/QA ratio is the only ratio out of the five ratios that is used in the Stevens study. The other four ratios represented by the receivable turnover factor in the PMC and PEMC studies are not included in Stevens's principal component analysis. Consequently, the S/QA ratio will either correlate with one other ratio in a different factor or not be represented at all in the factors selected. Nevertheless, this evidence suggests that the activity factor of the Stevens study is represented by factors found in the PMC and PEMC studies.

Liquidity, Asset Balance, and Capital Turnover

Similar reasoning can be applied to the importance of the current assets/total assets (CA/TA) ratio.

Stevens does not include CA/TA as one of his ratios, but he does use net working capital/total assets (NWC/TA). This ratio loads heavily on the factor Stevens describes as his liquidity factor. This ratio is mentioned but is not included in the final factors in both the PMC and PEMC studies. A separate analysis, which will be discussed in detail later, reveals that the NWC/TA ratio is highly correlated (r = 0.80) with the current assets/total assets ratio (CA/TA). The result of a principal component analysis indicates that both NWC/TA and CA/TA ratios have high factor loadings, 0.85 and 0.91, respectively, on the same factor. This indicates that the NWC/TA ratio could be an important ratio in the same factor as the CA/TA ratio were it included in the same analysis.

In the PMC and PEMC studies, the CA/TA ratio is among the ratios with high loadings on the capital turnover factor. Thus, the liquidity factor in the Stevens study is similar to the capital turnover factor in the PMC and PEMC studies. Libby also uses the CA/TA ratio to represent one of his five factors. He denotes the factor best represented by CA/TA as his asset balance factor. This means that one ratio, CA/TA, is used to describe a capital turnover factor, an asset balance factor, and, if employed in the Stevens study, could even describe a liquidity factor.

At first it appears somewhat confusing that one ratio can represent three basically different factors. This again can be reconciled if one examines the original ratio sample for the three studies. Stevens includes only two ratios that are slightly related to liquidity — NWC/TA and NWC/S. As no other ratios could represent liquidity in his study, an obvious choice for the factor containing high loadings on these ratios has to be liquidity. If Stevens had started with a larger variable set, his liquidity factor could very well not have included NWC/TA. The ratios Stevens calls liquidity could actually represent capital turnover as described by PMC and PEMC.

Libby started with a 14–variable set. Six ratios had total assets as their denominator, and four of those ratios had a current asset item for their numerator. Three other ratios related current asset items to current liabilities, while four ratios used sales as the denominator base. Because of the restricted set of ratios employed and the predominate use of total assets as a denominator base, Libby's result was not surprising. Why he chose "asset balance" to describe the factor represented by CA/TA was not reported, nor were any of the ratios' factor loadings. Without detailed information about the ratios and the factors, further analysis is impossible.

Given the set of ratios included in both the Stevens and Libby studies, it is possible for the three factors — capital turnover, liquidity, and asset balance — to capture basically the same information even though their titles differ. The ratio CA/TA is common to two and significantly correlated with a ratio in the third factor. With this common bond, it is possible to reconcile Stevens's liquidity and Libby's asset balance factors with PMC's and PEMC's capital turnover factor.

Other Factors

Two other factors are quite easily reconciled. The leverage factors in the PMC, PEMC, and Stevens studies are virtually identical. In all three studies, the long–term debt/net worth, long–term debt/total assets, and total liabilities/total assets ratios have high loadings on the leverage factor. The ratio with a high loading on Libby's liquidity factor is current assets/current liabilities. This same ratio also has a high loading on the short–term liquidity factor in the PMC and PEMC studies.

The final factor to reconcile is Libby's activity factor. The ratio designated by Libby to represent this factor is current assets/sales. This same ratio has a high loading on the inventory turnover factor in the PMC and PEMC studies. The cash position factor is common to the PMC and PEMC studies as well as to Libby's study. The ratio in Libby's study, cash/total assets, is also highly loaded on the cash position factor in both the PMC and PEMC studies. Results of the above analyses suggest that factors found in the Stevens and the Libby studies, although different in name, are included in the PMC and PEMC factors.

The evidence we have described so far confirms that financial ratios can be grouped and represented by the seven common factors defined in the PMC and PEMC studies. Each factor represents a unique dimension in the description of financial characteristics of a business firm. This finding offers a possible reconciliation of the diverse results of various empirical studies. This result can be applied to reconcile the seemingly disorganized state of useful financial ratios in the several studies on the prediction of firm failure reported in the literature.

Important Factors in Firm—Failure Prediction

Thirty-four financial ratios have been found by researchers to be significant variables in the prediction of firm failure in recent studies. If a smaller number of ratios could still convey substantially the same amount of information, the task of using them would be easier.

If the seven–factor space from the PMC and PEMC studies is used as the basis for classifying financial ratios, all but ten of the ratios found useful in the firm failure prediction studies can be classified by one of the seven factors. Exhibit 5 summarizes the seven studies and their ratios. Ten ratios could not be classified without further analysis because they were not included in the final factors of the PMC or PEMC study. They are quick assets/inventory, net income/common equity, quick flow ratio,[2] funds flow/current liabilities, net income/sales, funds flow/total debt, working capital/total assets, long–term debt/current assets, no–credit interval, and retained earnings/total assets.

---

[2]Blum [4, p. 16] defines quick flow as [Cash + Notes Receivable + Market Securities + (Annual Sales ÷ 12)] ÷ [(Cost of Goods Sold − Depreciation Expense + Selling and Administration Expense + Interest) ÷ 12].

Exhibit 5. Factor Classification of Important Ratios for Predicting Firm Failure as Found in Recent Empirical Studies

Factor	Ratio	Beaver	Altman	Deakin	Study by Edmister	Blum	Elam	Libby
Return on Investment	Net Income/Sales*						X	
	Funds Flow/NW						X	
	Funds Flow/TA						X	
	Net Income/TA	X		X				X
	Net Income/NW						X	
	EBIT/Sales						X	
	EBIT/TA		X					
	NI/Common Equity**					X		
Capital Turnover	QA/TA			X				
	Funds Flow/Sales						X	
	Current Assets/TA			X				X
	Net Worth/Sales				X			
	Sales/TA		X				X	
	WC/TA*	X	X	X				
Financial Leverage	Total Liabilities/TA	X		X			X	
	Total Liabilities/NW					X	X	
	Long–Term Debt/CA**						X	
	Funds Flow/TD**	X		X		X	X	
	Funds Flow/CL**				X			
	Retained Earnings/TA**		X					
Short–Term Liquidity	Current Assets/CL	X		X			X	X
	Quick Assets/CL			X	X		X	
	Current Liabilities/NW				X			
	Current Liabilities/TA						X	
Cash Position	Cash/Sales			X				
	Cash/Total Assets			X				X
	Cash/Current Liabilities			X			X	
	No Credit Interval**	X						
	Quick Flow**					X		
Inventory Turnover	Current Assets/Sales			X				X
	Inventory/Sales				X			
	Sales/Working Capital			X	X			
Receivables Turnover	Quick Assets/Inventory**					X		
	Quick Assets/Sales			X				

*Ratio not included in the final factors of the PEMC studies.
**Ratio not in the 48 ratios included in the PEMC study.

Empirical Results

To study the relationship of the ten ratios to the other ratios included in the factors, we conducted a principal component analysis of 39 ratios for the firms included in the COMPUSTAT tape. A total of 1,053 firms with complete data for both total assets and net sales in 1977 was included. The results from the test are summarized in Exhibit 6. Each of the ten ratios is paired with the ratio from the PEMC study for which its product moment correlation is the highest. The factor loadings of the paired ratios on a common factor are also reported.

Net Income/Sales, Net Income/Common Equity, and Return on Investment

The result of the analysis shows that two of the ten ratios correlate highly with ratios representing the return on investment factor in the PEMC study. Net income/sales is highly correlated (r = .98) with

Exhibit 6. Factor Loading and Product-Moment Coefficient of Correlation of Selected Ratios in 1977

Unclassified Ratio	Factor Loading	Classified Ratio	Factor Loading	Factor	Correlation Coefficient	Level of Significance
Net Income / Sales	.90	EBIT / Sales	.86	Return on Investment	.98	.001
Net Income / Common Equity	.62	Net Income / Net Worth	.87	Return on Investment	.39	.001
Working Capital / Total Assets	.85	Current Assets / Total Assets	.91	Capital Turnover	.80	.001
Funds Flow / Total Debt	.92	Net Worth / Total Debt	.89	Financial Leverage	.88	.001
Funds Flow / Current Liabilities	.91	Net Worth / Total Debt	.89	Financial Leverage	.84	.001
Long–Term Debt / Current Assets	–.81	Long–Term Debt / Total Assets	.63	Financial Leverage	–.31	.001
Retained Earnings / Total Assets	.62	Total Debt / Total Assets	–.71	Financial Leverage	–.72	.001
No Credit Interval	.82	Cash / Sales	.85	Cash Position	.80	.001
Quick Flow	–.86	Cash / Sales	.85	Cash Position	–.58	.001
Quick Assets / Inventory	.98	Receivables / Inventory	.97	Receivable Turnover	.98	.001

EBIT/Sales with factor loadings of .90 and .86, respectively, on the same factor. Net income/common equity and net income/net worth have high loadings (.62 and .87, respectively) on the same factor and are significantly correlated (r = .39). This is not surprising, since common equity and net worth differ only by the amount of preferred stock outstanding. The ratios EBIT/Sales and net income/net worth have high loadings on PEMC's return on investment factor. Thus the two ratios that correlate with these ratios could be classified as ratios exhibiting return on investment characteristics.[3]

Working Capital/Total Assets and Capital Turnover

The ratio, working capital/total assets, does not have a high factor loading score on any of the factors in the PEMC study. The ratio is significantly correlated with the ratio, current assets/total assets. The current asset/total assets ratio is represented in the

capital turnover factor in the PEMC study. The ratio WC/TA is thus classified as a capital turnover ratio.

Ratios Pertaining to Financial Leverage

Four of the unclassified ratios correlate and load highly with ratios classified in the financial leverage factor of the PMC and PEMC studies. Two of these ratios, funds flow/total debt and funds flow/current liabilities, are highly correlated (.88 and .84, respectively) with the net worth/total debt ratio. Their loadings on a common factor are .92 for funds flow/total debt, .91 for funds flow/current liabilities, and .89 for net worth/total debt. The two ratios, long–term debt/current assets and retained earnings/total assets, can also be regarded as representative of the financial leverage factor. They load and are significantly correlated with ratios that are part of PEMC's financial leverage factor.

The ratio, retained earnings/total assets, was one of Altman's [1] most significant ratios in predicting bankruptcy, but it has not been incorporated in any other study on firm failure. The results of factor analysis applied to the 1977 data confirm its importance in the financial leverage factor.

---

[3] In the present analysis, all but net income/common equity and net income/net worth load on the same factor. These two ratios load on a separate factor. This slight difference can be attributed to differences in the original variable space.

No—Credit Interval, Quick Flow, and Cash Position

Two previously unclassified ratios, no—credit interval and quick flow, correlate with cash/sales. The coefficients of correlation are .80 and −.58, respectively. Further evidence that these two ratios can be grouped with ratios that measure cash position is provided in their factor loadings. The factor loadings of these two ratios on the cash position factor are .82 and −.86, respectively.

Quick Asset/Inventory and Receivables Turnover

The last ratio to classify is quick assets/inventory. This ratio correlates highly with receivables/inventory (r = .98), and both ratios have high loadings on the same factor. The ratio, receivables/inventory, loads heavily on the receivables turnover factor in the PEMC study. Because of this relationship, the ratio quick assets/inventory is classified in Exhibit 6 as belonging to the receivables turnover factor.

Based on the PMC and PEMC results and supplemented with the analysis of the 1977 data, all 34 financial ratios that were found useful in the various predictive studies on bankruptcy can be assigned by one of the seven major factors. Because ratios belonging to the same factor are highly correlated and reveal primarily the same information, a decision-maker can select an appropriate set of financial ratios that best represents these seven factors for the prediction of firm failure.

Conclusions

This paper demonstrates that the financial ratios investigated in previous predictive studies of bankruptcy can be classified by a substantially reduced number of factors. The ratios classified by the same factor are highly correlated, and the selection of one ratio to represent a factor can account for most of the information provided by all the ratios of that factor. Inclusion of more than one ratio from a factor leads to multicollinearity among ratios and distorts the relationship between the dependent and independent variables. In addition, high correlation between ratios causes the results to be sample-sensitive and possibly misleading. It is important then that a minimum number of ratios, one ratio in most cases, be selected to represent each factor for further statistical analysis.

Still, the question of which ratio should represent a factor has yet to be resolved. The popular procedure of selecting the ratio with the highest absolute factor loading makes the selection sensitive to the sample. Such a procedure may be satisfactory for data reduction purposes, but it is certainly not satisfactory for model building or theory construction. Concerted effort should be applied to the process of selecting the most representative ratios of these factors.

The selection of the best representative ratio for a factor is not independent of the ratios selected for other factors. Each ratio contains common as well as unique information. The common information contained in a ratio is represented by factors. The unique information is not shared by any other ratio in the factor. Consequently, the set of financial ratios used for further analysis should be selected in such a way that the ratios capture most of the common information contained in their factors and, as a group, contain more of the unique information than any other set of ratios. Unfortunately, such a theory is yet to be developed. Empirical evidence has so far been concerned with the extraction of common factors.

No study has reported on the type and amount of unique information contained in a ratio. Future studies on this problem will certainly enhance the usefulness of financial ratios and facilitate the selection of appropriate ratios for decision-making.

References

1. Edward I. Altman, "Financial Ratios, Discriminant Analysis and the Prediction of Corporate Bankruptcy," *Journal of Finance* (September 1968), pp. 589–609.
2. William H. Beaver, "Alternative Accounting Measures as Predictors of Failure," *The Accounting Review* (January 1968), pp. 113–122.
3. William H. Beaver, "Financial Ratios as Predictors of Failure," *Empirical Research in Accounting: Selected Studies, 1966, Journal of Accounting Research* (1967), pp. 71–111.
4. Marc P. Blum, "The Failing Company Doctrine," *Journal of Accounting Research* (Spring 1974), pp. 1–25.
5. William J. Breen and Eugene M. Lerner, "Corporate Financial Strategies and Market Measures of Risk and Return," *Journal of Finance* (May 1973), pp. 339–351.
6. Walter A. Chudson, *The Pattern of Corporate Financial Structure*, New York, National Bureau of Economic Research, 1945.
7. Edward B. Deakin, "A Discriminant Analysis of Predictors of Business Failure," *Journal of Accounting Research* (Spring 1972), pp. 167–179.
8. Robert O. Edmister, "An Empirical Test of Financial Ratio Analysis for Small Business Failure Prediction," *Journal of Financial and Quantitative Analysis* (March 1972), pp. 1477–1493.

9. Rick Elam, "The Effect of Lease Data on the Predictive Ability of Financial Ratios," *The Accounting Review* (January 1975), pp. 25–43.

10. Paul J. Fitzpatrick, *Symptoms of Industrial Failures,* Washington, D.C., Catholic University of America Press, 1931.

11. Richard Gorsuch, *Factor Analysis,* Philadelphia, W. B. Saunders Company, 1974.

12. W. Braddock Hickman, *Corporate Bond Quality and Investor Experience,* Princeton, N.J., Princeton University Press, 1958.

13. James O. Horrigan, "Some Empirical Bases of Financial Ratio Analysis," *The Accounting Review* (July 1965), pp. 558–568.

14. Nathanial Jackendoff, *A Study of Published Industry Financial and Operating Ratios,* Small Business Management Research Report, Philadelphia, Temple University, 1962.

15. Frank Chifeng Jen, "The Determinants of the Degree of Insufficiency of Bank Credit to Small Business," *Journal of Finance* (December 1963), pp. 694–695.

16. Robert Libby, "Accounting Ratios and the Prediction of Failure: Some Behavioral Evidence," *Journal of Accounting Research* (Spring 1975), pp. 150–161.

17. Alvin Martin, "An Empirical Test of the Relevance of Accounting Information for Investment Decisions," *Journal of Accounting Research,* Supplement (1971), pp. 1–31.

18. Charles L. Merwin, *Financing Small Corporations,* New York, National Bureau of Economic Research, 1942.

19. Geoffrey H. Moore and Thomas R. Atkinson, *Risks and Returns in Small Business Financing,* 41st Annual Report, New York, National Bureau of Economic Research, 1961.

20. Melvin C. O'Connor, "On the Usefulness of Financial Ratios to Investors in Common Stock," *The Accounting Review* (April 1973), pp. 339–352.

21. George E. Pinches and Kent A. Mingo, "A Multivariate Analysis of Industrial Bond Ratings," *Journal of Finance* (March 1973), pp. 1–18.

22. George E. Pinches, Kent A. Mingo, and J. Kent Caruthers, "The Stability of Financial Patterns in Industrial Organizations," *Journal of Finance* (May 1973), pp. 389–396.

23. George E. Pinches, A. A. Eubank, Kent A. Mingo, and J. Kent Caruthers, "The Hierarchical Classification of Financial Ratios," *Journal of Business Research* (October 1975), pp. 295–310.

24. T. F. Pogue and R. M. Soldofsky, "What's in a Bond Rating," *Journal of Financial and Quantitative Analysis* (June 1969), pp. 201–228.

25. Raymond I. Saulnier, Neil H. Jacoby, and Harold G. Halcrow, *Federal Lending and Loan Insurance,* Princeton, N.J., Princeton University Press, 1958.

26. Raymond F. Smith and Arthur H. Winakor, *Changes in the Financial Structure of Unsuccessful Corporations,* Urbana, Ill., Bureau of Business Research, University of Illinois, 1935.

27. D. L. Stevens, "Financial Characteristics of Merged Firms: A Multivariate Analysis," *Journal of Financial and Quantitative Analysis* (March 1973), pp. 149–158.

28. Meir Tamari, "Financial Ratios as a Means of Forecasting Bankruptcy," *Management International Review* (1966), pp. 15–21.

29. William D. Wells and J. N. Sheth, "Factor Analysis in Marketing Research," in *Multivariate Analysis in Marketing,* David A. Aaker, ed., Belmont, California, Wadsworth Publishing Company, Inc., 1971, pp. 212–227.

30. Richard R. West, "An Alternative Approach to Predicting Corporate Bond Ratings," *Journal of Accounting Research* (Spring 1970), pp. 15–21.

31. Albert M. Wojinlower, *The Quality of Bank Loans: A Study of Bank Examination Records,* New York, National Bureau of Economic Research, 1962.

Industry Averages as Targets for Financial Ratios

BARUCH LEV*

Introduction

The traditional literature of financial statement analysis often emphasizes the desirability of adjusting the firm's financial ratios to predetermined targets which are usually based on industry-wide averages.[1] This study considers the question of whether there is empirical evidence to suggest that firms do adjust their financial ratios to such targets. The results of the test, using the partial adjustment model, indicate that financial ratios are periodically adjusted to their industry means.

One way management can adjust the financial ratios to predetermined targets is to choose from the set of generally accepted accounting measurement rules (e.g., inventory valuation methods) those which affect the financial ratios in the desired direction. This technique—in the context of the income smoothing hypothesis—was proposed by Gordon as a means of maximizing management's utility:

> Given that the above four propositions are accepted or found to be true, it follows that a management should within the limits of its power, i.e., the latitude allowed by accounting rules, (1) smooth reported income, and (2) smooth the rate of growth in income. By smooth the rate of growth in income we mean the

* Assistant Professor, University of Chicago. The author is grateful to Professor Hector Anton, Peter Pashigian, and Henri Theil for their comments on this paper.

[1] A typical example is the popular text by R. Foulke, *Practical Financial Statement Analysis*, 6th ed. (McGraw-Hill Book Co., 1968). Foulke summarizes the discussion of each financial ratio by presenting the median ratios for a number of industries, implying that conformity with these standards is desirable. For example, "From the figures in the preceding paragraph [the industry medians] it is obvious that a ratio of total liabilities to tangible net worth in excess of 100.0 per cent is unusual. Rarely, if ever, *should* total liabilities of a commercial or industrial concern exceed the tangible net worth, . . ." p. 253 (emphasis supplied).

following: If the rate of growth is high, accounting practices which reduce it should be adopted and vice versa.[2]

The rate of income growth can be regarded as high or low only when compared with a standard. Gordon, in a later study, used the industry mean as one such standard:

> For the purpose of this study the smoothing theorem was tested by considering whether an accounting measurement rule was selected which tended to: (1) adjust the firm's percentage change in earnings per share to the average percentage change in the industry. . . .[3]

Smoothing is thus defined operationally: when the value of the ratio is above/below the standard (e.g., the industry mean), measurement rules which decrease/increase it will be used by management.

Gordon and others,[4] in investigating the income smoothing hypothesis, examined the effect on income of specific measurement rules. They outlined a certain pattern for the firm's income series as a standard and then tested whether the use of a specific measurement rule adjusted the data in the direction of the standard. However, despite the fact that net income is not the only item of interest to financial statement users, no attempt has yet been made to generalize the smoothing question to financial ratios. In addition, because the studies used small samples,[5] inferences could not be made as to the extent to which there is a *general* tendency for firms to adjust their ratios to equilibrium positions defined in terms of industry averages. The present study addresses itself to this general question.

The use of alternative accounting measurement rules is not the only way to adjust financial ratios to predetermined targets. Managers can include the desired ratios in their budgets and then regulate business operations such that the resultant ratios will conform with the budgeted ones. For example, a firm might change its terms of credit sales to achieve a more desirable current ratio. Moreover, when the target is an industry average, ratios can be adjusted to some extent by allowing industry-wide effects to operate on them. This might be termed a passive adjustment, as opposed to the active techniques mentioned above. No attempt has been made in this study to determine the technique, or combination of techniques, by which adjustment is achieved.

---

[2] M. J. Gordon, "Postulates, Principles and Research in Accounting," *The Accounting Review*, XXXIX (April, 1964), 261–62.

[3] M. J. Gordon, B. N. Horwitz, and P. T. Meyers, "Accounting Measurements and Normal Growth of the Firm," in *Research in Accounting Measurement*, ed. Jaedicke, Ijiri, and Nielsen (American Accounting Association, 1966), p. 224.

[4] For a comprehensive survey of the income smoothing studies, see R. M. Copeland, "Income Smoothing," *Empirical Research in Accounting: Selected Studies, 1968*, Supplement to Vol. 6, *Journal of Accounting Research*, pp. 101–16.

[5] For example, the sample used by Gordon, *et al.* included 21 firms in the chemical industry, and Copeland's sample consisted of 19 firms.

The Partial Adjustment Model

The partial adjustment model is employed by economists in a wide variety of empirical research concerned with the dynamic properties of the variables tested. Specifically, this model has been used to examine and describe investment, inventory, and dividend decisions by firms.[6] Following is a brief description of the model.

Let y be some relevant and observable variable which is adjusted over time to a target, denoted by y^*, according to

$$y_t - y_{t-1} = \beta(y_t^* - y_{t-1}), \qquad 0 < \beta \le 1. \qquad (1)$$

The behavioral function (1) postulates that at any particular time period t, only a fixed fraction of the desired adjustment is accomplished. This fixed fraction (i.e., the coefficient of adjustment β) reflects the fact that there are limitations to the periodic adjustment of y caused by technological and institutional constraints. Assume that the target, y_t^*, is determined by some other observable variable x_{t-1},

$$y_t^* = x_{t-1}. \qquad (2)$$

The combination of (1) and (2) defines the partial adjustment model

$$y_t - y_{t-1} = \beta(x_{t-1} - y_{t-1}). \qquad (3)$$

In the context of this study, y_t is the observed value of a financial ratio at time t, y_t^* is the value of the target ratio (i.e., the budgeted ratio) for time t, and x_{t-1} is the industry mean of the ratio which determines the target according to (2). The behavioral equation (3) therefore postulates that when the firm observes a deviation between its ratio and the industry mean (i.e., $x_{t-1} - y_{t-1}$), it will adjust its ratio in the next period (i.e., y_t) so that the observed deviation will be partially eliminated. For example, when the firm's ratio is above the industry mean and $\beta = .5$, it will decrease the value of the ratio in the next period by half the deviation. Generally, when (3) is applied to real data and the estimated β falls between 0 and 1, it is an indication that the firm adjusts the year-to-year differences in the ratio according to the industry mean. The speed of adjustment is determined by the size of β; the closer β is to 1, the faster the periodic adjustment. This model may therefore be used to test whether firms tend to adjust their financial ratios to the industry average.

The partial adjustment model poses several problems of estimation which are caused mainly by its autoregressive form, i.e., the presence in (3) of the lagged variable y_{t-1} as an explanatory variable. When such a lagged variable is included in the model there are reasons to expect a bias in the estimated regression coefficients and their standard errors.[7] However,

---

[6] For a comprehensive list of empirical studies using the model, see Zvi Griliches, "Distributed Lags: A Survey," *Econometrica*, 35 (January, 1967), 46–49.

[7] For a comprehensive discussion of the statistical issues concerning the model, see Griliches, *ibid.*

despite these statistical problems, economists still use the model extensively mainly because of its mathematical convenience and the absence of more adequate models.

The Sample and Test Procedures

The source of data for this study was Standard and Poor's Compustat tape. This tape contains annual financial statements for about 900 major U. S. firms for the period 1947–1966; however, data are not available for all firms for the entire period.[8] The firms are organized on the tape by industries. The Compustat's four-digit industrial classification was used for this study.

The sample was restricted to those firms which met the following two requirements: (a) the full 20 years' financial data are available, and (b) the firm belongs to an industry consisting of at least 10 firms. The first requirement was set because least-squares regressions are applied in this study to each individual firm. A small number of observations (because of the missing data) would render the results statistically meaningless. The second requirement which restricts the sample to large industries,[9] was imposed so that the industry mean would not be sensitive to the individual ratios which are used to compute the mean. In the case of large industries, the effect of any firm's ratio on the mean is negligible, and the latter may be regarded as an exogenous variable to the firm. 245 firms in 18 four-digit industries met the two requirements, and they comprise the sample for this study.

Six financial ratios were chosen to represent the well-known categories of ratios:

Category	Ratio Chosen[10]
1. Short-term liquidity ratios	1. Current assets less inventory to current liabilities (quick ratio)
	2. Current assets to current liabilities (current ratio)
2. Long-term solvency ratios	3. Equity to total debt
3. Short-term capital turnover ratios	4. Sales to inventory
4. Long-term capital turnover ratios	5. Sales to total assets
5. Return on investment ratios	6. Net operating income to total assets

Since ratios within a category were found to be highly intercorrelated with each other, one representative of each category should be sufficient.[11]

---

[8] The main reasons: missing data and firms which started operations after 1947.

[9] The cut-off point of 10 firms was chosen to keep the sample fairly large. A cut-off point of 15 firms, for example, would reduce the sample by more than a half.

[10] Balance sheet items used for calculating the ratios refer to end-of-year figures.

[11] For empirical evidence on this point, see J. O. Horrigan, "The Determination of Long-Term Credit Standing with Financial Ratios," *Empirical Research in Accounting: Selected Studies, 1966*, Supplement to Vol. 4, *Journal of Accounting Research*, pp. 44–62.

However, two ratios from the short-term liquidity category were chosen to focus on the effect of inventory on the adjustment.

Least-square regressions were used to estimate the coefficients of

$$\log y_{k,t} - \log y_{k,t-1} = \alpha + \beta(\log x_{k,t-1} - \log y_{k,t-1}) + u_t \qquad (4)$$

$$t = 1, \cdots, 20$$

$$k = 1, \cdots, 6$$

for each of the 245 firms in the sample. $y_{k,t}$ is the firm's financial ratio k for the year t, $x_{k,t-1}$ is the arithmetic mean of the ratio k for the industry in year $t - 1$, u_t is an error term assumed to meet the least-squares model requirements, and $k = 1, \cdots, 6$ represents the six financial ratios tested. Equation (4) differs from (3) in its logarithmic form and in the addition of the constant term α. The logarithmic form[12] is used to capture the *relative* yearly change in the ratio. Since we are dealing with adjustments of deviations from a target, it seems reasonable to assume that the relative deviations are more significant to the firm than the absolute ones. For example, the absolute deviation between a firm's ratio of .20 and an industry mean of .10 is equal to the deviation between a ratio of 2.10 and a mean of 2.00. Yet, the former deviation would certainly be regarded as far more serious than the latter. The logarithmic deviation reflects this difference: $\log_e (.20/.10) = .69$, while $\log_e (2.10/2.00) = .05$. A constant term α was added to equation (4) to test the hypothesis that $\alpha = 0$.

Summary of Results

Table 1 summarizes the cross-sectional distribution of parameter estimates obtained when equation (4) was applied to the data. The six panels of the table correspond to the six ratios tested. Column 1 shows the distribution of the coefficient of determination, R^2. Columns 2 and 4 show the distribution of the estimated regression coefficients, and columns 3 and 5 show the distribution of their t-values (i.e., ratios of coefficients to estimated standard errors). Six summary statistics are shown for each parameter: the mean and the five fractiles (.10, .25, .50, .75, and .90).

The following comments relate to the findings of Table 1.

1. This study focuses on the partial adjustment coefficient β. It was stated earlier that $0 < \hat{\beta} \leq 1$ is an indication that the firm periodically adjusts its ratio to the industry mean. The data in Table 1 strongly confirm the periodic adjustment hypothesis; the mean and the five fractiles of $\hat{\beta}$ for all the ratios tested lie between 0 and 1. The individual exceptions (i.e., $\hat{\beta} < 0$ or $\hat{\beta} > 1$) are very rare: out of 245 firms only 17, 16, 13, 23, 18, and 25 exceptions were noted for the six ratios respectively.

2. The statistical significance of the adjustment coefficient may be inferred from the $t(\hat{\beta})$ values. The coefficients for the quick and current ratios

---

[12] Natural logarithms are used throughout this study.

18

TABLE 1

Cross-Sectional Distribution of Regression Coefficients for Equation (4)

Ratio	Mean and fractiles	(1) R^2	(2) $\hat{\alpha}$	(3) $t(\hat{\alpha})$	(4) $\hat{\beta}$	(5) $t(\hat{\beta})$
Quick ratio	Mean	.22	−.04	−.43	.51	2.10
	.10	.04	−.23	−2.27	.12	.82
	.25	.10	−.10	−1.48	.29	1.33
	.50	.20	−.01	−.31	.50	2.09
	.75	.32	.04	.65	.72	2.81
	.90	.43	.10	1.44	.95	3.60
Current ratio	Mean	.19	−.02	−.33	.48	1.93
	.10	.02	−.13	−1.96	.10	.53
	.25	.08	−.07	−1.27	.24	1.14
	.50	.20	−.02	−.31	.46	1.97
	.75	.29	.03	.67	.67	2.65
	.90	.36	.09	1.33	.84	3.12
Equity/Total debt	Mean	.16	−.06	−.43	.30	1.64
	.10	.01	−.26	−2.16	.05	.40
	.25	.06	−.11	−1.38	.12	.97
	.50	.12	−.03	−.47	.25	1.52
	.75	.24	.04	.75	.42	2.30
	.90	.34	.12	1.43	.65	2.94
Sales/Total assets	Mean	.17	−.01	−.29	.37	1.75
	.10	.01	−.11	−2.29	.06	.43
	.25	.05	−.06	−1.42	.16	.95
	.50	.13	−.01	−.36	.33	1.57
	.75	.27	.03	.80	.59	2.48
	.90	.37	.10	1.67	.80	3.19
Sales/Inventory	Mean	.19	−.02	−.24	.38	1.78
	.10	.02	−.20	−2.32	.07	.46
	.25	.07	−.09	−1.31	.19	1.12
	.50	.16	−.01	−.42	.37	1.78
	.75	.27	.05	.95	.58	2.49
	.90	.39	.12	1.80	.82	3.28
Net operating income/Total assets	Mean	.17	−.06	−.35	.43	1.75
	.10	.02	−.28	−2.02	.10	.46
	.25	.07	−.12	−1.26	.23	1.09
	.50	.15	−.03	−.51	.40	1.71
	.75	.25	.03	.51	.60	2.36
	.90	.37	.16	1.63	.91	3.15

are statistically significant (at the 5 per cent level) for about half the firms in the sample. The significance of the $\hat{\beta}$ values for the other ratios is lower. Note, however, that the importance of this significance test should not be overemphasized. Given the estimation problems of our model (alluded to earlier), the t-values provide only a rough indication of the "importance" of the variable.

3. The α coefficient (constant) was found in all cases to be very small and statistically insignificant, leading to the conclusion that the original model (i.e., without the constant) fits the data well.

4. The coefficient of determination, R^2, is not large for any of the ratios tested. The quick and current ratios had the largest coefficients (median $R^2 = .20$). This indicates the existence of additional explanatory variables which are not included in (4). But the objective of this study was to examine the periodic adjustment hypothesis and not to develop a prediction model for financial ratios. Therefore, we can concentrate on the β coefficients, and the modest R^2's need not be of great concern.[13]

The Speed of Adjustment

The speed of adjustment to the target is indicated by the size of the β coefficient; the closer β is to 1, the faster the periodic adjustment. The extent of partial adjustment is rationalized by economists in terms of two conflicting types of costs: (a) the cost of adjustment and (b) the cost of being out of equilibrium. In our context, the cost of adjustment reflects the degree of difficulty in a quick adjustment of the financial ratio to a predetermined target. Some ratios (e.g., the current ratio) involve short-term items and are under the direct control of management; therefore, they can be adjusted in the short run more easily (with less cost) than other ratios. The cost of being out of equilibrium reflects the importance to the firm of the conformity of a ratio with a target. If, for example, lenders insist on a 2:1 current ratio, then the cost to a firm not conforming with this standard will be the higher interest rates charged. Consequently, the speed of adjustment of a ratio will depend on the relative significance of these two cost items.

The differences in the sizes of the $\hat{\beta}$ coefficients in Table 1 can be rationalized by the cost arguments given above. The adjustment coefficient is largest for the short-term liquidity ratios (the medians: .50 for the quick ratio and .46 for the current ratio) and smallest for the equity/debt ratio and sales/total assets ratio (the medians: .25 and .33 respectively). The former ratios involve current items only and hence are less costly to adjust rapidly.[14] However, the latter ratios involve long-term items (e.g., equity and long-term debt) and variables which are not under the complete control of management (e.g., sales). Hence, they should be more difficult to adjust. Moreover, the traditional emphasis on the importance of the current ratios to lenders increases the cost of being out of equilibrium for these ratios, thus inducing management to adjust them more rapidly. The out-of-equilibrium cost argument may also explain the relatively large adjustment

---

[13] This point is pursued later.

[14] One such adjustment, which is under the direct control of management and can be done in a very short time is to offset cash and accounts payable.

coefficient for the operating income/total assets ratio, even though the ratio incorporates exogenous and long-term items.

The cost involved in the adjustment process is only one of the factors determining the size of the β coefficient. Another factor is the *stability* of the target—the industry mean. The major question facing the firm is the interpretation of any recent change in the industry mean: Is it due to some fundamental change which may be expected to persist, or is it nothing more than a transitory (random) fluctuation? The firm's adjustment would depend on how confidently it expects the change to persist since it is useless to adjust the ratio to random fluctuations in the target. Accordingly, we would expect that when the industry mean is highly variable, and thus reflective of a large random component, the adjustment coefficient would be relatively small. Our results are consistent with this hypothesis—the correlation coefficient of the variances of the 18 industry means[15] with the means of the $\hat{\beta}$ coefficients for the current ratios was found to be about $-.20$.[16]

The size of the firm might also affect the periodic adjustment coefficient. We would expect that because of the indivisibilities (lumpiness) of assets and liabilities, a large firm would find it easier to adjust its ratios to a target than a small firm in a given time period. This expectation is also consistent with the data; the correlation coefficient of the median assets size of the industries with the average $\hat{\beta}$ coefficient for the current ratio is .25.

Extensions

The present study can be extended in several directions:

Improvement of the model. The original model can be modified to reflect a broader definition of the target for financial ratio adjustment. Our model assumes that the target ratio y_t^* is adjusted to the industry mean according to

$$y_t^* = x_{t-1}.$$

This seems to be an oversimplification since management wants to adjust to the *current* mean x_t rather than to the most recent mean x_{t-1}. The current mean is, of course, unknown to most firms when they plan (budget) their ratios, but they can probably improve on the naive prediction x_{t-1}. An improved model would therefore replace the observed x_{t-1} by some prediction x_t^* based on the historical behavior of the industry means (e.g., an exponential smoothing prediction). An indication of the improved performance of such a model was obtained when x_{t-1} in (4) was replaced

---

[15] The $\hat{\beta}$ coefficients for each firm were aggregated by industries, and the mean of the coefficient for the industry was calculated and correlated with the variance of the industry mean.

[16] According to the "stability of the target" argument, we would expect small adjustment coefficients for industries experiencing fast technological changes. This is also indicated by the data; the aerospace industry has the smallest $\hat{\beta}$ coefficient (.36 for the current ratio) of the 18 industries in the sample.

by x_t. As a result of the modified model, the median R^2 for the quick ratio increased from .20 to .40, and about 85 per cent of the $\hat{\beta}$ coefficients were found to be statistically significant.

Another improvement of the model involves the introduction of an additional coefficient b in equations (2) and (3):

$$y_t^* = bx_{t-1}$$

and (5)

$$y_t - y_{t-1} = \beta(bx_{t-1} - y_{t-1}).$$

This coefficient will indicate whether firms tend to maintain a *fixed deviation* from the industry mean in their adjustment process. However, the introduction of an additional variable may be undesirable in our case, considering the relatively small number of observations per firm.

The adjustment coefficient was considered in this study to be a constant over the 20-year period. However, this coefficient may change over time reflecting changes in the economic environment and in the objectives of the firm. These changes may be examined by substituting the β coefficient in (4) with a β_t which will change over the 20-year period. Here again, the small number of observations per firm may pose estimation difficulties.

Predicting the level of the ratios. The current study was not directly concerned with the prediction of future financial ratios. However, since the industry mean was found to be an important variable in adjusting the ratio, we would expect it to assist in such a prediction. Specifically, a model which attempts to predict the level of a ratio should include the recent industry mean and a lagged variable of the ratio among the explanatory variables. To obtain an indication of the predictive ability of these two explanatory variables, the following equation was applied to the data for the current ratio

$$y_t = \alpha + \beta_1 x_{t-1} + \beta_2 y_{t-1} + u_t, \tag{6}$$

where y_t is the value of the current ratio at time t, and x_{t-1} is the industry mean at time $t - 1$. The median coefficient of determination, R^2, for the whole sample was .41, a substantial improvement over the R^2's in Table 1 (90 firms had an R^2 larger than .50). Thus, the results of this study should be useful in developing a prediction model for ratios.

Summary

The objective of this study was to test the hypothesis, often suggested by financial analysts, that firms adjust their financial ratios according to industry-wide averages. The empirical results are consistent with this hypothesis.

The techniques by which firms adjust their ratios were not investigated here. This is a very complex problem since ratio adjustment may be achieved in several ways. Even some passive adjustment by allowing industry-wide effects to operate on the ratios is not precluded. Moreover, in such a large and heterogeneous sample there is no way to identify specific techniques which probably differ from firm to firm. However, irrespective of the adjustment techniques employed, the usefulness of this study mainly lies in its contribution to the development of a *general* model describing the behavior of financial ratios. Such a model will permit prediction of ratios on the basis of the variables investigated above.

ASSOCIATIONS BETWEEN ALTERNATIVE ACCOUNTING
PROFITABILITY MEASURES AND SECURITY RETURNS

*Cheng-Few Lee and J. Kenton Zumwalt**

I. Introduction

The importance of accounting information on security price determination is
of interest to both security analysts and accountants. Beaver [3], Downes and
Dyckman [6], Gonedes [12], Beaver and Manegold [4], and others have investigated
the possible relationships between accounting information and market information. Rosenberg [26] has shown the existence of extra-market components of covariance in security returns while Simkowitz and Logue (S-L) [28] have derived
the interdependent structure of security returns. However, none of this research has explicitly investigated how the empirical results can be affected by
alternative accounting profitability measures within an industry simultaneously.

The main purpose of this paper is to investigate the impact of different
profitability measures on security rates of return determination. The model
used in this empirical study is a simultaneous equation model developed by Lee
and Vinso (L-V) [19, 20]. In the second section, previous research is reviewed
and the model used in this paper is specified. In the third section, annual
financial data of the 35 largest industries are used to estimate the empirical
results. In the fourth section, a simulation technique is used to test whether
there exists a statistical bias associated with the small sample size used in
the empirical study. Implications of the results obtained from both actual data
and the simulation are presented in Section V. Finally, the results of this
paper are summarized and some concluding remarks are presented.

*
*Both authors, the University of Illinois at Urbana-Champaign. The authors
gratefully acknowledge the assistance of Professor Thomas A. Yancey in setting
up and interpreting the simulation procedure. The authors would like to thank
an anonymous referee for suggesting the simulation approach and a new method
for obtaining the mean response across all firms.*

II. Specification of the Model

The familiar capital asset pricing model developed by Sharpe [27] and others assumes that the relationship between any two securities i and j is completely described by their relationship to the market. This means the covariances between securities' returns should be zero after the effect of the market has been removed.

Several studies have examined the extra-market components of the covariance in security returns. Cohen and Pogue [5] examined the relationships between securities after the market component had been removed and found many nonzero correlations. They then employed a multi-index model and found that an industry index is relatively important in reducing the interrelationship among the ordinary least squares associated with the market model. King [15] and Meyers [23] used factor analysis in examining the impact of industry effects on security returns. Both concluded that industry factors were an important source of interdependence among security returns, but differed as to the magnitude of the influence.

Simkowitz and Logue [28] used a simultaneous equation approach in examining the interdependent structure of security returns. Their model assumed the returns on a security were a function of the returns on other similar securities (i.e., same industry), the return on the market portfolio, and firm related variables. They found that there exists extra explanatory power associated with some firm related variables in equity rates of return determination.

Rosenberg [26] utilized a multiple-factor model in examining the "extra-market components of covariance in security returns." He concluded there are "highly significant" extra-market components which could be at least partially explained by particular firm characteristics, industry factors, and historical return behavior of the security.

Livingston [22] analyzed the covariance among securities after the market influence was removed. He concluded there existed considerable "residual industry comovements" and suggested analysis of industry groups should be important in portfolio construction.

We are analyzing a similar problem, but are using a more powerful tool. Specifically, a simultaneous equation model, three stage least squares, is used to examine the impact of accounting profitability determination on security returns. Because measurement problems arise in the determination of profitability, six different profitability measures are examined. Leverage and dividend policy variables are included in the model to account for different financing and dividend strategies among firms.

One of the primary concerns of both security analysts and managerial accountants is the measurement of income. From an economic viewpoint, income for any period is represented by the change in a firm's net worth. While security analysts or accountants strive to produce an accounting income which accurately reflects economic income, many essentially arbitrary judgments are necessary in reaching the accounting income figure. Among the arbitrary judgments are the problems of allocation of receipts and expenditures, methods of depreciation, capitalization versus expensing of research and development expenditures, the meeting of pension fund obligations, valuation of inventory, and inflation. As a security analyst or accountant examines a firm's income statement, it becomes obvious that different measures of income are subject to different degrees of arbitrary judgments. In addition, different industries may follow different accounting practices and in some industries different regulatory agencies may prescribe different methods of accounting. For these reasons, different earnings or profitability measures may be important in different industries for security price determination.

As values are determined for Sales, Operating Income, Earnings Before Taxes, Earnings After Taxes, and Net Income, it becomes difficult to determine which of the reported earnings figures most accurately reflect the economic profitability of the firm.

This paper examines six alternative profitability measures for each of 35 industries. From the results derived from the overall spectrum of possible income measures, the impact of accounting profitability measures on security returns will be analyzed.

Following Lee and Vinso (L-V) [19, 20] the basic model used in this empirical study can be defined as:

(1) $$R_{jt} = a_j + \beta_j R_{mt} + b_{j1} X_{j1t} + b_{j2} X_{j2t} + b_{j3} X_{j3t} + \epsilon_{jt}$$

where

R_{jt} = the return on the jth security over time interval t in a group classified by a reasonable classification scheme, $(j = 1, 2, \ldots, I_k)$, $(t = 1, 2, \ldots, T)$,

R_{mt} = the return on a market index over time interval t,

X_{j1t} = the profitability variable of jth firm over time interval t, $(j = 1, 2, \ldots, I_k)$,

X_{j2t} = the leverage variable of jth firm over time period t, $(j = 1, 2, \ldots, I_k)$, $(t = 1, 2, \ldots, T)$,

X_{j3t} = the dividend policy variable of jth firm over time period t, $(j = 1, 2, \ldots, I_k)$, $(t = 1, 2, \ldots, T)$,

b_{jn} = the coefficient of the nth firm related variable in the jth
    equation, $(n = 1, 2, 3)$,

β_{mj} = the coefficient of the market rate of return in the jth equation, and

ε_{jt} = the disturbance term for j^{th} equation.

Equation (1) represents a linear relationship between the rates of return
on the jth security, the market rates of return, and three firm related variables. The relationship between the model and the S-L model and the strength
of this model relative to the other models can be found in the Lee and Vinso
[19, 20] papers.

III. Empirical Results

To test empirically the impact of different profitability measures on
security rate of return determination, annual data from the 35 largest industries during 1960-1975 are used (see Appendix A). Annual stock prices of 495
firms are used to calculate the rates of return with appropriate adjustment
for both dividends and stock splits. The Standard and Poor's 500 (S & P) index
is used to calculate the annual market rate of return.

As noted by Simkowitz and Logue, a good case can be made for including
profitability, financing, and dividend policy variables in security valuation
models. Because this study focuses essentially on the impact of accounting
profitability measures on security returns, this paper analyzes six profitability measures in an attempt to determine which measure provides the best
specification for the model. The six profitability measures used were (A)
Total Asset Turnover, (B) Gross Return on Total Assets, (C) Net Return on Total
Assets, (D) Return on Common Equity, (E) Gross Profit Margin, and (F) Net Profit
Margin.[1] Each of these six variables was used in turn as the profitability
index in equation (1). While Sales/Total Assets is typically referred to as a
turnover or activity ratio, it is included here because it is a frequently used
measure of the efficiency of a firm.

Further justification of using several profitability measures is now explored. Miller and Modigliani [24], Francis [9], and others have argued that

-----

[1]It is well known that security return data generally used are based on
the calendar year while, for some firms, accounting data are based on fiscal
years different from the calendar year. In this study only firms with fiscal
years ending in the June through December period are utilized to minimize the
possible bias caused by the inconsistency of the ending period. The reason
for including the firms with fiscal years not corresponding with the calendar
year is an attempt to capture the overall interaction within each industry.
It should be noted that about 80 percent of the sample (396 firms) has fiscal
years ending in December.

there exist some measurement errors in the accounting profit measures. In other words, the accounting profit measure can generally be decomposed into transitory and permanent components. Following the concept developed by Friedman [10], the transitory component of the accounting profit measure can be regarded as the measurement error of the expected earnings of a company.[2] Following the errors-in-variables regression theory, the measurement errors of a regressor will make the estimated regression coefficient become biased and inconsistent. Six different profit measures are used to reflect the possible differential measurement errors associated with alternative accounting profit measures.

The explanatory power of alternative income measures on the annual equity rates of return will shed some light to accountants and financial analysts as to the relative importance of different income information disclosure.

Because leverage and dividend policy variables are often examined in security analysis, a leverage and a dividend policy variable were included in the model. Following Simkowitz and Logue, the leverage variable is defined as the annual change of long-term debt plus the annual change of outstanding preferred stock divided by total assets, while the dividend policy variable is defined as the annual change of total dividends divided by the book value of equity. By using the annual changes in computing these variables, changes in financing and dividend policies which might influence security returns are taken into account.

It should be noted that the pay-out ratio can be used as an alternative dividend policy measure (see Bar-Yosef and Koldony [2]). In addition, it should also be noted that interest charge/total returns can be used as an alternative leverage measure (see Krainer [17]). However, the impacts of dividend and leverage policies are not the main concern of this study.

Based upon the specification of equation (1), the OLS was used to estimate the related parameters for individual firms. Residual correlation coefficient matrices are estimated for each of the 35 industries. Because it was found that the residuals within the industry were generally highly correlated, Zellner's Seemingly Unrelated Regression (SUR) method was used to estimate simultaneously all the equations within an industry. Due to the large number of firms in several of the industries, Zellner's Generalized Least Squares (GLS) could not be directly applied to obtain efficient estimators. Under this circumstance, cluster analysis was used to classify the firms into several appropriate subgroups.[3] Zellner's GLS method was then used to obtain efficient

---

[2]Friedman [10] has decomposed the current income of a consumer into permanent income and transitory income and regarded the transitory income as the measurement errors of expected income.

[3]Farrell [8] and Lee and Lloyd [18] have used the cluster analysis technique to obtain homogenous stock groupings.

estimators within each subgroup.

The metal mining industry is used as an example to show how the L-V model can be used to analyze the impacts of alternative profitability measure on security rate of return determination. First the return on equity is used as the profitability index and the OLS is used to estimate the L-V model. The results are presented in Table 1. As can be seen, the income variable, NI/CEq, is significant for three of the nine firms at the .05 level. The leverage and dividend variables are significant for three and two of the nine firms, respectively. The coefficient indicating the importance of market information, β_j, is significant for five of the firms.

To investigate the possible interrelationship among the OLS residuals of (1) within an industry, a 9 x 9 OLS residual correlation coefficient matrix was calculated and the results are presented in Table 2. Using Fisher's Z test, it was found that 14 of the 36 residual correlation coefficients were significantly different from zero at the .05 level. This implies that Zellner's SUR method can be used to obtain more efficient estimates than those of the OLS procedure.

The SUR results associated with these nine firms are also presented in Table 1 beneath the OLS results. From the empirical results in this Table it is found that six out of nine regression coefficients associated with market rates of return were significantly different from zero at the .05 level. With respect to the coefficients related to accounting based variables, five regression coefficients associated with the profitability index, five coefficients associated with the leverage index, and four coefficients associated with the dividend policy index were significantly different from zero at the .05 level. These results imply that there exist some extra-market components for the metal mining industry as demonstrated by Rosenberg [26].[4] The sign of the regression coefficients associated with each firm related variable must also be analyzed. All of the significant coefficients of the income variables are positive, indicating that higher reported return on common equity will result in higher investor returns.

----

[4]As was noted by the referee, the explanatory variables in Rosenberg's study were predetermined while in the present study the explanatory variables are synchronous with the observed returns. In this context, two different elements of extra-market covariance can be identified; one element is explained by accounting variables and the other is not. The first element is the covariance due to the correlation among the contemporaneous explanatory variables, which results in correlation of security returns that is explained by the regressions; and the second element is the covariance from the residual correlation in the regressions not explained by the regressions.

Of the five significant leverage coefficients, one is negative and of the four significant dividend coefficients, three are negative.[5]

The standard errors of the estimated regression coefficients associated with the SUR results are generally smaller than those associated with the OLS results. This implies that the SUR estimation method has improved the efficiency of the estimated regression coefficients (see Theil [29, pp. 298-302]).

In addition to the return on equity, similar procedures were utilized for each of the other five profitability measures.[6]

In each industry the regression coefficients associated with different profitability measures were significant for different companies. For example, in the Metal Mining Industry, the Sales/TA and EBIT/TA coefficients are both significant for five firms, but not the same five firms. (Only three firms have both measures significant.) Furthermore, the gross profit margin, EBDT/Sales, was significant in only two instances. Also of interest is the fact that one firm exhibited a significant negative correlation coefficient when EBIT/TA was utilized as the profitability measure.[7] Theoretically, the negative relationship between market rates of return and the overall accounting rates of return measure is hard to justify. This problem will be explored in Section IV.

It may also be observed that the different profitability measures have little impact on the relationship between market return and the return on the individual security. The same six firms exhibited significant market return coefficients for each of the alternative profitability measures. As alternative profitability measures are used in the regression procedure, different companies exhibit significant regression coefficients for the leverage and/or

---

[5]Overall, for the 495 companies 45 percent of the significant leverage variable coefficients were negative while 69 percent of the significant dividend variable coefficients were negative. Explanation for these results includes the possibility of imprecise measurement of the leverage and dividend variables as well as the possibility that investors perceive "optimal" leverage and dividend policies. For example, if a firm has reached its optimal leverage ratio, an increase of debt will reduce the value of a firm and the sign associated with leverage variable will be negative. (See either Gale [11] or Hurdle [13]). A similar argument can be used to determine the sign associated with the dividend policy variable.

[6]Ball and Brown [17] have used the relationship between the residual of the market model and the net income number to evaluate the importance of accounting information disclosure to the value of the security. Our model can be used as an alternative for Ball and Brown's model. One of the strengths of our model is the consideration of the relationship of individual firms within an industry simultaneously.

[7]These results are available from the authors.

30

dividend measures. This implies that the impact of financing and/or dividend policies on alternative return measures is not necessarily identical. Sample correlation coefficients among the explanatory variables, the market rate of return, the profitability index, the leverage index, and the dividend policy index revealed that the problem of multicollinearity associated with the multi-index model used in this study is relatively trivial.

All 35 industries were examined in a similar manner, and the aggregated results are presented in Table 3. For five out of six profitability measures, the regression coefficients indicated a significant relationship existed at the .05 level for approximately 50 percent of the firms. The sixth profitability measure, Sales/Total Assets, exhibited significance for 35.9 percent of the firms. The proportion of significantly negative profitability coefficients to the total number of coefficients ranged from a low of 7.5 percent (37/495) for Sales/TA and EBIT/TA, to a high of 11.5 percent (57/495) for EBDT/Sales. (An industry-by-industry comparison is presented in Table 4 and discussed in the next section.)

Generally, between 40 and 50 percent of the significant leverage coefficients were negative and between 65 and 75 percent of the significant dividend coefficients were negative. These results suggest that optimal leverage and dividend policies exist on an industry basis (see footnote 5).

In the following section a simulation study will be used to test the possible statistical bias associated with using only 16 observations to estimate the profitability coefficients. Implications related to the empirical results of this section will be explored in Section V.

IV. Simulations

To our knowledge, this paper represents the first major study using the SUR methodology to examine the association among alternative accounting profitability measures and security returns. The simulation study which follows attempts to achieve two purposes. First, it indicates how a simulation procedure may technically be used to resolve some of the problems faced by the empirical work in finance.[8] Secondly, this specific simulation is used to test for the possible existence of bias associated with the estimated profitability coefficients which were reported in the previous section.

The reason to believe that the sampling theory used here may be biased is now discussed. With 16 observations per firm and five coefficients being estimated, only 11 residual degrees of freedom remained for each firm in the ordinary

[8] Fama and Babiak [7] have used the simulation technique to investigate some potential bias caused by sample size. However, their model is a single equation model and, therefore, it is much simpler than what we have faced.

least squares regression. Since the correlation matrix used in the SUR equations utilizes information from the OLS regression, with the relatively few degrees of freedom for each firm, it is possible that a substantial proportion of the apparent disturbance variance was attributed to the residual correlation. This would result in the apparent standard errors for the estimated coefficients being too small, and would increase the number of apparently significant coefficients, both positive and negative. Additional bias may result if the disturbances do not meet the assumption of being normally distributed.[9]

The simulation study was carried out in the following manner:[10]

(1) A residual variance-covariance matrix was constructed from the residuals of the OLS regressions. This resulted in a square symmetric postive definite matrix.[11] A Cholesky decomposition was performed on the residual variance-covariance matrix. This procedure decomposed the residual variance-covariance matrix, Σ, into a lower triangular matrix, L, and its transpose, L', such that $\Sigma = LL'$.

(2) Since each of the j firms in an industry had 16 residual terms (one for each year), 1000 jx16 matrices of random numbers, U, were generated from a log-normal distribution with mean $e^{1/2}$ and variance $e(e-1)$.[12]

(3) The triangular matrix L was multiplied by each of the 1000 U matrices (i.e., $V^*_{jt} = LU$) resulting in simulated residual terms similar in distribution to the residuals observed in the actual case.

(4) To generate one set of simulated rates of return (R'_{jt}), one set of estimated residual terms as indicated in (3) were added to the estimated rates of return determined by the SUR procedure.

$$R'_{jt} = \hat{a}_j + \hat{\beta}_j R_{mt} + \hat{b}_{j1} X_{j1t} + \hat{b}_{j2} X_{j2t} + \hat{b}_{j3} X_{j3t} + v^*_{jt}$$

where $\hat{a}_j$, $\hat{\beta}_j$, $\hat{b}_{j1}$, $\hat{b}_{j2}$, $\hat{b}_{j3}$ are the coefficients from the original SUR procedure,

---

[9] These potential problems were pointed out by the referee.

[10] A more detailed description and justification of the simulation data generation procedures can be found in Nerlove ([25, pp. 366-371]). We are grateful to Professor Nagesh S. Revankar for pointing out this information.

[11] As simulations were performed on two separate industries, the matrix was 7x7 for the nonclustered industry and 15x15 for the clustered industry.

[12] The residual terms were generated from a log-normal distribution of total rates of return from which unity was subtracted. This resulted in a rate of return residual distribution with a zero mean and a variance of 1.0.

R_{mt}, X_{j1t}, X_{j2t} and X_{j3t} are the original variable data, and v_{jt}^* is the jth column of V_j^*. This procedure was repeated 1000 times resulting in 1000 sets of simulated returns.

(5) These 1000 sets of simulated returns were used in the OLS regression procedure resulting in 1000 jx16 residual matrices.

(6) The 1000 jx16 residual matrices were used to estimate 1000 jxj variance-covariance matrices.

(7) The 1000 sets of simulated returns, R'_{jt}, the original variables, R_{mt}, X_{1t}, X_{2t}, X_{3t}, and the 1000 estimated variance-covariance matrices were used in the SUR procedure to produce 1000 sets of estimates of the coefficients of the model.

This procedure was performed for each of two industries and the frequency of significant coefficients, both positive and negative, was recorded.

Table 5 presents the results related to the percentage of significant coefficients obtained from the original model and those obtained from the simulation. Furthermore, both the original results and the simulation results are classified into total significant, positive significant, and negative significant. Table 5 indicates that the number of significant coefficients from the simulations is greater than the original model in 11 out of 12 cases if the 1 percent significant level is used. Therefore, the conjectured bias is present in an important degree. However, it is also the case that the change in the fraction of significant coefficients is not enough to grossly affect the results. Thus the bias seems to be substantial but acceptable.

In the following section, results reported in Sections III and IV will be used to draw implications concerning the association between alternative profitability measures and security returns.

V. Implications

Now, the implications associated with Table 4 are analyzed. From Table 4 the proportion of negative coefficients significant at the 5 percent level ranges from a low of 3.7 percent to a high of 5.8 percent as opposed to an expectation of a 2.5 percent.[13] Now, the possible reasons for these findings are explored. In Section IV, we have argued that the six different measures used in this study may contain different degrees of measurement errors. It is well known that the measurement error in a regression may make the sign of a regression coefficient change from positive to negative (see Johnston [14]).

_____

[13]The referee has suggested using the simulation as indicated in the previous section to resolve this issue. However, the simulation results cannot be used to explain these findings.

Therefore, it can be argued that the negative significant coefficients associated with profitability measure may be partially due to the measurement errors. In addition, the possible multicollinearity between the profitability index and the dividend policy index can also cause the sign of estimated coefficients to switch from positive to negative (see Klein and Nakamura [16]). A major reason for multicollinearity is due to the number of observations being too small. One way of increasing the sample size is to utilize quarterly instead of annual data. Recent work by Lee and Zumwalt [21] furnishes some support for this argument. If we carefully examine the percentage of signficant negative coefficients associated with every industry, it is found that both the percentage of significant positive coefficients and the percentage of significant negative coefficients are different among different profitability index measurements. It is interesting to note that only four industries--SIC code 29, 30, 36 and 37-- have the percentage of significant negative coefficients greater than 5 percent for all of the six profitability measures. In sum, it can be concluded that the profitability of a firm has some positive impact to the individual firm's rates of return determination. While the aggregation shows that accounting income information has a significant impact on the return of a security, closer examination reveals that the impact is not uniform across industries, and that different profitability measures are important for different industries. In Table 4 the proportion of significant regression coefficients for the profitability measures is presented for each of the 35 industries. It may be observed that some industries exhibit little or no relationship between the profitability measure and the return on the security while other industries show a substantial proportion of the firms do exhibit a significant relationship. For example, none of the three firms in the Heavy Construction Industry (SIC code 16) shows any significant profitability regression coefficients while the Printing and Publishing Industry (SIC code 27) has 50 to 90 percent of the firms showing a significant relationship, depending on the profitability measure used.

The relative importance of alternative accounting profitability measures on the security rates of return determination is thus indicated. It is found that overall Sales/TA is not as important as the other five profitability measures. The extra explanatory power associated with alternative accounting profitability measures adding to the capital asset pricing determination is not independent of the industry. These results imply that the security analyst or investors cannot always use one particular accounting profit measure to predict the security rates of return.

To estimate the mean response and the underlying variance of the true parameter across firms, the mean response, the sample variance of the estimate, and the average estimation error variance for each parameter are calculated and presented in Table 6. From Table 6, it is found that the mean responses for Sales/TA, EBIT/TA, NI/TA, NI/CEq, EBDT/Sales and NI/Sales are .399, 2.840, 4.316, 2.123, 3.753 and 6.974, respectively. By subtracting the average estimation error variance (column c) from the sample variance of the estimate (column b), we obtain the underlying variance (column d) and standard deviation (column e) of the true parameter across firms. The mean response and its standard deviation as listed in Table 6 allows the practitioner to determine the average impact of each profitability measure on the security rates of return and the variation of this mean response.[14] As can be seen, the standard deviation of the true parameter across firms is greater than the mean in every case. The mean value approaches the standard deviation for the EBIT/TA and NI/CEq profitability measures. This indicates these two measures are the most consistent of the six profitability measures. This is consistent with the results shown in Table 3 for the EBIT/TA measure. That is, the ratio of significant positive coefficients to significant negative coefficients also indicates the EBIT/TA parameter is one of the best profitability measures. However, from Table 6, it appears that the NI/CEq is the best parameter when comparing the mean response to the standard deviation of true parameter values, but is not as good when comparing the significant positive and significant negative coefficients from Table 3. One possible explanation is that the NI/CEq measure may have fewer extreme values of the estimated parameter and, as a result, the standard deviation of true parameters across firms is reduced without reducing the number of significant negative coefficients.

VI. Summary and Concluding Remarks

Based upon an efficient estimation model for capital asset pricing developed by Lee and Vinso [20, 21], the importance of accounting profitability measures in explaining security returns is empirically examined. Six alternative profitability measures are used in the analysis. The results suggest accounting profitability information is an important source of extra-market component information in asset pricing. Further, it is shown that different accounting profitability measures should be used by security analysts or investors to determine the equity rates of return for different industries. In general, however, it appears that the EBIT/TA and the NI/CEq provide the most consistent

---

[14]An anonymous referee suggested this approach to provide an overall view in relating security returns to alternative profitability measures.

results.

To investigate the possible bias associated with the small sample, approximately 1000 simulation runs are performed for two industries. It is found the SUR model is not sensitive to the small sample size. To supply the practitioner some guidelines, the mean response and its standard deviation for six profitability measures are also reported.

Finally, quarterly accounting information will be used to test the importance of accounting information on security returns in future research. In addition, the advantage of the model used in this study relative to Ball and Brown's model in testing the importance of accounting information for capital asset pricing will be explored in the near future.

TABLE 1

ESTIMATES OF REGRESSION COEFFICIENTS USING THE OLS AND THE SUR PROCEDURES

THE ACCOUNTING PROFITABILITY MEASURE IS NET INCOME/COMMON EQUITY

Industry Name   Metal Mining
Industry Code   10
Number of Firms   9

Company		Constant	NI/CEq	Leverage	Dividends	Rm
Amax, Inc.	OLS	1.315*	1.829	-1.512*	-15.833*	1.793**
	SUR	1.164*	.004	-1.096*	-11.235**	1.493**
Asarco, Inc.	OLS	-.419	3.479	1.816	-.845	1.690*
	SUR	-.742**	3.996*	2.674*	2.395	1.714**
Cleveland-Cliffs Iron Co.	OLS	-.490	-.491	-1.443	21.668	1.174
	SUR	-.649*	4.109	-1.031	11.514	1.221*
Foote Mineral Co.	OLS	-.371	8.341*	-1.008*	5.931	.039
	SUR	-.481	8.355*	-.586	5.553	-.002
Inco, Ltd.	OLS	.186	2.676	-.743	-5.453	1.239*
	SUR	1.063	3.404**	-.476	-6.118*	1.412**
Texasgulf, Inc.	OLS	.827	-1.362	-.367	-.866	1.171
	SUR	.592	-.068	-.083	8.833*	1.474
Cominco, Ltd.	OLS	-.379	.342	1.086	3.111	1.644**
	SUR	-.331*	-.388	1.164*	3.597	1.604**
Hudson Bay Mining and Smelting	OLS	-.493*	2.004*	1.876*	1.640	1.605**
	SUR	-.441**	2.302**	1.809**	.611	1.668**
Homestake Mining	OLS	-.392	1.133**	2.305	-15.804**	1.657
	SUR	-.244	9.802**	2.479**	-15.574**	1.271

Remarks: * indicates significance at the .05 level.
          ** indicates significance at the .01 level.

TABLE 2

RESIDUAL CORRELATION MATRIX FOR THE METAL MINING INDUSTRY
WITH NET INCOME/COMMON EQUITY AS THE PROFITABILITY VARIABLE

	1	2	3	4	5	6	7	8	9
1	1.000	.241	.306	-.311	.459	.320	.500*	.433	.531*
2		1.000	.718*	-.016	-.185	.156	.706*	.527*	.464
3			1.000	-.062	.081	.304	.592*	.584*	.602*
4				1.000	-.588*	.209	-.088	-.512*	-.203
5					1.000	.148	-.121	.212	.219
6						1.000	.393	-.052	.548*
7							1.000	.623*	.539*
8								1.000	.511*
9									1.000

*Indicates significance at the .05 level.

TABLE 3

A SUMMARY OF THE SIGNIFICANT REGRESSION COEFFICIENTS

FOR SIX ALTERNATIVE INCOME MEASURES FOR 495 COMPANIES

Variable	Level of Significance		Variable	Level of Significance	
	.01	.05		.01	.05
Sales/TA	99	139	NI/TA	154	212
	(20)[a]	(37)		(30)	(39)
Leverage[b]	58	87	Leverage	72	111
	(49)	(88)		(53)	(78)
Dividends[c]	38	62	Dividends	37	58
	(69)	(113)		(96)	(138)
Rm[d]	144	284	Rm	147	275
		(A)			(B)
EBIT/TA	151	209	NI/CEq	140	199
	(22)	(37)		(34)	(45)
Leverage	68	109	Leverage	48	87
	(49)	(62)		(56)	(85)
Dividends	33	52	Dividends	22	55
	(91)	(144)		(99)	(146)
Rm	154	283	Rm	156	288
		(C)			(D)
EBDT/Sales	117	178	NI/Sales	107	206
	(35)	(57)		(26)	(38)
Leverage	59	99	Leverage	64	106
	(65)	(94)		(58)	(87)
Dividends	54	60	Dividends	43	72
	(85)	(134)		(89)	(134)
Rm	145	259	Rm	139	259
		(E)			(F)

(a) Significant negative coefficients are in parentheses.

(b) Leverage = (Long-Term Debt + Preferred Stock)/Total Assets.

(c) Dividends = Common Stock Dividends/Common Stock Equity.

(d) Rm - return on S & P 500.

TABLE 4

THE PROPORTION OF PROFITABILITY MEASURES WITH REGRESSION COEFFICIENTS
SIGNIFICANT AT THE .05 LEVEL FOR EACH OF THE 35 INDUSTRIES
USING THE SEEMINGLY UNRELATED REGRESSION PROCEDURE*

2-Digit SIC Code	Number of Firms	Sales/TA	EBIT/TA	NI/TA	NI/CEq	EBDT/Sales	NI/Sales
10	9	.556	.444(.111)	.556	.556	.222	.556
12	4	.250	.500	.500	.500	.250	.750
13	3	.333	.333	.333	.333	.000	.333
16	3	.000	.000	.000	.000	.000	.000
20	38	.289(.053)	.474	.368(.026)	.395(.053)	.368(.105)	.395(.105)
21	7	.143	.714	.143	.714	.286	.143
22	9	.444(.111)	.222(.111)	.333	.333	.556(.111)	.444
23	9	.333	.222(.111)	.222(.111)	.222(.111)	.222(.111)	.444
24	7	.286(.143)	.286	.286	.286	.286	.429
25	3	.333	.333	.333	.333	.333	.333
26	16	.375	.750(.063)	.563	.625	.500(.126)	.500(.063)
27	10	.500	.500(.300)	.500(.200)	.500(.200)	.500(.400)	.500(.200)
28	59	.373(.119)	.569(.034)	.569(.085)	.475(.102)	.322(.186)	.373(.085)
29	28	.179(.205)	.179(.205)	.205(.333)	.250(.370)	.222(.250)	.321(.250)
30	12	.250(.083)	.333(.333)	.416(.333)	.250(.250)	.333(.500)	.416(.250)
31	3	.000	.333	.333	.333	.667	.667
32	20	.350(.150)	.500(.200)	.600(.050)	.550(.250)	.400(.200)	.450(.150)
33	32	.375(.031)	.531	.656	.688	.438(.031)	.594
34	17	.294	.235(.059)	.235(.059)	.294(.059)	.176	.118(.059)
35	42	.190(.071)	.426(.071)	.476(.048)	.405(.048)	.500(.071)	.548(.048)
36	27	.259(.148)	.481(.074)	.481(.074)	.519(.074)	.481(.111)	.444(.074)
37	39	.147(.147)	.382(.176)	.382(.147)	.382(.206)	.324(.206)	.353(.118)
38	15	.533(.067)	.400	.400	.400	.333	.267
39	8	.000	.250	.250	.125(.125)	.250	.125
42	3	.333	.000	.000(.333)	.333	.333	.000
45	12	.333(.083)	.500(.083)	.583	.500(.167)	.500(.083)	.583(.167)
48	7	.000	.429	.143	.286	.143	.429
50	2	.000	1.000	.000	1.000	.500	1.000
51	4	1.000	.250(.250)	.000	.250	.250	.250
53	17	.235	.471	.353(.235)	.294	.471	.353(.117)
54	11	.364	.545(.091)	.545(.091)	.545	.636(.091)	.454(.091)

40

TABLE 4 (Cont.)

THE PROPORTION OF PROFITABILITY MEASURES WITH REGRESSION COEFFICIENTS
SIGNIFICANT AT THE .05 LEVEL FOR EACH OF THE 35 INDUSTRIES
USING THE SEEMINGLY UNRELATED REGRESSION PROCEDURE*

2-Digit SIC Code	Number of Firms	Sales/TA	EBIT/TA	NI/TA	NI/CEq	EBDT/Sales	NI/Sales
56	4	.250	.250	.500	.500	.500	.250
59	5	.600	.400	.400	.400	.200(.200)	.200
78	2	.500	1.000	1.000	.000(.500)	.200(.200)	1.000
99	8	.000	.250	.250(.250)	.250	.259	.250(.125)
Total	495	.281(.075)	.422(.075)	.428(.079)	.402(.091)	.360(.115)	.416(.077)

*values without parentheses indicate the proportion positive and values in parentheses indicate the proportion negative at the .05 level.

41

TABLE 5

RESULTS OF SIMULATION

Industry: Lumber and Wood Products   No. of Simulations: 949
SIC: 24   No. of Regressions: 6,643
No. of Companies: 7

VARIABLE: Sales/Total Assets

Original Results Significance Level	Total Significant No.	%	Positive Significant No.	%	Negative Significant No.	%
.01	2	28.6	1	14.3	1	14.3
.05	3	42.9	2	28.6	1	14.3

Simulations Results Significance Level	Total Significant No.	%	Positive Significant No.	%	Negative Significant No.	%
.01	2559	38.5	1690	25.4	869	13.1
.05	3006	45.3	1937	29.2	1069	16.1

Industry: Instruments & Related Products   No. of Simulations: 1,008
SIC: 38   No. of Regressions: 15,120
No. of Companies: 15 (clustered)

VARIABLE: EBIT/Total Assets

Original Results Significance Level	Total Significant No.	%	Positive Significant No.	%	Negative Significant No.	%
.01	4	26.7	4	26.7	0	0
.05	6	40.0	6	40.0	0	0

Simulation Results Significance Level	Total Significant No.	%	Positive Significant No.	%	Negative Significant No.	%
.01	6061	40.1	5840	38.6	221	1.5
.05	7219	47.7	6732	44.5	487	3.2

42

TABLE 6

MEAN RESPONSE, SAMPLE VARIANCE AND AVERAGE ESTIMATION ERROR VARIANCE

	Mean Response (a)	Sample Variance (b)	Average Estimation Error Variance (c)	(b) - (c) (d)	Standard Deviation of True Parameters Across Firms (e)
Sales/TA	.399	1.310	.574	.736	.858
EBIT/TA	2.840	22.804	7.706	15.098	3.886
NI/TA	4.316	93.028	26.750	66.287	8.141
NI/CEq	2.123	17.092	11.453	5.639	2.375
EBDT/Sales	3.753	94.949	30.178	64.771	8.048
NI/Sales	6.974	377.548	122.944	254.604	15.956

REFERENCES

[1] Ball, R., and P. Brown. "An Empirical Evaluation of Accounting Income Numbers." *Journal of Accounting Research*, Vol. 6 (1968), pp. 159-178.

[2] Bar-Yosef, Sassom, and R. Koldony. "Dividend Policy and Capital Market Theory." *Review of Economics and Statistics* (May 1976), pp. 181-190.

[3] Beaver, W. H. "The Behavior of Security Price and Its Implications for Accounting Research (Methods)." Supplement to *The Accounting Review* (1975), pp. 407-437.

[4] Beaver, W., and J. Manegold. "The Association between Market-Determined and Accounting-Determined Measures of Systematic Risk: Some Further Evidence." *Journal of Financial and Quantitative Analysis*, Vol. 10 (1975), pp. 231-284.

[5] Cohen, K. J., and J. A. Pogue. "An Empirical Evaluation of Alternative Portfolio Selection Models." *Journal of Business*, Vol. 40 (1967), pp. 166-193.

[6] Downes, D., and T. Dyckman. "Efficient Market Research and Accounting Information." *Accounting Review*, Vol. 48 (1973), pp. 300-317.

[7] Fama, E. F., and H. Babiak. "Dividend Policy: An Empirical Analysis." *The Journal of American Statistical Association*, Vol. 63 (1968), pp. 1132-1161.

[8] Farrell, J. L., Jr. "Homogeneous Stock Groupings: Implications for Portfolio Management." *Financial Analysts Journal*, Vol. 31 (1975), pp. 50-62.

[9] Francis, J. C. "Analysis of Equity Returns: A Survey with Extension." *Journal of Economics and Business*, Vol. 29 (1977), pp. 181-192.

[10] Friedman, M. *A Theory of the Consumption Function*. Princeton: Princeton University Press (1955).

[11] Gale, B. T. "Market Share and Rate of Return." *Review of Economics and Statistics*, Vol. 54 (November 1972).

[12] Gonedes, N. J. "Evidence on the Information Content of Accounting Numbers: Accounting-Based and Market-Based Estimates of Systematic Risk." *Journal of Financial and Quantitative Analysis*, Vol. 8 (1973), pp. 438-443.

[13] Hurdle, G. J. "Leverage, Risk, Market Structure and Profitability." *The Review of Economics and Statistics*, Vol. 56 (1974), pp. 478-485.

[14] Johnston, J. *Econometric Methods*, 2nd ed. New York: McGraw-Hill (1972).

[15] King, B. F. "Market and Industry Factors in Stock Price Behavior." *Journal of Business*, Vol. 39 (1966), pp. 139-190.

[16] Klein, L. R., and Mitsugu Nakamura. "Singularity in the Equation Systems of Econometrics: Some Aspects of the Problem of Multicollinearity." *International Economic Review*, Vol. 3 (1962), pp. 274-299.

[17] Krainer, R. E. "Interest Rates, Leverage, and Investor Rationality." *Journal of Financial and Quantitative Analysis*, Vol. 12 (1977), pp. 1-31.

[18] Lee, C. F., and W. P. Lloyd. "Block Decursive Systems in Asset Pricing Models: An Extension." *Journal of Finance*, Vol. 33 (1978), pp. 640-644.

[19] Lee, C. F., and J. D. Vinso. "Simultaneous Equation Market Models: A New Approach to the Problem of Multicollinearity." Working Paper No. 11-76, Rodney L. White Center for Financial Research, University of Pennsylvania (1976).

[20] _____. "The Single vs. Simultaneous Equation Model in Capital Asset Pricing." *Journal of Business Research*, Vol. 10 (1980), pp. 65-80.

[21] Lee, C. F., and J. K. Zumwalt. "Alternative Specifications and Estimations of the Capital Asset Pricing Process: An Empirical Analysis." *Business and Economic Statistics Section, 1978 American Statistical Association Proceedings* (1978), pp. 389-394.

[22] Livingston, M. "Industry Movements of Common Stocks." *Journal of Finance*, Vol. 32 (1977), pp. 861-874.

[23] Meyers, S. L. "A Re-examination of Market and Industry Factors in Stock Price Behavior." *Journal of Finance*, Vol. 28 (1973), pp. 695-705.

[24] Miller, M. H., and F. Modigliani. "Some Estimates of the Cost of Capital to the Electric Utility Industry, 1954-57." *American Economic Review*, Vol. 56 (1966), pp. 333-391.

[25] Nerlove, M. "Further Evidence on the Estimation of Dynamic Economic Relations from a Time Series of Cross Sections." *Econometrica*, Vol. 39 (1971), pp. 359-382.

[26] Rosenberg, B. "Extra-Market Components of Covariance in Security Analysis." *Journal of Financial and Quantitative Analysis*, Vol. 9 (1974), pp. 275-284.

[27] Sharpe, W. F. "Capital Asset Prices: A Theory of Market Equilibrium under Conditions of Risks." *Journal of Finance*, Vol. 19 (1964), pp. 425-442.

[28] Simkowitz, M. A., and D. E. Logue. "The Interdependent Structure of Security Returns." *Journal of Financial and Quantitative Analysis*, Vol. 8 (1973), pp. 259-272.

[29] Theil, H. *Principles of Econometrics*. New York: John Wiley & Sons, Inc. (1971).

[30] Zellner, A. "An Efficient Method of Estimating Seemingly Unrelated Regressions and Tests for Aggregation Bias." *Journal of the American Statistical Association*, Vol. 57 (1962), pp. 348-368.

Industry Listing

2-Digit SIC Code	Industry Title	Number of Firms
10	Metal Mining	9
12	Bituminous Coal and Lignite Mining	4
13	Oil and Gas Extraction	3
16	Heavy Construction Contractors	3
20	Food and Kindred Products	38*
21	Tobacco Manufactures	7
22	Textile Mill Products	9
23	Apparel and Other Textile Products	9
24	Lumber and Wood Products	7
25	Furniture and Fixtures	3
26	Paper and Allied Products	16*
27	Printing and Publishing	10
28	Chemicals and Allied Products	59*
29	Petroleum and Coal Products	28*
30	Rubber and Misc. Plastics Products	12
31	Leather and Leather Products	3
32	Stone, Clay, and Glass Products	20*
33	Primary Metal Industries	32*
34	Fabricated Metal Products	17*
35	Machinery, Except Electrical	42*
36	Electric and Electronic Equipment	27*
37	Transportation Equipment	39*
38	Instruments and Related Products	15*
39	Miscellaneous Manufacturing Industries	8
42	Trucking and Warehousing	3
45	Transportation By Air	12
48	Communication	7
50	Wholesale Trade--Durable Goods	2
51	Wholesale Trade--Nondurable Goods	4
53	General Merchandise Stores	17*
54	Food Stores	11
56	Apparel and Accessory Stores	4
59	Miscellaneous Retail	5
78	Motion Pictures	2
99	Nonclassifiable Establishments	8

*Indicates the clustering procedure was utilized.

The Journal of FINANCE

| Vol. XXIII | September 1968 | No. 4 |

FINANCIAL RATIOS, DISCRIMINANT ANALYSIS AND THE PREDICTION OF CORPORATE BANKRUPTCY

EDWARD I. ALTMAN*

ACADEMICIANS SEEM to be moving toward the elimination of ratio analysis as an analytical technique in assessing the performance of the business enterprise. Theorists downgrade arbitrary rules of thumb, such as company ratio comparisons, widely used by practitioners. Since attacks on the relevance of ratio analysis emanate from many esteemed members of the scholarly world, does this mean that ratio analysis is limited to the world of "nuts and bolts"? Or, has the significance of such an approach been unattractively garbed and therefore unfairly handicapped? Can we bridge the gap, rather than sever the link, between traditional ratio "analysis" and the more rigorous statistical techniques which have become popular among academicians in recent years?

The purpose of this paper is to attempt an assessment of this issue—the quality of ratio analysis as an analytical technique. The prediction of corporate bankruptcy is used as an illustrative case.[1] Specifically, a set of financial and economic ratios will be investigated in a bankruptcy prediction context wherein a multiple discriminant statistical methodology is employed. The data used in the study are limited to manufacturing corporations.

A brief review of the development of traditional ratio analysis as a technique for investigating corporate performance is presented in section I. In section II the shortcomings of this approach are discussed and multiple discriminant analysis is introduced with the emphasis centering on its compatibility with ratio analysis in a bankruptcy prediction context. The discriminant model is developed in section III, where an initial sample of sixty-six firms is utilized to establish a function which best discriminates between companies in two mutually exclusive groups: bankrupt and non-bankrupt firms. Section IV reviews empirical results obtained from the initial sample and several secondary samples, the latter being selected to examine the reliability of the discriminant

* Assistant Professor of Finance, New York University. The author acknowledges the helpful suggestions and comments of Keith V. Smith, Edward F. Renshaw, Lawrence S. Ritter and the *Journal's* reviewer. The research was conducted while under a Regents Fellowship at the University of California, Los Angeles.

1. In this study the term bankruptcy will, except where otherwise noted, refer to those firms that are legally bankrupt and either placed in receivership or have been granted the right to reorganize under the provisions of the National Bankruptcy Act.

model as a predictive technique. In section V the model's adaptability to practical decision-making situations and its potential benefits in a variety of situations are suggested. The final section summarizes the findings and conclusions of the study, and assesses the role and significance of traditional ratio analysis within a modern analytical context.

I. TRADITIONAL RATIO ANALYSIS

The detection of company operating and financial difficulties is a subject which has been particularly susceptible to financial ratio analysis. Prior to the development of quantitative measures of company performance, agencies were established to supply a qualitative type of information assessing the creditworthiness of particular merchants.[2] Formal aggregate studies concerned with portents of business failure were evident in the 1930's. A study at that time[3] and several later ones concluded that failing firms exhibit significantly different ratio measurements than continuing entities.[4] In addition, another study was concerned with ratios of large asset-size corporations that experienced difficulties in meeting their fixed indebtedness obligations.[5] A recent study involved the analysis of financial ratios in a bankruptcy-prediction context.[6] This latter work compared a list of ratios individually for failed firms and a matched sample of non-failed firms. Observed evidence for five years prior to failure was cited as conclusive that ratio analysis can be useful in the prediction of failure.

The aforementioned studies imply a definite potential of ratios as predictors of bankruptcy. In general, ratios measuring profitability, liquidity, and solvency prevailed as the most significant indicators. The order of their importance is not clear since almost every study cited a different ratio as being the most effective indication of impending problems.

II. MULTIPLE DISCRIMINANT ANALYSIS

The previous section cited several studies devoted to the analysis of a firm's condition prior to financial difficulties. Although these works established certain important generalizations regarding the performance and trends of particular measurements, the adaptation of their results for assessing bankruptcy

2. For instance, the forerunner of well known Dun & Bradstreet, Inc. was organized in 1849 in Cincinnati, Ohio, in order to provide independent credit investigations. For an interesting and informative discussion on the development of credit agencies and financial measures of company performance, see, Roy A. Foulke, *Practical Financial Statement Analysis*, 5th Ed., (New York, McGraw-Hill, 1961).

3. R. F. Smith and A. H. Winakor, *Changes in the Financial Structure of Unsuccessful Corporations.* (University of Illinois: Bureau of Business Research, 1935).

4. For instance, a comprehensive study covering over 900 firms compared discontinuing firms with continuing ones, see C. Merwin, *Financing Small Corporations* (New York: Bureau of Economic Research, 1942).

5. W. B. Hickman, *Corporate Bond Quality and Investor Experience* (Princeton, N.J.: Princeton University Press, 1958).

6. W. H. Beaver, "Financial Ratios as Predictors of Failure," *Empirical Research in Accounting, Selected Studies, 1966* (Institute of Professional Accounting, January, 1967), pp. 71-111. Also a recent attempt was made to weight ratios arbitrarily, see M. Tamari, "Financial Ratios as a Means of Forecasting Bankruptcy," *Management International Review,* Vol. 4 (1966), pp. 15-21.

potential of firms, both theoretically and practically, is questionable.[7] In almost every case, the methodology was essentially univariate in nature and emphasis was placed on individual signals of impending problems.[8] Ratio analysis presented in this fashion is susceptible to faulty interpretation and is potentially confusing. For instance, a firm with a poor profitability and/or solvency record may be regarded as a potential bankrupt. However, because of its above average liquidity, the situation may not be considered serious. The potential ambiguity as to the relative performance of several firms is clearly evident. The crux of the shortcomings inherent in any univariate analysis lies therein. An appropriate extension of the previously cited studies, therefore, is to build upon their findings and to combine several measures into a meaningful predictive model. In so doing, the highlights of ratio analysis as an analytical technique will be emphasized rather than downgraded. The question becomes, which ratios are most important in detecting bankruptcy potential, what weights should be attached to those selected ratios, and how should the weights be objectively established.

After careful consideration of the nature of the problem and of the purpose of the paper, a multiple discriminant analysis (MDA) was chosen as the appropriate statistical technique. Although not as popular as regression analysis, MDA has been utilized in a variety of disciplines since its first application in the 1930's.[9] During those earlier years MDA was used mainly in the biological and behavioral sciences.[10] More recently this method had been applied successfully to financial problems such as consumer credit evaluation[11] and investment classification. For instance in the latter area, Walter utilized a MDA model to classify high and low price earnings ratio firms,[12] and Smith applied the technique in the classification of firms into standard investment categories.[13]

MDA is a statistical technique used to classify an observation into one of several *a priori* groupings dependent upon the observation's individual characteristics. It is used primarily to classify and/or make predictions in problems

7. At this point bankruptcy is used in its most general sense, meaning simply business failure.

8. Exceptions to this generalization were noted in works where there was an attempt to emphasize the importance of a group of ratios as an indication of overall performance. For instance, Foulke, *op. cit.,* chapters XIV and XV, and A. Wall and R. W. Duning, *Ratio Analysis of Financial Statements,* (New York: Harper and Row, 1928), p. 159.

9. R. A. Fisher, "The Use of Multiple Measurements in Taxonomic Problems," *Annals of Eugenics,* No. 7 (September, 1936), pp. 179-188.

10. For a comprehensive review of studies using MDA see W. G. Cochran, "On the Performance of the Linear Discriminant Function," *Technometrics,* vol. 6 (May, 1964), pp. 179-190.

11. The pioneering work utilizing MDA in a financial context was performed by Durand in evaluating the credit worthiness of used car loan applicants, see D. D. Durand, *Risk Elements in Consumer Installment Financing,* Studies in Consumer Installment Financing (New York: National Bureau of Economic Research, 1941), pp. 105-142. More recently, Myers and Forgy analyzed several techniques, including MDA, in the evaluation of good and bad installment loans, see H. Myers and E. W. Forgy, "Development of Numerical Credit Evaluation Systems," *Journal of American Statistical Association,* vol. 50 (September, 1963), pp. 797-806.

12. J. E. Walter, "A Discriminant Function for Earnings Price Ratios of Large Industrial Corporations," *Review of Economics and Statistics,* vol. XLI (February, 1959), pp. 44-52.

13. K. V. Smith, *Classification of Investment Securities Using MDA,* Institute Paper #101 (Purdue University, Institute for Research in the Behavioral, Economic, and Management Sciences, 1965).

where the dependent variable appears in qualitative form, e.g., male or female, bankrupt or non-bankrupt. Therefore, the first step is to establish explicit group classifications. The number of original groups can be two or more.

After the groups are established, data are collected for the objects in the groups; MDA then attempts to derive a linear combination of these characteristics which "best" discriminates between the groups. If a particular object, for instance a corporation, has characteristics (financial ratios) which can be quantified for all of the companies in the analysis, the MDA determines a set of discriminant coefficients. When these coefficients are applied to the actual ratio, a basis for classification into one of the mutually exclusive groupings exists. The MDA technique has the advantage of considering an entire profile of characteristics common to the relevant firms, as well as the interaction of these properties. A univariate study, on the other hand, can only consider the measurements used for group assignments one at a time.

Another advantage of MDA is the reduction of the analyst's space dimensionality, i.e., from the number of different independent variables to G - 1 dimension(s), where G equals the number of original *a priori* groups.[14] This paper is concerned with two groups, consisting of bankrupt firms on the one hand, and of non-bankrupt firms on the other. Therefore, the analysis is transformed into its simplest form: one dimension. The discriminant function of the form $Z = v_1 x_1 + v_2 x_2 + \ldots + v_n x_n$ transforms individual variable values to a single discriminant score or Z value which is then used to classify the object

$$\text{where } v_1, v_2, \ldots v_n = \text{Discriminant coefficients}$$

$$x_1, x_2, \ldots x_n = \text{Independent variables}$$

The MDA computes the discriminant coefficients, v_j, while the independent variables x_j are the actual values

$$\text{where, } j = 1, 2, \ldots n.$$

When utilizing a comprehensive list of financial ratios in assessing a firm's bankruptcy potential there is reason to believe that some of the measurements will have a high degree of correlation or collinearity with each other. While this aspect necessitates careful selection of the predictive variables (ratios), it also has the advantage of yielding a model with a relatively small number of selected measurements which has the potential of conveying a great deal of information. This information might very well indicate differences between groups but whether or not these differences are significant and meaningful is a more important aspect of the analysis. To be sure, there are differences between bankrupt firms and healthy ones; but are these differences of a magnitude to facilitate the development of an accurate prediction model?

Perhaps the primary advantage of MDA in dealing with classification problems is the potential of analyzing the entire variable profile of the object simultaneously rather than sequentially examining its individual characteristics.

14. For a formulation of the mathematical computations involved in MDA, see J. G. Bryan, "The Generalized Discriminant Function, Mathematical Foundation & Computational Routine," *Harvard Educational Review,* vol. XXI, no. 2 (Spring, 1951), pp. 90-95, and C. R. Rao, *Advanced Statistical Methods in Biometric Research* (New York: John Wiley & Sons, Inc., 1952).

Just as linear and integer programming have improved upon traditional techniques in capital budgeting[15] the MDA approach to traditional ratio analysis has the potential to reformulate the problem correctly. Specifically, combinations of ratios can be analyzed together in order to remove possible ambiguities and misclassifications observed in earlier traditional studies.

Given the above descriptive qualities, the MDA technique was selected as most appropriate for the bankruptcy study. A carefully devised and interpreted multiple regression analysis methodology conceivably could have been used in this two group case.

III. DEVELOPMENT OF THE MODEL

Sample Selection. The initial sample is composed of sixty-six corporations with thirty-three firms in each of the two groups. The bankrupt group (1) are manufacturers that filed a bankruptcy petition under Chapter X of the National Bankruptcy Act during the period 1946-1965.[16] The mean asset size of these firms is $6.4 million, with a range of between $0.7 million and $25.9 million. Recognizing that this group is not completely homogeneous, due to industry and size differences, a careful selection of non-bankrupt firms was attempted. Group 2 consisted of a paired sample of manufacturing firms chosen on a stratified random basis. The firms are stratified by industry and by size, with the asset size range restricted to between $1-$25 million.[17] Firms in Group 2 were still in existence in 1966. Also, the data collected are from the same years as those compiled for the bankrupt firms. For the initial sample test, the data are derived from financial statements one reporting period prior to bankruptcy.[18]

An important issue is to determine the asset-size group to be sampled. The decision to eliminate both the small firms (under $1 million in total assets) and the very large companies from the initial sample essentially is due to the asset range of the firms in Group 1. In addition, the incidence of bankruptcy in the large asset-size firm is quite rare today while the absence of comprehensive data negated the representation of small firms. A frequent argument is that financial ratios, by their very nature, have the effect of deflating statistics by size, and therefore a good deal of the size effect is eliminated. To choose Group 1 firms in a restricted size range is not feasible, while selecting firms for Group 2 at random seemed unwise. However, subsequent tests to the original sample do not use size as a means of stratification.[19]

15. H. M. Weingartner, *Mathematical Programming and the Analysis of Capital Budgeting, Budgeting Problems,* (Englewood Cliffs, New Jersey: Prentice-Hall, 1963).

16. The choice of a twenty year period is not the best procedure since average ratios do shift over time. Ideally we would prefer to examine a list of ratios in time period t in order to make predictions about other firms in the following period (t + 1). Unfortunately it was not possible to do this because of data limitations. However, the number of bankruptcies were approximately evenly distributed over the twenty year period in both the original and the secondary samples.

17. The mean asset size of the firms in Group 2 ($9.6 million) was slightly greater than that of Group 1, but matching exact asset size of the two groups seemed unnecessary.

18. The data was derived from Moody's Industrial Manuals and selected Annual Reports. The average lead time of the financial statements was approximately seven and one-half months prior to bankruptcy.

19. One of these tests included only firms that experienced operating losses (secondary sample of non-bankrupt firms).

After the initial groups are defined and firms selected, balance sheet and income statement data are collected. Because of the large number of variables found to be significant indicators of corporate problems in past studies, a list of twenty-two potentially helpful variables (ratios) is compiled for evaluation. The variables are classified into five standard ratio categories, including liquidity, profitability, leverage, solvency, and activity ratios. The ratios are chosen on the basis of their 1) popularity in the literature,[20] 2) potential relevancy to the study, and a few "new" ratios initiated in this paper.

From the original list of variables, five variables are selected as doing the best overall job together in the prediction of corporate bankruptcy.[21] In order to arrive at a final profile of variables the following procedures are utilized: (1) Observation of the statistical significance of various alternative functions including determination of the relative contributions of each independent variable; (2) evaluation of inter-correlations between the relevant variables; (3) observation of the predictive accuracy of the various profiles; and (4) judgment of the analyst.

The variable profile finally established did not contain the most significant variables, amongst the twenty-two original ones, measured independently. This would not necessarily improve upon the univariate, traditional analysis described earlier. The contribution of the entire profile is evaluated, and since this process is essentially iterative, there is no claim regarding the optimality of the resulting discriminant function. The function, however, does the best job among the alternatives which include numerous computer runs analyzing different ratio-profiles. The final discriminant function is as follows:

(I) $\quad Z = .012X_1 + .014X_2 + .033X_3 + .006X_4 + .999X_5$
where $X_1 =$ Working capital/Total assets
$\qquad X_2 =$ Retained Earnings/Total assets
$\qquad X_3 =$ Earnings before interest and taxes/Total assets
$\qquad X_4 =$ Market value equity/Book value of total debt
$\qquad X_5 =$ Sales/Total assets
$\qquad Z =$ Overall Index

X_1—*Working Capital/Total Assets.* The Working capital/Total assets ratio, frequently found in studies of corporate problems, is a measure of the net liquid assets of the firm relative to the total capitalization. Working capital is defined as the difference between current assets and current liabilities. Liquidity and size characteristics are explicitly considered. Ordinarily, a firm experiencing consistent operating losses will have shrinking current assets in relation to total assets. Of the three liquidity ratios evaluated, this one proved to be the most valuable.[22] Inclusion of this variable is consistent with the Merwin study which

20. The Beaver study (cited earlier) concluded that the cash flow to debt ratio was the best single ratio predictor. This ratio was not considered here because of the lack of consistent appearance of precise depreciation data. The results obtained, however (see section IV), are superior to the results Beaver attained with his single best ratio, see Beaver, *op. cit.,* p. 89.

21. The MDA computer program used in this study was developed by W. Cooley and P. Lohnes. The data are organized in a blocked format; the bankrupt firms' data first followed by the non-bankrupt firms'.

22. The other two liquidity ratios were the current ratio and the quick ratio. The Working capital/Total assets ratio showed greater statistical significance both on a univariate and multi-variate basis.

rated the net working capital to total asset ratio as the best indicator of ultimate discontinuance.[23]

X_2—*Retained Earnings/Total Assets*.[24] This measure of cumulative profitability over time was cited earlier as one of the "new" ratios. The age of a firm is implicitly considered in this ratio. For example, a relatively young firm will probably show a low RE/TA ratio because it has not had time to build up its cumulative profits. Therefore, it may be argued that the young firm is somewhat discriminated against in this analysis, and its chance of being classified as bankrupt is relatively higher than another, older firm, *ceteris paribus*. But, this is precisely the situation in the real world. The incidence of failure is much higher in a firm's earlier years.[25]

X_3—*Earnings Before Interest and Taxes/Total Assets*. This ratio is calculated by dividing the total assets of a firm into its earnings before interest and tax reductions. In essence, it is a measure of the true productivity of the firm's assets, abstracting from any tax or leverage factors. Since a firm's ultimate existence is based on the earning power of its assets, this ratio appears to be particularly appropriate for studies dealing with corporate failure. Furthermore, insolvency in a bankruptcy sense occurs when the total liabilities exceed a fair valuation of the firm's assets with value determined by the earning power of the assets.

X_4—*Market Value of Equity/Book Value of Total Debt*. Equity is measured by the combined market value of all shares of stock, preferred and common, while debt includes both current and long-term. The measure shows how much the firm's assets can decline in value (measured by market value of equity plus debt) before the liabilities exceed the assets and the firm becomes insolvent. For example, a company with a market value of its equity of $1,000 and debt of $500 could experience a two-thirds drop in asset value before insolvency. However, the same firm with $250 in equity will be insolvent if its drop is only one-third in value. This ratio adds a market value dimension which other failure studies did not consider.[26] It also appears to be a more effective predictor of bankruptcy than a similar, more commonly used ratio: Net worth/Total debt (book values).

X_5—*Sales/Total Assets*. The capital-turnover ratio is a standard financial ratio illustrating the sales generating ability of the firm's assets. It is one measure of management's capability in dealing with competitive conditions. This final ratio is quite important because, as indicated below, it is the least

23. Merwin, *op. cit.*, p. 99.

24. Retained Earnings is the account which reports the total amount of reinvested earnings and/or losses of a firm over its entire life. The account is also referred to as Earned Surplus. It should be noted that the Retained Earnings account is subject to manipulation via corporate quasi-reorganizations and stock dividend declarations. While these occurrences are not evident in this study it is conceivable that a bias would be created by a substantial reorganization or stock dividend.

25. In 1965, over 50 per cent of all manufacturing firms that failed did so in the first five years of their existence. Over 31 per cent failed within three years. Statistics taken from *The Failure Record, Through 1965* (New York: Dun & Bradstreet, Inc., 1966), p. 10.

26. The reciprocal of X_4 is the familiar Debt/Equity ratio often used as a measure of financial leverage. X_4 is a slightly modified version of one of the variables used effectively by Fisher in a study of corporate bond interest rate differentials, see Lawrence Fisher, "Determinants of Risk Premiums on Corporate Bonds," *Journal of Political Economy*, LXVII, No. 3 (June, 1959), pp. 217-237.

significant ratio on an individual basis. In fact, based on the statistical significance measure, it would not have appeared at all. However, because of its
unique relationship to other variables in the model, the Sales/Total assets ratio
ranks second in its contribution to the overall discriminating ability of the
model.

To test the individual discriminating ability of the variables, an "F" test is
performed. This test relates the difference between the average values of the
ratios in each group to the variability (or spread) of values of the ratios within
each group. Variable means one financial statement prior to bankruptcy and
the resulting "F" statistics are presented in Table 1.

TABLE 1

VARIABLE MEANS AND TEST OF SIGNIFICANCE

Variable	Bankrupt Group Mean	Non-Bankrupt Group Mean	F Ratio
	$n = 33$	$n = 33$	
X_1	− 6.1%	41.4%	32.60*
X_2	−62.6%	35.5%	58.86*
X_3	−31.8%	15.3%	26.56*
X_4	40.1%	247.7%	33.26*
X_5	150.0%	190.0%	2.84

* Significant at the .001 level.

$$F_{1,60} (.001) = 12.00$$
$$F_{1,60} (.01) = 7.00$$
$$F_{1,60} (.05) = 4.00$$

Variables X_1 through X_4 are all significant at the .001 level, indicating extremely significant differences in these variables between groups. Variable X_5
does not show a significant difference between groups and the reason for its
inclusion in the variable profile is not apparent as yet. On a strictly univariate
level, all of the ratios indicate higher values for the non-bankrupt firms. Also,
the discriminant coefficients of equation (I) display positive signs, which is
what one would expect. Therefore, the greater a firm's bankruptcy potential,
the lower its discriminant score.

One useful technique in arriving at the final variable profile is to determine
the relative contribution of each variable to the total discriminating power of
the function, and the interaction between them. The relevant statistic is observed as a scaled vector which is computed by multiplying corresponding elements by the square roots of the diagonal elements of the variance-co-variance
matrix.[27] Since the actual variable measurement units are not all comparable to
each other, simple observation of the discriminant coefficients is misleading.
The adjusted coefficients shown in Table 2 enable us to evaluate each variable's
contribution on a relative basis.

The scaled vectors indicate that the large contributors to group separation

27. For example, the square root of the appropriate variance-covariance figure (standard deviation) for X_1 is approximately 275 and when multiplied by the variable's coefficient (.012) yields a
scaled vector of 3.29.

of the discriminant function are X_3, X_5, and X_4, respectively. The profitability ratio contributes the most, which is not surprising if one considers that the incidence of bankruptcy in a firm that is earning a profit is almost nil. What is surprising, however, is the second highest contribution of X_5 (Sales/Total assets). Recalling that this ratio was insignificant on a univariate basis, the multivariate context is responsible for illuminating the importance of X_5.[28] A probable reason for this unexpected result is the high negative correlation $(-.78)$ we observe between X_3 and X_5 in the bankruptcy group. The negative correlation is also evident in subsequent bankrupt group samples.

TABLE 2
RELATIVE CONTRIBUTION OF THE VARIABLES

Variable	Scaled Vector	Ranking
X_1	3.29	5
X_2	6.04	4
X_3	9.89	1
X_4	7.42	3
X_5	8.41	2

In a recent evaluation of the discriminant function, Cochran concluded that most correlations between variables in past studies were positive and that, by and large, negative correlations are more helpful than positive correlations in adding new information to the function.[29] The logic behind the high negative correlation in the bankrupt group is that as firms suffer losses and deteriorate toward failure, their assets are not replaced as much as in healthier times, and also the cumulative losses have further reduced the asset size through debits to Retained Earnings. The asset size reduction apparently dominates any sales movements.

A different argument, but one not necessarily inconsistent with the above, concerns a similar ratio to X_5, Net Sales to Tangible Net Worth. If the latter ratio is excessive the firm is often referred to as a poor credit risk due to insufficient capital to support sales. Companies with moderate or even below average sales generating lower (low asset turnover, X_5) might very well possess an extremely high Net Sales/Net Worth ratio if the Net Worth has been reduced substantially due to cumulative operating losses. This ratio, and other net worth ratios, are not considered in the paper because of computational and interpretive difficulties arising when negative net worth totals are present.

It is clear that four of the five variables display significant differences between groups, but the importance of MDA is its ability to separate groups using multivariate measures. A test to determine the overall discriminating power of the model is the common F-value which is the ratio of the sums-of-squares

28. For an excellent discussion of how a seemingly insignificant variable on a univariate basis can supply important information in a multivariate context see, W. W. Cooley and P. R. Lohnes *Multivariate Procedures for the Behavioral Sciences* (New York: John Wiley and Sons, Inc., 1962), p. 121.

29. Cochran, *op. cit.*, p. 182.

between-groups to the within-groups sums-of-squares. When this ratio of the form,

$$\lambda = \frac{\displaystyle\sum_{g=1}^{G} N_g [\bar{y}_g - \bar{y}]^2}{\displaystyle\sum_{g=1}^{G} \sum_{p=1}^{N_g} [y_{pg} - \bar{y}_g]^2}$$

where

G = Number of groups
g = Group g, g = 1 ... G
N_g = Number of firms in group g
y_{pg} = Firm p in group g, p = 1 ... N_g
$\bar{y}_g$ = Group mean (centroid)
$\bar{y}$ = Overall sample mean

is maximized, it has the effect of spreading the means (centroids) of the G groups apart and, simultaneously, reducing dispersion of the individual points (firm Z values, y_{pg}) about their respective group means. Logically, this test (commonly called the "F" test) is appropriate because one of the objectives of the MDA is to identify and to utilize those variables which best discriminate *between* groups and which are most similar *within* groups.

The group means, or centroids, of the original two-group sample of the form

$$\bar{y}_g = \frac{1}{N_g} \sum_{p=1}^{N_g} y_{pg}$$

are

Group 1 = —0.29   F = 20.7
Group 2 = +5.02 $F_{5,60}$ (.01) = 3.34

The significance test therefore *rejects* the null hypothesis that the observations come from the same population. With the conclusion that *a priori* groups are significantly different, further discriminatory analysis is possible.

Once the values of the discriminant coefficients are estimated, it is possible to calculate discriminant scores for each observation in the sample, or any firm, and to assign the observations to one of the groups based on this score. The essence of the procedure is to compare the profile of an individual firm with that of the alternative groupings. In this manner the firm is assigned to the group it most closely resembles. The comparisons are measured by a chi-square value and assignments are made based upon the relative proximity of the firm's score to the various group centroids.

IV. EMPIRICAL RESULTS

At the outset, it might be helpful to illustrate the format for presenting the results. In the multi-group case, results are shown in a classification chart or "accuracy-matrix." The chart is set up as follows:

Actual Group Membership	Predicted Group Membership	
	Bankrupt	Non-Bankrupt
Bankrupt	H	M_1
Non-Bankrupt	M_2	H

The actual group membership is equivalent to the *a priori* groupings and the model attempts to classify correctly these firms. At this stage, the model is basically explanatory. When new companies are classified, the nature of the model is predictive.

The H's stand for correct classifications (Hits) and the M's stand for mis-classifications (Misses). M_1 represents a Type I error and M_2 a Type II error. The sum of the diagonal elements equals the total correct "hits," and when divided into the total number of firms classified (sixty-six in the case of the initial sample), yields the measure of success of the MDA in classifying firms, that is, the per cent of firms correctly classified. This percentage is analogous to the coefficient of determination (R^2) in regression analysis, which measures the per cent of the variation of the dependent variable explained by the independent variables.

The final criterion used to establish the best model was to observe its accuracy in predicting bankruptcy. A series of six tests were performed.

(1) *Initial Sample (Group 1)*. The initial sample of 33 firms in each of the two groups is examined using data one financial statement prior to bankruptcy. Since the discriminant coefficients and the group distributions are derived from this sample, a high degree of successful classification is expected. This should occur because the firms are classified using a discriminant function which, in fact, is based upon the individual measurements of these same firms. The classification matrix for the initial sample is as follows:

				Predicted	
			Actual	Group 1	Group 2
			Group 1	31	2
			Group 2	1	32

	Number Correct	Per cent Correct	Per cent Error	n
Type I	31	94	6	33
Type II	32	97	3	33
Total	63	95	5	66

The model is extremely accurate in classifying 95 per cent of the total sample correctly. The *Type I error* proved to be only 6 per cent, while the *Type II error* was even better at 3 per cent. The results, therefore, are encouraging, but the obvious upward bias should be kept in mind and further validation techniques are appropriate.

(2) *Results Two Years Prior to Bankruptcy*. The second test is made to observe the discriminating ability of the model for firms using data from two

years prior to bankruptcy. The two year period is an exaggeration since the average lead time for the correctly classified firms is appoximately twenty months with two firms having a thirteen month lead. The results are:

	Predicted	
	Group 1 (Bankrupt)	Group 2 (Non-Bankrupt)
Group 1	23	9
Group 2	2	31

	Number Correct	Per cent Correct	Per cent Error	n
Type I	23	72	28	32
Type II	31	94	6	33
Total	54	83	17	65

The reduction in the accuracy of group classification is understandable because impending bankruptcy is more remote and the indications are less clear. Nevertheless, 72 per cent correct assignment is evidence that bankruptcy can be predicted two years prior to the event. The Type II error is slightly larger (6 per cent vs. 3 per cent) in this test but still is extremely accurate. Further tests will be applied below to determine the accuracy of predicting bankruptcy as much as five years prior to the actual event.

(3) *Potential Bias and Validation Techniques.* When the firms used to determine the discriminant coefficients are re-classified, the resulting accuracy is biased upward by (a) sampling errors in the original sample and (b) search bias. The latter bias is inherent in the process of reducing the original set of variables (twenty-two) to the best variable profile (five). The possibility of bias due to intensive searching is inherent in any empirical study. While a subset of variables is effective in the initial sample, there is no guarantee that it will be effective for the population in general.

The importance of secondary sample testing cannot be over-emphasized and it appears appropriate to apply these measures at this stage. A method suggested by Frank et al.[30] for testing the extent of the aforementioned search bias was applied to the initial sample. The essence of this test is to estimate parameters for the model using only a subset of the original sample, and then to classify the remainder of the sample based on the parameters established. A simple t-test is then applied to test the significance of the results.

Five different replications of the suggested method of choosing subsets (sixteen firms) of the original sample are tested, with results listed in Table 3.[31]

The test results reject the hypothesis that there is no difference between the groups and substantiate that the model does, in fact, possess discriminating

30. R. E. Frank, W. F. Massy, and G. D. Morrison, "Bias in Multiple Discriminant Analysis," *Journal of Marketing Research,* vol. 2 (August 1965), pp. 250-258.

31. The five replications included (1) random sampling (2) choosing every other firm starting with firm number one, (3) starting with firm number two, (4) choosing firms 1-16, and (5) firms 17-32.

power on observations other than those used to establish the parameters of the model. Therefore, any search bias does not appear significant.

TABLE 3
ACCURACY OF CLASSIFYING A SECONDARY SAMPLE

Replication	Per cent of Correct Classifications	Value of t
1	91.2	4.8*
2	91.2	4.8*
3	97.0	5.5*
4	97.0	4.5*
5	91.2	4.8*
Average	93.5	5.1*
Total number of observations per replication		34

* Significant at the .001 level.

$$t = \frac{\text{proportion correct} - .5}{\sqrt{\dfrac{.5(1 - .5)}{n}}}$$

(4) *Secondary Sample of Bankrupt Firms.* In order to test the model rigorously for both bankrupt and non-bankrupt firms two new samples are introduced. The first contains a new sample of twenty-five bankrupt firms whose asset-size range is the same as that of the initial bankrupt group. Using the parameters established in the discriminant model to classify firms in this secondary sample, the predictive accuracy for this sample as of one statement prior to bankruptcy is:

		Predicted	
		Bankrupt	Non-Bankrupt
Bankrupt Group (Actual)		24	1

	Number Correct	Per cent Correct	Per cent Error	n
Type I (total)	24	96	4	25

The results here are surprising in that one would not usually expect a secondary sample's results to be superior to the initial discriminant sample (96 per cent vs. 94 per cent). Two possible reasons are that the upward bias normally present in the initial sample tests is not manifested in this investigation, and/or the model, as stated before, is something less than optimal.

(5) *Secondary Sample of Non-Bankrupt Firms.* Up to this point the sample companies were chosen either by their bankruptcy status (Group 1) or by their similarity to Group 1 in all aspects except their economic well-being. But what of the many firms which suffer temporary profitability difficulties, but in actuality do not become bankrupt. A bankruptcy classification of a firm from this group is an example of a *Type II error.* An exceptionally rigorous

59

test of the discriminant model's effectiveness would be to search out a large sample of firms that have encountered earnings problems and then to observe the MDA's classification results.

In order to perform the above test, a sample of sixty-six firms is selected on the basis of net income (deficit) reports in the years 1958 and 1961, with thirty-three from each year. Over 65 per cent of these firms had suffered two or three years of negative profits in the previous three years reporting. The firms are selected regardless of their asset size, with the only two criteria being that they were manufacturing firms which suffered losses in the year 1958 or 1961.[32] The two base years are chosen due to their relatively poor economic performances in terms of GNP growth. The companies are then evaluated by the discriminant model to determine their predictive bankruptcy potential.

The results, illustrated below, show that fifteen of the sixty-six firms are classified as bankrupts with the remaining fifty-one correctly classified. The number of misclassifications is actually fourteen, as one of the firms went bankrupt within two years after the data period.

		Predicted		
		Bankrupt		Non-Bankrupt
Non-Bankrupt Group Actual		14		52
	Number Correct	Per cent Correct	Per cent Error	n
Type II (total)	52	79	21	66

Therefore, the discriminant model correctly classified 79 per cent of the sample firms. This percentage is all the more impressive when one considers that these firms constitute a *secondary* sample of admittedly *below average* performance. The t-test for the significance of this result is t = 4.8; significant at the .001 level.

Another interesting facet of this test is the relationship of these "temporarily" sick firms' Z scores, and the "zone of ignorance" or gray-area described more completely in the next section. Briefly, the "zone of ignorance" is that range of Z scores (see Chart I) where misclassifications can be observed. Chart I illustrates some of the individual firm Z scores (initial sample) and the group centroids. These points are plotted in one dimensional space and, therefore, are easily visualized.

Of the fourteen misclassified firms in this secondary sample, ten have Z scores between 1.81 and 2.67, which indicates that although they are classified as bankrupts, the prediction of bankruptcy is not as definite as the vast majority in the initial sample of bankrupt firms. In fact, just under one-third of the sixty-six firms in this last sample have Z scores within the entire overlap area, which emphasizes that the selection process is successful in choosing firms which showed signs (profitability) of deterioration.

32. The firms were selected at random from all the firms listed in *Standard and Poor's Stock Guide,* January 1959, 1962, that reported negative earnings.

Chart I

INDIVIDUAL FIRM DISCRIMINANT SCORES AND GROUP CENTROIDS--ONE YEAR PRIOR TO BANKRUPTCY

$$(Z = .012 \, X_1 + .014 \, X_2 + .033 \, X_3 + .006 \, X_4 + .999 \, X_5)$$

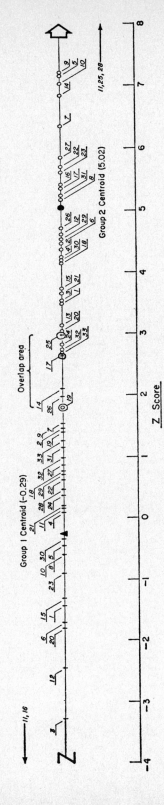

KEY:

t	= Discriminate Points (Group 1 - Bankrupt Firms)	n = 33
o	= Discriminate Points (Group 2 - Non-bankrupt Firms)	n = 33
①	= Misclassified Firms (Group 1) = 2	} one year prior
⊚	= Misclassified Firms (Group 2) = 1	

61

(6) *Long-Range Predictive Accuracy.* The previous results give important evidence of the reliability of the conclusions derived from the initial sample of firms. An appropriate extension, therefore, would be to examine the firms to determine the overall effectiveness of the discriminant model for a longer period of time prior to bankruptcy. Several studies, e.g., Beaver and Merwin, indicated that their analyses showed firms exhibiting failure tendencies as much as five years prior to the actual failure. Little is mentioned, however, of the true significance of these earlier year results. Is it enough to show that a firm's position is deteriorating or is it more important to examine when in the life of a firm does its eventual failure, if any, become an acute possibility? Thus far, we have seen that bankruptcy can be predicted accurately for two years prior to failure. What about the more remote years?

To answer this question, data are gathered for the thirty-three original firms from the third, fourth, and fifth year prior to bankruptcy. The reduced sample is due to the fact that several of the firms were in existence for less than five years. In two cases data were unavailable for the more remote years. One would expect on an *a priori* basis that, as the lead time increases, the relative predictive ability of any model would decrease. This was true in the univariate studies cited earlier, and it is also quite true for the multiple discriminant model. Table 4 summarizes the predictive accuracy for the total five year period.

TABLE 4
FIVE YEAR PREDICTIVE ACCURACY OF THE MDA MODEL
(Initial Sample)

Year Prior to Bankruptcy	Hits	Misses	Per cent Correct
1st n = 33	31	2	95
2nd n = 32	23	9	72
3rd n = 29	14	15	48
4th n = 28	8	20	29
5th n = 25	9	16	36

It is obvious that the accuracy of the model falls off consistently with the one exception of the fourth and fifth years, when the results are reversed from what would be expected. The most logical reason for this occurrence is that after the second year, the discriminant model becomes unreliable in its predictive ability, and, also, that the change from year to year has little or no meaning.

Implications. Based on the above results it is suggested that the bankruptcy prediction model is an accurate forecaster of failure up to two years prior to bankruptcy and that the accuracy diminishes substantially as the lead time increases. In order to investigate the possible reasons underlying these findings the trend in the five predictive variables is traced on a univariate basis for five years preceding bankruptcy. The ratios of four other important but less significant ratios are also listed in Table 5.

The two most important conclusions of this trend analysis are (1) that all of the observed ratios show a deteriorating trend as bankruptcy approached,

62

TABLE 5
Average Ratios of Bankrupt Group Prior to Failure—Original Sample

Ratio	Fifth Year		Fourth Year		Third Year		Second Year		First Year	
	Ratio	Change[a]	Ratio	Change[a]	Ratio	Change[a]	Ratio	Change[a]	Ratio	Change[a]
Working Capital/Total Assets (%) (X_1)	19.5		23.2	+ 3.6	17.6	− 5.6	1.6	−16.0[b]	(6.1)	− 7.7
Retained Earnings/Total Assets (%) (X_2)	4.0		(0.8)	− 4.8	(7.0)	− 6.2	(30.1)	−23.1	(62.6)	−32.5[b]
EBIT/Total Assets (%) (X_3)	7.2		4.0	− 3.2	(5.8)	− 9.8	(20.7)	−14.9[b]	(31.8)	−11.1
Market Value Equity/Total Debt (%) (X_4)	180.0		147.6	−32.4	143.2	− 4.4	74.2	−69.0[b]	40.1	−34.1
Sales/Total Assets (%) (X_5)	200.0		200.0	0.0	166.0	−34.0[b]	150.0	−16.0	150.0	0.0
Current Ratio (%)	180.0		187.0	+ 7.0	162.0	−25.0	131.0	−31.0[b]	133.0	+ 2.0
Years of Negative Profits (yrs.)	0.8		0.9	+ 0.1	1.2	+ 0.3	2.0	+ 0.8[b]	2.5	+ 0.5
Total Debt/Total Assets (%)	54.2		60.9	+ 6.7	61.2	+ 0.3	77.0	+15.8	96.4	+19.4[b]
Net Worth/Total Debt (%)	123.2		75.2	−28.0	112.6	+17.4	70.5	−42.1[b]	49.4	−21.1

[a] Change from previous year.
[b] Largest yearly change in the ratio.

and (2) that the most serious change in the majority of these ratios occurred between the third and the second years prior to bankruptcy. The degree of seriousness is measured by the yearly change in the ratio values. The latter observation is extremely significant as it provides evidence consistent with conclusions derived from the discriminant model. Therefore, the important information inherent in the individual ratio measurement trends takes on deserved significance only when integrated with the more analytical discriminant analysis findings.

V. Applications

The use of a multiple discriminant model for predicting bankruptcy has displayed several advantages, but bankers, credit managers, executives, and investors will typically not have access to computer procedures such as the Cooley-Lohnes MDA program. Therefore, it will be necessary to investigate the results presented in Section IV closely and to attempt to extend the model for more general application. The procedure described below may be utilized to select a "cut-off" point, or optimum Z value, which enables predictions without computer support.[33]

By observing those firms which have been misclassified by the discriminant model in the initial sample, it is concluded that all firms having a Z score of greater than 2.99 clearly fall into the "non-bankrupt" sector, while those firms having a Z below 1.81 are all bankrupt. The area between 1.81 and 2.99 will be defined as the "zone of ignorance" or "gray area" because of the susceptibility to error classification (see Chart I). Since errors are observed in this range of values, we will be uncertain about a *new* firm whose Z value falls within the "zone of ignorance." Hence, it is desirable to establish a guideline for classifying firms in the "gray area."

The process begins by identifying sample observations which fall within the overlapping range. These appear as in Table 6. The first digit of the firm

TABLE 6
FIRM WHOSE Z SCORE FALLS WITHIN GRAY AREA

Firm Number Non-Bankrupt	Z Score	Firm Number Bankrupt
2019*	1.81	
	1.98	1026
	2.10	1014
	2.67	1017*
2033	2.68	
2032	2.78	
	2.99	1025*

* Misclassified by the MDA model; for example, firm "19" in Group 2.

number identifies the group, with the last two digits locating the firm within the group.

33. A similar method proved to be useful in selecting cut-off points for marketing decisions, see R. E. Frank, A. A. Kuehn, W. F. Massy, *Quantitative Techniques in Marketing Analysis* (Homewood, Ill.: Richard D. Irwin, Inc., 1962), pp. 95-100.

Next, the range of values of Z that results in the *minimum number of misclassifications* is found. In the analysis, Z's between (but not including) the indicated values produce the following misclassifications as shown in Table 7.

TABLE 7
NUMBER OF MISCLASSIFICATIONS USING VARIOUS Z SCORE CRITERIONS

Range of Z	Number Misclassified	Firms
1.81-1.98	5	2019, 1026, 1014, 1017, 1025
1.98-2.10	4	2019, 1014, 1017, 1025
2.10-2.67	3	2019, 1017, 1025
2.67-2.68	2	2019, 1025
2.68-2.78	3	2019, 2033, 1025
2.78-2.99	4	2019, 2033, 2032, 1025

The best critical value conveniently falls between 2.67-2.68 and therefore 2.675, the midpoint of the interval, is chosen as the Z value that discriminates best between the bankrupt and non-bankrupt firms.

Of course, the real test of this "optimum" Z value is its discriminating power not only with the initial sample, but also with the secondary samples. The results of these tests are even slightly superior to the job done by the computer assignments, with the additional benefit of practical applicability.

Business Loan Evaluation. Reference was made earlier to several studies which examined the effectiveness of discriminant analysis in evaluating *consumer-loan* applications and, perhaps, these suggest a useful extension of the bankruptcy-prediction model. The evaluation of *business-loans* is an important function in our society, especially to commercial banks and other lending institutions. Studies have been devoted to the loan offer function[34] and to the adoption of a heuristic-bank-loan-officer model whereby a computer model was developed to simulate the loan officer function.[35] Admittedly, the analysis of the loan applicant's financial statements is but one section of the entire evaluation process, but it is a very important link. A fast and efficient device for detecting unfavorable credit risks might enable the loan officer to avoid potentially disastrous decisions. The significant point is that the MDA model contains many of the variables common to business-loan evaluation and discriminant analysis has been used for consumer-loan evaluation. Therefore, the potential presents itself for utilization in the business sector.

Because such important variables as the purpose of the loan, its maturity, the security involved, the deposit status of the applicant, and the particular characteristics of the bank are not explicitly considered in the model, the MDA should probably not be used as the only means of credit evaluation. The discriminant Z score index can be used, however, as a guide in efforts to lower

34. D. D. Hester, "An Empirical Examination of a Commercial Loan Offer Function," *Yale Economic Essays,* vol. 2, No. 1 (1962), pp. 3-57.

35. K. Cohen, T. Gilmore, and F. Singer, "Banks Procedures for Analyzing Business Loan Applitions," *Analytical Methods in Banking,* K. Cohen and F. Hammer (eds.) (Homewood, Ill.: Richard D. Irwin, Inc., 1966), pp. 218-251.

the costs of investigation of loan applicants. Less time and effort would be spent on companies whose Z score is very high, i.e., above 3.0, while those with low Z scores would signal a very thorough investigation. This policy would be advisable to the loan officer who had some degree of faith in the discriminant analysis approach, but who did not want his final decision to depend solely on a numerical score. Also, the method would be particularly efficient in the case of short-term loans or relatively small loans where the normal credit evaluation process is very costly relative to the expected income from the loan. Herein lie important advantages of the MDA model—its simplicity and low cost.

Internal Control Considerations and Investment Criteria. An extremely important, but often very difficult, task of corporate management is to periodically assess honestly the firm's present condition. By doing so, important strengths and weaknesses may be recognized and, in the latter case, changes in policies and actions will usually be in order. The suggestion here is that the discriminant model, if used correctly and periodically, has the ability to predict corporate problems early enough so as to enable management to realize the gravity of the situation in time to avoid failure. If failure is unavoidable, the firm's creditors and stockholders may be better off if a merger with a stronger enterprise is negotiated before bankruptcy.

The potentially useful applications of an accurate bankruptcy predictive model are not limited to internal considerations or to credit evaluation purposes. An efficient predictor of financial difficulties could also be a valuable technique for screening out undesirable investments. On the more optimistic side it appears that there are some very real opportunities for benefits. Since the model is basically predictive the analyst can utilize these predictions to recommend appropriate investment policy. For instance, observations suggest that while investors are somewhat capable of anticipating declines in operating results of selective firms, there is an overwhelming tendency to underestimate the financial plight of the companies which eventually go bankrupt. Firms in the original sample whose Z scores were below the so-called "zone of ignorance" experienced an average decline in the market value of their common stock of 45 per cent from the time the model first predicted bankruptcy until the actual failure date (an average period of about 15 months).

While the above results are derived from an admittedly small sample of very special firms, the potential implications are of interest. If an individual already owns stock in a firm whose future appears dismal, according to the model, he should sell in order to avoid further price declines. The sale would prevent further loss and provide capital for alternative investments. A different policy could be adopted by those aggressive investors looking for short-sale opportunities. An investor utilizing this strategy would have realized a 26 per cent gain on those listed securities eligible for short-sales in the original sample of bankrupt firms. In the case of large companies, where bankruptcy occurs less frequently, an index which has the ability to forecast downside movements appears promising. This could be especially helpful in the area of efficient portfolio selection. That is, firms which appear to be strongly susceptible to downturns, according to the discriminant model, would be rejected regardless of any positive potential. Conversely, firms exhibiting these same downside characteristics could be sold short, thereby enabling the portfolio manager to be more aggressive in his other choices.

VI. CONCLUDING REMARKS

This paper seeks to assess the analytical quality of ratio analysis. It has been suggested that traditional ratio analysis is no longer an important analytical technique in the academic environment due to the relatively unsophisticated manner in which it has been presented. In order to assess its potential rigorously, a set of financial ratios was combined in a discriminant analysis approach to the problem of corporate bankruptcy prediction. The theory is that ratios, if analyzed within a multivariate framework, will take on greater statistical significance than the common technique of sequential ratio comparisons. The results are very encouraging.

The discriminant-ratio model proved to be extremely accurate in predicting bankruptcy correctly in 94 per cent of the initial sample with 95 per cent of all firms in the bankrupt and non-bankrupt groups assigned to their actual group classification. Furthermore, the discriminant function was accurate in several secondary samples introduced to test the reliability of the model. Investigation of the individual ratio movements prior to bankruptcy corroborated the model's findings that bankruptcy can be accurately predicted up to two years prior to actual failure with the accuracy diminishing rapidly after the second year. A limitation of the study is that the firms examined were all publicly held manufacturing corporations for which comprehensive financial data were obtainable, including market price quotations. An area for future research, therefore, would be to extend the analysis to relatively smaller asset-sized firms and unincorporated entities where the incidence of business failure is greater than with larger corporations.

Several practical and theoretical applications of the model were suggested. The former include business credit evaluation, internal control procedures, and investment guidelines. Inherent in these applications is the assumption that signs of deterioration, detected by a ratio index, can be observed clearly enough to take profitable action. A potential theoretical area of importance lies in the conceptualization of efficient portfolio selection. One of the current limitations in this area is in a realistic presentation of those securities and the types of investment policies which are necessary to balance the portfolio and avoid downside risk. The ideal approach is to include those securities possessing negative co-variance with other securities in the portfolio. However, these securities are not likely to be easy to locate, if at all. The problem becomes somewhat more soluble if a method is introduced which rejects securities with high downside risk or includes them in a short-selling context. The discriminant-ratio model appears to have the potential to ease this problem. Further investigation, however, is required on this subject.

For Further Study

1. Eisenbeis, R.A. (1977), "Pitfalls in the Application of Discriminant Analysis in Business, Finance, and Economics". *Journal of Finance* (June 1977), pp. 875-900.

2. Hilliard, J.E. and R.A. Leitch (1975). "Cost-Volume-Profit Analysis Under Uncertainty: A Log Normal Approach". *The Accounting Review* (January 1975), pp. 69-80.

3. Johnson, W.B. (1979). "The Cross-sectional Stability of Financial Ratio Patterns". *Journal of Financial and Quantitative Analysis* (December 1979) pp. 1035-1048.

4. Pinches, G.E. and K.A. Mingo (1973). "A Multivariate Analysis of Industrial Bond Ratings". *Journal of Finance* (March 1973), pp. 1-18.

5. _____ and J.S. Trieschman (1977). "Discriminant Analysis, Classification Results and Financially Distressed P-L Insurers". *Journal of Risk and Insurance* (June 1977), pp. 289-298.

6. Sinkey, J.F. (1975). "A Multivariate Statistical Analysis of the Characteristics of Problem Banks". *Journal of Finance* (March 1974), pp. 21-36.

Part II

Valuation Theory
and the Capital Structure

Introduction

Bond valuation and equity valuation are important to security analysts and financial managers. Classical valuation theory, the M&M theory, the capital asset pricing model (CAPM), and the option pricing model (OPM) are four important theories of financial analysis and asset valuation. The models are reviewed and discussed in the various papers presented in this section. The issue of corporate capital structure is also discussed.

The basic differences between the classical valuation theory and M&M's theory are: the specific impacts of leverage policy and dividend policy on the market value of the firm, and the assertion of the existence of an optimal capital structure. Both financing policy and the existence of an optimal capital structure are discussed in this section; dividend policy will be analyzed in Part IV.

In their seminal papers (1958, 1963), M&M considered the cost of capital, corporate valuation, and capital structure. Under certain simplifying assumptions (capital markets are frictionless; firms and individuals can borrow and lend at the risk-free rate; there are no bankruptcy costs; firms issue only two instruments, risk-free debt and equity; there are only corporate taxes; and all cash flow streams are perpetuities (i.e., no growth), M&M argued that the corporation will use 100 percent debt. In his 1977 presidential address paper, Miller reconsiders the issue of optimal capital structure and generalizes the relationship between the market value of an unlevered firm (V^U) and the market value of a levered firm (V^L) as:

$$V^L = V^U + \frac{[1-(1-t_c)(1-t_{ps})]\ B}{(1-t_{pB})}$$

where B = total risk-free debt issue by the firm

t_c, t_{ps}, and t_{pB} are the corporate tax rate, personal tax rate on the income from stock, and the personal tax rate on the income from bonds.

Thus, the issue of an optimal structure hinges on certain tax considerations. If both t_{ps} and t_{pB} are 0, then the above equation reduces to $V^L = V^U + t_{cB}$, the primary finding of the two earlier papers by M&M. Further, assuming that $t_{ps} = 0$, Miller argues that the aggregate equilibrium tax advantage can disappear if the bond's supply rate (r_s) is equal to demand rate (r_0), or

$$r_s = \frac{r_0}{1- t_c} = r_0 = \frac{r}{t- t_{pB}}$$

where r_0 is the rate paid on the debt of a tax free institution, (e.g., municipal bonds).

Thus, there will be no optimal capital structure for firms, but perhaps an optimal amount of debt for the aggregate. It should be noted, however, that DeAngelo and Masulis (1980) (DM) have shown that Miller's results are relatively restricted. With more general assumptions, DM show that the optimal capital structure does exist for the individual firm.

To round out an examination of M&M's contribution to this topic, M&M's 1961 article (Part VI) carefully discusses and integrates the four alternative valuation approaches: the stream of dividends; the stream of earnings; the discount cash flow; and the investment opportunity approach. The investment opportunity approach explicitly allows for the growth opportunities of a firm; thus, this 1961 paper can be read in conjunction with Miller's 1977 article and the other articles in this section to gain a fuller understanding of the valuation process.

The Capital Asset Pricing Model (CAPM) and Option Pricing Model are two particularly important interrelated valuation models. Using an integrated graphical and mathematical method, Sharpe (1964) was one of the first scholars to derive the CAPM used in Sharpe's paper. The derivation and the specification of the CAPM used by Sharpe are generally discussed in the first course in financial management. The Option Pricing Model was first derived by Black and Scholes (1973) in terms of stochastic differential equations. However, the degree of mathematical sophistication required to fully appreciate the derivation is beyond the experience of both undergraduate and master's students. Hence, Rendleman and Batter (1979) develop a two-state option pricing determination process and derive a discrete (binomial) option pricing model (OPM).

The binomial OPM introduced here can be utilized to derive Black and Scholes' continuous option pricing model as defined in Galai and Masulis (1976). This is accomplished by letting the length of the period between up or down movements in price become very small and hence the number of periods becomes very large. Galai and Masulis take the insight of the OPM provided by Black and Scholes and show how it may be applied to many of the traditional issues of corporate finance such as dividend policy, acquisitions, divestiture, conglomerate mergers, and investment decisions of various kinds.

Rubenstein (1973) shows how the CAPM can be used to estimate the cost of capital; determine the value of a firm; determine the relationship between the leverage ratio and beta coefficient; and show how business risk and financial risk can jointly affect the beta coefficient estimate. In addition, Rubenstein also explicitly discusses the relationship between the CAPM and M&M's propositions.

In their review article, Barnes, Haugen and Senbet (BHS) (1981) discuss the issues related to market imperfections, agency problems and capital structure in detail. They use M&M's valuation theory and the option pricing theory to reconcile the differences between academicians and practitioners about the effectiveness of financing and dividend policies. Their main conclusions are:

1. If frictions exist in capital markets, then agency problems may give rise to potential costs. These costs can be minimized through complex contractual arrangements between the parties in conflict.
2. Agency problems may be used to explain the evolution of complexities in capital structure such as conversion and call privileges in corporate debt.
3. Financial contracts which differ in terms of their inherent ability to resolve agency problems may sell at differential equilibrium prices (or yields) in the marketplace. The financial manager reaches an optimal capital structure when, at the margin for each class of contract, the costs associated with each agency problem are balanced by the benefits associated with existing yield differentials and tax exposure.

Overall, BHS shows an optimal capital structure does exist for a firm. This is consistent with classical financial theory.

It is well known that the financial analysis of unregulated firms is not necessarily equivalent to that undertaken for regulated firms. Litzenberger and Sosin (LS) (1979) do some conceptual and empirical comparisons of capital structure decisions in the regulated and unregulated firm. Using the idea of a trade-off between business risk and financial risk developed by Litzenberger and Tuttle (1968), LS conclude that the tax advantage might discourage the industries from undertaking riskier investment opportunities.

In real-world financial management, the problem of bankruptcy cannot be avoided. Part of this issue has been discussed in Part I (Altman (1968)). Scott (1976) shows that optimal leverage may be related to the collateral value of the tangible assets held by the firm. In particular, if the firm goes bankrupt, the losses of bondholders are limited by the salvage value of the property held in the firm. Under a no-tax assumption, Scott shows that the optimal amount of debt in the capital structure is the discounted value of the liquidity price of the firm's assets in bankruptcy. If the probability of bankruptcy is nil, then Scott's model is formally identical to M&M's (1958, 1963) mentioned above. Scott also discusses the debt policy for both unregulated and regulated firms.

Author's Note: Two minor corrections should be noted in Scott's paper. First, Equation 1, when X is specified to be normally distributed, is given in the original paper as:

$$V = (1-t) \frac{[(\overline{X}-R)(1-F) + \sigma f(b)]}{\rho + f}$$

This equation should be modified so that $f(b)$ becomes $n[(b-\overline{X})/\sigma]$, where $n[\ ]$ is the density function of a standardized normally distributed random variable.

Secondly, equation 14 should be modified to read:

$$\frac{\partial^2 V}{\partial R \partial A} = \frac{\rho(1 + \rho)f}{(\rho + F)^3} > 0$$

The Journal of FINANCE

| VOL. XXXII | MAY 1977 | NO. 2 |

DEBT AND TAXES*

MERTON H. MILLER**

THE SOMEWHAT HETERODOX VIEWS about debt and taxes that will be presented here have evolved over the last few years in the course of countless discussions with several of my present and former colleagues in the Finance group at Chicago— Fischer Black, Robert Hamada, Roger Ibbotson, Myron Scholes and especially Eugene Fama. Charles Upton and Joseph Williams have also been particularly helpful to me recently in clarifying the main issues.[1] My long-time friend and collaborator, Franco Modigliani, is absolved from any blame for the views to follow not because I think he would reject them, but because he has been absorbed in preparing *his* Presidential Address to the American Economic Association at this same Convention.

This coincidence neatly symbolizes the contribution we tried to make in our first joint paper of nearly twenty years ago; namely to bring to bear on problems of corporate finance some of the standard tools of economics, especially the analysis of competitive market equilibrium. Prior to that time, the academic discussion in finance was focused primarily on the empirical issue of what the market *really* capitalized.[2] Did the market capitalize a firm's dividends or its earnings or some weighted combination of the two? Did it capitalize net earnings or net operating earnings or something in between? The answers to these questions and to related questions about the behavior of interest rates were supposed to provide a basis for choosing an optimal capital structure for the firm in a framework analogous to the economist's model of discriminating monopsony.

We came at the problem from the other direction by first trying to establish the propositions about valuation implied by the economist's basic working assumptions of rational behavior and perfect markets. And we were able to prove that when the full range of opportunities available to firms and investors under such conditions

* Presidential Address, Annual Meeting of the American Finance Association, Atlantic City, N.J., September 17, 1976.

** University of Chicago.

1. More than perfunctory thanks are also due to the many others who commented, sometimes with considerable heat, on the earlier versions of this talk: Ray Ball, Marshall Blume, George Foster, Nicholas Gonedes, David Green, E. Han Kim, Robert Krainer, Katherine Miller, Charles Nelson, Hans Stoll, Jerold Warner, William Wecker, Roman Weil, and J. Fred Weston. I am especially indebted (no pun intended) to Fischer Black.

2. To avoid reopening old wounds, no names will be mentioned here. References can be supplied on request, however.

are taken into account, the following simple principle would apply: in equilibrium, the market value of any firm must be independent of its capital structure.

The arbitrage proof of this proposition can now be found in virtually every textbook in finance, followed almost invariably, however, by a warning to the student against taking it seriously. Some dismiss it with the statement that firms and investors can't or don't behave that way. I'll return to that complaint later in this talk. Others object that the invariance proposition was derived for a world with no taxes, and that world, alas, is not ours. In our world, they point out, the value of the firm can be increased by the use of debt since interest payments can be deducted from taxable corporate income. To reap more of these gains, however, the stockholders must incur increasing risks of bankruptcy and the costs, direct and indirect, of falling into that unhappy state. They conclude that the balancing of these bankruptcy costs against the tax gains of debt finance gives rise to an optimal capital structure, just as the traditional view has always maintained, though for somewhat different reasons.

It is this new and currently fashionable version of the optimal capital structure that I propose to challenge here. I will argue that even in a world in which interest payments are fully deductible in computing corporate income taxes, the value of the firm, in equilibrium will still be independent of its capital structure.

I. Bankruptcy Costs in Perspective

Let me first explain where I think the new optimum capital structure model goes wrong. It is not that I believe there to be no deadweight costs attaching to the use of debt finance. Bankruptcy costs and agency costs do indeed exist as was dutifully noted at several points in the original 1958 article [28, see especially footnote 18 and p. 293]. It is just that these costs, by any sensible reckoning, seem disproportionately small relative to the tax savings they are supposedly balancing.

The tax savings, after all, are conventionally taken as being on the order of 50 cents for each dollar of permanent debt issued.[3] The figure one usually hears as an estimate of bankruptcy costs is 20 percent of the value of the estate; and if this were the true order of magnitude for such costs, they would have to be taken very seriously indeed as a possible counterweight. But when that figure is traced back to its source in the paper by Baxter [5] (and the subsequent and seemingly confirmatory studies of Stanley and Girth [36] and Van Horne [39]), it turns out to refer mainly to the bankruptcies of individuals, with a sprinkling of small businesses, mostly proprietorships and typically undergoing liquidation rather than reorganization. The only study I know that deals with the costs of bankruptcy and reorganization for large, publicly-held corporations is that of Jerold Warner [40]. Warner

---

3. See, among others, Modigliani and Miller [27]. The 50 percent figure—actually 48 percent under present Federal law plus some additional state income taxes for most firms—is an upper bound that assumes the firm always has enough income to utilize the tax shield on the interest. For reestimates of the tax savings under other assumptions with respect to availability of offsets and to length of borrowing, see Kim [21] and Brennan and Schwartz [12]. The estimate of the tax saving has been further complicated since 1962 by the Investment Tax Credit and especially by the limitation of the credit to fifty percent of the firm's tax liability. Some fuzziness about the size of the tax savings also arises in the case of multinational corporations.

tabulated the direct costs of bankruptcy and reorganization for a sample of 11 railroads that filed petitions in bankruptcy under Section 77 of the Bankruptcy Act between 1930 and 1955. He found that the eventual cumulated direct costs of bankruptcy—and keep in mind that most of these railroads were in bankruptcy and running up these expenses for over 10 years!—averaged 5.3 percent of the market value of the firm's securities as of the end of the month in which the railroad filed the petition. There was a strong inverse size effect, moreover. For the largest road, the costs were 1.7 percent.

And remember that these are the *ex post*, upper-bound cost ratios, whereas, of course, the *expected* costs of bankruptcy are the relevant ones when the firm's capital structure decisions are being made. On that score, Warner finds, for example, that the direct costs of bankruptcy averaged only about 1 percent of the value of the firm 7 years before the petition was filed; and when he makes a reasonable allowance for the probability of bankruptcy actually occurring, he comes up with an estimate of the expected cost of bankruptcy that is, of course, much smaller yet.

Warner's data cover only the *direct* costs of reorganization in bankruptcy. The deadweight costs of rescaling claims might perhaps loom larger if measures were available of the indirect costs, such as the diversion of the time and energies of management from tasks of greater productivity or the reluctance of customers and suppliers to enter into long-term commitments.[4] But why speculate about the size of these costs? Surely we can assume that if the direct and indirect deadweight costs of the ordinary loan contract began to eat up significant portions of the tax savings, other forms of debt contracts with lower deadweight costs would be used instead.[5]

An obvious case in point is the income bond. Interest payments on such bonds need be paid in any year only if earned; and if earned and paid are fully deductible in computing corporate income tax. But if not earned and not paid in any year, the bondholders have no right to foreclose. The interest payments typically cumulate for a short period of time—usually two to three years—and then are added to the principal. Income bonds, in sum, are securities that appear to have all the supposed tax advantages of debt, without the bankruptcy cost disadvantages.[6] Yet, except for a brief flurry in the early 1960's, such bonds are rarely issued.

The conventional wisdom attributes this dearth to the unsavory connotations that surround such bonds.[7] They were developed originally in the course of the railroad bankruptcies in the 19th century and they are presumed to be still associated with that dismal process in the minds of potential buyers. As an

4. For more on this theme see Jensen and Meckling [20].

5. A similar argument in a somewhat different, but related, context is made by Black [6, esp. pp. 330–31]. Note also that while the discussion has so far referred exclusively to "bankruptcy" costs fairly narrowly construed, much the same reasoning applies to the debt-related costs in the broader sense, as in the "agency" costs of Jensen and Meckling [20] or the "costs of lending" of Black, Miller and Posner [9].

6. Not quite, because failure to repay or refund the principal at maturity could trigger a bankruptcy. Also, a firm may have earnings, but no cash.

7. See Esp. Robbins [31], [27].

investment banker once put it to me: "They have the smell of death about them." Perhaps so. But the obvious retort is that bit of ancient Roman wisdom: *pecunia non olet* (money has no odor). If the stakes were as high as the conventional analysis of the tax subsidy to debt seems to suggest, then ingenious security salesmen, investment bankers or tax advisers would surely long since have found ways to overcome investor repugnance to income bonds.

In sum, the great emphasis on bankruptcy costs in recent discussions of optimal capital structure policy seems to me to have been misplaced. For big businesses, at least (and particularly for such conspicuously low-levered ones as I.B.M. or Kodak), the supposed trade-off between tax gains and bankruptcy costs looks suspiciously like the recipe for the fabled horse-and-rabbit stew—one horse and one rabbit.[8]

II. TAXES AND CAPITAL STRUCTURES: THE EMPIRICAL RECORD

Problems arise also on the other side of the trade-off. If the optimal capital structure were simply a matter of balancing tax advantages against bankruptcy costs, why have observed capital structures shown so little change over time?[9]

When I looked into the matter in 1960 under the auspices of the Commission on Money and Credit (Miller [24]), I found, among other things, that the debt/asset ratio of the typical nonfinancial corporation in the 1950's was little different from that of the 1920's despite the fact that tax rates had quintupled—from 10 and 11 percent in the 1920's to 52 percent in the 1950's.[10] Such rise as did occur, moreover, seemed to be mainly a substitution of debt for preferred stock, rather than of debt for common stock. The year-to-year variations in debt ratios reflected primarily the cyclical movements of the economy. During expansions debt ratios tended to fall, partly because the lag of dividends behind earnings built up internally generated equity; and partly because the ratio of equity to debt in new financings tended to rise when the stock market was booming.

My study for the CMC carried the story only through the 1950's. A hasty perusal of the volumes of Statistics of Income available for the years thereafter suggests that some upward drift in debt ratios did appear to be taking place in the 1960's, at least in book-value terms. Some substantial portion of this seeming rise, however, is a consequence of the liberalization of depreciation deductions in the early 1960's. An accounting change of that kind reduces reported taxable earnings and, barring an induced reduction in dividend policy, will tend to push accumulated retained earnings (and total assets) below the levels that would otherwise have been

8. In this connection, it is interesting to note that the optimal debt to value ratio in the hypothetical example presented in the recent paper by E. Han Kim [21] turns out to be 42 percent and, hence, very substantially higher than the debt ratio for the typical U.S. corporation, even though Kim's calculation assumes that bankruptcy costs would eat up no less than 40 percent of the firm's assets in the event of failure.

9. A related question is why there appears to be no systematic cross-sectional relation between debt ratios and corporate tax rates in the countries of the European Economic Community. See Coates and Wooley [13].

10. The remarkable stability of corporate debt ratios in the face of huge increases in tax rates was noted by many other writers in this period. See, e.g., Sametz [22, esp. pp. 462–3] and the references there cited.

recorded.[11] Thus, without considerable further adjustment, direct comparison of current and recent debt ratios to those of earlier eras is no longer possible. But suppose we were to make the extreme assumption that all the rise in debt ratios genuinely reflected policy decisions rather than changes in accounting rules. Then that would still have meant that the average nonfinancial corporation raised its ratio of long-term debt from about one-fifth to only about one-fourth of total assets during the decade.[12]

Whatever may have been the case in the 1960's, the impression was certainly widespread in the early 1970's that corporate debt ratios were rising rapidly and ominously. This was a period, after all, in which *Business Week* could devote an entire and very gloomy issue (October 12, 1974) to the theme "The Debt Economy."

Looking back now, however, with all the advantages of hindsight, the increases in debt of such concern in 1974 can be seen to be a transitory response to a peculiar configuration of events rather than a permanent shift in corporate capital structures.[13] A surge in inventory accumulation was taking place as firms sought to hedge against shortages occasioned by embargoes or price controls or crop failures. Much of this accumulation was financed by short-term borrowing—a combination that led to a sharp deterioration in such conventional measures of financial health as "quick ratios" and especially coverage ratios (since little of the return on the precautionary inventory buildup was showing up in current earnings and since inflation *per se* will automatically reduce the ratio of earnings to interest payments even with no change in the interest burden in real terms).

But this inventory bubble burst soon after the famous doomsday issue of *Business Week* hit the stands—providing one more confirmation of Allen Wallis' dictum that by the time journalists become interested in an economic problem, the worst is already over. In the ensuing months, inventories have been pared, bank loans have been repaid and conventional measures of corporate liquidity have been restored to something closer to their old-time vigor. New common stock issues have been coming briskly to market as always in the past when the stock market was bouyant. Thus, when the returns for the first half of the 1970's are finally in, we are likely to be facing the same paradox we did in the 1950's—corporate debt ratios only marginally higher than those of the 1920's despite enormously higher tax rates.[14]

11. Also acting in the same direction were the liberalized rules for expensing rather than capitalizing outlays for research and development. On the other hand, debt ratios would tend to be understated by the growth during the decade of off-balance-sheet debt financing, such as leasing and unfunded pension liability.

12. For manufacturing corporations, Federal Trade Commission reports indicate that long-term debt rose during the 1960's from 12.2 percent of reported total assets to 16.6 percent. Short-term debt rose from about 7 percent to 12 percent of reported total assets over the same period. The corresponding figures for the end of 1975 were 17.9 percent for long-term debt and 10.2 percent for short-term debt. The figures here and throughout refer of course, to gross debt without allowing for the substantial amounts of debt securities that are owned by manufacturing and other nonfinancial corporations.

13. For an independent reading of these events that is similar in most essential respects, see Gilbert [16].

14. The discussion in the text has focused mainly on debt/asset ratios at book value, in the hope that

Actually, the cognitive dissonance is worse now than it was then. In the 1950's it was still possible to entertain the notion that the seeming failure of corporations to reap the tax advantages of debt financing might simply be a lag in adjustment. As corporate finance officers and their investment bankers sharpened their pencils, the tax savings they discovered would eventually wear down aversions to debt on the part of any others in the Boardroom still in a state of shock from the Great Depression. But hope can no longer be expected from that quarter. A disequilibrium that has lasted 30 years and shows no signs of disappearing is too hard for any economist to accept.[15] And since failure to close the gap cannot convincingly be attributed to the bankruptcy costs or agency costs of debt financing, there would seem to be only one way left to turn: the tax advantages of debt financing must be substantially less than the conventional wisdom suggests.[16]

III. The Tax Advantages of Debt Financing Reexamined

That the solution might lie in this direction was hinted at, but alas only hinted at, in the original 1958 MM paper. If I may invoke the Presidential priviledge of being allowed to quote (selectively) from my earlier work, we said there in the 57th footnote:

> It should also be pointed out that our tax system acts in other ways to reduce the gains from debt financing. Heavy reliance on debt in the capital structure, for example, commits a company to paying out a substantial proportion of its income in the form of interest payments taxable to the owners under the personal income tax. A debt free company, by contrast, can reinvest in the business all of its (smaller) net income and to this extent subject the owners only to the low capital gains rate (or possibly to no tax at all by virtue of the loophole at death).

We alluded to the same line of argument again briefly in the correction paper in 1963.[17] The point was developed in a more extensive and systematic way by Farrar and Selwyn [15]. Further extensions were made by Myers [30], Stapleton [37],

---

book value measures might give better insight to corporate capital structure objectives than would market value measures of leverage, which are highly sensitive to changes in the level of stock prices. As of the end of 1975, tabulations prepared by Salomon Brothers in their volume *The Supply and Demand for Credit, 1976*, indicate a ratio of long-term debt to market value for all U.S. corporations (including public utilities) of 27.1 percent. (Actually, even this is a bit on the high side since the debt is measured at face value and thus does not reflect the substantial fall in the value of outstanding debt in the 1st half of the 1970's.) In 1972, at the height of the boom, the long-term debt ratio at market value was only about 17 percent. The highest recent level reached in recent years was 30 percent at the end of 1974 after a two-year fall of $500 billion in the market value of common and preferred stock.

15. There are certainly few signs that firms were rushing to close the gap by methods as direct as exchanges of debt for their common shares. Masulis [22] was able to find only about 60 such cases involving listed corporations in the 1960's and 1970's. Most of these were concentrated during an 18-month period after the drop in the stock market in 1973; and some of these, in turn, appear more to be attempts to "go private" than to adjust the capital structure.

16. The resolution of the paradox offered in the CMC paper [24] was essentially one of agency costs and, in particular, that the costs of monitoring risky debt made such debt uneconomic as a market instrument.

17. In that paper, the major weight in resolving the paradox was placed on what might be called a "precautionary" motive. Corporations were presumed to want to maintain substantial reserves of high-grade borrowing power so as not to be forced to float common stocks when they believe their stock to be undervalued. Such motives are by no means inconsistent with the explanation to be offered here.

Stiglitz [38], and in two important papers by Fischer Black [7], [8]—papers still unpublished but whose contents were communicated to me, sometimes in very forceful fashion, in the course of many arguments and discussions.

When the personal income tax is taken into account along with the corporation income tax, the gain from leverage, G_L, for the stockholders in a firm holding real assets can be shown to be given by the following expression:

$$G_L = \left[1 - \frac{(1 - \tau_C)(1 - \tau_{PS})}{1 - \tau_{PB}}\right] B_L$$

where τ_C is the corporate tax rate, τ_{PS} is the personal income tax rate applicable to income from common stock, τ_{PB} is the personal income tax rate applicable to income from bonds and B_L is the market value of the levered firm's debt. For simplicity at this stage of the argument, all the taxes are assumed to be proportional; and to maintain continuity with the earlier MM papers, the expression is given in its "perpetuity" form.[18]

Note that when all tax rates are set equal to zero, the expression does indeed reduce to the standard MM no-tax result of $G_L = 0$. And when the personal income tax rate on income from bonds is the same as that on income from shares—a special case of which, of course, is when there is assumed to be no personal income tax at all—then the gain from leverage is the familiar $\tau_C B_L$. But when the tax rate on income from shares is less than the tax on income from bonds, then the gain from leverage will be less than $\tau_C B_L$. In fact, for a wide range of values for τ_C, τ_{PS} and τ_{PB}, the gain from leverage vanishes entirely or even turns negative!

Let me assure you that this result is no mere sleight-of-hand due to hidden trick assumptions. The gain evaporates or turns into a loss because investors hold securities for the "consumption possibilities" they generate and hence will evaluate them in terms of their yields net of all tax drains. If, therefore, the personal tax on income from common stocks is less than that on income from bonds, then the *before-tax* return on taxable bonds has to be high enough, other things equal, to offset this tax handicap. Otherwise, no taxable investor would want to hold bonds. Thus, while it is still true that the owners of a levered corporation have the advantage of deducting their interest payments to bondholders in computing their corporate income tax, these interest payments have already been "grossed up," so to speak, by any differential in the taxes that the bondholders will have to pay on their interest income. The advantage of deductibility at the one level thus merely

18. The expression can be derived in a number of ways of which the simplest is perhaps the following variant on the MM reply to Heins and Sprenkle [29]. Ownership of the fraction α of the levered corporation yields a return to the investor of $\alpha(\tilde{X} - rB_L)(1 - \tau_C)(1 - \tau_{PS})$ where $\tilde{X}$ is the uncertain return on firm's real (as opposed to financial) assets. This can be duplicated by the sum of (a) an investment of αS_U in the shares of the twin unlevered corporation, which yields $\alpha X(1 - \tau_C)(1 - \tau_{PS})$; plus (b), borrowing $\alpha B_L[(1 - \tau_C)(1 - \tau_{PS})/(1 - \tau_{PB})]$ on personal account. Since interest is deductible under the personal income tax, the net cost of the borrowing is $\alpha r B_L(1 - \tau_C)(1 - \tau_{PS})$ and thus the original levered stream has been matched.

Here and throughout, the tax authorities will be presumed to have taken the steps necessary to prevent taxable individuals or firms from eliminating their tax liabilities or converting them to negative taxes by "tax arbitrage" dodges (such as borrowing to hold tax-exempt securities) or by large-scale short-selling.

serves to offset the disadvantages of includability at the other.[19] When the rates happen to satisfy the equation $(1 - \tau_{PB}) = (1 - \tau_C)(1 - \tau_{PS})$, the offset is one-for-one and the owners of the corporation reap no gain whatever from their use of tax-deductible debt rather than equity capital.

But we can say more than this. Any situation in which the owners of corporations could increase their wealth by substituting debt for equity (or vice versa) would be incompatible with market equilibrium. Their attempts to exploit these opportunities would lead, in a world with progressive income taxes, to changes in the yields on stocks and bonds and in their ownership patterns. These changes, in turn, restore the equilibrium and remove the incentives to issue more debt, even without invoking bankruptcy costs or lending costs as a *deus ex machina*.

IV. Taxes and Market Equilibrium

Like so many other propositions in financial economics this, too, is "obvious once you think of it." Let me belabor the obvious a bit, however, by a simple graphical example that will serve, I hope, both to illustrate the mechanism that brings the equilibrium about and to highlight some of the implications of that equilibrium.

Suppose, for simplicity that the personal tax rate on income from stock were zero (and we'll see later that this may be a less outrageous simplification than it looks). And suppose further, again strictly for simplicity of presentation, that all bonds are riskless and that there are no transaction costs, flotation costs or surveillance costs involved in their issuance. Then in such a world, the equilibrium of the market for bonds would be that pictured in Figure 1. The quantity of bonds outstanding is measured along the horizontal axis and the rate of interest along the vertical. The demand for bonds by the investing public is given by the upward sloping curve labeled $r_d(B)$. (Yes, it *is* a demand curve even though it slopes up.) Its intercept is at r_0 which measures the equilibrium rate of interest on fully tax-exempt bonds (such as those of state and local governments). The flat stretch of the curve immediately to the right represents the demand for fully taxable corporate bonds by fully tax-exempt individuals and organizations. Clearly, these investors would be the sole holders of corporate bonds if the market interest rate on corporate debts were only r_0. Any taxable investor who wanted to hold bonds in his or her portfolio would find it preferable to buy tax-exempt bonds.

To entice these taxable investors into the market for corporate bonds, the rate of interest on such bonds has to be high enough to compensate for the taxes on interest income under the personal income tax. More precisely, for an individual whose marginal rate of personal income tax on interest income is τ_{PB}^α, the "demand rate of interest" on taxable corporate bonds would be the rate on tax exempts grossed up by the marginal tax rate, i.e., $r_0(1/(1 - \tau_{PB}^\alpha))$. Since the personal income tax is progressive, the demand interest rate has to keep rising to pull in investors in

19. An analogous argument in the context of the lease-or-buy decision is given in Miller and Upton [26]. Reasoning of essentially this kind has also long been invoked to explain the otherwise puzzling survival of preferred stock (see, among many others, Miller [24, esp. note 40, p. 431]). The fact that 85 percent of any dividends received by a taxable corporation can be excluded in computing its taxable income, pushes down the yields on preferred stocks and thereby offsets the disadvantage of nondeductibility.

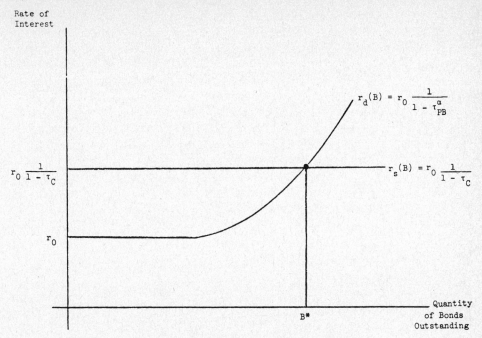

Rate of
Interest

$$r_d(B) = r_0 \frac{1}{1 - \tau_{PB}^\alpha}$$

$$r_0 \frac{1}{1 - \tau_C}$$

$$r_s(B) = r_0 \frac{1}{1 - \tau_C}$$

r_0

B^*

Quantity
of Bonds
Outstanding

FIGURE 1. Equilibrium in the Market for Bonds

higher and higher tax brackets, thus giving the continuous, upward sloping curve
pictured.

The intersection of this demand curve with the horizontal straight line through
the point $r_0/1 - \tau_C$, i.e., the tax-exempt rate grossed up by the corporate tax rate,
determines the market equilibrium. If corporations were to offer a quantity of
bonds greater than B^*, interest rates would be driven above $r_0/1 - \tau_C$ and some
levered firms would find leverage to be a losing proposition. If the volume were
below B^*, interest rates would be lower than $r_0/1 - \tau_C$ and some unlevered firms
would find it advantageous to resort to borrowing.

The market equilibrium defined by the intersection of the two curves will have
the following property. There will be an equilibrium level of aggregate corporate
debt, B^*, and hence an equilbrium debt-equity ratio for the corporate sector as a
whole. *But there would be no optimum debt ratio for any individual firm.* Companies
following a no-leverage or low leverage strategy (like I.B.M. or Kodak) would find
a market among investors in the high tax brackets; those opting for a high leverage
strategy (like the electric utilities) would find the natural clientele for their securities at the other end of the scale. But one clientele is as good as the other. And in
this important sense it would still be true that the value of any firm, in equilibrium,
would be independent of its capital structure, despite the deductibility of interest
payments in computing corporate income taxes.[20]

One advantage of graphical illustration is that it makes it so easy to see the

20. The details of corporate strategy and investor valuation at the micro level implied by this model
are interesting in their own right, but further analysis is best deferred to another occasion.

answer to the following inevitable question: If the stockholders of levered corporations don't reap the benefits of the tax gains from leverage, who does? Professors of finance, of course—though only indirectly and only after cutting in their colleagues in other departments. As Figure 1 shows, universities and other tax exempt organizations, as well as individuals in low tax brackets (widows and orphans?) benefit from what might be called a "bondholders' surplus." Market interest rates have to be grossed up to pay the taxes of the marginal bondholder, whose tax rate in equilibrium will be equal to the corporate rate.[21] Note that this can cut both ways, however. Low bracket individuals (and corporations) have to *pay* the corporate tax, in effect, when they want to borrow.

An equilibrium of the kind pictured in Figure 1 does not require, of course, that the effective personal tax rate on income from shares of the marginal holder be literally zero, but only that it be substantially less than his or her rate on income from bonds. As a practical matter, however, the assumption that the effective rate at the margin is close to zero may not be so wide of the mark. Keep in mind that a "clientele effect" is also at work in the market for shares. The high dividend paying stocks will be preferred by tax exempt organizations and low income investors; those stocks yielding more of their return in the form of capital gains will gravitate to the taxpayers in the upper brackets.[22] The tax rate on such gains is certainly greater than zero, in principle. But holders need pay no taxes on their gains until realized and only a small fraction of accumulated gains are, in fact, realized and taxed in any year (see, e.g., Bhatia [4, esp. note 12] and Bailey [2]). Taxes on capital gains can not only be deferred at the option of the holder—and remember that by conventional folk wisdom, 10 years of tax deferral is almost as good as exemption —but until the recent Tax Reform Act of 1976, could be avoided altogether if held until death, thanks to the rules permitting transfer of the decedent's tax basis to his or her heirs.

To the extent that the effective tax rate on income from shares is greater than zero, the horizontal line defining the equilibrium interest rate will be above that pictured in Figure 1. In the limiting case where the tax concessions (intended or unintended) made to income from shares were either nonexistent or so small that $(1 - \tau_C)(1 - \tau_{PS})$ implied a value for τ_{PB}^{α} greater than the top bracket of the personal

21. In point of fact, the spread between municipals and corporates has typically been within shouting distance of the corporate rate, though comparisons are difficult because of differences in risk (including, of course, the risk that the tax status of municipals will be changed) and though, admittedly, mechanisms of a different kind might also be producing that result. The recent study of the yield curve of U.S. Government securities by McCulloch [23] gives estimates of the marginal tax rate of holders of such bonds that are close to, but usually somewhat below the corporate rate.

22. The data presented in the study of stock ownership by Blume, Crockett and Friend [11, esp. Table G, p. 40] are consistent with this form of clientele effect, though its magnitude is perhaps somewhat smaller than might have been expected *a priori*. They estimate, for example, that in 1971, the ratio of dividends to the market value of holdings was about 2.8 percent for individual investors with adjusted gross income of less than $15,000 as compared to 2.1 percent for those with adjusted gross incomes of $100,000 or more.

By invoking this dividend clientele effect, an argument analogous to that in Figure 1 can be developed to show that the value of a firm could be invariant to its dividend policy despite the more favorable tax treatment of capital gains than of dividends. Some gropings in that direction were made in the MM dividend paper [25, esp. pp. 431-2]. A more explicit analysis along those lines was given by Black and Scholes [10]. For a related model dealing with tax shelters on real investment see Bailey [3].

income tax, then no interior market equilibrium would be possible. Common stock would indeed be a dominated security from the purely financial point of view, exactly as the standard micro model of the tax effect suggests. Common stock could continue to exist only by virtue of special attributes it might possess that could not be duplicated with bonds or with other forms of business organization, such as co-ops.

The analysis underlying Figure 1 can be extended to allow for risky borrowing, but there are complications. What makes things difficult is not simply a matter of risk *per se*.[23] Default risk can be accommodated in Figure 1 merely by reinterpreting all the before-tax interest rates as risk-adjusted or certainty-equivalent rates. The trouble is, rather, that bonds of companies in default will not, in general, yield the issuing stockholders their full tax shield (see MM [27, esp. note 5], Kim [21] and Brennan and Schwartz [12]). Unless the firm has past profits against which its current losses can be carried back, or unless it can escape the vigilance of the I.R.S. and unload the corporate corpse on a taxable firm, some of the interest deduction goes to waste. To entice firms to issue risky bonds, therefore, the risk-adjusted supply-rate would have to be less than $r_0(1/(1 - \tau_C))$, and presumably the more so the greater the likelihood of default.[24]

An essentially similar effect will be produced by the bankruptcy costs discussed earlier. And this will imply, among other things, that the full burden of the bankruptcy costs or lending costs is not necessarily borne by the debtors as is frequently supposed. Part of the costs are shifted to the bond buyers in the form of lower risk-adjusted rates of interest in equilibrium.

A model of the kind in Figure 1 could, in principle, clear up most of the puzzles and anomalies discussed in Sections I and II above—the seeming disparity between the tax gains of debt and the costs of bankruptcy particularly for large low-levered corporations; the lack of widespread market interest in income bonds; and especially the failure of the average corporate debt ratio to rise substantially in response to the enormous increase in tax rates since the 1920's (because these increases in rates in the late 1930's as well as subsequent decreases and reincreases have generally moved both the corporate and individual rate schedules in the same direction). The model could also account as well for other of the stylized facts of corporate finance such as the oft-remarked dramatic transition of the bond market from an individual to an institution-dominated market in the late 1930's and early 1940's.[25] On the other hand, many questions clearly still remain to be answered.

23. For the specialists in these matters, suffice it to say that in the equilibrium of Figure 1, the capital markets are, of course, assumed to be "complete." For a discussion of some of the implications of corporate taxes the deductibility of interest payments under conditions of "incomplete markets" see Hakansson [18].

24. These effects, however, do not imply the existence of "super-premiums" for riskless bonds of the kind visualized recently by Glenn [17] and earlier by Durand [14]. Those were presumed to arise from the segmentation of the bond market and especially from the strong preferences of the institutional sector for low-risk securities. In terms of Figure 1, any such increase in the demand for safe securities would show up in the first instance as a lower value for r_0 and, hence, a lower value for the equilibrium corporate borrowing rate, $r_0/1 - \tau_C$. (See the MM 1958 article [28, especially pp. 279–80]. See also Hamada's discussion of Glenn's paper [19].)

25. For an early account of that transition that stresses precisely the kind of tax effects that underlie Figure 1, see Shapiro [35].

What about cross-sectional variations in debt ratios, for example—a subject on which surprisingly little work has yet been done?[26] Can they be explained convincingly by the market equilibrium model presented here or some variant of it? Or do the variations observed reflect some systematic part of the equilibrating process that escapes the kind of aggregate market models discussed here? What about the distribution of stocks and bonds among investors? Does ownership sort out in terms of tax status as sharply as emphasized here? Or does the need for diversification swamp the tax differences and thereby throw the main burden of the equilibration onto other factors, such as agency costs?

The call for more research traditionally signals the approaching end of a Presidential Address; and it is a tradition that I know you will want to see preserved. Let me conclude, therefore, by trying to face up, as I promised in the beginning, to the kind of complaint so often raised against market equilibrium analysis of financial policy of the type here presented: "But firms and investors don't behave that way!"

V. MARKET EQUILIBRIUM AND THE BEHAVIOR OF FIRMS AND INDIVIDUALS

If the phrase "don't behave that way" is taken to mean that firms and individuals don't literally perform the maximizing calculations that underlie the curves in Figure 1, then it is most certainly correct. No corporate treasurer's office, controller's staff, or investment banker's research team that I have ever encountered had, or could remotely be expected to have, enough reliable information about the future course of prices for a firm's securities to convince even a moderately skeptical outside academic observer that the firm's value had indeed been maximized by some specific financial decision or strategy. Given the complexities of the real-world setting, actual decision procedures are inevitably heuristic, judgmental, imitative and groping even where, as with so much of what passes for capital budgeting, they wear the superficial trappings of hard-nosed maximization. On this score, has there ever been any doubt that the Harvard cases (and the work of Herbert Simon and his followers) give a far more accurate picture of the way things really look and get done out on the firing line than any maximizing "model of the firm" that any economist ever drew?

Why then do economists keep trying to develop models that assume rational behavior by firms? They are not, I insist, merely hoping to con their business school deans into thinking they are working on problems of business management. Rather they have found from experience—not only in finance, but across the board —that the rational behavior models generally lead to better predictions and descriptions at the level of the industry, the market and the whole economy than any alternatives available to them. Their experience, at those levels, moreover, need involve no inconsistency with the heuristic, rule-of-thumb, intuitive kinds of decision making they actually observe in firms. It suggests rather that evolutionary mechanisms are at work to give survival value to those heuristics that are compat-

26. One of the few studies of cross-sectional differences in debt ratios is that of Schwartz and Aronson [34], but it really does little more than document the fact that utilities and railroads have substantially higher debt ratios than firms in manufacturing and mining.

ible with rational market equilibrium, however far from rational they may appear to be when examined up close and in isolation.[27]

But we must be wary of the reverse inference that merely because a given heuristic persists, it must have some survival value and, hence, must have a rational "explanation." The MM and related invariance propositions, for example, are often dismissed on grounds that corporate finance officers would surely not show so much concern over decisions that really "don't matter." The most, however, that we can safely assert about the evolutionary process underlying market equilibrium is that harmful heuristics, like harmful mutations in nature, will die out. Neutral mutations that serve no function, but do no harm, can persist indefinitely. Neither in nature nor in the economy can the enormous variation in forms we observe be convincingly explained in simple Darwinian terms.[28]

To say that many, perhaps even most, financial heuristics are neutral is not to suggest, however, that financial decision making is just a pointless charade or treat the resources devoted to financial innoviations are wasted. A mutation or a heuristic that is neutral in one environment may suddenly acquire (or lose) survival value if the environment changes. The pool of existing neutral mutations and heuristics thus permits the adaptation to the new conditions to take place more quickly and more surely than if a new and original act of creation were required. Once these types and roles of heuristics in the equilibrating process are understood and appreciated, the differences between the institutionalist and theorist wings of our Association may be seen to be far less fundamental and irreconcilable than the sometimes ferocious polemics of the last 20 years might seem to suggest.

REFERENCES

1. Victor L. Andrews. "Captive Finance Companies," *Harvard Business Review*, Vol. 42 (July-August 1964), 80–92.
2. Martin J. Bailey. "Capital Gains and Income Taxation," In *The Taxation of Income From Capital*. Edited by A. Harberger and M. Bailey. (Washington, D.C.: The Brookings Distribution, 1969).
3. ———. "Progressivity and Investment Yields under U.S. Income Taxation," *Journal of Political Economy*, Vol. 82, No. 6 (Nov./Dec. 1974), 1157–75.
4. Ku B. Bhatia. "Capital Gains and Inequality of Personal Income: Some Results From Survey Data," *Journal of the American Statistical Association*, Vol. 71, No. 355 (September 1976), 575–580.
5. Nevins Baxter. "Leverage, Risk of Ruin and the Cost of Capital," *Journal of Finance*, Vol. 22, No. 3 (September 1967), 395–403.
6. Fischer Black. "Bank Funds Management in an Efficient Market," *Journal of Financial Economics*, Vol. 2, No. 4 (December 1975).
7. ———. "Taxes and Capital Market Equilibrium." Working Paper No. 21A, Associates in Finance, Belmont, Massachusetts, April 1971 (mimeo).
8. ———. "Taxes and Capital Market Equilibrium under Uncertainty," Working Paper No. 21B, Chicago, May 1973 (mimeo).

27. Has anyone a better explanation for the puzzle of why the pay-back criterion continues to thrive despite having been denounced as Neanderthal in virtually every textbook in finance and accounting over the last 30 years?

28. Any experienced teacher of corporate finance can surely supply numerous examples of such neutral variations. My own favorite is the captive finance company. See, e.g., the perceptive discussion in Andrews [1].

9. ———, Merton H. Miller and Richard A. Posner. "An Approach to the Regulation of Bank Holding Companies," University of Chicago, April 1976 (multilith).

10. ——— and Myron Scholes. "The Effects on Dividend Yield and Dividend Policy on Common Stock Prices and Returns," *Journal of Financial Economics*, Vol. 1, No. 1 (May 1974), 1–22.

11. Marshall E. Blume, Jean Crockett and Irwin Frend. "Stock Ownership in The United States: Characteristics and Trends," *Survey of Current Business* (November 1974), 16–40.

12. M. J. Brennan and E. S. Schwartz. "Corporate Income Taxes, Valuation and the Problem of Optimal Capital Structure," University of British Columbia, Vancouver, B.C., Canada, multilith, August 1976 (revised).

13. J. H. Coates and P. K. Wooley. "Corporate Gearing in the E.E.C.," *Journal of Business Finance and Accounting*, Vol. 2, No. 1 (Spring 1975), 1–18.

14. David Durand. "The Cost of Capital, Corporation Finance and the Investment: Comment," *American Economic Review*, Vol. 49, No. 4 (Sept. 1959), 39–55.

15. Donald Farrar and Lee L. Selwyn. "Taxes, Corporate Policy, and Returns to Investors," *National Tax Journal*, Vol. 20, No. 4 (December 1967), 444–54.

16. R. Alton Gilbert. "Bank Financing of the Recovery," *Federal Reserve Bank of St. Louis Review*, Vol. 58, No. 7, 2–9.

17. David W. Glenn. "Super Premium Security Prices and Optimal Corporate Financial Decisions," *Journal of Finance*, Vol. 31, No. 2 (May 1976), 507–24.

18. Nils Hakansson. "Ordering Markets and the Capital Structures of Firms, with Illustrations," Working Paper No. 24, Institute of Business and Economic Research, University of California, Berkeley, October 1974 (multilith).

19. Robert Hamada. "Discussion," *Journal of Finance*, Vol. 31, No. 2 (May 1976), 543–46.

20. Michael C. Jensen and William H. Meckling. "Theory of the Firm: Managerial Behavior, Agency Costs and Capital Structure," University of Rochester, August 1975 (multilith).

21. Han E. Kim. "A Mean-Variance Theory of Optimum Capital Structure and Corporate Debt Capacity," Ohio State University, undated (multilith).

22. Ronald W. Masulis. "The Effects of Capital Structure Change on Security Prices," Graduate School of Business, University of Chicago, May 1976 (multilith).

23. J. Huston McCulloch. "The Tax Adjusted Yield Curve," *Journal of Finance*, Vol. 30, No. 3 (June 1975), 811–30.

24. Merton H. Miller. "The Corporation Income Tax and Corporate Financial Policies," In *Stabilization Policies*, Commission on Money and Credit, Prentice Hall, 1963.

25. ——— and Franco Modigliani. "Dividend Policy, Growth and the Valuation of Shares," *Journal of Business*, Vol. 34, No. 4 (October 1961), 411–33.

26. ——— and Charles W. Upton. "Leasing, Buying and the Cost of Capital Services." *Journal of Finance* (June 1976).

27. Franco Modigliani and Merton H. Miller. "Corporate Income Taxes and the Cost of Capital: A Correction," *American Economic Review*, Vol. 53, No. 3 (June 1963), 433–43.

28. ——— and ———. "The Cost of Capital, Corporation Finance and the Theory of Investment," *American Economic Review*, Vol. 48, No. 3 (June 1958), 261–97.

29. ——— and ———. "Reply to Heins and Sprenkle," *American Economic Review*, Vol. 59, No. 4, Part I (September 1969).

30. Stewart C. Myers. "Taxes, Corporate Financial Policy and the Return to Investors: Comment," *National Tax Journal*, Vol. 20, No. 4 (Dec. 1967), 455–62.

31. Sidney M. Robbins. "A Bigger Role for Income Bonds," *Harvard Business Review* (November-December 1955).

32. ———. "An Objective Look at Income Bonds," *Harvard Business Review* (June 1974).

33. Arnold W. Sametz. "Trends in the Volume and Composition of Equity Finance," *Journal of Finance*, Vol. 19, No. 3 (September 1964), 450–469.

34. Eli Schwartz and J. Richard Aronson. "Some Surrogate Evidence in Support of the Concept of Optimal Financial Structure," *Journal of Finance*, Vol. 22, No. 1 (March 1963), 10–18.

35. Eli Shapiro. "The Postwar Market for Corporate Securities: 1946–55," *Journal of Finance*, Vol. 14, No. 2 (May 1959), 196–217.

36. D. T. Stanley and M. Girth. *Bankruptcy: Problem, Process, Reform.* (Washington, D.C.: The Brookings Institution, 1971).

37. R. C. Stapleton. "Taxes, the Cost of Capital and the Theory of Investment," *The Economic Journal*, Vol. 82 (December 1972), 1273–92.

38. Joseph Stiglitz. "Taxation, Corporate Financial Policy, and the Cost of Capital," *Journal of Public Economics*, Vol. 2, No. 1 (February 1973), 1–34.

39. James C. Van Horne. "Corporate Liquidity and Bankruptcy Costs," Stanford University, Graduate School of Business, Research Paper No. 205, undated (multilith).

40. Jerold Warner. "Bankruptcy Costs, Absolute Priority and the Pricing of Risky Debt Claims," University of Chicago, July 1976 (multilith).

THE OPTION PRICING MODEL AND THE RISK FACTOR OF STOCK*

Dan GALAI

Hebrew University, Jerusalem, Israel

Ronald W. MASULIS

University of Chicago, Chicago, Ill. 60637, U.S.A.

Received February 1975, revised version received May 1975

In this paper a combined capital asset pricing model and option pricing model is considered and then applied to the derivation of equity's value and its systematic risk. In the first section we develop the two models and present some newly found properties of the option pricing model. The second section is concerned with the effects of these properties on the securityholders of firms with less than perfect 'me first' rules. We show how unanticipated changes in firm capital and asset structures can differentially affect the firm's debt and equity. In the final section of the paper we consider a number of theoretical and empirical implications of the joint model. These include investment policy as well as the causes and effects of non-stationarity in the systematic risk of levered equity and risky debt.

1. Introduction

The basic premise of this paper is that combining the option pricing model (OPM) with the capital asset pricing model (CAPM) yields a theoretically more complete model of corporate security pricing.[1] From this vantage point we focus upon the issue of risk in corporate stock. We show that this synthesis of models leads to a number of insights regarding stock risk and changes in corporate asset structure and capital structure. In the process, we consider some important issues in corporate finance, illustrating the analytical advantages of this combined pricing model. Among these advantages is the ability to treat many of the issues in the corporate finance literature in a consistent and unified manner that can be easily quantified. Essentially, this paper is an attempt to gain a clearer focus, both theoretically and empirically, on the question of corporate stock risk and how the OPM adds to its understanding.

*We would like to thank J. Babad, F. Black, E. Fama, L. Fisher, N. Hakansson, M. Jensen, M. Miller, M. Rubinstein, M. Scholes and the participants in the Workshop in Finance at the Graduate School of Business, University of Chicago, 1974, for helpful comments on earlier drafts. We are especially grateful to N. Gonedes and R. Hamada for their help and encouragement. All remaining errors are ours.

[1] Many of the theoretical results concerning the OPM used in our paper have their origin in Black–Scholes (1973) and Merton (1973a and 1974).

To simplify the analysis, we will consider a firm with one pure-discount bond issue and one common stock issue. The bond with face value C will mature at T (i.e., T periods from the current period which is denoted by 0) and at that time, the firm will liquidate itself. Up to T, the firm does not experience any net cash flows and pays no dividends to its shareholders. Under this set of simplifying assumptions, Black–Scholes (1973) observed that common stock can be regarded as a European call option.[2]

After listing the assumptions needed, the capital asset pricing model and the option pricing model are presented in their continuous time framework. We explain how the firm's equity can be viewed as a call option when the underlying asset is the firm. From this perspective, the CAPM and the OPM yield the equilibrium value and expected rate of return of the firm and its equity (and debt) simultaneously. The implications of this interpretation of equity will be illustrated by a number of case studies, considering differences in firm asset and capital structures. In addition, we consider some portfolio rebalancing rules for firms, which protect the interests of all its securityholders. The final part will be devoted to implications – theoretical and empirical – of pricing corporate stock.[3]

2. The assumptions

Under the following set of assumptions both the capital asset pricing model and the option pricing model can be derived.[4]

(a) All individuals have a strictly concave von Neuman–Morgenstern utility function and are expected utility maximizers.
(b) There are homogeneous expectations about the dynamics of firm asset values and of security prices.
(c) The capital markets are perfect: there are no transaction costs or taxes and all traders have free and costless access to all available information. Traders are price takers in the capital markets, i.e., they are atomistic competitors.[5]
(d) There are no costs of voluntary liquidation or bankruptcy, e.g., court or reorganization costs, where bankruptcy is defined as the state when the value of the firm's assets is less than the face value of the maturing debt.

---

[2]See Masulis (1975) for an application of the OPM to firms with more complex capital structures.
[3]Those familiar with the CAPM and the OPM may prefer to go directly to section 5 entitled 'Risk of equity', ignoring the description of the models in the preceding two sections.
[4]Note that this set of assumptions is a sufficient set; specifically, assumptions (a) and (b) are not required for the derivation of the OPM. Some assumptions are stronger than needed. Merton, for example, proves that the CAPM can be derived for a more general case where the dynamics of the price change can be described by the instantaneous expected rate of return $\bar{r}_i$ and the instantaneous standard deviation of return σ_i and a simple Gauss–Wiener process (Gaussian 'white noise'). The parameters $\bar{r}_i$ and σ_i are not necessarily constant over time; if they are, then we have a log-normal distribution as assumed above [i.e., assumption (g)]. For further details, see Merton (1973b).

(e) There is a known instantaneously riskless interest rate which is constant through time and is equal for borrowers and lenders.

(f) Borrowing and short-selling by all investors and free use of all proceeds are allowed.

(g) The distribution of firm asset value at the end of any finite time interval is log normal. The variance of the rate of return on the firm is constant.

(h) Trading takes place continuously, price changes are continuous and assets are infinitely divisible.

3. The capital asset pricing model and the valuation of the firm[6]

It is implicit in the CAPM that investors differentiate assets only according to the assets' expected rates of return and their contribution to the variance of investors' efficient portfolios. According to the continuous time CAPM, the capital market will be in equilibrium only if at each instant of time assets are priced so that

$$\bar{r}_i = r_F + \beta_i(\bar{r}_M - r_F). \tag{1}$$

The instantaneous expected rate of return of asset i, $\bar{r}_i$, is a linear function of its instantaneous systematic risk β_i. The slope is determined by the instantaneous market risk premium $(\bar{r}_M - r_F)$ and the intercept is the instantaneous riskless interest rate r_F, where $\bar{r}_M$ is the instantaneous expected rate of return on the market. The instantaneous systematic risk is defined as

$$\beta_i \equiv \text{cov}\,(\tilde{r}_i, \tilde{r}_M)/\sigma^2(\tilde{r}_M), \tag{2}$$

the instantaneous covariability of asset i's percentage return with the percentage return on the market, standardized by the instantaneous variance of the market's percentage return. It should be noted that the instantaneous expected rate of return $\bar{r}_i$ is not a direct function of the instantaneous variance of the *asset's* rate of return. This variance includes non-systematic risk which can be costlessly diversified away; therefore, the market price for bearing this risk is zero.

We have assumed that our firm J expects to realize all its cash flows at the end

[5]We do not interpret perfect capital markets as implying the existence of side payments between classes of securityholders or of perfect 'me first' rules. For our purposes, we define perfect 'me first' rules as rules restricting the firm's management from changing its asset or capital structure in any way that improves the value of one class of securities at the expense of another class. It should be obvious that perfect 'me first' rules would, in general, severely restrict the actions of a firm. For a further discussion of perfect competition in the capital market see Merton–Subrahmanyam (1974).

[6]The derivation of the CAPM in a discrete time framework can be found in Sharpe (1963 and 1964), Lintner (1965a and 1965b), Mossin (1966), and Fama–Miller (1972, chs. 6 and 7); and in a continuous time framework in Merton (1970 and 1973b). Jensen (1972) summarizes the different approaches and provides a survey of empirical tests of the model.

of a discrete period of length T. Given the finite life of the firm, the equilibrium present value of the firm can be written as follows:

$$V_0^J = \left[\, \bar{V}_T^J - \frac{\lambda \, \text{cov}\,(\tilde{V}_T^J, \; \tilde{V}_T^M)}{\sigma(\tilde{V}_T^M)}\,\right]\bigg/ (1+R_F). \tag{3}$$

The present value of firm J, V_0^J, is equal to the expected terminal value of the firm $\bar{V}_T^J$ minus a premium for bearing non-diversifiable risk, all discounted at the discrete time riskless rate of return R_F,[7] where $\tilde{V}_T^M$ is the market value at T of the aggregate value of all risky firms (assuming all of them liquidate their assets at T), and cov $(\tilde{V}_T^J, \tilde{V}_T^M)$ is the covariance of firm asset value with total market value over T. A unit of risk is measured by cov $(\tilde{V}_T^J, \tilde{V}_T^M)/\sigma(\tilde{V}_T^M)$; and λ, which is the market price per unit of risk, is defined by $(\bar{R}_M - R_F)/\sigma(\bar{R}_M)$, where $\bar{R}_M$ is defined as the discrete time expected market rate of return.[8] Note that while we assume the firm's cash flow is discrete, trading in the firm's securities is continuous throughout the period.

4. The option pricing model and the valuation of equity

The option pricing model as derived by Black–Scholes (1973) applies to European-type options.[9] They create a perfect hedge, at each instant of time, composed of one unit long (short) of the underlying security and a short (long) position on a number of options. The return on a completely hedged position should be equal to the riskless return on the investment in order to eliminate arbitrage opportunities. The resulting value for a European call option is[10]

$$S = VN(d_1) - C\,e^{-r_F T}N(d_2), \tag{4}$$

where V is the current value of the underlying asset, σ^2 is the instantaneous variance of percentage returns on V, C is the exercise price of the option, T is the time to maturity, r_F is the riskless interest rate, $N(\cdot)$ is the standardized normal cumulative probability density function, and

$$d_1 \equiv \frac{\ln(V/C) + (r_F + \tfrac{1}{2}\sigma^2)T}{\sigma\sqrt{T}},$$

[7] R_F is the instantaneous riskless rate of return r_F, continuously compounded over period T.
[8] $\bar{R}_M$ is the instantaneous expected market rate of return $\bar{r}_M$, continuously compounded over period T.
[9] European-type options are options that cannot be exercised before the expiration date. For a basic description of options see Kruizenga (1967) and Galai (1974a and 1974b).
[10] Assuming the firm's asset value is unaffected by its capital structure it can be shown that the debt of our firm has the value

$$D = V - S = VN(-d_1) + C\,e^{-r_F T}N(d_2).$$

and

$$d_2 \equiv d_1 - \sigma\sqrt{T}.$$

For the kind of firm which we have hypothesized above, it was shown by Black–Scholes (1973) that the firm's equity can be regarded as a European call option. To see this note that the owner of a call option has claim to the slice of a stock's price distribution to the right of the exercise price at maturity date T. Similarly, a firm's stockholders have claim to the slice of the firm's price distribution to the right of the face value of the firm's debt at its maturity date. To complete the analogy we view the stockholders as having an option to buy back the firm (whose current market value is V) from the bondholders for an exercise price equal to the face value of the firm's debt C at time T. If the value of the firm at maturity V_T is above C, the equity will have a positive value; if it is below, the stock is valueless. In other words, the stockholders have protection against depreciation of the firm's value below C (this is the 'limited liability' nature of equity) and have a right to the appreciation in the firm's value above C.

We can apply the comparative static results derived for call options by Black–Scholes (1973) and Merton (1973a) for our model to show the effect of the parameters in eq. (4) on the value of the stock. It can be shown that[11]

$$1 \geq \frac{\partial S}{\partial V} \geq 0, \quad \frac{\partial S}{\partial C} < 0, \quad \frac{\partial S}{\partial r_F} > 0, \quad \frac{\partial S}{\partial \sigma^2} > 0, \quad \frac{\partial S}{\partial T} > 0. \tag{5}$$

In words, the value of the stock is an increasing function of the value of the firm, the riskless interest rate, the variance of the percentage return of the firm and the time to liquidation; and it is a decreasing function of the face value of the debt.[12]

The above formulation requires only partial equilibrium. Given the current market value of the firm V, eq. (4) tells us the equilibrium value of the equity; however, this does not require that V be the equilibrium value of the firm. Nevertheless, as was indicated above, we can find the equilibrium value of the firm using the CAPM. It should be noted again that while S is a function of the firm's current market value and the variance of the firm's rate of return, it is not directly a function of the firm's expected rate of return or systematic risk, as will be explained in the next section.

[11] See appendix I for actual values of the partial derivatives. From the equation in footnote 10 it was shown by Merton (1974) that

$$\frac{\partial D}{\partial V} = 1 - \frac{\partial S}{\partial V}, \quad \frac{\partial D}{\partial C} = -\frac{\partial S}{\partial C}, \quad \frac{\partial D}{\partial r_F} = -\frac{\partial S}{\partial r_F}, \quad \frac{\partial D}{\partial \sigma^2} = -\frac{\partial S}{\partial \sigma^2}, \quad \frac{\partial D}{\partial T} = -\frac{\partial S}{\partial T}.$$

[12] For comparative static purposes these changes of variables can be either anticipated or unanticipated, but for dynamic analysis they must be unanticipated by the market.

5. The risk of equity[13]

Now we will show that if the systematic risk of the firm β_V is constant over time, the instantaneous risk of the equity β_S will not necessarily be stable or known with certainty for the time period in question. Therefore, determining the current value of the equity from the CAPM, even when its expected value at the horizon point T is known, is not a facile procedure.

From stochastic calculus and our assumptions, the dollar return on an option, and thus the dollar return on the equity, can be described as

$$\Delta S = S_V \Delta V + \tfrac{1}{2} S_{VV} \sigma^2 V^2 \Delta t + S_t \Delta t,$$

where $S_V \equiv \partial S / \partial V$, $S_{VV} \equiv \partial^2 S / \partial V^2$ and $S_t \equiv \partial S / \partial t$. Dividing ΔS by S and substituting for $\tilde{r}_S$ we obtain in the limit (as $\Delta t \to 0$)

$$\frac{\Delta S}{S} = \frac{S_V}{S} V \frac{\Delta V}{V} \quad \text{or} \quad \tilde{r}_S = \frac{S_V}{S} V \tilde{r}_V. \tag{6}$$

Defining β_S according to (2) and substituting into the instantaneous covariance term of definition (6) yields[14]

$$\beta_S \equiv \frac{\text{cov}(\tilde{r}_S, \tilde{r}_M)}{\sigma^2(\tilde{r}_M)} = \frac{S_V}{S} V \frac{\text{cov}(\tilde{r}_V, \tilde{r}_M)}{\sigma^2(\tilde{r}_M)} \equiv \frac{S_V}{S} V \beta_V. \tag{7}$$

In words, the systematic risk of equity is the product of the firm's systematic risk and the elasticity of equity value with respect to firm value.

Taking the derivative of stock value with respect to firm value in the OPM equation (4), Black–Scholes (1973) found that $S_V = N(d_1)$. So combining the CAPM with the OPM yields[15,16]

$$\beta_S = N(d_1) \frac{V}{S} \beta_V \equiv \eta_S \beta_V. \tag{8}$$

---

[13] Parts of the analysis here are based on Black–Scholes (1973).
[14] See Black–Scholes (1973, eq. 15).
[15] The partial derivative of the debt value with respect to the firm value is shown in the equation in footnote 11 to be

$$D_V = 1 - S_V = N(-d_1).$$

Repeating the arguments used to prove eq. (7) we obtain the relationship between the systematic risk of the bond and of the firm,

$$\beta_D = D_V \frac{V}{D} \beta_V = N(-d_1) \frac{V}{D} \beta_V \equiv \eta_D \beta_V.$$

[16] Given $\sigma_S^2 \equiv \text{cov}(\tilde{r}_S, \tilde{r}_S)$, we can also show that $\sigma_S = S_V(V/S)\sigma_V \equiv \eta_S \sigma_V$.

Substituting eq. (4) into the definition of the elasticity term η_S in eq. (8), we obtain

$$\eta_S \equiv \frac{VN(d_1)}{S} = \frac{VN(d_1)}{VN(d_1) - C e^{-r_F T} N(d_2)}$$

$$= \frac{1}{1 - (C/V) e^{-r_F T}(N(d_2)/N(d_1))} .$$

The limited liability characteristic of options $0 \leqq S = VN(d_1) - C e^{-r_F T} N(d_2)$ implies

$$\frac{C e^{-r_F T} N(d_2)}{VN(d_1)} \leqq 1 ,$$

so the denominator of the right-hand term of the definition of η_S is less than one. Since $\eta_S \geqq 1$, the systematic risk of equity is greater than or equal to the systematic risk of the firm (for $\beta_V > 0$).

In the case where the firm's systematic risk is stationary, the implication of eq. (8) is that its equity's systematic risk will generally be non-stationary.[17] That is, for the vector of parameters V, C, r_F, σ^2 and T denoted as K,

$$\frac{\partial \beta_S}{\partial K} = \frac{\partial \eta_S}{\partial K} \beta_V + \frac{\partial \beta_V}{\partial K} \eta_S . \tag{9}$$

But by the assumption of stationarity for β_V, we then obtain

$$\frac{\partial \beta_S}{\partial K} = \frac{\partial \eta_S}{\partial K} \beta_V .$$

We have proved that (when $\beta_V > 0$)[18]

$$\frac{\partial \beta_S}{\partial V} < 0, \quad \frac{\partial \beta_S}{\partial C} > 0, \quad \frac{\partial \beta_S}{\partial r_F} < 0, \quad \frac{\partial \beta_S}{\partial \sigma^2} < 0, \quad \frac{\partial \beta_S}{\partial T} < 0. \tag{10}$$

The analysis indicates that the relationship between the systematic risk of the firm β_V and of its equity β_S is not only a positive function of the firm's leverage

[17]Even with a non-stationary β_V, this conclusion will generally be correct. However, we need to replace the Black–Scholes OPM with the more general formulation. See Merton (1973a).

[18]See appendix I for the proofs. For $\beta_V < 0$, the signs of the partial derivatives are reversed. Generally, a firm's systematic risk can be stationary only when the firm's asset structure is composed entirely of physical assets. This excludes all financial assets with the exception of riskless debt and unlevered equity.

V/S as shown by Hamada (1972),[19] but that it is a positive function of the face value of debt C and a negative function of the value of the firm V, the riskless interest rate r_F, the variance of the firm's percentage returns σ^2 and the time to maturity of the firm's debt T.[20] Since β_S is a function of the time to maturity of the debt and the realizations of V at each instant, it will usually change from instant to instant.

The factors determining the expected rate of return on equity have been extensively analyzed in the existing literature. A few of the more important results will be reinterpreted and extended below, utilizing the option characteristics of equity.

The instantaneous expected rate of return of a firm is equal to the instantaneous expected rates of return of its securities (debt and equity) weighted by the relative value of their claims on the firm,[21]

$$\bar{r}_V = \frac{S}{V}\bar{r}_S + \frac{D}{V}\bar{r}_D, \tag{11}$$

so that

$$\bar{r}_S = \bar{r}_V + [\bar{r}_V - \bar{r}_D]\frac{D}{S}. \tag{12}$$

Eq. (12) is proposition II of Modigliani–Miller generalized to risky debt where the CAPM has replaced the risk class assumption.[22,23] Defining $\bar{r}_S$ from eq. (1) and substituting for β_S from eq. (8) and for $\beta_V = (\bar{r}_V - r_F)/(\bar{r}_M - r_F)$ from eq. (1), we obtain an alternative expression of the instantaneous expected rate of return on equity,

$$\bar{r}_S = r_F + N(d_1)[\bar{r}_V - r_F]\frac{V}{S}. \tag{13}$$

[19] $\beta_S = (V/S)\beta_V$ (Hamada's equation 4a) which assumed that the debt was riskless. Hence, eq. (8) is a generalization of the Hamada result.

[20] It is also shown in appendix I that for $\partial\beta_V/\partial K = 0$ and $\beta_V > 0$,

$$\frac{\partial\beta_D}{\partial V} < 0, \quad \frac{\partial\beta_D}{\partial C} > 0, \quad \frac{\partial\beta_D}{\partial r_F} < 0, \quad \frac{\partial\beta_D}{\partial\sigma^2} \gtrless 0, \quad \frac{\partial\beta_D}{\partial T} \gtrless 0.$$

These results are consistent with Merton's (1974) results,

$$\frac{\partial\beta_D}{\partial\sigma^2 T} \gtrless 0 \quad \text{and} \quad \frac{\partial\beta_D}{\partial g} > 0, \quad \text{where} \quad g \equiv \frac{C\,e^{-r_F T}}{V}.$$

[21] The instantaneous expected rate of return defined in eq. (1) holds for any asset including options.

[22] See Modigliani–Miller (1958) and Fama–Miller (1972, ch. 4).

[23] For riskless debt $\bar{r}_D = r_F$, which substituted into eq. (12) yields Hamada's (1969) equation 13. Merton (1974) shows eq. (12) to be a concave function of D/S.

Rubinstein (1973) interprets the first term on the right-hand side of eq. (12) to represent the expected rate of return for the operating risk and the second term to represent the financial risk of a levered firm borne by its stockholders. Eq. (13) can also be written as

$$\bar{r}_S = \bar{r}_V + (\bar{r}_V - r_F)(\eta_S - 1), \tag{14}$$

and the second term on the right-hand side of the equation stands for that part of the shareholder's return due to financial risk. Hence the expected rate of return due to financial risk can be written as follows:

$$(\bar{r}_V - \bar{r}_D)\frac{D}{S} = (\bar{r}_V - r_F)(\eta_S - 1) = (\bar{r}_V - r_F)\frac{C\,e^{-r_F T}N(d_2)}{S}. \tag{15}$$

From this expression we can see explicitly the terms that contribute to the higher required expected rate of return by stockholders due to leverage.

By using eq. (1) with our previous results for β_S in (10) we can show that

$$\frac{\partial \bar{r}_S}{\partial V} < 0, \quad \frac{\partial \bar{r}_S}{\partial C} > 0, \quad \frac{\partial \bar{r}_S}{\partial r_F} \gtreqless 0, \quad \frac{\partial \bar{r}_S}{\partial \sigma^2} < 0, \quad \frac{\partial \bar{r}_S}{\partial T} < 0, \tag{16}$$

for the instantaneous expected rate of return on equity.[24]

In the next section we will utilize the above analysis to explore a number of important questions in corporate finance. The implications of this analysis for empirical investigations of the CAPM will be emphasized in the last section.

6. Case studies

Throughout these case studies we will take a comparative-static approach. To do this we will first compare two, initially identical, firms (A and B) after changing one or more of firm B's relevant characteristics. The comparative firm analysis will be accompanied by numerical examples which can help to explain some observed differences in equity across firms. This will be followed by a comparative-static analysis of a single firm where firm B will now represent firm A at a second point in time.

We will consider, in the course of each case study, the effects of unanticipated changes in specific variables upon the systematic risk, the expected rate of return and the market value of a single firm's debt and equity. The analysis highlights the potential for a redistribution of wealth from one security class to another

---

[24]For $\beta_V < 0$ the signs of the partial derivative are reversed, with the exception that $\partial \bar{r}_S / \partial r_F > 0$.

E

when perfect 'me first' rules[25] or side payments between security classes are non-existent or prohibitively expensive. From this analysis, we can better understand the motivations for indenture restrictions[26] and a number of firm asset and capital structure changes.

Strictly speaking, while these redistribution effects exist in the Sharpe–Lintner CAPM, they will be irrelevant. This follows from the property of the CAPM that all investors hold the market portfolio; therefore, all investors hold equal proportions of each firm's debt and equity. Consequently, shifts of wealth from one class of securities to another leave all investors indifferent.[27] Thus, protection or 'me first' rules are not needed and serve no economic purpose under these conditions. Such indifference to redistributions will not exist if investors do not all hold the market portfolio.[28] We believe that our comparative-static analysis can, despite its limitations, serve a useful purpose in highlighting some of the potential effects of alternative corporate policies.

We will begin by comparing two levered firms (A and B) which in each case study differ in one or more relevant variables. The two firms have the same liquidation date, which is T periods from now, and at that time the pure discount bonds of both will mature. The parameters of the firms A and B are given in table 1. Throughout the discussion tildes will denote stochastic variables and bars will denote expected values of variables.

Table 1

Variables of the firm	Firm A	Firm B	General
Current market value of firm	V_0^A	V_0^B	V_0
Terminal market value of firm	V_T^A	V_T^B	V_T
Current market value of shares	S_0^A	S_0^B	S_0
Current market value of debt	D_0^A	D_0^B	D_0
Systematic risk of firm	β_V^A	β_V^B	β_V
Systematic risk of shares	β_S^A	β_S^B	β_S
Variance of rate of return of the firm	σ_A^2	σ_B^2	σ^2
Rate of return of the firm	r_V^A	r_V^B	r_V
Rate of return of the shares	r_S^A	r_S^B	r_S
Face value of debt maturing at T	C_A	C_B	C

Case I. Rate of return variability and changes due to acquisitions and divestitures

Assume that

(a) $C_A = C_B,$

[25] See footnote 5 for a clarification of this assumption and the definition of 'me first' rules.
[26] For an earlier qualitative analysis of this conflict of interest among securityholders, see Fama–Miller (1972, pp. 150–156, 178–180).
[27] For that matter, shifts of wealth between firms also leave investors indifferent.
[28] This is true of the Mayers (1973) CAPM with non-marketable human capital, which otherwise exhibits the major properties of the Sharpe–Lintner CAPM.

(b) $\qquad \bar{V}_T^A = \bar{V}_T^B,$

(c) $\qquad \text{cov}\,(\tilde{V}_t^A, \tilde{V}_t^M) = \text{cov}\,(\tilde{V}_t^B, \tilde{V}_t^M), \qquad 0 \leq t \leq T.$

$\tilde{V}_t^M$ is defined at the end of section 3, and

(d) $\qquad \sigma_A^2 > \sigma_B^2.$

From assumptions (b) and (c), and using eq. (3), we find that the market value of the two firms is identical, $V_0^A = V_0^B$. The two firms are in the same risk class with the same systematic risk. They differ in their total variability of returns. How will this affect the market value of the shares of firms A and B?

If $\sigma_A^2 > \sigma_B^2$, then we can prove, using the OPM, that $D_0^A < D_0^B$ and $S_0^A > S_0^B$.[29] The proof is based on the fact that options' values will be an increasing function of the variance of the underlying security, ceteris paribus. With the exception of rate of return variability, the parameters that determine the equity value of firms A and B are identical in terms of eq. (4) [note, however, that the *equities'* co-variability with the market is not assumed to be the same]. We showed before that equity can be regarded as a call option, and thus we can apply the result $\partial S_0 / \partial \sigma^2 > 0$ directly.[30] We conclude that firms with apparently similar characteristics with regard to face value of debt, total market value and profitability, but with a different variance of rate of return, will have a different capital structure in market value terms. The market value of the debt–equity ratio (D/S) will be greater for the firm with lower variance. In our example, it will be true that $D_0^A / S_0^A < D_0^B / S_0^B$.

To see the effect more clearly, we will assume that

$$V_0^A = V_0^B = \$1{,}000,$$

$$C_A = C_B = \$500,$$

$$\sigma_A^2 = 0.10\,(10\%), \qquad \sigma_B^2 = 0.05\,(5\%),$$

$$R_F = 0.08\,(8\%).$$

Then, for $T = 5$ (e.g., five years) we find, using eq. (4), that

$$S_0^A = \$675, \qquad S_0^B = \$666,$$

[29]See the derivatives in eq. (5) and footnote 11.
[30]For the derivation see appendix I.

and therefore,

$$D_0^A = \$325, \qquad D_0^B = \$334.$$

If we raise the variance of the rate of return of firm A to $\sigma_A^2 = 0.15$, then

$$S_0^A = \$688, \qquad D_0^A = \$312.$$

Alternatively, if we lowered the face value of the debt of both firms to $400, we obtain (for $\sigma_A^2 = 0.10$ and $\sigma_B^2 = 0.05$)

$$S_0^A = \$736, \qquad S_0^B = \$732,$$

and

$$D_0^A = \$264, \qquad D_0^B = \$268.$$

Differences in the variance of the rate of return of *firms* cause differences in the market value of the firm's equity and debt, and such differences can be quantified (at least for our simplified world). We see from the last example that the effect of such a difference in the variance on the value of the debt and equity is diminished by a decline in the debt–equity ratio.

Given the assumptions of this case study another prediction can be made with respect to the differences in the expected rates of return on the shares of the two firms. We previously showed that[31] $\partial \beta_S / \partial \sigma^2 < 0$, so we can expect to obtain lower rates of return on the equity of firms with larger rate of return variances σ^2 (i.e., firm A in our example). So the value of a firm's equity will be higher while its expected rate of return will be lower as a function of the firm's rate of return variance σ^2, ceteris paribus.

In the context of a single firm, consider management making an unanticipated acquisition, divestiture or other investment decision which changes the variance of the firm's rate of return.[32] To keep the presentation simple, view an acquisition as an exchange of riskless assets (riskless government securities) for risky physical assets, and a divestiture as just the reverse. Then it should be obvious that in a world of imperfect 'me first' rules, such an unanticipated investment decision will indeed change the market values of the firm's debt and equity.

Case II. Changes in the scale of a firm and the problem of dilution

Assume that

(a) $\qquad \tilde{V}_t^A = \alpha \tilde{V}_t^B, \qquad 0 \leqq t \leqq T.$

This implies

$$\bar{V}_T^A = \alpha \bar{V}_T^B,$$

[31] For firms with positive systematic risk, see appendix I.

[32] Assume for simplicity that the assets acquired or divested are economically independent of the other assets of the firm.

99

and

$$\text{cov}\,(\tilde{V}_t^A,\ \tilde{V}_t^M) = \alpha\,\text{cov}\,(\tilde{V}_t^B,\ \tilde{V}_t^M), \qquad 0 \leqq t \leqq T,$$

which together with the valuation eq. (3) yields

(b) $\qquad V_0^A = \alpha V_0^B.$

Assumption (a) also implies that the two firms' rates of return have perfect positive correlation and therefore

(c) $\qquad \sigma_A^2 = \sigma_B^2,$

and

(d) $\qquad \beta_V^A = \beta_V^B.$

If we further assume that

(e) $\qquad C_A = \alpha C_B,$

then from eq. (4) we see that $d_1^A = d_1^B$ and $d_2^A = d_2^B$, so

$$S_0^A = (\alpha V_0^B) N(d_1^B) - (\alpha C_B)\,e^{-r_F T} N(d_2^B) = \alpha S_0^B.$$

Hence, if two firms are identical except that they differ by the same proportion in terms of firm asset value and face value of debt, then their equities' (debts') value will also differ by this proportion. Using eq. (8) and then substituting in the above relationship yields

$$\beta_S^A = \frac{\alpha V_0^B}{\alpha S_0^B}\,N(d_1^B)\beta_V^B = \beta_S^B.$$

The systematic risk of the two firms' debt and equity are identical. They are unaffected by the proportional differences in the two firms.

We can reach the same conclusion for an unanticipated change in the scale of an individual firm, externally financed.[33] From the option pricing model alone, it can easily be shown that the value of equity and debt can be written as[34]

$$S = S_V V + S_C C, \tag{17}$$

---

[33] For simplicity we assume stochastic constant returns to scale, which is consistent with a perfectly competitive capital market as shown by Merton–Subrahmanyam (1974).

[34] Note that $S_V \equiv \partial S/\partial V = 1 - D_V$ and $S_C \equiv \partial S/\partial C = -D_C$, as defined in appendix I and footnote 11. Also see Merton (1973a, theorem 9).

and

$$D = D_V V + D_C C, \tag{18}$$

both of which are first-degree homogeneous functions of V and C. It can also be shown from the OPM that the systematic risk of the equity and debt are zero-degree homogeneous functions of V and C,[35] hence

$$\frac{\partial \beta_S}{\partial V} V + \frac{\partial \beta_S}{\partial C} C = 0, \tag{19}$$

and

$$\frac{\partial \beta_D}{\partial V} V + \frac{\partial \beta_D}{\partial C} C = 0. \tag{20}$$

The content of the above results is that there is a financing policy devoid of redistribution effects. For a proportional rise in the firm's scale of operations of $\Delta V/V$, the firm can issue debt until $\Delta C/C = \Delta V/V$ and then raise the remaining capital with new equity. This is equivalent to increasing the firm's debt and equity proportionately with the rise in the firm's scale.[36] If the firm's unanticipated expansion is financed in any other combination of debt and equity, there will be a 'watering down' or dilution effect on one or the other class of securities.[37]

Case III. Conglomerate mergers

In this case, we want to investigate the effects of a pure conglomerate merger, in a perfect capital market, on the values of the equity and debt of the two firms that are involved. Because the merger is defined as a conglomerate type, we are assuming that there is no economic 'synergy' effect.[38] Merger of two firms with less than a perfect correlation of their returns will decrease the variance of the new firm (assuming initially, without loss of generality, that $\sigma_A^2 = \sigma_B^2$), and thus reduce the value of the unprotected equity and increase the market value of debt.

We will assume that firm G owns exactly the same assets as held by firms A and B and that there is no economic dependence between the assets of the two firms. Specifically, we assume

(a) $\qquad \tilde{V}_t^G = \tilde{V}_t^A + \tilde{V}_t^B, \qquad 0 \leqq t \leqq T,$

[35]See appendix I for the partial derivatives.
[36]Since $\Delta D/D = \Delta C/C$, then $\Delta D/D = \Delta V/V$ which implies $\Delta S/S = \Delta V/V$.
[37]If the expansion is financed with only equity $\Delta V = \Delta S$, the old stock will be diluted. If the expansion is financed with debt (of the same seniority) the old debt's value is diluted. An equity-financed expansion decreases the systematic risk of the debt and equity since $\partial \beta_S/\partial V < 0$ and $\partial \beta_D/\partial V < 0$. A debt-financed expansion increases the systematic risk of the debt and equity since $\partial \beta_S/\partial C > 0$ and $\partial \beta_D/\partial C > 0$, and this dominates the effect of a rise in V for $\Delta C/C > \Delta V/V$, by the zero-degree homogeneity of eqs. (19) and (20) with respect to V and C.
[38]See Levy–Sarnat (1970), Lewellen (1971) and Lintner (1971).

which can be seen from the analysis of Case II to imply

(a') $V_0^G = V_0^A + V_0^B$,

and

(a") $\beta_V^G = \gamma\beta_V^A + (1-\gamma)\beta_V^B$,   where $\gamma = V_0^A/V_0^G$,

(b) $C_G = C_A + C_B$,

(c) $\rho(\tilde{r}_V^A, \tilde{r}_V^B) < 1$,

where ρ is the correlation coefficient.

For expositional simplicity we will further assume

(d) $\sigma_A^2 = \sigma_B^2$,

(e) $V_0^A/C_A = V_0^B/C_B$.

Assumptions (c) and (d) imply that[39]

(f) $\sigma_G^2 < \sigma_A^2 = \sigma_B^2$,

while assumptions (a'), (b) and (e) yield[40]

(g) $V_0^G/C_G = V_0^A/C_A = V_0^B/C_B$.

From the results (f) and (g) combined with the analysis of Case I, we see that eq. (4) implies

$$S_0^G < S_0^A + S_0^B \quad \text{and} \quad D_0^G > D_0^A + D_0^B.$$

The risk of ruin of firm G is smaller than that facing A or B separately ($\sigma_G^2 < \sigma_A^2 = \sigma_B^2$). Therefore the market value of firm G's bonds is greater than the sum of the market values of the bonds of firms A and B. Their promised terminal values are the same as shown in (b) above. On the other hand, the market value of firm G's stock is smaller than the sum of the values of firms A and B's stock by an equal amount.

This analysis can be applied to the case of a conglomerate merger. If investors are unprotected against changes in the volatility of their holdings, the value of

---

[39]Since $\sigma_G^2 = \gamma^2\sigma_A^2 + (1-\gamma)^2\sigma_B^2 + 2\gamma(1-\gamma)\sigma_A\sigma_B\rho(\tilde{r}_V^A, \tilde{r}_V^B)$, where $\gamma \equiv V_0^A/V_0^G$.

[40]From assumptions (a) and (b) we have $V_0^G/C_G = \delta(V_0^A/C_A) + (1-\delta)(V_0^B/C_B)$, where $\delta \equiv C_A/C_G$.

their holdings might be changed. It is assumed here that each bond of the two original firms is exchanged for a bond of identical face value, with the same seniority and maturity, and guaranteed by the new firm. This assumption, which will be discussed further at a later point, is made in order to emphasize the concept of 'debt capacity' in the firm. Stock in the new firm is distributed according to the relative equity value of the two firms before the merger is announced. Under the above assumptions the stockholder's position can be expected to deteriorate with the unanticipated announcement of a merger between A and B, due to the lower variance of the new firm's (denoted hereafter by G) rate of return. The bondholders of the merged firm G are better off since the risk of bankruptcy has decreased. What is taking place, as Rubinstein (1973) points out,[41] is that the bondholders receive more protection since the stockholders of each firm have to back the claims of the bondholders of both companies. The stockholders are hurt since their limited liability is weakened. An alternative solution to this refinancing problem is to retire the existing debt of firms A and B at their market value (assuming the market anticipates no redistribution effects) and then to issue debt in firm G with a market value equal to the preexisting debt of firms A and B. Other solutions are also possible.

In our world of no transaction costs of bankruptcy [assumption (d) of the OPM] there is no financial synergy which increases the value of the merged firm G as Lewellen (1971) and Lintner (1971, p. 107) assert, nor any economies of scale associated with the cost of capital as suggested by Levy–Sarnat (1970, p. 801). This can be seen once one recognizes that investors in the marketplace could have created an identical financial position by purchasing equal proportions of the debt and equity of the two firms. The value of the sum of all the merged firm's liabilities equals the sum of its assets, the latter being a function of the firm's production-investment policy. But firm G's production-investment policy is only the sum of the policies of the original two firms which are unchanged since there is no economic synergy in a pure conglomerate merger. So the value of firm G's liabilities is simply the sum of the asset values of firms A and B, which in turn are equal to the sum of their liabilities.[42] This result does not necessarily hold for the value of debt or equity alone because they are functions of the volatility of the firm's returns, and the volatility is not an additive function when assets are not perfectly positively correlated. Hence, changes in the values of specific liabilities can be expected to occur under mergers.

This case describes a situation where securityholders (i.e., stockholders, in our specific example) do not have adequate protection against financial policy that can change their wealth.[43] A more interesting question is how securityholders will be compensated so that they will have no incentive to block a conglomerate

---

[41]A similar, but rather qualitative, claim can be found in Higgins' comments (1971) to Lewellen's paper.

[42]This point is proved by Levy–Sarnat (1970).

[43]See Stiglitz (1969 and 1972), and Fama–Miller (1972, ch. 4, pp. 150–156).

type merger. In our example above, one way to do this is by issuing more debt with the same seniority and retiring a certain fraction of the merged firm's equity. By doing so, the value of the original bonds will decline. This process can be continued until the original bondholders' holdings have a market value identical to their combined market value before the merger took place. The result of this process is an increase in the debt–equity ratio of the merged firm. In other words, by increasing the debt–equity ratio of the merged firm, the market values of the original securityholders can be restored to their pre-merger levels. This result is consistent with the claim that mergers 'allow' the firms to increase their 'debt capacity'.[44] For some numerical examples of this type, see appendix II. As was mentioned previously, this process of refinancing is not unique – other alternatives also exist. Under our assumptions, the 'debt capacity' of the firm has increased, while the wealth of individual securityholders remains unchanged. In a world with corporate taxes where interest payments on debt are tax deductible, increases in 'debt capacity' increase the after tax value of the firm. This may help explain the motivations behind the conglomerate merger movement of recent years.

Case IV. Spin-offs[45]

The obverse of a merger is a spin-off: the division of a single firm into two separate corporate entities. The conventional procedure is to take a portion of a firm's assets, often a division relatively unrelated to the remaining operations of the firm, and create a legally independent firm with these assets. The crucial facet of the procedure hinges on distributing the shares of this new equity solely to the *stockholders* of the parent corporation. In effect, the stockholders have 'stolen away' a portion of the bondholders' collateral since they no longer have any claim on the assets of the new firm.

To illustrate this we will assume

(a) $\qquad \tilde{V}_t^G = \tilde{V}_t^A + \tilde{V}_t^B, \qquad 0 \leq t \leq T,$

implying no economic dependence between A and B. Assumption (a) implies

(b) $\qquad V_0^G = V_0^A + V_0^B.$

We can view firm G as being composed of two economically independent divisions A and B.[46] At time 0 firm G unexpectedly spins off division B, so that firm G is now composed solely of division A. Hence,

(c) $\qquad C_G = C_A.$

[44]See Lewellen (1971).
[45]Dividends can be treated similarly [as shown by Black–Scholes (1973)], as can the firm's repurchase of its own stock in the capital market (treasury stock).
[46]Note that in this case study we have gone directly to a comparative-static framework, omitting initial development of the comparative firm analysis.

As a result of the spin-off the debtholders of A (debtholders of firm G after the spin-off) find that their position has deteriorated because less assets now serve as collateral for the debt. Furthermore, the leverage V/C of the firm has gone up due to the loss in assets, so $\beta_S^A > \beta_S^G$ and $\beta_D^A > \beta_D^G$.[47] Moreover, the variance of the firm's rate of return will, in general, change ($\sigma_A^2 \neq \sigma_G^2$) due to the spin-off.[48] This would give the additional results illustrated in Case Study I. For simplicity, we will assume that this variance remains constant.

Hence, we observe that

$$D_0^A \lesseqgtr D_0^G,$$

which combined with the assumption (b) yields

$$S_0^A + S_0^B > S_0^G.$$

In words, the value of the holdings of the equityholders of firm G, who are now the equityholders of firms A and B, will increase at the expense of firm G's debtholders who are now the debtholders of firm A. This is just another case where the lack of protection against investment and financial decisions of the firm by classes of securityholders may result in deterioration of their positions. The qualitative analysis in all of the above cases can be quantified and thus illustrate more powerfully the extent of deterioration in the positions of specific classes of securityholders.

If, in any of the above cases, the firm's decision had been anticipated by the market, there would be no redistribution effects. However, if the market over-anticipates the magnitude of the firm's change in policy, the redistribution effects among the classes of securityholders would be *reversed*.

7. An application to corporate investment decisions

One question not considered in our case studies is that of corporate investment decision making. We continue to assume in this section that no side payments or perfect 'me first' rules are allowed or that the transactions costs of affecting such actions are prohibitively large.[49] Jensen–Long (1972) and Merton–Subrahman-yam (1974) proved that an unlevered firm in a perfectly competitive environment under uncertainty acts to maximize its current value. They implicitly, if not

[47]See the partial derivatives for V in eq. (10) and footnote 20.

[48]By substituting $\sigma_A{}^2$ for $\sigma_G{}^2$ in the equation

$$\sigma_G{}^2 = \alpha\sigma_A{}^2 + (1-\alpha)\sigma_B{}^2 + 2(1-\alpha)\alpha \operatorname{cov}(\tilde{r}_V{}^A, \tilde{r}_V{}^B),$$

where $\alpha \equiv V_0{}^A/V_0{}^G$, we see that $\sigma_G{}^2 \gtreqless \sigma_A{}^2$ if $\sigma_A{}^2 \lesseqgtr \sigma_B{}^2 + 2\alpha \operatorname{cov}(\tilde{r}_V{}^A, r_V{}^B)$.

[49]See footnote 5 for a further discussion of this assumption.

explicitly, assumed that this result would also hold for levered firms.[50] But in a world of imperfect 'me first' rules where the stockholders control the investment decisions of the firm, this may not be the case.[51] Consider a firm which unexpectedly finds a new investment opportunity. It has a choice between two mutually exclusive projects of equal profitability in terms of expected net cash flow (discounted for systematic risk), but one project has a higher variance of percentage returns. Then from our earlier analysis, it should be clear that the firm controlled by its stockholders will invest in the project of higher variance. Moreover, it is even possible that a more profitable investment project will be rejected in favor of a project with a higher variance of percentage returns. While a pure equity firm will accept a project if the market value of the firm is increased by the investment ($dV/dI \geq 0$), a levered firm will accept the project only if $dS/dI = (\partial S/\partial V)(dV/dI) + (\partial S/\partial \sigma^2)(d\sigma^2/dI) \geq 0$.[52] One interpretation of this is that the cost of capital used in making the firm's investment decisions is a negative function of the change in the firm's rate of return variance if the investment is accepted. The reason why the levered firm does not maximize the market value of the firm is due to an externality affecting the securityholders of the firm. For an unanticipated rise in the firm's variance of percentage returns due to a new investment project, there will be a fall in the value of the bonds and a rise in the value of the stock. This will also cause a rise in the systematic risk borne by the bondholders and a fall in that borne by the stockholders.[53]

8. Implications for empirical studies of debt and equity

A number of empirical implications can be derived from our model. Most of these implications are based on the result that the systematic risk and rate of return variance of levered equity and risky debt are in general non-stationary. Hence, the rate of return distributions of this debt and equity will generally also be non-stationary. This will present a number of statistical difficulties in measuring security risk and in testing the efficiency of the capital market or the validity of the CAPM, which we will now detail.

[50]Both the above studies utilized the simple CAPM which implies that everyone holds the market portfolio and therefore everyone holds an equal proportion of each firm's debt and equity. Hence there is no motive for affecting a redistribution of wealth without the introduction of a more 'realistic' asset pricing model.

[51]For an earlier treatment of this possibility using a state preference model, see Fama–Miller (1972, pp. 178–181).

[52]This assumes no change in firm scale. It is, rather, a change in asset composition, e.g., a change in the holdings of riskless government debt. For external financing or a dividend reduction the decision rules are as follows: for unlevered firms $dV/dI \geq 1$, and for levered firms $dS/dI = (\partial S/\partial V)(dV/dI) + (\partial S/\partial \sigma^2)(d\sigma^2/dI) + (\partial S/\partial C)(dC/dI) \geq 1$, where the third term only appears if there is some debt financing. This assumes that there is no effect on the total supply or composition of the capital market's assets.

[53]Actually, this result is an example of the moral hazard problem [see Arrow (1970)].

There is a great deal of empirical evidence by Blume (1968 and 1971), Gonedes (1973), Bachrach–Galai (1974) and others indicating that individual common stock β's are non-stationary. Surprisingly, little empirical work has been done, utilizing information concerning changes in the firm's asset and capital structure, to predict changes in its securities' risk. One notable exception is Hamada (1972). Utilizing a model which allows a firm only riskless debt, Hamada found that changing a firm's leverage may cause the systematic risk of the stock to be non-stationary.[54] 'The total firm's systematic risk may be stable (as long as the firm stays in the same risk class), whereas the common stock's systematic risk may not be stable merely because of unanticipated capital structure changes.'[55] He then went on to test this empirically and found that taking account of leverage improves the estimation of β (the variance of the estimates was lowered). This would seem to be only one of many possible sets of information concerning firm asset and capital structure changes which could help predict changes in the risk of individual securities.

In an efficient capital market, any new information reaching the market concerning asset values is immediately impounded into security prices. From our previous analysis of the variables causing redistribution effects, we should expect to find an empirical relationship between changes in security prices or in their systematic risk and the appearance of new information in the market concerning the variance of the firm's rate of return, the riskless interest rate, the time to maturity of its debt and the face value of debt to asset value ratio. So new information concerning changes in a firm's asset structure or financial structure as they affect the above variables should be seen to simultaneously change the prices and systematic risk of the firm's securities.

One implication of this is that one can expect on average that the realized rate of return on securities will be affected not only by changes in the expected terminal value but also by changes in their systematic risk. Unfortunately, this compounds the problem of measuring and interpreting the excess realized rates of return due to information effects such as the study done by Fama–Fisher–Jensen–Roll (1969). A more complete way of measuring the effects of information would be to devise a joint test of changes in systematic risk and excess realized rates of return. Aside from this methodological criticism of Fama–Fisher–Jensen–Roll, we also would like to suggest an alternative interpretation of their statistical results. They studied the information effects of stock splits and found that stocks which split and later had increases in dividends also had positive excess realized rates of return. They concluded that this shows that dividends give positive information about the firm to the market. From our earlier analysis, we would conclude that this phenomena may be due, at least in part, to the positive

---

[54]The option pricing model, in addition, implies that changes in the firm's variance of percentage returns, the remaining life of the debt, and riskless interest rate also affect the systematic risk of a firm's debt and equity.

[55]Hamada (1972, p. 443).

redistribution effect of the unanticipated dividend rise.[56] Moreover, we would predict an adverse effect upon the value of the firm's debt while the information hypothesis would predict the reverse.

Much of the empirical work testing the efficient capital market assumption has assumed that the distribution of common stock returns behaves as a random walk.[57] A necessary ingredient for this to be true is stationarity of the returns distribution. This, however, is generally not possible since the rate of return of common stock $\tilde{r}_S$ (in a levered firm) is a non-stationary function of the rate of return on the assets of the firm $\tilde{r}_V$.[58] As has been previously explained, this is because each time there is a change in η_S (e.g., a change in V, σ^2, r_F or T), the relationship between $\tilde{r}_V$ and $\tilde{r}_S$ changes. Consequently, even if the expected rate of return on the firm's assets $\bar{r}_V$ is a stationary process, the variable $\bar{r}_S$ will not follow a stationary process. Hence, the random walk assumption for common stock is at best a first approximation, and for a certain class of firms it is simply incorrect. This analysis is consistent with the empirical findings of Officer (1971) and the theoretical probability model of Press (1967). Officer found that common stock returns have a fat-tailed distribution (relative to a normal distribution) with a stable and finite variance which converges toward normality with additional observations. Such a random process is consistent with a non-stationary normal process, as shown by Press.

Our model has important implications for tests of the validity of the CAPM using returns data of levered equity. In Merton (1970) there is a warning about using equity returns in empirical studies:

> Although the value of the firm follows a single dynamic process with constant parameters . . . the individual component securities follow a more complex process with changing expected returns and variances. Thus, in empirical examination using a regression . . . , if one were to use equity instead of firm values, systematic biases will be introduced.[59]

Black–Jensen–Scholes (1972) and Fama–MacBeth (1973) have developed techniques for testing the CAPM which avoid selection bias due to the regression phenomenon. Essentially, they estimate common stock β's in one period and then use these estimates to test the CAPM on a later period of data. In addition, they aggregate individual securities which have non-stationary β's into portfolios with more stationary β's. These portfolios' β's are then estimated over an average of nine years of monthly data, implying that the portfolio β's are indeed stationary

[56]Also, there would be a rise in systematic risk and, therefore, in expected rate of return of both debt and equity due to the rise in leverage resulting from the dividend payments. See Case Study IV and substitute dividend payment for spin-off.

[57]Fama (1970) rightfully pointed out that stationarity is not a necessary condition for the existence of an efficient capital market.

[58]The generality of this conclusion depends on the assumption of stationarity for the firm's systematic risk. Also see footnote 17.

[59]See Merton (1970, p. 35).

over that period. This should be tested, not assumed. But more importantly, the aggregation of non-stationary individual securities to obtain stationary portfolios of securities should be closely scrutinized to see if this is eliminating the problem or only obscuring it. One alternative statistical technique which shows promise is a random coefficient model which Rosenberg (1973), among others, has recently been studying.

Turning once again to the measurement of market risk, our analysis suggests that the proxy for the market index of asset returns should not consist entirely of equity. Such a market index can be expected to be an upward biased estimate of market risk.[60] This, in turn, causes a downward bias in the estimates of individual asset's systematic risk.[61] One would suspect that more stable estimates of assets' systematic risk could be obtained by using a market index including firm debt.

The conclusion from this discussion is that the statistical methodology generally used to estimate corporate securities' risk has much to be desired. The problems associated with non-stationary security return distributions have rarely been faced directly; this is especially important when major asset or capital structure changes occur in the period in which the firms are being studied. It is hoped that our analysis will provide some structure in the pursuit of better techniques of estimating market risk.

Appendix I

(A) *Partial derivatives of the option pricing equation*

Partial derivatives of the option pricing equation,

$$S = VN(d_1) - C e^{-r_F T} N(d_2) > 0,$$

are as follows:

$$S_V = N(d_1) > 0,$$

$$S_C = -e^{-r_F T} N(d_2) < 0,$$

$$S_{\sigma^2} = C e^{-r_F T} Z(d_2) \frac{\sqrt{T}}{2\sigma} > 0,$$

---

[60] See footnote 16.

[61] This can be clearly seen if we assume that there exists only one representative firm. Using eq. (7), we can show that the systematic risk of any asset i is

$$\beta_{iV} \equiv \frac{\text{cov}(r_i, \tilde{r}_V)}{\sigma^2(r_V)} = \frac{\eta_S^2}{\eta_S} \frac{\text{cov}(\tilde{r}_i, r_S)}{\sigma^2(\tilde{r}_S)} \equiv \eta_S \beta_{iS}, \quad \text{where} \quad \eta_S \geq 1.$$

β_{iS} is the measured systematic risk of asset i when the equity of our representative firm is used as a proxy for the entire firm.

$$S_{r_F} = TC\,e^{-r_F T}N(d_2) > 0,$$

$$S_T = C\,e^{-r_F T}\left[Z(d_2)\frac{\sigma}{2\sqrt{T}} + r_F N(d_2)\right] > 0,$$

where

$$Z(d_1) = \frac{1}{\sqrt{(2\pi)}}\,e^{-d_1^2/2} = \text{the standard normal density at } d_1.$$

For the partial derivatives of debt see footnote 11.

(B) *Partial derivatives of* β_D

The partial derivatives of the systematic risk of debt where the firm's systematic risk is stationary and positive,[62] i.e., $\partial\beta_V/\partial K = 0$ and $\beta_V > 0$ are as follows:

$$R \equiv \frac{VN(-d_1)C\,e^{-r_F T}N(d_2)}{D^2\sigma\sqrt{T}},$$

$$\frac{\partial\beta_D}{\partial V} = -\frac{R}{V}\left[\frac{Z(-d_1)}{N(-d_1)} + \frac{Z(d_2)}{N(d_2)} - \sigma\sqrt{T}\right]\beta_V < 0,$$

$$\frac{\partial\beta_D}{\partial C} = \frac{R}{C}\left[\frac{Z(-d_1)}{N(-d_1)} + \frac{Z(d_2)}{N(d_2)} - \sigma\sqrt{T}\right]\beta_V > 0,$$

$$\frac{\partial\beta_D}{\partial r_F} = -RT\left[\frac{Z(-d_1)}{N(-d_1)} + \frac{Z(d_2)}{N(d_2)} - \sigma\sqrt{T}\right]\beta_V < 0,$$

$$\frac{\partial\beta_D}{\partial\sigma^2} = \frac{R\sqrt{T}}{2\sigma}\left[d_2\frac{Z(-d_1)}{N(-d_1)} + d_1\frac{Z(d_2)}{N(d_2)}\right]\beta_V \gtreqless 0,$$

$$\frac{\partial\beta_D}{\partial T} = R\left[-r_F\left(\frac{Z(-d_1)}{N(-d_1)} + \frac{Z(d_2)}{N(d_2)} - \sigma\sqrt{T}\right)\right.$$

$$\left. + \frac{\sigma}{2\sqrt{T}}\left(d_2\frac{Z(-d_1)}{N(-d_1)} + d_1\frac{Z(d_2)}{N(d_2)}\right)\right]\beta_V \gtreqless 0,$$

where

(A) $$\frac{Z(-d_1)}{N(-d_1)} + \frac{Z(d_2)}{N(d_2)} - \sigma\sqrt{T} > 0,$$

[62]We also assume that the firm is composed of physical assets, riskless debt or unlevered equity but not other financial assets. See footnote 18.

(B) $\qquad d_2 \dfrac{Z(-d_1)}{N(-d_1)} + d_1 \dfrac{Z(d_2)}{N(d_2)} \gtreqqless 0,$

and $Z(d_1) = Z(-d_1)$.

(C) Partial derivatives of β_S

The partial derivatives of the systematic risk of a call option where the underlying asset's systematic risk is stationary and positive,[63] i.e., $\partial \beta_V / \partial K = 0$ and $\beta_V > 0$ are as follows:

$$Q \equiv \frac{V N(d_1) C\, e^{-r_F T} N(d_2)}{S^2 \sigma \sqrt{T}} > 0,$$

$$\frac{\partial \beta_S}{\partial V} = -\frac{Q}{V}\left[\frac{Z(d_1)}{N(d_1)} - \frac{Z(d_2)}{N(d_2)} + \sigma\sqrt{T}\right]\beta_V < 0,$$

$$\frac{\partial \beta_S}{\partial C} = \frac{Q}{C}\left[\frac{Z(d_1)}{N(d_1)} - \frac{Z(d_2)}{N(d_2)} + \sigma\sqrt{T}\right]\beta_V > 0,$$

$$\frac{\partial \beta_S}{\partial r_F} = -QT\left[\frac{Z(d_1)}{N(d_1)} - \frac{Z(d_2)}{N(d_2)} + \sigma\sqrt{T}\right]\beta_V < 0,$$

$$\frac{\partial \beta_S}{\partial \sigma^2} = -\frac{Q\sqrt{T}}{2\sigma}\left[d_1\frac{Z(d_2)}{N(d_2)} - d_2\frac{Z(d_1)}{N(d_1)}\right]\beta_V < 0,$$

$$\frac{\partial \beta_S}{\partial T} = -Q\left[r_F\left(\frac{Z(d_1)}{N(d_1)} - \frac{Z(d_2)}{N(d_2)} + \sigma\sqrt{T}\right)\right.$$

$$\left. + \frac{\sigma}{2\sqrt{T}}\left(d_1\frac{Z(d_2)}{N(d_2)} - d_2\frac{Z(d_1)}{N(d_1)}\right)\right]\beta_V < 0,$$

where

(C) $\qquad d_1\dfrac{Z(d_2)}{N(d_2)} - d_2\dfrac{Z(d_1)}{N(d_1)} > 0,$

(D) $\qquad \dfrac{Z(d_1)}{N(d_1)} - \dfrac{Z(d_2)}{N(d_2)} + \sigma\sqrt{T} > 0,$

and $VZ(d_1) = C\,e^{-r_F T} Z(d_2)$.

[63]See preceding footnote.

(D) *Proofs of the inequalities*

Using the upper bound of the Mills ratio,[64] we can show that

(E) $\qquad \dfrac{Z(d)}{N(d)} > -d, \qquad$ for $\quad -\infty < d < \infty.$

From this inequality we can see that

(A) $\qquad \dfrac{Z(-d_1)}{N(-d_1)} + \dfrac{Z(d_2)}{N(d_2)} - \sigma\sqrt{T} > d_1 - d_2 - \sigma\sqrt{T} = 0.$

Transforming eq. (B) we see that

(B) $\qquad d_2 \dfrac{Z(-d_1)}{N(-d_1)} + d_1 \dfrac{Z(d_2)}{N(d_2)}$

$$= [d_2 C e^{-r_F T} N(d_2) + d_1 V N(-d_1)]$$

$$\times [C e^{-r_F T} N(d_2)(Z(-d_1))^{-1} N(-d_1)]^{-1}$$

$$= [d_1 D - \sigma\sqrt{T} C e^{-r_F T} N(d_2)]$$

$$\times [C e^{-r_F T} N(d_2)(Z(-d_1))^{-1} N(-d_1)]^{-1} \gtreqless 0,$$

since

$$d_1 \gtreqless \sigma\sqrt{T}\left(\frac{C e^{-r_F T} N(d_2)}{D}\right), \quad \text{where} \quad 0 \leqq \left(\frac{C e^{-r_F T} N(d_2)}{D}\right) \leqq 1.$$

So expression (B) is always greater than zero, for $d_1 > \sigma\sqrt{T}$ or $V > C e^{-(r_F + \frac{1}{2}\sigma^2)T}$.

Transforming eq. (C) we find

(C) $\qquad d_1 \dfrac{Z(d_2)}{N(d_2)} - d_2 \dfrac{Z(d_1)}{N(d_1)} = [d_1 V N(d_1) - d_2 C e^{-r_F T} N(d_2)]$

$$\times [C e^{-r_F T} N(d_2)(Z(d_1))^{-1} N(d_1)]^{-1}$$

$$= [d_1 S + \sigma\sqrt{T} C e^{-r_F T} N(d_2)]$$

$$\times [C e^{-r_F T} N(d_2)(Z(d_1))^{-1} N(d_1)]^{-1}.$$

[64]See Gordon's (1941) upper bound on the Mill's ratio, $N(-t)/Z(-t)$ for $t > 0$.

F

This will be positive if

$$d_1 > -\sigma\sqrt{T}\left[\frac{C\,e^{-r_FT}N(d_2)}{S}\right], \quad \text{where} \quad \left[\frac{C\,e^{-r_FT}N(d_2)}{S}\right] \geq 0.$$

Therefore, eq. (C) will always be positive for firms where $V \geq C\,e^{-(r_F+\frac{1}{2}\sigma^2)T}$, the firm's asset value at least equals the discounted face value of its debt; or, equivalently, when $d_1 \geq 0$. The only exception is the case where the firm experiences extreme losses causing $V \leq C\,e^{-(r_F+\frac{1}{2}\sigma^2+k\sigma^2)T}$, where $k \equiv (C\,e^{-r_FT}N(d_2))/S$.

Defining

$$h(d) \equiv \frac{Z(d)}{N(d)} + d,$$

we know that $h(d)$ is always positive from (E). Furthermore, it can be shown[65] that $h'(d) \geq 0$ for all d, which means that $h(d)$ is a monotone strictly increasing function of d. Now $d_1 > d_2$, so $h(d_1) - h(d_2) > 0$.

(D)
$$\frac{Z(d_1)}{N(d_1)} - \frac{Z(d_2)}{N(d_2)} + \sigma\sqrt{T} = \left(\frac{Z(d_1)}{N(d_1)} + d_1\right) - \left(\frac{Z(d_2)}{N(d_2)} + d_2\right)$$

$$= h(d_1) - h(d_2) > 0.$$

The first equality is based on the definition of d_2 at the beginning of section 4.

Appendix II

Numerical examples of the case of conglomerate merger

In our analysis of Case III, we showed how the value of equity of the merged firm G (denoted by S_0^G) can be derived by using eq. (4). From a merger of A and B, when $C_G = C_A + C_B$, the equityholders will suffer a loss of $L_S = S_0^A + S_0^B - S_0^G$. Their position can be restored by increasing the face value of debt C_G to C_G' (where primes denote the firm with the new capital structure) so that $D_0^{G'}(C_G/C_G') - D_0^G$ is equal to L_S.

For example, assume

$$V_0^A = V_0^B = \$1000,$$

$$S_0^A = S_0^B,$$

$$\sigma_A^2 = \sigma_B^2 = \sigma^2,$$

[65]A more detailed proof will be supplied by the authors upon request.

$$C_A = C_B = \$500,$$

$$T = 5 \quad \text{(e.g., 5 years),}$$

$$r = 0.08.$$

If $\sigma^2 = 0.10$, then

$$S_0^A = S_0^B = \$675.2 \quad \text{and} \quad S_0^A + S_0^B = \$1350.4.$$

If the correlation between the percentage return on A and B is $\rho = 0$, then for the merged firm ($C_G = C_A + C_B = \$1000$),

$$S_0^G = \$1332.5 \quad \text{and} \quad D_0^G = \$667.5,$$

and hence

$$L_S = \$1350.4 - \$1332.5 = \$17.9.$$

If we issue additional debt with face value of \$560 and with the proceeds retire part of the equity[66] we obtain

$$S_0^{G'} = \$1013.27 \quad \text{and} \quad D_0^{G'} = \$986.7.$$

The market value of the old bonds is \$986.7 (1000/1560) = \$649.6, exactly like their combined value before the merger (i.e., $D_0^A + D_0^B = 2 \times 324.8 = \$649.6$). The wealth of the equityholders is now composed of the current market value of equity (\$1013.3) plus the amount of cash they have received, which is equal to the market value of the new debt (\$337.1), together totaling \$1350.4. By the merger, the 'debt capacity' of the firm has increased by approximately 50 percent.[67] The following table gives the amount by which C_G should increase, in order to restore previous values, for a few values of σ^2 and ρ.

	$\rho =$	
	0.0	0.5
$\sigma^2 = 0.05$	48.0%	20.0%
$= 0.10$	56.0%	23.6%

[66]Before the debt is issued it is announced that an equal dollar amount of equity will be retired.

[67]It should be noted that in an economy with perfect capital markets, where securityholders have complete protection against deterioration of their positions, the debt capacity of the firm is not an operative term, as the firm is indifferent to its capital structure [Modigliani–Miller (1958)]. Also refer to footnote 5.

References

Arrow, K., 1970, Essays in the theory of risk-bearing (North-Holland, Amsterdam).

Bachrach, B. and D. Galai, 1974, Risk-return relationship and stock prices, Working Paper 28 (Research Program in Finance, University of California, Berkeley).

Black, F. and M. Scholes, 1973, The pricing of options and corporate liabilities, Journal of Political Economy 81, 637–654.

Black, F., M.C. Jensen and M. Scholes, 1972, The capital asset pricing model: Some empirical tests, in: M.C. Jensen, ed., Studies in the theory of capital markets (Praeger, New York).

Blume, M., 1968, The assessment of portfolio performance: An application of portfolio theory, unpublished Ph.D. dissertation (University of Chicago, Chicago).

Blume, M., 1971, On the assessment of risk, Journal of Finance, 1–10.

Fama, E., 1970, Efficient capital markets: A review of theory and empirical work, Journal of Finance, 383–417.

Fama, E. and J. MacBeth, 1973, Risk, return and equilibrium: Empirical tests, Journal of Political Economy 81, 607–636.

Fama, E. and M. Miller, 1972, The theory of finance (Holt, Rinehart and Winston, New York).

Fama, E., L. Fisher, M. Jensen and R. Roll, 1969, The adjustment of stock prices to new information, International Economic Review, 1–21.

Galai, D., 1974a, Characterization of options, or, options – are they 'insurance' or 'gambling'? Report 7405 (Center for Mathematical Studies in Business and Economics, University of Chicago, Chicago).

Galai, D., 1974b, The Boness and Black–Scholes models for valuation of call options: Presentation and synthesis, mimeo. (University of Chicago, Chicago).

Gonedes, N., 1973, Evidence of the information content of accounting numbers: Accounting-based and market-based estimates of systematic risk, Journal of Financial and Quantitative Analysis, 407–444.

Gordon, R.D., 1941, Values of Mill's ratio of area to bounding ordinate and of the normal probability integral for large values of the arguments, Annals of Mathematical Statistics 12, 364–366.

Hamada, R., 1969, Portfolio analysis, market equilibrium and corporate finance, Journal of Finance, 13–31.

Hamada, R., 1972, The effects of the firm's capital structure on the systematic risk of common stocks, Journal of Finance, 435–452.

Higgins, R.C., 1971, Discussion, Journal of Finance, 543–545.

Jensen, M.C., 1972, Capital markets: Theory and evidence, Bell Journal of Economics and Management Science 3, 357–398.

Jensen, M.C. and J. Long, 1972, Corporate investment under uncertainty and pareto optimality in the capital markets, Bell Journal of Economics and Management Science 3, 151–174.

Kruizenga, R.J., 1967, Introduction to the option contract, in: P.A. Cootner, ed., The random character of stock market prices (M.I.T. Press, Cambridge).

Levy, H. and M. Sarnat, 1970, Diversification, portfolio analysis and the uneasy case for conglomerate mergers, Journal of Finance, 795–802.

Lewellen, W.G., 1971, A pure financial rationale for the conglomerate merger, Journal of Finance, 521–537.

Lintner, J., 1965a, The valuation of risk assets and the selection of risky investments in stock portfolios and capital budgets, Review of Economics and Statistics, 13–37.

Lintner, J., 1965b, Security prices, risk and maximal gains from diversification, Journal of Finance, 587–616.

Lintner, J., 1971, Expectations, mergers and equilibrium in pure competitive securities markets, American Economic Review 61, 101–111.

Masulis, R., 1975, The pricing of subordinate debt and convertible debt, mimeo. (University of Chicago, Chicago).

Mayers, D., 1973, Nonmarketable assets and the determination of capital asset prices in the absence of a riskless asset, Journal of Business 46, 258–267.

Merton, R.C., 1970, A dynamic general equilibrium model of the asset market and its application to the pricing of the capital structure of the firm, Working Paper no. 497-70 (Sloan School of Management, M.I.T., Cambridge).

Merton, R.C., 1973a, Theory of rational option pricing, Bell Journal of Economics and Management Science 4, 141–183.

Merton, R.C., 1973b, An intertemporal capital asset pricing model, Econometrica 41, 867–888.

Merton, R.C., 1974, On the pricing of corporate debt: The risk structure of interest rates, Journal of Finance, 449–470.

Merton, R.C. and M. Subrahmanyam, 1974, The optimality of a competitive stock market, Bell Journal of Economics and Management Science, 145–170.

Modigliani, F. and M. Miller, 1958, The cost of capital, corporation finance, and the theory of investment, American Economic Review, 261–297.

Mossin, J., 1966, Equilibrium in a capital asset market, Econometrica, 768–783.

Officer, R., 1971, An examination of the time series behavior of the market factor of the New York Stock Exchange, unpublished Ph.D. dissertation (University of Chicago, Chicago).

Press, J., 1967, A compound events model for security prices, Journal of Business, 317–335.

Rosenberg, B., 1973, A survey of stochastic parameter regression, Annals of Economic and Social Measurement 2, 381–397.

Rubinstein, M.E., 1973, A mean variance synthesis of coporate financial theory, Journal of Finance, 165–181.

Sharpe, W.F., 1963, A simplified model for portfolio analysis, Management Science, 377–392.

Sharpe, W.F., 1964, Capital asset prices: A theory of market equilibrium under conditions of risk, Journal of Finance, 429–442.

Stiglitz, J., 1969, A reexamination of the Modigliani–Miller theorem, American Economic Review 59, 78–93.

Stiglitz, J., 1972, On some aspects of the pure theory of corporate finance: Bankruptcies and take-overs, Bell Journal of Economics and Management Science 3, 458–482.

The Journal of FINANCE

Vol. XXXIV   December 1979   No. 5

Two-State Option Pricing

RICHARD J. RENDLEMAN, JR. and BRIT J. BARTTER*

I. Introduction

IN THIS PAPER WE present an elemental two-state option pricing model (TSOPM) which is mathematically simple, yet can be used to solve many complex option pricing problems.[1] In contrast to widely accepted option pricing models which require solutions to stochastic differential equations, our model is derived algebraically. First we present the mathematics of the model and illustrate its application to the simplest type of option pricing problem. Next, we discuss the statistical properties of the model and show how the parameters of the model can be estimated to solve practical option pricing problems. Finally, we apply the model to the pricing of European and American put and call options on both non-dividend and dividend paying stocks. Elsewhere, we have applied the model to the valuation of the debt and equity of a firm with coupon paying debt in its capital structure [9], the valuation of options on debt securities [7], and the pricing of fixed rate bank loan commitments [1, 2]. In the Appendix we derive the Black-Scholes [3] model using the two-state approach.

II. The Two-State Option Pricing Model

Consider a stock whose price can either advance or decline during the next period. Let H_t^+ and H_t^- represent the returns per dollar invested in the stock if the price rises (the + state) or falls (the − state), respectively, from time $t - 1$ to time t, and V_t^+ and V_t^- the corresponding end-of-period values of the option. With the assumption that the prices of the stock and its option follow a two-state process, it is possible to form a riskless portfolio with the two securities. [See Black and Scholes [3] for the continuous time analog of riskless hedging.] Since the end-of-period value of the portfolio is certain, the option should be priced so that the portfolio will yield the riskless interest rate.

The riskless portfolio is formed by investing one dollar in the stock and

---

* Both Assistant Professors of Finance, Graduate School of Management, Northwestern University.
[1] Since the original writing of this paper, the authors have learned that a similar procedure has been suggested by Rubinstein [10], Sharpe [11], and Cox, Ross, and Rubinstein [5].

purchasing α units of the option at a price of P_{t-1}. The value of α is chosen so that the portfolio payoffs are the same in both states, or

$$H_t^+ + \alpha V_t^+ = H_t^- + \alpha V_t^-. \tag{1}$$

Solving for α we obtain the number of units of the option to be held in the portfolio per \$1 invested in the stock.

$$\alpha = \frac{H_t^- - H_t^+}{V_t^+ - V_t^-} \tag{2}$$

A negative value of α implies that the option is sold short (written) with the proceeds being used to partially fund the purchase of the stock.

The time $t - 1$ value of portfolio is $1 + \alpha P_{t-1}$. The end-of-period value is given by either side of (1). Discounting the left-hand side by the riskless interest rate, R, and setting the discounted value equal to the present value of the portfolio, a pricing equation for the option is obtained.

$$1 + \alpha P_{t-1} = \frac{H_t^+ + \alpha V_t^+}{1 + R}. \tag{3}$$

Substituting the value of α from (2) into (3), the price of the option can be solved in terms of its end-of-period values.

$$P_{t-1} = \frac{V_t^+(1 + R - H_t^-) + V_t^-(H_t^+ - 1 - R)}{(H_t^+ - H_t^-)(1 + R)} \tag{4}$$

Equation 4 is a recursive relationship that can be applied at any time $t - 1$ to determine the price of the option as a function of its value at time t.

Note that in equation (4) we make a notational distinction between an option's value (V) and its price (P). Assuming that an investor will exercise an option when it is in his best interest to do so,

$$V_t = \text{MAX}[P_t, \text{VEXER}_t], \tag{5}$$

where VEXER_t is the value of exercising the option at time t.

The distinguishing feature among American and European puts and calls is in the definition of their exercisable values. American options can be exercised at any time whereas European options can only be exercised at maturity. Calls are options to buy stock at a set price whereas puts are options to sell. Letting S_t represent the time t price of the stock, X the option's exercise price, and T the maturity date of the option, we obtain

American:

Call	$\text{VEXER}_t = S_t - X$	for all t,	
Put	$\text{VEXER}_t = X - S_t$	for all t,	

European:

Call	$\text{VEXER}_t = S_t - X$	for $t = T$	
	$\text{VEXER}_t = 0$	for $t < T$,	
Put	$\text{VEXER}_t = X - S_t$	for $t = T$	
	$\text{VEXER}_t = 0$	for $t < T$.	

Recognizing that for both American and Euopean puts and calls

$$P_T = 0, \tag{7}$$

since there is no value associated with maintaining an option position beyond maturity, (4-7) represent the formal specification of the two-state model. Through repeated application of (4), subject to (5-7), one can begin at an option's maturity date and recursively solve for its current price.

To illustrate the model, consider a call option on a stock with an exercise price of $100. The current price of the stock is $100 and the possible prices of the stock on the option's maturity date are $110 and $90, implying $H_1^+ = 1.10$ and $H_1^- = .90$. Assuming that the option is exercised if the stock price rises to $110 and is allowed to expire worthless if the stock price falls to $90, the present prices and the end-of-period payoffs of the stock and option can be represented by the following two-branched tree diagram.

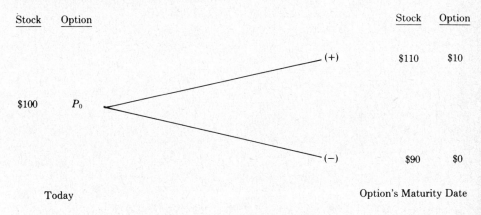

Stock	Option		Stock	Option
		(+)	$110	$10
$100	P_0			
		(−)	$90	$0

Today   Option's Maturity Date

If an investor purchases the stock and writes two call options, the end-of-period portfolio value will be $90 in both states. Equivalently, for every $1 invested in the stock, a riskless hedge requires that $\alpha = (.90 - 1.10)/(10 - 0) = -.02$, or that .02 options are written. Assuming a risk free interest rate of 5%, the present value of the riskless portfolio should be $90/1.05 or $85.71 to ensure no riskless arbitrage opportunities between the stock-option portfolio and a riskless security. Since the riskless portfolio involves a $100 investment in the stock which is partially offset by the two short options, an option price of $7.14 is required to obtain an $85.71 portfolio value. The option price can also be obtained directly from (4):

$$P_0 = \frac{\$10(1 + .05 - .90) + \$0(1.10 - 1.05)}{(1.10 - .90)(1 + .05)}$$

$$= \frac{\$10(.15)}{.2(1.05)} = \$7.14.$$

Although this example is unrealistic, it nevertheless illustrates two of the most important features of the TSOPM. We can observe that the option price does not depend upon the probabilities of the up (+) or down (−) states occurring or the risk preferences of the investor. Two investors who agreed that the stock price is in equilibrium, but had different probability beliefs and preferences, would both view $7.14 as the equilibrium option price. As long as they agreed on the magnitudes of the underlying stock's holding period returns (H^+ and H^-), they would agree on the price of the option.

The example can be extended to a multiperiod framework in which the price of the underlying stock can take on only one of two values at any time t given the price of the stock at $t - 1$. Consider the case in which a non-dividend paying stock's holding period return is 1.175 in all up states and .85 in all down states. Given an initial stock price of $100, these return parameters imply the four-period price pattern shown in Figure 1.

Assume that we wish to value a call option which matures at the end of period 4 and has an exercise price of $100. Given a riskless interest rate of 1.25% per period (5% per year, assuming a one-year maturity), the sequence of option values corresponding to the stock prices in Figure 1 is given in Figure 2.

In Figure 2 the prices $90.61 and $37.89 are the values of the call obtainable by exercising at maturity. For those states at maturity where the price of the stock falls below the exercise price of $100, the option expires worthless. Each of the time 3 option prices is obtained from (4). Similarly, the prices at time 2, 1, and 0 are obtained by recursive application of (4) resulting in a current call option price of $14.41.

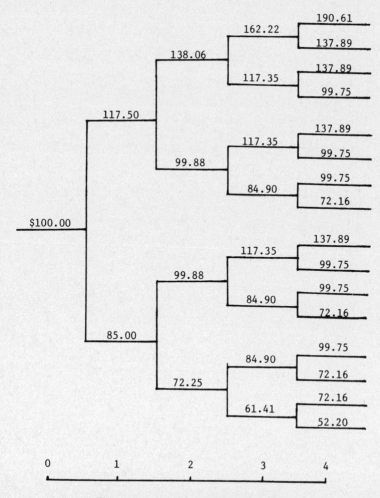

Figure 1. Price Path of Underlying Stock

120

Although the above example considers only four periods of time, one can always choose an interval of time to recognize price changes that more realistically captures expected stock price behavior. In Section IV we demonstrate the sensitivity of option prices to the choice of the time differencing interval under the assumption that H^+ and H^- are chosen to hold the mean and variance of the distribution of stock price changes constant over the life of the option. In the Appendix, a generalized formula for the multiperiod case is derived for the situation where R, H^+, and H^- are constant. This formula is extended under the assumption that the two-state process evolves over an infinitesimally small interval of time.

III. Operationalizing the TSOPM

In the TSOPM, the only parameters describing the probability distribution of returns of the underlying stock are the magnitudes of the holding period returns, H^+ and H^-. Although our examples assume that H^+ and H^- remain constant

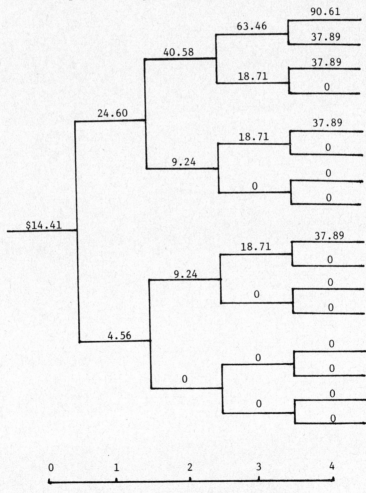

Figure 2. Price Path of European Call Option

through time, this is not a necessary assumption for the implementation of the model. Thus, if one can simply specify the pattern of H^+ and H^- through time, it is possible to value the option.

The TSOPM can be used as a method for obtaining exact values of options when the magnitudes of H^+ and H^- are known in advance. As a practical matter, the values of H^+ and H^- will not be known, but must be estimated. For example, if the probabilities associated with the occurrence of the + and − states remain stable over time along with the magnitudes of H^+ and H^-, then the two-state model implies a binomial distribution for the returns of the stock. It is well known that both the Normal and Poisson distributions can be viewed as limiting cases of the Binomial. Thus, the Binomial distribution can be employed as an approximation procedure for deriving option prices when the actual distribution of returns is assumed to be either Normal or Poisson. We will illustrate how the values of H^+ and H^- can be determined when the binomial distribution is used as an approximation to the lognormal distribution.

If the magnitudes of the relative price changes in our model and their associated probabilities remain stable from one period to the next, then the distribution of returns which is generated after T time periods will follow a log-binomial distribution with a mean

$$\mu = T[h^+ \theta + h^-(1 - \theta)] = T[(h^+ - h^-)\theta + h^-], \tag{8}$$

and variance

$$\sigma^2 = T(h^+ - h^-)^2\theta(1 - \theta), \tag{9}$$

where:

θ = the probability that the price of the stock will rise

in any period,

$h^+ = \ln(H^+)$,

$h^- = \ln(H^-)$.

In the last four-period example where $H^+ = 1.175$ and $H^- = .85$, the value of σ and μ for the entire four periods would be .324 and −.003, respectively, if a value of θ equal to .5 is assumed.

It is also possible to determine the values of H^+ and H^- that are implied by the values of μ, σ, θ, and T. By solving (8) and (9) in terms of these parameters and recognizing that $H = \exp(h)$, we obtain the following implied values of H^+ and H^-.

$$H^+ = \exp\left(\mu/T + (\sigma/\sqrt{T})\sqrt{\frac{(1 - \theta)}{\theta}}\right) \tag{10}$$

$$H^- = \exp\left(\mu/T - (\sigma/\sqrt{T})\sqrt{\frac{\theta}{(1 - \theta)}}\right) \tag{11}$$

As T becomes large, the log-binomial distribution will approximate a lognormal distribution with the same mean and variance.

IV. Applications of the Model

European Puts and Calls on Non-Dividend Paying Stocks

In this section we price European put and call options on non-dividend paying stocks using the two-state model as an approximation procedure for the case in which stock prices are assumed to follow a lognormal distribution.[2] Given the assumptions of no dividends and lognormal returns, the Black-Scholes [3] model provides the exact values for both types of options, thereby serving as a benchmark to assess the accuracy of the two-state model as a numerical procedure.

In Table 1, we present prices of one-year European put and call options with exercise prices of $75, $100, and $125 assuming a current stock price of $100. The riskless interest rate is assumed to be 5% per year. To conform with the Black-Scholes model, continuous compounding of interest is assumed. Thus, $R = e^{.05/N} - 1$, where N is the number of time intervals per year employed in the analysis. The values of H^+ and H^- are chosen so that the annual standard deviation of the logarithmic return is .324 as in the previous four-period example. The expected value of the logarithmic return is assumed to take on values of .5, .1, 0, −.1 and −.5 per year, and a value of θ equal to .5 is assumed. Finally, option prices are calculated by partitioning the year into 12, 52, and 100 time periods.

Consider the panel of Table 1 in which the stock's growth rate (μ) is assumed to be 0%. When the year is divided into 100 time intervals, the two-state prices of all the put and call options are quite close to their corresponding Black-Scholes prices. With these two parameters ($\mu = 0$, $T = 100$), the greatest absolute percentage difference between the Black-Scholes and two-state prices is .6%. Even if only 12 time differencing intervals are assumed, the two-state and Black-Scholes prices are remarkably close.

For growth rates of 10% and −10%, the two-state prices do not appear to be significantly different from those obtained when a zero growth rate is assumed. Thus, within this range of growth rates, the option price does not appear to be significantly affected by the growth rate.

If extreme growth rates are assumed ($\mu = .5$ and $\mu = −.5$), the two-state model does not appear to provide an accurate approximation to the Black-Scholes price for low T values. However, for 100 time intervals, the two-state and Black-Scholes prices are reasonably close.

The entries in Table 1 reveal that the option price is slightly dependent upon the stock's growth rate. In addition, if θ were varied, we would also discover a slight dependence on investor probability beliefs. These findings seem to contradict the earlier observation that two-state prices are independent of both investor preferences (which would be revealed through μ) and probability beliefs.

This dependence results from the fact that H^+ and H^- are chosen in the two-state model to conform with a given continuous distribution. Since the two-state model is only an approximation, the values of μ and θ implicit in the continuous distribution may be reflected in the two-state solution. In the limit as $T \to \infty$, the two distributions will be identical, and therefore, preferences and probabilities

---

[2] See Brennan and Schwartz [4] and Parkinson [7] for descriptions of alternative numerical procedures for solving option pricing equations.

Table 1

Comparison Between TSOPM and Black-Scholes Option Prices[a]
(European)

Option Parameters			TSOPM		Black-Scholes Model		Percent Difference[b]	
μ	X	T	Call	Put	Call	Put	Call	Put
.5	75	12	29.94	1.28	30.74	2.08	− 2.6	−38.7
		52	30.57	1.91			− .5	− 8.2
		100	30.65	1.99			− .3	− 4.6
	100	12	14.23	9.35	15.14	10.26	− 6.0	− 8.9
		52	14.95	10.07			− 1.3	− 1.9
		100	15.03	10.16			− .7	− 1.1
	125	12	6.05	24.96	6.58	25.48	− 7.9	− 2.1
		52	6.38	25.28			− 3.0	.8
		100	6.50	25.41			− 1.1	− .3
.1	75	12	30.58	1.93	30.74	2.08	− .5	− 7.6
		52	30.74	2.09			0	0
		100	30.72	2.06			− .1	− 1.1
	100	12	15.37	10.50	15.14	10.26	+ 1.5	+ 2.3
		52	15.12	10.25			− .1	− .2
		100	15.17	10.29			+ .2	+ .3
	125	12	6.78	25.69	6.58	25.48	+ 3.1	+ .8
		52	6.62	25.53			+ .7	+ .2
		100	6.57	25.47			− .1	0
.0	75	12	30.85	2.19	30.74	2.08	− .4	+ 5.2
		52	30.74	2.09			0	0
		100	30.75	2.10			0	+ .6
	100	12	14.88	10.00	15.14	10.26	− 1.7	− 2.5
		52	15.08	10.20			− .4	− .6
		100	15.11	10.23			− .2	− .3
	125	12	6.55	25.46	6.58	25.48	− .3	− .1
		52	6.62	25.52			+ .7	+ .2
		100	6.60	25.50			+ .3	+ .1
−.1	75	12	30.60	1.94	30.74	2.08	− .5	− 7.0
		52	30.73	2.07			− .1	− .8
		100	30.74	2.08			0	− .3
	100	12	15.31	10.43	15.14	10.26	+ 1.1	+ 1.6
		52	15.11	10.23			− .2	− .3
		100	15.16	10.28			+ .1	+ .2
	125	12	6.55	25.43	6.58	25.48	− .8	− .2
		52	6.62	25.48			− .1	0
		100	6.60	25.43			− .8	− .2
−.5	75	12	30.25	1.59	30.74	2.08	− 1.6	−23.6
		52	30.65	2.00			− .3	− 4.2
		100	30.69	2.04			− .2	− 2.4
	100	12	13.85	8.97	15.14	10.26	− 8.6	−12.6
		52	14.87	10.00			− 1.8	− 2.6
		100	14.99	10.12			− 1.0	− 1.5
	125	12	4.65	23.55	6.58	25.48	−29.4	− 7.6
		52	6.12	25.02			− 7.0	− 1.8
		100	6.36	25.27			− 3.4	− .8

[a] $S_0 = 100$, $R = e^{05/N} - 1$, $\sigma = .324$, $\theta = .5$. In this table, $N = T$ in all cases.

[b] Percent difference between the TSOPM and Black-Scholes (BS) prices is computed according to: (TSOPM-BS)/BS, rounded to the nearest one-tenth of one percent.

should not be reflected in option prices. In the Appendix, we derive the Black-Scholes equation using the two-state model. As expected, neither the growth rate nor probabilities enter the final solution. For practical applications, the two-state model appears to provide an accurate approximation to the Black-Scholes model if 100 or more time differencing intervals are assumed along with any reasonable growth rate. As we show below, however, it is possible to select a growth rate that will closely approximate the value of μ that minimizes the error in the two-state approximation.

Finding the Best Approximation

According to equation (A.11) in the Appendix, the price of a call option in the two-state model can be stated in terms of two binomial pseudo probability distributions. In each distribution, ψ and ϕ are the pseudo probabilities that the price of the underlying stock will rise. These pseudo probabilities are not necessarily equal to the true probability, θ, but nevertheless, the mathematics of probability theory are still applicable.

According to the Laplace-DeMoivre Limit Theorem, it can be shown that the best fit between the binomial and normal distributions occurs when the binomial probability (or pseudo probability in this case) is $\frac{1}{2}$. As a general rule, ψ and ϕ will not be identical. Therefore, it will usually be impossible to simultaneously set both pseudo probabilities to $\frac{1}{2}$. However, since $\psi = \phi(H^+/(1 + R))$, and the term in parenthesis will generally be close to unity, the parameters of the underlying distribution that sets ϕ to $\frac{1}{2}$ will set ψ to approximately $\frac{1}{2}$.

By expanding ϕ in Taylor's series, we find that ϕ is approximately $\frac{1}{2}$ when

$$\mu = \frac{r - \frac{1}{2}\sigma\sqrt{T}\left[\sqrt{\frac{1-\theta}{\theta}} - \sqrt{\frac{\theta}{1-\theta}}\right] - \frac{1}{4}\sigma^2\left[\frac{1-\theta}{\theta} + \frac{\theta}{1-\theta}\right]}{\left[1 + \left(\sqrt{\frac{1-\theta}{\theta}} - \sqrt{\frac{\theta}{1-\theta}}\right)\Big/\sqrt{T}\right]}. \tag{12}$$

If the true probability, θ, is $\frac{1}{2}$, this expression simplifies to[3]

$$\mu = r - \frac{1}{2}\sigma^2. \tag{13}$$

For the parameters underlying Table 1, we find that (approximately) the best two-state approximation occurs when $\mu = -.002488$. The reasonableness of this result is confirmed by the $\mu = 0$ panel of Table 1.[4]

---

[3] We wish to acknowledge the referee for suggesting that the best approximation would occur if $\mu = r - \frac{1}{2}\sigma^2$.

[4] We repeated the analysis of Table 1 by setting μ to $-.002488$. Although the prices were almost identical to those obtained by setting μ to zero, they were slightly more accurate.

Pricing American Puts and Non-Dividend Paying Stocks

Table 2 shows the prices of American put options along with the value of the premature exercise privilege for the same parameters underlying Table 1, except that only a zero growth rate is assumed. Prices of American call options are not shown since, with no dividends, there will be no added value associated with the ability to exercise the call prior to maturity (see Merton [6]). Prices are shown for put options with exercise prices of 75, 100, and 125 under the assumption that the time differencing interval is 12, 52, 100, and 500 times per year. The differencing interval of 500 times is used as a proxy for the continuous case.

The prices in Table 2 suggest that the two-state model provides a fairly accurate approximation to the value of the premature exercise privilege, even for T values as low as 12. For all practical purposes, 100 time periods appears to provide sufficient accuracy for determining actual American put prices using the two-state model. For the options in Table 2, the prices obtained when $T = 100$ are within $.01 of the $T = 500$ prices.

American and European Puts and Calls on Dividend Paying Stocks

If a stock pays a dividend, it may sometimes pay to prematurely exercise a call option on the stock before the dividend is paid rather than hold the option when the stock is almost certain to decline in value. Thus, one would expect American call options on dividend paying stocks to be worth more than their European counterparts. On the other hand, if a stock is expected to pay a dividend, it is less likely that an American put option will be exercised prematurely since the stock is likely to decrease in value when the dividend is paid due to the ex-dividend effect. The Black-Scholes model has been extended by Merton [6] to price

Table 2

American Put Prices Using the TSOPM[a]

Option Parameters				Dollar Value
			American	of Premature
μ	X	T	Put	Exercise[b]
.0	75	12	2.26	$ .05
		52	2.15	.06
		100	2.16	.06
		500	2.15	.07
	100	12	10.65	.65
		52	10.75	.55
		100	10.77	.54
		500	10.78	.52
	125	12	27.42	1.96
		52	27.40	1.88
		100	27.38	1.88
		500	27.37	1.89

[a] $S_0 = 100$, $R = e^{.05/T} - 1$, $\sigma = .324$, $\theta = .5$.

[b] Dollar value of premature exercise is computed as:

$$\begin{matrix} \text{TSOPM} & \text{TSOPM} \\ \text{[American]} & - \text{[European]}, \text{assuming } \mu = .0 \text{ in both cases.} \\ \text{Put Price} & \text{Put Price} \end{matrix}$$

126

European puts and calls when dividends are paid continuously at a constant rate. This model is used in Table 3 as a benchmark for determining the accuracy of the two-state model for pricing European puts and calls.

In Table 3 the prices of European and American puts and calls are shown under the assumption that the underlying stock is expected to pay a quarterly dividend at an annual rate of 4%. The assumptions underlying Tables 1 and 2 are maintained.

The two-state prices of European puts and calls are all within $.03 of the corresponding dividend-adjusted Black-Scholes-Merton prices when the life of the options are partitioned into 100 time intervals. Therefore, with dividends, the two-state model appears to provide an accurate approximation to the lognormal model.

As one would expect, the ability to exercise an American call option on a dividend paying stock prior to maturity can carry a significant premium. For example, for $X = 75$ and $T = 100$, the difference between the prices of American and European calls is $1.03. This premium declines as the option's exercise price increases.

In contrast to the call option, the payment of a 4% dividend significantly lowers the value associated with the ability to exercise the put option prematurely. For example, for $T = 100$ and $X = 100$, the premature exercise premium is $.54 for a non-dividend paying stock but only $.16 if the stock pays a quarterly dividend at an annual rate of 4%.

V. Conclusions

This paper develops a simple two-state option pricing model and demonstrates the application of the model to several complex option pricing problems. Although the mathematics of the model are quite simple, especially when compared to the more conventional continuous time approach, the economics of both approaches to option pricing are essentially the same. Thus, the two-state approach opens the door to the understanding of modern option pricing theory without the added complications associated with the solutions to stochastic differential equations.

In addition to its pedagogic features, the two-state approach can be used as a numerical procedure for solving continuous time option pricing problems for which closed form solutions are unattainable. Moreover, the Black-Scholes equation can be derived from the two-state model as a special case. Admittedly, the mathematics of this derivation are as difficult as stochastic calculus itself, yet one need not carry the two-state model to its continuous limit to derive many interesting insights into both theoretical and practical applications of modern option pricing theory.

Appendix

Derivation of the Continuous Time Version of the TSOPM

In this Appendix we determine the value of a European call option, w_0, using the TSOPM, assuming that the interval of time over which price changes in the underlying stock are recognized is infinitesimally small. This is equivalent to

Table 3

Comparison Between TSOPM and Black-Scholes-Merton Option Prices Including Dividends[a]

Option Parameters				TSOPM European Prices		TSOPM American Prices		Dollar Value of Premature Exercise[d]		Black-Scholes-Merton Prices[c]	
μ	X	T	INTVL[b]	Call	Put	Call	Put	Call	Put	Call	Put
.0	75	12	3	27.37	2.66	28.15	2.67	$ .78	$ .01	27.30	2.58
		52	13	27.32	2.59	28.29	2.61	.97	.02		
		100	25	27.30	2.59	28.33	2.60	1.03	.01		
	100	12	3	12.85	11.92	13.14	12.10	.29	.18	12.78	11.84
		52	13	12.83	11.89	13.33	12.05	.50	.16		
		100	25	12.80	11.86	13.35	12.02	.55	.16		
	125	12	3	5.40	28.24	5.52	28.93	.12	.69	5.27	28.11
		52	13	5.22	28.07	5.50	28.74	.28	.67		
		100	25	5.24	28.09	5.53	28.75	.29	.66		

[a] $S = 100$, $R = e^{.05/T} - 1$, $\sigma = .324$, $\theta = .5$ and annual dividend yield $= .04$ for all contracts.

[b] For $T = 12$, a dividend interval (INTVL) of 3 means that a dividend payment is made every 3rd period. If the entire time horizon is one year, then each (T, INTVL) pair implies a typical quarterly dividend payment.

[c] Dividend adjusted Black-Scholes prices are computed by substituting $100 (1 - .04/4)^4$ for the stock price in the Black-Scholes model.

[d] Dollar value of premature exercise is computed as: [TSOPM American price] − [TSOPM European price].

allowing the number of time differencing intervals to become infinite over the fixed life of the option. Before deriving the continuous time version of the model, we will develop a valuation equation for the discrete time case under the assumptions that the distribution of returns of the stock is stationary over time and the stock pays no dividends.

The Discrete Time Model

When the option matures, there will be a one-to-one correspondence between the value of the option and the value of its underlying stock. The value of a call option at maturity, w_T, is $\max(0, S_T - X)$, where S_T is the value of the underlying stock at the maturity date, T, and X is the exercise price of the option. At the period prior to the option's maturity date, the value of the option is given by

$$w_{T-1} = \frac{w_T^+(1 + R - H^-) + w_T^-(H^+ - (1 + R))}{(H^+ - H^-)(1 + R)}. \tag{A.1}$$

Similarly, the value of the option two periods prior to maturity is

$$w_{T-2} = \frac{w_{T-1}^+(1 + R - H^-) + w_{T-1}^-(H^+ - (1 + R))}{(H^+ - H^-)(1 + R)}. \tag{A.2}$$

By substituting equation (A.1) into (A.2) and noting that the term w_t^{+-} is the option value at maturity, given that the price of the underlying stock advances in period $T - 1$ and falls in period T, the value of the option at period $T - 2$ becomes:

$$w_{T-2} = \frac{(w_T^{++}(1 + R - H^-) + w_T^{+-}(H^+ - (1 + R)))(1 + R - H^-)}{(H^+ - H^-)^2(1 + R)^2}$$

$$+ \frac{(w_T^{-+}(1 + R - H^-) + w_T^{--}(H^+ - (1 + R)))(H^+ - (1 + R))}{(H^+ - H^-)^2(1 + R)^2}. \tag{A.3}$$

Equation (A.3) can be simplified by noting that $w_T^{+-} = w_T^{-+}$, since the value of the underlying stock at maturity will be the same whether or not it advances first and then declines, or declines first and then advances. With this substitution, equation (A.3) can be restated as:

w_{T-2}

$$= \frac{w_T^{++}(1 + R - H^-)^2 + 2w_T^{+-}(H^+ - (1 + R))(1 + R - H^-) \atop {+w_T^{--}(H^+ - (1 + R))^2}}{(H^+ - H^-)^2(1 + R)^2}. \tag{A.4}$$

If this same type of procedure is repeated for a total of T periods, there will always be $T + 1$ terms in the numerator of the option valuation equation. After T periods, there are exactly $\binom{T}{0}$ ways that a sequence of T pluses can occur, there are $\binom{T}{1}$ ways that $T - 1$ pluses can occur along with one minus, there are $\binom{T}{2}$ ways for $T - 2$ pluses and 2 minuses, and so on. In addition, the power to which a term $(H^+ - (1 + R))$ associated with a particular w_T is raised is equal to the number of minus signs associated with the w_T. Therefore, if the valuation procedure is carried back to the present, the value of the option becomes:

$$w_0 = \left[\binom{T}{0} w_T^{+\cdots+}(1 + R - H^-)^T(H^+ - (1 + R))^0 \right.$$

$$+ \binom{T}{1} w_T^{+\cdots+-}(1 + R - H^-)^{T-1}(H^+ - (1 + R))^1 + \cdots$$

$$\cdots + \binom{T}{T-1} w_T^{+-\cdots-}(1 + R - H^-)^1(H^+ - (1 + R))^{T-1}$$

$$\left. + \binom{T}{T} w_T^{-\cdots-}(1 + R - H^-)^0(H^+ - (1 + R))^T \right] \Bigg/ [(H^+ - H^-)(1 + R)]^T.$$

$$(A.5)$$

Next, we must determine the value of the option at maturity. If the stock advances i times and declines $(T - i)$ times, the price of the stock will be $S_0 H^{+^i} H^{-^{(T-i)}}$ on the expiration date. The option will be exercised if

$$S_0 H^{+^i} H^{-^{(T-i)}} > X, \tag{A.6}$$

in which case, the maturity value of the option will be

$$w_T = S_0 H^{+^i} H^{-^{(T-i)}} - X.$$

Otherwise, the option will expire worthless.

Let the symbol a denote the minimum integer value of i in (A.6) for which the inequality is satisfied. This value is given by:

$$a = 1 + \text{INT} \left[\frac{\ln(X/S_0) - T \cdot \ln(H^-)}{\ln(H^+) - \ln(H^-)} \right], \tag{A.7}$$

where $\text{INT}[\cdot]$ denotes the integer operator. Thus, the maturity value of the option is given by

$$w_T = S_0 H^{+^i} H^{-^{(T-i)}} - X \quad \text{if} \quad i \geq a$$

$$w_T = 0 \qquad\qquad\qquad \text{if} \quad i < a. \tag{A.8}$$

By substituting (A.8) into (A.5), one obtains a generalized option pricing equation for the discrete time case.

$$w_0 = \frac{\sum_{i=a}^{T} \binom{T}{i}(S_0 H^{+^i} H^{-^{(T-i)}} - X)(1 + R - H^-)^i(H^+ - (1 + R))^{T-i}}{(H^+ - H^-)^T(1 + R)^T}. \tag{A.9}$$

The Continuous Time Model

In the derivation of the continuous time model, we will determine the option price when $T \to \infty$ assuming that the mean and variance of logarithmic returns of the stock are held constant over the life of the option.

Note that (A.9) can be rewritten as

$$w_0 = S_0 \sum_{i=a}^{T} \binom{T}{i} \left[\frac{(1 + R - H^-)H^+}{(1 + R)(H^+ - H^-)} \right]^i \left[\frac{(H^+ - 1 - R)H^-}{(H^+ - H^-)(1 + R)} \right]^{T-i}$$

$$\frac{-X}{(1 + R)^T} \sum_{i=a}^{T} \binom{T}{i} \left[\frac{1 + R - H^-}{H^+ - H^-} \right]^i \left[\frac{H^+ - 1 - R}{H^+ - H^-} \right]^{T-i}. \quad \text{(A.10)}$$

The two bracketed terms in each term in (A.10) sum to unity and therefore can be interpreted as "pseudo probabilities." Although these pseudo probabilities do not represent the true probabilities that the price of the stock will either advance or decline, we can still apply the mathematics of probability theory to the solution of the problem. Let these pseudo probabilities be represented by

$$\psi = \frac{(1 + R - H^-)H^+}{(1 + R)(H^+ - H^-)}, \quad \text{and}$$

$$\phi = \frac{1 + R - H^-}{H^+ - H^-}.$$

The option price can now be stated as:

$$w_0 = S_0 B(a, T, \psi) - \frac{X}{(1 + R)^T} B(a, T, \phi), \quad \text{(A.11)}$$

where $B(a, T, (\cdot))$ is the cumulative binomial probability that the number of successes will fall between a and T after T trials, where $(\cdot)$ is the probability associated with a success after one trial.

As T becomes large, the cumulative binomial density function can be approximated by the cumulative normal density function. The approximation will be exact in the limit as $T \to \infty$. Therefore,

$$w_0 \sim S_0 N(Z_1, Z_1') - \frac{X}{(1 + R)^T} N(Z_2, Z_2'), \quad \text{(A.12)}$$

where $N(Z, Z')$ is the probability that a normally distributed random variable with zero mean and unit variance will take on values between a lower limit of Z and an upper limit of Z', and

$$Z_1 = \frac{a - T\psi}{\sqrt{T\psi(1 - \psi)}}, \quad Z_1' = \frac{T - T\psi}{\sqrt{T\psi(1 - \psi)}}$$

$$Z_2 = \frac{a - T\phi}{\sqrt{T\phi(1 - \phi)}}, \quad Z_2' = \frac{T - T\phi}{\sqrt{T\phi(1 - \phi)}}.$$

Thus, the price of the option that will obtain when the two-state process evolves continuously is given by:

$$w_0 = S_0(\text{Lim}_{T \to \infty} Z_1, \text{Lim}_{T \to \infty} Z_1') - \frac{X}{\text{Lim}_{T \to \infty} (1 + R)^T} N(\text{Lim}_{T \to \infty} Z_2, \text{Lim}_{T \to \infty} Z_2').$$

$$\text{(A.13)}$$

Let $1 + R = e^{r/T}$ to reflect the continuous compounding of interest. Then,

$$\text{Lim}_{T \to \infty} (1 + R)^T = e^r.$$

We will state without proof that

$$\text{Lim}_{T \to \infty} Z_1' = \text{Lim}_{T \to \infty} Z_2' = \infty.$$

Thus, all that remains in the derivation of the continuous time version of the two-state model is to determine $\text{Lim}_{T \to \infty} Z_1$ and $\text{Lim}_{T \to \infty} Z_2$.

In determining both limits, we will assume that both H^+ and H^- are chosen to hold the logarithmic mean and variance of returns of the stock constant over the option's life. Therefore, we make the following substitutions derived earlier in the text.

$$H^+ = e^{\mu/T + (\sigma/\sqrt{T})\sqrt{(1-\theta)/\theta}}$$

$$H^- = e^{\mu/T - (\sigma/\sqrt{T})\sqrt{\theta/(1-\theta)}}$$

Substituting H^+ and H^- into a,

$$Z_1 = \frac{1 + \text{INT}\left[\dfrac{\ln(X/S_0) - \mu + \sigma\sqrt{T}\,\sqrt{\theta/(1-\theta)}}{\sigma/\sqrt{T\theta(1-\theta)}}\right] - T\psi}{\sqrt{T\psi(1-\psi)}}.$$

In the limit, the term $1 + \text{INT}[\cdot]$ will simplify to the term in brackets. To simplify the exposition, we will replace $1 + \text{INT}[\cdot]$ with $[\cdot]$ at this point. With this substitution Z_1 can be restated as

$$Z_1 \sim \frac{\ln(X/S_0) - \mu}{\sigma\sqrt{\dfrac{\psi(1-\psi)}{\theta(1-\theta)}}} + \frac{\sqrt{T}(\theta - \psi)}{\sqrt{\psi(1-\psi)}}. \tag{A.14}$$

Substituting H^+, H^-, and $1 + R = e^{r/T}$ in the expression for ψ and expanding in Taylor's series in T, we obtain

$$\psi \sim \frac{1}{\sqrt{T}} \, \frac{r - \mu - \dfrac{1}{2}\sigma^2\left(\dfrac{\theta}{1-\theta}\right) + \sigma^2}{\sigma\left(\sqrt{\dfrac{1-\theta}{\theta}} + \sqrt{\dfrac{\theta}{1-\theta}}\right) + \dfrac{1}{2}(\sigma^2/\sqrt{T})\left(\dfrac{1-\theta}{\theta} - \dfrac{\theta}{1-\theta}\right) + o\left(\dfrac{1}{T}\right)}$$

$$+ \frac{\sqrt{\dfrac{\theta}{1-\theta}}}{\sqrt{\dfrac{1-\theta}{\theta}} + \sqrt{\dfrac{\theta}{1-\theta}} + \dfrac{1}{2}\left(\dfrac{\sigma}{\sqrt{T}}\right)\left(\dfrac{1-\theta}{\theta} - \dfrac{\theta}{1-\theta}\right) + o\left(\dfrac{1}{T}\right)} + o\left(\dfrac{1}{T}\right),$$

where $o\left(\dfrac{1}{T}\right)$ denotes a function tending to zero more rapidly than $\dfrac{1}{T}$. [The derivation of the Taylor's series expansions of ψ and ϕ as well as the derivation of the limits below will be made available by the authors upon request.] It can be shown that

$$\text{Lim}_{T\to\infty}\,\psi = \theta \quad \text{and}$$

$$\text{Lim}_{T\to\infty}\,\sqrt{T}\,(\theta - \psi) = -\frac{\sqrt{\theta(1-\theta)}}{\sigma}\left(r - \mu + \frac{1}{2}\sigma^2\right)$$

Substituting $\text{Lim}_{T\to\infty}\,\psi$ for ψ and $\text{Lim}_{T\to\infty}\,\sqrt{T}\,(\theta - \psi)$ for $\sqrt{T}\,(\theta - \psi)$ into (A.14), we obtain:

$$\text{Lim}_{T\to\infty}\,Z_1 = \frac{\ln(X/S_0) - \mu}{\sigma\sqrt{\dfrac{\theta(1-\theta)}{\theta(1-\theta)}}} - \frac{\sqrt{\theta(1-\theta)}\left(r - \mu + \dfrac{1}{2}\sigma^2\right)}{\sigma\sqrt{\theta(1-\theta)}}\,.$$

$$= \frac{\ln(X/S_0) - r - \dfrac{1}{2}\sigma^2}{\sigma}\,.$$

The derivation of $\text{Lim}_{T\to\infty}\,Z_2$ closely parallels the corresponding derivation for Z_1. It can be shown that

$$\text{Lim}_{T\to\infty}\,Z_2 = \frac{\ln(X/S_0) - r + \dfrac{1}{2}\sigma^2}{\sigma}\,.$$

Recognizing that $N(Z, \infty) = N(-\infty, -Z)$, and letting

$$D_1 = -\text{Lim}_{T\to\infty}\,Z_1$$

$$D_2 = -\text{Lim}_{T\to\infty}\,Z_2,$$

the continuous time version of the two-state model is obtained:

$$w_0 = S_0 N(-\infty, D_1) - Xe^{-r}N(-\infty, D_2)$$

$$D_1 = \frac{\ln(S_0/X) + r + \dfrac{1}{2}\sigma^2}{\sigma}$$

$$D_2 = D_1 - \sigma.$$

The above equation is identical to the Black-Scholes model.

REFERENCES

1. Brit J. Bartter and Richard J. Rendleman, Jr.. "Free-Based Pricing of Fixed Rate Bank Loan Commitments." *Financial Management*, forthcoming (Spring, 1979).
2. Brit J. Bartter and Richard J. Rendleman, Jr.. "Pricing Fixed Rate Bank Loan Commitments." (Northwestern University, 1978, unpublished working paper).
3. Fischer Black and Myron Scholes. "The Pricing of Options and Corporate Liabilities." *Journal of Political Economy* (May/June, 1973).

4. Michael Brennan and Eduardo Schwartz. "The Valuation of American Put Options." *Journal of Finance* (May, 1977).

5. John C. Cox, Stephen Ross, and Mark Rubinstein, "Option Pricing: A Simplified Approach." (University of California at Berkeley, September, 1978, Working paper No. 79).

6. Robert C. Merton. "Theory of Rational Option Pricing." *Bell Journal of Economics and Management Science* (Spring 1973).

7. Michael Parkinson. "Option Pricing: The American Put." *Journal of Business* (January, 1977).

8. Richard J. Rendleman, Jr. and Brit J. Bartter. "The Pricing of Options on Debt Securities." *Journal of Financial and Quantitative Analysis*, forthcoming (March, 1980).

9. Richard J. Rendleman, Jr. "Corporate Income Taxes, Valuation, and the Problem of Optimal Capital Structure: A Closer Look." (Northwestern University, 1978, unpublished working paper).

10. Mark Rubinstein. *Option Markets* unpublished book (1977).

11. William F. Sharpe. *Investments* (Englewood Cliffs, New Jersey, Prentice Hall, 1978).

A MEAN-VARIANCE SYNTHESIS OF CORPORATE FINANCIAL THEORY

MARK E. RUBINSTEIN*

IN RECENT YEARS the elaboration of portfolio theory has shattered the conventional partitions within the field of finance. While it has always been desirable, it is now possible to treat security valuation, asset expansion decision rules, and capital structure policies as derivatives of market equilibrium models under uncertainty. Additionally, these models provide benchmarks for measuring the efficiency of markets and investment performance. Portfolio theory, providing as it does, theories of individual choice of securities and the determination of their market prices, therefore comprises the theoretical substructure of finance. The objective of this essay is to demonstrate that an integration of much of the subject matter of finance is possible at a relatively introductory level. No attempt is made to cover all the applications of portfolio theory; I have rather concentrated on the contributions of the popular mean-variance theory[1] to corporate finance, and consequently this essay is divided into three parts treating the three major problems of corporate finance: security valuation, asset expansion, and capital structure, in that order.

Much of the theory, informally treated in the text with formal arguments banished to footnotes, is contained in the existing literature, in particular Sharpe [15] on security valuation, Mossin [11] on asset expansion and Stiglitz [16] on capital structure.[2] However, several results will not be found in the published literature: (1) development of mean-variance capital budgeting criteria for mutually exclusive projects, capital rationing, and mutually interdependent projects; (2) proof that although non-synergistic merging typically reduces the probability of bankruptcy, shareholders will nonetheless be indifferent; (3) proof of the Modigliani-Miller Proposition I with risky corporate debt and corporate taxation; (4) proof of the Modigliani-Miller Proposition II revised for risky corporate debt; (5) analysis of the separate effects of operating risk and financial risk on equity risk premiums; (6) analysis of the components of operating risk; and (7), in the Appendix, a relatively elegant proof of the mean-variance security valuation theorem.

* Assistant Professor of Finance, University of California, Berkeley. Thanks are due to Professor Fred Weston for many helpful discussions and the opportunity to test and refine the pedagogic approach in this essay in the classroom.

1. The state-preference theory, developed for example by Myers [12], from which this theory can be derived as a special case, is omitted from this synthesis. However, while empirical tests of the more general theory are lacking, they are available for the mean-variance theory in increasing abundance in recent years. Jensen [4] provides an excellent summary of these results. He concludes that the model in its simplest form fails to explain adequately the structure of security returns; however, slightly generalized forms of the model which do not destroy its basic features appear more promising.

2. Portions of several other papers are summarized in the text, including those of Hamada [3], Lintner [5], Modigliani and Miller [9], and Mossin [10].

I. SECURITY VALUATION

Let us start from the familiar mean-variance security valuation theorem that under certain assumptions[3] it follows that for any security j

$$E(R_j) = R_F + \lambda \, \text{Cov}\,(R_j, R_M) \tag{1}$$

3. The most important assumptions are (1) its single-period context, (2) no restrictions on short-selling and borrowing, and (3) a perfect and competitive securities market. However, Fama [1] has demonstrated that even though an individual has a concave multiperiod utility function, he will nonetheless behave in the first period as if he possesses some concave single-period utility function. This theorem is significant since if security returns are assumed normally distributed and intertemporally statistically independent, equation (1) applies even in a multiperiod setting where R_j represents a first period rate of return. Nonetheless, the model remains incapable of valuing irregular or non-perpetual income streams over time and hence has not rigorously been applied to the analysis of dividend policy and capital budgeting projects with multiperiod receipts. Only if firms can in some way estimate the probability distribution of the market value of a project at the end of the first period (without knowing future discount rates) and sale of the project at that time does not result in synergistic losses will the mean-variance model be appropriate. However, this model should not be criticized too heavily on this account since the present failure of theorists to produce any multiperiod (i.e., permitting portfolio revision over time) security valuation model under uncertainty consistent with maximizing expected utility (see Hakansson [2]) is very likely the most pressing theoretical problem in the field of finance.

The assumption of a *perfect* securities market precludes personal or corporate taxes, brokerage fees, underwriting costs, bankruptcy penalties, or other types of transactions costs as well as indivisibilities of securities. Relaxation of this assumption provides no analytical complications provided the imperfection is confined to a proportional reduction (possibly different for different securities) in the rate of return on a security; that is, stochastic constant returns must prevail. Otherwise, the necessary first order conditions in the Appendix must be drastically revised. However, if certain imperfections are admitted (as we will do in the case of proportional corporate income taxes) the capital structure and merger irrelevancy propositions do not strictly hold. Bankruptcy penalties, though not proportional corporate income taxes, create an incentive to merge since mergers almost invariably diminish the probability of bankruptcy. However, proportional personal income taxes do not affect any of the conclusions in this essay.

With a *competitive* securities market, the same security investment opportunities are available to all investors and no investor believes he can influence the rate of return on any security by his market transactions. No such assumption is made for firms in Sections I and III. However, in Section II, a firm's capital budgeting decisions are assumed to have negligible impact on the capitalized opportunities of other firms. The implications of relaxing the assumption of a competitive securities market have received little attention in the theoretical literature.

Rubinstein [13] demonstrates that the assumption of (4) the existence of a risk-free (i.e. zero variance) security is not substantive provided at least two risky securities exist in which case the symbol R_F in this paper may be replaced at every point by $E(R_p)$, where p is a portfolio with Cov $(R_p, R_M) = 0$. The strong short-selling assumption, by circumventing the issue of personal bankruptcy, makes this possible. Restrictions on short-selling leading to Kuhn-Tucker conditions have been examined by Lintner [5,6].

If the assumption of (5) homogeneous subjective probabilities is omitted, as Lintner [6] has shown, a concept similar to λ remains well-defined. However expected rates of return and covariances must be replaced by weighted averages. Furthermore, the convenient separation property of the model (i.e. all individuals regardless of differences in wealth levels or preferences, divide their wealth between the same two mutual funds, one of which is risk-free and the other the market portfolio of risky securities) no longer holds. As Stiglitz [16] proves, this failure of the separation property invalidates the Modigliani-Miller Proposition I in the presence of risky corporate borrowing. However, if corporate debt is risk-free, the proposition still holds. A similar qualification applies to the asset expansion propositions; see Lintner [8] and Myers [12].

The assumption that (6) all individuals evaluate portfolios by only two parameters, expectation and variance of future wealth, if omitted leads to a more complex security valuation equation which nonetheless preserves many of the characteristics of the simpler mean-variance case; see Rubinstein [13]. However, in this case the separation property is more difficult to obtain. Finally, if the assumption of (7) risk aversion is omitted, equation (1) remains necessary but no longer sufficient for market equilibrium.

where R_j (random variable) is the rate of return on security j,
$\quad$ R_F is the rate of return on a risk-free security,
$\quad$ R_M (random variable) is the rate of return on the market portfolio of risky securities, and
$\quad$ λ is a positive constant.

See the Appendix for a short proof of this theorem. This market equilibrium relationship between security risk and return may be interpreted in perhaps more familiar language by defining $R_j \equiv \tilde{P}_j/P_j$ where P_j is the present price of security j and P_j (random variable) is the change in price of security j.[4] With this definition it follows immediately that

$$P_j = \frac{E(\tilde{P}_j)}{R_F + \lambda \operatorname{Cov}(R_j, R_M)} = \frac{E(\tilde{P}_j) - \lambda \operatorname{Cov}(\tilde{P}_j, R_M)}{R_F},$$

the first equality representing a risk-adjusted discount rate formula, the second equality a certainty-equivalent formula.[5] Equation (1) is illustrated graphically in Figure 1. Since λ and R_F are market parameters, all securities have risk and return characteristics which fall along the "λ market line" in equilibrium. Define α_j as the proportion of the value of an arbitrary portfolio p assigned to security j. Observing that $R_p = \Sigma_j \alpha_j R_j$, it is easily demonstrated that all possible portfolios of securities fall along this same market line;[6] that is, for any portfolio p,

$$E(R_p) = R_F + \lambda \operatorname{Cov}(R_p, R_M).$$

Further since the market portfolio of risky securities is itself a portfolio, its risk and return characteristics fall along the market line; that is,

$$E(R_M) = R_F + \lambda \operatorname{Cov}(R_M, R_M) = R_F + \lambda \operatorname{Var} R_M$$

or alternatively,

$$\lambda = \frac{E(R_M) - R_F}{\operatorname{Var} R_M}.$$

Two popular alternative formulations of the equation (1) are

4. If R_j is defined as a *rate* of return, $\tilde{P}_j$ must be interpreted as a perpetual flow. Alternatively, R_j can be regarded as *one plus* the rate of return in which case $\tilde{P}_j$ must be interpreted as the future price of security j, a stock variable. With this latter definition of $\tilde{R}_j$ all equations in the text remain unchanged; however, all flow variables must be regarded as stock variables and, in particular, τ_j must be considered as a *wealth* tax rate on equity. To see this, observe that equation (1) holds if and only if

$$E(1 + R_j) = (1 + R_F) + \lambda \operatorname{Cov}(1 + R_j, 1 + R_M).$$

5. In the traditional risk-adjusted discount rate and certainty-equivalent dividend capitalization equations, the relationship between the risk premium or certainty-equivalent factor in each period and the risk characteristics of the dividend stream are unspecified. Unless some relationship is postulated, the equations remain merely *definitions* of the risk premiums or certainty-equivalent factors. In this context, the contribution of the mean-variance security valuation *theorem* is to provide the needed specification of the risk premium and certainty-equivalent factor.

6. To see this, merely multiply equation (1) by α_j and take the summation over all j.

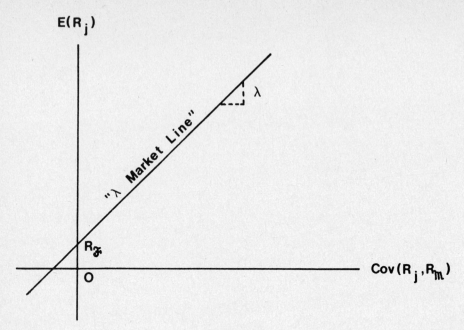

FIGURE 1

$$E(R_j) = R_F + \lambda^* \rho(R_j, R_M) \sqrt{\text{Var } R_j} \qquad (2)$$

$$E(R_j) = R_F + \lambda^{**} \beta_j \qquad (3)$$

where $\lambda^* \equiv \lambda \sqrt{\text{Var } R_M} = [E(R_M) - R_F] \sqrt{\text{Var } R_M}$,
$\lambda^{**} \equiv \lambda \text{ Var } R_M = E(R_M) - R_F$,
$\beta_j \equiv \text{Cov}(R_j, R_M)/\text{Var } R_M$, and
$\rho(R_j, R_M)$ is the correlation coefficient between R_j and R_M.

Unlike λ and λ^{**}, λ^* is dimensionless. These equations are derived from the definition of correlation coefficient and the result that the market portfolio of risky securities falls along the market line. These results can be described by similar graphical representations (see Figure 2). Equation (2) permits convenient distinctions between types of risk. Held alone as a portfolio, the risk of security j to an individual can be measured by $\sqrt{\text{Var } R_j}$; in a market or well-diversified portfolio context, the risk is measured by $\rho(R_j, R_M)\sqrt{\text{Var } R_j}$ (see equation (2)). The former may be called the *total risk* and the latter the *nondiversifiable* or *systematic risk*. Since $-1 \leqslant \rho(R_j, R_M) \leqslant 1$, $\rho(R_j, R_M)$ may be interpreted as the percentage of total risk that cannot be eliminated by diversification without sacrificing expected rate of return. The difference between total and nondiversifiable risk, $[1 - \rho(R_j, R_M)]\sqrt{\text{Var } R_j}$, measures the portion of the total risk that can be eliminated by diversification and hence can be called *diversifiable* or *nonsystematic risk*. All these results can, of course, be shown to hold for portfolios as well as securities.

If all diversifiable risk has been eliminated from a portfolio, we define that portfolio to be *efficient*. In this case

$$[1 - \rho(R_\epsilon, R_M)] \sqrt{\text{Var } R_\epsilon} = 0$$

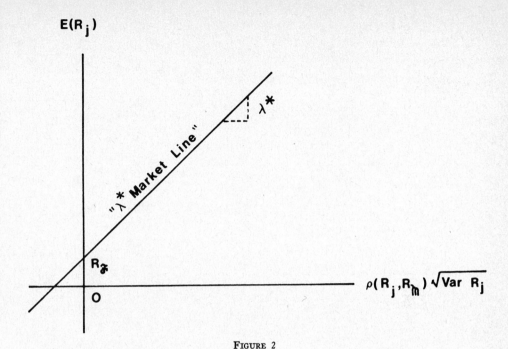

E(R$_j$)

"λ* Market Line"

λ*

R$_{\mathcal{F}}$

O

$\rho(R_j, R_m)\sqrt{Var\ R_j}$

FIGURE 2

where subscript ϵ denotes an efficient portfolio. For this equation to hold, $\rho(R_\epsilon, R_M) = 1$; or, in other words, all efficient portfolios are perfectly positively correlated with the market portfolio of risky securities (with the exception of the efficient portfolio containing only risk-free securities). It follows that $\rho(R_p, R_M)$ may be interpreted as a dimensionless measure of the degree of diversification of any portfolio p. This analysis provides a method of segregating the efficient portfolios from other portfolios and securities which fall along the "λ* market line" by noting that an "efficient portfolio market line" is described by setting the correlation coefficient equal to 1 in equation (2), and hence

$$E(R_\epsilon) = R_F + \lambda^* \sqrt{Var\ R_\epsilon}.$$

This, by the way, is the same line each individual will derive in a Markowitz efficient set analysis with the existence of a risk-free security and homogeneous subjective probabilities.

II. Asset Expansion

The mean-variance security valuation theorem is readily applied to capital budgeting decisions for share price maximizing firms.[7] Consider j now as referring to firm j and R$_j$ as representing the rate of return on the equity of firm j. It is easily demonstrated that firm j should accept a project only if

$$E(R_j^o) > R_F + \lambda\ Cov\ (R_j^o, R_M)^{[8]}$$

7. The following theory does not actually require share price maximizing behavior for firms; it merely indicates the influence of capital budgeting decisions on share prices.

8. Alternative present value risk-adjusted discount rate and certainty-equivalent forms of this criterion are easily derived. Further, the criterion also has alternative formulations analogous to

139

where X_j° (random variable) is the dollar return of the project,
$COST_j^\circ$ is the cost of the project,[9] and
$R_j^\circ \equiv X_j^\circ/COST_j^\circ$ (random variable) is the rate of return of the project.

This decision rule advises acceptance of a project only if its expected internal rate of return $E(R_j^\circ)$ exceeds the appropriate risk-adjusted discount rate for the project, $R_F + \lambda\, Cov(R_j^\circ, R_M)$; this discount rate is equal to the expected rate of return on a security with the same risk as the project. Graphically, in Figure 3, the acceptance criterion implies a firm should accept

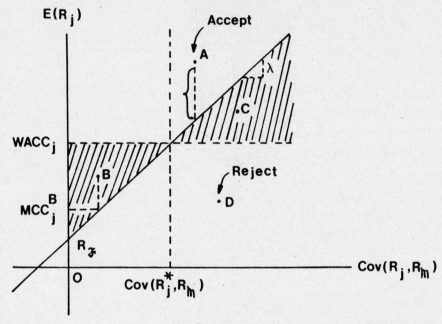

FIGURE 3

a project only if the *project's* risk-return order pair plots above the market line, such as projects A and B. In this case, when the firm accepts such favorable projects, there must be an upward revision of the firm's share price. To see this, after acceptance of a favorable project but before the price adjustment, the firm can be viewed in temporary disequilibrium with the firm's risk-return ordered pair temporarily plotting above the line. To restore equilibrium, individuals cause $E(R_j)$ to be lowered to the market line by bidding up the share price of firm j.[10]

equations (2) and (3). However, the version given by Mossin [11, p. 755] similar to $[E(R_j^\circ) - R_F]/Cov\,(R_j^\circ, R_M) > \lambda$ is only correct provided $Cov\,(R_j^\circ, R_M) > 0$.

9. X_j° and $COST_j^\circ$ should be understood to represent, respectively, the entire marginal dollar return and cost of the project to the firm. Synergistic benefits could clearly cause the same project to have different marginal dollar returns and costs to different firms. Again, X_j° may be interpreted as a perpetual flow of income or as the future market value of the project, with corresponding interpretations for R_j°; see footnote 4.

10. The asset expansion criterion is demonstrated formally under the convenient, though unnecessary, assumption of all-equity financed firms and projects. Consider firm j for which

The constant slope of the market line, λ, may be interpreted as the *risk-standardized cost of capital* appropriate to all firms and all projects since, if $\text{Cov}(R_j^o, R_M) > 0$, then a firm should accept a project only if

$$\frac{E(R_j^o) - R_F}{\text{Cov}(R_j^o, R_M)} > \lambda.$$

We will call this result the "market price of risk" (MPR) asset expansion criterion. All firms in the economy may use λ as a cutoff value for all projects; [11] this contrasts with the traditional "weighted average cost of capital" (WACC) criterion which must be computed separately for each firm, and as we will shortly show, is generally invalid. Further, since the contribution of the project to the firm's variance of equity rate of return does not affect the accept or reject decision given by the MPR criterion, *diversification* (i.e., reduction of Var R_j) can be ignored in capital budgeting decisions. That is, in the absence of *synergy* (i.e., if $R_j^o = R^o$, the rate of return if the project were itself a firm), each project is evaluated on its own merits without reference to the firm's existing investments.[12] This conclusion also follows from the observation that individuals, by their own diversification, can costlessly eliminate any diversifiable risk present in a firm's investment portfolio so that the firm need not diversify for individuals.[13]

P'_j is the revised present price after acceptance of the new project,

N_j is the number of shares before acceptance of the new project,

N_j^o is the additional shares issued at price P'_j to finance the project, and

X_j (random variable) is the dollar value of net operating income before acceptance of the new project.

From equation (1), before acceptance of the project since $R_j = X_j/(N_j P_j)$

$$E(X_j) = R_F N_j P_j + \lambda \, \text{Cov}(X_j, R_M). \tag{a}$$

After acceptance of the project

$$E(X_j + X_j^o) = R_F(N_j + N_j^o)P'_j + \lambda \, \text{Cov}(X_j + X_j^o, R_M). \tag{b}$$

Since by definition $X_j^o = R_j^o(\text{COST}_j^o)$ and $\text{COST}_j^o = N_j^o P'_j$, from equations (a) and (b)

$$R_F N_j(P_j - P'_j) = (\text{COST}_j^o)[R_F + \lambda \, \text{Cov}(R_j^o, R_M) - E(R_j^o)]. \tag{c}$$

The asset expansion criterion follows since both $R_F N_j$ and COST_j^o are positive. This analysis, however, ignores second order effects on R_M, and hence on λ. In U.S. capital markets such effects are likely to be insignificant. See Myers [12, pp. 12,13] for a more probing discussion of this point.

11. λ, therefore, is an important economy-wide variable. Several studies have attempted to measure the related λ^* from *ex-post* data; and the comparative statics analyses of Lintner [7] and Rubinstein [14] permit a theoretical examination of the determinants of λ^* and its behavior over time.

12. Since R_M reflects the existing investments of firm j as well as all other firms, this statement is not formally accurate. However, in U.S. capital markets the influence of a single firm's investments on R_M is likely to be insignificant.

13. The "homemade diversification" theorem should be regarded as one of the major discoveries in corporate financial theory. Despite lack of recognition in several recent papers, the theorem was first formally proven by Mossin [10, pp. 779-781]. Myers [12] has demonstrated a similar proposition with a state-preference model under complete (i.e., Arrow-Debreu) markets for securities and under incomplete (i.e., generalized) markets with the existence of security risk classes.

A common interpretation of the WACC criterion can easily be shown to be generally invalid. This interpretation advises that a project should be accepted only if $E(R_j^o) > WACC_j$, that is, graphically, only if it falls above the horizontal dotted line in Figure 3, such as projects A and C. Therefore, for projects that fall in the shaded areas, such as B and C, the WACC and MPR criteria lead to contradictory decisions. The WACC criterion is obviously invalid because it fails to consider the risk of projects. For example, projects with $E(R_j^o) > WACC_j$ but with very high risk, such as C, will be improperly accepted. In fact, the WACC criterion will only lead to the correct cut-off rate for projects in the same "risk class" as the firm; that is, projects for which $Cov(R_j^o, R_M) = Cov(R^*_j, R_M)$ where R^*_j (random variable) is the rate of return shareholders would earn if the firm kept its existing investments intact but altered its capital structure so that it became debt free. $Cov(R^*_j, R_M)$ therefore reflects only the "business" or "operating risk" of the firm as distinct from its "financial risk." In Section III, we will show that the ordered pair $(Cov(R^*_j, R_M), WACC_j)$ falls on the market line. Graphically, a project will be in the same "risk class" as the firm only if it plots on the vertical dotted line in Figure 3, from which it can be visually verified that only for such projects will the WACC criterion provide the appropriate cut-off rate. A second explanation of the failure of the WACC criterion is that it is not a marginal criterion. The appropriate marginal cost of capital (MCC_j^B) for project B is indicated on the vertical axis in Figure 3. The MCC_j^o depends on the risk of a project and is equal to the appropriate discount rate for the project, $R_F + \lambda Cov(R_j^o, R_M)$.

Mutually exclusive projects, capital rationing and mutually interdependent projects are easily treated in this framework. Suppose projects A and B in Figure 3 are mutually exclusive. It can be readily shown that the firm should accept the project with the highest excess expected internal rate of return weighted by its cost,[14] that is, the highest $(COST_j^o)[E(R_j^o) - R_F - \lambda Cov(R_j^o, R_M)]$. Note that the excess expected internal rate of return for project A, for example, is measured graphically by the vertical distance between A and the market line in Figure 3. With capital rationing, the proper procedure is again to reject all projects falling below the line. Of the remaining projects consider all possible bundles of projects satisfying the rationing constraint. These bundles are in effect mutually exclusive; therefore the firm should accept the bundle with the highest excess expected internal rate of return weighted by its cost. If n superscripts projects in a feasible bundle, this is equivalent to accepting that bundle for which $\Sigma_n(COST_j^n)[E(R_j^n) - R_F - \lambda Cov(R_j^n, R_M)]$ is the highest. With mutually interdependent projects, selection is determined by appropriately increasing the number of mutually exclusive projects. Assume, for example, that projects A and C are mutually interdependent; in this case in addition to projects A and C treated separately, the joint acceptance of A and C is considered as a single project.

Decision rules regarding mergers are easily derived. Consider firms j and

---

14. This result follows immediately from equation (c) of footnote 10 and is equivalent to accepting the project with the highest net present value.

k which are contemplating merger. Let X_j, X_k, and X_{jk} (random variables) be the net operating income (EBIT) of firms j, k, and the pro-forma post-merger firm, respectively. In the absence of *synergy*, that is, if $X_{jk} = X_j + X_k$, the post-merger firm can be considered equivalent to a portfolio containing all the securities of firms j and k. Since all possible portfolios, as well as securities, fall along the market line, the post-merger firm will fall along the market line and it will be impossible for the shareholders of both j and k to benefit from the merger. Again, the intuitive reason for this result is costless "homemade diversification." Alternatively, since an individual could have held the stock of both j and k in his portfolio before the merger, his portfolio becomes no more diversified if he holds the post-merger firm.[15] Therefore, as in capital budgeting, the diversification effects of a merger will not affect equity values. However, mergers with synergy will affect equity values and such mergers can be analyzed similarly to capital budgeting projects, since with synergy, *from the point of view of firm j*, the risk-return ordered pair of firm k may not plot on the market line.

It has been argued (see Lintner [8, p. 107]) that with risky corporate borrowing, merging decreases the probability of bankruptcy (provided the separate net operating incomes of the merging firms are not perfectly correlated). As a result, the merged firm can borrow on more favorable terms thereby increasing the value of equity. However, an offsetting consequence of merging is overlooked in this argument. The effects of bankruptcy are double-edged since mergers also have the unfavorable consequence of removing the separated limited liabilities of the merging firms. Consider two firms j and k: prior to merger bankruptcy of k does not affect the returns to shares of j; subsequent to merger, the returns from j's portion of the merged firm would be reduced by the requirement of meeting k's defaulted portion of the merged firm's obligations.[16]

15. Before the merger, the shares of firms j and k could have been held in any proportion in an individual's portfolio; however, after the merger, shares in firms j and k can, in effect, be held only in a fixed proportion. It may be argued, therefore, that mergers destroy opportunities for individual portfolio selection and hence even a merger with positive synergy could reduce equity values. However, the portfolio separation property of the mean-variance model insures that relevant opportunities will remain intact.

16. The irrelevancy of mergers is formally demonstrated even where corporate debt is explicitly risky. Define R_{F_j}, R_{F_k}, and $R_{F_{jk}}$ (random variables) as the borrowing rates for firms j, k, and jk. To reflect the influence of bankruptcy, for example, the probability distribution of R_{F_j} could be defined such that $\bar{R}_{F_j} \equiv R_{F_j}$ if $X_j \geqslant \bar{R}_{F_j} B_j$ and $R_{F_j} \equiv X_j / B_j$ if $X_j \leqslant \bar{R}_{F_j} B_j$ where $\bar{R}_{F_j}$ is the promised or contracted rate of interest (see text for definitions of B_j and V_j). From equation (1) and since $R_j = (X_j - R_{F_j} B_j)/(V_j - B_j)$, $E(X_j) - B_j E(R_{F_j}) = R_F V_j - B_j \bar{R}_F + \lambda \, \text{Cov}(X_j, R_M) - B_j \lambda \, \text{Cov} \, (R_{F_j}, R_M)$. Since risky debt is also a security, $E(R_{F_j}) = R_F + \lambda \, \text{Cov} \, (R_{F_j}, R_M)$; therefore

$$E(X_j) = R_F V_j + \lambda \, \text{Cov} \, (X_j, R_M). \tag{a}$$

Similar arguments may also be made for firms k and jk, so that

$$E(X_k) = R_F V_k + \lambda \, \text{Cov} \, (X_k, R_M) \text{ and (c) } E(X_{jk}) = R_F V_{jk} + \lambda \, \text{Cov} \, (X_{jk}, R_M). \tag{b}$$

These equations will hold regardless of the effects of reduced probability of bankruptcy on $R_{F_{jk}}$. Since $X_{jk} = X_j + X_k$, adding equations (a) and (b) and comparing the sum to equation (c) yields the result $V_{jk} = V_j + V_k$.

III. Capital Structure

The mean-variance security valuation theorem is also readily applied to the effect of capital structure on the value of a firm. Consider firm j for which

X_j (random variable) is the dollar value of net operating income,
B_j is the present dollar value of debt,
S_j is the present dollar value of equity,
$V_j \equiv B_j + S_j$ is the present total dollar value of the securities of the firm, and
$R_j \equiv (X_j - R_F B_j)/S_j$ (random variable) is the rate of return on equity.

Define these variables for a second firm denoted by a * superscript for which $B^*_j = 0$. Since the risk-return ordered pairs of all securities fall along the market line,

$$\frac{E(R_j) - R_F}{\rho(R_j, R_M)\sqrt{\text{Var } R_j}} = \frac{E(R^*_j) - R_F}{\rho(R^*_j, R_M)\sqrt{\text{Var } R^*_j}} = \lambda^*. \tag{4}$$

If $X_j = X^*_j$, it follows that $V_j = V^*_j$ by substituting the definitions of R_j and R^*_j in equation (4).[17] Interpreting this result, as a firm alters its capital structure, but before price adjustment, the firm moves along, not off, the market line achieving the precise risk-return trade-off which leaves the market indifferent and hence its stock price unchanged.[18]

---

17. This proposition is demonstrated formally in the presence of corporate taxes and risky corporate debt where superscript ^ denotes after tax variables, τ_j is the corporate income tax rate for firm j, and R_{F_j} (random variable) denotes the rate of return on the risky debt of firm j. Since $E(R_j) = R_F + \lambda \, \text{Cov } (R_j, R_M)$ and $R_j \equiv (X_j - R_{F_j}B_j)(1 - \tau_j)/S_j$, it follows in the levered case that

$$E(X_j)(1 - \tau_j) - E(R_{F_j})B_j(1 - \tau_j) = R_F S_j + \lambda(1 - \tau_j) \, \text{Cov } (X_j, \hat{R}_M)$$
$$- \lambda(1 - \tau_j)B_j \, \text{Cov } (R_{F_j}, \hat{R}_M). \tag{a}$$

By similar reasoning since in the unlevered case $\hat{R}^*_j \equiv X_j(1 - \tau_j)/V^*_j$

$$E(X_j)(1 - \tau_j) = R_F V^*_j + \lambda(1 - \tau_j) \, \text{Cov } (X_j, \hat{R}_M). \tag{b}$$

Further since risky debt is also a security, $E(R_{F_j}) = R_F + \lambda \, \text{Cov } (R_{F_j}, R_M)$. Substituting this equation and equation (b) into equation (a) and recalling that by definition $V_j \equiv S_j + B_j$, it follows that $V_j = V^*_j + \tau_j B_j$. This is the familiar result of Modigliani-Miller which holds even the presence of risky debt.

It should be emphasized, as Stiglitz [16] has shown, for more general models which lack the separation property, the Modigliani-Miller Proposition I, with or without taxes, will not hold in the presence of risky debt. The separation property in the mean-variance model insures that changes in capital structure will not alter relevant opportunities available to individuals.

18. It is not difficult to demonstrate that if $V_j = V^*_j$, then $P_j = P^*_j$ where P_j and P^*_j refer to share prices. Imagine that a firm is first in an unlevered position so that $V^*_j = S^*_j = N^*_j P^*_j$ where N^*_j is the number of shares. The firm now levers its capital structure without affecting its net operating income by purchase of ΔN shares of equity at price P_j (a priori, possibly different from P^*_j) and financing $(\Delta N)P_j$ with debt so that $(\Delta N)P_j = B_j$. Hence

$$V_j \equiv S_j + B_j = (N^*_j - \Delta N)P_j + (\Delta N)P_j = N^*_j P_j,$$

and since $V_j = V^*_j$, then $P_j = P^*_j$.

To show that the ordered pair $(\rho(R^*_j, R_M)\sqrt{\text{Var } R^*_j}, \text{WACC}_j)$ falls on the "λ^* market line" (or, alternatively, that $(\text{Cov}(R^*_j, R_M), \text{WACC}_j)$ falls on the "λ market line") we need only recall that by definition

$$\text{WACC}_j \equiv R_F \left[\frac{B_j}{V_j} \right] + E(R_j) \left[\frac{S_j}{V_j} \right] = \frac{E(X_j)}{V_j}$$

and since $X_j = X^*_j$ and $V_j = V^*_j$,

$$\text{WACC}_j = \frac{E(X_j)}{V_j} = \frac{E(X^*_j)}{V^*_j} = E(R^*_j).$$

Since R^*_j is independent of capital structure, it follows that the weighted average cost of capital is also.

The precise relationship between expected rate of return to equity and capital structure is easily demonstrated since by substitution of $R_j \equiv (X_j - R_F B_j)/S_j$ and $R^*_j = X_j/V_j$:

$$\rho(R_j, R_M) = \rho(R^*_j, R_M) \quad \text{and} \quad \sqrt{\text{Var } R_j} = \sqrt{\text{Var } R^*_j} \left[1 + \frac{B_j}{S_j} \right]. \tag{5}$$

Therefore, from equation (2),

$$E(R_j) = R_F + \lambda^* \rho(R^*_j, R_M) \sqrt{\text{Var } R^*_j} \left[1 + \frac{B_j}{S_j} \right]. \tag{6}$$

Equation (6) quantifies the effect of financial leverage on the risk of a firm and hence on its expected rate of return to equity. Equation (5) indicates that since the correlation coefficient is invariant to changes in financial leverage, the full impact of financial risk is absorbed by the standard deviation $\sqrt{\text{Var } R_j}$. Further, since both λ^* and $\sqrt{\text{Var } R^*_j}$ are positive, the direction of the influence of changes in financial leverage on $E(R_j)$ depends on the sign of $\rho(R^*_j, R_M)$, so that $E(R_j)$ could conceivably decrease with increased financial leverage. In more familiar terms, equation (6) is a specialization of the Modigliani-Miller Proposition II,

$$E(R_j) = E(R^*_j) + [E(R^*_j) - R_F] \left[\frac{B_j}{S_j} \right], \tag{7}$$

for the attitudes toward risk implied by the mean-variance security valuation theorem.[19] Both equations (6) and (7) permit separate analysis of operating risk and financial risk. Equation (6) can be written

19. If corporate debt is risky, equation (7) is generalized by replacing the symbol R_F with $E(R_{F_j})$. To see this, applying the definitions $R_j \equiv (X_j - R_{F_j} B_j)/S_j$, $R^*_j \equiv X_j/V^*_j$ and $V_j \equiv B_j + S_j$, it is easy to demonstrate that the revised equation (7) holds if and only if $V_j = V^*_j$, but this last equality has already been demonstrated in the absence of taxes in footnote 17. Since $E(R_{F_j})$ exceeds R_F for most firms in U.S. capital markets, the consideration of risky debt will cause $E(R_j)$ to be less than it would otherwise be if debt were assumed risk-free. This is intuitively plausible since with risky debt, the total risk of net operating income is shared by both equity and debt holders.

$$E(R_j) = R_F + \lambda^* \rho(R^*_j, R_M) \sqrt{Var\ R^*_j} + \lambda^* \rho(R^*_j, R_M) \sqrt{Var\ R^*_j} \left[\frac{B_j}{S_j} \right], \quad (8)$$

thereby separating the effects of the risk-free rate of return, operating risk, and financial risk on the expected rate of return to equity.[20]

It is further interesting to develop the components of operating risk. Consider, for firm j, product m for which

Q_m (random variable) is the output in units,
v_m is the variable cost per unit,
p_m is the sales price per unit,
F_m is the fixed cost, and
α_m is the proportion of assets (i.e., V_j) devoted to its production.

Therefore, assuming all fixed costs of the firm can be allocated, $X_j = \Sigma_m (Q_m p_m - Q_m v_m - F_m)$. Since $R^*_j = \alpha_m X_j / \alpha_m V_j$, it is not difficult to demonstrate that operating risk

$$\rho(R^*_j, R_M) \sqrt{Var\ R^*_j} = \Sigma_m [\alpha_m(p_m - v_m)\rho\ (Q_m, R_M) \sqrt{Var\ (Q_m/\alpha_m V_j)}]$$

where α_m measures the relative influence of each product line (assuming all assets of the firm can be allocated to products), $p_m - v_m$ reflects operating leverage, $\rho(Q_m, R_M)$ the pure influence of economy-wide events on output, and $\sqrt{Var\ (Q_m/\alpha_m V_j)}$ the uncertainty of output per dollar of assets which could be interpreted as a measure of the uncertainty of "operating efficiency."

Illustration of the effect of corporate income taxes on the relationship between capital structure and firm values is easily analyzed by equation (4) upon substitution of

20. This result can be used to explain the size of observed *ex post* values of β_j in equation (3). Defining $\beta^*_j \equiv Cov\ (R^*_j, R_M)/Var\ R_M$, it can be shown with adjustment for corporate income taxes that

$$\beta_j = \beta_j^* \left[1 + \frac{B_j(1 - \tau_j)}{S_j} \right].$$

From data in *Moody's Handbook of Common Stocks:* First Quarter, 1971, on General Motors (GM) and Chrysler (C) for 1960-1969, $\beta^*_{GM} = .77$ and $\beta^*_C = 1.69$ with $\beta_{GM} = .86$ and $\beta_C = 2.48$. We might infer that not only was Chrysler's "operating risk" about double General Motors' but the substantially higher financial leverage ratio for Chrysler ($B_{GM}/S_{GM} = .2$ and $B_C/S_C = 1.0$) caused Chrysler's nondiversifiable risk (operating plus financial) to be about triple General Motors'.

An alternative approach is to use equation (8) directly. The results for General Motors and Chrysler (adjusted for corporate income taxes) are summarized in the following table:

	$E(R_j)$	Risk-Free Rate R_F	Operating Risk $\lambda^* \rho(R^*_j, R_m) \sqrt{Var\ R^*_j}$	Financial Risk $\lambda^* \rho(R^*_j, R_m) \sqrt{Var\ R^*_j} \left[\frac{B_j(1 - \tau_j)}{S_j} \right]$
GM	.10	.045	.050	.005
C	.21	.045	.110	.055

146

$$R_j = \frac{(X_j - R_F B_j)(1 - \tau_j)}{V_j - B_j} \text{ and } R^*_j = \frac{X_j(1 - \tau_j)}{V^*_j}$$

where τ_j is the corporate income tax rate of firm j.[21] We immediately derive the familiar result $V_j = V^*_j + \tau_j B_j$. This result can be given a similar interpretation to the acceptance of a project with a risk-return ordered pair falling above the market line. After an increase in financial leverage, but before price adjustment, the risk-return ordered pair of the firm's equity moves temporarily above the market line. To restore equilibrium, individuals cause $E(R_j)$ to be lowered to the market line by bidding up the share price of the firm.

In contrast to Modigliani and Miller [9], whose ingenious "risk class" assumption insulated their partial equilibrium approach from a need to provide a theory of the market risk premium, at some sacrifice of generality (see footnote 3), the mean-variance market equilibrium model provides this theory. By straightforward extensions, the most important concepts of corporate finance can be demonstrated by use of virtually a single diagram. Furthermore, quantification of risk premiums supplies the key to practical implementation.

APPENDIX[22]

A short proof of the mean-variance security valuation theorem follows under the special case of quadratic utility.[23] In addition to the variables already used in this paper consider individual i for which

S_{ij} is his present dollar value holdings of risky security j,

B_i is his present dollar value holdings of risk-free securities,

$W_i = \Sigma_j S_{ij} + B_i$ is his present wealth,

$\widetilde{W}_i = \Sigma_j S_{ij} R_j + B_i R_F$ (random variable) is his future wealth (interpreting R as 1 + rate of return), and

$U_i(\widetilde{W}_i)$ is his twice continuously differentiable measurable utility of future wealth function where $U'_i > 0$.

21. The corporate income tax is assumed to be proportional and with full loss offset. See footnote 17 for formal proof for the more general case of risky corporate debt.
In general, with the introduction of taxes, while all securities still fall along the market line, the slope of the line will change; see Rubinstein [14].

22. This proof as well as other arguments in this essay utilize freely and without comment basic properties of expectation operators. Specifically, if X and Y are any two random variables, a and b are nonrandom parameters, and i is an index, then (1) $E(a + bX) = a + bE(X)$, (2) $E(\Sigma_i X_i) = \Sigma_i E(X_i)$, (3) $Var(a + bX) = b^2 Var\ X$, (4) $Cov(X,Y) = Cov(Y,X)$, (5) $Cov(a + bX,Y) = b\ Cov(X,Y)$, (6) $Cov(\Sigma_i X_i,Y) = \Sigma_i\ Cov(X_i,Y)$, (7) $Cov\ (X,Y) = E(XY) - E(X)E(Y)$, and (8) if $b > 0$, $\rho(a + bX,Y) = \rho(X,Y)$. It is, of course, assumed that all random variables have finite variances (and hence finite means).

23. Mossin [10] provides a more general proof assuming only ordinal utility functions with future value portfolio mean and variance as arguments. In a more recent paper, Mossin [11] offers another proof which sacrifices generality by assuming all individuals have measurable quadratic utility functions for future wealth; however, Mossin's new proof has the virtue of simplicity and provides detailed information about the determinants of λ. Nonetheless, as this appendix demonstrates, his new proof is needlessly lengthy. For the mean-variance security valuation equation to be consistent with measurable utility, one can alternatively assume that all securities have normally distributed rates of return; see Rubinstein [14].

In this context, closure requires $S_j = \Sigma_j S_{ij}$ and $R_M = \Sigma_j S_j R_j / \Sigma_j S_j$. These definitions imply the simple Lagrangian form of optimization

$$\max_{\{S_{ij}\}, B_i} \quad E[U_i(\widetilde{W}_i)] + L_i[W_i - \Sigma_j S_{ij} - B_i]$$

with first order conditions[24]

$$E[U'_i R_j] = E[U'_i R_F] = L_i \quad \text{for all} \quad j \quad \text{and} \quad W_i = \Sigma_j S_{ij} + B_i.$$

These conditions imply $E[U'_i(R_j - R_F)] = 0$ which in turn implies $E(U'_i)E(R_j - R_F) + \text{Cov}(U'_i, R_j - R_F) = 0$. If $U_i = W_i - a_i W_i^2$ where a_i is a nonrandom parameter, then $U'_i = 1 - 2a_i W_i$ and therefore

$$[E(R_j) - R_F] \frac{E(U'_i)}{2a_i} = \text{Cov}(R_j, W_i).$$

Since this equation will hold for all individuals in the market,

$$[E(R_j) - R_F] \Sigma_i \frac{E(U'_i)}{2a_i} = \Sigma_i \text{Cov}(R_j, \widetilde{W}_i) = \text{Cov}(R_j, \Sigma_i \widetilde{W}_i).$$

Closure requires that $\Sigma_i \widetilde{W}_i = \Sigma_j S_j R_j + \Sigma_i B_i R_F = R_M \Sigma_j S_j + R_F \Sigma_i B_i$; however, since $\Sigma_j S_j$ and $R_F \Sigma_i B_i$ are nonrandom, $\text{Cov}(R_j, \Sigma_i W_i) = \text{Cov}(R_j, R_M \Sigma_j S_j) = (\Sigma_j S_j) \text{Cov}(R_j, R_M)$. Therefore,

$$E(R_j) = R_F + \left[\frac{\Sigma_j S_j}{\Sigma_i \dfrac{E(U'_i)}{2a_i}} \right] \text{Cov}(R_j, R_M);$$

and if the quantity in brackets is identified with λ,[25] then

$$E(R_j) = R_F + \lambda \, \text{Cov}(R_j, R_M).$$

REFERENCES

1. E. F. Fama. "Multiperiod Consumption-Investment Decisions," *American Economic Review*, March, 1970.
2. N. H. Hakansson. "On the Dividend Capitalization Model under Uncertainty," *Journal of Financial and Quantitative Analysis*, March, 1969.
3. R. S. Hamada. "Portfolio Analysis, Market Equilibrium, and Corporation Finance," *Journal of Finance*, March, 1969.
4. M. C. Jensen. "The Foundations and Current State of Capital Market Theory," ed. M. C. Jensen, *Studies in the Theory of Capital Markets* (forthcoming).
5. J. Lintner. "The Valuation of Risk Assets and the Selection of Risky Investments in Stock Portfolios and Capital Budgets," *Review of Economics and Statistics*, February, 1965.
6. —————. "The Aggregation of Investor's Diverse Judgments and Preferences in Purely Competitive Markets," *Journal of Financial and Quantitative Analysis*, December, 1969.
7. —————. "The Market Price of Risk, Size of Market, and Investor's Risk Aversion," *Review of Economics and Statistics*, February, 1970.
8. —————. "Expectations, Mergers and Equilibrium in Purely Competitive Securities Markets," *American Economic Review*, May, 1971.
9. F. Modigliani and M. H. Miller. "The Cost of Capital, Corporation Finance, and the Theory of Investment," *American Economic Review*, June, 1958.
10. J. Mossin. "Equilibrium in a Capital Asset Market," *Econometrica*, October, 1966.

24. These first order conditions will be necessary and sufficient for a unique global maximum if $U''_i(\widetilde{W}_i) < 0$ and no security rate of return is perfectly correlated with the rate of return of any portfolio excluding it.

25. If $U''_i < 0$, then $2a_i > 0$. From this it follows that $\lambda > 0$ since both $\Sigma_j S_j$ and U'_i are assumed positive.

11. —————. "Security Pricing and Investment Criteria in Competitive Markets," *American Economic Review*, December, 1969.
12. S. C. Myers. "Procedures for Capital Budgeting under Uncertainty," *Industrial Management Review*, Spring, 1968.
13. M. E. Rubinstein. "The Fundamental Theorem of Parameter-Preference Security Valuation," *Journal of Financial and Quantitative Analysis*, January, 1973.
14. —————. "A Comparative Statics Analysis of Risk Premiums," (forthcoming in *Journal of Business*).
15. W. F. Sharpe. *Portfolio Theory and Capital Markets*, McGraw-Hill, 1970.
16. J. E. Stiglitz. "A Re-Examination of the Modigliani-Miller Theorem," *American Economic Review*, December, 1969.

Market Imperfections, Agency Problems, and Capital Structure: A Review

Amir Barnea, Robert A. Haugen, and Lemma W. Senbet

*Amir Barnea is on the Faculty of Management at Tel-Aviv
University. During the writing of this paper, he was visiting at the
Graduate School of Business at the University of Wisconsin
at Madison, where his co-authors teach. The authors wish to
acknowledge many helpful comments and suggestions from a reader
for this journal and from the participants in the Finance Workshop
at the University of Wisconsin-Madison. This tutorial article
was solicited by the editors, who are grateful for the authors'
response.*

Introduction

Prediction of the effect of capital structure on the
market value of the firm remains elusive despite much
research over the past three decades. On the one hand,
Modigliani and Miller [35] demonstrate that under
perfect capital markets — free entry, equal access to
information, and absence of transaction costs and taxes — the choice among various financial instruments
is inconsequential to the value of the firm. This powerful result is reinforced by Stiglitz [45], who shows that
financial policies are irrelevant even with risky debt,
provided the investment opportunity set remains unchanged by financial policy. His proof further implies
that corporate decisions relating to the maturity structure of debt as well as other complexities which
characterize financial instruments do not affect firm
value.[1] On the other hand, real world corporations
engage in active financial management which
manifests itself in the form of cross-sectional

variations in debt ratios, differing debt maturity structures across industries, and complex financial contractual arrangements (*e.g.*, call provisions, convertibility
features, sinking fund arrangements, warrants, or

---

[1]Many apparent explanations of the observable complex structure
of financial instruments are not consistent with the Stiglitz framework. For example, *call provisions* on corporate debt are commonly
attributed to interest rate uncertainty, suggesting that since stockholders are able to reap the added value of the bond caused by a
decrease in interest rates, they gain, and bondholders lose commen-
surately, in an *ex ante* sense. However, in the Stiglitz framework,
when arbitrage profits are fully exploited, the value of a non-callable
bond will always equal the value of a callable bond plus the value of
the call privilege. That is, stockholders pay at issuance an amount
which reflects the full value of the call privilege. Also the common
explanation of the *maturity structure* of debt is a "habitat" argument, which implies that "optimal" debt maturity is achieved at the
point where debt and asset maturities are matched so as to minimize
the uncertainty associated with interest rate fluctuations [36].
Again, however, in the framework of perfect markets, there is no
basis for an "optimal" maturity structure.

preferred stock).

There are two alternative explanations for the discrepancy between theory and reality. The first asserts that corporate reliance on complex financial instruments is merely an artifact of market equilibrium and by itself does not provide evidence for the relevance of the corporate financial policies. According to this argument, the multiplicity of financial instruments emerges from situations of disequilibrium in which (certainty equivalent) yield differentials temporarily exist. Corporations engage in activities that are aimed to capture arbitrage profits by providing more of the desired instrument. These supply adjustments continue until equilibrium is reached where the choice among financial arrangements no longer affects the market value of the firm. Still, at this point, corporations are financed by a variety of financial instruments so that complex financial structures may be observed. The second explanation of complex financial structures centers on imperfections in the functioning of the capital market. The link between specific types of market imperfections and corporate financial policies is the subject of this paper.

The introduction of imperfections to rationalize corporate decisions is not new. Finance texts provide criteria for optimal capital budgeting decisions. But such criteria can be justified only if the product and factor markets are imperfect in the sense that they are subject to barriers to entry, scale economies, information monopoly, and so on. Only then can positive net present values occur. By the same token, an explanation for the resources expended to identify optimal financial decisions must rely on market imperfections or frictions. One example of an imperfection is the tax code which, in recognizing interest as an allowable expense, favors debt over equity financing.[2] The focus of our paper is on *another* class of market imperfections, namely, agency problems stemming from the ownership structure of the firm.

Agency problems may exist when a principal, or group of principals, employs an agent to perform a service which necessitates delegating decision-making authority to the agent. These problems arise from conflicts of interests between the agent and the principal, or they can occur among the principals themselves. The analysis of the impact of these conflicts of interest on corporate decisions is based on two fundamental

assumptions. First, owners and agents behave according to their own self-interest; and second, each of the participants in the activities of the firm is rational and capable of forming unbiased expectations regarding the future wealth. The agency literature identifies situations where conflicts of interest coupled with self interested behavior and rational expectations result in suboptimal business decisions. When this occurs, agency problems create "agency costs."

The agency problems considered in this paper arise from three sources. *First,* market imperfections may lead to an inability of management (the agent) to reveal the exact nature of the firm to debt and equity financiers (the principals) costlessly. This is a problem of informational asymmetry [20, 29, 39, 40, 44].

Second, the existence of debt financing under limited liability generates 1) stockholder incentives to accept suboptimal and high-risk projects which transfer wealth from bondholders to stockholders [15, 23], 2) stockholder incentives to forgo new profitable investments when previously issued debt is supported by the existing assets and the option to undertake these investments [8, 37], and 3) bankruptcy costs associated with resolving stockholder–bondholder disputes if insolvency occurs [5, 19, 23, 24, 27, 28, 42, 48].

Third, partial ownership of the firm by an owner–manager may provide him or her an incentive to consume non-pecuniary benefits or perquisites beyond that which a manager who is the sole owner of the firm would consume [21, 23].

Agency problems result in a reduction in market value *if* the markets for financial and human capital are unable to resolve the problems costlessly. One market mechanism that can mitigate agency problems is the takeover process. An impediment to this mechanism exists in the form of the "free rider" problem (see [16]). While we discuss the "free rider" problem in detail later, our analysis focuses on the agency problems that remain unresolved after natural market forces have operated to the full extent possible. Attempts to control these residual problems yield 1) complex contracts which may partially resolve them, 2) differential yields among various types of financial instruments, and 3) complex (and possibly optimal) capital structure.

The Nature of Agency Problems

Debtholders are assumed to be rational in anticipating agency problems and in pricing agency costs into the value of their financial claims. In this framework, it should come as no surprise that stockholders might bear the full consequences of all unresolved agency

---

[2]Differential tax treatment of equity and debt *by itself* is not sufficient to explain observed corporate financial policies since it implies either the dominance of debt over equity financing or, as Miller [31] has recently shown, supply adjustments by value-maximizing corporations can eliminate any gain from leverage at a particular firm level.

problems.

The Agency Problem of Informational Asymmetry

Consider a management that seeks to finance a project by selling securities, while the true nature of the return distribution of the project is unknown to the outside market. Management possesses valuable information about the project which is unavailable to the market. If this information were revealed to the market without ambiguity, the market would value the project at V_A. Otherwise, the market is unable to distinguish this project from another *less* profitable project with a value of V_B. This is a problem of informational asymmetry. It does not imply that management has better or more information than the market, but that it possesses some information that is valuable but unavailable to the market, without which the market cannot identify the true nature of the project before it is undertaken.

This asymmetry may be resolved, at a cost, through various "signaling mechanisms." In the absence of an unambiguous signal, however, management will obtain less for securities sold than their "fair value" reflected in the true nature of project A. The difference between the "fair" price and the actual price is the agency cost associated with informational asymmetry, and it exists for the issuance of debt as well as new equity securities, provided that there is a differential probability of bankruptcy for the two projects.

It should perhaps be noted here that this particular agency problem is unique, because unlike the others, it cannot be resolved costlessly through arbitrage in the financial markets. Consequently, this problem may be more significant than the others in terms of inducing yield differentials between securities and optimal capital structure. We wish to emphasize that a going concern faces a continuing problem of informational asymmetry. The problem is not merely one of identifying the nature of new projects, but also one of identifying the nature of the current distribution of returns to the entire firm whenever additional financing is needed.

Agency Problems Associated With Debt Financing Under Limited Liability

The Incentive of Stockholders to Bear Unwarranted Risk

The fact that stockholders may benefit by investing in high-risk projects is best demonstrated by consider-

ing equity as a European-type call option to buy back the entire firm from the debtholders at maturity, at an exercise price equal to the face value of the debt. The debtholders can be viewed as buying the assets of the firm and issuing the call option (equity) on these assets. It is easy to understand this if the debt is in the form of pure discount bonds so that the time to expiration of the option (equity) is the maturity date of the bonds. As (in the framework of the option pricing model of Black and Scholes [7]) the value of this call option increases with the variance of the cash flows of the underlying assets, stockholders will increase the market value of equity, at the expense of debtholders, by selecting high-risk projects. For expositional purposes, suppose that two projects with differing risks are available to the firm. If both low- and high-risk projects available to the firm have the same market value, the choice does not affect the total value of the firm. It affects only the distribution of the value between bondholders and stockholders. Rational bondholders recognize the investment alternatives and stockholder risk incentives, and thus offer a price for the debt that reflects the distribution of wealth given adoption of the high-variance project. In any case, because both projects command the same value, no cost is incurred by either party.

The situation is more serious, however, if the high-variance project commands a lower market value, say $9 as opposed to $10 for the low-variance project. Suppose that for a given face value and coupon, the price of debt is $5 if priced in accordance with the adoption of the superior (but low-risk) project but $3 if priced with the presumption that the inferior (but high-risk) project is adopted. If bondholders have no means of neutralizing the stockholder incentive for risk shifting, they would presume that the inferior (but higher-risk) project will be adopted, and hence offer a price of $3. Unlike the previous case, the price reflects not only the higher-risk from which equityholders benefit but also the inferiority of the project in terms of current value. If stockholders wish to finance the superior project, they will lose, because the bond price will go up to $5 from $3, and commensurately the stock price will decline from $6 to $5. Thus, they are forced to adopt the inferior project with a value differential of $1. This differential is an agency cost which, on the surface, appears to be borne by stockholders.

The Incentive of Stockholders to Forgo Profitable Investments

This case considers a firm that holds an option on future investment opportunities [37]. Based on those opportunities, the firm issues debt (at time t = 0) with a face value of D which matures (at t = 2) *after* the true market value of the investments is revealed (at t = 1). This debt is *entirely* supported by future investment opportunities. At t = 1 the firm faces a decision whether to exercise the option (*i.e.*, undertake the investment). In the absence of debt financing, the firm accepts any investment for which the market value net of the required dollar investment is positive. But given the outstanding debt, stockholders maximize their wealth by accepting an investment only if its *net* market value exceeds D. Otherwise, it is in their best interests to default. Thus, the presence of debt in the capital structure causes the firm to forgo any investments for which the (positive) net market value is lower than D. Obviously rational bondholders recognize the increased probability of default on their claims and discount it in the price they are willing to offer the firm for its bonds. Consequently, the stockholders, once again, are apparently forced to suffer the full burden of this agency cost.

Suboptimal future investments can also occur when the currently outstanding debt is issued against the currently held assets [8]. This is unlike the previous case in which debt is entirely supported by future investments. Stockholders, however, cannot capture the full benefits of future investment opportunities, because they partially accrue to bondholders in the form of a reduction in the probability of default. Consequently, investment incentives may be curtailed despite the possibility that these opportunities generate a positive net present value for the firm as a whole. As before, equityholders suffer the full burden of the associated agency cost, because bondholders are unwilling to pay for future benefits due to the moral hazard problem.

Bankruptcy Costs

It is well known that if the transfer of ownership from stockholders to bondholders under default is costless, the mere possibility of bankruptcy should have no impact on the capital structure decision [3, 4, 13, 18, 33, 45]. Since it is impossible, though, to write contracts which specify, clearly and unambiguously, the rights of claimholders under all contingencies, one or more of the parties may precipitate a dispute that may be resolved in the process of formal bankruptcy proceedings. These proceedings are not costless; they involve a legal process which itself consumes a portion of the remaining value of the firm's assets. Moreover, the formal process of transferring ownership may disrupt the normal activities of the firm, precipitating a deterioration in long-standing customer and supplier relationships.

As significant as the costs associated with formal bankruptcy proceedings may be, they should not be confused with the costs associated with *liquidating* the firm's assets [19]. Bankruptcy and liquidation are best considered as distinct and independent events. Neither event is necessarily sufficient to trigger the other. The firm liquidates if and only if the market value of the firm as a going concern falls below its dismantled value under liquidation. Many authors have attributed the costs associated with distress sale of the assets of the firm to the event of bankruptcy [24, 27, 28, 42]. This is inappropriate, because while the proportion of debt in the capital structure affects the probability of bankruptcy, in no way does it affect the probability of liquidation. Liquidation is, in a complete sense, a mere capital budgeting decision. There is no *necessary* link between the decision to liquidate and the ability to pay off debt claims. A firm on the brink of bankruptcy should be liquidated only if the value of its assets as a going concern net of the reorganization costs is below the dismantled value under liquidation. By the same token, a non-bankrupt which fits this same test must be liquidated. At any rate, the expected value of bankruptcy costs, if any, can be said to be borne by equityholders if debt is sold to rational investors. Bankruptcy costs are identical to other agency costs in this respect.

The Agency Problem Associated with Partial Ownership with Controlling Interests

Consider an owner–manager who uses external equity financing but retains complete control of the firm [23]. The manager behaves so as to maximize his utility from 1) money wages (which are assumed to be fixed), 2) the market value of his firm, and 3) on-the-job perquisites (which are assumed to be *inseparable* from the firm).[3] *As sole owner,* the manager fully bears the cost associated with additional perquisite consumption, and he seeks a utility maximizing combination of the rewards described above. This balance is upset, however, once the manager sells a fraction of

---

[3]A good example of a "perk" of this type is expanding the owner–manager's span of control beyond the level that would maximize firm value. The manager may value the social prestige and power accompanying his position as chief executive officer and may be hesitant to delegate authority, even when it would increase the market value of the firm to do so.

his common shares to outsiders. This is the case, because, while he continues to enjoy the full benefit of additional perquisite consumption, he bears only *his* proportional ownership fraction of the associated reduction in the value of the firm's stock.

With rational expectations, outsiders are aware of the owner–manager's incentive to increase "perk" consumption. They make unbiased estimates of the costs associated with the increased perk consumption, and they pass these costs back to the owner–manager in full, in the form of a commensurate reduction in the price they are willing to pay for the securities he initially desires to sell. The manager is left with a combination of benefits in the form of dollar wealth and perquisites that is undesirable relative to his optimal combination as sole owner. Thus, in attempting to finance the firm through sale of common stock, he suffers a welfare loss that may be described as an agency cost. A similar problem occurs if the owner–manager seeks financing through debt securities. Given limited liability, if the probability of default on the debt increases with increased perk consumption, the manager bears only a (decreasing) fraction of the associated cost. Again, however, with symmetric rationality, that portion of the costs not borne directly will be incurred when the securities are issued in the form of lowered proceeds of sale.

Agency problems have been classified in this section by their origin. A related classification emphasizes the financial asset (equity or debt) which is subject to a particular agency problem. The agency problems of equity appear under informational asymmetry and under excessive perk consumption. The agency problems of debt are associated with these as well as with risk incentives and bankruptcy problems. The fixed nature of the debt claim in conjunction with limited liability is the prime source for the risk incentive and bankruptcy problems.

Market Solutions to Agency Problems

Here we will assess the role that well-functioning markets for capital and labor may play in reducing or eliminating the costs involved in specific agency problems. In essence, we argue that, if markets are well-functioning, sufficient pressures are present to force management to carry out decisions on the basis of the interests of all securityholders. Thus, costs arising from conflicts of interest are resolved.

The Market for Financial Capital

Agency problems associated with debt financing

under limited liability may be resolved by natural forces in the capital market. Assume management seeks to maximize stockholder welfare by switching to projects characterized by relatively high variance and relatively low value. In anticipation of these decisions, the total value of the firm declines as a net result of an increase in the value of the common stock and a more than proportionate decrease in the value of the outstanding debt. It is now in the interests of bondholders to acquire controlling interest in the common stock and to make decisions that maximize *firm* value [2, 13]. In doing so, they capture a pure benefit (an arbitrage profit) from increased value.

Existing common stockholders, of course, may also force management into a decision to maximize firm value. In fact, in view of possible impediments to "market pressure" that we shall discuss, stockholders seem to have a *comparative advantage* in carrying out the process. If each individual stockholder imputes rationality to other stockholders, it is in his interests to acquire debt in the firm (at a reduced price which reflects the impending *suboptimal* investment decision) in proportion to the fractional amount of debt contained in the firm's capital structure. Once a controlling majority of stockholders have done this, management must shift to an optimal investment decision, and these rational stockholders reap arbitrage profits.

When equityholders buy up the bonds of the firm on a *pro rata* basis, debt possibly loses its economic distinction and bondholders essentially become equityholders. However, for a firm with dispersed ownership, the Internal Revenue Code recognizes the debt as legitimate, and hence tax deduction of interest payments is still intact. Moreover, as far as an owner–manager is concerned, purchasing debt in proportion to his equity share has no impact on his propensity to consume perks if the debt is riskless, and it actually reduces the propensity if the probability of default on the debt is positive.[4]

A similar arbitrage argument can be evoked in the context of the agency cost associated with bankruptcy [19]. The argument states that if the costs of *formal* reorganization are indeed significant, it is in the interest of managers to adjust to an optimal capital structure by reorganizing the firm *informally* through purchase and sale of the bonds and the stock of the firm at prevailing capital market prices. If the

---

[4]On the other hand, if investors are forced to hold fixed proportions of debt and equity, they may suffer diversification costs as their portfolios deviate from the desired, utility-maximizing, weights.

154

manager fails to do so and the market values of the securities of the firm are reduced to reflect the costs of formal bankruptcy, it is in the interests of outsiders to take over the firm and initiate an informal reorganization. This can be accomplished by buying the bonds and the stock at their discounted market values. By acquiring all the claims to the firm, the dispute can be avoided and the expected bankruptcy cost can be captured as an arbitrage profit.

The Market for Human Capital

Agency problems associated with informational asymmetry and managerial perk consumption may be resolved via the operation of well-functioning markets for human capital. Consider the problem of excessive perk consumption. This problem must be of no consequence if the managerial labor market is efficient in the sense that the managerial wage reflects an unbiased estimate of his expected marginal product. In this case, the present value of the manager's future wages adjusts fully to reflect "shirking" or excessive perk consumption. In such an efficient labor market, the adjustment in the manager's wage provides for a full *ex post* settling up, so that the manager is disciplined to behave in the optimal interests of the firm [12].

It doesn't seem to be widely recognized that discipline in this form by the labor market provides a solution to the problem of informational asymmetry as well. In this case, the manager has a problem of communicating the true nature of the firm without moral hazard. If the manager fully suffers the consequences of attempts to deceive the market through changes in the value of his human capital, the moral hazard problem disappears. This may explain why managers want the Board of Directors to verify their honesty. The Board may be viewed as improving the functioning of labor markets in resolving the problem of informational asymmetry. Therefore, in the presence of a well-functioning labor market, managers are motivated to tell the truth with or without a specific managerial incentive compensation scheme that is tied to bankruptcy such as discussed in [39]. Thus, the link between financial structure and informational asymmetry disappears.

Impediments to Spontaneous Market Solutions of Agency Problems

Impediments may exist which serve to block a natural and costless resolution to agency problems in the *capital* market. Consider first the agency problem associated with excessive perk consumption by an owner–manager. It would seem at first that outsiders are in a position to capture an arbitrage profit by purchasing all the securities of the firm and replacing the owner with a manager who will run the firm to maximize shareholder wealth. It must be remembered, however, that in order to surrender his controlling interest in the firm, the owner–manager demands compensation, over and above the fair market value of his securities, for his "managerial rights." Recall, that the manager derives utility from perk consumption as well as from the dollar wealth represented by his security holdings. Moreover, the combined utility from both exceeds the utility he can derive from reducing perk consumption to zero and maximizing the value of the firm. Consequently, he will not surrender the firm at a price that reflects this maximized value, and hence the natural capital market mechanism is impeded.

The nature of the personal income tax may also impede the market mechanism. Capital gains are taxed when realized and, if the market value of the stock has appreciated, a controlling majority of stockholders may be locked into their existing investment in the firm. By holding their shares they are in effect benefiting from an interest-free loan from the government (the capital gains tax they do not have to pay) and they will demand a price for their stock that is higher than the prevailing equilibrium market price in order to surrender this benefit. One may counter this argument with an assumption of unlimited short selling, but it is difficult to imagine how one can force a takeover of *controlling interest* in the shares of the firm even when the potential acquirer is aided by additional supply brought on by short selling.

This impediment is not as effective in blocking market mechanisms as solutions to the agency problems of debt associated with bankruptcy. The securityholders of a bankrupt firm are likely to have already suffered accrued capital losses, and hence they are not "locked in" in terms of taxes.

Still another impediment to the threat of takeover, which underlies many of the market solutions to agency problems, is implied by the "free rider" problem [16, 17]. In a standard definition, a free rider is one who benefits from actions or costs borne by others. In other words, a free rider gets a "free lunch," so to speak. In the context of this paper, a free rider is an individual who attempts to benefit at the expense of his fellow securityholders by blocking a process which is in the general interests of all parties. It is not surprising that free riders themselves are discouraged through the legislative and judicial process. Consider the case where the takeover process is initiated by an outsider, say another firm. Suppose the target firm's bankruptcy is imminent and that the total value of all securities of the firm reflects the expected costs of formal bankruptcy. Corporate charters commonly provide for acceptance of merger bids by majority vote of existing stockholders. Free riders can be prevented from blocking the takeover process by tendering an offer to existing stockholders at a slight premium over the prevailing market price. A controlling majority of stockholders need only respond favorably to the offer in order to formally merge the two firms. In legal terms, minority stockholders may now be "cashed out" of the arrangement on the basis of the market value of the firm prior to merger. In fact, if one assumes that the capital market functions perfectly, it is in the interest of securityholders to write corporate charters that severely restrict the ability of shareholders to "free ride." By allowing successful raiders to "cash out" free riders at unfavorable terms, securityholders increase the probability of attempted takeovers, and motivate existing management to maximize the value of the firm and thus reduce agency costs.

On the other hand, if the market for takeovers is not perfectly competitive, such charters may not be optimal, as they may reduce the expected value of the takeover bid. The importance of the "free rider" problem thus hinges on the functioning of the capital market. It is worth noting that an unimpeded operation of the takeover mechanism is the cornerstone of all financial theories which produce valuation models based on the elimination of arbitrage profits. In this regard, the importance of the "free rider" problem as an impediment in the capital market extends beyond the issue of agency problems.

Impediments may also block managerial discipline arising from the market for *human capital*. For example, senior corporate officers are usually not individuals in the early stages of their career. If retirement is a relatively short period away, a *simple* contract which specifies the manager's wage as his expected marginal product may be inappropriate to ensure a complete *ex post* settling up. A more complex contract which makes the manager's retirement benefits a function of his *ex post* marginal products may be required. In addition, a complete *ex post* settling up for a wage readjustment depends on perfect and costless information in the labor market on past performance of each and every executive. If such information is not available, or if it is costly, firms may err in assessing managers,

and a complete *ex post* settling up is no longer achieved for managers who change employers. Finally, we note the difficulty in assessing top level management given the sweeping impact of their decisions on corporate performance. It is possible that the magnitude and variability of corporate performance measures may not allow for meaningful estimation of managers' excessive perk consumption. In this case, managers are able to consume perks without the threat of an accompanying loss in the value of their human capital.

In the face of these impediments, one must admit some possibility of a blockage to natural resolution of agency problems by markets.

Agency Problems and Optimal Capital Structure

Marginal agency costs of debt are commonly considered to be an increasing function of the amount of debt employed in the capital structure. This is true in the case of bankruptcy, as the expected marginal costs associated with bankruptcy depend on the probability of bankruptcy, which is an increasing function of the amount of debt relative to equity. In terms of the risk incentive and the forgone growth opportunities problems, *marginal* agency costs of debt depend on the investment opportunity set facing the firm. For the risk incentive problem [15] this is immediately observed by ordering projects according to their net market value and level of risk. The change in net market value which is associated with a shift to a higher risk project will determine the magnitude of marginal agency costs.

On the other hand, if debt is used to signal the true nature of the firm [39] an increase in the amount of debt may *reduce* the agency costs associated with informational asymmetry. The rate of reduction, *i.e.,* the marginal agency costs associated with informational asymmetry, depends on the distribution of capital structures among firms which remain undistinguished by the market. This distribution determines the signaling value of marginal units of debt which are used to identify the true value of the firm.

These relationships between the agency costs of debt and the amount of debt give rise to an optimal capital structure in three distinct ways. *First,* agency costs (in particular bankruptcy costs) may serve as an offset against the tax advantage of debt financing, and hence the corner solution (99.99 . . . % debt in capital structure) implied by the traditional Modigliani-Miller [34] tax-adjusted valuation model breaks down.

The interior optimum arises from the tradeoff between the tax subsidy which is an increasing function (at a decreasing rate) of the amount of debt employed and the agency costs which are also an increasing function (at an increasing rate) of the amount of debt. *Second,* an optimal capital structure can result from the tradeoff between agency costs of debt on the one hand and agency costs of equity on the other hand, even in a taxless world. *Third,* a positive theory of capital structure can emerge in the process of signaling to the market the true nature of the firm when there is informational asymmetry.

The Tradeoff Between Tax Savings and Bankruptcy Costs

For some 15 years, agency costs in the form of bankruptcy costs have been offered as a link between observed firm debt policies and the Modigliani–Miller theorem under corporate taxes. The MM theorem depicted in Exhibit 1 predicts that the value of the levered firm, V_L, increases linearly with debt, D, so as to exceed the value of the unlevered (but otherwise equivalent) firm by a tax subsidy, $T_C D$, where T_C is the marginal corporate tax rate uniform across all cor-

Exhibit 1. Firm Value and Optimal Capital Structure

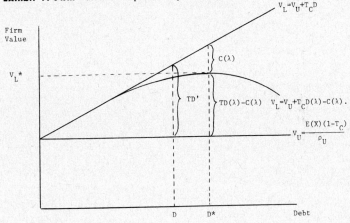

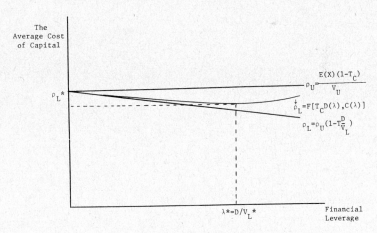

porations. Thus this theorem leads to a corner solution in which a nearly 100% debt/value ratio is desirable. Given possibility of costly bankruptcy, however, an optimal capital structure obtains when the present value of expected tax savings is offset at the margin by the present value of expected incremental bankruptcy costs [5, 25, 27, 42]. Assuming that bankruptcy costs exist, the value of the firm, V_L, is shown in Exhibit 1 as a concave function of the amount of debt employed. The present value of expected bankruptcy costs, C, is an increasing function (at an *increasing* rate) of the financial leverage, λ, while the tax subsidy $T_C D(\lambda)$ is also increasing with D. These phenomena manifest themselves in both the value and the cost of capital of the firm. At the optimum, the level of debt, D^*, maximizes the value of the firm (V^*) or equivalently minimizes the cost of capital (ρ_L^*).

It should be noted here that this tradeoff results in an (interior) optimal capital structure regardless of the magnitude of bankruptcy costs. This is true because, even if these costs are small, at some finite degree of leverage the present values of expected bankruptcy cost and the expected value of the tax subsidy may offset each other at the margin. However, the preceding arguments have been employed in order to reconcile existing financial theory with contemporary financial structures for observed firms. In the context of the actual probabilities of default, and the models employed by those advocating a bankruptcy cost–tax subsidy tradeoff, one must allege that the costs associated with bankruptcy are large. Limited efforts have been made to document their magnitude [48], but in any case the *traditional* arguments concerning bankruptcy costs and the tax subsidy rest on a significant breakdown of the arbitrage process described earlier. However, as we shall see below, if one evokes arguments pursuant to an equilibrium [31] in which bond yields are grossed up to reflect the tax advantage of debt at the corporate level, one *begins* from a position of indifference to debt *vis-à-vis* equity financing. This being the case, even an expected agency cost which is relatively small can result in an optimal capital structure, assuming that transaction costs associated with search for an optimal capital structure are negligible. However, it is still the case that agency costs of small magnitude have low impact on the *value of the firm*.

The Tradeoff Between Agency Costs of Debt and Agency Costs of Equity

It would seem that, in a taxless world with agency

problems of debt financing, we should have a corner solution to the capital structure decision in which equity financing dominates debt. This view is limited, because it ignores the possibility that equity financing may be characterized by significant agency costs. Agency problems of informational asymmetry and managerial perquisite consumption are endemic to equity financing as well. Capital structure policies that merely substitute equity for debt are trading off agency costs of debt against agency costs of equity [23].

The tradeoff is depicted in Exhibit 2 in which marginal agency costs of equity and debt are shown as rising functions of equity and debt, respectively. It is no longer necessary that debt financing have a tax advantage for an optimal capital structure. The advantage here is the reduction in the agency cost of equity. This advantage is offset at the margin by the incremental disadvantage of debt financing in the form of its own agency costs. In Exhibit 2 the optimum, λ^*, is reached when the present value of the sum of the expected agency costs of equity and debt is minimized. Thus, agency costs alone without tax considerations may give rise to an optimal capital structure.

Financial Signaling and Optimal Capital Structure

Various signaling mechanisms may be used to resolve the problem of informational asymmetry. The capital structure itself may be used as a signaling device to convey, without moral hazard, the true nature of the projects (firms). For instance, a proper

Exhibit 2. Optimal Capital Structure With Agency Costs of Equity and Debt

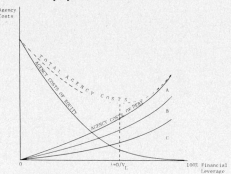

A Bankruptcy Costs
B Investment Incentive Costs
C Risk Incentive Costs

role of financial structure as a signal can be ensured through a managerial incentive schedule with an associated penalty tied to the occurrence of bankruptcy [39]. The "bankruptcy" penalty, which is built into the schedule, ensures a truthful signal by a manager who behaves rationally. The incentive problem associated with managerial announcements relating to firm profitability is resolved. In this framework, debt financing allows firms to signal the quality of their projects. For a firm with superior projects, additional debt financing is beneficial as it reduces the costs associated with informational asymmetry.

Another approach asserts that the entrepreneur's fractional equity ownership signals his personal evaluation of the project [29]. It is argued that there exists an optimal fractional ownership that correctly signals the true return stream of the project. This mechanism requires a prespecified schedule depicting the expected return on the project as a function of the entrepreneur's fractional ownership and an assumption that his utility function is known to the market.

While in the first two explanations of optimal capital structure the relationship between the capital structure and the value of the firm is *causal,* the signaling explanation suggests merely a *statistical* relationship. In the latter case, if financial structure serves as a signal, the value of the firm would respond to changes in financial structure caused by a change in the market's *perceptions* and not because of a *real* change in the return stream.

Complex Financial Contracts as Solutions to Agency Problems

The failure of markets to provide complete and costless solutions to agency problems suggests that a class of securityholders may require additional assurances against possible expropriation of their wealth by another class. Such assurances, and a commensurate reduction in agency costs, can be obtained through complex financial (and management compensation) contracts. Our discussion of the role of complex financial contracts in reducing agency costs covers call provisions, conversion privileges, income bonds, and the maturity structure of debt. By no means is this list exhaustive. For instance, we do not discuss avenues such as debt renegotiations or leasing arrangements which may be useful in resolving agency problems of debt financing.

The notion that complex contracts evolve in order to reduce agency problems has the potential to explain many real world contractual arrangements. The literature includes analyses of bond covenants (*e.g.,* contractual limitations on managers' incentive to take unwarranted risk) as a means of reducing the agency problems associated with risk incentives. Management compensation contracts are known as examples of arrangements that are beneficial in reducing agency problems when labor markets fail to provide appropriate solutions. Corporate bylaws include provisions that limit minority stockholders' options to block prospective takeovers or to act as "free riders" as discussed earlier.

Call Provisions in Corporate Debt

The call provision can be explained as a means of resolving the agency problems associated with informational asymmetry and risk incentives.[6] Consider first the case of informational asymmetry. Managers know that the firm is worth V(A); the market, however, is uncertain about the firm's worth and hence is unable to distinguish it from the worth of an alternative firm, V(B), where V(B) < V(A). Management seeks to finance the firm with debt maturing in T periods. The true nature of the firm will be revealed to the market at some point prior to T. If the debt is risky, it must be sold in the market at less than its true value. The agency cost associated with the asymmetry is $V_D(A) - V_D(B)$, where $V_D(\cdot)$ is the market value of the debt, given the information set.

Management can mitigate the agency cost by attaching a call provision which provides the right to repurchase the bond at a specified price at a point in time immediately following the point at which the true nature of the firm is revealed. Thus, the stockholders of the firm take a long position in the call option and a short position in the debt. Note that the market undervalues both the call option and the debt, because they are both valued with the presumption that the value of firm is V(B). The stockholders suffer a cost in amount $V_D(A) - V_D(B)$, but they recapture it, in part, through the undervaluation of the call option, $V_C(A) - V_C(B)$, where $V_C(A)$ and $V_C(B)$ are the values of call provisions associated with V(A) and (B), respectively. The partial recapture is possible because of a lag in the revelation of the true nature of the firm. The call is effective in mitigating the transfer of wealth, however,

---

[6]It should be pointed out that, with respect to all the agency problems discussed above, shortening the maturity of the debt accomplishes the same task as the call strategy does. The issues of debt maturity structure and call provisions belong to the same family in that both are alternative solutions to specific agency problems [2].

only to the extent that the true nature of the firm is revealed prior to the maturity date of the debt. If the maturity and revelation dates coincide, there will be no recapture of the agency cost.

The call provision can also be used to eliminate the incentive to shift to high-risk (but low-value) investments in order to transfer wealth from bondholders to stockholders. In the absence of a call provision, the shift to a high-risk investment may reduce the total value of the firm but may alter the relative values of debt and equity such that the value of equity is actually greater after the shift. The presence of a call option may eliminate the incentive entirely, because the value of this option declines with the value of the debt. Given that stockholders have a long position in this option, the option may be designed so that the decline in its value more than offsets the increase in the value of the stock that would take place. In this way, the risk incentive problem is neutralized, and the agency cost disappears.

The call provision may also be used to eliminate the incentive to forgo otherwise profitable investment opportunities. If the debt matures after the future investment decision is to be made, the benefits of the decision partly accrue to debtholders by a reduction in the probability of default and a corresponding increase in the value of the debt. This benefit may once again be recaptured by attaching a call provision to the debt, which gives management the right to recall the debt at a stated price at the time when the investment decision is made.

While callable debt may not restore the value of the firm to the value which exists under all equity financing, the issuance of callable debt can be shown to dominate the issuance of non-callable debt [8]. It should be noted that call provisions may also resolve the agency problems associated with forgone growth opportunities if the debt issued is supported entirely by these opportunities [2, 37].

Convertible Securities

Convertible securities may reduce agency problems associated with excessive perk consumption by an owner–manager. Suppose the manager sells a fraction $(1-\alpha)$ of the stock to outsiders, and he retains a fraction α of the stock for himself. The change in the manager's wealth, V_w, in response to a change in the value of the firm, V, is now given by $\frac{\partial V_w}{\partial V} = \alpha$, and the smaller α, the less the effect of his perk consumption on his own *monetary* wealth. The manager, though,

can align his own interests with those of external securityholders if he raises capital by offering to outside capital contributors the following financial instruments.

The manager holds a positive position in a call option along with his positive position in $\alpha\%$ of the outstanding common stock. He holds a negative position in a put option which is to be held long by outsiders. If the manager increases consumption of perks, he will a) decrease the value of his common stock, b) decrease the value of his call option, and c) increase the value of the put option which can be viewed as the manager's liability. The options can be designed so that the following condition holds: $\partial V_w/\partial V = \alpha + \partial V_c/\partial V - \partial V_P/\partial V = 1$, where V_c and V_p are the values of the call and the put options, respectively. In this sense the manager's incentive to consume perks is restored to that of his original position as sole owner. Outsiders will recognize that the manager will consume perks at a level consistent with that of sole ownership, and hence price the securities accordingly. Once again the agency cost is reduced.

It should be apparent that if the contract is *continuously* readjusted, outside capital contributors end up holding a riskless position in the firm. However, the solution does not call for continuous readjustments. The contract may be viewed as a solution to the single-period world of Jensen and Meckling in which decisions relating to investment, financing, and the nature of the productive process are made simultaneously at the beginning of the period and are not altered throughout the productive period. Moreover, the contract is readily generalizable to a multiperiod framework where *discrete* time readjustments of contractual positions are feasible, given that the productive decisions and the corresponding incentive problems occur through discrete time.

While the issuance of stock options may be used to resolve the agency problem associated with the consumption of perquisites, stock options may create an incentive for the manager to engage in either high- or low-risk investment programs. This incentive problem is analogous to the wealth transfer problem associated with the existence of risky debt in the capital structure. It can be shown, however, that the stock options can be designed so as to simultaneously solve the problems associated with perk consumption and risk-taking [21].

The put–call financial package may seem unusual, but it actually represents a financial strategy that is often observed. The use of the call option is analogous to the actual use of executive stock options in managerial compensation. The put option, in combination with the fraction of the stock held by the outsiders, can be thought of as a surrogate for the convertible bond. If the terminal value of the firm exceeds the exercise price of the put, the put is worthless, and the outsiders remain as common stockholders holding a fractional interest in the common stock of the firm. This outcome represents conversion of the bond into a fractional interest in the firm's common stock. If, on the other hand, the firm value falls below the exercise price, the outsiders exercise their claim and sell the firm to the manager at the exercise price. This represents the case where conversion is unprofitable and bondholders exercise their fixed claim.

Income Bonds

The agency cost associated with bankruptcy may also call for the issuance of a complex debt instrument [31]. The obvious analogue of this complexity in the context of bankruptcy problems is the issuance of income bonds. Interest payments on these bonds are required only if earned. Income bonds can, however, trigger bankruptcy at maturity from the firm's failure to meet principal payments. Perpetual income bonds would seem to satisfy this deficiency, but, even prior to maturity, income bonds can trigger technical default if available cash is incommensurate with current earnings and hence is insufficient to meet current interest payments. Income bonds are rarely issued by firms, possibly because 1) they are unable to fully resolve bankruptcy problems, and 2) natural market mechanisms are relatively efficient in resolving these problems.

Unlike income bonds, interest on conventional coupon bonds is payable irrespective of the level of current earnings, or default would occur. Because each coupon payment can be regarded as a bond, there is a higher probability of bankruptcy with conventional bonds than with income bonds. Income bonds are similar to preferred stock, but, unlike the latter, they carry the tax benefit of interest payment deduction.

The Effect of Agency Problems on Equilibrium Pricing in Financial Markets

Miller [31] has extended the notion of tax-induced differential returns into a general equilibrium framework in which firms adjust the amount of bonds offered in response to differential yields on equity and debt. He shows that, in the presence of the corporate income tax subsidy on debt financing, yields on corporate debt are "grossed up" to reflect the tax subsidy in such a way as to cause individual firms to be indifferent between debt and equity financing. There is, nonetheless, an economy-wide optimal debt outstanding. As a direct result of the equilibrating process, the tax subsidy that is shifted away from the stockholders is captured by bondholders in the form of increased yields on corporate debt.

This equilibrium can be explained in terms of Exhibit 3, which plots *certainty equivalent* interest rates on the vertical axis and quantities of total corporate debt demanded and supplied on the horizontal axis. Assume two types of securities are available: common stock whose returns are tax-exempt and bonds whose returns are taxable at varying rates. The certainty equivalent return on common stock is given by r^*. Tax-exempt institutions may exist that are willing to demand corporate debt as an investment in aggregate amount D'' at a certainty equivalent rate equal to that available on common stock. Additional demand, stemming from investment by individual investors in progressively higher tax brackets, can be generated by offering progressively higher yields on corporate bonds. The upward sloping demand curve reflects the progressive nature of the personal income tax.

The supply curve for corporate debt is horizontal at a rate of interest equal to $r^* (1 - \tau_c)$ where τ_c is the corporate income tax rate, which is presumed to be uniform. The supply curve is horizontal, because corporations are assumed to be wealth maximizers, and because the corporate tax rate is uniform across all corporations. Consequently, if the yield on corporate debt falls slightly below $r^*/(1 - \tau_c)$, it is in the interest of all wealth maximizing firms to finance their investments entirely with debt. On the other hand, if the yield rises slightly above $r^*/(1 - \tau_c)$, corporate debt

Exhibit 3. Equilibrium in Corporate Bond Market

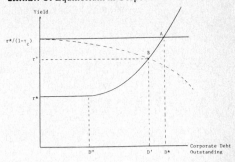

completely disappears from the market. The horizontal supply curve intersects the upward-sloping demand curve at A, and the equilibrium yield is given by $r^*/(1 - \tau_c)$. At this rate individual firms are indifferent between issuing debt or equity to finance their investments.

The Miller equilibrium follows only in the absence of agency problems associated with debt financing. If agency costs are not completely resolved by natural market forces, it can be shown [1, 10] that they will manifest themselves in yield differentials between securities which differ in terms of their inherent ability to resolve the problems. To illustrate this point, suppose that equity financing involves no agency cost, but that debt financing involves firm-specific agency costs which increase with the relative amount of debt in the capital structure. If firms face agency costs of this type, they are no longer indifferent between equity and debt financing when debt yields $r^*/(1 - \tau_c)$, and the supply curve is no longer horizontal. For each rate of interest on corporate debt, $r_c < \dfrac{r^*}{(1 - \tau_c)}$, firms increase the amount of debt in their capital structures until the agency cost as a percent of marginal debt financed, $\theta(D)$, is equal to $r^*/(1 - \tau_c) - r_c$. As long as rates are lower, it pays each firm to issue more debt so that aggregate supply is increased. Every point on the broken, downward-sloping supply curve of Exhibit 3 represents the quantity of debt supplied as firms optimize their capital structures. As the interest rate on corporate debt falls, there is a general increase across all firms in the optimal amount of debt in capital structures. Equilibrium occurs at B, the intersection of the upward-sloping demand curve with the downward-sloping supply curve.

Unlike the Miller equilibrium, optimal capital structures exist for individual firms as well as for the corporate sector as a whole as denoted by D'. While the analysis here is carried out in terms of pure debt and equity instruments, the analysis may be generalized to equilibrium yield differentials and optimal capital structure proportions involving a wide variety of financial contracts.

The expected value of the agency costs need not be large to induce complexity in financial contracts and optimal capital structure. In the absence of agency problems, management faces alternative contracts and capital structures with indifference. The presence of even minor residual costs associated with agency problems may serve to explain the complexity of capital structure, as managers attempt to balance these costs with yield differentials on alternative contracts. Thus, it is possible to observe corporations engaging in capital structure decisions even if markets are reasonably (but not strictly) proficient in disciplining managers to act in the interest of all securityholders. The effect of financial decisions on the value of the firm may be *insignificant* but still *sufficient* to explain a) why corporations engage in capital structure decision-making, b) complexities in financial contracts, and c) clustering of capital structure characteristics by industry so long as there are no costs involved in financial contracting.

Another property of our equilibrium relates to a sharing of the agency costs among the securityholders. It is apparent from Exhibit 3 that the agency costs associated with debt financing may be shifted to the bondholders in the form of reduced equilibrium yields on corporate debt. This conclusion stands in direct contradiction to the long held point of view that stockholders bear the agency costs of debt financing. The reader should recall that the belief that stockholders reap the tax subsidy associated with debt financing was also long held, until Miller's equilibrium analysis showed that the tax subsidy, like the agency cost, is shifted to bondholders.

We emphasize that this equilibrium analysis is still partial in the sense that the equity rate of return is taken as given. This is similar to the Jensen–Meckling [23] agency cost incidence analysis where the interest rate (state prices) for bond payoffs is taken as given. Obviously, any definite statement regarding the final incidence of agency costs and debt tax subsidy must rely on a general equilibrium analysis where the rate of return on equity is endogenously determined.

Policy Implications of the Shifting of Agency Costs

Agency costs are real factor costs that affect production decisions. Optimal resource allocation in the economy requires that firms act to reduce agency costs up to the level where the marginal costs associated with the reduction are equal to the marginal benefits. If the agency costs associated with debt financing are shifted to bondholders, what are the benefits associated with reducing agency costs to those who control production and financing decisions?

Consider Exhibit 4 which depicts the relationship between marginal and average agency costs as a function of the amount of debt in the capital structure of an individual firm. Given a particular (certainty-equivalent) rate of interest on corporate debt, one can compute the differential, θ^*, between this rate and the rate required to induce debt financing in the absence of agency costs $r^*/(1 - \tau_c)$. The differential, θ^*, may be interpreted as the benefit of debt financing associated with the tax subsidy. The individual firm issues debt until the marginal agency cost associated with the last unit of debt issued is equal to this (constant) marginal benefit. The amount of debt issued is thus D^*, and the stockholders of the firm gain a surplus associated with debt financing which is represented by the shaded area of Exhibit 4.

Suppose that the firm now acts to reduce its agency costs by introducing some mechanism by which its management can be costlessly monitored by securityholders. Presume also that this mechanism cannot be imitated by other firms. In this case, the agency costs of debt financing are reduced, as represented in Exhibit 5, and the magnitude of the financiers' surplus is increased as long as the differential θ^* remains intact. In this case, stockholders have an incentive to institute the monitoring activity.

Suppose, instead, that the monitoring mechanism is easily imitated by other firms. Note that this represents a departure from our initial assumption that individual firms are price takers in the capital market. The adoption of the new mechanism by all firms will shift the supply curve of Exhibit 3 upward in the direction of the horizontal supply curve at $r^*/(1 - \tau_c)$. The equilibrium rate of interest on corporate debt rises to reflect the diminished importance of the agency problems. Consequently, the differential, θ^*, falls to some level θ'. The change in the magnitude of the financiers' surplus is determined by two offsetting effects: The reduction in agency costs, which increases the surplus, and the reduction in the yield differential, which decreases the surplus. As was shown in [1], the dollar change in the surplus depends on the elasticities of the demand and supply curves for corporate debt. It is possible that the surplus will fall below its initial level of Exhibit 5. In this special case, stockholders are actually penalized by introducing the costless monitoring mechanism.

It would seem that stockholder incentives to reduce agency problems are related to the speed at which other firms can imitate the financial innovation. Most financial innovations are easily imitated by other firms, which would seem to be true especially for modifications in generally accepted accounting principles. Accounting is one of many monitoring systems that may serve to reduce agency problems. It would appear that, as acceptance of modifications in this system is by definition widespread, improvements in accounting designed solely to increase its effective-

Exhibit 4. Determination of the Financiers' Surplus

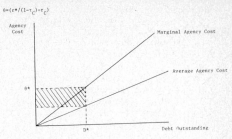

Exhibit 5. Determination of the Financiers' Surplus

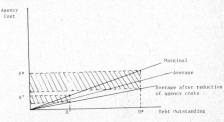

ness in monitoring management may not be in the interest of managers attempting to maximize stockholder wealth, even if these modifications are *costless*. This same point would seem to hold for some government regulations of the securities markets such as prospectus requirements, full disclosure provisions, and mandatory provisions in indentures associated with debt financing. One may expect to see managerial opposition to these requirements even if such requirements are considered desirable on the basis of social costs and benefits.

Conclusion

Agency problems derive from conflicts of interest between individuals associated with the firm. Many of these conflicts can be resolved in a spontaneous and costless fashion by the markets for financial and human capital. If frictions exist in these markets, however, the agency problems may give rise to potential costs.

These costs can be minimized through complex contractual arrangements between the parties in conflict. Thus, agency problems may explain the evolution of complexities in capital structure such as conversion and call privileges in corporate debt. Financial contracts which differ in terms of their inherent ability to resolve agency problems may sell at differential equilibrium prices or yields in the market place. The financial manager reaches an optimal capital structure when, at the margin for each class of contract, the costs associated with agency problems are balanced by the benefits associated with existing yield differentials and tax exposure.

References

1. A. Barnea, R. Haugen, and L. Senbet, "An Equilibrium Analysis of Debt Financing Under Costly Tax Arbitrage and Agency Problems," forthcoming in the *Journal of Finance* (June 1981).

2. A. Barnea, R. Haugen, and L. Senbet, "A Rationale for Debt Maturity Structure and Call Provisions in the Agency Theoretic Framework," *Journal of Finance* (December 1980), pp. 1223–1234.

3. D. Baron, "Default Risk, Home-made Leverage, and the Modigliani–Miller Theorem," *American Economic Review* (March 1974), pp. 176–182.

4. D. Baron, "Default Risk and the Modigliani–Miller Theorem: A Synthesis," *American Economic Review* (March 1976), pp. 204–212.

5. N. Baxter, "Leverage, Risk of Ruin and the Cost of Capital," *Journal of Finance* (September 1967), pp. 395–404.

6. S. Bhattacharya, "Imperfect Information, Dividend Policy, and the 'Bird in the Hand' Fallacy," *Bell Journal of Economics* (Spring 1979), pp. 259–270.

7. F. Black and M. Scholes, "The Pricing of Options and Corporate Liabilities," *Journal of Political Economy* (May-June 1973), pp. 637–654.

8. Z. Bodie and R. Taggart, "Future Investment Opportunities and the Value of the Call Provision on a Bond," *Journal of Finance* (September 1978), pp. 1187–1200.

9. W. Boyce and A. Kalotay, "Tax Differentials and Callable Bonds," *Journal of Finance* (September 1979), pp. 825–838.

10. H. DeAngelo and R. Masulis, "Optimal Capital Structure Under Corporate and Personal Taxation," *Journal of Financial Economics* (March 1980), pp. 3–30.

11. E. Elton and M. Gruber, "The Economic Value of the Call Option," *Journal of Finance* (September 1972), pp. 891–901.

12. E. Fama, "Agency Problems and the Theory of the Firm," *Journal of Political Economy* (April 1980), pp. 288–307.

13. E. Fama, "The Effects of a Firm's Investment and Financing Decisions on the Welfare of its Security Holders," *American Economic Review* (June 1978), pp. 272–284.

14. E. Fama and M. Miller, *The Theory of Finance*, New York, Holt, Rinehart and Winston, 1972.

15. D. Galai and R. Masulis, "The Option Pricing Model and the Risk Factor of Stock," *Journal of Financial Economics* (January-March 1976), pp. 53–81.

16. S. Grossman and O. Hart, "Take-Over Bids, The Free-Rider Problem and the Theory of the Corporation," *Bell Journal of Economics* (Spring 1980), pp. 42–64.

17. S. Grossman and J. Stiglitz, "On Value Maximization and Alternative Objectives of the Firm," *Journal of Finance* (May 1977), pp. 389–402.

18. K. Hagen, "Default Risk, Home-made Leverage, and the Modigliani–Miller Theorem: A Note," *American Economic Review* (March 1976), pp. 199–203.

19. R. Haugen and L. Senbet, "The Insignificance of Bankruptcy Costs to the Theory of Optimal Capital Structure," *Journal of Finance* (May 1978), pp. 383–393.

20. R. Haugen and L. Senbet, "New Perspectives on Informational Asymmetry and Agency Relationships," *Journal of Financial and Quantitative Analysis* (November 1979), pp. 671–694.

21. R. Haugen and L. Senbet, "Resolving the Agency Problems of External Capital through Stock Options," forthcoming in the *Journal of Finance*.

22. R. Higgins and L. Schall, "Corporate Bankruptcy and Conglomerate Merger," *Journal of Finance* (March 1975), pp. 93–113.

23. M. Jensen and W. Meckling, "Theory of the Firm: Managerial Behavior, Agency Costs and Ownership Structure," *Journal of Financial Economics* (October 1976), pp. 305–360.

24. E. Kim, "A Mean–Variance Theory of Optimal Capital Structure and Corporate Debt Capacity," *Journal of Finance* (March 1978), pp. 45–64.

25. E. Kim, W. Lewellen, and J. McConnell, "Financial Leverage Clienteles: Theory and Evidence," *Journal of Financial Economics* (March 1979), pp. 83–109.

26. A. Kraus, "The Bond Refunding Decision in an Efficient Market," *Journal of Financial and Quantitative Analysis* (December 1973), pp. 793–806.

27. A. Kraus and R. Litzenberger, "A State–Preference Leverage," *Journal of Finance* (September 1973), pp. 911–922.

28. W. Lee and H. Barker, "Bankruptcy Costs and the Firm's Optimal Debt Capacity: A Positive Theory of Capital Structure," *Southern Economic Journal* (April 1977), pp. 1453–1465.

29. H. Leland and D. Pyle, "Informational Asymmetries, Financial Structure, and Financial Intermediation," *Journal of Finance* (May 1977), pp. 371–387.

30. J. McCulloch, "The Tax-Adjusted Yield Curve," *Journal of Finance* (June 1975), pp. 811–830.

31. M. Miller, "Debt and Taxes," *Journal of Finance* (May 1977), pp. 261–275.

32. M. Miller and M. Scholes, "Dividends and Taxes," *Journal of Financial Economics* (March 1978), pp. 333–364.

33. F. Milne, "Choice Over Assets Economies: Default Risk and Corporate Leverage," *Journal of Financial Economics* (June 1975), pp. 165–185.

34. F. Modigliani and M. Miller, "Corporation Income Taxes and the Cost of Capital: A Correction," *American Economic Review* (June 1963), pp. 433–443.

35. F. Modigliani and M. Miller, "The Cost of Capital, Corporation Finance, and the Theory of Investment," *American Economic Review* (June 1958), pp. 261–297.

36. F. Modigliani and R. Sutch, "Innovations in Interest Rates Policy," *American Economic Review* (May 1966), pp. 178–197.

37. S. Myers, "Determinants of Corporate Borrowing," *Journal of Financial Economics* (November 1977), pp. 147–176.

38. G. Pye, "The Value of Call Deferment on a Bond: Some Empirical Results," *Journal of Finance* (December 1967), pp. 623–636.

39. S. Ross, "The Determination of Financial Structure: The Incentive-Signalling Approach," *The Bell Journal of Economics* (Spring 1977), pp. 23–40.

40. S. Ross, "The Economic Theory of Agency: The Principal's Problem," *American Economic Review* (May 1973), pp. 134–139.

41. S. Ross, "Some Notes on Financial Incentive-Signalling Models," *Journal of Finance* (June 1978), pp. 777–792.

42. J. Scott, "A Theory of Optimal Capital Structure," *Bell Journal of Economics* (Spring 1976), pp. 33–54.

43. C. Smith and J. Warner, "On Financial Contracting: An Analysis of Bond Covenants," *Journal of Financial Economics* (June 1979), pp. 117–161.

44. M. Spence, *Market Signalling: Information Transfer in Hiring and Related Processes,* Cambridge, Harvard University Press, 1974.

45. J. Stiglitz, "On the Irrelevance of Corporate Financial Policy," *American Economic Review* (December 1974), pp. 851–866.

46. J. Stiglitz, "A Re-examination of the Modigliani-Miller Theorem," *American Economic Review* (December 1979), pp. 784–793.

47. R. Taggart, "Taxes and Corporate Capital Structure in an Incomplete Market," *Journal of Finance* (June 1980), pp. 645–659.

48. J. Warner, "Bankruptcy Costs: Some Evidence," *Journal of Finance* (May 1977), pp. 239–276.

49. H. Weingartner, "Optimal Timing of Bond Refunding," *Management Science* (March 1967), pp. 511–524.

A Comparison of Capital Structure Decisions of Regulated and Non-Regulated Firms

Robert H. Litzenberger and Howard B. Sosin

Robert H. Litzenberger is Professor of Finance at the Graduate School of Business at Stanford University. Howard B. Sosin is a member of the Technical Staff at Bell Labs and is also an Associate Professor at the Columbia University Business School. The authors acknowledge with thanks the helpful comments of the anonymous reviewers. They are of course (jointly) equally and solely responsible for the contents of the paper.

Introduction

This note contrasts the financial leverage decision of a regulated firm with that of a non-regulated firm, illustrating the influence of regulation on debt policy. We will examine the effects of corporate taxes, insolvency costs, and institutional portfolio restrictions in light of national and regional regulation.

Debt Financing and the Non-Regulated Sector

Debt financing by a non-regulated firm results in a tax savings under the current tax system, because the firm may deduct interest charges from profits before computing its tax liability. This saving, analogous to a subsidy from the federal government to the firm, equals the corporate tax rate times the firm's interest charges. The favorable tax treatment of debt financing over other sources of capital financing (*e.g.*, common stock, preferred stock, and income bonds) is a positive inducement for firms to add debt to their capital structure. When non-default-free debt is included in a firm's capital structure, however, there is an increase in the risk of insolvency and its concomitant costs brought about by the firm's inability to meet or difficulty in meeting its interest obligation.

Insolvency costs may be dichotomized into direct and indirect costs. Direct insolvency costs include legal costs, court fees, and diminution in value caused by liquidation sales. Estimates of the direct costs of bankruptcy range from an average of 2.5% for railroads (Warner [27]) to 20% for smaller corporate entities and individuals (Baxter [2], Stanley and Girth [4], and Van Horne [25]). Jensen and Meckling [11] note that, in addition to costs associated with insolvency, agency costs of non-default-free debt include the reduction in the value of the firm and monitoring costs caused by the manager's incentive to reallocate wealth from bondholders to stockholders (and thereby to himself by increasing his equity claim). They also note that these costs are directly related to the amount of debt in the firm's capital structure.

Indirect insolvency costs are less obvious, more prevalent, potentially of much larger magnitude, and often occur prior to an actual bankruptcy. These costs include operating inefficiencies induced by the deferral of maintenance expenditure, and loss of sales due to the deterioration of the quality of the firm's services and/or deterioration in the perceived reliability of the firm as a permanent source of supply. Insolvency costs may also be divided another way: into one component that redistributes wealth among consumers, and another that represents a dead-weight loss to society. The loss of customers (for reasons related to financial stress) to competitors who have excess capacity is an example of a predominantly redistributive effect of insolvency. Operating inefficiencies, increased future capital outlays resulting from deferral of preventive maintenance during periods of financial stress, and legal costs and court fees (to the extent that the resources expended could be gainfully employed elsewhere) are examples of dead-weight social losses.

For the loss of customers to be a purely redistributive effect of insolvency, the firm's competitors must have identical cost functions, and there must be no proportional economies or diseconomies of scale in production. The substitution of truck transport for train transport caused by the deterioration in the quality of rail services is an example of a predominantly redistributive effect of Penn Central's financial distress. The higher cost of shipping by truck relative to the cost of shipping by rail (ignoring the insolvency-induced decline in the quality of rail services) is an example of a dead-weight loss to society. The deferral of maintenance by Penn Central prior to its collapse and the resulting deterioration in the quality of its rail services illustrate social costs of insolvency, costs that were borne, in large measure, by the consumers of rail services and by the general taxpayer. These costs may be measured in part by the huge capital expenditure required by Conrail to replace and repair neglected equipment.

It is useful to distinguish between the dead-weight social losses from insolvency that are internalized by the firm's security holders and those that are externalities directly borne by consumers. If close sub-stitutes for the firm's final products or services do not exist, a large portion of the dead-weight social loss may be in the form of an externality resulting from the decline in the quality and/or supply of the respective good or service.

Several authors have illustrated how, under the current tax system, when economy-wide investment and operating decisions of firms are held constant, a non-regulated firm can maximize its aggregate market value by trading off the tax advantage of debt against the risk and costs of insolvency. The basic conclusion of these studies is that, *ceteris paribus*, judicious use of debt, which usually involves some amount of non-default-free debt, may increase the value of a firm.[1]

Viewed nationally, however, the advantages of non-default-free debt are less persuasive. Holding economy-wide investment and operating decisions of firms constant, a reduction in one corporation's tax liability necessitates either an increase in the federal deficit, an increase in taxes paid by individuals and/or other corporations, a decrease in the level of public goods and services, or some combination of these. This conservation relationship implies that a reduction in corporate taxes resulting from an increase in leverage is a zero sum game. The firm's tax saving merely results in a redistribution of income and wealth across individuals.

It should be noted that even in the absence of insolvency costs it is not generally the case that all shareholders within a firm would desire an increase in leverage — even if it resulted in an increase in the firm's value. That is, when individuals hold different ratios or quantities of securities across firms in their portfolios and/or consume different quantities of public goods relative to private goods, increases in wealth brought about by having a firm increase its financial leverage could be more than offset for some individuals (in particular, those holding small positions in securities of the firm in question) because of the increased tax liability of other firms and/or by

---

[1]See, for example, Kraus and Litzenberger [12], Modigliani and Miller [19, 20], Scott [21], Van Horne [26], Arditti *et al.* [1], or Brennan [3] for discussions of the effects of the current tax system on the value of the firm.

Taking cognizance of personal taxes, Miller [19] has argued that in equilibrium there will be no tax advantage to debt financing. Litzenberger and Van Horne [16] argue that when dividend and interest income is taxed at the same personal tax rate, there is a tax incentive to debt financing. Given the estimate of the weighted average tax rate on dividend income of 0.23 estimated by Litzenberger and Ramaswamy [15] and the implied tax rate on corporate debt of between 0.22 and 0.30 estimated by McCulloch [18], the Litzenberger and Van Horne assumption seems to be a reasonable first order approximation.

their exposure to inflation or by decreases in government services.

Unlike accelerated depreciation allowances and the investment tax credit, the tax deductibility of interest does not affect all investment capital identically, which may lead to socially non-optimal investment decisions by firms. This possibility arises because firms with differing operating risks may choose to use different amounts of debt in their capital structures, although it should be noted that competition would tend to force firms with similar operating risk to assume similar capital structures. (For a discussion of output effects of leverage see Hite [10].)

Firms with differing operating risks would receive different tax subsidies from the government. The government, in essence, would be subsidizing capital investment for the production of different commodities at different rates. In the goods market, this may distort quantities produced, prices charged, and levels consumed when compared to those which would obtain if all capital were taxed equally.

Further, the tax deductibility of interest combined with the double taxation of corporate dividends does not encourage investment in newer, high-risk industries, because the debt capacities of firms in these industries would be expected to be low relative to the debt capacity of firms in mature industries with more stable streams of earnings.

One of the major advantages cited for the existence of debt of varying riskiness is that it allows firms to partition their streams of earnings into flows that are desirable to investors who have differing preferences for risk. The notion here is that, when markets are incomplete, securities offering patterns of payout not currently available may be desirable to some investors.[2]

Low-grade debt may appeal to a particular class of investors. However, the major demanders of corporate debt (pension funds and insurance companies) have traditional preferences and/or operate under legal restrictions that limit the amount of low-grade debt that they may hold. These considerations suggest that the judicious use of financial leverage (*i.e.,* only issuing high-grade debt) may reduce the firm's cost of capital even in the absence of tax considerations. More importantly, the preference for high-grade debt by major demanders of corporate bonds implies that excessive additions of debt that result in a down-grad-

ing of the firm's bonds may make the firm's bonds less desirable to these institutional investors.[3]

Debt Financing and the Regulated Sector

Like its non-regulated counterpart, a regulated firm can reduce its tax liability by increasing the amount of debt in its capital structure. However, subject to a regulatory lag, a tax saving resulting from an increase in the financial leverage of a regulated firm would be expected to be passed on to the firm's customers. That is, regulatory commissions would be expected to set prices in such a way as to capture for the consumers of the regulated good any tax advantage associated with leverage. (A similar argument can be found in Gordon [7].) In the absence of a regulatory lag, such action by a regulatory commission would, in the long run, make it impossible for the shareholders of a regulated firm to receive any of the incremental tax savings associated with an increased level of debt. Thus, shareholders would not have a long-run incentive to encourage management to increase the leverage of the firm.

As long as debt financing remains free of default risk, however, increased leverage would not adversely affect the value of the firm; it would simply lower prices (and tax revenues), thus redistributing income among consumers.[4] A resulting leverage ratio for a regulated firm in excess of the economy-wide average may be viewed as a subsidy to individuals who spend a higher-than-average fraction of their income on the goods produced by the firm, a subsidy paid by individuals who spend a lower-than-average fraction of their income on the goods produced by the firm. (Strictly speaking, this result holds only under a proportional income tax.)

Increased leverage also implies that the goods of highly-levered firms are being subsidized relative to the goods of other firms. In this context, it should be noted that regulated firms, and utilities in particular, tend to have larger-than-average amounts of debt in their capital structures. It would, therefore, be difficult to argue that under-investment in productive

---

[2]See Hirshleifer [9] for a description of incomplete markets and Litzenberger and Sosin [15] and Sosin [23] for a discussion of the creation of new securities and their influence on valuation and welfare.

[3]Glenn [5, 6] discusses the restrictions placed on the portfolios of the major purchasers of corporate debt. He also provides a rigorous derivation of a "premium for safety" in the context of a capital asset pricing model where there are restrictions on short sales. Lintner [13] provides extensions to Glenn's work.

[4]It should be noted that increases in leverage would increase the systematic risk (beta) of the equity of the firm. In the absence of bankruptcy costs, leverage would not affect the total risk of the firm (its variance).

facilities for the regulated good would take place if utilities were not forced to issue low-grade debt. Furthermore, the issuance of excessive amounts of debt by a regulated firm may make its bonds less desirable to institutional investors, resulting in higher interest costs. Subject to a regulatory lag, these higher interest costs would be passed on to consumers of the regulated product through higher prices.

Requiring regulated firms to issue non-default-free debt[5] must be viewed as a particularly costly method of redistributing income and one that is undesirable from a national perspective. In analyzing these costs, it is interesting to compare how they are borne when the insolvent firm is a small firm in a competitive industry and when it is a natural monopolist. If, as is the case in a competitive industry, there tend to be readily-available substitutes for the goods of an insolvent firm, then the actual occurrence of a bankruptcy will be felt primarily by the shareholders and creditors of the insolvent firm. Here, insolvency costs represent a cost that is internalized by the firm's security holders rather than an externality imposed on the firm's customers. That is, the threat of insolvency and its concomitant costs may raise capital costs and hence prices to consumers. However, the actual occurrence of a single bankruptcy would have little or no visible impact on the firm's customers. If, as is frequently the case, a small, competitive, and insolvent firm is allowed to fail, its customers will simply shop elsewhere. When the firm is a natural monopolist, insolvency costs are borne directly by both the firm's shareholders and creditors, and by its customers. Here, while the courts are unlikely to let such a firm actually fail (*e.g.*, Penn Central), they are also unlikely to be able to stem a decline in the quality of service.

In the short run, increased leverage by a state or regionally regulated firm that was associated with non-default-free debt could be associated with lower rates in that jurisdiction. In effect, this short-run

---

[5]What constitutes default-free debt is somewhat debatable. However, Hickman [8] and Fraine and Mills [4] have shown that, for the period from 1900 to 1943, default rates on corporate bonds are inversely related to bond ratings:

Bond Rating	% Default Prior to Maturity
Aaa	5.9
Aa	6.0
A	13.4
Baa	19.1
below Baa	42.4

While these data are illustrative, it should be noted that they come from a particularly turbulent period of financial history and need not characterize present-day experience.

reduction in local rates, which is financed out of general tax revenues, is traded off against the increased risk of financial stress and the resulting decline in the quality of the locally-regulated good or service. Any regulatory authority that takes cognizance of social costs and benefits from a national perspective should realize that forcing a locally-regulated firm to issue low-grade debt is a particularly costly way to subsidize the price of the regulated good or service within its jurisdiction. Further, during periods of financial distress, any resulting decline in the quality of services of a regionally-regulated firm would be a cost borne directly by consumers in that jurisdiction. It may be, for example, that the weak financial position of Consolidated Edison Corporation was a contributing factor in the decline in quality of electrical services to residents of New York City.

Conclusion

While the present tax system may provide a private incentive for the issuance of debt by non-regulated firms, we have argued that the issuance of non-default-free debt by regulated and non-regulated firms may be socially non-optimal. That is, the existence of dead-weight social losses associated with insolvency implies that there are no public incentives for firms issuing non-default-free debt. Furthermore, since regulatory commissions would be expected to capture for the consumers of the regulated good any tax advantage associated with debt financing, there is no private incentive for regulated firms to use any debt financing. Thus, the issuance of other than high-grade debt by a regulated firm is undesirable from the perspective of both the firm's shareholders and its customers.

References

1. F. Arditti, H. Levy, and M. Sarnat, "Taxes, Capital Structure and the Cost of Capital: Some Extensions," *Quarterly Review of Economics and Business* (Summer 1977), pp. 89–95.
2. N. Baxter, "Leverage, Risk of Ruin, and the Cost of Capital," *Journal of Finance* (September 1967), pp. 395–404.
3. M. Brennan, "Taxes, Market Valuation and Corporate Financial Policy," *National Tax Journal* (December 1970), pp. 417–427.
4. H. Fraine and R. Mills, "The Effect of Defaults and Credit Deterioration on Yields of Corporate Bonds," *Journal of Finance* (September 1961), pp. 423–434.
5. D. Glenn, "Institutional Portfolio Restrictions, Capital Market Equilibrium, and Corporate Financing

Decisions," unpublished dissertation, Stanford University (August 1974).

6. D. Glenn, "Super Premium Security Prices and Optimal Corporate Financing Decisions," *Journal of Finance* (May 1976), pp. 507–524.

7. M. Gordon, "Some Estimates of the Cost of Capital to the Electric Utility Industry, 1954–57: Comment," *American Economic Review* (December 1967), pp. 1267–1277.

8. W. Hickman, *Corporate Bond Quality and Investor Experience,* Princeton, N.J., Princeton University Press, 1958.

9. J. Hirshleifer, *Investment, Interest and Capital,* Englewood Cliffs, N.J., Prentice-Hall, Inc., 1970.

10. G. Hite, "Leverage, Output Effects, and the M-M Theorem," *Journal of Financial Economics* (March 1977), pp. 177–202.

11. M. Jensen and W. Meckling, "Theory of the Firm: Managerial Behavior, Agency Costs and Capital Structure," *Journal of Financial Economics* (October 1976), pp. 305–361.

12. A. Kraus and R. Litzenberger, "A State-Preference Model of Optimal Capital Structure," *Journal of Finance* (September 1973), pp. 911–922.

13. J. Lintner, "Bankruptcy Risk, Market Segmentation, and Optimal Capital Structure," in *Risk and Return in Finance,* vol. 2, eds. Friend and Bickler, Cambridge, Mass., Ballinger, 1977, pp. 1–128.

14. R. Litzenberger and K. Ramaswamy, "The Effect of Personal Taxes and Dividends on Capital Asset Prices: Theory and Empirical Evidence," forthcoming in the *Journal of Financial Economics.*

15. R. Litzenberger and H. Sosin, "The Theory of Recapitalizations and the Evidence of Dual Purpose

Funds," *Journal of Finance* (December 1977), pp. 1433–1456.

16. R. Litzenberger and J. Van Horne, "Elimination of the Double Taxation of Dividends and Corporate Financial Policy," *Journal of Finance* (June 1978), pp. 737–749.

17. H. McCulloch, "The Tax-Adjusted Yield Curve," *Journal of Finance* (June 1975), pp. 811–839.

18. M. Miller, "Debt and Taxes," *Journal of Finance* (May 1977), pp. 261–276.

19. F. Modigliani and M. Miller, "Taxes and the Cost of Capital: A Correction," *American Economic Review* (June 1963), pp. 433–443.

20. F. Modigliani and M. Miller, "The Cost of Capital, Corporate Finance, and the Theory of Investment," *American Economic Review* (June 1958), pp. 261–297.

21. J. Scott, Jr., "A Theory of Optimal Capital Structure," *The Bell Journal of Economics* (Spring 1976), pp. 33–54.

22. W. Sharpe, *Portfolio Theory and Capital Markets,* New York, McGraw-Hill Book Co., 1970.

23. H. Sosin, "Neutral Recapitalizations: Predictions and Tests Concerning Valuation and Welfare," *Journal of Finance* (September 1978), pp. 1228–1234.

24. David T. Stanley and Marjorie Girth, "Bankruptcy: Problem, Process, Reform," Washington, D.C., The Brookings Institution, 1971.

25. J. Van Horne, "Corporate Bankruptcy and Liquidation Costs," Research Paper #205, Graduate School of Business, Stanford University, 1976.

26. J. Van Horne, "Optimal Initiation of Bankruptcy Proceedings by Debt Holders," *Journal of Finance* (June 1976), pp. 897–910.

27. J. Warner, "Bankruptcy Costs: Some Evidence," *Journal of Finance* (May 1977), pp. 337–347.

A theory of optimal capital structure

James H. Scott, Jr.

Assistant Professor
Graduate School of Business
Columbia University

This paper presents a multiperiod model of firm valuation derived under the assumptions that bankruptcy is possible and that secondary markets for assets are imperfect. Given the assumption that the probability of bankruptcy is zero, the model is formally identical to that proposed by Modigliani and Miller. Under plausible conditions the model implies a unique optimal capital structure. Comparative statics analysis is used to obtain a number of testable hypotheses which specify the parameters on which optimal financial policy depends. Implications for the debt policy of the regulated firm are also considered.

■ This paper presents a multiperiod model of firm valuation which captures the costs of bankruptcy and implies the existence of a unique optimal capital structure. The interest of financial economists in this topic was stimulated by the 1958 publication of a path breaking article by Modigliani and Miller. Their work presented a logically consistent proof that, given unfettered arbitrage opportunities, no possibility that firms could go bankrupt, and no corporate taxes, the total market value of the firm is unaffected by the amount of debt that it issues. A number of later authors have obtained the same result under different and often more general assumptions.[1]

The proof brought clarity, precision, and controversy to theoretical inquiries concerning the optimal debt policy of corporations. The controversy was heightened by the fact that under the assumption that the corporate tax rate is positive and that interest payments are deductible from taxable income, the Modigliani-Miller analysis implies that an optimal capital structure consists entirely of debt. This implication of their analysis generated a good deal of comment, since an infinite debt-equity ratio is inconsistent with both common sense and established practice. Indeed even Modigliani and Miller did not advocate the exclusion of equity financing and argued that a number

1. Introduction

James H. Scott, Jr., received the B.A. from Rice University (1967) and the M.S. and Ph.D. from Carnegie-Mellon (1970 and 1975, respectively). His research centers on firm valuation, corporate finance, and capital market theory.

A number of people have offered useful suggestions on earlier drafts of this paper. In particular I would like to thank J. Walter Elliot, David Glenn, Nils Hakansson, Miles Livingston, a referee, the editor, and especially Robert E. Lucas, Jr. and Richard Roll, who both served on my thesis committee. Remaining errors are my responsibility.

[1] See Fama and Miller (1972), Hirshleifer (1966), and Stiglitz (1969, 1974). A fuller discussion of the effects of taxation on capital structure where there is no possibility of bankruptcy can be found in Stiglitz (1973).

of considerations outside of their model render such a policy unsuitable.

Recently the topic of optimal capital structure and the Modigliani-Miller paradigm in particular have gained increased importance in the study of the regulated firm, as such firms have been encouraged to increase their levels of debt.[2] Theoretically the Modigliani-Miller analysis implies that regulators can pass the resulting tax savings on to consumers by lowering the maximum price they allow a regulated firm to charge. However, the use of this theory in such a manner can be dangerous because it fails to consider the detrimental effects increased debt can have upon a firm. What is required is a more powerful theory that accounts for the costs as well as the benefits of debt within a useful framework.

By weakening the assumptions required by Modigliani and Miller, a number of authors have been able to show that the total market value of the firm is affected by changes in its level of debt apart from the tax effect. Modigliani and Miller (1958) demonstrated that higher levels of debt can increase the value of the firm if corporations can borrow at a lower rate of interest than can investors. Baumol and Malkiel (1967) have argued that capital structure will not be irrelevant if investors incur transactions costs when engaging in arbitrage activities. Rubinstein (1973) has shown that if security markets are partially segmented, i.e., "if the sets containing both investors and available securities in each market are disjoint," (p. 749) and if debt is traded in a separate market where traders are more risk averse than are investors in the firm's equity, then increases in the level of debt can lower the total value of the firm. Similarly, Stiglitz (1972) demonstrated that if debt is traded in a separate market in which investors are more pessimistic about the firm than its equity holders, then a sufficiently large increase in debt can lower the total value of the firm.[3] Finally and perhaps more plausibly, if there are costs associated with bankruptcy and reorganization, Baxter (1967), Bierman and Thomas (1972), Kraus and Litzenberger (1973), and Robichek and Myers (1966) have argued that debt policy is not irrelevant and that an internal optimal capital structure can exist.

Collectively, these studies indicate progress in the theory of cor-

---

[2] See Davis and Sparrow (1972), who argue that the assumptions upon which the Modigliani-Miller analysis rests underlie virtually all of the financial models used in regulatory hearings.

[3] Stiglitz (1972) does not explicitly cast his analysis within the framework of a partially segmented market although that appears to be what he has assumed. As Rubinstein (1973, footnote 2) points out, Stiglitz' assumption of no short selling is crucial to his argument. In Stiglitz' Section 3, if short selling were permitted, the bondholders would enter the equity market. Although he does not recognize it, Stiglitz also implicitly assumes that equity holders cannot buy the firm's debt, for it they can, it is easy to show that, given the investment decision, capital structure is irrelevant. However, under the assumption of partially segmented markets, his conclusion that capital structure matters is correct.

In a reply to a recent comment by Richard Stapleton, Stiglitz (1975) has reacted to the observations in the above paragraph. He argues that even in the absence of partial segmentation, results similar to those in his original article can be obtained. Nevertheless, for the specific model set forth in his 1972 article, the argument presented above remains relevant. In particular, the "equilibrium" prices in equations (4) and (6) of that article are not stable; at those prices all equity holders would want to sell their equity and buy risky debt. As far as equity holders are concerned, the risky debt has a higher expected return than does the equity. Given partial segmentation, the prices will be stable.

porate capital structure. However, the models set forth to date have been too complex or insufficiently concrete to answer the practical questions of managers or regulators. In addition, Stiglitz (1974, p. 866) has recently called for a better understanding of the implications of assumptions which imply the existence of an optimal capital structure, so that sharper empirical tests can be conducted.[4]

This paper attempts to lay some of the foundations for a theoretical framework which is complex enough to yield an optimal capital structure, yet simple enough to provide testable hypotheses for empirical researchers, as well as useful insights for managers and regulators. Debt is valuable within this framework primarily because interest payments are tax deductible. It is detrimental to the extent that increases in the level of debt increase the probability that the firm will incur bankruptcy costs.

In the next section the models of equity, debt, and firm valuation which lie at the heart of the analysis are presented. What distinguishes these models from others which have incorporated bankruptcy costs is the fact that the formulas presented here are explicitly multiperiod, but still relatively simple. They incorporate a multiperiod definition of bankruptcy which surmounts the difficulties raised by Stiglitz (1972, pp. 459–462, and 1974, pp. 856–857), and, because they are mathematically tractible, they can be used to analyze a number of important, but neglected, theoretical issues.

In the third section the capital structure properties of the model are derived. Not only is it shown that an optimal capital structure can exist, but conditions which guarantee the existence of a unique internal optimal level of debt are set forth. Throughout the model is compared with that set forth by Modigliani and Miller. In Section 4 a comparative statics analysis is used to determine how shifts in various external parameters affect the optimal level of debt. Section 5 relates the paper's findings to the regulated firm and in particular to the recent proposal made by Leland (1974). A short summary concludes the paper.

2. Valuation formulas

■ It is assumed that the securities market consists of a large number of buyers, sellers, and issuers of financial instruments, none of whom is large enough for his transactions to have an appreciable impact on current prices. Securities are completely divisible and there are no brokerage charges, transfer taxes, or flotation costs. All traders have equal and costless access to all relevant information. In addition, and partially as a consequence of the preceding, they share the same subjective probability distribution of future events (i.e., they possess homogeneous expectations). The default free rate of interest equals ρ and the term structure of interest rates is flat. The personal tax rate of investors is assumed equal to zero, and investors are assumed to be indifferent to risk, i.e., they maximize expected future wealth.

Firms issue only debt and equity, both of which have limited

---

[4] Empirical studies by Schwartz and Aronson (1967) and by Scott (1972) have shown that there are often striking cross industry differences in capital structure. None of the theories mentioned above appear to be capable of explaining these differences. In fact, many of the models are built upon assumptions so weak that they yield few, if any, testable hypotheses.

liability. Corporate profits are taxed at a constant rate, t, and the interest payments on the debt, R, are deductible for corporate tax purposes. As long as they do not go bankrupt, firms can exist indefinitely. In each period earnings before interest and taxes but after depreciation ($EBIT$) will be represented by the random variable X which is assumed to have a temporally independent, identical (subjective) probability distribution in all future periods as long as the firm remains solvent. Upon bankruptcy the assets are sold and the earnings cease. The range of X is such that it may be possible for the firm to go bankrupt even if it has no debt, e.g., the firm may lose an expensive law suit. Once financial policy has been determined, investors expect that the current financial policy of the firm (as measured by R) will not be altered.[5]

The market value of the firm, V, will be derived by developing the market value of its equity, V_e, and of its debt, V_d, and then summing the two ($V = V_e + V_d$). However, in order to develop either, it is necessary to specify the protective covenants included in the bond indenture, which are similar to the "me first" rules proposed by Fama and Miller (1972, pp. 151–152).

(1) Interest payments must be made at the end of each period.

(2) Changes in financial or investment policy which would decrease the value of existing debt are not permitted without adequate compensation to debtholders.

(3) Failure to comply with provision 1 or 2 results in firm bankruptcy.

(4) Upon bankruptcy the claims of the bondholders equal the par value of their debt plus interest currently due.

If the firm is declared bankrupt, its assets are sold and the proceeds are distributed to its creditors according to their order of priority. Bankruptcy costs are introduced by the assumption that the productive assets of the firm are sold in imperfect secondary markets.[6] This implies that the liquidation value of the firm's assets, lA, is always less than the market value of a well-managed nonbankrupt firm, V.

□ **The market value of equity.** Under the assumption of a frictionless capital market peopled by risk neutral investors, there will be equilibrium only if all securities are expected to earn the same rate of return. Therefore, the equilibrium market value of the common stock equals its expected end of period value to current stockholders discounted at the default-free rate of interest. This value can arise from three different sources. If the firm does not go bankrupt, then stockholders (1) may receive dividends and (2) their stock will have a value based on its expected dividends in subsequent period. If the firm does go bankrupt, then the equity holders share in (3) the liquidating value of

---

[5] Given that future earnings are identically and independently distributed and that the capital stock and risk free rate of interest remain constant, this assumption is reasonable. If the current capital structure is perceived as optimal, then unless perceptions change, the same capital structure will be viewed as optimal in future periods as well.

[6] See Karlin (1962) and Nichols (1970) for discussions of asset sales in such markets.

the assets, if there is any value left after the firm's creditors have been satisfied.

If at the end of next period X equals or exceeds contractual interest payments, R, then dividends equaling current earnings, $(1-t)(X \times R)$, could be paid stockholders. Since the assumption that the distribution of X is the same in all future periods implies that the firm's investment decision is fixed and since there is no informational content to dividend policy, whether next period's dividends actually equal after tax profits or whether the firm engages in share repurchase will not affect the current value of equity.[7]

In addition to receiving the dividend, stockholders still own their original equity. Since, ρ, t, R, and the distribution of X remain fixed over time, if V_e represents the current expected dividend value of equity, then the value next period of expected dividends payable in succeeding periods will also equal V_e. In sum, if at the end of the first period $X \geq R$, the total value of equity owners' holdings will equal current earnings plus the value of expected future earnings, $(1-t)(X-R) + V_e$.

On the other hand if X is less than R, then stockholders must raise enough money to pay the interest or the firm will go bankrupt. Basically they have three ways to avoid bankruptcy: they can sell additional equity, sell additional debt, or sell assets. If they choose to sell equity, they must sell an amount equal to their after tax losses, $(1-t)(X-R)$.[8] The proceeds from the sale of stock are used to pay the firm's creditors, after which the total market value of the equity again equals V_e, the present value of expected future earnings. However, because new equity was sold, the wealth of the original stockholders is less than V_e and equals $V_e + (1-t)(X-R)$, the current loss plus the present value of future earnings.

Since there are no flotation costs, it is possible to argue that it is always optimal to cover losses by the sale of equity.[9] For example, assume that the firm has an optimal level of debt and (as will be shown later) that the sale of more debt would decrease the total value of the firm. Since the sale of additional debt would decrease the value of the existing debt, stockholders would also have to compensate the existing bondholders in accordance with provision two of the bond indenture. Thus, stockholders would have to sell enough new debt not only to cover the interest payments, but also to obtain funds to compensate bondholders. This alternative costs more than the sale of equity, since the sale of equity does not alter the current value of the firm's debt.

Similarly, if it is assumed that the firm follows an optimal investment policy, and given that secondary markets for assets are imper-

---

[7] See Miller and Modigliani (1961).

[8] This formulation implies that the government pays the firm a rebate of $-t(X-R)$ which is used to pay the bondholders, i.e., it is always possible for the firm to use its tax loss carry overs immediately. The above argument implicitly assumes that the tax rebate is received before the interest must be paid. However, the formulation still holds if the tax rebate is received shortly after the interest payment. Since all investors recognize that the rebate is forthcoming, it will be reflected in the value of the equity, and hence additional equity in the amount of $-t(X-R)$ can be sold. Again the wealth of original stockholders will equal $V_e + (1-t)(X-R)$.

[9] Strictly interpreted, the assumptions that R and the distribution of X are fixed eliminate the possibility of a sale of debt or assets so that the only way stockholders can avoid bankruptcy is by a sale of equity.

fect, the proceeds from a sale of assets will bring less than the assets are worth in the firm. Since provisions two and three of the bond indenture stipulate that stockholders must compensate bondholders for any resulting decrease in the value of the outstanding bonds, it follows that the sale of assets will cost stockholders more than the sale of equity.

There is a limit on how much equity can be sold to meet losses. If *EBIT* is so low that stockholder wealth, $(1-t)(X-R) + V_e$, is negative, then it is impossible to sell enough new equity to pay the firm's debts. Stockholders are prohibited from selling assets or additional debt, for to do so would violate covenant 2 of the bond indenture. Since the claims of creditors exceed the resources of the firm, it is declared bankrupt and stockholders, who are protected by limited liability, receive nothing.[10]

If Y_e denotes the value next period of the equity held by current stockholders, the above discussion can be summarized as follows

$$Y_e = \begin{cases} 0 & \text{if } X \le R - V_e/(1 - t) \\ V_e + (1 - t)(X - R) & \text{if } X > R - V_e/(1 - t). \end{cases}$$

Since investors are indifferent to risk, in equilibrium the total market value of the equity is equal to the expected value of Y_e discounted by the default-free rate of interest, ρ. Let $f[\cdot]$ be the continuous, differentiable probability density function of X and let E represent the expectations operator, then since V_e represents the total value of the equity (minus current net earnings) of the solvent firm in any period,

$$V_e = \frac{E[Y_e]}{1 + \rho}$$

$$V_e = \frac{(1 - F)V_e + (1 - t)E_b[X - R]}{1 + \rho}$$

$$V_e = \frac{(1 - t)E_b[X - R]}{\rho + F}, \tag{1}$$

where $F = \int_{-\infty}^{b} f(X)dX$,

$E_b[X - R] = \int_{b}^{\infty} (X - R)f[X]dX$,

and the limit of integration, $b \equiv R - V_e/(1 - t)$. In general, the following notation will be used:

$$E_a^b[g[X]] \equiv \int_{a}^{b} g[X]f[X]dX.$$

The absence of subscript (superscript) implies that the limit of integration is $-\infty(\infty)$. In what follows, F written with or without its argument, e.g., $F[b]$, will always represent the probability of bankruptcy.

The numerator on the right-hand side of (1) is the expected per period earnings available to holders of equity. The first term in the denominator is the default-free rate of interest and is properly viewed as a discount rate for what is possibly a perpetual stream of div-

[10] Upon bankruptcy, the stockholders' portion of the liquidating proceeds equals $lA + X - V_d - R$ (assuming V_d equals the par value of the debt). Since $V > lA$ and $R > 0$, this term is negative, so stockholders are protected by limited liability and receive nothing. If $lA > V$, then stockholders might receive a liquidation payment. However, in this case the firm is acting suboptimally and should have liquidated before the low *EBIT* was realized.

idends. The second term is the probability of bankruptcy, i.e., the chance that the equity will become completely worthless. F is not a risk premium in the sense that risk averting investors require an expected rate of return in excess of ρ because of the possibility of bankruptcy. Investors have been assumed indifferent to risk and, as equation (1) implies, expect only to earn ρ per period. F can be considered a default premium since, given a positive probability of bankruptcy, its inclusion is required so that the expected return will equal ρ.

Because (1) represents a multiperiod valuation formula which explicitly recognizes the possibility of bankruptcy, it is more complex than traditional equity valuation formulas. As Stiglitz (1974, p. 856) has recognized, when a firm has insufficient current earnings to meet its debt payments, it can resort to the capital market. In this model it will sell additional equity so that the probability of bankruptcy depends on the value of the equity of the going concern. As a result, V_e appears in the limits of integration on the right-hand side of (1), and thus the equation defines V_e only implicitly.

If X is normally distributed with mean $\overline{X}$ and variance σ^2, the numerator of the formula can be expressed more simply so that (1) becomes,

$$V_e = \frac{(1 - t)[(\overline{X} - R)(1 - F) + \sigma f[b]]}{\rho + F}$$

If $\overline{X} = 100$, $R = 20$, $t = 0.5$, $\sigma = 400$, and $\rho = 0.1$, then $b = -2.24$ and $V_e = 408$. If bankruptcy were ignored as in traditional theory, then $V_e = 40/0.1 = 400$. Equation (1) gives a higher valuation because unlike the traditional theory, it explicitly recognizes that stockholders are protected by limited liability and can lose no more than their initial investment.

□ **The market value of debt.** Upon bankruptcy a firm's assets are sold and the proceeds are distributed to its creditors. In the U.S. there are three major classes of creditors: secured, priority, and unsecured. Secured creditors (e.g., mortgage bondholders) are paid first out of the proceeds from the assets in which they hold a secured interest. If these proceeds exceed the amount owed the secured creditors, then they are paid in full and the excess is returned to the estate of the bankrupt. If the proceeds are insufficient, then the secured creditors receive the total amount of the proceeds and become unsecured creditors for the balance due them.

Priority creditors are paid next and must be paid in full before unsecured creditors can receive any of the liquidation proceeds. Priority claims include the administration costs of the bankruptcy process, taxes due the Internal Revenue Service, and certain wages due employees. Unlike secured and unsecured claimants, priority creditors are not security holders of the firm. Because order of priority upon bankruptcy is valuable, the firm can increase the total market value of its securities by issuing secured as opposed to unsecured debt.[11] For this reason two formulas will be developed for the total

---

[11] For example, one of the hazards of running a business is that a disgruntled customer, supplier, or other individual may file suit against the business and win legal damages. Secured debt is more valuable than unsecured debt since, should the firm lose a lawsuit and be forced into bankruptcy, the firm's secured bondholders will receive all

market value of the firm's debt, one if all of the firm's debt is fully secured, a second if all of the firm's assets have been pledged as security and additional, unsecured, debt has been issued as well.

Upon bankruptcy the claims of the firm's bondholders equal $V_d + R$. If $lA > V_d + R$, then it is assumed that the debt is fully secured, in which case the value of the bonds at the end of the period will equal $V_d + R$ regardless of whether the firm goes bankrupt or not. For simplicity, it is assumed that the interest payments on the debt are set so that the bonds sell at par. Given that either secured or unsecured bonds are issued at par, they will continue to sell at par as long as the firm remains solvent, since ρ, t, lA, R, and the distribution of X remain fixed over time. Thus, in the case of fully secured debt,

$$V_d = \frac{R + V_d}{1 + \rho}$$

$$V_d = \frac{R}{\rho}.$$

If the firm issues additional debt, it will reach a point where it no longer has enough assets to secure the debt fully. Beyond that point (i.e., when $R + V_d > lA$) some of the debt will be unsecured. If Y_d (a random variable) represents the end of period value of the debt, then[12]

$$Y_d = \begin{cases} R + V_d & \text{if } X > R - V_e/(1 - t) \\ lA & \text{otherwise} \end{cases}$$

and in equilibrium,

$$V_d = \frac{E[Y_d]}{1 + \rho} = \frac{(R + V_d)(1 - F) + lAF}{1 + \rho}$$

$$V_d = \frac{R(1 - F) + lAF}{\rho + F}. \tag{2}$$

The first term in the numerator of the bond valuation formula (2) is the expected coupon payment. The second term is the expected proceeds payable upon bankruptcy; if the firm had enough assets to secure the debt fully, then this term would be $(V_d + R)F$ and $V_d = R/\rho$ as before. The first term in the denominator is the appropriate discount rate for the expected payments to bondholders. The second, F, is a default premium[13] and represents the probability that

---

of its assets if they have been pledged as collateral for the loan. If only unsecured debt had been issued, bondholders must share the proceeds from the sale of the assets with the victor in the lawsuit. Stockholders benefit from the sale of secured versus unsecured debt because they receive more dollars per dollar of promised interest payment when the debt is secured. For a fuller discussion of the effect of secured debt on the market value of the firm see Scott (1975b).

[12] This formulation is correct if any tax rebates are lost upon bankruptcy. It is also appropriate if a tax rebate, $t(R - X)$, is paid to the bankrupt estate under the assumptions that (1) it is not possible to promise a tax rebate as security to bondholders and (2) the rebate is exhausted by the priority creditors. Furthermore, in the unlikely event that $R > V_e/(1-t)$, then bankruptcy is possible even when $X > 0$. The analysis presented here tacitly assumes that in this case a positive X is used up in administrative costs upon bankruptcy. Note that since the debt sells at par and all relevant variables are constant over time, it is not necessary to specify whether the debt is single period or multiperiod since the formulas are the same in either case.

[13] Usually, however, a default premium is defined only in terms of a bond's market price and its promised payments, i.e., normally terms like lA do not enter the definition.

the bond will fail to make its promised payments.[14] Note that as long as $V_d + R > lA$ and $F > 0$, the "yield to maturity," R/V_d, on the debt will exceed the default-free rate of interest.

If X is normally distributed as in the previous example with $\bar{X} = 100$ and $\sigma = 400$, and if $\rho = 0.1$, and $R = 20$, then $F = 0.0125$. If $lA = 175$, then formula (2) implies $V_d = 195$. Had there been no probability of bankruptcy, the value of the debt would have been 20/0.1 or 200.

It is relatively easy to use this framework to derive valuation formulas for different classes of debt. For example, assume that the value of the debt represented by equation (2) consists of two types of debt, the senior of which, V_d^s, is fully secured, the other V_d^u, being completely unsecured. The formula for the secured debt is the same as that for a default: free security, i.e., $V_d^s = R^s/\rho$. Since it is fully secured while the other is completely unsecured, upon bankruptcy, all of the firm's assets will be delivered to the secured creditors or $V_d^s + R^s = lA$. This implies that $V_d^u = (1 - F)R^u/(\rho + F)$, where[15] $R = R^s + R^u$. Upon bankruptcy, the claims of the unsecured bondholders (who will receive nothing) equal $V_d + R - lA$. This latter quantity is important within the context of the firm's optimal structure, which will be discussed below.

☐ **The market value of the firm.** If the firm has issued a relatively small amount of debt so that all of it is fully secured, then the total value of the firm is given by

$$V = V_d + V_e = \frac{R}{\rho} + \frac{(1 - t)E_b[X - R]}{\rho + F}. \tag{3}$$

If the firm has issued so much debt that part of it is unsecured (i.e., if $V_d + R > lA$), then

$$V = V_d + V_e = \frac{(1 - t)E_b[X] + tR(1 - F) + lAF}{\rho + F}. \tag{4}$$

Equations (3) and (4) can be viewed as generalizations of the firm valuation formula derived by Modigliani and Miller,[16] which assumed that the probability of bankruptcy is zero. If that is the case, then both (3) and (4) become

$$V = \frac{(1 - t)\bar{X}}{\rho} + tV_d, \tag{5}$$

which, given risk neutrality, is equivalent to the Modigliani-Miller formula.

[14] It is possible to modify the above derivation along the lines followed in Scott (1975a) under the assumption that investors are the risk averse and maximize the expected value of their quadratic utility functions, that the term structure is flat, and that the market price of risk is constant over time. In that case, a third term depending on the bond's covariance with the market can appear in the denominator. Such a term represents a true risk premium. The formula for equity can be modified as well.

[15] For the numerical example considered above, $R^s = 15.9$, $V_d^s = 159.1$; $R^u = 4.1$, $V_d^u = 36$. In order for this unsecured debt to sell at par, the coupon must be set so that $R^u = \text{Par } (\rho + F)/(1 - F)$. For the example, $R^u/\text{Par} = 0.113$, while $R^s/\text{Par} = 0.10$.

[16] Modigliani and Miller (1963), equation (3). As shown in note 14, (3) and (4) can be generalized to a setting where investors are risk averse and maximize expected (quadratic) utility. Given $F = 0$ these generalized formulas are equivalent to the model derived by Hamada (1969), which is itself an extension of the Modigliani-Miller model.

3. The optimal mix of debt and equity

■ The purpose of this section is to find that level of contractual coupon payments which will maximize the total value of the firm's debt plus its equity. Since there are two firm valuation formulas, equation (3) for $0 \le R \le lA\rho/(1 + \rho)$, and (4) for higher levels of R, both must be examined. To determine whether it is optimal for R to be fixed in the first range, the following derivative of (3) can be evaluated:[17]

$$\frac{\partial V}{\partial R} = \frac{1}{\rho} - \frac{(1 - t)(1 - F)}{\rho + F} \tag{6}$$

$$\frac{\partial V}{\partial R} = \frac{1}{\rho + F}\left[t(1 - F) + \left(\frac{1 + \rho}{\rho}\right)F \right] > 0. \tag{7}$$

Since (7) is strictly positive, it is always optimal to increase debt as long as the debt is fully secured, i.e., if $R < lA\rho/(1 + \rho)$. The first term within the brackets of (7) is the expected per period tax saving resulting from a unit increase in interest payments. Dividing this term by $\rho + F$ yields the present value of such savings. The second term within the brackets when divided by $\rho + F$ represents the increase in the value of the firm which results from the issuance of $\$1/\rho$ worth of fully secured debt.[18]

Since V is a continuous function of R, it would be optimal to issue at least some unsecured debt if $\partial V/\partial R > 0$ at $R = lA\rho/(1 + \rho)$. However, because the derivative does not exist at that point, $\partial V/\partial R$ must be evaluated as R approaches $lA\rho/(1 + \rho)$ from above. It is shown in Appendix 1 that the derivative of (4) is given by the following formula

$$\frac{\partial V}{\partial R} = \frac{1}{\rho + F}\left[t(1 - F) - (V_d + R - lA)\left(\frac{1 + \rho}{\rho + F}\right)f \right], \tag{8}$$

where $f = f[b]$.

As R approaches $lA\rho/(1 + \rho)$, $V_d = R/\rho$ and $V_d + R - lA = 0$, so that $\partial V/\partial R > 0$ if $t > 0$.[19] This implies that if $t > 0$, it is optimal for a firm that has exhausted its secured debt capacity to issue at least some amount of unsecured debt. In fact the result implies that even if a firm has no assets with any collateral value ($lA = 0$), the firm should issue some positive amount of unsecured debt as long as $t > 0$. If $t = 0$, then equations (7) and (8) imply that the optimal level of debt is given by $V_d + R = lA$, or equivalently $V_d = lA/(1 + \rho)$.

If the tax rate is positive and an internal optimal capital structure exists, then $\partial V/\partial R$ as given by equation (8) will equal zero at that R which maximizes V. To interpret this condition note that the first term within the brackets equals the tax rate multiplied by the probability that the firm does not go bankrupt in a given period. Holding the probability of bankruptcy constant, the term represents the marginal

---

[17] The derivation of $\partial V_e/\partial R$ is somewhat complex and can be found in Appendix 1.

[18] By changing the order of priority upon bankruptcy, the issuance of fully secured debt increases the total value of the firm more than it does in the no bankruptcy model of Modigliani and Miller (equation (5)). If $t = .05$ and $p = 0.1$, then a $\$1$ increase in R will raise the value of the Modigliani-Miller firm by $\$5$. However, by using (7), if $F = 0.01$, such an increase will raise V by $\$5.50$. See also note 11.

[19] It can also be shown that $\partial^2 V/\partial R^2$ is positive for $R < lA\rho/(1+\rho)$ and that its right-hand limit is negative at $R = lA\rho/(1+\rho)$.

increase in expected per period tax savings resulting from a \$1 increase in contractual interest payments. Dividing $t(1 - F)$ by $\rho + F$ gives the present value of those expected tax savings.

The second term within the brackets captures the effect of the concomitant increase in the probability of bankruptcy on the total value of the firm. The first part, $V_d + R - lA$, represents the bankruptcy costs to the firm's security holders due to a unit increase in R, while $(1 + \rho)f/(\rho + F)$ is the change in the probability of bankruptcy resulting from a \$1 increase in r. That $V_d + R - lA$ represents the cost of bankruptcy to the firm's security holders follows from the fact that upon bankruptcy stockholders and secured creditors lose nothing, while unsecured creditors lose everything. Secured creditors are protected since they receive lA, which equals the non-bankruptcy value of their debt plus accrued interest. While it is true that after bankruptcy the value of current equity is worthless, stockholders do not lose because of the bankruptcy process *per se*. They had already lost everything because the firm's earnings were so disastrously low. In fact bankruptcy occurs precisely because the outstanding equity is worthless; it does not cause it to become worthless.

On the other hand, at the end of each period the value of the unsecured debt is $V_d + R - lA$ as long as the firm continues in operation. However, upon bankruptcy its value falls to zero, i.e., unsecured creditors lose $V_d + R - lA$. Viewing the payments to security holders as a function of X, that function is continuous at the level of X where the firm goes bankrupt for both secured creditors and stockholders, while it is discontinuous for unsecured creditors.

Next it will be shown that under plausible conditions the model presented here has a unique optimal capital structure. Rewriting (8) and setting it equal to zero, one obtains

$$\frac{\partial V}{\partial R} = \frac{1 - F}{\rho + F} \left[t - (V - V_e + R - lA) \left(\frac{1 + \rho}{\rho + F} \right) \left(\frac{f}{1 - F} \right) \right] = 0. \quad (9)$$

At a point where $\partial V/\partial R = 0$,

$$\frac{\partial^2 V}{\partial R^2} = \frac{1 - F}{\rho + F} \left\{ \left(\frac{\partial V_e}{\partial R} - 1 \right) \left(\frac{1 + \rho}{\rho + F} \right) \left(\frac{f}{1 - F} \right) \right.$$

$$\left. + (V_d + R - lA) \left(\frac{1 + \rho}{\rho + F} \right) \left[\frac{(1 + \rho)f^2}{(\rho + F)^2(1 - F)} - \frac{\partial f/(1 - F)}{\partial R} \right] \right\}. \quad (10)$$

Since

$$\frac{\partial V_e}{\partial R} - 1 = - \left(\frac{1 + \rho}{\rho + F} \right) + \frac{t(1 - F)}{\rho + F}$$

and, since at $\partial V/\partial R = 0$

$$\left(\frac{1 + \rho}{\rho + F} \right) \frac{f}{1 - F} (V_d + R - lA) = t,$$

it follows that

$$\frac{\partial^2 V}{\partial R^2} = \frac{1 - F}{\rho + F} \left\{ -(V_d + R - lA) \left(\frac{1 + \rho}{\rho + F} \right) \frac{\partial f/(1 - F)}{\partial R} \right.$$

$$\left. - \frac{2f(1 + \rho)}{(\rho + F)^2} \left[\frac{1 + \rho}{2(1 - F)} - t \right] \right\}. \quad (11)$$

Since

$$\frac{\partial f/(1-F)}{\partial R} = \frac{\partial f/(1-F)}{\partial b}\frac{\partial b}{\partial R}$$

$$= \frac{\partial f/(1-F)}{\partial b}\left(\frac{1+\rho}{\rho+F}\right),$$

(11) will be negative and the second-order conditions for a local maximum will be satisfied if the following two (sufficient) conditions hold whenever $\partial V/\partial R = 0$, i.e., if

$$\frac{\partial f(z)/1-F(z)}{\partial z} = \frac{f'[z](1-F[z]) + f[z]^2}{(1-F[z])^2} \geq 0, \tag{12}$$

where $f'[z] = df[z]/dz$, and if

$$t < \frac{1+\rho}{2(1-F)}. \tag{13}$$

Condition (12) holds throughout their range for the uniform and, more realistically, the normal distributions.[20] Condition (13) will always hold if the tax rate is less than 0.5. If when $\partial V/\partial R = 0$, $F = 0.05$ and $\rho = 0.1$, then (13) requires $t < 0.58$. If these conditions do not hold, then V may have several local maxima. [21]

Given (12), Appendix 2 shows that $\partial V/\partial R < 0$ for R sufficiently large. Since $\partial V/\partial R$ is positive in the neighborhood of $R = \rho lA/(1+\rho)$ and is continuous on the interval $(\rho lA/(1+\rho),\infty)$, it follows that $\partial V/\partial R = 0$ at some point, say R^*, within the interval. Conditions (12) and (13) imply that V must be a local maximum at R^*, so that V has a unique internal maximum and is a strictly quasi-concave function of R.[22]

Table 1 contains a numerical example under the assumptions used previously. Given the same assumptions Table 2 presents equity, debt, and total firm values using the Modigliani-Miller valuation equations. Graphs of the various formulas are presented in Figure 1. While the firm valuation formula presented here reaches an internal maximum at $R = 50$, the value of the Modigliani-Miller firm rises throughout. This difference arises because while the Modigliani-Miller analysis recognizes the tax deductibility of interest payments, it fails to capture the fact that an increase in the level of debt also increases the probability of incurring the costs of bankruptcy. As a result, the Modigliani-Miller analysis vastly overstates the value of debt at high levels of R.[23]

---

[20] It may not hold for some distributions within the range where they are falling, e.g., for $z > 0$, (12) does not hold for $f[z] = 1/2(|z| + 1)^{-2}$, which is defined on the entire real line. However (12) does hold for the exponential distribution which falls throughout. For the normal density $f'[z] = zf[z]$, so (12) implies $f[z] \geq z(1 - F[z])$. That this latter inequality holds strictly can be proven by squaring both sides and transforming to polar coordinates.

[21] If one is willing to make a stronger assumption about the distribution of X, then weaker but still sufficient conditions on t are derivable. For example, if

$$\frac{1-F}{f}\frac{\partial f/(1-F)}{\partial z} = f, \text{ then } t < \frac{1+\rho}{(2-\rho-F)(1-F)}.$$

A still more restrictive condition of f is $f' \geq 0$, in which case (11) will be negative if

$$t < \frac{1 + \rho}{2(1-F) - (\rho+F)}.$$

[22] A function $q[z]$ is strictly quasi-concave if $g[\lambda z + (1 - \lambda)z'] > \min [g[z],g[z']]$.

[23] Nevertheless, it is interesting that a slightly different valuation equation suggested by the Modigliani-Miller analysis comes very close to the total firm values in Table 1 when R is less than or equal to its optimal value. If V_d is taken to the market

TABLE 1

NUMERICAL EXAMPLE: VALUATION EQUATIONS (3) AND (4)

R	V_e	V_d	V	V_d/V_e	F	"COST" OF DEBT (R/V_d)	"COST" OF EQUITY $(\rho+F)/(1-F)$
0	501	0	501	0	0.001	0.10	0.10
10	454	100	554	0.22	0.006	0.10	0.11
20	409	195	604	0.48	0.012	0.10	0.11
30	367	272	639	0.74	0.022	0.11	0.12
40	329	329	658	1.0	0.036	0.12	0.14
50	304	375	679	1.2	0.050	0.13	0.16
60	267	391	658	1.5	0.076	0.15	0.19
70	243	405	648	1.7	0.099	0.17	0.22
80	221	410	631	1.9	0.124	0.20	0.26
90	204	412	616	2.0	0.149	0.22	0.29
100	188	413	601	2.2	0.174	0.24	0.33

ASSUMPTIONS: X IS DISTRIBUTED NORMALLY WITH $\bar{X} = 100$; $\sigma = 400$; $\rho = 0.1$; $t = 0.5$; $\ell A = 175$.

TABLE 2

NUMERICAL EXAMPLE: VALUATION EQUATION (5) (MODIGLIANI–MILLER)

R	V_e	V_d	V	V_d/V_e
0	500	0	500	0
10	450	100	550	0.22
20	400	200	600	0.50
30	350	300	650	0.86
40	300	400	700	1.3
50	250	500	750	2.0
60	200	600	800	3.0
70	150	700	850	4.7
80	100	800	900	8.0
90	50	900	950	18.0
100	0	1000	1000	∞

ASSUMPTIONS: $\bar{X} = 100$; $\rho = 0.1$; $t = 0.5$.

This overvaluation of debt is slightly offset by the fact that the Modigliani-Miller formulation undervalues equity. Bankruptcy is actually beneficial to stockholders because it provides them with the protection of limited liability. This protection becomes more valuable the greater probability that earnings will be low enough to force bankruptcy.

The last two columns of Table 1 relate to conventionally used methods of determining the cost or rate of return on different instruments issued by the firm. Since the debt in Table 1 is assumed to be selling at par, yield to maturity is simply R/V_d. Yield to maturity rises with increases in R even though the expected return required by investors remains equal to ρ.

If an estimate of the cost of equity is obtained by using past data, then an overestimate is likely to be obtained here as well. If the firm

value of debt as given by the analysis of this paper rather than the Modigliani-Miller value of debt (R/ρ), then the following approximation

$$V \cong V_{eo} + tV_d,$$

where V_{eo} is the market value of the all equity firm, is within 1 percent of the market value of the firm given in Table 1 for $R \leq 50$.

FIGURE 1

MARKET VALUE OF SECURITIES AS A FUNCTION OF THE LEVEL
OF INTEREST PAYMENTS

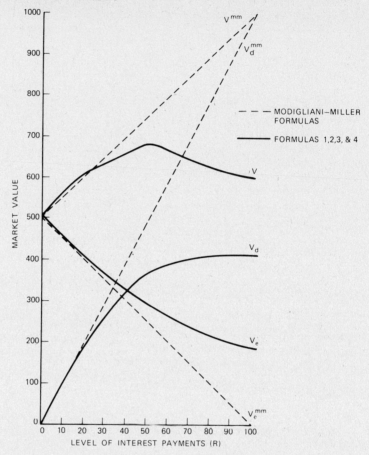

has not gone bankrupt, then an average of past increments in stockholder wealth will have the following conditional expectation,
$(1-t)E_b[X-R]/(1-F)$. Dividing this by the value of equity, one
obtains $(\rho+F)/(1-F)$ as an estimate of the cost of equity, even
though its true cost is ρ.[24]

☐ **Comparative statics analysis.** Because of the complexity of modeling bankruptcy and optimal capital structure within a multiperiod

---

[24] This suggests a possible explanation for the well-known empirical finding that *ex
post* rates of return on common stocks are positively related to the variance of their
rate of return. This finding is in conflict with the implications of the capital asset pricing
model. See Jensen (1972), for a review of this literature. The empirical studies generally
eliminate bankrupt firms from the data base or drop them from the sample before the
firms go bankrupt. As a result, the formula for the cost of equity presented above is
appropriate. It is probably true that in most cases F is positively related to the variance
of X. Given that this variance is positively related to the variance of the investors' rate
of return on equity, a positive relationship between the mean and variance of *ex post*
rates of return is not surprising.

framework it is not possible to derive closed form solutions for R^*, nevertheless, it is possible to conduct comparative statics analysis. Differentiating the first-order conditions for a maximum, $\partial V/\partial R$, with respect to R and some exogenous parameter, say δ, yields

$$\frac{\partial^2 V}{\partial R^2}\ \partial R + \frac{\partial^2 V}{\partial R \partial \delta}\ \partial \delta = 0.$$

Since (12) and (13) imply that $\partial^2 V/\partial R^2$ is negative, $\partial R/\partial \delta$ has the same sign as $\partial^2 V/\partial R \partial \delta$.

The effects of changes in the liquidating value of the firm's assets and in the tax rate are easy to determine:

$$\frac{\partial^2 V}{\partial R \partial lA} = \frac{(1+\rho)f}{(\rho+F)^3} > 0. \tag{14}$$

Equation (14) implies that an increase in lA increases R^*. This occurs because an increase in lA decreases the cost of going bankrupt. Next for the tax rate, note that

$$\frac{\partial^2 V}{\partial R \partial t} = \frac{1-F}{\rho+F} > 0. \tag{15}$$

An increase in t increases the tax savings which result from higher levels of debt and thus raises $R.^*$

It can also be shown that a proportional increase in both X and lA increases R^* proportionally, i.e., big firms differ from small firms only in terms of scale.[25] This follows from the implicit assumption that there are no economies of scale in financing.

Shifts solely in the distribution of X lead to ambiguous effects on R^*. Consider, for example, a simple shift in the mean of X which leaves the shape of the distribution unchanged. If X' represents the shifted variable, then $X' = X + \alpha$, where α is the shift parameter. If Y represents the payments per period to security holders, given the exhaustion of the secured debt capacity, then

$$Y = \begin{cases} lA & \text{if} & X \le R - \alpha - V_e/(1-t) \\ V + X + \alpha - t(X+\alpha-R) & \text{if} & X > R - \alpha - V_e/(1-t) \end{cases}$$

and

$$V = \frac{(1-t)E_b[X+\alpha] + tR(1-F) + lAF}{\rho + F},$$

where $b = R - \alpha - V_e/(1-t)$ and $F = [b]$. It can be shown that

$$\frac{\partial V}{\partial \alpha} = \frac{1-F}{\rho+F} - \frac{\partial V}{\partial R} > 0$$

and

$$\frac{\partial^2 V}{\partial R \partial \alpha} = \frac{\partial (1-F)/(\rho+F)}{\partial R} - \frac{\partial^2 V}{\partial R^2}. \tag{16}$$

Since the first term on the right-hand side of (16) is negative, the positivity of $\partial R/\partial \alpha$ (as conventional wisdom dictates) requires conditions stronger than (12) and (13), the conditions which guarantee the existence of a unique optimal capital structure. However, for the numerical example shown in Table 1, it can be shown that a small increase in α increases the optimal level of interest payments.

Other shifts in the distribution of X can be analyzed in a similar

---

[25] A proof of this statement can be found in Scott (1975a).

manner. If $X' = \lambda X$, then an increase in λ increases both the mean and variance of *EBIT* and can be shown to have an ambiguous effect on R^*.[26] If $X' = \delta(X-\overline{X}) + \overline{X}$, an increase in δ increases the variance of *EBIT*. Conventional wisdom indicates that such an increase should reduce R^*, however, it can be shown[27] that the result is ambiguous. Finally, the effect of changes in the risk-free rate of interest can be analyzed. While an increase in ρ reduces V, the effect on R^* is again ambiguous.[28]

□ **Reorganization.** In this section it is assumed that a firm need not go bankrupt but can be reorganized. Reorganization will be more profitable than bankruptcy as long as the value of the reorganized firm (assumed to be V) less the implicit and explicit costs of reorganization, C, exceeds the value of the firm upon bankruptcy, i.e., as long as $V - C > lA$.

For simplicity assume that the computation of taxes is unaltered by reorganization and that any unsecured debt is subordinated in the sense that upon reorganization the holders of the unsecured debt receive max $[0, V + (1-t)X + tR - (C+lA)]$. In this and other frameworks it is relatively easy to show that a firm should exhaust its secured debt capacity. Assuming that is the case and that lA of the firm's assets are available to secure debt, the end of period wealth of the firm's security holders can be represented as follows:

$$Y = \begin{cases} V + (1-t)X + tR & \text{if} \quad X > R - V_e/(1-t), \\ V + (1-t)X + tR - C & \text{if} \quad R - V_e/(1-t) \\ & \qquad \geq X \geq (C+lA-tR-V)/(1-t), \\ lA & \text{otherwise.} \end{cases}$$

Thus in equilibrium,

$$V = \frac{(1-t)E_a[X] + tR(1-F[a]) + lAF[a] - C(F[b] - F[a])}{\rho + F[a]}, \quad (17)$$

where $a = (C+lA-tR-V)/(1-t)$, $F[b]$ is the probability of reorganization, and $F[a]$ is the probability that unsecured bondholders will receive nothing.

Equation (17) can be analyzed in the same manner used to investigate (4). Just as the costs of bankruptcy were important in that framework, the cost of reorganization plays a major role in the present case. At one extreme, if reorganization is costless ($C=0$) and the tax rate is positive, then the optimal level of R is infinite. Given that second-order conditions hold, as C increases, the optimal level of R falls until it reaches that level which would be optimal if reorganization were impossible and only bankruptcy occurred. It is interesting that under current assumptions this point is reached while it is still optimal for the firm to reorganize rather than to go bankrupt. In other

---

[26] See Scott (1975a). For the numerical example in Table 1 $\partial R^*/\partial \lambda > 0$.

[27] See Scott (1975a). For the numerical example $\partial R^*/\partial \delta < 0$.

[28] See Scott (1975a). For the numerical example $\partial R^*/\partial \rho > 0$.

Preliminary empirical evidence in Scott (1975a) is consistent with the comparative statics propositions of the theory. Aggregated industry data from U.S. corporate tax returns suggest a strong positive relationship between the amount of debt a firm carries and the value of its assets. On the other hand, the coefficients reflecting the effect of the mean and variability of *EBIT* were statistically insignificant and of changing sign. These results are similar to those of Chudson (1945, p. 103), who reports "evidence of the existence of a relationship between long-term debt and fixed capital assets."

words the analysis of the previous sections can be strictly correct even though firms reorganize rather than declare bankruptcy.

In order to see this, note that (17) is valid only if it is possible for the firm's security holders (or more precisely, its unsecured bondholders) to gain as a result of reorganization, i.e., only if

$$R - V_e/(1-t) \geqslant (C + lA - tR - V)/(1-t)$$
$$V_d + R - lA \geqslant C.$$

If the above inequality does not hold then (4) is the appropriate valuation formula, yet the firm will still be reorganized as long as $C < V - lA$.[29]

☐ **A note on debt policy for the regulated firm.** The above analysis concerns unregulated firms, but it can be used to provide some insights useful for the regulatory process. Leland (1974) has recently argued that optimal regulation results if output price is set so that the financial value of the firm equals its real asset value, or in the terminology used here, so that $V = A$. The strength of Leland's argument derives from the fact that it rests on a model of production and stock market equilibrium under uncertainty. It differs from the model presented here in that it is based on assumptions which imply that capital structure is irrelevant. Although the analysis in this paper is not well adapted to deal precisely with questions of social optimality, it does suggest some plausible conjectures relating to Leland's proposal and regulatory debt policy in general.

Because capital structure is irrelevant in Leland's model, V is uniquely determined once output price (and thus the distribution of X) is fixed, as long as the firm pursues optimal investment and operating policies. On the other hand in models where there are corporate taxes as well as chance of incurring bankruptcy costs, V is not fixed when output price is set, even if the firm follows optimal investment and operating policies. In general, and certainly in the model presented here, V is a function of R as well.

One possible escape from this indeterminacy would set output price such that $V = A$ only if the firm followed an optimal debt policy as well. However, this raises an additional problem. The more debt a company carries, the greater is the probability that it will incur bankruptcy costs. Should a competitive firm fail, its stockholders and creditors can be expected to bear the bulk of these costs. Accordingly, their decision to incur debt will reflect these costs. The firm's customers will not suffer from the loss of the opportunity to buy the firm's output, since the firm's competitors will be able to meet the demand.

On the other hand, if a regulated monopoly fails, customers have few alternatives, if at all. This implies that there may be additional social costs of bankruptcy if there is a disruption of service to customers, or if public funds must be spent to prevent such a disruption. In addition, the intricacies of the bankruptcy process are likely to require additional attention by the regulatory authority, and thereby increase the costs of regulation. These additional bankruptcy costs of the regulated firm are not borne by the firm's security holders, since

---

[29] If upon reorganization unsecured bondholders were to receive $V - C - lA$, then (4) would hold only when bankruptcy was preferable to reorganization.

stockholders are protected by limited liability and bondholders are protected both by limited liability and the value of their security. Thus these costs will be ignored by the value maximizing firm when it sets its optimal level of debt, but they should not be ignored by regulators interested in the public welfare. *Ceteris paribus,* regulators should prefer a level of debt lower than that which maximizes the market value of the firm.

The effect of this divergence of social and private costs is exacerbated by the fact that the government subsidizes the use of debt through the tax structure. This creates a private benefit of debt financing for which there is no corresponding social benefit.[30] The most obvious and perhaps the best way for the regulator to eliminate this spurious benefit is to place an upper limit on the amount of debt regulated firms are permitted to incur. If $t=0$, the privately optimal level of debt is given by $V_d = lA(1+\rho)$. Thus, if the regulator was unconvinced by the arguments of the preceding paragraph and felt that except for the tax incentive favoring debt, the private costs of bankruptcy accurately reflected its social costs, he could require that $V_d = lA/(1+\rho)$ and set output price such that if the firm followed optimal operating and investment policies, $V = A$. However, if it is felt that bankruptcy would create the additional social costs of the previous paragraph, then debt should be set at a lower level.

4. Summary

■ This paper has presented a multiperiod model of debt, equity, and firm valuation. Under the assumption that the market for real assets was imperfect, the model implied that the value of the nonbankrupt firm was a function not only of expected future earnings but also of the liquidating value of its assets. Conditions were presented which guaranteed the existence of a unique optimal capital structure.

Comparative statics analysis yielded three clear-cut results. The optimal level of debt (as measured by the interest payments per period) was an increasing function of the liquidation value of the firm's assets, the corporate tax rate, and the size of the firm. Sharp results were not obtainable with respect to changes in the mean and/or the variance of earnings before interest and taxes and in the default-free rate of interest. Implications for the regulated firm were briefly discussed.

Appendix 1

■ As noted in the text V_e is only implicitly defined by equation (1). As a result, finding the derivatives of V_e and V with respect to, say, R is more complex than usual. Fortunately the general form of Leib-

---

[30] It has been argued that since interest payments are tax deductible, a regulator, by forcing a firm to carry additional debt, can lower its costs and thus the regulator can set a lower output price. Even apart from its effect on expected bankruptcy costs, this type of proposal is questionable. If the total amount of government spending is unaffected by the action, then the tax bill would merely be redistributed. If the reduction in the tax of the regulated firm resulted in an equal increase in the taxes of all individuals, then the higher debt and lower prices of the regulated firm would simply redistribute wealth in favor of individuals who consume relatively more of the regulated good.

nitz' rule handles the task.[31] Let $a(Z)$, $b(Z)$ be differentiable functions on the interval $[C_o,C_1]$ such that $b[Z] \geqq a[Z]$. Let $g[Z,X]$ and $\partial g[Z,X]/\partial Z$ exist and be continuous on the rectangle $C_1 \geqq Z \geqq C_o$, $b[Z] \geqq X \geqq a[Z]$. Define

$$G[Z] = \int_{a[Z]}^{b[Z]} g[Z,X]dX.$$

Then for any Z in $[C_o,C_1]$

$$\frac{dG[Z]}{dZ} = g[Z,b[Z]]\frac{db[Z]}{dZ} - g[Z,a[Z]]\frac{da[Z]}{dZ}$$

$$+ \int_{a[Z]}^{b[Z]} \cdot \frac{\partial g[Z,X]}{\partial Z} dX.$$

If $b[Z] = \infty$ ($a[Z] = -\infty$), then the last term in the above equation must be uniformly convergent for Z in $[C_o,C_1]$. Given that, the first (second) term in the above equation equals zero and the above formula is appropriate.

Now $V_e = q/p$, where

$$q = (1 - t)\int_{R-V_e/(1-t)}^{\infty} (X - R)f[X]dX$$

$$p = \rho + \int_{-\infty}^{R-V_e/(1-t)} f[X]dX.$$

Thus, given the above continuity conditions,

$$\frac{\partial V_e}{\partial R} = \frac{1}{p}\left[\frac{\partial q}{\partial R} - \frac{q}{p}\frac{\partial p}{\partial R}\right]. \tag{A1}$$

Using Leibnitz' rule,

$$\frac{\partial q}{\partial R} = -(1 - t)(R - V_e/(1 - t) - R)f[b]\partial b/\partial R$$

$$-(1 - t)\int_{R-V_e/(1-t)}^{\infty} f[X]dX = V_e f[b]\frac{\partial b}{\partial R} - (1 - t)(1 - F), \tag{A2}$$

where $b = R - V_e/(1 - t)$ and $(1 - F)$ is the above integral. Similarly,

$$\frac{\partial p}{\partial R} = f[b]\frac{\partial b}{\partial R}. \tag{A3}$$

Substituting (A2) and (A3) into (A1) yields the desired result

$$\frac{\partial V_e}{\partial R} = \frac{1}{P + F}\left\{ V_e f[b]\frac{\partial b}{\partial R} - (1 - t)(1 - F) - V_e f[b]\frac{\partial b}{\partial R}\right\}$$

$$\frac{\partial V_e}{\partial R} = \frac{-(1 - t)(1 - F)}{\rho + F} \leqq 0. \tag{A4}$$

The derivative of V with respect to R can be obtained in a similar fashion. For this derivation let

$$q = (1 - t)E_b[X] + tR(1 - F) + lAF$$

$$p = \rho + F.$$

Thus $V = q/p$, and $\partial V/\partial R$ is given by the right-hand side of (A1).

---

[31] See, for example, Buck (1965).

$$\frac{\partial q}{\partial R} = -(1 - t)\left(R - \frac{V_e}{1 - t}\right)f[b]\frac{\partial b}{\partial R} + t(1 - F) - tRf[b]\frac{\partial b}{\partial R}$$

$$+ \, lAF[b]\frac{\partial b}{\partial R} = t(1 - F) + (V_e - R + lA)f[b]\left(1 - \frac{1}{1 - t}\frac{\partial V_e}{\partial R}\right).$$

Using (A4)

$$\frac{\partial q}{\partial R} = t(1 - F) + (V_2 - R + lA)f[b]\left(\frac{1 + \rho}{\rho + F}\right). \tag{A5}$$

Since $\partial p/\partial R$ is given by (A3), substituting (A3), (A5), and the re-defined q/p into the right-hand side of (A1) yields

$$\frac{\partial V}{\partial R} = \frac{1}{\rho + F}\left\{t(1 - F)\right.$$

$$\left. + (V_e - R + lA)f[b]\left(\frac{1 + \rho}{\rho + F}\right) - Vf[b]\left(\frac{1 + \rho}{\rho + F}\right)\right\}.$$

Now $V = V_e + V_d$, so

$$\frac{\partial V}{\partial R} = \frac{1}{\rho + F}\left[t(1 - F) - (V_d + R - lA)f[b]\left(\frac{1 + \rho}{\rho + F}\right)\right]. \tag{8}$$

Appendix 2

■ This appendix shows that $\partial V/\partial R < 0$ for R sufficiently large. There are two cases to be considered, one if the distribution of X is such that the domain of feasible X is bounded from above, another if it is not. First assume that X is bounded and represent the highest level of X with positive probability as X_{max}. Let $R' \equiv X_{max}$, then at R' equation (8) becomes

$$\frac{\partial V}{\partial R} = \frac{-f(R')}{1 + \rho}\left(R' - \frac{\rho lA}{1 + \rho}\right),$$

which is negative if $R' > \rho lA/(1 + \rho)$, which is reasonable to assume. (If $X_{max} < \rho lA/(1 + \rho)$, then it is *always* optimal to disband the firm and invest the proceeds at the risk-free rate of interest.)

If X is not bounded from above, then $\partial V/\partial R$ will be negative for finite R if and only if (from equation (8)).

$$(V_d + R - lA)\left(\frac{1 + \rho}{\rho + F}\right)\left(\frac{f}{1 - F}\right) > t. \tag{A6}$$

Since $f/(1 - F) > 0$ and nondecreasing by condition (12), there exists some k such that $f/(1 - F) \geq k$ for all $R \geq R'$ (where $R' = M < \infty$). Using this information plus the fact that $F < 1$ and $V_d + R - lA = \frac{(1 + \rho)R - \rho lA}{\rho + F}$, inequality (A6) will always hold if

$$\left(R - \frac{\rho lA}{1 + \rho}\right)k > t$$

$$R > \frac{\rho lA}{1 + \rho} + \frac{t}{k}.$$

Therefore, a finite $R \geq R'$ can be found to satisfy the above inequality. This proves that $\partial V/\partial R < 0$ for some R sufficiently large.

References

BAUMOL, W. AND MALKIEL, B. "The Firm's Optimal Debt-Equity Combination and the Cost of Capital." *Quarterly Journal of Economics*, Vol. 91, No. 4 (November 1967), pp. 547–578.

BAXTER, N. "Leverage, Risk of Ruin, and the Cost of Capital." *Journal of Finance*, Vol. 22, No. 3 (September 1967), pp. 395–404.

BIERMAN, H. AND THOMAS, J. "Ruin Considerations and Debt Issuance." *Journal of Financial and Quantitative Analysis*, Vol. 7, No. 1 (January 1972), pp. 1361–1378.

BUCK, R. C. *Advanced Calculus*, 2nd ed. New York: McGraw-Hill, 1965.

CHUDSON, W. A. *The Pattern of Corporate Financial Structure*. New York: National Bureau of Economic Research, 1945.

DAVIS, B. E. AND SPARROW, F. T. "Valuation Models in Regulation." *The Bell Journal of Economics and Management Science*, Vol. 3, No. 2 (Autumn 1972), pp. 544–67.

FAMA, E. AND MILLER, M. *The Theory of Finance*. New York: Holt, Rinehart, and Winston, 1972.

HAMADA, R. "Portfolio Analysis, Market Equilibrium, and Corporation Finance." *Journal of Finance*, Vol. 24, No. 1 (March 1969), pp. 13–31.

HIRSHLEIFER, J., "Investment Decision under Uncertainty: Applications of the State-Preference Approach." *Quarterly Journal of Economics*, Vol. 80, No. 2, (May 1966), pp. 252–277.

JENSEN, M. C. "Capital Markets: Theory and Evidence." *The Bell Journal of Economics and Management Science*, Vol. 3, No. 2 (Autumn 1972), pp. 357–398.

KARLIN, S. "Stochastic Models and Optimal Policy for Selling an Asset," in K. J. Arrow *et al.*, eds., *Studies in Applied Probability and Management Science*, Stanford: Stanford University Press, 1962.

KRAUS, A. AND LITZENBERGER, R. "A State-Preference Model of Optimal Financial Leverage." *Journal of Finance*, Vol. 28, No. 4 (September 1973), pp. 911–922.

LELAND, H. "Regulation of Natural Monopolies and the Fair Rate of Return." *The Bell Journal of Economics and Management Science*, Vol. 5, No. 1 (Spring 1974), pp. 3–15.

MILLER, M. AND MODIGLIANI, F. "Dividend Policy, Growth, and the Valuation of Shares." *Journal of Business*, Vol. 34, No. 4 (October 1961), pp. 411–433.

MODIGLIANI, F. AND MILLER, M. "The Cost of Capital, Corporation Finance, and the Theory of Investment." *The American Economic Review*, Vol. 48, No. 3 (June 1958), pp. 261–297.

———— AND ————. "Corporate Income Taxes and the Cost of Capital: A Correction." *The American Economic Review*, Vol. 53, No. 3 (June 1963), pp. 433–443.

NICHOLS, D. "Market Clearing for Heterogeneous Capital Goods," in E. Phelps *et al.*, eds., *Microeconomic Foundations of Employment and Inflation Theory*. New York: W. W. Norton and Co., 1970.

ROBICHEK, A. AND MYERS, S. "Problems in the Theory of Optimal Capital Structure." *Journal of Financial and Quantitative Analysis*, Vol. 1 (June 1966), pp. 1–35.

RUBINSTEIN, M. "Corporate Financial Policy in Segmented Markets." *Journal of Financial and Quantitative Analysis*, Vol. 8, No. 5 (December 1973), pp. 749–761.

SCHWARTZ, E. AND ARONSON, B. "Some Surrogate Evidence in Support of Concept of Optimal Financial Structure." *Journal of Finance*, Vol. 22, No. 1 (March 1967), pp. 10–18.

SCOTT, D. "Evidence on the Importance of Financial Structure." *Financial Management*, Vol. 50, No. 2 (Summer 1972), pp. 45–50.

SCOTT, J. "Bankruptcy, Firm Valuation, and Optimal Capital Structure." Unpublished Ph.D. dissertation, Carnegie-Mellon University, 1975.

————. "Bankruptcy, Secured Debt, and Optimal Capital Structure." Graduate School of Business, Columbia University, Research Paper No. 101, 1975b, *Journal of Finance*, forthcoming.

STIGLITZ, J. "A Reexamination of the Modigliani-Miller Theorem." *The American Economic Review*, Vol. 59, No. 5 (December 1969), pp. 784–793.

————. "Some Aspects of the Pure Theory of Corporate Finance: Bankruptcies and Take-Overs." *The Bell Journal of Economics and Management Science*, Vol. 3, No. 2 (Autumn 1972), pp. 458–482.

————. "Taxation, Corporate Financial Policy, and the Cost of Capital." *Journal of Public Economics*, Vol. 2, No. 1 (February 1973), pp. 1–34.

————. "On the Irrelevance of Corporate Financial Policy." *The American Economic Review*, Vol. 64, No. 6 (December 1974), pp. 851–866.

————. "Some Aspects of the Pure Theory of Corporate Finance: Bankruptcies and Take-Overs: Reply." *The Bell Journal of Economics*, Vol. 6, No. 2 (Autumn 1975), pp. 711–714.

For Further Study

Additional references which the reader may find useful include:

1. Arditti, F.D. (1980), "A Survey of Valuation and Cost of Capital". *Research in Finance*, vol. 2, pp. 1–56.
2. Brigham, E.F. and M.J. Gordon (1968). "Leverage, Dividend Policy, and Cost of Capital". *Journal of Finance* (March 1968), pp. 85–103.
3. Haley, C.W. and L.D. Schall (1979). *The Theory of Financial Decisions*, 2nd ed., New York: McGraw Hill.
4. Miller, M.H. and F. Modigliani (1966). "Some Estimates of the Cost of Capital for the Electrical Utility Industry, 1954–75. *American Economic Review* (June 1966), pp. 333–391.
5. Ohlson, J.A. (1979). "Risk, Return, Security Valuation and the Stochastic Behavior of Accounting Numbers". *Journal of Financial and Quantitative Analysis* (June 1979), pp. 317–336.
6. Scapens, R.W. (1978). "A New Classical Measure of Profit," *The Accounting Review* (April 1978), pp. 448–469.
7. Van Horne, J.C., Jr. (1980). *Financial Management and Policy*, Prentice-Hall, Englewood Cliffs, New Jersey.
8. Weston, J.F. and E.F. Brigham (1981). *Managerial Finance*, seventh ed., The Dryden Press: Hinsdale, Ill.

Part III

Cost of
Capital Determination

Introduction

The cost of capital of a firm is an important factor in determining the value of a firm. Basic financial management texts (e.g., Weston and Brigham (1981), Van Horne (1980)) have extensively discussed four alternative cost of capital estimation methods: the weighted average cost of capital, the average earnings yield, the discounted cash flow (DCF), and the CAPM. Rubenstein (1973) (Part II) carefully discusses the concepts and applications of the weighted average cost of capital and the CAPM methods. He graphically demonstrates that the CAPM method, rather than the weighted average cost of capital, explicitly takes the systematic risk of investment projects into account.

In the paper entitled, "Problems with the Concept of the Cost of Capital", Haley and Schall (HS) (1978) indicate that the concept of the cost of capital has historically served three purposes: as a guide for financial decisions, as a standard for investment decisions, and as a link between financing and investment decisions. They carefully investigate the conditions under which certain cost of capital concepts can become either misleading or irrelevant. By reviewing M&M's cost of capital definitions, HS demonstrate that the weighted cost of capital can be misleading and inefficient since income streams may not be perpetual, discount rates may change over time, and a firm's risk class is not independent of its financial structure.

In addition, HS demonstrates that there are two possible problems in using the cost of capital as an indicator of investment decisions:

1. There may be a different cost of capital for different risk levels and for different time periods.
2. If the rate of return an investment must earn in order to be justified differs when calculated for internal and for external financing, a unique cost of capital does not exist for the investment.

Henderson (1979) uses the CAPM and M&M theory, which have been discussed in Part II, to show that the weighted average cost of capital is an acceptable estimation method. In addition, Henderson discusses the conceptual relationship between the average cost of capital and the marginal cost of capital.

M&M (1966) develop a cross-sectional method to estimate the cost of capital for the utility industry. Higgins (1974) uses a finite growth valuation theory to integrate the DCF cost of capital with M&M's method to derive a generalized cost of capital estimation model for the utility industry. In Higgins' model, finite growth potential is explicitly considered. The dividend policy issue is also empirically examined.

The debt cost of capital, an integrated part of a firm's cost of capital, is defined as the equilibrium required rate of return on a risk-free corporate bond and on a risky corporate bond. Chen (1978) reviews some recent developments in the theory of risky debt and examines more systematically the determinants of the cost of debt capital. Both static and dynamic models are used to determine the cost of debt capital. Both a single period CAPM model and the Option Pricing Model are said to show that the market value of a leveraged firm is the sum of four components:

1. the market value of the unlevered firm plus
2. the present value of the tax shelter generated by the tax deductibility of interest payments,
3. minus the present value of the costs associated with bankruptcy, and
4. minus a term that summarizes the limited liability of bondholders.

This result is different from that of M&M's Proposition I with taxes which was discussed in Part II. In addition, Chen also uses a multiperiod model to generalize the cost of debt capital determination. Finally, Chen concludes that the more rigorous theories of the cost of debt capital will provide a better framework for empirical work on the risky premium of corporate bonds.

In addition to issues pertaining directly to the cost of capital, there has been extensive work done on defining and clarifying the concept of the "earnings" of a firm. Earnings can be classified as either accounting earnings or economic earnings. Haley and Schall (1979) discuss the difference between these two alternative earnings measurements in detail, and Scapens (1978) has developed methods for relating accounting earnings to economic earnings. Ohlson (1979) has shown mathematically that accounting figures are random variables that can be used to determine the market value of a firm. Thus, it has been shown that accounting earnings can be used as a proxy for economic earnings to determine both the value of a firm and the cost of capital.

Cost of capital estimation should be based upon the valuation theory discussed in Part II as well as considerations of practical usefulness. In addition, a practical market value determination for both equity and debt and capital budgeting decisions will generally rely upon accurate cost of capital estimates. Therefore, papers in this part should be jointly read with those listed in Parts II and IV.

PROBLEMS WITH THE CONCEPT OF THE COST OF CAPITAL

*Charles W. Haley and Lawrence D. Schall**

The cost of capital concept has for some years permeated both finance
theory and textbook treatments of capital structure and business investment
decisions. This has been due, to a major extent, to the important works of
Modigliani and Miller [10,11] and Solomon [16], among others. In recent years,
however, the concept has been the subject of some controversy. A number of
authors have shown that the cost of capital, as usually computed, can produce
errors except under highly restrictive assumptions and that there continues to
be some debate over its proper definition and use.[1] Our purpose in the present
paper is to explicate more fully the source of the difficulties with the cost
of capital and to suggest that, despite the initial usefulness of the concept,
the field of finance would be better off now if it were relegated to history.
Both the perfect and imperfect market cases will be considered. We propose
that the term "cost of capital" be eliminated from textbooks and research
papers and be replaced by superior concepts.

That the cost of capital is currently one of the most heavily emphasized
and important concepts in finance cannot be disputed. Innumerable research
papers published in the last 25 years are devoted in whole or in part to it.
Furthermore, a leading textbook (Weston and Brigham [19]) has a single chapter
on the topic which comprises 10 percent of the book. The cost of capital is
used in three ways:

(1) As a criterion for financing decisions where the optimal mix of
financing sources is defined as that mix which minimizes the cost of
capital to the firm. Our major criticism of the concept is directed
toward its use in this way.

---

*
Both, University of Washington.

[1]See, for example, Myers [12] and Ang [1] for a discussion of some difficulties. Nantell and Carlson [13] argue in favor of using the weighted average
cost of capital as a guide to optimal capital structure and as a criterion for
investment decisions.

(2) As a standard for investment decisions where the minimum acceptable rate of return or discount rate on proposed new investments is defined as the cost of capital. We will argue that this use is simply poor terminology.

(3) As a link between investment decisions and financing decisions, where the minimum acceptable rate of return on new investment is measured as a function of the rates of return required by investors in the firm's securities. We believe that the cost of capital concept is appropriate here as a first approximation; however the term "cost of capital" leads to so much confusion with respect to items (1) and (2) that it should be abandoned.[2]

In Section I and Appendix A we examine the firm's financing problem and observe that a minimum cost of capital is not an appropriate criterion for the optimal use of debt even under highly restrictive assumptions. We then argue that under more general and realistic assumptions, the "cost of capital" is irrelevant to the problem. The application of cost of capital approaches to business investment is discussed in Section II. We suggest that such approaches will likely require modification as financial theory increases in realism and complexity. Appendix B explores the conditions under which the weighted average cost of capital is a valid discount rate for valuing the firm's cash flows. New results are derived which indicate that the conditions are especially restrictive. We conclude that no useful purpose is served by retaining the term "cost of capital" to refer to a minimum rate of return required on investment, since the term is both ambiguous and unnecessary.

I. The Cost of Capital and Firm Financial Structure

To explain the deficiencies of each of the cost of capital formulations, we will assume the simplest of worlds, specifically, that all flows are level perpetuities, that all assets are nondepreciating, that discount rates are constant over time (same rate to discount cash flows of year t as those of year t+1, all t), that the firm has only two classes of outstanding securities (stocks and bonds), and that all firm cash flow is paid out as dividends or interest (on perpetual debt). It is also assumed that firm value maximization and shareholder wealth maximization are consistent goals (more on this later).

---

[2]Our views are counter to those expressed in a highly regarded book on investment decisions by Bierman and Smidt [4, page v], who state, "The cost of capital is a useful concept in handling the capital mix problem, but it is not useful in evaluating investment alternatives."

The following terms will be used:

      V = firm market value (= $S + B$)

      S = market value of the firm's stock

      B = market value of the firm's bonds

      D = expected dividends per period

      R = expected interest on debt per period

      τ = the corporate tax rate

      X = firm pretax net cash flow (before interest payments)

      k_s = market rate on stock = D/S

      k_b = market rate on bonds = R/B

The M-M Cost of Capital

One definition of the cost of capital, used by Modigliani and Miller (M-M) and most often seen in finance textbooks, is the interest rate that discounts the after-tax cash flow the firm would have in the absence of debt (Z_u) to equal the total value of the firm (the value of equity plus debt). Denote this cost of capital as k_v^a. Thus,

$$(1) \qquad V = \frac{Z_u}{k_v^a}$$

or,

$$(2) \qquad k_v^a = \frac{Z_u}{V}$$

Since, by assumption, Z_u does not vary with the amount of debt used by the firm, it must necessarily be true that maximum firm value is achieved when k_v^a is at its minimum. We show in Appendix A that k_v^a can be expressed (with suitable assumptions) as a function of the component "costs" of debt and equity; that is

$$(3) \qquad k_v^a = k_s(S/V) + (1 - \gamma)k_b(B/V).$$

Equation (3) takes the form of a weighted average cost of capital. The $(1 - \gamma)$ term adjusts the rate paid on debt, k_b, for costs associated with financial distress or bankruptcy, restrictions embodied in debt agreements, and the tax-deductibility of interest. If debt financing involves no costs other than interest expense, $\gamma = \tau$ and, with other costs, $\gamma < \tau$ and may be negative. If $\gamma = \tau$, equation (3) becomes

$$(4) \qquad k_v^a = k_s (S/V) + (1 - \tau) k_b (B/V)$$

where $(1 - \tau) k_b$ is the "after-tax cost" of debt. Equation (4) is the standard version of the cost of capital as found in textbook discussions. Observe, however, that regardless of whether equation (3) or (4) is appropriate, in order to determine k_v^a, one must first compute V. Finding the debt ratio (B/V) that maximizes V requires the determination of V for each level of debt, then the computation of k_v^a using either equation (3) or equation (4) (as appropriate) and finally the identification of the level of debt that minimizes k_v^a and hence maximizes V. But this is clearly a circuitous and inefficient way to determine the debt level that maximizes V. It would be more direct and would necessarily involve fewer steps to simply employ the first step noted above; specifically, to estimate V for each level of debt and choose the level that maximizes V. Computation of k_v^a is completely unnecessary.

A second difficulty with k_v^a as defined in equation (2) is that Z_u is not an operational concept. If the firm uses debt, Z_u is not observable directly (even historically) unless the firm has been historically debtfree in which case Z_u is the after-tax cash flow. Z_u is difficult to estimate for firms using debt since Z_u is purely hypothetical, i.e., it is the cash flow *if* the firm had no debt. It is generally not correct to simply identify Z_u as equal to $(1-\tau)X$ where X is the pre-tax cash flow of the firm (earnings before interest and taxes under our assumptions) unless one is willing to assume that the use of debt has and will not change any of the operating or investment decisions of the firm. This assumption, while perhaps useful as an approximation in developing investment criteria, avoids basic issues concerning the interactions between investment and financing decisions. Different financing may imply different investment and therefore a different X.

In the absence of noninterest costs associated with debt financing, equation (4) is valid under perfect and imperfect capital markets. But its use is still circuitous and inefficient as explained above.

It might occur to some that if the firm identifies its financial structure in terms of book values rather than market values, minimization of a weighted average cost of capital would be computationally direct since the book values are under the control of management. Unfortunately, however, minimizing a cost of capital computed using book values weights is not ordinarily consistent with maximization of shareholder wealth or firm market value (see Brennan [5]).

The After-Tax Cost of Capital

A second definition of the cost of capital avoids some of the problems of the one expressed by (3). Define k_v as the interest rate that discounts the after-tax payments to shareholders and bondholders to the value of the firm; that is

$$(5) \qquad V = \frac{\text{Dividends Plus Interest}}{k_v} = \frac{D + R}{k_v}$$

or

$$(6) \qquad k_v = \frac{D + R}{V} .$$

Since dividends and interest payments are made exclusive of any taxes or non-interest costs associated with debt, we can express equation (6) readily as

$$(7) \qquad k_v = k_s (S/V) + k_b (B/V) .$$

Equation (7) follows since $D = k_s S$ and $R = k_b B$ by the definitions of k_s and k_b above. This definition of the cost of capital does not suffer from the lack of operationality of the M-M definition; however as is discussed in Appendix A, minimizing k_v does not necessarily result in maximizing V. Consequently this definition of the cost of capital cannot be used as a criterion for the optimal financial structure.

More Complex Situations

Use of the cost of capital as a guide to financial structure optimization was shown above, under highly idealized conditions, to be either misleading or circuitous and inefficient. This holds, *a fortiori*, in situations in which streams are not perpetuities, discount rates vary over time, flotation and other transaction costs are incurred in securing external capital, and the firm's risk class is not independent of financial structure. In such a complex situation, just as in the simple case considered earlier, an alternative to a cost of capital formulation is to deal directly with firm value (or equity value if this is the preferred goal and if equity value maximization is not consis- tent with firm value maximization) as a function of the various financial vari- ables controllable by management (e.g., the level of debt, the types of firm investments, dividend policy, etc.). In any case, a cost of capital computa- tion is at best inefficient and at worst misleading.

II. The Cost of Capital and Investment Policy

For investment purposes, the "cost of capital" is used as a guide for the selection of projects that will increase the value of the firm's shares. The cost of capital is used either as a discount rate for computing present values or for comparison with an investment's internal rate of return. However, there are problems with this use of a cost of capital rate:

(a) There may be a different cost of capital for different risk levels and for different time periods. Beranek [3] provides sufficient conditions for use of a cost of capital which may vary over time.

(b) If the rate of return an investment must earn in order to be justified differs between internal and external financing, a unique cost of capital does not exist for an investment. Furthermore, if capital not used in period t can be held for investment in period t+j, $j \geq 1$, there is interperiod dependency between investments since not using internal funds at time t may obviate the need to resort to external funds in a future period. Evaluation of individual investments becomes very difficult in this case and can only be accomplished if the future need for funds for investments is estimated (so as to be able to determine how much of current funds will eliminate the need for future external funds).

An approach for dealing with the above situation is to express firm value (or share value) as a function of the total future returns to investors discounted at a rate that reflects the riskiness of the returns (dividends, interest, etc.), where the returns are net of all costs including transaction costs associated with external financing. That is,

$$(8) \qquad\qquad S = \Sigma \; \frac{D_t}{(1+k_t)^t} = \text{share value}$$

where D_t is expected dividends (which depends on investment) and k_t is the discount rate for period t which depends on the probability distribution of D_t. An investment is evaluated in terms of its impact on (8) where that impact will depend on financing costs, personal taxes (which affect the k_t), etc.

It should be noted that even if problems (a) and (b) are considered to be negligible or worth ignoring as an approximation, a cost of capital defined as a weighted average of rates on the firm's securities (such as equations 3, 4, or 7) is subject to restrictive and highly unrealistic assumptions. We explore this issue in some depth in Appendix B.

Current usages of the term "cost of capital" with regard to investment decisions recognize the above points. However, in this context the term loses its original meaning as the return (price) required by investors on invested capital. Financial theorists have devoted much attention to the appropriate discount rate to be used to evaluate a risky investment. Calling this rate the "cost of capital" does not appear to serve any useful purpose. Other terms such as "minimum acceptable rate of return," "required rate of return," or simply the "discount rate" are more descriptive of what is actually being done. It is better to consider directly the problem of interdependencies between financing and investment than to submerge it through the concept of the cost of capital.

III. Conclusion

The concept of the cost of capital has historically served three purposes: as a guide to financing decisions, as a standard for investment decisions, and as a link between financing and investment decisions. Under highly restrictive assumptions all three purposes can be well served through its use. However, as our understanding of more realistic and complex situations increases, the concept of the cost of capital becomes either irrelevant, misleading, or both. Its current use in textbooks has some merit given the long history of the concept and its familiarity to practitioners. However, even in textbooks, to the extent that it is used as a decision criterion, it should be confined to the investment decision. The cost of capital concept offers no advantages in research and, in the long run, the term cost of capital might best be abandoned.

FINANCING DECISIONS AND THE COST OF CAPITAL

Assume perfect capital markets and perpetuities. Assume that there may
be noninterest costs of debt financing signified by F. These costs may arise
due to financial distress where the costs of financial distress include accounting and legal costs and increased operating costs or lost revenues due to
creditor takeover of the firm in the event of bankruptcy. Noninterest costs
F also include any costs imposed on the firm by creditors due to restrictions
in loan agreements, collateral, transaction costs, etc.[3] Define $Z = X -
\tau(X-R-F) - F$ = expected after-tax returns of the firm (going to shareholders
and bondholders). We can separate Z into parts where

$$(A.1) \qquad\qquad Z = (1-\tau)X + g(B) = Z_u + g(B)$$

and where

$$(A.2) \qquad\qquad g(B) = \tau R - (1-\tau)F.$$

All effects on Z of varying leverage (B) are included in $g(B)$; Z_u is the part
of Z that is independent of leverage. In this perpetuity model we assume no
tax depreciation; therefore X is both pre-tax cash flow and taxable income for
the firm if it has no debt.

Using the after-tax definition of the cost of capital in (6), k_v, it follows that $V = Z/k_v$, and therefore

$$(A.3) \qquad\qquad k_v = Z/V = [Z_u + g(B)]/V.$$

Several situations involving (A.3) can be distinguished:

(i) *The maximum value of V involves $0 < B < V$ (a firm with some debt and
some equity)*: To see that V is not maximized when k_v is minimized, note that
at a maximum for V, $dV/dB = 0$, and at a minimum for k_v, $dk_v/dB = 0$. Therefore, with $V = Z/k_v$, at a maximum V:

$$(A.4) \qquad\qquad \frac{dV}{dB} = \frac{k_v \frac{dZ}{dB} - Z \frac{dk_v}{dB}}{k_v^2} = 0$$

and for $dk_v/dB = 0$ to be simultaneously satisfied, it follows that by substituting $dk_v/dB = 0$ into (A.4) and solving for (dZ/dB) using (A.1) and (A.2),

(A.5)
$$\frac{dV}{dB} = \frac{dZ/dB}{k_v} = \frac{\tau dR/dB - (1-\tau)\ dF/dB}{k_v}$$

which implies for a finite k_v that

(A.6)
$$\tau(dR/dB\ ) = (1-\tau)(dF/dB).$$

Equation (A.6) must hold (with perfect or imperfect capital markets) if the same level of B maximizes V and simultaneously minimizes k_v; satisfaction of this condition is extremely unlikely. If F = 0 (no noninterest costs of debt) *and* capital markets are perfect (no government constraints on trading and no trading costs), then by the M-M proposition the maximum V is at V = B (all debt firm); in this case of a corner solution, minimizing k_v does not maximize V. If F = 0 with *imperfect capital markets*, the left-hand side of (A.6) must equal zero at maximum V; this will occur only if interest is not tax-deductible at that point and this is contrary to assumptions that are consistent with existing tax laws.

(ii) *The maximum value of V involves B = 0 or B = V:* Two situations are of interest:

    (a) Perfect capital markets with F = 0: This is the familiar M-M case. Maximum firm value occurs if the firm is all debt, assuming that all interest is tax-deductible. It has been shown elsewhere that in this case k_v is minimized for a B < V.[4]

    (b) Perfect capital markets with F $\neq$ 0 or imperfect capital markets (with $F \gtrless 0$). With Z in the numerator of (A.3) varying with B, the standard assumptions regarding perfect or imperfect markets are insufficient to insure that the same level of B will maximize V and minimize k_v. It is a straightforward exercise to produce examples for which k_v is minimized at a 0 < B < V even though V is maximized at B = 0 or B = V.

The M-M Cost of Capital

Equation (A.3) provides the bridge between the after-tax cost of capital (k_v) and the M-M cost of capital (k_v^a) as defined in equation (2).

(2)
$$k_v^a = Z_u/V$$

---

[4] See Arditti [2] and Haley and Schall [6, Chap. 12].

(A.3)
$$k_v = [Z_u + g(B)]/V$$

(A.7)
$$k_v^a = k_v - g(B)/V$$

Furthermore, by the definition of g(B), equation (A.2),

$$k_v^a = k_v - [\tau R - (1-\tau)F]/V$$

$$= k_v - \tau R/V + (1-\tau)F/V$$

but

$$R = k_b B, \text{ so}$$

(A.8)
$$k_v^a = k_v - \tau k_b(B/V) + (1-\tau)F/V.$$

If we assume there are no noninterest costs of debt (F = 0), and substitute for k_v an average of the rates on the firm's securities, we obtain the conventional average cost of capital,

$$k_v^a = k_s(S/V) + k_b(B/V) - \tau k_b(B/V)$$

(A.9)

$$= k_s(S/V) + (1-\tau)k_b(B/V)$$

We see here the critical nature of the assumption that F = 0. In the absence of this condition, equation (A.9) is not a valid "cost of capital" for use in capital structure decisions, nor, is it a valid criterion for investment decisions. This is true regardless of whether capital markets are perfect or imperfect, since F includes real costs imposed on the firm due to financial distress or debt transactions.

APPENDIX B

INVESTMENT DECISIONS AND THE COST OF CAPITAL

There continues to be some debate as to the "correct" specification of the minimum required rate of return for investment decisions.[5] Here we show the necessary conditions for a single-valued rate to be consistent with shareholder wealth maximization. Beranek [3] has provided sufficient conditions for a set of rates (k_t) which are less restrictive than those derived here. However, a single-valued rate is still of considerable interest to academics, especially teaching faculty, and to practitioners. We find that the conditions required for k_v^a, the conventional cost of capital as defined in equations 4 and A.9, to be an appropriate standard for investment decisions are quite unrealistic. Therefore, more complex criteria are desirable in most cases.

The appendix is divided into three sections. Section B.I provides the basic criterion for investment decisions from which cost of capital formulations are normally derived. Our purpose in this section is to briefly define the setting of the problem. The major findings of Sections B.II and B.III have not previously appeared in the literature. Section B.II establishes the conditions for k_v^a to be the appropriate rate for discounting the firm's future cash flows. We also comment briefly on the alternative specification for the cost of capital, k_v, and note that one of the conditions validating k_v^a does not apply to k_v. Therefore k_v can be applied under less restrictive assumptions than can k_v^a. The development in B.II also addresses the issue of a constant cost of capital over time; however, no explicit analysis of risk is made. In Section B.III we use the single-period mean-variance model of capital market equilibrium to develop a complete condition for the use of k_v^a in terms of fundamental economic variables. Throughout we focus on the structure of the arguments and results. Detailed algebraic proofs will be supplied on request.

B.1 The Basic Criterion

This section examines the question of when firm value maximization (the goal applying to a weighted average cost of capital formulation) is consistent with share value maximization as a goal of investment policy.[6] Given an independent investment opportunity requiring initial outlay I_0 at time 0, we wish

---

[5] A recent paper by Nantell and Carlson [13] reviews several of the issues.

[6] See Haley and Schall [6, Chap. 17] for a more extensive discussion and references to the literature in this area.

to know whether the investment will benefit current (time 0) stockholders. The market values of the firm's outstanding common stock and bonds if the investment is not undertaken ("pre-investment") are $\hat{S}_0^o$ and $\hat{B}_0^o$ respectively. The pre-investment value of all firm securities is V_0,

(B.1)
$$\hat{V}_0 = \hat{S}_0^o + \hat{B}_0^o.$$

The superscript "o" refers to the "old" securities of the firm; for example, $\hat{S}_0^o$ does not include any stock sold to finance I_0. The "^" is used to indicate the pre-investment values. Assume for simplicity that the investment outlay, I_0, is financed entirely by issuing new stock S_0^N and bonds B_0^N such that[7]

(B.2)
$$I_0 = S_0^N + B_0^N$$

The value of the firm if the investment is adopted will be

(B.3)
$$V_0 = S_0^o + B_0^o + S_0^N + B_0^N$$

where S_0^o and B_0^o are the post-investment values of the old shares and bonds.

Using (B.2) and (B.3) it follows that

(B.4)
$$V_0 = S_0^o + B_0^o + I_0 \ .$$

In order for the original stockholders to be benefited by the investment, it is necessary that their stock increase in value since, by assumption, no changes in current (t = 0) dividends have occurred because of the investment (since the investment is entirely externally financed). Thus, the basic criterion for investment at time 0 is

(B.5)
$$S_0^o - \hat{S}_0^o > 0.$$

Although it is entirely possible and may be desirable to evaluate the change in share values from investment decisions directly, conventional cost-of-capital approaches are based on a somewhat different criterion, namely

(B.6)
$$V_0 - \hat{V}_0 > I_0.$$

_____

[7] The conclusions here also hold with retained earnings financing although the analysis is slightly more complicated, even assuming no personal taxes or transaction costs.

To determine the conditions under which (B.6) is consistent with (B.5), note that from (B.1) and (B.4) we can solve for $\hat{S}_0^o$ and S_0^o and substitute the results in (B.5):

$$(V_0 - B_0^o - I_0) - (\hat{V}_0 - \hat{B}_0^o) > 0$$

where the above can also be expressed as:

(B.7)
$$V_0 - \hat{V}_0 > I_0 + (B_0^o - \hat{B}_0^o).$$

Since (B.7) is equivalent to (B.5), for criterion (B.6) to be consistent with (B.7) (and therefore with (B.5)), it is necessary in general that the value of outstanding bonds not change as a result of undertaking the investment, i.e., in (B.7)

(B.8)
$$B_0^o - \hat{B}_0^o = 0.$$

If (and generally only if) condition (B.8) holds will investment decisions based on total value maximization ((B.6)) result in optimal decisions from the viewpoint of the stockholder ((B.5)). Since average cost of capital formulations are based on the equivalence of (B.5) and (B.6), we assume that (B.8) does hold in Section B.II below.

The interesting thing about condition (B.8) is the possibility that it not hold. There may be investment-cum-financing plans which benefit current bondholders, but not current stockholders, yet which would be indicated as desirable by capital budgeting procedures based on (B.6). This might happen, if the investment were a low-risk and low-return type financed largely with new common stock. Such decisions would reduce the risk of default on the debt at the expense of a reduction in the expected income of the original stockholders. The value of the outstanding bonds could well increase by a greater amount than the loss in value of the stock so that the total value of the firm would increase. Alternatively some options might well be rejected using (B.6) which are desirable according to (B.5). This is likely to be a time of high risk-return projects. The current bondholders would share the risk but not the returns.

B.II Defining the Cost of Capital

Earlier we examined two alternative definitions of the cost of capital, k_v and k_v^a. Here we focus on the conditions necessary for k_v^a to be the proper rate for discounting all future firm cash flows. Later, we comment briefly on the alternative definition, k_v.

We wish to determine the conditions under which k_v^a as defined in Equations

(4) and (A.9) capitalizes the stream $X_t(1-\tau) - I_t$ to produce the value of the firm at $t = 0$, V_0. That is, k_v^a should be that value of k such that

(B.9)
$$V_0 = \sum_{t=1}^{\infty} \frac{X_t(1-\tau) - I_t}{(1+k)^t}$$

where

(B.10)
$$k = k_v^a \equiv k_s(S_0/V_0) + (1-\tau)k_b(B_0/V_0).$$

We are capitalizing $X_t(1-\tau) - I_t$ because this is the cash flow paid to security holders of the firm in the absence of debt. As discussed in Appendix A, k_v^a is based on the capitalization of this cash flow. Here we are including future investment outlays, I_t, but assuming no tax depreciation deduction for simplicity. Any flotation costs or underpricing on future securities issues in period t are assumed either to be zero or, depending on their tax deductibility, to be included in I_t (if not tax-deductible) or deducted from X_t (if tax-deductible). The rates k_s and k_b, are defined as the (current) market discount rates for stocks and bonds, respectively, and are assumed constant over time. That is,

(B.11a)
$$S_0 = \sum_{t=1}^{\infty} \frac{D_t^o}{(1+k_s)^t}$$

(B.11b)
$$B_0 = \sum_{t=1}^{T} \frac{R_t^o}{(1+k_b)^t} + \frac{B_T^o}{(1+k_b)^t}.$$

The superscripts o indicate payment made to those securities outstanding at time 0 (i.e., not including new securities issued at time 0). The term B_T^o is included to provide for the possibility of retiring the bonds at time T.

Proposition I. Relations (B.9) and (B.10) are satisfied if (a), (b), and (c) below all hold:

(a) k_s, k_b and τ are expected to remain constant for all t,

(b) $B_t/V_t = B_0/V_0$ for all t, and

(c) $B_{t+1}^t + P_{t+1}^t = B$ for all t,

where B_t and V_t are the expected (as of time 0) time t bond and firm values; B_{t+1}^t is the expected t+1 market value of all bonds outstanding at time t (not including any new bonds issued at time t+1); and P_{t+1}^t are the expected principal payments at t+1 on bonds outstanding at time t.

Condition (b) is the well-known requirement that the ratio of debt to total value be a constant over time. Condition (c) states that the market value of bonds outstanding at time t equals the market value plus principal payments on the bonds at time t+1. This condition implies that bondholders in aggregate at any time t are expected to have no capital gains or losses on their bonds in the coming period. It is interesting that (a) and (b) alone are not in general sufficient for $k = k_v^a$; (c) must also hold.

We shall develop the proof of Proposition I by first examining a single period. The single period results generalize easily to n periods.

Define rate k_t such that the expected value of the firm at time t, V_t, is

$$\text{(B.12)} \qquad V_t = \frac{(1-\tau)X_{t+1} - I_{t+1}}{(1+k_t)} + \frac{V_{t+1}}{(1+k_t)}$$

or

$$\text{(B.13)} \qquad k_t \equiv \frac{(1-\tau)X_{t+1} - I_{t+1}}{V_t} + \frac{V_{t+1}}{V_t} - 1.$$

By beginning at t = 0 with (B.12) and successively substituting for V_1, V_2, etc., using (B.13), it follows that

$$\text{(B.14)} \qquad V_0 = \sum_{t=1}^{\infty} \frac{X_t(1-\tau) - I_t}{\prod_{j=1}^{t}(1+k_j)}$$

For (B.9), (B.10), and (B.14), it is sufficient that $k_t = k_v^a$ in (B.10), all t. We now examine the conditions under which $k_t = k_v^a$.

The expected rate of return for period t+1 on stock outstanding at time t, $k_{s,t}$ is

$$\text{(B.15)} \qquad k_{s,t} = \frac{D_{t+1}^t + S_{t+1}^t}{S_t} - 1$$

where D_{t+1}^t is the expected dividend paid on time t shares and S_{t+1}^t is the expected value of time t shares at time t+1. Similarly, the expected rate of return on time t bonds, $k_{b,t}$ is

$$\text{(B.16)} \qquad k_{b,t} = \frac{R_{t+1}^t + B_{t+1}^t + P_{t+1}^t}{B_t} - 1$$

where R_{t+1}^t is the expected interest payment at time t+1 to bonds outstanding at time t, B_{t+1}^t is the expected time t+1 market value of time t bonds after any principal payments P_{t+1}^t on these bonds.

We first must show that, given the existence of corporate income taxes and the tax-deductibility of interest payments (R),

(B.17) $$k_t = k_{s,t}(S_t/V_t) + (1-\tau)k_{b,t}(B_t/V_t)$$

if and only if $B_{t+1}^t + P_{t+1}^t = B_t$. For brevity only the general structure of the proof is provided here.

First, note that the dividends in period t+1 paid to t stockholders will be

(B.18) $$D_{t+1}^t = (1-\tau)(X_{t+1}-R_{t+1}) - I_{t+1} + S_{t+1}^N + B_{t+1}^N - P_{t+1}^t \ .$$

This follows from the cash flow relationships. The term $(1-\tau)(X_{t+1}-R_{t+1})$ is the after-tax operating cash flow available for dividends or investment, given the absence of tax depreciation (only for simplicity we assume depreciation to be zero). S_{t+1}^N and B_{t+1}^N are the values of any new stocks and bonds issued at time 1. Any flotation costs or underpricing are assumed to be included in I_{t+1} or deducted from X_{t+1} depending on their tax-deductibility.

At this point we use equations (B.15) and (B.16) to solve for D_{t+1}^t and R_{t+1}^t in terms of the rates and security values. Equation (B.18) is rearranged to express $X_{t+1}(1-\tau) - I_{t+1}$ in terms of the other variables. Making the appropriate substitutions into (B.13) we arrive at the following relationship:

(B.19)
$$k_t = k_{s,t}(S_t/V_t) + (1-\tau)k_{b,t}(B_t/V_t) + \frac{V_{t+1}}{V_t}$$
$$- \frac{\tau(B_t-B_{t+1}^t-P_{t+1}^t) + (S_{t+1}^t+B_{t+1}^t+S_{t+1}^N+B_{t+1}^N)}{V_t} \ .$$

By our definitions of S_{t+1}^t, B_{t+1}^t, S_{t+1}^N, and B_{t+1}^N, it must be true that

(B.20) $$S_{t+1}^t + B_{t+1}^t + S_{t+1}^N + B_{t+1}^N = V_{t+1} \ .$$

Therefore, substituting (B.20) into the numerator of the last expression in (B.19), it follows that

(B.21) $$k_t = k_{s,t}(S_t/V_t) + (1-\tau)k_{b,t}(B_t/V_t) + \tau(B_t-B_{t+1}^t-P_{t+1}^t)/V_t \ .$$

Thus,

(B.22)
$$k_t = k_{s,t}(S_t/V_t) + (1-\tau)k_{b,t}(B_t/V_t) + \tau(B_t-B_{t+1}^t-P_t)/V_t$$
$$= k_{s,0}(S_0/V_0) + (1-\tau)k_{b,0}(B_0/V_0) = k_v^a, \text{ all } t$$

if (a), (b), and (c) of Proposition I hold. Note that no subset of conditions (a), (b), and (c) is sufficient for (B.22). The interpretation of condition (c) is quite simple if (B.16) is examined. For $k_{b,t}$ (the expected rate of return on the bonds from time t to time t+1) to be used in the average cost of capital on a tax-adjusted basis (multipled by $(1-\tau)$), there must not be any expected capital gains or losses on those bonds.[8] That is, all the returns on the bonds must be in the form of tax-deductible (by the firm) payments R. There are many circumstances under which this will be true. For example:

(1) The bonds are perpetual *and* no changes in their risk or in market interest rates are expected; hence no changes in market values are expected.

(2) The bonds are currently selling at par (principal value) *and* no changes in their risk or in market interest rates are anticipated from t to t+1 *and* any principal payments scheduled are considered certain to be paid.

(3) The bonds mature at time t+1, principal and interest are certain, and the coupon rate equals the riskless rate of interest for the period from t to t+1.

Note that merely assuming the bonds to be "riskless" in the sense of no uncertainty in the promised stream of principal and interest payments is not sufficient. It is necessary that there be no expected changes in market value due to changes in market interest rates as well, unless all the bonds will be retired at time t+1. In the case of complete retirement of riskless bonds, the bonds must be selling at par at time t.

The question arises as to what happens if one or more of conditions (a), (b), and (c) do not hold. First, observe that for any *particular stream* of expected cash flows $[X_t(1-\tau) - I_t]$ it is possible (although very unlikely) that (B.9) and (B.10) (using k_v^a for k in (B.9)) produces the same V_0 as does (B.14) even though the true k_t do not all equal k_v^a, i.e., the k_t can vary around k_v^a (some lower and some higher than k_v^a). But for this to occur the terms in (B.19) must vary in just the proper fashion (and what is proper will depend on the $[X_t(1-\tau) - I_t]$). If conditions (a) and (b) hold but (c) does not, the last term in (B.21) must fluctuate between positive and negative values in such a way that k_v^a could have been used instead for all t (a very improbable situation).

---

[8]This condition applies only in aggregate; a particular bond issue outstanding at time t might be expected to have a capital gain; however, there must be an equal capital loss expected on another bond issue. The sum of all expected gains and losses for bonds included in B_t must equal zero for all t.

If, on the other hand, we want (B.9) and (B.10) to produce the same post investment V_0 as does correct formula (B.14), and if this is to hold *regardless of the time pattern of a new investment's cash flows*, then $k_t = k_v^a$, all t [(B.22)] must hold. This imposes an even more stringent restriction on the terms comprising k_t in (B.22). Although it is possible that (a), (b), and (c) do not hold, precise offsetting effects *in each period* would have to apply, an extremely unlikely occurrence.

Before proceeding to Section B.III, which examines the economic conditions justifying assumptions (a) and (b) of Proposition I, we briefly review the comparable results for the alternative cost of capital definition.

$$\text{(B.23)} \qquad\qquad k_v = k_s (S/V) + k_b (B/V).$$

This cost of capital can be shown by similar arguments to be the rate k that discounts the net cash flow paid by the firm to its security holders to arrive at the total value of the firm:

$$
\begin{aligned}
V_0 &= \sum_{t=1}^{\infty} \frac{(1-\tau)(X_t - R_t) + R_t - I_t}{(1+k)^t} \\
&= \sum_{t=1}^{\infty} \frac{(1-\tau)X_t - I_t + \tau R_t}{(1+k)^t}.
\end{aligned}
$$

(B.24)

It is easily shown that an advantage of k_v over k_v^a is that condition (c), the absence of capital gains or losses on bonds, is not necessary for k_v (conditions (a) and (b) are sufficient).[9] This is so because the tax deductibility feature of debt interest is not incorporated into an adjusted rate of debt $((1-\tau)k_b)$, but rather is handled directly. The drawback to this definition in evaluating investment opportunities is that the tax impact of debt financing resulting from the adoption of the opportunity must be included in the cash flow from the investment. Whether the modest increase in complexity in analyzing investment using k_v is outweighed by the more stringent theoretical requirements of k_v^a must be assessed by the reader. Of course both k_v and k_v^a suffer from conditions (a) and (b) which we now assess via the capital asset pricing model.

---

[9] To prove this, use equations (B.21) and (B.22) instead of (B.10) and (B.9) and follow the arguments of Proposition I. Equation (B.22) becomes

$$
\begin{aligned}
k_t &= k_{s,t}(S_t/V_t) + k_{b,t}(B_t/V_t) \\
&= k_{s,0}(S_0/V_0) + k_{b,0}(B_0/V_0) = k_v
\end{aligned}
$$

(i)

where term $\tau(B_t - B_{t+1}^t - P_{t+1}^t)$ in equations (B.19) and (B.22) no longer appears. Conditions (a) and (b) of Proposition I are sufficient to produce (i).

B.III Risk and the Average Cost of Capital

Given the setting of the single period capital asset pricing model, we wish to determine necessary and sufficient conditions for the use of a weighted average cost of capital in making optimal investment decisions from the viewpoint of the firm's existing (pre-investment) stockholders. The assumptions and application of this model to corporate financial decisions are developed in [6, Chap. 7 and 8]. Here, for ease of analysis, we assume that investment outlays are financed externally through issues of new stocks and bonds. Our conditions are unaffected by this assumption as dividend policy is irrelevant under the general assumptions of the model.

First, define "net present value," NPV, as

$$(B.25) \quad NPV = \frac{\Delta X_1 (1-\tau)}{1 + k} - I_0 \qquad k \equiv \hat{k}_s (\hat{S}_0 / \hat{V}_0) + (1-\tau)\hat{k}_b (\hat{B}_0 / \hat{V}_0)$$

where ΔX_1 is the incremental pre-tax cash flow at time 1 resulting from an investment outlay of I_0 at time 0 and the other variables are as defined earlier. Note here that we are explicitly defining k in terms of the pre-investment variables as denoted by the "$\hat{\ }$".

Proposition II

Given that the firm will liquidate one period from the present at time 1, investment selection based on NPV as defined in (B.25) will be consistent with shareholder wealth maximization, if and only if, the following conditions hold

$$(B.26) \qquad\qquad A + B - C - D = 0$$

where

$$A = \lambda(\text{Cov } [\hat{\tilde{X}}_1 / \bar{\hat{X}}_1, \tilde{r}_m] - \text{Cov } [\Delta\tilde{X}_1 / \Delta\bar{X}_1, \tilde{r}_m])$$

$$B = \tau \frac{\bar{R}_1^N - \lambda \text{ Cov } [\tilde{R}_1^N, \tilde{r}_m]}{\Delta\bar{X}_1 (1-\tau)} - \frac{\bar{\hat{R}}_1 - \lambda \text{ Cov } [\hat{\tilde{R}}_1, \tilde{r}_m]}{\bar{\hat{X}}_1 (1-\tau)}$$

$$C = \frac{\Delta\bar{R}_1^0 (1-\tau) + \Delta\bar{P}_1^0 - \lambda \text{ Cov } [\Delta\tilde{R}_1^0 (1-\tau) + \Delta\tilde{P}_1^0, \tilde{r}_m]}{}$$

$$D = \tau(\bar{P}_1 - \hat{B}_0) \left\{ \frac{1 - \lambda \text{ Cov } [\Delta\tilde{X}_1 / \Delta\bar{X}_1, \tilde{r}_m]}{(1-\tau)\bar{\hat{X}}_1} + \tau \frac{\bar{R}_1^N - \lambda \text{ Cov } [\tilde{R}_1^N, \tilde{r}_m]}{\bar{\hat{X}}_1 \bar{\hat{X}}_1 (1-\tau)^2} - \frac{C}{\hat{X}_1} \right\}.$$

The variables in the expressions are defined as:

λ: The slope of the security market line

Cov[ ]: Covariance between the variables in brackets

r_m: The rate of return on the market portfolio

215

$\hat{X}_1$: The liquidating pre-tax cash flow of the firm at time 1 if the investment is not made

ΔX_1: The Pre-tax incremental cash flow to the firm at time 1 resulting from the investment

R_1^N: The tax-deductible (interest) payments made at time 1 to new bonds issued at time 0

$\hat{R}$: The tax-deductible (interest) payments made at time 1 to bonds outstanding (pre-investment) at time 0, if investment is not made

$\hat{P}_1$: The non-tax deductible (principal) payments made to old bonds at time 1 if investment is not made

ΔR_1^0: The change in interest payments to old bonds at time 1 resulting from investment, $\Delta R_1^0 = R_1^0 - \hat{R}_1$

ΔP_1^0: The change in principal payments at time 1 to old bonds as a result of the investment $\Delta P_1^0 = P_1^0 - \hat{P}_1$

$\sim$: Indicates a random variable

$-$: Indicates the expected value of the random variable.

First, we note that condition (B.26) may hold even if the individual components A - D are nonzero. However, generally it will be necessary and certainly sufficient that each term will be zero since identical, offsetting values are highly unlikely.

Term A compares the risk of the pre-investment, pre-tax cash flow $\hat{X}_1$ with the risk of the investment's cash flow ΔX_1. For this term to be zero, the risks of the two cash flows must be the same. We measure risk by the "adjusted" covariance of the cash flow with the return on the market portfolio. The cash flows are adjusted for scale by dividing by their expected values. Therefore term A indicates, as is generally known, that an average cost of capital based on pre-investment security values and rates requires an assumption that the risk of the investment is the same as the pre-investment cash flow (before interest and taxes) of the firm.

Term B compares a scaled certainty equivalent of the interest payments R_1^N on new bonds issued by the firm with the certainty equivalent of the pre-investment interest payments $\hat{R}_1$ to be paid to the bonds outstanding prior to the issue of the new bonds. This term implies that the investment is financed with bonds which are comparable to the pre-investment bonds of the firm. The basic sense of this term is that the value of the tax advantage from issuing new bonds relative to investment income is the same as for the pre-investment bonds. Note that the term is zero, if the tax-rate τ is zero.

Term C involves the changes in interest payment ΔR_1^0 and principal payments

ΔP_1^0 at time 1 resulting from the investment and its associated financing. This term, therefore, has to do with potential gains or losses imposed on the pre-investment bondholders by reason of the firm's decisions. The issues here were discussed in Section B.I above.

Term D is the product of $\tau(\bar{P}_1 - \hat{B}_0)$ with a variety of components resulting from the investment and its financing. The net value of the components within the braces will generally be nonzero. To guarantee that term D is zero, the expected pre-investment principal payment $\bar{P}_1$ must equal the pre-investment market value of the firm's bonds. Again this is a sufficient condition and likely to be necessary to guarantee a zero value for term D. This requirement is identical to condition (c) of Proposition I. Here again, in the absence of corporate taxes (or tax-deductibility of interest), this term will be zero.

The proof of Proposition II is algebraically complicated and does not involve any special assumptions beyond those associated with the capital asset pricing model itself. We do assume that undertaking the investment does not affect equilibrium conditions in the capital markets. The proof will be provided on request.

A comparable condition can be developed for k_v which differs from (B.24) in that, as for Proposition I, term D does not enter. This is the only significant difference between the two definitions of the cost of capital.

A final point of interest gleaned from (B.26) is that, in a single period world of perfect markets, it does not appear necessary or sufficient to maintain a constant ratio of debt to value in order to apply an average cost of capital. In the absence of corporate taxes ($\tau = 0$), only terms A and C remain. Term A concerns only the risk of the investment's cash flows and is independent of financing. Term C concerns the impact of the investment and its financing on the old bonds. For term C to be zero old bonds must neither gain nor lose in value as a result of the investment-financing. Maintenance of a constant ratio of debt to value is neither necessary nor sufficient for term C to be zero since for any given debt-value ratio, the amount of new bonds issued can be adjusted to compensate for any given loss on the old bonds and for any gains up to the point where no new bonds could be issued at all. Of course, this amounts to Proposition I of Modigliani and Miller [10].

With corporate income taxes, terms B and D may also be nonzero. We have discussed term D, so we need only consider B. Term B concerns the tax-deductible (interest) payments to the old and the new bonds. Although the value of old and new bonds is likely to be affected by the division between tax-deductible and non-tax-deductible payments (because those payments which are tax-deductible for the firm are apt to be taxable income to the bondholders),

without additional assumptions there is no reason why the assumption of a constant debt-value ratio would imply any particular division between tax-
deductible and non-tax-deductible returns to each set of bonds. Thus the debt-
value ratio has no special significance under the assumptions of the single-
period capital asset pricing model and condition (b) of our Proposition I does
not apply here.

SELECTED REFERENCES

[1] Ang, James. "Weighted Average versus True Cost of Capital." *Financial Management* (Autumn 1973), pp. 56-60.

[2] Arditti, Fred D. "The Weighted Average Cost of Capital: Some Questions on its Definition, Interpretation and Use." *Journal of Finance* (September 1973), pp. 1001-1008.

[3] Beranek, William. "Some New Capital Budgeting Theorems." *Journal of Financial and Quantitative Analysis* (December 1978).

[4] Bierman, Harold, and Seymour Smidt. *The Capital Budgeting Decision.* New York: Macmillan, 4th ed. (1976).

[5] Brennan, Michael. "A New Look at the Weighted Average Cost of Capital." *Journal of Business Finance,* Vol. 5, No. 1 (1973), pp. 24-30.

[6] Haley, Charles W., and Lawrence D. Schall. *The Theory of Financial Decisions,* 2nd ed. New York: McGraw-Hill (1979).

[7] Kraus, Alan. "The Bond Refunding Decision in an Efficient Market." *Journal of Financial and Quantitative Analysis,* Vol. 8 (December 1973).

[8] Litzenberger, Robert H., and Alan P. Budd. "Corporate Investment Criteria and the Valuation of Risk Assets." *Journal of Financial and Quantitative Analysis,* Vol. 4 (December 1970), pp. 395-419.

[9] Litzenberger, Robert H., and David P. Rutenberg. "Size and Timing of Corporate Bond Flotations." *Journal of Financial and Quantitative Analysis,* Vol. 7 (January 1972), pp. 1343-1360.

[10] Modigliani, France, and Merton Miller. "The Cost of Capital, Corporation Finance, and the Theory of Investment." *American Economic Review* (June 1958).

[11] _____. "Corporation Income Taxes and the Cost of Capital: A Correction." *American Economic Review* (June 1963).

[12] Myers, Stewart C. "Interactions of Corporate Financing and Investment Decisions--Implications for Capital Budgeting." *Journal of Finance* (March 1973), pp. 1-26.

[13] Nantell, T. J., and C. R. Carlson. "The Cost of Capital as a Weighted Average." *Journal of Finance,* Vol. 30 (December 1975), pp. 1343-1355.

[14] Pye, Gordon. "Preferential Tax Treatment of Capital Gains, Optimal Dividend Policy, and Capital Budgeting." *Quarterly Journal of Economics* (July 1972).

[15] Robichek, A. A., and Stewart C. Myers. "Problems in the Theory of Optimal Capital Structure." *Journal of Financial and Quantitative Analysis,* Vol. 1 (June 1966), pp. 1-35.

[16] Solomon, Ezra. *The Theory of Financial Management.* New York: Columbia University Press (1963).

[17] Stapleton, Richard C. "Portfolio Analysis, Stock Valuation and Capital Budgeting Decision Rules for Risky Projects." *Journal of Finance,* Vol. 26

(March 1971), pp. 95-117.

[18] _____. "Taxes, the Cost of Capital and the Theory of Investment." *The Economic Journal* (December 1972).

[19] Weston, J. Fred, and Eugene F. Brigham. *Managerial Finance,* 6th ed. Hinsdale, Ill.: Dryden Press (1978).

In Defense of the Weighted Average Cost of Capital

Glenn V. Henderson, Jr.

Glenn V. Henderson, Jr., is Associate Professor of Finance at Louisiana Tech University, where he holds the Burton R. Risinger Faculty Chair.

■ Despite the availability of more elegant alternatives, protestations of the measure's *ad hoc* nature, and suggestions as to biases inherent in its calculation, the weighted average method of calculating the cost of capital is the one most often found in finance texts [12, pp. 175–189; 21, pp. 209–213; 22, pp. 609–611]. From a pedagogical perspective, this is quite understandable. The calculation *per se* is quite simple. Given the normal disclaimers as to difficulty of measuring the cost of the components (primarily equity), the interpretation is also straightforward. That is, the weighted average cost of capital is the rate that must be earned by a corporation to satisfy the return expectations of its investors.

In addition to its pedagogical value, the measure is also defensible pragmatically. Even if the weighted average cost of capital is not the best possible measure, it may well be the best measure possible. However, the weighted average needs little, if any, defense as a pragmatic choice. Its virtually universal use in textbooks, its use in utility rate making, and its longevity attest to its acceptance on that basis. This paper proposes to provide a more rigorous defense.

The purposes of this paper are: 1) to derive a generalized weighted average cost of capital (WACC) that reduces, as a special case, to the so-called classical WACC, and 2) to show that the generalized WACC is consistent with equity cost of capital expressions that emerge from the Modigliani and Miller (MM) treatment as well as from the CAPM. In particular, the cost of capital, K_0, is defined as the after-tax required rate of return on an investment which renders the increase in firm value exactly equal to the investment outlay. I will show that K_0 can be expressed in terms of 1) a generalized WACC, 2) the MM leverage-adjusted cost of equity formulation, and 3) the expected rate of return given by the security-market line (SML) from the standard CAPM treatments. Since each of these forms is equal to K_0, they are equal to each other and hence equivalent.

Theoretical Foundation

As normally presented, the WACC formulation is not derived but presented on an *ad hoc* basis as simply a weighted average calculation. In the procedure, the cost of each component (debt, common equity, and possibly preferred) is multiplied by the percentage of the long-term financing normally derived from each component source. The weighted costs are then summed to get an average, or overall, cost of capital.

Simply because the WACC is presented without rigorous development does not mean such a derivation does not exist. The development can be accomplished in a manner analogous to the procedure used by MM [16].

First, a valuation model for the firm must be specified. This value can then be optimized subject to a minimum valuation change requirement.

Assuming depreciation allowances would be reinvested to maintain productive capacity makes the cash flow of an unlevered firm equal to its after-tax earnings, $X(1-t)$, where X is earnings before interest and taxes, and t is the corporate tax rate — assumed constant.

If a firm were leveraged by selling D dollars worth of debt at a rate r, the total cash flows to investors would be

$$(X-rD)(1-t) + rD. \qquad (1)$$

Assuming that the market capitalizes equity flows such as $[(X-rD)(1-t)]$ by a cost of equity, K, and debt-related flows such as rD by the market rate r, the value of the firm (V) can be specified. Assuming that $[(X-rD)(1-t)]$ and rD are both perpetual streams simplifies the matter. (The result holds for finite-lived firms, also.) If the flows are perpetual, the value of the firm is

$$V = \frac{(X-rD)(1-t)}{K} + \frac{rD}{r}. \qquad (2)$$

From this point on, the derivation is identical to the MM derivation [16] (see Appendix A):

$$K_o = K\frac{\partial S}{\partial I} + r(1-t)\frac{\partial D}{\partial I} + \frac{\partial K}{\partial I}S + \frac{\partial r}{\partial I}(1-t)D. \qquad (3)$$

This then is the generalized form of the WACC formulation. As a minimum, new investments of the firm must earn a weighted average of the cost of equity (K) and the after-tax cost of debt $(r(1-t))$. In addition, if the firm's new investment changes the cost of equity, investments must earn an amount (plus or minus) sufficient to offset that effect $(\partial K/\partial I \cdot S)$. The same is true for investments that alter debt costs. That is the effect of the last term.

In this generalized form, WACC can handle investments of other than average riskiness, contrary to what is sometimes suggested [18, p. 174]. The weakness of the WACC is not the basic theory or the method of calculation. The problem is one of completeness. There was originally no method of specifying the determinants of K. This is the void filled by the capital asset pricing model (CAPM) and its associated security market line. Assuming the CAPM is valid, the derived cost of capital is equivalent to the WACC. Regardless of the accuracy of the CAPM, Equation (3) remains valid.

Generally, textbooks qualify their explanation as being appropriate only for investments of average riskiness [12, p. 189; 21, p. 213]. Such investments would not alter the firm's riskiness; therefore, $\partial K/\partial I$ and $\partial r/\partial I$ are zero, and the last two terms vanish. What is left is the traditional WACC as normally presented in beginning texts:

$$K_o = K\frac{\partial S}{\partial I} + r(1-t)\frac{\partial D}{\partial I}. \qquad (4)$$

Of course, the normal *caveats* about measurement problems are still appropriate, but these reservations apply to all cost of capital calculations.

One of the major unresolved measurement problems is how to determine the weights. It appears that the majority favors the use of market value weights based on the arguments of MM [16] and their supporters. However, there are proponents of book value weighting [3, 4, 5]. Some theorists argue that all historical weights, market or book, are irrelevant, and that the cost of capital determination should use the proportions associated with the financing of new investments [13, 19]. There appears to be a recent trend in textbooks to discuss a variety of alternatives, allowing users of the texts some flexibility in the way they present the cost of capital concept [7, 14]. However, these same texts generally acknowledge the theoretical superiority of market value weights [7, p. 490; 14, p. 386].

The model presented here, by definition, uses marginal, market value weights. Each weight is the proportion of new investment financed with debt $(\partial D/\partial I)$ and/or equity $(\partial S/\partial I)$. However, the starting point for the derivation is a market valuation model for the firm. This model implies that debt is cheaper than equity because of its tax deductibility. The demonstrated equivalence of the WACC and MM models that follows makes this implication apparent. The tax induced bias for total debt financing is constrained by an externally imposed limit (L) on borrowing. As MM have shown, under such conditions, current market value weights and marginal weights are identical. That is, if the firm's outstanding debt and equity prices are in equilibrium (which is consistent with both MM and CAPM assumptions), they reflect a constrained optimum, and the current market value proportions will also represent the optimal proportions for financing new investments.

More Elegant Equivalents

Some of the dissatisfaction with WACC may be attributed to its lack of complexity. It seems very pedestrian when compared to the Modigliani-Miller and CAPM security market line model (SML) approaches.

Regardless of their differences in appearances, it can be shown that they are equivalent. The MM model is as follows:

$$K_0 = \rho \left(1 - t\frac{\partial D}{\partial I} \right). \tag{5}$$

We have already used all the symbols in this model except ρ. This is MM's notation for the discount rate that the market applies to all equity streams. MM provide the relationship between ρ and K [16, p. 439]. It is

$$K = \rho + (1-t) [\rho - r]D/S. \tag{6}$$

Substituting for K in the WACC equation and rearranging will result in the MM equation. Appendix B traces this trip through the algebraic forest.

The same type of thing can be done using the SML valuation approach. In the context of the capital asset pricing model [20], the expected return on any capital asset would be a function of the covariance of the asset's returns with market returns. The relationship can be written as follows:

$$R_i = r + \lambda \, cov(R_i, R_m), \tag{7}$$

where R_i is the expected return on any risk asset, r is the risk-free rate (which can be treated as equivalent to the firm's r under CAPM assumptions), λ is the market price of risk, and $cov(R_i, R_m)$ is the covariance of return R_i, with market returns, R_m. There are a number of versions of λ (see [18]); the one used here is $\lambda = (R_m - r)/\sigma_m^2$ where σ_m^2 is the variance of market returns.

A derivation (see Appendix C) similar to the previous two provides another cost of capital measure:

$$K_0 = [r + \lambda \, cov(R_i, R_m)] \, (1 - t \cdot \partial D/\partial I). \tag{8}$$

Comparing Equation (8) to Equation (5) should satisfy the reader that (8) is a specific form of the more general model in (5), where ρ in this case is defined by the SML as $r + \lambda \, cov(R_i, R_m)$. Equation (5) has been shown to be equivalent to the WACC calculation in

Equation (4); therefore another algebraic exercise to demonstrate equivalence is unnecessary.

Summary

I hope this paper has demonstrated that the generally taught, but often maligned, WACC rests on as sound a theoretical foundation as one of the currently in vogue alternatives. Further, it is equivalent to them. It appears that text writers' loyalty to the WACC is well founded.

References

1. J. S. Ang, "Weighted Average vs. True Cost of Capital," *Financial Management* (Autumn 1973), pp. 56–65.
2. F. D. Arditti and H. Levy, "The Weighted Average Cost of Capital as a Cut-off Rate: A Critical Analysis of the Classical Textbook Weighted Average," *Financial Management* (Fall 1977), pp. 24–34.
3. W. Beranek, "Some New Capital Budgeting Theorems," *Journal of Financial and Quantitative Analysis* (December 1978), pp. 809–823.
4. W. Beranek, "The Weighted Average Cost of Capital and Shareholder Wealth Maximization," *Journal of Financial and Quantitative Analysis* (March 1977), pp. 17–31.
5. R. H. Bernhard, "Some New Capital Budgeting Theorems: Comment," *Journal of Financial and Quantitative Analysis* (December 1978), pp. 825–829.
6. E. J. Elton and M. J. Gruber, *Finance as a Dynamic Process,* Englewood Cliffs, N.J., Prentice-Hall, Inc., 1975.
7. L. J. Gitman, *Principles of Managerial Finance,* New York, Harper & Row, 1979.
8. M. J. Gordon, *The Investment, Financing, and Valuation of the Corporation,* Homewood, Ill., Richard D. Irwin, Inc., 1962.
9. C. W. Haley and L. D. Schall, *The Theory of Financial Decisions,* New York, McGraw-Hill Book Company, 1973.
10. R. S. Hamada, "Portfolio Analysis, Market Equilibrium, and Corporation Finance," *Journal of Finance* (March 1969), pp. 13–31.
11. R. A. Haugen and J. L. Pappas, "Equilibrium in the Pricing of Capital Assets, Risk Bearing Debt Instruments, and the Question of Optimal Capital Structure," *Journal of Financial and Quantitative Analysis* (June 1971), pp. 943–953.
12. O. M. Joy, *Introduction to Financial Management,* Homewood, Ill., Richard D. Irwin, Inc., 1977.
13. W. G. Lewellen, "A Conceptual Reappraisal of Cost of Capital," *Financial Management* (Winter 1974), pp. 63–70.
14. J. D. Martin, J. W. Petty, A. J. Keown, and D. F. Scott, Jr., *Basic Financial Management,* Englewood Cliffs,

N.J., Prentice-Hall, Inc., 1979.

15. R. C. Merton and M. G. Subrahmanyam, "The Optimality of a Competitive Stock Market," *Bell Journal of Economics and Management Science* (Spring 1974), pp. 145–170.

16. F. Modigliani and M. H. Miller, "Corporate Income Taxes and the Cost of Capital: A Correction," *American Economic Review* (June 1963), pp. 433–443.

17. J. Mossin, *Theory of Financial Markets,* Englewood Cliffs, N.J., Prentice-Hall, Inc., 1973.

18. M. E. Rubinstein, "A Mean-Variance Synthesis of Corporate Financial Theory," *Journal of Finance* (March 1973), pp. 167–181.

19. L. D. Schall, "Asset Valuation, Firm Investment, and Firm Diversification," *Journal of Business* (January 1972), pp. 11–28.

20. W. Sharpe, "Capital Asset Prices: A Theory of Market Equilibrium Under Conditions of Risk," *Journal of Finance* (September 1964), pp. 425–442.

21. J. C. Van Horne, *Financial Management and Policy,* 4th ed., Englewood Cliffs, N.J., Prentice-Hall, Inc., 1977.

22. J. F. Weston and E. F. Brigham, *Managerial Finance,* 5th ed., Hinsdale, Ill., The Dryden Press, 1975.

Appendix A. Derivation of WACC

The cost of capital is defined as the minimum after-tax return $\partial X(1-t)/\partial I$ on I dollars of investment such that the value of the firm is undiminished, $(\partial V/\partial I = 1)$ [8, p. 218; 16, pp. 439–440]. Recalling Equation (2),

$$V = \frac{(X-rD)(1-t)}{K} + \frac{rD}{r}.\qquad (A-1)$$

Note that in this derivation equity flows, $(X-rD)(1-t)$, are discounted at an equity cost, K, that considers the interest-related tax saving, rDt, and debt flows, rD, are capitalized at a pre-tax rate, r. However, in the final calculation, the cost of debt, $r(1-t)$, is the after-tax cost — contrary to the suggestion in [2, p. 27].

Rewriting and rearranging gives

$$V = \frac{X(1-t)}{K} - \frac{rD(1-t)}{K} - D.\qquad (A-2)$$

Differentiating with respect to I,

$$\frac{\partial V}{\partial I} = \frac{K\frac{\partial X}{\partial I}(1-t) - \frac{\partial K}{\partial I}(X(1-t))}{K^2} - (1-t)$$

$$\left[\frac{K\left(\frac{\partial r}{\partial I}D + \frac{\partial D}{\partial I}r\right) - \frac{\partial K}{\partial I}(rD)}{K^2}\right] + \frac{\partial D}{\partial I}.\qquad (A-3)$$

Recalling that the acceptance criterion requires $\partial V/\partial I = 1$ and by definition the incremental stock financing plus the incremental debt financing are complementary $(\partial S/\partial I + \partial D/\partial I = 1)$ allows the above equation to be rewritten as

$$\frac{\partial S}{\partial I} = \frac{\partial X}{\partial I}\frac{(1-t)}{K} - \frac{\partial K}{\partial I}\frac{X(1-t)}{K^2}$$

$$-\frac{(1-t)}{K}\left(\frac{\partial r}{\partial I}D + \frac{\partial D}{\partial I}r\right) + \frac{(1-t)}{K^2}\frac{\partial K}{\partial I}rD.\qquad (A-4)$$

Multiplying both sides of the equation by K, and recognizing $\partial X(1-t)/\partial I$ as our variable of interest, the overall cost of capital (K_0), allows further rewriting as

$$K\frac{\partial S}{\partial I} = K_0 - \frac{\partial K}{\partial I}\frac{(X(1-t))}{K} - (1-t)\frac{\partial r}{\partial I}D$$

$$-(1-t)r\frac{\partial D}{\partial I} + \frac{\partial K}{\partial I}\frac{(1-t)rD}{K}.\qquad (A-5)$$

Solving for K_0 and collecting terms on the factor $\partial K/\partial I$ results in Equation (A-6).

$$K_0 = K\frac{\partial S}{\partial I} + (1-t)r\frac{\partial D}{\partial I} + \frac{\partial K}{\partial I}\frac{(X-rD)(1-t)}{K}$$

$$+ \frac{\partial r}{\partial I}(1-t)D.\qquad (A-6)$$

Comparing Equation (A-6) with Equation (A-1) will disclose that the third term in the cost of capital definition is the change in the equity capitalization rate $\partial K/\partial I$ times the original value of the firm's stock $[(X-rD)(1-t)]/K = S$, where S is the value of the firm's total outstanding shares. Therefore

$$K_0 = K\frac{\partial S}{\partial I} + r(1-t)\frac{\partial D}{\partial I} + \frac{\partial K}{\partial I}S + \frac{\partial r}{\partial I}(1-t)D.\qquad (A-7)$$

Appendix B. MM and WACC Equivalence

Using Equation (6)

$$K = \rho + (1-t)[\rho-r]D/S\qquad (B-1)$$

and substituting in (4) (which is appropriate because MM's derivation assumes K and r constant) gives

$$K = \left(\rho + (\rho-r)(1-t)\frac{D}{S}\right)\frac{\partial S}{\partial I} + r(1-t)\frac{\partial D}{\partial I}.\ (B-2)$$

In the MM paper it was argued that the tax deductibility of interest payments would encourage firms to make maximum use of debt. Subsequent work has generally supported this conclusion [6, 10]. If firms maintain reserve borrowing capacity, they will endeavor to maintain a target debt ratio. In either case, $L = D/D+S$, where L denotes either a target leverage ratio or a binding constraint. Given that firms maintain this ratio $\partial D/\partial I$ also equals L and $\partial S/\partial I = (1-L)$ and, additionally, $D/S = L/(1-L)$.

Making these substitutions gives

$$K_0 = \left[\rho + (\rho-r)(1-t)\frac{L}{1-L} \right] (1-L) + r(1-t)L. \tag{B-3}$$

Expanding the equation,

$$K_0 = \rho - \rho L + \rho(1-t)L - r(1-t)L + r(1-t)L, \tag{B-4}$$

and combining terms

$$K_0 = \rho(1-tL) = \rho\left(1 - t\frac{\partial D}{\partial I}\right). \tag{B-5}$$

Appendix C. Derivation of SML Cost of Capital

Under CAPM equilibrium, the SML defines the valuation mechanism for all capital assets, separately or in combinations. Therefore, the valuation of the firm may be expressed in terms of its components. A form similar to Equation (A-2) would be

$$V = \frac{X(1-t)}{r + \lambda\, cov(R_i, R_m)} - \frac{rD(1-t)}{r + \lambda\, cov(r, R_m)} + D. \tag{C-1}$$

This formulation, a perpetuity model, assumes r, λ, and $cov(R_i, R_m)$, the riskiness of $X(1-t)$, are constant over time. For further elaboration as to when the SML may be used in a multiperiod context see [18, p. 168, n. 1]. (Note that the assumption of constant riskiness and capitalization rates is not unique to the SML model. The use of a single K in the WACC derivation, or ρ in the MM model, imply the same. The greater precision of the SML-CAPM model simply forces explicit recognition of these assumptions.)

Under the CAPM, interest flows are assumed to be riskless. Therefore, they do not covary with the market. This allows Equation (C-1) to be rewritten as

$$V = \frac{X(1-t)}{r + \lambda\, cov(R_i, R_m)} - \frac{rD(1-t)}{r} + D, \tag{C-2}$$

which simplifies to

$$V = \frac{X(1-t)}{r + \lambda\, cov(R_i, R_m)} + tD. \tag{C-3}$$

Again differentiating and finding $\partial X(1-t)/\partial I$ such that $\partial V/\partial I = 1$ defines the cost of capital. The derivation is simplified by explicitly assuming r and λ are invariant with respect to individual investments — a standard analytical simplification [15].

$$1 = \frac{\partial X}{\partial I} = \frac{Z\frac{\partial X}{\partial I}(1-t) - \frac{\partial Z}{\partial I}(X(1-t))}{Z^2} + t\frac{\partial D}{\partial I} \tag{C-4}$$

where $\quad Z = r + \lambda\, cov(R_i, R_m)$, and

$$\frac{\partial Z}{\partial I} = \lambda\,\frac{\partial cov(R_i, R_m)}{\partial I}.$$

Simplifying and rearranging

$$Z\left(1 - t\frac{\partial D}{\partial I}\right) = \frac{\partial X}{\partial I}(1-t) - \frac{\partial Z}{\partial I}\frac{(X(1-t))}{Z}. \tag{C-5}$$

Further, $X(1-t)/Z$ is by definition the value of this firm if it were not leveraged. This is denoted with the symbol V_u. Therefore, the cost of capital under this valuation model is

$$K_0 = [r + \lambda\, cov(R_i, R_m)]\left(1 - t\frac{\partial D}{\partial I}\right)$$

$$+ \lambda\,\frac{\partial cov(R_i, R_m)}{\partial I} V_u. \tag{C-6}$$

Again, for investments that do not change firm riskiness, the last term vanishes. That is, if $\partial cov(R_i, R_m)/\partial I = 0$, the last term in total is zero leaving

$$K_0 = [r + \lambda\, cov(R_i, R_m)](1 - t \cdot \partial D/\partial I). \tag{C-7}$$

This same formulation can be derived from the Hamada criterion [10, p. 27, Eq. 30], which is a special case of the MM model [10, pp. 26–27, n. 27].

To simplify the SML derivation, based on the WACC value specification, riskless debt was assumed. However, a more generalized model is equivalent.

The MM cost of capital model previously cited is from their 1963 article and was presented without derivation. That article assumes riskless debt [16, p. 436]. However, it has since been shown that the MM model also holds under CAPM equilibrium [9, 10, 11, 17]. More specifically, the MM valuation model, from which Equation (5) was derived, holds where firms issue risky debt, with taxes, under CAPM conditions [18, p. 176, n. 17]. By induction, the SML cost of capital model can be derived with risky debt via a MM-CAPM valuation model.

GROWTH, DIVIDEND POLICY AND CAPITAL COSTS IN THE ELECTRIC UTILITY INDUSTRY

ROBERT C. HIGGINS*

IN [11] Miller and Modigliani, hereinafter MM, used a finite-growth valuation model to estimate the cost of capital to the electric utility industry and to test their controversial propositions on the role of capital structure and dividend policy in the valuation of shares. Published criticisms of the study [3], [6], and [12] argued that it was flawed in several respects and that consequently neither the cost of capital estimates nor the valuation evidence was as convincing as might be supposed.

Recently, Litzenberger and Rao [8] and McDonald [9] have extended and adapted the original finite-growth model to investigate related topics. Litzenberger and Rao explicitly introduced intra-firm differences in risk to estimate the marginal rate of time preference and average risk aversion of investors in utility shares; and McDonald employed nonlinear regression techniques to estimate the national and regional cost of equity capital to public utilities.

While these studies are unquestionably worthwhile, they have left unanswered, and in some instances even exacerbated, several significant issues raised in response to the original MM study. One is the recurring concern that a finite-growth model cannot adequately represent the value of future growth to current shareholders, even in the highly stable utility industry. As witness, some of McDonald's cost of equity capital estimates are actually below comparable earnings to price ratios—a finding which is valid only if future investment has a negative present worth. Another more theoretical issue is whether share prices are truly independent of dividend policy as assumed in the finite growth model. In addition to its importance for valuation theory, this issue is central to the continued use of the finite-growth model, because if independence does not exist, the model in any of its variations is necessarily misspecified.

Because growth, dividend policy and capital costs are central to much of modern valuation and regulatory theory, it is deemed important to examine them anew in light of existing criticism. The purpose of this paper is, therefore, threefold: to derive and test a finite-growth model for electric utility shares which accurately reflects the present value of future investment, to provide new evidence on the dividend policy-share price controversy, and to present estimates of the required rate of return, or cost of equity capital, to the electric utility industry over the period 1960-68.

Basic to the model described here is the use of population growth trends, rather than capital formation rates, as surrogates for the expected rate of utility investment. Evidence presented suggests that the extrapolation of historical

* Associate Professor of Finance, University of Washington.
  I wish to express my gratitude to Hugh Cunningham, Charles Steward, and Bob Howard for computational assistance, and to Professors A. A. Robichek, J. G. McDonald and R. H. Litzenberger for many useful discussions.

population trends is superior to the conventional use of past capital formation rates in terms of both statistical significance and the plausibility of the resulting cost of capital estimates. Regarding dividend policy, evidence also suggests that share prices are not a positive function of dividends as often suggested. In fact, if there is any correlation at all, it seems to be in the opposite direction, with dividends exerting a depressing effect on share prices.

I. The Valuation Model

Think of the market value of a firm's equity as coming from two sources: the present value of income to shareholders from existing capital, and the present value of new investment. Assuming that depreciation is just sufficient to maintain the value of existing assets, the present value of the income from existing capital is simply Y_0/k, where Y_0 is current earnings to common, and k is the required return on equity—or the cost of equity capital.

To represent the present value of new investment, suppose that from $t = 0$ to T, net investment, I_t, is expected to grow (decline) at a constant exponential rate g and is expected to yield an average return to equity of r% per year in perpetuity. For $t > T$, suppose that opportunities to invest at returns above costs disappear, and $r = k$. Then, as shown below,[1] the present value of future growth to equity shareholders can be represented as

$$\frac{(r - k)\pi I_0}{k} \int_0^T e^{(g-k)t}\, dt. \tag{1}$$

In this expression, π is the proportion of total assets financed by equity, which for simplicity is assumed constant over time. Assuming that $(g - k)T$ is small, (1) simplifies to $(r - k)\pi I_0 T/k$, and the market value of equity is

$$S_0 = \frac{Y_0}{k} + \frac{(r - k)\pi I_0 T}{k} \tag{2}$$

The implications of this finite-growth model for the firm's cost of equity capital can be seen more readily by solving (2) for k,

$$k = \frac{Y_0 + r\pi I_0 T}{S_0 + \pi I_0 T}.$$

In the absence of extraordinary investment opportunities $(r > k)$, k is simply the earnings to price ratio, Y_0/S_0. In the presence of extraordinary investments, k differs from the earnings to price ratio in two respects: the prospective income stream increases by an amount equal to the income from new investment, $r\pi I_0 T$, and the cost of acquiring the income stream rises by an amount equal to the equity financed portion of the investment, $\pi I_0 T$.

1. For $t < T$, equity investment is $\pi I_0 e^{gt}$. The annual value of this investment to equity is $(r - k)\pi I_0 e^{gt}$; and because it is a perpetuity, its present value at time t is $(r - k)\pi I_0 e^{gt}/k$. Taking the present value at $t = 0$ and summing over all $t < T$ yields equation (1). If $(g - k)T$ is small, a Taylor series expansion yields $1 - e^{(g-k)T} \cong (k - g)T$. Performing the indicated integration in (1) and making the Taylor series substitution yields (2).

Perpetual Growth

To reconcile this model with the perpetual growth model common to the literature, it is necessary only to restrict new equity financing to internal sources, and to set $T = \infty$ in equation (1). Assuming that $k > g$, equation (1) yields

$$S_o = \frac{Y_o}{k} + \frac{(r-k)\pi I_o}{k(k-g)}.$$

To simplify this, represent the amount retained at $t = 0$ as bY_o, where b is the retention rate. In the absence of external equity financing, $bY_o = \pi I_o$, and $rbY_o = r\pi I_o$. But rb equals g in the perpetual growth model, so $gY_o = r\pi I_o$. Using this relationship,

$$S_o = \frac{Y_o - \pi I_o}{k-g}.$$

Since $Y_o - \pi I_o$ equals current dividends, D_o, this equation becomes the familiar perpetual-growth model

$$S_o = \frac{D_o}{k-g}.$$

The perpetual-growth model can thus be viewed as a special case of the finite-growth model in which $T = \infty$ and all equity financing is internal.

Equation (2) is one of a class of finite-growth models discussed by McDonald [9]. It differs structurally from the model McDonald actually tested in that, by including π, it explicitly allows for differences in firm capital structure. Other more substantive statistical differences will be discussed below.

II. The Statistical Model

Provided that k and T are the same for all sample firms, equation (2) is suitable as a statistical model for the estimation of the cost of equity capital. Deleting the time subscripts, the test model is

$$S = a_2 Y + a_3 r\pi I + a_4 \pi I + \mu, \tag{3}$$

where $a_2 = 1/k$, $a_3 = T/k$ and $a_4 = -T$. An estimate of cost of equity capital is then $1/\hat{a}_2$, or $-\hat{a}_4/\hat{a}_3$. Note that the equation is nonlinear in the coefficients since $a_2 = -a_3/a_4$.

The presumption that k is constant in equation (3) is analogous to the usual constant risk class assumption except that here the notion of proportionality among returns applies to equity returns rather than total capital returns. Such an assumption is warranted, or at least superior to the conventional risk class assumption, to the extent that the level of financial risk a firm bears is inversely related to the level of business risk it faces. That is, returns to equity capital will be approximately proportional, or at least more so than returns to total capital, if managements react to differences in product and factor market risk by maintaining compensating financial risks.[2] That such a tendency is at least broadly consistent with observation can be seen by comparing the capital structures of, say, public utilities, with their low business risk and high leverage ratios, and industrials, with their higher business risk and correspondingly lower leverage ratios. Whether this tendency also holds for companies within a given industry is more difficult to determine, but in the absence of evidence to the contrary, the proposition is plausible enough that accepting it will probably not affect our results significantly.

There is no similar reason to suppose, *a priori*, that the time horizon for extraordinary growth is constant for all firms in a sample. Consequently, in the absence of any meaningful theory of what determines T, particularly for a regulated firm, ad hoc tests were conducted first on the assumption that T is proportional to r and then on the assumption that T is proportional to I. In neither case were the results superior to, or even very much different from, those in which T is assumed to be the same for all firms.[3]

Size and Value

Ignoring investment for the moment, previous studies [11] suggest that the relationship between firm value and earnings is nonlinear in the range of small firms. Due presumably to reduced shareholder liquidity, the indication is that the cost of equity capital for small firms exceeds that for large firms. A failure to anticipate this nonlinearity in the estimation of equation (3) would bias our estimates of k, even though none of the firms in our sample could be construed as very small. A convenient solution to this problem is simply to add a constant term to (3), and to interpret k as the marginal cost of equity capital applicable to large firms.

It is further suggested by some, [3], that size in a valuation equation such as ours may act as a surrogate for omitted risk variables. In this event, size itself would presumably be positively correlated with equity value. Adding a size variable and the indicated constant term and dividing the equation by total assets, A, to reduce heteroscedasticity yields

$$\frac{S}{A} = a_0 + a_1 \frac{1}{A} + a_2 \frac{Y}{A} + a_3 \frac{r\pi I}{A} + a_4 \frac{\pi I}{A} + e. \tag{4}$$

Here, a_0 is the size variable, A, in the unnormalized equation and a_1 is the constant term. If the effect of size on value is as others suggest, $\hat{a}_0$ should be positive and $\hat{a}_1$ negative.

Extraordinary Growth

A persistent problem with finite-growth models has been the specification of the growth term. In their initial study, MM [11] simply used the 5 year aver-

---

2. It should be noted here that the maintenance of compensating financial risk is not a purely mechanical task. Since financial risk depends, at least in part, on the market value of the firm's shares, the level of financial risk borne by the firm is not completely within management control.

3. $(r - k)\pi I$ is a measure of the rent earned by the firm on new investment. In a competitive industry it would only be a matter of time before this rent was eliminated. In assuming that T is proportional to r and I we are assuming that the time required to eliminate the rent is related to its magnitude.

age of past investment as a surrogate for the entire growth term. In extending their results to additional years, Robichek, McDonald and Higgins [12] cited theoretical and empirical reasons to suspect that the MM growth term was misspecified. McDonald [9] and Litzenberger and Rao [8] corrected the most obvious shortcoming in the MM growth term by including some measure of the profitability of new investment as well as its magnitude. But even then, McDonald's growth term, for instance, was statistically significant in only 4 of the 12 years tested and his cost of equity capital estimates averaged only 40 basis points above the "no-growth" earnings to price. ratio.[4] Litzenberger and Rao's estimates were much the same, averaging only about 50 basis points above the earnings to price ratio for the years tested.

One explanation for these results is that the historical investment figures commonly employed as a measure of I are poor surrogates for the investment term actually required by the model. Specifically, recall that for purposes of simplification, it was convenient in deriving the model to assume that the firm's investment stream would grow at a constant rate g over time. But even casual observation indicates that the actual values of investment do not display the uniform pattern over time required by the model. In particular, the "lumpiness" of physical investment in the electric utility industry means that actual investment in any given year may differ substantially from the steady-state or "warranted" figure relevant to the model. If this is the case, use of historical investment figures, even when averaged over several years, can introduce measurement errors which bias downward the estimated growth coefficients.

To explore this possibility, we examined two alternative definitions of I. In the first, I was defined conventionally as an extrapolation of the past several years investment. This is referred to subsequently as I_a. In the second, we assumed that the warranted but unobservable growth in assets was proportional to underlying historical growth in population in the franchise area served by the utility, G_p. Specifically, our assumption was that $G_p = \alpha\, I/A$, where α is the constant of proportionality. The overwhelming superiority of G_p in terms of significance and explanatory power strongly suggests that the use of historical investment figures does introduce substantial measurement error into the growth term.[5]

Variable Definitions

Definitions of the variables used in the empirical estimation of equation (4) appear below. The statement that a variable is a trend value means that it is equal to the estimated value for the current period derived from a regression

---

4. Technically, the usual tests of significance do not apply for a nonlinear model such as McDonald's. We interpret his statement to mean that the growth term would have been significant in 4 of the 12 years tested had the model been ordinary least squares.

5. As an intermediate step, we also defined I as proportional to the historical change in sales. Change in sales generally performed better than I_a but not as well as G_p. Change in sales is not subject to the discontinuities affecting I_a, but it is still not as stable as G_p. In particular, annual electricity sales in the high residual southern states are dependent upon weather conditions via the demand for air conditioning. This dependence may introduce a random pattern in the sales figures and result in measurement error.

of the most recent 5 years of the variable against time.[6] This smoothing is done to reduce potential errors in measurement. The reasoning is that annual observations of a variable can be viewed, to a first approximation, as observations about a trend consisting of a true component and a random element. If these random elements have zero mean and are serially uncorrelated, use of the trend value of the variable, rather than the current observed value, will tend to reduce errors in measurement.

S = market value of equity = end of year price per share $\times$ number of common shares outstanding.

A = book value of total assets.

Y = trend value of "flow through" earnings available to common. Flow through earnings are defined as earnings available for common + charges in lieu of income taxes + deferred income taxes.[7]

r = trend value of "flow through" earnings to common divided by book value of equity.

I_a = trend value of the change in net assets.

G_p = annualized growth in population in utility's service area in the period 1950-60.[8] For a given utility, G_p is constant in all test years.

π = book value of equity/total assets.[9]

Except for the population figures, data for the study came from the Compustat Annual Utility Tape. The final sample of 81 companies included all of the electric utilities on the tape for which the required information was available. Development of the data on historical growth rates of population in individual utility service areas required two steps. First, we found the service area of each utility, usually by county in *Moody's Utility Manual*. Then we calculated the change in population in each franchise area in the decade 1950-1960 from Bureau of the Census data. When the service areas were discrete counties or other recognized geographic subdivisions, these calculations were exact. In other instances, some degree of approximation was required.[10]

III. EMPIRICAL RESULTS

Table 1 presents ordinary least squares estimates of equation (4) employing G_p. The column labeled $\hat{k}$ is an estimate of the cost of equity capital equal to the reciprocal of the earnings coefficient, $\hat{a}_2$.

6. That is, if $Y = a + bt + e$, where t is time in years and a and b are constants, the trend value of Y is $\hat{a} + \hat{b}t_0$, where t_0 is the current year and $\hat{a}$ and $\hat{b}$ are estimates of a and b.

7. Similar results were obtained when earnings available to common were used instead of flow-through earnings in Y and r.

8. Annualized growth rates are used here because it is logical to suppose that warranted investment is proportional to the annual growth rate in population rather than the ten year growth rate. That these rates are not proportional can be seen by considering the annualized rate, r_1, as a function of the ten year rate r_{10}; $1 + r_1 = (1 + r_{10})^{1/10}$.

9. π in our model measures the expected percentage of new investment to be financed by equity. To the extent that firms seek to maintain a stable capital structure measured in terms of book values rather than market values, the use of book weight is appropriate here.

10. *Moody's Manual* contains the number of customers for some utilities in some years, but the data are sufficiently spotty that no attempt was made to employ them.

TABLE 1
ORDINARY LEAST SQUARES ESTIMATES DEPENDENT VARIABLE: S/A

Year	Coefficients of*								Earnings¹ Price	Bond²² Yield	k̂(NL)
	Cons't	1/A	Y/A	rπG_p	πG_p	R²	k̂	T̂			
1960	.07	−10.9	16.7	280	−17.0	.78	6.0%	3.6	5.9%	4.5%	6.0
t	.61	− 2.69*	6.61*	2.96*	− 1.52						
1961	.01	− 4.9	17.4	300	−14.1	.72	5.8	3.7	4.8	4.5	5.8
t	.04	.88	5.64*	2.36*	− .96						
1962	.02	−11.7	16.7	279	−17.1	.71	6.0	3.6	5.2	4.4	6.0
t	.17	− 2.30*	6.31*	2.73*	− 1.49						
1963	.01	−11.9	17.7	300	−22.5	.72	5.7	3.7	4.9	4.3	5.5
t	.10	− 2.20*	7.17*	3.29*	− 2.11*						
1964	.04	−17.2	18.7	392	−34.4	.80	5.4	4.5	5.0	4.4	4.8
t	.40	− 3.19*	8.63*	4.58*	− 3.42*						
1965	.16	−19.7	14.8	329	−29.3	.75	6.8	4.8	5.1	4.5	6.5
t	1.67*	− 3.35*	7.12*	3.88*	− 2.86*						
1966	.15	−28.0	12.9	278	−24.3	.72	7.8	4.6	6.1	5.3	8.1
t	1.66*	− 4.36*	6.59*	3.23*	− 2.34*						
1967	.13	−24.5	10.9	206	−16.4	.65	9.2	4.1	6.5	5.7	8.6
t	1.53	− 3.88*	5.71*	2.42*	− 1.60						
1968	.09	−13.3	12.0	121	−7.9	.72	8.3	2.2	6.8	6.4	8.3
t	1.28	− 2.67*	7.42*	1.64*	− .91						

* Significant at the 5% confidence level.
1 Moody's Public Utility Manual.
2 Moody's Public Utility Manual, Rating Aa.

Considered in total, these results are generally as predicted by theory. In particular, all of the coefficients have the anticipated signs and the great majority are statistically significant at the 5% confidence level. Further, as witnessed by the multiple correlation coefficient, almost 75% of the variation in the dependent variable is accounted for by the model. This compares with a figure of about 54% for McDonald who used the same dependent variable and approximately the same number of independent variables.

Looking in more detail at the size variable, the indication is that the relation between total assets and equity value is nonlinear. For small firms, increasing size does increase value. This is borne out by the sign and significance of $\hat{a}_1$. However, once the firm exceeds a certain minimum size, further increases in total assets do not affect equity value. This is evidenced by the fact that the constant term, while consistently positive, is significant in only two years.[11]

The efficacy of representing the impact of future growth on current value by the two terms $r\pi G_p$ and πG_p is also supported by the evidence. Although $r\pi G_p$ and πG_p are very highly correlated, averaging .97 over the 9 test years, the coefficient of $r\pi G_p$ is significantly positive in every year, and that of πG_p is significantly negative in 4 years. Tests for the joint significance of the two terms are positive at the 1% level in every year.

Some measure of the importance of historical population trends relative to past investment rates in the valuation of utility shares can be seen by comparing Tables 1 and 2. Table 2 contains ordinary least squares estimates of equa-

TABLE 2

ORDINARY LEAST SQUARES ESTIMATES I_a/A REPLACING G_p DEPENDENT VARIABLE: S/A

Year	Cons't	1/A	Y/A	$r\pi I_a/A$	$\pi I_a/A$	R^2	$\hat{k}$
	\multicolumn{3}{l}{Coefficients of*}				
1961	−.19	4.0	25.2	17.4	—	.49	4.0
t	−.38	.67	8.13*	1.45			
1965	.05	15.0	17.8	170.7	−16.2	.71	5.6
t	.17	2.50*	9.36*	2.89*	− 2.24*		

* Significant at 5%.

tion (4) which are comparable to those in Table 1, except that I_a/A replaces G_p in the growth terms. The coefficient estimates for 1965 might appear reasonable except the coefficient of $1/A$ is significantly positive, implying a smaller cost of capital for small firms than large firms. It is, however, in 1961 where the model truly breaks down. In that year, neither of the growth terms is significant, the multiple correlation coefficient is reduced by almost one third, and $\hat{k}$ is 50 basis points below the A_a utility bond yield for the same period.

Examining finally the cost of equity capital estimates, $\hat{k}$ averages 6.8% over the test period and ranges from a low of 5.4% in 1964 to a high of 9.2% in 1967. For comparison, the estimates of McDonald were on the order of 50 to

11. In [11], MM argue that a_0 should be suppressed. However to the extent that equity value for large firms does depend on size, it should be included; and to the extent that it does not, a_0 is a superfluous variable which cannot bias the other coefficients significantly. See Rao and Miller, *Applied Regression Analysis,* pp. 35-37.

100 basis points below these figures in comparable years. To what extent these estimates are "correct" cannot be answered definitely, of course, but certain rough benchmark tests of plausibility are nonetheless applicable. The first of these is simply that $\hat{k}$ should exceed the utility bond yield and, as previously indicated, should also exceed the earnings to price ratio in the presence of opportunities for extraordinary growth. As shown in Table 1, our $\hat{k}$ meets both of these requirements in every year.[12] In terms of averages, $\hat{k}$ exceeds the A_a utility bond yield by 1.9% and the earnings/price ratio by 1.2%.

A second test of plausibility is that, provided assessments of risk do not change materially over the period, $\hat{k}$ should vary over time roughly in accordance with changes in the yields on competitive market instruments. Comparing $\hat{k}$ with the A_a bond yield once again, it is apparent that $\hat{k}$ meets this expectation as well. Thus $\hat{k}$ and the bond yield trend slightly downward until 1964. Then with $\hat{k}$ preceding the bond yield by one year, both turn sharply upward. This upward adjustment in k may have been excessive in 1967 because a decline in 1968 reduces the yield differential to a more typical 1.5% spread from the 3.25% figure prevailing in 1967. On both counts then, magnitude and trend, $\hat{k}$ appears to be a reasonable estimate of the cost of equity capital.

The Time Horizon for Extraordinary Growth

An important determinant of equity value in finite-growth models is the time horizon over which extraordinary growth is expected to continue. To estimate the values of T implicit in our model, note that the coefficients of $r\pi G_p$ in Table 1 are estimates of $\alpha T/k$. Multiplying these coefficients by $\hat{k}$ and dividing by an exogenously determined α yields the estimates of T shown in Table 1. The α used in this calculation was the ratio of the annual growth rate in U.S. population to the growth rate in electric utility net assets over the period 1950-60. Its value was .216. The estimates of T are generally above those found by Litzenberger and Rao, and except for 1968, are quite stable, varying in a range of 3.6 to 4.8 years with a noticeable increase of 1 year in 1964.

Nonlinear Estimates

In addition to ordinary least squares estimates, the predicted multiplicative relationship among the coefficients in equation (4) suggests the possibility of calculating a second set of cost of capital estimates. Known as nonlinear regression, this is done in the present instance by solving iteratively for the coefficient values which minimize the sum of the squared residuals in (4) subject to the constraint that $\hat{a}_2 = -\hat{a}_3/\hat{a}_4$.[13] The resulting cost of equity capital estimates appear in Table 1 as $\hat{k}(NL)$.

---

12. Note that these plausibility tests are not symmetric. Had $\hat{k}$ been less than the Aa bond yield, or the earnings to price ratio, this would have been strong evidence of misspecification. However, the opposite is not true. The fact that k exceeds these lower limits is not conclusive proof that the model is correctly specified; for similar results could occur with many misspecified models. All that can be said statistically, therefore, is that the tests do not show any evidence of misspecification.

13. The program used here was MXLE written by Potluri Rao at the University of Washington.

Nonlinear regression has the virtue of producing maximum likelihood estimates of the coefficients for a correctly specified model. It has an equally significant drawback however: the usual measures of significance, such as t statistics and multiple correlation coefficients, are not valid for nonlinear estimating techniques.[14] It is therefore impossible to judge the specification of a nonlinear model without referring to ordinary least squares estimates as well as the nonlinear estimates. For this reason, and because of the added computational difficulties, nonlinear regression has not been used very often in finance or economics. In this same light, a significant criticism of McDonald's study is that his complete reliance on nonlinear estimates makes it impossible to appraise the specification of his model.

Our use of the nonlinear estimates is primarily as a check on the ordinary least squares model. Of particular interest, therefore, is the magnitude of the difference between the two estimates of k. A sizeable difference would suggest that the constraint on the coefficients is fundamentally inconsistent with the valuation equation and would, in turn, cast doubt on the validity of the equation and/or its specification. But as can be seen, the two estimates are reassuringly similar, differing by an average of only 20 basis points. Which set of estimates is superior is difficult to determine. On a practical level, the only appreciable differences occur in 1964 and 1967 when $\hat{k}$ exceeds $\hat{k}(NL)$ by 60 basis points. In 1964, $\hat{k}(NL)$ is slightly less than the earnings to price ratio, leading one to prefer $\hat{k}$, but in 1967, $\hat{k}(NL)$ has the virtue of implying a somewhat more consistent spread between k and the interest rate. In either case, the two estimates are close enough to lend support to equation (4) and its specification.

IV. Dividend Policy and Equity Value

The fact that neither dividends nor the payout ratio appear in equation (4) as an explanatory variable is consistent with the view that the proportion of earnings distributed by a firm as dividends does not significantly affect the value of its equity shares. That this proposition is not universally accepted is well attested to by the existence of numerous theoretical and empirical studies to the contrary. For examples, see [1] and [7].

MM first addressed this issue within the context of a finite-growth model in [11]. Recall that MM first ran an ordinary least squares model with the addition of a dividend term and found results which they interpreted to be consistent with the traditional view that dividend payments and share values are positively correlated. Then arguing that these results were due to measurement errors in the earnings term, they adopted a two stage least squares estimating procedure designed to purge the earnings term of measurement errors. In the first stage, measured earnings were regressed against a number of

---

It is based on the Generalized Gauss-Newton iteration procedure developed by Rao and combines the Gauss-Newton and the Cochrane-Orcutt estimation procedures to compute maximum likelihood estimates.

14. When the error term of a nonlinear model is assumed to be normally distributed, the coefficient estimates are no longer normally distributed, and the conventional estimate of the variance of the error term is biased. Consequently, the usual tests of significance are not strictly appropriate. See [4] for a more complete discussion of nonlinear estimating techniques.

instrumental variables, including dividends. Then, the estimate of earnings from this regression was used in the second stage valuation equation.

The effect of this procedure, according to Gordon [6], was to substitute a ". . . *multiple* of the dividend . . ." for earnings in the second stage. To the extent that dividends were thus already in the second stage under the guise of estimated earnings, the explicit introduction of a second dividend term was a rather empty exercise since it could only prove to be superfluous. This is indeed what MM found. Whether this finding is indicative of the independence of share values and dividend policy, or is simply the result of improper testing, is unclear.

To examine the question and to test further the specification of our model, let us add a dividend term to the test equation. Denoting the total dividends distributed by the firm as D, the test equation employed is

$$S/A = a_0 + a_1 1/A + a_2 Y/A + a_3 r\pi G_p + a_4 \pi G_p + a_5 D/A + \mu.$$

Considering the unnormalized equation for a moment, a_5 can be interpreted as $\partial S/\partial D$ with all other variables held constant. Inasmuch as earnings and the equity portion of new investment are among those variables held constant, a_5 measures the effect on equity value of increasing dividends solely at the expense of retained earnings.

The results of this exercise are presented in Table 3. Looking first at the es-

TABLE 3
ADDITION OF DIVIDEND VARIABLE DEPENDENT VARIABLE: S/A

Year	Coefficients of*						R²	k̂
	Cons't	1/A	Y/A	rG_p	πG_p	D/A		
1960	− .06	− 5.06	16.5	285	−17.4	− 1.75	.79	6.1
t	− .59	− .90	6.58*	3.03*	− 1.56	− 1.51		
1961	.00	− .77	17.7	285	−12.7	− 2.30	.73	5.7
t	.02	− .11	5.71*	2.22*	− .86	− 1.00		
1962	.01	− 1.80	17.3	254	−15.3	− 6.11	.73	5.8
t	.08	− .25	6.62*	2.52*	− 1.35	− 1.97*		
1963	.00	− 1.44	18.2	269	−19.6	− 6.60	.74	5.5
t	.00	− .19	7.47*	2.93*	− 1.86*	− 2.02*		
1964	.00	− 8.45	18.7	380	−33.4	− 5.48	.80	5.4
t	.42	− 1.07	8.74*	4.45*	− 3.33*	-- 1.50		
1965	.16	−21.42	14.8	333	−29.7	1.42	.75	6.8
t	1.68*	− 2.56*	7.03*	3.85*	− 2.85*	.26		
1966	.14	−10.30	13.8	226	−19.1	−19.3	.73	7.3
t	1.53	− .84	6.89*	2.51*	− 1.79*	− 1.71*		
1967	.13	− 7.20	11.5	174	− 13.5	−18.3	.67	8.7
t	1.52	− .60	5.99*	2.02*	1.31	− 1.75*		
1968	.08	7.77	12.7	92	− 6.0	−20.5	.74	7.9
t	1.25	.69	7.86*	1.24	− .70	− 2.09*		

* Significant at 5%.

timates of a_5, it is apparent that, unlike the great majority of studies relating dividend policy to equity value, dividends do not appear to have a positive effect on value. In fact, $\hat{a}_5$ is actually negative in eight of the nine test years,

236

significantly so in 5. Moreover, in the one year in which $â_5$ is positive, it has a t value of only .26. While this is probably not sufficient to conclude that dividends depress equity values, it does seem safe to conclude that at least within the context of this model, dividends do not add to value. Coupled with the additional fact that the introduction of D/A has only a marginal impact on $\hat{k}$, it would appear that dividends can be safely ignored without seriously distorting the model.[15]

The observed insignificance of dividends is particularly interesting here in view of the fact that no elaborate precautions were taken to purge the earnings variable of measurement errors foreseen by MM. The now standard criticism of test equations containing some form of measured earnings and dividends is that the greater stability of the dividend stream imbues the dividend variable with an "informational content" and thereby imparts a positive bias to the estimate of the dividend coefficient. That is, dividends are thought to act in some degree as a surrogate for the unmeasurable "true" earnings. Here, the dividend coefficient is often negative in spite of this potential countervailing bias. Results comparable to MM's are thus obtainable without resorting to more complicated and controversial estimating techniques.

V. Summary and Conclusion

The purpose of this paper has been to derive and test a finite-growth model for the valuation of electric utility shares in the years 1960 to 1968. Primary attention has focused on the cost of equity capital to the industry, the specification of the growth term, and the relationship between dividend policy and share prices.

For the most part, the results of this exercise have been satisfactory. In particular, the estimates of the cost of equity capital are measurably above the finite-growth estimates of others for comparable periods and are quite plausible in terms of magnitude and variation over time. Moreover, these estimates change very little when a nonlinear constraint among the coefficients is enforced.

A finding of particular significance for utility shares is the apparent importance of basic population trends, as opposed to historical capital investment, in determining the value of future extraordinary growth. Growth variables incorporating historical changes in franchise population performed satisfactorily in all test years and proved measurably superior to growth variables based on changes in net assets. This accounts, at least in part, for the observed increase in the cost of equity capital.

Finally, tests of the importance of dividend policy for share valuation corroborate MM in strongly suggesting that dividends do not increase share prices. In fact, the indication is that if there is any relationship at all between the variables, it is in the opposite direction. This finding is particularly significant

---

15. Crockett and Friend [3] argue that tests of the kind reported here are inappropriate because the relation between equity value and dividend policy is likely to be nonlinear. As at least a partial test of this proposition, the model was also run with D^2/A added as a second dividend term. The results of this test are consistent with those already reported; equity value is not significantly dependent upon dividend policy.

when one realizes that it arises in the face of at least two unfavorable conditions: it relates to an industry in which dividends and dividend yield are conventionally presumed to be major shareholder concerns, and it occurs in spite of the potential bias inherent in the "informational content" of dividends. The result is also centrally important for the continued use of finite-growth models in valuation or regulation, since all such models are premised on the independence of dividend policy and equity values.

REFERENCES

1. E. Brigham and M. Gordon. "Leverage Dividend Policy, and the Cost of Capital," *Journal of Finance,* March 1968.
2. *County and City Data Book 1965: A Statistical Abstract Supplement,* U.S. Department of Commerce.
3. J. Crockett and I. Friend. "Some Estimates of the Cost of Capital to the Electric Utility Industry, 1954-57: Comment," *American Economic Review,* December 1967.
4. N. R. Draper and H. Smith. *Applied Regression Analysis,* New York: John Wiley and Sons, Inc., 1966.
5. E. J. Elton and M. J. Gruber. "Valuation and the Cost of Capital for Regulated Industries," *Journal of Finance,* June 1971.
6. M. J. Gordon. "Some Estimates of the Cost of Capital to the Electric Utility Industry, 1954-1957: Comment," *American Economic Review,* December 1967.
7. —————. *The Investment, Financing and Valuation of a Corporation.* Homewood, Ill.: Irwin, 1962.
8. R. H. Litzenberger and C. U. Rao. "Estimates of the Marginal Time Preference and Average Risk Aversion of Investors in Electric Utility Shares 1960-66," *The Bell Journal of Economics and Management Science,* Spring 1971.
9. J. G. McDonald. "Required Return on Public Utility Equities: A National and Regional Analysis, 1958-69," *The Bell Journal for Economics and Management Science.* Autumn 1971.
10. M. H. Miller and F. Modigliani. "Dividend Policy, Growth and the Valuation of Shares," *Journal of Business,* October 1961.
11. —————. "Some Estimates of the Cost of Capital to the Electric Utility Industry, 1954-57," *American Economic Review,* June 1966.
12. A. A. Robichek, J. G. McDonald and R. C. Higgins. "Some Estimates of the Cost of Capital to the Electric Utility Industry, 1954-57: Comment," *American Economic Review,* December 1967.

RECENT DEVELOPMENTS IN THE COST OF DEBT CAPITAL

ANDREW H. CHEN*

I. INTRODUCTION

THE IRRELEVANCE OF financial policy was first noted by J. B. Williams [46] some forty years ago, as he stated that "no change in the investment value of the enterprise as a whole would result from a change in its capitalization."[1] In 1952, Durand [9], in contrasting the Net Operating Income and the Net Income approaches to market valuation, demonstrated that the value of a firm is independent of its capital structure under the Net Operating Income theory of market valuation. However, it was not until after the publication of Modigliani and Miller's (MM) [31] classic paper in 1958 that the theory of financial leverage began to attract a great deal of attention among researchers in finance and economics. In their paper, Modigliani and Miller first brought out more explicitly the relationship between market valuation and individual portfolio decisions under uncertainty and proved, based upon the risk-class assumption and the arbitrage argument, the famous proposition that the value of a firm is invariant to its capital structure in the absence of corporate income taxes and bankruptcy risk. Several subsequent studies have shown that the same result can be obtained under more general conditions.[2]

The meaning and the measure of a firm's cost of capital have been the subject of numerous theoretical and empirical inquiries in the past two decades, and the theory of financial leverage has now become an essential part of the modern theory of corporation finance.

The cost of debt capital, an integral part of a firm's cost of capital, is defined as the equilibrium required rate of return on a risky corporate bond. Therefore, understanding the theory of corporate bankruptcy and the pricing of risky debt in an equilibrium capital market is the key to a better understanding of the determinants of a firm's cost of debt capital. The purpose of this paper is to review some recent developments in the theory of pricing risky debt and to examine more systematically the determinants of the cost of debt capital.

In Section II, we review and discuss the pricing of risky bonds and the determination of the cost of debt capital within a framework of one-period capital asset pricing model under uncertainty. In Section III, the mathematically more elegant models of pricing risky bonds based upon the continuous-time option pricing model are reviewed and discussed. The determinants of the risk premiums

* Professor of Finance, College of Administrative Science, The Ohio State University. The author wishes to thank S. A. Buser, M. J. Gordon, E. H. Kim, W. Y. Lee, G. A. Racette, J. H. Scott and especially J. B. Yawitz, the discussant of this paper, for valuable comments on earlier versions of the paper.

1. See Williams [46], p. 72–73.

2. See, for example, Baron [1], Hamada [18], Rubinstein [36] and Stiglitz [42, 44].

on bonds based on the option pricing model are then compared with that derived in Section II. In Section IV, we reveiw and discuss some recent developments in the theory of firm valuation and the cost of debt capital in a mutliperiod context.

II. The Cost of Debt Capital in Static Models

In order to understand more fully the determinants of the cost of debt capital and the effects of financial leverage on the values of debt and equity of a levered firm subject to bankruptcy risk, we analyze in this section the cost of debt capital using a simple static two-parameter model of asset valuation under uncertainty.

A. *A Simple Capital Asset Pricing Model*

Under three key assumptions [(1) there exists a fixed risk-free interest rate in perfectly competitive capital markets; (2) all investors have homogeneous expectations with respect to the probability distributions of future yields on risky assets;[3] and (3) all investors are risk-averse and the expected utility of terminal wealth maximizers], Sharpe [40], Lintner [24], and Mossin [33] have derived the following two-parameter equilibrium valuation equation:

$$V_j = (R)^{-1} \left[\bar{Y}_j - \lambda \operatorname{Cov}(\tilde{Y}_j, \tilde{R}_m) \right],$$ (1)

where

V_j = the equilibrium value of asset j;

$\bar{Y}_j = E(\tilde{Y}_j)$ = the expected value of the end-of-period cash flows to the owners of asset j;

$R = 1 + R_f$, where R_f is the risk-free interest rate;

$\operatorname{Cov}(\tilde{Y}_j, \tilde{R}_m)$ = the covariance between the total cash flows of asset j and the return on the market portfolio;

λ = the market price of risk (a composite risk aversion of all investors).

Equation (1) states that in equilibrium the value of asset j is the present value of the certainty-equivalent (CEQ) of the asset's random cash flow. The certainty-equivalent is derived by subtracting the asset's risk premium (the product of the market price of risk and the asset's systematic risk) from its expected end-of-period cash flow.

B. *Effects of Corporate Taxes and Bankruptcy Costs*

MM [32] have shown that in the presence of corporate income taxes but in the absence of bankruptcy risk there is a linear relationship between the value of the levered firm and that of its debt. This implies that a firm should maximize its use of debt in order to capture the benefit of tax subsidy on interest payments.

Several recent studies have shown that in the presence of both corporate income taxes and costly bankruptcy there exists an optimal capital structure for a firm.[4] The debt is utilized up to the point where the gain from tax savings on the debt is

---

3. Lintner [25] has demonstrated that a relaxation of this assumption does not change the equilbirium risk-return relation in any significant way.

4. See, for example, Baxter [3], Chen [6 and 7], Elton *et al.* [10], Jensen and Meckling [20], Kim [21], Kraus and Litzenberger [22], Lee and Barker [23], Robichek and Myers [35], Scott [38], and Turnbull [45].

just offset by the expected cost of bankruptcy. In the following we utilize a static two-parameter valuation model to present the essentials of the theory of financial leverage in the presence of corporate income taxes and bankruptcy costs.

B.1. *The Market Value of All-Equity Firm.* Denote X as the firm's operating income which is assumed to be jointly normally distributed with the return on the market portfolio so that

$$X = N(\overline{X}, \sigma_X^2), \tag{2}$$

for any given assessment of $\overline{R}_m$ and σ_m^2. The after-tax total return to the owners of the unlevered firm is $\tilde{Y}_u = \tilde{X}(1-\tau)$ when $X > 0$ and zero when $X \leqslant 0$, where τ is the proportional corporate income tax. Therefore, the market value of the unlevered firm is given by

$$V_u = (R)^{-1} \left[\overline{Y}_u - \lambda \operatorname{Cov}(\tilde{Y}_u, \tilde{R}_m) \right]$$

$$= (R)^{-1}(1-\tau)\left[E_0(\tilde{X}) - \lambda \operatorname{Cov}_0(\tilde{X}, \tilde{R}_m) \right]. \tag{3}$$

where

$$E_0(\tilde{X}) = \int_0^\infty \tilde{X} f(\tilde{X}) \, d\tilde{X};$$

$$\operatorname{Cov}_0(\tilde{X}, \tilde{R}_m) = E\left\{ \left[\tilde{X}_0 - E_0(\tilde{X}) \right] \left[\tilde{R}_m - E(\tilde{R}_m) \right] \right\},$$

the partial covariance between $\tilde{X}$ (truncated from zero upward) and $\tilde{R}_m$.[5]

B.2. *The Market Value of Debt.* To analyze the effects of financial leverage on the value of a firm, we assume for simplicity that the total contractual payments to the bondholders are tax deductible.[6] The bondholders receive their contractual claims of D at the end of the period if the firm is solvent, and the shareholders receive the after-tax residual value of the firm. If, however, the firm is declared bankrupt at the end of the period, the entire after-tax value of the firm is transferred to the bondholders who have to incur the bankruptcy penalties, K,[7] and the shareholders receive nothing. The total returns to the bondholders at the end of the period are given below:

$$\tilde{Y}_D = \begin{cases} D & \text{if } X \geqslant D, \\ (1-\tau)\tilde{X} - K & \text{if } D > X > K/(1-\tau) \equiv Z, \\ 0 & \text{if } X \leqslant Z. \end{cases} \tag{4}$$

Therefore, the market value of the firm's debt, V_D, can be expressed as follows:

$$V_D = (R)^{-1} \left\{ D[1 - F(D)] + (1-\tau)\left[E_Z^D(\tilde{X}) - \lambda \operatorname{Cov}_Z^D(\tilde{X}, \tilde{R}_m) \right] \right.$$

$$\left. - K[F(D) - F(Z)] \right\} \tag{5}$$

---

5. Several useful properties of the partial moments are presented in the Appendices to Lintner's [26] paper.

6. A more elaborate tax treatment in the event of bankruptcy similar to that in Baron [2] can be incorporated at the expense of increasing the complexity of the analysis.

7. This includes the direct costs to lawyers, trustees and referees and the costs arising from liquidating the firm's assets at "distress" price.

where

$$F(Z) = \int_{-\infty}^{K/(1-\tau)} f(\tilde{X})\, d\tilde{X},$$

the probability that the bondholders will receive nothing from the firm.

From the total returns available to the bondholders given in (4), we know that the equilibrium required rate of return on the risky debt of the firm, $E(\tilde{R}_d)$, must be such that

$$V_D = \left[1 + E(\tilde{R}_d)\right]^{-1} \overline{Y}_D. \tag{6}$$

Therefore, we can express $E(\tilde{R}_d)$ as follows:

$$E(\tilde{R}_d) = (1 + R_f)\frac{D[1 - F(D)] - K[F(D) - F(Z)] + (1 - \tau)E_Z^D(\tilde{X})}{D[1 - F(D)] - K[F(D) - F(Z)] + (1 - \tau)CEQ_Z^D(\tilde{X})} - 1 \tag{7}$$

Note that $E(\tilde{R}_d)$ in (7) is the required rate of return on the firm's risky debt demanded by the bond-investors in the equilibrium capital market, which is the firm's *cost of debt capital*. Thus, a firm's cost of debt capital is shown to be a function of the risk-free interest rate, the firm's systematic business (operating) risk measured by $\mathrm{Cov}(\tilde{X}, \tilde{R}_m)$, the probability of bankruptcy ($F(D)$), the corporate income tax rate and the costs of bankruptcy.

If we denote $\hat{R}_d$ for the *yield to maturity*, then

$$\hat{R}_d = (V_D)^{-1}D - 1$$

$$= (1 + R_f)\left\{\left[1 - F(D)\right] - (K/D)\left[F(D) - F(Z)\right]\right.$$

$$\left. + \left[(1 - \tau)/D\right]CEQ_Z^D(\tilde{X})\right\}^{-1} - 1 \tag{8}$$

Therefore, the yield to maturity on a risky bond is also a function of the firm's systematic business risk and the probability of bankruptcy. Note, however, that the yield on a risky bond is the maximum possible return to the bondholders. It is not the firm's cost of debt capital. The relationship between the two can be derived as follows using (7) and (8).

$$E(\tilde{R}_d) = (1 + \hat{R}_d)\left\{\left[1 - F(D)\right] - (K/D)\left[F(D) - F(Z)\right]\right.$$

$$\left. + \left[(1 - \tau)/D\right]E_Z^D(\tilde{X})\right\} - 1 \tag{9}$$

B.3. *Market Values of Equity and the Firm.* At the end of the period the shareholders receive the after-tax residual value of the firm if it remains solvent, and they receive nothing if the firm goes bankrupt. Therefore, the end-of-period after-tax total returns to the shareholders are given as follows:

$$\tilde{Y}_E = \begin{cases} (\tilde{X} - D)(1 - \tau) & \text{if } X > D, \\ 0 & \text{if } X \leqslant D. \end{cases} \tag{10}$$

Thus, the market value of the firm's equity, V_E, is given by

$$V_E = (R)^{-1}(1 - \tau)\left\{\left[E_D(\tilde{X}) - \lambda\,\mathrm{Cov}_D(\tilde{X}, \tilde{R}_m)\right] - D[1 - F(D)]\right\}. \tag{11}$$

242

The *cost of equity capital* can be expressed as

$$E(\tilde{R}_e) = (V_E)^{-1}(1-\tau)\{E_D(\tilde{X}) - D[1-F(D)]\} - 1. \tag{12}$$

It is important to note that a firm's systematic business risk, its level of total promised payment and the associated probability of bankruptcy are the key determinants of the firm's cost of equity capital; a result which has been overlooked in the cost of equity literature.

The market value of the levered firm is simply the sum of market values of its equity and debt. Therefore, adding V_D in (5) and V_E in (11), and using V_u in (3), we can express the market value of the levered firm as follows:

$$V_L = V_u + (R)^{-1}\{\tau D[1-F(D)] - K[F(D) - F(Z)]$$
$$- (1-\tau)[E_0^Z(\tilde{X}) - \lambda \text{Cov}_0^Z(\tilde{X}, \tilde{R}_m)]\} \tag{13}$$

Equation (13) shows that the market value of the levered firm is equal to the market value of the unlevered firm plus the present value of tax subsidy on debt payments, minus the present value of the expected bankruptcy costs, and minus the present value of the after-tax operating earnings the bondholders lose when they are not sufficient to cover the costs of bankruptcy.

If bankruptcy is costless (i.e., $K = 0$), the value of the levered firm in (13) reduces to $V_L = V_u + (R)^{-1}\tau D[1 - F(D)]$, which is similar to the result of the MM tax-model. However, note that the present value of tax savings on interest payments in this special case is smaller than that in the MM tax-model because of our assumptions of the one-period world and the existence of bankruptcy risk.

It can be easily seen that in the absence of corporate income taxes and bankruptcy costs the value of the levered firm reduces to $V_L = V_u$. Thus, the market value of a levered firm is the same as an otherwise identical unlevered firm in an *unsegmented* perfect capital market.[8] Costless bankruptcy does not invalidate the well-known MM theorem of the irrelevance of financial policy.

Differentiating V_L in (13) with respect to D and setting the result equal to zero, we can derive the value-maximizing level of debt as follows:[9]

$$D^* = [1 - F(D^*)]/f(D^*) - K/\tau. \tag{14}$$

It has been pointed out in Chen [7] that D^* which satisfies Eq. (14) brings the firm's total value to a maximum and its average cost of capital to a minimum. Therefore, a firm's cost of capital is a U-shaped function of its leverage factor in the presence of corporate income taxes and bankruptcy costs.

III. The Pricing of Risky Debt Using the Option Pricing Model

In their path-breaking paper, Black and Scholes [4] provide a general equilibrium approach to the valuation of stock options and derive a simple formula for the value of a European call option. The Black-Scholes option valuation indicates that

---

8. It has been shown that a unique optimal value-maximizing capital structure for a firm exists even in the absence of corporate income taxes and bankruptcy costs if the capital markets are either weakly or partially segmented. See, for example, Stiglitz [43], Rubinstein [37] and Lintner [26].

9. See Chen [7] for the derivation. Kim [21] has shown the existence of optimal capital structure under different conditions.

the option price is determined only by the observable variables. Merton [27] has generalized the Black-Scholes option pricing model to the cases of a stochastic interest rate and payments of dividends.

A. The Case of No Corporate Taxes and Bankruptcy Costs

The Black-Scholes and Merton option pricing models have laid the foundation for several recent advancements in the theories of pricing complex contingent claims such as equity and bonds of a levered firm. Black and Scholes [4] first suggested in their paper on option pricing that common equity can be regarded as a call option to buy back the firm from the bondholders at a price equal to the total promised payment. Thus, the market value of equity of a levered firm can be derived based on the Black-Scholes option pricing formula for the European calls, and hence the market value of the risky debt with a balloon payment can also be derived. In a recent study, Merton [28] uses the Black-Scholes option pricing formula to express the value of the equity of a firm with one senior balloon-payment bond as follows:

$$
V_E = V\Phi\left\{ \frac{\ln(V/D) + \left[r + (1/2)\sigma^2\right]T}{\sigma\sqrt{T}} \right\}
$$

$$
- e^{-rT}D\Phi\left\{ \frac{\ln(V/D) + \left[r - (1/2)\sigma^2\right]T}{\sigma\sqrt{T}} \right\}, \tag{15}
$$

where

V = the value of the firm;
r = the risk-free rate of interest;
σ^2 = the instantaneous variance rate on the value of the firm;
T = the length of time until maturity;
D = the total promised payments;
$\Phi(\cdot)$ = the cumulative standard normal distribution function.

Since $V_D = V - V_E$, the market value of the risky balloon-payment debt can be derived as follows:[10]

$$
V_D = V\Phi\left\{ \frac{-\ln(V/D) - \left[r + (1/2)\sigma^2\right]T}{\sigma\sqrt{T}} \right\}
$$

$$
+ e^{-rT}D\Phi\left\{ \frac{\ln(V/D) + \left[r - (1/2)\sigma^2\right]T}{\sigma\sqrt{T}} \right\} \tag{16}
$$

To examine the risk structure of interest rates, Merton has transformed the price of risky debt into an expression in terms of the yield on the bond as follows:

$$
e^{-R(T)T} \equiv V_D/D \tag{17}
$$

where $R(T)$ is the *yield to maturity* on the risky debt with a balloon payment of D and time to maturity T, provided that the firm does not default.

---

10. Merton [28] has pointed out that no closed-form solution for coupon-bearing bond can be derived under general conditions.

Thus, the *risk premium* on a balloon-payment risk bond can be expressed as

$$R(T) - r = [-\ln(V_D/D)]/T - r. \tag{18}$$

As Merton has pointed out, for a given maturity the risk premium is a function of the variance of the firm's value and the ratio of the present value of the promised payment to the current value of the firm. Note that the total risk is the relevant risk factor in the option pricing model, while the systematic risk is the relevant risk factor in the capital asset pricing model. Thus, the determinants of risk premium on risky bond based upon these two models of market valuation are similar but not identical. Furthermore, the following points are also worth noting.

First, one of the key assumptions in deriving (15) and (16) is that the value of the firm follows a diffusion process with continuous sample path. In other words, it is assumed that the firm can exist safely (with a zero probability of bankruptcy) until the maturity date of its bond. As noted earlier, all firms are subject to business risk. Thus, it is possible for a firm to go bankrupt prior to the maturity of its balloon-payment debt. Consequently, alternative processes for the value of a firm allowing positive probability of bankruptcy prior to the maturity of the bond are needed to derive a more general theory of pricing risk debt and the risk premium.

In their recent works, Merton [29] and Cox and Ross [8] have developed theories of option pricing when the prices of the underlying stock follow jump processes. Merton has pointed out that the Black-Scholes option pricing formula remains valid if the jump process involves a positive probability that the stock price drops to zero. Therefore, one can still apply the Black-Scholes option pricing to derive the value of risky debt and the risk premium, simply "adding" the jump intensity to the interest rate.[11]

Second, the simple formulas for the values of equity and risky debt given in (25) and (16) are derived based upon the assumptions that there are no corporate income taxes and no bankruptcy costs. As we shall see next, an explicit consideration of the market imperfections such as the presence of corporate income taxes and bankruptcy costs will result in a different valuation formula for risky debt using the option pricing model.

B. The Case with Corporate Taxes and Bankruptcy Costs

Most recently Turnbull [45] has incorporated corporate income taxes and bankruptcy cost into Merton's model of pricing equity and risky debt of a levered firm.

In order to facilitate some direct comparisons of the new results with that in Section II, we slightly modify Turnbull's assumptions and specify the total returns to the bondholders at the time of maturity as

$$\tilde{Y}_D = \begin{cases} D & \text{if} \quad V(T) \geqslant D, \\ (1-\tau)\tilde{V}(T) - K & \text{if} \quad D > V(T) > K/(1-\tau) \equiv Z, \\ 0 & \text{if} \quad V(T) \leqslant Z, \end{cases} \tag{19}$$

where

$$\tilde{V}(T) = \text{the random value of the firm at the time of maturity } (T).$$

11. As we shall see later, the probability of bankruptcy enters as a part of discount factor in the discrete-time multiperiod model also.

Therefore, the market value of the firm's debt can be shown as follows:

$$V_D = e^{-rT} D \Phi(d_1) + (1-\tau) V [\Phi(d_2) - \Phi(d_3)] - e^{-rT} K [\Phi(d_4) - \Phi(d_1)] \quad (20)$$

where

V = the value of the unlevered firm;

$d_1 = [\ln(V/D) + (r - (1/2)\sigma^2) T]/\sigma\sqrt{T}$;

$d_2 = [\ln(V/Z) + (r + (1/2)\sigma^2) T]/\sigma\sqrt{T}$;

$d_3 = [\ln(V/D) + (r + (1/2)\sigma^2) T]/\sigma\sqrt{T}$;

$d_4 = [\ln(V/Z) + (r - (1/2)\sigma^2) T]/\sigma\sqrt{T}$.

The first term on the RHS of (20) is the present value of the total promised payments to the bondholders times the probability that the firm will remain solvent. The second term is the after-tax value of the firm to be transferred to the bondholders in the event the firm is declared bankrupt, and the last term is the present value of the bankruptcy cost to be borne by the shareholders. Therefore, the economic interpretations of (20) are the same as that of (5).

Similar to Merton [28], we can derive the risk premium on a balloon-payment risky bond in the presence of corporate income taxes and bankruptcy costs.

Furthermore, we can derive the market values of equity and the firm. As Turnbull has shown, the market value of the levered firm is equal to the market value of the unlevered firm, plus the present value of the tax shelter generated by the tax deductibility of interest payments, minus the present value of the costs associated with bankruptcy, and minus a term that arises because of the limited liability of the bondholders. Therefore, the expression for the market value of the firm using the option pricing model is the same as that given in (13) using the static capital asset pricing model.

IV. THE COST OF DEBT CAPITAL IN MULTIPERIOD CONTEXT

A. *A Multiperiod CAPM and Definition of Bankruptcy for an On-going Firm*

Under the assumption that the Sharpe-Lintner-Mossin CAPM holds in every period, Fama [12] and Myers and Turnbull [34] have recently developed methods of evaluating a stream of uncertain cash flows in a multiperiod context. Fama has pointed out that the only admissible risk under this assumption is the uncertainty associated with the reassessments of expectations, and that the market parameters (the market price of risk and the future risk-free interest rates) can not be stochastic. He has shown that the value of any future cash flow is the current expected value of the flow discounted at non-stochastic risk-adjusted discount rates for each of the periods until the flow is realized. Myers and Turnbull, on the other hand, have applied the certainty-equivalent approach to derive their asset valuation model and to show that the risk associated with revision of expectations complicates the real determinants of beta in capital budgeting.

To examine the effects of financial leverage on the value of a firm and the cost of capital we can conveniently assume that the parameters of expectations are known in all relevant periods, since for a given investment plan the firm's *basic* cash flows are not affected by its financial choices. Thus, for our present purpose, the equilibrium market value of an asset is simply the sum of the certainty-equivalents of the asset's future cash flows discounted at the risk-free interest rates. The risk-adjustment factor is simply a product of the market price of risk and the systematic risk of the cash flow.

The definition of bankruptcy for a firm in a single-period model is relatively simple. A firm is declared bankrupt if the terminal value of the firm is less than the total promised payments to the bondholders. However, this definition of bankruptcy is not appropriate for an on-going firm. Stiglitz [42] defines bankruptcy for an on-going firm as follows: "A firm is bankrupt if the value of its equity is zero (it cannot be negative under conditions of limited liability), or equivalently, if the value of its future income streams, assuring it does not go bankrupt, is less than the value of its outstanding debt."[12] Therefore, an on-going firm can only be declared bankrupt if it is unable to meet its fixed obligations. A firm can have income less than its fixed obligations and yet remains solvent, because it can obtain more funds in a perfect capital market.

The bankruptcy for an on-going firm will be described more fully in the following. At time t, if the firm's net operating income $X(t)$ exceeds the interest payment $I(t)$, then $(1-\tau)[X(t)-I(t)]$ is the after-tax net income available to the firm's shareholders. Let the equilibrium ex-dividend market value of equity at time t be $V_E(t)$, then the shareholder's wealth at time t is equal to $V_E(t)+(1-\tau)[X(t)-I(t)]$. However, if $X(t)$ is less than $I(t)$, the firm must obtain enough money to meet the interest payments or the firm will be declared bankrupt. A firm can sell additional equity in a perfect capital market to meet its interest payments as long as the shareholders' wealth is positive, that is $V_E(t)+(1-\tau)[X(t)-I(t)]>0$.[13] Therefore, within a multiperiod framework, an on-going firm is declared bankrupt at time t if

$$X(t) \leqslant I(t) - V_E(t)(1-\tau)^{-1}. \tag{21}$$

B. The Market Value of All-Equity Firm

In the presence of business risk, it is assumed that the unlevered firms are also subject to the risk of bankruptcy. Under the assumption that corporate securities are traded in an efficient and perfect capital market, the impact of future possible bankruptcy will be fully reflected in the security prices. Since the shareholders receive nothing if a firm is declared bankrupt, they will first attempt to avoid bankruptcy by issuing additional equity as long as shareholder wealth is positive. An on-going firm is declared bankrupt if the wealth of shareholders is equal to or less than zero. Thus, shareholder wealth at the end of period t is given by

$$Y_u(t) = \begin{cases} (1-\tau)\tilde{X}(t) + V_u(t) & \text{if} \quad X(t) > -V_u(t)(1-\tau)^{-1} \equiv b(t) \\ 0 & \text{otherwise} \end{cases} \tag{22}$$

12. See Stiglitz [43], p. 460.

13. With the full enforcement of "me-first" rule, issuing equity is the most convenient way to obtain additional capital needed.

where $\tilde{X}(t)$ denotes the before-tax earnings in period t and $V_u(t)$ the market value of the unlevered firm at the end of period t, respectively.

Therefore, the equilibrium market value of the unlevered firm at the beginning of period t (or equivalently, at the end of period $t-1$) is

$$V_u(t-1) = \frac{1}{1+r(t)} \{ CEQ[\,\tilde{Y}_u(t)\,] \}$$

$$= \frac{1}{1+r(t)} \{ (1-\tau)[\, E_{b(t)}(\tilde{X}(t)) - \lambda(t)\mathrm{Cov}_{b(t)}(\tilde{X}(t), \tilde{R}_m(t)) \,]$$

$$+ V_u(t)[\, 1 - F(b(t)) \,] \} \tag{23}$$

where $r(t)$ = the risk-free rate of interest in period t;

Using the recursive relations in dynamic programming, we can express the *current* equilibrium market value of the unlevered firm as

$$V_u = \sum_{t=1}^{\infty} \frac{\prod_{s=1}^{t} \{1 - F[b(s-1)]\} \{(1-\tau)[\, E_{b(t)}[\tilde{X}(t)] - \lambda(t)\mathrm{Cov}_{b(t)}(\tilde{X}(t), \tilde{R}_m(t)) \,]\}}{\prod_{s=1}^{t} [1 + r(s)]} \tag{24}$$

For expositional simplicity, we shall assume in the following analysis a zero-growth firm with the net operating incomes identically and temporally independently distributed. We further assume that the term structure of interest rates is flat and that the market price of risk is constant over time. As a result, the expression for the market value of the unlevered firm in (24) can be greatly simplified to

$$V_u = \frac{(1-\tau)[\, E_b(\tilde{X}) - \lambda \mathrm{Cov}_b(\tilde{X}, \tilde{R}_m) \,]}{r + F(b)} \tag{25}$$

where $F(b) = \int_{-\infty}^{b} f(\tilde{x})\, d\tilde{X}$, the identical probability that the firm will not survive at the end of each period;

$$b = -V_u(1-\tau)^{-1}.$$

The numerator on the RHS of (25) is the per period risk-adjusted expected returns to the shareholders of the firm. The first term in the denominator is the risk-free interest rate and the second term can be regarded as a default premium.

Define $E(\tilde{R}_e)$ as the equilibrium required rate of return on the securities of the zero-growth all-equity firm such that

$$V_u = \frac{(1-\tau)E_b(\tilde{X})}{E(\tilde{R}_e) + F(b)}. \tag{26}$$

From (25) and (26), we can derive

$$E(\tilde{R}_e) = [\, r + F(b) \,][\, 1 - \lambda \mathrm{Cov}_b(\tilde{X}, \tilde{R}_m)/(E_b(\tilde{X})) \,]^{-1} - F(b). \tag{27}$$

248

Therefore, the *cost of equity capital* for an all-equity zero-growth firm is a function of its systematic business risk, its default premium and the risk-free interest rate.

C. The Market Value of Equity of a Levered Firm

For simplicity, the stationarity assumption in the preceding section will be maintained. Assume, for the moment, that the debt is a perpetual bond with coupon interest, I, which is tax-deductible. Under these circumstances, shareholder wealth at the end of any period is given by

$$\tilde{Y}_E = \begin{cases} (1-\tau)(\tilde{X} - I) + V_E & \text{if } X > I - V_E(1-\tau)^{-1} \equiv h \\ 0 & \text{otherwise} \end{cases} \tag{28}$$

Therefore, we can derive the *current* market value of the firm's equity as follws:

$$V_E = \frac{(1-\tau)\left[E_h(\tilde{X} - I) - \lambda \operatorname{Cov}_h(\tilde{X}, \tilde{R}_m)\right]}{r + F(h)} \tag{29}$$

Thus, the value of a zero-growth firm's equity is simply the risk-adjusted expected net income available for the shareholders divided by the sum of the risk-free interest rate and the default premium.

The cost of equity capital for a levered firm can be expressed as

$$E(\tilde{R}_e) = \left[r + F(h)\right]\left\{1 - \lambda \operatorname{Cov}_h(\tilde{X}, \tilde{R}_m)/\left[E_h(\tilde{X}) - I(1 - F(h))\right]\right\}^{-1} - F(h) \tag{30}$$

D. The Market Value of Risky Debt

If a firm is declared bankrupt because the shareholders are not capable of meeting the fixed obligations to the bondholders, one of the following two possible situations will occur to the bankrupt firm: (1) straight (or ordinary) bankruptcy, and (2) corporate reorganization. These are two different events in which bondholder wealth is not the same. In the following analysis, it is assumed that upon bankruptcy the total assets of the firm are liquidated and the business enterprise is terminated.[14]

D.1. The Case of Perpetual Bond. If the firm is declared bankrupt, the bondholders receive the net proceeds from the liquidation of assets and will have to cover the losses which the firm has incurred and the expenses associated with bankruptcy proceedings. Therefore, bondholder wealth at the end of any period can be expressed as

$$Y_D = \begin{cases} I + V_D & \text{if } X > I - V_E(1-\tau)^{-1} \equiv h \\ (1-\tau)\tilde{X} + V - K & \text{if } h \geqslant X > (K - V)(1-\tau)^{-1} \equiv W \\ 0 & \text{if } X \leqslant W \end{cases} \tag{31}$$

---

14. The different effects of bankrutcy-liquidation and bankruptcy-reorganization are examined in Chen [6].

249

Thus, the market value of debt is given by

$$V_D = \frac{[1-F(h)]I + [F(h)-F(W)](V-K) + (1-\tau)\left[E_w^h(\tilde{X}) - \lambda \operatorname{Cov}_w^h(\tilde{X},\tilde{R}_m)\right]}{r+F(h)}$$

(32)

The first term in the numerator on the RHS of (32) represents the expected per period coupon interest payments to the bondholders, and the sum of the second and the third terms in the numerator represents the expected net liquidation value of the bankrupt firm to the bondholders.

It can be shown from (32) that the cost of debt capital is given by

$$E(\tilde{R}_d) = [r+F(h)]\left(\frac{H}{H-q}\right) - F(h)$$

(33)

where

$$H = [1-F(h)]I + [F(h)-F(W)](V-K) + (1-\tau)E_w^h(\tilde{X});$$

$$q = (1-\tau)\lambda \operatorname{Cov}_W^h(\tilde{X},\tilde{R}_m).$$

Note that in a risk-neutral world q in (33) equals zero and the cost of debt capital is equal to the risk-free interest rate.

D.2 *The Case of Finite Maturity Bond.* Assume that the firm issues a T-period balloon-maturity bond with face value B and coupon interest I.[15] The returns to the bondholders are given as follows:
For $t < T$,

$$\tilde{C}(t) = \begin{cases} I & \text{if } X \geqslant I - V_E(t)(1-\tau)^{-1} \equiv h(t) \\ (1-\tau)\tilde{X}+V-K & \text{if } h(t) > X > (K-V)(1-\tau)^{-1} \equiv W \\ 0 & \text{if } X \leqslant W \end{cases}$$

(34)

and for $t = T$,

$$\tilde{C}(t) = \begin{cases} I+B & \text{if } X \geqslant I - [V_E(T)-B](1-\tau)^{-1} \equiv h(t) \\ (1-\tau)\tilde{X}+V-K & \text{if } h(t) > X > (K-V)(1-\tau)^{-1} \equiv W \\ 0 & \text{if } X \leqslant W \end{cases}$$

(35)

Therefore, the market value of the firm's finite maturity debt is given by

$$V_D = \sum_{t=1}^{T} \frac{\displaystyle\prod_{s=1}^{t}[1-F(h(s-1))]\left\{[1-F(h(t))]I + [F(h(t))-F(W)](V-K) + (1-\tau)\left[CEQ_W^{h(t)}(\tilde{X})\right]\right\}}{(1+r)^t}$$

$$+ \frac{\displaystyle\prod_{t=1}^{T}[1-F(h(t))]B}{(1+r)^T}$$

(36)

15. The formulation can easily be extended to serial retirement bond.

where

$$CEQ_W^{h(t)}(\tilde{X}) = E_W^{h(t)}(\tilde{X}) - \lambda \text{Cov}_W^{h(t)}(\tilde{X}, \tilde{R}_m).$$

Note that the probability of bankruptcy for a firm with finite-maturity bond depends on the time to maturity of its debt. From (36), we know that the market value of a finite-maturity coupon-bearing bond and the cost of debt capital are functions of the time to maturity, the systematic business risk and the probability of bankruptcy. As $T \to \infty$, $V_E(t) = V_E$ and $F[h(t)] = F(h)$ for all t, and thus (36) reduces to (32), which is the value of a perpetual risky bond.

Finally, in order to see more clearly the difference between the cost of debt capital in one-period context and that in multiperiod context, we derive the market value of a finite-maturity and non-coupon-bearing bond in the absence of taxes and bankruptcy costs as follows

$$V_D = (1+r)^{-T}\left\{\prod_{t=1}^{T-1}\left[1 - F(b(t))\right]\right\}\left\{D\left[1 - F(b(T))\right] + CEQ_0^{b(T)}(\tilde{X})\right\} \quad (37)$$

where

$b(t) \equiv -V_E(t)$ for all $t < T$;
$b(T) \equiv D - V_E(T)$;
$D \equiv$ the total promised payment at the end of period T.

Thus, in multiperiod context the value of a non-coupon-bearing bond depends also on the firm's probability of survival prior to the maturity of its debt.

We can derive the cost of debt capital in this special case as follows:

$$E(\tilde{R}_d) = (1+r)(\theta)^{1/T} - 1, \quad (38)$$

where

$$\theta = \frac{D\left[1 - F(b(T))\right] + E_0^{b(T)}(\tilde{X})}{D\left[1 - F(b(T))\right] + CEQ_0^{b(T)}(\tilde{X})}.$$

Furthermore, the yield to maturity on this non-coupon-bearing bond is given as

$$\hat{R} = (1+r)(H)^{1/T} - 1, \quad (39)$$

where

$$H = D/\left[\prod_{t=1}^{T-1}\left[1 - F(b(t))\right]\left\{D\left[1 - F(b(T))\right] + CEQ_0^{b(T)}(\tilde{X})\right\}\right].$$

Equations (38) and (39) indicate that both the cost of debt capital and the yield to maturity on a finite-maturity and non-coupon-bearing bond depend on its time to maturity.

It is interesting to note that if we assume that the probabilities of the firm's survival are exogeneously given and identical in all periods and ignore the possible payment to the bondholders upon bankruptcy, (39) reduces to $\hat{R} = (1+r)[1 - F(b)]^{-1} - 1$, which is the same as Eq. (6) in Yawitz [47]. Therefore, the proposition that risk differentials (or risk premiums) are independent of maturity given in Bierman and Hass [5] and Yawitz [47] is derived under rather special conditions.

V. Conclusions

The recent developments in the pricing of risky debt within various frameworks have been reviewed and discussed in the paper. Thus, we have rigorously examined the determinants of the cost of debt capital. It is hoped the more rigorous theories of the cost of debt capital will provide a better framework for empirical work on the risk premiums on corporate bonds. There are a number of interesting problems, such as how the explicit consideration of other agency costs, the managerial incentive, and the differential personal taxes might affect the determinants of the cost of debt capital, which deserve our futher attention.

REFERENCES

1. D. P. Baron. "Default Risk, Homemade Leverage, and the Modigliani-Miller Theorem," *American Economic Review* (March 1974).
2. ———. "Firm Valuation, Corporate Taxes, and Default Risk," *Journal of Finance* (December 1975).
3. N. Baxter. "Leverage, Risk of Rein and the Cost of Capital," *Journal of Finance* (September 1967).
4. F. Black and M. Scholes. "The Pricing of Options and Corporate Liabilities," *Journal of Political Economy* (May-June 1973).
5. H. Bierman, Jr. and J. E. Hass. "An Analytic Model of Bond Risk Differentials," *Journal of Financial and Quantitative Analysis* (December 1975).
6. A. H. Chen. "A Theory of Corporate Bankruptcy and Optimal Capital Structure," in *Handbook of Financial Economics* (ed. by J. Bicksler) to be published by North-Holland Publishing Co. (1978).
7. ———. "Bankruptcy and Corporate Investment-Financing Decisions," Working Paper, Ohio State University (October 1977).
8. J. C. Cox and S. A. Ross. "The Valuation of Options for Alternative Stochastic Processes," *Journal of Financial Economics* (January-March 1976).
9. D. Durand. "Cost of Debt and Equity Funds for Business: Trends and Problems of Measurement," *Conference on Research on Business Finance, New York: National Bureau of Economic Research,* (1952).
10. E. J. Elton, M. J. Gruber and J. B. Lightstone. "The Impact of Bankruptcy on the Firm's Capital Structure, the Reasonableness of Mergers and the Risk Independence of Projects," mimeo, New York University (1977).
11. E. F. Fama and M. H. Miller. *The Theory of Finance*, Holt, Rinehart, and Winston, New York (1972).
12. E. F. Fama. "Risk-Adjusted Discount Rates and Capital Budgeting Under Uncertainty," *Journal of Financial Economics* (August 1977).
13. L. Fisher. "Determinants of Risk Premiums on Corporate Bonds," *Journal of Political Economy* (June 1959).
14. D. Galai and R. W. Masulis. "The Option Pricing Model and the Risk Factor of Stock," *Journal of Financial Economics* (January-March 1976).
15. M. J. Gordon. "Towards a Theory of Financial Distress," *Journal of Finance* (May 1971).
16. ——— and L. I. Gould. "The Cost of Equity Capital: A Reconsideration," this issue, pp. 849–861.
17. ——— and C. Y. Kwan. "Towards an Empirically Relevant Theory of Corporate Leverage," mimeo, University of Toronto (September 1977).
18. R. Hamada. "Portfolio Analysis, Market Equilibrium and Corporation Finance," *Journal of Finance* (March 1969).
19. J. Hirschleifer. *Investment, Interest and Capital*, Englewood Cliffs, New Jersey: Prentice-Hall, (1970)
20. M. Jensen and W. Meckling. "Theory of the Firm: Managerial Behavior, Agency Costs and Ownership Structure," *Journal of Financial Economics* (October 1976).
21. E. H. Kim. "A Mean-Variance Theory of Optimal Capital Structure and Corporate Debt Capacity," *Journal of Finance* (March 1978).

22. A. Kraus and R. Litzenberger. "A State-Preference Model of Optimal Financial Leverage," *Journal of Finance* (September 1973).

23. W. Y. Lee and H. H. Barker. "Bankruptcy Costs and the Firm's Optimal Debt Capacity: A Positive Theory of Capital Structure," *Southern Economic Journal* (March 1977).

24. J. Lintner. "The Valuation of Risk Assets and the Selection of Risky Investments in Stock Portfolios and Capital Budgets," *Review of Economics and Statistics* (February 1965).

25. ———. "The Aggregation of Investor's Diverse Judgments and Preferences in Purely Competitive Securities Markets," *Journal of Financial and Quantitative Analysis* (December 1969).

26. ———. "Bankruptcy Risk, Market Segmentation, and Optimal Capital Structure," in *Risk and Return in Finance*, I. Friend and J. L. Bicksler (eds.), Ballinger Publishing Co., Massachusetts, (1977).

27. R. C. Merton. "Theory of Rational Option Pricing," *Bell Journal of Economics and Management Science* (Spring 1973).

28. ———. "On the Pricing of Corporate Debt: The Risk Structure of Interest Rates," *Journal of Finance* (May 1974).

29. ———. "Option Pricing When Underlying Stock Returns Are Discontinuous," *Journal of Financial Economics* (January 1976).

30. M. Miller. "Debt and Taxes," Presidential Address, *Journal of Finance* (May 1977).

31. F. F. Modigliani and M. H. Miller. "The Cost of Capital Corporation Finance, and the Theory of Investment," *American Economic Review* (June 1958).

32. ——— and ———. "Corporation Income Taxes and the Cost of Capital: A Correction," *American Economic Review* (June 1963).

33. J. Mossin. "Equilibrium in a Capital Asset Market," *Econometrica* (October 1966).

34. S. C. Myers and S. M. Turnbull. "Capital Budgeting and the Capital Asset Pricing Model: Good News and Bad News," *Journal of Finance* (May 1977).

35. A. A. Robichek and S. C. Myers. "Problems in the Theory of Optimal Capital Structure," *Journal of Financial and Quantitative Analysis* (June 1966).

36. M. Rubinstein. "A Mean-Variance Synthesis of Corporate Financial Theory," *Journal of Finance* (March 1973).

37. ———. "Corporate Financial Policy in Segmented Security Markets," *Journal of Financial and Quantitative Analysis* (December 1973).

38. J. H. Scott. "A Theory of Optimal Capital Structure," *The Bell Journal of Economics and Management Science* (Spring 1976).

39. ———. "Bankruptcy, Secured Debt, and Optimal Capital Structure," *Journal of Finance* (March 1977).

40. W. F. Sharpe. "Capital Asset Prices: A Theory of Market Equilibrium under Conditions of Risk," *Journal of Finance* (September 1964).

41. C. W. Smith, Jr.. "Option Pricing: A Review," *Journal of Financial Economics* (January-March 1976).

42. J. Stiglitz. "A Re-Examination of the Modigliani-Miller Theorem," *American Economic Review* (December 1969).

43. ———. "Some Aspects of the Pure Theory of Corporate Finance: Bankruptcies and Takeovers," *The Bell Journal of Economics and Management* (Autumn 1972).

44. ———. "On the Irrelevance of Corporate Financial Policy," *American Economic Review* (December 1969).

45. S. M. Turnbull. "Capital Structure, Debt Capacity and the Investment Decision," Working Paper, Department of Political Economy, University of Toronto (September 1977).

46. J. B. Williams. *The Theory of Investment Value*, Harvard University Press (1938), pp. 72–73.

47. J. B. Yawitz. "An Analytical Model of Interest Rate Differential and Different Default Recoveries," *Journal of Financial and Quantitative Analysis* (September 1977).

For Further Study

Besides the papers collected in this section, some other suggested references are:

1. Black, F. and M. Scholes (1973). "The Pricing of Options and Corporate Liabilities". *Journal of Political Economy* (May-June 1973), pp. 637–654.
2. DeAngelo, H. and R. Masulis (1980). "Optimal Capital Structure Under Corporate and Personal Taxation". *Journal of Financial Economics* (March 1980), pp. 3–30.
3. Kim, E. (1978). "A Mean Variance Theory of Optimal Capital Structure and Corporate Debt Capacity". *Journal of Finance* (March 1978), pp. 45–64.
4. Modigliani, F. and M. Miller (1963). "Corporation Income Taxes and the Cost of Capital: a Correction". *American Economic Review* (June 1963), p. 433–443.
5. _____ , "The Cost of Capital, Corporate Finance, and the Theory of Investment". *American Economic Review* (June, 1958), pp. 261–297.
6. Myers, S. (1977). "Determinants of Corporate Borrowing". *Journal of Financial Economics* (November 1977), pp. 147–176.
7. Reilly, F.K. and R.S. Sidhu (1980). "The Many Uses of Bond Duration". *Financial Analysts Journal* (July-August, 1980), pp. 2–16.
8. Roll, R. (1977). "A Critique of Asset Pricing Theory's Tests". *Journal of Financial Economics* (March 1977), pp. 129–176.
9. Sharpe, W.F. (1964). "Capital Asset Prices: a Theory of Market Equilibrium Under Conditions of Risk". *Journal of Finance* (September 1964), pp. 425–442.
10. Taggert, R. (1980). "Taxes and Corporate Capital Structure in an Incomplete Market". *Journal of Finance* (June 1980), pp. 645–659.
11. Tuttle, D.L. and R.H. Litzenberger (1968). "Leverage, Diversification and Capital Market Effects on a Risk-adjusted Capital Budgeting Framework". *Journal of Finance* (June, 1968), pp. 427–443.

Part IV

Capital Budgeting
Decision Making

Introduction

The capital budgeting decision is one of the most important topics in financial management education. Basic accounting, economics, and finance courses discuss capital budgeting methods in some detail. Various methods generally introduced to the student include: the payback method, the net present value (NPV) method, the internal rate of return (IRR) method, as well as the decision-tree method and simulation. These methods are applied to various examples of cash flows from investment projects. Thus, the first finance course generally introduces many of the concepts and procedures necessary to make investment decisions. However, issues relating to the uncertainty of cash flows, inflation, and the intertemporal nature of capital budgeting decisions are generally left to a second course in financial management. The six papers in Part IV allow the student in a second corporate finance course to review topics covered in previous courses as well as to explore some new capital budgeting concepts and methods.

Hastie (1974) reviews current alternative capital budgeting methods and summarizes managers' opinions on their advantages and disadvantages. The paper serves to bridge the separate concerns of academicians and practitioners and can aid the student in constructing a compromise view of theory and practice in capital budgeting.

255

The CAPM can be used to estimate the required rates of return or risk-adjusted discount rate for capital budgeting decisions (see Rubenstein (1973) in Part II). Myers and Turnbull (1977) investigate the advantages and disadvantages associated with use of the CAPM in capital budgeting decisions. The good news is that it is possible to use the CAPM in capital investment decisions provided that the right asset beta is used to calculate the discount rate. The bad news is that the right asset beta depends on project life, the growth trend of expected cash flow as well as other variables. The actual market value of a firm can be decomposed into a "perpetual" value and a value associated with the growth opportunities discussed by M&M (1961) (Part VI). Since growth opportunities affect observed systematic risk, the correct beta is thus not easily obtained. A more theoretical interpretation of corporate borrowing, real options, the cost of capital and beta estimation can be found in Myers (1977). In a similar but more complicated paper, Fama (1977) investigates the potential problems of using the CAPM estimated risk-adjusted discount rate for multi-period capital budgeting decisions.

In an innovative paper, Van Horne (1969) uses the concept of a product life cycle to resolve the uncertainty in cash flows for new products. This paper points to the fruitful result which can arise when concepts from marketing are incorporated into finance and accounting problems to improve the precision of decisions on new projects under uncertainty.

The relationship between inflation and capital budgeting has been extensively investigated by academicians and practitioners. Cooley, Roenfelt, and Chew (1975) (CRC) present a normative capital budgeting procedure that explicitly incorporates anticipated inflation and allows for uncertainties in real cash flows. Using the NPV method, CRC suggested that real net cash inflow or an inflation- and risk-adjusted discount rate can be used to incorporate the impacts of known inflation on the capital budgeting decision. Some issues related to uncertain inflation are also discussed.

By incorporating uncertain inflation into the CAPM, Chen and Boness (1975) express expected rate of return for a common stock as

risk-free rate + (market price of risk) (the covariance between the stock's rate of return and that of the market portfolio) − (the covariance between the stock's rate of return and the inflation rate).

The term in brackets is the beta, or the measure of systematic risk of the stock. There are two covariance terms in brackets. If the latter covariance is positive (negative), then the real beta will be smaller (larger) than the nominal beta. Therefore, uncertain inflation will affect the beta and through it the risk-adjusted discount rate estimate.

Following Nelson's (1976) theoretical analysis of the impacts of inflation on the capital budgeting process and capital/labor mix decision, Kim (1978) empirically demonstrates that inflation has an important impact on the aggregate investment decision.

The capital budgeting decision process for a regulated firm is not exactly identical to that of the unregulated firm. Regulations may lag for a regulated firm. The possible implications of regulation lag on capital budgeting decisions can be found in Brigham and Pettway (1973) and Elton and Gruber (1977).

Finally, the investment decision may be interrelated with the financing decision as well as the dividend payment decision. These issues can be referred to in Myers (1974) listed in Part V and Spies' paper listed in Part IX.

ONE BUSINESSMAN'S VIEW OF CAPITAL BUDGETING

K. LARRY HASTIE

Dr. Hastie is Assistant Treasurer of The Bendix Corporation in Southfield,
Michigan. Formerly he was Director, International Finance and Director,
Financial Studies at Monsanto Company and Manager, Budgeting at
Boise Cascade. He received the MBA and PhD degrees from Cornell
University and has published articles in Managerial Planning, Journal of
Financial and Quantitative Analysis *and* Management Science.

I am continually amazed at the academic community's preoccupation with refining capital expenditure analyses rather than with improving decision making. Unlikely business examples are often emphasized to demonstrate that less refined measurement techniques are unreliable and result in the misranking of projects. This implies that the use of less refined techniques is the most important weakness in the investment decision making process. Further it presumes that the utilization of more refined techniques will improve decision making and corporate profitability. My experience indicates that this assumption is unwarranted.

Because there are many more "apparently acceptable" projects than a company can approve — either because of limited capital or raw materials or because of limited management or engineering talent — elimination of apparently profitable projects becomes the key element of investment decision making. Elimination based on a simple ranking of the projects by the company's preferred evaluation criterion is inappropriate, regardless of the criterion's refinement. In fact, a review of bad investment decisions would probably indicate that the use of more refined evaluation techniques would have changed very few of them.

It is suggested here that use of incorrect assumptions has been a more significant source of bad investment decisions than has the use of simple measurement techniques. Investment decision making could be improved significantly if the emphasis were placed on asking the appropriate strategic questions and providing better assumptions rather than on increasing the sophistication of measurement techniques. While this suggested change in emphasis does not mean that refined evaluation techniques should be discarded, it does mean that their adoption may not result in the desired improvement in corporate profitability.

The following observations are derived from conversations with consultants, professors, and practicing decision makers over a number of years. Necessarily, the observations do not represent scientific evidence; they are reflections. While most of the comments refer to profit oriented businesses, they apply equally to investment decisions in universities, government agencies, or other non-profit organizations.

Survey Results

Studies in the early 1960's indicated that relatively few firms were using discounted cashflow (DCF) and other refined techniques to measure the benefits of proposed capital expenditures. By the late 1960's and early 1970's, studies showed increasing use. However, Thomas Klammer's study [3] showed that as late as 1970, 43% of the firms in his study were not using DCF techniques. These results continue to puzzle researchers and academicians, who find it difficult to understand why corporations use measurement techniques from the "dark ages." From my viewpoint, the answer is fairly simple. It is not clear that more refined techniques lead to better "go-no-go" decisions. While it is generally true that more refined techniques will lead to better project ranking, it has not been demonstrated that better ranking of projects is the key to improved decision making.

To gain a perspective on the importance of measuring the benefits of a project, it is useful to list nine steps in the investment decision making process. They are to (1) determine the alternative investments available; (2) weigh the strategic aspects of the alternatives; (3) collect data and information on the viable alternatives; (4) develop assumptions and calculate the incremental income and cashflow benefits; (5) measure the net benefits; (6) assess the effect that different assumptions have on the project's measured results; (7) analyze the risks of the project; (8) weigh the benefits and strategic purpose of the project against its risks and the constraints of the corporation; and (9) communicate the relevant information to top management in a manner that facilitates effective decision making.

In general, most academicians and many practitioners have overestimated the importance of the fifth step, and academic work over the last two decades has concentrated on improving the techniques that "measure net benefits." Actually, measuring net benefits is one of the least important steps, but at the same time it is one of the easiest areas for which to recommend and implement changes.

Practitioner Problems

Generally speaking, most corporations are dissatisfied with their record of capital investment decisions. Undoubtedly, more corporations would adopt DCF or any other technique if they were convinced that it would improve their decision making ability. To understand why business has resisted wholesale adoption of the techniques so strongly advocated by the academic world, one must understand: (1) the problems of project rationing, (2) the value of project ranking, (3) the problems of single point estimates of profitability, and (4) the characteristics of those who prepare capital expenditure requests.

Project Rationing

In many corporations, a large majority of the approved capital expenditures have pro forma returns that significantly exceed the firm's cost of capital or internal hurdle rate. (Let's ignore for the moment the mandatory or nonearnings projects.) In these cases, almost all measurement criteria — simple or more refined — would lead to the same "go" decision. In addition, in many companies the last project approved (lowest return on discretionary projects) is several percentage points above the firm's cost of capital or average return on investment. This means that the company is project rationing — either for strategic purposes or because of scarce capital or materials or limited management or engineering talent.

Frequently, raising the hurdle rate is suggested as the most appropriate means of solving the project rationing problem. However, this recommendation ignores the strategic importance of projects and the timing of use and return of corporate resources; it does not consider different risk levels; and equally important, it assumes that the quality of the analytical support is the same for all projects. Corporate staffs with experience in reviewing capital expenditure requests know well the difficulty of ranking projects with different risks, strategic purposes, and quality of analytical support.

Ranking or "Go-No Go" Classification

The adoption of refined techniques will not solve the rationing problem. While the use of DCF techniques − as compared to ROI or cash payback − may change the ranking of projects slightly, the decision maker is not concerned with ranking *per se*. He is concerned with whether or not the project should be approved, and I believe that ranking by ROI or cash payback would put 90-95% of the projects in the same "Go" or "No Go" category as would a DCF method of ranking. Moreover, ranking the projects by the preferred criterion − be it a refined or simple criterion − is not a sufficient basis for making the decision; projects should receive more thoughtful review of their risk and strategic purpose. It would be unreasonable to suggest that the accuracy of pro forma projections and the viability of assumptions would warrant one project to be chosen over another simply because its return − DCF, ROI, or cash payback − is several percentage points higher than another. Potential errors in the assumptions tend to overwhelm the errors caused by using less sophisticated evaluation techniques.

The emphasis on simple "Go-No Go" decisions rather than on ranking implies that before new measurement techniques are adopted, they must hold significant promise for different and better decisions. Before one can determine whether different and better decisions will result, it is necessary to understand the causes of bad investment decisions. My own experience suggests that bad decisions are more often caused by using incorrect assumptions than by use of crude measures of benefits.

Errors in Assumptions

In developing a single point estimate of a project's profitability, the choice of assumptions is usually critical. Since a single set of assumptions is typically used in expenditure requests, it is likely that some of them will be wrong. There are two kinds of errors in assumptions — those derived from excessive conservatism or optimism and those caused by poor judgments concerning future uncertainties. These points are not the same.

For example, consider a firm that decided to manufacture products in Germany in 1971 for export into the United States. Given reasonable foreign exchange expectations at that time, it is doubtful that any analyst would have suggested that there was a significant chance of a 50% devaluation of the dollar relative to the German mark over the next few years. In 1971, the projected 20% return of the project compared to the company's 10% cost of capital made the project acceptable. However, following the devaluations the project could well be losing money in 1975 or returning significantly less than the cost of capital. This is not the fault of the capital budgeting method because the DCF, payback or ROI criteria would have yielded the same "Go" decision.

Similarly, a company that evaluated a new product in 1970 and projected significant price appreciation of the product may have realized significantly different results because of the U.S. price freezes starting in 1971. The company may have appropriately estimated product acceptability and inflation rates in the United States but failed to anticipate government price freezes. Similarly, who forecasted in 1972 that crude oil prices would quadruple by 1974?

These examples represent poor judgment of future events rather than excessive optimism. An example of excessive optimism might be assuming that sales of a product will grow at a rate of 15% per year simply because they have over the last three years. Assuming that sales will not increase in the future, in spite of recent growth, thus making the audit results look good, may represent excessive conservatism. It is necessary to understand the difference between these errors in assumption in order to improve decision making.

Since results in most corporations usually fall below pro forma returns in the expenditure requests, top executives tend to be less concerned about eliminating excessive conservatism than they are about improving the corporation's ability to eliminate over-optimism (without stifling aggressiveness) and improving their managers' ability to assess future uncertainties.

Post-Audit Reviews

Traditionally, audit reviews are suggested as the prime restraint against over-optimism. While a post-audit system may help to eliminate some over-optimism, the value of such a system is overly touted. While audits can be effective in reviewing isolated, non-interdependent projects, audits of expansions, replacements, or other interdependent projects require the same type of subjective assumptions used for the expenditure request. Take, for example, the question, "How many times will the replaced machine break down?" It is impossible to audit how many times it would have broken down had it not been replaced. Similarly, "What would have been the sales prices or costs without the expansion?" Obviously, approval of the expansion makes it impossible to determine objectively what the sales would have been had it not been approved.

In most corporations, a majority of the important projects are interdependent; acceptance of a project will affect the sales, costs and/or profitability of other operations. For many projects, the range of reasonably acceptable assumptions for the audit is wide — so wide that the audit can either commend or condemn the original decision. Therefore, the audits do not represent an objective judgment of the quality of past capital expenditure decisions. On the contrary, they can become a game of providing reasonably acceptable assumptions to create the desired "answer" of the auditor. This does not necessarily mean that audits are not beneficial and should be discontinued. However, the threat of audits should not be expected to serve as the primary check on submitting overly optimistic or conservative capital expenditure requests since they can be as poorly conceived and misused as the capital expenditure request itself. They are more effective as a review of the engineering cost group and the team charged with preparing capital expenditure requests than they are as a review of the senior executive acting as the project's proponent.

Expenditure Request Preparers

Given quality performance in the rest of the investment decision making process, more refined techniques will unquestionably lead to better ranking of projects. However, before adopting a more refined technique, the company must determine whether the more correct and more complicated criterion can be successfully implemented within the organization. With regard to the question of whether DCF techniques should be adopted, it is important that all participants in the investment decision making process understand the characteristics and meaning of DCF techniques. Proponents of DCF techniques should be aware that the ability of individuals preparing capital expenditure analyses varies significantly among companies and from division to division. Moreover, some expenditure request preparers do not have access to a computer. Therefore, the cost of educating the corporation and of using the techniques may be significant — especially in light of other flaws in decision making. This is especially true in terms of opportunity costs. Before DCF and other refined methods are adopted, the company must determine whether its effort should be directed at refining the measurement techniques or at improving other steps in the investment decision making process.

These comments do not imply that companies should discontinue the use of DCF or other refined techniques in all cases; once the educational process has been undertaken, the refined approaches should remain in use for large projects. However, lower level staffs should first learn to perform sensitivity analysis with ROI or cash payback and then learn how to read present value tables. For small projects at lower levels of the organization, simple criteria will provide good decisions as often as will cumbersome refined techniques. When more refined techniques are used, the company should be (1) performing good incremental analysis, (2) considering the strategic aspects of the investment, and (3) communicating the impact different assumptions have on the project.

The adoption of refined measurement techniques is easier to implement than any of the three preceding steps, but is also the least productive for improved decision making. This may explain why many companies who have refined their measurement criteria are unhappy with the results and why it is not realistic to expect more widespread use of these refined techniques in the future.

Dealing with Uncertainty

In part, the failure of investment decision making relates to the emphasis corporations have placed on "single point estimate" presentations, e.g., "the project's return is 15.2%." The calculation of this estimated return — either in terms of ROI or DCF — requires many assumptions, no single set of which is "correct." The expenditure request reviewers are, at best, shooting in the dark unless they know the key assumptions and their impacts on profitability.

The key problem is how to communicate the uncertainty to top management so they can make intelligent decisions. Certainly a single point estimate — be it a simple or refined criterion — does not communicate enough information. The textbook answer to this uncertainty assessment has been risk analysis or sensitivity analysis. Although neither is purported to be widely used in companies, it is suggested here that risk analysis has failed to improve decision making, and it will later be shown that the use of sensitivity analysis is the key to improving the communication of uncertainty to decision makers.

Risk Analysis

In the risk analysis popularized by Hertz [2], individuals are asked to place probabilities on certain events or variables. Unfortunately, the businessman is working with the same forecasting uncertainty or bias in risk analysis as that used to develop assumptions for single point estimates. In many cases, events occur that few businessmen expect; yet they have significant impacts upon the project's profitability.

In the case of many "bad" decisions, unfavorable profit results have been caused by events which are difficult to assess in the year prior to their occurrence, e.g., U.S. price freezes in 1971 and the doubling of crude oil prices. Not only would such events have been allotted small probabilities, but most managers would have considered them unimportant because they were not among the key elements of uncertainty being assessed. Moreover, the possibility of these events may have been dismissed as irrelevant. The investment decision affected by them would probably have been the same if DCF criteria had been used instead of a simple cash payback or ROI.

In addition, the optimism of managers affects the determinations of probabilities in risk analysis in the same way assumptions are determined for single point estimates. In the experience of this author, no matter how much the risk analysis coordinator tries to solicit information that would indicate losses, the final reports underestimate their probability. While no scientific data are offered here to prove this, it is believed that the probability of losing money in a project must be greater than 0%, 5%, or 15%, whatever estimated results typically showed. The past record of poorly performing divisions, plants, or products indicates that the probabilities were much higher. Other individuals experienced in risk analyses share these views.

Evidence of the failure of risk analysis is seen by the number of companies that have formally adopted it and have since ceased using it in a meaningful way. While early critics of risk analysis may question how well it was originally accepted by senior executives, the fact remains that even corporate staff members have become disenchanted. As a result, risk analysis has received criticism from all sides — senior management, operating management, and corporate staff members; consequently, its use will probably continue to decline. While it has the potential to be usefully applied, most corporations are not ready for such a refined technique at this time. For a more comprehensive discussion of the problems associated with using risk analysis, see [1].

Recent papers and articles on portfolio analysis and other highly refined techniques provide little value for current and future capital expenditure decisions. A discussion of certainty equivalents and complex probability distributions may have certain pedagogical value for students, but it is wishful thinking for authors to suggest that these can be practically applied to real capital budgeting situations. It is necessary to learn to apply the simplest of the "Hertz" risk analyses before seriously considering application of portfolio analysis and especially the more refined types being discussed, promoted, and published today. To be more direct, in the area of capital budgeting, more calculus will be of little or no value to the real world of business.

Recommendations

It is my belief that the solution to these problems will result from: (1) utilizing existing analytical techniques more effectively in order to communicate relevant information to top management, and (2) developing a comprehensive understanding of the corporate strategy. The necessary tools have all been invented—the problem is how to utilize them to expose the key assumptions and subjective judgments to management review. Many corporations excel in providing pages of numerical support in capital expenditure requests, but even so, fail to communicate relevant information to management. In addition,

corporations must spend more time and effort determining corporate strategy. Why spend money on engineering and financial analysis when the decision will be "no" because the company does not want to expand in this business, independent of the fact that the project earns more than the cost of capital?

Weighing Strategic Aspects

One of the keys to different and better decisions is development of comprehensive understanding of the corporation's strategy. Even though the overall strategy of the corporation may be well considered and communicated, it is unlikely that the micro-strategic aspects of specific investments have been considered. While frequently overlooked by middle levels of management, these strategic aspects must be weighed once alternative investments have been determined. Examples of these considerations might include whether or not to remain dependent upon this community's labor market, whether or not the political and/or socio-economic climate of the country is conducive to new or additional investments or what the long-term business climate is in Germany, the United Kingdom, or Argentina. If such considerations give the investment a low priority, there is no reason to collect information and prepare an analysis.

After the initial steps of the investment decision making process are completed, the company must again ask strategic questions from a macro-corporate viewpoint that can be answered only at the top levels of the company. Such questions might include: Why not "milk" a mature business rather than expand? Do we, as a company, wish to remain so dependent on Saudi Arabian crude oil? Do we want to remain or grow in this business? Will we be competitive in this business five years from now? Are we expanding in areas of our competitive advantages? Do we wish to increase the corporation's dependence upon earnings from this industry?

One way to clarify the strategy of the corporation and define each division's relationship to the overall strategy is to segregate the divisions into one of three categories—businesses in which the corporation wants to expand aggressively, those in which it wants to maintain its current position, and those to be divested or liquidated. This segregation should be completed prior to the review of any capital expenditures. For each of these categories, acceptable returns and risks may be significantly different. In the first, it may be desirable to accept lower returns initially in order to get a "foot in the door" or in order to grow to a size significant within the company or industry. In the second category, replacement expenditures are normally approved and expansions must exceed corporate hurdle rates. In the third category, capital expenditures must significantly exceed corporate hurdle rates or directly enhance the liquidation or divestiture position.

In effect, the strategy process establishes different standards for different businesses. One project may be rejected despite its high returns, while another may be accepted even though its returns are far below a corporate hurdle rate. Once the corporation has developed and communicated the overall strategy to appropriate management, management can direct its attention to generating and evaluating proposed capital expenditures.

Adoption of New Analytical Techniques

Many corporations have been too quick to adopt new evaluation techniques without a clear understanding of weaknesses in the overall investment decision making process. The assessment of the existing process should be directed at making better rather than more "sophisticated" decisions. The corporation must first ask: What are the weaknesses of the current investment process? Is the company faced with project rationing so that it must concentrate on eliminating many apparently desirable projects? Or, is it unable to generate enough acceptable projects to be reviewed? These are far different problems and warrant far different remedies. One of the most effective ways to determine real weaknesses is to study past decisions, especially those later proved to have been incorrect.

Sensitivity Analysis

In contrast to the view of risk analysis, more positive statements can be made about the use and acceptance of sensitivity analysis. "Sensitivity analysis" refers here to the process of changing variables or assumptions to determine their impact on a project's profitability. It does not involve the use of probabilities.

There appear to be more corporations using sensitivity analysis than surveys indicate. In some cases firms may not know that what they are undertaking is called "sensitivity analysis," and it probably is not in the sophisticated, computer-oriented sense. However, most individuals charged with preparing capital expenditure requests do consider various prices, volumes, and growth rates, and a variety of these assumptions are tried before establishing the final ones for the expenditure request. Typically, analysts or middle managers eliminate the alternative assumptions and solutions in order to simplify the decision making process for higher management.

It is my impression that many companies are presenting the results of sensitivity analysis on their capital expenditure requests, and it is becoming more widely accepted and used by senior executives. Its presentation might be in the form of Exhibit 1 or 2. Exhibit 1 indicates that price and life of the project are the key factors determining its profitability. The most vertical line in the graph indicates the most profit sensitive factor. Volume is shown to have almost no impact on the profitability of the project.

There are several reasons why sensitivity analysis is helpful to investment decision making. First, the results of sensitivity analysis indicate to the expenditure request preparer the key factors to be analyzed and supported. Second, it enables the senior executive or line manager to understand which variables are the most critical. If the senior executive knows that volume is the key factor, he can demand that the sponsoring manager justify his price assumptions; and he can avoid wasting his own time attempting to understand or question the aspects with little impact on the project's profitability. Third, it forces the reviewers to recognize the wide or narrow range of potential profitability and encourages explicit discussion of risks and uncertainties. To the extent that the key factors are controllable, it also indicates the areas in which the project manager must concentrate his efforts subsequent to the project's approval. Further, it is a learning technique to help managers understand the situation and explain the project to others. Additionally, it may enable management to better understand the factors that determine the profitability of existing investments related to the project but unaffected by the expenditure decision.

One of the keys to better use of sensitivity analysis lies in package computer models from outside consulting firms or internal computer systems having capabilities to enable fast start-up and minimum programming changes. The more cases that can be run with the least "start-up" problems, the more valuable sensitivity analysis can be.

Communicating Assumptions

In effect, part of the decision making process involves simplifying reality to a small package of information that facilitates effective decision making by top management. In doing so, it is necessary to prevent biasing of the information in favor of the project. While analysts and middle managers must eliminate some alternative assumptions and solutions, many corporations attempt to oversimplify decisions by eliminating all alternative assumptions and ignoring the key assumptions for the single point estimate of profitability.

Exhibit 1. Sensitivity Analysis Summary

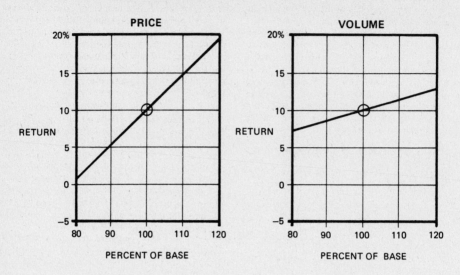

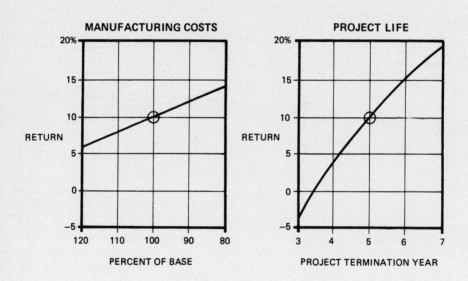

Exhibit 2. Sensitivity Analysis

Project Return in Capital Expenditure Request: 10.0%

Project Returns Under Various Assumptions:

Prices	Return
Down 20%	1.0%
Down 10%	5.5%
Up 10%	14.5%
Up 20%	19.0%

Volume	Return
Down 20%	7.5%
Down 10%	8.8%
Up 10%	11.2%
Up 20%	12.5%

Manufacturing Costs	Return
Up 20%	8.4%
Up 10%	7.8%
Down 10%	12.2%
Down 20%	14.6%

Life of Project	Return
3 Years	−3.0%
4 Years	4.0%
5 Years	10.0%
6 Years	15.0%
7 Years	19.0%

A surprising number of corporations provide many pages of figures, yet do not provide a listing or description of the key assumptions. One possible way of eliminating or questioning these potentially incorrect assumptions is to ensure that they are given proper review by top management, which has a broader perspective of the corporation than other levels of management. It certainly gives top management a better opportunity to question the viability of the project in a meaningful way.

The key question relates to how involved top management is in capital expenditure decisions. There is a natural tendency for division managers to want to obviate the decision making role of top management. Because lower level managements want to gain approval of their projects, they tend to emphasize their strengths and fail to raise important questions so that the system tends to ignore key factors and assumptions. In effect, top management determines its decision making role by allowing the investment process to oversimplify the information it reviews. If top management is to have a key role in the investment decision, it must necessarily be provided with the assumptions and the relevant information.

It was argued earlier that project rationing was one of the key factors in investment decision making. The problem of determining which projects to approve may be alleviated by: (1) eliminating the constraints on the corporation—such as limited capital or raw materials or limited management or engineering talent—or (2) improving the quality of the assumptions. The latter point suggests that the projects may not be as desirable as the single point estimates might indicate. In the short run, there may be little the corporation can do to eliminate the constraints; even so, significant steps can be taken to improve the quality of the assumptions.

Once the corporate strategy has been defined and communicated, the capital expenditure prepared must determine the key factors affecting the profitability of the project, justify the assumptions that have been chosen for those factors and communicate the relevant information to top management. By giving the assumptions on key factors good visibility, the corporation increases the opportunity for questioning poor assumptions and investigating alternatives.

Conclusion

It should be clear that "measuring the benefit of projects"—as DCF, ROI, or payback approaches attempt to do—is only one step in the investment decision making process. We have erred too long by exaggerating the "improvement in decision making" that might result from the adoption of DCF or other refined evaluation techniques. What is needed are approximate answers to the precise problem rather than precise answers to the approximate problem. There is little value in refining an analysis that does not consider the most appropriate alternative and does not utilize sound assumptions. Management should spend its time improving the quality of the assumptions and assuring that all of the strategic questions have been asked, rather than implementing and using more refined evaluation techniques. The selection of better assumptions can be facilitated through making the assumptions more visible and asking the right strategic questions. In most capital expenditure analyses, the major assumptions are either not provided or they are buried in the supporting detail. More attention should be directed toward improved use of sensitivity analysis and the communication of its results to top management. This would enable executives to direct their review of projects to areas that are key to profitability and enable them to demand more detailed justification of crucial assumptions.

REFERENCES

1. E. Eugene Carter, "What are the Risks in Risk Analysis?" *Harvard Business Review* (July 1972).

2. David B. Hertz, "Risk Analysis in Capital Investment," *Harvard Business Review* (January 1964).

3. Thomas P. Klammer, "Empirical Evidence of the Adoption of Sophisticated Capital Budgeting Techniques," *Journal of Business* (July 1972).

CAPITAL BUDGETING AND THE CAPITAL ASSET PRICING MODEL: GOOD NEWS AND BAD NEWS

Stewart C. Myers and Stuart M. Turnbull*

I. Introduction

This paper derives and presents expressions for the market value of a long-lived capital investment project, assuming that the capital asset pricing model (CAPM) holds in each period. We use these expressions to examine the determinants of beta and to evaluate traditional capital budgeting procedures based on the discounted cash flow formula and the opportunity cost of capital.

The good news is that it is possible to value capital investments using relatively simple formulas derived from the CAPM. Also, the traditional procedures give close-to-correct answers, provided that the right asset beta is used to calculate the discount rate.

The bad news is that the right asset beta depends on project life, the growth trend of expected cash flows, and other variables which are not usually considered important in assessing business risk. Moreover, for growth firms the right discount rate cannot be inferred from the observed systematic risk of the firm's stock, even if the firm invests only in projects of a single risk class. The reason is that growth opportunities affect observed systematic risk.

II. Using the CAPM to Value Long Lived Assets

The methodology of using the CAPM to value long lived assets is not new. Bogue and Roll [1], and independently Hamada [5], use the CAPM in a multi-period context. Merton [8] derives a relatively simple valuation formula by assuming that cash flows are auto-correlated and that the interest rate and the market price of risk are constant over time. Myers [11], who also keeps the market price of risk and the interest rate constant, assumes that investors forecast the firm's cash flows using a simple adaptive expectations model. He derives an expression for the value of a firm's assets and its systematic risk.

Treynor and Black [16] argue that the value of an uncertain cash flow should be related to underlying economic variables. They work in continuous time, and derive a partial differential equation describing the market value of the cash flow, given an exogenous risk premium. Brennan [2] derives an expression for this risk premium by assuming the validity of the continuous time analog of the CAPM. Turnbull [17] has generalized and extended the work of Brennan [2] and examined the explicit determinants of systematic risk.

Fama's recent paper [4] starts with the CAPM and derives conditions under

* Massachusetts Institute of Technology and University of Toronto, respectively. The authors are grateful to the London Graduate School of Business Studies for research support, and to Fischer Black, Richard Brealey, Michael Brennan, Robert Merton, and Mark Rubinstein for helpful criticism of early drafts of the paper.

which it is valid to discount a stream of cash flows at a single risk-adjusted rate. The goal of his paper is similar to the goal of ours, but the two papers are based on different assumptions about the stochastic process generating the cash flows.

We now present a generalized model which incorporates the work of Myers [11] and Turnbull [17]. Myers's discrete time framework is used. This sacrifices some of the rigor and generality of Turnbull's results, but is adequate for present purposes, which are to develop the specific implications of the CAPM for capital budgeting.

Assumptions and Notation

Let us suppose that the capital asset pricing model is true now and will be in every relevant future period. Consider a real asset which generates an uncertain stream of cash flows $\tilde{X}_1, \tilde{X}_2, \ldots, \tilde{X}_t$ out to some terminal point $t = T$. The problem is to determine the current equilibrium value of the asset, P_0.

Since the CAPM holds, we know that P_t will be given by

$$P_t = \left[E(\tilde{X}_{t+1} + \tilde{P}_{t+1} | \phi_t) - \lambda \operatorname{cov}(\tilde{X}_{t+1} + \tilde{P}_{t+1}, \tilde{R}_{M,t+1}) \right] / (1 + r), \tag{1}$$

where $E(\tilde{X}_{t+1} | \phi_t)$ represents investors' expectations of $\tilde{X}_{t+1}$ based on the information set, ϕ_t, at time t; $E(\tilde{P}_{t+1} | \phi_t)$ represents investors' expectations of $\tilde{P}_{t+1}$, given the information set at time t; $\tilde{R}_{M,t+1}$ is the return on the market portfolio composed of all risky securities; λ is an exogenous parameter interpreted as the market price of risk, assumed constant over time;[1] and r is the one period risk free rate of interest, also assumed constant over time.[2] Equation (1) illustrates the usual problem with the CAPM: today's price cannot be calculated without knowing the probability distribution of tomorrow's price. The key to solving this problem is to specify how investors' expectations are formed.

We assume that investors attempt to forecast future cash flows from current information. Actual and expected cash flows differ, however:

$$\tilde{X}_t = E(\tilde{X}_t | \phi_{t-1})(1 + \tilde{\delta}_t), \tag{2}$$

where $\tilde{\delta}_t$ is a random disturbance term representing the proportional difference between the actual cash flow and its expected value based upon past information. Realized values of the disturbance term will, in general, depend upon unanticipated events specifically affecting the cash flows, and also upon unanticipated events external to the firm. We assume that the disturbance term can be expressed as a linear combination of a component which is purely firm specific (μ_t), and a second component measuring unanticipated changes in the economy:

$$\tilde{\delta}_t = b\tilde{I}_t + \tilde{\mu}_t. \tag{3}$$

1. Assuming that the market price of risk is constant achieves a great simplification in the valuation formula. However, it is an approximation, for as wealth changes over time, it can affect the market price of risk. See Rubinstein [14] for an extensive discussion of this point.

2. There are two reasons for keeping λ and r constant. The first is a desire for simplicity. The second is the fact that CAPM is not generally correct in a multi-period world if the investment opportunity set is changing stochastically over time. See Fama [3] and Merton [7].

$\tilde{I}_t$ represents the unanticipated changes in some general economic index, and b is a firm-specific constant measuring the sensitivity of the disturbance term to unanticipated changes in the economic index.[3]

We assume, for the present, that the cash flows have no systematic growth, so that $E(\tilde{X}_{t+j}|\phi_{t-1}) = E(\tilde{X}_t|\phi_{t-1})$ for all j and all t. Forecasted values of the expected future cash flows are assumed to be generated by the process[4]

$$E(\tilde{X}_{t+1}|\phi_t) = a_1 X_t + a_2 X_{t-1} + \cdots \tag{4}$$

where $a_1, a_2, \ldots$ are constants summing to unity.

Now, if the weights $a_1, a_2, \ldots$ decline geometrically, then (4) implies that expectations are revised by the simple adaptive expections model

$$E(\tilde{X}_{t+1}|\phi_t) = E(\tilde{X}_t|\phi_{t-1})(1 + \eta\delta_t), \tag{5}$$

where $\eta \equiv a_1$. η, the elasticity of expectations, will normally lie in the range $0 \leqslant \eta \leqslant 1$. We adopt this model of expections for its simplicity and for the intuitively attractive valuation formulas it leads to. However, the qualitative properties discussed below do not appear to depend on the specific model used. Computer simulations indicate that the qualitative results hold when expected values are forecast using the general process described by (4).

Derivation of the Valuation Formula

The price of the asset at any time t, given expected income at that time, can be determined by dynamic programming—that is, by using (1) at the terminal point and working "backwards." Recall that the cash flow streams stops at time T, implying that $P_T \equiv 0$. Therefore, P_{T-1} can be determined from (1), given $E(\tilde{X}_T|\phi_{T-1})$ and using (3):

$$P_{T-1} = E(\tilde{X}_T|\phi_{T-1})(1 - \lambda b\sigma_{IM})/(1 + r), \tag{6}$$

where $\sigma_{IM} \equiv \mathrm{cov}(\tilde{I}_T, \tilde{R}_{MT})$.[5]

At time $T-2$ the present value of the cash flows will depend upon $\tilde{X}_{T-1}$ and $\tilde{P}_{T-1}$. The present value of $\tilde{X}_{T-1}$ is given by $E(\tilde{X}_{T-1}|\phi_{T-2})(1 - \lambda b\sigma_{IM})/(1 + r)$. (We assume that σ_{IM} is constant over time, thus implying a stationary probability distribution for the unanticipated changes in the economic index.) The present value of P_{T-1} will depend upon how expectations are revised at $T-1$, given the information conveyed by observing the discrepancy between the actual value of $\tilde{X}_{T-1}$ and its expected value based on the information set ϕ_{T-2}. The present value of $\tilde{P}_{T-1}$ as of $T-2$ is $E[\tilde{P}_{T-1}|\phi_{T-2}](1 - \lambda\eta b\sigma_{IM})/(1 + r)$. The expectation of $\tilde{P}_{T-1}$ can be expressed in terms of $E[\tilde{X}_T|\phi_{T-2}]$ by using (6).

---

3. We are simplifying by omitting a time subscript from the constant b.

4. As there is only a finite number of observations for the cash flow, the last term in the series is the initial expectation of the cash flow for the first period: $E(\tilde{X}_1|\phi_0)$.

5. We assume that $\tilde{\mu}_t$ is uncorrelated with the market return $\tilde{R}_{Mt}$.

Thus the present value of the asset as of $T-2$ is given by:

$$P_{T-2} = E(\tilde{X}_{T-1}|\phi_{T-2})(1-\lambda b\sigma_{IM})/(1+r)$$

$$+ E(\tilde{X}_{T-1}|\phi_{T-2})(1-\lambda b\sigma_{IM})(1-\lambda \eta b\sigma_{IM})/(1+r)^2. \tag{7}$$

The first term on the right hand side of (7) is the present value of $\tilde{X}_{T-1}$. The second is the present value of $\hat{P}_{T-1}$.

Applying the same methodology, we can find P_{T-3}, P_{T-4}, etc. Eventually we arrive at the current equilibrium value:

$$P_0 = E(\tilde{X}_1|\phi_0)q \sum_{t=0}^{T-1} z^t, \tag{8}$$

where $q = (1-\lambda b\sigma_{IM})/(1+r)$ and $z = (1-\lambda \eta b\sigma_{IM})/(1+r)$. Note that q and z are each less than one.[6] For a very long-lived asset ($T \to \infty$), value is given by

$$P_0 = E(\tilde{X}_1|\phi_0)(1-\lambda b\sigma_{IM})/(r+\lambda \eta b\sigma_{IM}). \tag{9}$$

Equations (8) and (9) are the most basic part of the theory presented in this paper. They are two valuation formulas for single assets (or for firms that can be regarded as single assets), given investors' current expectation for the asset's future cash flow.

Multiple Cash Flow Streams

An obvious extension if the case in which the cash flow $\tilde{X}_t$ can be decomposed into a number of components.[7] If there are two components[7] such that $\tilde{X}_t = \tilde{X}_{1t} + \tilde{X}_{2t}$, $t=1,2,\ldots,T$, then, in general, we will have a double set of variables and parameters: δ_{1t} and δ_{2t}, b_1 and b_2, and η_1 and η_2.[8] The asset can be regarded as a portfolio of claims to two separate cash flow streams $\{X_{1t}\}$ and $\{X_{2t}\}$. The present value of the two components is given by

$$P_0 = E(\tilde{X}_{11}|\phi_0)q_1 \sum_{t=0}^{T-1} z_1^t + E(\tilde{X}_{21}|\phi_0)q_2 \sum_{t=0}^{T-1} z_2^t, \tag{10}$$

6. Providing that σ_{IM} is positive. We assume this throughout the paper.

7. A possible example would be a firm operating in two different industries.

8. One might introduce two underlying indices, I_1 and I_2. This does not change the algebra of our derivations, but it does raise a difficult conceptual problem: how can covariances between the indexes and the market return be constant if there is more than one index?

Suppose there are two indices, I_1 and I_2. Unanticipated changes in these indices affect forecast errors (δ's) for all assets in the economy. Consider the stream of cash flows generated by the market portfolio of all assets, $\{\tilde{X}_t^M\}$. The present value of this stream will obviously depend on $\sigma_{I_1M}, \sigma_{I_2M}$ and the variance of the market asset's rate of return, σ_M^2. But these parameters are almost certainly not constant. If, for example, I_1 is more volatile than I_2, and in a given period there is an unanticipated increase in I_1 and a decrease in I_2, then σ_M^2 will be higher at the start of the next period. The reason is that the part of $\tilde{X}_t^M$ contingent on I_1 will account for a greater proportion of the value of the market portfolio.

In other words, assumptions which appear sensible for a single firm or asset, analyzed in a partial equilibrium context, may be inconsistent in a general equilibrium model.

However, we believe our models are consistent with general equilibrium providing that there is only one underlying index that is systematically related to the market return.

where $q_i = (1 - \lambda b_i \sigma_{IM})/(1 + r)$ and $z_i = (1 - \lambda \eta_i b_i \sigma_{IM})/(1 + r)$. If one of the cash flows, say $\tilde{X}_{2t}$, is uncorrelated with the market portfolio,[9] implying that $b_2 \sigma_{IM} = 0$, then (10) simplifies to

$$P_0 = E(\tilde{X}_{11}|\phi_0) q_1 \sum_{t=1}^{T-1} z_1^t + E(\tilde{X}_{21}|\phi_0) \sum_{t=1}^{T} 1/(1+r)^t. \tag{11}$$

The second component is discounted at the risk free rate of interest.

Growth

Suppose that expected cash flows grow at the exogenous, known rate g.[10] This requires a change in the way expectations are revised:

$$E(\tilde{X}_{t+1}|\phi_t) = E(\tilde{X}_t|\phi_{t-1})(1+g)(1+\eta\delta_t). \tag{12}$$

However, the valuation formulas can be obtained by the same route used above. It turns out that the present value of the cash flows is given by (8), although z must be redefined as $z = (1+g)(1 - \lambda \eta b \sigma_{IM})/(1+r)$.

For a very long lived asset ($T \to \infty$), value is given by

$$P_0 = E(\tilde{X}_1|\phi_0)(1 - \lambda b \sigma_{IM})/[r - g + \lambda \eta b \sigma_{IM}(1+g)]. \tag{9a}$$

In the absence of uncertainty, this reduces to the well-known constant growth formula of Williams [18] and Gordon and Shapiro [6].

III. Determinants of Asset Betas

The valuation formulas imply a theory of the real determinants of systematic risk, —i.e., of beta. Beta depends on the cyclicality of the component cash flows (measured by $b_i \sigma_{IM}$), on the growth rate of the cash flows, on the elasticities of expectation (η_i), and on the duration of the asset's cash flow (T).

It is helpful to start with a single cash flow stream with no growth ($g = 0$). We are concerned with beta in the interval $t = 0$ to $t = 1$. (Later periods' betas will generally differ, providing T is finite.) The first step in computing β is to write down an expression for R_1, the rate of return for this period.

Define Q_t as a cash flow multiplier for period t: $Q_t = P_t/E(\tilde{X}_{t+1}|\phi_t)$. Then

$$1 + \tilde{R}_1 = \frac{\tilde{X}_1 + E(\tilde{X}_2|\phi_1)Q_1}{E(\tilde{X}_1|\phi_0)Q_0}$$

$$= \left[E(\tilde{X}_1|\phi_0)(1 + \tilde{\delta}_1) + E(\tilde{X}_1|\phi_0)(1 + \eta\tilde{\delta}_1)Q_1\right] / \left[E(\tilde{X}_1|\phi_0)Q_0\right]. \tag{15}$$

From (15) and the definition of β,

$$\beta = \left[(1 + \eta Q_1)/Q_0\right] b \sigma_{IM}/\sigma_M^2. \tag{16}$$

9. This would correspond to a "firm effect" which generates only unsystematic risk.

10. If growth is stochastic, the random part can be incorporated into the uncertain cash flow.

For a project of infinite life, $Q_0 = Q_1$, and

$$\beta = [(r+\eta)/(1-\lambda b\sigma_{IM})]b\sigma_{IM}/\sigma_M^2. \tag{17}$$

As might be expected, β is positively related to $b\sigma_{IM}$. Also, $\delta\beta/\delta\eta > 0$, although this result holds, in general, only for $T > 1$. There is no revision of expectations for a single period project. Finally, it can be shown that $\delta\beta/\delta T < 0$ for $0 \leqslant \eta < 1$; this occurs essentially because an increase in asset life increases the cash flow multiplier Q_0 relative to Q_1.

The relationship of beta to T and η is illustrated by the numerical results in the top panel of Table 1. These were calculated from (16), given a risk free rate of $r = 0.05$, an expected return on the market of $E[\tilde{R}_M] = 0.12$, a market variance of $\sigma_M^2 = .02$ and a covariance term of $b\sigma_{IM} = .025$. The impact of asset life on beta is dramatic for low values of η. However, for assets of moderately long life (say $T > 10$), beta is approximately proportional to η.

TABLE 1

CALCULATED BETAS

1. Asset beta as a function of asset life (T) and elasticity of expectations (η).

	$T=1$	2	5	10	20	40	∞
$\eta = 0$	1.438	.737	.316	.177	.110	.080	.068
$\eta = .5$	1.438	1.080	.866	.797	.766	.755	.753
$\eta = 1.0$	1.438	1.438	1.438	1.438	1.438	1.438	1.438

2. Asset beta as a function of growth rate (g) and elasticity of expections (η), for infinite-lived project ($T = \infty$).

	$g=0$	.02	.04	.08	.12
$\eta = 0$	.068	.041	.014	a	a
$\eta = .5$	.753	.740	.726	.699	a
$\eta = 1.0$	1.438	1.438	1.438	1.438	1.438

a Asset value not defined.

Assumptions

$$r = .05, \quad \sigma_M^2 = .02, \quad b\sigma_{IM} = .025, \quad E[\tilde{R}_M] = .12.$$

Some find it difficult to understand how longer-lived projects can be safer in the sense of having a lower β. They forget that β depends on the systematic risk borne over the single period from $t = 0$ to $t = 1$. The investor at $t = 0$ looks forward to cash return $\tilde{X}_1$ and also an asset value $\tilde{P}_1$.

You can think of an asset's beta as a weighted average of a cash beta, $\beta(X)$, and a price beta, $\beta(P)$. These apply to $\tilde{R}(X)$, the rate of return generated by cash, and $\tilde{R}(P)$, the rate of return generated by capital gains or losses. $\tilde{R}(X)$ is proportional to the underlying cash flow $\tilde{X}_1$ and $\tilde{R}(P)$ is proportional to shifts in investors' expectations of the cash flows' future values. So long as $\eta < 1$, $\tilde{R}(P)$ will be less volatile than $\tilde{R}(X)$. Thus, $\text{Cov}(\tilde{R}(P), \tilde{R}_M) < \text{Cov}(\tilde{R}(X), \tilde{R}_M)$ and $\beta(P) < \beta(X)$.

Since β is a weighted average of $\beta(P)$ and $\beta(X)$ it declines as the future price $\tilde{P}_1$

accounts for more of the present value P_0. This is what occurs as project life (T) is lengthened. The only exception is when $\eta = 1$ and $\beta(X) = \beta(P)$.

The Relation Between Growth and Beta

Exogenous growth in the cash flows will in general affect systematic risk. The derivation for beta as a function of g is similar to that used for (15). The rate of return is

$$1 + \tilde{R}_1 = \left[(1 + \tilde{\delta}_1) + (1 + g)(1 + \eta\tilde{\delta}_1)Q_1\right]/Q_0.$$

Hence, beta is defined by

$$\beta = \{[1 + \eta(1 + g)Q_1]/Q_0\}b\sigma_{IM}/\sigma_M^2. \tag{18}$$

The beta of a perpetuity is

$$\beta = \{[r - g + \eta(1 + g)]/(1 - \lambda b\sigma_{IM})\}b\sigma_{IM}/\sigma_M^2. \tag{19}$$

Increasing the growth rate decreases β, provided $\eta < 1$:

$$\delta\beta/\delta g = -[(1 - \eta)/(1 - \lambda b\sigma_{IM})]b\sigma_{IM}/\sigma_M^2. \tag{20}$$

If $\eta = 1$, then $\delta\beta/\delta g = 0$, and growth has no effect on β. The explanation of these results is similar to that given for the effects of maturity upon beta. The relationship between beta and growth for various levels of η is illustrated in the bottom panel of Table 1.

Determinants of Beta in a Multi-Cash Flow Model

Suppose the asset's cash flow can be decomposed into different components. Each component is like a distinct asset, with a beta determined by the factors discussed just above. The composite asset's beta is a weighted average of each component's own beta.

$$\beta = \sum_j w_j \beta_j, \tag{21}$$

where β_j is the beta for the jth component of the cash flow and w_j is the proportional contribution of the jth component to P_0.

The effect of asset life on beta when there are two component cash flows is shown in Table 2. The elasticities of expectations, η_1 and η_2, are assumed to be equal to one, so that β_1 and β_2 are independent of T. β_2 is held constant at 1.0 and β_1 varied from 0 to 2.0. The table shows that beta is again a declining function of asset life whenever $\beta_1 \neq \beta_2$. (The expected annual cash flow generated by each component is held constant.) The reason is that the weights w_1 and w_2 depend on T.[11] As the horizon is extended, the present value of each stream increases, but not at the same rate. The cash flows of the stream having the higher β are "discounted" at a higher rate, and thus the weight put on high-β stream declines as T increases.

11. Each cash flow is assumed to end in the same period T.

273

The longer the horizon, the greater the proportion of P_0 generated by the safer stream and the lower the asset's beta.

TABLE 2

CALCULATED BETAS FOR ASSET YIELDING TWO-COMPONENT CASH FLOW STREAM

Asset beta as a function of asset life (T) and betas of component cash flows (β_1, β_2).

β_1	$T=1$	2	5	10	20	40	∞
0	.484	.476	.454	.423	.375	.325	.294
.5	.746	.744	.739	.731	.721	.711	.707
1.0	1.0	1.0	1.0	1.0	1.0	1.0	1.0
1.5	1.246	1.244	1.239	1.233	1.225	1.219	1.218
2.0	1.485	1.478	1.459	1.434	1.406	1.389	1.387

Assumptions

1. $\beta_2 = 1.0$ and $\eta = 1.0$ in all cases.
2. $r = .05$, and $E[\tilde{R}_M] = .12$.
3. $E(\tilde{X}_1 | \phi_0) = E(\tilde{X}_2 | \phi_0)$ and $g_1 = g_2 = 0$. Thus each component generates one half of the asset's expected cash flow.

Capital Budgeting

Capital budgeting is essentially a problem of valuation; the point of the exercise is to find assets that are worth more than they cost. The most-used valuation standard is to accept investment projects if

$$\mathrm{PV} = \sum_{t=1}^{T} E\left(\tilde{X}_t | \phi_0\right)/(1+R)^t > -X_0, \tag{22}$$

where PV is the present value of the future cash flows and R is the opportunity cost of capital appropriate to the project. Usually X_0 is the required investment and thus is negative.

In a certain world with perfect capital markets, this procedure is exactly right. The $\{X_t\}$ are not random variables and R is simply the rate of interest.[12] In an uncertain world, it may or may not be correct. It is plausible enough to replace the known with expected cash flows, and to add a risk premium to the discount rate. But these modifications lack rigorous support.

We are now in a position to evaluate the present value formula against a more rigorous standard. We begin with our single cash flow model. First return to equation (8) and substitute for q and z:

$$P_0 = E\left(\tilde{X}_1 | \phi_0\right)\left(\frac{1 - \lambda b \sigma_{IM}}{1+r}\right) \sum_{t=0}^{T-1} \frac{(1 - \lambda \eta b \sigma_{IM})^t}{(1+r)^t}. \tag{8}$$

This formula in effect discounts the expected future cash flows for two separate sources of risk: first, the risk associated with next period's actual cash flow, and,

---

12. We assume a flat term structure of interest rates throughout this paper.

second, for the risk associated with revision of expectations. Note that if $\eta = 0$, the second source of risk disappears. In this case normal earnings never change and there are no unanticipated capital gains or losses.

We can write (8) in terms of certainty equivalents:

$$P_0 = \sum_{t=1}^{T} \alpha_t E(\tilde{X}_1 | \phi_0)/(1+r)^t \tag{23}$$

where $\alpha \equiv CEQ[\tilde{X}_t]/E(\tilde{X}_t | \phi_0)$. The coefficients α_t are given by $(1 - \lambda b \sigma_{IM}) \cdot (1 - \lambda \eta b \sigma_{IM})^{t-1}$. Now in order for (22) and (8) to be equivalent, there must exist a rate R such that[13]

$$1/(1+R)^t = \alpha_t/(1+r)^t, \tag{24}$$

for each future period $t = 1, 2, \ldots, T$. Such a rate exists only if $\eta = 1$, that is, the cash flows follow a pure random walk, or if $T = 1$ or infinity. Otherwise equation (22), the conventional capital budgeting criterion, is wrong.[14]

There are further difficulties when the cash flow can be decomposed into several components. For the case of two components, a two-part discounting process is appropriate, that is

$$PV = \sum_{t=1}^{T} E(\tilde{X}_{1t} | \phi_0)/(1+R_1)^t + \sum_{t=1}^{T} E(\tilde{X}_{2t} | \phi_0)/(1+R_2)^t, \tag{25}$$

where R_1 and R_2 are the discount rates appropriate to each component.

Suppose that η_1 and η_2 each equal 1.0, so that it makes sense to discount the streams $\{\tilde{X}_{1t}\}$ and $\{\tilde{X}_{2t}\}$ at risk-adjusted rates R_1 and R_2. There is still the question of whether a single discount rate R can be used to discount both components; that is, whether it makes sense to write

$$PV = \sum_{t=1}^{T} E(\tilde{X}_{1t} + \tilde{X}_{2t} | \phi_0)/(1+R)^t. \tag{26}$$

It is possible to define an average rate R which discounts the two components properly, but unfortunately it depends on project life, as well as the relative present values of the two streams.

Before going any further, however, let us ask whether the difficulties with the conventional discounted present value formula are serious. Suppose you know the exact value of beta for an investment project. Moreover, you know the exact value of $E(\tilde{R}_M | \phi_0)$ and use it in the CAPM to calculate the equilibrium, one-period, expected rate of return for the project: $R = r + \beta[E(R_M | \phi_0) - r]$. Then you use this R in (22) to calculate the project's value. Will you get the right answer?

Your answer will be wrong, but close. The top panel of Table 3 shows percentage errors of estimated versus true values, assuming various values of T and η in a

13. See Robichek and Myers [13].

14. Of course, one can usually find a rate R that gives the right answer when plugged into (22). But it is not helpful to define the opportunity cost of capital as the discount rate that gives the right answer.

single-cash flow model.[15] The bottom panel shows the errors when the cash flow can be decomposed into two components.[16]

TABLE 3

Errors From Discounting Cash Flows at Risk-Adjusted Rates Calculated from Observed Betas and the CAPM Formula

Error = Percentage overestimate, estimated present value vs. true value.
Assets assumed to offer level expected cash flow from $t = 1$ to $t = T$.
Other assumptions as in Tables 1 and 2.

A. Single cash flow model.

	$T = 1$	2	5	10	20	40	∞
$\eta = 0$	0	2.07	3.20	3.27	2.78	1.69	0
$\eta = .5$	0	1.04	1.50	1.38	.908	.279	0
$\eta = 1.0$	0	0	0	0	0	0	0

B. Two-component cash flow stream, with $\eta = 1$ and $\beta_2 = 1.0$.

β_1	$T = 1$	2	5	10	20	40	∞
0	0	.02	.17	.55	1.34	5.91	0
.5	0	.006	.04	.12	.25	.23	0
1.0	0	0	0	0	0	0	0
1.5	0	.005	.04	.09	.15	.07	0
2.0	0	.02	.12	.13	.48	.17	0

For the single cash flow model, the discount rate R is too low when the duration of the project is greater than one period but less than infinite. The error is at first an increasing function of asset life, since the sensitivity of estimated present value to a given error in the discount rate increases as T increases. But increasing T, given η, decreases the error in the discount rate. These two effects work against each other for any asset of intermediate life ($1 < T < \infty$). The net error does not appear to be serious.

There is an additional error introduced when the asset's cash flow reflects two underlying components. The observed beta is a weighted average of the two components' betas, and the corresponding expected, one-period rate of return is a weighted average of the rates appropriate to each component. Discounting the sum of the expected component cash flow streams at the weighted average discount rate does not give exactly the right answer, but as Panel B of Table 3 shows, the error is small.

Our tentative conclusion, therefore, is that no serious errors are introduced by discounting cash flow streams at one-period expected rates of return inferred from observed betas. Of course this statement rests on a long list of simplifying assumptions, including constant market parameters, validity of the CAPM, and the ability of financial managers to estimate betas for specific assets. But we have shown that conventional valuation formulas based on discounting expected cash

---

15. Estimates are from equation (22), and true values from equation (8).
16. Estimates are from equation (26), and true values from equation (10).

flows give a good approximation to asset values derived from rigorous analysis of equilibrium market values. We have uncovered no evidence that conventional valuation models are unsafe for management consumption.

IV. GOOD NEWS AND BAD NEWS

The good news is that relatively simple and general valuation formulas can be developed from the CAPM. These formulas may find direct use in capital budgeting. In this paper, however, we have used these formulas to examine traditional valuation procedures based upon the discounted cash flow formula and risk-adjusted discount rates. Although we show that these procedures are not exact, we also show that they give close-to-correct answers providing that the CAPM holds, and that the project beta and the expected market return are known.

The bad news is that the real determinants of beta are more complicated than is generally suspected. Beta depends on the link between cash flow forecast errors and forecast errors for the market return. It depends on asset life, the growth trend in the cash flows, and on the pattern of expected cash flows over time.[17] It depends on the procedure by which investors forecast asset cash flows.

If we could *observe* the appropriate beta, it would be unnecessary to explain it. A firm might take the following alternative approach. It could observe the actual beta of its common stock, or the stock of other firms believed to be in the same "risk class,"[18] and substitute it into the CAPM to obtain a project's hurdle rate or "cost of capital."

But there are three serious problems with this approach. First is the inevitable measurement error in any statistical measure of β. Second, the firms used as a sample for estimating β must actually have the same β as the project under consideration. They should be matched on asset life, growth, patterns of expected cash flows over time, the characteristics of each component of the cash flows, the relative contribution of the components to the firm's value, and possibly on other factors.

These are problems of classification and measurement. The third problem seems more fundamental.[19] It is that the observed β will generally lead to biased hurdle rates if the firms examined have valuable growth opportunities.

Miller and Modigliani (MM) [8] showed that a firm's market value represents two components: the present value of (cash flows generated by) assets in place and the present value of growth opportunities. In MM's certainty model, growth opportunities have positive value only if the rate of return on future investments exceeds the rate of interest.

If we apply this idea to an uncertain world, then the firm should be considered as a portfolio of tangible and intangible assets. The tangible assets are units of productive capacity in place—real assets—and the intangible assets are *options* to

17. We have not discussed the role of the pattern of cash flows in this paper, but its importance is obvious from our discussion of project life.

18. Adjustments for financial leverage would also be necessary. The relevant beta is that of the unlevered firm, not of the common shares.

19. This was first noted by Myers [10]. See [12] for a fuller discussion.

purchase additional units of productive capacity in future periods. The market value of the firm is (1) the present value of the tangible assets, plus (2) the sum of the option values, which corresponds to the "present value of growth." The risk (β) of an option is not the same as the risk of the asset the option is written on. Usually it is greater.[20] If so, the larger the option value, relative to the value of assets in place, the greater is the systematic risk of the firm's stock. Thus, the systematic risk of the firm's stock is an over-estimate of the beta for tangible assets, and a rate of return derived from observed common stock β's will be an overestimate of the appropriate hurdle rate for capital investment whenever firms have valuable growth options. The practical and theoretical difficulties created by this phenomenon are obvious.

REFERENCES

1. M. Bogue and R. Roll. "Capital Budgeting for Risky Projects with 'Imperfect' Markets for Physical Capital," *Journal of Finance*, 29 (May 1974), 601–13.
2. M. J. Brennan. "An Approach to the Valuation of Uncertain Income Streams," *Journal of Finance*, 28 (June 1973), 661–74.
3. E. Fama. "Multiperiod Consumption-Investment Decisions," *American Economic Review*, LX, No. 1 (March 1970).
4. ———. "Risk-Adjusted Discount Rates and the Cost of Capital in a Two-Parameter World," Working Paper, European Institute for Advanced Studies in Management, April 1976.
5. R. S. Hamada. "Multiperiod Capital Asset Prices in an Efficient and Perfect Market: A Valuation or Present Value Model Under Two Parameter Uncertainty," Unpublished ms., University of Chicago, 1972.
6. M. J. Gordon and E. Shapiro. "Capital Equipment Analysis: The Required Rate of Profit," *Management Science*, 3 (October 1956), 102–10.
7. R. C. Merton. "An Intertemporal Capital Asset Pricing Model," *Econometrica*, Vol. 45, No. 5 (September 1973), 867–87.
8. ———. "Capital Budgeting in the Capital Asset Pricing Model," Unpublished note. 1973.
9. M. H. Miller and F. Modigliani. "Dividend Policy, Growth and the Valuation of Shares," *Journal of Business*, 34 (October 1961), 411–53.
10. S. C. Myers. "A Note on the Determinants of Corporate Debt Policy," Unpublished ms., London Graduate School of Business Studies, 1975.
11. ———. "The Relationship Between Real and Financial Measures of Risk and Return," Forthcoming in J. Bicksler and I. Friend, eds., *Studies in Risk and Return* (Cambridge, Mass.: Ballinger, 1977).
12. ———. "Determinants of Corporate Debt Policy," Working Paper, Sloan School of Management, M.I.T., 1976.
13. A. A. Robichek and S. C. Myers. "Conceptual Problems in the Use of Risk-Adjusted Discount Rates," *Journal of Finance*, 21 (December 1966), 727–30.
14. M. Rubinstein. "A Comparative Statics Analysis of Risk Premiums," *Journal of Business*, Vol. 46 (October 1973).

20. In an earlier version of this paper we said "always" instead of "usually." Michael Brennan pointed out our mistake: there are cases in which options are safer than the assets they are written on.

Consider an asset with $g = 0$, $T = 2$ and $\eta = 0$, and a European call option expiring at $t = 1$. Moreover, suppose the option expires *after* $\tilde{X}_1$ is revealed and distributed to the asset's owners. Now, the asset itself has a positive β, providing σ_{IM} is positive, but the option is a risk-free asset! Since $\eta = 0$, there is no uncertainty about the "ex-dividend" value of the asset at $t = 1$. The option is essentially written on a safe asset. Therefore the option is itself a safe asset.

15. ———. "Valuation of Uncertain Income Streams and the Pricing of Options," Working Paper No. 57, Research Program in Finance, University of California at Berkeley. (August 1975).

16. J. Treynor and F. Black. "Corporate Investment Decisions," in S. C. Myers, ed., *New Developments in Financial Management* (New York: Praeger, 1976).

17. S. M. Turnbull. "Market Value and Systematic Risk," forthcoming in the *Journal of Finance*.

18. J. B. Williams. *The Theory of Investment Value*. (Cambridge, Mass.: Harvard University Press, 1938).

THE ANALYSIS OF UNCERTAINTY RESOLUTION IN CAPITAL BUDGETING FOR NEW PRODUCTS*

JAMES C. VAN HORNE†

Stanford University

In this paper, a method is developed for analyzing the resolution of uncertainty over time for the individual new product and for combinations of existing and new products, or the firm's over-all product mix. Probability concepts are employed, and it is shown that new products can be evaluated according to their marginal impact upon the resolution of the uncertainty pattern for the firm's total product mix. The analysis of this dimension is undertaken within a capital-budgeting framework, allowing a GO or NO decision to be reached for the new product under consideration. Information about when uncertainty is expected to be resolved enables management to evaluate more realistically the effect of a new-product decision on the riskiness of the firm's entire product mix. This knowledge is valuable in planning for new products and in balancing the firm's risk over time. As a result, more rational capital budgeting for new products is possible.

Methods for capital allocation to new products have been confined mainly to the evaluation of the expected return from the product and possible deviations from this return.[1] Little attention has been paid to when uncertainty is expected to be resolved, either for the individual product or for the product mix of the firm as a whole. To ignore this dimension may lead to new-product decisions which are less than optimal and to a resulting sacrifice in flexibility with respect to future new-product decisions. In this paper, we develop a framework for analyzing risk and uncertainty resolution for the new product and for a combination of existing and new products. Given this information, management is able to make more rational new-product decisions.

Uncertainty Resolution for the New Product

For most new products, uncertainty is not resolved at a constant rate over time, as implied by conventional capital-budgeting procedures. Frequently, these procedures call for discounting all expected cash flows by a risk-adjusted rate to obtain the net-present value of the product, which is

$$(1) \qquad NPV = \sum_{t=0}^{n} \frac{A_t}{(1 + k)^t},$$

where A_t is the expected cash inflow or outflow in period t, and k is the risk-adjusted discount rate—the required rate of return. If the net-present value of the product is positive, the product should be accepted; if not, it should be rejected. The discount rate, k, represents the time value of money plus a premium for risk.

It is implied that uncertainty will be resolved at a constant rate over time by discounting with k.[2] However, for the typical new product, the greater portion of un-

* Received April 1968; revised September 1968.

† I am grateful to Professors Henry J. Claycamp, William F. Massy, Alexander A. Robichek and the referees of this journal for their helpful suggestions.

[1] For an analysis of the collection of new-product information and the economic analysis of expected returns and risk, see Pessemier [10]. See also Urban [13] and [14].

[2] For an analysis of this point, see Robichek and Myers [11]. For additional analysis of the use of discount rates embodying a risk premium, see Chen [2].

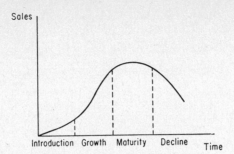

FIGURE 1. Product life cycle

certainty is resolved in the early life of the product, after which the cash flows become more certain. To illustrate briefly, consider the life cycle of a brand product. This life cycle is characterized by four phases: introduction, growth, maturity, and decline. These phases are shown in Figure 1. In the introductory phase, the product is developed, tested, and brought to market, usually with high promotional costs. During the initial part of the growth phase, sales increase at an increasing rate as acceptance is built with promotion and expansion of distribution. In the maturity phase, the market becomes saturated. By this time, competition is keen and takes its toll on profit margins. As competition increases and "new" products increasingly come into the market, the product enters the decline phase. Sales drop off rather sharply, and the product is phased out, completing its life cycle.[3]

For many new products, the major portion of uncertainty is resolved in the introductory phase and in the early part of the growth phase. The more innovative the product and the more it falls outside existing product classes, the greater the probability of rapid uncertainty resolution. As the product moves into the latter part of its growth phase and into its maturity phase, the predictability of future outcomes becomes ever more certain. The ability to predict here is clouded primarily by competitive factors. To illustrate uncertainty resolution for a new product, suppose that management formulated the probability tree shown in Table 1. For simplicity, we assume that the cash flows occur at the end of each of the periods. Moreover, we assume that $1 million will need to be expended at time zero and that this amount is known with certainty.

As seen in Table 1, there are 27 cash-flow series. At time 0, any of these cash flows is possible. As we move to period 1, however, much of the initial uncertainty with respect to future cash flows will be resolved. Suppose, for example, that the net cash flow in period 1 proved to be $-\$600,000$. For future periods, then, our concern would be with only cash flow series 1 to 9; the number of possible outcomes has been reduced considerably. Thus, for many new products, a large portion of uncertainty tends to be resolved in the introductory and early growth phases of their lives. The question is how should the expected resolution of uncertainty be measured so that it is useful to management in new-product decisions.

Measuring Risk for the Single New Product

A risky investment often is evaluated by determining the expected value of net-present value for the product and the dispersion of the probability distribution of possible

---

[3] For a discussion of the product life cycle and an analysis of its implications for marketing, see Patton [8] and Levitt [6].

TABLE 1

Period 1		Period 2		Period 3		Cash Flow Series
Initial Probability $P(1)$	Net Cash Flow	Conditional Probability $P(2 \mid 1)$	Net Cash Flow	Conditional Probability $P(3 \mid 2, 1)$	Net Cash Flow	
		.30	−$200,000	.25	$500,000	1
				.50	700,000	2
				.25	900,000	3
.25	−$600,000	.40	100,000	.25	700,000	4
				.50	900,000	5
				.25	1,100,000	6
		.30	400,000	.25	900,000	7
				.50	1,100,000	8
				.25	1,300,000	9
		.25	300,000	.30	1,000,000	10
				.40	1,200,000	11
				.30	1,400,000	12
.50	−400,000	.50	600,000	.30	1,200,000	13
				.40	1,400,000	14
				.30	1,600,000	15
		.25	900,000	.30	1,400,000	16
				.40	1,600,000	17
				.30	1,800,000	18
		.30	800,000	.25	1,500,000	19
				.50	1,700,000	20
				.25	1,900,000	21
.25	−200,000	.40	1,100,000	.25	1,700,000	22
				.50	1,900,000	23
				.25	2,100,000	24
		.30	1,400,000	.25	1,900,000	25
				.50	2,100,000	26
				.25	2,300,000	27

net-present values about this expected value.[4] For our purposes, the expected value of net-present value at time 0 is

$$(2) \qquad \overline{NPV} = \sum_{t=0}^{n} \frac{\bar{A}_t}{(1 + i)^t},$$

where $\bar{A}_t$ is the expected value of net cash flow in period t; and i is the risk-free rate. The risk-free rate is used as the discount rate in this analysis because we attempt to isolate the time value of money. To include a premium for risk in the discount rate would result in double counting with respect to our evaluation of risk.

As a measure of absolute risk, we employ the standard deviation of the probability distribution of net-present values. Given the cash flow information in Table 1, the

[4] See, for example, Hillier [5]; Payne [9]; and Hertz [4].

standard deviation at time 0 can be determined by

$$(3) \qquad S_0 = [\sum_x NPV_x^2 P_x - (\overline{NPV})^2]^{\frac{1}{2}},$$

where NPV_x is the net-present value for series x of net cash flows, covering all periods, and P_x is the probability of occurrence of that series. For our example in Table 1, there are 27 possible series of cash flows; the first series is represented by a net cash flow of $-\$1,000,000$ at time 0, $-\$600,000$ in period 1, followed by cash flows of $-\$200,000$ and $\$500,000$ in periods 2 and 3, respectively. The variance of a probability distribution, S_0^2, is, simply, the difference between the weighted sum of the squares and the expected value squared. While it is possible to calculate higher moments of the probability distribution, for simplicity we shall consider only one measure of risk—the standard deviation.[5]

In addition to calculating the expected value of possible net-present values and a measure of dispersion, the standard deviation, we wish to measure the expected resolution of uncertainty over time. The statistic we use to approximate relative uncertainty at a moment in time is the ratio

$$(4) \qquad CV_t = S_t / \overline{NPV},$$

where S_t represents the "average" standard deviation of the various branches of the probability tree at the end of period t.

The calculation of S_t involves the following steps:

1. Discount all expected cash flows to their present value at time 0, using i as the discount rate. Thus, the entire probability tree is expressed in terms of present values of cash flows. These are labeled y_{gt}, indicating the gth discounted cash flow in period t.

2. Determine the total node value (TNV) for each node and branch tip in the probability tree by the following method:

    a. For each node, compute the expected value of all future y_{gt} in that branch.

    b. For each node and each branch tip, sum the y_{gt} involved in reaching that node or tip from time zero.

    c. Add (a) and (b) to obtain the total node value (TNV) for each node and tip.

3. Compute the weighted sum of the squares of the total node values for each period by

$$V_t = \sum_h TNV_{ht}^2 P_{ht},$$

where TNV_{ht} is the hth total node value at the end of period t, and P_{ht} is the probability of reaching that node or branch tip. When $t = 0$, there is but one total node value— the expected value of net-present value of the product. The probability of occurrence of this node, of course, is 1.00.

4. Determine the S_t for each period by

$$S_t = [V_n - V_t]^{\frac{1}{2}},$$

where n is the last period in the probability tree.

To illustrate the calculation of CV_t, our measure of relative uncertainty, consider the probability tree in Table 1. If the discount rate, i, were 5 per cent, we first would discount all cash flows by this rate to their present value at time 0. Next, we would determine the total node values and calculate their sum of squares for each of the three periods. Then we would compute S_t by the method described above. The expected

[5] See Markowitz [7], for a measure of relative skewness.

value of net-present value of the product at time 0, which is obtained in step 2, when we calculate TNV_0, is \$372,642. The V_t, S_t^2, S_t, and CV_t for the probability tree are shown in Table 2.

Given the CV_t for a product, we can approximate the expected resolution of uncertainty for that product. This is done simply by plotting the CV_t over time and studying the pattern of relationship. The relationship between the CV_t and length of time in the future for the example problem is shown in Figure 2. The pattern of uncertainty resolution gives management considerable insight into the duration of risk for a product. In the case of Figure 2, we see that uncertainty is expected to be resolved at a very fast rate through period 1, after which it is expected to be resolved more slowly.

Suppose that the firm were comparing this product with another possible new product and that the two were mutually exclusive. Assume for now that both products are independent of the firm's existing product mix. Suppose further that expectations for the second product under consideration resulted in the following:

$$\overline{NPV} = 372,642$$

$$S_0 = 839,083$$

$$CV_0 = 2.25$$

$$CV_1 = 1.38$$

$$CV_2 = .73$$

$$CV_3 = 31$$

$$CV_4 = 0$$

We see that both products have identical expected values of net-present value and dispersion about these expected values. On the basis of this information, management would be indifferent between the two. The risk, as measured by the standard deviation,

TABLE 2

Statistics for Example Problem

	t = 0	t = 1	t = 2	t = 3
V_t (in millions)	0	578,790	687,630	704,050
S_t^2 (in millions)	704,050	125,260	16,420	0
S_t	839,083	353,921	128,141	0
CV_t	2.25	.95	.34	0

$\overline{NPV} = 372,642.$

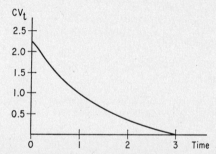

FIGURE 2. Uncertainty resolution example problem

284

is identical. However, the resolution of uncertainty is not the same. Uncertainty is expected to be resolved at a much faster rate for the first product than for the second. Given this additional information, management is unlikely to be indifferent between the products. Whether it prefers the first to the second, however, will depend upon the uncertainty resolution pattern of existing products and management's preferences. To evaluate this problem, we must consider combinations of products and the firm's over-all product mix.

Combination of Products

Because over-all business risk is what is important in the valuation of the firm, our concern is not with the resolution of the uncertainty pattern for a new product *per se*. Rather, it is with the *marginal* impact of a new product on the resolution of uncertainty for the firm's entire product mix. In this section, we propose a method for providing and analyzing this information. Given this information, together with information about the marginal effect of the new product on expected return and variance, management then must decide whether to introduce the product—the GO decision, or whether to reject it—a NO decision.[6] In the discussion that follows, we assume that new products are evaluated sequentially in time and that a GO or NO decision is reached.

In our cash flow estimates, it is important to take account of the effect that the new product will have on the cash flows of existing products. Given this adjustment of cash flows for existing products, the expected value of net-present value for a combination of products is the sum of the expected values of net-present value of the products making up the combination. The incremental profitability of a new product is, simply, the expected value of net-present value of the combination of existing products plus the new product less the expected value of net-present value for existing products alone.

To determine the risk of a combination, we must recognize covariances among the products in the combination. These interdependencies do not allow us to sum the variances of the individual products. Instead, the standard deviation of the probability distribution of possible total node values for a combination of m products at the end of period t is

$$(5) \qquad \sigma_t = [\sum_{j=1}^{m} \sum_{k=1}^{m} \sigma_{jkt}]^{\frac{1}{2}},$$

where σ_{jkt} is the covariance at time t between possible total node values of products j and k. The covariance is

$$(6) \qquad \sigma_{jkt} = r_{jkt} S_{jt} S_{kt},$$

where r_{jkt} is the expected correlation between possible total node values for products j and k. The four-step calculation of S_t for a product was described in the previous section. When $j = k$ in equation (6), σ_{jkt} becomes S_{jt}^2.

The expected correlation between possible total node values of various products may be positive, negative, or zero, depending upon the nature of the association.[7] The

---

[6] For a discussion of a third alternative, namely one where a product is investigated more thoroughly, see Urban [13, pp. 502–509].

[7] Cohen and Elton [3, pp. 8–9], propose a method whereby the functional interrelationships between cash flows over time and various factors giving rise to these cash flows are specified for each investment. The cash flows in each period then are simulated a number of times for each investment, with the net-present value for the investment calculated for each run. The variance-covariance matrix of the net-present values from a combination of investments is generated from the simulation runs. The difficulty, in either this case or the situation proposed in this paper, is in estimating the underlying functional interrelationships.

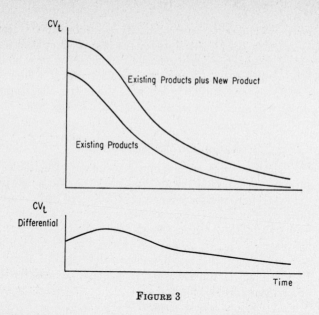

FIGURE 3

degree of correlation is estimated by management on the basis of past experience and forecasts of the future. When actual correlation differs from that which is expected, future correlation estimates should be revised in keeping with the learning process. Estimates of the cross response between products must be as accurate as possible for the standard deviation figure obtained in equation (5) to be meaningful. However, it is not unreasonable to assume that management is in the position to make fairly reliable estimates of the degree of interaction between products.[8]

The standard deviation at time 0 for a combination of products, σ_0, measures the dispersion of the probability distribution of net-present values for that combination about the expected value of the distribution. The incremental risk of taking on a new product is determined by subtracting the variance at time 0, σ_0^2, for the combination of existing products from the variance for the combination of existing products plus the new product and taking the square root of the difference.

Having considered the marginal impact of a new product on expected value of net-present value and on variance about this expected value, we must consider its marginal impact on the resolution of uncertainty. To do so, we compute the CV_t over time for the combination of existing products plus the new product under consideration. The numerator of the ratio is determined with equation (5), while the denominator is the sum of the expected values of net-present values of the products comprising the combination. When the CV_t are determined for the present and various future periods, we can graph the expected pattern of uncertainty resolution for the combination of products being studied in the same manner as we did for the single product. The resulting graph gives us the risk profile of the firm over time.

The marginal impact of a new product on the uncertainty resolution pattern of the firm is evaluated by comparing the risk profile for the combination of existing products plus the new product with that for the combination of existing products alone. To illustrate, consider the patterns of uncertainty resolution in the upper portion of Figure

[8] For further discussion of the procedure for collecting this information and estimating the correlation coefficient, see Van Horne [15, p. 87].

286

3. We see that the introduction of the new product is expected to lengthen the resolution of uncertainty for the firm as a whole. For a more exact measurement of the incremental impact, we can subtract the CV_t for the combination of existing products from the CV_t for the combination of existing products plus the new product. The differences for each time period then can be graphed, if desired. An example of the differential impact for the above example is shown in the lower portion of Figure 3.

Implications for New-Product Selection

The new-product decision should be made in keeping with information provided about the incremental impact of the new product on: (1) the expected value of net-present value of the firm as a whole; (2) the variance about this expected value; and (3) the resolution of uncertainty for the firm's total product mix. The GO-NO decision can be made on either an individual basis for each product, after evaluation of the above information, or according to some over-all set of constraints. The former, perhaps, is the more practical method. The emphasis is upon providing management with as clear a picture as possible of the risk and profitability involved with introducing a new product. Given this information, management then should introduce the new products that it feels will best fulfill corporate objectives with respect to the three factors listed above.

The second approach involves a set of constraints that delineate the GO from the NO areas. The simplest, and crudest, way is to establish minimum levels for each of the three factors. An example of such a policy might be:

1. Profitability index of at least 1.03. For our purposes, the profitability index is

$$P.I. = \frac{INPV + PVO}{PVO},$$

where $INPV$ is the incremental expected value of net-present value to the firm resulting from the introduction of the product; and PVO is the expected value of present value of cash outflows for the product.

2. No more than a .10 probability that the profitability index will be less than 1.00.
3. Incremental CV_t not to exceed:

$$CV_0 \qquad .15$$

$$CV_1 \text{ through } CV_5 \qquad .13$$

$$CV_6 \text{ through } CV_n \qquad .10$$

If the new product under consideration passes all of these screens, it should be introduced; if not, it should be rejected.

The difficulty with establishing separate screens for all three factors is that, typically, they involve a tradeoff. For example, management usually is able to tolerate more variance if the additional profitability is great enough. Consequently, the minimum for a GO decision should involve a tradeoff between the three factors. An illustration of a constraint involving tradeoffs is shown in Figure 4. The Figure is three-dimensional, and the constraint is denoted by the surface resembling an inverted spinnaker sail. For simplicity, uncertainty resolution is expressed as the average incremental CV_t for all periods. Any new product with incremental properties that place it either on the constraint surface or above and to the left is in the GO area. This occurrence means that the product should be introduced. Any new product lying to the right and below

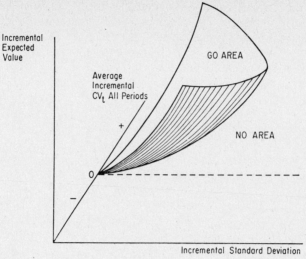

FIGURE 4

the constraint surface is in the NO area, indicating that the product should be rejected.

The configuration of the constraint surface suggests that management is risk adverse. Moreover, it indicates that management prefers to lengthen the uncertainty resolution pattern somewhat. In situations where management is concerned with only the ratio of standard deviation to expected value of net-present value, the constraint can be expressed more easily in only two dimensions. The constraint then would involve a tradeoff between the incremental $\sigma_0/\overline{NPV}$ and the incremental pattern of uncertainty resolution. Because of the loss of information involved in using an average incremental CV_t for all periods, it may be more feasible to choose new products on an individual basis, given information about the three factors. Here, management is able to judge the incremental effect of a new product on uncertainty resolution in each future period.

The selection of new products on an individual basis or the specification of a constraint surface separating the GO area from the NO area depends upon the risk preferences of management. Preferences as to the incremental pattern of uncertainty resolution are affected by considerations of flexibility of the firm for future new-product decisions and by the stability of the firm's net-present value over time. With respect to the former, the pattern of uncertainty resolution for a combination of products is important in that it gives management considerable insight into how much uncertainty it can add with future new-product decisions.

To illustrate, suppose that the present uncertainty resolution pattern for existing products were sharply downward-sloping, as illustrated by combination A in Figure 5. The bulk of the uncertainty for this combination is expected to be resolved in period 1. Suppose further that the firm had the policy of maintaining a given risk complexion, as denoted by the ratio, $\sigma_0/\overline{NPV}$, and of maximizing expected value of net-present value for all products subject to this constraint. If the pattern for combination A is realized, the firm would be able to add new products at time 1 that, on a marginal basis, raised $\sigma_0/\overline{NPV}$ of all products to approximately point y while maximizing the expected value of net-present value. Thus, the firm could take on new products with a high degree of marginal risk and still maintain its risk complexion. This information

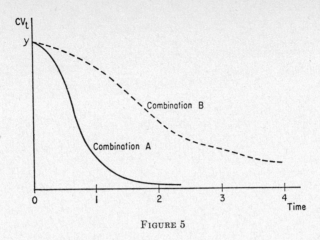

FIGURE 5

is valuable to a company in the generation of new products; it tells management what types of new products it should seek.

The pattern for combination A in Figure 5 suggests, for example, that the firm will have to generate new products in significant magnitude if it wishes to maximize its expected value of net-present value subject to maintaining its risk complexion. This information is important in planning for new products and for the acquisition of other companies and their products. The latter is applicable particularly if sufficient new products are not developed internally. If the firm is not able to generate new products in sufficient magnitude, either internally or externally, and wishes to maintain, roughly, a given risk complexion, it should strive for an uncertainty resolution pattern that is more spread out. An example of such a pattern is shown by combination B in Figure 5. A pattern of this sort would give the firm flexibility with respect to balancing risk from period to period; and, consequently, the firm would not be under the same degree of pressure to generate new products as it was in the previous example. Thus, management would prefer new products with a low degree of marginal relative uncertainty in the near future and greater marginal relative uncertainty in the more distant future. Such a marginal impact would result in a desired lengthening of the uncertainty resolution pattern for the firm's total product mix.

Another implication has to do with the stability of the net-present value of the firm over time. If the uncertainty associated with the product mix of the firm is expected to be resolved very quickly, and the firm periodically takes on new products that result in similar patterns of uncertainty resolution, the net-present value of the firm is likely to fluctuate considerably over time. With a rapid resolution of uncertainty, there is little opportunity to balance risk for various products from period to period. As a result, the actual net-present value of a product combination may differ significantly from the expected outcome. If the uncertainty-resolution pattern of the firm were more spread out, the firm would have greater opportunity to balance the risk of its various products so as to stabilize the trend of net-present value over time. To the extent that investors at the margin value stability over time, the flexibility afforded by spreading out the uncertainty resolution pattern of the product mix may enhance the market price of the firm's stock, all other things being the same.

Thus, it is important that management have information about the present uncertainty resolution pattern of the firm and the likely effect of a new product upon this pattern. Given this information, together with information about the impact of the new product on expected value of net-present value and variance, management then must decide whether to introduce the product—a GO decision, or to reject it—a NO decision. This decision can be made on either an individual basis or according to a set of constraints which define the GO and NO areas. In either case, the framework suggested in this paper enables management to analyze new products realistically, in keeping with a more complete portrayal of risk.

Conclusions

In this paper, we propose a method for providing information by which the resolution of uncertainty over time for a single new product and for the entire product mix of the firm may be analyzed. If the firm has existing products, it is important to evaluate the marginal impact of a new-product decision on the resolution of uncertainty for the firm as a whole. This impact can be judged by studying the differential pattern of expected uncertainty resolution for the firm's over-all product mix with and without the addition of the new product. Information about the resolution of uncertainty is valuable in planning for new products and in balancing the risk of the firm over time. Moreover, this information can be provided with the same basic data that is used to evaluate any risky investment. To ignore the implications of uncertainty resolution may result in unwanted fluctuations in the net-present value of the firm and less than optimal planning for future new products. Given the framework proposed in this paper, management can choose new products that best fulfill corporate objectives with respect to expected return, variance about this return, and the resolution of uncertainty over time.

References

1. CHARNES, A., COOPER, W. W., DeVOE, J. K., AND LEARNER, D. B. "DEMON, Mark II: an Extremal Equation Approach to New Product Marketing," *Management Science*, Vol. 14 (May 1968), pp. 513–524.
2. CHEN, HOUNG-YHI. "Valuation under Uncertainty," *Journal of Financial and Quantitative Analysis*, Vol. 2 (September 1967), pp. 313–325.
3. COHEN, KALMAN J. AND ELTON, EDWIN J. "Inter-Temporal Portfolio Analysis Based on Simulation of Joint Returns," *Management Science*, Vol. 14 (September 1967), pp. 5–18.
4. HERTZ, DAVID B. "Investment Policies that Pay Off," *Harvard Business Review*, Vol. 46 (January–February 1968), pp. 96–108.
5. HILLIER, FREDERICK S. "The Derivation of Probabilistic Information for the Evaluation of Risky Investments," *Management Science*, Vol. 9 (April 1963), pp. 443–457.
6. LEVITT, THEODORE. "Exploit the Product Life Cycle," *Harvard Business Review*, Vol. 43 (November–December 1965), pp. 81–94.
7. MARKOWITZ, HARRY M. *Portfolio Selection*, John Wiley & Sons, New York, 1959, Chapter IX.
8. PATTON, ARCH, "Top Management's Stake in the Product Life Cycle," *Management Review* (June, 1959), reprinted in Stuart H. Britt and Harper W. Boyd, Jr., eds: *Marketing Management and Administrative Action*, McGraw-Hill, New York, 1963, pp. 254–264.
9. PAYNE, NEIL R., "Uncertainty and Capital Budgeting," *Accounting Review*, Vol. 49 (April 1964), pp. 330–332.
10. PESSEMIER, EDGAR A., *New Product Decisions: An Analytical Approach*. New York: McGraw-Hill, 1966.
11. ROBICHEK, ALEXANDER A. AND MYERS, STEWART C. "Conceptual Problems in the Use of Risk-Adjusted Discount Rates," *Journal of Finance*, Vol. 21 (December 1966), pp. 727–730.
12. ROBICHEK, ALEXANDER A. AND VAN HORNE, JAMES C. "Abandonment Value and Capital Budgeting," *Journal of Finance*, Vol. 22 (December 1967), pp. 577–589.
13. URBAN, GLEN L. "A New Product Analysis and Decision Model," *Management Science*, Vol. 14 (April 1968), pp. 490–517.
14. ——, "SPRINTER: A Tool for New Product Decision Makers," *Industrial Management Review*, Vol. 8 (Spring 1967), pp. 43–54.
15. VAN HORNE, JAMES C. "Capital Budgeting Decisions Involving Combinations of Risky Investments," *Management Science*, Vol. 13 (October 1966), pp. 84–92.

CAPITAL BUDGETING PROCEDURES UNDER INFLATION

PHILIP L. COOLEY, RODNEY L. ROENFELDT, and IT-KEONG CHEW

*The authors are, respectively, Assistant Professor of Finance,
Associate Professor of Finance and doctoral candidate in finance at
the University of South Carolina.*

Significant increases in the general price level for goods and services necessitate modification of traditional capital budgeting procedures to avoid inefficient allocation of capital. During the 1960's, price levels as measured by the Consumer Price Index increased 2.8% per annum on average and thus far in the 1970's have increased an average of 6.2% per annum. A chronic inflationary environment diminishes the purchasing power of the monetary unit, causing large divergences between nominal and real future cash flows. Thus, since rational decision makers presumably are interested in real returns, they should explicitly include the impact of inflation on investment projects when making capital budgeting decisions.

The purpose of this paper is to present a normative framework, building on the traditional net present value model, that explicitly incorporates anticipated inflation and allows for uncertainties in real cash flows. Failure to consider the impact of inflation tends to produce suboptimal decisions for several reasons. For example, cash-flow estimates must embody anticipated inflation if the discount rate contains an element attributable to inflation [9, 13]. Ignoring this adjustment would result in either an upward or a downward appraisal bias depending on the relative responsiveness to inflation of the cash inflows and outflows. Even if cash expenses and revenues from an investment project were fully responsive to inflation, depreciation tax-shields would suffer diminution of real value since conventional accounting procedures base depreciation computations on historical cost [11].

Suboptimal decisions may also result from overlooking the synergistic reduction of real returns due to taxation and inflation [3]. With no inflation, a 50% tax bracket, and a before-tax return of 4%, real after-tax return equals 2%; if an inflation rate of 4% is introduced, before-tax return must be increased to 12% to completely offset the combined effects of taxation and inflation. Simply adding 4% to the before-tax return to counteract the 4% inflation is insufficient, and would cause a 2% reduction in real return because taxes are paid on nominal income, not real income.

Traditional Capital Budgeting Model

The traditional risk-adjusted discount-rate (RADR) capital budgeting model is represented as follows:

$$NPV_T = -C_o + \sum_{t=1}^{n} \frac{\overline{C}_t}{(1+k)^t} \qquad (1)$$

where NPV_T is the traditional net present value of the project, C_o is the initial cash outlay, $\overline{C}_t$ is the expected nominal net cash flows at the end of period t, n is the number of periods in which cash flows related to the project occur, and k is the risk-adjusted discount rate [12, 14].

The discount rate, k, can be considered as the sum of the risk-free rate, i^*, and a risk premium, ρ, associated with the uncertainty of receiving the expected nominal net cash flows, $\overline{C}_t$. That is, $k = i^* + \rho$. For projects with risk characteristics similar to the firm's, k becomes the marginal cost of capital, which represents the rate of return on a project required to leave the firm's market value unchanged. A lesser rate of return would cause a decline in market value, and, hence, owner's wealth. For projects with risk characteristics different from the firm's, the theoretically correct discount rate can be built up from the risk-free rate and risk premium; this discount rate may differ, reflecting differences in risk, from the firm's marginal cost of capital.

Although i^* might be estimated by the return on long-term U.S. Treasury securities, a reasonable estimate for ρ is more difficult. (Long-term treasuries, or treasuries approximating project-life, would reflect an element for inflation as well as time preference.) The risk-return trade-off might be determined subjectively by the financial manager or through policy decisions by executive consensus. Modern capital asset pricing theory provides the appropriate trade-off assuming, *inter alia*, competitive, efficient markets [15]. If the decision maker is competing in such a market, the market-determined trade-off becomes relevant, not the subjectively determined trade-off. While proper risk adjustments are controversial [2], clearly some adjustment, even though imprecise, should be made.

In the presence of inflation, the risk-free rate, i^*, being expressed in nominal terms, may be decomposed into the pure rate of return, i, and an element due to anticipated inflation, η. That is, $i^* = i + \eta$. The pure rate represents time value of real money and is used for discounting real cash flows. Evidence for investors in the aggregate suggests a value of 3 to 4% for the pure rate [18]. Thus, anticipated inflation might be obtained by subtracting i from the return on long-term U.S. Treasury securities, a surrogate for i^*. More directly, anticipated inflation might be estimated by averaging published forecasts of economists and/or econometric models. Finally, considerable historical data are available on price increases—consumer and wholesale prices in aggregate, by products, and commodities [5, 7, 10, and 16] and average wage increases [7, 10]—providing a basis for extrapolation techniques or more sophisticated forecasting procedures. Since management represents investors who are confronted with price increases probably best approximated by changes in the Consumer Price Index, it may be argued that expected percent increases in this index are the best proxy for the anticipated inflation rate. This ignores, of course, the well-known problems of price-index measurement [17]. Whatever procedures are deemed most appropriate in a particular situation for obtaining estimates, the discount rate used in the traditional model may be usefully considered as consisting of 3 elements:

$$k = i^* + \rho = i + \eta + \rho \qquad (2)$$

Equation (2) indicates that an inflation premium is normally included implicitly in the traditional RADR model. In practical usage of the model cash flows may also contain implicit adjustments for inflation. Both types of adjustments are theoretically correct but they deserve explicit recognition in the model. The traditional RADR model, requiring little computational effort, is a simplified representation of reality, which is both a virtue and a handicap. Unfortunately, in a risky world characterized by persistent and high inflation rates, the model becomes oversimplified and less useful and is unlikely to produce optimal investment decisions except under very restrictive conditions.

Characteristics of the traditional model (as defined by equation (1)) may be summarized as follows: (1) it discounts nominal cash flows; (2) the risk-adjusted discount rate is constant for cash flows of all time periods; (3) the inflation rate is contained implicitly in the overall discount rate and remains unchanged throughout the life of the project; (4) varying sensitivities of revenues and costs to inflation are unaccounted for; (5) depreciation tax shields are assumed to have the same amount of uncertainty as other cash flows associated with the project; and (6) the implicit inflation rate is known with certainty. When these restrictive characteristics are relaxed, the result is a more realistic model of real net present value. In the following sections the restrictions are relaxed one at a time until all are eliminated.

Net Present Value of Real Cash Flows

Viewing an investment as foregoing current for future consumption, the future values of importance are real, not nominal, and are determined by expressing nominal net cash flows in terms of dollars of the period in which the project is being considered. Thus, the nominal net cash flow expected in period n is discounted by one plus the anticipated inflation rate, η, raised to the power n. This procedure is illustrated for periods 0, 1, 2, . . ., n in Exhibit 1. The real net cash flows are then discounted at the real rate $(i+\rho)$, which excludes any inflationary element, to arrive at the real net present value of the project. This is illustrated by the following equation:

$$NPV_r = -C_o + \sum_{t=1}^{n} \frac{\bar{C}_t}{(1+\eta)^t \ (1+i+\rho)^t}, \qquad (3)$$

where NPV_r is the real net present value.

Exhibit 1. Real Net Present Value

End of period	Nominal net cash flow	Real net cash flow	Real present value
0	$-C_o$	$-C_o$	$-C_o$
1	$\bar{C}_1$	$\bar{C}_1/(1+\eta)$	$\bar{C}_1/[(1+\eta)(1+i+\rho)]$
2	$\bar{C}_2$	$\bar{C}_2/(1+\eta)^2$	$\bar{C}_2/[(1+\eta)^2(1+i+\rho)^2]$
.	.	.	.
.	.	.	.
.	.	.	.
n	$\bar{C}_n$	$\bar{C}_n/(1+\eta)^n$	$\bar{C}_n/[(1+\eta)^n(1+i+\rho)^n]$

Sum = NPV_r = Real net present value

Equation (3) makes clear the necessity of finding real cash flows, which are then discounted by the real rate, $r = i+\rho$. Embodied in the multiplicative denominator of NPV_r, $(1+\eta)^t (1+r)^t$, is the usual assumption that compounding periods correspond with the periods for which rates are stated and cash flows occur. If the denominator of equation (1), $(1+k)^t$, equals $(1+\eta)^t$ $(1+r)^t$, algebraic manipulation shows k equaling $(\eta+r+\eta r)$. Therefore, only if the product of the inflation rate and real rate were sufficiently small, could the traditional additive denominator—$k=i+\rho+\eta=r+\eta$—be

appropriate. For example, simply adding r to η when r equals 12% and η equals 8% understates the appropriate rate by roughly 1% ($\eta r = .08 \times .12$). Such disparities are not insignificant for large long-term projects as inspection of a present-value table will show. Larger precentages would increase the disparity although smaller percentages would improve $(r+\eta)$ as an approximation for k. Because of this potential disparity, the multiplicative form is used in subsequent discussion.

Varying Risk Premiums

Analysts frequently modify the traditional capital budgeting model given by equation (1) to account for different degrees of risk associated with cash flows of each period. This is accomplished by allowing the discount rate, k, to vary from period to period as shown in equation (4):

$$NPV_T = -C_o + \sum_{t=1}^{n} \frac{\bar{C}_t}{(1+k_t)^t}, \qquad (4)$$

where k_t is the discount rate that applies only to period t.

Although the certainty-equivalent approach for adjusting risk has been suggested as theoretically superior to the RADR approach [9], this is true only when the RADR model is misspecified [4; 8, p. 417]. Based on equation (4), the present value of the expected net cash flow at the end of the period t, $\bar{C}_t$, is given by

$$V_o = \bar{C}_t/(1+k_t)^t,$$

where $\bar{C}_t$ is the expected value of the uncertain cash flow, $\tilde{C}_t$. This implies that the risk-adjusted value of $\bar{C}_t$ at the end of period $t-1$ is

$$V_{t-1} = \bar{C}_t/(1+k_t).$$

V_o may be expressed in terms of V_{t-1} as follows:

$$V_o = V_{t-1}(1+k_t)/(1+k_t)^t = V_{t-1}/(1+k_t)^{t-1},$$

but V_{t-1} is already a risk-adjusted value, and $(1+k_t)^{t-1}$ will overadjust $\bar{C}_t$ by $t-1$ periods. The correct present value of $\bar{C}_t$, which avoids overadjustment through compounding the risk premium, requires discounting at the risk-free rate once the risk adjustment has been made:

$$V_o = \bar{C}_t / [(1+k_t)(1+i^*)^{t-1}],$$

where i^* is the risk-free rate. Note that $(1+k_t)(1+i^*)^{t-1} \neq (1+\rho_t)(1+i^*)^t$ and the latter will bias downward the present value of $\bar{C}_t$. These procedures suggest that the inferiority of the traditional RADR model relative to the certainty-equivalent model stems from misapplication, not an intrinsic conceptual defect. Thus equation (4) becomes

$$NPV_T = -C_o + \sum_{t=1}^{n} \frac{\bar{C}_t}{(1+k_t)(1+i^*)^{t-1}} \qquad (5)$$

where $k_t = i^* + \rho_t$ and ρ_t is the risk premium required for net cash flows of period t.

Using this more appropriate risk-adjusting procedure and incorporating it into equation (3), which uses real cash flows, the following model results:

$$NPV_r = -C_o + \sum_{t=1}^{n} \frac{\bar{C}_t}{(1+\eta)^t (1+i+\rho_t)(1+i)^{t-1}} \qquad (6)$$

In this formulation the first factor $(1+\eta)^t$ of the denominator transforms the nominal cash flows $\bar{C}_t$ into real cash flows; the second factor $(1 + i + \rho_t)$ adjusts for risk and accounts for time value of money for one period; and i in the third factor $(1+i)^{t-1}$ is the pure rate, which accounts solely for time value of money for (t−1) periods. Pure rate, i, is assumed invariant throughout the project life, which appears reasonable based on evidence for investors in the aggregate [18]. The assumption is easily relaxed, if necessary, using procedures analogous to those suggested in the following section for varying inflation rates.

Varying Inflation Rates

Inflation rates will undoubtedly vary from period to period throughout the life of a capital investment. At the time of investment evaluation, various scenarios might be envisioned by the analyst. For example, the current inflation rate may be anticipated to exist for the next 3 years, dropping to 4% thereafter. Whatever the scenario, its accomodation is easily achieved by adjusting η_j in the following equation:

$$NPV_r = -C_o + \sum_{t=1}^{n} \frac{\bar{C}_t}{(1+i+\rho_t)(1+i)^{t-1} \prod_{j=1}^{t}(1+\eta_j)}, \qquad (7)$$

where η_j is the anticipated inflation rate in period j. Allowing the inflation rate to vary from period to period makes the model more applicable to real-world conditions.

Exhibit 2 illustrates the procedural differences between equation (7) and the traditional model shown by equation (4). The example uses a project cost of $21,500 and expected receipts of $10,000 per year for 3 years. The pure rate is assumed constant at 5%; inflation is shown to decline from 10% to 6% for a 3-year average of 8%; and the risk premium, for ease of illustration, is assumed constant at 7%. Using traditional risk and inflation adjustments, net present value equals −$436, indicating the project should be rejected. Under the suggested procedures, however, net present value equals +$206, indicating the project should be accepted. The traditional procedure overadjusted for risk causing a downward bias in net present value. Using traditional risk-adjustment procedures with the theoretically correct treatment of inflation yields a NPV_r equal to −$1020. This bias, however, is offset in the traditional model by an upward bias due to simply adding the inflation rate to the real rate, bringing the net result to −$436. The difference between NPV_T and NPV_r—minus $436 versus $206—would be accentuated for longer time periods, riskier projects, higher inflation rates, and larger pure rates of return.

Effect of Inflation on Cash Flows

Explicitly adjusting the discount rate for inflation requires that the effects of inflation on cash flows also be accounted for in the model to prevent biased NPV results. To illustrate, suppose a single-period, risk-free investment costs $100 and will return $110 in the absence of inflation. Assume that a 5% rate of return is required when no risk or inflation exists (pure rate), but that an 8% increase in general price-level is anticipated. With no upward adjustment in cash flow to account for inflation, equation (7) yields the following:

$$NPV_r = -C_o + \frac{\bar{C}_1}{(1+i)(1+\eta_1)}$$

$$= -100 + \frac{110}{(1+.05)(1+.08)}$$

$$= -\$3.$$

If $\bar{C}_1$ were fully responsive to inflation, however, NPV_r would equal $4.76 (−100 + 110(1.08)/(1.05 × 1.08)). Furthermore, since $\bar{C}_1$ represents a nominal net cash

294

Exhibit 2. Numerical Comparison of NPV_T and NPV_r

Input Data:

Project cost: C_o = $21,500

Expected net cash inflows: $\overline{C}_t$ = $10,000 per year for 3 years

Pure rate: i = 5% assumed constant

Anticipated inflation: η_1 = 10%, η_2 = 8%, η_3 = 6% and $\overline{\eta}$ = 8%

Risk premium: ρ_t = 7% assumed constant for convenience

Traditional discount rate: $k_t = i + \overline{\eta} + \rho_t$ = 5% + 8% + 7% = 20%

(1) Yearend (t)	(2) $\overline{C}_t$	(3) $(1+k_t)^t$	(4) $(1+i+\rho_t)$	(5) $(1+i)^{t-1}$	(6) $\Pi(1+\eta_j)$	(7) (4)x(5)x(6)
0	−$21,500	--	--	--	-	-
1	+ 10,000	1.200	1.120	1.000	1.100	1.232
2	+ 10,000	1.440	1.120	1.050	1.188	1.397
3	+ 10,000	1.728	1.120	1.103	1.259	1.555

$NPV_T = -C_o + \Sigma \overline{C}_t /(1+k_t)^t$

$\qquad = -21,500 + 8,333 + 6,944 + 5,787$

$\qquad = -\$436$

$NPV_r = -C_o + \Sigma \overline{C}_t /[(1 + i + \rho_t) (1 + i)^{t-1} \Pi(1 + \eta_j)]$

$\qquad = -21,500 + 8,117 + 7,158 + 6,431$

$\qquad = +\$206$

---

flow—cash inflow minus cash outflow—multiplying $110 by 1.08 implicitly assumes equal, full responsiveness of both cash inflows and outflows to general price increases. Specific revenues and costs, however, may react differently to inflation [1, 6]. For example, wage costs may adjust differently than prices of raw materials or finished goods because of contractual agreements between labor and management. If labor expenses account for a major portion of operating expenses of a particular investment project and revenues are derived from sales of finished products, it may be improper to assume that cash inflows and cash outflows are affected equally by inflation.

Additionally, although percentage change in the Consumer Price Index may accurately reflect opportunity cost of most investors, it probably reflects inaccurately the true impact of inflation on most individual project revenues and expenses. Since construction of this index is based on only a portion of all goods and services at retail prices, the goods and services relevant to an investment project may be excluded, or only partially included, in the index. Estimates of the impact of inflation on project cash flows can be made more accurately from published data on the Wholesale Price Index and its component parts and indices on wage increases.

In the absence of inflation, expected gross cash inflow (I_t) and outflow for variable operating expenses (O_t) can be combined for period t with expected cash charges (F_t) fixed for subperiods of the project life, fixed non-cash charges (D_t), and the marginal corporate tax rate (T) to determine the net cash flow as follows:

$$[I_t - O_t - F_t - D_t] \ [1 - T] + D_t. \qquad (8)$$

Net cash flow, therefore, is computed by adding back fixed non-cash charges to after-tax earnings. A more commonly used form of equation (8) is obtained by rearranging terms as follows:

$$[I_t - O_t - F_t] \ [1 - T] + D_t T, \qquad (9)$$

where $D_t T$ represents the tax shield due to fixed non-cash charges. Since cash flow $D_t T$ is fixed through legal rules and F_t is fixed for subperiods of the project life—e.g., maintenance and rental contracts—only I_t and O_t will change each period with inflationary climate. For a particular project, I_t and O_t could be broken down into specific sources of revenue and cash outlays, and their respective reactions to price-level changes could be analyzed. For present purposes, however, I_t and O_t are each treated as homogeneous cash-flow groups in inflation.

Suppose that λ_j is the percentage change in expected cash inflow (I_t) induced by inflation in period j. λ_j may be more or less than the general price-level change. That is, λ_j is more than η_j if I_t overresponds to inflation in period j and less than η_j if I_t does not respond fully to inflation. Thus, the expected nominal cash inflow in period t is

$$I_t \prod_{j=1}^{t} (1 + \lambda_j).$$

Furthermore, let θ_j be the percentage change in O_t induced by inflation in period j. Again, θ_j may differ from η_j. Thus, the expected nominal cash outflow for variable operating expenses in period t is

$$O_t \prod_{j=1}^{t} (1 + \theta_j).$$

Adding fixed cash charges resulting from contractual agreements and restrictions on costs (F_t) and depreciation and other non-cash charges (D_t) yields the following:

$$[I_t \prod_{j=1}^{t} (1 + \lambda_j) - O_t \prod_{j=1}^{t} (1 + \theta_j) - F_t - D_t]$$

$$[1 - T] + D_t, \tag{10}$$

which represents the inflation-adjusted form of equation (8). Rearranging terms yields the inflation-adjusted form of equation (9):

$$[I_t \prod_{j=1}^{t} (1 + \lambda_j) - O_t \prod_{j=1}^{t} (1 + \theta_j) - F_t] \ [1 - T]$$

$$+ D_t T. \tag{11}$$

Responsiveness of revenues and variable costs to inflation have an important influence on the magnitude of the nominal net cash flows. A larger λ_j and smaller θ_j reflects a more attractive project. Similarly, if revenues rise with inflation, fixed cash costs have a more

favorable effect on cash flows than costs that rise with inflation, suggesting an advantage of higher operating leverage. Non-cash charges such as depreciation are also unresponsive to inflation. However, since these items are deductible for tax purposes but are non-cash expenses, larger deductions would result in a higher net cash inflow. The fact that these costs do not respond to inflation reduces the attractiveness of an investment project.

Discount Rates and Cash Flows

Since the cash flows are risky quantities occurring over time, they must be adjusted by appropriate rates reflecting time value of money, risk, and inflation. From results of the previous two sections, the first cash-flow term in equation (11) should be discounted as follows:

$$\sum_{t=1}^{n} \frac{[I_t \prod_{j=1}^{t} (1 + \lambda_j) - O_t \prod_{j=1}^{t} (1 + \theta_j) - F_t] \ [1 - T]}{(1 + i + \rho_t)(1 + i)^{t-1} \prod_{j=1}^{t} (1 + \eta_j)},$$

where ρ_t is the risk premium for net cash flow resulting from I_t, O_t, and F_t.

The second term in equation (11) represents tax shields of periodic depreciation charges, which are unresponsive to inflation once the purchase price of the project has been determined. Assuming that the firm has adequate revenue to cover depreciation charges, depreciation tax-shields may be considered as relatively certain. In fact, these shields depend only on the purchase price, salvage value, number of years over which depreciation is to be taken, method of computation, and tax rate. Hence, the depreciation tax-shields should be converted to real flows and then discounted at the pure rate, which, by definition, is independent of inflation effects and any risk factor:

$$\sum_{t=1}^{n} \frac{D_t T}{(1 + i)^t \prod_{j=1}^{t} (1 + \eta_j)}.$$

If F_t were also fixed for the life of the project, it would be included as $-F_t(1-T)$ along with $D_t T$ in the above expression.

Combining these two terms with the initial cash outlay, we have the model for evaluating real net present value of capital budgeting projects under anticipated inflation:

$$NPV_r = -C_o + \sum_{t=1}^{n} \left\{ \frac{[I_t \prod_{j=1}^{t} (1+\lambda_j) - O_t \prod_{j=1}^{t} (1+\theta_j) - F_t][1-T]}{(1+i+\rho_t)(1+i)^{t-1} \prod_{j=1}^{t} (1+\eta_j)} + \frac{D_t T}{(1+i)^t \prod_{j=1}^{t} (1+\eta_j)} \right\} \qquad (12)$$

Equation (12) improves upon the traditional capital budgeting model by explicitly incorporating inflation into both the cash flows and discount rates, modifying the risk adjustment to prevent overadjusting for risk, and discounting more certain flows at a lower discount rate. Only the allowance for risk in the inflation rate remains to be covered in the next section.

Before examining the effects of uncertain inflation, we numerically illustrate equation (12) in Exhibit 3, which builds upon the problem presented in Exhibit 2. A project costing $21,500 and generating net cash inflows of $10,000 per year for 3 years was shown in the original data. In Exhibit 3 these cash inflows are decomposed into their elemental parts, consisting of gross cash inflows, variable cash outflows, fixed cash outflows, and depreciation tax shields. Combining these cash flows into the two terms of equation (12) yields: $7,133 per year, the after-tax difference between cash inflows and outflows; and $2,867 per year, the tax shield for non-cash charges. Applying the discount factors in Exhibit 2 (column 7) to the 3-year $7,133 cash flow, and the discount factors indicated by equation (12) to the 3-year $2,867 tax shield, results in NPV_r equaling $621. The project would, therefore, be even more acceptable than suggested by the analysis of Exhibit 2, where NPV_r equals $206. The increase in NPV_r occurs in this case because the annual tax shield of $2,867 is discounted at a lower rate than was used in equation (7).

Exhibit 3. Expanded Numerical Comparison of NPV_T and NPV_r

Additional Input Data

Original input data contained in Exhibit 2

Cash inflow in absence of inflation: $I_1 = I_2 = I_3 = \$40,000$

Variable cash outflow in absence of inflation: $O_1 = O_2 = O_3 = \$28,000$

Fixed cash outflow: $F_1 = \$2,672$; $F_2 = \$5,338$; $F_3 = \$7,997$

Depreciation charges: $\$21,500/3 = \$7,167 = D_1 = D_2 = D_3$

Marginal tax rate: 40%

Inflation induced change in I_t: $\lambda_1 = 12\%$; $\lambda_2 = 10\%$; $\lambda_3 = 8\%$

Inflation induced change in O_t: $\theta_1 = 8\%$; $\theta_2 = 6\%$; $\theta_3 = 4\%$

Exhibit 3. (Continued)

Net Cash Flows

Yearend 1: $\bar{C}_1$

$\bar{C}_1 = [I_1(1+\lambda_1) - O_1(1+\theta_1) - F_1][1-T] + TD_1$

$\bar{C}_1 = [40,000(1+.12) - 28,000(1+.08) - 2,672][1-.4] + .4(7,167)$

$\bar{C}_1 = 7,133 + 2,867 = \$10,000$

Yearend 2: $\bar{C}_2$

$\bar{C}_2 = [I_2(1+\lambda_1)(1+\lambda_2) - O_2(1+\theta_1)(1+\theta_2) - F_2][1-T] + TD_2$

$\bar{C}_2 = [40,000(1+.12)(1+.10) - 28,000(1+.08)(1+.06) - 5,338][1-.4] + .4(7,167)$

$\bar{C}_2 = 7,133 + 2,867 = \$10,000$

Yearend 3: $\bar{C}_3$

$\bar{C}_3 = [I_3(1+\lambda_1)(1+\lambda_2)(1+\lambda_3) - O_3(1+\theta_1)(1+\theta_2)(1+\theta_3) - F_3][1-T] + TD_3$

$\bar{C}_3 = [40,000(1+.12)(1+.10)(1+.08) - 28,000(1+.08)(1+.06)(1+.04) - 7,997][1-.4] + .4(7,167)$

$\bar{C}_3 = 7,133 + 2,867 = \$10,000$

Model for NPV_r: equation (12)

$NPV_r = -21,500 + 7,133/1.232 + 7,133/1.397 + 7,133/1.555 + 2,867/(1+.05)(1+.10) + 2,867/(1+.05)^2(1+.10)(1+.08) + 2,867/(1+.05)^3(1+.10)(1+.08)(1+.06) = +\$621$

Uncertain Inflation

Over the past 15 years, annual inflation rates as measured by the Consumer Price Index have varied from 1.1 to 11.0%. Among the causes of variation in inflation—cost push, demand pull, and material shortages—there exist imperfectly understood principles governing observed inflation rates. This inability to accurately anticipate inflation rates is demonstrated by widely differing econometric forecasts and expert judgments at given points in time. Uncertainty in *ex ante* inflation rates, or inflation risk, can be incorporated into equation (12), which already adjusts the real cash flows for business risk.

Uncertainty in real net cash flows prevails for 3 reasons: (1) business risk, or uncertainty in the operation of the project, which causes variations in I_t, O_t, and F_t; (2) uncertainty in the anticipated inflation rate, η_j; and (3) uncertainty in cash-flow sensitivities (λ_j and θ_j) to general price changes. The appropriate adjustment for business risk is shown in the first expression of equation (12) by the inclusion of ρ_t in the denominator. The uncertainties in η_j, λ_j, and θ_j may be compensated for by further incrementing the denominator to read:

$$(1 + i + \rho_t + \psi_t)(1 + i)^{t-1} \prod_{j=1}^{t} (1 + \eta_j) ,$$

where ψ_t is an adjustment for the 3 inflationary uncertainties.

The second expression of equation (12) represents real present value of the depreciation tax-shields. Since tax-shields are assumed to be relatively certain for a going concern, no business-risk adjustment is included. Under uncertain inflation, however, their real values are uncertain, and should be adjusted as follows:

$$(1 + i + \phi_t)(1 + i)^{t-1} \prod_{j=1}^{t} (1 + \eta_j) ,$$

where ϕ_t is an adjustment for uncertainty in the anticipated inflation rate, η_j. Development of this adjustment is based on a derivation similar to that used for the business-risk adjustment.

Explicit recognition of the existence of ψ_t and ϕ_t is useful since they otherwise would be contained only implicitly or else ignored in the analysis. For the illustration presented in Exhibit 3, let ψ_t be constant at 2% and ϕ_t be constant at 1%. Incorporating these inflation risk premiums into equation (12) causes NPV_r to decline from $621 to $286. If the inflationary environment were more uncertain, warranting higher risk permiums, NPV_r would become negative and the project would be rejected.

The problems in obtaining reasonable estimates of ψ_t and ϕ_t are similar to those for ρ_t, but these difficulties obviously do not mandate their exclusion from analysis. Refined judgments based on repeated experience with specific project cash-flows should lead to improved estimates of ψ_t and ϕ_t, and a sufficient number of η_j estimates are frequently available enabling judgment of its uncertainty. For projects warranting the required resources, probability distributions of the random variables in equation (12) could be employed in a simulation of NPV_r. A computer program for computing NPV_r, which would also assist in a sensitivity analysis, is provided in the Appendix. Whatever level of analysis is used, the uncertainties of inflation in the 1970's suggest that without explicit adjustments for inflation risk, profitable decisions might not be reached.

REFERENCES

1. George L. Bach and Albert Ando, "The Redistributional Effects of Inflation," *Review of Economics and Statistics* (February 1957), pp. 1-13.

2. Richard S. Bower and Donald R. Lessard, "An Operational Approach to Risk-Screening," *Journal of Finance* (May 1973), pp. 321-337.

3. Gary P. Brinson, "The Synergistic Impact of Taxes and Inflation on Investment Return," *Financial Analysts Journal* (March-April 1973), pp. 74-75.

4. John R. Ezzell, "A Clarification and Reconciliation of the Risk Adjusted Discount Rate and the Certainty Equivalent Models in Capital Budgeting," presented at the Southern Finance Association Meeting in Atlanta, Georgia, November, 1974.

5. *Federal Reserve Bulletin*, Board of Governors of the Federal Reserve System, Washington, D. C., various issues.

6. Reuben A. Kessel and Armen A. Alchian, "The Meaning and Validity of the Inflation-Induced Lag of Wages Behind Prices," *American Economic Review* (March 1960), pp. 45-46.

7. *Monthly Labor Review*, U.S. Department of Labor, Bureau of Labor Statistics, Washington, D.C., various issues.

8. David E. Peterson, *A Quantitative Framework for Financial Management*, Homewood, Illinois, Richard D. Irwin, Inc., 1969.

9. Alexander A. Robichek and Stewart C. Myers, *Optimal Financial Decisions*, Englewood Cliffs, New Jersey, Prentice-Hall, Inc., 1965.

10. *Survey of Current Business*, United States Department of Commerce, Bureau of Economic Analysis, Washington, D. C., various issues.

11. George Terborgh, "Effect of Anticipated Inflation on Investment Analysis," (No. 2 in a series of studies in the *Analysis of Business Investment Projects*) copyrighted by Machinery & Allied Products Institute and Council for Technological Advancement, 1200 Eighteenth Street Northwest, Washington, D. C. Also appeared as Appendix G in *Engineering Economy: Analysis of Capital Expenditures* by G. W. Smith, The Iowa State Universtiy Press, Ames, Iowa, U.S.A., 1968.

12. James C. Van Horne, *Financial Management and Policy*, third edition, Englewood Cliffs, New Jersey, Prentice-Hall, Inc., 1974.

13. James C. Van Horne, "A Note on Biases in Capital Budgeting Introduced by Inflation," *Journal of Financial and Quantitative Analysis* (January 1971), pp. 653-758.

14. J. Fred Weston and Eugene F. Brigham, *Managerial Finance*, fifth edition, New York, Holt, Rinehart and Winston, 1975.

15. J. Fred Weston, "Investment Decisions Using the Capital Asset Pricing Model," *Financial Management* (Spring 1973), pp. 25-33.

16. *Wholesale Prices and Price Indexes*, U.S. Department of Labor, Bureau of Labor Statistics, Washington, D. C., various issues.

17. Taro Yamane, *Statistics, An Introductory Analysis*, second edition, New York, Harper and Row Publishers, 1967, chapter 11.

18. W. P. Yohe and D. S. Karnosky, "Interest Rates and Price Level Changes, 1952-1969," *Review*, Federal Reserve Bank of St. Louis (December 1969).

Appendix

The theoretically appropriate model of real net present value—equation (12) modified by ψ_t and ϕ_t for uncertainties in inflation—becomes computationally burdensome for projects with long lives. Written in APL for a time-sharing terminal, the program below relieves that burden (thanks to M. A. Foxworth of the U.S.C. Computer Center). The 3 major sections of the program perform the follwoing tasks, respectively: (1) requests input data from the user and performs the summation operation; (2) completes computations for each iteration in the summation operation, and (3) provides for input and input messages.

```
          ∇NETPV[□] ∇
      ∇   NETPV
[1]       'NUMBER OF PERIODS IN WHICH CASH FLOWS OCCUR '
[2]       N1←INPUTD 1
[3]       'INITIAL CASH OUTLAY'
[4]       NPVR←-CO←INPUTD 1
[5]       'EXPECTED CASH INFLOW IN ABSENCE OF FUTURE INFLATION (PER PERIOD)'
[6]       IN←INPUTD N1
[7]       'PERCENTAGE CHANGE IN EXPECTED CASH INFLOW (I) INDUCED BY INFLATION (PER PERIOD)'
[8]       LT←INPUTD N1
[9]       'EXPECTED CASH OUTFLOW FOR VARIABLE EXPENSES IN ABSENCE OF FUTURE INFLATION
          (PER PERIOD)'
[10]      ON←INPUTD N1
[11]      'PERCENTAGE CHANGE IN EXPECTED CASH OUTFLOW (O) INDUCED BY INFLATION (PER
          PERIOD)'
[12]      OBT←INPUTD N1
[13]      'FIXED CASH CHARGES FROM CONTRACTUAL AND OTHER RESTRICTIONS (PER PERIOD)'
[14]      FN←INPUTD N1
[15]      'MARGINAL CORPORATE TAX RATE'
[16]      TT←INPUTD 1
[17]      'PURE RATE OF RETURN; REPRESENTS TIME VALUE OF REAL MONEY'
[18]      I←INPUTD 1
[19]      'RISK PREMIUM FOR BUSINESS RISK OF NOMINAL NET CASH FLOW (PER PERIOD)'
```

```
[20]    PN←INPUTD N1
[21]    'RISK PREMIUM FOR UNCERTAINTIES IN INFLATION RATE AND CASH FLOW SENSITIVITIES
        (PER PERIOD)'
[22]    YN←INPUTD N1
[23]    'INFLATION RATE (PER PERIOD)'
[24]    NT←INPUTD N1
[25]    'DEPRECIATION AND OTHER FIXED NON-CASH CHARGES (PER PERIOD)'
[26]    DT←INPUTD N1
[27]    'RISK PREMIUM FOR UNCERTAIN INFLATION RATE (PER PERIOD)'
[28]    OMN←INPUTD N1
[29]    N←1
[30]    LOOP:NPVR←NPVR+PRODUCT N
[31]    N←N+1
[32]    →(N≤N1)/LOOP
[33]    'THE NET PRESENT VALUE IS'
[34]    NPVR
        ∇

        ∇PRODUCT[□]∇
     ∇  X←PRODUCT N
[1]     A←(1-TT)×((IN[N]××/1+LT[⍳N])-(ON[N]××/1+OBT[⍳N])+FN[N])
[2]     B←(1+I+PN[N]+YN[N])×B1←((1+I)*N-1)××/1+NT[⍳N]
[3]     C←(1+I+OMN[N])×B1
[4]     X←(A÷B)+(DT[N]×TT÷C)
        ∇

        ∇INPUTD[□]∇
     ∇  VEC←INPUTD N
[1]     VEC←,□
[2]     →(N=ρVEC)/0
[3]     →(N>ρVEC)/FEW
[4]     'TOO MANY NUMBERS. RETYPE THE ';N;' NUMBERS.'
[5]     →1
[6]     FEW:'TOO FEW NUMBERS. SUPPLY THE REMAINING ';(N-ρVEC);' NUMBERS.'
[7]     VEC←VEC,□
[8]     →2
        ∇
```

EFFECTS OF UNCERTAIN INFLATION ON THE INVESTMENT AND FINANCING DECISIONS OF A FIRM

A. H. Chen and A. J. Boness*

I. Introduction

In their classic paper, Modigliani and Miller [20], assuming the presence of risk classes of firms, first brought out the relationship between the value of shares and the firm's financial decisions without explicitly specifying an equilibrium market valuation model. By use of an arbitrage argument, they derived their three well-known propositions in the financial theory of the firm.

Indeed, if value-maximization is an appropriate goal of the firm, the development of any normative theories of the firm's financial policies requires a theoretically sound model of market share valuation. Fortunately, the capital asset pricing models of Sharpe [30], Lintner [13], and Mossin [22] have provided us with theoretically sound valuation equations for risky assets in an equilibrium capital market. The SLM capital asset pricing model has been applied to the problems of capital budgeting and capital structure decisions, and several significant implications for corporate financial decisions have been derived.[1] In particular, the cost of capital for an investment project has been shown to depend on its relevant risk and not on the particular firm which undertakes the project. With respect to the problem of a firm's capital structure, it has been demonstrated that the value of a firm is invariant with capital structure if corporate income taxes are not considered.

The traditional capital asset pricing models are derived without an explicit consideration of uncertain inflation. Thus, the effects of uncertain inflation upon the firm's investment and financing decisions have not been analyzed within the context of equilibrium market valuation models. The purpose of this paper is to investigate how the presence of uncertain inflation might affect a firm's investment and financing decisions. In Section II, assuming a specific preference structure for investors, we will derive and discuss an equilibrium capital asset pricing model under the condition of uncertain inflation. Based upon the derived model, the

* The authors are Associate Professors of Finance, SUNY/AB. They are indebted to E. T. Chen, M. J. Gordon, P. J. Halpern, F. C. Jen, M. C. Jensen, E. H. Kim and M. Rubinstein for valuable comments on an earlier draft of the paper. They also wish to acknowledge the financial support for this research from the Dean Witter Foundation to the first author while he was visiting at Graduate School of Business Administration, U.C., Berkeley.

1. See, for example, Hamada [10], Litzenberger and Budd [15], Mossin [23], Rubinstein [27], and Tuttle and Litzenberger [33]. It should be pointed out that the problem of Pareto optimality of stock market in investment allocation, which is beyond the scope of this paper, has been studied based upon the capital asset pricing model by Jensen and Long [11], Fama [7], Stiglitz [32], and most recently by Leland [12], Merton and Subrahmanyam [19], and Rubinstein [29].

effects of uncertain inflation upon the firm's investment decisions will be discussed in Section III; and its effects upon the firm's financing decisions will be analyzed in Section IV.

II. A Model of Market Equilibrium Asset Valuation Under Uncertain Inflation

A. Assumptions

We make the following assumptions in deriving an equilibrium capital asset pricing model under uncertain inflation:

(1) A perfectly competitive capital market exists, in which both stocks and bonds are traded. This implies that there are no transaction costs and no taxes, and that investors are price-takers.[2]
(2) Investors have homogeneous expectations with respect to the probability distributions of future rates of return on risky securities and the rate of inflation.
(3) Investors are risk-averse, single-period expected utility of real terminal wealth maximizers.

B. Notation

The following notation is employed in subsequent analysis:

S_{ij} = the market value of the ith investor's holding of the jth stock.

$S_j = \sum_i S_{ij}$, the aggregate market value of the jth stock.

$S = \sum_j S_j = \sum_i \sum_j S_{ij}$, the aggregate market value of all stocks.

B_{ij} = the market value of the ith investor's holding of the jth firm's bond.

$B_i = \sum_j B_{ij}$, the aggregate market value of bonds held by the ith investor.

$B_j = \sum_i B_{ij}$, the aggregate market value of the jth firm's bond.

$B = \sum_i B_i = \sum_j B_j$, the aggregate market value of all bonds.

$W_i = \sum_j (S_{ij} + B_{ij}) = \sum_j S_{ij} + B_i$, the ith investor's investable wealth.

$W = \sum_i W_i$, the aggregate investable wealth.

$\tilde{R}_j$ = the random *nominal* rate of return on the jth stock, with mean $E(\tilde{R}_j)$ and variance $Var(\tilde{R}_j)$.

$Cov(\tilde{R}_j, \tilde{R}_k)$ = the covariance between the nominal rates of return on stocks j and k.

R_f = the nominal risk-free rate of return on bonds.

$\tilde{R}_a$ = the random rate of inflation, with mean $E(\tilde{R}_a)$ and variance $Var(\tilde{R}_a)$.

$Cov(\tilde{R}_j, \tilde{R}_a)$ = the covariance between the random nominal rate of return on stock j and the rate of inflation.

2. Without considering the consumption decisions in the model, we are, in essence, assuming that the nominal risk-free rate of return on bonds is exogenously determined. It can be shown, however, that in an equilibrium model which includes consumption decisions the risk-free interest rate is endogenously determined by the marginal rate of substitution between the current and future consumptions. See, for example, Rubinstein [29].

$$\tilde{r}_j = \tilde{R}_j - \tilde{R}_a, \text{ the random } \textit{real} \text{ rate of return on the } j^{th} \text{ stock.}[3]$$
$$\tilde{r}_b = R_f - \tilde{R}_a, \text{ the random } \textit{real} \text{ rate of return on bonds.}$$

C. *The Model*

With the above notation, the ith investor's *real* ending wealth can be expressed as:

$$\begin{aligned}
\tilde{Y}_i &= \sum_j S_{ij}(1 + \tilde{r}_j) + B_i(1 + \tilde{r}_b) \\
&= \sum_j S_{ij}(1 + \tilde{R}_j - \tilde{R}_a) + (W_i - \sum_j S_{ij})(1 + R_f - \tilde{R}_a) \qquad (1) \\
&= W_i(1 + R_f - \tilde{R}_a) + \sum_j S_{ij}(\tilde{R}_j - R_f).
\end{aligned}$$

If we assume that each investor is rational in the von Neumann-Morgenstern sense and is maximizing the expected utility of real ending wealth, then for each investor the demands for stocks are given by the following relations,

$$\frac{\partial E[U_i(\tilde{Y}_i)]}{\partial S_{ij}} = E[U'_i(\tilde{Y}_i)(\tilde{R}_j - R_f)] = 0 \qquad \text{(all j)} \qquad (2)$$

In order to characterize the quilibrium relationship between the risk and the expected return of stocks, it is necessary to specify the investors' preference structure. Assume that investors have quadratic utility functions of terminal wealth in real terms of the following form:

$$U_i(\tilde{Y}_i) = \tilde{Y}_i - C_i \tilde{Y}_i^2, \qquad (3)$$

where the coefficient $C_i > 0$ for risk-averse investors. Then, the expected utility to be maximized by each investor can be expressed as

$$E[U_i(\tilde{Y}_i)] = E_i(\tilde{Y}_i) - C_i\{V_i(\tilde{Y}_i) + [E_i(\tilde{Y}_i)]^2\}, \qquad (4)$$

where $E_i(\tilde{Y}_i)$, the expected value of the ith investor's real ending wealth, can be expressed as

$$E_i(\tilde{Y}_i) = W_i[1 + R_f - E(\tilde{R}_a)] + \sum_j S_{ij}[E(\tilde{R}_j) - R_f]$$

and $V_i(\tilde{Y}_i)$, the variance of the ith investor's real ending wealth, can be expressed as

$$V_i(\tilde{Y}_i) = W_i^2 \text{Var}(\tilde{R}_a) + \sum_j \sum_k S_{ij}S_{ik}\text{Cov}(\tilde{R}_j, \tilde{R}_k) - 2W_i \sum_j S_{ij}\text{Cov}(\tilde{R}_j, \tilde{R}_a)$$

3. The rate of inflation is defined as $R_a = \frac{I_1}{I_0} - 1$, where I_0 and I_1 are the general price levels at the beginning and the end of the period. Let S_j and S_{1j} be the nominal values of the jth stock at the beginning and the end of the period. Therefore, one plus the *real* rate of return on the jth stock can be expressed as

$$1 + r_j = (S_{1j}/I_1)/(S_j/I_0)$$

$$= (1 + R_j)\left(\frac{1}{1 + R_a}\right)$$

$$= (1 + R_j)(1 - R_a + R_a^2 - R_a^3 + \ldots)$$

$$= (1 + R_j - R_a - R_jR_a + R_a^2 + \ldots)$$

Hence,

$$r_j \doteq R_j - R_a.$$

As given in (2), the first-order condition for optimization requires that $\partial E[U_i(\tilde{Y}_i)]/\partial S_{ij} = 0$. The chain rule yields the following first-order condition:

$$\frac{\partial E[U_i(\tilde{Y}_i)]}{\partial S_{ij}} = \frac{\partial E[U_i(\tilde{Y}_i)]}{\partial E_i(\tilde{Y}_i)} \cdot \frac{\partial E_i(\tilde{Y}_i)}{\partial S_{ij}} + \frac{\partial E[U_i(\tilde{Y}_i)]}{\partial V_i(\tilde{Y}_i)} \cdot \frac{\partial V_i(\tilde{Y}_i)}{\partial S_{ij}} = 0. \quad (5)$$

From this, we derive for each investor the following demand relation on stock j:

$$[E(\tilde{R}_j) - R_f]\left[\frac{1}{2C_i} - E_i(\tilde{Y}_i)\right] = \sum_k S_{ik} Cov(\tilde{R}_j, \tilde{R}_k) - W_i Cov(\tilde{R}_j, \tilde{R}_a) \quad \text{(all i, j).} \quad (6)$$

Thus a system of linear equations with constant coefficients is given for each investor. Taking the jth equation for each investor and summing over all i, we have

$$[E(\tilde{R}_j) - R_f]\left[\sum_i \frac{1}{2C_i} - \sum_i E_i(\tilde{Y}_i)\right] = \sum_i \sum_k S_{ik} Cov(\tilde{R}_j, \tilde{R}_k) - \sum_i W_i Cov(\tilde{R}_j, \tilde{R}_a) \quad \text{(all j)}$$

which simplifies to[4]

$$E(\tilde{R}_j) = R_f + \frac{S\,Cov(\tilde{R}_j, \tilde{R}_m) - W\,Cov(\tilde{R}_j, \tilde{R}_a)}{\sum_i \frac{1}{2C_i} - \sum_i E_i(\tilde{Y}_i)}. \quad (7)$$

This is an equilibrium capital asset pricing model under uncertain inflation (CAPMUI).[5] Equivalently,

4. The rate of return on market portfolio of risky securities is given as $\tilde{R}_m = (\sum_j S_j \tilde{R}_j / \sum_j S_j)$, hence,

$$\sum_i \sum_k S_{ik}\,Cov(\tilde{R}_j, R_k) = \sum_k S_k\,Cov(\tilde{R}_j, \tilde{R}_k) = Cov(\tilde{R}_j, \sum_k S_k \tilde{R}_k)$$

$$= Cov(\tilde{R}_j, \sum_k S_k \tilde{R}_m) = S\,Cov(\tilde{R}_j, \tilde{R}_m).$$

5. Assuming a general preference function with the mean and variance of real terminal wealth as arguments, Chen [4] has derived and empirically tested the following alternative version of CAPMUI:

$$E(\tilde{R}_j) = R_f + \frac{S\,Cov(\tilde{R}_j, \tilde{R}_m) - W\,Cov(\tilde{R}_j, \tilde{R}_a)}{S\,Var(\tilde{R}_m) - W\,Cov(\tilde{R}_m, \tilde{R}_a)}\,[E(\tilde{R}_m) - R_f] \quad (7A)$$

It should be noted that the CAPMUI of (7) or (7A) has a certain similarity to Mayers' [17, 18] extension of the SLM model to include non-marketable assets.

Lintner [14], Roll [26] and Gaviria [8] have, under different assumptions, derived different versions of CAPMUI. However, the key parameters of their models are still in real rather than nominal terms, and hence the effects of uncertain inflation on financial decisions can not be explicitly analyzed. Gordon and Halpern [9] have explored the micro and macro implications of their CAPMUI. Finally, in a most recent article, Long [16] has studied the effects of inflation on stock prices and the term structure of interest rates in a multi-period framework.

$$E(\tilde{R}_j) = R_f + R^* b^*_j \qquad (8)$$

where

$$R^* = \cfrac{1}{\displaystyle\sum_i \frac{1}{2C_i} - \sum_i E_i(\tilde{Y}_i)}$$

and

$$b^*_j = S\,\mathrm{Cov}(\tilde{R}_j, \tilde{R}_m) - W\,\mathrm{Cov}(\tilde{R}_j, \tilde{R}_a).$$

We now have a simple formula showing that the equilibrium expected nominal rate of return on stock (or risky asset) equals the nominal rate of return on bond (or risk-free asset) plus a risk premium. The risk premium consists of two factors. The first, b^*_j, often referred to as "systematic risk," is the relevant risk measure associated with stock j. It is of interest to note that when uncertain inflation is explicitly considered in the model, the systematic risk of each stock contains two elements: (1) the covariance between the stock's rate of return and the rate of return on the market portfolio of stocks, and (2) the covariance between the stock's rate of return and the rate of inflation. We shall call the former *"the variability risk"* and the latter *"the inflation risk."* A positive value of $\mathrm{Cov}(\tilde{R}_j, \tilde{R}_a)$ indicates that stock j is likely to have a higher return when inflation exists. Such a stock will be called an *"inflation-preferred"* stock. Likewise, we shall call a stock whose return is uncorrelated with inflation as *"inflation-neutral"* and that whose return is negatively correlated with inflation as *"inflation-averse."* Since not all stocks are inflation-preferred, it is clear that not all common stocks can be used to hedge against inflation.

The second factor, R^*, is the same for all firms and serves as a weighting factor for the firm's risk factor b^*_j. It is the *market* risk aversion factor and has been referred to as "the market price of risk." R^* is the harmonic mean of the investors' expected Pratt-Arrow absolute risk aversion measures.[6]

Let R_i be the ith investor's absolute risk aversion, that is,

$$R_i = -\frac{U''_i(Y_i)}{U'_i(Y_i)}$$

where U'_i and U''_i are the first and second derivatives of the ith investor's utility function with respect to *real* wealth. Then,

$$R^* = \cfrac{1}{\displaystyle\sum_i E\left(\frac{1}{R_i}\right)}. \qquad (9)$$

The traditional version of the capital asset pricing model, which has

6. See Arrow [2] and Pratt [25] for various measures of risk-aversion.

not explicitly taken uncertain inflation into account, can be obtained by setting $E(\tilde{R}_a) = 0$ and $Cov(\tilde{R}_j, \tilde{R}_a) = 0$ in (8). Then,

$$E(\tilde{R}_j) = R_f + Rb_j \tag{10}$$

where

$$R = \frac{1}{\sum_i \dfrac{1}{2C_i} - \Sigma E_i(\tilde{Z}_i)}$$

$b_j = S\, Cov(\tilde{R}_j, \tilde{R}_m)$

$\tilde{Z}_i = W_i(1 + R_f) + \sum_j S_{ij}(\tilde{R}_j - R_f)$, the ith investor's nominal ending wealth.

Equation (10) is the same result obtained by Mossin [23]. Comparing (8) and (10), we see that the traditional capital asset pricing model *overstates* the market price of risk if an uncertain inflation is expected; and it *understates* the market price of risk if an uncertain deflation is expected.

The measure of systematic risk has changed from $S\, Cov(\tilde{R}_j, \tilde{R}_m)$ in the traditional model to $[S\, Cov(\tilde{R}_j, \tilde{R}_m) - W\, Cov(\tilde{R}_j, \tilde{R}_a)]$ in the modified model. Therefore, the traditional capital asset pricing model *overstates* the firm's relevant risk if its return is positively correlated with the rate of inflation, and it *understates* the firm's relevant risk if its return is negatively correlated with the rate of inflation.

III. The Firm's Investment Decisions

The effects of uncertain inflation upon a firm's capital investment decisions are analyzed in this section.

Equation (10) is the security valuation equation under the traditional capital asset pricing model. It can be expressed alternatively as

$$E(\tilde{R}_j) = R_f + \lambda\, Cov(\tilde{R}_j, \tilde{R}_m) \tag{11}$$

where

$$\lambda = SR = \frac{S}{\sum_i \dfrac{1}{2C_i} - \{W(1 + R_f) + S[E(\tilde{R}_m) - R_f]\}}.$$

Using (11), Rubinstein [27], has derived the following capital budgeting criterion for a value-maximizing firm:[7] an investment project z should be accepted if and only if

$$E(\tilde{R}_z) > K_z = R_f + \lambda\, Cov(\tilde{R}_z, \tilde{R}_m). \tag{12}$$

where $\tilde{R}_z \equiv (\tilde{X}_z/I_z) - 1$, is the random (internal) rate of return of project z. $\tilde{X}_z$ is the random gross cash inflow and I_z is the cost of the project z.

In words, the criterion states that an investment project should be accepted if its internal rate of return is greater than its cost of capital, K_z,

7. See also Jensen and Long [11] and Merton and Subrahmanyam [19].

which equals the risk-free rate of return plus a risk premium appropriate to the project.

If $Cov(\tilde{R}_z, \tilde{R}_m) > 0$, the project acceptance criterion is changed to the following: an investment project should be accepted only if

$$\frac{E(\tilde{R}_z) - R_f}{Cov(\tilde{R}_z, R_m)} > \lambda. \tag{13}$$

Here, λ is interpreted as "the risk-standardized cost of capital" appropriate to all firms and all projects.[8]

To see the effects of uncertain inflation upon the firm's criterion for capital budgeting, we rewrite (8) as

$$E(\tilde{R}_j) = R_f + \lambda^*[Cov(\tilde{R}_j, \tilde{R}_m) - g\ Cov(\tilde{R}_j, \tilde{R}_a)] \tag{14}$$

where

$$\lambda^* = SR^* = \frac{S}{\sum_i \dfrac{1}{2C_i} - \{W[1 + R_f - E(\tilde{R}_a)] + S[E(\tilde{R}_m) - R_f]\}}$$

$$g = W/S = 1 + B/S.$$

Therefore, the project selection criterion for a value-maximizing firm under uncertain inflation is as follows: an investment project should be accepted if and only if

$$E(\tilde{R}_z) > K^*_z = R_f + \lambda^*[Cov(\tilde{R}_z, \tilde{R}_m) - g\ Cov(\tilde{R}_z, \tilde{R}_a)]. \tag{15}$$

Alternatively, if $[Cov(\tilde{R}_z, \tilde{R}_m) - g\ Cov(\tilde{R}_z, \tilde{R}_a)] > 0$, the capital investment should be accepted only if

$$\frac{E(\tilde{R}_z) - R_f}{Cov(\tilde{R}_z, \tilde{R}_m) - g\ Cov(\tilde{R}_z, \tilde{R}_a)} > \lambda^*. \tag{16}$$

Here, λ^* is interpreted as "the risk-standardized cost of capital under uncertain inflation" and is appropriate to all firms and all projects when uncertain inflation exists. Thus, λ, derived under the traditional capital asset pricing model, *overstates* the true risk-standardized cost of capital if uncertain inflation is expected; it *understates* the true risk-standardized cost of capital if uncertain deflation is expected. Therefore, in using λ as an investment criterion, the level of total investments by firms tends to be lower than warranted if uncertain inflation is expected, and it tends to be higher than warranted if uncertain deflation is expected. Note that the "market price of risk" criterion for capital investment selection obtained from the traditional CAPM, biased as it might be when uncertain inflation or deflation exists, does provide an automatic counter-cyclical adjustment mechanism. The cost of capital is biased upward in an inflationary period, as a result it tends to discourage capital expansion; and it is

8. See Rubinstein [27], p. 173.

biased downward in a deflationary period, therefore, it tends to encourage capital expansion. Of course, the degree of biases in the cost of capital depends also upon what types (inflation-preferred or inflation-averse) of investment projects are under consideration.

The traditional market price of risk criterion for project selection requires that any project with a return-risk combination plotted above the market line (with the slope of λ) should be accepted and any project plotted below the market line should be rejected. For example, A in Figure 1 should be accepted, while C in Figure 1 should be rejected. However, the traditional criterion which considers only variability risk but not inflation risk might result in an incorrect investment decision for the firm. Let λ^* be the market price of risk when an uncertain inflation is expected. Then, $\lambda^* < \lambda$.

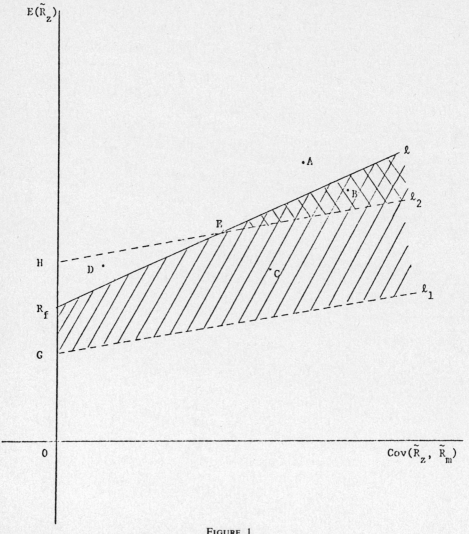

FIGURE 1
Project Selection in an Inflationary Period

The project selection criterion for an inflationary period is shown in Figure 1. In the figure, there are two market lines, l_1 and l_2, and they both have the same slope of λ^*. l_1 is for the selection of inflation-preferred projects (those with the same $Cov(\tilde{R}_z, \tilde{R}_a) > 0$) and l_2 is for the selection of the inflation-averse projects (those with the same $Cov(\tilde{R}_z, \tilde{R}_a) < 0$). Note that the market line l_1 intercepts the vertical axis at $G = R_f - \lambda^* g$ $Cov(\tilde{R}_z, \tilde{R}_a)$, and line l_2 intercepts the vertical axis at $H = R_f + \lambda^* g |Cov(\tilde{R}_z, \tilde{R}_a)|$. In an inflationary period, the traditional market price of risk criterion (using λ) is always biased upward for the inflation-preferred projects in the sense that it rejects some desirable projects. As shown in Figure 1, all the inflation-preferred projects plotted within the shaded area between lines 1 and l_t should have been accepted, but will be rejected using the traditional criterion. For example, the inflation-preferred project C should have been accepted, but will be rejected if λ is used as criterion. On the other hand, λ tends to be biased upward for inflation-averse projects with *higher* variability risk and biased downward for inflation-averse projects with *lower* variability risk. For example, the inflation-averse project B, which has a relatively higher variability risk, should have been accepted but will be rejected if λ is used as selection criterion; whereas the inflation-averse project D, which has a relatively lower variability risk, should be rejected, but will be accepted if λ is used.

Similarly, we can analyze the project selection criterion for a deflationary period.

If the new projects are of the same risk as the firm's existing assets, the firm's cost of equity capital can then be used as the cut-off rate for investment decisions. Under such a condition, we have

$$K^*_z = R_f + \lambda^*[Cov(\tilde{R}_z, \tilde{R}_m) - g\, Cov(\tilde{R}_z, \tilde{R}_a)]$$
$$= R_f + \lambda^*[Cov(\tilde{R}_j, \tilde{R}_m) - g\, Cov(\tilde{R}_j, \tilde{R}_a)]$$
$$= E(\tilde{R}_j).$$

This is the special case of scale expanding investment projects which has been discussed extensively in Modigliani and Miller's studies.

The problems of selecting among mutually exclusive projects and capital rationing can be easily handled within the framework of the equilibrium capital asset pricing model. For example, between two mutually exclusive projects, the one with a higher expected risk-adjusted net future value, that is, the higher $I_z\{E(\tilde{R}_z) - R_f - \lambda^*[Cov(\tilde{R}_z, \tilde{R}_m) - g\, Cov(\tilde{R}_z, \tilde{R}_a)]\}$, should be accepted.

The cost of capital for specific investment projects in the presence of corporate income taxes will be analyzed in the next section.

IV. The Firm's Financing Decisions

In the preceding section we have seen that the presence of uncertain inflation has significant impact upon a firm's investment decisions and that ignoring its presence can lead to incorrect decisions in project selection. In this section, we examine the effects of uncertain inflation upon the firm's financing decisions. The following additional notational will be employed:

$\tilde{X}_j$ = the random dollar value of net operating income of the jth firm.

$V_j = S_j + B_j$, the total market value of firm j.

$\tilde{R}_j = (\tilde{X}_j - R_f B_j)/S_j$, the random nominal rate of return on the jth firm's equity.

All symbols with a superscript "u" denote the variables of an unlevered or pure-equity firm. Hence, $B_j{}^u = 0$, $S_j{}^u = V_j{}^u$, and $\tilde{R}_j{}^u = \tilde{X}_j{}^u/S_j{}^u = \tilde{X}_j{}^u/V_j{}^u$.

A. The Financing Decision Without Corporate Income Taxes

Using the definition of rate of return on equity and the valuation equation of (14), we have the following relation for a levered firm:

$$E(\tilde{X}_j) = R_f(S_j + B_j) + \lambda^*[\text{Cov}(\tilde{X}_j, \tilde{R}_m) - g\,\text{Cov}(\tilde{X}_j, \tilde{R}_a)]. \tag{17}$$

Similarly, we have the following relation for a pure-equity firm:

$$E(\tilde{X}_j{}^u) = R_f V_j{}^u + \lambda^*[\text{Cov}(\tilde{X}_j{}^u, \tilde{R}_m) - g\,\text{Cov}(\tilde{X}_j{}^u, \tilde{R}_a)]. \tag{18}$$

If $\tilde{X}_j = \tilde{X}_j{}^u$, then (17) and (18) imply that

$$V_j = V_j{}^u. \tag{19}$$

The proposition that the value of a firm is independent of its capital structure is derived within the framework of the equilibrium capital asset pricing model under uncertain inflation. Therefore, the existence of uncertain inflation, which changes the market price of risk and affects the firm's investment criterion, will not change MM's basic proposition on capital structure.

The MM proposition II, which indicates the effect of leverage on the equilibrium rate of return on the equity of a firm, can also be derived using CAPMUI. From the definitions of $\tilde{R}_j$ and $\tilde{R}_j{}^u$, we have

$$\tilde{R}_j = \tilde{R}^u(1 + h_j) - R_f h_j \tag{20}$$

where

$$h_j = B_j/S_j.$$

Taking the expectations of both sides of (20) and rearranging yields the MM proposition II in a special form,

$$E(\tilde{R}_j) = E(\tilde{R}_j{}^u) + [E(\tilde{R}_j{}^u) - R_f]h_j. \tag{21}$$

Using the valuation equation (14), we can derive an alternative expression of (21), which enables us to see the effect of financial leverage on the risk premium of a firm's equity. Equation (21) can be expressed as

$$E(\tilde{R}_j) = R_f + (1 + h_j)\lambda^*[\text{Cov}(\tilde{R}_j{}^u, \tilde{R}_m) - g\,\text{Cov}(\tilde{R}_j{}^u, \tilde{R}_a)] \tag{22}$$

or,

$$E(\tilde{R}_j) = R_f + \theta + \Psi \tag{23}$$

where

$\theta = \lambda^* \sigma(\tilde{R}_j^u)[\rho_{jm}\sigma(\tilde{R}_m) - g\rho_{ja}\sigma(\tilde{R}_a)]$, the premium for business risk of firm j.

$\Psi = \lambda^* \sigma(\tilde{R}_j^u)[\rho_{jm}\sigma(\tilde{R}_m) - g\rho_{ja}\sigma(\tilde{R}_a)]h_j$, the premium for financial risk of firm j.

$\sigma(\cdot)$ = the standard deviation of the random variate.

ρ_{jm} = the correlation coefficient between the rate of return on the jth firm's equity and that of the market portfolio of risky securities.

ρ_{ja} = the correlation coefficient between the rate of return on the jth firm's equity and the rate of inflation.

Thus, the equilibrium expected rate of return on a firm's equity can be decomposed into a risk-free rate, a premium for its business risk, and a premium for its financial risk. A firm's financial risk consists of the variability-risk and the inflation-risk components.

From (22) or (23), we see that other things being equal the premium for financial risk of an inflation-preferred firm (the one with $Cov(\tilde{R}_j, \tilde{R}_a) > 0$) is relatively lower than that of an inflation-averse firm (the one with $Cov(\tilde{R}_j, \tilde{R}_a) < 0$). Thus, the securities of an inflation-preferred firm will gain more than that of an inflation-averse firm do with an increase in the firm's leverage in an inflationary period. This suggests why many previous empirical studies, which have not distinguished whether the firms are inflation preferred or averse, obtain inconclusive results in testing the "net-debtor/net-creditor hypothesis."[9]

B. *The Financing Decision with Corporate Income Taxes*

In the presence of corporate income taxes, the rate of return must be defined on an after-tax basis, since investors make their portfolio decisions using the expected after-tax rates of return and the riskiness of these after-tax rates of return on securities. With corporate income taxes, the rate of return on equity for a levered firm can be expressed as

$$\tilde{R}_j^\tau \equiv \frac{(\tilde{X}_j - R_f B_j)(1 - \tau)}{S_j},$$

and for an unlevered firm,

$$\tilde{R}_j^{u\tau} \equiv \frac{\tilde{X}_j^u(1 - \tau)}{V_j^u}$$

where τ = the constant marginal (and average) corporate income tax rate.

Using these definitions of after-tax rates of return on equity and the valuation equation,[10] we have the following relation for a levered firm,

---

9. See, for example, Alchian and Kessel [1], Bach and Ando [3] and DeAlessi [5].

10. Note that the valuation equation of (14) should be expressed in after-tax terms.

$$E(\tilde{X}_j)(1 - \tau) = R_f[S_j + B_j(1 - \tau)]$$
$$+ \lambda^*(1 - \tau)[\text{Cov}(\tilde{X}_j, \tilde{R}_m{}^\tau) - g\,\text{Cov}(\tilde{X}_j, \tilde{R}_a)]. \quad (24)$$

and the following relation for a pure-equity firm,

$$E(\tilde{X}_j{}^u)(1 - \tau) = R_f V_j{}^u + \lambda^*(1 - \tau)[\text{Cov}(\tilde{X}_j{}^u, \tilde{R}_m{}^\tau) - g\,\text{Cov}(\tilde{X}_j{}^u, \tilde{R}_a)]. \quad (25)$$

where $\tilde{R}_m{}^\tau$ is the after-tax return on market portfolio. If $\tilde{X}_j = \tilde{X}_j{}^u$, then (24) and (25) imply that

$$V_j = V_j{}^u + \tau B_j. \quad (26)$$

Thus, MM's result with corporate income taxes is derived within the framework of the equilibrium capital asset pricing model under uncertain inflation. Equation (26) states that the value of a firm increases as its leverage factor increases, since the government subsidy is given to a firm's debt capital through the tax-deductibility of interest payments. Hence, the entity value theorem no longer holds with the presence of corporate income taxes.

MM's after-tax earnings yield (i.e., the ratio of interest payments plus profits after taxes to total market value) can be derived using the equilibrium model with uncertain inflation. Let after-tax earnings be $E(\tilde{X}_j{}^\tau)$ = $(1 - \tau)E(\tilde{X}_j) + \tau R_f B_j$, we know from (26) that

$$V_j = \frac{(1 - \tau)E(\tilde{X}_j)}{E(\tilde{R}_j{}^{u\,\tau})} + \tau B_j$$

$$= \frac{E(\tilde{X}_j{}^\tau)}{E(\tilde{R}_j{}^{u\,\tau})} + \frac{[E(\tilde{R}_j{}^{u\,\tau}) - R_f]\tau B_j}{E(\tilde{R}_j{}^{u\,\tau})}.$$

Hence,

$$\frac{E(\tilde{X}_j{}^\tau)}{V_j} = E(\tilde{R}_j{}^{u\,\tau}) - \tau[E(R_j{}^{u\,\tau}) - R_f]H_j \quad (27)$$

where $H_j = B_j/V_j$.

Equation (27) (which is the same as Eq. (11.c) in Modigliani and Miller [21]) states that a firm's after-tax earning yield is a decreasing function of its leverage factor. As noted by MM, however, the effect of leverage on the after-tax earning yield is solely a matter of the tax deductibility of interest payments.

The after-tax earning yield of (27) can also be expressed as

$$\frac{E(\tilde{X}_j{}^\tau)}{V_j} = R_f + (1 - \tau H_j)\lambda^*[\text{Cov}(\tilde{R}_j{}^{u\,\tau}, \tilde{R}_m{}^\tau) - g\,\text{Cov}(\tilde{R}_j{}^{u\,\tau}, \tilde{R}_a)]. \quad (28)$$

MM's after-tax yield on equity capital (i.e., the ratio of net profits after taxes to value of the shares) can also be derived. From the definitions of $\tilde{R}_j{}^\tau$ and $\tilde{R}_j{}^{u\,\tau}$, we have

$$\tilde{R}_j{}^\tau = \tilde{R}_j{}^{u\,\tau} + (1 - \tau)[\tilde{R}^{u\,\tau} - R_f]h_j$$

which yields MM's result,

$$E[\tilde{R}_j^{*\tau}] = E(\tilde{R}_j^{u\,\tau}) + (1 - \tau)[E(\tilde{R}_j^{u\,\tau}) - R_f]h_j. \tag{29}$$

In terms of the equilibrium return-risk relationships, (29) becomes

$$E(\tilde{R}_j^{\,\tau}) = R_f + [1 + (1 - \tau)h_j]\lambda^*[\mathrm{Cov}(\tilde{R}_j^{u\,\tau}, \tilde{R}_m^{\,\tau}) - g\,\mathrm{Cov}(\tilde{R}_j^{u\,\tau}, \tilde{R}_a)]. \tag{30}$$

Equation (30) shows that, in the presence of corporate income taxes, the premium for financial risk in the expected after-tax rate of return on equity is an increasing function of the firm's leverage factor, but is a decreasing function of the corporate income tax rate.

Finally, MM's net-of-tax cost of capital can also be derived using the CAPMUI. From the definition of $\tilde{R}_j^{u\,\tau}$ and Equation (26), we have

$$\tilde{R}_j^{u\,\tau} = \frac{(1 - \tau)\,\tilde{X}_j^u}{V_j^u} = \frac{(1 - \tau)\tilde{X}_j}{V_j(1 - \tau H_j)}. \tag{31}$$

And since $(1 - \tau)\,E(\tilde{X}_j) = E(\tilde{X}_j^{\,\tau}) - \tau R_f B_j$, we have

$$\frac{(1 - \tau)E(\tilde{X}_j)}{V_j} = \frac{E(\tilde{X}_j^{\,\tau})}{V_j} - \tau R_f H_j. \tag{32}$$

Substituting (28) and (31) into (32) and rearranging, we derive the net-of-tax cost of capital as below:

$$\frac{(1 - \tau)E(\tilde{X}_j)}{V_j} = R_f(1 - \tau H_j) + \lambda^*\left[\mathrm{Cov}\left(\frac{(1 - \tau)\tilde{X}_j}{V_j}, \tilde{R}_m^{\,\tau}\right)\right.$$

$$\left. - g\,\mathrm{Cov}\left(\frac{(1 - \tau)\tilde{X}_j}{V_j}, \tilde{R}_a\right)\right]. \tag{33}$$

From (33) we see that, in the presence of corporate income taxes, the firm's investment criterion is influenced by the way in which a specific project is financed. Thus, we derive the following project selection criterion: a capital project is acceptable only if

$$E(_\tau\tilde{R}_z) > {_\tau}K^*_z = R_f(1 - \tau H_z) + \lambda^*[\mathrm{Cov}(_\tau\tilde{R}_z, \tilde{R}_m^{\,\tau}) - g\,\mathrm{Cov}(_\tau\tilde{R}_z, \tilde{R}_a)] \tag{34}$$

where

$_\tau\tilde{R}_z$ = the net-of-tax random internal rate of return of project z.

H_z = the ratio of debt financing used to total cost of the investment project.

Modigliani and Miller [21] suggest that if the firm has a long-run "target" leverage ratio H^*_j, then it can be substituted for H_z in (34) for project selection. Hence, the cost of capital for an investment project is not independent of the particular firm undertaking it, if both corporate income taxes and long-run target leverage ratios exist and are different among firms.

V. Conclusion

Our analyses, based upon an equilibrium capital asset pricing model under uncertain inflation, indicate that uncertain inflation affects the cost of capital of a specific project through the market price of risk and the systematic risk of the project, and hence the firm's investment decisions. However, in the absence of corporate income taxes, the Modigliani-Miller proposition on capital structure holds even under uncertain inflation. Our analyses also indicate that the leverage factor affects the premium for a firm's financial risk through the components of variability and inflation risks.

REFERENCES

1. A. A. Alchian and R. Kessel. "Redistribution of Wealth Through Inflation." *Science*, September 1959.
2. K. J. Arrow. *Aspects of the Theory of Risk Bearing*, Helsinki, 1965.
3. G. L. Bach and A. Ando. "The Redistribution Effects of Inflation." *Review of Economics and Statistics*, February 1957.
4. E. T. Chen. "Capital Asset Prices Under Uncertain Inflation." Ph.D. thesis in progress, Graduate School of Business Administration, University of California, Berkeley, 1974.
5. L. DeAlessi. "Do Business Firms Gain From Inflation?" *Journal of Business*, April 1964.
6. E. F. Fama. "Multiperiod Consumption-Investment Decisions." *American Economic Review*, March 1970.
7. ————. "Perfect Competition and Optimal Production Decisions Under Uncertainty." *Bell Journal of Economics and Management Science*, Autumn 1972.
8. N. G. Gaviria. "Inflation and Capital Asset Market Prices: Theory and Tests." Ph.D. thesis, Stanford University, 1973.
9. M. J. Gordon and P. J. Halpern. "Capital Asset Pricing Under Inflation." Working Paper, The University of Toronto, 1974.
10. R. S. Hamada. "Portfolio Analysis, Market Equilibrium, and Corporation Finance." *Journal of Finance*, March 1969.
11. M. C. Jensen and J. B. Long. "Corporate Investment Under Uncertainty and Pareto Optimality in the Capital Market." *Bell Journal of Economics and Management Science*, Spring 1972.
12. H. E. Leland. "Production Theory and the Stock Market." *Bell Journal of Economics and Management Science*, Spring 1974.
13. J. Lintner. "The Valuation of Risk Assets and the Selection of Risky Investments in Stock Portfolios and Capital Budgets." *Review of Economics and Statistics*, February 1965.
14. ————. "The Aggregation of Investor's Diverse Judgments and Preferences in Purely Competitive Security Markets." *Journal of Financial and Quantitative Analysis*, December 1969.
15. R. H. Litzenberger and A. P. Budd. "Corporate Investment Criteria and the Valuation of Risk Assets." *Journal of Financial and Quantitative Analysis*, December 1970.
16. J. B. Long. "Stock Prices, Inflation, and The Term Structure of Interest Rates." *Journal of Financial Economics*, July 1974.
17. D. Mayers. "Non-Marketable Assets and Capital Market Equilibrium Under Uncertainty." in M. C. Jensen, ed., *Studies in The Theory of Capital Markets*, New York: Praeger Publishers, 1972.
18. ————. "Non-Marketable Assets and the Determination of Capital Asset Prices in the Absence of a Riskless Asset." *Journal of Business*, April 1973.
19. R. C. Merton and M. G. Subrahmanyam. "The Optimality of A Competitive Stock Market." *Bell Journal of Economics and Management Science*, Spring 1974.
20. F. Modigliani and M. H. Miller. "The Cost of Capital, Corporation Finance, and the Theory of Investment." *American Economic Review*, June 1958.
21. ————. "Corporate Income Taxes and the Cost of Capital: A Correction." *American Economic Review*, June 1963.
22. J. Mossin. "Equilibrium in a Capital Asset Market." *Econometrica*, October 1966.
23. ————. "Security Pricing and Investment Criteria in Competitive Markets." *American Economic Review*, December 1969.
24. S. C. Myers. "Procedures for Capital Budgeting Under Uncertainty." *Industrial Management Review*, Spring 1968.
25. J. W. Pratt. "Risk Aversion in the Small and in the Large." *Econometrica*, January 1964.
26. R. Roll. "Assets, Money, and Commodity Price Inflation Under Uncertainty: Demand Theory." *Journal of Money, Credit and Banking*, November 1973.
27. M. E. Rubinstein. "A Mean-Variance Synthesis if Corporate Financial Theory." *Journal of Finance*, March 1973.

28. ————. "A Comparative Statics Analysis of Risk Premium." *Journal of Business*, October 1973.
29. ————. "An Aggregation Theorem For Securities Markets." *Journal of Financial Economics*, September 1974.
30. W. F. Sharpe. "Capital Asset Prices: A Theory of Market Equilibrium Under Condition of Risk." *Journal of Finance*, September 1964.
31. J. E. Stiglitz. "A Re-examination of the Modigliani-Miller Theorem." *American Economic Review*, December 1969.
32. ————. "On the Optimality of the Stock Market Allocation of Investment." *Quarterly Journal of Economics*, February 1972.
33. D. L. Tuttle and R. H. Litzenberger. "Leverage, Diversification and Capital Market Effects on a Risk-Adjusted Capital Budgeting Framework." *Journal of Finance*, June 1968.

Inflationary Effects in the Capital Investment Process: an Empirical Examination

MOON K. KIM*

I. Introduction

IT HAS BEEN SHOWN that correct capital budgeting decisions only can be made based on the real net present value (*NPV*) derived from inflation-adjusted cash flows and discount rates and that disregarding such inflationary impacts will result in suboptimal decisions in capital budgeting [2, 3, 12]. In regard to inflationary impacts on the amount invested by firms under a specific assumption that both cash revenue and costs are in exactly the same proportion as the general price level, Nelson [10] has recently stated that "The optimal level of capital investment will depend in general on the rate of inflation. The amount invested will typically be smaller the higher the rate of inflation." The principal reason for this decreasing investment under inflation is the overstatement of net income before taxes due to historical depreciation charges. Since there will be an additional tax, so called inflation tax, on this inflated income, the nominal cash flow does not increase in proportion to the general price level. Therefore the real *NPV* becomes less than before, thereby projects become less attractive. Under this perfect net operating income (*NOI*) sensitivity to inflation assumption, Nelson's analysis is correct.

In general, economic activities are more sluggish in periods of deflation than inflation. A mild inflation (say, 3%) has been thought of as a driving force to booming economic and investment activities. These observations indicate that the ceteris paribus negative relationship between the rate of inflation and the amount of investment shown by Nelson may not hold true in the real world. It is the intention of this paper to theoretically and empirically investigate the inflation-investment relationship under more general conditions.

The hypothesis that wages, which take a large portion of cash costs, lag behind the general price level is well known even though Kessel and Alchian [7] conclude that this hypothesis remains untested. Under the validity of the wage-lag hypothesis or for some reasons such as output excess demand, net operating income may increase at a higher rate than the rate of inflation and such an increase also may be large enough to offset any adverse inflationary effects of depreciation on investments. Van Horne and Glassmire [13] have noticed, in their analysis of inflationary impacts of depreciation, *NOI*, and others on the value of the firm, that the inflationary impact of *NOI* is more significant than the negative impact of depreciation.

In this paper the assumption of the perfect *NOI* sensitivity to inflation is relaxed and then a model regarding the inter-firm differences in investment activities under inflation is developed and empirically tested. In the next section

* Syracuse University

316

a model is presented to analyze aggregate inflationary impacts on investment, and several hypotheses are shown. Empirical tests and results are presented in Section III and conclusions and implications are discussed in the last section.

II. A Model and Hypotheses

The net present value of a project without inflation (NPV_0) is determined as

$$NPV_o = -X_o + \sum_{i=1}^{n} \frac{X_i(1 - T) + DT}{(1 + r)^i}, \tag{1}$$

where X_i = NOI before depreciation, interest, and taxes without inflation in year i
X_o = initial cash outflow
D = straight-line depreciation charges
r = real discount rate which is assumed constant over time periods
T = income tax rate
n = life of the project.

For the analytical purposes, suppose that only in the first year there is a $p\%$ expected rate of inflation. If the NOI from the project in the first year increases at the rate of $\lambda(1 + p)$, where λ is a measure of the NOI sensitivity to inflation, the real NPV under inflation (NPV_p) becomes[1]

$$NPV_p = -X_o + \frac{X_1\lambda(1 + p)(1 - T) + DT}{(1 + p)(1 + r)} + \sum_{i=2}^{n} \frac{X_i(1 - T) + DT}{(1 + r)^i}. \tag{2}$$

Then the changes in the real NPV, ΔNPV, of the project under inflation is found from equations (1) and (2):

$$\Delta NPV = NPV_p - NPV_o$$

$$= \frac{X_1\lambda(1 + p)(1 - T) + DT}{(1 + p)(1 + r)} - \frac{X_1(1 - T) + DT}{(1 + r)}$$

$$= \frac{X_1(1 - T)}{(1 + r)} \left(\lambda - 1 - \frac{D}{X_1} \frac{T}{1 - T} \frac{p}{1 + p} \right). \tag{3}$$

In theory, the amount invested is determined at the point where the marginal rate of return (MRR) is equal to the marginal cost of capital (MCC). When the real discount rate is assumed invariant to inflation following Fisher [4] and if a positive ΔNPV results due to inflation, the optimal amount of investment increases from I_o to I_1 as illustrated in Figure 1 since the positive ΔNPV causes the MRR curve to shift upward. This indicates that the direction of ΔNPV is directly related to that of the amount invested. Intuitively, the positive ΔNPV implies more investment because the attractiveness of overall projects is enhanced due to inflation, thereby projects that are not acceptable without inflation will increase their chances to be accepted under inflation.

[1] The nominal cash flow in year 1 is transformed into the real cash flow, dividing it by $(1 + p)$. It is assumed that cash flows for $t = 2, 3, \ldots$ are not affected by inflation in the first year.

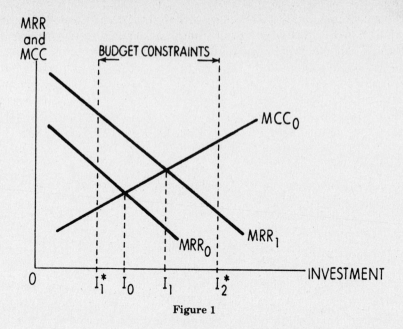

Figure 1

Under capital rationing, however, this result is not always true. If equilibriums occur beyond the budget constraint I_1^*, the optimal investment is at I_1^*. If the budget constraint is greater than the equilibrium points as at I_2^* or there is no capital rationing, the direction of changes in investments is positively related to that of changes in ΔNPV. In this paper no capital rationing is assumed and its implications are discussed later in the paper.

A. *The Zero Inflationary Impact Condition*

When $\Delta NPV = 0$, the attractiveness of the project is not altered by inflation. Then, the zero inflationary impact condition is found in (3) as:

$$\lambda^* = 1 + \frac{D}{X_1}\frac{T}{1-T}\frac{p}{1+p} > 1. \tag{4}$$

Since the variables on the right-hand side of (4) have all positive values, the *NOI* sensitivity coefficient, λ^*, at which the attractiveness of the project is not altered, is always greater than 1.

Under the perfect *NOI* sensitivity assumption ($\lambda = 1$), it is easy to confirm Nelson's conclusion that the amount invested declines as the rate of inflation increases or the attractiveness of the project becomes less than before, simply because $\lambda < \lambda^*$. This result is more obvious if we directly analyze the inflationary impact when $\lambda = 1$ in (3) as:

$$\Delta NPV = -\frac{X_1(1-T)}{1+r}\left(\frac{D}{X_1}\frac{T}{1-T}\frac{p}{1+p}\right) < 0. \tag{5}$$

The ΔNPV is always negative because the variables on the right-hand side of (5) are all positive.

If, however, λ is assumed to be greater (less) than λ^*, projects become more (less) attractive and the amount invested will increase (decrease). That is, from (3), $\Delta NPV \gtreqless 0$ if $\lambda \gtreqless \lambda^*$. For example, if $D/X_1 = .3$, $T = .5$, and $p = 6\%$, then $\lambda^* = 1 + .3$ $(.06/1.06) = 1.017$. In this case, λ over 1.017 will make the project more attractive. The faster increase in nominal NOI beyond λ^* $(1 + p)$ offsets any inflationary tax burden due to historical depreciation charges. Relaxing the perfect NOI sensitivity assumption results in a conclusion that the amount invested increases (decreases) if λ is greater (less) than λ^*. (See Figure 2.)

B. *Cross-Sectional Inflationary Impacts*

In order to examine inter-firm differences in investment activities under a certain inflation, equation (3) is divided by total assets at the beginning of year 1 (TA):

$$\frac{\Delta NPV}{TA} = \frac{X_1}{TA} \frac{1 - T}{1 + r} \left(\lambda - 1 - \frac{D}{X_1} \frac{T}{1 - T} \frac{p}{1 + p} \right). \tag{6}$$

The TA variable is added to eliminate any size effects on inter-firm differences in investment activities. Since inflation-favored firms would engage in more active investments or ΔNPV directly causes the amount of investments to change in the same direction, the ratio $\Delta NPV/TA$ will be henceforth interpreted as the growth rate of total assets. Thus, the cross-sectional difference in the growth rate of total assets under inflation is determined by not only the relative strength of λ and λ^*, but also the size of the NOI to TA ratio, the discount rate, and the depreciation to NOI ratio.

Now, the cross-sectional inflationary impacts of X_1/TA, r, λ and D/X_1 on investment can be isolated by taking the partial derivative of $\Delta NPV/TA$ with respect to each variable.

(a) The NOI/TA Ratio Impact

Taking the partial derivative of $\Delta NPV/TA$ in (6) with respect to X_1/TA results in

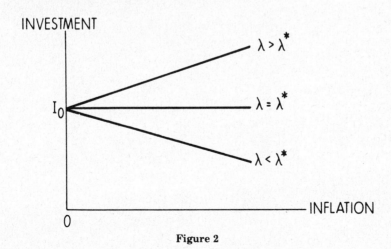

Figure 2

319

$$\frac{\partial(\Delta NPV/TA)}{\partial(X_1/TA)} = \frac{1-T}{1+r}\left(\lambda - 1 - \frac{D}{X_1}\frac{T}{1-T}\frac{p}{1+p}\right) \gtreqless 0 \tag{7}$$

$$\text{if } \lambda \gtreqless \lambda^*.$$

Therefore, a firm which has a higher NOI/TA ratio, if $\lambda > \lambda^*$, would have a higher growth of TA, ceteris paribus. If $\lambda < \lambda^*$, there is a negative relationship between NOI/TA and the growth in TA. The impact of the NOI/TA ratio on investment is positive or negative depending on the relation between λ and λ^*.
(b) The Discount Rate Impact
   From (6),

$$\frac{\partial(\Delta NPV/TA)}{\partial(1+r)} = -\frac{X_1}{TA}\frac{1-T}{(1+r)^2}\left(\lambda - 1 - \frac{D}{X_1}\frac{T}{1-T}\frac{p}{1+p}\right) \gtreqless 0 \tag{8}$$

$$\text{if } \lambda \gtreqless \lambda^*.$$

As with the NOI to TA ratio, the impact of the discount rate depends on the relation between λ and λ^*. A firm which has a higher r, if $\lambda > \lambda^*$, would have a lower growth rate of TA, ceteris paribus. If $\lambda < \lambda^*$, the growth of TA increases as r increases.
(c) The NOI Sensitivity Coefficient Impact
   From (6),

$$\frac{\partial(\Delta NPV/TA)}{\partial\lambda} = \frac{X_1}{TA}\frac{1-T}{1+r} > 0. \tag{9}$$

There is always a positive relationship between the growth in TA and λ. As λ becomes larger, the growth rate of TA increases.
(d) The Depreciation to NOI Ratio Impact
   Again, from (6)

$$\frac{\partial(\Delta NPV/TA)}{\partial(D/X_1)} = -\frac{X_1}{TA}\frac{T}{1+r}\frac{p}{1+p} < 0. \tag{10}$$

The relation between the size of the depreciation to NOI ratio and the growth of TA is negative. The higher the depreciation to NOI ratio, the lower the growth in total assets. This adverse inflationary impact of depreciation on the firm in general has already been most widely recognized through theoretical analyses and empirical tests [5, 6, 8, 9, 11].
   The above analyses of cross-sectional impacts of four variables on investment activities under inflation are summarized in Table 1.

C. *A Cross-Sectional Inflationary Impact Model*

   Based upon the previous analyses, an empirically testable model can be derived as below:

$$g_j = a_o + a_1 XTA_j - a_2 r_j + a_3\lambda_j - a_4 DX_j + u_j \quad \text{if} \quad \lambda_j > \lambda_j^*, \tag{11-a}$$

Table 1

Direction of the Ceteris Paribus
Inflationary Impact of Each Variable
on Investments

Condition	NOI/TA	Discount rate	NOI Sensitivity	DEP./ NOI
$\lambda > \lambda^*$	+	−	+	−
$\lambda = \lambda^*$	0	0	+	−
$\lambda < \lambda^*$	−	+	+	−

$$g_j = a_o \qquad\qquad\qquad + a_3\lambda_j - a_4 DX_j + u_j \quad \text{if} \quad \lambda_j = \lambda_j^*, \qquad (11\text{-b})$$

$$g_j = a_o - a_1 XTA_j + a_2 r_j + a_3\lambda_j - a_4 DX_j + u_j \quad \text{if} \quad \lambda_j < \lambda_j^*, \qquad (11\text{-c})$$

where
$$a_1, a_2, a_3, a_4 > 0$$

$$g_j = \text{the growth rate of } TA \text{ of firm } j$$

$$XTA_j = \text{the } NOI \text{ to } TA \text{ ratio of firm } j$$

$$DX_j = \text{the depreciation to } NOI \text{ ratio of firm } j.$$

Combining (11-a), (11-b), and (11-c) results in

$$g_j = a_o + a_1 XTA_j z_j - a_2 r_j z_j + a_3\lambda_j - a_4 DX_j + u_j, \qquad (12)$$

where z_j is a dummy variable for firm j which has a $(1, 0, -1)$ value;

$$z_j = \begin{pmatrix} 1 \\ 0 \\ -1 \end{pmatrix} \quad \text{if} \quad \lambda_j \gtreqless \lambda_j^*.$$

The NOI sensitivity coefficient (λ_j) can be estimated from the following time series equation:

$$(NOI_i/NOI_o)_j = c_o + \lambda_j(PI_i/PI_o) + w_j, \qquad (i = 1, 2, \cdots), \qquad (13)$$

where PI_i is a general price level index in year i and w_j is the standard random error.

In sum, if the model is correct, each of the four coefficients a_1, a_2, a_3 and a_4 should have a significant positive value.

D. *A Test of the Perfect NOI Sensitivity Coefficient*

If $\lambda = 1$, equation (6) reduces to

$$\frac{\Delta NPV}{TA} = -\frac{X_1}{TA}\frac{T}{1+r}\frac{D}{X_1}\frac{p}{1+p}. \qquad (14)$$

Thus, inter-firm inflationary impacts on investment are determined by only three variables X_1/TA, r, and D/X_1 excluding λ. Similarly to the previous analyses, we may take the partial derivative of $\Delta NPV/TA$ with respect to each of the three variables to examine the impact of each variable on investment under inflation. Or since this is the same case as $\lambda < \lambda^*$ (note that $\lambda^* > 1$) in (11-c) except that λ should not appear in the equation, (11-c) can be directly utilized. Thus, if $\lambda =$

1, the following model exists:

$$g_j = a_0' - a_1'XTA_j + a_2'r_j + a_3'\lambda_j - a_4'DX_j + u_j', \qquad (15)$$

where a_1', a_2', $a_4' > 0$ and $a_3' = 0$. If λ is indeed equal to 1, empirical tests should show that each of a_1', a_2', and a_4' is significantly positive and a_3' is not different from zero.

III. Empirical Tests

The time period chosen for the study was the 1965–1976 period, during which time both mild and high rates of inflation had been experienced. The 1965–76 period was divided into two subperiods, 1965–70 and 1971–76.

One may debate the use of a proper general price index among the Wholesale Price Index, the GNP Deflator, and the Consumer Price Index. In this study, the Consumer Price Index is simply chosen as the general price level indicator. In period 1 (1965–76) the consumer prices rose at the rate of 5.19% per annum; in period 2 (1965–70), 3.82%; and in period 3 (1971–76), 6.58%. (Two subperiods are conveniently designated as periods 2 and 3.)

Sample firms were drawn from the COMPUSTAT tapes using the following criteria: (i) income statement data are available in the COMPUSTAT Industrial file from 1964 through 1976; (ii) monthly stock price data from 1964 through 1976 are also available in the COMPUSTAT PDE file; (iii) the size of total assets is greater than $1 million; and (iv) the fiscal year starts on January 1. The third condition is to eliminate any possible effects from erratic behaviors of small-sized firms and the fourth condition is to match price indexes and financial data to calendar years. A total of 317 firms were thus selected.

In each of the three periods studied the average g_j, XTA_j, and DX_j for each firm were obtained. The mean monthly rate of return on common stock including dividends for the firm in question was used as a proxy of its discount rate. The estimates of λ_j and λ_j^* for each firm in each period were obtained according to (13) and (4), respectively. The income tax rate was conveniently assumed to be 50%.

The sample means of the variables and the partial correlation matrix in each period are shown in Table 2. An interesting observation is that the partial correlation coefficients between DX_j and the other variables are all negative and those among the variables excluding DX_j are all positive. The sample mean of λ_j is far greater than 1 in each of the three periods. It is proper at this point to briefly discuss the conventional test of the null hypothesis of $\lambda_j = 1$ for all j against $\lambda_j \neq 1$ before proceeding to the formal regression test of the hypothesis.

Using the usual t-statistics $t = (\bar{\lambda}_j - 1)/s(\bar{\lambda}_j)$ and $s(\bar{\lambda}_j) = s(\lambda_j)/\sqrt{m}$, where $s(\lambda_j)$ is the sample standard deviation, $s(\bar{\lambda}_j)$ the standard error of the sampling distribution of the mean ($\bar{\lambda}_j$), and m the size of the sample, the null hypothesis is rejected at the 1% level in each of the three periods as shown below:

Period	$\bar{\lambda}_j$	$s(\bar{\lambda}_j)$	t
1	2.746	0.136	12.84[a]
2	2.264	0.162	7.80[a]
3	2.091	0.110	9.92[a]

[a] Indicates significance at the 1% level on a two-tail test.

Since λ_j is not equal to 1 and is widely dispersed among the sample firms, the dispersion should be able to explain the inter-firm differences in g_j if the model (12) is valid.

The regression results of equation (12) are shown in Table 3. The signs of the regression coefficients in period 1 (1965–76) are as hypothesized and significant at the 1% level. (The sign of the coefficient of a variable and that of a_k (k = 1, 2, 3, 4) should not be confused.) The variable XTA_jz_j has a positive coefficient, r_jz_j

TABLE 2

Correlation Matrices and Sample Means

Period		Correlation Matrix								Sample Mean	Standard Deviation
		g_j	XTA_j	XTA_jz_j	r_j	r_jz_j	λ_j	DX_j	z_j		
1 (1965–76) $\bar{p}$ = 5.19%	g_j	1								.106	.041
	XTA_j	.36	1							.161	.068
	XTA_jz_j	.55	.47	1						.106	.139
	r_j	.40	.42	.37	1					.008	.005
	r_jz_j	.53	.32	.80	.67	1				.006	.007
	λ_j	.68	.28	.51	.63	.69	1			2.746	2.423
	DX_j	−.34	−.42	−.29	−.11	−.18	−.16	1		.276	.133
	z_j	.51	.13	.87	.24	.78	.48	−.19		.615	.790
2 (1965–70) $\bar{p}$ = 3.82%	g_j	1								.110	.059
	XTA_j	.24	1							.167	.074
	XTA_jz_j	.40	43	1						.063	.171
	r_j	.46	.39	.45	1					.008	.008
	r_jz_j	.48	.36	.71	.73	1				.005	.010
	λ_j	.65	.24	.61	.65	.73	1			2.264	2.879
	DX_j	−.23	−.45	−.32	−.20	−.27	−.26	1		.266	.131
	z_j	.38	.19	.90	.36	.66	.61	−.25	1	.300	.956
3 (1971–76) $\bar{p}$ = 6.58%	g_j	1								.104	.054
	XTA_j	.26	1							.155	.067
	XTA_jz_j	.42	.35	1						.089	.144
	r_j	.19	.23	.39	1					.009	.006
	r_jz_j	.30	.16	.71	.58	1				.007	.008
	λ_j	.45	.17	.54	.51	.60	1			2.091	1.951
	DX_j	−.34	−.36	−.17	−.06	−.08	−.11	1		.285	.166
	z_j	.45	.08	.88	.36	.73	.60	−.13	1	.546	.839

TABLE 3

Cross-Sectional Tests on Inflationary Impacts on Investments:

$$g_j = a_0 + a_1XTA_jz_j - a_2r_jz_j + a_3\lambda_j - a_4DX_j + u_j$$

(Figures in parentheses are t-values.)

Period	a_0	a_1	$-a_2$	a_3	$-a_4$	R^2
1	.0884	.0957	−1.0007	.0103	−.0545	0.55
(1965–76)		(4.88)[a]	(2.35)[a]	(14.74)[a]	(4.42)[a]	
2	.0882	−.0079	.0670	.0131	−.0297	0.43
(1965–70)		(0.37)	(0.15)	(9.93)[a]	(1.46)	
3	.1044	.1046	−.8642	.0097	−.0870	0.33
(1971–76)		(4.05)[a]	(1.87)[b]	(5.90)[a]	(5.63)[a]	

[a] Significant at the 1% level on a one-tail test.
[b] Significant at the 5% level on a one-tail test.

a negative coefficient, λ_j a positive coefficient, and DX_j a negative coefficient. In period 2 the results are not significant to support the hypotheses except λ_j which has a correct sign and is significant at the 1% level; the coefficient of DX_j is not significant but negative. These insignificant results in period 2 may be due to the fact that the relatively lower rate of inflation in this period could not produce sufficient differential impacts through such variables on investments. The results in period 3 are similar to those in period 1; each coefficient is as hypothesized and significant.

The presence of the significant, positive coefficient of λ_j in (12) confirms that the *NOI* sensitivity is an important variable in explaining inter-firm differences in investment activities under inflation and not constant at 1. The regression test of the hypothesis $\lambda_j = 1$ of (16) also shows similar results. If $\lambda_j = 1$, the coefficient of λ_j should not be different from zero. However, it has significant, positive signs through all three periods studied as shown in Table 4. The hypothesis that the coefficient of XTA_j is negative is not supported. The coefficient has positive signs through all three periods even though it is not significant in period 2. The sign of r_j is significantly negative in period 1 but in other periods the signs are mixed and not significant. The signs of DX_j are negative and similar to the results of the previous test. Again, the results do not support the perfect *NOI* sensitivity hypothesis.

IV. Conclusions

The results found in this paper consistently show that the *NOI* sensitivity to inflation and the size of depreciation are two major determinants of inter-firm differences in investments under inflation. Historical depreciation charges incur additional burdens, thus deterring investment activities. On the other hand, a favorable *NOI* response to inflation encourages investment activities. Effects of the earnings power and discount rate on investments appear to depend upon the net effect of the *NOI* sensitivity and depreciation charges on investment activities. The earnings power of assets tends to amplify the net effect of the *NOI* sensitivity and depreciation on investments. Instead, the size of the discount rate tends to dampen such a net effect.

TABLE 4

Tests on the Perfect NOI Sensitivity Hypothesis:
$$g_j = a'_0 - a'_1 XTA_j + a'_2 r_j + a'_3 \lambda_j - a'_4 DX_j + u'_j$$
(Figures in parentheses are t-values.)

Period	a'_0	$-a'_1$	a'_2	a'_3	$-a'_4$	R^2
1	.0843	.0811	−.9345	.0116	−.0563	.53
(1965–76)		(2.85)[b]	(2.02)[c]	(13.45)[a]	(4.21)[b]	
2	.0750	.0582	.0071	.0128	−.0147	.43
(1965–70)		(1.43)	(0.02)	(10.83)[a]	(0.67)	
3	.0948	.0842	−.6776	.0123	−.0848	.30
(1971–76)		(2.01)[c]	(1.38)	(8.03)[a]	(5.10)[b]	

[a] Significant at the 1% level on a two-tail test.
[b] Significant at the 1% level on a one-tail test.
[c] Significant at the 5% level on a one-tail test.

The presence of the strong positive relationship between the *NOI* sensitivity and the growth rate of *TA* does not support the hypothesis that the *NOI* sensitivity coefficient is constant at 1. The wage-lage hypothesis or specific characteristics existing in a firm seem to cause the coefficient to be greater or less than 1. Notwithstanding the worry about the small observations in the estimation process of λ_j, the regression coefficients of λ_j of equations (12) and (16) are relatively stable throughout the three periods tested.

If strict capital rationing is maintained and the equilibrium positions between the marginal rate of return and cost of capital curves occur beyond the budget constraint, the amount of investment will be invariant to changes in the variables included in (12). It is not an easy task to conclude whether or not all firms operate under capital rationing before we directly investigate individual firms. However, from the results found in this study that the amount of investment responds, to a certain degree, to changes in earnings power, discount rate, *NOI* sensitivity to inflation, and depreciation charges, it is most likely that the budget constraint partially exists or exists beyond the equilibrium points of investment.

REFERENCES

1. Brant Allen. "Evaluating Capital Expenditures under Inflation: A Premier." *Business Horizons* (December 1976).
2. A. D. Bailey, Jr., and D. L. Jensen. "General Price Level Adjustments in the Capital Budgeting Decision." *Financial Management* (Spring 1977).
3. P. L. Cooley, R. L. Roenfeldt, and I. Chew. "Capital Budgeting Procedures under Inflation." *Financial Management* (Winter 1975).
4. Irving Fisher. *The Theory of Interest* (New York: Macmillan Co., 1930).
5. Hai Hong. "Inflation and the Market Value of the Firm: Theory and Tests." *Journal of Finance* (September 1977).
6. ———— "Inflationary Tax Effects on the Assets of the Business Corporations." *Financial Management* (Fall 1977).
7. R. A. Kessel, and A. A. Alchian. "The Meaning and Validity of the Inflation-Induced Lag of Wages Behind Prices." *American Economic Review* (March 1960).
8. J. Lintner. "Inflation and Security Returns." *Journal of Finance* (May 1975).
9. Brian Motley. "Inflation and Common Stock Values: Comment." *Journal of Finance* (June 1969).
10. C. R. Nelson. "Inflation and Capital Budgeting." *Journal of Finance* (June 1976).
11. D. A. Nichols. "A Note on Inflation and Common Stock Values." *Journal of Finance* (September 1968).
12. J. Van Horne. "A Note on Biases in Capital Budgeting Introduced by Inflation." *Journal of Financial and Quantitative Analysis* (January 1971).
13. ————, and W. F. Glassmire, Jr. "The Impacts of Changes in Inflation on the Value of Common Stocks." *Journal of Finance* (September 1972).

For Further Study

1. Brigham, E.F. and R. Pettway (1973), "Capital Budgeting by Utilities". *Financial Management* (Autumn 1973), pp. 11–22.

2. Elton, E.J. and M.J. Gruber (1977), "Optimal Investment and Financing Patterns for a Firm Subject to Regulation with a Lag". *Journal of Finance* (December 1977), pp. 1485–1500.

3. Fama, E.F. (1977), "Risk-adjusted Discount Rate and Capital Budgeting Under Uncertainty". *Journal of Financial Economics*, 5, pp. 3–24.

4. Myers, S.C. (1977), "Determinants of Corporate Borrowing". *Journal of Financial Economics*, 5, pp. 147–175.

5. Nelson, C.R. (1976). "Inflation and Capital Budgeting". *Journal of Finance*, 31. (June 1976), pp. 923–931.

6. Schall, L.D., G.L. Sundem, and W.R. Geijsheek, Jr. (1978). "Survey and Analysis of Capital Budgeting Methods." *The Journal of Finance* (March 1978), pp. 281–287.

Part V

Financing Decisions

Introduction

Financing, investment, and dividend decisions are three important areas in financial management. In analyzing the theoretical aspects of these decisions, financial economists have derived ideal conditions for firm operations in which both financing and dividend decisions become irrelevant. Unfortunately, the ideal conditions used by financial economists are not indicative of real world conditions. Therefore, it is important for students of finance to understand how financing and dividend decisions can affect the market value of a firm. The financing decision is discussed in this part and the dividend decision is discussed in Part VI.

Myers (1974) presents a general approach for the analysis of the interaction between a firm's financing and investment decisions. M&M's theories relating financing policy to dividend policy are considered in Myers' capital budgeting decision. He finds that the corporate investment and financing decisions should be made simultaneously, since the decisions interact in important ways. (See also Spies' (1974) paper in Part IX). This paper presents an interactive framework that has also been used to analyze the widely accepted average cost of capital formula discussed in Part III. A general and flexible capital budgeting rule is also derived.

Rendleman (1978) extends Merton's (1974) risky perpetual bond valuation model to an analysis of corporate financing and investment policy.

Rendleman's conclusions are similar to those obtained by Galai and Masulis (Part II). In addition, he finds that the risk characteristics of capital investment projects and the method by which it is financed can affect the value of the firm's existing debt and market value of equity. Further discussion on the implications of debt capacity on financing and investment policies can be found in Kim (1978) and Martin and Scott (1976, 1980).

In an imperfect market, new equity financing and dividend policy are interrelated. Due to flotation costs for new issues, internal financing is generally cheaper than new equity financing. However, a low dividend yield may result in a greater portion of return being taxed at the lower capital gains rate. Van Horne and McDonald (1971) consider the issues involved in using new equity vs. internal financing. The paper uses a cross-sectional model to demonstrate that share value is adversely affected by new equity financing in the presence of cash dividends except for those firms in the group with the highest number of new issues.

The decision to lease or buy is an important financing decision. Using perfect capital market assumptions, Lewellen, Long and McConnell (1976) (LLM) conclude that environmental factors which can bring about significant differences in the costs of asset purchase vs. asset leasing seldom exist for a firm, especially since the tax rate effect on such transactions can affect them in either way. In addition to this paper, Miller and Upton (1976) have used CAPM to analyze the lease vs. buy decision; Gordon (1974) uses a capital budgeting decision procedure and M&M's basic valuation model to derive a general solution to lease vs. buy decisions.

Papers in previous parts have also considered the financing and dividend decisions. Galai and Masulis (Part II) use Black and Scholes' (1973) option pricing model to examine the firm's investment and financing decisions. Galai and Masulis demonstrate that such decisions are interrelated, even in the absence of bankruptcy costs and tax deductibility of interest. Chen (Part V) carefully discusses the cost of risky debt and its relation to the financing decision.

The Journal of FINANCE

| Vol. XXIX | March 1974 | No. 1 |

INTERACTIONS OF CORPORATE FINANCING AND INVESTMENT DECISIONS—IMPLICATIONS FOR CAPITAL BUDGETING

Stewart C. Myers*

I. Introduction

EVERYONE seems to agree that there are significant interactions between corporate financing and investment decisions. The most important argument to the contrary—embodied in Modigliani and Miller's (MM's) famous Proposition I—specifically assumes the absence of corporate income taxes; but their argument implies an interaction when such taxes are recognized. Interactions may also stem from transaction costs or other market imperfections.

The purpose of this paper is to present a general approach for analysis of the interactions of corporate financing and investment decisions, and to derive the approach's implications for capital investment decisions. Perhaps the most interesting implication is that capital budgeting rules based on the weighted average cost of capital formulas proposed by MM and other authors are not generally correct. Although the rules are reasonably robust, a more general "Adjusted Present Value" rule should, in principle, be used to evaluate investment opportunities.

The paper is organized as follows. Section II presents the framework for my analysis, which is a mathematical programming formulation of the problem of financial management. The conditions for the optimum and the implications for corporate investment decisions are derived. In Section III, the usual weighted average cost of capital rules are derived as special cases of the more general analysis. Section IV examines the errors that can occur if weighted average cost of capital rules are used in practice, and evaluates the rules' robustness. Finally, I discuss the Adjusted Present Value rule as an alternative for practical applications.

It must be emphasized that this paper is not intended to catalogue or deal with all possible interactions of financing and investment decisions; in other words, there is no attempt to specify the problem of financial management in

* Associate Professor of Finance, Sloan School of Management, Massachusetts Institute of Technology. This paper was greatly improved by comments of G. A. Pogue. I also thank Mr. Swaminathan Iyer for programming assistance. Any deficiencies in the paper are my own.

full detail. I present an *approach* to analyzing interactions and a specific analysis of the most important ones.

Another limitation is that the model developed in the paper is static—that is, it does not consider how future financial decisions might respond to information which will become available in future periods. Instead the model specifies a financial plan which is optimal given that current expectations are realized. Since there is no assurance that sequential application of a static model constitutes optimal strategy under uncertainty, this paper is only of intermediate generality. In this respect it is no better or worse than the existing theory of financial management, which is likewise static.

The analysis is nevertheless of immediate interest. As far as I know the literature of finance contains no full analysis of the use of the weighted average cost of capital as a standard for capital budgeting. Most authors present sufficient conditions for its use, and are careful to warn the reader against assuming it to be generally valid.[1] They clearly regard it as a special case of some more general standard. But they do not specify the general standard in operational form, and therefore cannot offer much perspective on how special the special case really is, or on how dangerous it is to use the special rule generally. This paper, on the other hand, formulates a general model, states its implications in reasonably operational form (as the Adjusted Present Value rule), and then goes on to evaluate traditional procedures as special cases.

I do not mean this to minimize previous work on capital budgeting and the weighted average cost of capital, but simply to designate this paper's contribution.[2] My debt to the literature—particularly the Modigliani-Miller papers[3] —will be evident throughout.

II. BASIC FRAMEWORK

We will consider the firm's problem in the following terms. It begins with a certain initial package of assets and liabilities. For a brand-new firm, this will be simply money in the bank and stock outstanding. For a going concern, the package will be much more complicated. Any firm, however, has the opportunity to change the characteristics of its initial package by transactions in real or financial assets—i.e., by investment or financing decisions. The problem is to determine which set of current and planned future transactions will maximize the current market value of the firm. Market value is taken to be

1. See, for example, Miller and Modigliani [14], esp. pp. 346-343; Fama and Miller [7], pp. 170-175; Haley and Schall [9], ch. 13; Vickers [28] and Beranek [2].

Other authors who have expressed concern about the general applicability of the weighted average cost of capital include Robichek and McDonald [21], Arditti [1], and Tuttle and Litzenberger [26].

2. The paper most similar to this one is Beranek's [2]. He analyzes the necessary conditions for use of the weighted average cost of capital, and obtains a list of conditions essentially equivalent to the one presented below. However, his method of analysis is different, he is concerned only with the "textbook" formula (defined below), and he does not go on to evaluate robustness or propose general procedures. His paper does cover certain other issues not addressed here, for example the proper definition of "cash flow" for an investment project.

3. Miller and Modigliani [14] contains the most precise and compact exposition of their theory. See also their other papers, [15] and [16].

an adequate proxy for the firm's more basic objective, maximization of current shareholders' wealth.

This type of problem can be approached by (1) specifying the firm's objective as a function of investment and financing decisions and (2) capturing interactions of the financing and investment opportunities by a series of constraints.

General Formulation

Consider a firm which has identified a series of investment opportunities. It must decide which of these "projects" to undertake.[4] At the same time it wishes to arrive at a financing plan for the period $t = 0, 1, \ldots, T$. The financing plan is to specify for each period the planned stock of debt outstanding, cash dividends paid, and the net proceeds from issue of new shares.

Let: x_j = proportion of project j accepted.

y_t = stock of debt outstanding in t.

D_t = total cash dividends paid in t.

E_t = net proceeds from equity issued in t.

C_t = expected net after-tax cash inflow to the firm in t, with net outflow (i.e. investment) represented by $C_t < 0$.

Z_t = debt capacity in t, defined as the limit on y_t. Z_t depends on firm's investment decision,[5] i.e., $\delta Z_t / \delta x_j$ will normally be positive.

Also, let ψ equal ΔV, the change in the current market value of the firm, evaluated cum dividend at the start of period $t = 0$. In general, ψ is a function of the x's, y's, D's and E's.

The problem is to maximize ψ, subject to:

$$\phi_j = x_j - 1 \leqslant 0, \qquad j = 1, 2, \ldots, J. \tag{1a}$$

$$\phi_t^F = y_t - Z_t \leqslant 0, \qquad t = 0, 1, \ldots \ T. \tag{1b}$$

$$\phi_t^C = -C_t - [y_t - y_{t-1}(1 + (1 - \tau)r)] + D_t - E_t = 0 \tag{1c}$$
$$t = 0, 1, \ldots, T.$$

$$x_j, y_t, D_t, E_t \geqslant 0. \tag{1d}$$

The borrowing rate, r, is assumed constant for simplicity, as is the corporate tax rate τ. In general, r will be a function of the other variables.

This formulation of the firm's financial planning problem is perfectly general in the sense of not imposing restrictions (e.g., linearity) on the functions determining ψ or Z_t. It is by no means a *detailed* formulation. The maturity structure of the planned stock of debt is not treated, for example. Stock repurchases are not allowed. These "details," while important to the firm's overall financial plan,[6] are not critical to this paper.

4. Some projects may be future investment opportunities anticipated for $t = 1, 2, \ldots$. Accepting such a project does not imply immediate investment, but simply that the project is included in the firm's financial plan.

5. The limit may be imposed by capital markets or it may simply reflect management's judgment as to the best level of debt.

6. These "details" are considered in Myers and Pogue [20], who develop mathematical programming models for overall financial planning.

Conditions for the Optimum

Eqs. (1) define the nature of the interactions between the firm's financing and investment decisions. The effects of the interactions can be better understood by examining the necessary conditions for the optimal solution.

In order to simplify notation define $A_j \equiv \delta\psi/\delta x_j$, $F_t \equiv \delta\psi/\delta y_t$, $Z_{jt} \equiv \delta Z_t/\delta x_j$, and $C_{jt} \equiv \delta C_t/\delta x_j$. Also, note that each of the following equals 1: $\delta\phi_j/\delta x_j$, $\delta\phi_t^F/\delta y_t$ and $-\delta\phi_t^C/\delta y_t$. Finally, note that $\delta\phi_t^C/\delta x_j = -C_{jt}$. The shadow prices are λ_j for ϕ_j, λ_t^F for ϕ_t^F and λ_t^C for ϕ_t^C.

With these simplifications, the necessary conditions for the optimum can be written as follows. For each project:

$$A_j + \sum_{t=0}^{T} [\lambda_t^F Z_{jt} + \lambda_t^C C_{jt}] - \lambda \leqslant 0. \tag{2a}$$

For debt in each period,

$$F_t - \lambda_t^F + \lambda_t^C - [1 + (1-\tau)r]\lambda_{t+1}^C \leqslant 0. \tag{2b}$$

For dividends in each period,

$$\delta\psi/\delta D_t - \lambda_t^C \leqslant 0. \tag{2c}$$

For equity issued in each period,

$$\delta\psi/\delta E_t + \lambda_t^C \leqslant 0. \tag{2d}$$

In each of these equations a strict equality holds if the corresponding decision variable is positive in the optimal solution.

Eq. (2a) is particularly interesting because it states the condition for evaluating a marginal investment in a project. Marginal investment is justified if project j's "Adjusted Present Value" (APV_j) be positive, i.e.,

Expand
Investment if:
$$APV_j \equiv A_j + \sum_{t=0}^{T} [\lambda_t^F Z_{jt} + \lambda_t^C C_{jt}] > 0. \tag{3}$$

In the optimal solution $APV_j = \lambda_j$ if the project is accepted ($x_j = 1$). If it is rejected ($x_j = 0$) then APV_j is negative and $\lambda_j = 0$. If it is partially accepted, then $APV_j = \lambda_j = 0$.

The term adjusted present value is used because in the optimal solution A_j, the project's direct contribution to the objective, is "adjusted for" the project's side effects on other investment and financing options. The side effects occur because of the project's effects on the debt capacity and sources/uses constraints.

Effects of financial leverage when dividend policy is irrelevant.—Suppose that dividend policy is irrelevant, in the sense that $\delta\psi/\delta E_t = \delta\psi/\delta D_t = 0$ for all T.[7] Then $\lambda_t^C = 0$, from Eqs. (1c) and (1d).

---

7. This defines irrelevance of dividend policy in the same way as Miller and Modigliani [14]. That is, *given* values for the x_j's and y_t's, a marginal change in D_t and an offsetting change in E_t will not affect shareholder's wealth.

Also, assume that $\delta\psi/\delta y_t$ is positive—which is realistic, given the tax deductibility of debt, regardless of whether one agrees with MM. Then the constraints ϕ_t^F will always be binding, Eqs. (2b) will be strict equalities, and λ_t^F for all t.

Substituting in Eq. (3),

$$APV_j = A_j + \sum_{t=0}^{T} Z_{jt}F_t. \qquad (4)$$

Eq. (4) implies that APV_j, the contribution of a marginal investment in j to the firm's value, is measured by A_j, plus the present value of the additional debt the project supports.

Effects of dividend policy.—In practice, however, dividend policy may not be completely irrelevant. At very least, $\delta\psi/\delta E_t$ will be negative because of transaction costs associated with stock issues. It is not clear whether $\delta\psi/\delta D_t$ is positive, negative or zero in real life.[8]

Suppose that the optimal solution calls for an equity issue in a period t. Then $\lambda_t^c = -\delta\psi/\delta E_t$ and $\lambda_t^c > 0$. Examination of Eq. (2a) shows that this is reflected in the optimal solution in two ways. First, project j is penalized if $C_{jt} < 0$. On the other hand, the project is relatively more attractive if $C_{jt} > 0$: in this case the project generates funds and this reduces the need for a stock issue. Second, if the project contributes to debt capacity in t, this in turn reduces the need for the stock issue. This is evident in Eq. (2b), which shows that λ_t^F, the marginal value of debt capacity in t, depends on λ_t^c as well as on $\delta\psi/\delta y_t$.

The same type of interactions exists if dividends are paid in t and $\delta\psi/\delta D_t \neq 0$.

Conditions for independence of financing and investment decisions.—In a world with no taxes and perfect capital markets, both debt policy and dividend policy are irrelevant, i.e., $F_t = \delta\psi/\delta D_t = \delta\psi/\delta E_t = 0$. In this case the investment and financing decisions are independent, and APV_j equals simply A_j.

The independence of financing and investment decisions in a "pure MM world" is well known, but worth mentioning here because it reveals the economic interpretation of A_j. A_j is the contribution to firm value of marginal investment in project j, assuming all-equity financing and irrelevance of dividend policy. In a pure MM world that is all the financial manager needs to know. In effect, the APV concept first evaluates the project in this base case and then makes appropriate adjustments (via the shadow prices λ_t^F and λ_t^c) when debt and/or dividend policy is relevant and influenced by adoption of the project.

---

8. It can be argued that dividends decrease shareholder wealth because dividends are taxed more heavily than capital gains. On the other hand, it is possible that some investors positively prefer dividends because of the convenience of having a regular, "automatic" cash income, or for other reasons.

Although the matter of dividend policy is still controversial, recent evidence does not indicate that it is all that important, apart from the "informational content" of dividends which is not germane here. (See [15], pp. 367-70, [3] and [8] for empirical evidence consistent with the irrelevance of dividend policy.) Thus most of the analysis later in the paper assumes $\delta\psi/\delta D_t = 0$.

Decentralized capital budgeting systems.—The shadow prices λ_t^F and λ_t^C can, in principle, be used as a basis for a decentralized capital budgeting system. Consider the accept-reject decision on an individual project j. The first step is to estimate the project's contribution to firm value in the base case just described; call this ΔV_o. Then, given estimates of the project's year-by-year contribution to debt capacity (ΔZ_t) and after-tax cash flow (ΔC_t), the decision is:

Accept if:
$$\Delta \psi = \Delta V_o + \sum_{t=0}^{T} (\Delta Z_t \lambda_t^F + \Delta C_t \lambda_t^C) > 0.$$

This may be written in the same form as Eq. (3), i.e.,

Accept if:
$$APV_j = A_j + \sum_{t=0}^{T} (Z_{jt} \lambda_t^F + C_{jt} \lambda_t^C) > 0, \tag{3a}$$

with the understanding that APV_j, A_j, Z_{jt} and C_{jt} are interpreted as discrete amounts rather than partial derivatives.

The distinction between Eqs. (3) and (3a) is important. The discrete form (3a) is relevant for the simple accept-reject choice, given the project's scale. The continuous version (3) is relevant to the choice of optimal scale. The APV's computed according to the two formulas will not be the same unless the various partial derivatives in (3) are constants.

The remainder of the paper is concerned with the discrete accept-reject decision. This was done solely to simplify exposition. The reader can verify that the formal argument could just as well have been based on Eq. (3) as (3a); and that the major results also apply to the problem of determining optimal project scale.

It is, of course, necessary to take λ_t^F and λ_t^C as given regardless of the interpretation. This may be justified in two ways. One assumption is that project j is "small." Another is that the project, regardless of size, does not affect F_t, $\delta\psi/\delta D_t$ or $\delta\psi/\delta E_t$.

The second assumption requires further explanation. Inspection of Eqs. (2c) and (2d) shows that λ_t^C will equal either $\delta\psi/\delta D_t$ or $-\delta\psi/\delta E_t$ at the optimum, depending on whether the optimal plan calls for issuing stock or paying dividends. Thus, so long as $\delta\psi/\delta D_t$ or $\delta\psi/\delta E_t$ is constant, λ_t^C is independent of the decision to accept or reject j. This could be entirely realistic: $\delta\psi/\delta E_t$ might reflect a constant transaction cost per dollar of equity issued, for example.

If the debt constraint (1b) is binding, then Eq. (2b) will be an equality, and λ_t^F will be a constant if F_t, λ_t^C and λ_{t+1}^C are constants. Again, this seems plausible: for example, in an MM world with corporate taxes, F_t is simply present value of the tax shield generated per dollar of debt outstanding at t.

The practical implications of APV for project by project capital budgeting decisions are discussed in more detail later in the paper. Before that I will use the APV concept to analyze capital budgeting rules based on the weighted average cost of capital.

III. A Reexamination of the Weighted Average Cost of Capital Concept

Introduction and Definitions

It is widely accepted that the accept/reject decision for investment projects ought to be evaluated on a "DCF," or discounted cash flow, basis. This is done by one of two decentralized rules. The first is to compute project j's internal rate of return, R_j, from the formula

$$\sum_{t=0}^{T} \frac{C_{tj}}{(1+R_j)^t} = 0, \tag{5}$$

and to accept the project if R_j exceeds ρ_j^*, the "cost of capital" for j. The second rule is to compute the net present value of j's cash flows, discounted at ρ_j^*, and accept j if this figure is positive. Thus, j is accepted if

$$\text{NPV}_j = \sum_{t=0}^{T} \frac{C_{jt}}{(1+\rho_j^*)^t} > 0. \tag{6}$$

In either rule, ρ_j^* is the "hurdle rate" or minimum acceptable expected rate of return.

Comparing Eq. (3a) to (5) and (6), it is evident that NPV_j and APV_j are intended to measure the same thing: the net contribution of j to market value, taking account of the interactions of j with other investment and financing opportunities. There is always some value of ρ_j^* which will insure that $\text{NPV}_j = \text{APV}_j$, or that

$$\sum_{t=0}^{T} \frac{C_{jt}}{(1+\rho_j^*)^t} = A_j + \sum_{t=0}^{T} [\lambda_j^F Z_{jt} + \lambda_t^C C_{jt}] \equiv \text{APV}_j. \tag{7}$$

Eq. (7) may be regarded as an implicit definition of ρ^*. An analogous, but narrower definition is

$$\sum_{t=0}^{T} \frac{C_{jt}}{(1+\rho_j^*)^t} > 0 \quad \begin{array}{l} \text{if and} \\ \text{only if} \end{array} \quad \text{APV}_j > 0. \tag{7a}$$

This interprets ρ_j^* simply as a hurdle rate, or minimum acceptable expected rate of return. A ρ_j^* derived from Eq. (7a) does not necessarily give a correct valuation (i.e., $\text{NPV}_j = \text{APV}_j$) for projects of more than minimum profitability. The conditions under which Eqs. (7) and (7a) are consistent are given later in this paper. For the moment we will work with Eq. (7a). The problem is, how should ρ_j^* be computed, if not directly from Eq. (7a)?

Of the many procedures for calculating ρ_j^*, two are of particular interest. The first is MM's. They propose[9]

$$\hat{\rho}_j^* = \rho_{oj}(1 - \tau L), \tag{8}$$

9. [15], p. 342. In MM's notation ρ^* is C(L) and ρ_{oj} is simply ρ_j.

335

where: ρ_{oj} = The appropriate discount rate assuming all-equity financing;

τ = The corporate tax rate;

L = The firm's "long-run" or "target" debt ratio; and

$\hat{\rho}^*_j$ = A proposed value for ρ^*_j.

MM interpret ρ_{oj} as the rate at which investors would capitalize the firm's expected average after-tax income from currently-held assets, if the firm were all-equity financed.[10] This would restrict application of the formula to projects whose acceptance will not change the firm's risk characteristics. (However, we will see that this is an unnecessarily narrow interpretation of the MM formula.)

The second proposed formula is:

$$\hat{\rho}^*_j = (1 - \tau)r \frac{B}{V} + k \frac{S}{V} \tag{9}$$

where: r = the firm's borrowing rate at t = 0;

k = "the cost of equity capital"—that is, the expected rate of return required by investors who purchase the firm's stock;

B = market value of currently outstanding debt;

S = market value of currently outstanding stock, and

V = B + S, the total current market value of the firm.

I will refer to Eq. (9) as the "textbook formula," for lack of a better name. (The formula, or some variation on the same theme, appears in nearly all finance texts.)[11] It is not necessarily inconsistent with the MM formula, but it is recommended by many who explicitly disagree with MM's view of the world.

The task now is to determine what assumptions are necessary to derive Eqs. (8) and/or (9) from Eq. (3a), the general condition for the optimal investment decision. I will present a set of sufficient conditions, and then argue that, in most cases, the conditions are necessary as well.

Derivation of the MM Cost of Capital Rule

If MM's view of the world is correct, then the value of the firm will be V_0, the value of the firm assuming all-equity financing, plus PVTS, the present value of tax savings due to debt financing actually employed. Dividend policy is irrelevant. Assuming this view is correct, the objective function in the mathematical programming formulation is:

$$\psi = \Delta V_0 + \sum_{t=0}^{T} y_t F_t = \Delta V_0 + \sum_{t=0}^{T} \frac{y_t r \tau}{(1 + r)^{t+1}}. \tag{10a}$$

10. Ibid., pp. 337, 340.

11. See Johnson [11], Ch. 11; Weston and Brigham [29], Ch. 11; Van Horne [27], Ch. 4.

That is, F_t is $r\tau$, the tax saving per dollar of debt outstanding in t, discounted to the present. (It is assumed that the interest is paid at $t + 1$.) Second, assume that

$$A_j = C_j/\rho_{oj} - I_j. \tag{10b}$$

That is, project j is expected to generate a constant, perpetual stream of cash returns.[12]

The third assumption is that undertaking project j does not change the risk characteristics of the firm's assets. That is,

$$\rho_{oj} = \rho_o, \tag{10c}$$

where ρ_o is the firm's cost of capital given all-equity financing.

Fourth, assume that project j is expected to make a permanent and constant contribution to the firm's debt capacity:

$$Z_{jt} = Z_j, \quad t = 0, 1, \ldots, \infty. \tag{10d}$$

Finally assume

$$Z_j = LI_j, \tag{10e}$$

where L is the long-run "target" debt ratio which applies to the firm overall. Eq. (10e) implies that adoption of project j will not change this target.

Rewriting Eq. (3a) using Eqs. (10a) through (10e), we have:

$$APV_j = \frac{C_j}{\rho_o} - I_j + LI_j \sum_{t=0}^{\infty} F_t$$

$$= \frac{C_j}{\rho_o} - I_j + LI_j\tau. \tag{11}$$

From Eq. (7a), the cost of capital is the project's internal rate of return (C_j/I_j) when $APV_j = 0$. Eq. (11) implies that this is given by MM's formula:

$$\rho_j^* = C_j/I_j = \rho_o(1 - \tau L).$$

Extension of MM's Result to Projects of Varying Risk

Let us make one further assumption, that ΔV_o is a linear function of the present values of accepted projects:

$$\Delta V_o = \sum_{j=1}^{J} x_j A_j. \tag{10f}$$

Eq. (10f) assumes that projects are *risk-independent*, in the sense that there are no statistical relationships among projects' returns such that some

12. If $C_{jt} = C_j$, a constant for $t = 1, 2, \ldots, \infty$, then Eq. (10b) simply states the project's net present value when discounted at ρ_{oj}, the "appropriate rate" for j given all-equity financing. However, MM interpret C_j as the expectation of the *mean* of the series $\tilde{C}_{j1}, \tilde{C}_{j2}, \ldots, \tilde{C}_{j\infty}$. See [14], p. 337. This does not require that C_{jt} is constant, but there must be conditions to insure that this mean is finite. The reader may choose the interpretation he likes best. The form of the argument to follow is not affected.

combinations of projects affect stock price by an amount different than the sum of their present values considered separately. In particular, risk-independence implies that there is no advantage to be gained by corporate diversification. Risk-independence is a necessary condition for equilibrium in perfect security markets.[13]

Eq. (10f) also assumes that projects are "physically independent" in the sense that there are no *causal* links between adoption of project j and the probability distribution of cash returns to other projects—that is, it rules out "competitive" or "complementary" projects. Such interactions make it impossible to specify an unique hurdle rate for project j, since the minimum acceptable rate of return on j may depend on whether or not other projects are accepted. However, I am not concerned with this problem in this paper.

Let us adopt Eq. (10f) and drop Eqs. (10c) and (10e). We can recalculate the minimum acceptable rate of return on the project.

$$\rho_j^* = \rho_{oj}(1 - \tau Z_j/I_j). \tag{12}$$

This has the same form as Eq. (8) but is not restricted to projects within a single risk class. However, it is not plausible to identify Z_j/I_j, project j's *marginal* contribution to debt capacity, with L, the firm's overall target capitalization ratio. Presumably Z_j/I_j will be more or less than L, depending on the risk or on other characteristics of the project in question.

In short, MM's formula can be extended to independent projects which differ in risk and in their impact on the firm's target debt ratio.

What If Investment Projects Are Not Perpetuities?

So far we have established that Eqs. (10a, b, d and f) are sufficient for the generalized MM formula, Eq. (12). Eqs. (10a) and (10f) are clearly necessary as well. But what about (10b) and (10d), which require all projects to be perpetuities?

In general, they are necessary: Eq. (13) does not give the correct "hurdle rate" for projects of limited life.[14] (The question of whether the resulting errors are serious is taken up in the next section.)

This can be shown by a simple example. Consider a point-input, point-output project requiring an investment of I_j and offering an expected cash flow of C_{j1} in t = 1, and $C_{jt} = 0$ for t > 1. Assume $\rho_{oj} = \rho_o$ and $Z_{j1} = LI_j$ (and, of course, $Z_{jt} = 0$ for t > 1). Then

$$APV_j = \frac{C_{j1}}{1 + \rho_o} - I_j + LI_j \left(\frac{r\tau}{1 + r}\right).$$

The internal rate of return on the project is given by $R_j = C_{ij}/I_j - 1$, and the cost of capital is given by R_j when $APV_j = 0$. Thus

13. Myers [19] and Schall [24]. See Merton and Subramanyam [13] for a recent review of work relating to this aspect of capital market equilibrium.

14. Of course, the importance of project life has been recognized by MM (in [17], for example) and others (e.g., [1], [2], and [7], esp. p. 173n). But the implications for the cost of capital ρ_j^* have not been developed in the literature.

$$\rho_j^* = \rho_o - Lr\tau \left[\frac{1+\rho_o}{1+r}\right]. \tag{13}$$

Eqs. (12) and (13) are equivalent only in the uninteresting case of $\rho_o = r$.

The Textbook Formula

Let us reconsider Eq. (9),

$$\hat{\rho}_j^* = r(1-\tau)B/V + k(S/V). \tag{9}$$

Probably it is intuitively clear from the foregoing that $\hat{\rho}_j^* = \rho_j^*$ only under very restrictive assumptions. First, let us assume that Eqs. (10a) through (10e) hold.[15] (Remember that (10a) implies that dividend policy is irrelevant.) Also, assume that

$$V_o = \frac{C}{\rho_o}. \tag{14a}$$

That is V_o, the current market value of the firm if it were all equity financed, is found by capitalizing the firm's after-tax operating income at ρ_o. C is, of course, calculated assuming all-equity financing. Also Eq. (14a) presumes $C_t = C, t = 1, 2, \ldots, \infty$.[16]

Finally, assume that the firm is already at its target debt ratio.

$$L_j = B/V. \tag{14b}$$

Note that Eqs. (14a) and (14b) constrain the initial characteristics of the firm's assets and financing mix, whereas the assumptions underlying MM's cost of capital formula relate only to the marginal effects of adopting the project in question.

Now the task is to show that $\hat{\rho}_j^* = \rho_j^*$ under assumptions (10a-e) and (14a-b). Note first that the sum of payments to bondholders and earnings after interest and taxes is $rB + kS = C + \tau rB$, so that $C = r(1-\tau)B + kS$ and

$$V = \frac{C}{\hat{\rho}_j^*}. \tag{15}$$

In an MM world, V is also given by

$$V = \frac{C}{\rho_o} + \tau B, \tag{16}$$

which is equivalent to Eq. (11). We now combine Eqs. (15) and (16) and solve for $\hat{\rho}_j^*$:

15. Eq. (10f) is not relevant, since Eq. (10c) implies that project j will not change the risk characteristics of the firm's assets.

16. Alternatively, we could regard C as the expected value of the mean of the stream $\tilde{C}_1$, $\tilde{C}_2, \ldots, \tilde{C}_\infty$. See fn. 12 above.

$$\hat{\rho}_j^* = \rho_o\left(1 - \tau B\left(\frac{\hat{\rho}_j^*}{C}\right)\right).$$

But $\hat{\rho}_j^*/C = 1/V$, and $B/V = L_j$, so

$$\hat{\rho}_j^* = \rho_o(1 - \tau L_j),$$

which was previously demonstrated to be the correct value.

Thus we have shown that the textbook formula gives the correct cutoff rate for projects under a long list of assumptions, one of which is that MM are correct. However, it can be readily shown that the formula is correct even if MM are wrong, providing the other assumptions hold.[17]

To summarize, the textbook formula gives the correct hurdle rate if:

1. The project under consideration offers a constant, perpetual stream of cash flows, and is expected to make a permanent contribution to debt capacity.
2. The project does not change the risk characteristics of the firm's assets.
3. The firm is already at its target debt ratio, and adoption of the project will not lead the firm to change the ratio.
4. The firm's currently-held assets are expected to generate a constant after-tax cash flow C per annum. This stream is expected to continue indefinitely.

The last of these assumptions may be surprising. We know from Eq. (7) or (7a) that the cost of capital ρ_j^* does not depend on the pattern of expected cash flows offered by the firm's existing assets. But it can be readily shown that the pattern does affect the observed value $\hat{\rho}_j^*$. Let us assume that the life of the firm's existing assets will end at the close of $t = 1$. Retain all the other assumptions for the textbook formula, and assume MM are right. We must thus replace Eq. (14a) with

17. If MM are wrong, then

$$V = \frac{C}{\rho_o} + B\sum_{t=0}^{\infty} F_t \tag{N1}$$

where F_t reflects not only the present value of tax savings but also the impact of any relevant market imperfections. Then it is readily shown that the true cost of capital is

$$\rho_j^* = \rho_o\left(1 - L_j\sum_{t=1}^{\infty} F_t\right). \tag{N2}$$

Proceeding as before, we observe

$$V = \frac{C}{\rho_o} + B\sum_{t=0}^{\infty} F_t = \frac{C}{\hat{\rho}_j^*}.$$

Solving for $\hat{\rho}_j^*$ we find it to be the value given by Eq. (N2).

Incidentally, Eq. (N2) is an attractive alternative for those who disagree with MM but are also uncomfortable with the textbook formula.

$$V_o = \frac{C_1}{1 + \rho_o}. \qquad (17)$$

Also,

$$V = V_o + \text{PVTS} = \frac{C_1}{1 + \rho_o} + \frac{\tau r L V}{1 + r}. \qquad (18)$$

Observe that $rB + kS$, the total return received by stock and bondholders is equal to $C_1 + \tau r B - V$. This implies

$$r(1 - \tau)B + kS = C_1 - V = \hat{\rho}_j^* V.$$

Thus:

$$V = \frac{C_1}{1 + \rho_o} + \frac{LV\tau r}{1 + r} = \frac{C_1 - V}{\hat{\rho}_j^*}.$$

Now we can solve for $\hat{\rho}_j^*$:

$$\hat{\rho}_j^* = \rho_o - L\tau r \left(\frac{1 + \rho_o}{1 + r} \right). \qquad (21)$$

This establishes that the pattern of expected cash flows offered by the firm's existing assets does affect the observed value $\hat{\rho}_j^*$, which in this case is simply the hurdle rate for a one-period project. (See Eq. (13).)[18]

Summary

Table 1 summarizes the necessary and sufficient conditions for the derivation of MM's cost of capital formula, the generalized MM formula, and the textbook formula. Obviously, these conditions are quite stringent, particularly in the case of the textbook formula. The next section considers whether serious errors result when the conditions do not hold.

IV. How Robust are the Weighted Average Cost of Capital Formulas?

Introduction

The derivation of a cost of capital ρ_j^* for practical use involves two steps. The first is to measure the ρ_{oj}'s, the market opportunity costs of investing in assets of different levels of risk. The second is to adjust these opportunity costs to reflect the tax effects of debt financing, transaction costs of external financing, etc. These two steps are explicit in the MM cost of capital formulas and implicit in the textbook formula.

The difficulties in step (1) are notorious. My experience suggests that the confidence limit on empirical and/or subjective estimates of ρ_{oj} is at least a

---

18. This leads to the conjecture that the textbook rule is valid if, instead of Eqs. (14a) and (14b), it can be assumed that the stream of expected cash flows is strictly proportional over time to the cash flows of the firm's existing assets. However, I have not proved this generally. In any case, if $C_{jt} = h_j C_t$, where h_j is a constant, then we hardly need worry about the cost of capital. It suffices to determine whether $I_j < h_j V$, where I_j is the initial investment required for the project.

TABLE 1

NECESSARY AND SUFFICIENT CONDITIONS FOR COST OF CAPITAL FORMULAS

(Equation)	Condition	MM	Generalized MM	Textbook
—	Dividend policy irrelevant	x	x	x
(11a)	Leverage irrelevant except for corporate income taxes	x	x	
(11b)	Investment projects are perpetuities	x	x	x
(11c)	Project does not change firm's risk characteristics	x		x
(11d)	Project makes a permanent contribution to debt capacity	x	x	x
(11e)	Acceptance of project does not lead to shift of target debt ratio	x		x
(11f)	Risk-independence	n.a.*	x	n.a.*
(15a)	Firm's assets expected to generate a constant and perpetual earnings stream			x
(15b)	Firm is already at target debt ratio			x

* n.a. = not applicable.

percentage point under the most favorable conditions. This implies a certain tolerance for minor errors in step (2). How serious can these errors be, considered relative to the possible errors in step (1)? The purpose of this section is to begin exploring this question.

There are eight distinct assumptions listed in Table 1. Any one or any combination of them could be violated in practice. It is not feasible to compute the error for all possible cases. Instead, I will focus on assumptions (10b) and (10d), which require that the project being considered is expected to make a permanent contribution to the firm's earnings and debt capacity. These are the only assumptions necessary for all three cost of capital rules.

The decision to concentrate on (10b) and (10d) was based on several points concerning the other assumptions.

1. Assumptions (10a) and (10f) were not considered because they may well hold in fact. The empirical evidence to date does not lead to rejection of the MM and risk-independence hypotheses, and a strong theoretical case can be made for them.[19]

19. Probably the most extensive and sophisticated test or the MM propositions is MM's own study of the electric industry [15]. This study supports their theory. There is controversy about MM's tests: see, for example, Robichek, McDonald and Higgins [22], Crockett and Friend [5], Brigham and Gordon [4] and Elton and Gruber [6]. There clearly is room for a good deal more work, but despite the problems, we can at least say that recent work is not inconsistent with the MM hypotheses.

The proposition of risk independence is even harder to test directly. There is circumstantial evidence indicating that diversification is not an appropriate goal for the firm—for example, if investors were willing to pay for diversification would not closed-end mutual funds sell at a premium over asset value? And there is certainly no lack of diversification opportunities—even the small investor can buy mutual funds.

2. Assumptions (10c) and (10e) are not necessary for the generalized MM formula. It is clear, of course, that substantial errors can result if either assumption is violated and either the original MM or textbook formula is used. But the extent of the error can be readily estimated by comparing the rate obtained from the original MM formula or textbook formula with the rate obtained from the MM formula.

Note that if (10c) does not hold, (10e) is not likely to hold either. A low-risk project will probably also make a large contribution to the firm's debt capacity.

3. Assumptions (14a) and (14b) were not analyzed explicitly because the results of violating them will be similar in magnitude to the results of violating (10b) and (10d) respectively.

Effects of Expected Project Life

I will start with an extreme case, by comparing the cost of capital obtained via the MM rule with the true cost of capital for a one-period project.

Remember that the MM formula generates a proposed value $\hat{\rho}^*_j$, given by

$$\hat{\rho}^*_j = \rho_{oj}(1 - \tau L). \tag{8}$$

The correct value is

$$\overset{\wedge}{\rho}^*_j = \rho_{oj} - L r \tau \left(\frac{1 + \rho_{oj}}{1 + r} \right). \tag{13}$$

For simplicity, we will omit the j's henceforth.

Comparing Eqs. (9) and (14), it is clear that $\rho^* > \hat{\rho}^*$ for reasonable values of L and ρ_o. The error, ϵ, is

$$\epsilon = \rho^* - \hat{\rho}^* = L\tau \left[\rho_o - r \left(\frac{1 + \rho_o}{1 + r} \right) \right]. \tag{22}$$

From this we see that $\delta\epsilon/\delta L > 0$ and that $\delta\epsilon/\delta\rho_o = L\tau(1 - \dfrac{r}{1 + r}) > 0$. The error in $\hat{\rho}^*$ is highest for high-risk projects that can be heavily debt financed.

Table 2 consists of values of ϵ computed for values of ρ_o from 8 per cent to 25 per cent and for debt to value ratios of 10 to 60 per cent. ϵ ranges from .1 per cent to about 5 per cent. The errors shown in the bottom right of the table are dramatic, but the figures in the center, top right and bottom left of the table reflect the most reasonable combinations of capitalization rates and debt ratios. These errors are on the order of one percentage point, which is not serious. (Note that a one percentage point error in ρ^* for a one period project implies an error in NPV of only about one per cent of project investment.)

Tests of the "capital asset pricing model" of Sharpe [25], Lintner [12] and Mossin [18] may shed light on the risk-independence hypothesis. (The capital asset pricing model is sufficient but not necessary for risk-independence.) The empirical work to date indicates that the capital asset pricing model is probably an oversimplification, but it is too early to say for sure. Jensen [10] reviews the theory and evidence.

TABLE 2
Error[a] in MM Cost of Capital Formula for One-Period Project

ρ_o, Cost of Capital for all-equity financing	L, Target Debt Ratio					
	.1	.2	.3	.4	.5	.6
.08	.000	.001	.001	.002	.002	.003
.10	.002	.003	.004	.006	.007	.008
.12	.002	.005	.007	.009	.012	.014
.16	.004	.008	.013	.017	.021	.025
.20	.006	.012	.018	.024	.031	.037
.24	.008	.016	.024	.032	.040	.048

[a] Rounded to third decimal place.

The risk-free rate is assumed to be r = .07 and the tax rate is assumed to be τ = .5.

Evidently the error in $\rho*$ will be smaller, the longer the life of the project under consideration. However, a more important statistic is the error in NPV caused by use of an incorrect discount rate. This error at first increases as a percentage of project investment as project life is lengthened but finally decreases to zero for projects of infinite life.

Take, for example, a ten-year opportunity requiring investment of $1000 at t = 0 and offering a constant expected cash return for t = 1, 2, . . . , 10. Table 3 shows the difference between (1) NPV computed using $\hat{\rho}*$ from the MM or textbook formulas and (2) the projects' true APV.[20] The errors in this case are more serious than for a one-period project, but still on the order of two to four per cent of project investment.

These mental experiments indicate that the MM or textbook rules are reasonably robust with respect to variations in project life. An unqualified endorsement is not in order, however. First, use of these rules makes invest-

TABLE 3
Error[a] in Indicated NPV from Using MM Cost of Capital Formula to Evaluate Ten-Period Project Requiring $1000 Investment[b,c]

ρ_o, Cost of Capital for all-equity financing	L, Target Debt Ratio					
	.1	.2	.3	.4	.5	.6
.08	$ 2	4	6	8	10	12
.10	5	9	15	20	26	32
.12	7	14	21	29	38	47
.16	9	19	30	42	54	68
.20	10	22	34	48	63	79
.24	11	23	36	50	67	84

[a] Project investment and cash flows were taken as given—see note b below. Figures shown are NPV computed at $\hat{\rho}* = \rho_o(1 - T_cL)$, minus APV. Figures rounded to nearest dollar.

[b] The risk-free rate is assumed as r = .07 and the tax rate is assumed to be τ = .5. The project's expected cash flows are $150.00 per period from t = 1 to t = 10, and zero for t > 10.

[c] APV calculated by procedure described at pp. 27-28 below.

20. APV was computed by the procedure described at pp. 27-28 below.

ment projects look more valuable than they actually are. Second, the seriousness of the error depends on the specific pattern of project cash flows; the fact that the error was minor for the cases investigated does not prove the financial manager is safe in using the rules for projects with unusual patterns of cash flow over time.

Weak and Strong Definitions of the Cost of Capital

Let us suppose we have used Eq. (7a) to calculate the correct value of ρ^* for project j using the weak definition of the cost of capital. Then we can be assured that the project is a good one if NPV computed at ρ^* is positive. However, if projects j and k are mutually exclusive, and both have positive NPV's computed at correct hurdle rates, it is *not* generally correct to accept j over k if $NPV_j > NPV_k$. The general rule is to compare APV_j and APV_k, but Eq. (7a) insures that $NPV_j = APV_j$ only when $APV_j = 0$.

Under what conditions will discounting at the correct hurdle rate give correct value for NPV_j when project j is more than minimally profitable? To put it another way, under what conditions is ρ^*, calculated according to the strong definition of Eq. (7), independent of project profitability?

Assume the pattern of project cash flows over time is fixed. That is, $C_t = \gamma_t C$, for $t \geq 1$, where the γ_t's are constants, and C is varied to reflect changes in project profitability. C_o, project investment, is a fixed number, and the project's "risk class" is taken as given.

Now consider Eq. (7):

$$\sum_{t=0}^{T} \frac{C_t}{(1+\rho^*)^t} = A_j + \sum_{t=0}^{T} [\lambda_t^F Z_{jt} + \lambda_t^C C_{jt}] = APV_j. \tag{7}$$

Now divide through by C, after representing A_j by the usual present value formula and subtracting C_o from both sides

$$\sum_{t=1}^{T} \frac{\gamma_t}{(1+\rho^*)^t} = \sum_{t=1}^{T} \frac{\gamma_t}{(1+\rho_o)^t} + \sum_{t=0}^{T} \left[\lambda_t^F \left(\frac{Z_{jt}}{C} \right) \right]$$
$$+ \lambda_o^C \left(\frac{C_o}{C} \right) + \sum_{t=1}^{T} \lambda_t^C \gamma_t. \tag{23}$$

Eq. (23) is an alternative definition of ρ^*. C can be eliminated if the following conditions hold.

1. The project's expected period-by-period contributions to debt capacity are proportional to C.
2. $\lambda_o^C = 0$. That is, the dividend reduction (or stock issue) required to supply equity financing for the project must not affect shareholders' wealth; $\delta\psi/\delta D_o$ (or $\delta\psi/\delta E_o$) must equal zero.
3. The shadow prices λ_t^F and λ_t^C must be independent of C.

The third condition is not implausible.[21] In any case, a violation of it will under-

---

21. See p. 6 above.

mine *any* decentralized capital budgeting rule. The second condition could be handled by redefining the project's required investment as $C_o(1 + \lambda_o^C)$, in which case the term $\lambda_o^C(C_o/C)$ would not appear in Eq. (23).

The first condition is more interesting. It will clearly *not* be satisfied if the firm's target debt ratio is specified in book terms, since in that case Z_{jt} is independent of C. It will be satisfied if planned debt is related to the project's *market value*. Specifically, suppose

$$Z_t = L_t(APV_t - C_t), \tag{24}$$

that is, the firm's planned borrowing in t is a given proportion L_t of APV_t, the project's contribution to firm value in t, after receipt of project cash flow in t.[22] In this case ρ^* is independent of C, as is shown in the Appendix.

Thus, we can add one more condition to the list of assumptions in Table 1: weighted average cost of capital formulas give correct project valuation (i.e., NPV @ $\hat{\rho}^* = $ APV) only if the firm's target debt levels are specified in market value terms, or if the project has APV $= 0$. If the firm specifies target debt levels in book terms, then discounting at the $\hat{\rho}^*$'s will, other things equal, overstate project APV if APV > 0, and understate APV if APV < 0.[23]

The magnitude of possible error may be illustrated by the following numerical example. A project requires investment of $C_o = -1000$, but offers a constant expected stream of cash returns, C. The target debt ratio is L $= .4$, $\rho_o = .12$ and $\tau = .5$. Dividend policy is irrelevant as is financial leverage except for corporate taxes.

In this case the correct ρ^* is given by Eq. (8), the MM formula. It is

$$\rho^* = \rho_o(1 - \tau L) = .12(1 - .5(.4)) = .096.$$

The project's APV is $-1000 + C/.096$.

Another alternative would be to compute APV directly, as the sum of the project's value assuming all equity financing and the present value of tax savings generated due to the project's contribution to debt capacity.

$$APV = \left(\frac{C}{\rho_o} + C_o\right) + \tau L(APV - C_o)$$

$$APV = \left(\frac{C}{.12} - 1000\right) + .5(.4)(APV + 1000).$$

22. An alternative rule,

$$Z_t = L_t(A_t - C_t)$$

would also allow ρ^* to be calculated independent of project profitability. A_t is defined by

$$A_t = \sum_{1-t}^{T} \frac{C_1}{(1 + \rho_o)^{1-t}}.$$

23. This, of course, assumes debt capacity is valuable. It should also be noted that the level of profitability consistent with APV $= 0$ will depend on whether debt targets are in book or market terms, since book and economic depreciation are not generally equivalent.

Now compare this result to APV if the target debt ratio is set in book terms:

$$\underset{\substack{\text{(book debt} \\ \text{target)}}}{\text{APV}} = \left(\frac{C}{.12} - 1000 \right) + .5(.4)(1000).$$

The difference is $.5(.4)(\text{APV})$, that is 20 per cent of APV. This seems to me a serious error—although the error would be less for shorter-lived projects or for lower debt ratios.

Summary

Whether capital budgeting rules based on the weighted average cost of capital deserve the label "robust" depends entirely on one's tolerance for error. I would consider the generalized MM formula acceptably accurate for accept-reject decisions on run-of-the-mill projects. The original MM formula is acceptably accurate if attention is restricted to projects which do not shift the firm's risk class or target debt ratio. The textbook rule is inferior on all counts[24] if used directly[25] as a standard for investment decisionmaking.

Of course, it is always possible to find the correct value of ρ^* from Eqs. (7) or (7a). The procedure is relatively simple: first, calculate APV, and then find the discount rate which gives the correct NPV, i.e., NPV = APV. But once a project's APV is known, there is no need to calculate its ρ^*; it is sufficient to know whether APV > 0. Why not forget about ρ^* and use APV as the capital budgeting standard? The next section considers whether this is a practical alternative.

V. Adjusted Present Value as an Operational Capital Budgeting Standard

An alternative procedure is clearly needed for cases in which one or more of the assumptions underlying the weighted average cost of capital formulas are seriously violated. The natural choice is to accept project j if its adjusted present value is positive, i.e., if:

24. It might be argued that the textbook formula should be used by those who disagree with MM. But it is entirely feasible to develop a formula exactly like the MM formulas except for the assumed benefit of debt financing. See Eq. (N2), fn. 17 above.

25. The textbook formula may be helpful in *measuring* ρ_o. Suppose a firm can estimate k, the expected rate of return investors in the firm's stock. Then ρ^* can be directly calculated.

$$\hat{\rho}^* = (1 - \tau)\, r\frac{B}{V} + k\frac{S}{V} \tag{9}$$

This value is not an appropriate standard for capital budgeting unless a variety of conditions hold, among them the equality of target and actual debt ratios ($L = B/V$). However, if the target were B/V, then, assuming MM are correct,

$$\hat{\rho}^* = \rho_o \left(1 - \tau \left(\frac{B}{V} \right) \right) = (1 - \tau) r\frac{B}{V} + k\frac{S}{V} \tag{N3}$$

So an estimate of $\hat{\rho}^*$ can be translated into an estimate of ρ_o.

$$APV_j = A_j + \sum_{t=0}^{T} Z_{jt}F_t > 0. \qquad (4)$$

In the event that dividend policy is relevant and/or there are significant transaction costs in new external financing, the criterion should be expanded to:

$$APV_j = A_j + \sum_{t=0}^{T} [Z_{jt}\lambda_t^F + C_{jt}\lambda_t^C] > 0. \qquad (3a)$$

Calculating APV

The general procedure for calculating APV is obvious from the definition of the concept. First, A_j, the project's base case value, has to be calculated. This can be done by the usual NPV formula, except that the discount rate is ρ_{oj}. However, if the discounting procedure is inappropriate,[26] then any other procedure for estimating value may be followed. (This is a further advantage of the APV rule.)

The next step is to estimate the project's contribution to firm debt capacity, assign a value to this contribution and add it to A_j. (In an MM world, this amounts to adding the present value of tax shields generated by debt supported by the project. However, the APV rule does not *assume* MM are right.)

The third step is to determine whether the marginal source of equity financing is additional retained earnings, additional stock issue or a reduction in share repurchases. If there are special costs or benefits associated with the source (vs. the base case of irrelevance of dividend policy) then these can be incorporated in the λ_t^C's and the project value adjusted by adding ΣC_{jt}.

Perhaps the most difficult step in this process is to determine the Z_{jt}'s. This is simple if the firm's debt limits are determined by book debt ratios, since the Z_{jt}'s are then fixed ex ante and independent of project profitability or value (given book depreciation policy).

Calculating a project's adjusted present value turns out to be a moderately complex task when Z_{jt} is related to market value. The problem is that APV_{jo}, adjusted present value of project j as of $t = 0$, depends on estimated values of APV_{jt} for later periods. If the horizon is $t = T$, we have to calculate $APV_{j,T-1}$, $APV_{j,T-2}$, etc., and then finally APV_{jo}. For present purposes we will drop the j's and assume that Z_t is a constant proportion L of $APV_t - C_t$, except that $Z_T = 0$. We also assume that λ^C's are zero. That is, it is assumed that the firm plans to readjust its debt level at the end of every period in terms of its value at that time, and that this level is maintained during the next period. Also we assume that MM are right, i.e., that $F_t = \dfrac{\tau r}{(1+r)^{t+1}}$. Thus

26. Due to the problems cited by Robichek and Myers [23], for example.

$$APV_o = A_o + \sum_{t=0}^{T-1} \frac{\tau r L (APV_t - C_t)}{(1+r)^{t+1}}. \qquad (24)$$

Let $f = \dfrac{\tau r L}{1+r}$. Then

$$APV_{T-1} = A_{T-1} + f(APV_{T-1} - C_{T-1})$$
$$= \frac{A_{T-1} - f C_{T-1}}{1-f} = \frac{C_T/(1+\rho_o)}{1-f}. \qquad (25)$$

Having calculated APV_{T-1} we can determine APV_{T-2} from:

$$APV_{T-2} = A_{T-2} + f(APV_{T-2} - C_{T-2}) + \frac{f}{1+r}(APV_{T-1} - C_{T-1}). \qquad (26)$$

The general formula for any interim period $t = T - S$ is

$$APV_{T-s} = A_{T-s} + f(APV_{T-s} - C_{T-s}) + f\left[\sum_{t=T-S+1}^{T-1} \frac{(APV_t - C_t)}{(1+r)^{t-T+s}}\right]. \qquad (27)$$

Of course Eq. (26) reduces to (24) when $S = T$.

This backwards-iteration procedure is tedious to work through manually, but I did not find it difficult to construct a computer program to do the calculations. Also, note that the calculations are done as a by-product of the linear programming models of Myers and Pogue.[27]

Comments

This calculation procedure leads to two interesting theoretical observations. First, we might question the rationality of planning to keep L constant over time. Consider an equity investor in a single project firm with bonds B outstanding and equity worth S. Note $V = B + S = APV = A + PVTS$, where PVTS is the present value of the tax shield due to debt financing. The equity may be thought of as a portfolio long in assets A, long in the tax shield PVTS and short in debt B. If PVTS and B are equivalent-risk assets, then the portfolio weights are as follows.

Long position in firm's assets:

$$\frac{A}{APV}\left(1 + \frac{B}{S}\right)$$

Short position in B, net of PVTS:

$$\frac{B}{S} - \frac{APV - A}{APV}\left(1 + \frac{B}{S}\right)$$

27. See [20].

where APV − A ≡ PVTS. If the investor wants to maintain a constant degree of financial risk, he will set $\dfrac{A}{APV}(1 + \dfrac{B}{S}) = Q$, a constant. This implies

$$L_t \equiv \frac{Z_t}{APV_t} = 1 - \frac{1}{Q}\left(\frac{A}{APV}\right). \tag{28}$$

Thus we would expect L_t to decline as the project ages and $\dfrac{A}{APV}$ approaches 1. The empirical prediction is that firms with long-lived assets would have higher debt ratios.

The second observation concerns the discount rate used in computing PVTS. I have followed MM who argue that it should be the risk-free rate r. This is clearly appropriate if the debt levels Z_{jt} are fixed at t = 0 and not changed thereafter. If Z_{jt} is determined by book debt ratios, for example, then there is no uncertainty about future tax shields, since there is no uncertainty about future profitability. On the other hand, suppose management wishes to maintain a constant ratio $L_j \equiv \dfrac{Z_{jt}}{APV_{jt}}$ over time. This means that Z_{jt} is a random variable that is perfectly correlated with APV_{jt} and *thus has the same risk characteristics*. The implication is that PVTS should be computed at ρ_o, not r. The intuitive meaning of this is that, although the tax shield associated with any debt instrument is safe, the aggregate value of instruments obtainable is uncertain. We have in effect a compound lottery; the fact that the second stage is risk-free does not mean that the lottery itself is safe.

There are a number of reasons why firms do not immediately adjust the value of bonds outstanding to every change in project or firm value. But to the extent that future debt capacity is contingent on future value of the firm's assets, the debt tax shield takes on the assets' risk characteristics. This is another reason why use of, say, the generalized MM formula for ρ^* would tend to overestimate APV. (So would use of Eq. (3a) or (4) unless the F_t's were computed using a discount rate greater than r.)

Using APV

Objections to the practical use of APV might be made on the basis of lack of realism, increased complication, the unfamiliarity of managers with the concept and the deficiencies of a static model.

Realism is not a valid objection relative to traditional rules. As was shown above, APV is a more general concept and therefore is more adaptable to whatever assumptions are considered "realistic."

The extra complication of the APV rule is a valid point for decisionmakers concerned with run-of-the-mill projects. However, for large and/or unusual projects the extra effort involved in using APV does not seem large relative to the magnitude of errors that might be avoided.

Lack of familiarity is a valid temporary objection. Understanding and interpreting the concept does require financial sophistication—although I have found it easier to explain to beginning finance students than to sophisticated financial managers who have "learned" the concept of discounting at "the" cost of capital.

The static assumptions underlying APV are a real liability, although it is no worse than traditional approaches on this dimension. Whether to advise use of APV in spite of its static assumptions is a question that requires balancing possible errors due to the deficiencies of APV against the improved decisions stemming from its use. But it would seem that anyone who now advises use of traditional capital budgeting rules should be willing to advise a definite improvement.

Perhaps the greatest advantage of the APV concept is that it guides the corporate financial manager through various problems that turn into a can of worms when analyzed by any approach relying on the cost of capital. Here are some examples.

1. APV provides a natural basis for analysis of the lease vs. buy or lease vs. borrow decision.
2. APV can readily incorporate the impact of dividend policy, if relevant, without making awkward distinctions between the cost of retained earnings vs. the cost of stock issue. Transaction costs in financing can also be accommodated. (The effect of transaction costs on the cost of capital is a relatively complicated function of project life. Under the APV rule, dollar transaction costs are simply subtracted.)
3. Suppose subsidized borrowing is available for certain investments (e.g., for pollution control facilities). How does this affect the investments' value? The impact is clear in the APV framework.

I suggest the reader analyze these cases with and without APV and make his or her own judgment about the concept's usefulness.

V. Concluding Comments

In principle corporate investment and financing decisions should be made simultaneously, since the decisions interact in important ways. This paper presents a framework in which the interactions can be analyzed. Further, the framework has been used to evaluate the most widely accepted weighted average cost of capital formulas, and to derive a more general and flexible capital budgeting rule.

There are other uses for the framework. Specifically, it is possible—given some additional assumptions—to develop a linear programming model that can be of direct assistance to management responsible for overall financial planning. This model is described in another paper written jointly with Professor G. A. Pogue [20].

APPENDIX

PROOF THAT ρ^* IS INDEPENDENT OF PROJECT PROFITABILITY WHEN DEBT TARGETS ARE SPECIFIED IN TERMS OF MARKET VALUES

Once APV_0 is calculated for a project, then the true cost of capital ρ^* can be calculated via Eq. (7). But there is nothing evident in Eq. (7) that rules out the possibility of ρ^* being a function of the C_t's. It turns out that ρ^* is independent of project profitability only under certain special conditions.

We can restate the cash flows in terms of a scale factor and a pattern over time. That is, $C_t = \gamma_t C$ where $\gamma_1, \gamma_2, \ldots, \gamma_T$ are weight summing to 1. Also, let ρ_t^* be the true cost of capital, under the strong definition of Eq. (7), for the project at some intermediate point $0 < t < T$.

From Eq. (25) and (7), we have for $t = T - 1$

$$APV_{T-1} \equiv C\left[\gamma_{T-1} + \frac{\gamma_T}{1 + \rho_{T-1}^*} \right] = \frac{\gamma_T C/(1 + \rho_o)}{1 - f}. \tag{A.1}$$

Note that this assumes dividend policy is irrelevant (λ_t^C's $= 0$) and that MM are correct—see Eq. (24). The first assumption is necessary to the following proof, but the second is not.

Dividing both sides of Eq. (A.1) by C, we have an expression for ρ_{T-1}^* that is independent of C. Now consider ρ_{T-2}^*, which is defined by

$$APV_{T-2} = C\left[\gamma_{T-2} + \frac{\gamma_T}{1 + \rho_{T-1}^*} + \frac{\gamma_T}{(1 + \rho_{T-2}^*)^2} \right] \tag{A.2}$$

But from Eq. (26),

$$APV_{T-2} = \frac{1}{1 - f}\left[A_{T-2} - fC_{T-2} + \frac{f}{1 + r}(APV_{T-1} - C_{T-1}) \right]. \tag{A.3}$$

However, all terms within the brackets in Eq. (A.3) are proportional to C. (This is obviously true for A_{T-2}, C_{T-2} and C_{T-1}; we have just shown it to be true for APV_{T-1}). Thus, we can equate Eqs. (A.2) and (A.3), divide through by C, and obtain a definition of ρ_{T-2}^* that is independent of C.

Similarly, ρ_{T-3}^* can be defined in terms of ρ_{T-2}^*, ρ_{T-1}^* and the γ's. By working backwards we eventually find that ρ^* evaluated at $t = 0$ is independent of C. It is also independent of C_o, the initial investment, since C_o is not discounted.

The same result follows if L_t is variable and defined by Eq. (28).

REFERENCES

1. F. D. Arditti. "The Weighted Average Cost of Capital: Some Questions on its Definition, Interpretation and Use." *Journal of Finance,* Vol. XXVIII (September 1973), 1001-08.
2. W. Beranek. "The Cost of Capital, Capital Budgeting and the Maximization of Shareholder Wealth." Unpublished manuscript, University of Pittsburgh, 1973.
3. F. Black and M. Scholes. "Dividend Yields and Common Stock Returns: A New Methodology." Working paper, Sloan School of Management, M.I.T. (1971).
4. E. Brigham and M. J. Gordon. "Leverage, Dividend Policy and the Cost of Capital," *Journal of Finance,* Vol. XXIII (March 1968), pp. 85-104.
5. J. Crockett and I. Friend. "Some Estimates of the Cost of Capital to the Electric Utility Industry 1954-57: Comment," *American Economic Review,* Vol. 57 (December 1957), pp. 1259-67.
6. E. J. Elton and M. J. Gruber. "Valuation and the Cost of Capital in Regulated Industries," *Journal of Finance,* Vol. XXVI (June 1971), pp. 661-70.
7. E. F. Fama and M. H. Miller. *The Theory of Finance* (New York: Holt, Rinehart and Winston, 1972).

8. I. Friend and M. Puckett. "Dividends and Stock Prices," *American Economic Review,* Vol. 54 (September 1964), pp. 656-82.

9. C. W. Haley and L. D. Schall. *The Theory of Financial Decisions* (New York: McGraw-Hill, 1973).

10. M. E. Jensen. "The Foundations and Current State of Capital Market Theory," in M. C. Jensen, Ed., *Studies in the Theory of Capital Markets* (New York: Praeger, 1972).

11. R. W. Johnson. *Financial Management,* Fourth Edition (Boston: Allyn and Bacon, 1971).

12. J. Lintner. "The Valuation of Risk Assets and the Selection of Risky Investments in Stock Portfolios and Capital Budgets," *Review of Economics and Statistics,* Vol. 47 (February 1965), pp. 13-17.

13. R. Merton and M. Subramanyam. "The Optimality of a Competitive Stock Market." Forthcoming in the *Bell Journal of Economics and Management Science.*

14. M. H. Miller and F. Modigliani. "Dividend Policy, Growth and the Valuation of Shares," *Journal of Business,* Vol. XXXIV (October 1961), pp. 411-33.

15. —————. "Some Estimates of the Cost of Capital to the Electric Utility Industry: 1954-57," *American Economic Review,* Vol. LVI (June 1966), pp. 333-91.

16. F. Modigliani and M. H. Miller. "Corporate Income Taxes and the Cost of Capital: a Correction," *American Economic Review,* Vol. 53 (June 1963), pp. 333-91.

17. —————. "The Cost of Capital, Corporation Finance and the Theory of Investment," *American Economic Review,* Vol. 48 (June 1958), pp. 261-97.

18. J. Mossin. "Equilibrium in a Capital Asset Market," *Econometrica,* Vol. 34 (October 1966), pp. 768-83.

19. S. C. Myers. "Procedures for Capital Budgeting under Uncertainty," *Industrial Management Review,* Vol. 9 (Spring 1968), pp. 1-20.

20. ————— and G. A. Pogue. "A Programming Model for Corporate Financial Management." Working Paper, Sloan School of Management, M.I.T., November 1972. Revised version forthcoming in *Journal of Finance* (May 1974).

21. A. A. Robichek and J. G. McDonald. "The Cost of Capital Concept: Potential Use and Misuse." *Financial Executive,* Vol. 33 (June 1965), pp. 2-8.

22. ————— and R. C. Higgins. "Some Estimates of the Cost of Capital to the Electric Utility Industry 1954-57: Comment," *American Economic Review,* Vol. 57 (December 1957), pp. 1278-88.

23. A. A. Robichek and S. C. Myers. "Conceptual Problems in the Use of Risk-Adjusted Discount Rates." *Journal of Finance,* Vol. XXI (December 1966), pp. 727-30.

24. L. D. Schall. "Asset Valuation, Firm Investment and Firm Diversification," *Journal of Business,* Vol. 45 (January 1972), pp. 11-28.

25. W. F. Sharpe. "Capital Asset Prices: A Theory of Market Equilibrium Under Conditions of Risk," *Journal of Finance,* Vol. 19 (September 1964), pp. 425-42.

26. D. L. Tuttle and R. H. Litzenberger. "Leverage, Diversification and Capital Market Effects in a Risk-Adjusted Capital Budgeting Framework," *Journal of Finance,* Vol. XXIII (June 1968), pp. 429-43.

27. J. C. Van Horne. *Financial Management and Policy,* Second Edition (Englewood Cliffs, New Jersey: Prentice-Hall, Inc. 1971).

28. D. Vickers. "The Cost of Capital and the Structure of the Firm," *Journal of Finance,* Vol. XXV (March 1970), 35-46.

29. J. F. Weston and E. F. Brigham. *Managerial Finance* (New York: Holt, Rinehart and Winston, 1971).

The Effects of Default Risk on the Firm's Investment and Financing Decisions

Richard J. Rendleman, Jr.

Richard J. Rendleman is Assistant Professor of Finance at the Graduate School of Management at Northwestern University.

■ This paper analyzes the firm's investment and financing decisions under the assumptions that shareholders have limited liability for the firm's debt obligations and that interest on debt is tax deductible. The limited liability of equity ownership can often create a conflict of interest between a firm's stockholders and bondholders. With limited liability, and in the absence of legal restrictions, shareholders might be encouraged to pursue investment and financing policies in which they have nothing to lose and everything to gain. (See Fama and Miller [4, pp. 178-81], Black and Scholes [3, pp. 650-51] and Galai and Masulis [5, p. 71].) Presumably such actions should increase the value of the firm's equity relative to its debt. Therefore, the traditional view that financial structure does not play a role in corporate investment and financing decisions can often be inapplicable.

Dealing with Limited Liability and Default Risk

Black and Scholes [3] suggest that their option pricing model can serve as the basis for a theory of equity valuation assuming limited shareholder liability. For the simple case in which a firm has pure discount debt in its capital structure, equity can be viewed as an option to buy the assets of the firm from the bondholders for an amount equal to the face value of the bonds (principal plus interest). If the value of the firm's assets is greater than the debt's face value when the debt becomes due, the debt will be paid and the shareholders will have a claim on the residual value of the firm's assets. Otherwise, bankruptcy will occur, and shareholders will receive nothing. In this situation shareholders receive payoffs identical to those of an option to purchase the firm's assets with an exercise price equal to the debt's face value. The Modigliani-Miller [11] theorem that the total value of a firm's financial claims is invariant to its capital structure can be used to determine the value of the pure discount bond as the difference between the firm's asset and equity values.

Galai and Masulis [5] apply the Black-Scholes model to equity valuation to examine the firm's investment and financing decisions. They demonstrate that such decisions are interrelated, even in the absence of bankruptcy costs and the tax deductibility of interest. New projects cannot be evaluated independently of a firm's existing financial structure and asset composition when there is a possibility that the firm will default on its bonds. For example, projects which reduce the firm's operating risk will tend to decrease the probability of default and therefore increase the value of the firm's debt. Given the fact that the total value of the firm's financial claims does not depend upon its financial structure, an increase in the value of the firm's bonds must be accompanied by a corresponding decrease in the value of its stock. Similarly, projects that are financed in such a way as to reduce a firm's reliance on debt should increase the value of existing debt at the expense of equity. As a result, it is in the best interest of the shareholders to pursue investment and financing policies that will reduce the value of a firm's existing debt relative to its equity. Although the insights Galai and Masulis provide are quite useful, they do not consider tax effects, and their analysis is applicable only to firms which employ pure discount debt financing.

Merton's [8] approach to the valuation of risky consol (perpetual) bonds is more generally applicable to the analysis of corporate financing and investment policy. Although consols are not used in this country, they are similar to the long-term debt that corporations typically employ, especially when the market anticipates that a firm is likely to refinance its final debt obligation. Moreover, much of the theory of corporate finance is based upon the simplifying assumption that firms employ perpetual debt financing.

The Merton Model

The Merton bond valuation model serves as the basis for the remaining analysis. There is no claim that the values of actual corporate bonds reflect the Merton model, but to the extent that the values of corporate bonds reflect default risk, the insights provided by the Merton model can be quite useful. The existence of a perfectly competitive and efficient securities market in which costless trading can take place in continuous time is assumed. The term structure of riskless interest rates is flat and known with certainty. The dynamics of the value of the firm through time can be described by a diffusion-type stochastic process. Finally, the total value of the firm's financial claims is assumed to be independent of the firm's capital structure.

As in the Black and Scholes analysis, it is useful to view Merton's stock and bond valuation models in terms of option pricing theory. Consider an option on a non-dividend paying stock with an infinitely distant maturity date that gives one the right to purchase the stock at any particular striking price on that date. Given any striking price, the amount of present funds needed to eventually exercise the option approaches zero if the option's maturity date is infinitely distant, and as a result, the equilibrium value of the option is identical to that of the stock (see Merton [9]).

If the stock is expected to pay a dividend over the life of the option, then the option's value is reduced. The higher the expected dividend rate, the lower the value of the option. At the extreme, if a dividend equal to the value of the stock were expected to be paid, then the ex-dividend values of both the option and stock would be zero.

Suppose that a constant dividend is expected to be paid on the stock. In such a situation, both the option buyer and writer, who we will assume owns the stock, would hope that the value of the stock remains sufficiently high that the probability of an eventual ex-dividend price of zero is remote. This will depend upon the value of the stock as well as its volatility. As long as the probability is less than one that the stock price will eventually fall to zero, the perpetual option will have some positive value. Since the option is certain to be exercised if the stock price does not fall to zero prior to the maturity date, the value of the covered option writing position is simply the present value of the expected dividend stream.

Consider a corporation that is partially capitalized by perpetual bonds carrying a coupon payment of $C per period. Assume that no dividends are paid on the firm's stock. The shareholders of this company in essence have a perpetual option to buy the firm's assets from the bondholders by paying the face value of the debt when it matures. Until this option is exercised, stockholders can expect to have the value of their underlying asset reduced by $C per period, just as the owner of a perpetual option on a dividend-paying stock would expect the value of the underlying stock to be reduced each period by the amount of the dividend. If the value of the firm's assets becomes less than the required interest payment, bankruptcy will occur, and the "option" associated with equity ownership will become worthless. Otherwise, the firm's equity should have some positive value. This analysis suggests that a valuation model for a perpetual option on a stock paying a constant dividend per unit of time can be utilized to price the equity of a firm which employs consol debt financing. In an earlier study, Merton [9] derived such a model which, when applied to equity valuation, can be stated as:

$$S = V - \frac{C}{r}[1 - \lambda],$$

$$\lambda = \frac{b^a}{\Gamma(2+a)} M(a, 2 + a, -b), \quad a = \frac{2r}{\sigma^2}, \quad b = \frac{2C}{\sigma^2 V}, \quad (1)$$

where V is the value of the firm's assets, C, r and σ^2 are the coupon payment on debt, the riskless interest rate, and the variance of the rate of return on the firm's assets, respectively, all expressed with reference to the same unit of time. $\Gamma(.)$ is the gamma function, and $M(.,.,.)$ is the confluent hypergeometric function. (The confluent hypergeometric function is described in Korn and Korn [6, pp. 262-65].) By subtracting the value of the stock from the value of the assets, Merton derived the following equation for the value of the firm's bonds:

$$B = \frac{C}{r}[1 - \lambda]. \quad (2)$$

In Equation (2), the term λ can be viewed as a risk premium which reflects the probability that the firm will default on its bonds. The value of λ approaches zero (i.e., the debt is riskless) when either σ^2 approaches zero or C/V approaches zero. Similarly, the value of the risk premium approaches one (i.e., the bond is infinitely risky) when σ^2 becomes infinitely large or C/V approaches one.

The values of various consol bonds are presented in Exhibit 1. For all bonds under consideration it is assumed that the value of the firm's assets is $100 and the annual riskless interest rate is 5%. The annual rate of interest payment and the standard deviation of the returns from the firm's assets are varied in the table.

Consider the value of a bond in which interest payments are paid at an annual rate of $3.00. Assume that the annual standard deviation of returns on the issuing firm's assets is .30. From Exhibit 1, the price of the bond is $46.27. If there were no possibility of default, (i.e., $\sigma \rightarrow 0$ or C/V $\rightarrow$ 0), the value of the bond would

be 3.0/.05, or $60. Therefore, the discount of $13.73 from $60 and the associated nominal interest rate of $3/$46.27 = 6.48% reflects the risk that the firm will eventually default on the bonds. Note that the bond prices in Exhibit 1 are inversely related to the magnitude of the standard deviation. For example, if the standard deviation were .50 for the above bond, its price would be $33.75 rather than $46.27. Thus, the riskier the assets backing up the bond (where risk is measured in terms of the standard deviation), the lower the value of the bond.

Again, consider the bonds of a firm in which the annual standard deviation of the returns from the firm's assets is .30. If the annual coupon on the bond is $0.50, rather than $3.00 as in the earlier example, the nominal rate of interest on the bond is 5.2%. This example illustrates the fact that the riskiness of a bond decreases as the annual debt service requirement decreases relative to the value of the firm's assets.

Pricing Perpetual Debt When Interest Is Tax Deductible

In the following analysis, Merton's bond valuation model is modified to reflect the tax deductibility of interest payments. To simplify the analysis, it is assumed that the firm can always obtain a tax refund in the amount of $ t C per period, where t denotes the corporate tax rate, as long as interest is paid, even if the firm's taxable income is negative. Although this might appear to be a restrictive assumption, the three-year operating loss carryback provision of the tax code often permits a firm to obtain such a refund. When the entire loss cannot be offset against prior years' income, the tax loss might be "sold" to another company by means of a merger. In any event, it is assumed that the firm can always obtain a refund if interest is paid. As a result, the net cost of servicing debt becomes $C (1 − t) per unit of time.

Exhibit 1. Prices of Consol Bonds When Interest Is Not Tax Deductible

Asset Value = $100.00, Interest Rate = 5.00

| Annual Standard Deviation | Annual Coupon | | | | | | | | |
	$0.5	$1.0	$1.5	$2.0	$2.5	$3.0	$3.5	$4.0	$4.5
.10	$10.00	$20.00	$30.00	$39.96	$49.78	$59.23	$67.99	$75.74	$82.27
.20	9.98	19.77	29.16	37.98	46.12	53.50	60.11	65.98	71.12
.30	9.62	18.43	26.45	33.73	40.31	46.27	51.65	56.50	60.88
.40	8.80	16.37	23.08	29.11	34.56	39.53	44.06	48.20	52.00
.50	7.79	14.21	19.86	24.93	29.53	33.75	37.63	41.21	44.54

The tax deductibility of interest payments affects a firm's stock and bond values in basically two ways. First, the net debt service requirement is reduced, allowing the firm to build a more valuable asset base over the long run. Given a larger asset base, the probability of default on the debt is reduced, and as a result the value of the firm's bonds should be higher than that which obtains in the non-deductibility case. Also, the anticipation of a higher asset base obviously gives rise to a higher equity value.

The second effect is to delay the firm's bankruptcy. Without the tax deductibility of interest, bankruptcy is forced whenever the value of the firm's assets, V, is less than the required coupon payment. Since interest is tax deductible, V can fall as low as $(1 - t)C$ before bankruptcy occurs.

From this analysis it should be clear that the value of the firm's equity is the same as that which would obtain if interest were *not* tax deductible, and the coupon rate on the firm's debt were $(1 - t)C$. In such a situation, the net depletion of the firm's asset value per unit of time due to the payment of interest would be $(1 - t)C$. Also, bankruptcy would occur when $V \leq (1 - t)C$.

In Equation (1) the value of the equity of a firm that pays $C per unit of time to bondholders was presented. This equation is modified below to reflect a tax savings of $ t C per period when interest is tax deductible.

$$S = V - \frac{C(1 - t)}{r}[1 - \lambda']$$

$$\lambda' = \frac{b^a}{\Gamma[2 + a]} M[a, 2 + a, -b],$$

$$a = 2r/\sigma^2, \qquad b = 2C(1 - t)/\sigma^2 V. \qquad (3)$$

The only difference between Equations (1) and (3) is that all terms involving coupon payments are mul-tiplied by $(1 - t)$ in Equation (3).

Assuming that interest payments on debt are tax deductible, Modigliani and Miller [10] demonstrate that the value of the financial claims of a levered firm is equal to the value of the firm if it were all equity-fi-nanced plus the present value of the tax savings asso-ciated with the deductibility of interest. For a per-petual bond, the present value of the tax savings is the tax rate times the value of the bond. Therefore the value of the financial claims of the levered firm is given by:

$$S + B = V + tB. \qquad (4)$$

By substituting the value of the equity from Equation (3) and solving for B, the value of the debt is deter-mined:

$$B = \frac{C}{r}[1 - \lambda']. \qquad (5)$$

In Exhibit 2, the prices of the bonds given in Exhibit 1 are recomputed using Equation (5). Note that the bond prices in Exhibit 2 are never less than their cor-responding values in Exhibit 1. This is due to the fact that the tax deductibility of interest payments reduces the amount of the firm's resources that must be com-mitted to servicing debt, and as a result the risk of default is reduced. For those situations in which the risk of default is negligible, even when interest is not tax deductible, the bond prices in both exhibits are vir-tually the same. When default risk cannot be ignored, however, the tax deductibility of interest can have a significant impact on bond values. For example, con-sider the situation in which $\sigma = .30$ and $C = 3$. If in-terest payments were not tax deductible, the price of the bond would be $46.27, as compared with $52.90. The price difference of $6.63 reflects the fact that the risk of default is decreased when the government funds part of the firm's interest costs.

Exhibit 2. Prices of Consol Bonds When Interest Is Tax Deductible

Asset Value = $100.00, Interest Rate = 5%, Tax Rate = 50%

Annual Standard Deviation	Annual Coupon								
	$0.5	$1.0	$1.5	$2.0	$2.5	$3.0	$3.5	$4.0	$4.5
.10	$10.00	$20.00	$30.00	$40.00	$50.00	$59.99	$69.97	$79.92	$89.80
.20	10.00	19.95	29.82	39.54	49.05	58.32	67.30	75.96	84.28
.30	9.82	19.25	28.26	36.87	45.08	52.90	60.36	67.45	74.20
.40	9.22	17.61	25.41	32.73	39.63	46.15	52.34	58.21	63.80
.50	8.32	15.59	22.24	28.43	34.24	39.72	44.92	49.86	54.57

An Analysis of Investment and Financial Decisions

Case 1: Interest is not tax deductible

According to Modigliani and Miller [11], if interest on debt is not tax deductible, the firm's decision to invest in a project is independent of the method by which the project is financed. Their theory implies that a firm should invest in a new project if and only if the capitalized value of its expected unlevered income stream is greater than its cost. Presumably, if securities markets are efficient, such action should increase the market value of the firm's existing equity by the net present value of the project. However, this decision rule can be misleading if the new investment affects the value of the firm's debt.

If the firm invests in a new project, and the value of the firm's financial claims changes by an amount, ΔV, which represents the capitalized value of the project, then the change in the value of the firm's equity will be

$$\Delta S = \Delta V - \Delta B. \tag{6}$$

The market value of a project is determined by capitalizing the project's expected after tax cash flows at the rate of return that reflects their risk characteristics. Thus, the project is valued as a pure income stream independently of the method by which it is financed. In addition, it is assumed throughout that bankruptcy costs are inconsequential.

If the goal of the firm is to maximize the value of its equity, the project should be accepted if and only if the change in the value of the equity is greater than the amount of new equity employed in financing the project. Letting I represent the cost of the project, S_1 the cost financed by stock, and B_1 the cost financed by bonds, $S_1 = I - B_1$, and the firm should accept a project if and only if

$$\Delta S > S_1, \text{ or} \tag{7}$$

$$\Delta V - \Delta B > I - B_1. \tag{8}$$

The Modigliani-Miller proposition that the investment and financing decisions are independent implies that the firm should accept a project if and only if $\Delta V > I$. In Equation (8), ΔV is unambiguously greater than I only when $\Delta B = B_1$. Therefore, the Modigliani-Miller theorem is only valid when the value of the firm's bonds changes by exactly the amount of new bond financing.

The change in the bond value will obviously be equal to the value of new bonds issued when there is no debt in the firm's initial capital structure. Also, if the firm's existing debt is riskless, and the total debt obligation is expected to be riskless after the project is implemented, then the value of the firm's existing bonds will not be changed as a result of the new investment-financing decision. Therefore, any change in the value of the firm's debt will arise from the new debt issue.

If a firm has debt in its capital structure and the risk characteristics of the new investment when combined with the method of financing change the value of the firm's existing debt, ΔB will not equal B_1, and the Modigliani-Miller proposition becomes inapplicable. Given the fact that the total value of the firm's securities is invariant to its capital structure, any change in the value of existing bonds will be accompanied by an equal, but opposite, change in the equity value.

Letting $\Delta B = \Delta B_0 + B_1$, where ΔB_0 is the change in the value of the firm's present debt, Equation (8) can be reexpressed as

$$\Delta V - \Delta B_0 > I. \tag{9}$$

In other words, the firm should accept a project if and only if the unlevered capitalized value of the project less the change in the value of the firm's existing bonds is greater than the project's cost. If it is anticipated that an investment in a new project will give rise to an increase in the value of the debt (and therefore a decrease in equity value), the firm must be able to purchase the project for a price less than that indicated by the Modigliani-Miller criterion. Similarly, if a project decreases the value of the firm's existing debt, the project could be purchased at a price which is greater than that which the Modigliani-Miller criterion would suggest. Thus, the investment and financing decisions are interrelated, even in the absence of the tax deductibility of interest. Moreover, a project cannot be evaluated independently of its effects on the risk characteristics of the firm's present assets, since projects that change the firm's operating risk will affect the value of its debt.

The following examples illustrate the problems that might arise when there is a possibility that a firm will default on its existing debt. Assume that the annual riskless interest rate is 5%, the current asset value of XYZ, Inc., is $100, and the standard deviation of the rate of return of XYZ's assets is .40 per year. Part of the assets are financed by perpetual bonds with an annual coupon of $2. From Exhibit 1, the value of the bonds is $29.11. Therefore, the value of XYZ's equity is $100 − $29.11, or $70.89.

Consider a situation in which XYZ plans an expansion that should double the market value of its financial assets. Initially, assume that the standard deviation of the returns from the assets is not expected to be affected by the expansion. If the investment, which is assumed to have a capitalized market value of $100, is financed entirely by equity, at what price must XYZ purchase the new plant in order to maintain the value of its existing equity?

After the project is purchased, the value of the firm's bonds will be twice that of a $100 firm paying $1.0 per year to service its debt, or $2 \times \$16.37 = \$32.74$. Thus, when the anticipated investment in the project becomes certain, the value of XYZ's bonds will rise to $32.74, causing the value of its equity to decline to $67.26 ($70.89 − ($32.74 − $29.11) = $70.89 − $3.63 = $67.26). In order to compensate current shareholders for this potential loss, the project must be purchased for $3.63 less than its capitalized market value, $100 − $3.63, or $96.37.

Suppose that this project is partially financed by debt which is not subordinated to the previous debt issue.* The annual interest payment on the new debt is expected to be $4, bringing the total debt service to $6/year. In this situation, the total value of the firm's bonds would be $2 \times \$39.53$ (the value of a $3 coupon bond), or $79.06, one-third of which would represent the value of the firm's present debt, or $26.35. The value of the bonds would decline by $29.11 − $26.35, or $2.76, and as a result, XYZ could pay up to $102.76 for the project.

In the last example it is possible that the value of the debt could actually increase if the new project reduced the variability of the asset's returns. For instance, if it is expected that the standard deviation of the returns of the firm's assets will decline to .30 after the new project is purchased, the value of the firm's existing debt should rise to one-third of $(2 \times \$46.27)$, or $30.85. As a result, the project should be purchased at a price of $100 − ($30.85 − $29.11), or $98.26 or less.

Case 2: Interest is Tax Deductible

After considering the impact of the tax advantage associated with the deductibility of interest payments,

*The valuation of subordinated debt is very complex and depends to a large extent upon the provisions of the firm's bond indentures. Black and Cox [2] have developed an approach to the valuation of subordinated and unsubordinated financial claims by extending Merton's initial model. It would appear that their models could be extended to the situation in which interest is tax deductible in order to deal more explicitly with the issues that are addressed in this analysis.

Modigliani and Miller [10] conclude that the firm's investment decisions depend upon its financing methods, since the value of a project is enhanced by the present value of the tax refund associated with interest payments. Their theory implies that a new project should be accepted if and only if

$$\Delta V + tB_1 > I. \qquad (10)$$

Again, ΔV is the change in the value of the firm's assets that would occur if the firm were unlevered and B_1 is the amount of new debt financing.

As in the case in which interest is not tax deductible, this decision rule will not maximize equity value if the value of the firm's existing debt is changed as a result of the new investment. The total value of the firm's stock and bonds will change by $\Delta V + t\Delta B$, implying that the change in the firm's equity value will be $\Delta V + t\Delta B − \Delta B$. The new project should be accepted if the change in the equity value is greater than the new amount of equity financing, or

$$\Delta V + t\Delta B − \Delta B > I − B_1. \qquad (11)$$

Letting $\Delta B = \Delta B_0 + B_1$, Equation (11) can be restated as

$$\Delta V + tB_1 − (1 − t)\Delta B_0 > I. \qquad (12)$$

The discrepancy between Equation (12) and the Modigliani-Miller criterion, Equation (10), is not nearly as great as that which obtains when interest is not tax deductible. Shareholders need only be compensated by an amount equal to the after tax change in the value of existing debt. Furthermore, with the risk reduction associated with the deductibility of interest payments, the magnitude of such a change is not as large.

Consider the investment and financing decisions of XYZ, Inc., when interest is tax deductible. Again, assume that the annual riskless interest rate is 5%, the unlevered capitalized value of XYZ's assets is $100, and the standard deviation of the unlevered returns on the assets is .40 per year. The assets are partially financed by debt with a coupon of $2 per year. From Exhibit 2, the value of the debt is $32.73, which is $3.62 higher than the corresponding value from Exhibit 1. With an assumed tax rate of 50%, the value of XYZ's equity is $100 − (1 − .5) \times \$32.73$, or $83.64 [see Equation (4)].

As in the previous analysis, if XYZ doubles the market value of its assets (if they were unlevered) without changing their risk composition, and the expansion is financed entirely by equity, the value of XYZ's bonds will increase at the expense of equity.

When a commitment is made to expand, the value of the debt will increase to $2 \times \$17.61$, or \$35.22. This will result in a decline in the value of the current equity position to $\$83.64 - (1 - .5) \times (\$35.22 - \$32.73) = \$82.40$. To maintain the original equity value, XYZ should not pay more than $\$100 - (1 - .5) \times \$2.49$, or \$98.76 for the new assets. This can be confirmed by noting from Equation (4) that the total value of XYZ's financial assets will be $\$200 + .5 \times \$35.22 = \$217.61$ after the expansion takes place. Of this amount, $\$217.61 - \$35.22$, or \$182.39, represents the value of XYZ's stock, \$98.76 of which represents new equity capital. The remainder, \$83.64, is the value of the original equity position.

If part of the expansion is financed by issuing unsubordinated debt with an annual coupon of \$4, the total debt service for XYZ will increase to \$6 per year. This will cause the value of XYZ's existing debt to fall to one-third of $(2 \times \$46.15)$, or \$30.77. As a result, the project could be purchased for a price as high as \$131.75 without lowering the value of XYZ's current equity position.

Finally, assume that additional unsubordinated debt with an annual coupon of \$4 is issued to finance the project, and the standard deviation of the returns on the firm's assets is expected to fall to .30 due to the expansion. In this situation, the value of XYZ's debt would be higher than in the previous example since the expansion would be expected to reduce the firm's operating risk. The value of the existing debt would rise to \$35.27, causing the value of XYZ's equity to fall to $\$82.37$ $(\$83.64 - (1 - .5)(\$35.27 - \$32.73) = \$82.37)$. However, the increased tax break associated with the additional debt financing would cause the equity value to increase to $\$82.37 + .5 \times \$70.54 = \$117.64$. As a result, XYZ could pay up to $\$100 + (\$117.64 - \$83.64)$, or \$134 before the equity would decline in value. In this example, the increase in the tax break associated with the additional debt more than offsets the decline in equity value that results from the reduction in the firm's operating risk and the associated increase in the value of the debt.

Further Implications for Investment and Financing Decisions

The analysis thus far suggests it is in the best interest of shareholders that a firm pursue investment and financial policies that serve them rather than the firm's creditors. In general, creditors will be hurt if the financial policies of the firm tend to increase the probability of default on its debt. This may happen when the firm invests in projects that increase the riskiness of the firm's asset base and/or increase the amount of unsubordinated debt in the firm's capital structure. The complex covenants of bond indentures are often designed to discourage this type of activity by the firm. In the absence of such provisions, however, it is in the shareholders' best interest that management attempts to enhance the economic position of shareholders instead of the firm's creditors.

Suppose that a firm is able to issue debt with no restrictive covenants. If the prospective bondholders expect that their economic position will be placed in jeopardy, it is likely that the amount of debt that can be issued will reflect the anticipated risk characteristics and financial structure of the firm, rather than the firm's current financial position. Therefore, any subsequent action management takes that hurts creditors will not affect the value of its bonds as long as such action was anticipated initially. However, if shareholders do not attempt to pursue the type of financial policies anticipated by its bondholders, they will have had part of their economic claim "stolen" out from under them. As a result, it appears that it is still in the shareholders' best interest to jeopardize the economic position of its bondholders, even if such action is fully anticipated and reflected in bond prices.

Dividend Policy

Perhaps one of the best ways for a firm to transfer its economic resources to stockholders is to pay as generous dividends as possible. Black [1, p. 7] has pointed out that "there is no better way for a firm to escape the burden of a debt than to pay out all its assets in the form of a dividend, and leave the creditors holding an empty shell." Although this is an extreme position, it is obvious that a depletion of the firm's asset base through the payment of dividends tends to increase the firm's debt to asset ratio through time, and, in so doing, increases the probability of default on its bonds. Given such an increase in the probability of default, the economic position of the firm's shareholders is enhanced relative to that of its creditors.

The Financial Rationale for Mergers and Acquisitions

If there are no economic synergies provided by a merger, it is often said that a merger will have no effect on the value of the acquiring or acquired firm's shares, provided that the terms of the merger are fair.

Lintner [7, p. 107] has argued that if either firm is partially financed by debt, the diversification provided by the merger will lower the probability of default on the merged firm's debt, and accordingly provide higher equity values than those which could be obtained without the merger. However, it has been subsequently pointed out by Rubinstein [13, p. 175] that this argument is in error.

If the merger decreases the probability of default on the merged firm's bonds, the value of the bonds should increase at the expense of the equity position. According to Rubinstein [13, p. 175],

> The effects of bankruptcy are double edged since mergers also have the unfavorable consequence of removing the separated limited liabilities of the merging firms. Consider two firms j and k: prior to merger bankruptcy of k does not affect the returns to shares of j; subsequent to merger, the returns from j's portion of the merged firm would be reduced by the requirement of meeting k's defaulted portion of the merged firm's obligations.

It is also argued, however, that if the risk of default on debt obligations is reduced through a merger, it is possible for the merged firm to obtain additional credit to take advantage of the tax break associated with the deductibility of interest payments. (See, for example, Myers [12, p. 636].) Thus, the debt capacity of the merged firm may be higher than that of the two separate firms.

By employing the tax-adjusted bond values in Exhibit 2, an example is presented to illustrate the benefits that arise from the increase in the merged firm's debt capacity. In the example, it is assumed that the merger is not expected to provide any economic synergies. Consider two firms, both identical in size of their asset bases, capitalizations, and operating risks (as measured by σ). If both firms were unlevered, their equity values would be $100. The standard deviation of the returns on the unlevered asset base of both firms is .40. Both firms are capitalized by equity and consol bonds with an annual coupon rate of $1.0. From Exhibit 2, the values of the bonds would be $17.61 for both firms, implying that the value of each equity position would be $100 − (1 − .5) $17.61, or $91.20. The bonds carry a nominal interest rate of 5.68% ($1.0/$17.61) per year.

Assume that, if a merger takes place, the post-merger standard deviation of returns from the unlevered asset base is expected to be reduced to .30. This reduction in risk would result in an increase in the value of the merged firm's bonds to 2 × $19.25, or

$38.50, and result in a post-merger equity value of $200 − (1 − .5) × $38.50 = $180.75, which is less than the total value of the two separate pre-merger equity positions ($182.40).

Without explicitly considering the nature of the merged firm's bankruptcy costs compared to those of the individual firms, it seems reasonable to assume that if the individual firms could obtain credit at a nominal rate of interest of 5.68%, the merged firm should also be able to obtain credit at that rate. From Exhibit 2, it can be shown that if the merged firm had a total of $52.90 × 2 = $105.80 of debt in its capital structure, it would be paying a nominal interest rate of $6/$105.80, which is approximately 5.68%. The $105.80 represents a potential increase in the firm's debt capacity of $105.80 − $17.61 × 2, or $70.58. By issuing $70.58 of additional debt, the firm could repurchase $70.58 of equity, leaving the total value of the remaining equity position at $200 − (1 − .5) × 105.80 = $147.10. Thus, the total value of the merger to the stockholders would be $147.10 + $70.58, or $217.68, which is clearly greater than the combined pre-merger equity values. In this example, the tax benefit from the increase in the merged firm's debt capacity more than offsets the initial decline in equity values that results from a reduction in the probability of bankruptcy for the merged firm.

Summary and Conclusions

In this study, Merton's [8] model for the valuation of consol bonds is extended for the situation in which interest payments on debt are tax deductible. Both Merton's original model and the extended model are employed to illustrate the problems involved in a firm's investment and financing decisions when there is a possibility that the firm might default on its existing debt. As in Galai and Masulis [5], it is shown that a firm cannot consider its investment and financing decisions independently, even when interest payments on debt are not tax deductible. It is possible that the risk characteristics of a capital investment project and the method by which it is financed can affect the value of a firm's existing debt, and, as a result, cause the value of the firm's equity to change in the opposite direction. Therefore, if management attempts to act in the best interest of shareholders, it should consider these effects when determining the maximum purchase price of a new project.

When interest payments on debt are tax deductible, these effects are not nearly as great due to the fact that the risk associated with meeting the firm's debt obligations is significantly reduced. If a possibility exists that a firm might default on its debt, however, management must not only consider the tax savings associated with new debt financing, but they must also attempt to compensate shareholders in the event that investment in a new project affects existing debt and equity values.

Once the effects of default risk are considered, it appears that a firm should attempt to pay as high a dividend as its creditors will allow in order to avoid the possibility that today's earnings might eventually wind up in the hands of the creditors. In addition, it appears that the negative effect of a merger (resulting from the loss of two separated limited liabilities) is inconsequential when compared with the potential tax benefits made available by the merged firm's increased debt capacity.

References

1. Fischer Black, "The Dividend Puzzle," *Journal of Portfolio Management* (Winter 1976), pp. 5–8.
2. Fischer Black and John C. Cox, "Valuing Corporate Securities: Some Effects of Bond Indenture Provisions," *Journal of Finance* (May 1976), pp. 351–68.
3. Fischer Black and Myron Scholes, "The Pricing of Options and Corporate Liabilities," *Journal of Political Economy* (May/June 1973), pp. 637–54.
4. Eugene F. Fama and Merton H. Miller, *The Theory of Finance*, New York, Holt, Rinehart and Winston, 1972, pp. 178–81.
5. Dan Galai and Ronald W. Masulis, "The Option Pricing Model and the Risk Factor of Stock," *Journal of Financial Economics* (January/March 1976), pp. 53–81.
6. G. A. Korn and T. M. Korn, *Mathematical Handbook for Scientists and Engineers*, New York, McGraw Hill, 1968, pp. 262–65.
7. John Lintner, "Expectations, Mergers, and Equilibrium in Purely Competitive Securities Markets," *American Economic Review* (May 1971), pp. 101–11.
8. Robert C. Merton, "On the Pricing of Corporate Debt: The Risk Structure of Interest Rates," *Journal of Finance* (May 1974), pp. 449–70.
9. Robert C. Merton, "Theory of Rational Option Pricing," *The Bell Journal of Economics and Management Science* (Spring 1973), pp. 141–83.
10. Franco Modigliani and Merton H. Miller, "Corporate Income Taxes and the Cost of Capital: A Correction," *The American Economic Review* (June 1963), pp. 433–43.
11. Franco Modigliani and Merton H. Miller, "The Cost of Capital, Corporate Finance, and the Theory of Investment," *The American Economic Review* (June 1958), pp. 261–97.
12. Stewart C. Myers, *Modern Developments in Financial Management*, New York, Praeger Publishers, Inc., 1976, pp. 633–45.
13. Mark Rubinstein, "A Mean-Variance Synthesis of Corporate Financial Theory, *Journal of Finance* (March 1973), pp. 167–81.

DIVIDEND POLICY AND NEW EQUITY FINANCING

JAMES C. VAN HORNE AND JOHN G. McDONALD*

THE PURPOSE OF THIS PAPER IS to investigate the combined effect of dividend policy and new equity financing decisions on the market value of the firm's common stock. Some basic aspects of a conceptual framework are explored, and empirical tests are performed with year-end 1968 cross sections for two industries, using a well-known valuation model. The results must be considered exploratory, but the method of analysis should prove useful in future investigations.

Dividends, New Equity Issues and Value

The notion of an optimal dividend policy implies a dividend payout rate which, *ceteris paribus,* maximizes shareholder wealth. Any normative approach to dividend policy intended to be operative under real world conditions should consider the firm's investment opportunities, any preferences that investors have for dividends as opposed to capital gains or vice versa, and differences in "cost" between retained earnings and new equity issues. The extent to which dividends and new issues affect stock price is at this date an unresolved empirical question.

Nearly a decade ago, Modigliani and Miller demonstrated the irrelevance of dividend payout under one set of assumptions as to perfectly competitive financial markets, where the investment decision and total earnings of the firm are given and there exists a frictionless trade-off between dividends and new equity issues.[1] Some key conditions in this analysis include the exogenous investment variable, a constant discount rate applicable to expected future flows, and the absence of taxes, transaction costs, and flotation costs. If these conditions hold, the way in which the current earnings stream is split between dividends and retained earnings (or the extent to which new investment is financed with retained earnings or new equity issues) does not affect the value of the firm to existing stockholders.

As these perfect market assumptions are relaxed, arguments that dividend policy may affect value can be viewed in two categories: (1) investors may have a net preference for dividends relative to capital gains or vice-versa owing to uncertainty resolution, transaction and inconvenience costs, and differential tax rates; (2) costs associated with the sale of new issues of equity securities may make these issues a more "costly" source of equity financing than retained earnings.

Some of the considerations which may be sufficient for a net preference

* Stanford University. We are indebted to Michael Kinsman for his programming assistance in the preparation of this paper. This study was supported by the Dean Witter Foundation. The conclusions, opinions, and other statements are those of the authors.

1. See Merton H. Miller and Franco Modigliani. "Dividend Policy, Growth and the Valuation of Shares," *Journal of Business,* XXXIV (October 1961), pp. 411-33.

of investors for either dividends or capital gains are briefly reviewed. Gordon has alleged that the required rate of return used by investors to discount dividends expected in future periods increases with time, t.[2] If the level of investment depends on financing from retained earnings, retention for current investment implies that current dividends are foregone in order to increase the future growth of dividends. The implication of Gordon's construct is that the required rate of return, which represents a weighted average of future period required rates, rises with the proportion of earnings retained. As a result, investors would value current dividends over capital gains, *ceteris paribus*.

The existence of transaction costs and any aversion to the inconvenience of selling shares tends to favor current dividends over capital gains. The irrelevance doctrine implies that investors with a preference for current income above the current dividends can always sell stock to obtain additional income. However, with transaction costs and the inconvenience of selling stock periodically, the investor with a desire for consumption in excess of current dividends will prefer incremental current dividends to capital gains. Some institutional investors may favor dividends, owing to legal constraints or tax considerations. For example, universities often prefer dividend income to capital gains on endowment investments because of restrictions on expenditures of capital gains. For corporate investors, inter-company dividends are taxed at rates below that applicable to capital gains. However, the more favorable tax rate on capital gains relative to that on dividends for most investors creates a powerful bias in favor of the retention of earnings.[3] Thus, the first three factors suggest a preference for current dividends as opposed to capital gains while the tax effect favors the latter. Whether there is a net preference among investors for current dividends as opposed to capital gains or vice versa depends on the combined influence of these factors.

Flotation costs and the necessity to "underprice" a stock issue are factors tending to favor earnings retention rather than dividend payout and concurrent new equity financing, *ceteris paribus*. Under the assumption that the investment decision and capital structure of the firm are given, dividend payments must be offset exactly by new equity issues when desired investment exceeds internally generated funds. Flotation costs may be significant if the equity financing alternative is chosen. In addition, the firm may face a downward sloping demand curve for new shares when it appeals to existing investors to increase their holdings or tries to attract new investors. Lintner contends that with divergent investor expectations, the equilibrium price of shares will decline as the firm sells additional shares to offset current divi-

2. See Myron J. Gordon. "Optimal Investment and Financing Policy," *Journal of Finance*, XVIII (May, 1963), pp. 264-72; and "The Savings Investment and Valuation of a Corporation," *Review of Economics and Statistics*, XLIV (February, 1962), pp. 37-51. See also Houng-Yhi Chen, "Valuation Under Uncertainty," *Journal of Finance and Quantitative Analysis*, II (September, 1967), pp. 313-25, and Robert C. Higgins, "Time, Uncertainty and Corporate Dividend Policy," unpublished working paper, University of Washington.

3. For an empirical test dealing with this notion, see Edwin J. Elton and Martin J. Gruber, "Marginal Stockholder Tax Rates and the Clientele Effect," *Review of Economics and Statistics*, LII (February, 1970), pp. 68-74.

dends.[4] With underpricing of this sort, there will be additional dilution of earnings, which, in turn, will result in a lower share value than would obtain in the absence of such underpricing. In sum, any net preference among investors for current dividends, as opposed to the capital gains associated with retention of earnings, is subject to the countervailing influence of flotation costs and underpricing which make new security issues a more expensive form of equity financing than retained earnings.

If there existed a net preference among investors for capital gains as opposed to dividends, then the firm's dividend policy would be a residual decision determined by the profitability of its investments. If we invoke the assumption of an investment decision which is exogenously given, then only if the firm has earnings remaining after financing all "acceptable" investment opportunities would it distribute dividends to stockholders.

Justification for paying a dividend in excess of unused earnings requires a net preference among investors for current dividends as opposed to capital gains, and this net preference must more than offset the difference in "cost" between retained earnings and new equity financing. For example, consider a firm which has a capital structure consisting entirely of equity and has acceptable investment opportunities exactly sufficient to exhaust its earnings. If dividends are irrelevant, representing only the distribution of unused funds after all investment opportunities were financed, the firm obviously would pay no dividend. If it did pay a dividend, the payment would have to be financed with new equity at a "cost" disadvantage relative to retained earnings.

Contrarily, if there exists among investors a net preference for current dividends as opposed to capital gains which more than offsets the "cost" disadvantage of new equity financing, share price could be raised at least initially by increasing the dividend payout ratio. This phenomenon would be due to investors placing considerable importance at first on the resolution of uncertainty and other factors favoring current dividends relative to the differential tax treatment of dividends and capital gains. If, as the payout ratio increases, the importance of the former factors diminishes relative to the tax disadvantage of current dividends, the tax disadvantage might cause a change in the net preference of investors toward capital gains as opposed to current dividends, implying an optimal dividend policy. If the firm had earnings remaining after commitments to all acceptable investment projects, it would distribute a greater portion of its earnings than in the case above.

Empirical Test Methodology

In this paper, we specify a cross-section regression model and suggest a method for treating inter-company differences in new equity financing.[5] The

4. John Linter, "Dividends, Earnings, Leverage, Stock Prices and the Supply of Capital to Corporations," *Review of Economics and Statistics,* XLIV (August, 1962), pp. 256-59.

5. As an alternative to a cross-section approach, Fischer Black and Myron Scholes, "Dividend yields and Common Stock Returns: A New Methodology," Working Paper, Sloan School of Management, MIT, September, 1970, employed a time series methodology to test the effect of differential dividend yields on common stock returns. They found that dividend yield was insignificant in explaining security returns.

valuation of firms which both pay dividends and engage in new equity financing is compared with that of other companies in an industry sample. We hypothesize that the value of the first set of companies is greater than the second, other factors being equal, if investors have a systematic net preference for current dividends relative to capital gains and this net preference more than offsets the "cost" disadvantage of new equity financing relative to the retention of earnings. In lieu of new equity financing, the first set of companies could reduce or eliminate cash dividends, thereby retaining a greater portion of earnings. Instead, these companies behave in a manner that is consistent with the belief that there is a net preference of investors for current dividends as opposed to capital gains and that this net preference exceeds the difference in "cost" described above. In view of the greater cost of new equity financing, a finding of no essential difference in valuation between the two sets of companies may be considered weak support of the idea of a net preference of investors for current dividends as opposed to capital gains. However, such an inference would require a reasonably well-specified valuation model.

We begin with a traditional share-price model, which represents a solution in price of a capital market equilibrium equation under idealized uncertainty: share price, P_0, equals the present value of a future stream of expected dividends, discounted at a market rate k that depends on the risk-free rate and the riskiness of the security.[6] The share-price model implies that the ratio of current price to earnings, P_0/E_0, is a function of expected growth rate in dividends, g, the dividend payout ratio, D_0/E_0, and a measure of risk of the security, R:

$$P_0/E_0 = f(g, D_0/E_0, R). \tag{1}$$

Models of this general form have been formulated for empirical purposes by Malkiel and Cragg, Bower and Bower, and Brigham and Gordon.[7] We propose to use this model as a point of departure to investigate whether firms which pay dividends and engage in new equity financing have higher price-earnings ratios than other firms in an industry sample.

Two samples of firms are employed: the 86 electric utilities in the continental U.S. which are included on the COMPUSTAT utility data tape; and

---

6. The equilibrium equation under certainty is as follows
$$k_t = D_t/P_t + d(\log P_t)/dt.$$
Under conditions of idealized uncertainty, k_t is assumed to be a constant rate of return for all securities of "equivalent risk." A solution of this equation for current market price P_0 is
$$P_0 = \int_0^\infty D_t e^{-kt} dt,$$
the familiar formulation of price as the present value of expected future dividends discounted at k. In the special case of "golden age" growth at rate g from the current dividend level D_0, one can divide both sides by current earnings E_0 to obtain
$$P_0/E_0 = (D_0/E_0) \int_0^\infty e^{(g-k)t} dt.$$
The implication is that P_0/E_0 varies directly with dividend payout and growth, and inversely with risk, as reflected in the discount rate, k.

7. See Burton G. Malkiel and John Cragg. "Expectations and the Structure of Share Prices," *American Economic Review*, LX (September, 1970), pp. 601-17; Richard S. Bower and Dorothy H. Bower, "Risk and the Valuation of Common Stock," *Journal of Political Economy*, LXXVII (May-June, 1969), pp. 349-62; and Eugene F. Brigham and Myron J. Gordon, "Leverage, Dividend Policy, and the Cost of Capital," *Journal of Finance*, XXIII (March, 1968), pp. 85-103.

39 companies in the electronics and electronic-component industries as listed on the COMPUSTAT industrial data tape. The companies in the two samples are shown in Table 5. The industries were chosen on the basis of frequency of new equity issues and our desire to test both a regulated and an unregulated industry.

Tests in the Electric Utility Industry

For the electric utility industry, two regression models were tested. The first reflects structural model (1) in the following form:

$$P_o/E_o = a_0 + a_1(g) + a_2(D_o/E_o) + a_3(\text{Lev}) + u \qquad (2)$$

where

$P_o/E_o =$ Closing market price in 1968 divided by average earnings per share for 1967 and 1968, adjusted to a consistent "flow through" accounting basis by adding back deferred taxes to reported earnings for each firm.[8]

$g =$ Expected growth rate, measured by the compound annual rate of growth in assets per share for 1960 through 1968, where the first three years and last three years were each normalized and the growth rate computed for the resulting six-year span.

$D_o/E_o =$ Dividend payout, measured by cash dividends in 1968 divided by earnings in 1968, adjusted to a consistent "flow through" basis by adding back deferred taxes to reported earnings.

$\text{Lev} =$ Financial risk, measured by interest charges divided by the difference of operating revenues and operating expenses.

$u =$ Error term.

A number of alternative historical growth rates were considered as measures of expected future growth in earnings and dividends. The best measure for both industries, in terms of correlation with price-earnings ratios in 1968, was the compound growth rate of assets per share. Capital market theory suggests that an appropriate risk measure is a company parameter, called beta by Sharpe, representing the slope of a regression of returns from a firm's shares on returns from a market index over comparable holding periods.[9] Recent results by Malkiel,[10] however, suggest that for utility firms a flow measure of leverage is a satisfactory proxy for the over-all risk of the security.[11] Accord-

---

8. Models (2) and (3) were also estimated with average (unadjusted) reported earnings in the denominator of the dependent variable. The resulting R^2 was lower; however, the coefficient estimates were not materially different. Hence, the conclusions of this analysis were the same as those drawn below.

9. William F. Sharpe. "A Simplified Model for Portfolio Analysis," *Management Science,* IX (January, 1963), pp. 122-136.

10. Burton G. Malkiel. "The Valuation of Public Utility Equities," *Bell Journal of Economics and Management Science,* I (Spring, 1970), pp. 143-160.

11. An operating risk variable like that used in electronic-electronic component industry regressions was added to equation (2). As the estimated coefficient was quite insignificant and of positive sign, it was excluded in the final run.

ingly, we shall use this measure inasmuch as our purpose is not to test for risk but to avoid specification bias. The results of estimation of equation (2) are shown in Table 1. All coefficient estimates have the correct sign and the growth and leverage estimates are significant.[12]

TABLE 1

REGRESSION ESTIMATES FROM MODEL (2): ELECTRIC UTILITIES, 1968

	Constant	g	D_o/E_o	Lev
Regression coefficient	9.37	114.	7.02	−18.2
Standard error	(3.11)	(17.1)	(3.86)	(7.06)
t-ratio	3.01	6.66	1.82	− 2.58

$R^2 = .36$ $F = 15.5 (3;82)$

Dependent variable: P_o/E_o
Sample size: 86 firms

Of the 86 utility firms, 37 had one or more new equity issues during the five-year period, 1964-68. New equity financing is defined here as the sale of common stock or securities convertible into common stock where the proceeds represent new money. All firms in the sample paid a dividend in every year. As a first test of the extent to which firms which both pay dividends and raise new equity differ in value from other firms in the industry, we employed a t-test of the two sets of residuals. The mean residual for firms with new equity issues was larger than that for firms which did not issue stock (.08 versus −.06). This difference, however, is not significant, as reflected by a t-ratio of 0.23. Therefore, we are unable to reject the null hypothesis that these two sets of companies come from the same population. As discussed earlier, given the "cost" disadvantage of new equity financing relative to retained earnings, a finding of no essential difference in value between the two sets of companies gives weak support to the idea of a net preference for current dividends as opposed to capital gains.

The prevalence of new issues among public utilities enables us to devise a cardinal measure of new equity financing for firms in this industry. For each firm, "new issue ratio" (NIR) was computed which represents total common shares, including the fully converted equivalent of convertible issues, divided by total shares outstanding at year-end 1968. The firms were grouped in five categories by NIR, as shown in Table 2. This table indicates that the mean dividend payout is slightly higher among those firms in groups D and E— companies which have the highest new issue ratios.

To assess the impact of level of new issue financing on value, we added four dummy variables F_a through F_d corresponding to NIR groups A through D

---

12. The positive sign for the dividend payout variable may be due to spurious correlation. Both the dependent and the independent variable contain earnings per share in the denominator. To the extent that errors of measurement are independent of the numerators, a positive bias in the regression coefficient for the dividend-payout variable would result. However, with a correlation coefficient for the two variables of −.01 in the utility sample, spurious correlation is unlikely to be a serious problem. For a discussion of spurious correlation, see Edwin Kuh and John R. Meyer, "Correlation and Regression Estimates When the Data are Ratios," *Econometrica*, XXIII (October, 1955), pp. 400-16.

TABLE 2
New Issue Ratios (NIR) of Electric Utility Firms

	A	B	C	D	E
NIR: New issues/shares outstanding, 1968	0	.001-.05	.05-.10	.10-.15	greater than .15
Number of firms	49	16	11	6	4
Mean dividend payout, D_o/E_o	.681	.679	.678	.703	.728

in Table 2. A coefficient for the last group, F_e, cannot be estimated simultaneously with the other four dummy-variable coefficients, as it is a linear function of the other four and would result in singularity. For each firm, the value of the dummy variable representing its NIR group is one and the values of the remaining dummy variables are zero. For example, the value of F_b would be one for a firm whose NIR falls between .001 and .05 (Group B) and the value of the other three variables for this firm would be zero. The resulting valuation model is:

$$P_o/E_o = a_o + a_1(g) + a_2(D_o/E_o) + a_3(Lev) \qquad (3)$$
$$+ a_4(F_a) + a_5(F_b) + a_6(F_c) + a_7(F_d) + u$$

At high levels of new equity financing, we would expect underpricing effects and flotation costs to be relatively important, resulting in a negative coefficient. The greater the amount of new equity financing, the greater its percentage "cost" is likely to be relative to retained earnings.

Regression results for the estimation of Model (3) are shown in Table 3. The estimated coefficients of growth, dividend payout, and leverage are significant and have correct signs. The coefficient estimate for F_b is positive and significant, supporting the notion that at moderate levels of new equity financing, the net preference of investors for dividends more than offsets the "cost" disadvantage of new issues relative to the retention of earnings. Coefficient estimates for the other three dummy variables are positive but not significant. The coefficients decline with increasing employment of new equity financing, from group B to C to D. When we omit any one of the four dummy variables discussed above and add a dummy variable for the last NIR group, E, the estimate of its coefficient is found to be negative. This is consistent with the "cost" disadvantage of new equity financing relative to the retention of earnings widening with high levels of new equity financing.[13]

Two caveats seem obvious. First, the results for one year do not permit us to generalize beyond the present findings for 1968. Secondly, with less than one-half of the total variance explained, we cannot be sure that all factors other than those being investigated are held constant. Criticisms of specifica-

13. It is conceivable that the new issue variable captures an aspect of growth not measured in variable g. As indicated near the bottom of Table 2, the correlation coefficient between the new issue variables for firms that engage in external equity financing (F_b through F_e) and the growth variables are small and positive, ranging from .06 to .15. Except for the four firms in group E, the bi-variate correlations between the new issue variables and dividend payout are consistently small, less than .05.

369

TABLE 3

REGRESSION ESTIMATES FROM MODEL (3): ELECTRIC UTILITES 1968

	Constant	g	D_o/E_o	Lev	Dummy Variables Representing Level of New Equity Financing			
					F_a	F_b	F_c	F_d
Regression coefficient	6.45	115	8.03	−15.3	1.86	3.23	1.26	0.89
Standard error	(3.75)	(17.4)	(3.85)	(7.39)	(1.40)	(1.44)	(1.50)	(1.64)
t-ratio	1.72	6.60	2.08	−2.22	1.33	2.25	0.84	0.54

$R^2 = .42$
Sample Size: 86 firms

$F = 7.04\ (8;77)$

Bi-variate correlation
coefficients:

	F_a	F_b	F_c	F_d	F_e
Between growth (g) and	−.32	.15	.16	.14	.06
Between dividend payout (D_o/E_o) and	−.04	−.03	−.02	.05	.12

tion, as to omitted variables, and measurement errors may be applicable to these results.[14]

Tests in the Electronics—Electronic Components Industry

For tests with a sample of firms in the electronics and electronic components industry, the following regression form of structural valuation equation (1) was employed.[15]

$$P_0/E_0 = a_0 + a_1(g) + a_2(D_0/E_0) + a_3(Lev) + a_4(OR) + u \qquad (4)$$

where

$P_0/E_0 =$ Average of high and low market price per share in 1968 divided by average earnings per share in 1967 and 1968.

$g =$ Expected growth rate, measured by compound annual rate of growth of assets per share for 1960 through 1968, where the first three years and the last three years were each normalized and the growth rate computed for the resulting six-year span.[16]

$D_0/E_0 =$ Dividend payout, measured by the average of earnings per share in 1967 and 1968 divided by the average of dividends per share in 1967 and 1968.

$Lev =$ Financial risk, measured by long-term debt plus preferred stock divided by net worth as of the end of 1968.

$OR =$ Operating risk, measured by the standard error for the regression of operating earnings per share on time for 1960 through 1968, using a second degree polynominal equation, over average operating earnings per share for nine years.

$u =$ Error term.

In order to test whether companies which both pay dividends and engage in new equity financing differ significantly in value from other companies in the sample, we test the hypothesis that the two sets of residuals come from the

14. For a discussion of such biases, see Irwin Friend and Marshall Puckett, "Dividends and Stock Prices," *American Economic Review*, LIV (September, 1964), pp. 656-82.

15. Because the dependent variable in the regression model is the price/earnings ratio, it was necessary to exclude companies in this sample whose average earnings were negative in 1967 or 1968, or whose earnings were abnormally low during this period of time. The latter was effected by excluding companies whose price/earnings ratios were 60 or above. While the use of 60 is arbitrary, some upper limit was necessary in view of the erratic earnings performance of some of the companies in the electronics and electronic components industry. Also excluded were companies whose average market price per share during 1967 and 1968 was less than $10. Finally, companies whose growth in assets per share was negative were eliminated because, in all three cases, the shrinkage in assets was due to factors that would not be expected to occur in the future. For these firms, historical growth in assets per share would be a poor proxy for the expected growth in the stream of future income available to stockholders. The companies in this sample are shown in Table 5.

16. For Solitron Devices, the growth in sales per share for the five year period 1964-1968, was employed. As this company was started in 1959, the percentage growth in assets per share from 1960 to 1968 was much larger than could be expected in the future. In addition, the acquisition of a division of another company for stock in 1967 resulted in an extraordinary increase in assets per share. For these reasons, growth in sales per share over the most recent five years was felt to be more representative of expected future growth.

371

same population. The first set consisted of companies which both paid dividends throughout the period 1964-1968 and issued new equity one or more times during the period; the second set comprised all other firms in the sample. New equity financing again included common stock and securities convertible into stock.[17] As only seven companies of the 39 in this industry both paid dividends and issued new equity, it did not seem feasible to develop a cardinal measure, such as the new issue ratio employed with the utility sample. Owing to this small number of companies, only crude insight into the question of the relevance of dividends is possible with this industry sample.

TABLE 4

REGRESSION ESTIMATES FROM MODEL (4): ELECTRONICS AND ELECTRONIC COMPONENTS, 1968

	Constant	g	D_0/E_0	Lev	Risk
Regression Coefficient	16.87	56.68	1.08	2.72	−2.31
Standard Error	(2.21)	(10.35)	(4.56)	(8.17)	(2.47)
t Ratio	7.64	5.47	0.24	0.33	−0.93
$R^2 = .52$		$F = 9.33\ (4;34)$			

Dependent variable: P_0/E_0
Sample size: 39 firms

The results using regression equation (4) are shown in Table 4.[18] We see that the variables employed explain about one-half of the variance in the price-earnings ratios. As expected, the growth variable is highly significant and positive. None of the other explanatory variables is significant,[19] and the leverage variable has an unexpected positive sign. The nonparametric Mann-Whitney U test is used to test whether the residuals for the seven companies that paid dividends and engaged in new equity financing were from the same population as the residuals for the other 32 companies in the sample.[20] This test revealed that the bulk of the first set of residuals was higher than the bulk of the second set. However, at the customary .05 level of significance, we are unable to reject the null hypothesis that the two sets of residuals came from the same population.

While the evidence does not support the idea that companies which pay dividends and engage in equity financing have a higher value than other companies, *ceteris paribus*, it is not inconsistent with the notion that investors at the margin prefer current dividends to capital gains despite the latter's tax advantage for most investors. Because of the "cost" disadvantage of financing

17. New issue data were obtained from the *Investment Dealers Digest*.

18. In general, homoscedasticity for the variance of the error terms prevailed when price-earnings ratios were regressed against the growth variable. Equation (4) was also run in logarithmic form; as the R^2 was somewhat lower, these results are not shown.

19. As discussed for the utility industry sample, the positive sign for the dividend payout variable may be due to spurious correlation. However, since the correlation coefficient for dividend payout and dependent variables is only 0.01 in this electronics industry sample, it is unlikely that spurious correlation is a serious problem. See footnote 12.

20. This test is described in Sidney Siegel, *Nonparametric Statistics* (New York: McGraw-Hill, 1956), pp. 116-27.

with new equity as opposed to retained earnings, any net preference for current dividends must exceed this "cost" disadvantage in order for the financing of dividend payments with new equity to be a thing of value. Therefore, a finding of a neutral effect with respect to value is consistent with there being a net preference by investors for current dividends as opposed to capital gains.

At best, however, the results in Table 4 offer very weak support for this notion. The proportion of explained variation is not large enough to assure us that the variables other than expected growth are correctly measured or that other relevant variables have not been omitted. The issue of new equity and payment of dividends may be a proxy for other factors affecting value. Moreover, the small number companies which fell into this classification, namely seven, does not permit us to make broad generalizations. Thus, the insights provided with this industry sample are crude at best.

Conclusions

The methodology in this study compares the valuation of firms which both pay dividends and engage in new equity financing with other firms in an industry sample. For electric utility firms in 1968, the findings indicate that share value is not adversely affected by new equity financing in the presence of cash dividends, except for those firms in the highest new-issue group. This evidence is consistent with the existence of a net preference for current dividends, despite the differential tax advantage of capital gains for most investors. For electric utilities, except those in the highest new-issue group, this net preference for dividends appears to offset the flotation costs and underpricing effects that make new equity a more costly form of financing than the retention of earnings. The findings indicate that the "cost" disadvantage of new equity issues relative to retained earnings widens as relatively large amounts of new equity are raised, so that the payment of dividends through excessive equity financing reduces share price. For firms in the electronics-electronic component industry, a significant relationship between new equity financing and value was not demonstrated. While the evidence is less than conclusive, the findings are consistent with the existence of a net preference by investors for current dividends as opposed to capital gains, assuming that dividends at the margin are financed with new equity.

The generalizations that can be made from these findings are limited, as tests were undertaken in only two industries for a single year. Moreover, the regression models explained only about one half of the total variance and exhibited other empirical shortcomings. Nevertheless, we feel that the proposed approach of comparing companies that both pay dividends and engage in new equity financing with other companies in a sample offers considerable promise in testing for the relevance of dividends. In a world of market imperfections, it is useful to view separately the net preference of investors for dividends or for capital gains and the fact that new equity financing is more "costly" than the retention of earnings. As additional years are tested and the number of companies investigated is expanded, greater insight into the effect of dividend policy on value may be gained.

TABLE 5
SAMPLES OF COMPANIES

Electric Utility Industry	
Allegheny Power System, Inc.	Minnesota Power & Light
American Electric Power Co.	Montana-Dakota Utilities
Arizona Public Service Co.	Montana Power Co.
Atlantic City Electric Co.	Nevada Power Co.
Baltimore Gas & Electric Co.	New England Electric System
Boston Edison Co.	New England Gas & Electric
Carolina Power & Light Co.	New York State Electric & Gas Co.
Central Hudson Gas & Electric	Niagara Mohawk Power Corp.
Central Illinois Light	Northeast Utilities
Central Illinois Public Service Co.	Northern Indiana Public Service Co.
Central Louisiana Electric	Northern States Power Co. (Minn.)
Central Maine Power Co.	Ohio Edison Co.
Central & Southwest Corp.	Oklahoma Gas & Electric Co.
Cincinnati Gas & Electric Co.	Orange & Rockland Utilities
Cleveland Electric Illuminating Co.	Pacific Gas & Electric Co.
Columbus & Southern Ohio Electric Co.	Pacific Power & Light
Commonwealth Edison Co.	Pennsylvania Power & Light
Consolidated Edison Co.	Philadelphia Electric Co.
Consumers Power Co.	Potomac Electric Power
Dayton Power & Light Co.	Public Service Co. of Colorado
Delmarva Power & Light Co.	Public Service Co. of Indiana, Inc.
Detroit Edison Co.	Public Service Co. of New Hampshire
Duke Power Co.	Public Service Co. of New Mexico
Duquesne Light Co.	Public Service Electric & Gas Co.
El Paso Electric Co.	Puget Sound Power & Light
Florida Power Corp.	Rochester Gas & Electric
Florida Power & Light Co.	San Diego Gas & Electric Co.
General Public Utilities Corp.	Sierra Pacific Power Co.
Gulf States Utilities Co.	South Carolina Electric & Gas Co.
Houston Lighting & Power Co.	Southern California Edison Co.
Idaho Power Co.	Southern Co.
Illinois Power Co.	Southwestern Public Service Co.
Indianapolis Power & Light	Tampa Electric Co.
Interstate Power Co.	Texas Utilities Co.
Iowa-Illinois Gas & Electric	Toledo Edison Co.
Iowa Power & Light	Tucson Gas & Electric Co.
Iowa Public Service Co.	Union Electric Co.
Kansas City Power & Light Co.	United Illuminating Co.
Kansas Gas & Electric	Utah Power & Light
Kentucky Utilities Co.	Virginia Electric & Power Co.
Long Island Lighting Co.	Washington Water Power
Louisville Gas & Electric Co.	Wisconsin Electric Power Co.
Middle South Utilities, Inc.	Wisconsin Public Service

TABLE 5 (*Continued*)
Electronic—Electronic Components Industry

AMP Inc.	IMC Magnetics
Alloys Unlimited	Lear Siegler
Ambac Industries	P.R. Mallory Co.
Ampex Corp.	Microdot, Inc.
Avnet Inc.	Microwave Associates
Burndy Corp.	Nytronics, Inc.
Collins R	Oak Electro/netics
Conrac Corp.	Oxford Electric
CTS Corp.	Pacific Industries
Dynamics Corp. of America	Pepi Inc.
Edo Corp.	Raytheon Co.
Electronic Assistance Corp.	Sanders Associates
Electronic Engnr. Cal.	Sola Basic
General Instrument	Solitron Devices
General Signal	Sparton Corp.
Genisco Technology	Systron-Donner Corp.
Gulton Industries	Tektronix
Hazeltine Corp.	Vernitron Corp.
Hewlett Packard	Victoreen Leece Neville
Hydrometals Inc.	

ASSET LEASING IN COMPETITIVE CAPITAL MARKETS

WILBUR G. LEWELLEN, MICHAEL S. LONG AND JOHN J.
MCCONNELL*

OVER THE SPAN of the last several years, there has been substantial interest evidenced in the finance literature in asset leasing as a corporate decision problem. Indeed, given the sheer volume of published papers on the topic,[1] the casual reader might be tempted to conclude that leasing is at least one of the two or three most inportant issues in the theory of the firm. Some portion of this activity would appear to be attributable to a widespread feeling that certain outrages were perpetrated in an early paper in the area [8]. A more neutral view, however, suggests that the intriguing characteristic of the leasing problem is the fact that it forces one to confront along the way most of the difficult and subtle issues of asset-and-liability valuation under uncertainty which have veen the general concern of the finance theorist in recent times. For this reason, it holds particular fascination as an analytical challenge. We hope in the present paper to shed additional light on the relevant issues by approaching the analysis from a somewhat different perspective than has thus far been attempted. Our debt to various writers, notably Gordon [5] and Schall [21], will be evident in that undertaking.

I.

We begin, as an expositional strategy, with the situation of an unlevered enterprise having a specified set of production and investment plans, all of which have been announced to investors. Those plans embody a policy of relying solely on internally-generated funds to support future years' additions to the firm's real-asset base, and the distribution of all residual cash flows to shareholders as dividends. If we let $\bar{R}_t$ denote pre-tax net cash operating revenues expected by investors to occur in year t—given the announced corporate plan—let $\bar{D}_t$ be year t's anticipated asset depreciation charges, $\bar{I}_t$ be the expected size of cash reinvestments in additional assets for the year, and $\bar{S}_t$ be the cash salvage value of assets to be disposed of during the year, the cash dividend expectation visualized by shareholders for the year will be

$$\bar{X}_t = \bar{R}_t - \tau\left(\bar{R}_t - \bar{D}_t\right) - \bar{I}_t + \bar{S}_t \tag{1}$$

$$\bar{X}_t = \bar{R}_t(1 - \tau) + \tau\bar{D}_t - \bar{I}_t + \bar{S}_t \tag{2}$$

* Respectively: Professor of Industrial Management, Purdue University; Assistant Professor of Industrial Management, Georgia Institute of Technology; Assistant Professor of Finance, Ohio State University.

1. See, for example: Beechy [1], Bierman [2], Bower [3], Clark, Jantorni, and Gann [4], Gordon [5], Johnson and Lewellen [8] [9], Lev and Orgler [10], Lusztig [13], Mitchell [14], Nantell [17], Roenfeldt and Osteryoung [18], Sartoris and Paul [19], Schall [21], and Wyman [22].

where τ is the applicable corporate income tax rate, and $\bar{S}_t$ is defined for convenience to be net of whatever tax levies are associated with asset retirement. Clearly, a more concise notational scheme would be feasible, but the intent is to identify explicitly the several cash flow elements that may individually be affected (transferred) if a leasing arrangement is entered into by the firm for certain of the relevant assets.

The market value of the shares of such a firm will thereupon depend on investors' reactions to the constituents of the indicated dividend stream. As Schall [20] has demonstrated in his "value additivity principle," the value of the total stream must, in a transaction-costless competitive capital market, be equal to the sum of the respective values of its individual components. That is,

$$V_U = \sum_{t=0}^{\infty} \bar{R}_t(1-\tau)/(1+k_1)^t + \sum_{t=0}^{\infty} \tau \bar{D}_t/(1+k_2)^t$$

$$- \sum_{t=0}^{\infty} \bar{I}_t/(1+k_3)^t + \sum_{t=0}^{\infty} \bar{S}_t/(1+k_4)^t \tag{3}$$

in which $k_1, \ldots, k_4$ are capitalization rates commensurate with the risk features of the separate elements, in the light of investor opportunities to trade in similar such streams elsewhere in the market.

Consider then the consequences should the firm elect to obtain a portion of the assets it requires by arranging to lease them from another enterprise rather than purchasing them directly, but in the context of an unchanged over-all production and asset-employment strategy. If those assets would have cost an amount $\bar{I}_t^L$ in year t if purchased, and would have given rise to depreciation deductions $\bar{D}_t^L$ and salvage recoveries $\bar{S}_t^L$, and will necessitate lease payments of size $\bar{L}_t$, the revised cash dividend expectations of shareholders become:

$$\bar{X}_t' = (\bar{R}_t - \bar{L}_t) - \tau \left[\bar{R}_t - \bar{L}_t - (\bar{D}_t - \bar{D}_t^L) \right] - (\bar{I}_t - \bar{I}_t^L) + (\bar{S}_t - \bar{S}_t^L) \tag{4}$$

$$\bar{X}_t' = \bar{X}_t - \bar{L}_t(1-\tau) - \tau \bar{D}_t^L + \bar{I}_t^L - \bar{S}_t^L. \tag{5}$$

To this point, the analysis has the normal form. What has been omitted in prior treatments, however, is a consideration of the other side of the transaction—and its market implications. Thus, the cash dividend prospects of the owners of the *lessor* firm pursuant to the arrangement are

$$\bar{X}_t^L = \bar{L}_t - \tau(\bar{L}_t - \bar{D}_t^L) + \bar{S}_t^L - \bar{I}_t^L \tag{6}$$

$$\bar{X}_t^L = \bar{L}_t(1-\tau) + \tau \bar{D}_t^L + \bar{S}_t^L - \bar{I}_t^L \tag{7}$$

since they must bear the burden of the outlays $\bar{I}_t^L$ to purchase the assets which now are leased, but, in return, are entitled to claim the depreciation tax savings and any available salvage opportunities.

Inevitably, therefore, the *total* dividend flows to be generated for the owners of the two firms come to

$$\bar{X}_t' + \bar{X}_t^L = \bar{X}_t \tag{8}$$

and the net result is a combined income prospect exactly like that which was available to investors before the lease was written. If we then invoke the value additivity principle—or even simple intuition—we must conclude that the total market value of the shares of the lessee firm, V_S, and the shares of the lessor firm, V_L, together can only match the original pre-lease V_U, and, thereupon, that the leasing contract will have no impact on aggregate share valuation—so long as the tax rate on corporate income is the same for lessee and lessor enterprises. Note also that this conclusion holds, whether the lease identified is the *only* activity of the lessor or is just one of many such lease contracts it has outstanding, since the value additivity principle would assert that the addition of one more set of income flows to an existing base would have a market value impact precisely like that of the same set of flows valued in isolation.

What, therefore, would be expected to occur under the press of competition in the leasing market? No firm will be willing to become a lessee at the sacrifice of any of its shareholders' market wealth positions, i.e., will not be amenable to lease payment obligations whose present value exceeds the benefit derived from avoiding the direct expenditures on the assets involved, net of the attendant depreciation tax savings and salvage values. Accordingly, its decision rule will be

$$\sum_{t=0}^{\infty} \bar{L}_t(1-\tau)/(1+k_L)^t \leqslant \sum_{t=0.}^{\infty} \bar{I}_t^L/(1+k_5)^t - \sum_{t=0}^{\infty} \tau\bar{D}_t^L/(1+k_6)^t$$

$$- \sum_{t=0}^{\infty} \bar{S}_t^L/(1+k_7)^t \tag{9}$$

where the capitalization rates at issue are left in their most general notational form to allow for the possibility that the mode of the market's valuation of the $\bar{D}_t^L$, $\bar{S}_t^L$, and $\bar{I}_t^L$ may differ from that of the counterpart flows associated with the remaining, non-leased assets of the firm.[2]

By the same token, of course, investors in the lessor firm will be unwilling to provide the $\bar{I}_t^L$ cash inputs to permit the purchase-and-subsequent-lease of the relevant assets unless the value of the lease payment prospects generated is at least as great as that of the asset expenditures, also net of depreciation and salvage. In short, the decision rule from the lessor firm's standpoint is exactly as in equation (9), with the inequality condition reversed. But, since $V_S + V_L = V_U$, and V_U is

---

2. And, obviously, the various $\bar{L}_t$, $\bar{I}_t^L$, and $\bar{S}_t^L$ will be zero for values of t beyond the termination date of the lease.

unaffected by the division of the income streams between the two firms because $\overline{X}_t$ is unaffected, any increment in value realized by *either* firm's shareholders requires a corresponding sacrifice on the part of the *other* firm's owners, whatever may be the applicable k_L, k_5, k_6, k_7. Hence, only one set of leasing terms can satisfy both entities' acceptance criteria—that array of $\overline{L}_t$ for which the left and right hand sides of equation (9) are equal. Such terms will leave shareholders, in the aggregate, just as well off as if leasing were not undertaken. Therefore, in a competitive capital market comprised of completely equity-financed firms, an enterprise can expect to confront leasing opportunities which are fully as expensive as outright asset purchases;[3] the lease-or-buy choice will be a matter of indifference.

This conclusion, it may be noted, applies as well to the situation where the assets involved are new ones under consideration as *additions* to the firm's existing capital stock. The capital-budgeting hurdle criterion $dV_U \geqslant dI$ for purchase must be imposed in precisely the same form on potential leased-asset expansions, given that leasing terms of a size just sufficient to induce the lessor firm to commit its funds to assume the burden dI will inevitably be quoted.

II.

However, the more intriguing circumstance, is that in which it is possible for both lessor and lessee enterprises to lever themselves and exploit the tax-deductibility features of interest obligations, to the benefit of shareholders. Let us suppose that our hypothetical corporation had, as part of its original financing-and-investment scenario, arranged for total borrowings in the amount $\overline{B}_t$ to be outstanding during year t and that the rate of interest charged for those loans was set at r by the pertinent lenders. In such a case, stockholder dividend prospects would be:

$$\overline{X}_t^S = \left(\overline{R}_t - r\overline{B}_t\right) - \tau\left(\overline{R}_t - r\overline{B}_t - \overline{D}_t\right) - \overline{I}_t + \overline{S}_t - \overline{M}_t \tag{10}$$

where the term $\overline{M}_t$ denotes the loans which are scheduled to mature at the end of the year. These repayment obligations, of course, diminish the cash available for dividend distributions to shareholders, dollar for dollar, and are equal simply to $\overline{B}_t - \overline{B}_{t+1}$. Thus

$$\overline{X}_t^S = \overline{R}_t(1 - \tau) - r\overline{B}_t(1 - \tau) + \tau\overline{D}_t - \overline{I}_t + \overline{S}_t - \overline{M}_t \tag{11}$$

$$\overline{X}_t^S = \overline{X}_t - r\overline{B}_t(1 - \tau) - \overline{M}_t \tag{12}$$

where the $\overline{X}_t$ is that of equation (2) above. Correspondingly, the lenders involved can look forward to cash flows of size

$$\overline{X}_t^B = r\overline{B}_t + \overline{M}_t \tag{13}$$

and the resulting combined income prospect for both classes of securityholders is

$$\overline{X}_t^* = \overline{X}_t^S + \overline{X}_t^B = \overline{X}_t + \tau r\overline{B}_t. \tag{14}$$

3. We shall examine the effect of certain market peculiarities and tax differences below.

This stream must sell in the market for a present price of

$$V^* = V_U + \sum_{t=1}^{\infty} \tau r \overline{B}_t / (1+r)^t \tag{15}$$

pursuant to the value additivity principle,[4] given that r is unambiguously the capitalization rate appropriate to flows of the risk character of the borrowings in question, since it is the observable yield demanded by the relevant market participants—the lenders—in return for providing the funds.[5] Accordingly, the market value of the common shares of the firm will be

$$V_S^* = V^* - \sum_{t=1}^{\infty} r \overline{B}_t / (1+r)^t + \sum_{t=1}^{\infty} \overline{M}_t / (1+r)^t \tag{16}$$

$$V_S^* = V^* - B_0, \tag{17}$$

the difference between the total value of the enterprise and the value of lender claims to it, B_0.

If equipment leasing possibilities are introduced in such a context, then, we must recognize not only the direct cash flow impact of the lease contract but also any potential indirect consequences on borrowing capacities. Certainly, the amount that lenders would be willing to advance to the firm *at the interest rate r* cannot help but be diminished by commitments made to lessors, so long as the operating cash flow stream available to meet the company's total senior obligations remains unchanged. Whatever the perceived contingencies which caused the yield r to be required on the loans, those contingencies can only be exacerbated by the firm's assumption of competing concurrent lease obligations. While we might consider how *much* of a loss in (rate r) borrowing capacity would be entailed, it will suffice for the moment simply to denote the ensuing reductions in available loan balances by the generalized sequence $\overline{B}_t^L$ and the accompanying lower principal repayments $\overline{M}_t^L$.

On that basis, and continuing our prior notation, the dividend expectations of the shareholders of the leveraged lessee firm become

$$\overline{X}_t^{SL} = \left[\overline{R}_t - \overline{L}_t - r\left(\overline{B}_t - \overline{B}_t^L\right) \right] - \tau \left[\overline{R}_L - \overline{L}_t - r\left(\overline{B}_t - \overline{B}_t^L\right) - \left(\overline{D}_t - \overline{D}_t^L\right) \right]$$

$$- \left(\overline{I}_t - \overline{I}_t^L\right) + \left(\overline{S}_t - \overline{S}_t^L\right) - \left(\overline{M}_t - \overline{M}_t^L\right) \tag{18}$$

$$\overline{X}_t^{SL} = \overline{X}_t^S - \overline{L}_t(1-\tau) + r\overline{B}_t^L(1-\tau) - \tau \overline{D}_t^L + \overline{I}_t^L - \overline{S}_t^L + \overline{M}_t^L. \tag{19}$$

---

4. The $t=0$ interval for the summation in the second term of (15) is dropped, on the conventional assumption of end-of-period interest-and-principal payment schedules.

5. On the assumption that the bonds carry a coupon rate sufficient to permit them to sell at par. Such an assumption simplifies the algebra of the expressions, although it is by no means essential. Whatever the coupon, the bonds need not be riskless for the arguments to hold; a required market yield r above the riskless rate preserves the form of equation (15), as demonstrated in [7], [15], [20].

For the same reason that borrowing opportunities are somewhat diminished for the lessee, of course, they are correspondingly—and equivalently—enhanced for the lessor, given that the incremental net cash inflow of the latter enterprise is the mirror image of the outflow of the former. The lessor therefore can avail itself of those opportunities and create for shareholders the dividend prospect

$$\overline{X}_t^{LL} = \left(\overline{L}_t - r\overline{B}_t^L\right) - \tau\left(\overline{L}_t - r\overline{B}_t^L - \overline{D}_t^L\right) - \overline{I}_t^L + \overline{S}_t^L - \overline{M}_t^L \tag{20}$$

$$\overline{X}_t^{LL} = \overline{L}_t(1 - \tau) - r\overline{B}_t^L(1 - \tau) + \tau\overline{D}_t^L - \overline{I}_t^L + \overline{S}_t^L - \overline{M}_t^L \tag{21}$$

which maintains for lenders in the aggregate a cash flow expectation of

$$\overline{X}_t^{BL} = r\left(\overline{B}_t - \overline{B}_t^L\right) + \left(\overline{M}_t - \overline{M}_t^L\right) + r\overline{B}_t^L + \overline{M}_t^L = \overline{X}_t^B \tag{22}$$

and thereby a total set of flows to the three groups of securityholders amounting to

$$\overline{X}_t^{SL} + \overline{X}_t^{LL} + \overline{X}_t^{BL} = \overline{X}_t^S + \overline{X}_t^B = \overline{X}_t + \tau r\overline{B}_t \tag{23}$$

matching that generated in the absence of the lease arrangement. Hence, total market value must remain at its pre-lease level V^*. Leasing, in short, will not alter the price which investors will pay for the underlying productive income stream even when leverage possibilities are present, since any loss in debt capacity on the part of lessee firms will necessarily be offset by commensurate increases in the capacity of lessors.

The competitive-market equilibrium implications of such a circumstance are obvious. As in the unlevered-firm case, if total security values are invariant to leasing, any future-period commitments made under leasing contracts will occasion a transfer of market worth to the lessor matching that relinquished by the lessee. Only if the lessee obtains asset expenditure savings of at least equal value for its owners, will it concur in the arrangement. Similarly, the lessor cannot offer terms which provide a net gain to the lessee without harming its own shareholders—put differently, cannot induce them to supply the capital to purchase and then rent the assets unless the resulting cash income prospects are as attractive as those they could obtain by investing directly in the potential lessee enterprise. Therefore, there is only one lease price that can satisfy both constraints—the price which will render leasing and buying equally worthwhile.

III.

The profile of the associated managerial decision rule, however, is of interest, both because it has been a subject of contention in the literature and because it permits us to pinpoint the conditions under which certain market peculiarities could interfer with the indicated competitive equivalent-price outcome. From equations (19) and (22), it is clear that the total cash flows to the stockholders *and* creditors of the *lessee* firm will differ in year t by the amount

$$\overline{L}_t(1 - \tau) + \tau r\overline{B}_t^L + \tau\overline{D}_t^L + \overline{S}_t^L - \overline{I}_t^L$$

381

from those that would be in prospect for securityholders of a similar firm in the absence of leasing. Its aggregate market value therefore will be

$$V^{*L} = V^* - \sum_{t=0}^{\infty} \bar{L}_t(1-\tau)/(1+k_L)^t + \sum_{t=0}^{\infty} \bar{I}_t^L/(1+k_5)^t$$

$$- \sum_{t=0}^{\infty} \tau\bar{D}_t^L/(1+k_6)^t - \sum_{t=0}^{\infty} \bar{S}_t^L/(1+k_7)^t$$

$$- \sum_{t=1}^{\infty} \tau r\bar{B}_t^L/(1+r)^t \tag{24}$$

relying once more on the value additivity prescription. The resulting equity market value is

$$V_S^{*L} = V^{*L} - (B_0 - B_0^L) \tag{25}$$

since loans smaller by B_0^L will be outstanding due to the reduction in borrowing power, where B_0^L is the present worth of the $r\bar{B}_t^L$ and $\bar{M}_t^L$, capitalized at r. That foregone immediate loan inflow, of course, must be made up for directly by shareholders out of what would otherwise have been larger cash dividend receipts at $t=0$. Accordingly, in order for shareholders to be well-served by a leasing arrangement, management must require that V_S^{*L} be greater than the original V_S^* by at least enough to compensate for the immediate dividend reduction. Thus, the acceptance criterion is

$$V_S^{*L} \geqslant V_S^* + B_0^L \tag{26}$$

which, upon substitution from (17), (24), and (25), resolves to

$$\sum_{t=0}^{\infty} \bar{L}_t(1-\tau)/(1+k_L)^t \leqslant \sum_{t=0}^{\infty} \bar{I}_t^L/(1+k_5)^t - \sum_{t=0}^{\infty} \tau\bar{D}_t^L/(1+k_6)^t$$

$$- \sum_{t=0}^{\infty} \bar{S}_t^L/(1+k_7)^t$$

$$- \sum_{t=1}^{\infty} \tau r\bar{B}_t^L/(1+r)^t. \tag{27}$$

In words, the market value of the lease promises made cannot exceed that of the asset expenditure flow saved, net of salvage and depreciation tax recoupments and the valuation consequences of the lessee firm's reduced borrowing power—the latter being purely a tax phenomenon.[6]

The cash flow impact of the arrangement from the lessor firm's standpoint is exactly symmetrical. It receives the indicated $\bar{L}_t$, bears the outlays $\bar{I}_t^L$, and claims the $\tau\bar{D}_t^L$ and $\bar{S}_t^L$. Similarly, it can borrow B_0^L to help finance the activity but, in so

---

6. In effect, equation (27) is Schall's [21] criterion cast in standard expected-return-discounting form.

doing, incures repayment obligations having the same present value, leaving it with only the incremental tax-benefit stream $\tau r \overline{B}_t^L$ as a net valuation gain. Only, therefore, if the lease contract receipts plus these other inflows equal or exceed the $\overline{I}_t^L$ will the contract be attractive. Further, since the capitalization rates applicable to the various streams involved are not firm-specific in a rational securities market, the appropriate decision criterion for the lessor *is* simply equation (27) in reverse. Once more, then, only one figure for the present value of the $\overline{L}_t$ can meet both parties' conditions for a willingness to transact, and price competition in the leasing market must yield that outcome.

At such a price, of course, the cost of leasing is the same as that of direct asset acquisition, and the same discounted-cash-flow test for new investment project acceptability should be imposed by the lessee firm *regardless* of the manner of acquisition. The acceptance test for asset purchase—that is, $dV^* \geqslant dI$, where the V^* is that of equation (15) above—will have imbedded in it the valuation effect of the accompanying increase in corporate borrowing power.[7] The competitive equilibrium implication of equation (27), however, is an alteration in that borrowing power, when leasing is undertaken, the valuation consequence of which will be just offset by the present worth of the other cash flows involved. The lessee's decision problem in such an environment, therefore, is the normal one of "expand or not," examined in the light of the normal debt financing policy the firm has established.[8]

IV.

On the other hand, there may occasionally be some differences in the *cirsumstances* of lessor and lessee enterprises which, even in a competitive market framework, could lead to differentially attractive asset acquisition opportunities. While none of these are especially startling, their role in the present valuation portrayal merits attention since it is only through that mechanism that their impact can be rigorously defined.

The basic question is easily posed: under what conditions can the market value of two firms, combined—a lessor and lessee—exceed that of a single enterprise, given a fixed array of underlying production and investment activities? Only if such an enhancement of total value is possible can leasing bargains be struck that will offer an advantage to one of the parties without harming the other—and an acquiescence to harm is inconsistent both with rationality and market competition.

In that regard, certain assumptions were implicit in the derivations above: (1) that the tax rates of lessor and lessee were equal, (2) that the assets involved would cost the lessor the same amount to purchase as they would the lessee, (3) that depreciation deductions were realizable on the same terms by both, (4) that the

---

7. As formally delineated in Haley and Schall [7], Lewellen and Racette [11], Lewellen [12], Myers [16], and Schall [20].

8. And the decision is definitely lease-or-buy rather than lease-or-borrow. The so-called "effective interest rate" on the obligations $\overline{L}_t$ in (27) which equates their present value to that of the purchase costs $\overline{I}_t^L$ is a meaningless concept for decision purposes, because the $\overline{I}_t^L$ are not the only cash flows affected by the lease contract and thereby the debt capacity change involved is nowhere automatically tied just to the $\overline{I}_t^L$ alone.

salvage potential of the assets would be unaffected by the arrangement, and (5) that borrowing *policies*—as distinct from *capacities*—were identical in the two companies. We may therefore examine the implications of any departures from these stipulations.

In order to do so in a way that permits a convenient paraellel with the leasing treatments of the recent literature, let us cast the decision criterion of equation (27) in the mold of the "standard" lease contract typically assayed: one in which the lease payments occur at year's end, where the contract has a specified term T, where the assets acquired would have necessitated expenditures entirely out of the current year's ($t=0$) capital budget, where the term of the lease coincides with the period over which the lessee firm planned to employ the assets if it purchased them,[9] and where the borrowing affected would have had a finite balloon maturity N.[10] Under that scenario, consider the case wherein the lease arrangement is *just* acceptable from the standpoint of the lessee. That is, the firm finds that

$$(1-\tau)\sum_{t=1}^{T} \bar{L}_t/(1+k_L)^t - I_0^L + \tau \sum_{t=1}^{T} \bar{D}_t^L/(1+k_6)^t$$

$$+ \bar{S}_T^L/(1+k_7)^T + \tau r B_0^L A_{N:r} = 0 \tag{28}$$

where $A_{N:r}$ denotes the present value of a one-dollar annuity of N years' duration, discounted at r. If, then, this same contract is *more* valuable to the lessor—in the one relevant sense that the external securities market puts a price higher than zero on that firm's counterpart cash flows—total market values *will* rise as a result of the transaction and some viable contract bargaining room on lease terms, under which both enterprises can gain, will exist.

The requisite conditions are obvious. The $\bar{L}_t$ and the applicable capitalization rates—whatever they may be—are the same as in (28) for the lessor's side of the contract, but the other elements may not be. In particular, if the lessor (a) can acquire the assets at a price below I_0^L, (b) can realize salvage proceeds greater than $\bar{S}_T^L$, (c) can depreciate the assets more rapidly or more reliably than the lessee, or (d) levers the transaction to a greater extent than B_0^L, the market price associated with the lessor's equivalent of (28) will indeed be positive.[11] The tax effect, interestingly, can go either way. Thus, if some $\tau^* > \tau$ applied to the lessor, the first term in (28) would fall, but the third and fifth would increase, and the net change would depend on the specific asset life (lease period), depreciation schedule, capitalization rates, and leverage possibilities involved.[12] Therefore, the standard

9. Indeed, this is a necessary condition, if we are to remain in the context of a particular set of production-and-investment plans for the firm.

10. There is, of course, in principle no requirement that the lease and these borrowings have the same maturity ($T=N$), as there is no requirement in general that a particular asset be financed with loans having a maturity matched to the asset's economic life.

11. Note that, while the tax savings on the $\bar{D}_t^L$ decline when I_0^L falls, the present-value impact of the former is always less than that of the latter, as long as $\tau < 1$ and $k_6 > 0$.

12. In particular, the shorter the lease term and the greater the alteration in debt capacity, the more likely is the lessor's higher tax rate to generate valuation gains.

wisdom that high-tax-rate lessors are a rich potential source of lucrative leasing deals, is not necessarily borne out. The reverse may easily be true; a high tax rate may actually induce a firm to be a lessee rather than a lessor. In any case, we see that differences in the two parties' circumstances *could* at times generate market valuation benefits that would make leasing attractive, and the framework encompassed in (28) identifies those dimensions. One could readily insert representative numerical values therein and quantify the possible scope of the relevant opportunities.

Some commentary on the likelihood—and the origin—of such differences in a competitive market economy, on the other hand, seems warranted. It is conceivable that a lessor firm which buys assets in volume from their manufacturers could negotiate for lower average prices than would be quoted for single purchases by lessees. Savings of this sort, however, can only be attributable to reduced transactions costs since the underlying manufacturing economics are not affected, i.e., no change in total *supplier* output is occasioned by a mere re-routing of the assets through intermediaries to their ultimate users. We therefore suspect that the savings are apt to be rather modest, if they exist at all. The same goes for resale/salvage values. The lessor may be more active or more skillful in dealing in the associated second-hand asset market; his specialized knowledge may give him an edge. But if that market is itself reasonably competitive, lowered transactions costs (from information acquisition perhaps) again are the one legitimate source of potential savings. To the extent that many leasing arrangements involve assets manufactured for quire specific purposes, of course, few of these transaction efficiencies are likely to emerge—indeed, they may be more than offset by the extra transactions costs of the intervening lease contract. Only in the case of leases of very standard, high-volume asset items do any benefits appear to be realizable.

Whether the depreciation tax savings stream offers any corresponding opportunities is equally problematical. These could arise in principle from more *rapid* write-off patterns by lessors, but it stretches credulity to believe that the IRS would sanction differences of this sort on any systematic large scale, given the demonstrated sensitivity of the tax authorities to the obvious adverse revenue consequences. Alternatively, the lessor's depreciation deductions may be more "attainable" in the sense that the lessee may not as consistently have taxable income against which to claim the deductions. This argument is often made particularly in connection with accelerated depreciation schedules that could exceed lessee income in the early years of asset life. We do not rule out such possible differences—in effect, they connote more rapid *de facto* lessor write-off profiles—but the carry-forward and backward corporate income averaging provisions of the tax law should substantially diminish their impact for all but the most marginal lessee enterprises. Note that the realization of these tax benefits by the lessor depends on the existence of additional taxable income from other sources on his part; if his only business is leasing the one asset, the lease payments he receives are his only taxable earnings as well, and he confronts precisely the same deduction limits as would the lessee. For that matter, many lessees may be in a *better* position to take the deductions—against other income—than would be the lessors, depending upon the specific earnings time patterns of the respective enterprises. In any

385

case, the less effective in practice are the income-smoothing provisions of the revenue code, the more likely are the tax deduction transfers associated with lease contracts to provide some occasional opportunities for net valuation gains.

Finally, there is the issue of differences in borrowing policies between lessor and lessee firms. As was discussed earlier, it is inevitable that any debt *capacity* increments generated for lessors will be matched by reductions for lessees, given that the (debt-supporting) cash flow receipts of the former are the mirror image of the cash flow losses of the latter. So long as both enterprises exploit such borrowing capacities to the fullest—as they should be led to do by competitive conditions— the valuation effects cancel out. Nonetheless, it could occur that the lessee firm may not be so diligent and thereupon that the B_0^L of equation (28) which that firm actually relinquishes, according to its policies, is below the figure the enlightened lessor takes advantage of in the transaction. To the degree, then, that leasing results in improved aggregate capital structures in the community, some lease-price bargaining room becomes available. It should be stressed, however, that the lease does not *create* this effect; its origin is simply the ineptitude of the lessee, and that ineptitude can be remedied without entering into a rental arrangement.

We therefore are led to conclude that environmental factors which can bring about significant differences in the costs of asset purchase and asset leasing will seldom prevail, especially since the tax *rate* effect on the transaction can go either way. Perturbations from equilibrium cannot be ruled out, certainly, but market pressures can be expected to eliminate most of these fairly quickly. The corporate decision rule for testing those possibilities has been portrayed above, and the securities market context of such decisions identified. The implication of that framework is that subsequent investigations of the leasing phenomenon might most profitably focus on the role of market imperfections as qualifying influences, and on the *empirical* prevalence of the factors discussed which could lead to exploitable profit opportunities. It appears to us that, in an idealized competitive milieu, a reliable rationale for leasing attractiveness cannot reasonably be maintained.

REFERENCES

1. T. Beechy. "Quasi-Debt Analysis of Financial Leases," *Accounting Review*, April 1969, pp. 375–381.
2. H. Bierman. "Analysis of the Lease-or-Buy Decision: Comment," *Journal of Finance*, September 1973, pp. 1019–1021.
3. R. Bower. "Issues in Lease Financing," *Financial Management*, Winter 1973, pp. 25–34.
4. R. Clark, J. Jantorni, and R. Gann. "Analysis of the Lease-or-Buy Decision: Comment," *Journal of Finance*, September 1973, pp. 1015–1016.
5. M. Gordon. "A General Solution to the Buy or Lease Decision," *Journal of Finance*, March 1974, pp. 245–250.
6. ———— and P. Halpern. "Cost of Capital for a Division of a Firm," *Journal of Finance*, September 1974, pp. 1153–1163.
7. C. Haley and L. Schall. *The Theory of Financial Decisions*, New York, McGraw-Hill, 1973.
8. R. Johnson and W. Lewellen. "Analysis of the Lease-or-Buy Decision," *Journal of Finance*, September 1972, pp. 815–823.
9. ———— and ————. "Reply," *Journal of Finance*, September 1973, pp. 1024–1028.
10. B. Lev and Y. Orgler. "Analysis of the Lease-or-Buy Decision: Comment," *Journal of Finance*, September 1973, pp. 1022–1023.

11. W. Lewellen and G. Racette. "Convertible Debt Financing," *Journal of Financial and Quantitative Analysis*, December 1973, pp. 777–792.

12. ———. "A Conceptual Reappraisal of Cost of Capital," *Financial Management*, Winter 1974.

13. P. Lusztig. "Analysis of the Lease-or-Buy Decision: Comment," *Journal of Finance*, September 1973, pp. 1017–1018.

14. G. Mitchell. "After-Tax Cost of Leasing," *Accounting Review*, April 1970, pp. 308–314.

15. J. Mossin. *Theory of Financial Markets*, Englewood Cliffs, N. J., Prentice-Hall, 1973.

16. S. Myers. "Interactions of Corporate Investment and Financing Decisions—Implications for Capital Budgeting," *Journal of Finance*, March 1974, pp. 1–25.

17. T. Nantell. "Equivalence of Lease vs. Buy Analyses," *Financial Management*, Autumn 1973, pp. 61–65.

18. R. Roenfeldt and J. Osteryoung. "Analysis of Financial Leases," *Financial Management*, Spring 1973, pp. 74–87.

19. W. Sartoris and R. Paul. "Lease Evaluation—Another Capital Budgeting Decision," *Financial Management*, Summer 1973, pp. 46–52.

20. L. Schall. "Asset Valuation, Firm Investment, and Firm Diversification," *Journal of Business*, January 1972, pp. 11–28.

21. ———. "The Lease-or-Buy and Asset Acquisition Decisions," *Journal of Finance*, September 1974, pp. 1203–1214.

22. H. Wyman. "Financial Lease Evaluation Under Conditions of Uncertainty," *Accounting Review*, July 1973, pp. 489–493.

For Further Study

In addition to the papers included in this section, the reader may want to refer to the following papers:

1. Black, F. and M. Scholes (1973). "The Pricing of Option and Corporate Liabilities", *Journal of Political Economy* (May/June 1973), pp. 637–654.
2. Gordon, M.J. (1974). "A General Solution to the Buy vs. Lease Decision: a Pedagogical Note", *Journal of Finance* (March 1974), pp. 245–250.
3. Kim, E.H. (1978). "A Mean Variance Theory of Optimal Capital Structure and Corporate Debt Capacity", *Journal of Finance* (March 1978), pp. 45–64.
4. Martin, J.D. and D.F. Scott (1976). "Debt Capacity and the Capital Budgeting Decision", *Financial Management*, (Summer 1976), pp. 7–14.
5. _____ (1980). "Debt Capacity and the Capital Budgeting Decision: a Revisitation", *Financial Management*, (Spring 1980), pp. 23–26.
6. Merton, R.C. (1974). "On the Pricing of Corporate Debt: The Rate of Interest Rates", *Journal of Finance* (May 1974), pp. 449–470.
7. Miller, M.H. (1976). "Leasing, Buying and Cost of Capital Service", *Journal of Finance* (June 1976), pp. 761–786.

Part VI

Dividend Policy

Introduction

Both empirical and theoretical issues in dividend policy have been discussed indirectly in Parts I through V. Dividend policy is interrelated with both investment and financing policy. Hence, it is important for a student of finance to understand the theoretical and empirical results of some dividend policy studies.

In their well-known article "Dividend Policy, Growth, and the Valuation of Shares", Modigliani and Miller (M&M) (1961) examine a wide variety of issues concerning dividend policy. They use a recursive valuation formula to show the irrelevance of dividend policy to sharcholders in a world without taxes. They also show that the "dividend stream" valuation approach is equivalent to three other valuation approaches, i.e., the income stream approach, the discount cash flow approach, and the investment opportunity approach. M&M analyze the relationship between the growth rates of price per share, earnings per share, and dividend per share. They use the concept of the "informational content" of dividends to explain why, under the assumption of uncertainty, a change in a firm's dividend rate is often followed by a change in the market price of a firm's stock. In addition, M&M use the concept of a "clientele effect" to argue that each corporation will tend to attract to itself a "clientele"; those preferring the particular pay-out ratio of the firm. Finally, M&M argue that the favorable tax treatment on capital gains is undoubtedly the primary systematic imperfection in the market.

In his paper entitled, "The Dividend Puzzle", Black (1976) discusses some inconsistencies between practitioners and academicians. Academicians such as M&M use quite restrictive assumptions to show analytically that dividend policy does not matter. However, almost all successful firms pay dividends, and dividend policy is of major concern to financial managers. Black concludes that we are presently unable to show that dividends matter, though we are also not willing to assert that dividends definitely do not matter. Therefore, the effectiveness of dividend policy must still be regarded as a puzzle.

In the real world, both the corporate tax rate and the personal tax rate are important in financial management decisions. The possible impacts of the favorable tax treatment of capital gains was first investigated by Farrar and Selwyn (1967) and Brennan (1970). The results of these two papers are reviewed and extended by Litzenberger and Ramaswamy (1979) (LR). LR derive the CAPM with tax. The main difference between the CAPM with tax and without is that the dividend yield is an additional determinant of capital asset pricing. Several relatively complicated econometric models are used by LR to show that dividend yields are indeed important for explaining the market value of a firm. This detailed estimation procedure can be omitted without losing the essence of the paper. It should be mentioned that there are methods other than those used by LR to investigate the importance of dividend policy on financial analysis and planning. For example, two early studies, Gordon (1959) and Friend and Puckett (1964) investigated empirically the relationship between price per share, dividend per share and retained earnings per share. Though there are some problems associated with these approaches, they remain among the primary alternative methods to understand the impact of dividends on the market value of a firm. Lee and Forbes (1980) (LF) use the above-mentioned two alternative models to test the impacts of dividend policy on both stock price and stock rates of return for property and liability insurance industry. They have found that the dividend policy is relevant in equity value determination. In addition, LF also estimate the cost of capital for the non-life insurance industry.

Lee (1976) reviews the results obtained by Gordon (1959) and Friend and Puckett (1964) and generalizes their cross-sectional model by using a generalized functional form specification model. The paper shows that the decision concerning dividend payments will simultaneously affect both dividends per share and retained earnings per share.

Rappaport (1981) analyzes the potential impact of inflation on the earnings power of a firm and on its dividend payment decision. He concludes that a company's maximum affordable dividend depends on its financing policy and the projected cash flow consequences of its planned growth in investment rather than on last year's accrued accounting earnings performance, whether calculated on an inflation-adjusted basis or not.

More recently, Litzenberger and Ramaswamy, Bar-Yosef and Kolodny (1976), Blume (1981), Lee and Forbes (1981), and Djarraya and Lee (1980) have used different methods to show empirically that dividend policy matters. It should also be noted that Miller and Scholes (1978, 1981) have theoretically as well as empirically re-examined the yield-related tax effect of dividends.

DIVIDEND POLICY, GROWTH, AND THE VALUATION OF SHARES*

MERTON H. MILLER† AND FRANCO MODIGLIANI‡

THE effect of a firm's dividend policy on the current price of its shares is a matter of considerable importance, not only to the corporate officials who must set the policy, but to investors planning portfolios and to economists seeking to understand and appraise the functioning of the capital markets. Do companies with generous distribution policies consistently sell at a premium over those with niggardly payouts? Is the reverse ever true? If so, under what conditions? Is there an optimum payout ratio or range of ratios that maximizes the current worth of the shares?

Although these questions of fact have been the subject of many empirical studies in recent years no consensus has yet been achieved. One reason appears to be the absence in the literature of a complete and reasonably rigorous statement of those parts of the economic theory of valuation bearing directly on the matter of dividend policy. Lacking such a statement, investigators have not yet been able to frame their tests with sufficient precision to distinguish adequately between the various contending hypotheses. Nor have they been able to give a convincing explanation of what their test results do imply about the underlying process of valuation.

In the hope that it may help to overcome these obstacles to effective empirical testing, this paper will attempt to fill the existing gap in the theoretical literature on valuation. We shall begin, in Section I, by examining the effects of differences in dividend policy on the current price of shares in an ideal economy characterized by perfect capital markets, rational behavior, and perfect certainty. Still within this convenient analytical framework we shall go on in Sections II and III to consider certain closely related issues that appear to have been responsible for considerable misunderstanding of the role of dividend policy. In particular, Section II will focus on the long-standing debate about what investors "really" capitalize when they buy shares; and Section III on the much mooted relations between price, the rate of growth of

* The authors wish to express their thanks to all who read and commented on earlier versions of this paper and especially to Charles C. Holt, now of the University of Wisconsin, whose suggestions led to considerable simplification of a number of the proofs.

† Professor of finance and economics, University of Chicago.

‡ Professor of economics, Northwestern University.

profits, and the rate of growth of dividends per share. Once these fundamentals have been established, we shall proceed in Section IV to drop the assumption of certainty and to see the extent to which the earlier conclusions about dividend policy must be modified. Finally, in Section V, we shall briefly examine the implications for the dividend policy problem of certain kinds of market imperfections.

I. EFFECT OF DIVIDEND POLICY WITH PERFECT MARKETS, RATIONAL BEHAVIOR, AND PERFECT CERTAINTY

The meaning of the basic assumptions. —Although the terms "perfect markets," "rational behavior," and "perfect certainty" are widely used throughout economic theory, it may be helpful to start by spelling out the precise meaning of these assumptions in the present context.

1. In "perfect capital markets," no buyer or seller (or issuer) of securities is large enough for his transactions to have an appreciable impact on the then ruling price. All traders have equal and costless access to information about the ruling price and about all other relevant characteristics of shares (to be detailed specifically later). No brokerage fees, transfer taxes, or other transaction costs are incurred when securities are bought, sold, or issued, and there are no tax differentials either between distributed and undistributed profits or between dividends and capital gains.

2. "Rational behavior" means that investors always prefer more wealth to less and are indifferent as to whether a given increment to their wealth takes the form of cash payments or an increase in the market value of their holdings of shares.

3. "Perfect certainty" implies complete assurance on the part of every investor as to the future investment program and the future profits of every corporation. Because of this assurance, there is, among other things, no need to distinguish between stocks and bonds as sources of funds at this stage of the analysis. We can, therefore, proceed as if there were only a single type of financial instrument which, for convenience, we shall refer to as shares of stock.

The fundamental principle of valuation.—Under these assumptions the valuation of all shares would be governed by the following fundamental principle: the price of each share must be such that the rate of return (dividends plus capital gains per dollar invested) on every share will be the same throughout the market over any given interval of time. That is, if we let

$d_j(t)$ = dividends per share paid by firm j during period t

$p_j(t)$ = the price (ex any dividend in $t-1$) of a share in firm j at the start of period t,

we must have

$$\frac{d_j(t)+p_j(t+1)-p_j(t)}{p_j(t)} \qquad (1)$$

$$= \rho(t) \text{ independent of } j \text{ ;}$$

or, equivalently,

$$p_j(t) = \frac{1}{1+\rho(t)}[d_j(t)+p_j(t+1)] \quad (2)$$

for each j and for all t. Otherwise, holders of low-return (high-priced) shares could increase their terminal wealth by selling these shares and investing the proceeds in shares offering a higher rate of return. This process would tend to drive down the prices of the low-return shares and drive up the prices of high-return shares until the differential in rates of return had been eliminated.

The effect of dividend policy.—The implications of this principle for our problem of dividend policy can be seen somewhat more easily if equation (2) is restated in terms of the value of the enterprise as a whole rather than in terms of the value of an individual share. Dropping the firm subscript j since this will lead to no ambiguity in the present context and letting

$n(t)$ = the number of shares of record at the start of t

$m(t+1)$ = the number of new shares (if any) sold during t at the ex dividend closing price $p(t+1)$, so that

$n(t+1) = n(t) + m(t+1)$

$V(t) = n(t) \, p(t)$ = the total value of the enterprise and

$D(t) = n(t) \, d(t)$ = the total dividends paid during t to holders of record at the start of t,

we can rewrite (2)

$$V(t) = \frac{1}{1+\rho(t)} \, [\, D(t) + n(t) \, p(t+1) \,]$$

$$= \frac{1}{1+\rho(t)} \, [\, D(t) + V(t+1)$$

$$- m(t+1) \, p(t+1) \,] . \quad (3)$$

The advantage of restating the fundamental rule in this form is that it brings into sharper focus the three possible routes by which current dividends might affect the current market value of the firm $V(t)$, or equivalently the price of its individual shares, $p(t)$. Current dividends will clearly affect $V(t)$ via the first term in the bracket, $D(t)$. In principle, current dividends might also affect $V(t)$ indirectly via the second term, $V(t+1)$, the new ex dividend market value. Since $V(t+1)$ must depend only on future and not on past events, such could be the case, however, only if both (a) $V(t+1)$ were a function of future dividend policy and (b) the current distribution $D(t)$ served to convey some otherwise unavailable information as to what that future dividend policy would be. The first possibility being the relevant one from the standpoint of assessing the effects of dividend policy, it will clarify matters to assume, provisionally, that the future dividend policy of the firm is known and given for $t+1$ and all subsequent periods and is independent of the actual dividend decision in t. Then $V(t+1)$ will also be independent of the current dividend decision, though it may very well be affected by $D(t+1)$ and all subsequent distributions. Finally, current dividends can influence $V(t)$ through the third term, $-m(t+1) \, p(t+1)$, the value of new shares sold to outsiders during the period. For the higher the dividend payout in any period the more the new capital that must be raised from external sources to maintain any desired level of investment.

The fact that the dividend decision effects price not in one but in these two conflicting ways—directly via $D(t)$ and inversely via $-m(t) \, p(t+1)$—is, of course, precisely why one speaks of there being a dividend policy *problem*. If the firm raises its dividend in t, given its investment decision, will the increase in the cash payments to the current holders be more or less than enough to offset their lower share of the terminal value? Which is the better strategy for the firm in financing the investment: to reduce dividends and rely on retained earnings or to raise dividends but float more new shares?

In our ideal world at least these and related questions can be simply and immediately answered: the two dividend effects must always exactly cancel out so that the payout policy to be followed in t will have *no* effect on the price at t.

We need only express $m(t+1) \cdot p(t+1)$ in terms of $D(t)$ to show that such must indeed be the case. Specifically, if $I(t)$ is the given level of the firm's investment or increase in its holding of physical assets in t and if $X(t)$ is the firm's total net profit for the period, we know that the amount of outside capital required will be

$$m(t+1) p(t+1) = I(t)$$
$$- [X(t) - D(t)].$$
(4)

Substituting expression (4) into (3), the $D(t)$ cancel and we obtain for the value of the firm as of the start of t

$$V(t) \equiv n(t) p(t)$$
$$= \frac{1}{1 + \rho(t)} [X(t) - I(t) + V(t+1)].$$
(5)

Since $D(t)$ does not appear directly among the arguments and since $X(t)$, $I(t)$, $V(t+1)$ and $\rho(t)$ are all independent of $D(t)$ (either by their nature or by assumption) it follows that the current value of the firm must be independent of the current dividend decision.

Having established that $V(t)$ is unaffected by the current dividend decision it is easy to go on to show that $V(t)$ must also be unaffected by any future dividend decisions as well. Such future decisions can influence $V(t)$ only via their effect on $V(t+1)$. But we can repeat the reasoning above and show that $V(t+1)$—and hence $V(t)$—is unaffected by dividend policy in $t+1$; that $V(t+2)$—and hence $V(t+1)$ and $V(t)$—is unaffected by dividend policy in $t+2$; and so on for as far into the future as we care to look. Thus, we may conclude that given a firm's investment policy, the dividend payout policy it chooses to follow will affect neither the current price of its shares nor the total return to its shareholders.

Like many other propositions in economics, the irrelevance of dividend policy, given investment policy, is "obvious, once you think of it." It is, after all, merely one more instance of the general principle that there are no "financial illusions" in a rational and perfect economic environment. Values there are determined solely by "real" considerations—in this case the earning power of the firm's assets and its investment policy—and not by how the fruits of the earning power are "packaged" for distribution.

Obvious as the proposition may be, however, one finds few references to it in the extensive literature on the problem.[1] It is true that the literature abounds with statements that in some "theoretical" sense, dividend policy ought not to count; but either that sense is not clearly specified or, more frequently and especially among economists, it is (wrongly) identified with a situation in which the firm's internal rate of return is the same as the external or market rate of return.[2]

A major source of these and related misunderstandings of the role of the dividend policy has been the fruitless concern and controversy over what investors "really" capitalize when they buy shares. We say fruitless because as we shall now proceed to show, it is actually possible to derive from the basic principle of valuation (1) not merely one, but several valuation formulas each starting from one of the "classical" views of what is being capitalized by investors. Though differing somewhat in outward appearance, the various formulas can be shown to be equivalent in all essential respects including, of course, their implication that dividend policy is irrelevant. While the

[1] Apart from the references to it in our earlier papers, especially [16], the closest approximation seems to be that in Bodenborn [1, p. 492], but even his treatment of the role of dividend policy is not completely explicit. (The numbers in brackets refer to references listed below, pp. 432–33).

[2] See below p. 424.

controvery itself thus turns out to be an empty one, the different expressions do have some intrinsic interest since, by highlighting different combinations of variables they provide additional insights into the process of valuation and they open alternative lines of attack on some of the problems of empirical testing.

II. WHAT DOES THE MARKET "REALLY" CAPITALIZE?

In the literature on valuation one can find at least the following four more or less distinct approaches to the valuation of shares: (1) the discounted cash flow approach; (2) the current earnings plus future investment opportunities approach; (3) the stream of dividends approach; and (4) the stream of earnings approach. To demonstrate that these approaches are, in fact, equivalent it will be helpful to begin by first going back to equation (5) and developing from it a valuation formula to serve as a point of reference and comparison. Specifically, if we assume, for simplicity, that the market rate of yield $\rho(t) = \rho$ for all t,[3] then, setting $t = 0$, we can rewrite (5) as

$$V(0) = \frac{1}{1+\rho}[X(0) - I(0)]$$
$$+ \frac{1}{1+\rho} V(1). \qquad (6)$$

Since (5) holds for all t, setting $t = 1$ permits us to express $V(1)$ in terms of $V(2)$ which in turn can be expressed in terms of $V(3)$ and so on up to any arbitrary terminal period T. Carrying out these substitutions, we obtain

$$V(0) = \sum_{t=0}^{T-1} \frac{1}{(1+\rho)^{t+1}}[X(t) - I(t)]$$
$$+ \frac{1}{(1+\rho)^T} V(T). \qquad (7)$$

In general, the remainder term $(1+\rho)^{-T} \cdot V(T)$ can be expected to approach zero

as T approaches infinity[4] so that (7) can be expressed as

$$V(0) = \lim_{T \to \infty} \sum_{t=0}^{T-1} \frac{1}{(1+\rho)^{t+1}} \qquad (8)$$
$$\times [X(t) - I(t)],$$

which we shall further abbreviate to

$$V(0) = \sum_{t=0}^{\infty} \frac{1}{(1+\rho)^{t+1}}[X(t) - I(t)]. \qquad (9)$$

The discounted cash flow approach.— Consider now the so-called discounted cash flow approach familiar in discussions of capital budgeting. There, in valuing any specific machine we discount at the market rate of interest the stream of cash receipts generated by the machine; plus any scrap or terminal value of the machine; and minus the stream of cash outlays for direct labor, materials, repairs, and capital additions. The same approach, of course, can also be applied to the firm as a whole which may be thought of in this context as simply a large, composite machine.[5] This ap-

---

[3] More general formulas in which $\rho(t)$ is allowed to vary with time can always be derived from those presented here merely by substituting the cumbersome product

$$\prod_{\tau=0}^{t} [1 + \rho(\tau)] \qquad \text{for} \qquad (1+\rho)^{t+1}.$$

[4] The assumption that the remainder vanishes is introduced for the sake of simplicity of exposition only and is in no way essential to the argument. What is essential, of course, is that $V(0)$, i.e., the sum of the two terms in (7), be finite, but this can always be safely assumed in economic analysis. See below, n. 14.

[5] This is, in fact, the approach to valuation normally taken in economic theory when discussing the value of the *assets* of an enterprise, but much more rarely applied, unfortunately, to the value of the liability side. One of the few to apply the approach to the shares as well as the assets is Bodenhorn in [1], who uses it to derive a formula closely similar to (9) above.

proach amounts to defining the value of the firm as

$$V(0) = \sum_{t=0}^{T-1} \frac{1}{(1+\rho)^{t+1}}$$
$$\times [\mathcal{R}(t) - \mathcal{O}(t)] + \frac{1}{(1+\rho)^T} V(T), \quad (10)$$

where $\mathcal{R}(t)$ represents the stream of cash receipts and $\mathcal{O}(t)$ of cash outlays, or, abbreviating, as above, to

$$V(0) = \sum_{t=0}^{\infty} \frac{1}{(1+\rho)^{t+1}} [\mathcal{R}(t) - \mathcal{O}(t)]. \quad (11)$$

But we also know, by definition, that $[X(t) - I(t)] = [\mathcal{R}(t) - \mathcal{O}(t)]$ since, $X(t)$ differs from $\mathcal{R}(t)$ and $I(t)$ differs from $\mathcal{O}(t)$ merely by the "cost of goods sold" (and also by the depreciation expense if we wish to interpret $X(t)$ and $I(t)$ as net rather than gross profits and investment). Hence (11) is formally equivalent to (9), and the discounted cash flow approach is thus seen to be an implication of the valuation principle for perfect markets given by equation (1).

The investment opportunities approach. —Consider next the approach to valuation which would seem most natural from the standpoint of an investor proposing to buy out and operate some already-going concern. In estimating how much it would be worthwhile to pay for the privilege of operating the firm, the amount of dividends to be paid is clearly not relevant, since the new owner can, within wide limits, make the future dividend stream whatever he pleases. For him the worth of the enterprise, as such, will depend only on: (*a*) the "normal" rate of return he can earn by investing his capital in securities (i.e., the market rate of return); (*b*) the earning power of the physical assets currently held by the firm; and (*c*) the opportunities, if any, that the firm offers for making additional

investments in real assets that will yield more than the "normal" (market) rate of return. The latter opportunities, frequently termed the "good will" of the business, may arise, in practice, from any of a number of circumstances (ranging all the way from special locational advantages to patents or other monopolistic advantages).

To see how these opportunities affect the value of the business assume that in some future period t the firm invests $I(t)$ dollars. Suppose, further, for simplicity, that starting in the period immediately following the investment of the funds, the projects produce net profits at a constant rate of $\rho^*(t)$ per cent of $I(t)$ in each period thereafter.[6] Then the present worth as of t of the (perpetual) stream of profits generated will be $I(t) \rho^*(t)/\rho$, and the "good will" of the projects (i.e., the difference between worth and cost) will be

$$I(t) \frac{\rho^*(t)}{\rho} - I(t) = I(t) \left[\frac{\rho^*(t) - \rho}{\rho} \right].$$

The present worth as of now of this future "good will" is

$$I(t) \left[\frac{\rho^*(t) - \rho}{\rho} \right] (1+\rho)^{-(t+1)},$$

and the present value of all such future opportunities is simply the sum

$$\sum_{t=0}^{\infty} I(t) \frac{\rho^*(t) - \rho}{\rho} (1+\rho)^{-(t+1)}.$$

Adding in the present value of the (uniform perpetual) earnings, $X(0)$, on the as-

<hr/>

[6] The assumption that $I(t)$ yields a uniform perpetuity is not restrictive in the present certainty context since it is always possible by means of simple, present-value calculations to find an equivalent uniform perpetuity for any project, whatever the time shape of its actual returns. Note also that $\rho^*(t)$ is the *average* rate of return. If the managers of the firm are behaving rationally, they will, of course, use ρ as their cut-off criterion (cf. below p. 418). In this event we would have $\rho^*(t) \geq \rho$. The formulas remain valid, however, even where $\rho^*(t) < \rho$.

sets currently held, we get as an expression for the value of the firm

$$V(0) = \frac{X(0)}{\rho} + \sum_{t=0}^{\infty} I(t)$$

$$\times \frac{\rho^*(t) - \rho}{\rho}(1+\rho)^{-(t+1)}. \tag{12}$$

To show that the same formula can be derived from (9) note first that our definition of $\rho^*(t)$ implies the following relation between the $X(t)$:

$$X(1) = X(0) + \rho^*(0) I(0),$$

$$\cdots \cdots \cdots \cdots \cdots \cdots \cdots \cdots$$

$$X(t) = X(t-1) + \rho^*(t-1) I(t-1)$$

and by successive substitution

$$X(t) = X(0) + \sum_{\tau=0}^{t-1} \rho^*(\tau) I(\tau),$$

$$t = 1, 2 \ldots \infty.$$

Substituting the last expression for $X(t)$ in (9) yields

$$V(0) = [X(0) - I(0)] (1+\rho)^{-1}$$

$$+ \sum_{t=1}^{\infty} \left[X(0) + \sum_{\tau=0}^{t-1} \rho^*(\tau) I(\tau) \right.$$

$$\left. - I(t) \right] (1+\rho)^{-(t+1)}$$

$$= X(0) \sum_{t=1}^{\infty} (1+\rho)^{-t}$$

$$- I(0) (1+\rho)^{-1}$$

$$+ \sum_{t=1}^{\infty} \left[\sum_{\tau=0}^{t-1} \rho^*(\tau) I(\tau) - I(t) \right]$$

$$\times (1+\rho)^{-(t+1)}$$

$$= X(0) \sum_{t=1}^{\infty} (1+\rho)^{-t}$$

$$+ \sum_{t=1}^{\infty} \left[\sum_{\tau=0}^{t-1} \rho^*(\tau) I(\tau) - I(t-1) \right.$$

$$\left. \times (1+\rho) \right] (1+\rho)^{-(t+1)}.$$

The first expression is, of course, simply a geometric progression summing to $X(0)/\rho$, which is the first term of (12). To simplify the second expression note that it can be rewritten as

$$\sum_{t=0}^{\infty} I(t) \left[\rho^*(t) \sum_{\tau=t+2}^{\infty} (1+\rho)^{-\tau} \right.$$

$$\left. - (1+\rho)^{-(t+1)} \right].$$

Evaluating the summation within the brackets gives

$$\sum_{t=0}^{\infty} I(t) \left[\rho^*(t) \frac{(1+\rho)^{-(t+1)}}{\rho} \right.$$

$$\left. - (1+\rho)^{-(t+1)} \right]$$

$$= \sum_{t=0}^{\infty} I(t) \left[\frac{\rho^*(t) - \rho}{\rho} \right] (1+\rho)^{-(t+1)},$$

which is precisely the second term of (12).

Formula (12) has a number of revealing features and deserves to be more widely used in discussions of valuation.[7] For one thing, it throws considerable light on the meaning of those much abused terms "growth" and "growth stocks." As can readily be seen from (12), a corporation does not become a "growth stock" with a high price-earnings ratio merely because its assets and earnings are growing over time. To enter the glamor category, it is also necessary that $\rho^*(t) > \rho$. For if $\rho^*(t) = \rho$, then however large the growth in assets may be, the second term in (12) will be zero and the firm's price-earnings ratio would not rise above a humdrum $1/\rho$. The essence of "growth," in short, is not expansion, but the existence of opportunities to invest significant quantities of funds at higher than "normal" rates of return.

[7] A valuation formula analogous to (12) though derived and interpreted in a slightly different way is found in Bodenhorn [1]. Variants of (12) for certain special cases are discussed in Walter [20].

Notice also that if $\rho^*(t) < \rho$, investment in real assets by the firm will actually reduce the current price of the shares. This should help to make clear among other things, why the "cost of capital" to the firm is the same regardless of how the investments are financed or how fast the firm is growing. The function of the cost of capital in capital budgeting is to provide the "cut-off rate" in the sense of the minimum yield that investment projects must promise to be worth undertaking from the point of view of the current owners. Clearly, no proposed project would be in the interest of the current owners if its yield were expected to be less than ρ since investing in such projects would reduce the value of their shares. In the other direction, every project yielding more than ρ is just as clearly worth undertaking since it will necessarily enhance the value of the enterprise. Hence, the cost of capital or cut-off criterion for investment decisions is simply ρ.[8]

Finally, formula (12) serves to emphasize an important deficiency in many recent statistical studies of the effects of dividend policy (such as Walter [19] or Durand [4, 5]). These studies typically involve fitting regression equations in which price is expressed as some function of current earnings and dividends. A finding that the dividend coefficient is significant—as is usually the case—is then interpreted as a rejection of the hypothesis that dividend policy does not affect

[8] The same conclusion could also have been reached, of course, by "costing" each particular source of capital funds. That is, since ρ is the going market rate of return on equity any new shares floated to finance investment must be priced to yield ρ; and withholding funds from the stockholders to finance investment would deprive the holders of the chance to earn ρ on these funds by investing their dividends in other shares. The advantage of thinking in terms of the cost of capital as the cut-off criterion is that it minimizes the danger of confusing "costs" with mere "outlays."

valuation.

Even without raising questions of bias in the coefficients,[9] it should be apparent that such a conclusion is unwarranted since formula (12) and the analysis underlying it imply only that dividends will not count given current earnings *and growth potential*. No general prediction is made (or can be made) by the theory about what will happen to the dividend coefficient if the crucial growth term is omitted.[10]

The stream of dividends approach.—From the earnings and earnings opportunities approach we turn next to the dividend approach, which has, for some reason, been by far the most popular one in the literature of valuation. This approach too, properly formulated, is an entirely valid one though, of course, not the only valid approach as its more enthusiastic proponents frequently suggest.[11] It does, however, have the disadvantage in contrast with previous approaches of obscuring the role of dividend policy. In particular, uncritical use of the

[9] The serious bias problem in tests using current reported earnings as a measure of $X(0)$ was discussed briefly by us in [16].

[10] In suggesting that recent statistical studies have not controlled adequately for growth we do not mean to exempt Gordon in [8] or [9]. It is true that his tests contain an explicit "growth" variable, but it is essentially nothing more than the ratio of retained earnings to book value. This ratio would not in general provide an acceptable approximation to the "growth" variable of (12) in any sample in which firms resorted to external financing. Furthermore, even if by some chance a sample was found in which all firms relied entirely on retained earnings, his tests then could not settle the question of dividend policy. For if all firms financed investment internally (or used external financing only in strict proportion to internal financing as Gordon assumes in [8]) then there would be no way to distinguish between the effects of dividend policy and investment policy (see below p. 424).

[11] See, e.g., the classic statement of the position in J. B. Williams [21]. The equivalence of the dividend approach to many of the other standard approaches is noted to our knowledge only in our [16] and, by implication, in Bodenhorn [1].

dividend approach has often led to the unwarranted inference that, since the investor is buying dividends and since dividend policy affects the amount of dividends, then dividend policy must also affect the current price.

Properly formulated, the dividend approach defines the current worth of a share as the discounted value of the stream of dividends to be paid on the share in perpetuity. That is

$$p(t) = \sum_{\tau=0}^{\infty} \frac{d(t+\tau)}{(1+\rho)^{\tau+1}}. \quad (13)$$

To see the equivalence between this approach and previous ones, let us first restate (13) in terms of total market value as

$$V(t) = \sum_{\tau=0}^{\infty} \frac{D_t(t+\tau)}{(1+\rho)^{\tau+1}}, \quad (14)$$

where $D_t(t+\tau)$ denotes that portion of the total dividends $D(t+\tau)$ paid during period $t+\tau$, that accrues to the shares of record as of the start of period t (indicated by the subscript). That equation (14) is equivalent to (9) and hence also to (12) is immediately apparent for the special case in which no outside financing is undertaken after period t, for in that case

$$D_t(t+\tau) = D(t+\tau)$$
$$= X(t+\tau) - I(t+\tau).$$

To allow for outside financing, note that we can rewrite (14) as

$$V(t) = \frac{1}{1+\rho} \Big[D_t(t)$$

$$+ \sum_{\tau=1}^{\infty} \frac{D_t(t+\tau)}{(1+\rho)^{\tau}} \Big]$$

$$\quad (15)$$

$$= \frac{1}{1+\rho} \Big[D(t)$$

$$+ \sum_{\tau=0}^{\infty} \frac{D_t(t+\tau+1)}{(1+\rho)^{\tau+1}} \Big].$$

The summation term in the last expression can be written as the difference between the stream of dividends accruing to all the shares of record as of $t+1$ and that portion of the stream that will accrue to the shares newly issued in t, that is,

$$\sum_{\tau=0}^{\infty} \frac{D_t(t+\tau+1)}{(1+\rho)^{\tau+1}} = \Big(1 - \frac{m(t+1)}{n(t+1)}\Big)$$

$$\quad (16)$$

$$\times \sum_{\tau=0}^{\infty} \frac{D_{t+1}(t+\tau+1)}{(1+\rho)^{\tau+1}}.$$

But from (14) we know that the second summation in (16) is precisely $V(t+1)$ so that (15) can be reduced to

$$V(t) = \frac{1}{1+\rho} \Big[D(t)$$

$$+ \Big(1 - \frac{m(t+1)p(t+1)}{n(t+1)p(t+1)}\Big)$$

$$\times V(t+1) \Big] \quad (17)$$

$$= \frac{1}{1+\rho} [D(t) + V(t+1)$$

$$- m(t+1)p(t+1)],$$

which is (3) and which has already been shown to imply both (9) and (12).[12]

There are, of course, other ways in which the equivalence of the dividend approach to the other approaches might

[12] The statement that equations (9), (12), and (14) are equivalent must be qualified to allow for certain pathological extreme cases, fortunately of no real economic significance. An obvious example of such a case is the legendary company that is expected *never* to pay a dividend. If this were literally true then the value of the firm by (14) would be zero; by (9) it would be zero (or possibly negative since zero dividends rule out $X(t) > I(t)$ but not $X(t) < I(t)$); while by (12) the value might still be positive. What is involved here, of course, is nothing more than a discontinuity at zero since the value under (14) and (9) would be positive and the equivalence of both with (12) would hold if that value were also positive as long as there was some period T, however far in the future, beyond which the firm would pay out $\epsilon > 0$ per cent of its earnings, however small the value of ϵ.

have been established, but the method presented has the advantage perhaps of providing some further insight into the reason for the irrelevance of dividend policy. An increase in current dividends, given the firm's investment policy, must necessarily reduce the terminal value of existing shares because part of the future dividend stream that would otherwise have accrued to the existing shares must be diverted to attract the outside capital from which, in effect, the higher current dividends are paid. Under our basic assumptions, however, ρ must be the same for all investors, new as well as old. Consequently the market value of the dividends diverted to the outsiders, which is both the value of their contribution and the reduction in terminal value of the existing shares, must always be precisely the same as the increase in current dividends.

The stream of earnings approach.— Contrary to widely held views, it is also possible to develop a meaningful and consistent approach to valuation running in terms of the stream of earnings generated by the corporation rather than of the dividend distributions actually made to the shareholders. Unfortunately, it is also extremely easy to mistake or misinterpret the earnings approach as would be the case if the value of the firm were to be defined as simply the discounted sum of future total earnings.[13] The trouble with such a definition is not, as is

often suggested, that it overlooks the fact that the corporation is a separate entity and that these profits cannot freely be withdrawn by the shareholders; but rather that it neglects the fact that additional capital must be acquired at some cost to maintain the future earnings stream at its specified level. The capital to be raised in any future period is, of course, $I(t)$ and its opportunity cost, no matter how financed, is ρ per cent per period thereafter. Hence, the current value of the firm under the earnings approach must be stated as

$$V(0) = \sum_{t=0}^{\infty} \frac{1}{(1+\rho)^{t+1}}$$

$$\times \left[X(t) - \sum_{\tau=0}^{t} \rho I(\tau) \right].$$

(18)

That this version of the earnings approach is indeed consistent with our basic assumptions and equivalent to the previous approaches can be seen by regrouping terms and rewriting equation (18) as

$$V(0) = \sum_{t=0}^{\infty} \frac{1}{(1+\rho)^{t+1}} X(t)$$

$$- \sum_{t=0}^{\infty} \left(\sum_{\tau=t}^{\infty} \frac{\rho I(t)}{(1+\rho)^{\tau+1}} \right)$$

$$= \sum_{t=0}^{\infty} \frac{1}{(1+\rho)^{t+1}} X(t) \qquad (19)$$

$$- \sum_{t=0}^{\infty} \frac{1}{(1+\rho)^{t+1}}$$

$$\times \left(\sum_{\tau=0}^{\infty} \frac{\rho I(t)}{(1+\rho)^{\tau+1}} \right).$$

Since the last inclosed summation reduces simply to $I(t)$, the expression (19) in turn reduces to simply

$$V(0) = \sum_{t=0}^{\infty} \frac{1}{(1+\rho)^{t+1}} [X(t) - I(t)], \quad (20)$$

[13] In fairness, we should point out that there is no one, to our knowledge, who has seriously advanced this view. It is a view whose main function seems to be to serve as a "straw man" to be demolished by those supporting the dividend view. See, e.g., Gordon [9, esp. pp. 102–3]. Other writers take as the supposed earnings counter-view to the dividend approach not a relation running in terms of the *stream* of earnings but simply the proposition that price is proportional to current earnings, i.e., $V(0) = X(0)/\rho$. The probable origins of this widespread misconception about the earnings approach are discussed further below (p. 424).

which is precisely our earlier equation (9).

Note that the version of the earnings approach presented here does not depend for its validity upon any special assumptions about the time shape of the stream of total profits or the stream of dividends per share. Clearly, however, the time paths of the two streams are closely related to each other (via financial policy) and to the stream of returns derived by holders of the shares. Since these relations are of some interest in their own right and since misunderstandings about them have contributed to the confusion over the role of dividend policy, it may be worthwhile to examine them briefly before moving on to relax the basic assumptions.

III. EARNINGS, DIVIDENDS, AND GROWTH RATES

The convenient case of constant growth rates.—The relation between the stream of earnings of the firm and the stream of dividends and of returns to the stockholders can be brought out most clearly by specializing (12) to the case in which investment opportunities are such as to generate a constant rate of growth of profits in perpetuity. Admittedly, this case has little empirical significance, but it is convenient for illustrative purposes and has received much attention in the literature.

Specifically, suppose that in each period t the firm has the opportunity to invest in real assets a sum $I(t)$ that is k per cent as large as its total earnings for the period; and that this investment produces a perpetual yield of ρ^* beginning with the next period. Then, by definition

$$X(t) = X(t-1) + \rho^* I(t-1)$$
$$= X(t-1)[1 + k\rho^*] \quad (21)$$
$$= X(0)[1 + k\rho^*]^t$$

and $k\rho^*$ is the (constant) rate of growth of total earnings. Substituting from (21) into (12) for $I(t)$ we obtain

$$V(0) = \frac{X(0)}{\rho} + \sum_{t=0}^{\infty} \left(\frac{\rho^* - \rho}{\rho}\right)$$
$$\times kX(0)[1 + k\rho^*]^t$$
$$\times (1 + \rho)^{-(t+1)} \quad (22)$$
$$= \frac{X(0)}{\rho} \left[1 + \frac{k(\rho^* - \rho)}{1 + \rho}\right.$$
$$\left. \times \sum_{t=0}^{\infty} \left(\frac{1 + k\rho^*}{1 + \rho}\right)^t\right].$$

Evaluating the infinite sum and simplifying, we finally obtain[14]

$$V(0) = \frac{X(0)}{\rho} \left[1 + \frac{k(\rho^* - \rho)}{\rho - k\rho^*}\right]$$
$$= \frac{X(0)(1 - k)}{\rho - k\rho^*}, \quad (23)$$

which expresses the value of the firm as a function of its current earnings, the rate of growth of earnings, the internal rate of return, and the market rate of return.[15]

[14] One advantage of the specialization (23) is that it makes it easy to see what is really involved in the assumption here and throughout the paper that the $V(0)$ given by any of our summation formulas is necessarily finite (cf. above, n. 4). In terms of (23) the condition is clearly $k\rho^* < \rho$, i.e., that the rate of growth of the firm be less than market rate of discount. Although the case of (perpetual) growth rates greater than the discount factor is the much-discussed "growth stock praradox" (e.g. [6]), it has no real economic significance as we pointed out in [16, esp. n. 17, p. 664]. This will be apparent when one recalls that the discount rate ρ, though treated as a constant in partial equilibrium (relative price) analysis of the kind presented here, is actually a variable from the standpoint of the system as a whole. That is, if the assumption of finite value for all shares did not hold, because for some shares $k\rho^*$ was (perpetually) greater than ρ, then ρ would necessarily rise until an over-all equilibrium in the capital markets had been restored.

[15] An interesting and more realistic variant of (22), which also has a number of convenient features from the standpoint of developing empirical tests, can be obtained by assuming that the special invest-

(2) the stream of dividends to the original owners (or dividends per share) in the special case in which all financing is internal. The slope of B is, of course, the same as that of A and the (constant) difference between the curves is simply $\ln(1 - k)$, the ratio of dividends to profits. Line C shows the growth of dividends per share when the firm uses both internal and external financing. As compared with the pure retention case, the line starts higher but grows more slowly at the rate g given by (25). The higher the payout policy, the higher the starting position and the slower the growth up to the other limiting case of complete external financing, Line D, which starts at $\ln X(0)$ and grows at a rate of $(k/1 - k) \cdot (\rho^* - \rho)$.

The special case of exclusively internal financing.—As noted above the growth rate of dividends per share is not the same as the growth rate of the firm except in the special case in which all financing is internal. This is merely one of a number of peculiarities of this special case on which, unfortunately, many writers have based their entire analysis. The reason for the preoccupation with this special case is far from clear to us. Certainly no one would suggest that it is the only empirically relevant case. Even if the case were in fact the most common, the theorist would still be under an obligation to consider alternative assumptions. We suspect that in the last analysis, the popularity of the internal financing model will be found to reflect little more than its ease of manipulation combined with the failure to push the analysis far enough to disclose how special and how treacherous a case it really is.

In particular, concentration on this special case appears to be largely responsible for the widely held view that, even under perfect capital markets, there is an optimum dividend policy for the firm that depends on the internal rate of return. Such a conclusion is almost inevitable if one works exclusively with the assumption, explicit or implicit, that funds for investment come *only* from retained earnings. For in that case *dividend policy* is indistinguishable from *investment policy;* and there *is* an optimal investment policy which does in general depend on the rate of return.

Notice also from (23) that if $\rho^* = \rho$ and $k = k_r$, the term $[1 - k_r]$ can be canceled from both the numerator and the denominator. The value of the firm becomes simply $X(0)/\rho$, the capitalized value of current earnings. Lacking a standard model for valuation more general than the retained earnings case it has been all too easy for many to conclude that this dropping out of the payout ratio $[1 - k_r]$ when $\rho^* = \rho$ must be what is meant by the irrelevance of dividend policy and that $V(0) = X(0)/\rho$ must constitute the "earnings" approach.

Still another example of the pitfalls in basing arguments on this special case is provided by the recent and extensive work on valuation by M. Gordon.[18] Gordon argues, in essence, that because of increasing uncertainty the discount rate $\hat{\rho}(t)$ applied by an investor to a future dividend payment will rise with t, where t denotes not a specific date but rather the distance from the period in which the investor performs the discounting.[19]

[18] See esp. [8]. Gordon's views represent the most explicit and sophisticated formulation of what might be called the "bird-in-the-hand" fallacy. For other, less elaborate, statements of essentially the same position see, among others, Graham and Dodd [11, p. 433] and Clendenin and Van Cleave [3].

[19] We use the notation $\hat{\rho}(t)$ to avoid any confusion between Gordon's purely subjective discount rate and the objective, market-given yields $\rho(t)$ in Sec. I above. To attempt to derive valuation formulas under uncertainty from these purely subjective discount factors involves, of course, an error essentially

Hence, when we use a single uniform discount rate ρ as in (22) or (23), this rate should be thought of as really an average of the "true" rates $\hat{\rho}(t)$ each weighted by the size of the expected dividend payment at time t. If the dividend stream is growing exponentially then such a weighted average ρ would, of course, be higher the greater the rate of growth of dividends g since the greater will then be the portion of the dividend stream arising in the distant as opposed to the near future. But if all financing is assumed to be internal, then $g = k_r\rho^*$ so that given ρ^*, the weighted average discount factor ρ will be an increasing function of the rate of retention k_r which would run counter to our conclusion that dividend policy has no effect on the current value of the firm or its cost of capital.

For all its ingenuity, however, and its seeming foundation in uncertainty, the argument clearly suffers fundamentally from the typical confounding of dividend policy with investment policy that so frequently accompanies use of the internal financing model. Had Gordon not confined his attention to this special case (or its equivalent variants), he would have seen that while a change in dividend policy will necessarily affect the size of the expected dividend payment on the share in any future period, it need not, in the general case, affect either the size of the *total* return that the investor expects during that period or the degree of uncertainty attaching to that total return. As should be abundantly clear by now, a change in dividend policy, given investment policy, implies a change only in the distribution of the total return in any period as between dividends and capital gains. If investors behave rationally, such a change cannot affect market valuations. Indeed, if they valued shares according to the Gordon approach and thus paid a premium for higher payout ratios, then holders of the low payout shares would actually realize consistently higher returns on their investment over any stated interval of time.[20]

Corporate earnings and investor returns. —Knowing the relation of g to $k\rho^*$ we can answer a question of considerable interest to economic theorists, namely: What is the precise relation between the earnings of the corporation in any period $X(t)$ and the total return to the owners of the stock during that period?[21] If we let $G_t(t)$ be the capital gains to the owners during t, we know that

$$D_t(t) + G_t(t) = X(t) \times (1 - k_r) + gV(t) \qquad (26)$$

[20] This is not to deny that growth stocks (in our sense) may well be "riskier" than non-growth stocks. But to the extent that this is true, it will be due to the possibly greater uncertainty attaching to the size and duration of future growth opportunities and hence to the size of the future stream of total returns quite apart from any questions of dividend policy.

[21] Note also that the above analysis enables us to deal very easily with the familiar issue of whether a firm's cost of equity capital is measured by its earnings/price ratio or by its dividend/price ratio. Clearly, the answer is that it is measured by neither, except under very special circumstances. For from (23) we have for the earnings/price ratio

$$\frac{X(0)}{V(0)} = \frac{\rho - k\rho^*}{1 - k},$$

which is equal to the cost of capital ρ, only if the firm has no growth potential (i.e., $\rho^* = \rho$). And from (24) we have for the dividend/price ratio

$$\frac{D(0)}{V(0)} = \rho - g,$$

which is equal to ρ only when $g = 0$; i.e., from (25), either when $k = 0$; or, if $k > 0$, when $\rho^* < \rho$ and the amount of external financing is precisely

$$k_e = \frac{\rho^*}{\rho} k [1 - k_r],$$

so that the gain from the retention of earnings exactly offsets the loss that would otherwise be occasioned by the unprofitable investment.

analogous to that of attempting to develop the certainty formulas from "marginal rates of time preference" rather than objective market opportunities.

since the rate of growth of price is the same as that of dividends per share. Using (25) and (26) to substitute for g and $V(t)$ and simplifying, we find that

$$D_t(t)+G_t(t) = X(t)\left[\frac{\rho(1-k)}{\rho-k\rho^*}\right]. \quad (27)$$

The relation between the investors' return and the corporation's profits is thus seen to depend entirely on the relation between ρ^* and ρ. If $\rho^* = \rho$ (i.e., the firm has no special "growth" opportunities), then the expression in brackets becomes 1 and the investor returns are precisely the same as the corporate profits. If $\rho^* < \rho$, however, the investors' return will be less than the corporate earnings; and, in the case of growth corporations the investors' return will actually be greater than the flow of corporate profits over the interval.[22]

Some implications for constructing empirical tests.—Finally the fact that we have two different (though not independent) measures of growth in $k\rho^*$ and g and two corresponding families of valuation formulas means, among other things, that we can proceed by either of two routes in empirical studies of valuation. We can follow the standard practice of the security analyst and think in terms of price per share, dividends per share, and the rate of growth of dividends per

share; or we can think in terms of the total value of the enterprise, total earnings, and the rate of growth of total earnings. Our own preference happens to be for the second approach primarily because certain additional variables of interest—such as dividend policy, leverage, and size of firm—can be incorporated more easily and meaningfully into test equations in which the growth term is the growth of total earnings. But this can wait. For present purposes, the thing to be stressed is simply that two approaches, properly carried through, are in no sense *opposing* views of the valuation process; but rather equivalent views, with the choice between them largely a matter of taste and convenience.

IV. THE EFFECTS OF DIVIDEND POLICY UNDER UNCERTAINTY

Uncertainty and the general theory of valuation.—In turning now from the ideal world of certainty to one of uncertainty our first step, alas, must be to jettison the fundamental valuation principle as given, say, in our equation (3)

$$V(t) = \frac{1}{1+\rho(t)}\left[D(t)+n(t)p(t+1)\right]$$

and from which the irrelevance proposition as well as all the subsequent valua-

---

[22] The above relation between earnings per share and dividends plus capital gains also means that there will be a systematic relation between retained earnings and capital gains. The "marginal" relation is easy to see and is always precisely one for one regardless of growth or financial policy. That is, taking a dollar away from dividends and adding it to retained earnings (all other things equal) means an increase in capital gains of one dollar (or a reduction in capital loss of one dollar). The "average" relation is somewhat more complex. From (26) and (27) we can see that

$$G_t(t) = k_r X(t) + kX(t)\frac{\rho^*-\rho}{\rho-k\rho^*}.$$

Hence, if $\rho^* = \rho$ the total capital gain received will be exactly the same as the total retained earnings per share. For growth corporations, however, the

capital gain will always be greater than the retained earnings (and there will be a capital gain of

$$kX(t)\left[\frac{\rho^*-\rho}{\rho-k\rho^*}\right]$$

even when all earnings are paid out). For non-growth corporations the relation between gain and retentions is reversed. Note also that the absolute difference between the total capital gain and the total retained earnings is a constant (given, ρ, k and ρ^*) unaffected by dividend policy. Hence the *ratio* of capital gain to retained earnings will vary directly with the payout ratio for growth corporations (and vice versa for non-growth corporations). This means, among other things, that it is dangerous to attempt to draw inferences about the relative growth potential or relative managerial efficiency of corporations solely on the basis of the ratio of capital gains to retained earnings (cf. Harkavy [12, esp. pp. 289–94]).

tion formulas in Sections II and III were derived. For the terms in the bracket can no longer be regarded as given numbers, but must be recognized as "random variables" from the point of view of the investor as of the start of period t. Nor is it at all clear what meaning can be attached to the discount factor $1/[1 + \rho(t)]$ since what is being discounted is not a given return, but at best only a probability distribution of possible returns. We can, of course, delude ourselves into thinking that we are preserving equation (3) by the simple and popular expedient of drawing a bar over each term and referring to it thereafter as the mathematical expectation of the random variable. But except for the trivial case of universal linear utility functions we know that $V(t)$ would also be affected, and materially so, by the higher order moments of the distribution of returns. Hence there is no reason to believe that the discount factor for expected values, $1/[1 + \rho(t)]$, would in fact be the same for any two firms chosen arbitrarily, not to mention that the expected values themselves may well be different for different investors.

All this is not to say, of course, that there are insuperable difficulties in the way of developing a testable theory of rational market valuation under uncertainty.[23] On the contrary, our investigations of the problem to date have convinced us that it is indeed possible to construct such a theory—though the construction, as can well be imagined, is a

fairly complex and space-consuming task. Fortunately, however, this task need not be undertaken in this paper which is concerned primarily with the effects of dividend policy on market valuation. For even without a full-fledged theory of what *does* determine market value under uncertainty we can show that dividend policy at least is *not* one of the determinants. To establish this particular generalization of the previous certainty results we need only invoke a corresponding generalization of the original postulate of rational behavior to allow for the fact that, under uncertainty, choices depend on expectations as well as tastes.

"Imputed rationality" and "symmetric market rationality."—This generalization can be formulated in two steps as follows. First, we shall say that an individual trader "imputes rationality to the market" or satisfies the postulate of "imputed rationality" if, in forming expectations, he assumes that every other trader in the market is (*a*) rational in the previous sense of preferring more wealth to less regardless of the form an increment in wealth may take, and (*b*) imputes rationality to all other traders. Second, we shall say that a market as a whole satisfies the postulate of "symmetric market rationality" if every trader both behaves rationally and imputes rationality to the market.[24]

Notice that this postulate of sym-

[23] Nor does it mean that all the previous certainty analysis has no relevance whatever in the presence of uncertainty. There are many issues, such as those discussed in Sec. I and II, that really relate only to what has been called the pure "futurity" component in valuation. Here, the valuation formulas can still be extremely useful in maintaining the internal consistency of the reasoning and in suggesting (or criticizing) empirical tests of certain classes of hypotheses about valuation, even though the formulas themselves cannot be used to grind out precise numerical values for specific real-world shares.

[24] We offer the term "symmetric market rationality" with considerable diffidence and only after having been assured by game theorists that there is no accepted term for this concept in the literature of that subject even though the postulate itself (or close parallels to it) does appear frequently. In the literature of economics a closely related, but not exact counterpart is Muth's "hypothesis of rational expectations" [18]. Among the more euphonic, though we feel somewhat less revealing, alternatives that have been suggested to us are "putative rationality" (by T. J. Koopmans), "bi-rationality" (by G. L. Thompson), "empathetic rationality" (by Andrea Modigliani), and "pan-rationality" (by A. Ando).

metric market rationality differs from the usual postulate of rational behavior in several important respects. In the first place, the new postulate covers not only the choice behavior of individuals but also their expectations of the choice behavior of others. Second, the postulate is a statement about the market as a whole and not just about individual behavior. Finally, though by no means least, symmetric market rationality cannot be deduced from individual rational behavior in the usual sense since that sense does not imply imputing rationality to others. It may, in fact, imply a choice behavior inconsistent with imputed rationality unless the individual actually believes the market to be symmetrically rational. For if an ordinarily rational investor had good reason to believe that other investors would not behave rationally, then it might well be rational for him to adopt a strategy he would otherwise have rejected as irrational. Our postulate thus rules out, among other things, the possibility of speculative "bubbles" wherein an individually rational investor buys a security he knows to be overpriced (i.e., too expensive in relation to its expected *long-run* return to be attractive as a permanent addition to his portfolio) in the expectation that he can resell it at a still more inflated price before the bubble bursts.[25]

[25] We recognize, of course, that such speculative bubbles have actually arisen in the past (and will probably continue to do so in the future), so that our postulate can certainly not be taken to be of universal applicability. We feel, however, that it is also not of universal inapplicability since from our observation, speculative bubbles, though well publicized when they occur, do not seem to us to be a dominant, or even a fundamental, feature of actual market behavior under uncertainty. That is, we would be prepared to argue that, as a rule and on the average, markets do not behave in ways which do not obviously contradict the postulate so that the postulate may still be useful, at least as a first approximation, for the analysis of long-run tendencies in organized

The irrelevance of dividend policy despite uncertainty.—In Section I we were able to show that, given a firm's investment policy, its dividend policy was irrelevant to its current market valuation. We shall now show that this fundamental conclusion need not be modified merely because of the presence of uncertainty about the future course of profits, investment, or dividends (assuming again, as we have throughout, that investment policy can be regarded as separable from dividend policy). To see that uncertainty about these elements changes nothing essential, consider a case in which current investors believe that the future streams of total earnings and total investment whatever actual values they may assume at different points in time will be identical for two firms, 1 and 2.[26] Suppose further, provisionally, that the same is believed to be true of future total dividend payments from period one on so that the only way in which the two firms differ is possibly with respect to the prospective dividend in the current period, period 0. In terms of previous notation we are thus assuming that

$$\tilde{X}_1(t) = \tilde{X}_2(t) \qquad t = 0 \ldots \infty$$

$$\tilde{I}_1(t) = \tilde{I}_2(t) \qquad t = 0 \ldots \infty$$

$$\tilde{D}_1(t) = \tilde{D}_2(t) \qquad t = 1 \ldots \infty$$

capital markets. Needless to say, whether our confidence in the postulate is justified is something that will have to be determined by empirical tests of its implications (such as, of course, the irrelevance of dividend policy).

[26] The assumption of two identical firms is introduced for convenience of exposition only, since it usually is easier to see the implications of rationality when there is an explicit arbitrage mechanism, in this case, switches between the shares of the two firms. The assumption, however, is not necessary and we can, if we like, think of the two firms as really corresponding to two states of the same firm for an investor performing a series of "mental experiments" on the subject of dividend policy.

the subscripts indicating the firms and the tildes being added to the variables to indicate that these are to be regarded from the standpoint of current period, not as known numbers but as numbers that will be drawn in the future from the appropriate probability distributions. We may now ask: "What will be the return, $\tilde{R}_1(0)$ to the current shareholders in firm 1 during the current period?" Clearly, it will be

$$\tilde{R}_1(0) = \tilde{D}_1(0) + \tilde{V}_1(1) - \tilde{m}_1(1)\,\tilde{p}_1(1)\,. \quad (28)$$

But the relation between $\tilde{D}_1(0)$ and $\tilde{m}_1(1)\,\tilde{p}_1(1)$ is necessarily still given by equation (4) which is merely an accounting identity so that we can write

$$\tilde{m}_1(1)\,\tilde{p}_1(1) = \tilde{I}_1(0) - [\tilde{X}_1(0) - \tilde{D}_1(0)]. \quad (29)$$

and, on substituting in (28), we obtain

$$\tilde{R}_1(0) = \tilde{X}_1(0) - \tilde{I}_1(0) + \tilde{V}_1(1) \quad (30)$$

for firm 1. By an exactly parallel process we can obtain an equivalent expression for $\tilde{R}_2(0)$.

Let us now compare $\tilde{R}_1(0)$ with $\tilde{R}_2(0)$. Note first that, by assumption, $\tilde{X}_1(0) = \tilde{X}_2(0)$ and $\tilde{I}_1(0) = \tilde{I}_2(0)$. Furthermore, with symmetric market rationality, the terminal values $\tilde{V}_i(1)$ can depend only on prospective future earnings, investment and dividends from period 1 on and these too, by assumption, are identical for the two companies. Thus symmetric rationality implies that every investor must expect $\tilde{V}_1(1) = \tilde{V}_2(1)$ and hence finally $\tilde{R}_1(0) = \tilde{R}_2(0)$. But if the return to the investors is the same in the two cases, rationality requires that the two firms command the same current value so that $V_1(0)$ must equal $V_2(0)$ regardless of any difference in dividend payments during period 0. Suppose now that we allow dividends to differ not just in period 0 but in period 1 as well, but still retain the assumption of equal $\tilde{X}_i(t)$ and $\tilde{I}_i(t)$ in

all periods and of equal $\tilde{D}_i(t)$ in period 2 and beyond. Clearly, the only way differences in dividends in period 1 can effect $\tilde{R}_i(0)$ and hence $V_i(0)$ is via $\tilde{V}_i(1)$. But, by the assumption of symmetric market rationality, current investors know that as of the start of period 1 the then investors will value the two firms rationally and we have already shown that differences in the current dividend do not affect current value. Thus we must have $\tilde{V}_1(1) = \tilde{V}_2(1)$—and hence $V_1(0) = V_2(0)$—regardless of any possible difference in dividend payments during period 1. By an obvious extension of the reasoning to $\tilde{V}_i(2)$, $\tilde{V}_i(3)$, and so on, it must follow that the current valuation is unaffected by differences in dividend payments in *any* future period and thus that dividend policy is irrelevant for the determination of market prices, given investment policy.[27]

Dividend policy and leverage.—A study of the above line of proof will show it to be essentially analogous to the proof for the certainty world, in which as we know, firms can have, in effect, only two alternative sources of investment funds: retained earnings or stock issues. In an uncertain world, however, there is the additional financing possibility of debt issues. The question naturally arises, therefore, as to whether the conclusion about irrelevance remains valid even in the presence of debt financing, particularly since there may very well be inter-

[27] We might note that the assumption of symmetric market rationality is sufficient to derive this conclusion but not strictly necessary if we are willing to weaken the irrelevance proposition to one running in terms of long-run, average tendencies in the market. Individual rationality alone could conceivably bring about the latter, for over the long pull rational investors could enforce this result by buying and holding "undervalued" securities because this would insure them higher long-run returns when eventually the prices became the same. They might, however, have a long, long wait.

actions between debt policy and dividend policy. The answer is that it does, and while a complete demonstration would perhaps be too tedious and repetitious at this point, we can at least readily sketch out the main outlines of how the proof proceeds. We begin, as above, by establishing the conditions from period 1 on that lead to a situation in which $\bar{V}_1(1)$ must be brought into equality with $\bar{V}_2(1)$ where the V, following the approach in our earlier paper [17], is now to be interpreted as the total market value of the firm, debt plus equity, not merely equity alone. The return to the original investors taken as a whole—and remember that any individual always has the option of buying a proportional share of both the equity and the debt—must correspondingly be broadened to allow for the interest on the debt. There will also be a corresponding broadening of the accounting identity (4) to allow, on the one hand, for the interest return and, on the other, for any debt funds used to finance the investment in whole or in part. The net result is that both the dividend component and the interest component of total earnings will cancel out making the relevant (total) return, as before, $[\bar{X}_i(0) - \bar{I}_i(0) + \bar{V}_i(1)]$ which is clearly independent of the current dividend. It follows, then, that the value of the firm must also therefore be independent of dividend policy given investment policy.[28]

The informational content of dividends. —To conclude our discussion of dividend policy under uncertainty, we might take note briefly of a common confusion about the meaning of the irrelevance proposition occasioned by the fact that in the real world a change in the dividend rate is often followed by a change in the market price (sometimes spectacularly so). Such a phenomenon would not be incompatible with irrelevance to the extent that it was merely a reflection of what might be called the "informational content" of dividends, an attribute of particular dividend payments hitherto excluded by assumption from the discussion and proofs. That is, where a firm has adopted a policy of dividend stabilization with a long-established and generally appreciated "target payout ratio," investors are likely to (and have good reason to) interpret a change in the dividend rate as a change in management's views of future profit prospects for the firm.[29] The dividend change, in other words, provides the occasion for the price change though not its cause, the price still being solely a reflection of future earnings and growth opportunities. In any particular instance, of course, the investors might well be mistaken in placing this interpretation on the dividend change, since the management might really only be changing its payout target or possibly even attempting to "manipulate" the price. But this would involve no particular conflict with the irrelevance proposition, unless, of course, the price changes in such cases were not reversed when the unfolding of events had made clear the true nature of the situation.[30]

[28] This same conclusion must also hold for the current market value of all the shares (and hence for the current price per share), which is equal to the total market value minus the given initially outstanding debt. Needless to say, however, the price per share and the value of the equity at *future* points in time will not be independent of dividend and debt policies in the interim.

[29] For evidence on the prevalence of dividend stabilization and target ratios see Lintner [15].

[30] For a further discussion of the subject of the informational content of dividends, including its implications for empirical tests of the irrelevance proposition, see Modigliani and Miller [16, pp. 666–68].

V. DIVIDEND POLICY AND MARKET IMPERFECTIONS

To complete the analysis of dividend policy, the logical next step would presumably be to abandon the assumption of perfect capital markets. This is, however, a good deal easier to say than to do principally because there is no unique set of circumstances that constitutes "imperfection." We can describe not one but a multitude of possible departures from strict perfection, singly and in combinations. Clearly, to attempt to pursue the implications of each of these would only serve to add inordinately to an already overlong discussion. We shall instead, therefore, limit ourselves in this concluding section to a few brief and general observations about imperfect markets that we hope may prove helpful to those taking up the task of extending the theory of valuation in this direction.

First, it is important to keep in mind that from the standpoint of dividend policy, what counts is not imperfection per se but only imperfection that might lead an investor to have a systematic preference as between a dollar of current dividends and a dollar of current capital gains. Where no such systematic preference is produced, we can subsume the imperfection in the (random) error term always carried along when applying propositions derived from ideal models to real-world events.

Second, even where we do find imperfections that bias individual preferences —such as the existence of brokerage fees which tend to make young "accumulators" prefer low-payout shares and retired persons lean toward "income stocks"—such imperfections are at best only necessary but not sufficient conditions for certain payout policies to command a permanent premium in the market. If, for example, the frequency distribution of corporate payout ratios happened to correspond exactly with the distribution of investor preferences for payout ratios, then the existence of these preferences would clearly lead ultimately to a situation whose implications were different in no fundamental respect from the perfect market case. Each corporation would tend to attract to itself a "clientele" consisting of those preferring its particular payout ratio, but one clientele would be entirely as good as another in terms of the valuation it would imply for the firm. Nor, of course, is it necessary for the distributions to match exactly for this result to occur. Even if there were a "shortage" of some particular payout ratio, investors would still normally have the option of achieving their particular saving objectives without paying a premium for the stocks in short supply simply by buying appropriately weighted combinations of the more plentiful payout ratios. In fact, given the great range of corporate payout ratios known to be available, this process would fail to eliminate permanent premiums and discounts only if the distribution of investor preferences were heavily concentrated at either of the extreme ends of the payout scale.[31]

Of all the many market imperfections that might be detailed, the only one that would seem to be even remotely capable of producing such a concentration is the substantial advantage accorded to capital gains as compared with dividends un-

[31] The above discussion should explain why, among other reasons, it would not be possible to draw any valid inference about the relative preponderance of "accumulators" as opposed to "income" buyers or the strength of their preferences merely from the weight attaching to dividends in a simple cross-sectional regression between value and payouts (as is attempted in Clendenin [2, p. 50] or Durand [5, p. 651]).

der the personal income tax. Strong as this tax push toward capital gains may be for high-income individuals, however, it should be remembered that a substantial (and growing) fraction of total shares outstanding is currently held by investors for whom there is either no tax differential (charitable and educational institutions, foundations, pension trusts, and low-income retired individuals) or where the tax advantage is, if anything, in favor of dividends (casualty insurance companies and taxable corporations generally). Hence, again, the "clientele effect" will be at work. Furthermore, except for taxable individuals in the very top brackets, the required difference in before-tax yields to produce equal after-tax yields is not particularly striking, at least for moderate variations in the composition of returns.[32] All this is not to say, of course, that differences in yields (market values) caused by differences in payout policies should be ignored by managements or investors merely because they may be relatively small. But it may help to keep investigators from being too surprised if it turns out to be hard to

measure or even to detect any premium for low-payout shares on the basis of standard statistical techniques.

Finally, we may note that since the tax differential in favor of capital gains is undoubtedly the major *systematic* imperfection in the market, one clearly cannot invoke "imperfections" to account for the difference between our irrelevance proposition and the standard view as to the role of dividend policy found in the literature of finance. For the standard view is not that low-payout companies command a premium; but that, in general, they will sell at a discount![33] If such indeed were the case—and we, at least, are not prepared to concede that this has been established—then the analysis presented in this paper suggests there would be only one way to account for it; namely, as the result of systematic irrationality on the part of the investing public.[34]

To say that an observed positive premium on high payouts was due to irrationality would not, of course, make the phenomenon any less real. But it would at least suggest the need for a certain measure of caution by long-range policymakers. For investors, however naïve they may be when they enter the market, do sometimes learn from experience; and perhaps, occasionally, even from reading articles such as this.

[32] For example, if a taxpayer is subject to a marginal rate of 40 per cent on dividends and half that or 20 per cent on long-term capital gains, then a before-tax yield of 6 per cent consisting of 40 per cent dividends and 60 per cent capital gains produces an after-tax yield of 4.32 per cent. To net the same after-tax yield on a stock with 60 per cent of the return in dividends and only 40 per cent in capital gains would require a before-tax yield of 6.37 per cent. The difference would be somewhat smaller if we allowed for the present dividend credit, though it should also be kept in mind that the tax on capital gains may be avoided entirely under present arrangements if the gains are not realized during the holder's lifetime.

[33] See, among many, many others, Gordon [8, 9], Graham and Dodd [11, esp. chaps. xxxiv and xxxvi], Durand [4, 5], Hunt, Williams, and Donaldson [13, pp. 647–49], Fisher [7], Gordon and Shapiro [10], Harkavy [12], Clendenin [2], Johnson, Shapiro, and O'Meara [14], and Walter [19].

[34] Or, less plausibly, that there is a systematic tendency for external funds to be used more productively than internal funds.

REFERENCES

1. BODENHORN, DIRAN. "On the Problem of Capital Budgeting," *Journal of Finance*, XIV (December, 1959), 473–92.

2. CLENDENIN, JOHN. "What Do Stockholders Like?" *California Management Review*, I (Fall, 1958), 47–55.

3. CLENDENIN, JOHN, and VAN CLEAVE, M. "Growth and Common Stock Values," *Journal of Finance*, IX (September, 1954), 365–76.

4. DURAND, DAVID. *Bank Stock Prices and the Bank Capital Problem.* ("Occasional Paper," No. 54.) New York: National Bureau of Economic Research, 1957.

5. ———. "The Cost of Capital and the Theory of Investment: Comment," *American Economic Review*, XLIX (September, 1959), 639–54.

6. ———. "Growth Stocks and the Petersburg Paradox," *Journal of Finance*, XII (September, 1957), 348–63.

7. FISHER, G. R. "Some Factors Influencing Share Prices," *Economic Journal*, LXXI, No. 281 (March, 1961), 121–41.

8. GORDON, MYRON. "Corporate Saving, Investment and Share Prices," *Review of Economics and Statistics* (forthcoming).

9. ———. "Dividends, Earnings and Stock Prices," *ibid.*, XLI, No. 2, Part I (May, 1959), 99–105.

10. GORDON, MYRON, and SHAPIRO, ELI. "Capital Equipment Analysis: The Required Rate of Profit," *Management Science*, III, 1956, 102–10.

11. GRAHAM, BENJAMIN, and DODD, DAVID. *Security Analysis.* 3d ed. New York: McGraw-Hill Book Co., 1951.

12. HARKAVY, OSCAR, "The Relation between Retained Earnings and Common Stock Prices for Large Listed Corporations," *Journal of Finance*, VIII (September, 1953), 283–97.

13. HUNT, PEARSON, WILLIAMS, CHARLES, and DONALDSON, GORDON. *Basic Business Finance.* Homewood, Ill.: Richard D. Irwin, 1958.

14. JOHNSON, L. R., SHAPIRO, ELI, and O'MEARA, J. "Valuation of Closely Held Stock for Federal Tax Purposes: Approach to an Objective Method," *University of Pennsylvania Law Review*, C, 166–95.

15. LINTNER, JOHN. "Distribution of Incomes of Corporations among Dividends, Retained Earnings and Taxes," *American Economic Review*, XLVI (May, 1956), 97–113.

16. MODIGLIANI, FRANCO, and MILLER, MERTON. "'The Cost of Capital, Corporation Finance and the Theory of Investment,': Reply," *American Economic Review*, XLIX (September, 1959), 655–69.

17. ———. "The Cost of Capital, Corporation Finance and the Theory of Investment," *ibid.*, XLVIII (1958), 261–97.

18. MUTH, JOHN F. "Rational Expectations and the Theory of Price Movements," *Econometrica* (forthcoming).

19. WALTER, JAMES E. "A Discriminant Function for Earnings-Price Ratios of Large Industrial Corporations," *Review of Economics and Statistics*, XLI (February, 1959), 44–52.

20. ———. "Dividend Policies and Common Stock Prices," *Journal of Finance*, XI (March, 1956), 29–41.

21. WILLIAMS, JOHN B. *The Theory of Investment Value.* Cambridge, Mass.: Harvard University Press, 1938.

414

The dividend puzzle

"The harder we look at the dividend picture, the more it seems like a puzzle, with pieces that just don't fit together."

Fischer Black

Why do corporations pay dividends? Why do investors pay attention to dividends? Perhaps the answers to these questions are obvious. Perhaps dividends represent the return to the investor who put his money at risk in the corporation. Perhaps corporations pay dividends to reward existing shareholders and to encourage others to buy new issues of common stock at high prices. Perhaps investors pay attention to dividends because only through dividends or the prospect of dividends do they receive a return on their investment or the chance to sell their shares at a higher price in the future.

Or perhaps the answers are not so obvious. Perhaps a corporation that pays no dividends is demonstrating confidence that it has attractive investment opportunities that might be missed if it paid dividends. If it makes these investments, it may increase the value of the shares by more than the amount of the lost dividends. If that happens, its shareholders may be doubly better off. They end up with capital appreciation greater than the dividends they missed out on, and they find they are taxed at lower effective rates on capital appreciation than on dividends.

In fact, I claim that the answers to these questions are not obvious at all. The harder we look at the dividend picture, the more it seems like a puzzle, with pieces that just don't fit together.

THE MILLER-MODIGLIANI THEOREM

Suppose you are offered the following choice. You may have $2 today, and a 50-50 chance of $54 or $50 tomorrow. Or you may have nothing today, and a 50-50 chance of $56 or $52 tomorrow. Would you prefer one of these gambles to the other?

Probably you would not. Ignoring such factors

1. Footnotes appear at the end of the article.

as the cost of holding the $2 and one day's interest on $2, you would be indifferent between these two gambles.

The choice between a common stock that pays a dividend and a stock that pays no dividend is similar, at least if we ignore such things as transaction costs and taxes. The price of the dividend-paying stock drops on the ex-dividend date by about the amount of the dividend. The dividend just drops the whole range of possible stock prices by that amount. The investor who gets a $2 dividend finds himself with shares worth about $2 less than they would have been worth if the dividend hadn't been paid, in all possible circumstances.

This, in essence, is the Miller-Modigliani theorem.[1] It says that the dividends a corporation pays do not affect the value of its shares or the returns to investors, because the higher the dividend, the less the investor receives in capital appreciation, no matter how the corporation's business decisions turn out.

When we say this, we are assuming that the dividend paid does not influence the corporation's business decisions. Paying the dividend either reduces the amount of cash equivalents held by the corporation, or increases the amount of money raised by issuing securities.

IF A FIRM PAYS NO DIVIDENDS

If this theorem is correct, then a firm that pays a regular dividend equal to about half of its normal earnings will be worth the same as an otherwise similar firm that pays no dividends and will never pay any dividends. Can that be true? How can a firm that will never pay dividends be worth anything at all?

Actually, there are many ways for the stockholders of a firm to take cash out without receiving dividends. The most obvious is that the firm can buy back some of its shares. This has the advantage that most investors are not taxed as heavily on shares sold as they are on dividends received.

If the firm is closely held, it can give money to its shareholders by giving them jobs at inflated salaries, or by ordering goods from other firms owned by the shareholders at inflated prices.

If the firm is not closely held, then another firm or individual can make a tender offer which will have the effect of making it closely held. Then the same methods for taking cash out of the firm can be used.

Under the assumptions of the Modigliani-Miller theorem, a firm has value even if it pays no dividends. Indeed, it has the same value it would have if it paid dividends.

TAXES

In a world where dividends are taxed more heavily (for most investors) than capital gains, and where capital gains are not taxed until realized, a corporation that pays no dividends will be more attractive to taxable individual investors than a similar corporation that pays dividends. This will tend to increase the price of the non-dividend-paying corporation's stock. Many corporations will be tempted to eliminate dividend payments.

Of course, corporate investors are taxed more heavily on realized capital gains than on dividends. And tax-exempt investors are taxed on neither. But it is hard to believe that these groups have enough impact on the market to outweigh the effects of taxable individuals.

Also, the IRS has a special tax that it likes to apply to companies that retain earnings to avoid the personal taxation of dividends. But there are many ways to avoid this tax. A corporation that is making investments in its business usually doesn't have to pay the tax, especially if it is issuing securities to help pay for these investments.

If a corporation insists on paying out cash, it is better off replacing some of its common stock with bonds. A shareholder who keeps his proportionate share of the new securities will receive taxable interest but at least the interest will be deductible to the corporation. Dividends are not deductible.

With taxes, investors and corporations are no longer indifferent to the level of dividends. They prefer smaller dividends or no dividends at all.

TRANSACTION COSTS

An investor who holds a non-dividend-paying stock will generally sell some of his shares if he needs to raise cash. In some circumstances, he can borrow against his shares. Either of these transactions can be costly, especially if small amounts of money are involved. So an investor might want to have dividend income instead.

But this argument doesn't have much substance. If investors are concerned about transaction costs, the corporation that pays no dividends can arrange for automatic share repurchase plans, much like the automatic dividend reinvestment plans that now exist. A shareholder would keep his stock in trust, and the trustee would periodically sell shares back to the corporation, including fractional shares if necessary. The shareholder could even choose the amounts he wants to receive and the timing of the payments. An automated system would probably cost about as much as a system for paying dividends.

If the IRS objected to the corporation's buying back its own shares, then the trustee could simply sell blocks of shares on the open market. Again, the cost would be low.

Thus transaction costs don't tell us much about why corporations pay dividends.

WHAT DO DIVIDEND CHANGES TELL US?

The managers of most corporations have a tendency to give out good news quickly, but to give out bad news slowly. Thus investors are somewhat suspicious of what the managers have to say.

Dividend policy, though, may say things the managers don't say explicitly. For one reason or another, managers and directors do not like to cut the dividend. So they will raise the dividend only if they feel the company's prospects are good enough to support the higher dividend for some time. And they will cut the dividend only if they think the prospects for a quick recovery are poor.

This means that dividend changes, or the fact that the dividend doesn't change, may tell investors more about what the managers really think than they can find out from other sources. Assuming that the managers' forecasts are somewhat reliable, dividend policy conveys information.

Thus the announcement of a dividend cut often leads to a drop in the company's stock price. And the announcement of a dividend increase often leads to an increase in the company's stock price. These stock price changes are permanent if the company in fact does as badly, or as well, as the dividend changes indicated.

If the dividend changes are not due to forecasts of the company's prospects, then any stock price changes that occur will normally be temporary. If a corporation eliminates its dividend because it wants to save taxes for its shareholders, then the stock price might decline at first. But it would eventually go back to the level it would have had if the dividend had not been cut, or higher.

Thus the fact that dividend changes often tell us things about the corporations making them does not explain why corporations pay dividends.

HOW TO HURT THE CREDITORS

When a company has debt outstanding, the indenture will almost always limit the dividends the company can pay. And for good reason. There is no easier way for a company to escape the burden of a debt than to pay out all of its assets in the form of a dividend, and leave the creditors holding an empty shell.[2]

While this is an extreme example, any increase in the dividend that is not offset by an increase in external financing will hurt the company's creditors. A dollar paid out in dividends is a dollar that is not available to the creditors if trouble develops.

If an increase in the dividend will hurt the creditors, then a cut in the dividend will help the creditors. Since the firm is only worth so much, what helps the creditors will hurt the stockholders. The stockholders would certainly rather have $2 in dividends than $2 invested in assets that may end up in the hands of the creditors. Perhaps we have finally found a reason why firms pay dividends.

Alas, this explanation doesn't go very far. In many cases, the changes in the values of the stock and bonds caused by a change in dividend policy would be so small they would not be detectable. And if the effects are large, the company can negotiate with the creditors. If the company agrees not to pay any dividends at all, the creditors would presumably agree to give better terms on the company's credit. This would eliminate the negative effects of cutting the dividend on the position of the stockholders relative to the creditors.

DIVIDENDS AS A SOURCE OF CAPITAL

A company that pays dividends might instead have invested the money in its operations. This is especially true when the company goes to the markets frequently for new capital. Cutting the dividend, if there are no special reasons for paying dividends, has to be one of the lowest cost sources of funds available to the company.

The underwriting cost of a new debt or equity issue is normally several percent of the amount of money raised. There are no comparable costs for money raised by cutting the dividend.

Perhaps a company that has no profitable investment projects and that is not raising money externally should keep its dividend. If the dividend is cut, the managers may lose the money through unwise investment projects. In these special cases, there may be a reason to keep the dividend. But surely these cases are relatively rare.

In the typical case, the fact that cutting the dividend is a low cost way to raise money is another reason to expect corporations not to pay dividends. So why do they continue?

DO INVESTORS DEMAND DIVIDENDS?

It is possible that many, many individual investors believe that stocks that don't pay dividends should not be held, or should be held only at prices lower than the prices of similar stocks that do pay dividends. This belief is not rational, so far as I can tell. But it may be there nonetheless.

Add these investors to the trustees who believe it is not prudent to hold stocks that pay no dividends, and to the corporations that have tax reasons for preferring dividend-paying stocks, and you may have a substantial part of the market. More important, you may have a part of the market that strongly influences the pricing of corporate shares. Perhaps the best evidence of this is the dominance of this view in investment advisory publications.

On the other hand, investors also seem acutely aware of the tax consequences of dividends. Investors in high tax brackets seem to hold low dividend stocks, and investors in low tax brackets seem to hold high dividend stocks.[3]

Furthermore, the best empirical tests that I can think of are unable to show whether investors who prefer dividends or investors who avoid dividends have a stronger effect on the pricing of securities.[4]

If investors do demand dividends, then corporations should not eliminate all dividends. But it is difficult or impossible to tell whether investors demand dividends or not. So it is hard for a corporation to decide whether to eliminate its dividends or not.

PORTFOLIO IMPLICATIONS

Corporations can't tell what dividend policy to choose, because they don't know how many irrational investors there are. But perhaps a rational investor can choose a dividend policy for his portfolio that will maximize his after-tax expected return for a given level of risk. Perhaps a taxable investor, especially one who is in a high tax bracket, should emphasize low dividend stocks. And perhaps a tax-exempt investor should emphasize high dividend stocks.

One problem with this strategy is that an investor who emphasizes a certain kind of stock in his portfolio is likely to end up with a less well-diversified portfolio than he would otherwise have. So he will probably increase the risk of his portfolio.

The other problem is that we can't tell if or how much an investor will increase his expected return by doing this. If investors demanding dividends dominate the market, then high dividend stocks will have low expected returns. Even tax-exempt investors, if they are rational, should buy low dividend stocks.

On the other hand, it seems that rational investors in high brackets will do better in low dividend stocks no matter who dominates the market. But how much should they emphasize low dividend stocks? At what point will the loss of diversification offset the increase in expected return?

It is even conceivable that investors overemphasize tax factors, and bid low dividend stocks up so high that they are unattractive even for investors in the highest brackets.

Thus the portfolio implications of the theory are no clearer than its implications for corporate dividend policy.

What should the individual investor do about dividends in his portfolio? We don't know.

What should the corporation do about dividend policy? We don't know.

[1] See Merton H. Miller and Franco Modigliani, "Dividend Policy, Growth, and the Valuation of Shares." *Journal of Business* 34 (October, 1961): 411-433. Also Franco Modigliani and Merton H. Miller, "The Cost of Capital, Corporation Finance, and the Theory of Investment: Reply." *American Economic Review* 49 (September, 1959): 655-669.

[2] This issue is discussed in more detail in Fischer Black and Myron Scholes, "The Pricing of Options and Corporate Liabilities." *Journal of Political Economy* 81 (May/June, 1973): 637-654.

[3] See Marshall E. Blume, Jean Crockett, and Irwin Friend, "Stockownership in the United States: Characteristics and Trends." *Survey of Current Business* 54 (November, 1974): 16-40.

[4] See Fischer Black and Myron Scholes, "The Effects of Dividend Yield and Dividend Policy on Common Stock Prices and Returns." *Journal of Financial Economics* 1 (May, 1974): 1-22.

Dividend Policy, Equity Value, and Cost of Capital Estimates for the Property and Liability Insurance Industry

Cheng F. Lee and Stephen W. Forbes

ABSTRACT

Based upon the corporate finance theory and concept, possible impacts of dividend policy on the market value of equity for the property and liability insurance industry are theoretically and empirically investigated. The finding is that some effects of dividend policy on the market value of equity exist in the property and liability insurance industry. In addition, alternative methods for estimating cost of capital also are empirically applied to the property and liability insurance industry.

I. Introduction

The impacts of dividend policy upon the market value of equity and the cost of capital are of interest to financial managers and investors. These issues have been investigated by Bar-Yosef and Koldony [1], Black and Scholes [2] and others for industrial firms but not for financial institutions. That the financial management principles of financial institutions are not necessarily identical to those of industrial firms is well known among financial analysts. Specifically, the property and liability insurance company (hereafter called the non-life insurance company) deals with (1) different income measures which affect reported earnings and retained earnings, (2) unique borrowing-lending rate relationships [6], and (3) an asset portfolio comprised primarily of securities of industrial firms. In addition, most insurance stocks are traded over the counter. Therefore, an investigation of how some of the financial theories developed for and applied to industrial firms can be used to determine the dividend policy, the market equity value, and the cost of capital of this type of financial intermediary.

Cheng F. Lee is Professor of Finance at the University of Illinois, Urbana-Champaign. Professor Lee holds the Ph.D. degree from the State University of New York at Buffalo. He is an Associate Editor of the *Journal of Financial and Quantitative Analysis* and a member of the editorial board of the *Journal of Business Research*. He has published extensively with articles appearing in the *Journal of Finance*, the *Journal of Financial and Quantitative Analysis*, the *Review of Economics and Statistics*, and other scholarly journals.

Stephen W. Forbes was Associate Professor of Finance at the University of Illinois, Urbana-Champaign when this article was submitted. He is now Vice-President of the Life Office Management Association. Professor Forbes received his Ph.D. degree from the University of Pennsylvania, where he was an Heubner Fellow. He has published extensively in *The Journal of Risk and Insurance* and other scholarly journals.

The authors gratefully acknowledge the financial support of the S.S. Heubner Foundation for Insurance Education of the University of Pennsylvania. They also acknowledge the assistance of Mr. Dongsae Cho and the editorial comments of J. David Cummins.

In the next section of the paper, two methods are used to investigate the impact of dividend policy upon the market value of the equity of the non-life insurance firm. In the third section, Zellner's [20] seemingly unrelated regression [SUR] method is used to investigate the existence of time effect in testing the effectiveness of dividend policy. The SUR technique uses a generalized least squares method to recognize implicitly the possible impact of time upon cross-sectional estimates in terms of OLS estimators (see Section III for details on the methodology). In the fourth section, three methods are used to estimate the cost of capital in the non-life insurance industry. Finally, the results of the paper are summarized and some conclusions are indicated.

II. Dividend Policy and Equity Value

Two financial models are used to analyze the relationship between dividend policy and the market value of equity for the non-life insurance industry.

The first model involves the following equation:

$$P_{ti} = a + bR_{ti} + cD_{ti} \tag{1}$$

where,

P_{ti} = stock price per share for the ith firm in period t

D_{ti} = dividends per share for the ith firm in period t

R_{ti} = retained earnings per share for the ith firm in period t

Gordon [7, 8] has used the stock price valuation model to justify equation (1). Furthermore, he has discussed the potential usefulness of the relative magnitudes of the estimated b and c regression coefficients in (1) in testing the importance of dividends relative to retained earnings in the determination of equity value.

Friend and Puckett [5], Gordon [8] and others have carefully examined the possible problem associated with the model defined in equation (1). They have concluded that some potential misspecifications associated with this model exist. A misspecified model implies that the magnitude of the estimated regression coefficients cannot be used directly to make some comparisons. However, it can be used to perform null hypothesis tests.

Granger [9] also has used the dividend stream model and the dividend forecasting model proposed by Lintner [14, 16] to draw theoretical implications for equation (1). In addition, Granger has shown that the relative magnitude between the estimated b and c regression coefficients in (1) is an inappropriate index for determining the importance of dividends relative to retained earnings in determining equity value. Thus, the authors use only the t-values associated with both the estimated b's and estimated c's to investigate whether or not the split between retained earnings and dividends per share is important in determining the stock price.

Cross-sectional data associated with P_i, D_i, and R_i of non-life insurers are used to estimate the parameters of equation (1). Four income measures are used to determine D_i and R_i. These income measures are defined as (A)

420

earnings without the amortization of underwriting expenses and without the inclusion of unrealized capital gains and losses, (B) earnings without the amortization of underwriting expenses but with the inclusion of unrealized capital gains and losses, (C) earnings with the amortization of underwriting expenses but without the inclusion of unrealized capital gains and losses, and (D) earnings with the amortization of underwriting expenses and with the inclusion of unrealized capital gains and losses. Income measures C and D are theoretically superior because they match appropriate revenues and expenses. However, income measures A and C are empirically superior because they do not include the transitory component — the unrealized capital gain and loss factor. These results for the 21 years (1955-1975) are presented in Table 1. As some of the non-life insurers were acquired by other firms, the sample size does not remain the same over time. The sample size for each year is listed in Column 6 of Table 1. From the empirical results in Table 1, the relative importance of the dividends and retained earnings per share in determining equity value is found to vary through time. This variation may be due to the fact that the investment opportunities for non-life insurers and the investors' preferences for dividends relative to retained earnings changed over time. It is also of interest to observe that the estimated b's for 1964, 1966, 1969, 1973, and 1975 are significantly different from zero for one retained earnings definition but not for the others. A more detailed interpretation of the empirical results in Table 1 is explored in Section III. The negative coefficients of determination found for some income measures for 1969, 1974, and 1975 are due to the fact that the coefficients of determination have been adjusted for degrees of freedom. Thus, a negative adjusted coefficient of determination implies a very small nonadjusted coefficient of determination.

The second model used in this study is one developed by Bar-Yosef and Koldony [1]. This model, defined in equation (2), is applied to analyze non-life insurance company dividend policy.

$$\overline{r}_i = a_o + a_1 \beta_i + a_2 \left(\frac{\overline{D}_i}{E_i}\right) + \epsilon_i \qquad (2)$$

where,

$\overline{r}_i$ = average monthly rate of return for the ith firm for 21 years

β_i = the beta coefficient for the ith firm estimated from the capital asset pricing model using monthly data

$\left(\frac{\overline{D}_i}{E_i}\right)$ = the time-aggregated annual earnings payout ratio for 21 years.

The capital asset pricing model [CAPM], developed by Sharpe [19], Lintner [17], and Mossin [18], is defined in equation (3).

$$R_{jt} - R_{ft} = \alpha_j + \beta_j (R_{mt} - R_{ft}) + \epsilon_{jt} \qquad (3)$$

where,

R_{jt} = rate of return of ith firm's common stock in period t

R_{ft} = risk-free rate of return using monthly Treasury bill rates as a proxy

R_{mt} = market rate of return using Standard and Poor's index.

TABLE 1

EMPIRICAL RESULTS FOR CROSS-SECTIONAL
PRICE PER SHARE REGRESSIONS [EQ.(1)]
[1955-1975]

(1) Year		(2) Constant	(3) Retained Earnings Per Share	(4) Dividends Per Share	(5) $\overline{R}^2$	(6) Sample Size
1955	A[1]	26.668 (2.278)	1.67 (.46)	17.809 (2.729)	.257	21
	B[1]	27.471 (2.57)	1.889 (.947)	10.626 (1.011)	.283	
	C[1]	27.129 (2.348)	-.0719 (-.025)	18.768 (2.851)	.249	
	D[1]	26.746 (2.471)	1.258 (.641)	13.13 (1.227)	.265	
1956	A	16.163 (2.241)	1.4 (.832)	19.928 (4.691)	.528	23
	B	15.316 (2.106)	.209 (.184)	20.633 (4.747)	.513	
	C	15.276 (2.131)	1.214 (.631)	20.205 (4.747)	.521	
	D	15.173 (2.097)	.008 (.006)	20.855 (4.812)	.512	
1957	A	18.126 (2.595)	-.318 (-.247)	16.825 (4.026)	.375	25
	B	18.271 (2.609)	-.154 (-.182)	16.406 (3.358)	.374	
	C	18.17 (2.601)	-.303 (-.22)	16.900 (4.043)	.374	
	D	18.278 (2.606)	-.134 (-.156)	16.497 (3.438)	.374	
1958	A	17.531 (2.541)	.565 (.633)	19.036 (4.853)	.473	26
	B	18.574 (2.683)	.509 (.982)	15.239 (2.728)	.486	
	C	17.505 (2.549)	.659 (.774)	18.812 (4.787)	.478	
	D	18.615 (2.703)	.545 (1.072)	14.795 (2.627)	.49	
1959	A	25.653 (2.74)	2.369 (1.017)	16.561 (3.068)	.247	27
	B	28.043 (3.113)	3.083 (1.271)	9.685 (1.245)	.263	
	C	27.282 (2.906)	.833 (.384)	16.342 (2.886)	.22	
	D	28.304 (3.057)	1.453 (.591)	12.734 (1.432)	.227	

TABLE 1 (con't.)

Year		Constant	Retained Earnings Per Share	Dividends Per Share	$\overline{R}^2$	Sample Size
1960	A	16.33 (2.08)	4.143 (1.755)	18.307 (3.384)	.502	28
	B	16.618 (2.189)	4.413 (2.202)	18.116 (3.594)	.531	
	C	17.006 (2.195)	4.203 (2.023)	16.411 (2.898)	.519	
	D	16.437 (2.147)	3.372 (2.081)	17.892 (3.444)	.523	
1961	A	20.141 (2.121)	-.811 (-.604)	26.267 (4.754)	.429	29
	B	16.667 (1.781)	-.375 (-1.453)	31.911 (4.84)	.465	
	C	20.041 (2.101)	-.642 (-.442)	26.439 (4.764)	.425	
	D	16.65 (1.777)	-.379 (-1.44)	32.068 (4.8)	.464	
1962	A	14.678 (1.475)	-.38 (-.157)	31.395 (4.503)	.506	28
	B	14.923 (1.586)	-.452 (-.382)	29.78 (4.816)	.509	
	C	16.073 (1.684)	1.126 (.484)	28.965 (4.304)	.51	
	D	15.185 (1.614)	-.079 (-.062)	30.576 (4.831)	.506	
1963	A	38.902 (2.638)	11.366 (2.741)	12.461 (1.115)	.264	29
	B	50.868 (3.336)	5.79 (2.967)	-14.811 (-.909	.292	
	C	33.701 (2.235)	11.034 (2.463)	15.045 (1.342)	.231	
	D	48.369 (3.194)	5.874 (2.875)	-14.147 (-.858)	.281	
1964	A	7.617 (.602)	1.937 (.841)	40.946 (3.887)	.402	30
	B	9.906 (.912)	6.122 (3.145)	21.813 (1.971)	.551	
	C	10.419 (.846)	3.597 (1.678)	35.548 (3.308)	.444	
	D	11.97 (1.169)	6.262 (3.863)	16.958 (1.597)	.605	
1965	A	9.02 (.771)	8.324 (3.332)	28.629 (3.087)	.48	30
	B	1.897 (.161)	4.943 (3.037)	33.442 (3.629)	.453	
	C	7.958 (.653)	6.714 (2.827)	27.415 (2.762)	.433	
	D	2.103 (.173)	4.219 (2.704)	32.193 (3.365)	.422	

TABLE 1 (con't.)

Year		Constant	Retained Earnings Per Share	Dividends Per Share	$\overline{R}^2$	Sample Size
1966	A	9.956 (.688)	6.31 (2.054)	17.385 (1.149)	.36	28
	B	1.182 (.08)	.927 (.635)	40.98 (3.381)	.26	
	C	10.575 (.792)	8.24 (2.873)	11.125 (.79)	.435	
	D	.858 (.058)	1.318 (.911)	41.892 (3.481)	.273	
1967	A	3.331 (.365)	13.798 (6.558)	17.417 (2.305)	.717	28
	B	-1.124 (-.099)	6.14 (4.299)	16.17 (1.63)	.558	
	C	.339 (.041)	13.9 (7.497)	16.223 (2.341)	.763	
	D	-2.525 (-.228)	6.266 (4.603)	15.282 (1.586)	.584	
1968	A	8.79 (1.003)	14.269 (8.245)	11.87 (1.824)	.79	26
	B	-2.483 (-.25)	7.723 (7.037)	16.212 (2.277)	.737	
	C	6.393 (.768)	13.547 (8.828)	11.159 (1.801)	.811	
	D	-3.597 (-.375)	7.577 (7.416)	15.543 (2.258)	.755	
1969	A	21.043 (2.163)	19.168 (7.843)	-.285 (-.047)	.773	19
	B	26.168 (.985)	-3.141 (-.381)	9.661 (.706)	-.089	
	C	30.932 (2.711)	16.455 (6.256)	-16.519 (-2.032)	.681	
	D	29.87 (1.075)	-.997 (-.136)	9.715 (.563)	-.097	
1970	A	3.839 (.182)	16.306 (5.505)	9.229 (.498)	.663	18
	B	-4.056 (-.215)	14.667 (6.466)	16.645 (1.028)	.731	
	C	2.376 (.126)	14.986 (6.473)	5.176 (.31)	.732	
	D	-4.751 (-.28)	13.498 (7.431)	12.602 (.859)	.783	
1971	A	12.742 (.684)	15.357 (3.514)	-2.671 (-.147)	.4	19
	B	19.151 (.996)	9.518 (3.126)	-20.704 (-.938)	.336	
	C	8.063 (.436)	15.012 (3.703)	-1.275 (-.073)	.424	
	D	15.81 (.835)	9.664 (3.32)	-20.774 (-.976)	.367	

TABLE 1 (con't.)

Year		Constant	Retained Earnings Per Share	Dividends Per Share	$\bar{R}^2$	Sample Size
1972	A	-11.998 (-.607)	33.404 (6.45)	-18.724 (-.906)	.666	21
	B	12.938 (.511)	10.236 (3.851)	-3.639 (-.133)	.393	
	C	-14.862 (-.743)	31.461 (6.429)	-20.555 (-.99)	.664	
	D	10.655 (.426)	10.396 (4.009)	-5.037 (-.187)	.415	
1973	A	17.454 (.988)	10.438 (1.996)	-6.037 (-.338)	.095	20
	B	49.114 (2.366)	-9.464 (-1.685)	-45.617 (-1.36)	.043	
	C	15.022 (.85)	11.09 (2.153)	-8.131 (-.457)	.122	
	D	49.596 2.298	-9.034 (-1.569)	-42.168 (-1.257)	.025	
1974	A	18.903 (1.36)	.06 (.051)	3.234 (.238)	-.108	21
	B	22.921 (1.777)	-1.647 (-1.711)	-8.616 (-.601)	.029	
	C	18.71 (1.345)	.145 (.126)	3.315 (.244)	.047	
	D	22.934 (1.765)	-1.586 (-1.633)	-8.089 (-.561)	-.107	
1975	A	15.663 (1.214)	1.684 (.476)	4.218 (.313)	-.085	21
	B	12.711 (1.465)	8.162 (4.588)	-20.846 (-1.962)	.494	
	C	16.383 (1.307)	3.878 (1.026)	2.46 (.187)	-.038	
	D	10.822 (1.421)	8.868 (5.741)	-22.199 (-2.416)	.612	

[1]Income definitions (A), (B), (C), and (D) are found in the text.

This model can be used to estimate β_i in equation (2). The t-values associated with the a_2 regression coefficients in equation (2) then can be used to determine whether dividend policy affects the value of non-life insurance equity. The degree aggregation bias introduced by time-aggregated data is still an open question.

To estimate the empirical relationships in equation (2), monthly stock prices associated with the 34 firms were collected from New York Stock Exchange, American Stock Exchange, and over-the-counter trading records. Name of sample firms are identified in Table 2, Column 1. These data were adjusted for stock splits when the rates of return were calculated. The insurers were selected at random from the population of firms in *Best's Property Liability* (formerly *Best's Fire and Casualty*) *Insurance Reports* having a

TABLE 2

CAPM RESULTS FOR 34 NON-LIFE INSURERS

(1)	(2)	(3)	(4)
Name of firms	α_j	β_j	$\overline{R}^2$
1. Ohio Casualty	-.0370 (-1.2117)	.9008 (10.9193)	.32108
2. Government Employees	.01162 (1.5993)	1.10367 (20.8164)	.6336
3. Peerless	-1.4310 (-1.0020)	920974 (8.8381)	.2357
4. Employers Casualty	-.01705 (-2.3289)	.8979 (16.8137)	.5298
5. Hanover	-.00665 (-.21840)	.97981 (4.4044)	.0685
6. American Reinsurance	.00008 (.01390)	1.01186 (22.27882)	.66459
7. General Reinsurance Corporation	-.00324 (-.50865)	.96390 (20.73732)	.63183
8. Hartford Steam Boiler Inspection & Ins. Company	-.00945 (-1.14279)	.93706 (15.53732)	.49022
9. Northeastern Insurance Company of Hartford	-.00756 (-.64796)	.94324 (11.08314)	.32766
10. Limited State Fidelity and Guaranty	-.010831 (-2.3517)	.92272 (27.4544)	.7506
11. Western Casualty and Security	-.00489 (-.77861)	.96588 (21.0776)	.63939
12. INA	-.00573 (-.48697)	.95994 (7.05849)	.37320
13. Continental Insurance	-.01690 (-1.6245)	.81461 (4.76874)	.35339
14. Providence Washington	-.00899 (-1.01844)	.93329 (11.66852)	.4415
15. National Casualty	-.02164 (-1.5960)	.63575 (3.36616)	.34061
16. American General	.00364 (.27921)	1.04741 (12.12186)	.44367
17. American Banker	.005064 (.24745)	1.05495 (8.66406)	.36118
18. Excelsior	-.00847 (-1.27783)	.93629 (18.4566)	.5962
19. American Insurance	-.01776 (-1.5583)	.85299 (6.56839)	.20072
20. Cincinnati Insurance	-.05523 (-1.0853)	.58827 (1.59720)	.02331
21. Eagle Insurance	-.01142 (-1.80376)	.90504 (16.5585)	.60548
22. Fidelity and Deposit Comp. of Maryland	-.04294 (-5.61351)	.54486 (6.70682)	.25279
23. Firemen's Insurance of Washington, D.C.	-.00898 (-.97779)	.90359 (8.50678)	.46533

426

TABLE 2 (con't.)

Name of firms	α_j	β_j	$\bar{R}^2$
24. Germantown Insurance	−.016446 (−2.76785)	.86277 (17.50472)	.59511
25. Harbor	−.04347 (−1.78517)	.632165 (3.24843)	.11165
26. Interstate Fire and Casualty	−.020696 (−1.3388)	.820319 (6.77994)	.27258
27. Phoenix Insurance Company	−.01005 (−1.10792)	.93025 (10.09309)	.42228
28. Reinsurance Company of New York	−.012833 (−2.03977)	.88139 (14.85714)	.57562
29. Republic Insurance	−.00771 (−1.28416)	.95883 (18.33521)	.65442
30. Trinity Universal	−.019852 (−2.38160)	.852098 (11.36800)	.42711
31. United Fire Insurance	−.00987 (−.34752)	.98921 (6.33789)	.33429
32. Aetna Casualty and Surety	−.02620 (−3.4385)	.70124 (8.9312)	.38467
33. Federal	−.058592 (−10.82971)	.39363 (8.65567)	.32576
34. Westchester Fire	−.06815 (−7.36746)	.32933 (4.20722)	.099
Average β_j		.85356	

complete series of 1955-75 financial data. The stock price data were taken from the *Bank Quotation Record.*

As the first stage, the betas for equation (2) are estimated by using the CAPM as indicated by equation (3). The beta coefficients associated with these 34 firms are listed in Table 2, Column 2. Most of the estimated α_j's are negative. The implications of these results are explored in Section IV.

The results for equation (2) are shown in Table 3 for the four income measures as discussed in this section. The t-values associated with the a_2 coefficients provide an indication of the significance of dividend policy in determining the average monthly rates of return for the period. Table 3 shows that dividend policy was important in determining stock price behavior when using income measures B and D. These results are important because income measures B and D include unrealized capital gains and losses whereas income measures A and C do not include these gains and losses. Foster [4] has argued that the stock market considers unrealized capital gains and losses in pricing non-life insurance equity shares. He used an econometric valuation model in arriving at this conclusion. If one accepts his conclusion, then dividend policies are relevant in determining non-life insurance company equity values.

The findings of this section follow Bar-Yosef-Koldony [1] but differ from Black-Scholes [2]. The authors' results cannot be compared directly with the Black-Scholes results for the following reasons: (1) they use time series instead of cross-sectional data, and (2) they use stock portfolios instead of individual stocks. Blume [3] has reexamined the Black-Scholes results and

TABLE 3

REGRESSION RESULTS FOR (2) FOR AGGREGATE FIRMS

(1) Income Definition	Regression Coefficients		
	(2) a_0	(3) a_1	(4) a_2
A'	.965 (26.47)	.048 (1.16)	-.00004 (-.10)
B	.935 (28.51)	.039 (1.07)	.0608 (3.25)
C	.946 (23.69)	.049 (1.21)	.034 (1.06)
D	.937 (26.47)	.045 (1.17)	.056 (2.41)

'See text for definitions.

has reached a different conclusion regarding the impact of dividend policy and equity value. The present authors believe that cross-sectional modeling using individual securities is superior to time series modeling using securities portfolios.

III. Seemingly Unrelated Regression (SUR) and Aggregate Behavior for Shareholder Dividends

A pooled time series and cross-sectional simultaneous equation model is constructed using the following extensions of equation (1):

$$P_{11} = a_1 + b_1 D_{11} + C_1 R_{11} + \varepsilon_{11}$$
$$P_{12} = a_2 + b_2 D_{12} + C_2 R_{12} + \varepsilon_{12}$$
$$\begin{matrix} \bullet & \bullet & \bullet & \bullet \\ \bullet & \bullet & \bullet & \bullet \\ \bullet & \bullet & \bullet & \bullet \end{matrix} \qquad (4)$$
$$P_{in} = a_n + b_n D_{in} + C_n R_{in} + \varepsilon_{in}$$

where the equations are generated for each year and the subscript i refers to each of the insurers studied. The notation ε_{i1} represents the error terms in the tth period $(t = 1, 2, \ldots n)$. Zellner's [20] seemingly unrelated regression method is used to estimate these equation systems simultaneously. The strength of this method is in its ability to consider the time effect of dividend policy.

The SUR technique attempts to take into account the lead and lag effect of common stock price determination. Technically, one can perform SUR simultaneously for 21 years if a large enough number of observations exists. The authors did not have enough observations to provide the necessary degrees of freedom for estimating the variance-covariance matrix. Therefore, they divided the periods studied into 1955-64 and 1965-75. These periods were chosen because they were considered economically dissimilar. A residual correlation coefficient matrix was calculated for each group by using the ordinary least squares [OLS] residuals. Each matrix indicates that some relationship exists among the residuals over time. Therefore, the SUR technique generally can be used to increase the efficiency of estimators.

The t-values for income measurement (A) for the regression coefficients for the OLS and SUR techniques are presented in Table 4, Columns 3-5. The majority of the t-values in Table 4 are higher for the same regression coefficient using SUR rather than OLS.[1] Thus, the SUR technique appears to do a better job estimating the regression coefficients.

IV. Cost of Equity Capital of a Non-Life Insurer

The cost of capital for a mercantile or manufacturing firm may involve the (1) cost of debt, (2) cost of preferred stock, (3) cost of retained earnings, or (4) cost of a new issue of common stock. Items (3) and (4), when combined, are called the cost of equity. Launie [13] has tried to find cost of capital counterparts for insurance companies. Haugen and Kroncke [10] have investigated the relationship between the cost of capital and rate regulation in the insurance industry. While policyholder reserves may be viewed as a source of investable funds for the non-life insurance industry, assigning an explicit cost to these funds is debatable. Policyholder funds are not considered in this study.

Many ways are available to measure the cost of equity capital. In the present study, the authors examine three widely accepted ones: (1) the earning yield method [15], (2) Gordon's method [7, 8], and (3) the capital asset pricing model method.

The cost of capital of a non-life insurance company may be viewed as an opportunity cost involving the investment of shareholder funds in the insurer rather than an alternative investment of similar financial risk. This point of view follows the earning yield equation expressed as

$$k = \frac{E}{P} \tag{5}$$

where,

k = cost of capital

E = earnings available to shareholders

P = market price of outstanding common stock

The capital market adjusts this yield ratio in order to bring it into line with other investments of similar financial risk. The average yields in this study for

---

[1] SUR technique also has improved the estimates based upon other income measures.

TABLE 4

REGRESSION T-VALUES FOR CROSS-SECTIONAL RESULTS
FOR EQUATION (1) - INCOME MEASUREMENT (A)

(1) Year	(2)	(3) a_1	Regression Coefficients (4) b_1	(5) c_1
1955	OLS[1]	2.278	.46	2.729
	(SUR)[2]	(2.880)	(.303)	(2.509)
1956	OLS	2.241	.832	4.691
	(SUR)	(1.442)	(1.601)	(17.986)
1957	OLS	2.595	-.247	4.026
	(SUR)	(2.850)	(-.431)	(4.121)
1958	OLS	2.541	.633	4.853
	(SUR)	(3.609)	(1.454)	(3.270)
1959	OLS	2.74	1.017	3.068
	(SUR)	(1.133)	(2.094)	(11.336)
1960	OLS	2.08	1.755	3.384
	(SUR)	(1.347)	(1.016)	(6.907)
1961	OLS	2.121	-.604	4.754
	(SUR)	(1.819)	(-3.519)	(12.516)
1962	OLS	1.475	-.157	4.503
	(SUR)	(1.304)	(1.364)	(8.956)
1963	OLS	2.638	2.741	1.115
	(SUR)	(2.700)	(5.906)	(.544)
1964	OLS	.602	.841	3.887
	(SUR)	(.387)	(-.409)	(6.231)
1965	OLS	.771	3.332	3.087
	(SUR)	(1.095)	(6.090)	(1.617)
1966	OLS	.688	2.054	1.149
	(SUR)	(1.074)	(3.260)	(.089)
1967	OLS	.365	6.558	2.305
	(SUR)	(.301)	(8.467)	(3.005)
1968	OLS	1.003	8.245	1.824
	(SUR)	(.881)	(16.721)	(1.016)
1969	OLS	2.163	7.843	-.047
	(SUR)	(2.477)	(8.835)	(-.457)
1970	OLS	.182	5.505	.498
	(SUR)	(-.956)	(7.281)	(2.716)
1971	OLS	.684	3.514	-.147
	(SUR)	(1.017)	(4.659)	(-.158)
1972	OLS	-.607	6.45	-.906
	(SUR)	(-.376)	(8.403)	(-1.332)
1973	OLS	.988	1.996	-.338
	(SUR)	(.934)	(4.245)	(-.469)
1974	OLS	1.36	.051	.238
	(SUR)	(.482)	(-.098)	(2.322)
1975	OLS	1.214	.476	.313
	(SUR)	(.619)	(.705)	(1.323)

[1] Ordinary least squares regression.

[2] Seemingly unrelated regression.

430

income measures A, B, C, and D are 6.58, 6.51, 7.49, and 7.36 percent, respectively. The selective taking of realized capital gains and the arbitrary adjustment of loss and loss-adjustment expense reserves may distort the reported earnings in a given year; the investor in non-life insurance company equity may adjust the reported earnings in light of his or her awareness of these accounting manipulations. This adjustment may affect the precision of the yield ratio in equation (5) as a cost of capital measure.

The definition of insurer income also is potently important to this cost of capital definition. Foster [4] found that the capital market considers an insurer's realized and unrealized capital gains and losses in pricing its equity shares. It follows that the insurer's income should include these gains and losses in determining its cost of capital. The other question is whether the GAAP (generally accepted accounting principle) or the statutory basis of measuring underwriting results is appropriate for the determination of earnings. GAAP underwriting earnings are assumed to be the most relevant as they are reported to the shareholder and thus govern his or her investment decision.

Another point of view holds that the cost of capital is a function of the current dividend yield (dividends to shareholders divided by the price per common share) and an estimate of the future growth of dividends. In this model, retained earnings and dividends are viewed as financing substitutes. The model takes the following form:

$$P = \frac{d_o}{k - g} \tag{6}$$

where,

P = price per share of common stock

g = br, the growth rate of dividend payment

b = earnings retention rate = $1 -$ earnings payout ratio

r = internal rate of return

k = investor's required rate of return

d_o = dividend per share for current period

Equation (6) implies that a company's market price per share generally is determined by its dividend per share and required rate of return.

To use Gordon's model to estimate the cost of equity capital, both the dividend yield and the estimated growth rate of shareholder dividends are required. The dividend yield of non-life insurer equity is shown in Table 5. The F value of Table 5 indicates that the differences of the average dividend yield among different time periods are statistically significant.

Table 6 presents the continuous compound percentage growth rates in shareholder dividends for the insurers studied. The model used to calculate these growth rates is defined as follows:

$$\log D_{it} = A_0 + A_1 n_{it} + E_{it} \tag{7}$$

where,

D_{it} = total shareholder dividend for ith company in period t

n_{it} = number of years over which shareholder dividend growth is compounded

E_{it} = error term

A_0 = intercept

A_1 = growth rate estimator

Columns 3 and 4 in Table 6 show a frequency distribution of the shareholder dividend growth rates using a three-year moving average as the measurement base. The overall average growth rate under this method is 9.74 percent.

Columns 5 and 6 in Table 6 portray a frequency distribution of the dividend growth rates without using a moving average. The overall average growth rate under this method is 9.20 pecent, which is close to the results obtained under the moving average technique.

TABLE 5

NON-LIFE INSURER DIVIDEND YIELDS

(1) Year	(2) Annual Average Dividend Yield (%)	(3) Sample Size
1955	2.90%	22
1956	3.37	23
1957	3.63	25
1958	3.38	26
1959	3.04	28
1960	3.58	28
1961	2.79	29
1962	2.70	28
1963	2.36	29
1964	2.48	30
1965	3.14	30
1966	3.14	28
1967	3.43	28
1968	3.30	26
1969	4.40	19
1970	4.27	18
1971	2.90	19
1972	2.72	21
1973	3.68	20
1974	5.57	21
1975	6.03	20

Overall
Average   3.38%

F-test results for average dividend yields among years 1955-75,
F = 5.3006 (significant at 1 percent level).

TABLE 6

Shareholder Dividend Growth Rates

(1) Continuous Compounded Percentage Growth Rate		(2) Growth Rate With Moving Average		(3) Growth Rate Without Moving Average	
At Least	And Less Than	# of Insurers	% of Total	# of Insurers	% of Total
	0	9	14.8%	10	16.4%
0	6	12	19.7	11	18.0
6	12	22	36.1	26	42.6
12	18	8	13.1	9	14.8
18	24	4	6.6	1	1.6
24	30	2	3.3	2	3.3
30	36	3	4.9	2	3.3
36	42	1	1.6	0	0
Total		61	100.1[a]%	61	100.0%

[a]Total exceeds 100 percent due to rounding.

The overall average shareholder dividend yield in Table 5 is 3.38 percent. The addition of the authors' growth rate estimate to this yield results in a non-life insurance cost of capital estimate of approximately 12 percent over 1955-75.

A third approach to measuring the cost of equity capital of non-life insurer is offered by the following equation:

$$E(R_{jt}) = E(R_{ft}) + \beta_j [E(R_{mt}) - E(R_{ft})] \tag{8}$$

where,

E = expectation operator and the other variables are defined as in equation (3).

In order to estimate the cost of capital from equation (8), one needs to estimate $E(R_{ft})$, $E(R_{mt})$, and β. The average annual Treasury Bill rate of 5.28 percent for the period 1955-75 can be used as the proxy for a risk-free rate. The betas for the 34 insurers studied can be taken from Column 3 of Table 2. The average beta was .85356.

The cost of capital estimate in equation (8) is dependent upon the assumption regarding the expected market rate of return. If $E(R_{mt})$ is assumed to equal 10 percent, then an average cost of capital of 9.308 percent is obtained for the non-life insurers studied.

The results of equation 3 are analyzed in light of Jensen's investment performance measure α_j[2] from the second column in Table 2, and most of the estimated α_j's are found to be negative. This finding implies that the performances of non-life insurance equity shares have not been superior to the market average.

---

[2] Jensen's performance measure, one of several investment performance measures, can be used to measure the performance of either individual securities or portfolios. See Jensen [12].

In conclusion, the earnings yield method appears to be too difficult to apply as a cost of capital estimator for non-life insurance companies because of (1) widely fluctuating earnings and (2) the presence of negative earnings. The Gordon model, on the other hand, can be applied more successfully in estimating the non-life insurance cost of capital because shareholder dividends are more stable over time than earnings. Therefore, the authors had some success in using this model. The CAPM approach also provides some insight into the cost of capital in the non-life insurance industry. Theoretically the CAPM model provides the best measure of the cost of capital; however, as a practical matter the expected excess market rate of return is difficult to determine objectively. The difference between the dividend growth model and CAPM cost of capital estimates can be attributed to the problem of achieving objectivity with this latter measure.

V. Summary and Concluding Remarks

The share price determination model and the modified security market line model were used to study the impact of shareholder dividend policy upon the market value of non-life insurance equity for the four income definitions.

From 1955-68, shareholder dividends were found to have significant impacts upon non-life insurance equity values when the share determination model was used. However, the results were mixed for 1969-75. In years of high stock market volatility the impact of dividend policy upon equity value was masked by other influences (e.g., unrealized capital gains and losses and inflation).

The security market line model was different from the share price determination model in that the former was a temporal regression run for the combined sample of insurers whereas the latter was a cross-sectional year-by-year model. The authors found that shareholder dividends significantly influenced equity value for income measures including unrealized capital gains and losses in the security market line model. This finding is not entirely consistent with the results of the cross-sectional model because the latter is static whereas the former is dynamic.

When the OLS residuals among the firms within the group are correlated, the SUR is superior to the OLS regression method. The authors found that the SUR technique was superior to the OLS in investigating the cross-sectional relationship among stock price per share, dividend per share, and retained earnings per share.

Three widely accepted cost of capital models were applied to the sample insurers. Theoretically both the earnings yield model and CAPM model are superior to Gordon's model in estimating the cost of capital. However, the earnings yield model presented problems because of some negative and widely fluctuating non-life insurer incomes. The CAPM requires a good estimate of the expected market rate of return, which limits its usefulness. For these reasons, the cost of capital analysis in this paper concentrated on Gordon's model. The overall estimate of the cost of non-life insurer equity capital was approximately 12 percent for this model during 1955-75.

As a by-product of this research, empirical CAPM results produced Jensen performance measure information for 34 non-life insurers with monthly stock price information. It was found that 88 percent of the Jensen measures were moderately negative over 1955-75. This result implies that the common stocks of non-life insurers did not out-perform the overall market during this period.

References

1. Bar-Yosef, S. and R. Koldony. "Dividend Policy and Capital Market Theory," *Review of Economics and Statistics* (May 1976), pp. 181-190.

2. Black, F. and Scholes, M. "The Effects of Dividend Yield and Dividend Policy On Common Stock Prices and Returns," *Journal of Financial Economics*, 1 (May 1974), pp. 1-22.

3. Blume, M. E. "Some Further Evidence On Dividend Yield," Rodney L. White Center For Financial Research, University of Pennsylvania (February 1978).

4. Foster, F. "Valuation Parameters of Property-Liability Companies," *The Journal of Finance* (June 1977), pp. 823-35.

5. Friend, I. and M. Puckett. "Dividends, Earnings and Stock Prices," *American Economic Review*, 54 (September 1964), pp. 656-681.

6. Gordon, M. J. "A General Solution to the Buy or Lease Decision: A Redagogical Rate," *Journal of Finance*, 29 (September 1974), pp. 243-250.

7. _____. "Optimal Investment and Financing Policy," *Journal of Finance*, 18 (May 1963), pp. 264-272.

8. _____. "Dividends, Earnings, and Stock Prices," *Review of Economics and Statistics* (1959), pp. 99-105.

9. Granger, C. W. J. "Some Consequences of the Valuation Model When Expectations are Taken to be Optimum Forecasts," *The Journal of Finance*, (March 1975), pp. 135-45.

10. Haugen, R. A. and Kroncke, C. O. "Rate Regulation and the Cost of Capital in the Insurance Industry," *Journal of Financial and Quantitative Analysis* (December 1971), pp. 1283-1305.

11. Henderson, G. V. "In Defense of the Weighted Average Cost of Capital," *Financial Management*, 8 (Fall 1979), pp. 57-61.

12. Jensen, M. "The Performance of Mutual Funds in the Period 1954-1964," *Journal of Finance*, 23 (1968), pp. 389-416.

13. Launie, J. J. "The Cost of Capital of Insurance Companies," *The Journal of Risk and Insurance* (June 1971), pp. 263-68.

14. Lintner, J. "Distribution of Incomes Among Dividends, Retained Earnings and Taxes," *American Economic Review* (May 1956), pp. 97-113.

15. _____. "The Cost of Capital and the Optimal Financing of Corporate Growth," *The Journal of Finance*, 18 (May 1963), pp. 292-310.

16. _____. "The Determination of Corporate Savings," in *Savings in the Modern Economy*, edited by W. W. Heller (Minneapolis: University of Minnesota Press, 1963), pp. 230-55.

17. _____. "The Valuation of Risk Assets and the Selection of Risky Investments in Stock Portfolios and Capital Budgets," *The Review of Economics and Statistics* (February 1965), pp. 13-37.

18. Mossin, J. "Equilibrium in a Capital Asset Market," *Econometrica* (1966), pp. 768-783.

19. Sharpe, W. F. "Capital Asset Prices: A Theory of Market Equilibrium Under Conditions of Risk," *The Journal of Finance* (1964), pp. 425-42.

20. Zellner, A. "An Efficient Method of Estimating Seemingly Unrelated Regressions and Tests for Aggregation Bias," *J. of American Statist. Assn.* (1962), pp. 57, 348-68.

FUNCTIONAL FORM AND THE DIVIDEND EFFECT IN THE ELECTRIC UTILITY INDUSTRY

CHENG F. LEE*

GORDON [5], DURAND [3], AND OTHERS have employed either linear or logarithmic linear relationships between prices and both dividends and retained earnings to explain price variations in cross-section samples of companies drawn from a particular industry. They have concluded that the divident multiplier in general is several times the retained earning multiplier. However, Friend and Puckett [4] have detected the existence of possible specification biases in previous studies of the importance of the divident effect relative to the retained earning effect.[1] For the electric utility industry, they found that evidences of the relative importance between the dividend effect and the retained earning effect are not independent of the functional forms—linear and logarithmic—being employed to test the relationship among the price, dividends, and the retained earnings. They concluded that it is not possible to choose conclusively between the linear and the logarithmic results on statistical or *a priori* grounds. In addition, they concluded that the linearity assumption employed by them and others is relatively restrictive.

The main purpose of this paper is to determine the most appropriate functional form for investigating the dividend effect of the electricity industry in accordance with the generalized functional form (GFF) developed by Box and Cox [1]. Both linear and logarithmic functional forms are treated as a special case of the GFF. The GFF allows us to choose conclusively between the linear and the logarithmic results of the dividend effect wholly on statistical grounds. It also allows testing whether a nonlinear instead of a linear functional form should be used to investigate the dividend effect in the electric utility industry. In the first section, models are developed to test the dividend effect. The procedure employed to estimate the functional form parameter also is specified. In the second section, 116 electric utility companies from the Compustat are employed to investigate the importance of the dividend effect relative to the retained earning effect on the basis of the GFF. Logarithmic results are shown to be statistically more suitable for investigating the dividend effect. In addition, the nonlinear instead of the logarithmic linear functional form is found more suitable for investigating dividend effect. Furthermore, some implications of different functional forms in investigating the dividend effect are discussed. The last section provides a summary and concluding remarks.

I. THE MODEL

Following Box and Cox [1] and Zarembka [6], a generalized deterministic relationship between the stock price, dividends and retained earning is defined as

$$P_{ti}^{\lambda} = l_0 + l_1 D_{ti}^{\lambda} + l_2 R_{tt}^{\lambda} \tag{1}$$

* Associate Professor of Finance, The University of Illinois at Urbana-Champaign. The author thanks Robert R. Dince, and a referee of this *Journal*, Richard E. Quandt, for his helpful comments.
1. Their study covered chemical, electronic, electric utility, food and steel industries.

where P_{ti}, D_{ti}, and R_{ti} represent per share price, dividend, and retained of ith company earnings in the tth period respectively. λ is the functional form parameter to be estimated. Equation (1) will become a linear form when λ is equal to one; equation (1) will reduce to a logarithmic linear form when λ approaches zero.[2] In other words, equation (1) includes both the linear and the logarithmic form as a special case and provides a generalized functional form (GFF) for testing the dividend effect. In order for equation (1) to be continuous at $\lambda = 0$ and stochastic, it should be rewritten as

$$P_{ti}^{(\lambda)} = l_0' + l_1 D_{ti}^{(\lambda)} + l_2 R_{ti}^{(\lambda)} + \tau_{ti} \tag{2A}$$

where

$$P_{ti}^{(\lambda)} = \frac{P_{tt}^{\lambda} - 1}{\lambda}, \qquad D_{ti}^{(\lambda)} = \frac{D_{ti}^{\lambda} - 1}{\lambda},$$

$$R_{ti}^{(\lambda)} = \frac{R_{ti}^{\lambda} - 1}{\lambda}, \qquad l_0' = \frac{(l_0 + l_1 + l_2) - 1}{\lambda} \tag{2B}$$

and

$$\tau_{ti} \sim N\left(0, \sigma_{\tau}^2\right)$$

Using the maximum likelihood method, Box and Cox [1] derived a maximum logarithmic likelihood for determining the functional form parameter as

$$L \max (\hat{\lambda}) = -n \log \hat{\sigma}_{\tau}(\lambda) + (\lambda - 1) \sum_{i=1}^{n} \log P_{ti} \tag{3}$$

where n is the sample size, and $\hat{\sigma}_{\tau}(\lambda)$ is the estimated regression residual standard error of equation (2A). After the $\hat{\sigma}_{\tau}(\lambda)$ being estimated equation (3) is employed to determine the optimum value of the functional form parameter, λ. The optimum value of λ is obtained by plotting equation (3) for different values of λ to arrive at the maximized logarithmic likelihood over the whole parameter space. Using the likelihood ratio method, an approximate 95% confidence region for λ can be obtained from

$$L \max (\hat{\lambda}) - L \max (\lambda) < \tfrac{1}{2}\chi_1^2(.05) = 1.92 \tag{4}$$

The 95% confidence region for λ subsequently is used to determine the true functional form in investigating the divident effect.

II. Functional Form and the Dividend Effect

Some 116 electric utility companies are used to investigate the divident effect relative to the retained earnings effect. For determining the true functional form

2. Zarembka [6] has employed the generalized functional form technique to determine the true functional for money demand. The proof of this statement can also be found in his paper.

parameter, P_t, D_t and R_t are transformed in accordance with equation (2B) by λ's between -0.1 and 1.0 at intervals of length 0.1. Twelve different regressions are estimated for each year in accordance with the procedure described above.[3] The L max(λ) for 1960 is calculated using equation (3) and plotted in Figure I. Vertical lines are drawn to indicate the approximate 95% confidence region. Note that λ for 1960 is about .55 and is significantly different from both the linear ($\lambda = 1$) and logarithmic ($\lambda = 0$) forms. Following the similar procedure employed for 1960, the maximum likelihood estimates of λ for the period during 1961–1969 are estimated. The maximum likelihood estimates of λ and their confidence regions for ten sample years are given in Table 1. All the true functional forms in investigating the

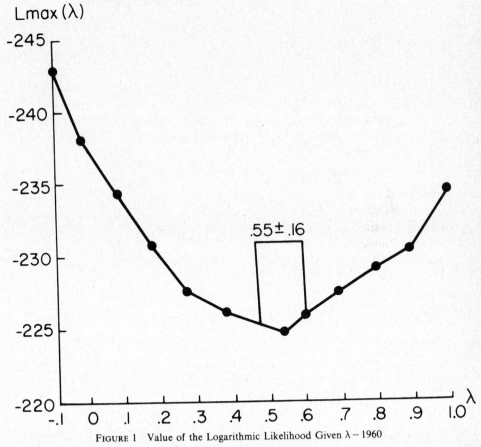

FIGURE 1   Value of the Logarithmic Likelihood Given $\lambda - 1960$

3. Since a company with negative retained earning is not included in the regression, therefore, the sample size is 110, 114, 115, 115, 115, 116, 116, 116, 116 and 116 for 1960, 1961, 1962, 1963, 1964, 1965, 1966, 1967, 1968 and 1969 respectively.

TABLE 1

THE MAXIMUM LIKELIHOOD ESTIMATES OF λ AND THEIR RELATED REGRESSION PARAMETERS

Years	$\hat{\lambda}$	95% Confidence Region for $\hat{\lambda}$	l_1	l_2
1960	.55	$.55 \mp .16$	2.85986	3.63352
1961	.55	$.55 \mp .01$	3.66002	4.13767
1962	.25	$.25 \mp .25$	1.11466	1.11100
1963	.35	$.35 \mp .30$	1.58914	1.63041
1964	.45	$.45 \mp .41$	2.32391	2.56805
1965	.35	$.35 \mp .29$	1.68970	1.70573
1966	.35	$.35 \mp .32$	1.61676	1.31104
1967	.05	$.05 \mp .10$	.66763	.34821
1968	.05	$.05 \mp .12$	.69266	.32054
1969	$-.10$	$-.10 \mp .18$	.42596	.17736

dividend effect for these ten sample years are all significantly different from the simple linear form. In addition, the true functional forms for 1960, 1961, 1963, 1964, 1965 and 1966 are also significantly different from the logarithmic linear form.

The regression coefficients associated with different λ's are employed to analyze the relationship between the functional form and the dividend effect. From the results of linear ($\lambda = 1$) form, the retained earning effect is stronger than the dividend effect for nine sample years; from the results of logarithmic linear ($\lambda = 0$) form, the dividend effect is stronger than the retained earning effect for all ten sample years. These inconsistent results are essentially identical to those found by Friend and Puckett [4]. However, if results from the true functional form are used to make comparisons, the dividend effect is almost identical to the retained earning effect for the years 1961, 1962, 1963, 1964, 1965 and 1966, and the dividend effect is different from the retained earning effect for the years 1960, 1967, 1968 and 1969 [See Table 2]. In sum, *a priori* (and arbitrary) choice of λ (e.g., one or zero) not only can lead to misspecification of the functional form but also can lead to an incorrect

TABLE 2

ANNUAL AVERAGED DIVIDEND AND RETAINED EARNING PDR SHARE DURING 1960–1969

Years	Averaged Dividend Per Share	Averaged Retained Earning Per Share
1960	1.47309	.75790
1961	1.43855	.69721
1962	1.31281	.68399
1963	1.24488	.62380
1964	1.22491	.65021
1965	1.21557	.65808
1966	1.23268	.68144
1967	1.29834	.69983
1968	1.33792	.64716
1969	1.37976	.70324

conclusion about the importance of dividend effects relative to the retained earning effects.

The main disadvantage of employing the simple linear regression to investigate the dividend effect is that the regression coefficients are not always free from the scale effect.[4] If the pay-out ratio is higher than the retention rate for most of the companies in a particular industry, then the coefficient of the dividend variable will be generally smaller than that of the retained earning variable. From Table 2, it can be shown that the averaged retention rate is about 1/2 of the average pay-out ratio for every sample year, therefore, the lower dividend effect, relative to the retained earning effect, may essentially be due to the scale effect of regression analysis. Similarly, if an industry's average retention rate is much higher than its pay-out ratio, then the scale effect may be so strong as to lead us to mistakenly conclude that the dividend effect is stronger than the retained earning effect.

The main advantage of the logarithmic relation is to reduce the problem of regression weights even though it fails to take care of negative retained earnings.[5] If the relation used to investigate the dividend effect for any year is significantly different from both the linear and the logarithmic relations, then one cannot separate the effects of the dividend on the stock price from those of the retained earning because the relation used to investigate the dividend effect is no longer linear in parameter. Hence, equation (1) is rewritten as

$$P_{ti} = \left[l_0 + l_1 D_{ti}^{\lambda} + l_2 R_{ti}^{\lambda} \right]^{1/\lambda} \tag{5}$$

Equation (5) implies that effects of the dividend and the retained earning on the stock price are interrelated. This specification is indeed consistent with the theoretical relationship between the dividend and the retained earning. For the GFF of (5), the statistical tests here have entirely rejected the linear ($\lambda = 1$) relation for all ten sample years being used in this paper. These findings imply that the traditional cross-section investigations of the dividend effect in the electric utility industry have failed to employ a correct functional form. Thus conclusions for the importance of the dividend effect relative to the retained earning effect are subject to specification bias. The functional form analysis of this paper is not identical to that of Friend and Puckett since the purposes of their studies are to investigate the effects of omitting variables on the regression coefficients while the main purpose of this study is to determine the true functional form which they have regarded as an open question.

III. Summary and Concluding Remarks

A generalized functional form is developed here in order to determine the relationship among the stock price, dividends and retained earnings. The linear form (sometimes even the logarithmic linear form) is not a correct functional form for

---

4. However, the linear regression can handle satisfactorily very small and negative retained earnings.

5. See Friend and Puckett [4, p. 672] for details. Draper and Cox [2] have shown that the failure of permitting the negative real value in power transformation does not reduce the usefulness of GFF.

investigating the dividend effect of the electric utility industry. Moreover, the dividend effect is not significantly different from the retained earning effect for 60% of the cross-section results after the true functional relationship has been determined. Essentially, the GFF explicitly takes the interrelation between dividends and retained earnings into account; the functional form parameter also reflects the different relationship among the stock price, dividends and retained earnings under different economic conditions.[6] In sum, it has been established that the previous studies of determining the dividend effect of the electric utility industry may have pre-judged an important issue—the correct functional form. While linear and logarithmic forms are easy to handle, this consideration alone is not enough to justify employment of either of these forms. In fact, it has been shown that there exists a generalized functional form which allows a compact analysis of the effects of choice of functional form on determining the dividend effect of the electric utility industry.

REFERENCES

1. G. E. P. Box and D. R. Cox. "An Analysis of Transformations," *Journal of the Royal Statistical Society, Series B*, 26, (1964), pp. 211–243.
2. N. R. Draper and D. R. Cox. "On Distributions and Their Transformation to Normality," *Journal of the Royal Statistical Society, Series B*, 31, (1969), pp. 472–476.
4. D. Durand "The Cost of Capital, Corporation Finance, and the Theory of Investment: Comment," *American Economic Review*, 49, (1959), pp. 639–654.
4. I. Friend and M. Puckett. "Dividends and Stock Prices," *American Economic Review*, 54, (1964), pp. 656–681.
5. J. J. Gordon. "Dividends, Earnings and Stock Prices," *Review of Economic and Statistics*, 41, (1959), pp. 99–105.
6. P. Zarembka. "Functional Form in the Demand for Money," *Journal of American Statistical Association*, 63, (1968), pp. 502–511.

6. This remark is based upon the classification of estimated λ's (See Table 1). For reflecting the impact of economic conditions on the dividend effect, Friend and Puckett [4] employed the data from 1956 and 1958 to represent a bear market and a bull market respectively. However, they could not find any evidence to support their assumption.

INFLATION ACCOUNTING AND CORPORATE DIVIDENDS

Rather than considering current cost income as an indicator of maximum affordable dividends, enlightened corporate policy should be conditioned by the interplay of planned growth, investment and financing.

ALFRED RAPPAPORT
Leonard Spacek Professor of
Accounting and Information Systems
Northwestern University

Inflation-adjusted income statements appeared for the first time in the 1979 annual reports of over 1,000 large public companies subject to the new Financial Accounting Standards Board (FASB) disclosure requirements. Since no meaningful consensus was achieved on the best approach to inflation accounting, the FASB mandated that during the current experimental period companies provide supplementary information using two fundamentally different methods for calculating income from continuing operations: constant dollar and current cost accounting. The constant dollar method adjusts traditional historical cost results for changes in the purchasing power of the dollar as measured by the Consumer Price Index for All Urban Consumers. Under the current cost method, results are restated for changes in specific rather than general prices, that is, the current costs of replacing the company's assets. For both methods adjustments are required for cost of goods sold and depreciation in the income statement. Because companies subject to the FASB disclosure requirements are permitted to defer disclosure of current cost information for one year, many companies reported only constant dollar information in their 1979 annual reports. Preliminary studies of sample 1979 data offer few surprises. Income computed in constant dollars was on average 40 percent less than the corresponding historical cost earnings figures. While the average decline in current cost earnings is about the same, there is substantially greater variability. The results range from very severe declines for capital intensive companies to increases over historical cost earnings for high technology companies on a decreasing cost curve.

Now that the dust has cleared on the new inflation accounting disclosures, it is time to focus on

EDITOR'S NOTE: An abbreviated version of this article, entitled "Affordable Dividends," appeared in the *Wall Street Journal*, Sept. 15, 1980.

how this information is being interpreted and used by the investment and business communities. Many financial analysts and corporate executives have dismissed constant dollar earnings as misleading because the adjustments resulting from using the consumer price index do not reflect the change in purchasing power experienced by specific companies. Some FASB members and well-known financial analysts attach great importance to the use of current cost earnings data for assessing a company's capacity for paying dividends. In brief, the argument is that dividends should be distributed from earnings, not from capital, and the current cost concept, which recognizes no income until provision is made for the maintenance of the company's physical capital, is the "best" measure of earnings in an environment of changing prices. Current cost income is then seen as an approximation of *distributable income* or the amount of cash dividends that can be distributed without reducing the operating capability of an enterprise. Thus, we see increasingly in the financial press, and undoubtedly in corporate boardrooms, presentation of dividend coverage ratios in terms of current cost earnings.

Current cost income (and most certainly historical cost income and constant dollar income) as an estimate of a company's maximum affordable dividend can be misleading for several reasons:

● It is based on the assumption that maintaining existing productive capacity is the appropriate corporate objective. In an economy characterized by increasing product turnover and corporate diversification, maintaining existing productive capacity is rarely the optimal way of preserving and enhancing the earning power of the business.

● It anticipates the increased cost of replacing facilities in the future, but anticipates no change in future selling prices.

● It does not account for the planned or expected rate of corporate sales growth and the corresponding working and fixed capital investment needed to fuel that growth.

● It does not account for the portion of investment to be financed by debt.

A company's maximum affordable dividend depends simply on its financing policy and the *projected* cash flow consequences of its *planned* growth-investment strategy rather than on *last year's* accrual accounting earnings performance, whether calculated on an inflation-adjusted basis.

Examples

To illustrate, suppose a company's business plan calls for annual sales growth of 15 percent, pre-tax return on sales of 12 percent, average investment of $0.40 per dollar of incremental sales, a current income tax rate of 46 percent, and maintenance of a 30 percent debt to equity ratio. This company can pay no more than 38.1 percent of its historical cost earnings as dividends. At the 38.1 percent payout rate, the cash earnings retained plus added available debt ca-

---

FIGURE I
Maximum Affordable Dividend Payout Rate

Sales growth rate			Working capital + Capital expenditures per Dollar of Incremental Sales								
			.350			.400			.450		
			Debt/Equity			Debt/Equity			Debt/Equity		
			0.250	0.300	0.350	0.250	0.300	0.350	0.250	0.300	0.350
.100		0.100	52.9%	54.7%	56.4%	46.1%	48.2%	50.1%	39.4%	41.7%	43.9%
	EBT/Sales	0.120	60.7%	62.2%	63.6%	55.1%	56.8%	58.4%	49.5%	51.4%	53.2%
		0.140	66.3%	67.6%	68.8%	61.5%	63.0%	64.4%	56.7%	58.4%	59.9%
.150		0.100	32.4%	35.0%	37.4%	22.7%	25.7%	28.4%	13.0%	16.4%	19.5%
	EBT/Sales	0.120	43.6%	45.8%	47.8%	35.6%	38.1%	40.4%	27.5%	30.3%	32.9%
		0.140	51.7%	53.5%	55.3%	44.8%	46.9%	48.9%	37.9%	40.3%	42.5%
.200		0.100	13.6%	16.9%	20.0%	1.2%	5.0%	8.6%	−11.1%	−6.8%	−2.9%
	EBT/Sales	0.120	28.0%	30.8%	33.3%	17.7%	20.9%	23.8%	7.4%	11.0%	14.3%
		0.140	38.3%	40.6%	42.8%	29.5%	32.2%	34.7%	20.6%	23.7%	26.5%

pacity are just equal to the investment dollars required to support the 15 percent growth in sales.

This result can easily be shown by assuming sales will grow at the stipulated 15 percent rate (from $100 million to $115 million). At $0.40 per dollar of incremental sales, capital expenditures (net of depreciation) plus working capital requirements will total $6 mil-

paid and reported earnings per share figures for a major manufacturing company and major chemical company (**Figure II**). For purposes of estimating maximum affordable dividends, values for pre-tax return on sales, effective tax rate and debt to equity ratio are assumed to remain at their 1979 levels. Sales growth rates and investment requirements per dollar of incremental sales are assumed

Conclusion

If the economy is to function effectively, it is essential for management and government, as well as investors, to understand the effects of inflation on the capital invested and its earning power. Managers and investors need this information in their respective resource allocation roles; government needs the information to assure itself that present taxation policies do not tax at levels that impair the capital of business and discourage investment. The task of developing useful and reliable measurements of the effects of inflation is extraordinarily complex and the FASB experiment represents a promising beginning.

	EPS from continuing operations			Dividend		Dividend as a % of historical cost EPS	
	Historical cost	Constant dollar	Current cost	Paid	Afford-able	Paid	Afford-able
Manufacturing company	$6.20	$4.68	$4.34	$2.75	$4.56	44%	73%
Chemical company	8.47	6.01	6.03	2.90	0.42	34	5

FIGURE II Maximum Affordable Dividend Payout Rate

lion. This amount will be financed as follows:

After-tax earnings ($115 million sales)	$7.45 mil.
Less: 38.1 percent dividend payout	(2.83)
Earnings retained (increase in equity)	4.62
Added debt capacity (30 percent of earnings retained)	1.38
	$6.00 mil.

The maximum affordable dividend payout rate table (**Figure I**) shows how sensitive this rate is to changes in growth, profitability, investment intensity and financial leverage. Note, for example, if sales growth is increased to 20 percent and investment requirements to 0.45, the maximum affordable dividend payout rate decreases from 38.1 to 11 percent.

Consider the comparison between the estimated affordable dividends and the dividends

as the average figures for the most recent five years.

Current cost earnings per share figures for both companies are 30 percent less than their historical cost figures. However, while the chemical company's estimated affordable dividends are substantially less than its actual dividends paid, the reverse is true in the case of the manufacturing company. Further, the latter's maximum affordable dividends are estimated to be somewhat greater than its current cost earnings. In contrast, the chemical company's affordable dividends are just 7 percent of its current cost income and its low affordable dividends relative to those of the manufacturing company are attributable to a combination of lower return on sales, higher sales growth and substantially higher investment requirements per dollar of incremental sales.

There is, however, a real danger that the newly available data might be misinterpreted and used improperly by decision-makers. The greatest concern lies with the emerging notion that current cost income is a reliable indicator of a company's maximum affordable dividend. As has been shown, this is simply not the case. Enlightened corporate dividend policy will continue to be conditioned by the interplay of planned growth, profitability, investment and financing. Government officials, particularly those concerned with the effect of tax policy on capital formation, must recognize that even without the exacerbating effects of inflation, growing capital-intensive companies need to withhold a significant portion of current earnings to finance the future. If government were to view inflation-adjusted earnings as distributable, it would seriously overestimate dividend paying capacity and seriously underestimate the tax remedies needed to promote capital formation in key sectors of the economy. □

For Further Study

1. Bar-Yosef, S., and R. Kolodny (1976). "Dividend Policy and Market Theory". *The Review of Economics and Statistics* (May 1976), pp. 181–190.

2. Blume, M. (1980). "Stock Returns and Dividend Yields: Some More Evidence", *The Review of Economics and Statistics* (November 1980), pp. 567–577.

3. Brennan, M.J. (1970). "Taxes, Market Valuation and Corporate Financial Policy". *National Tax Journal* (December 1970), pp. 417–427.

4. Djarraya, D. and C.F. Lee (1981). "Residual Theory, Partial Adjustment and Information Content of Dividend Payment Decision: An Integration and Extension", Working Paper, The University of Illinois at Urbana-Champaign.

5. Ehrber, A.F. (1979). "Building a Shelter for Dividends", *Fortune* (October 22, 1979), pp. 149–152.

6. Friend, I., and M. Puckett (1964). "Dividends and Stock Prices", *The American Economic Review* (September 1964), pp. 656–682.

7. Farrar D., and L. Selwyn (1967). "Taxes, Corporate Financial Policy and Return to Investors", *National Tax Journal* (December 1967), pp. 444–452.

8. Gordon, M. (1959). "Dividends, Earnings and Stock Prices", *Review of Economics and Statistics* (May 1959) pp. 99–105.

9. Lee, C.F. and S.W. Forbes (1981). "Income Measures, Ownership, Capacity Ratios and the Dividend Decision of the Non-life Insurance Industry: Some Empirical Evidence", *Journal of Risk and Insurance* (in press).

10. Litzenberger, R.H. and K. Ramaswamy (1979), "The Effect of Personal Taxes and Dividends on Capital Asset Prices: Theory and Empirical Evidence", *Journal of Financial Economics*, 7, pp. 163–195.

11. Miller, M.H. and M. Scholes (1978). "Dividends and Taxes", *Journal of Financial Economics* (December 1978), 6, pp. 333–364.

12. _____ (1981). "Dividends and Taxes: Some Empirical Evidence", *Journal of Political Economy* (forthcoming).

Part VII

Mergers:
Theory and Evidence

Introduction

Merger-related issues are of interest to both academicians and practitioners. A financial manager should know the possible implications of a merger to stockholders (both buyers and sellers) as well as in a broader sense to society. The three papers in Part VII demonstrate:

1. how the exchange ratio in a merger can be determined,
2. what kind of acceptable empirical methods can be used to investigate the relationship between tender offers and stockholder returns, and
3. what are the possible effects of a conglomerate merger.

To investigate the impacts of merger on stockholder returns, either the CAPM method or one of the non-CAPM methods can be used. A non-CAPM method has been used by Shick (1972), Shick and Jen (1974) and others. The CAPM approach has been used by Lev and Mandelker (1972), Halpern (1973), Mandelker (1974), and others; the various works and their findings are discussed in the review article by Mueller. Mueller carefully reviews the empirical research on the effects of conglomerate mergers in the last three decades. Mueller (1977) classifies major explanations concerning the benefits of mergers into two groups: the neo-classical explanations and the managerial explanations. The neo-classical explanations that can be used include:

a tax benefit,

a cost of capital benefit, bankruptcy cost reduction,

a positive diversification effect,

"P/E magic",

redeployment of corporate capital,

replacement of incompetent managers, and

economic disturbance.

Empirical evidence on the impacts of profitability, on stock returns, and on risk performance are also discussed.

To determine the merger benefits to shareholders of acquiring firms, Shick and Jen (1974) used a sample of 24 acquiring firms selected from three industries—chemicals, machinery and electric utilities—to do the empirical studies. Their empirical findings confirm that shareholders of acquiring firms benefit from mergers and acquisitions.

Mandelker (1974), Dodd and Ruback (1977) and others use a CAPM approach to study empirically the relationship between tender offers and stockholder returns. They find three distinct sets of empirical implications concerning the effects of tender offers on stock returns: each type of hypothesis can lead to differing empirical conclusions. The "monopolistic", "synergy", and "internal efficiency" hypotheses each predict non-negative abnormal performance for stockholders of firms engaged in successful tender offers. For an unsuccessful tender offer, the monopolistic and synergy hypotheses predict zero or negative returns for all stockholders. The internal efficiency hypothesis, on the other hand, predicts a non-negative return for stockholders of target firms in unsuccessful offers. Besides using the standard Cumulative Average Residual (CAR) technique to investigate the impacts of tender offers on stockholder returns, Dodd and Ruback also use a dummy regression technique to detect a possible shift of risk. Other kinds of updated switching regression techniques for detecting structural changes of rates of return for merging firms can be found in Lee, Shick and Jen (1977). The topics discussed in this section are interesting, however, they are not necessarily covered in the financial analysis and planning course.

Based upon two important determinants of the entity's value—the expected rate of earnings growth and the presumed risk of business operation—Larson and Gonedes (1969) derive an exchange ratio determination model.

In this model, both maximum and minimum exchange ratios are derived for the managers of acquiring and acquired firms to determine their bargaining ranges. This paper also discusses the basic stock valuation model and possible factors which influence the magnitude of an equity's earnings multiplier.

In sum, these three papers can give financial managers enough theoretical and empirical knowledge of conglomerate mergers to support their decisions concerning proposed mergers.

THE EFFECTS OF CONGLOMERATE MERGERS

A survey of the empirical evidence

Dennis C. MUELLER*

1. Introduction

The United States has experienced 3 large merger waves within the last century. Each has coincided with a period of strong economic and stock market advance. Each has come to an end along with the collapse of these bull markets and the recessions or depression that followed. The positive relationship between merger activity and stock market and economic advance is one of the well established if unexplained riddles of this literature [see, in particular, Nelson (1959, 1966); Reid (1968); and Beckenstein (1977)].

The first major merger wave has been described by Stigler as a wave to create monopolies; the second a wave to create oligopolies (1950). The third might be called a wave to create conglomerates. For the distinguishing feature of the mergers occurring in the 1960s was certainly the extent to which these mergers tended to diversify or extend the acquiring companies' product mixes.

Reid, Markham, and Steiner have all noted that many of these mergers were not between firms as unrelated in their business activities as the word 'conglomerate' or some of the literature discussing them might imply.[1] Their point is well taken. Nevertheless, a substantial difference does exist between the acquisitions characteristic of this most recent period, and the ones which brought the Standard Oil Company and General Motors together, in terms of both their potential market power advantages, and their potential for plant and production economies, as all observers of the recent wave have admitted. This difference has made it difficult to explain conglomerate mergers in terms of the market power and economic efficiency advantages that have traditionally been put forward as the motives behind mergers. Not surprisingly therefore a new set of hypotheses about the causes (and effects) of mergers has appeared to explain this new form of merger.

*This paper was written while the author was research fellow at the International Institute of Management, Berlin. Thanks are due for the support of this Institute and the helpful comments of John Cable, John Hiller, Thomas Hogarty, and Lee Preston.

[1]Reid (1968, pp. 74–77), Steiner (1975, pp. 17–22). These two books also present useful surveys of the earlier merger waves and the statistics on each. See, also Markham (1955, 1973).

This set is so large, however, that it is impossible to cover adequately both the recent theoretical literature on the causes of mergers, and the empirical evidence in support of these hypotheses. Fortunately, the former task has been admirably accomplished by Peter Steiner (1975). Thus, we are free here to focus upon the empirical literature, following a very brief review of the alternative hypotheses (section 2). Following this we review the empirical literature (section 3). Section 4 examines the evidence linking mergers to overall concentration changes. The last section draws the policy implications emerging from this review.

Although all Western countries experienced merger waves in the 1960s, and the conglomerate merger has been increasing in popularity in other countries too, it remains the dominant form of merger only within the U.S., and therefore we shall concentrate most of our attention on the literature concerning this country.

2. Hypotheses

It is convenient in reviewing the hypotheses about mergers to group them into those which predict that mergers generate profits to be shared between the two combining companies, and those claiming that mergers do not necessarily generate extra profits. The former we shall refer to as neoclassical theories of merger, since they are obviously consistent with the profit motive assumption. The latter we shall term managerial theories, since they are all based on the assumption that mergers are means by which managers pursue objectives other than profit or stockholder welfare maximization.

2.1. The neoclassical theories

Given the lack of a direct productive or technological relationship between the partners in a conglomerate merger, recent theories of this type of merger have often focussed on some form of *financial* economy to be gained from the merger. John Lintner has summarized the arguments for 5 such financial economies (1971), and we follow him over these.[2]

(1) *Taxes.* Lintner lists the tax exemption of corporate reorganizations, and the use of one firm's tax loss carryovers by its partner as possible stimulants to mergers (p. 107). He notes with respect to the former, however, that 'This "tax free" treatment . . . is not a positive incentive *relative to* continued independent operation.' [See, also, Sherman (1972).]

(2) *Leverage.* Borrowing costs decline with size of firm, and 'Large firms can thus refinance debt of small independent firms at lower economic cost resulting in a genuine capital gain through merger' [Lintner (1970, p. 107)].

[2]Lintner actually lists 'dirty pooling' and other accounting gimmicks as one of his 5 causes, and subsumes bankruptcy costs under leverage. For further discussion of these hypotheses, see again Steiner (1975, chs. 2, 4, 5).

(3) *Bankruptcy costs.* Both Levy and Sarnat (1970) and Lewellen (1971) have argued that mergers between companies whose income streams are not perfectly correlated reduces the profitability of bankruptcy and lenders' risk.

(4) *Diversification.* More generally, the pooling of imperfectly correlated income streams will produce a superior risk/return asset to the individual streams. Since the advantages of risk pooling can be achieved by individual stockholder portfolio diversification [Levy and Sarnat (1970)], this argument must be coupled with some restrictions on the stockholder's ability to form his own diversified portfolio (or buy into preformed portfolios like mutual funds) to justify mergers.

(5) *P/E Magic.* The argument was made that when a conglomerate acquired a firm with a lower *P/E* than its own, the market often evaluated the combined earnings of the two firms at the higher *P/E* of the conglomerate, rather than applying a weighted average of the two *P/E*'s, thus producing an instantaneous capital gain [Lintner (1971, p. 110); Mead (1969)].

(6) *Redeployment of corporate capital.* Oliver Williamson has emphasized the advantages of the *M*-form divisionalized organization for allocating capital [(1970, 1975), see also, Weston (1970)]. In this structure the central management moves capital from high average return, low marginal return divisions to those promising the highest marginal returns without undergoing the transactions costs of using the capital market [on these see, also, Sherman (1972)]. The conglomerates are prime examples of *M*-form organizations, and redeployment of capital in these ways was one of their stated goals.[3]

(7) *Replacement of incompetent managers.* Complementary to the achievement of a more efficient organizational form, conglomerate mergers are often seen as a method for replacing inefficient managements. Dewey's claim that mergers 'are merely a civilized alternative to bankruptcy or the voluntary liquidation that transfers assets from falling to rising firms' (1961, p. 257) has often been cited, and Henry Manne has generalized the argument in constructing a theory of 'the market for corporate control' (1965). In this market, firms compete for control of inefficiently managed companies via the takeover route. Thus, mergers are seen as an economical way of eliminating bad management, reorganizing corporate structures, and improving both allocational- and *X*-efficiency in the corporate sector.

(8) *Economic disturbances.* Michael Gort argues that mergers can be explained by the existence of economic disturbances which lead to a discrepancy between the value of a firm's assets placed on it by its managers or controlling stockholders, and the value placed on them by outsiders (1969). Gort cites three

---

[3]It should be noted that there are 2 separate issues involved here concerning *M*-form efficiency. The first is whether the *M*-form organization is superior to the *U*-form for managing a given set of diversified activities. The second is whether the *M*-form efficiency gains are sufficient to justify the transaction costs of acquiring a large number of *U*-form companies to create a conglomerate *M*-form. The first hypothesis could be valid even if the second is not. It is only the second which is addressed here.

specific types of economic disturbances that are likely to produce accelerated merger activity: rapid growth, technological change, and changes in stock market values.

2.2. The managerial theories

The managerial theories argue that the separation of ownership from control allows managers some discretion to pursue goals other than stockholder welfare maximization. The pursuit of growth, as hypothesized by Robin Marris (1964), seems the most natural managerial goal to be satisfied via mergers [Reid (1968); Mueller (1969); Singh (1971)]. From some of the empirical results has emerged the possibility that managers may be pursuing a speculative or risk-taking motive through mergers. But we shall discuss this hypothesis after reviewing the evidence supporting it.

2.3. Motives for mergers and merger waves

One of the difficulties with several of the neoclassical motives for mergers is that it is difficult to reconcile them with the occurrence of merger waves in times of economic prosperity and stock market advance. Why should mergers to avoid the transaction costs and taxes involved in bankruptcy reach a feverish pace during a broad, economic expansion when bankruptcies are on the decline? Why is it that the incompetencies of managers become most apparent when profits and stock prices are rising, and are immediately concealed once they begin to plummet? Nor does it seem logical that small firms should feel most compelled to merge with larger ones to obtain capital, at a time when their cash flows are likely to be high, and the demand for new equity issues is favorable.

Gort claims that his economic disturbance theory is consistent with the observed cyclic pattern of merger activity (1969, pp. 624–625). Logically, however, it would seem that valuation discrepancies would be as likely to arise in periods of rapid stock market decline and negative growth, as in periods of advance. Indeed, since stock prices usually fall faster following a boom than they rose during it, one might expect mergers to be counter cyclical under Gort's theory, and conclude, therefore, that the existing evidence runs counter to it.

Gort argues that mergers are more likely in upswings than in downturns, however, because

when security prices are low relative to their mean value over a period of years, managers and long-term investors will tend to consider the shares of their firm undervalued. The stockholders of firms that are potential acquirers, on the other hand, can be expected to resist acquisition prices that are far above those at which the individual investor can purchase securities in the open market on his personal account. Consequently, valuation discrepancies of the type needed for acquisitions to occur will be far more frequent in periods of high than in periods of low security prices. (p. 628)

Thus the economic disturbance theory assumes that stockholders and managers base their current valuations of their company's stock on the recent past, but nonholders do not. During an upswing stockholders undervalue their company's earnings' growth, i.e. they tend to be bearish relative to nonholders. During a downswing they are again looking backwards and are bullish relative to nonholders. Personally I find this assymetry in expectations an awkward assumption, but shall not pursue the matter here. For policy purposes, the relevant question is still whether these mergers generate any net efficiency gains.

P/E magic is also compatible with a cyclic-merger pattern. In a buoyant market, the kind of optimistic expectations which are necessary to bring about this magic are most likely to be present. Conversely, when the market breaks, the accompanying switch to pessimism may produce an opposing reevaluation of P/E's, and a sudden elimination of this possible advantage from mergers. If the merging companies have not achieved real efficiency gains to justify the high P/E's applied to their combined earnings, downward pressure on their stock will be intensified. Note that in this case P/E magic is only consistent with stockholder welfare maximization in the short run. Only the stockholders who sell out before the market breaks are likely to gain from the mergers.

The managerial theory is also consistent with a cyclical merger pattern. In an upswing corporate profits and cash flows are on the rise. Where ample opportunities for growth via internal expansion are lacking, the only alternatives may be higher dividend payments or growth through merger. Faced with these alternatives, 'it is not surprising that the "expansiveness" of the businessman during periods of prosperity often expresses itself in the merger movement and larger business organizations' as Thorp noted in commenting on the 1920s wave.[4]

The constraint upon managerial use of cash flows to achieve goals in conflict with stockholder goals is the threat of takeover [Marris (1964)]. But in periods of rising profits and stockmarket values this constraint is likely to weaken as rising returns to stockholders increase their optimism and confidence in their managers. Indeed, the most serious threat of takeover may come from other firms pursuing growth. But, as Singh has shown, growth in size, if it is not at too great of a cost in profits, may offer greater protection from takeover than maximizing profits (1971). Thus, while the desire to grow via mergers may be constant over time, the means and discretion to pursue this goal are likely to be greater with a rising economy and stock market.

But, prosperity may also provide a more conducive environment to consummate mergers in pursuit of some of the above listed neoclassical goals. Thus, a choice between these competing explanations must rest on an examination of their effects. If conglomerate mergers prove to be largely

[4]Thorp (1931, p. 86) as cited in Reid (1968, p. 67). See also Reid's discussion of the 'environment for mergers' and the managerial thesis (chs. 3, 4, 5, 7).

profitable ventures, we shall return to reexamine the set of neoclassical theories to see which is most compatible with the other evidence on their characteristics. If they are not profitable, we shall reexamine the managerial theories.

3. The evidence

3.1. Early evidence predating 1960s merger wave

Several good surveys of the evidence on the first two merger waves, as well as the merger history of the late 1940s and 1950s exist, and this literature need not be reviewed here [see in particular Markham (1955); Nelson (1959); Reid (1968) and most succinctly, Hogarty (1970a)]. Most of these studies compare profit rates before and after merger, and are thus somewhat difficult to compare with the more modern approach focussing on stockholder return on equity. Hogarty (1970a) concluded his survey of the early merger history thus:

> What can fifty years of research tell us about the profitability of mergers? Undoubtedly the most significant result of this research has been that no one who has undertaken a major empirical study of mergers has concluded that mergers are profitable, i.e., profitable in the sense of being 'more profitable' than alternative forms of investment. A host of researchers, working at different points of time and utilizing different analytic techniques and data, have but one major difference: whether mergers have a neutral or negative impact on profitability. (p. 389)

This conclusion seems fair based on this early evidence. It naturally raises the question of why so many mergers have taken place, and casts some doubt on the maximization of stockholder welfare hypothesis.

3.2. The recent evidence—Mergers and profitability

The first study to test for the effects of the conglomerate merger wave of the 1960s was by Weston and Mansinghka (1971). They compared the profitability of a sample of 63 conglomerates to that of a randomly selected sample of industrials, and a combined industrial–nonindustrial sample. The most interesting comparisons are between the conglomerates and the industrials and are reproduced in table 1. In 1958 the conglomerates, or rather the 63 firms that would become conglomerates, had profit rates significantly below the randomly selected sample of industrials. After 1968, the peak year of merger activity, the conglomerates had profit rates roughly equal to those of the industrials.[5] The fourth line of the table

---

[5] Holzmann, Copeland, and Hayya (1975) also found that a sample of 21 conglomerates had lower average profitability than a size matched sample of nonconglomerates for both the 1951–60 and 1961–70 periods, as well as over the entire 1951–70 period. They did not make before and after the merger wave comparisons.

gives an indication of how the conglomerates financed their growth. Although their leverage ratios were on average roughly 50% higher than those of the industrials in 1958, they increased to almost double the leverage ratios of the industrials by 1968. Thus, the conglomerates financed their growth in part by an aggressive increase in their leverage ratios. The last line of the table presents the not surprising result that conglomerates grew significantly faster than the industrials during the period of heavy merger activity.

Table 1

Major results from the Weston–Mansinghka study.[a]

	1958			1968		
	Sample means		F-statistic	Sample means		F-statistic
	C	R1		C	R1	
EBIAT/Total assets	5.8	9.2	9.83*	10.4	8.5	0.44
EBIT/Total assets	8.7	16.7	17.13*	15.1	15.6	0.02
Net income/Net worth	7.6	12.6	10.52*	13.3	12.4	0.81
Debt/Net worth	95%	56%	8.19*	169%	87%	10.25*
Growth in total assets 58–68				22.8%	12.6%	16.25*

[a]Notes: *Significant at 0.01 level.
   EBIAT is earnings before interest and preferred dividends, but after taxes.
   EBIT is earnings before interest, preferred dividends, and taxes.
   For a complete discussion of the variables see Weston and Mansinghka (1971).

To explain their results Weston and Mansinghka (1971) put forward a defensive diversification hypothesis:

Analysis of the backgrounds and acquisition histories of the conglomerate firms suggests that they were diversifying defensively to avoid (1) sales and profit instability, (2) adverse growth developments, (3) adverse competitive shifts, (4) technological obsolescence, and (5) increased uncertainties associated with their industries. (p. 928)

This hypothesis is also broadly consistent with the findings of Melicher and Rush (1974). They compared the profitability of 61 conglomerate firms with the firms they acquired. They found that the conglomerates acquired firms significantly more profitable than themselves. Conglomerates also acquired firms with significantly lower leverage ratios than themselves, suggesting a latent debt or leverage capacity motive (p. 145). These results are in contrast to those from a sample of 71 nonconglomerate acquirers, who Melicher and Rush found acquired firms with roughly the same profitability and leverage ratios as themselves.[6]

Similar findings to Melicher and Rush's were obtained by Boyle (1970). He compared the profitability of firms acquired in horizontal and vertical acquisitions to that of firms acquired by conglomerates. He found that the firms the conglomerates acquired had significantly higher profits than those acquired in horizontal and vertical acquisitions. Boyle specifically tested and rejected the hypothesis that the *acquired* companies were failing at the time of their acquisition, as did Conn (1976).

Weston and Mansinghka (1971) argue their 'data are consistent with the proposition that the conglomerate firms perform the economic function of preserving the values of ongoing organizations as well as restoring the earning power of the entities' (p. 928). This conclusion seems premature. That the profit levels of firms that merge with companies more profitable than themselves rise is no surprise. Whether this activity serves a useful economic function or is simply the result of the arithmetic of averaging depends on whether some additional economies are generated by joining the different sets of companies. If the defensive diversification of the conglomerates through the acquisition of relatively more profitable firms generated real economic efficiencies, the value of the resulting enterprises should exceed the value they would have attained in the absence of these mergers. Here it is particularly important to take into account the much higher leverage ratios the conglomerates developed as part of their acquisition strategies. While diversification reduces a company's risk against a downturn for any single line of activity, increased leverage by increasing fixed interest payments increases a company's risk in the face of a general downturn in economic activity. Thus, while the pre-interest payments profits of the conglomerates may have become more stable as a result of their merger programs, their post-interest payment profits may have become more volatile over the cycle. Given their heavy reliance on debt, a key performance question about the conglomerates is how they fare over the cycle.

The first suggestion that conglomerate acquisitions did not improve economic efficiency was presented by Reid (1971) in direct response to the Weston–Mansinghka article. Lags in publishing being what they are, Reid was able to base his comment on data extending up through mid-1970, and thus include the initial phase of the collapse of the 1960s bull market, while Weston and Mansinghka's data end in 1968 when the merger wave and the stock market were at their peaks. Reid reported a drop in the average price of the Weston–Mansinghka conglomerates between the end of 1968 and mid-1970 of 56%, compared with a drop in the average price of their industrials of 37%. Perhaps more dramatic and suggesting that the conglomerates had become highly risky

---

[6]Conn (1973, 1976) found no evidence of a difference between the profit rates of acquired and acquiring firms. But while the time periods and samples of Weston–Mansinghka and Melicher–Rush heavily overlap, that of Conn's does not so his results and theirs are difficult to compare.

due to their heavy levering was the drop in their bond prices of 45.6% over this period compared to a drop in the Dow-Jones Industrial Bond average 7.8% [Reid (1971, p. 945)].

3.3. The recent evidence—Returns on stocks

Regardless of whether the savings from a merger take the form of a tax gain, avoiding the costs of bankruptcy, diversification economies, superior deployment of capital or for some other reason, these gains should be reflected in the rate of return on the acquiring company's stock, unless the market was capable of fully anticipating the consequences of a merger or series of mergers long before they occurred. Thus, a direct test of the efficiency effects of conglomerate mergers net of the costs (including debt issues, premiums paid, etc.) of consummating them is to examine the returns on acquiring firms' stocks.

Hogarty was one of the first to use rate of return on equity as a performance measure using a sample of 43 firms engaging in substantial merger activity over 1953–64 (1970b). He specifically avoided choosing conglomerates since his point of comparison was the average firm in the acquiring company's industry. The bulk of the merging firms in his sample performed either no better or worse than the average company in their base industries.

Weston, Smith and Shrieves (1972) estimate rates of return on equity for a sample of 48 of the 63 conglomerates in the Weston–Mansinghka sample. Unfortunately they test the performance of the conglomerates against a random sample of 50 mutual funds rather than against the Weston–Mansinghka random samples of operating companies, so the two studies are not directly comparable. They find that the conglomerates outperform the mutual funds over the 1960–69 period on the basis of risk adjusted rates of return statistics proposed by Sharpe and Treynor, and Jensen's measure of portfolio performance.

In addition to their choice of control group, the Weston, Smith, Shrieves study suffers somewhat from its choice of time period. As noted above, the substantial increase in leverage the conglomerates incurred raises questions about their risk/return performance over the cycle. The period 1960–69 consists mostly of one long upswing, and the very beginning of a sharp drop. Thus, the time period chosen may have been particularly favorable to the aggressively managed conglomerates in a comparison with the conservatively managed mutual funds. This hypothesis is reinforced by the results Weston–Smith–Shrieves report. The average β for their sample of conglomerates is 1.928, nearly double the β expected on a fully diversified portfolio.[7] Thus, a one percentage point change in the returns on a diversified portfolio would be accompanied by a nearly two

[7]Brenner and Downes (1975) call into question the W–S–S estimates of β and conglomerate performance as well as those of Melicher and Rush, discussed below, on the basis of the data and statistical tests employed. Unfortunately, their call for new studies employing more refined techniques has yet to be answered, or perhaps even heard.

percentage points change for the average conglomerate. In contrast, the average β for the mutual funds was 0.878 suggesting quite a conservative management. Thus, the conglomerates were characterized by significantly higher market risk than the mutual funds, and were in a far weaker position to ride out the impeding storm in 1969.

Table 2

Main results of Melicher and Rush (1973) (C = conglomerate sample mean; N-C nonconglomerate sample mean; $F = F$-statistic).

Factors		6/66–12/71	6/66–2/69	3/69–12/71
Monthly returns	C	1.008	1.017	0.998
	N-C	1.007	1.011	1.030
	F	0.20	4.50**	11.05*
Standard deviation	C	0.102	0.099	0.105
	N-C	0.094	0.087	0.100
	F	1.95	4.13**	0.59
Beta values	C	1.335	1.522	1.204
	N-C	1.031	1.152	0.952
	F	9.00*	9.89*	4.63**
Jensen alpha	C	0.002	0.010	−0.006
	N-C	0.001	0.004	−0.002
	F	0.18	3.75	2.49
Sharpe variability	C	0.045	0.132	−0.041
	N-C	0.047	0.093	0.007
	F	0.03	1.91	4.31**
Treynor volatility	C	0.004	0.009	−0.004
	N-C	0.005	0.008	−0.029
	F	0.80	0.46	1.12

From the equation $R_i - R_f = \alpha_i + \beta_i(R_m - R_f)$, we obtain:

Sharpe variability $= \dfrac{\bar{R}_i - R_f}{\sigma_i}$,

Jensen alpha $= \alpha_i$,

Treynor volatility $= \dfrac{\bar{R}_i - R_f}{\beta_i}$,

where:
R_i = rate of return on equity of firm i,
R_f = risk free rate of return,
R_m = rate of return on the market portfolio.

Melicher and Rush (1973) test the performance of conglomerates against a sample of nonconglomerate firms over a period that does extend through the 'liquidity crisis' of 1970 and into 1971. Their main findings are summarized in table 2. The greater volatility of the conglomerates is again apparent. Their β values are significantly higher in both subperiods, and their standard deviations in returns are also higher in both subperiods, significantly so in the 6/66 to 2/69 subperiod. This volatility is also evidenced in the first row results presenting the average monthly returns for the two samples. For the period 6/66–2/69 covering the stock market's peak, the rate of return on conglomerate stocks was significantly higher than the average return for the sample of nonconglomerates. For the period 3/69–12/71 including the liquidity crisis and the market's initial phase of decline, the conglomerates earned a significantly lower rate of return than the nonconglomerates. Over the entire $5\frac{1}{2}$ year period the returns earned on the two stocks were nearly the same. The same conclusions emerge from an examination of the various risk adjusted measures. All 3 favor the conglomerates over the first period, two of the three favor the nonconglomerates in the second. Only one of these 6 comparisons is statistically significant, however, the nonconglomerates had a significantly higher risk adjusted rate of return than the conglomerates over the 3/69–12/71 using the Sharpe measure. All 3 statistics are virtually identical for the full period.

3.4. Risk performance

One of the few questions for which all of the existing evidence, and all of the authors' interpretations of their own evidence are in accord is that conglomerate mergers are not an efficient method for reducing risk. The theoretical argument for this proposition is well established [Levy and Sarnat (1970)]. Lintner's argument to the contrary assumes that stockholders are limited to fairly small portfolios. But Evans and Archer (1968) have shown that the bulk of the gains from diversification can be achieved with a portfolio of roughly 10 stocks, so the following results are not unexpected.

Smith and Schreives (1969) were the first to study the efficiency of conglomerate diversification directly. Using simulation techniques they compared the portfolio holdings of 19 conglomerates and 8 mutual funds. On average the mutual funds tended to be closer to the efficient portfolio frontier than the conglomerates.

The Weston, Smith, Shrieves (1972) study was in some ways a direct follow-up to Smith and Schrieves using data on actual conglomerate firm and mutual fund performances. As noted above, the β's for their conglomerates were more than double those of the mutual funds and they in fact reject 'diversification in a risk-reducing sense' as 'the major objective of conglomerate mergers' (p. 362). This conclusion has been further supported by several studies.

Melicher and Rush (1973) did not find β's as high as Weston, Smith, and Shrieves did, but they did find conglomerate firm β's to be significantly higher than for their nonconglomerate sample. The same was found by Joehnk and Nielsen (1974). They also tested for a change in β's as a result of mergers using both conglomerate and nonconglomerate firms. They found an insignificant effect on the β's for conglomerate companies making acquisitions. A similar result was also observed by Lev and Mandelker (1972), although their sample was not limited to conglomerate mergers. Their sample consisted of 69 companies making large acquisitions (more than 10% of their own size) over the period 1952–63. They found no significant difference between the changes in β's for acquiring firms over this period, and the changes in β's for a control group matched by industry, size, and time period.[8]

Thus, there is no evidence that conglomerate firms achieved superior risk spreading performance. Indeed, to the extent their higher β's are a result of their merger activity, the conglomerates became more risky and volatile than a comparable nonconglomerate.

Having rejected 'diversification in a risk-reducing sense' as the objective of conglomerate mergers, Weston, Smith and Schrieves go on to argue that it was the active management of the assets the conglomerates acquired that accounted for their superior performance (p. 362). This hypothesis was directly tested by Mason and Goudzwaard (1976). They compared the performance of 22 conglomerates with that of 22 portfolios of randomly selected stocks chosen to match the exact industries in which the conglomerates operated. Thus, the comparison was directly of whether the direct management of a portfolio of assets by conglomerate managers achieved significantly better performance than randomly chosen portfolios. It did not. Even after adjusting for the costs of buying and selling stocks, and paying a portfolio manager, the randomly selected portfolios had statistically higher rates of return on assets and accumulated stockholders' wealth over the 1962 to 1967 period. This result is all the more remarkable, because Mason and Goudzwaard end their comparison in 1967, the year Melicher and Rush (1973) found to be the peak performance year for the conglomerates.[9]

3.5. Characteristics of the acquired firms

If the benefits to the stockholders of acquiring firms are ambiguous at best, the same cannot be said for the stockholders of the acquired firms. Every study which has examined the latter has found that the stockholders of the acquired firms earn significantly higher rates of return on their shares than other shares are earning, both over the immediate period before the merger and including a reasonable period after the merger is consummated. The results seem robust to type of merger, time period, and the type of compensation the stockholders of the acquired firms accept in return for their shares [see Hogarty and Gort (1970); Lorie and Halpern (1970); Haugen and Udell (1972); and Halpern (1973)].

[8]The β's for acquiring firms in Mandelker's study fall significantly following the merger, but this fall seems to begin as much as 2 years before the merger takes place and does not seem directly related to the mergers, Joehnk and Nielsen (1974) note significant changes in the β's for nonconglomerate firms engaging in a single conglomerate merger over the period 1962–1969.

[9]Haugen and Langetieg (1975) follow a somewhat similar methodology, although they focus on the risk reduction effects of 59 large *nonconglomerate* mergers. They find no significant difference in the risk performance of the merging firms, and the matched nonmerging portfolios.

The reason the stockholders of acquired firms fare so well, of course, is that they are paid a substantial premium above the premerger price for their shares. Although estimates of the premium paid in a merger vary over a fairly wide range, the minimum average premiums that have been calculated run about 15 % [see Hayes and Taussig (1967); Gort (1969); Piper and Weiss (1974); and studies cited in Halpern (1973, pp. 556–557)].

What were the characteristics of these acquired firms, which made their merger partners willing to pay such large premiums for them? As already noted conglomerates acquired firms relatively more profitable than themselves. This characteristic appears to be entirely due to the lower profitability of the conglomerates. Melicher and Rush (1974) compared two samples of 61 conglomerate and 71 nonconglomerate acquisitions. The firms acquired by the conglomerates differed only in size (being larger) than those acquired by the nonconglomerates. But, since the conglomerate·acquirers were less profitable and more highly levered than nonconglomerate acquirers, the firms they acquired were relatively more profitable and less levered than themselves. Both conglomerate and nonconglomerate companies had higher P/E's than the firms they acquired so that P/E magic was listed as a possible motive for both types of acquisitions by Melicher and Rush.

Boyle (1970) compared the profitability of 698 large firms acquired in conglomerate, horizontal and vertical acquisitions between 1948–1968. He found that the companies acquired in conglomerate mergers had profit rates somewhat higher than those acquired in horizontal and vertical mergers, and roughly equal to the average over all manufacturing.

Stevens undertook a detailed multivariate discriminate analysis of the financial characteristics of 40 firms acquired in 1966 and 40 nonacquired firms matched by size (1973). Of the initial 20 factors investigated 6 were identified as making independent contributions to explaining whether a sample firm was acquired or not: '(1) leverage, (2) profitability, (3) activity, (4) liquidity, (5) dividend policy, and (6) price earnings' (p. 152). In the second phase of the discriminate analysis, only leverage and liquidity held up as significant discriminatory variables. Acquired firms had lower leverage ratios and higher liquidity than their matched nonacquired firms. The profits of acquired and nonacquired firms were the same. Acquired companies had higher dividend payout ratios and lower P/E's, although the differences in sample means were not significant. Additional evidence of P/E magic was obtained by Conn (1973) for pure conglomerate acquisitions over the 48–69 period, and Mead (1969).

Mandelker (1974) found that the 252 acquired firms in his sample earned significantly lower rates of return on equity than other firms over most of the period prior to their acquisition (table 2, p. 315). He interprets this to imply 'that mergers are a mechanism by which the market replaces incompetent management' (p. 324).

Smiley (1976) has come up with even more dramatic results. He estimates the decline in market value of a taken-over firm up to the date of takeover as from 50 to 60 percent of its potential maximum, and he estimates the start of this decline as occurring 10 years before takeover.

How can the results of Mandelker (1974) and Smiley (1976) indicating significant deterioration in rate of return on equity performance be reconciled with those studies indicating average profitability performance? Perhaps, they cannot. The differences may be due simply to differences in samples and time periods covered. Mandelker did not find an inferior rate of return performance for the subsample of 167 acquired firms listed on the NYSE, for example (table 6, p. 320). Since these are generally larger than the other firms in his sample, it appears that the lower than average performance of acquired firms was most pronounced among the smaller acquired companies.

Mandelker's study covers the period before the conglomerate merger wave, and includes many nonconglomerate acquisitions. Smiley's (1976) study includes the years up through 1968, but is not restricted to conglomerates. The Boyle (1970) study does suggest that a significant fraction of those companies involved in horizontal or vertical acquisitions were losing money or showing profit declines. These firms may be disproportionately represented in the Mandelker and Smiley samples.

Denis Binder (1973) also noted a change in the relative profitability of acquired firms over time. Acquired firms, *which contested acquisition*, were less profitable than average for the first half of the 1960s but *more* profitable over the 1965–69 period. Mandelker's, but not Smiley's, sample is restricted to firms in the first time period; Melicher and Rush's, and Boyle's samples span both periods.

But the two sets of conflicting findings can be reconciled in another way. Those studies, which have concluded that acquired firms are not badly managed, have based their conclusions on profit rate and other accounting data. Those, which have concluded they are, have based their conclusions on return on equity data. The picture of an acquired firm emerging from Boyle (1970), Melicher and Rush (1974), Conn (1976), and Stevens (1973) suggests an average (profitability, leverage) to somewhat conservatively (liquidity, dividend payouts) managed company. In a period of sustained stockmarket advance average/conservative financial policies may be under-rewarded by the market vis-à-vis more aggressive risk-oriented financial behavior. Thus, the lower return on equity and P/E performance of the acquired firms relative to the companies acquiring them may be explained by the former's more conservative financial policies and the market conditions fostering intensive merger activity.

This interpretation is further supported by the work of Piper and Weiss (1974) and Mingo (1976) on multibank holding company acquisitions. Piper and Weiss found that 'on average the 102 acquisitions [they] studied were breakeven investments that did not result in higher earnings per share for the holding companies in 1967 than would have been achieved in the absence of the acquisitions' (1974, p. 167). Mingo found that the only significant difference between the asset management policies of multibank holding companies and nonholding company banks was that the former held significantly riskier asset portfolios. Both studies concluded that their findings could be rationalized only in terms of a managerial or nonprofitmaximizing theory of the firm.

But further work on the characteristics of acquired firms is certainly needed.

3.6. Premiums and merger success

A few studies have tried to relate the success of a merger, from the point of view of the acquiring firm's stockholders, to various characteristics of the acquiring and acquired firms. The one variable that stands out above all in these analyses is the premium paid over the premerger price of the acquired company by its acquirer. The lower this premium is, the greater the likelihood that the acquiring firm's stockholders gain from the acquisition [Hogarty and Gort (1970); Nielsen and Melicher (1973); Piper and Weiss (1974).

Although this result is perhaps not surprising, it does seem inconsistent with those hypotheses which claim that mergers take place to eliminate inefficient managements or to bring about special matchings between the merger partners. If the mergers were to eliminate incompetent managers, the size of the premium would tend to reflect the potential gains to the acquiring firms from replacing the incompetent managers of the firms acquired. There would be no particular reason to expect a merger with a premium of 30 % to be more successful than one with 15 %. The higher premium in the former would reflect the greater potential gains following the merger, and the higher price the acquirer was forced to pay in a competitive acquisition market.[10] Similarly, under a special matchings thesis, higher premiums would reflect greater latent synergy.

The finding of an inverse relationship between merger success and the size of premium suggests instead that acquired firms do not have special characteristics (e.g. managements of varying qualities), which differ from firm to firm warranting different prices for each firm. Acquired companies would appear to be bundles of assets accurately priced in the market. The payment of a premium for these assets over their market value is on average at best a breakeven investment, and the smaller the premium one pays, the better the chance of doing better than breaking even.

Although Nielsen and Melicher (1973) are not able to relate differences in premiums paid to real or financial (P/E magic) gains *achieved through the merger*, they do find the acquiring firm's cash flow and P/E to be positively related to the size of the premium it is willing to pay. Together these studies of the premiums paid support rather consistently a managerial-motive thesis abour mergers. The higher a firm's cash flow or price/earnings ratio, i.e. the cheaper capital is to it, the

[10]Even in imperfect competitive markets premium sizes should reflect potential gains, if profitability is the goal, since the acquiring firm's managers and stockholders are then in somewhat of a monopsony situation, and can hold out for a greater share of the net gains.

more it is willing to pay to acquire other firms. The amount it is willing to pay does not reflect post-merger gains. Indeed, the more it pays the less likely it is that the merger will be a success.

Unfortunately, the above studies do not deal directly with the conglomerates. One study that did, Haugen and Udell (1972), found that conglomerate acquirers paid significantly higher premiums on average than nonconglomerate acquirers, but it did not relate premium size to acquiring firm profitability.

3.7. Studies which conclude that mergers improve economic efficiency

The pattern of results that has emerged up to this point seems more consistent with the managerial thesis than with the neoclassical alternative. But before examining this contention specifically, let us pause to consider directly those studies which claim to have rejected the managerial motive hypothesis.

Of the recent studies examined here 5 have concluded that mergers improve economic efficiency and seem to present evidence directly contradicting a managerial thesis. These are the two papers coauthored by Fred Weston (1971, 1972), and three stemming from the Ph.D. dissertations by Halpern and Mandelker at the University of Chicago [Halpern (1973); Lev and Mandelker (1972); Mandelker (1974)]. We have already discussed the Weston et al. studies in detail and seen that their results, when extended, are quite consistent with the general pattern emerging from the full set of studies, and are not inconsistent with a managerial theory interpretation. We shall focus here, therefore, on the 3 papers coming out of Chicago.

These studies are based on similar data samples. Halpern uses a sample of 78 mergers between January 1950 and July 1965 'composed of companies for which merging is an infrequent method of growth' (1973, p. 559); Lev and Mandelker have a sample of 69 firms undertaking a single large acquisition between 1952 and 1963; Mandelker has a sample of 241 mergers from November 1941 to August 1962. Thus, none of these studies covers the period of the conglomerate merger wave nor focusses on firms engaged in numerous, conglomerate-type mergers. Nevertheless, each claims that its results contradict some of the hypotheses put forward with respect to the conglomerates, and, since they have not been reviewed before, an examination of their results and claims seems warranted.

Halpern examines the rate of return performance of both partners in a merger up until the date of the merger. He does so by regressing the rate of return of an individual firm on the market return as in the equation presented on the bottom of table 2, and then cumulating the residuals from this equation. He finds that both the larger and the smaller of the two merger partners have positive, average, cumulative residuals up through the date of the merger. But the variances are large, and neither the larger nor the smaller firms involved in these acquisitions have an average cumulative residual as large as the sample standard deviations. An interesting aspect of Halpern's study is that much of the excess returns on the merging companies' stocks is earned in the months preceding the *announcement* of the merger. Halpern concludes that 'my results show that the larger company does not give away everything in a merger; the mean adjusted gain to the larger company is positive and the total adjusted gain is divided evenly, on average' (p. 572). This conclusion is stronger than warranted. As noted the positive returns earned by the acquiring firms are not statistically different from zero. In addition, since Halpern's study measures performance only *up to the date* of the merger, it is really a study of the market's *expected* gains from a merger, not of the actual gains.

The latter failing is corrected by Mandelker. He also employs a monthly-residual-approach, but extends his comparisons to up to 40 months after the merger takes place. As did Halpern, Mandelker finds a rise in the cumulative residuals of the acquiring firm up to the date of the merger (5.1 percent). Following the merger there is a drop-off in the cumulative residuals of 1.7 percent, indicating that the market was somewhat overoptimistic about the merger's success. The cumulative increase in residuals over the entire period remains positive, but the variance is again large and the average residual is not significantly different from zero.

A detailed comparison of the behavior of the returns on the acquired and acquiring firms' stocks before the merger reveals an important difference. For the acquired companies a significant and steady increase in cumulative residuals occurs over the 7 months preceding the merger indicating 'that for some mergers, positive information regarding acquisitions, or any other "good" news correlated with acquisitions, starts leaking out to the market about 7 months before the merger' (p. 314). For the acquiring firms, however, the rise in returns occurs long before the merger takes place, a phenomenon also observed by Ellert (1976). Over the 7 months preceding the merger the cumulative residuals for the acquiring firm exhibited a slight decline pointing 'to the possibility that for the stockholders of the acquiring firms, "news" of an acquisition may not be worthwhile news, since no abnormal behavior is in fact observed during the period (–7 to 0). The abnormal returns earned long before the merger may have nothing to do with the acquisition per se' (p. 321).

In fact, however, it may be the abnormal returns of the acquiring firm long before the merger which are causing the merger, rather than the other way round. The rise in returns on acquiring firms' stocks over the years preceding the merger suggests that these firms were experiencing higher than normal profits and/or P/E's over this period. And it might have been this abnormal prosperity which precipated the decision to undertake an acquisition. This interpretation is consistent with the Nielsen and Melicher (1973) findings relating high cash flows and P/E's for acquiring firms to the premiums they pay, and the more general phenomenon that merger waves occur in periods of prosperity. If the rise in residuals for the acquiring firms before the merger were the cause of the acquisition, and the *fall* in residuals *following* the merger a result of it,

Mandelker's findings would present a more negative view of the successfulness of mergers for the stockholders of the acquiring firms, and would be more in line with the managerial thesis than he is willing to conclude himself.

A closer look at Halpern's results suggests that they *may* follow the same pattern as Mandelker's and be amenable to the same interpretation. Unfortunately, Halpern does not report the monthly residual pattern for the larger and smaller of the two merging firms separately. But he does report these residuals for the two samples combined (1973, p. 567, table 2). These residuals show a noticeable rise over the period from 18 to 23 months before the merger, and again starting 7 months before the merger. If the latter reflected the gains from speculation in the to-be-acquired firm's stock, Halpern's results would conform exactly to Mandelker's. But, it is again hard to believe that the increases in returns being earned between a year and a half and two years before the merger were *caused* by the merger. Instead it is likely that these were higher returns earned by the acquiring firms, and if causality is involved at all it is these returns that caused the merger. Even if the latter conjecture is false, however, it seems unjustified to include as part of the gains *from* mergers, increases in returns on the stocks of acquiring companies earned more than a year and a half before the merger is announced.

The 69 firms making a single large acquisition which Lev and Mandelker study earned higher average returns on their stocks over the 5 years following the merger than before, as compared with a sample of companies matched by size and industry, but again the difference in sample means was statistically insignificant. Most of the other evidence in their study was also 'largely negative.'

All three of these studies conclude that their findings are inconsistent with the 'allegations' that mergers are not undertaken to improve the welfare of the acquiring firm's stockholders, or lead to real gains in economic efficiency. Halpern and Mandelker argue more specifically that their results suggest that mergers are a means of removing inefficient managements (of acquired companies). If we ignore the question of whether high returns cause firms to become acquirers or the reverse, this is a potentially legitimate interpretation of their findings. For the mergers do appear to have generated gains to the stockholders of the acquired firms. And if they did not do likewise for the stockholders of the acquirers they also did not generate negative returns. So at a minimum the mergers appear to have generated enough efficiency gains to have benefitted unambiguously the stockholders of the acquired firms. But this conclusion still raises some questions about the motives behind the mergers from the point of view of the acquiring firms.

For the mergers are not simply another form of *marginal* investment. The mergers examined in each of these 3 studies were between firms both of which were large enough to have listed securities. The acquiring firms in the Lev and Mandelker sample grew at roughly double the rate of their matched pairs over the same 11 year period, as did Weston and Mansinghka's conglomerates compared to their sample of industrials. Why should managers engage in acquisitions or series of acquisitions resulting in such dramatic increases in their company's size and perhaps character when their stockholders obtain no benefits from these changes, if the goal of the managers is to increase their stockholders' welfare? The interpretation of the Halpern, Mandelker and Lev and Mandelker findings these authors themselves give, leaves the managers of the acquiring firms as corporate good samaritans who go about bidding up the prices of badly managed firms and rescuing the stockholders of these firms from their managements, to the benefit of only the stockholders of the acquired firms. The acquiring company managers gain nothing, their stockholders a normal return.

The difficulty in reconciling normal returns to stockholders of acquiring companies, and supranormal returns to stockholders of acquired firms in a neoclassical framework is clearly evidenced in Mandelker's discussion of why it is that stockholders of *acquired* firms fair so well:

> When a firm is confronted with a tender offer a conflict of interest between management and shareholders may result. Although the stockholders of the acquired firm are likely to profit from the merger more than any other party involved, incumbent management may stand to lose the most, for they may forfeit their controlling position with all of the accompanying benefits (p. 326).

Earlier on the same page he notes that 'Indeed, it is very difficult to acquire a firm if its management resists forcefully,' citing B.F. Goodrich management's successful defeat of a merger bid that would have increased stockholder net worth by 30 percent. But a takeover fight is but a polar case and the most blatant example of a conflict of interest between managers and stockholders. And just as the existence of a separation between ownership and control can explain why managers reject merger proposals which would result in instantaneous capital gains of 30% and more for their stockholders, it can explain why managers make merger proposals resulting in no gains for their stockholders—and might even be willing to make such proposals if the stockholders suffered a loss. For the same strategems which allowed B.F. Goodrich's management to resist Northwest Industries' $1 billion tender offer were available to Northwest Industries management should they need them, to ward off unhappy stockholders who felt that was too much to pay for the assets of the Goodrich firm.

Thus, the conclusion that the stockholders of acquiring firms earned a normal return on their companies' acquisitions, even if warranted, does not in itself settle the issue as to why the managers of acquiring companies engage in this form of investment. We turn to this issue now.

3.8. The evidence as it relates to managerial motives for merger

Gort has noted with respect to earlier mergers that acquiring firms tend to be located in slow-growing sectors and enter fast growing ones (1966, p. 41). This strategy is consistent with Weston and Mansinghka's defensive diversification hypothesis, as is Gort's finding that *acquired* firms tend to be in R and D intensive industries (1969), and McGowan's that *acquiring* firms are in R and D *unintensive* industries (1971). These tendencies lead to a life-cycle view of the firm that is consistent with either a stockholder welfare maximization interpretation, as Weston and Mansinghka put forward, or a growth objective [see Mueller (1972); Grabowski and Mueller (1975)]. The conglomerates appear to have been located in industries in which technological maturity and competitive pressures inhibited internal growth.[11] If these firms wanted to grow fast, merger was the only feasible way. The evidence surveyed here indicates that whatever their objective, conglomerate mergers, like their predecessors, did not lead to significant improvements in the risk/return performance of the acquiring firms' stocks. Whether it was the objective sought or not, significant increases in growth were achieved via these mergers [Reid (1968); Weston and Mansinghka (1971); Mandelker (1974)].

The significantly higher leverage ratios of the conglomerates *before* they undertook their merger activity suggests that they did have more aggressive, expansion oriented managers than other companies. Singh also found that acquiring firms in the U.K. had higher leverage (gearing) ratios than nonacquirers, and in addition had higher retention ratios, lower liquidity, and faster growth rates (1971, pp. 160–161). Although Kuehn's results for the U.K. differ from Singh's in some respects, they are also consistent with the interpretation that acquiring company managers are more aggressive than other managers (1975, ch. 6).

Singh observed that acquired firms earned somewhat lower profits than nonacquired firms, and Kuehn observed both lower profits and valuation ratios for U.K. companies acquired (1975, ch. 3). Some studies in the U.S. from *before* the conglomerate merger wave have found similar patterns. But, no evidence has been gathered to suggest that acquired firms were to any degree in danger of bankruptcy, however, and the companies the *conglomerates* acquired were earning higher profits than themselves. Lynch has even argued on the basis of case study analysis of 28 conglomerates that they followed a strategy of acquiring 'successful, profitable companies' with 'capable management that can be retained' (1971, pp. 83–85). Indeed, to the extent that a failing-firm or alternative-to-bankruptcy motive for conglomerate mergers emerges at all from this literature, it is the *acquiring* firms that may be trying to improve their positions by *defensively* acquiring companies more profitable than themselves. This is ironic since the usual failing-firm defense of mergers has been couched in terms of rescuing acquired company stockholders from bad managers [e.g. Dewey (1961); Manne (1965)].

[11]A similar pattern of location for acquiring firms was observed by Kuehn for the U.K. (1975, pp. 16–24, ch. 4). Given the milder antitrust environment in the U.K., however, it was not necessary for these firms to go outside of their industries to achieve growth via mergers.

Several of the studies cited found that acquiring firms experienced periods of temporarily higher than normal returns preceding their acquisitions, returns that could not be in any sense 'caused' by the mergers. Nielsen and Melicher's finding that high P/E's and cash flows lead to higher offered premiums on mergers is also consistent with the view that it is 'cheap' internal and external capital which leads to mergers, capital which is cheap in the sense that management does not feel compelled to use it to maximize stockholder welfare. Beckenstein has observed a positive relationship between aggregate merger activity and the cost of external capital, which he interprets as supporting a managerial thesis (1977).

The would-be conglomerates did not have high cash flows and P/E's at the beginning of the 1960s. Nevertheless, the rise in profits and stock market values that occurred during this decade, and the relatively low interest rates prevailing throughout much of it, provided these firms with a more favorable environment to pursue growth through the most attractive avenue available to them: external expansion. The pursuit of this goal subsided at the end of the 1960s, when this environment changed.

Since growth must accompany any significant merger program, there is no way to establish whether this is the primary objective of these mergers, or auxiliary to some other(s). Space does not allow a review of all possible alternatives [but, see Steiner (1975, ch. 6)]. One does emerge from this survey, however, and since it has not received much attention in the literature it is worth discussing here.

Both Halpern (1973) and Mandelker (1974) provide evidence that the gains from mergers that do occur often come before the merger takes place or is even announced. This finding has been confirmed by Firth (1976) for the U.K. and Gagnon, Brehain, and Guerra (1976) for Belgium. Firth found a substantial rise in the stock prices for acquired firms over the 21 trading days preceding the announcement of the merger, peaking 4 days before the announcement (pp. 83–90). No change in the returns to stock on the acquiring firms was noted in this period, however.[12] Gagnon, et al. found a significant increase in the *volume* of trading in both the acquiring and acquired firms' stocks over the 10 *months* preceding a merger's announcement and concluded that information about the merger reached the market during this pre-announcement period.

None of these studies pursues the issue of who it is 'in the market' who has possession of this information about a forthcoming merger that causes an increase in trading volume and a rise, at least for the company to be acquired, in stock price. The most obvious group having access to this information is the management planning the merger. As Manne (1966) has emphasized the access to insider information is one of the important prerequisites managers have. And the knowledge that the shares of a to-be-acquired firm will soon rise by 15 percent or

[12](pp. 142–157) Some rise was noted if the acquiring firm financed the acquisition by a new equity issue, but this was attributed to the arrangement of 'some buying support for their securities' (p. 147). Interestingly enough, the acquiring firm's stock suffered a significant *decline* in value in the 30 trading days *following* the merger's announcement.

more, is a valuable piece of information. Thus, one possible explanation for why managers engage in mergers that have no benefit to their stockholders is that the mergers provide opportunities for possible gains from insider information.[13] This interpretation also seems easier to accept than that given by Hogarty (1970b) and Gort (1970), that the managers were risktakers maximizing stockholder welfare. For much of the risks arising from a merger fall to the stockholders, and access to insider information gives managers an opportunity to share disproportionately in the gains while avoiding some of the risks.

This interpretation also raises additional questions about studies such as Halpern's (1973) that base their conclusions solely on the gains from mergers on stock price data preceding the merger. To the extent managers do undertake mergers in anticipation of a favorable stockmarket reaction to the merger's announcement, an unfavorable reaction might be expected to lead to a cancellation of the merger bid. By focussing on stock market data for only successful bids up to the time of the merger, these studies choose the most favorable time period over which to judge the 'effects' from a merger.

Studies of previous merger waves have concluded that 'promoters profits' played a significant role in explaining the volume of merger activity.[14] The promoters of the conglomerate merger wave were the acquiring firms' managers themselves. The studies surveyed here suggest that someone was profiting on the information about the forthcoming merger, before it became public. Whether this was the managers, and to what extent these profits influenced their decisions, cannot be ascertained. But the hypothesis that speculation of this type may have been a significant factor is certainly consistent with the evidence surveyed here, and the more general phenomenon that merger waves accompany stock market advances.

4. The effects of conglomerate mergers on concentration

A fair consensus exists that conglomerate mergers have not contributed to increases in industry level concentration, at least at a low level of aggregation, and have not had serious anticompetitive effects [Markham (1973, ch. 5); Goldberg (1973, 1974); FTC (1972)]. But at the same time there appears to be little consensus as to what the effects of mergers have been on overall concentration. Thus, the FTC (1969) concluded:

There can be no doubt that mergers played a key role in increasing the share of manufacturing assets held by [the top 200] companies over the period [1947–

---

[13]Some of the rise in the acquired company's stock price may have been brought about through the acquiring firm's 'buying in' before the formal announcement. But Gagnon, et al. show that not all of the increase in *volume* of transactions can be explained in this way, and thus probably not all of the change in price. Any change in the volume traded or price of the acquiring firm's stock obviously cannot be explained in this way.

[14]For surveys of the early literature on this point, see Markham (1955) and Reid (1968, chs. 3, 4, 5).

1968]. Significantly, whereas industry growth effect played a role about equal in importance to mergers between 1947 and 1960, mergers have been almost exclusively responsible for the increase occurring since 1960. (p. 193)

While Jules Backman (1970) concluded:

Moreover, the growth of large companies is due primarily to internal expansion rather than to mergers. Thus, between 1948 and 1968, the total assets of the 200 largest manufacturing corporations increased by $242.4 billion . . . acquisitions accounted for $50.0 billion or 20.6 percent of this total increase. However, for the 10 largest companies, acquired assets were only 2.8 percent of the asset growth; for the second 10 largest it was (sic) 16.2 percent; and for the 21st to 50th largest, it was (sic) 24.3 percent. Clearly, for the very largest companies mergers have been a minor factor in their growth. (p. 122)

Surprisingly, these two sets of conclusions are not as irreconcilable as they appear. These and other similar studies have reached different conclusions because they have been answering different questions. Those studies which have attributed a substantial fraction of firm or overall concentration growth to mergers have been asking the question: What would the growth of large firms or increase in overall concentration have been had there been no mergers?[15]

The most systematic examination of this question is by John McGowan (1965). He found that:

. . . mergers appear to play a substantial role in allowing firms . . . to grow faster than the aggregate growth rate. Furthermore, though there are exceptions, the tendency appears to be that as the firm increases its size its ability to grow faster than the aggregate depends increasingly upon growth by merger . . . as the firm becomes relatively very large its ability just to maintain its position seems heavily dependent upon growth by merger. (p. 454)

McGowan concluded that mergers accounted for almost $\frac{2}{3}$ of the increase in the 500 firm concentration ratio between 1950 and 1960, and almost $\frac{3}{4}$ the increase in the 100 firm ratio (pp. 455–456).

The FTC study quoted above, also tried to answer the same question for the 1960s, although with less sophistication than McGowan, as did Lee Preston (1973). These studies confirm or even strengthen McGowan's conclusions as to the importance of mergers in explaining increases in overall concentration. The FTC's figures indicate an increase in the share the assets held by the largest 200 manufacturing corporations between 1960 and 1968 from 54.1 % to 60.9 % (1969, pp. 189–193). Over the same period the assets acquired by the largest 200 firms amounted to 10 % of total manufacturing assets. Thus, if no mergers had taken place, and other forms of growth were not fully substituted for mergers, overall concentration might have actually fallen over this period. This is in fact what one

[15]For a similar interpretation of these differences see Preston (1971, 1973).

would expect to have happened. In the absence of mergers overall concentration should rise during periods of contraction due to the greater vulnerability of smaller firms, and fall during upswings, due to new entry and the more rapid growth of smaller companies. This expectation was confirmed over the relatively merger free period of 1929–1947 when concentration rates increased substantially during the decline in business activity from 1929 to 1933, and then declined significantly during the economic recovery starting in 1933 and extending through World War II [Scherer (1971, pp. 41–45)]. Thus, one would expect overall concentration to have fallen over the sustained economic advance of the 1960s; that it did not is probably attributable to the merger wave.[16] Studies of the impact of mergers on concentration in the U.K. [Aaronovitch and Sawyer (1975); Hannah and Kay (1977)] and West Germany [Müller and Hochreiter (1976)] have reached similar conclusions.

Those authors who appear to have reached a different conclusion have in fact been asking the following question: What has been the ratio of assets acquired by the largest firms to their total growth? These studies have generally found this ratio to vary from 10 to 25 percent depending on the time period and group of firms covered [Bock (1970); Backman (1970); Piccini (1970); Markham (1973, pp. 114–124); Steiner (1975, pp. 289–307)]. That these are different questions, and that the answers obtained are consistent with one another can be most easily seen from the following example. Suppose the economy consisted of 1000 firms of equal size, each growing at 3 percent per year. In the absence of any mergers, entry or exit, overall concentration would remain unchanged. The 100 largest would always control 10 percent of assets. Suppose, however, 100 firms begin acquiring 1 percent of the total assets outstanding each year by acquiring 10 of the other 900 firms per year. This amounts to one acquisition per acquiring firm every 10 years. After 90 years all of the other firms are gone; the 100 largest possess all of the economy's assets. The percentage growth in assets of the top 100 accounted for by mergers would fall from 77 % in year one to 25 % in year 90. Yet, there would have been no increase in concentration had there not been any mergers. Thus, a falling and eventually relatively small ratio of growth via merger to total growth is consistent with the conclusion that all of the increase in concentration is a result of past mergers. Indeed, a falling ratio of merger to 'internal' growth is inevitable unless the largest firms follow a strategy of acquiring an ever-increasing percentage of the nation's total assets.

Those studies such as Backman (1970), Bock (1970, and earlier, Weston (1953), which adjust overall concentration or firm growth rates by past ratios of acquired to total asset growth, build in the questionable assumption that the acquired firm stopped growing at the time of its acquisition and that all subsequent growth is

[16]This is also consistent with McGowan's conclusion that overall concentration would eventually decline if all mergers were prohibited (1965). See also Preston (1973). There are various upward and downward biases in using the percentage of assets acquired as an indication of the importance of mergers, of course, but the figures give one a rough idea. See the FTC's discussion of these biases (1969) as well as Bock's (1970).

internal. Thus, over time, the contribution of any given merger to a firm's growth or the change in overall concentration under this procedure tends to zero. The conclusion that mergers are an unimportant source of growth or overall concentration change, which these studies draw, is thus not particularly surprising.

For policy purposes, the relevant question is what the level of concentration would be without any mergers. The answer seems fairly clear—significantly lower.

5. Policy implications

The evidence reviewed in this paper indicates that mergers result in no net gains to the acquiring firm's stockholders. Those studies which have drawn conclusions to the contrary have based these conclusions on profit and stock price increases occurring in the period of economic and stock market buoyancy, or on returns earned on stocks prior to the merger, and not always directly (or causally) related to the merger. Even then most of the positive results found have not been statistically significant at conventional confidence intervals. These positive results on mergers seem fully offset by those which have concluded on the basis of post merger results, or data extended beyond the stock market peak, that mergers are breakeven or unprofitable ventures. The results from the relevant studies are summarized in table 3.

This evidence is broadly consistent with the hypothesis that managers pursue corporate growth or other objectives that are not directly related to stockholder welfare and economic efficiency. This hypothesis can explain why managers of acquiring firms undertake mergers providing no benefits for their stockholders; why managers of acquisition targets vigorously resist bids which would greatly enrich their stockholders.

Nevertheless, one might argue that this literature presents no compelling case for government intervention. For there is no evidence that mergers now result in significant anticompetitive effects, and the studies suggesting that mergers are on average failures, are partially offset by those concluding that they are breakeven ventures. If mergers do not make things any better, they also do not make them much worse. Assuming the latter inference is valid, why not let managers pursue whatever goals they choose?

One cost of the pursuit of growth via external expansions, which has been cited in the literature, is that it is likely to come at the expense of more socially productive forms of growth [Reid (1968); Sichel (1970)]. Mergers compete directly with capital investment, R&D and other investment-type expenditures for cash flows and managerial decisionmaking capacities. While a manager is perhaps indifferent between whether a given rate of expansion is achieved through internal or external growth, society is likely to be better off through the creation of additional assets. Two of the studies discussed here present direct

Table 3

Summary of recent studies of returns from mergers for acquiring firms' stockholders.[a]

Author	Sample	Control group	Time period	Returns acquiring firms	Returns control group	Significance test
Hogarty (1970b)	43 nonconglomerates engaged in heavy merger activity	Firms in acquiring company's base industry	1953–64	−0.01 (one percent below returns of industry)		$\sigma = 0.11$ (difference from zero insignificant)
Lev and Mandelker (1972)	69 firms making large acquisitions (conglomerate and otherwise)	69 nonmerging firms matched by industry and size	1952–63	0.056 (05.6 percent above return of stock of matched sample)		$Z = 1.40$
Weston, Smith and Shrieves (1972)	48 conglomerates	50 mutual funds	1960–69	Ave. returns 1.262 Sharpe 0.364 Treynor 0.131 α/β 0.097	1.091 0.313 0.054 0.020	$F = 22.83$** 1.75 6.21* 6.21*
Melicher and Rush (1973)	45 conglomerates	45 nonconglomerates base industry as of 1960	6/66–12/71	Ave. returns 1.008 Sharpe 0.045 Treynor 0.004 Jensen α 0.002	1.007 0.047 0.005 0.001	$F = 0.20$ 0.03 0.80 0.18
Halpern (1973)	78 mergers by nonconglomerate firms	market portfolio	1/50–7/65	0.063 (mean cumulative residual of larger firm up to date of merger)		$\sigma = 0.31$ (difference from zero insignificant)

Study	Sample	Benchmark	Period	Results	Significance
Mandelker (1974)	241 large acquisitions (conglomerate and nonconglomerate)	market portfolio	1941–63	0.0005 (cumulative residual in 7 mos. preceding merger using premerger β).	$t = 0.04$
				0.0023 (cumulative residual in 20 mos. preceding merger using post-merger β)	$t = 1.73$
				0.0003 (cumulative residual in 20 mos. after the merger using post-merger β)	$t = 0.033$
Haugen and Langetieg (1975)	59 large nonconglomerate mergers	59 matched pairs of firms	1951–1968	$1 >$ *market index; $5 <$ *market index	$1 >$ *market index; $3 <$ *market index; No significant difference exists in the proportions of success and failures in the two groups
Mason and Goudzwaard	22 conglomerates	22 matched portfolios	1962–1967	0.0746	0.1275 SM portfolio $Z = 1.93$*; 0.1182 Mutual fund $Z = 1.59$; 0.1399 Buy and hold $Z = 2.33$*

[a]Notes: *indicates significant at the 0.05 level,
**indicates significant at the 0.01 level.

evidence that mergers do come at the expense of internal growth. Hogarty (1970a) found that the post merger sales of the merging firms were lower than predicted from their premerger sales.[17] Lev and Mandelker found that the *internal* growth rates of acquiring firms decreased in the post-merger period, a result they attributed to 'perhaps a "shakedown" or "digestion" effect' (1972, p. 97).

A second cost of mergers is the rise in overall concentration they bring about, as documented in the preceding section, and the reduction in the number of independent economic entities this entails [on the latter see Preston (1971, p. 21)]. The usual argument by economists is that increases in industry concentration constitute a potential economic (market power) problem, increases in overall concentration, if anything, a political (power) problem. Up until the 1970s the latter would then be quickly dismissed as unsubstantiated or beyond the bounds of economic analysis. But, I trust, the age of innocence regarding corporate power is now over. Large corporations both have and utilize political power. And it seems reasonable to assume that this power is positively related to company size.[18] A policy curtailing mergers and reversing upward trends in overall concentration would be a first step toward halting, if not reversing, increases in corporate power.

Space precludes a review of all the proposals to constrain merger activity that have been put forward [see Steiner (1975, ch. 12)]. The main issues can be illustrated, however, by focussing on the two polar extremes: maintenance of the present policy, or a flat ban on all mergers.

The *economic* rationale underlying the antitrust laws is based on a variant of the invisible hand argument as applied to price competition. If managers maximize profits then the allocation of resources is most efficiently achieved through the independently set prices of each firm. Government intervention is warranted only to prevent collusion and other efforts to monopolize. But the invisible hand analogy breaks down when one switches to investment-type activities, and allows for nonprofit maximization objectives. Just as there is no proof that competition for sales among firms via advertising results in improved allocational efficiency, there is no proof or evidence that the pursuit of growth via merger leads to anything more than external growth at the expense of internal growth.

Acceptance of this argument would suggest abandoning the invisible hand premise as an underpinning for some parts of antitrust legislation. With respect to mergers this could imply a ban on all mergers, perhaps limited to companies above a given size, and subject to an 'efficiencies defense.' The latter could be

[17]Because of this Hogarty rejects growth in sales as the motive for mergers (1970a, p. 389). His conclusion *ignores* the immediate growth of the acquiring company brought about by the merger. If this is the growth sought, Hogarty's results are not inconsistent with this objective.

[18]For a pioneering and largely successful effort to relate political power to *industry* concentration see Pittman (1976).

written fairly broadly to include explicitly replacement of bad managers (as well as rescue of failing firms), capital transfer efficiencies, and perhaps other efficiency gains put forward in the literature. The major difference between this law and the present one would be in locating the burden of proof. Instead of the government having to prove a substantial lessening of competition, the companies would have to prove likely efficiency gains.

Obviously if anything like the present number of mergers were to take place, such a law could be a tremendous administrative burden. The assumption is, based on the surveyed evidence regarding the number of successful mergers occurring, that only a small fraction of the mergers presently undertaken would promise sufficient efficiency gains to be capable of defending on these grounds in court.

It can be argued that such a law would reduce the threat of takeover and thereby increase the scope of managerial discretion and potentially lead to an even more inefficient allocation of resources than under the present law. Smiley (1976) explains the decline in share prices he observes before takeover as evidence of the exercise of managerial discretion, and other studies finding lower returns or profits before merger are consistent with this view. But as noted above, the evidence on this point is in conflict. In addition, Smiley's own results, and the data on returns to acquiring firms, suggests that the gains from replacing incompetent or nonstockholder welfare maximizing managers have not been all that large. Nevertheless, any effort to curtail the volume of merger activity should, to be consistent, be accompanied by other measures to improve the markets for capital and corporate control. More detailed accounting procedures, less costly procedures for engaging in proxy fights or direct takeovers, and perhaps even measures forcing a greater payout of profits and more reliance on the external capital market.

Some of the evidence surveyed here concerning the greater profitability of the target firms in conglomerate mergers is consistent with the capital redeployment thesis, and also suggests a possible worsening of efficiency from an effective curtailment of merger activity. Here the possibility of internal expansion and diversification should be kept in mind, as well as an 'efficiencies defense' for mergers. The usual argument for mergers over internal expansion is that they allow the firm to achieve the potential efficiency gain faster than if it must expand internally [Williamson (1968)]. But, the evidence cited here on profit and return on equity effects indicates that no efficiency gains are realized *or perceived* by the market in the first few years following the merger. Perhaps, this too is a result of the digestion problems Lev and Mandelker suspect are inhibiting post merger growth. But, whatever the cause, these results imply a small loss, if any, to society from waiting for the benefits from a redeployment of capital to follow internal diversification.[19]

[19]Internal expansion is not a viable alternative under Cable's 'information search' variant on the redeployment of capital thesis (1976).

Several writers have pointed out that growth through merger is not the only form of growth, and the conglomerates in particular are not the only or even necessarily the worst abusers of political power. [Steiner (1975, chs. 11, 12); Williamson (1975, pp. 170–171)]. Their points are well taken. The reasons for singling out growth through merger, conglomerate or otherwise, for discriminatory treatment is that it is the easiest form of growth to attack, it is a main contributor to increasing overall concentration, and we have good evidence that there will be negligible efficiency losses from such a policy. This policy need not be considered a substitute for or superior to a broad scale attack on existing market power. It is simply a place to start.

6. Conclusion

It has become customary to close a review of the merger literature by observing that the arguments are still in conflict, the main issues still in doubt, and from this draw the prudent conclusion that policy changes should proceed slowly and cautiously. True, the a priori theories of mergers' causes and effects are still in conflict, and will probably always remain so. But the empirical literature, upon which this survey focusses, draws a surprisingly consistent picture. Whatever the stated or unstated goals of managers are, the mergers they have consummated have on average not generated extra profits for the acquiring firms, have not resulted in increased economic efficiency. Admittedly some unsolved riddles remain, but all discussion of serious policy alternatives need not be set aside until these are resolved.

Although a recommendation to proceed cautiously in the face of conflicting evidence seems on the surface reasonable enough, it is in fact a recommendation to accept the neoclassical theories of mergers, stick with the status quo policy on mergers, and accept this policy's underlying premise of an invisible hand guiding the market for control.

We now have almost a century of accumulated evidence as to the effects of a laissez faire policy toward mergers. Enough time has elapsed and evidence been gathered that one can say that this policy experiment has not been a success. The time has come to try a new experiment. I think we can now legitimately ask managers to prove prior to a merger, that this merger is likely 'to substantially lessen' inefficiency.

References

Aaronovitch, S. and M.C. Sawyer, 1975, Mergers, growth and concentration, Oxford Economic Papers 27, 136–155, March.
Backman, J., 1970, Conglomerate mergers and competition, St. John's Law Review, special edition 44, 90–132, Spring.
Beckenstein, A.R., 1977, Merger activity and merger theories: An empirical investigation, mimeo, University of Virginia.

Binder, D., 1973, An empirical study of contested tender offers: 1960–1969, S.J.D. thesis, Law School, University of Michigan.

Bock, B., 1970, Statistical games and the '200 largest industrials,' 1954 and 1968, New York: National Industrial Conference Board, 1970.

Boyle, S.E., 1970, Pre-merger growth and profit characteristics of large conglomerate mergers in the United States 1948–68, St. John's Law Review, special edition 44, 152–70, Spring.

Brenner, M. and D.H. Downes, 1975, A critical evaluation of the measurement of conglomerate performance, using the capital asset pricing model, Berkeley, Research Program in Finance, Working Paper No. 35, May.

Cable, J., 1976, Searching by merger and the transfer of capital, IIM, Berlin.

Conn, R.L., 1973, Performance of conglomerate firms: Comment, Journal of Finance 28, 154–159, June.

Conn, R.L., 1976, The failing firm/industry doctrines in conglomerate mergers, Journal of Industrial Economics 24, 181–187, March.

Dewey, D., 1961, Mergers and cartels: Some reservations about policy, American Economic Review 51, 255–262, May.

Ellert, J.C., 1976, Mergers, antitrust law enforcement and stockholder returns, Journal of Finance 31, 715–732, May.

Evans, J.L. and S.H. Archer, 1968, Diversification and the reduction of dispersion: An empirical analysis, Journal of Finance 23, 29–40, December.

Federal Trade Commission, 1969, Economic report on corporate mergers, Washington, D.C.: United States Government Printing Office.

Federal Trade Commission, 1972, Economic report on conglomerate merger performance, an empirical analysis of nine corporations, Washington, D.C.: United States Government Printing Office, November.

Firth, M., 1976, Share prices and mergers, Westmead, England: Saxon House.

Gagnon, J.-M., P. Brehain and F. Guerra, 1976, Stock market behavior of merging firms: The Belgian experience: I, Mons, Belgium.

Goldberg, L.G., 1973, The effect of conglomerate mergers on competition, Journal of Law and Economics 16, 137–158, April.

Goldberg, L.G., 1974, Conglomerate mergers and concentration ratios, Review of Economics and Statistics 56, 303–309, August.

Gort, M., 1966, Diversification, mergers and profits, in: W. Alberts and J. Segall, eds., The corporate merger, Chicago: University of Chicago Press.

Gort, M., 1969, An economic disturbance theory of mergers, Quarterly Journal of Economics 83, 624–642, November.

Gort, M. and T.F. Hogarty, 1970, New evidence on mergers, Journal of Law and Economics 13, 167–184, April.

Grabowski, H.G. and D.C. Mueller, 1975, Life-cycle effects on corporate returns on retentions, Review of Economics and Statistics 57, 400–409, November.

Halpern, P.J., 1973, Empirical estimates of the amount and distribution of gains to companies in mergers, Journal of Business 46, 554–75, October.

Hannah, L. and J.A. Kay, 1977, Concentration in modern industry (Macmillan, London).

Haugen, R.A. and T.C. Langetieg, 1975, An empirical test for synergism in merger, Journal of Finance 30, 1003–1014, September.

Haugen, R.A. and J.G. Udell, 1972, Rates of return to stockholders of acquired companies, Journal of Financial and Quantitative Analysis 7, 1387–1398, January.

Hayes, S.L. III and R.A. Taussig, 1967, Tactics of cash takeover bids, Harvard Business Review 45, 135–148, March-April.

Hogarty, T.F., 1970a, Profits from Mergers: The evidence of fifty years, St. John's Law Review, special edition 44, 378–391, Spring.

Hogarty, T.F., 1970b, The profitability of corporate mergers, Journal of Business 43, 317–327, July.

Holzmann, O.J., R.M. Copeland and J. Hayya, 1975, Income measures of conglomerate performance, Quarterly Review of Economics and Business 15, 67–78, Autumn.

Joehnk, M.D. and J.F. Nielsen, 1974, The effects of conglomerate merger activity on systematic risk, Journal of Financial and Quantitative Analysis 9, 215–225, March.

Kuehn, D., 1975, Takeovers and the theory of the firm (Macmillan, London).

Lev, B. and G. Mandelker, 1972, The microeconomic consequences of corporate mergers, Journal of Business 45, 85–104, January.

Levy, H. and M. Sarnat, 1970, Diversification, portfolio analysis and the uneasy case for conglomerate mergers, Journal of Finance 25, 795–802, September.

Lewellen, W., 1971, A pure financial rationale for the conglomerate merger, Journal of Finance 26, 521–537, May.

Lintner, J., 1971, Expectations, mergers and equilibrium in purely competitive securities markets, American Economic Review 61, 101–111, May.

Lorie, J.H. and P. Halpern, 1970, Conglomerates: The rhetoric and the evidence, Journal of Law and Economics 13, 149–166, April.

Lynch, H.H., 1971, Financial performance of conglomerates (Harvard Business School, Boston).

Mandelker, G., 1974, Risk and return: The case of merging firms, Journal of Financial Economics 1, 303–335, December.

Manne, H., 1965, Mergers and the market for corporate control, Journal of Political Economy 73, 110–120, April.

Manne, H., 1966, Insider trading and the stock market (Free Press, New York).

Markham, J., 1955, Survey of the evidence and findings on mergers, Business concentration and public policy (National Bureau of Economic Research, New York).

Markham, J., 1973, Conglomerate enterprise and public policy (Harvard Business School, Boston, Mass.).

Marris, R., 1964, The economic theory of managerial capitalism (Free Press, Glencoe, Ill.).

Mason, R.H. and M.B. Goudzwaard, 1976, Performance of conglomerate firms: A portfolio approach, Journal of Finance 31, 39–48, March.

Mead, W.J., 1969, Instantaneous merger profit as conglomerate merger motive, Western Economic Journal 7, 295–306, December.

Melicher, R.W. and D.F. Rush, 1973, The performance of conglomerate firms: Recent risk and return experience, Journal of Finance 28, 381–388, May.

Melicher, R.M. and D.F. Rush, 1974, Evidence on the acquisition-related performance of conglomerate firms, Journal of Finance 29, 1941–1949, March.

Mingo, J.J., 1976, Managerial motives, market structures and the performance of holding company banks, Economic Inquiry 14, 411–424, September.

McGowan, J.J., 1965, The effect of alternative antimerger policies on the size distribution of firms, Yale Economic Essays 5, 423–474, Fall.

McGowan, J.J., 1971, International comparisons of merger activity, Journal of Law and Economics 14, 233–250, April.

Mueller, D.C., 1969, A theory of conglomerate mergers, Quarterly Journal of Economics 83, 643–659, November.

Mueller, D.C., 1972, A life cycle theory of the firm, Journal of Industrial Economics 20, 199–219, July.

Müller, J. and R. Hochreiter, 1975, Stand, entwicklung und konsequenzen der unternehmenskonzentration in der Bundesrepublik, IIM, Berlin.

Nelson, R., 1959, Merger movements in American industry 1895–1956 (Princeton University Press, Princeton).

Nelson, R.L., 1966, Business cyle factors in the choice between internal and external growth, in: W. Alberts and J. Segall, eds., The corporate merger (University of Chicago Press, Chicago).

Nielsen, J.F. and R.W. Melicher, 1973, A financial analysis of acquisition and merger premiums, Journal of Financial and Quantitative Analysis 8, 139–148, March.

Piccini, R., 1970, Mergers, diversification, and the growth of large firms: 1948–1965, St. John's Law Review, special edition 44, 171–192, Spring.

Piper, T.F. and S.J. Weiss, 1974, The profitability of multibank holding company acquisitions, Journal of Finance 29, 163–174, March.

Pittmann, R., 1976, The effects of industry concentration and regulation on contributions in three 1972 U.S. Senate campaigns, Public Choice 27, 71–80, Fall.

Preston, L.E., 1971, The industry and enterprise structure of the U.S. economy (General Learning Press, New York).

Preston, L.E., 1973, Giant firms, large mergers and concentration: Patterns and policy alternatives, 1954–1968, Industrial Organization Review 1, 35–46.

Reid, S.R., 1968, Mergers, managers and the economy (McGraw-Hill, New York).

Reid, S.R., 1971, A reply to the Weston/Mansinghka criticisms dealing with conglomerate mergers, Journal of Finance 26, 937–946, September.

Scherer, F.M., 1971, Industrial market structure and economic performance (Rand McNally, Chicago).

Sherman, R., 1972, How tax policy induces conglomerate mergers, National Tax Journal 25, 521–529, December.

Sichel, W., 1970, Conglomerateness: Size and monopoly control, St. John's Law Review, special edition 44, 354–377, Spring.

Singh, A., 1971, Takeovers: Their relevance to the stock market and the theory of the firm (Cambridge University Press, Cambridge).

Smiley, R., 1976, Tender offers, transactions costs and the firm, Review of Economics and Statistics 58, 22–32, February.

Steiner, P.O., Mergers (University of Michigan Press, Ann Arbor, Michigan).

Stevens, D.L., 1973, Financial characteristics of merged firms: A multivariate analysis, Journal of Financial and Quantitative Analysis 8, 149–158, March.

Stigler, G.J., 1950, Monopoly and oligopoly by merger, American Economic Review 40, 23–34, May.

Thorp, W.L., 1931, The persistence of the merger movement, American Economic Review 21, 77–89, March.

Weston, J.F., 1953, The role of mergers in the growth of large firms (University of California Press, Berkeley).

Weston, J.F., 1970, The nature and significance of conglomerate firms, St. John's Law Review, special edition 44, 66–80, Spring.

Weston, J.F. and S.K. Mansinghka, 1971, Tests of the efficiency performance in conglomerate firms, Journal of Finance 26, 919–936, September.

Weston, J.F., K.V. Smith and R.E. Shrieves, 1972, Conglomerate performance using the capital asset pricing model, Review of Economics and Statistics 54, 357–363, November.

Williamson, O.E., 1968, Economies as an antitrust defense: The welfare tradeoffs, American Economic Review 58, 18–36, March.

Williamson, O.E., 1970, Corporate control and business behavior: An inquiry into the effects of organization form on enterprise behavior (Prentice-Hall, New York).

Williamson, O.E., 1975, Markets and hierarchies: Analysis and antitrust implications (Free Press, New York).

MERGER BENEFITS TO SHARE-HOLDERS OF ACQUIRING FIRMS

RICHARD A. SHICK and
FRANK C. JEN

Dr. Shick is Assistant Professor of Banking and Finance at the University
of Georgia. Dr. Jen is The Manufacturers and Traders Trust Company
Professor of Banking and Finance at the State University of New York at
Buffalo.

Introduction

Recent empirical investigations show that shareholders receive benefits from mergers despite the fact that academicians traditionally have argued they do not. Unfortunately, these studies have been concentrated on conglomerate mergers rather than on more traditional forms. Moreover, very little attention has been given to identification of the point of the merger process where these benefits arise. This article measures the benefits received by shareholders of firms involved in horizontal acquisitions and identifies the point at which they occur.

Measuring Merger Benefits

The principal problems encountered in measuring merger benefits are establishment of a standard for their measurement and adjustment of measured benefits for changes in the firm's risk. To establish a standard, the firm's merger decision is viewed as one of external rather than internal expansion. Thus, the return received as a result of the acquisition must be compared to the return the shareholders would have received had there been no merger. The difference is the merger benefit. Since the hypothetical or non-merger return cannot be observed, it is necessary to find a reasonable proxy. Financial theory says that shareholders must be compensated if the merger makes the equity of the acquiring firm more risky. Therefore, the difference between the actual return at the new risk level and the hypothetical nonmerger return contains two elements — merger benefits and compensation for changed risk. To measure only the merger benefits risk compensation must be removed.

A Technique of Measurement

A diagram of the merger analysis problem over a three year period is presented in Exhibit 1. A beneficial merger is depicted in the first year for which there are two ways of measuring benefits. Consistent with previous studies, the first method compares the actual returns over the entire 3 year period with the hypothetical or nonmerger return. The alternative approach decomposes the larger period into 3 subperiods and calculates merger benefits for each one. Thus, the main merger branch is compared with the nonmerger branch for the first year only and with the

483

Exhibit 1. Merger Analysis Diagram

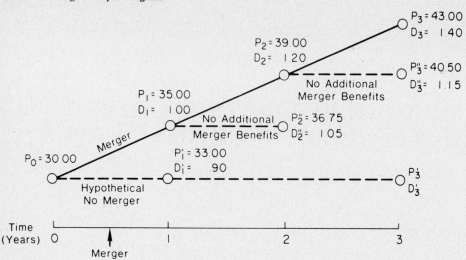

subbranches (shown by dotted lines) for years 2 and 3. One advantage to this approach is that it reduces the effect of risk differences by shortening the period (see the Appendix). Also, the shorter periods require predictions of hypothetical nonmerger performance for one year rather than 3 so that errors in the first years are not compounded.

The merger benefits for year 1 are measured by first calculating the actual return by adding the dividends paid during the year (D_1) to the ending price (P_1), subtracting the beginning price (P_0) from the sum, and dividing the result by the beginning price (P_0). In this example, $R_1 = (35.00 + 1.00 - 30.00)/30.00 = .200$. Both prices and dividends are observable and R_1 presents no calculation problems.

To complete the calculation, it is necessary to know the return that would have been received without a merger. This quantity is not observable for a completed merger, and a number of proxies have been proposed. Alternatives such as the average returns of firms in the acquirer's industry [3, 5] and those for an interindustry sample of nonmerging firms [8] are potentially poor substitutes because they do not account for the premerger return position of the acquiring firm. For example, if a firm is earning a return below its industry average, it must raise its return via the merger above the industry average to be considered successful.

Exhibit 1 indicates that the critical quantities for determining the nonmerger return in period 1 are the ending price (P_1') and the dividends paid during the

period (D_1') since neither is directly observable. The technique used here to predict these values [9] is described fully in the Appendix. Briefly, it allows a direct prediction of the unobservable quantities with a common stock valuation equation. This approach permits individual predictions for each firm analyzed; consequently, our results should be more sensitive to individual firm differences than those of previous studies.

Once nonmerging price and dividends are determined, the hypothetical nonmerger return (R_1') is calculated by summing the hypothetical ending price (P_1') and the hypothetical dividends (D_1'), subtracting the actual beginning price, and dividing by the actual beginning price, or as in Exhibit 1, $R_1' = (33.00 + .90 - 30.00)/30.00 = .130$. Finally, the merger benefit (MB_1) for period 1 is the difference between the actual return (R_1) and the hypothetical return (R_1') or $MB_1 = .200 - .130 = .070$.

Merger benefits for the second year are calculated in generally the same way. The actual return ($R_2 = .148$) is $P_2(39.00) + D_2(1.20) - P_1(35.00) / P_1(35.00)$. The hypothetical return ($R_2' = .145$) is slightly different for year 1 because of the interpretation of the hypothetical price (P_2'') and dividends (D_2'') at the end of the year. P_2'' is the price if *no additional* merger benefits are received from time 1 to time 2. That is, given the merger benefits and risk changes in the first period, P_2'' would be the price without further merger benefits. As described in the Appendix, this quantity can also be determined using the valuation equation approach. R_2^j is then calculated as $R_2^j =$ (36.75 + 1.05 − 33.00) / 33.00 = .145, and the merger benefit for year 2 is .003 (.148 − .145).

The same calculation method is repeated for year 3. The actual return is .138 [(43.00 = 1.40 − 39.00) / (39.00)]; the hypothetical return is .133 [(40.50 = 1.15 − 36.75) / (36.75)]; and the merger benefit is .005.

Data

A sample of 24 acquiring firms was selected from 3 industries — chemicals, machinery and electric utilities — for which names, acquisition dates, and types of payment are presented in Exhibit 2. These classifications represent a wide range of operating

Exhibit 2. Sample of Merging Firms

Acquiring firm	Acquired firm	Date of merger	Type of* payment
A. Chemical sample			
Air Products and Chemicals, Inc.	Houdry Process	2/1/62	C. Stock
Air Reduction Company	Speer Carbon	8/31/61	C. Stock
American Potash and Chemical Corporation	Lindsay Chemical	5/1/58	C. Stock
Atlas Chemical Industries, Inc.	Stuart Co.	6/1/61	C. Stock
Celanese Corp.	Devoe & Raynolds	8/4/64	Cash
	Champlin Oil	8/18/64	C. Stock & C. P. Stock
	Federal Enameling	11/27/64	C. Stock
Hooker Chemical	Parker Rustproof Co.	3/30/62	C. Stock & P. Stock
Reichhold Chemicals, Inc.	Alsynite	2/16/60	C. Stock
	Modiglas Fibers, Inc.	4/12/60	Cash
	Deecy Products	5/11/60	Cash
Stauffer Chemical Co.	Victor Chemical Works	11/1/59	C. Stock
B. Machinery sample			
American Chain & Cable Co., Inc.	Mechanical Handling Systems	12/31/65	C. Stock
Barber Greene	Smith Engineering	5/31/60	C. Stock
Bethlehem Corp.	Superior Tool & Dye Co.	8/31/62	C. Stock
Clark Equipment Co.	Tyler Refrigeration	9/30/63	C. Stock
Dresser Industries	Manning, Maxwell & Moore, Inc.	11/10/64	Cash
Koehring Co.	Thew Shovel	2/7/64	Cash & C. Stock
McNeil Co.	F. E. Myers Brothers	6/1/60	Cash
Midland Ross Corp.	Industrial Rayon	5/1/61	Cash
Rex Chainbelt	Mathews Conveyor	12/31/64	C. Stock
Wallace Murray Corp.	Wm. Wallace Corp.	9/1/65	C. Stock & P. Stock
	Simonds Saw and Steel	2/1/66	Cash
C. Utility sample			
Commonwealth Edison	Central Illinois Gas & Electric	5/1/66	C. P. Stock
Connecticut Light & Power Company	Housatonic Public Service	5/1/61	C. Stock
Orange & Rockland Utilities	Orange & Rockland Electric	2/1/58	C. Stock
Pacific Power and Light	California-Oregon Power	6/21/61	C. Stock
Public Service-Colorado	Colorado Central Power	12/29/61	C. Stock
Southern California Edison	California Electric Power	5/16/63	C. Stock

*C. Stock — Common Stock; C.P. Stock — convertible preferred stock; P. Stock — preferred stock.

environments, and each contains a relatively large number of nonmerging firms used to predict non-merger performance of the acquiring firm.

For merger benefits to be measurable, the acquired firm must be large enough to have a significant impact on the operations of the acquiring firm. As in other studies, the premerger market value of the acquired firm in this sample was required to be at least 5% of the premerger market value of the acquiring firm. To isolate the effects of the acquisition selected, it was required that no other firm meeting the 5% criterion had been acquired for a period of 3 years before and after the merger. Three exceptions to the last criterion were analyzed as single acquisitions.

Empirical Results

Merger benefits and geometric averages for all 3 periods are presented in Exhibit 3 for each firm. Summary figures including means, standard deviations, and t ratios are reported in Exhibit 4.

These results illustrate the success of the mergers. The 9.67 benefit in period 1 indicates that acquiring firms increased returns to shareholders by almost 10% over the estimated amount without the acquisition. Moreover, this figure is net of dilution effects since it looks at performance of a single share after adjustment for stock splits and stock dividends. The probability that the true merger benefit is zero and that the 9.67 value is due to chance is less than 2.5%. In addition, the results are not dominated by a few highly successful firms because 17 of 24, or 71%, exhibited positive merger benefits. It is also illustrated that all significant positive merger benefits occur during the first year. This indicates the efficiency with which investors evaluate the new information.

Further insights are gained by examining the behavior of firms with positive and with negative merger benefits in period 1. With respect to the overall benefits for the 3 year period, 12 of the 17 firms receiving positive merger benefits in period 1 continued to do so for the entire period. However, only 10 of the 17 successful firms in the second and only 6 of these 10 in the third period had positive merger

Exhibit 3. Merger Benefits by Firm and Period

[In Percent]

Firm	Period 1	Period 2	Period 3	Overall*
Connecticut L & P	.4	− 8.6	25.4	6.8
Orange & Rockland	− .9	5.1	19.8	4.5
Pacific P & L	15.0	− 7.8	38.5	13.6
Public Sev.-Col.	−14.6	29.2	35.8	14.3
So. Calif. Ed.	23.3	−39.0	− 4.9	−10.6
Comm. Edison	9.5	18.6	−31.5	− 7.7
Am. Chain & Cab.	2.9	10.6	1.3	4.7
Barber Greene	−26.0	−33.8	−32.4	−30.2
Bethlehem	−19.1	−15.9	31.7	− 3.6
Clark Equip.	20.5	15.6	10.3	15.3
Dresser	24.6	−12.0	13.5	7.5
Koehring	19.0	34.5	−29.6	3.9
McNeil	24.9	−22.0	−13.2	− 1.6
Midland Ross	22.5	12.8	14.4	16.5
Rex Chainbelt	36.6	39.0	38.2	37.9
Wallace-Murray	26.1	8.0	8.6	11.0
Am. Potash	−18.4	− 5.7	8.9	− 5.7
Air Products	25.1	.4	24.3	16.0
Air Reduction	−11.1	6.7	−11.5	− 5.7
Atlas	37.3	−44.4	−34.5	−20.6
Celanese	34.9	−29.3	−10.6	− 5.2
Hooker	0.0	24.9	− 3.5	6.3
Reichhold	25.9	1.5	− .7	8.0
Stauffer	−26.3	−44.7	−44.1	−38.9

*Computed as a geometric average of the returns for the first 3 periods.

Exhibit 4. A Summary of Merger Benefits

[In Percent]

	Mean	Standard deviation	t ratio
Three periods	1.52 (14)*	16.21	.46
Period 1	9.67 (17)	20.30	2.33 (.025)
Period 2	−2.68 (13)	24.22	.54
Period 3	2.68 (13)	25.58	.51

*Number of firms with positive merger benefits.

benefits. Thus, it cannot be inferred that a successful first period increases the probability of success in succeeding periods. It also appears that the probability of success decreases with succeeding periods.

The pattern is somewhat more favorable for firms with negative merger benefits in the first period. Four of the 7 show negative benefits overall, but while 5 of the 7 also have negative benefits in period 2, of these only two have negative benefits for period 3. The fact that the probability of positive merger benefits appears to increase after an unsuccessful beginning may indicate that some mergers are slow to reveal their benefits. However, it is dangerous to generalize from these results due to the smallness of the number involved.

There is no obvious reason for the lack of success of the 7 nonbeneficial mergers. They are fairly evenly distributed over the 3 industries, and 5 of them occurred during years in which the Standard and Poors Industrial Stock Average rose. Their only common characteristic was the use of common stock to pay shareholders of the acquired firm. While this type payment lowers benefits through dilution effects, the significance of its use is minimized since almost 50% of the beneficial mergers used common stock.

Some Caveats and Qualifications

The validity of the results of this study depends upon the ability to predict hypothetical nonmerger price and dividends. It is impossible to directly assess predictive ability, but some information as to how well the stock price equation predicts prices in general can be provided. After a thorough testing of the model the results were found to be highly satisfactory. Average R^2 values were over .82, and average standard errors of estimate for the firms were less than 6% of their share prices.

The high average explanatory power of the model

does not mean that relatively large individual errors cannot be made. In the chemical sample, for example, the standard error of prediction for an individual firm can approach 20% of its price. To test the model's validity for merging firms, the actual financial variables for acquiring firms were used to compare predicted with actual prices; no significant differences from the average results described above were discovered.

Significant gains are shown for a sample of firms who were not active acquirers, who generally paid for the acquired firms with common stock, acquired firms in the same or closely related industries, and paid an average premium of 35% based on share prices at the beginning of the first period. Benefits measured as the difference between actual common stock returns and predicted returns presumably represent changes in investor expectations about the firm and consequently could be regarded as expected or anticipated benefits. While there is no direct evidence on whether or not such expectations were realized, there do not appear to be any significant downward revaluations for positive benefits during the three years examined.

The positive merger benefit found here is contrary to some previous studies [3, 5, 8] and generally exceeds the positive benefits found in others [4, 6, 7, 10, 11]. This is partly explained by differences in the way merger benefits were measured. First, the valuation equation approach allows separate predictions for acquiring firms based on their premerger performance. It is more responsive to individual differences and does not require all firms to outperform a single standard to be judged successful as in [3, 5, 8]. Second, by decomposing the analysis period into 3 subperiods, it is possible to (1) minimize the risk change problem present in many studies and specifically recognized in [6], and (2) minimize the averaging effect that exists in most of the studies and is apparent in Exhibit 4. When the significant merger benefit in period 1 is combined with the two other periods the result is small and no longer significant; thus, the longer the period over which the benefits are measured, the greater will be the potential bias from averaging.

Implications

The findings have several implications for financial managers. First, the benefits were produced even though relatively large premiums were paid to the shareholders of the acquired firm proving that a high premium does not automatically imply an unsuccessful merger. Also, over 85% of the mergers involved the exchange of common stock and/or cash so that it was unnecessary to use hybrid securities to produce the benefits. Under these conditions, the only remaining source of merger benefits is operating economies of some form. Thus, a well-conceived and executed merger is possible and will yield substantial benefits for the firm's shareholders. Finally, although mergers are analyzed "after the fact," it is possible to analyze them "before the fact" as well and use the results to simulate outcomes from potential mergers.

REFERENCES

1. R. S. Bower and D. H. Bower, "Risk and the Valuation of Common Stock," *Journal of Political Economy* (May/June 1969), pp. 349-362.

2. M. J. Gordon, *The Investment, Financing and Valuation of the Corporation,* Homewood, Illinois, Richard D. Irwin, Inc., 1962.

3. M. Gort and T. F. Hogarty, "New Evidence on Mergers," *Journal of Law and Economics* (April 1970), pp. 167-184.

4. P. J. Halpern, "Empirical Estimates of the Amount and Distribution of Gains to Companies in Mergers," *Journal of Business* (October 1973).

5. T. F. Hogarty, "The Profitability of Corporate Mergers," *Journal of Business* (July 1970), pp. 317-327.

6. B. Lev and G. Mandelker, "The Microeconomic Consequences of Corporate Mergers," *Journal of Business* (January 1972), pp. 85-104.

7. R. W. Melicher and D. F. Rush, "The Performance of Conglomerate Firms: Recent Risk and Return Experience," *Journal of Finance* (May 1973), pp. 381-388.

8. S. R. Reid, *Mergers, Managers, and the Economy,* New York, McGraw-Hill Book Company, Inc., 1968.

9. R. A. Shick, "The Analysis of Mergers and Acquisitions," *Journal of Finance* (May 1972), pp. 495-502.

10. J. F. Weston and S. K. Mansinghka, "Tests of the Efficiency Performance of Conglomerate Firms," *Journal of Finance* (September 1971), pp. 919-936.

11. J. F. Weston, K. V. Smith and R. E. Schrieves, "Conglomerate Performance Using the Capital Asset Pricing Model," *Review of Economics and Statistics* (November 1972), pp. 357-363.

Appendix

Risk Change

Assume that (1) had no merger occurred, shareholders of acquiring firm X would require a return of 1.2% per month on their investment, (2) as a result of the merger, the firm's risk decreases and the required return drops to 1.0% and (3) the decrease in expected returns occurs at the end of month 1. This adjustment of returns will raise the price of X above its expected value at the end of the first month, thus producing a higher than expected return for that month, say 6%. Under these conditions, the actual return over a 3 year measurement period will be the product of the first month's return and 35 post adjustment returns of 1% per month. The predicted nonmerger return will be the product of 36 returns of 1.2% per month. When the merger benefit is computed as the difference between actual and predicted returns, it will reflect two factors — the true merger benefit and the difference in compensation for risk. The latter difference places a bias on the measure of merger benefits that increases with the length of the measurement period.

Dividing the 3 year period into 3 subperiods minimizes the risk adjustment bias. During the first year the actual return is compared to the nonmerger predicted return (1.2% per month in this case). In the second year, however, the actual return is in effect compared with the first year merger required return of 1% per month, and the second year merger required return is used as the nonmerger standard for the third year. In this example the actual return is 1%

per month in years 2 and 3, and the nonmerger standard is also 1% per month so that there are no merger benefits for the last two years.

It should be recognized that while this technique can minimize the risk effect it cannot eliminate it. To remove all bias it would be necessary to subdivide the analysis periods even further. In this case lack of firm data on less than an annual basis made this impossible.

Calculation of Merger Benefits

The actual calculation of the merger benefits required the following 5 step process.

Step 1: Valuation Equation and Parameter Estimates

The valuation equation was taken from [9] and expanded by adding a term reflecting the individual firm so that share price is a function of dividends (D), short-term growth (g_s), long-term growth (g_L), leverage (h), earnings variability (v), size (A) and firm effect (F) or,

$$\text{Log } P = \beta_0 + \beta_1 \log D + \beta_2 \log(g_s/g_L) + \beta_3 \log g_L +$$

$$\beta_4 \log h + \beta_5 \log V + \beta_5 \log A + \beta_7 \log F + \epsilon$$

As a derivative of Gordon's model [2], this equation is in logarithmic form, and the variable definitions are presented in Exhibit A-1.

At the outset it was believed that the equation's parameters were not constant across the 3 industries, and estimates were made for each separately. To obtain large enough samples for reliable estimates, the acquiring firms were supplemented with nonmerging companies from the same industry. The final samples contained 36 chemical firms, 38 machinery firms and 40 utility firms. Parameter sets were estimated for each industry in each year from 1957 to 1967 for a total of 33. (Tables of parameter estimates are available upon request from the first author.)

Step 2: Determine the Dates for the Merger Periods

Merger benefits were calculated for 3 subperiods rather than one long period to minimize the risk adjustment. Periods were either one year or multiples of one year in length since the valuation equation requires annual data. The first period begins a minimum of two months before the merger announcement as reported in the *Wall Street Journal* and ends at the first post-merger year-end date. It is

Exhibit A-1. Variable Definition for the Price Equation

P: The closing share price on the third Friday in January of the year following the cross-section year. That is, if the cross-section year is 1960, the price is measured in January, 1961.

D: The cash dividend payment per share in the cross-section year adjusted for any indicated increases as described by Gordon [2, p. 157].

g_s: The product of the retention rate (b) and the short-term return on equity r_s. The retention rate is a ten-year average of annual retention rate and r_s is the income available to common shareholders in the cross-section year divided by the book value of common equity in the cross-section year. 1.0 was added to the growth rate to remove the problem of negative values.

g_L: The product of b and r_L where b is defined as above and r_L is a ten-year average of r_s values. Like g_s, 1.0 was also added to g_L. Alternative definitions of g_L such as the slope of the log-linear trend line were also tested, but the definition used here produced the highest t values.

h: Sum of current liabilities, long-term debt and preferred stock (book values) divided by the book value of common equity. 1.0 was added to this ratio to insure that the logarithm of the variable would be uniformly positive across all cross-sectional samples.

v: Standard deviation of ten years' earnings before interest and taxes divided by the book value of common equity.

A: Book value of total assets in the cross-section year divided by 10^6.

F: Following [1] an exponentially weighted moving average of the 4 residuals immediately preceding the cross-section year. The residuals were obtained by estimating the equation without the firm effect term for each cross-section year of data available. Then, firm effect values were calculated using 3, 4 and 5 years of data with a weight of .4. Although there was very little difference in the R^2 of the equation with these 3 definitions, the 4 year average was the best.

important to set the starting date for the first period before the merger is anticipated to insure that no benefits have been reflected in the beginning price. While little is known about the time at which mergers are first recognized by the market, the minimum criterion employed here is consistent with other studies and the average lead time of 7.7 months before announcement is consistent with Halpern's findings [4].

Air Reduction's acquisition of Speer Carbon illustrates the method used to determine the merger periods. The acquisition was made on 8/31/61. The first available parameter set preceding the merger announcement by two months is the one using 12/31/60 financial information and prices in January,

1961. (See Exhibit A-1.) This cross-section will be denoted by 12/60 and is the beginning of period 1. Since the merger was completed in 1961 the first period ends at the 12/61 cross-section. When the merger announcement is near the beginning of the year (e.g., Air Products and Chemicals), the first period is two years long but the benefit is reported on a one year equivalent basis. The second period for Air Reduction runs from 12/61 to 12/62 and the third from 12/62 to 12/63. The second and third periods are one year in length for all mergers analyzed.

Step 3: Determine the Prices and Dividends of the Acquiring Firm

Beginning with period 1, actual price quotations for Air Reduction at the beginning (12/60) and at the end (12/61) of the period and dividends paid during 1961 must be obtained, all of which are available from published sources. Air Reduction's common sold for $82.375 at 12/60, $65.375 at 12/61 and common dividends of $2.50 per share were paid for 1961.

Step 4: Predict the Price and Dividend of the Acquiring Firm Without the Merger

Air Reduction's predicted price at the end of 1961 and the predicted dividends it would have paid if there had been no merger is calculated by substituting the set of financial variables for Air Reduction ($D, g_s, \ldots, F$) into the price equation and solving, assuming the error term is equal to its expected value of zero. Ideally, the financial variables necessary to calculate the 12/61 nonmerger price should not reflect any merger benefits occurring from 1960 to 1961. The last *observable* set of variables which contain no merger benefits are those for 12/31/60, and these must be adjusted for changes which would have occurred during 1961 without the merger.

The adjustment for other nonmerger changes was based on the average changes in the financial variable set for the nonmerging firms in the samples described in Step 1. The average change in the value of the corresponding variable for the nonmerging sample from 12/31/60 to 12/31/61 was added to each variable for Air Reduction at 12/31/60. For example, assume that Air Reduction's short-term growth rate (g_s) was 12% on 12/31/60 and 113 on 12/31/61. The value on 12/31/61 may already reflect some of the benefits from acquiring Speer Carbon. To determine what g_s would have been on 12/31/61 without the acquisition, it is first observed that the average g_s value for the nonmerging chemical firms in our sample decreased from 11% at 12/31/60 to 10% at 12/31/61. The change of -1% is then added to Air Reduction's actual growth rate value of 12% on 12/31/60 to obtain the estimated value of 11% for g_s on 12/31/61 without the merger. This procedure was performed for all variables in the model including the dividends. The key aspect of this adjustment is that it does *not* assume that the acquirer's data set will look like the industry average if there is no merger, but only that the changes in the set will approximate the industry average changes.

The same adjustment procedure is used for the second and third periods. In period 2 the actual g_s value of .13 for Air Reduction on 12/31/61 is added to the change in g_s values for the nonmerger sample from 12/31/61 to 12/31/62. Note that the base for 12/31/62 is the actual growth rate at the end of 12/31/61 instead of the predicted one. By adding the change on a year by year basis to the actual values at the beginning of the year, each period's merger benefit becomes an incremental one, and any past prediction errors are not compounded into the present merger benefit.

Following this procedure results in a predicted nonmerger price for 12/61 of $75.424 and predicted dividends for 1961 of $2.597.

Step 5: Calculate the Merger Benefits

Once the data on prices and dividends are generated in Steps 3 and 4, the merger benefits for period 1 are calculated as illustrated in Exhibit A-2, and the procedure is then repeated for periods 2 and 3.

Exhibit A-2. Calculation of Merger Benefits, Air Reduction Example

I. Data

	12/60	12/61
Actual prices	$82.375	$65.375
Predicted price without merger		74.424
Actual dividends		2.500
Predicted dividends without merger		2.597

II. Merger Benefits – Actual Prices

$$\text{Return with merger} = \frac{65.375 - 82.375 - 2.500}{82.375} = -.176$$

$$\text{Return without merger} = \frac{74.424 - 82.375 + 2.597}{82.375} = -.065$$

$$\text{Merger benefit} = -.176 - (-.065) = -.111$$

Business Combinations: An Exchange Ratio Determination Model

Kermit D. Larson and Nicholas J. Gonedes

Two of the important determinants of an entity's value are the expected rate of earnings growth and the presumed risk associated with its operations. Business combinations continue to be an increasingly popular means of achieving risk and growth objectives. The continuance of this trend, and the purposes for which such "external" means are utilized, were noted in a recent article by Smalter and Lancey:

[The use] of . . . mergers and acquisitions . . . has been increasing sharply during the past several years. Continued growth in its popularity is likely because it serves numerous corporate needs and growth motivations. An acquisition can strengthen a weakness; for instance, it can help to fill a raw material need or improve a vulnerable patent position. It can help management capitalize on the strengths of each partner, and utilize the synergistic possibilities which may arise in terms of geographic and product line expansion. It can provide diversification opportunities and it can enable a company to enter growth markets and reduce its dependence on existing activities for earnings growth.[1]

The use of mergers or combinations in order to achieve growth and risk objectives gives rise to a variety of managerial, financial, and accounting problems. Particular attention is being given in accounting literature to the problems of selecting between alternative methods of accounting for business combinations and, even more broadly, to the reporting and interpretive problems that issue from the complex nature of combined entities. On the other hand, the responsibility of accountants to provide relevant information to the negotiators of business combinations has not been adequately recognized. The information generating potential of accounting as it may apply to this vital area of contemporary business activity is in need of concerted research effort.

This paper relates to one of the many problems associated with negotiating a business combination, namely; the determination of an appropriate stock exchange ratio. The exchange ratio which is selected in order to effect a business combination may be expressed as the number of shares of the acquiring entity given in exchange for one share of the acquired entity.[2] The exchange ratio determines whether the

---

[1] Donald Smalter and R. C. Lancey, "P/E Analysis and Acquisition Strategy," *Harvard Business Review* (November–December 1966), p. 86.

[2] The preponderance of business combinations involves participants that may be appropriately described "acquiring" and "acquired" firms. In some cases of relatively equal sized participants, these terms may not be entirely descriptive. As employed in this paper, the "acquiring" term would apply to the surviving or parent firm and the "acquired" term would apply to the terminating or subsidiary firm.

Kermit D. Larson is Associate Professor of Accounting at The University of Texas at Austin, and Nicholas J. Gonedes is Assistant Professor of Accounting at the University of Chicago.

wealth positions of the parties to a proposed combination will experience improvement or diminution as a result of the combination. Accordingly, the exchange ratio is of crucial significance in assessing the desirability of a business combination from the perspectives of both negotiating parties.

The purpose of this paper is to develop a model that may be used to ascertain the exchange ratios which will leave the wealth positions of the parties *unchanged*, and to discern the range of exchange ratios which will result in *increases* in the wealth positions of the parties to a combination. Such a range would specify the limits of exchange ratio negotiation, given the prior selection of payment method.

The analysis will be limited to business combinations that are to be effected by an exchange of common stock for common stock. Market value of common stock is used to define the pre-combination wealth positions of the parties involved in a business combination. The assumption underlying the use of market value is that the objective of managements and owners is the maximization of owners' wealth.

Since an important factor in the model is the expected earnings multiple (price-earnings ratio) of a proposed combined entity, attention will be devoted first to the general factors that comprise the determinants of earnings multiples. A negotiating participant in a business combination may be capable of evaluating the prospects of the combined entity directly in terms of an expected earnings multiple. However, structuring the evaluation in terms of the basic determinants of earnings multiples probably conforms more closely to the evaluative thought patterns that are assumed by most investment decision models. Further, it facilitates the process of analysis by focusing attention on proximate causes, rather than on observed effects.

COMMENTARY ON EARNINGS MULTIPLES

The factors which influence the magnitude of an entity's earnings multiple may be discerned by focusing attention on a model of stock-price determination.[3] Assume that investors expect the annual per-share earnings, Y/S, of an entity to grow at a constant rate, g, over an investment horizon equal to n years. Assume, also, that the entity's dividend payout ratio, b, is expected to be constant over the n-year period. Finally, the minimum rate of return required by investors on an investment in the entity's common stock is denoted as k. Given the above assumptions, the current price of the entity's common stock may be represented as the present value of the investor's expected dividend receipts plus the capital return expected by the investor at the end of the investment horizon, n.

$$P_0 = \sum_{t=1}^{n} \frac{(1+g)^t b(Y/S)_0}{(1+k)^t} + \frac{P_n}{(Y/S)_n} \cdot \frac{(Y/S)_0(1+g)^n}{(1+k)^n}$$

The current earnings multiple, $P_0/(Y/S)_0$, of an entity may be represented by rearranging the terms of the above equation:

$$\frac{P_0}{(Y/S)_0} = \sum_{t=1}^{n} \frac{(1+g)^t b}{(1+k)^t} + \frac{P_n}{(Y/S)_n} \cdot \frac{(1+g)^n}{(1+k)^n}$$

As is suggested by the above formula-

[3] For more extensive discussions and alternative share-price determination models, see Eugene M. Lerner and Willard T. Carleton, *A Theory of Financial Analysis* (Harcourt, Brace & World, Inc., 1966); Myron J. Gordon, *The Investment Financing and Valuation of the Corporation* (Richard D. Irwin, 1962); and William R. Sloane and Arnold Reisman, "Stock Evaluation Theory: Classification, Reconciliation, and General Model," *Journal of Financial and Quantitative Analysis* (June 1968), pp. 171–204.

tion, an entity's current earnings multiple is a function of the expected growth rate and the rate of return required by investors. The growth rate is a function of the investment opportunities available to the entity and the reinvested earnings of the entity. The rate of return required by investors is a function of investors' opportunity costs and the riskiness associated with the entity's earnings stream by investors.

Theoretically, an entity's growth rate will vary directly with the fraction of total earnings reinvested and the profitability of available opportunities. The rate of return required by investors will vary directly with opportunity costs and risk.

It should be noted that the *current* earnings multiple of an entity will also be affected by the rate of growth and level of risk anticipated by investors with respect to the years after the nth year. These anticipations will affect the nth year earnings multiple, $P_n/(Y/S)_n$, and, thus, the capital return expected by investors at present.[4]

The above comments suggest that the earnings multiple of a combined entity will be a weighted average of its constituents' earnings multiples if (1) the growth rate of the combined entity is a weighted average of its constituents' growth rates, and (2) the riskiness of the combined entity's earnings stream is a weighted average of the riskiness of each of its constituents' earnings streams. Other things equal, the earnings multiple of a combined entity will exceed an average of its constituents' earning multiples if its expected growth rate exceeds an average of its constituents' growth rates. In addition, the earnings multiple of a combined entity will exceed an average of its constituents' earnings multiples if the level of risk associated with the combined entity's earnings stream is less than an average of the levels of risk associated with the earnings streams of its constituents, *ceteris paribus*.

An additional comment on the riskiness of a combined entity's earnings stream is warranted. Typically, the variance of an entity's earnings stream is utilized in order to represent risk. If the variance is used to represent risk, and if one assumes that the risk of a combined entity will equal a weighted sum of the levels of risk calculated for the constituents, then one must introduce the effects of covariance[5] in the summation process. A positive covariance will cause the variance ("risk") of the combined entity's earnings stream to *exceed* a weighted sum of the variances of the constituents' earnings streams; a negative covariance will have the reverse effect. Presumably, one of the objectives of diversification is a combination of earnings streams which have negative covariances. If the covariance between two earnings streams is zero, then the variance ("risk") of the combined entity's earnings stream will equal a weighted sum of the variances of

---

[4] The reader should note that

$$\frac{P_n}{(Y/S)_n}\cdot\frac{(Y/S)_0(1+g)^n}{(1+k)^n}$$

may be eliminated from the formula for P_0, simply by extending n to ∞ and assuming g to be constant throughout the infinite time horizon. Perhaps a more sophisticated formulation would employ some expected g for a reasonable time horizon (n) and utilize a different g (and corresponding b) for the periods $(n+1)\ldots\infty$. In these terms, the formulation would be as follows:

$$P_0 = \sum_{t=1}^{n}\frac{(1+g_1)^t b_1 (Y/S)_0}{(1+k)^t}$$
$$+ \sum_{t=n+1}^{\infty}\frac{(1+g_2)^{t-n} b_2 (Y/S)_n}{(1+k)^t}$$

[5] The covariance between earnings streams represents the degree to which the earnings streams vary together, in opposite directions, or independently of each other. If two earnings streams vary together in unison, then the covariance is positive; if the two earnings streams tend to vary in opposite directions, then the covariance is negative. If the earnings streams tend to vary independently of each other, then the covariance will tend to equal zero. Note, also, that the variance of the return on a given aggregation of wealth approaches zero if a diversification process embraces the inclusion of assets with identical or bounded variances and uncorrelated returns. An extensive discussion of covariance and diversification is presented in: Harry M. Markowitz, *Portfolio Selection* (John Wiley & Sons, Inc., 1959), Chs. 4, 5.

the constituent entities' earnings streams. Other things equal, a zero covariance implies that the earnings multiple of a combined entity will equal a weighted average of its constituents' earnings multiples; a negative covariance suggests that the earnings multiple will be higher than a weighted average of the constituent entities' earnings multiples.

AN EXCHANGE RATIO MODEL

The factor which determines the relative post-combination wealth positions of the parties to a business combination is the exchange ratio. Given the current price of the acquiring company's common stock, the total value of the common stock received by each stockholder of the acquired company will vary directly with the exchange ratio, i.e., the number of acquiring company shares received in exchange for each share of the acquired company. The post-combination wealth position of the acquiring firm's stockholders will vary inversely with the exchange ratio, since a higher exchange ratio will (1) cause the combined entity to have a greater number of shares outstanding and (2) cause the acquired company's stockholders to own a larger proportion of the combined entity. The following analysis presents a method of determining the maximum exchange ratio which will be acceptable to the acquiring company's stockholders and the minimum exchange ratio which will be acceptable to the acquired company's shareholders. The range of exchange ratios established by the aforementioned maximum and minimum consists of exchange ratios which will enhance (or leave unchanged) the wealth positions of the acquiring company's stockholders *and* the acquired company's stockholders. It, therefore, specifies a range of reasonable negotiation within which neither party incurs loss of wealth. Throughout the following discussion, the total earnings of the combined entity im-

mediately after the combination is assumed to equal the sum of the constituents' total earnings.[6]

The pre-combination wealth position of a holder of one share of the acquiring entity, A, is defined by the current earnings multiple of A's common stock and A's earnings per share:

$$(1) \qquad W_A = (M_A)(Y_A/S_A).$$

$W_A =$ The current wealth position of the holder of one share of A, equal to the price per share of A.
$M_A =$ The earnings multiple of A.
$Y_A =$ The total earnings of A.
$S_A = A$'s total outstanding common stock.

The pre-combination wealth position of a shareholder in the potential acquired firm, B, may be represented in a similar fashion:

$$(2) \qquad W_B = (M_B)(Y_B/S_B)$$

The expected post-combination wealth position of a stockholder in the combined entity may be defined by the anticipated market price of one share in the combined entity:

$$(3) \qquad W_{AB} = (\theta)(Y_A + Y_B)$$
$$\cdot \left(\frac{1}{S_A + (ER)S_B} \right)$$

$W_{AB} =$ Expected price per share of the combined entity
$\theta =$ Expected earnings multiple of the combined entity
$Y_A + Y_B =$ Total first period earnings of the combined entity, equal to A's total earnings, Y_A, plus B's total earnings, Y_B
$S_A + (ER)S_B =$ Total outstanding com-

[6] Surely this is a reasonable assumption; even those who proclaim the existence of "synergism" will admit that synergistic effects are not immediate.

mon stock of the com-
bined entity
$S_A = A$'s pre-combination shares
outstanding
$S_B = B$'s pre-combination shares
$ER =$ The exchange ratio

The wealth position of each stockholder of the acquiring firm will be enhanced if

(4) $$W_{AB} > W_A$$

and it will remain unchanged if

(5) $$W_{AB} = W_A.$$

The wealth position of each stockholder of the acquired firm will be enhanced if the value of a share in the combined entity is greater than the value of the number of shares given in exchange for one share of the combined entity:

(6) $$W_{AB} > \left(\frac{1}{ER}\right) W_B$$

and it will remain unchanged if

(7) $$W_{AB} = \left(\frac{1}{ER}\right)(W_B).$$

Given the expected earnings multiple of the combined entity, the exchange ratio which is consistent with condition (5)—which is a restatement of (3) and (1)—is the *maximum* exchange ratio which is acceptable to the stockholders of the acquiring firm; a higher exchange ratio will result in a diminution of the wealth positions of the acquiring firm's stockholders. By re-arranging the component factors of condition (5), we obtain the *maximum exchange ratio*, ER_A, which is acceptable to the ac-quiring firm's stockholders:

(8) $$ER_A = \frac{(\theta)(Y_A + Y_B) - (M_A)(Y_A)}{(M_A)(Y_A)(1/S_A)(S_B)}$$

The only variable in (8) is the expected earnings multiple, θ, of the combined en-tity; all of the other terms of (8) are given

constants in a particular situation. Thus, (8) expresses the maximum exchange ratio acceptable to the acquiring firm's stock-holders as a function of the expected earn-ings multiple of the combined entity. As was indicated in the preceding section, the earnings multiple of the combined entity will be determined by its expected rate of earnings growth and its risk characteris-tics.

Evaluating the first and second partial derivatives of ER_A with respect to θ, we may ascertain the shape of the curve which is used to represent ER_A as a function of θ. Since

$$\frac{\partial ER}{\partial \theta} > 0 \quad \text{and} \quad \frac{\partial^2 ER}{\partial \theta} = 0,$$

ER_A is represented as a linear function of θ, as is shown in Exhibit 1. Thus, the maxi-mum exchange rate acceptable to firm A stockholders is seen to increase at a con-stant rate as the expected earnings mul-tiple of the combined entity increases.

EXHIBIT 1

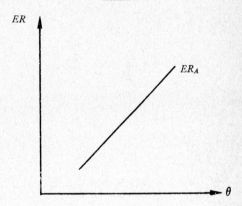

Since the wealth of the acquiring stock-holders will vary inversely with ER for a *given* θ, the acquiring company's stock-holders will desire an ER which is as far as possible below ER_A. If $ER = ER_A$, then the wealth positions of the acquiring company's stockholders will not be altered as a result of the combination. If $ER > ER_A$, then they will suffer wealth diminution. Thus, we may assert that the ER_A curve represents a *boundary condition* on ER which must not be violated if the wealth positions of the acquiring firm's stockholders are, at least, to remain undiminished.

The exchange ratio which is consistent with condition (7)—which is a restatement of (3) and (2)—represents the minimum exchange ratio which is acceptable to the acquired company's stockholders, given a particular θ; a lower exchange ratio will result in a diminution of their wealth positions. By rearranging the terms of which condition (7) is composed, we obtain the *minimum exchange* ratio, ER_B, that the acquired firm's stockholders will deem to be acceptable:

$$(9) \quad ER_B = \frac{(M_B)(Y_B/S_B)(S_A)}{(\theta)(Y_A + Y_B) - (M_B)(Y_B)}.$$

The only variable in (9) is θ; the additional terms are given constants in a particular situation. Hence, (9) expresses ER_B as a function of the expected earnings multiple of the combined entity, θ. An evaluation of the first and second partial derivatives of ER_B with respect to θ indicates the shape of the curve which may be used to represent ER_B as a function of θ:

$$\frac{\partial ER_B}{\partial \theta} < 0$$

and

$$\frac{\partial^2 ER}{\partial \theta^2} \begin{cases} > 0, & \text{if } (Y_A + Y_B)(\theta) > (M_B)(Y_B) \\ = 0, & \text{if } (Y_A + Y_B)(\theta) = (M_B)(Y_B) \\ < 0, & \text{if } (Y_A + Y_B)(\theta) < (M_B)(Y_B) \end{cases}$$

Obviously, a prospective business combination would not be consummated if the expected value of the combined entity was equal to or less than the current value of only *one* of the constituents. Thus, the sit-

uations in which $(Y_A + Y_B)\theta \le M_B(Y_B)$ need not be considered further. Correspondingly, the subsequent analysis relates to situations in which $\partial ER/\partial \theta^2 > 0$.

Given $\partial ER/\partial \theta > 0$ and $\partial^2 ER/\partial \theta^2 > 0$, the curve which represents ER_B as a function of θ will vary inversely with θ and will be concave upward, as is indicated in Exhibit 2.

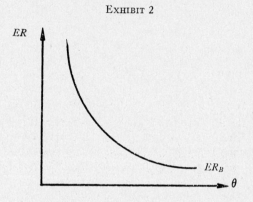

The post-combination wealth positions of the acquired firm's stockholders will vary directly with ER, given any θ. Thus, they will desire an ER which is as far as possible above ER_B. If $ER = ER_B$, then their wealth positions will not be altered as a result of the combination. If $ER < ER_B$, then they will suffer wealth diminution; thus, the ER_B curve represents a minimum boundary condition on ER which should not be violated if the wealth positions of the acquired company's common stockholders are to remain undiminished.

If a business combination is to be consummated, the selected exchange ratio must be consistent with the boundary condition imposed by the acquiring company's common stockholders *and* the boundary condition imposed by the acquired firm's common stockholders. The field of ER's which satisfy both boundary conditions may be ascertained by superimposing the ER_A curve on the ER_B curve, as is done in Exhibit 3.

EXHIBIT 3

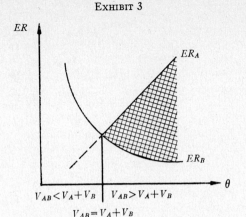

$V_{AB} < V_A + V_B$ | $V_{AB} > V_A + V_B$

$V_{AB} = V_A + V_B$

The shaded area of Exhibit 3, including its boundaries, represents the field of ER's which are consistent with the boundary conditions of *both* parties to the combination. For a given θ, the closed interval $[ER_A, ER_B]$ constitutes the *ER-Bargaining Range;* any ER which satisfies the condition $ER_A \geq ER \geq ER_B$ will not cause any party to the combination to experience wealth diminution as a result of the terms of the combination. Any ER within the closed interval $[ER_A, ER_B]$ but *not* equal to either endpoint of the interval will cause all parties to the combination to experience wealth accretion as a result of the terms of the combination. The particular ER which is finally agreed upon will be a function of the relative bargaining power of each party involved in the combination and the relative contribution which each party makes to the incremental value of the combined entity.

One should note that the intersection of the ER_A curve and the ER_B curve occurs at an earnings multiple for the combined entity, θ, which is equal to a weighted average of the constituent entities' earnings multiples, M_A and M_B. Given our assumption that the first period total earnings of the combined entity equals the sum of the constituents' pre-combination total

earnings, the intersection of the ER_A and ER_B curves occurs at the point at which the value of the combined entity, V_{AB}, is equal to the sum of the values of the constituent entities, V_A and V_B; at such a point, the incremental value of the combined entity equals zero: $(V_{AB}) - (V_A + V_B) = 0$. For all θ to the right of the intersection, the incremental value of the combined entity is greater than zero; the incremental value of the combined entity is negative for all θ to the left of the $ER_A - ER_B$ intersection.

As was suggested above, the earnings multiple of the combined entity will equal a weighted average of the constituents' pre-combination earnings multiples if the expected rate of earnings growth of the combined entity is equal to a weighted average of the constituent's expected rates of growth, and if the risk of the combined entity's earnings stream is evaluated as a weighted sum of the risks of each constituents' earnings stream. Decidedly, a business combination evidencing such conditions serves no apparent economic purpose.

The incremental value of the combined entity will be shared in proportion to the pre-combination values of the constituents if $(W_{AB} - W_A)$ is equal to $(W_{AB} - (1/ER) W_B)$. As is indicated below, such proportionality will exist if the selected exchange ratio equals the ratio of the constituents' precombination share prices:

$$W_{AB} - W_A = W_{AB} - (1/ER) W_B$$
$$W_A = (1/ER) W_B$$
$$ER = W_B/W_A = \frac{(M_B)(Y_B/S_B)}{(M_A)(Y_A/S_A)}.$$

If $ER > W_B/W_A$, the acquired firm gains proportionally more of the incremental value than does the acquiring firm. If $ER < W_B/W_A$, the acquiring firm gains proportionally more than the acquired firm. To reemphasize, the ER which is finally selected will depend upon the relative bargaining strength of each participant in a business combination, and the relative economic contribution of each participant.

Selected Parameter Changes

The sole variable in the exchange-ratio relationships formulated above is the expected earnings multiple of the combined entity, θ; all other terms are constants within the context of a particular business combination. Since it is probable that firms which are desirous of acquiring other firms, and firms which wish to be acquired, will consider a number of alternative combination participants, one might wish to inquire into the effects of several parameter changes on the *boundary conditions* discussed above. Specifically, one might desire answers to questions such as the following: How will the acquiring firm's, A's, boundary condition change if it considers the acquisition of an entity, C, which has a total current income in excess of the total current income of the entity, B, that is currently under consideration? Also, how will the acquiring firm's boundary condition change if C's total number of shares outstanding is in excess of B's?

Questions about the changes in a firm's boundary conditions which will be effected by considering different combination partners may be answered by differentiating each firm's boundary condition equation with respect to the parameters which relate to the characteristics of a combination

partner. As is indicated in equation (8), these parameters are Y_B and S_B for the acquiring firm. Equation (9) indicates that these parameters are Y_A and S_A for the potential acquired firm. A summary of the changes which will be associated with changes in each of the latter parameters is presented in Exhibit 4; it should be emphasized that *each* parameter change is treated under a *ceteris paribus* assumption.

The indicated boundary changes reveal the kinds of constraints which will be imposed upon acquiring firms and potential acquired firms in different situations. For example if, an acquiring firm, A, is considering the acquisition of one of three firms, B, C, D, and if B, C, and D are identical except that $Y_B > Y_C > Y_D$, then A's boundary conditions, ER_A, for each potential combination will assume the following relative positions.

In Exhibit 5, (ER_A/Y_B) represents the boundary condition of the acquiring firm with respect to firm B; (ER/Y_C) refers to firm C; and (ER_A/Y_D) refers to firm D. Firms B, C, D are identical except for their respective amounts of total current income. The relationships manifested in this exhibit indicate that the maximum exchange ratio which would be acceptable to the stockholders of an acquiring firm should vary directly with the current income of potential acquisitions.

The effects of changes in the additional selected parameters need not be discussed

Exhibit 4

Effects of Selected Parameter Changes on Boundary Conditions

Parameter	Associated Changes in *Acquiring Firm's* Boundary Conditions
Potential Acquired Firm's Total Income	Direct Changes ($\partial ER/\partial Y_B > 0$)
Potential Acquired Firm's Total Shares Outstanding	Inverse Changes ($\partial ER/\partial S_B < 0$)

Parameter	Associated Changes in Potential *Acquired* Firm's Boundary Conditions
Acquiring Firm's Total Income	Inverse Changes ($\partial ER/\partial Y_A < 0$)
Total Shares Outstanding of Acquiring Firm	Direct Changes ($\partial ER/\partial S_A > 0$)

EXHIBIT 5

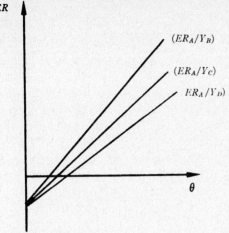

individually; they may be ascertained by examining the contents of Exhibit 4.

SUMMARY

The model presented herein may be employed in order to determine the exchange ratios which will leave the wealth positions of the parties in a business combination unchanged. The model indicates the *maximum* exchange ratio which will be acceptable to an acquiring company and the *minimum* exchange ratio which will be acceptable to a potential acquired firm, thereby specifying a bargaining range. The independent variable to which exchange ratios were related within the context of a particular business combination is the expected earnings multiple of the combined business entity.

The discussion was limited to business combinations which are consummated by exchanges of common stock. However, if appropriate adjustments are made in the terms of the exchange-ratio models presented, the models may be rendered applicable to situations in which other media

of exchange are employed. For example, if debentures *and* common stock are offered to the stockholders of a potential acquired firm, the necessary wealth transfer which is indicated by the models presented herein must be reduced by the value of the debentures. Also, the effects of the debentures on the growth and risk characteristics of the combined entity would have to be incorporated into our exchange-ratio models. The specific adjustments which must be made for combinations involving common stock and other media of exchange are topics for future research.

The model presented herein does not solve the exchange-ratio problem of any specific business combination. It does, however, indicate the kinds of constraints which are operative in the exchange ratio selection process. In addition, it indicates the interval of exchange ratios which will enhance, or *at least* not cause any diminution in, the wealth positions of all parties to a proposed business combination. Also, the terms which constitute our symbolic expressions indicate the kinds of information that are relevant to the determination of an exchange ratio.[7] Finally (though not considered explicitly in this paper), the model presented may be instrumental in determining the risk and growth expectations which are consistent with a given proposed exchange-ratio. The latter determination would involve the derivation of levels of risk and return from an exchange ratio, rather than the derivation of exchange ratios from levels of risk and return.

---

[7] Those who are interested in additional discussions of exchange ratios may find the following to be of interest: J. Fred Weston, "The Determination of Share Exchange Ratios in Mergers," pp. 117–138, and Samuel Schwartz, "Merger Analysis as a Capital Budgeting Problem," pp. 139–150, in: William W. Alberts and Joel E. Segall, etc., *The Corporate Merger* (The University of Chicago Press, 1966); and Irwin H. Silberman, "A Note on Merger Valuation," *Journal of Finance* (June 1968), pp. 528–534.

For Further Study

Additional references to which the reader may refer include:

1. Halpern, P.J. (1973). "Empirical Estimates of the Amount and the Distribution of Gains to Companies in Merger". *Journal of Business* (October 1973), pp. 554–575.
2. Lee C.F., R.A. Shick and F.C. Jen (1977). "A Comparison of Alternative Switching Regression Techniques for Detecting Structural Changes Using Common Stock Returns for Merging Firms". Working Paper, The University of Illinois at Urbana-Champaign.
3. Dodd, P. and R. Ruback (1977), "Tender Offers and Stockholder Returns". *Journal of Financial Economics*, 5, pp. 351–373.
4. Lev, B. and G. Mandelker (1972). "The Microeconomic Consequences of Corporate Mergers". *Journal of Business* (January 1972), pp. 85–104.
5. Mandelker, G. (1974). "Risk and Return: the Case of Merging Firms". *Journal of Financial Economics*, 1974, pp. 303–335.
6. Shick, R.A. (1972). "The Analysis of Mergers and Acquisitions". *Journal of Finance* (May 1972), pp. 495–502.
7. Higgins, R.C. and L.D. Schall (1975). "Corporate Bankruptcy and Conglomerate Merger". *Journal of Finance* (March 1975), pp. 93–113.

Part VIII

Working
Capital Management

Introduction

Financial planning and analysis can be either for the short term or the long term. Short-term analysis is generally referred to as working capital management. This area includes the management of cash, short term securities, inventory control, and accounts receivables collection. Long-term financial planning, on the other hand, essentially refers to the determination of a firm's investment, financing, and dividend policies. There is, of course, some interaction between short-term and long-term planning.

The four papers in Part VIII demonstrate basic concepts and procedures for short-term planning and discuss the relationship between short-term and long-term planning.

Stone (1973) uses some long-term financial planning models (discussed in Part IX) and computer simulation techniques to develop a cash planning and credit-line determination model. A financial statement simulation is also developed. The basic modeling concept used by Stone will help the reader understand the long-term planning models examined in Part IX. Stone also demonstrates some interactions between long-term and short-term planning, due in most part to errors in short-term borrowing, of credit line determination, and of short-term securities management.

Sartoris and Spruill (1974) show that goal programming can be used in working capital decisions to achieve the two essentially conflicting goals of profitability and liquidity. A model is developed, and a numerical illustration of its application is presented. The sensitivity of its results to priority parameters is also investigated.

Quarterly accounting data becomes more important in working capital management. Gentry and Lee (1981) use an X-11 time series decomposition model to analyze quarterly income statement data. They find that there are time, firm, and ledger effects in quarterly accounting data. These results shed some light on the possible applications of both short-term and long-term financial planning models in financial management.

In their paper, Stone and Hill (1980) discuss the problems associated with the timing and amount of cash transfers, concentrating on cash transfer scheduling for cash concentration. Overall, this paper presents a useful background to the problem, reviews contemporary practice and its deficiencies, formulates the task as an optimization problem, and discusses the solution's advantages. Additional information related to cash management can be found in Stone and Hill (1981).

CASH PLANNING AND CREDIT-LINE DETERMINATION WITH

A FINANCIAL STATEMENT SIMULATOR:

A CASE REPORT ON SHORT-TERM FINANCIAL PLANNING

Bernell K. Stone

I. Introduction

The use of computerized financial statement simulators in financial
planning has become widespread, particularly for long-range planning. Most
large firms have some form of financial statement simulator, although there
appears to be wide variation among firms in their sophistication, degree of
use, and acceptance by management.[1]

Problem Overview

Financial planning is often separated into problems of long-term planning
and short-term planning. The focus of long-term planning is the financing
plan for periods beyond one year. It involves developing and evaluating schedules of long-term borrowing, dividend payment, and equity issuance subject to

---

*Cornell University. This paper is based on a financial planning model
built for General Recreation, Inc. In working on the General Recreation model,
I worked extensively with Mr. J. Frederick Pingree, Vice President, Chief
Financial Officer, and Director of General Recreation. The opportunity of
interacting with a financial practitioner responsible for solving the problem
of cash planning and credit-line determination was invaluable in both structuring the problem and formulating the solution. David H. Downes and Robert
P. Magee (Ph.D. candidates at Cornell University who have respectively accepted
appointments at the School of Business Administration, University of California,
Berkeley, and the Graduate School of Business, University of Chicago) were
partners with the author in developing the General Recreation planning model.
Both contributed to the design and programming of the system. Despite this
acknowledgement of help gratefully received, I am, however, solely responsible
for the defects and limitations of this particular exposition of the use of
the General Recreation financial statement simulator for cash planning and
credit-line determination.

[1]See, for instance, Schrieber [9], which contains reports on a wide
variety of planning models. Gershefski [7] reports on a survey of the planning models of over 100 firms, over 95 percent of which were based on financial statement simulators. Dickson *et al.* [4] provide a detailed comparison
of the planning models of 20 firms. Naylor [8] also surveys a number of
planning models.

a variety of constraints such as (1) upper and lower limits on the firm's debt-equity ratio; (2) consistency of the dividend schedule with the firm's earnings pattern and dividend payout policy; (3) minimum acceptable earnings and cash flow coverage ratios for interest payments; (4) conformity to debt covenants; etc.

A central problem of short-term planning is the determination of an appropriate schedule of short-term borrowing (where short-term borrowing is borrowing that will be repaid in less than a year from the initiation of the loan). The usual vehicles for short-term borrowing are typically a bank credit line (or credit agreement) and the issuance of commercial paper. Associated with the problem of short-term borrowing is the problem of ensuring that month-to-month cash balances are positive, are sufficiently large to provide for firm transaction requirements, and are in conformity with the compensating balance requirement associated with the borrowing schedule and credit line. The schedule of investment in short-term securities is also closely related to the short-term borrowing problem, since holding short-term securities is an alternative to relying on credit-line borrowing for funds and since cash balances in excess of the firm's transaction and compensating balance require-ments are typically invested in short-term securities. The process of finding consistent schedules of cash balances, investment in short-term securities, and short-term borrowing is typically referred to as *cash planning*.

The problem of credit-line determination is closely connected to cash planning since: (1) the size of the required credit line depends on the peak level of short-term borrowing;[2] (2) the size of the credit line affects the compensating balance requirement and thus the level of required cash balances.[3]

The solution to both the cash planning and credit-line determination problems requires projections of both a firm's cash needs and its ability to generate cash. These cash projections are clearly dependent on a long-term financial plan, since cash levels are affected by the schedule of dividend payments, interest payments on long-term debt, and so on. The natural frame-work for solving the problem is the projection of future financial statements.

---

[2]This is true whether the borrowing involves the use of the bank credit line or the issuance of commercial paper, since the commercial paper of most nonfinancial corporations must be backed by an unused bank credit line.

[3]Many financial practitioners jointly characterize cash planning and credit-line determination as "the short-term financial planning problem." How-ever, despite its widespread popular usage, this author is somewhat averse to such a general term since there are many other aspects to short-term financial planning, such as short-term forecasting, working capital planning, credit granting policy, etc.

Purpose and Format

The purpose of the paper is to present a model for solving the problem of cash planning and credit-line determination. The model presented is based on one that has been in active use at General Recreation, Inc., for over two years as a major subsystem of the firm's financial planning model. However, the intent is not simply to describe cash planning and credit-line determination at General Recreation, but rather to present and explain the essential features of the model that are applicable to most firms.

In the remainder of this paper, we provide a brief overview of the General Recreation financial statement simulator, develop a quantitative statement of the cash planning and credit-line determination problem, present and explain the model for solution of the problem, discuss the interaction between the short-term and long-term planning processes, and finally outline simple extensions of the basic model that may be required to apply it to other firms.

II. The Problem Situation at General Recreation

General Recreation, an American Stock Exchange firm with sales of about $30 million, is a producer of a variety of leisure time products.[4] Like many producers of seasonal goods, General Recreation makes extensive use of dating plans and thus has seasonally large levels of accounts receivable that are financed with short-term borrowing on bank credit lines. In some past years, both peak accounts receivable and peak credit-line borrowing have been as large as 50 percent of sales. Because of its extensive use of credit-line borrowing, accurate cash planning and credit-line determination are critical problems for General Recreation.

Before the development of the financial planning model, cash planning and credit-line determination involved the projection of financial statements, generally on a quarterly basis. The essence of the financial statement projection was first to make good guesses of the appropriate credit-line and borrowing schedule, compute the financial statements, compare actual cash levels with the desired level, and then revise the borrowing schedule and possibly the credit line to eliminate the discrepancies between the actual and target balances.

---

[4]Major subsidiaries of General Recreation include Ithaca Gun Co., Alpine Designs, 10-X Manufacturing, American Fiberglass Corp., Gerico Inc. (formerly Gerry Designs), and Rich-Moor. Major product lines include sporting firearms; camping equipment; clothing, and related accessories for hunting, camping, and skiing; fiberglass boats and catamarans; infant back carriers; dried foods for camping; and a variety of related leisure-time products.

General Recreation found the execution of these *pro forma* statements by this trial and error technique to be a complex, time consuming, and computationally burdensome task. As a consequence of the required computational effort, the accuracy of cash planning was less than that desired by General Recreation. Moreover, it was difficult to evaluate very many alternative plans or to carry out extensive sensitivity analysis for a given plan. These limitations extended beyond cash planning per se. For instance, the critical evaluation of alternative credit granting policies requires the projection of accounts receivable and the assessment of the effect on earnings via the borrowing required to finance the accounts receivable, which in turn requires accuracy of the cash plan.

Because of General Recreation's extensive use of credit-line borrowing, the importance of accurate cash planning, and the computational effort associated with the task, the need to accomplish cash planning and credit-line determination quickly, efficiently, and accurately was a major impetus to the creation of a conversational financial statement simulator for financial planning. Automating this task was a major design objective along with long-range planning, merger evaluation, and accounts receivable forecasting and control.

Since compensating balance requirements are typically defined on a monthly basis and since it is necessary to know the peak monthly borrowing requirement, the logical time unit for projecting both cash balances and borrowing is a month. General Recreation felt that it was necessary to carry out its cash planning and credit-line determination 24 months in advance because: (1) a cash plan for which the short-term borrowing was not completely repaid for at least part of the year (as required by the banks for credit-line borrowing) meant that additional long-term financing was necessary,[5] (2) credit lines and changes in credit lines are negotiated well in advance of usage of the line, and frequent or unforeseen changes in the line are regarded as bad financial practice.

In addition to 24 months of future projections, General Recreation felt that other key aspects of the problem were (1) the ability to perform extensive sensitivity analysis with respect to the adequacy of a given credit line, (2) the accurate reflection of the timing of tax payments, (3) the ability to iterate between long-term and short-term plans where iteration between plans

---

[5]The implicit assumption here is that long-term financing requires a lead time of at least one year for intelligent planning and consummation, and that the long-term financing should be in hand before discussing short-term credit requirements with the banks.

means the ability to develop and evaluate a short-term plan conditional on a long-term plan, and vice versa.

The General Recreation financial planning model is a conversational financial statement simulator that enables the user to define accounting structure and convert assumptions about the environment, the operating plan, and the financial plan into projected financial statements.[6] While the model is capable of treating any number of variable length periods (that are integer multiples of a month), typical usage involves two years of monthly projections and five years of annual projections. When focusing on short-term planning, the user can suppress the long-term part of the model; similarly, the user can suppress monthly detail in long-term planning and, for instance, simply obtain seven years of annual statements. One feature of the model is the ability to do short- and long-term planning within the framework of a single model. (The importance of iteration between the short- and long-term plans is discussed subsequently.)

III. Problem Quantification

This section structures the relationship between the variables and specifies constraints ("consistency conditions" and "feasibility requirements") that an acceptable solution must satisfy.

The Interdependence of the Variables

The level of cash required in each month is the maximum of the level required for transaction purposes and the level required to provide compensating balances associated with borrowing and credit lines. Let $\hat{C}(t)$ be the target level of cash balances in month t. Then $\hat{C}(t)$ will be given by

$$(1) \qquad \hat{C}(t) = \max \{CMIN(t), CBR(t)\}$$

where $CMIN(t)$ is the minimum acceptable level for cash balances[7] and $CBR(t)$ is the compensating balance requirement in month t. The level of required compensating balances is a function of a firm's short-term borrowing and its line of credit. A common form of this function is[8]

$$(2) \qquad CBR(t) = A_o(t) + a_1 B(t) + a_2 CLINE$$

_____

[6]For further details on model features, see [10].

[7]Minimum acceptable level means the level required if there were no compensating balances associated with the credit line. This is the larger of the needs for transaction requirements and balances maintained to pay for tangible bank services.

[8]Equation (2) is a complete description of the usual compensating balance arrangement with a given bank. For a firm with several banks with different values for these parameters, it is necessary to specify rules for the order in which the firm will borrow from the various banks, as indicated in the section

509

where $B(t)$ is the short-term borrowing in period t, CLINE is the size of the firm's credit line, and $A_o(t)$, a_1, and a_2 are parameters of the firm's banking relationship. The variable a_1 is the rate of required balances per dollar of short-term borrowing and a_2 is the rate of required balances per dollar of credit line. A typical compensating balance requirement is that the firm maintain balances equal to 10 percent of the credit and 10 percent of the actual use of the credit line. For this case, the values of a_1 and a_2 are both .10. The parameter $A_o(t)$ allows management to add a constant amount to the balance requirement in any month. Provision for adding a constant allows the firm to compensate the bank for intangible services, to maintain "supporting balances" in anticipation of future credit needs, or to pay fixed charges such as commitment fees via balances rather than cash payments.

The required size of the credit line depends on the schedule of short-term borrowing. The peak level of borrowing cannot exceed the credit line. However, to allow for the uncertainty associated with the projected level of peak borrowing, a firm wants its actual credit line to exceed the projected peak borrowing requirement in the expected state of the world by an appropriate margin of safety. Let b, a so-called "buffer parameter," represent the fractional amount by which the credit line exceeds the projected peak borrowing requirement. Then

(3)
$$\text{CLINE} = (1 + b) \max_{t} \{B(t)\} \quad .$$

An alternative to scaling the peak projected borrowing upward is to simply add a fixed amount to the projected peak need, i.e.,

(3')
$$\text{CLINE} = \max_{t} \{STB(t)\} + \text{SLINE}$$

where SLINE represents the "safety line," i.e., the dollar amount of the line in excess of the projected need.

In addition to providing for actual projected borrowing requirements and a safety cushion, it is common to provide a call on credit for unanticipated needs and unforeseen opportunities such as an acquisition. Let OPLINE be the dollar amount of the credit line obtained for this purpose. Then the total credit line is given by

(4)
$$\text{CLINE} = (1 + b) \max_{t} \{B(t)\} + \text{OPLINE} \quad .$$

The reason for separating the credit line held for opportunities is that corporate financial officers usually structure credit-line specification problems

on extensions. This expression may also become more complex if average balances can be met over a period longer than a month. However, all that the cash planning model requires is an appropriate expression for CBR(t) as a function of the borrowing schedule and credit line. Thus, we shall use equation (2) throughout this paper as an illustrative expression that is typical of most firms.

in these terms and the explicit separation allows an easy assessment of the cost of the line held for opportunities.

Both the safety buffer b (or SLINE) and the reserve for opportunities, OPLINE, are financial policy parameters of the firm. The appropriate values for these parameters are a matter for management judgment given the perceived uncertainty in borrowing requirements, the firm's willingness to tolerate risk, and the value of a reserve for unexpected opportunities. Within the framework of the planning model, the adequacy of a given value of the buffer is determined by an assessment of the uncertainty of the peak borrowing requirement via sensitivity analysis as described subsequently.

Consistency Conditions and Feasibility Requirements

Let $C(t)$ be the cash level in month t computed by generating monthly financial statements using some schedule of short-term borrowing and investment in short-term securities. There is no guarantee that the cash level $C(t)$ will be consistent with the target cash level $\hat{C}(t)$ that represents the cash balance necessary for the firm to conform to its transaction and compensating balance requirements.

The problem of cash planning is to find a schedule of credit-line borrowing and security investment such that $C(t)$ equals $\hat{C}(t)$, or at least has equality to within allowable error tolerances. Let $e(t)$ be the allowable deviation of $C(t)$ from $\hat{C}(t)$ in month t. Then consistency between the firm's cash balances, short-term securities, credit-line borrowing, and level of the credit line occurs when:

(C1) $$\left| C(t) - \hat{C}(t) \right| < e(t) \quad ,$$

(C2) $$S(t) \geq SMIN(t) \quad , \text{ and}$$

(C3) $$CLINE = (1 + b) \max_{t} \left\{ STB(t) \right\} + OPLINE \quad ,$$

where $S(t)$ is the value of investment in short-term securities and $SMIN(t)$ is the minimum acceptable value of $S(t)$.

In addition to these three conditions, a feasible solution requires:

(C4) That short-term borrowing be completely repaid for at least some part of the year;

(C5) That investment in short-term securities not be at excessively high levels in all or even most time periods;

(C6) That the planned level of the credit line not exceed upper limits that either the firm or the banks regard as imprudent.

Given the information needed to project future financial statements, the algorithm presented in the next section finds schedules of $C(t)$, $S(t)$, and $B(t)$ and a value of the credit line that satisfies Conditions C1, C2, and C3. The conformity of this solution to Conditions C4, C5, and C6 is assessed by the model user from system output. Conformity to these latter conditions is obtained via changes in either the long-term financial plan or the operating plan since failure to satisfy these feasible conditions means that the long-term plan and operating plan are incompatible with the short-term constraints.

IV.   The Consistency Algorithm

The financial statement relations that relate the values of $C(t)$ to the values of $S(t)$ and $B(t)$ are a set of nonlinear, coupled difference equations for which a closed-form solution is not viable. As is usual in the solution of such a system of equations, iterative techniques are employed to obtain consistent values. The next section describes the solution procedure.

Overview of the Algorithm

The essence of the solution procedure is to start with trial schedules for $S(t)$ and $B(t)$, to generate financial statements to obtain $C(t)$, to compare $C(t)$ with the target balance in each time period, and, if $C(t)$ does not equal $\hat{C}(t)$ to within allowed error tolerances, to revise the values of $S(t)$ and $B(t)$ and possibly CLINE in such a way as to shift the new value of $C(t)$ toward $\hat{C}(t)$ while simultaneously ensuring that consistency conditions (C2) and (C3) are satisfied. This process of revising $S(t)$ and $B(t)$ and then comparing the new value of $C(t)$ with the (possibly revised) value of $\hat{C}(t)$ continues until $C(t)$ equals $\hat{C}(t)$ to within allowed error tolerances in every month.

Figure I is a logic diagram of the major steps in the adjustment procedure. The initial data required by the algorithm are:
1. the parameters CMIN(t), SMIN(t), $A_o(t)$, a_1, a_2, b, and OPLINE, which characterize management policy and the firm's banking relations;
2. the error tolerances, e(t);
3. an initial trial schedule for $S(t)$ and $B(t)$.

The initial values of the schedules for $S(t)$ and $B(t)$ do not affect the final values of $S(t)$, $B(t)$, or $C(t)$ but only the rate of convergence of the consistent set of values. A good set of starting values means quick convergence.[9]

---

[9]A simple choice of values that imposes a low data-entry burden on the system user is to employ the historical values of the variables or (as done in the General Recreation system) a scale factor (to allow for growth) times the historical values.

From this data and other information required for financial statement projection, the system finds the schedule C(t) by projecting monthly balance sheets, book income statements, and tax income statements. Then the system uses the peak borrowing requirement and user-specified parameters to compute the appropriate value of the credit line and target balances. The actual and target balances are checked for consistency. If actual and target values are not sufficiently close, the values of S(t) and B(t) are revised appropriately. If all actual and target balances are equal to within allowed error tolerances, then the system asks the user if he wishes to perform sensitivity analysis.

If the user answers "yes" to the query on sensitivity analysis, the system transfers him to the credit-line sensitivity analysis subsystem described subsequently; otherwise, it returns control to the user for further interaction with the planning system.

The Adjustment Algorithm

The requirement for the successful execution of the cash planning process depicted in Figure I is a systematic procedure for adjusting the schedules S(t) and B(t) to ensure the eventual congruence of the actual and target cash balances along with compliance to Conditions C2 and C3.

Figure II provides a detailed description of the adjustment algorithm that revises S(t) and B(t) at each iteration of the cash planning process. Figure II shows four distinct cases for which a different adjustment is made.

Case 1: Cash Deficit and No Securities Available for Sale. When $C(t) < \hat{C}(t)$ and $S(t) = \text{SMIN}(t)$, then additional cash must be provided by borrowing. In this case, the adjustment in short-term borrowing is given by

$$(5) \qquad\qquad \Delta B(t) = \frac{\hat{C}(t) - C(t)}{1 - a_1 - i_b(1-T)}$$

where $\Delta B(t)$ is the change in $B(t)$, i_b is the interest rate on short-term debt, and T is the effective income-tax rate. The adjustment of equation (5) is used instead of simply borrowing the amount $\hat{C}(t) - C(t)$ to increase the rate of convergence of the algorithm to a consistent set of values. To see the rationale for equation (5), we note that the total required change in borrowing

FIGURE I

MACROLOGIC OF THE CASH PLANNING PROCESS

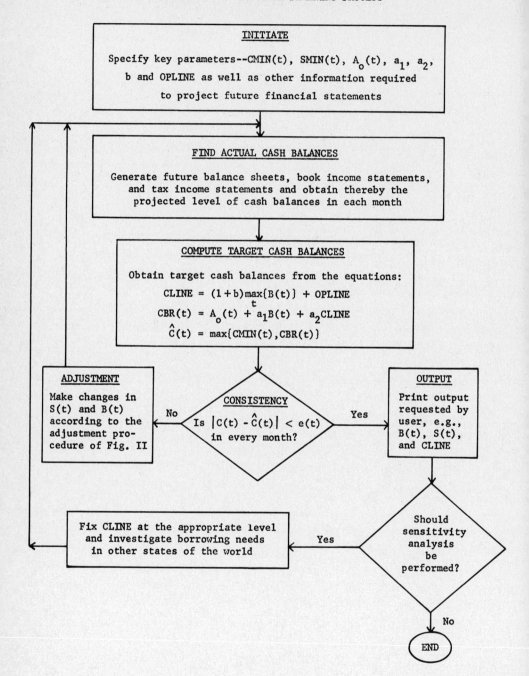

FIGURE II

THE ADJUSTMENT ALGORITHM FOR A GIVEN MONTH

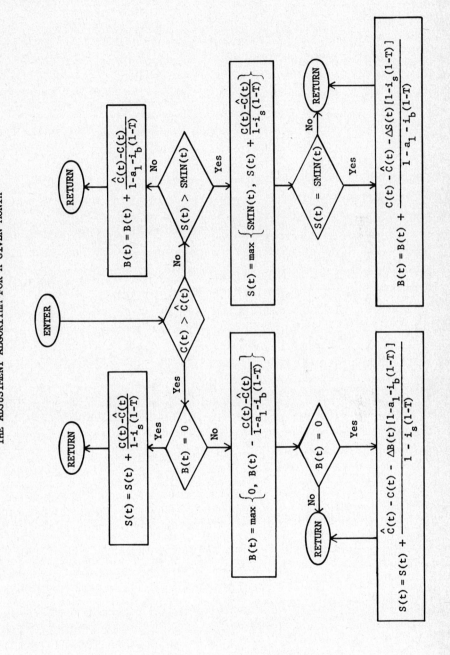

515

will be the sum of the difference in the target and expected balance, $\hat{C}(t) - C(t)$, plus the additional compensating balances required for the increased borrowing plus additional cash for payment of interest net of income taxes, i.e.,

$$\Delta B(t) = \hat{C}(t) - C(t) + a_1 \Delta B(t) + i_b(1-T)\Delta B(t) \quad .$$

When solved for $\Delta B(t)$ this expression gives equation (5).

Case 2: Inadequate Cash Balances and No Securities Available for Sale. When $C(t) < \hat{C}(t)$ and $S(t) > SMIN(t)$, then the short-term securities are reduced before credit-line borrowing is used as a source of cash. The formula for the amount of short-term securities to be sold is given by

(6) $$\Delta S(t) = \frac{\hat{C}(t) - C(t)}{1 - i_s(1-T)}$$

where $i_s(t)$ is the interest rate on short-term securities.

The adjustment in equation (6) is used instead of simply selling an amount equal to the required cash to account for the loss of interest income from the short-term securities. The actual adjustment consists of the cash deficit to be eliminated plus the interest income lost on the securities sold, i.e.,

$$\Delta S(t) = \hat{C}(t) - C(t) + i_s(1-T)\Delta S(t)$$

where the term $(1-T)$ corrects for the effect of taxes. Solving this expression for $\Delta S(t)$ gives equation (6).

Case 3: Cash Excess and No Credit-Line Borrowing in Month t. When $C(t) > \hat{C}(t)$ and $B(t) = 0$, the excess cash is invested in short-term securities. The change in the level of short-term securities is given by

(7) $$\Delta S(t) = \frac{C(t) - \hat{C}(t)}{1 - i_s(1-T)} \quad .$$

Equation (7) is analogous to the adjustment given in equation (6) in that the term in the denominator reflects an adjustment for the after-tax income on the short-term securities.

Case 4: Cash Excess and Credit-Line Borrowing in Time Period t. When $C(t) > \hat{C}(t)$ and there is also credit-line borrowing in month t, the excess cash is first used to reduce the borrowing rather than to purchase short-term securities. However, if there is still excess cash after eliminating the credit-line borrowing, then the remaining cash excess is invested in short-term securities. The logic for the adjustments to both credit-line borrowing and short-term securities depicted in Figure II for this case is analogous to that discussed previously.

Adjustment Priorities

The algorithm of Figure II contains assumptions about the relative attractiveness of securities and borrowing to adjust cash levels. To provide cash, the system first reduces securities to the minimum acceptable level before borrowing; to eliminate excess cash, the system first reduces borrowing to zero before investing in securities. The justification for these priorities is that the yield on securities is always less than the effective cost of borrowing.

The use of these priorities means that the final cash plan is the best plan that satisfies Conditions C1, C2, and C3 given the long-term financing plan. The use of priorities plus the guarantee within the algorithm that Conditions C2 and C3 are always met avoids the need to solve a nonlinear mathematical programming problem to find the best cash plan that satisfies Conditions C1, C2, and C3.

Convergence Properties

Since the cash-adjustment subsystem is part of a conversational planning model, the rate of convergence is important not only for the usual reason of computational efficiency but also for quick response time.

The particular formulas used for adjustment in $S(t)$ and $B(t)$ are designed to enhance the rate of convergence to a consistent set of values. For $B(t)$ the formula corrects for both adjustments in the compensating balance requirement and the after-tax debt interest. For $S(t)$ the formula corrects only for after-tax security interest.

The adjustments in $S(t)$ and $B(t)$ are on a period-to-period basis. They do not attempt to reflect the effect of the adjustment on the cash level in subsequent periods. In addition, the tax adjustment is only an approximation, since taxes will correspond to an actual cash flow only in the months in which tax payments actually occur.

While it is possible to carry cash changes forward and to incorporate the actual timing of tax payments, the increase in algorithmic complexity is not justified. Carrying out a more complex algorithm involves incorporating in the adjustment process much of the financial statement and tax law structure that is already part of the simulator. In fact, recomputing C(t) by returning to the simulator after these simple adjustments in S(t) and B(t) is *de facto* incorporation of the more complex structure.

The most critical factor for rate of convergence is quickly obtaining the appropriate value of the peak borrowing requirement since this stabilizes the credit line, which affects the target balance in all time periods.

With error tolerances set at 1 percent in the General Recreation system, a stable value for the credit line is typically obtained in two to three iterations of the algorithm. Obtaining consistency of cash balances in all 24 months typically requires another two to four iterations. Thus, a consistent set of values is typically found in four to seven iterations. More than seven iterations is rare with error tolerances set at 1 percent.

The efficiency of the system is such that there is no degradation of system response time in carrying out the 24-month short-term financial statement projection which involves the use of the cash planning subsystem with error tolerances set at 1 percent, the usual value for the General Recreation system.

If there were no discontinuities in the tax structure,[10] then the algorithm would always converge to a consistent set of values (where consistency here means that Conditions C1, C2, and C3 are satisfied).

Although nonconvergence is a potential theoretical problem, experimentation with the General Recreation system has revealed that it is not a practical problem for "reasonable" error tolerances. Here reasonable means .1 percent or larger, a level that considerably exceeds the accuracy with which most firms estimate cash position and which has negligible effect on the determination of the required credit line. Even though nonconvergence does not appear to be a practical problem, the system contains a counter that monitors the number of passes through the algorithm. If the number of passes should exceed a user-specified level, then the system prints a warning message and various diagnostics concerning the source of the problem.

Sensitivity Analysis for Credit-Line Adequacy

Part of the credit line includes a safety cushion to provide for credit needs when expectations are not completely met. To assess the adequacy of the safety cushion, one projects financial statements for other possible

---

[10]Discontinuities arise when tax credits or tax-loss carry-forwards are used up, which amounts to an effective jump discontinuity in tax rates. In addition, the tax laws on the timing of estimated, actual, and make-up taxes also involve effective discontinuities.

states of the world, e.g., a "worst case" and "best case" analysis. While one could simply rerun the system for these alternative cases and compare the various credit-line requirements, a preferable approach is to fix the credit line at its tentative value and assess the adequacy of the line in these other states. This is accomplished by eliminating the credit line of equation (4) and simply setting CLINE equal to a specific value. The adequacy of this particular value is assessed by comparing the peak borrowing requirement in other states of the world with the current value of CLINE or possibly the current value of CLINE - OPLINE.

V. Plan Feasibility and the Interaction of Long-Term and Short-Term Planning

When the system finds a consistent cash plan, it prints the schedules $C(t)$, $S(t)$, $B(t)$, and the value of the credit line.

Borrowing Infeasibility. The short-term plan is feasible in terms of the borrowing schedule if the borrowing is completely repaid for the required number of months in each year. If the borrowing is not repaid, then, since the cash plan has provided minimum levels of borrowing in each month, it is necessary either to provide additional long-term funds or to revise the operating plan.

Credit-Line Infeasibility. If the credit line required by the cash plan is greater than the firm feels it can reasonably negotiate with its banks, then (since the cash plan minimizes the credit line given the values of b and OPLINE), the firm must either provide additional long-term financing, revise the parameters b and OPLINE, or change its operating plan.

Short-Term Security Infeasibility. If $S(t)$ is substantially greater than SMIN(t), then the firm has a possible excess of short-term securities. This result implies that it is possible to reduce long-term financing, a generally profitable action since the cost of long-term funds exceeds the yield on short-term securities.

These feasibility conditions must be regarded as fuzzy constraints. For instance, borrowing infeasibility may occur, but at such a low level that a planner finds it tolerable. Or, the borrowing may be feasible in the most likely state of the world, but be so close to infeasibility that the ability to repay debt in adverse states is questionable.

The point here is that the actual assessment of feasibility is a judg-mental problem that requires interaction of the system with the planner.

While infeasible short-term plans necessitate revision of the long-term plan or change in the operating plan, the financial planning process generally involves interaction between short-term and long-term plans even when feas-ibility occurs. The assessment of the percent of total financing that is long-term and short-term is a judgmental problem that is typically solved by con-sidering alternative allocations and assessing their implications for firm performance in a variety of environments. The ability to obtain quickly the best cash plan that corresponds to any given long-term plan greatly facili-tates this process. Thus, this subsystem actually facilitates meaningful long-term planning.

VI. Extensions

As presented, the model is applicable to the cash planning and credit-line determination of most firms. Probably the major limitations are that it does not explicitly allow for the issuance of commercial paper and may require more detail for a firm with a variety of credit-line or compensating balance agreements. This section outlines procedures to cope with these problems.

Extension to a Commercial Paper Issuing Firm

Let CPI(t) be the current liability account that represents the amount of commercial paper issued in month t.

Since most industrial firms have their credit line backed by an unused bank credit line, the revised expression for the credit line is

$$\text{CLINE} = (1 + b) \max_{t} \{\gamma \text{ CPI}(t) + B(t)\} + \text{OPLINE}$$

where γ is the fraction of the firm's commercial paper that is backed by an unused credit line. For most firms, the appropriate value of γ is 1.0; how-ever, including the rate of backing as a parameter provides for those cases in which full backing is not required or where the firm maintains more than full backing as a matter of policy. Of course, a firm for which no credit-line backing is required would simply set γ equal to zero.

The availability of commercial paper means that a third asset is available for making adjustments in the level of cash balances. In eliminating a cash deficiency, the priority ordering for making adjustments in fund sources is: (1) sell short-term securities; (2) issue commercial paper; (3) borrow on the credit line. In eliminating a cash surplus, the priority ordering is reversed, i.e., (1) reduce outstanding borrowing; (2) reduce commercial paper issued; (3) invest in short-term securities.

The implicit assumption in these priority orderings is that the yield on short-term securities is less than the cost of issuing commercial paper which in turn is less than the cost of credit-line borrowing.

With these priority rules and the extended formula for specifying the credit line, the basic logic of the cash-notes-borrowing adjustment process can be extended to a commercial paper issuing firm.

Extension to Allow for Credit-Line Shifts

As formulated, the model assumes one level for the credit line over the entire planning horizon. To allow for one level for the first T months and another for the final months, equation (4) should be replaced by

$$CLINE(t) = \begin{cases} (1 + b) \max_{0 < t < T} \{ \gamma\, CPI(t) + B(t) \} + OPLINE & t \leq T \\[2em] (1 + b) \max_{t > T} \{ \gamma\, CPI(t) + B(t) \} + OPLINE & t > T \ . \end{cases}$$

It is possible to allow the parameters b and OPLINE to vary in each subperiod.

Extension to allow further changes in the level of the credit line is straightforward generalization of this procedure. However, changing a credit line more often than once a year is unusual practice.

Extension to Treat a Variety of Credit-Line Terms

Some firms, particularly very large firms with many banks, may have several arrangements available for borrowing that are characterized by different rates and/or different compensating balance agreements. To extend the model to this case, one needs only to define a borrowing account that corresponds to each distinct credit agreement and to specify the priority rules for borrowing by type of credit terms. One then computes compensating balance requirements by type. The total compensating balance agreement and total borrowing are the sum of these quantities over all credit types. Then the basic logic of the cash-notes-borrowing system carries over with the only complexity being the incorporation of the borrowing priorities in the adjustment procedure.

VII. Summary and Conclusions

This paper has presented a model for solving a central problem of short-term financial management -- cash planning and credit-line determination. The core of the model is an algorithmic procedure for finding the best cash plan and the associated credit line for a given operating plan and long-term financial plan. Since the model requires a computation of cash balances, it must be embedded in a financial statement simulator.

The two keys to the model are:

1. the use of priority rankings in specifying the order in which assets and liabilities are used to change cash balances;
2. the separation of solution constraints into two classes--consistency conditions given by C1, C2, and C3 and feasibility conditions stated in C4, C5, and C6. The latter conditions require changes in the long-term plan (or the operating plan) to obtain feasibility of the short-term plan.

The use of priority rankings and the separation of solution constraints into these two classes makes possible the formulation of an algorithmic procedure that is computationally efficient and that avoids having to solve a mathematical programming problem.

The benefits of the model are: (1) saved time; (2) increased accuracy in cash planning; (3) quick determination of infeasibility with respect to the short-term plan. For a firm already using financial statement simulation, the model is sufficiently easy to program and implement so that saved user time and system expense alone easily justify the cost of developing the system. Finally, a system that automatically handles short-term cash planning is critical for other areas of short-term planning, for meaningful sensitivity analysis, and for long-term financial planning for firms (such as General Recreation) for which a substantial part of the total financing is provided by either credit-line borrowing or commercial paper issuance.

Because of the similarity of both banking and financial practice across firms and banks, the basic approach used in this model is applicable to most nonfinancial corporations.

REFERENCES

[1] Ackoff, Russell L. *A Concept of Corporate Planning.* New York: John Wiley & Sons, Inc., 1970.

[2] Carleton, Willard T. "An Analytical Model for Long Range Financial Planning." *Journal of Finance,* May 1970, pp. 291-315.

[3] Carleton, Willard T.; Charles L. Dick, Jr.; and David H. Downes. "Converting Finance Theory into Practice: Observations from Case Histories." Working Paper.

[4] Dickson, G. W.; J. J. Muriel; and J. C. Anderson. "Computer Assisted Planning Models: A Functional Analysis." In *Corporate Simulation Models,* edited by Albert N. Schrieber. Seattle, Wash.: College of Business Administration of the University of Washington and the College on Gaming and Simulation of the Institute of Management Science, 1970.

[5] Gershefski, George W. *The Development and Application of a Corporate Financial Model.* Oxford, Ohio: The Planning Executive Institute, 1968.

[6] _____. "Building a Corporate Financial Model." *Harvard Business Review,* July-August 1969, pp. 61-72.

[7] _____. "The State of the Art." In *Corporate Simulation Models,* edited by Albert N. Schrieber. Seattle, Wash.: College of Business Administration of the University of Washington and the College on Gaming and Simulation of the Institute of Management Science, 1970.

[8] Naylor, Thomas H. *Computer Simulation Experiments of Models of Economic Systems.* New York: John Wiley and Sons, 1971.

[9] Schrieber, Albert N., ed. *Corporate Simulation Models.* Seattle, Wash.: College of Business Administration of the University of Washington and the College on Gaming and Simulation of the Institute of Management Science, 1970.

[10] Stone, Bernell K.; David H. Downes; and Robert P. Magee. "Computer-Assisted Financial Planning: The User Interface." Working Paper, July 1973.

[11] Warren, James M., and John P. Shelton. "A Simultaneous Equation Approach to Financial Planning." *Journal of Finance,* December 1971, pp. 1123-1142.

GOAL PROGRAMMING AND WORKING CAPITAL MANAGEMENT

WILLIAM L. SARTORIS and
M. L. SPRUILL

Dr. Sartoris is Associate Professor of Finance at the University of Kentucky. He received his Ph.D. from Purdue University and is the author of articles appearing in the Journal of Financial and Quantitative Analysis, Financial Management [11] and other academic journals. Dr. Spruill is Assistant Professor of Business Administration at the University of Kentucky. He received his Ph.D. from the University of Michigan and is the author of articles appearing in Decision Sciences and the proceedings of serveral national meetings.

Introduction

In normative financial theory it is usually assumed that the firm has the overall objective of the maximization of the present worth with appropriate consideration of risk. A finer breakdown of this general objective results in more specific and sometimes opposing objectives. Of these specific objectives, two common ones (but certainly not the only ones of importance) are profitability and liquidity. In most financial decision models that have been developed the dominant objective is profitability with minimal, if any, consideration given to liquidity. Specifically, in working capital models for the determination of the optimal level of a current asset, the liquidity objective is often ignored (see, for example, Soldofsky [12] or Hadley and Whitin [4]).

In an article published in the Spring 1972 issue of *Financial Management*, Knight [6] has argued that it is inappropriate to examine the optimal level of the several current assets independently. He also argued that when the investments in these assets are viewed jointly the decision must become one of satisficing rather than optimizing. He suggests a simulation procedure to develop several possible investment alternatives with the manager then choosing the alternative that best satisfies his objectives.

Proposals for the application of mathematical programming techniques in financial decision making are abundant, examples being given in Beranek [1], Mao [9], Quirin [10], and Weingartner [13]. However, most of the applications include only the profitability objective.

Beranek [1] attempted to investigate the liquidity and profitability objectives jointly by using a linear programming (LP) model. The profitability objective is incorporated in the objective function while the liquidity objective is expressed as a constraint on the level of cash and the quick ratio. There are two problems with this approach. First, no effect is given to the implications of investment in working capital for the profitability objective. Secondly, the liquidity objective need not necessarily be a strict constraint. Rather, management may have a desired level of working capital, and might like to minimize large deviations from this goal in either the positive or the negative direction.

It would be possible to solve the first difficulty by including the effect on profitability of investment in the various current assets in the objective function of the LP model. However, in an LP model the liquidity objective must still be expressed as a constraint with deviation from the objective possible in only one direction and with the amount of the deviation being of no consequence. In addition, all sacrifice in the model must be in the reduction of the level of achievement of the profitability objective, for the liquidity objective is treated as an inviolable constraint.

Lee [8] and Mao [9] have discussed the use of goal programming (GP), a relatively unexplored mathematical programming method developed by Charnes and Cooper [2] and Ijiri [5], in determining the optimal level of profit. Mao has suggested using GP to incorporate the liquidity and profitability objectives as goals for the model. However, he does not include the effects of investment in current assets on profitability.

Mathematical Programming Techniques

LP is a technique used to allocate scarce resources in order to maximize or minimize some mathematical function. This function usually represents either profit or cost in a financial decision context. The general LP problem with n variables and m constraints is stated mathematically as

$$\text{maximize} \quad C_1X_1 + C_2X_2 + \ldots + C_nX_n \tag{1a}$$

$$\text{subject to} \quad A_{j1}X_1 + A_{j2}X_2 + \ldots$$
$$+ A_{jn}X_n \leqslant b_j, j = 1, \ldots, m \tag{1b}$$

$$X_i \geqslant 0, i = 1, \ldots, n, \tag{1c}$$

where (1a) represents the objective function, with $X_1, \ldots, X_n$, representing levels of each of n decision variables and $C_1, \ldots, C_n$, representing per-unit contributions for each decision variable; where (1b) represents the constraint matrix, with $b_1, \ldots, b_m$, representing levels of available scarce resources and with the A_{ji}'s representing technology coefficients; and where (1c) represents the non-negativity restrictions.

The standard method of solving a problem of this form is the simplex method (see Dantzig [3]).

In contrast to LP, GP does not use only one goal or measure of performance (e.g., profit or cost) which is optimized subject to a set of constraints. Rather, use of GP assumes there are multiple goals (e.g., attaining a certain level of profitability *and* attaining a certain level of utilization of a scarce resource). Then, rather than maximizing or minimizing, an objective function is formulated which

measures the absolute deviations from desired goals; this objective function is then minimized. In an LP formulation the value of the objective function is found and may be reduced so that the minimum or maximum values of the constraints are not violated. In a GP formulation priorities are established for each of the goals explicitly by the penalties assigned to violations of the goal, and goals are satisfied in a manner that results in a minimum penalty.

Krouse [7] has suggested a somewhat different multiple objective programming technique for working capital management. His procedure utilizes a hierarchical ordering of objectives and requires that they be satisfied sequentially in the implied order. First, the optimal solution is obtained with only the objective having the highest priority being considered. Since it is generally not possible for the other objectives to be satisfied when the first objective is at this optimum level, it is necessary to determine some acceptable suboptimal level. Next, a solution is obtained with consideration being given to the second objective and with the additional requirement that the first objective at least achieve this suboptimal level. If an acceptable solution is not obtainable for both objectives, it is necessary to revise the initial constraining level for the first objective and resolve the problem. When an acceptable solution is obtained for both objectives, an acceptable suboptimal value is specified for the second objective and the solution proceeds to the third objective. This procedure continues until all objectives are considered. In a goal programming formulation priority weights establish the importance of the various goals rather than the order in which they must be satisfied; thus, a trade-off between violations of the different objectives is automatically allowed in the solution.

Perhaps an example will best illustrate the concepts of GP. Consider a new company which produces 2 products, X and Y. The company has a total of 15 production hours available; each unit of product X requires 3 hours of production time, while each unit of product Y requires 1 hour. The company will allow the use of overtime, but prefers to use at most 15 hours of production time. The company's marketing department has determined that the company could sell, at most, 10 units of product X and, at most, 6 units of product Y. Since one goal of the new company is market penetration, the company would like to sell as close to the maximum number of units of each product as possible. Finally, each unit of product X generates a revenue of $10, while each unit of product Y generates a revenue of $8. The goal that the company's stockholders consider most important is net revenue. In fact, they expect a revenue of $75 and are averse to any less.

Three goals can be distinguished: (1) minimizing the amount of overtime; (2) maximizing market penetration; and (3) attaining a revenue as close as possible to $75. In terms of importance to the company, goal 3 is more important than goal 2, which is more important than goal 1.

Let d_i^+ represent an upside deviation from goal i and d_i^- a downside deviation, where both d_i^+ and d_i^- are non-negative numbers. Let the P_1, P_2, and P_3 multipliers in the objective function express the priority relationship described in the preceding paragraph, where $P_3 >>> P_2 >>> P_1$. (The P values allow us to treat incommensurable goals, that is, those which cannot be compared directly. For a more complete discussion of this, see Lee [8].) With these definitions the model for our problem is

$$\text{minimize} \quad P_1 d_1^+ + P_2 d_2^- + P_2 d_3^- + P_3 d_4^- \qquad (2a)$$

$$\text{subject to} \quad 3X + Y + d_1^+ \qquad = 15 \text{ (hours)} \qquad (2b)$$

$$X + d_2^- \qquad = 10 \text{ (units of product X)} \qquad (2c)$$

$$Y + d_3^- \qquad = 6 \text{ (units of product Y)} \qquad (2d)$$

$$10X + 8Y + d_4^- \qquad = 75 \text{ (revenue)} \qquad (2e)$$

$$X, Y, d_1^+, d_2^-, d_3^-, d_4^- \geq 0. \qquad (2f)$$

This problem can now be solved using the ordinary simplex method for solving LP problems. It should be noted that the d_i^+ are not slack variables in the usual LP sense since their coefficients in the objective function are non-zero. The implication is that all constraints in the program are equality constraints, and there is a penalty if the constraints are not met exactly.

Application of GP to Working Capital Management

The following illustration uses LP and GP together to develop a one-period financial decision model that includes both the profitability and liquidity objectives. One of the goals used in the GP formulation will be derived from a standard linear programming model used to maximize net present value of the firm subject only to technical constraints.

The ABC Company manufactures two products, Y and Z, which can be sold either for cash or on credit. The sales can be made either from production during the period or from beginning inventory. See Exhibit 1 for information on costs, demand, inventory, etc.

The firm has available a maximum of 1000 hours for production. The company incurs a carrying cost of 10% of the value of the ending inventory. ABC can obtain a loan secured by the ending inventory which has a cost of 5% for the period and which can have a maximum value of 75% of the ending inventory. The sale of one unit for cash creates a net cash inflow equal to the profit on the sale, while a sale of one unit on credit creates a net cash outflow equal to the production costs plus the credit costs. The carrying cost for the ending inventory is a cash drain for the period. An additional cash inflow of 95% of the value of the loan (the value of the loan minus the 5% interest cost) can also be obtained.

ABC managers would like to obtain as much profit during the period as possible. However, they also want an ending cash balance of $75 with downside deviations from this amount being less desirable than upside deviations. At the same time they feel that an opportunity cost of 5% exists for carrying an ending cash balance. In addition, the management would like to obtain an end-of-period current ratio of 2:1 and a quick ratio of 1:1, with either upside or downside deviations from these goals being possible but undesirable. For simplicity only, the firm presently has $150 in current liabilities, not expected to change throughout the period unless the firm obtains an inventory loan.

Before this set of goals can be incorporated in a GP formulation, it is necessary to specify some quantified goal for profit. The managers could choose some arbitrary profit figure as their goal, but this would not be consistent with the actual goal of maximum possible profit. A method of quantifying the profit goal is first to determine the maximum

Exhibit 1. Data for ABC Company

Product	Maximum sales (units)		Price per unit ($)	Cost/unit ($)		Profit/unit ($)		Beginning inventory (units)	Hours used per unit produced
	Cash	Credit		Production cost	Credit cost	Cash	Credit		
Y	150	100	40	35	0.50	5	4.5	60	2
Z	175	250	52.50	45	1.00	7.5	6.5	30	4

profit that could be obtained if the working capital goals were not present. An LP formulation is particularly appropriate for this purpose.

For the above illustration the objective function for the LP formulation would be

max profits = revenue for the period less any costs charged to the period.

max profits = $5 (units Y sold for cash) + $4.5 (units Y sold for credit)

$+$7.5 (units Z sold for cash) + $6.5 (units Z sold for credit)

$-(.1)$ ($35) (ending inventory of Y) - (.1) ($45) (ending inventory of Z)

$-(.05)$ (value of loan) - (.05) (ending cash balance)

This objective function is to be maximized subject to the following constraints: sales $\leqslant$ production capacity plus beginning inventory; sales $\leqslant$ maximum demand; ending cash balance $\geqslant$ 0; value of the loan $\leqslant$ (.75) (value of ending inventory); and number of units withdrawn from inventory must be less than or equal to number of units sold.

Solution of this LP problem resulted in a profit of $2,698.94 for the period, obtained by selling 150 units of Y for cash, 175 units of Z for cash, and 44.8 units of Z on credit. The ending inventory, cash balance, and loan are all zero. Since the inventory is zero, the current ratio and the quick ratio are equal at a value of 15.69. The maximum profit of $2,698.94 physically possible for the firm results, and thus becomes the profit goal for the GP formulation.

We are now ready to use GP to incorporate into the decision process the conflicting goals specified by ABC management. The firm's goals are (1) the maximum possible profit of $2,698.94, (2) an ending cash balance of $75, (3) an ending current ratio of 2:1, and (4) an ending quick ratio of 1:1. As explained earlier, these goals are incorporated in the model by creation of variables representing deviations from the goal and use of the simplex method to minimize these deviations. For illustration we used three possible sets of priorities: (1) the profit goal has a much higher priority than any of the working capital goals; (2) the working capital goals have a much higher priority than the profit goal; and (3) all goals have relatively similar priorities. (See the appendix for a mathematical formulation of the GP problem for this illustration.)

It should be noted here that in actual practice ABC managers may or may not have a feel for the priority of each goal. If they do have this feel, they could simply assign coefficients for the deviation variables based on these priorities. However, if these priorities do not clearly exist in the mind of the managers, the goal programming approach is still extremely useful. In a very short period of time, with the aid of a computer, the managers can see an entire range of possible priority situations and associated goal trade offs. By selecting the solution that best meets their needs they are implicitly establishing a set of priorities after the fact. Whether before or after the fact, the optimal solution for the managers, determined after examining a set of alternatives and associated goal trade offs, is useful. Thus, the method can be used for situations where the manager knows the exact weights to be placed on deviation variables, where he knows only relative priorities, and finally, where he knows nothing about his priorities. The three sets of priorities chosen to illustrate the method should adequately represent a series of alternatives that would be presented to management.

To show the effects of these three sets of priorities on the profitability and liquidity goals, arbitrary values were assigned to the coefficients of the variables representing deviations from the goals. See Exhibit 2 for the values for the coefficients that were used.

Exhibit 2. Coefficients for Deviation Variables Associated with Three Sets of Priorities in GP

Deviation variable	Coefficient value		
	Set 1*	Set 2**	Set 3***
Downside profit	999.0	0.05	6.0
Downside cash	4.0	999.0	5.0
Upside cash	3.5	999.0	2.5
Downside current ratio	40.0	999.0	5.0
Upside current ratio	40.0	999.0	5.0
Downside quick ratio	40.0	999.0	5.0
Upside quick ratio	40.0	999.0	5.0

*Profit has a much higher priority than the working capital goal.
**The working capital goals have a much higher priority than the profit goal.
***The priorities for all goals are similar.

The effects of the three different sets of priorities are given in Exhibit 3. For set 1, where profit has highest priority, results are identical to the LP solutions. In effect, the priority of the profit goal is so high in relation to the working capital goals that these lower priority goals are ignored in practical effect. When the liquidity goals have much higher priorities than the profit goal, the cash and the quick ratio are at their desired values, while the

Exhibit 3. Results of the Goal Programming Solution Using Three Sets of Priorities

Goal	Actual value		
	Set 1	Set 2	Set 3
Profit = $2,698.94	$2,698.94	$491.25	$857.84
Cash = $75	$0	$75	$75
Current Ratio=2:1	15.7:1	2.2:1	3.4:1
Quick Ratio=1:1	15.7:1	1:1	3.4:1

current ratio is 10% higher and profit is only $491.25 (see Exhibit 3). When the priorities are similar for all goals, the cash balance is equal to the goal of $75, the quick current ratios have risen to 3.4:1, and the profit is $857.84 (see Exhibit 3).

Exhibit 4 gives the sales and end-of-period balances resulting from use of the three different sets of priorities in the GP problem. Results generated with the second set of priorities indicate that to approach the desired values of the current and quick ratios, it is necessary to increase the level of current liabilities. This necessitated some ending inventory to support the inventory loan.

A comparison of the results for Set 2 and Set 3 indicates that when the priority on the working capital goals is high, the penalty for upside deviations forces the current and quick ratios down, but

Exhibit 4. Sales and End-of-Period Balances Associated With the Three Sets of Priorities Used in the Goal Programs

Item	Value		
	Set 1	Set 2	Set 3
Cash sales Y(units)	150.00	40.52	60.00
Credit sales Y(units)	-----	19.48	----
Cash sales Z(units)	175.00	----	21.59
Credit sales Z(units)	44.84	3.56	8.41
Ending inventory Y(units)	----	----	----
Ending inventory Z(units)	----	26.42	--
Cash balance ($)	----	75.00	75.00
Loan outstanding ($)	----	891.83	----

it also reduces the profit. At this point the management of ABC might want to reconsider specification of their set of goals with particular attention to the undesirability of too high a current and quick ratio.

Summary

For illustration, we have used different sets of priorities to demonstrate their effect on the attainment of profitability and liquidity goals. In a practical application of this technique, managers presumably would have some subjective priorities they would attach to their goals. However, while their priorities might not be so concretely formed that they could specify absolute weights, they would probably be able to specify some relative priorities, such as upside deviations from cash being 1/2 to 1/3 as bothersome as downside deviations from the current ratio, and downside deviations from the current ratio being only 1/2 as important as the downside deviations from profit. The use of relative priorities allows the problem of meeting profitability and liquidity goals to be approached simultaneously in a manner similar to that employed in this paper. In other words, managers choose some arbitrary set of values that approximate the importance of various goals, and observe the result when these values are used as coefficients in the objective function of the GP. Then the managers allow these values to change and determine the sensitivity of the final result. The managers can then choose the particular mix they feel best achieves their desired goals. This approach may help managers understand which of their specified goals are hardest to attain and may even cause them to reassess goals and/or priorities.

A logical extension of the simplified model utilized here, but by no means a simple one, would be to make it a multiperiod model incorporating discounting for the time value of money. Since a realistic model must deal with uncertainty, it would be necessary to adjust for varying degrees of risk. A possible, but to our knowledge yet unexplored, extension would be for different aspects of risk to be employed in a goal framework.

REFERENCES

1. W. Beranek, *Analysis for Financial Decisions*, Homewood, Illinois, Richard D. Irwin, Inc., 1963.

2. A. Charnes and W.W. Cooper, *Management Models and Industrial Applications of Linear Programming*, Vols. I, II, New York, John Wiley & Sons, 1961.

3. G.B. Dantzig, *Linear Programming and Extension*, Princeton, New Jersey, Princeton University Press, 1963.

4. G. Hadley and T.M. Whitin, *Analysis of Inventory Systems*, Englewood Cliffs, New Jersey, Prentice-Hall, Inc., 1963.

5. Y. Ijiri, *Management Goals and Accounting for Control*, Chicago, Illinois, Rand McNally & Co., 1965.

6. W.D. Knight, "Working Capital Management—Satisficing Versus Optimization," *Financial Management*, (Spring 1972), p. 33.

7. C.G. Krouse, "Programming Working Capital Management," in *Management of Working Capital*, ed. by K.V. Smith, St. Paul, Minnesota, West Publishing Company, 1974.

8. Sang Lee, "Decision Analysis Through Goal Programming," *Decision Sciences*, (April, 1971), p. 172.

9. J.C.T. Mao, *Quantitative Analysis of Financial Decisions*, New York, The Macmillan Company, 1969.

10. C.D. Quirin, *The Capital Expenditure Decision*, Richard D. Irwin Inc., Homewood, Illinois, 1967.

11. William L. Sartoris and Ronda S. Paul, "Lease Evaluation—Another Capital Budgeting Decision," *Financial Management* (Summer 1973), p. 46.

12. R.M. Soldofsky, "A Model for Accounts Receivable Management," *Management Accounting* (January, 1966), p. 55.

13. H.M. Weingartner, *Mathematical Programming and the Analysis of Capital Budgeting Problems*. Chicago Illinois, Markham Publishing Company, 1967.

Appendix.

Following is a list of definitions of all variables used in the GP formulation of the working capital problem:

X_1 = unit sales of Y for cash

X_2 = unit sales of Y on credit

X_3 = unit sales of Z for cash

X_4 = unit sales of Z on credit

X_5 = unit sales of Y from inventory

X_6 = unit sales of Z from inventory

X_7 = dollar value of loan secured by inventory

X_8 = ending cash balance

X_9 = downside difference from profit goal

X_{10} = downside difference from cash goal

X_{11} = upside difference from cash goal

X_{12} = function of downside difference in current ratio

X_{13} = function of upside difference in current ratio

X_{14} = function of downside difference in quick ratio

X_{15} = function of upside difference in quick ratio

P_i, $i = 1, \ldots, 7$ = weights on the deviations from goals. These weights are defined in Exhibit 2 for each of the three sets of priorities.

Using these definitions, the GP problem is formulated as follows:

minimize: $P_1X_9 + P_2X_{10} + P_3X_{11} + P_4X_{12} + P_5X_{13} + P_6X_{14} + P_7X_{15}$

subject to:

$$
\begin{array}{ll}
5X_1 + 4.5X_2 + 7.5X_3 + 6.5X_4 + 3.5X_5 + 4.5X_6 - .05X_7 - .05X_8 + X_9 & = 2698.94 \\
2X_1 + 2X_2 + 4X_3 + 4X_4 - 2X_5 - 4X_6 - & \leqslant 1000.00 \\
X_5 & \leqslant 60 \\
X_6 & \leqslant 30 \\
X_1 & \leqslant 150 \\
X_2 & \leqslant 100 \\
X_3 & \leqslant 175 \\
X_4 & \leqslant 250 \\
5X_1 - 35.5X_2 + 7.5X_3 - 46X_4 + 3.5X_5 + 4.5X_6 + .95X_7 + X_{10} - X_{11} & = 420 \\
26.25X_5 + 33.75X_6 + X_7 & \leqslant 2587.50 \\
-40X_2 - 52.5X_4 + 35X_5 + 45X_6 + 2X_7 - X_8 - X_{12} + X_{13} & = 3150 \\
40X_2 + 52.5X_4 - X_7 + X_8 + X_{14} - X_{15} & = 150 \\
5X_1 - 35.5X_2 + 7.5X_3 - 46X_4 + 3.5X_5 + 4.5X_6 + .95X_7 - X_8 & = 345 \\
-X_1 \quad X_2 + X_5 & \leqslant 0 \\
-X_3 - X_4 + X_6 & \leqslant 0 \\
X_i \geqslant 0, \ i = 1, \ldots, 15 &
\end{array}
$$

The following list defines the constraint given by each row in the constraint matrix:

Row 1 - profit plus downside deviation = $2698.94

Row 2 - time used in production at most 1000 hours

Row 3 - at most 60 units of Y drawn from inventory

Row 4 - at most 30 units of Z drawn from inventory

Row 5 - at most 150 units of Y sold for cash

Row 6 - at most 100 units of Y sold on credit

Row 7 - at most 175 units of Z sold for cash

Row 8 - at most 250 units of Z sold on credit

Row 9 - total cash goals*

Row 10 - inventory loan constraint*

Row 11 - current ratio goal*,**

Row 12 - quick ratio goal*,**

Row 13 - constraint requiring cash to be non-negative

Row 14 - sales of Y for cash plus sales of Y for credit must be greater than or equal to Y drawn from inventory

Row 15 - sales of Z for cash plus sales of Z for credit must be greater than or equal to Z drawn from inventory

Finally, the following equations represent the goals prior to their being put into appropriate format for the goal program:

1) Cash: $X_8 = 5X_1 - 36X_2 + 7.5X_3 - 47X_4 - 3.5(60-X_5) - 4.5(30-X_6) + .95X_7 = 75$

2) Current ratio: $\dfrac{X_8 + 40X_2 + 52.5X_4 + 35(60-X_5) + 45(30-X_6)}{150 + X_7} = 2$

3) Quick ratio: $\dfrac{X_8 + 40X_2 + 52.5X_4}{150 + X_7} = 1.$

---

*The numbers on the right-hand side include not only the goal but also constants carried to right-hand side of the equality from left-hand side.
**Both ratio goals have been linearized by multiplying right-hand side by denominator of ratio.

MEASURING AND INTERPRETING TIME, FIRM AND
LEDGER EFFECTS: METHOD AND IMPLICATIONS

by

James A. Gentry
and
Cheng-few Lee

Professor of Finance
University of Illinois, Urbana-Champaign

MEASURING AND INTERPRETING TIME, FIRM AND LEDGER EFFECTS: METHOD AND IMPLICATIONS

ABSTRACT

The objectives of this paper are to use a relatively unknown and useful feature of the X-11 model to measure the relative percentage contribution of each trend-cycle (C), seasonal (S) and irregular (I) component to changes in the original series of income statement variables; to show that the trend of the percentage contribution of each component results in a time, firm and ledger effect for five income statement variables; to draw forecasting implications for financial managers and analysts and to develop modeling implications for financial theorists.

Improving the forecast of future earnings is a primary concern of financial analysts. Deschamps and Mehta [7] recently made a significant contribution by comparing the effectiveness of different extrapolation methods used to forecast earnings. Corporate financial managers are also searching for forecasting methods that will aid in improving their financial predictions and overall performance. Methodologies that decompose time series data can provide information that may improve management performance. The decomposition methods such as the X-11 have a long history of application by government and business macroeconomic forecasters. The X-11 program was designed by the Bureau of the Census [19] to analyze historical time series and determine seasonal adjustments and growth trends. To adjust the seasonal components of the data, the X-11 program first decomposes the time series data into trend (C), seasonal (S) and irregular (I) components. Subsequently, the trend and irregular components are used to construct a seasonally adjusted series.

Although time series decomposition methods are not generally problem free, Burman [4] and Chambers, Mullick and Smith [5] have found the X-11 provides a unique and highly useful approach for forecasting and monitoring sales and determining turning points in sales. Alternatively, the Box-Jenkins [3] overall autoregressive integrated moving average (ARIMA) seasonal model can be used to decompose data time series. Cleveland and Tiao [6] have found the X-11 approximation model is generally a good proxy for the ARIMA seasonal model.

In addition to its forecasting feature, the X-11 calculates the percentage contribution of each S, C and I component to the relative changes in the original time series.[1] Equipped with information concerning the relative percentage contribution each component makes to a series, financial managers can better understand the composition of the data, evaluate the predictive quality of a financial planning variable and assess potential causes of forecasting errors. Additionally, building an industry index for key financial planning variables would provide a quantitative measure of the relative percentage contribution of each component. The availability of index information would supply a benchmark against which the forecasting quality of a firm's planning variables can be compared. The results can be used to improve operating performance and forecasting success.

The objectives of this paper are to use a relatively unknown feature of the X-11 model to measure the relative percentage contribution
of each S, C and I component to changes in the original series of income
statement variables; to show that the trend of the percentage contribution
of each component results in a time, ledger and firm effect for each
income statement variable; and finally, to draw forecasting implications
for financial managers and analysts, and develop modeling implications
for theorists.

Section I introduces the X-11 model as a tool for financial analysis. Measuring and interpreting the percentage contribution of each
S, C and I component is presented in Section II. In Section III we
explain and measure the presence of time, ledger and firm effects and
show the affect these three effects have on the percentage contribution
of each component for five income statement variables. Section IV demonstrates how the relative percentage contribution of the irregular (random)
components can aid financial forecasters and managers, and, also provide
insight to financial model builders. The conclusions are presented in
Section V.

I.   THE X-11 AND FINANCIAL ANALYSIS

Monthly and quarterly economic and business data are widely used in
short-run financial planning. The quality of the information contained
in a monthly or quarterly time series is unique when compared to a series
of annual data. Extracting these unique properties of monthly or quarterly data can provide substantive insight to management.

Two major approaches to time series analysis are the component
analysis and sample function analysis. The component analysis regards
the time series as being composed of several influences or components
which are generally taken to be trend-cycle (C), seasonal (S), and
irregular (I), or random movements. In component analysis, C and S
influences are modeled in a deterministic manner; C may be regarded
as a polynomial of a given degree and the seasonal component may be
modeled by a trigonometric function with a given period and amplitude.
Random influences are usually assumed to have a sample probability
structure and are treated as independent, identically distributed
random variables having zero mean and finite variance.

The sample function analysis regards a time series as an observed
sample function representing a realization of an underlying stochastic
process. Complicated parametric statistical estimation procedures
are used to determine the properties of time series data. Cleveland
and Tiao [6] have shown that the X-11 component analysis is generally
a good approximation for the ARIMA type of sample function analysis.
Theoretically, the results obtained from sample function analysis are
more precise than those obtained from component analysis. However, the
empirical results obtained from the component analysis are easier to
understand and interpret than those from sample function analysis.
Therefore, the X-11 analysis technique has occupied an important place
in applied time series analysis for over 20 years.

Dunn, Williams and Spivey [8] have used both component analysis
and sample function analysis techniques to analyze and predict telephone

demand in local geographical areas. Bonin and Moses [2] have used the component analysis methods to determine the evidence of seasonal variations in prices of individual Dow Jones Industrial stocks. Chambers, Mullick and Smith [5] have extensively discussed the possible usefulness of the X-11 decomposition technique for business analysis and forecasting. In summary, the preceding discussion provides the justification for utilizing the X-11 method to analyze corporate quarterly accounting data.

II.   MEASUREMENT AND INTERPRETATION

A.   Identifying the Components

The X-11 program is based on the premise that seasonal fluctuations can be measured in an original series of economic data and separated from trend, cyclical, trading-day and irregular fluctuations. The seasonal component (S) reflects an intrayear pattern of variation which is repeated constantly or in an evolving fashion from year to year. The trend-cycle component (C) includes the long-term trend and the business cycle. The trading day component (TD) consists of variations which are attributed to the composition of the calendar. The irregular component (I) is composed of residual variations that reflect the effect of random or unexplained events in the time series [19, p. 1].

Decomposing past time series and discovering the relative percentage contribution of the C, S and I components to changes in the series provides invaluable insight to management and financial analysts. The trend-cycle (C) component reflects permanent information in both a short- and long-run economic time series. The seasonal component is considered to represent a permanent pattern underlying the short-run time series. Although the percentage contribution of the seasonal component may be quite high in the short-run, it contains permanent type information that management can take into account for short and intermediate-run planning. The uncertainty arising from the seasonal component is relatively low.

The irregular (I) component contains the randomness that exists in the time series for both short and long-run analysis. This I component can be interpreted as noise in the information system. The higher the relative percentage contribution of the I component in a time series the greater the noise and/or uncertainty. Large forecasting errors can occur when the percentage contribution of the I component is high. Additionally, the irregular component of accounting earnings can bias the cost of capital estimate which was of concern to Miller and Modigliani [14]. They used a cross sectional regression method to estimate the cost of capital for the utility industry. M & M used the instrumental variable method to remove the random component in annual accounting earnings data.

B.   Measuring Component Contribution

For quarterly forecasting the X-11 generates a seasonal forecast of the next four quarters and computes the percentage contribution of the C, S and I components relative to the change in the original data series. The relative percentage contribution of the C, S and I components is calculated for a time span of one, two, three and four quarters. This calculation provides the statistical information utilized in this study. It is structured on the following relationship [19, pp. 18-19].

$$\overline{0}_t^{\,2} = \overline{I}_t^{\,2} + \overline{C}_t^{\,2} + \overline{S}_t^{\,2} + \overline{P}_t^{\,2} + \overline{TD}_t^{\,2} \tag{1}$$

where each symbol represents the mean of the absolute changes in a series:

$\overline{0}_t$ = original series;

$\overline{I}_t$ = final irregular series;

$\overline{C}_t$ = final trend cycle;

$\overline{S}_t$ = final seasonal factors

$\overline{P}_t$ = prior monthly adjustment factors, (not applicable to the quarterly model);

$\overline{TD}_t^{\,2}$ = Final trading day adjustment factors (not applicable to the quarterly model).

Since the sum of squares of the percent changes does not exactly equal $\overline{0}_t^{\,2}$, $(\overline{0}_t^{\,\prime})^2$ is substituted, where $(\overline{0}_t^{\,\prime})^2 = \overline{I}_t^{\,2} + \overline{C}_t^{\,2} + \overline{S}_t^{\,2}$. The relative contribution of the changes in each component for each time span is the ratio $\overline{I}_t^{\,2}/(\overline{0}_t^{\,\prime})^2$, $\overline{C}_t^{\,2}/(\overline{0}_t^{\,\prime})^2$ or $\overline{S}_t^{\,2}/(\overline{0}_t^{\,\prime})^2$, [19, p. 19].

C. Underline An Example

An example will illustrate the statistical computation of the relative contribution of each C, S and I component to the percentage change in the original time series. The quarterly sales of Caterpillar Tractor Company from the IQ 1969 to the IVQ 1980 are the data used in the example. These original sales data are found in Exhibit 1 and are graphically presented in Exhibit 2.

The relative contribution of each component for a one-quarter time span is calculated in the following manner. The first step is to determine the absolute change in the original sales series (0_t) between each quarter, e.g., $|0_1 - 0_2|$. Sales in the first and second quarters $(0_1$ and $0_2)$ of 1969 were $500.4 million and $558.9 million, respectively. The absolute change in sales between the first and second quarters was $58.4 million. The absolute difference in sales between the third

and fourth quarters $|O_3 - O_4|$, was $23.1 million, $|\$482.7 - \$459.6|$.
Thus for the original sales series (O_t) the X-11 routine calculates
the absolute change in sales between each of the 36 quarters, i.e.,
$|O_1 - O_2|$, $|O_2 - O_3|$, $|O_3 - O_4|$, ..., $|O_{34} - O_{35}|$, $|O_{35} - O_{36}|$.
The mean of the changes in the original sales series ($\overline{O_t}$) was $1.091

billion, which is shown in Exhibit 3.
 The X-11 routine also calculates the absolute change in the
original sales for a time span of two, three and four quarters. Because the computation methodology is similar for each time span, the
four quarter time span is used to illustrate the technique. The absolute change in sales every four quarters is calculated by the model.
All possible four quarter time period combinations of changes in sales
are computed, e.g., $|O_1 - O_5|$, $|O_5 - O_9|$, $|O_9 - O_{13}|$, ..., $|O_{29} - O_{33}|$,
$|O_2 - O_6|$, $|O_6 - O_{10}|$, ..., $|O_{30} - O_{34}|$, $|O_3 - O_7|$, ..., $|O_{31} - O_{35}|$,
$|O_4 - O_8|$, ..., $|O_{32} - O_{36}|$. The same procedure is utilized to calculate a two and a three quarter time span. The means of the changes in
the original series (O_t) for a two, three and four quarter time span

were $1.419 billion, $1.534 billion and $1.908 billion. These values
are also presented in Exhibit 3.

D.   The Final Measurement

 The next step in the process is to calculate the mean absolute
change in the final adjusted time series for the C, I and S components.
The X-11 computes a final adjusted table for each component. A brief
review of the process used to calculate the final estimated C, I and
S components follows.
 The moving average used to estimate the C component is selected
on the basis of the amplitude of the irregular variations in the data
relative to the amplitude of long-term systematic variations. The
routine selects a moving-average that provides a suitable compromise
between the need to smooth the irregular with a long-term inflexible
moving average and the need to reproduce accurately the systematic
element with a short-term flexible moving average [19, p. 3].
 The selection of the appropriate moving average for estimating
the trend cycle (C) component is made on the basis of a preliminary
estimate of the I/C rate (the ratio of the mean absolute quarter-
to-quarter change in the irregular to the trend-cycle). A 13-term
Henderson average of the preliminary seasonally adjusted series is used
as the preliminary estimate of C and the ratio of the preliminary seasonally adjusted series to the 13-term average used as the estimate of
the I component [19, p. 3]. The extreme value of the series are replaced
with a smoothing routine. Finally a 5-term Henderson curve is used to
modify the seasonally adjusted series to obtain the final trend cycle

(C) and irregular (I) series [19, pp. 3-4]. A graphic presentation of the final trend-cycle, 5-term Henderson curve is presented in Exhibit 2. In general, Exhibit 2 shows the C component tracks the original time series reasonably close.

The S-I ratios for each quarter are smoothed by a 3x5-term moving average (a 3 term average of a 5-term average) to estimate final seasonal factors. Because the statistical calculations of the final C, S and I components are lengthy and complex, the numerous tables generated by the model are not presented. The final S and I series are graphically presented in Exhibit 2. The irregular component is substantially more volatile than the seasonal component for Caterpillar sales. A strike in the IVQ 1979 caused a substantial deviation from the original series and had a profound affect on the I component. A summary of the mean absolute changes in sales in the C, S and I series for one, two, three and four quarter time series are presented in Exhibit 3. The calculation of these mean absolute changes follows the same procedure used in computing the change in the original sales series. These mean values in Exhibit 3 provide the base for computing the relative contribution of each component to changes in the original series.

A revision to equation 1 presented earlier specifies the relationship involved in calculating the relative contribution of the C, S and I components. The calculations utilize the data in Exhibit 3. An example that computes the relative contribution of each component to changes in the original Caterpillar sales series for a one quarter time span follows. The revision to equation 1 is

$$(\overline{O}')^2 = \overline{I}^2 + \overline{C}^2 + \overline{S}^2. \tag{1a}$$

Substituting the appropriate values from Exhibit 3 into (1a) produces

$$(99.508)^2 = (72.358)^2 + (42.051)^2 + (53.831)^2. \tag{1b}$$

For a one quarter time span the relative contribution of each component is ...

$$\text{I component} = \frac{\overline{I}^2}{(\overline{O}')^2} = \frac{(72.358)^2}{(99.508)^2} = 52.88\%$$

$$\text{C component} = \frac{\overline{C}^2}{(\overline{O}')^2} = \frac{(42.051)^2}{(99.508)^2} = 17.86\%$$

$$\text{S component} = \frac{\overline{S}^2}{(\overline{O}')^2} = \frac{(53.831)^2}{(99.508)^2} = \underline{29.27\%}$$

$$100.00\%$$

of each component to a percentage change in sales in a one-quarter time
span. The I component is signaling random noise or transitory information, and it accounts for 18 percent of the series trend. The trend-
cycle and seasonal components are carrying permanent information that
contribute 82 percent of the change in the sales trend. The composition
of the information in the one-quarter sales data is heavily loaded with
permanent signals and modestly affected by random signals. In contrast
when annual data are decomposed a vastly different structure emerges.
There is a telescopic expansion of the contribution of the C component,
and the reverse of the seasonal contribution. The C component contributes 95 percent of the change in annual sales data and only 5 percent
is related to the I component. There is no seasonal component in annual
data. Exhibit 6 also shows the time effect is present in the other
income statement variables.

In Exhibit 5 the means and standard deviations of the relative
contributions of each component have unique patterns for each time
span. The relative contribution of the seasonal components decline
as the time span increases, which indicates a decreasing effect.
The relative contribution of the trend-cycle component increases with
the length of the time span, which reflects an increasing time effect.
The pattern of the relative contribution of the irregular component
oscillates over the length of the time spans. With the exception of the
one quarter time span, the contribution of the I component is always
smaller than the means of S and C. There is a significant drop in the
relative information of the I component in one, two and three quarter
time spans and a slight increase when all four quarters are included.

D.   Ledger Effect

In observing the ledger effect in Exhibit 5, one finds each I, C
and S component takes a unique path. In general the percentage contribution of the I component increases in size as one moves from sales to
net income. This portrays an increasing ledger effect and indicates
one explanation as to why forecasting net income is more difficult than
sales. In Exhibit 5 there is no consistent linear ledger effect present
in the percentage contributions of seasonal components. However, the
contributions of the trend-cycle component reflect an increasing effect.
These ledger effects are graphically presented in Exhibit 6 for the
five income statement variables and for a one and four quarter time span.

E.   Firm Effect

Porter [19] shows there is a substantial difference in the financial and production characteristics of industries and firms. We refer
to these differences as firm effects. The following ANOVA tests show
the presence of firm effects in the I, C and S components for cash income statement variable.

541

F.   ANOVA Tests[2]

A two-way ANOVA model was used to test the impact of the time, ledger and firm effects on the S, C and I components. The two-way ANOVA test can be defined as

$$X_{ijk} = U + T_i + B_j + (TB)_{ij} + e_{ijk} \tag{2}$$

where:

X_{ijk} = kth observation in a cell representing the intersection of the ith and jth factors;

U = overall mean;

T_i = sub-group mean associated with the first factor effect, which is time effect;

B_j = sub-group mean associated with second factor effect, which is either the firm effect or ledger effect;

TB_{ij} = interaction.

In this paper, the two factor pairwise combinations are (1) time and firm effects and (2) time and ledger effects.

There are three hypotheses to be tested with the analysis of variance as indicated in Equation 2. The hypotheses and their corresponding regions of rejection with α = .05 (or .01) are as follows:

H_{01}: there are no time effects H_a: there are time effects

H_{02}: there are no firm (or ledger) effects H_a: there are firm (or 1 ledger) effects

H_{03}: there are no interaction effects H_a: there are interaction effects

These two-way ANOVA techniques are used to analyze

(1) the impacts of time and firm effect on the percentage contribution of S, C and I components;

(2) the impacts of time and ledger effect on the percentage change contribution of S, C and I components.

The ANOVA tests used 68 firms, five ledgers and four time horizons to
analyze the fluctuation of the S, C and I components. The F values of
these tests are listed in Exhibit 7. The method of calculating the
degrees of freedom for F test in the two way analyses of variance with
interaction can be found in Neter and Wasserman [17]. F values in Exhibit
7 show that time, firm and ledger effects are all important in determining the relative percentage change of the S, C and I components. The
interaction between time and ledger effects are statisically different
from zero except for the C component. In conclusion the empirical study
supported the presence of a time, ledger and firm effect on the S, C
and I components for all but one test.

In investigating the association between alternative profitability
measures and security rates of return, Lee and Zumwalt [10] found security
rates of return are affected ky the location of a variable on the income
statement as well as the industry. The empirical results on the ledger
effect provide a direct explanation rf the Lee and Zumwalt findings.
However, the time effect implies that the Lee and Zumwalt results may
be dependent on length of time measurement.

IV.   FORECASTING IMPLICATIONS

A.   Financial Forecasting

The method presented in this study can be used to develop a quantitative index measure for the use of internal management and external
analysts. The quantitative measure is an industry index of the percentage contribution of the random component for a key financial planning
variables. The basic idea of the index is that the higher the contribution of the I component the greater the potential to produce forecasting
errors. Many types of comparisons can result from an industry index.
One example would be comparing the percentage contribution of the random
component of a variable for a firm to a comparable industry index. Such
a comparison provides insightful information to management. For example,
assuming the past time series of net income is a good indicator of a
future series, companies A, M and N listed below would be expected to
have more predictable net income results than companies C, O, X, Y and Z.

Relative Percentage
Contribution of the I Component
for ...

Company Name	Company	Industry P	Industry Q	Industry R
A	18	40		
B	38	40		
C	61	40		
M	15		59	
N	25		59	
O	75		59	
X	81			30
Y	92			30
Z	49			30

A second comparison shows that the industry indicies vary widely. For example, the relative contribution of the random component for net income is 30% for Industry R, 40% for Industry P and 59% for Industry Q. The industry indicies make it possible to rank the predictability of net income, where the Industry with the highest rank would be considered the most difficult to forecast and, naturally, vice versa.

Another comparison is to create an index for each income statement variable and for each industry. This can happen by calculating for each industry the relative percentage contribution of the I component for each income statement variable. Each index could be used as a benchmark to identify the variables within a firm that contain the greatest uncertainty. Management can use the information from each index to identify below average performance and work to improve internal operating performance. Finally, each index provides management and external analysts a measure to determine or verify the variables within a company that are the most difficult to forecast. This new information should serve as an aid for improving management performance. For external analysts each index provides clues to the difficult forecasting problems confronting management.[3]

B. Earnings Prediction Studies

Studies have found changes in earnings and earnings per share of American and British companies follow a random walk [11, 12, 13, 15]. Lintner and Glauber [13] also discovered that changes on sales, operating income and EBIT followed a random walk. Because the data sample and the methodologies used in these previous studies are not comparable to the sample and methodology used in this study, it is impossible to determine objectively if the magnitude of the I component is sufficiently large to generate a random walk process. Because this comparison is extremely important and will require substantial testing and analysis, the authors plan a separate empirical study to discover the results.

V.   CONCLUSIONS

Financial planning and forecasting are dependent on past data as a first approximation of future performance. One way to improve the planning and forecasting process is to provide management a tool that will generate greater insight into the secrets contained within the data. The X-11 time series decomposition program is a tool well known to analysts of macro economic data, but it is not widely used in analyzing firm data. The X-11 program makes it possible to determine the seasonal (S), trend-cycle (C) and irregular (I) components in a data time series. Additionally the program calculates the relative percentage contribution of the S, C and I components to the original time series.

Our analysis of five income statement accounts shows that S and C components provide permanent information trends to management; the irregular component contains temporary information. The larger the relative percentage contribution of the I component the greater the potential of forecasting or planning errors. Alternatively, the larger the permanent component the greater the potential of stable planning results. Creating an industry index of the percentage contribution of random components will provide a useful benchmark for management and external analysts.

To the best of our knowledge, we are the first to decompose accounting data into I, C and S components and to measure the relative contribution of each component for the five income statement variables. Acquiring the relative contribution of the I, C and S components provides the mechanism to measure the magnitude of the time, ledger and firm effects. This information may shed some light to academicians about the importance of a more dynamic and robust valution theory and also how to improve financial analysis and planning. The time effect showed the relative percentage contribution of the S, C and I components were directly affected by the length of the time period of the data. The shorter the time period of the data, the greater the relative percentage contribution of the irregular component. The longer the time period the greater the relative contribution of the C component and the smaller the S component. The analysis also discovered the relative percentage contribution of the S, C and I components varied widely among companies for all of the income statement variables tested. Finally, the study found the relative percentage contribution of the random component was markedly greater for net income than the variables that precede it in the income statement. That is the ledger effect.

In conclusion, an industry index of the percentage contribution of the random components for each income statement variable will provide a useful benchmark for internal management and external analysts. Also the availability of a measure of the relative percentage contribution of each S, C and I component provides a fresh dimension for financial research.

Exhibit 1. Original Quarterly Sales Data for Caterpillar Tractor,
           I 1969 to IV 1980
                           (in millions $)

Original Series Year	1st Quar	Quarterly Sales Data 2nd Quar	3rd Quar	4th Quar	Total
1969	500.4	558.9	482.7	459.6	2001.6
1970	524.6	537.0	579.1	487.1	2127.8
1971	564.4	585.1	522.3	503.4	2175.2
1972	620.8	653.6	678.5	649.3	2602.2
1973	751.8	800.2	823.4	807.0	3182.4
1974	822.4	956.8	1081.7	1221.2	4082.1
1975	1125.8	1328.7	1293.0	1216.2	4963.7
1976	1199.8	1266.6	1312.9	1263.0	5042.3
1977	1363.5	1454.6	1513.2	1517.6	5848.9
1978	1630.1	1843.7	1816.8	1928.6	7219.2
1979	1923.7	2136.7	2232.2	1320.6	7613.2
1980	2100.4	2316.3	2085.7	2095.4	8597.8

EXHIBIT 6. CONTRIBUTIONS OF SEASONAL, TREND-CYCLE AND IRREGULAR COMPONENTS

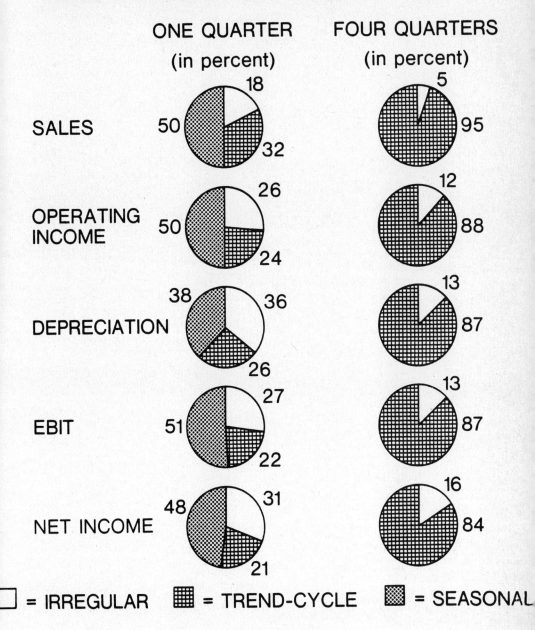

ONE QUARTER (in percent)   FOUR QUARTERS (in percent)

SALES

OPERATING INCOME

DEPRECIATION

EBIT

NET INCOME

☐ = IRREGULAR   ▦ = TREND-CYCLE   ▨ = SEASONAL

Exhibit 3. Mean of the Absolute Changes in Sales Related to Trend-
Cycle, Seasonal and Irregular Components For One, Two,
Three and Four Quarter Time Spans Without Regard to Sign

Mean Values (in millions of dollars)

Span in Quarters	Original	Trend Cycle	Seasonal	Irregular
1	109.12	92.35	53.83	72.36
2	141.93	114.51	64.72	60.22
3	153.38	146.92	52.22	61.98
4	190.84	191.05	6.49	69.67

Exhibit 4. Relative Contributions of Components to Changes in Caterpillar
Sales for One, Two, Three and Four Quarter Time Spans

Relative Contribution
(in percent)

Span in Quarters	Trend Cycle	Seasonal	Irregular	Total
1	17.86	29.27	52.88	100.00
2	46.94	28.44	24.62	100.00
3	68.50	13.08	18.42	100.00
4	82.58	0.15	17.27	100.00

Exhibit 5. Means and Standard Deviations of the Relative Contributions
of the I, C and S Components of Five Income Statement
Variables for 68 Companies, 1970–1978
(in percent)

Time Span in Quarters	Irregular		Trend–Cycle		Seasonal	
	Mean	S.D.	Mean	S.D.	Mean	S.D.
Sales						
1	17.71	11.82	32.42	18.76	49.87	22.76
2	6.59	5.80	60.15	23.52	33.26	23.69
3	4.35	3.94	72.65	20.09	23.00	19.58
4	4.71	4.83	95.11	4.99	.18	.33
Operating Income						
1	26.21	15.59	23.55	16.88	50.24	23.50
2	12.49	9.12	48.53	21.43	38.97	23.88
3	8.49	6.27	60.39	22.65	31.12	22.94
4	11.78	7.66	87.92	7.74	.30	.25
Depreciation						
1	36.13	18.35	25.59	15.09	36.80	23.58
2	15.66	10.97	51.10	22.31	31.77	23.32
3	11.77	9.30	65.92	21.69	20.84	19.06
4	13.46	11.47	84.87	15.48	.20	.27
EBIT						
1	27.04	15.59	21.95	15.50	51.01	23.09
2	12.70	8.62	46.95	20.98	40.34	23.90
3	9.08	5.99	58.30	21.77	32.62	22.76
4	13.11	7.28	86.54	7.35	.35	.31
Net Income						
1	30.63	19.09	21.41	14.64	47.96	25.27
2	15.17	11.23	47.10	21.50	37.73	24.02
3	11.33	10.19	57.35	22.88	31.33	24.04
4	15.80	12.49	83.83	12.55	.37	.49

EXHIBIT 2. ORIGINAL SALES AND THE X-11 FINAL COMPONENT SERIES OF CATERPILLAR 1969-1980

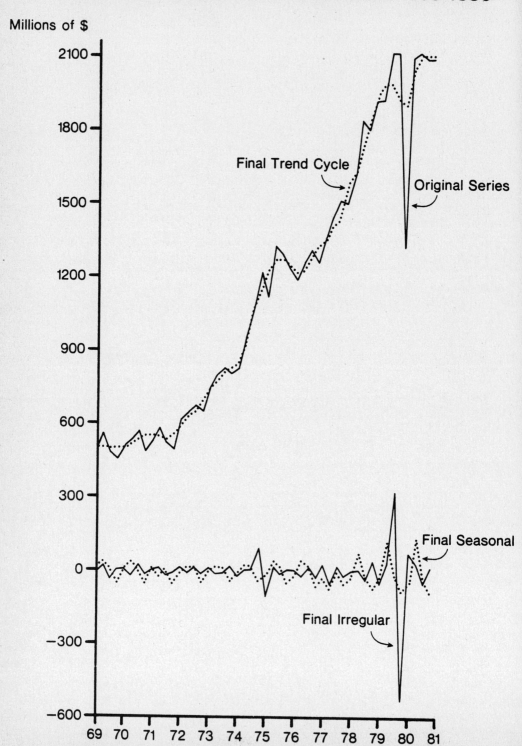

Millions of $

Final Trend Cycle

Original Series

Final Seasonal

Final Irregular

Exhibit 7. F Ratios for Analysis of Variance Tests Measuring the
Significance of Time, Ledger and Firm Effects

Single Variable Effect and Interaction Effects	SEASONAL COMPONENTS 68 Company Sample
Ledger	3.17*
Time	725.92**
Ledger and Time	2.48**
Firm	6.83**
Time	1449.50**
Firm and Time	6.23**
	CYCLICAL TREND COMPONENTS
Ledger	7.15**
Time	1810.85**
Ledger and Time	1.58
Firm	4.52**
Time	3624.71**
Firm and Time	6.13**
	IRREGULAR COMPONENTS
Ledger	13.45**
Time	539.76**
Ledger and Time	6.15**
Firm	3.40**
Time	411.83**
Firm and Time	5.00**

*significant at .05 level.
**significant at .01 level.

REFERENCES

[1]Ray Ball, "Anomalies in Relationships Between Securities' Yields and Yield-surrogates," Journal of Financial Economics, 1978, Vol. 6, pp. 5-25.

[2]Joseph M. Bonin and Edward A. Moses, "Seasonal Variation in Prices of Individual Dow Jones Industrial Stocks," Journal of Financial and Quantitative Analysis, December 1974, Vol. 9, pp. 963-991.

[3]G. E. P. Box and G. M. Jenkins, Time Series Analysis: Forecasting and Control. San Francisco: Holden-Day, 1970.

[4]J. Peter Burman, "Seasonal Adjustment--A Survey," in S. Makridakis and S. C. Wheelwright (editors), Studies in the Management Sciences: Forecasting, Amsterdam, North-Holland Publishing Company, 1979, pp. 45-57.

[5]John C. Chambers, Satinder K. Mullick and Donald D. Smith, An Executive's Guide to Forecasting, New York: John D. Wiley & Sons, 1974.

[6]W. P. Cleveland and G. C. Tiao, "Decomposition of Seasonal Time Series: A Model for the Census X-11 Program," Journal of American Statistical Association, 1976, Vol. 71, pp. 581-598.

[7]Benoit Deschamps and Dilee R. Mehta, "Productive Ability and Descriptive Validity of Earnings Forecasting Models," Journal of Finance, (September 1980), Vol. 35, pp. 933-949.

[8]D. M. Dunn, W. H. Williams and W. A. Spivey, "Analysis and Prediction of Telephone Demand in Local Geographical Areas," The Bell Journal of Economics and Management Science, 1971, Vol. 2, pp. 561-576.

[9]Domodas Gujarati, "Use of Dummy Variables in Testing for Equality Between Sets of Coefficients in Linear Regressions: A Generalization," The American Statistican, (December 1970), Vol. 24, pp. 18-22.

[10]C. F. Lee and J. K. Zumwalt, "Association Between Alternative Accounting Profitability Measures and Security Returns," Journal of Financial and Quantitative Analysis, forthcoming.

[11]Ian M. D. Little, "Higgledy Piggledy Growth," Institute of Statistics, Oxford, Vol. 24, No. 4 (November 1962).

[12]Ian M. D. Little and D. C. Rayner, Higgledy Piggledy Growth Again, Oxford: Basil Blackwell, 1966.

[13]John Lintner and Robert Glauber, "Higgledy Piggledy Growth in America," in James Lorie and Richard Brealey (editors), Modern Developments In Investment Management, New York: Praeger Publishers, 1972, pp. 645-662.

[14] M. H. Miller and F. Modigliani, "Some Estimates of the Cost of Capital to the Electric Utility Industry, 1954-57," *American Economic Review*, 1966, Vol. 56, pp. 333-391.

[15] Joseph E. Murphy, Jr., "Relative Growth in Earnings Per Share-- Past and Future," *Financial Analysts Journal*, (November/December 1966), pp. 73-76.

[16] Mark Nerlove, "Further Evidence on the Estimation of Dynamic Relations from a Time Series of Cross Sections," *Econometrica*, (March 1971), Vol. 39, pp. 359-382.

[17] John Neter and William Wasserman, *Applied Linear Statistical Models*. Homewood: Richard D. Irwin, Inc., 1974.

[18] Michael E. Porter, *Competitive Strategy, Techniques for Analyzing Industries and Competitors*. New York: The Free Press, 1980.

[19] Julius Shiskin, Allan H. Young and John C. Musgrave, "The X-11 Variant of the Census Method 11 Seasonal Adjustment Program." Technical Paper No. 15, U.S. Department of Commerce, February 1967.

FOOTNOTES

[1]To the best of our knowledge this feature of the X-11 has not been previously reported or used in the finance literature as a tool for financial planning and analysis.

[2]ANOVA is one of the possible methods that can be used to test the significance of time, firm and ledger effects. Alternatively, the dummy variable approaches developed by Gujarati [9] and Nerlove [16] can also be used to test for the three effects.

[3]An information file on each firm would provide another basis for intercompany comparison. The development of an information file on a large number of companies that contained the relative contribution of the random component for key income statement variables would permit intercompany comparisons and rankings within an industry group.

M/E/206

Cash Transfer Scheduling for Efficient Cash Concentration

Bernell K. Stone and Ned C. Hill

Bernell K. Stone is Mills B. Lane Professor of Banking and Finance at Georgia Institute of Technology. Ned C. Hill is Associate Professor of Finance at Indiana University.

Introduction

The essence of the cash allocation problem is moving money from a company's depository banks into a central cash pool in the company's concentration bank and moving money from the concentration bank to fund disbursing accounts. Moving money from depository banks to the concentration bank is called cash concentration. Moving money into disbursing accounts is called disbursement funding.

Cash transfer scheduling concerns the timing and amount of cash transfers. Solving a cash transfer scheduling problem answers the questions of when transfers should be initiated and how much should be transferred. Its logical objective is to minimize the transfer scheduling cost (direct cost of transfers, opportunity cost of excess and/or under-utilized balances tied up in the banking system, and administrative-control costs) while conforming to a variety of restrictions imposed by the banking system, a company's information system, and its administrative-control policies.

This paper deals with cash transfer scheduling for cash concentration. It presents problem background, reviews contemporary practice and its deficiencies, properly formulates the task as an optimization problem, and describes the solution benefits.

While its basic approach is also amenable to disbursement funding, differences in the problems, in institutional restrictions, and in typical company practice require separate formulations. Therefore, this paper will not discuss disbursement funding further.

Transfer Mechanisms

There are three mechanisms for moving money between accounts at two different banks — wires, depository transfer checks (DTCs), and electronic image transfers. A DTC is an ordinary check restricted "for deposit only" at a designated bank. The third transfer mechanism has only recently come into existence, namely, an electronic check image processed through automated clearing houses rather than through a wire network. It has a one business–day clearing time rather than the same–day transfer time of wires. It costs less than a DTC and is often called a "paperless DTC" or an "electronic DTC." Readers are referred to Stone and Hill [3] for more on transfer mechanisms, alternative ways to use them, comparative costs and transfer times, and to [2, 3] for procedures to decide on the appropriate mechanism. In this paper, it is assumed that the transfer method and the company's banking system are given. The problem is to specify a schedule of initiation times and amounts.

Cash Transfer Scheduling: Contemporary Practice

Most companies, probably more than 80% of the 1,200 largest industrial firms, make a daily transfer of each day's reported deposits. This is an outgrowth of most of the third–party information gathering services and most bank transfer preparation–initiation services. Daily transfer of whatever is deposited is a simple solution to the scheduling problem. This simplicity may, however, be attained at considerable cost.

In recent years, progressive companies have taken advantage of centralized information systems to move away from simple daily transfer schedules. By using various rules of thumb, such as managing about a target, anticipation, and weekend timing, a number of companies have realized substantial reductions in scheduling costs. A number of banks have also adapted their transfer preparation services to accommodate non–daily transfers using some of these rule-of-thumb scheduling procedures.

Managing About a Target

Exhibit 1 depicts a daily transfer of each day's deposits. It shows a cash build-up during the day and then a transfer that leaves a $20,000 target closing balance. Exhibit 2 depicts managing about the $20,000 target. The balance starts at zero and builds above the target so that the average closing balance is $20,000 over the transfer period. Both schedules give the same average balance, but the schedule of Exhibit 2 involves one-fifth the transfers. While the illustration is over-simplified in using a uniform deposit schedule and ignoring both transfer time delays and weekends, it suggests the potential for significant cost reductions. Moreover, note that, in addition to reducing transfers, managing about the target enables an initial withdrawal of the company's investment in the target balance. The target balance is then provided on average by using the deposit flow. Hence, managing about a target means more cash sooner.

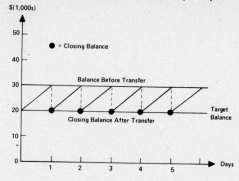

Exhibit 1. A Daily Transfer of Each Day's Deposits

Balance Table (in $1,000s)

Day	1	2	3	4	5
Starting Balance	20	20	20	20	20
Deposit Inflow	10	10	10	10	10
Transfer Amount	10	10	10	10	10
Closing Balance	20	20	20	20	20

$$\text{Average Closing Balance} = \frac{20 + 20 + 20 + 20 + 20}{5} = 20$$

There are several popular variants of managing about a target.

1. Trigger Point. Initiate a transfer whenever cumulative deposits exceed a prespecified level. This procedure is characterized by a trigger point and return point.

2. Periodic. Transfer at periodic intervals, e.g., every third business day.

3. Whole–Day Assignment. Assign each day's deposits to certain transfer days. An example involving two transfers per week is to assign Friday, the weekend, and Monday deposits to Monday and to assign Tuesday, Wednesday, and Thursday deposits to Thursday.

Anticipation

Anticipation is the initiation of a transfer before formal notice of a balance addition at the depository bank. Anticipation can eliminate communication, processing, and/or clearing delays. Hence, it can reduce or eliminate excess balances. The process can accelerate transfers by one to three days' deposits

Exhibit 2. Managing About the Target Balance

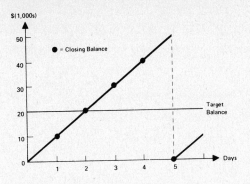

$(1,000s)

Balance Table (in $1,000s)

Day	1	2	3	4	5
Starting Balance	0	10	20	30	40
Deposit Inflow	10	10	10	10	10
Transfer Amount	0	0	0	0	50
Closing Balance	10	20	30	40	0

Average Closing Balance =
$$\frac{10 + 20 + 30 + 40 + 0}{5} = 20$$

when cleverly employed. It may but does not necessarily mean writing checks before funds are in the depository bank.

The most common use of anticipation is the "adjusted field target" technique. To illustrate, assume that a company wants to maintain an average field balance of $8,000, but it observes from its bank statement that the combination of communication, processing, and clearing delays leaves on average $7,000 of deposits in the process of being transferred. Hence, its actual average balance is $15,000. To hit the $8,000 target, the cash manager makes a one-time transfer of $7,000 from the field bank and runs with an "adjusted field target" or "effective field target" of $1,000. Because of the $7,000 average transfer-in-process, the actual average balance is the true target of $8,000. This procedure implicitly assumes an average level of transfers-in-process of $7,000. The ability, however, to extract the entire average transfer-in-process is limited by the variability in the deposits, especially by cycles such as a strong weekly cycle.

As an extreme case, suppose the $15,000 balance

was the result of a single deposit of $105,000 on Monday which is transferred out on Tuesday (105,000/7 = 15,000). No other deposits are made during the week. It would be impossible to remove the average excess of $7,000 with a one-time transfer, since that would result in an overdraft.

In this case, the company could employ "time-varying anticipation," which reflects variation in the deposit pattern. While there are many versions, most add to the known balance available for transfers some fraction of the additional deposits expected before the transfer clears. For example, if a weekend deposit of $105,000 is expected to be received at the deposit bank on Monday morning, a DTC for $105,000 could be deposited the previous Friday. By the time the DTC clears, the deposit will have been received.

Weekend Timing and Dual Balances

When the DTC availability time granted at the concentration bank is less than the clearing time back to the depository bank, there is an opportunity for a dual balance benefit. To illustrate, assume a $10,000 DTC transfer initiated on Tuesday with one business–day availability but two business–day clearing. On Wednesday, the company receives a $10,000 available addition at the concentration bank, but the funds are not removed from the depository bank until Thursday. The company has a "dual balance" on Wednesday in the sense that the same funds are available balances in two banks. The source of the dual balance might be Federal Reserve float arising from slow check clearings. Or, it could result from the concentration bank's granting faster availability than its actual clearing.

The dual balance benefit can be increased by weekend timing. For instance, if the $10,000 DTC transfer were initiated on Thursday, there would be a $10,000 available addition at the concentration bank on Friday, with the clearing delayed until Monday. Hence, with Thursday initiation, there would be three days of dual balances (Friday, Saturday, Sunday) rather than one.

While the more common situation is for the clearing time to exceed the availability time, the opposite can occur. Clearing time could be faster than granted availability; then the company will have a balance in neither bank. In this case, weekend timing means avoiding weekends.

Limitations of the Popular Techniques

Each of the three techniques — managing about a

target, anticipation, and weekend timing — focuses on a different component of the transfer scheduling cost. Managing about a target primarily reduces transfers, thereby reducing direct transfer costs. Anticipation takes advantage of time delays to get money out faster. It is appropriate when there is an "excess field balance," *i.e.* greater balance than is necessary to compensate the field bank. (In contrast, managing about a target balance implicitly assumes no excess balance, or at least no significant one.) Weekend timing increases the dual balances that arise from differences between actual clearing times and granted availability times. Such extra balances have value, however, only if they can be removed from the depository bank. Simply adding to an existing excess balance to obtain a larger excess does nothing for a company.

The difference in these objectives points up an obvious need to resolve conflicts. Some of the simpler versions of each technique actually preclude the use of the others. More sophisticated versions, while not mutually exclusive, conflict.

For instance, use of the popular trigger point rules precludes use of weekend timing, because the balance level determines the transfer initiation time. Likewise, use of periodic frequency also precludes systematic use of weekend timing unless the transfer frequency is one week or a multiple of a week. Using the simple adjusted field target version of anticipation also precludes using weekend timing, because the same amount is anticipated on each day of the week.

Anyone trying to resolve conflicts between the various versions of each rule-of-thumb technique quickly finds that trial-and-error transfer scheduling is a difficult task, especially when various constraints such as no overdraft and an appropriate average balance are explicitly recognized. The task is, in fact, logically equivalent to finding solutions to a larger number of simultaneous equations and then systematically comparing the solutions.

Finding good solutions is a difficult task even for one single depository bank. Finding good solutions for dozens or hundreds of depository banks clearly requires some kind of systematic procedure. Such a procedure should incorporate sophisticated versions of each scheduling technique and appropriately reflect trade-offs between direct transfer cost, excess balances, and any dual balances.

The mathematical program formulated in the next section is such a procedure. Its solution provides not just a good but an optimal schedule.

Mathematical Programming Formulation

We have used a one-week period to formulate the problem. Besides being simple for exposition, use of the one-week solution period is consistent with current practice, the often strong weekly cycle in field deposits, and the role of weekends.

The Objective Function

As noted already, there are three considerations in cash transfer scheduling — the direct transfer charges, the value of any excess balances, and any dual balance value. If CPT is the cost per transfer, and I is the appropriate daily interest rate for assessing the value of excess field deposits, the transfer scheduling cost (TSC) is the direct cost plus the interest value of excess field balances less the interest value of any dual balances:

$$TSC = CPT \,(\#transfers) + 7 \cdot I \,(EXCESS - ADBAL). \qquad (1)$$

EXCESS is the average excess balance over the solution period. ADBAL is the average dual balance. This formulation says a dual balance has value only if it can be removed from the depository bank. The interest rate provides a basis for comparing transfer charges and balances. The seven reflects the one-week solution period.

To express the objective function in terms of the transfer schedule and known parameters, let i be an index denoting days of the week. Let i be 1 on Monday, 2 on Tuesday, and so on, up to 7 for Sunday. The decision of cash transfer scheduling is when to transfer and how much. Let δ_i be a zero-one decision variable that is one only if there is a transfer on day i and zero otherwise. Let T_i be the amount transferred. Of course, T_i must be zero unless δ_i is one. The number of transfers over the week is $\sum_{i=1}^{7} \delta_i$ since δ_i is one whenever there is a transfer and zero otherwise.

To express the average dual balance in terms of the transfer schedule, let A_i denote the number of calendar days (not business days) by which the clearing time exceeds the granted availability time when a transfer is initiated on day i. The A_i's are called availability advantage coefficients. To illustrate, assume that the granted availability is one business day and the clearing time is two business days on Monday, Tuesday, Wednesday, and Thursday, but one business day on Friday. Then, the schedule of availability advantage coefficients is $A_1 = A_2 = A_3 = 1$, $A_4 = 3$, and $A_5 = 0$. In addition, we set A_6 and A_7 at zero, since there are no Saturday or Sunday transfers. For wires and electronic DTCs, all the A_i's are zero. For DTCs with faster clearing than granted availability, the A_i's would be negative.

With T_i denoting the amount transferred on day i, the dollar days of availability advantage is A_iT_i. The total dollar days of dual balances from a given week's transfers are the sum from each day's transfers: $\sum\limits_{i=1}^{7} A_iT_i$. The weekly average dual balance is one-seventh this amount.

The objective function of (1) can now be restated. Using $\sum\limits_{i=1}^{7} \delta_i$ for the number of transfers and

$(1/7) \sum\limits_{i=1}^{7} A_iT_i$ for the average dual balance gives:

$$TSC = CPT \cdot \sum\limits_{i=1}^{7} \delta_i +$$

$$7 \cdot I\,(EXCESS - 1/7 \sum\limits_{i=1}^{7} A_iT_i). \qquad (2)$$

The objective function is now expressed in terms of cost parameters (CPT and I), parameters of the banking system (the A_i's), and the decision variables characterizing the transfer schedule. The quantity EXCESS will be defined shortly in terms of the compensating balance constraint.

Constraints

Constraints on transfers include: average balance, flow balance, minimum balance, and maximum transfer.

Assume for the moment that a company pays its depository banks for services with balances. Hence, the average balance at the depository bank must be at least as large as the level necessary to pay for services. Let $ABAL_i$ be the available balance on day i. Then, the requirement that the average available balance be at least as large as the required balance for compensation means:

$$1/7 \sum\limits_{i=1}^{7} ABAL_i \geq REQUIRED\ BALANCE. \qquad (3)$$

It is necessary to reflect the fact that the required

balance depends on the number of transfers. Let TAB denote the average available balance necessary before compensation for transfers. If TCDB is the transfer cost of the depository bank and ECRDB is the earnings credit rate, then TCDB/ECRDB is the required balance per transfer. TAB and (TCDB/ECRDB) (# of transfers) are the two components of the average balance. Constraint (3) can be rewritten as:

$$1/7 \sum\limits_{i=1}^{7} ABAL_i \geq TAB +$$

$$(TCDB/ECRDB) \sum\limits_{i=1}^{7} \delta_i. \qquad (4)$$

Again, use has been made of the fact that the number of transfers is the sum of the δ_i's.

By definition, EXCESS is the amount by which the average available balance exceeds the required balance. With the additional requirement that EXCESS be non-negative, Constraint (4), the average balance constraint, can be written as:

$$1/7 \sum\limits_{i=1}^{7} ABAL_i - EXCESS =$$

$$TAB + (TCDB/ECRDB) \sum\limits_{i=1}^{7} \delta_i. \qquad (5)$$

Several special cases are pertinent. When a company pays its depository banks fees for their transfer services, the charge is included in CPT in the objective function, but TCDB is set equal to zero in (5). If balances are not used for compensation at all, set both TAB and TCDB at zero. In this case, any positive available balance is an excess. By appropriate choice of parameters, Expression (5) handles all cases of deposit bank compensation, namely: 1) all balances, 2) some fees and some balances, and 3) all fees.

A stable solution is one in which there is no period-to-period increase or decrease in balances at the depository bank. Requiring a stable solution prevents distortion from building up or drawing down balances. To ensure a stable solution requires that the sum of each week's transfers equal the sum of each week's available additions. This is the flow balance constraint, which can be expressed as:

$$\sum\limits_{i=1}^{7} T_i = \sum\limits_{i=1}^{7} AA_i. \qquad (6)$$

The ledger balance can never be negative; ledger overdrafts are prohibited. In addition, some banks may even require a positive available balance. Some companies may also want minimum balance restrictions. Let $LMIN_i$ and $AMIN_i$, respectively, denote the *pro forma* values of the minimum allowable ledger and available balances on day i. Let $LBAL_i$ and $ABAL_i$, respectively, denote the ledger balance and available balance on day i. Minimum balance constraints that reflect both bank restrictions and any company policy limits are:

$$LBAL_i \geq LMIN_i \text{ and } ABAL_i \geq AMIN_i. \quad (7)$$

In the absence of anticipation, the maximum amount that can be transferred without a *pro forma* violation of the minimum balance restriction is the closing balance on the previous day, less any transfers made but not yet cleared, less the minimum balance when the transfer clears in c days. The maximum transfer constraint in the absence of anticipation is:

$$T_i \leq LBAL_{i-1} -$$
$$[\text{TRANSFERS YET TO CLEAR}] -$$
$$LMIN_{i+c}. \quad (8)$$

The quantity $LBAL_{i-1} - [\text{TRANSFERS YET TO CLEAR}]$ is an effective start-of-day balance. It is what the company knows about. The amount by which this balance exceeds the minimum on the clearing day is the amount available for transfer before anticipation. It is assumed that deposits for day i are not known. If known, or if known in part, these balances would be added to the right-hand side of (8).

Anticipation increases the amount available for transfer so that the maximum transfer constraint becomes:

$$T_i \leq LBAL_{i-1} -$$
$$[\text{TRANSFERS YET TO CLEAR}] -$$
$$LMIN_{i+c} +$$
$$[\text{AMOUNT ANTICIPATED}]. \quad (9)$$

An analogous constraint can be written in terms of available balances and AMIN.

One possible constraint has not yet been mentioned or included — "whole-day assignment." For reasons of control, implementation ease, or compatibility with current information-control systems, some companies want all the deposits of a given day assigned to a particular transfer day. Or, alternatively, in the case of multiple deposits per day, they want all the deposits in a given time slot to be assigned to a particular transfer day.

An example of whole-day assignment would be to transfer the Monday and Tuesday deposits on Tuesday, transfer the Wednesday and Thursday deposits on Thursday, and transfer Friday's deposit on Friday. A whole-day restriction would preclude transferring some of Tuesday's deposits on Tuesday and some on Thursday. Whole-day assignment considerably complicates the formulation. It means adding a set of integer assignment constraints to the mathematical program.

Formulation Summary

Exhibits 3 and 4 summarize notation and the mathematical programming formulation, adding some technical constraints such as integer restrictions and non-negativity. Additional restrictions such as no Saturday or Sunday transfers and company-specific restrictions are ignored in these exhibits, although there would be no problem to include them in the analysis. This formulation generalizes to an H-day solution horizon by replacing 7 by H.

Deposit Variation

The mathematical programming formulation develops a transfer schedule for an average deposit pattern, but it can reflect deposit variation. First, the parameters LMIN and AMIN can create a buffer balance to allow for deposit variation. Second, anticipation is generally limited to the fraction of yet-unknown deposits that a company is certain to receive before the transfer clears so that anticipation incurs no exposure to an overdraft. Third, with daily deposit reporting, the usual information-control system records the daily error and cumulative variation between actual and *pro forma* deposits before a transfer clears. If any correction is necessary, it can always be done in time. The daily reporting and control means that a company need never be exposed to an overdraft by the schedules developed on the basis of an average deposit schedule, just as no overdraft exposure need occur when companies use any of the rule-of-thumb scheduling techniques for managing about a target. Fourth, translating the mathematical program's solution into transfer procedures includes adaptivity rules to reflect deposit variation. It is, for instance, straightforward either to reduce or to increase a planned transfer by an appropriate amount to reflect deviation from the *pro forma* deposit pattern. Hence, it is possible to have a system always tracking

Exhibit 3. Notation Summary: Key Variables and Parameters

Active Decision Variables

δ_i $\equiv$ 0-1 transfer initiation variable for day i
T_i $\equiv$ the transfer amount on day i

Implicit Decision Variables

$LBAL_i$ $\equiv$ ledger balance for day i
$ABAL_i$ $\equiv$ available balance for day i
$EXCESS \equiv$ average available balance in excess of the required compensating balance

Objective Function Parameters

CPT $\equiv$ cost per transfer
I $\equiv$ interest value of balances (rate per day)
H $\equiv$ number of days in decision horizon
A_i $\equiv$ expected clearing time less granted availability time in calendar days

Policy Variables

TAB $\equiv$ target average balance before transfer compensation
$LMIN_i$ $\equiv$ minimum ledger balance
$AMIN_i$ $\equiv$ minimum available balance

Deposit Schedule Parameters

AA_i $\equiv$ available addition on day i
LA_i $\equiv$ ledger addition on day i

Other Deposit Bank Parameters

TCDB $\equiv$ direct transfer cost per deposit at the depository bank
ECRDB $\equiv$ earnings credit rate at the depository bank
c(i) $\equiv$ business-day clearing time for transfers initiated on day i

the *pro forma* balance of the model solution and, in general, averaging the transfer scheduling cost of the objective function. Finally, a sense of ability to tolerate deposit variations can be obtained by simulating the solution and adaptivity rules over past deposit data to test robustness and even to make sure that the average improvement in scheduling cost is consistent with the improvement indicated by the objective function.

Relation of Model Formulation to Current Practice

Managing about a target balance is accomplished in the model by two constraints — the average balance and flow balance restrictions. In contrast, a daily transfer to each day's deposits would force the required compensating balance to be provided daily rather than on average; flow balance would also be a daily restriction (*e.g.*, a transfer equal to each day's reported deposits) rather than an average over the solution period.

Exhibit 4. A Summary Statement of the Mathematical Program

$$\text{Minimize TSC} \equiv CPT \cdot \sum_{i=1}^{H} \delta_i + H \cdot I \cdot EXCESS - I \cdot \sum_{i=1}^{H} A_i T_i$$

Subject To:

(C1) $(1/H) \sum_{i=1}^{H} ABAL_i - EXCESS = TAB + (TCDB/ECRDB) \sum_{i=1}^{H} \delta_i$

(C2) $\sum_{i=1}^{H} T_i = \sum_{i=1}^{H} AA_i$

(C3) $LBAL_i \geq LMIN_i$ $i = 1, \ldots, H$

(C4) $ABAL_i \geq AMIN_i$ $i = 1, \ldots, H$

(C5) $T_i \leq LBAL_{i1} - LMIN_{i+c(i)} -$ [TRANSFERS YET TO CLEAR] + [AMOUNT ANTICIPATED]

(C6) $T_i \leq M\delta_i$ $i = 1, \ldots, H$

(C7) $\delta_i = 0$ or $\delta_i = 1$ $i = 1, \ldots, H$

(C8) $EXCESS \geq 0; T_i \geq 0$ $i = 1, \ldots, H.$

Notes
1. This formulation is for an H-day solution period; for the weekly solution H = 7.
2. For any days in which transfers are not permitted, T_i and δ_i are both set at zero in advance.
3. This formulation includes the balances $ABAL_i$ and $LBAL_i$ and TRANSFERS YET TO CLEAR. Equations relating these variables to starting balance should be added for completeness. Or, the defining equations should be substituted for these variables.
4. In an operational formulation, AMOUNT ANTICIPATED would be replaced by incorporating anticipation policy, *e.g.*, a proportion of ledger additions over the anticipation period.
5. In (C6), M is a large number that is greater than any possible transfer. This constraint ensures that T_i is zero whenever δ_i is zero and unconstrained when δ_i is one. This constraint could also be $T_i (1 - \delta_i)$, which is nonlinear but easier to use in a branch-and-bound framework.
6. To eliminate Saturday, Sunday, and holiday transfers, δ_i is set equal to zero for appropriate values of i.

This mathematical programming method of managing about a target allows the target balance to adjust to reflect the transfer frequency. It is more general than any of the specific versions such as trigger point or periodic frequency. Typical programming solutions to actual problems rarely have a uniform trigger level. Likewise, they rarely have a periodic frequency except in the unusual case of a single transfer per week. Therefore, the restrictions of these rule-of-thumb methods of scheduling about a target involve some profit sacrifice.

As already pointed out, anticipation is reflected in the mathematical programming formulation by the maximum transfer constraint. By allowing the amount anticipated to vary, the formulation permits the most general form of time-varying anticipation.

Dual balances are counted in the objective function of the mathematical programming model and, as a result, the model will systematically shift transfers to pick up weekend effects only if the increased balance can be removed from the system and will exceed in value any increase in transfer costs. This formulation of dual balances is more general than simple weekend timing. It allows for variation in the clearing time over each day of the week. For instance, it can reflect expected differences in the Monday and Tuesday clear times. Thus, the formulation actually provides for general dual balance timing with the usual weekend timing being a special case.

To summarize, the formulation properly trades-off the components of transfer scheduling cost. The model also includes each of the three generic scheduling procedures in their most general form. As a result, the transfer schedule from the mathematical program can never be worse than the schedules obtained from the rule-of-thumb procedures, and it is reasonable to expect model solutions to be significantly better.

Implementation Tests

The authors have worked with The First National Bank of Chicago to develop a special-purpose solution algorithm and the necessary reports to implement the model. During 1979, The First National Bank of Chicago tested the model on a number of companies. Most of the tests were based on a subsample of each company's banks. Two classes of concentration problems were studied — field concentration and lockbox concentration.

Field Concentration Tests

Field concentration is moving money from depository banks used by cash generating field units. For companies making daily transfers of each day's deposit and using no systematic scheduling except possibly an adjusted field target, the model solution provided significant improvement over daily transfers. In particular, the model solutions were able to free up the equivalent of at least two days' average deposits.

Several test companies already practiced systematic scheduling. Some had even previously worked with The First National Bank of Chicago in applying the rule-of-thumb scheduling procedures, attaining significant improvement over daily transfers. Therefore, these companies provided a test of the value of the mathematical programming formulation versus sophisticated use of rule-of-thumb procedures. The model solutions indicated improvements at least equivalent to freeing up one day's average deposits in every case. In some cases, improvements equivalent to two days' average deposits were still found beyond those already obtained.

Skilled use of rule-of-thumb procedures was able to obtain only 40% to 60% of the total possible improvement over daily transfers. Moreover, very simple scheduling procedures, such as a trigger point with an adjusted target, typically could obtain only 15% to 30% of the total possible improvement.

Lockbox Concentration

Lockbox concentration is moving money from a firm's lockbox banks. There were not many tests of lockbox concentration. While the model did generally find opportunities for significant cost improvements, there were also many cases where daily transfers were optimal. Moreover, in other cases, skillful use of rule-of-thumb procedures could produce solutions very close to the optimal solution of the mathematical program.

Summary and Conclusions

Most efforts to move away from daily transfers involve special versions of three generic scheduling procedures — managing about a target, anticipation, and dual balance timing. Simply using the rule-of-thumb procedures is difficult and may not permit achieving the best solution, because each technique focuses primarily on different components of the transfer scheduling cost, and because the specialized versions of the techniques often conflict with each other. The formulation presented here combines the most general version of each technique and appropriately trades off the components of the transfer scheduling cost.

References

1. Bernell K. Stone, Daniel M. Ferguson, and Ned C. Hill, "Cash Transfer Scheduling: An Overview," *The Cash Manager,* (March 1980), pp. 3–8.
2. Bernell K. Stone and Ned C. Hill, "Cash Concentration Design," Georgia Institute of Technology, Working Paper No. MS-79-7, presented at the annual meeting of the Western Finance Association, San Francisco (June 1979).
3. Bernell K. Stone and Ned C. Hill, "Alternative Cash Transfer Mechanisms and Methods: Evaluation Frameworks," forthcoming in *Journal of Bank Research.*

For Further Study

Additional references to which the reader may wish to refer:

1. Gentry, J. (1973). "Integrating Working Capital and Capital Investment Processes". In K.V. Smith (1980), *Readings on the Management of Working Capital*, Second Edition, St. Paul: West Publishing Company, pp. 585–608.
2. Lewellen, W.G., J.J. McConnell, and J.A. Scott (1981). "Capital Market Influences on Trade Credit Policies". *The Journal of Financial Research* (Summer 1980), pp. 105–113.
3. Maier, S.F., D.W. Robinson, and J.H. Vander Weide (1981). "A Short-term Disbursement Forecasting Model". *Financial Management* (Spring 1981), pp. 9–20.
4. Pan, J., D.R. Nichols, and O.M. Joy (1977). "Sales Forecasting Practices of Large U.S. Industrial Firms". *Financial Management* (Fall 1977), pp. 72–77.
5. Stone, B.K. N.C. Hill (1981). "The Design of Cash Concentration System." *Journal of Financial and Quantitative Analysis*. (September 1981), pp. 301–322.

Part IX

Financial Planning and Forecasting

Introduction

Financial planning and forecasting is the synthesis of theory and practice. A programming approach and a simultaneous equation approach are two major alternatives for performing financial planning and analysis. In the programming model, an objective function is maximized and different constraints are introduced. The simultaneous equation model does not explicitly maximize an objective function; it does, however, explicitly specify the interrelationship between investment, financing, and dividend policy. To specify the above mentioned models, all material discussed in Parts I through IX are used either explicitly or implicitly.

In his paper, Eckstein (1981) discusses the importance of corporate planning. He suggests six factors as the most important in performing strategic financial planning in the 1980's: monitoring the environment; growth market identification; cost and productivity analysis; target setting; business portfolio analysis; and international strategy analysis. Eckstein then demonstrates the importance of linking individual firm analysis and forecasting to aggregate economic forecasting.

Carleton, Dick and Downes (1973) discuss and review the theory and practice of alternative financial policy models. They classify the models used in financial planning as either computer-based budget compilation or financial statement simulation. After a discussion of the possible weaknesses of the various financial planning models, the authors use an example to show how contemporary finance theory and programming tools can be used to improve financial model specifications.

Stern (1980) evaluates the use of conventional accounting tools as measures of corporate performance. He then develops an analytical framework for financial management in accordance with M&M's theories and other financial valuation theories.

Both Spies (1974) and Stern show the importance of explicitly considering the dynamic characteristics of financial planning. Spies proposes a simultaneous capital budgeting model. Five endogenous variables are used: cash dividends, net investment in short-term assets, gross investment in long-term assets, net proceeds from new debt and proceeds from new equity. Spies' model simultaneously takes investment, financing, and dividend policy into account. Dynamic simulation processes for investigating the impacts of three alternative policies is also discussed.

Carleton (1970) integrates finance and economic theory in developing a linear objective function and related constraints. A dividend stream valuation model is first used to develop a linear objective function. Basic finance concepts and theories are then used to linearize the objective function. To develop the related constraints, accounting information, economic theory and finance theory are jointly employed to justify the specifications. The constraints used by Carleton can be classified as either definitional constraints or policy constraints. This model can be used to forecast important financial variables, and to perform related sensitivity analysis.

Using simultaneous equations, Warren and Shelton (1970) (WS) construct a twenty equation system to describe the interrelation among different financial decision variables. This equation system contains four sections:

1. generation of sales and EBIT;
2. generation of total assets required;
3. financing for the desired level of assets; and
4. generation of per share data.

This model can be used to either forecast the basic finance variables or to perform related sensitivity analyses. (WS's computer program is available from C.F. Lee upon request.)

Francis and Rowell (1978) extend Warren and Shelton's model from four sections to ten. Concepts related to product market share, capacity utilization, and inflation are directly introduced into the model. Both business and financial risk concepts are used to determine the cost of debt and equity capital.

(Author's Note: Three minor corrections should be noted in Francis and Rowell's paper. First, depreciation (D) and interest expense (I) should be eliminated from the definition of OC in Appendix A. Second, in Equation 19 depreciation (D) should be subtracted. Third, in the AAE/RMSE computations, the AAE errors should not be negative.)

DECISION SUPPORT SYSTEMS FOR CORPORATE PLANNING by Otto Eckstein

A speech given to the Joint Meeting of New York City Chapter of The Institute of Management Sciences and The North American Society for Corporate Planning, Inc., on January 22, 1981.

The use of quantitative analysis to improve corporate planning in an increasingly complex environment is mushrooming. According to a recent survey,[1] 61% of all corporate planning groups use the services of Data Resources, Inc., and our competitors provide service to additional units. Econometric models play a central role in this work, but unlike earlier product line forecasting applications, the models today are part of an elaborate system of data bases, analytical software capable of producing planning analyses, and consulting support.

As I observe these planning activities, I am very pleased that the information system for which I have responsibility is achieving such widespread use, but it is also evident to me that the typical planning process of our users does not yet analyze the external environment efficiently, and that quantitative analysis must still be fully integrated into the work of business planning; the goal of such quantitative systems is, after all, to help produce the best possible business decisions for large organizations in a changing and unstable economic environment.

In my talk today I shall cover seven of the principal corporate planning functions and show how a full decision support system can contribute to each of them. To lend concreteness to the presentation, I shall draw on various examples out of DRI's econometric modeling work, and in the process also sketch for you the kind of economy that DRI projects for the 1980s.

---

[1]Thomas H. Naylor, "Experience with Corporate Econometric Models: The Results of a Survey of Users," presented at Duke University, December 4-5, 1980.

MONITORING THE ENVIRONMENT

Monitoring the environment, sometimes called environmental scanning, has always been a principal function of the corporate planner, and typically contains two quite distinct elements. The first monitors the short-run business cycle situation which frequently dominates the current year's plan achievements. Table 1 shows a typical short-term monitoring report for a fictitious corporation, utilizing the current DRI forecast. As most of you probably know, DRI projects a little recession in the first half of this year because of the Federal Reserve's determined effort to reverse a worsening inflation trend and bring the monetary aggregates under control. The interest rates of the last few months assure a decline in housing and other construction activity, which, when combined with a continued weak performance of auto sales, suffices to produce the little recession. Thereafter, the near-term outlook is dominated by the beginnings of the large tax cuts promised by the Reagan Administration, which will lift consumer purchasing power quite substantially, and which will begin an acceleration of business fixed investment and capital formation. This particular use of economic information systems is well established, of course, and in some companies is performed by groups other than planners, such as the economists, commercial research groups, or market analysis staffs. I shall say little more about it.

The second kind of environmental monitoring focuses on the longer term parameters of the business environment. In an era of high and rising core inflation and a period of increasingly costly and insecure energy supplies, rational strategic decisions for large corporations will depend significantly on the actual developments in the economy. In the longer term scanning, decisions must be supported by the best possible monitoring of the key assumptions about the environment. These assumptions do change as additional information becomes available and as political events at home and abroad alter the prospects.

Table 1
Summary Table for NFG Corporation
Economy Monitoring Report

	Quarterly Forecast			Annual Forecast	
	1981:1	1982:2	1981:3	1981:4	1981
KEY ECONOMIC INDICATORS (Annualized Rates of Change)					
Gross National Product - 1972 Dollars	-0.9	-2.1	3.3	3.0	0.5
Disposable Personal Income - 1972 Dollars	-2.1	-2.3	10.2	0.1	1.0
Consumer Durable Goods - 1972 Dollars	-4.3	1.0	9.5	7.4	2.7
Consumer Durable Goods excluding Motor Veh. & Pts. - 1972 Dollars	-4.2	-6.1	6.6	4.7	1.5
KEY INFLATION INDICATORS (Annualized Values at Seasonally Adjusted Rates)					
Consumer Price Index	12.9	11.8	10.7	10.5	11.5
Prime Rate on Short-Term Business Loans	18.4	14.7	13.6	14.5	15.3
Wholesale Price Index - Fuels Products and Power	38.4	34.3	26.5	20.0	25.2
KEY MARKET INDICATORS (Annualized Values - Millions of Units Seasonally Adjusted)					
Housing Starts	1.314	1.279	1.416	1.559	1.392
Shipments of Mobile Homes	.219	1.505	1.653	1.810	1.625
Retail Unit Sales of New Passenger Cars - Total					
Domestic	6.6	6.9	7.1	7.4	7.0
Imports	2.4	2.4	2.5	2.4	2.4
KEY CYCLICAL INDICATORS (Annualized Values Seasonally Adjusted)					
Index of Consumer Sentiment 1966=1.0	0.640	0.631	0.678	0.664	0.63
Vendor Performance - Companies Reporting					
Slower Deliveries Proportion of Total	0.393	0.416	0.491	0.508	0.452
Change in Business Inventories	-0.6	-1.7	1.2	2.4	0.342

*Source: Data Resources, Inc., National Forecasting Group

Let me illustrate what might be called long-term assumptions monitoring. Table 2 shows just a few of the numerous parameters routinely produced by the DRI Macro Model of the U.S. Economy and updated every month. The table shows the forecasts of two years ago, one year ago, and during the last quarter. It can be seen that some of the key magnitudes of the macroeconomy which are important parameters for corporate planning have been revised substantially over the two years because of new information, new political developments, and additional analytical insights. Other parameters have remained little changed. The table also shows the 1986 values of one of the alternative scenarios that we maintain on the computer systems, a more cyclical alternative in which the year 1986 happens to be a year of recession.

The DRI estimate of potential GNP growth was lowered from 2.8% to 2.4%, principally because of the mounting evidence that the traditional productivity trend has been partially lost. 'n the cyclical alternative, potential GNP grows even less because the stop-go economy disrupts capital formation. The inflation rate assumption has deteriorated from 5.4% to 8.0% because of the poor experience of the last two years and the worsening energy outlook. In the cyclical alternative, there is still worse inflation. Interest rates on bonds look more costly in the trend scenario, and still more costly under the cyclical scenario despite the economic downswing in the year we are examining. The profit share has been lowered somewhat on the basis of recent evidence; the cyclical alternative would be somewhat worse, of course.

Table 2
Monitoring Planning Parameters

	Characteristics of the 1986 Economy as Forecast at Various Points in Time			
	12/78 Trend Estimate	12/79 Trend Estimate	12/80 Trend Estimate of 1986	12/80 Cyclical Estimate of 1986
Potential Real GNP Growth	2.8	2.6	2.4	2.2
Inflation Rate (Deflator)	5.4	7.6	8.0	11.3
Bond Yields (Seasoned AAA Bonds)	8.36	10.06	11.37	13.48
After-Tax Profit Share (%GNP)	5.4	6.1	4.4	4.0
Auto & Light Truck Sales (Millions)	16.34	16.14	15.25	12.41
Housing Starts (Millions of units)	2.136	2.491	2.085	1.656
Unemployment (%)	5.1	6.3	6.2	6.2
Govt. Deficit (NIA billions)	-2.4	5.8	-71.5	-111.3

The outlook for auto and light truck sales has been reduced from 16.34 to 15.25 million units, and to 12.41 million units under the cyclical scenario. This is an important planning parameter for many industries. The reduction had to be made because the deteriorating energy outlook and other inflationary factors have substantially boosted our estimates of operating costs of automobiles as well as reduced the projected mileage driven. This is a typical case where the inputs to the analysis have changed for political and economic reasons, requiring significant change in an important planning parameter.

The forecast for housing starts is little changed from the forecast of December 1978 because, in the long run, the demographic factor of family formation is the basic driving force. It is only the imposition of restrictive credit conditions that pushes housing off its demographic trend as the cyclical alternative indicates. But even in this sector, rising energy and other costs have lowered our nearer term forecasts below the trend levels, and in the various alternative scenarios, whether cyclical, worsened energy, or lowered productivity alternatives, the housing figures for 1986 are lower. Housing is a high-risk market sector.

One of the more interesting revisions in the parameters is in the unemployment rate. Even two years ago, it still seemed possible to manage the economy with a 5% unemployment rate, at that time the conventional measure of "full" employment. However, in the last two years it has become abundantly clear that the noninflationary unemployment rate is much higher, and, as I have argued at length in my recent studies of core inflation, we do not seem to be able to manage the economy and keep unemployment rates much below 7%. As this reality gradually seeps through the political process, we assume that the goals of policy are in the 7% range for unemployment, improving by 1986 because of demographic trends and a more efficient labor market.

Finally, the later projection shows a substantially larger government deficit. We would like to assume that the political thrust demonstrated in the 1980 presidential election is going to prove effective: the public wants to slow the growth of government and to move toward budget balance. But our trend projection shows a big deficit, and it is even larger in the cyclical alternative, of course.

Table 2 shows only a few highlights from DRI's U.S. macro model. Let me illustrate the planners' use of other models with some pivotal energy matters forecast by our energy group. The projection for total energy demand has been reduced substantially in the last two years because the public has demonstrated an extraordinary ability to reduce total energy use in response to higher prices, and there will be plenty of additional higher prices to keep the conservation efforts going. The energy-GNP relationship has been improving by at least 2% a year, and we expect it to continue to do so. The production of natural gas also looks a lot more promising now than earlier. Whereas the best estimates looked for stagnant or declining natural gas production two years ago, the initial response of natural gas supplies to higher prices has been so favorable that there now really is a better prospect. On the other hand, domestic production of crude oil has not shown a comparable upward revision despite the more rapid path to decontrol. The volume of drilling activity is much larger than it was, but the success rate has not yet shown the kind of response that would prompt the energy experts, both at DRI and in the industry, to mark up the prospective domestic crude oil production from current levels. Finally, the power demonstrated by OPEC in 1979 and 1980 has, inevitably, led to massive upward revisions of the prospects for world oil prices. This key parameter underlies many changes in the planning assumptions, both in the price level generally and in the optimal absolute and relative uses of different energy sources.

GROWTH MARKET IDENTIFICATION (GMI)

The economic information component of a decision support system clearly must provide projections of long-term market growth in order to help companies identify the most

desirable areas of development for their given capabilities. This kind of work has also long been established. Table 3 shows an illustration out of the most recent DRI long-range macro forecast, using a few of our 79 industrial production indexes as indicators of growth. This type of relative growth analysis can be done on many data sets, including the 480 industry input-output breakdown, the 81 company product groups of the DRI Industry Financial Service, and the detailed consumer expenditure projections prepared by our consumer group, to name a few possibilities.

Besides identifying projected growth trends for different markets, it is also important to assess their volatility. Unfortunately, higher growth rates are produced in part by strong responses to real income growth, along with the innovational factors such as new technologies, new products, and new markets. Usually the high income elasticity items are the most cyclical, because they depend upon the growth of income and the degree of consumer confidence. During credit crunches and recessions, income growth goes into reverse and consumer confidence collapses. Consequently, it is wise to attach a measure of risk to the

Table 3
Growth Market Identification

	Real Production Growth Rate (1979-1989)			
	Trend Forecast	Cyclical Forecast	Low Trend Forecast	Historical Variability Relative to all Industries*
Rapid Growth Markets				
. Electronic Components	7.6	7.5	6.7	4.2
. Engines	4.4	4.1	3.6	1.1
. Synthetic Materials	4.7	4.3	3.9	3.9
Slow Growth Markets				
. Petroleum Products	0.1	-0.3	-0.2	0.6
. Paints	3.0	3.0	2.6	0.7
. Apparel Products	2.3	1.9	1.9	0.8

*1.0 indicates moves with Industry Average; less than 1.0 indicates less volatility than industry average; greater than 1.0 indicates more volatility than industry average.

Source: Data Resources, Inc.
National Forecasting Group

growth coefficients, measures which can be calculated from alternative model simulations or from the historical record.

It is as important for a company to understand the underlying forces determining relative market growth as it is to consider actual projections. The outside information will always provide data of greater generality than the actual market opportunities for an individual company would show. Products are not uniform across companies, and typically each business has carved out particular niches in the marketplace. It is therefore important to consider some of the fundamental driving forces of growth of markets in terms of demography, technology, and international competitiveness. To illustrate this point, Table 4 shows some summary results of DRI's DECO Model, which analyzes the age composition of consumer purchasing power. The table shows that the consumer groups with the largest increases in purchasing power over the next 10 years will be families in the 35 to 44 age group and singles between 25 and 44 years. These age groups represent a rising share of the total population with the largest probable income gains per capita.

COST AND PRODUCTIVITY ANALYSIS

In an increasingly supply-affected environment, the management of costs has assumed a renewed importance. Few long-term business decisions can be made sensibly without a sophisticated view of future cost patterns, and many of these decisions will focus on the reduction of costs through choice of new materials, energy savings, and programs to boost labor productivity.

Absolute Cost Increases—The Inflation: The inflation rate is one of the critical planning parameters because it helps define financing requirements, pricing strategies, interest rates, and, of course, future monetary and fiscal policies. To distinguish the systematic and therefore more predictable elements of inflation from the more politically and nature-determined elements, DRI has developed the core inflation analysis. Chart 1 shows the history of core inflation, defined as the trend increase in labor and capital costs, and Chart 2 shows two projections of the core inflation rate under alternative macroeconomic scenarios. The forecast projection is drawn from the Trendlong scenario, the alternative is based on

Table 4
Demographic Changes in 1980s: Spending Power By Age Group (Census Money Income, billions of 1972 dollars)

	1980	1985	1990	Compound Annualized Growth Rate 1980-1990 (Percent)
Families by Age of Head				
Under 24	32.467	32.124	30.464	(.5)
25 to 34	177.743	209.382	236.896	2.7
35 to 44	186.057	239.832	292.669	4.2
45 to 54	178.542	196.063	246.693	3.2
55 to 64	143.794	155.529	165.583	1.3
65 +	82.083	90.997	107.971	2.5
Individuals by Age				
Under 24	23.528	27.274	30.360	2.3
25 to 34	48.327	69.956	93.259	6.2
35 to 44	20.119	26.884	35.025	5.2
45 to 54	14.940	17.023	22.458	3.8
55 to 64	20.020	21.952	23.816	1.6
65+	36.778	43.673	52.361	3.3
Total All Families and Individuals	964.353	1,133.641	1,351.253	3.1

Source: Data Resources Inc. Consumer Research Division

worsening energy prices with monetary and fiscal policies which keep fanning the fires of inflation. Both solutions benefit from a 1981 capital cost reduction created by supply-side tax cuts.

Chart 1
Core Inflation: The Increase in
Labor and Capital Costs
(Year-over-year percent change)

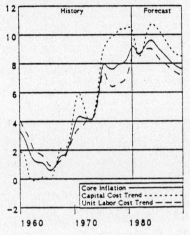

Chart 2
Two Scenarios for Inflation Shocks

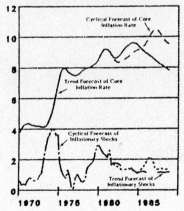

The demand element in inflation, the direct impact on the price level created by the overall unemployment and industrial utilization rates, is projected by DRI to be near zero over the next decade. The swing toward more conservative economic policies, as well as the recent lessons learned by the country, make us assume that fiscal and monetary policies will be substantially more cautious than what we have been suffering in the last 15 years.

The shock element of inflation—energy, crop yields, minimum wages, payroll taxes and the exchange rate—is forecast to average 1.34% over the next decade, with most of the shock originating in the world oil situation.

The DRI long-term forecast is on the gloomy side. Our econometric work still persuades us that the inflation expectations of businesses and households are determined by actual experience rather than by any pronouncements about policy by the Federal Reserve, the President, or any other high official. So long as expectations are based on actual experience, the poor historical record remains the dominant influence and puts a tremendous persistence factor into the system, thereby largely creating the continued high core inflation rate.

Relative Costs: Long-term production decisions require analysis of detailed input costs of the sort projected by our Cost Forecasting Service. For present purposes, and thinking more of the strategic decision level, let me use a macroeconomic illustration. Chart 3 shows the relative prices of energy, labor, and capital equipment over the next eight years. Energy costs rise much the most rapidly, of course; investments to economize on energy use, and selection of areas of expansion in which the energy component is unimportant should be favored. The chart also shows that equipment costs will be rising somewhat less rapidly than labor costs. This relative cost behavior implies improved labor productivity in the 1980s. It will not pay business to continue to hire people, and to expand activities that are highly labor intensive. Increased capital intensity, however, must combine with increased energy efficiency, if costs per unit of output are to be controlled.

Chart 3
Energy Labor and Capital Costs

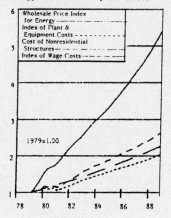

TARGET SETTING

Most corporations have a set of long-term growth targets expressed in terms of revenue and Net Operating Income (NOI). These targets are derived from the more successful periods of the company's own history and from a loose kind of analysis of the company's stock price behavior. The whole logic of today's tax and financial systems requires corporations to grow in NOI, even at the expense of incurring high risks. Companies are reluctant to change their long-term targets, and frequently tie the long-term incentive plans of their executives to their achievement.

However, long-term corporate targets deserve reexamination at this time. The high inflation means that all nominal magnitudes tend to swell at the inflation rate. Thus, the traditional 10-15% profit targets are not as impressive as they used to be, and indeed represent little more than the economy's average. Table 5 shows growth of net income for 81 industries as well as DRI Industry Financial Service projections through 1987. The table shows what we expect to be accomplished by the 551 large companies that make up the Industry Financial Service, as aggregated to the sector level.

Peer Group Analysis: Target setting also requires peer group analysis, the careful quantitative comparison with companies situated in the same industry. Since the security analysts on Wall Street evaluate company performance at least in part by looking within each industry group, the quality of management is assessed by this form of peer group comparison. It is not surprising, therefore, that most companies feel the need to engage in the peer group analysis themselves, to summarize the historical performance of their competitors, and to set sufficiently ambitious targets to make their companies emerge as industry leaders. In the context of the DRI decision support system, peer group analysis is performed using the Compustat (or Value Line) data. A typical set of comparisons is presented in Table 6.

Table 5
Inflation and Profit Growth
Compound Growth Rates

	1965-1973	1973-1980	1980-1987
Net Income for 81 Industries	8.8	11.3	13.2
GNP Deflator	4.5	7.7	9.0
Real Net Income for 81 Industries	4.1	3.3	3.9

Source: Data Resources, Inc., Industrial Financial Service
and National Forecasting Group

Table 6
Peer Group Analysis Report Comparison
of Companies Within Textile Industry

| | Growth and Profitability Highlights | | | | | | |
Firm Name	Sales In 1979 (Mil.$)	Change From Previous Year	Net Income 1979 (Mil.$)	Change From Previous Year	Profit % Sales 1979	Change From Previous Year	(P/E) Mkt. Value to Income Ratio*
Burlington Industries Inc.	2676.3	10.5%	76.2	8.4%	2.8	(1.9)%	7.2
Collins & Aikman Corp	599.5	4.0%	16.4	(31.4)%	2.7	(34.3)%	7.7
Cone Mills Corp	681.3	10.2%	43.8	21.7%	6.4	10.4%	4.6
Dan River Inc.	579.2	9.2%	22.1	9.3%	3.8	51.0%	4.4
Fieldcrest Mills	517.7	11.7%	24.8	9.3%	4.8	(2.2)%	5.7
Graniteville Co.	294.5	10.5%	8.6	NM	2.9	NM	4.3
Lowenstein (M) Corp	644.6	3.9%	(3.4)	NM	(0.5)	NM	NM
Reeves Brothers Inc	336.9	9.0%	16.3	35.8%	4.8	24.6%	4.9
Springs Mills Inc.	827.9	20.9%	35.1	23.2%	4.2	1.9%	4.5
Stevens (J.P.) & Co.	1833.1	11.0%	47.7	31.0%	2.6	18.1%	4.7
West Point-Pepperell	1012.6	14.4%	27.4	(15.4)%	2.7	(26.1)%	5.6
Industry Total	10,003.1	10.8	315.0	9.8	3.1	(0.9)	5.7

*Average 1971 to 1979
Note: NM indicates not measured because of fluctuations in the data

BUSINESS PORTFOLIO ANALYSIS

The repositioning of a company through acquisition and divestiture is, perhaps, the dominant theme of strategic planning. A good portfolio of businesses diversifies against such risks as the business cycle, credit crunches, oil crises, changes in international costs and exchange rates, and shifts of technology. A good business portfolio also has the proper balance between mature, cash-producing units and high-growth potential cash-absorbing units. Finally, the portfolio must have an overall level of risk which is consistent with the financial community's expectations of earnings stability and with management's staying power to survive through surprisingly tough times. If there is a substantive business synergism, such as the application of a new technology to old businesses, shared marketing organizations or production facilities, or the achievement of economies of vertical or horizontal integration, so much the better, but that is not usually the focus of the strategic planning portfolio optimizing work.

The decision support systems for business portfolio analysis have consisted mainly of the ability to do elaborate financial modeling, to condense large amounts of information in intricate graphics displays, and to access lots of data and scenarios to test out the portfolios created by the strategy. One example of such graphics is displayed in Chart 4, the typical "bubble" chart, here produced by the DRI EPS Graphics Package, using models and databanks for sales and return on net assets to provide the information inputs.

Once the basic strategy is developed, the enterprise turns to acquisition analysis. The Compustat (or Value Line) data, searched by a program such as DRI's DRISCAN, can identify companies that have the desired requisites. In the example chosen (Table 7), the criteria selected for the search were a company with sales in the $100-500 million range, a profit margin in excess of 5%, and an exceptionally low sensitivity to financial conditions. The latter criterion was expressed by requiring a strong balance sheet, defined as debt less than

Chart 4
Business Portfolio Analysis
Growth versus Profitability
of Business Units

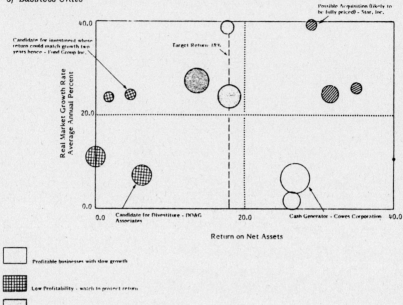

Return on Net Assets

Profitable businesses with slow growth

Low Profitability - watch to protect return

Companies experiencing mediocre returns at high growth

Potential acquisition candidates

Note: EPS Graphics software circles indicate magnitude of gross revenue

Source: Data Resources, Inc.

30% of sales, with short-term debt less than 10% of sales. Criteria can of course be more complicated. The particular search that was run turned up a number of very conservative and closely-held companies that might prove difficult or costly to acquire.

Divestiture has usually not received comparable quantitative attention. Because of the desire to grow, companies have a lot more enthusiasm for acquisitions than for selling operating units. Sales usually occur under distress conditions, with the modest volume of business sales in ordinary times reflecting a company's failure to

make a success of a particular unit or to integrate that unit successfully into the company's business structure. Nonetheless, it must be recognized that the analysis of potential sales is as challenging a task as the analysis of potential acquisitions, and that the tools are similar. Of course the data are internal, and it is elaborate financial modeling and projections of sales, costs, capital charges, and NOI which are the ingredients of the quantitative support system for the sales decision. Econometric projections of markets, costs, and interest rates are inputs to that work.

Table 7
Set of Firms Selected from Compustat
Based upon Financial Criteria

Ticker	Firm Name
RUSS	Russell Stover Candies, Inc.
DOC	Dr. Pepper Co.
CRC	Crompton Co, Inc.
GFD	Guilford Mills, Inc.
RML	Russell Corp.
TCX	Ti-Caro, Inc.
MEG.A	Media General - CL A
FRK	Florida Rock Inds.
VAC.A	Vermont American - CL A
FLS	Florida Steel Corp.
PRE	Premier Industrial Corp.
MYG	Maytag Co.
OVT	Overnite Transportation
SBP	Standard Brands Paint Co.
MLW	Miller-Wohl Co.
PST	Petrie Stores Corp.
CHU	Church's Fried Chicken, Inc.

Criteria for selection:
. Sales between $100 and $500 million
. Profits in excess of 5%
. Low sensitivity to financial conditions

INTERNATIONAL STRATEGY ANALYSIS

The large, successful company is likely to be multinational, and to be continually reassessing its strategy in terms of international composition. Should expansion of marketing programs shift toward foreign markets? What countries offer the greatest sales potential, and markets big enough to achieve a viable scale? What countries should be the location for future production facilities? What products would be most successful in foreign countries? Questions such as these rarely receive the attention they deserve, and many companies have seen their international success impaired by an initial poor choice of countries and an unwillingness to correct such mistakes later on.

Even the most sophisticated multinational companies tend to employ less than complete quantitative support systems for their decisions about foreign operations. Quite apart from the cost of replicating a full national information system for foreign markets, one must also recognize the harsh reality that the statistical systems of most countries are not up to the standard of the United States, and that the information industry is not as highly developed elsewhere as here. In recent years, DRI has invested heavily in the development of information systems for the major foreign countries, which begin to be comparable to our U.S. offerings. The DRI information offering in the international area consists mainly of elaborate statistics on international trade flows and on the dimensions of the foreign economies, as well as econometric forecasting services, both at the macro and micro levels, for the principal economies. However, it must still be recognized that foreign operations involve greater risks than domestic, and that the less complete availability of information is one of those risks.

To illustrate the use of some of the information which is available for strategic decisions, Table 8 shows some international dimensions

Table 8
Seven Potential Markets

Country	Population			Share of World GNP[1] (%)	
	1978 Million	1990 Million	Annual Change (%)	1978	1990
-------	--------	--------	------	----	----
USA	218.55	237.56	0.7	24.94	22.19
Britain	55.90	56.57	0.1	3.31	2.62
Brazil	119.37	166.28	2.8	2.20	2.69
Mexico	65.52	96.86	3.3	0.99	1.29
Nigeria	81.56	111.00	2.6	0.54	0.75
South Africa	27.70	37.70	2.6	0.48	0.50
Saudi Arabia	7.87	11.22	3.0	0.75	1.10

[1] In U.S. Dollars

Source: Data Resources, Inc., International Trade Information Service & World Service

pertinent to a company looking for export markets. The table shows the population and the share of world GNP for seven countries for the years 1978 and 1990. Even this little example shows that Nigeria, an oil-producer, has a larger GNP than South Africa, and is growing much more rapidly. Nigeria is the biggest economy on the African continent and will be our prime market there. This economic fact can already be seen as influencing United States foreign policy in Africa.

Table 9 looks at foreign markets from another point of view, ranking the world's economy by import volumes. The top 10 countries account for 64% of all imports. It might be added that a comparable table for exports would show Germany ahead of the United States, and leading the world. Data such as these can help a company assess whether there is a proper balance in its current worldwide marketing efforts. Projections of these data can help identify where on the world map additional emphasis should be placed.

Another kind of international strategic analysis focuses on the relative costs of production. Chart 5 shows the results of a DRI study[2] of the relative cost per unit of output in six major industrial countries. The chart shows quite dramatically that United States costs were too high in the 1960s and early 1970s, largely explaining the dramatic decline of the American position in the world economy. Since the dollar began to be devalued, this situation

Table 9
Noncommunist World Imports
Ranked by Size in 1979
(Billions of U.S. dollars, compound
Annual rates of growth)

	Levels	Compound Annual Rates of Growth	
	1979	1960-1973	1974-1979
Noncommunist World	1,546.0	12.1	14.5
Industrialized Countries	1,142.0	12.9	14.2
Other Europe	47.9	13.3	12.3
Oil Exporting Countries	101.8	10.8	25.9
Other Western Hemisphere	79.4	9.1	10.7
Other Middle East	24.2	10.4	12.1
Other Asia	100.5	9.3	17.2
Other Africa	37.1	7.6	8.7
Countries			
United States	218.9	12.3	15.2
W. Germany	159.7	13.8	18.1
Japan	109.8	18.0	12.1
France	107.0	14.8	15.1
United Kingdom	102.9	8.9	13.4
Italy	78.0	14.6	13.7
Netherlands	68.2	13.9	15.1
Belgium	60.9	14.1	15.3
Canada	56.8	11.3	10.6
Switzerland	29.4	13.6	15.2
Sweden	28.7	10.7	11.4
Saudi Arabia	25.4	17.8	54.8
Spain	25.4	22.1	10.5
Korea	20.3	21.3	24.3
Austria	20.3	13.2	17.6
Brazil	19.8	12.8	6.9
Denmark	18.4	11.9	13.1
Australia	18.2	8.5	7.9
Singapore	17.6	11.0	16.0
Taiwan	14.8	21.7	16.2
Norway	13.7	11.9	10.2
Nigeria	10.9	9.1	31.6
Yugoslavia	12.9	13.9	11.3
Venezuela	10.7	6.8	20.8
Israel	8.6	17.0	9.6
India	8.8	2.6	11.4
South Africa	9.0	9.3	2.7
Ireland	9.9	12.1	20.9
Mexico	12.1	9.4	14.8
New Zealand	4.6	8.2	4.5

Source: Data Resources Inc.,
International Trade Information Service.

[2] D. McLagan, R. Brinner, and M. Ellyne, "Should U.S. Firms make a Strategic Commitment to Exports?" Data Resources U.S. Long-Term Review, Winter 1980-81.

Chart 5
Relative Cost per Unit Output
for Six Major Industrial Countries
(Index: U.S. = 1.0)

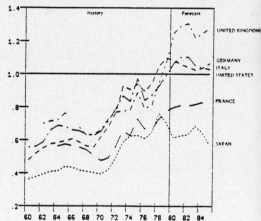

has been largely rectified. Indeed, at this time, only the costs of Japan and France are lower than our own, suggesting that the exchange rates for these countries require further appreciation. Data such as these are clearly pertinent for determining plant locations. Much more important, however, charts such as these are a strong warning where the keenest future competition is likely to be coming from.

STRATEGIC FINANCIAL PLANNING FOR THE 1980s

Let me conclude with what may well be for many companies the most important component of corporate planning in the 1980s, the planning of the company's finances. In a period of rapid inflation, with the central bank the focal point of the society's struggle against inflation, financial capital will be costly and financial markets unstable. This is the probable environment of the first half of the 1980s, and will be the decisive element for the fate of many companies.

The development of financial strategy has many elements, including the development of a good business portfolio which allows high growth without exceeding the corporation's ability to obtain external financing.

Internal management and financial controls, including elaborate systems for managing receivables and quickly varying spending commitments for plant and equipment and personnel, as well as systems for adjusting sales prices quickly in response to surprising cost increases are necessary to provide a strong internal business underpinning to a company's finances. But there is one decision which most companies make on the basis of short-run analysis alone, but which in truth is a long-term strategic choice. That decision is the choice of method of external financing.

Traditionally, in the United States, it has been cheaper to obtain capital in the short-term money markets through commercial paper, bank loans, and trade credit. Long-term debt financing and the issuance of stock have generally been triggered by the criteria of the financial community which enforce certain rules on the composition of a company's balance sheet. Short-term debt has offered a greater

flexibility because it can both be pared down in profitable times and expanded in rather precise quantities for short periods. But in addition to the flexibility, short-term financing has also been cheaper. As Chart 6 shows, the 3-month commercial paper rate has averaged 115 basis points below the AA-utility corporate bond rate over the last 27 years. Admittedly, there were some 8 awkward moments of credit crunches, when the availability of short-term credit was threatened and costs became very high. We are in the midst of such an episode just now. But for the company that was able to roll over short-term debt, it was a bargain, and indeed the actual interest payments fell short of the inflation rate for most of the last decade.

Chart 6
Historical Comparison of Short and Long Term Rates

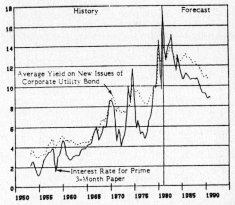

The DRI forecast projects an end to this situation. For the next several years, we project short-term interest rates to exceed long-term interest rates, even on average, and it will take one of the more favorable of the long-term scenarios to lead to a return of the historical relationship by the second half of the 1980s (Table 10).

The reason for this important conclusion is simple enough: the society has entered an

Table 10
*Forecast Cost of Rolling Over
Short-Term versus Long-Term Debt*

Average Prime Rate Through 1990	12.705
Interest Rate on New Issue of 10-Year High-Grade Corporate Bonds	12.577

extended period of struggle against inflation. The Federal Reserve is the principal instrument for achieving this goal, and the Fed acts on the economy principally through the short-term money market. Thus, the short-term money market becomes the battleground between the tremendous inflationary forces of the economy and the political will, exercised through the central bank, to stabilize and reverse those forces. The short-term money market will therefore see frequent periods of difficulty. Indeed, it is likely that the Federal Reserve will avoid the mistake made in 1976-77 and 1980 of lowering short-term interest rates substantially below the inflation rate even during recession and its aftermath, and will keep short-term interest rates above the inflation rate even in the near term.

Bond yields have tended to average 2 to 3 percentage points above the inflation rate, and there is little reason to think that this relationship will change in the future. Short-term interest rates have averaged less than the inflation rate, but we project this period to be finished. Therefore, the spread between long- and short-term interest rates on average will be quite small, and in the current DRI forecasts, there is enough pressure from the Federal Reserve to keep short-term rates above the long-term.

If this analytical conclusion is accepted as a planning parameter, it has very direct and important implications for corporate planning. It means that corporations must seize the opportunity to acquire long-term capital through bond or stock sales when the capital markets provide them the opportunity and when their internal financial conditions make it feasible to do so. In DRI's inflation projections and assumptions about Federal Reserve policy, high quality bonds sold for yields below 13% will be a bargain, and will allow a company to grow more smoothly and at lower cost than a strategy of heavier reliance on short-term debt. The more negative the long-term economic scenario that is assumed, the stronger becomes this conclusion.

Concluding Comment

My paper has covered a lot of ground, perhaps rather more than you bargained for. But there is a good reason: the potential role of quantitative analysis based on economic information systems and economic logic is enormous. The tools that are now available are very elaborate and bring an enormous store of information to bear on a great variety of strategic decisions confronting a large enterprise. The strategic planning task is more complicated than short-run analyses for market forecasting, cost analysis, and financial projections. In this paper, I have tried to give you an illustrative but quite comprehensive overview of the use of an economic information system such as that provided by DRI in corporate planning. I hope you will study the exhibits and come closer to realizing the full potential of these techniques in helping your companies reach the difficult strategic decisions that you must make correctly if you are to be among the winners of the 1980s.

FINANCIAL POLICY MODELS: THEORY AND PRACTICE

Willard T. Carleton, Charles L. Dick, Jr.,
David H. Downes*

Intelligent corporate financial planning has been necessary for as long as the corporate form of business enterprise has existed. Only in recent years, however, have computer technology and academic theorizing been harnessed to meet this practical need. Without wishing to minimize the impact and value of these efforts on the practice of corporate finance, we do think there are grounds for believing that the new finance "tools" have been less than maximally effective. In this article we contrast typical financial modeling theory in order to interpret the gap between the two. Then we describe a financial policy model whose characteristics might be expected to be more acceptable in practice. Finally, we discuss the implications of the theory/practice gap and our experience with this model for future scholarly activities in the modeling of financial policies.

I. Contemporary Financial Modeling Practice

By far the most popular recent innovation in financial models, which might be described as state-of-the-art practice, is the computer-based budget compiler, or financial statement simulator. While these simulation models vary tremendously in scale and detail[1] there are some features common to

*The Amos Tuck School of Business Administration, Dartmouth College; Cresap, McCormick and Paget, Inc.; and University of California, respectively. The views expressed in this paper reflect exposure in a number of professional meetings, university seminars, and consulting situations in the last few years. The people to whom our gratitude is due are therefore too numerous to name individually. On the other hand, some of our conclusions, especially with respect to the directions academic finance should take, are admittedly idiosyncratic, and for these we accept full responsibility. Finally, the Tuck Associates Program has been a source of financial support for this work, which we most willingly and gratefully acknowledge.

[1]The plethora of models developed by First National City Bank of New York, a major innovator in this field, as well as George Gershefski's efforts, come readily to mind. See George Gershefski [5] and Warren and Shelton [9].

virtually all. Presumably, these model features are well known to readers of this journal, but they bear repeating because of the light they shed on how financial planners and managers view their functions:

(a) "Bottom-up" rather than "top-down" approach. The inputs to most of these models include decisions and forecasts made at a variety of organizational levels within the firm, for example, divisional sales forecasts and desired capital structure. The computer is then used as an electronic clerk which adds up the effects of all these disparate inputs.

(b) Accounting rather than finance, the underlying frame of reference is **a sour**ce -and-uses-of-funds equation. All but one of the sources and uses are *inputs*, direct or indirect, to the computer; the last one is an output of the process indicating a net funds need or surplus for each year being planned.

(c) Deterministic rather than probabilistic approach. To the best of the authors' knowledge, no working simulators and very few experimental ones are probabilistic.

(d) Iterative use of trial and error rather than optimizing solutions. In fact, these models appear to avoid not only the techniques of optimization but even its language in their description.

These points are easily illustrated with the simulation model of a hypothetical firm. Details are kept at a minimum in order to highlight important features. Consider the sources-and-uses-of-funds statement for Firm X, whose balance sheet is as follows:

Firm X Balance Sheet

Current Assets (CA)	Current Liabilities (CL)
Fixed Assets (FA)	Long-term Debt (L)
	Equity (E)

Forming first differences, we have as our summary statement of financial flows between end of year t-1 and end of year t:

(1) $$\Delta CA(t) + \Delta FA(t) - \Delta CL(t) - \Delta L(t) - \Delta E(t) = 0 \quad .$$

Under the assumption that Firm X does not, as a matter of policy, ever sell new equity issues, the change in equity, $\Delta E(t)$, must equal profits less dividends, or

$$(2) \qquad \Delta E(t) = PR(t) - D(t)$$

where $PR(t)$ = after-tax profits and $D(t)$ = dividends paid. Furthermore, profits are also describable as earnings before interest and taxes ($EBIT(t)$) less interest ($iL(t)$, where i = interest rate), all times 1 less the corporate income tax rate, T:

$$(3) \qquad PR(t) = (1-T) [EBIT(t) - iL(t)] \qquad .$$

If equation (3) is substituted into (2), and (2) into (1), we are left with the funds-flow statement which forms the basis of a statement simulator:

$$(1)' \qquad \Delta CA(t) + \Delta FA(t) - \Delta CL(t) - \Delta L(t)$$
$$- (1-T) [EBIT(t) - iL(t)] + D(t) = 0 \qquad .$$

Note that up to this point we have merely been describing accounting equations that always hold true. In order to generate forecasts of future financial statements, all the elements of equation (1)' have to be forecasted or planned, either explicitly or implicitly. The underlying driving forecast for most simulators is of sales. Inputs of sales forecasts for all planning years together with ratios of the relevant operating expenses to sales result in derived EBIT forecasts for each year. Next, capital requirements are also forecasted implicitly, predicated on sales and forecasted asset turnover ratios. Thus we have $\Delta FA(t)$ produced as model output. Finally, current liabilities are usually expressed as a function of sales so that $\Delta CL(t)$ can also be known.[2]

The result of these inputs is that the funds-flow equation becomes the algebraic sum of "knowns" or "knowables" ($\Delta FA(t)$, $\Delta CL(t)$, and $(1-T)EBIT(t)$, which are derived from sales forecasts) and unknowns ($\Delta CA(t)$, $L(t)$, $\Delta L(t)$ and $D(t)$, which are financial decision variables). How are these decisions (which by their nature reflect policy choices) produced as output of the statement generator? The answer is: by simple rules of thumb. Typically, the dividend decision, $D(t)$, is input directly. If one does this, then equation (1)' can be rewritten as:

$$(1)'' \qquad \Delta CA(t) - \Delta L(t) + (1-T)iL(t)$$
$$= -\Delta FA(t) + \Delta CL(t) + (1-T)EBIT(t) - D(t) \qquad , \text{ or as}$$

---

[2]In large models, sales forecasts, operating ratio forecasts, and the forecasts of financial variables derived from these are usually generated in a decentralized, or "bottom-up," fashion.

$$\Delta CA(t) + [(1-T)i - 1]\ \Delta L(t)$$

$$= - (1-T)i\ L(t-1) - \Delta FA(t) + \Delta CL(t)$$

$$+ (1-T)EBIT(t) - D(t)$$

since $L(t) = L(t-1) + \Delta L(t)$. The right-hand side is the net "knowable" financial source (if > 0) or need (if < 0) for Firm X during year t. ($L(t-1)$ appears on the right-hand side because at the beginning of year t it is already known.) The usual rule of thumb is to allocate all of any net financial source to the current assets account and all of any net financial need to long-term indebtedness. More complicated rules of thumb can be employed, but they all share a common characteristic: they produce planned financial decisions independent (except in a very limited sense) both of the earnings outcome of the model and of one another.

Thus, to the extent that finance theory deals with choices (such as whether to increase dividends or retire debt), budget compilers contain little finance since they only trace out (simulate) the financial and operating consequences of choices already made.

The ever-widening use of statement simulators is testimony to their practicality. For purposes of this paper, however, they represent a challenge to the finance theorist or operations researcher to whom they are incomplete, albeit valid, devices.

In the first place, "bottom-up" modeling, by treating lower and higher level management concerns jointly, can easily produce a "trees versus forest" problem. In any iterative use of such a model, in which forecasts and decisions are varied to answer a series of "what if?" questions, it is easy to focus on lower level and less important inputs (e.g., a single division's sales forecasts) to the exclusion of major corporate financial policies (e.g., capital structure or dividends). Of course, financial models are created for many uses, including testing the sensitivity of operating results to different sales forecasts. On the other hand, most people seem to prefer to avoid being confronted by difficult choices, such as the tradeoffs among major financial decisions, so that users of simulators can easily concentrate on forecasts to the exclusion of decisions. Additionally, the mere burdening of such a model with financial details is distracting to top management planning committees concerned with major decisions such as capital expansion, dividends, and financing. More than one budget compiler has acquired enough details to be described as a corporate model but then has fallen into disuse except by planning staff as a computerized toy [Hall 6].

A couple of strategic lessons seem to emerge from this aspect of corporate modeling practice. Most importantly, despite occasional rhetoric, corporate managements do not like to deal head on with major decisions, especially tradeoffs among them. Therefore, if a financial policy model is to be used as designed, its orientation must be "top-down" and aggregative, so as to force attention to higher level rather than lower level matters. That is, from a standpoint which includes operationality, as well as completeness and elegance, there may be an optimum degree of disaggregation in financial policy models. The other lesson also derives from behavioral considerations. Since the major financial decisions being modeled can bring large payoffs/penalties *both to the firm and to the decision makers*, faith in the model-builder (or in the model as "black box") is not enough; some understanding is required. Pursuit of model inclusiveness (or, from the finance theorist's perspective, analytical elegance) without regard to human limitations has been the Waterloo of many modeling efforts.

Secondly, corporate financial simulation models deliberately avoid formal treatment of uncertainty, even though what seems to motivate the design and use of such models in the last analysis is uncertainty itself. The preferred mode is to simulate the effects of a discrete number of alternative "scenarios" (without the attachment of probabilities to these as uncertain states of nature) as a sensitivity test for financial policies and to incorporate policy objectives (e.g., limits on working capital ratios) as a way of limiting the firm's risk exposure. A crude criticism of such practice is that it is not very sophisticated and could stand some improvement. While this may be valid, a more profound evaluation is that the finance theoretical treatment of uncertainty is not sufficiently robust to provide guidance at this time; practitioner skepticism is eminently sensible. In other words, our "under uncertainty" efforts share features that interfere with operationality: (1) they blur the distinction between frequency and subjectivist interpretations of probability, among other things leading to the legitimate issue of whose probability assessments should be employed as model inputs; (2) except for the simplest cases they raise model complexity beyond the limits of managerial comprehension; (3) they beg the question of the best corporate objective function and decision structure once the conditional nature of future decisions upon sequences of random outcomes and prior decisions is admitted. Among other things, it is obvious that zero-order decision rules (in which decisions are committed now for the future on the basis that no new information will be forthcoming) are inappropriate once the event-time nature of uncertainty (and attendant benefits/costs to firms' owners, managers, and creditors) is admitted to the model. We think it is not an overstatement that economic theory has not produced any uniformly accepted normative corporate finance framework which admits event-time uncertainty and, more importantly, which admits such uncertainty joined to the effects of market imperfections financial managers have to face (restrictions imposed by loan agreements, transactions costs, and the like).[3]

The third feature of budget compilers is that they simply are not very efficient screeners of financial plans. This also is easily illustrated. Assume that Firm X would like to incorporate in its financial plans the following policy objectives (some of which may have originated with the firm and some with its creditors).

One policy objective is maximum leverage, in the form of an upper limit on the ratio of long-term debt to equity of 100 percent:

$$L(t) \leq 1.0 \ E(t)$$

$$\text{or} \quad L(t-1) + \Delta L(t) \leq E(t-1) + PR(t) - D(t)$$

but since $PR(T) = (1-T) \ [EBIT(t) - iL(t)]$

$$= (1-T)EBIT(t) - (1-T)iL(t-1) - (1-T)i \ \Delta L(t)$$

$$L(t-1) + \Delta L(t) \leq E(t-1) + (1-T)EBIT(t) - (1-T)iL(t-1)$$

$$- (1-T)i \ \Delta L(t) - D(t) \quad , \text{or}$$

(2) $$[1 + (1-T)i]\Delta L(t) + D(t) \leq E(t-1) - [1 + (1-T)i]L(t-1)$$

$$+ (1-T)EBIT(t)$$

with the decision variables on the left-hand side.

Another policy objective is minimum debt service coverage, in the form of a rule that EBIT be at least five times as large as interest payments, is:

$$EBIT(t) \geq 5i \ L(t) \quad , \text{or}$$

(3) $$\Delta L(t) \leq \frac{EBIT(t)}{5i} - L(t-1) \quad .$$

Still another policy objective is minimum working capital ratio of 2:

$$CA(t) \geq 2 \ CL(t) \quad , \text{or}$$

(4) $$\Delta CA(t) \geq 2 \ CL(t) - CA(t-1) \quad .$$

Another objective is dividends per share (hence total dividends, with no new equity) that are at least as large as in the prior year:

---

[3]On this point, see Carleton [1].

(5) $$D(t) \geq D(t-1) \qquad .$$

And another policy objective is earnings per share (hence earnings) growing at least 10 percent per year:

$$PR(t) \geq 1.1\ PR(t-1) \qquad , \text{ or}$$

$$(1-T)\ [EBIT(t) - i\ L(t)] \geq 1.1\ PR(t-1) \qquad , \text{ or}$$

(6) $$(1-T)i\ \Delta L(t) \leq (1-T)\ [EBIT(t)-iL(t-1)] - 1.1\ PR(t-1)$$

with the expression simplified and the decision variable, $L(t+1)$, on the left-hand side.

Finally, sources of funds equal uses, or equation (1)" must hold:

$$(1)" \qquad \Delta CA(t) + [(1-T)i - 1]\ \Delta L(T) + D(t)$$

$$= - (1-T)iL(t-1) - \Delta FA(t) + \Delta CL(t)$$

$$+ (1-T)\ EBIT(t) \qquad .$$

In order to attach numbers to these goals, or requirements, assume the following year $t-1$ results and year to forecasted values:

$CA(t-1) = 100$	$T = .5$
$FA(t-1) = 900$	$i = .08$
$CL(t-1) = 50$	$EBIT(t) = 225$
$L(t-1) = 450$	$C(t) = 60$
$E(t-1) = 500$	$\Delta FA(5) = 100 \qquad .$
$D(t-1) = 20$	

The consequences are:

(1)" $$\Delta CA(t) - .96\Delta L(t) + D(t) = 40.5 \qquad ,$$

(2) $$1.04\Delta L(t) + D(t) \leq 144.5 \qquad .$$

(3) $$\Delta L(t) \leq 112.5 \qquad .$$

(4) $$\Delta CA(t) \geq 20 \qquad ,$$

(5) $$D(t) \geq 20 \qquad ,$$

(6) $$\Delta L(t) \leq 107.5 \qquad .$$

There are a couple of things to note about this representation of Firm X's objectives. In the first place, it describes a feasible region containing a potentially infinite number of solutions. In the second place, with the possible exception of (6), none of these objectives automatically suggests itself as a higher level goal or objective function to drive the policy model. Typical corporate practice, especially in the context of statement simulators, removes this uncomfortable indeterminacy by assumptions which convert policy requirements from inequalities to equalities. The result is a crude satisficing model, in which objectives neither appear directly nor are separated into higher level objectives (goals) and lower level objectives (constraints).

Most typically, $D(t)$ and $\Delta CA(t)$ are fixed arbitrarily. Assume for example, that $\Delta CA(t)$ and $D(t)$ are set at their lower limits (given by inequalities (4) and (5) of 20). From the sources and uses equation, (1)", incremental borrowing, $\Delta L(t)$, will then be slightly more than 5. It can be seen that this amount is well within the limits given by inequalities (2), (3), and (6) of 124.5, 112.5, and 107.5, respectively. In effect, Firm X has planned current assets and dividends in a conservative fashion, so as to be "safe" on its other objectives. The conversion of financial policies as boundary conditions into exact targets is satisfying because it produces exact answers, but of course the benefits may be illusory inasmuch as an infinite number of $\Delta CA(t)$, $\Delta L(t)$, $D(t)$ combinations will also be "safe." Worse yet, in more complex simulators involving several time periods, the ad hoc reduction of broad policy requirements to exact targets may produce simulation results that violate some of the objectives, but without that fact being perceived except upon very close examination.[4]

The operations researcher or academic in such a situation would instinctively try to separate policy objectives into one major goal and several constraints, then call upon some constrained optimization technique for solution. It seems to be the case, however, that those who construct computerized budget compilers usually eschew any attempts to let the program seek decisions through optimization techniques such as linear programming.

As Gershefski [5, p. 64] noted:

---

[4]Sometimes inconsistency among objectives is a matter of accounting, but all too frequently it is compounded by bad economics. For example, (6) above *might* be defended on the grounds that, since we don't know enough about the dynamics of shareholder expectations, it is appropriate to try to put a floor under year-by-year EPS experience. Unfortunately, all too often (6) becomes a higher level objective, or goal, in its own right -- not traded off against others -- to which merger activities are directed. It may be obvious to academics, but frequently it is not so to practitioners, that maintenance of any EPS growth rate presupposes basic investment (rate of return) opportunities, or compensating adjustments to earnings retention and/or leverage policies.

> The case-study approach budget compiler, unlike
> linear programming, makes it possible to develop
> a hierarchy of objectives, with the weights of
> emphasis on these objectives left up to manage-
> ment. The model provides management with the
> information to help it decide what trade-offs
> must be made in determining weights of emphasis.

Unfortunately, an unguided "hunt and peck" series of reruns of the
budget compiler may not easily (if at all) produce satisfactory financial
plans for the intuitive, or nonoptimizing, user. Moreover, such a process,
conducted by a staff assistant with a highly detailed model, runs the danger
of producing a final plan which is either ignored by top management or else
reflects too much of the staff assistant's own sense of policy emphases. This
latter danger is a direct consequence of not embedding top management policy
objectives in the model itself. If financial planning methodologies are to
be truly useful, they should invite the participation of top management by
focusing on major financial decisions and providing some guidance in the "hunt
and peck" process. Budget compilers are powerful tools, but they have serious
inherent limitations.

II. Contemporary Finance Theory

It would appear to be a natural step to incorporate into planning models
both accepted criteria of normative finance theory (such as maximizing expected
present value of owners' equity) and the kinds of objectives described above.
In fact, a number of commercial banks have done so, pioneering the way in
developing large-scale linear programming models as aids to asset-and-
liability management (Cohen and Hammer [4]; Chervany, Strom and Boehlke [3];
and Komar [7]). This innovation is as significant as that of the budget compiler. From the standpoint of model structure, however, this effort reflects
a philosophy which appears at first glance to be quite opposite that of the
budget simulators. Given a set of interest rate forecasts as the key input,
the typical bank LP model selects a program of asset purchases and sales,
issuance of time certificates of deposit, and the like for each of the planning
periods. The selected program maximizes profits while at the same time obeying
management's preferences (input as constraints) regarding liquidity position,
capital adequacy, and so forth. By requiring top management emphasis to be
input explicitly, the LP procedure is then able to screen out undesirable
(or even unattainable) financial plans efficiently. In fact, if the best use
of such a model is regarded as iterative, one still may wish to explore "what
ifs?" by varying, for instance, minimum required liquidity ratios. Then the
procedure is one of deterministic simulation different from the budget compiler

only in that for each run only best plans are produced. It is useful to remember that any analytical closure of the firm as a financial system is somewhat arbitrary and that the firm's objectives are inherently multidimensional, not necessarily capable of a complete mapping into a scalar objective. Consequently, when one utilizes a model that employs a single objective (e.g., expected present value) as the *summum bonum*, one should not forget that the feasible region is in part defined by the imposition of other policy objectives as constraints.[5] If we are to be honest at this point we have to avoid imbuing the term *optimization* with too much philosophical meaning while at the same time using as much finance theory as seems reasonable and operational.

The analogous situation for the Firm X objectives described previously would exist if that company could make one of its objectives overriding for purposes of speeding up the "hunt and peck" process. With the relative value of, e.g., $\Delta CA(t)$, $\Delta L(t)$, and $D(t)$ thus treated quantitatively, the model would then find the best among possible combinations of these decisions.[6] Since each

---

[5]It has been suggested that goal programming is an appropriate modeling technique where corporate finance objectives are multidimensional. (See Mao [8]). In our judgment, the informational benefits from such an approach are less than those obtained using LP, for the following reasons. (1) Goal programming requires that corporate financial objectives treated as constraints be viewed as upper or lower bounds, with implied zero cost for solutions in which strict inequalities hold. But, corporate financial objectives treated as "goals" are symmetric; solutions on either side of exact fulfillment are considered costly. This nonsymmetric handling of objectives makes interpretation of solutions ambiguous, especially since managements are not always able to separate objectives naturally into goals and constraints. (2) If the objective function in a goal program has more than one argument, absolute priorities have to be imposed arbitrarily. Consequently, nonachievability of all of the goals, when such is the program solution, leaves unanswered the important economic question of how objectives trade off against one another. In other words, finance theory, even applied gently, has something to contribute to management's undertaking of how financial policy requirements fit together. And goal programming is a substantially less powerful tool than linear programming for accomplishing this.

[6]The objectives for Firm X -- relationships (1)", (2), (3), (4), (5), and (6) -- are linear combinations of financial decision variables. If the financial objective which is accepted as most important for Firm X's planning is also describable as a linear combination of the decision variables, then linear programming can be used. In fact, as will be described below, goals such as maximizing present value of owner equity or maximizing cumulative earnings per share can be so described although the algebra occasionally gets tedious. Consequently, and as will be seen, plans of companies like Firm X can easily be generated as financial statement simulations, but simulations in which all the policy objectives are recognized explicitly.

run is a simulation for given policy objectives, subsequent simulation runs could also be made under different policy mixes. The principal point in such procedures is that each run or solution utilizes all the constraints bearing on financial decisions *explicitly* and *jointly*.

Unfortunately, Gershefski's misconception that LP approaches to financial planning do not permit management to develop an "hierarchy of objectives" is a widespread one. Operations research writing on linear programming models all too frequently focus on the mathematics of a problem, or on the characteristics of a particular LP solution. The fact that this tool can be a powerful aid to a manager by allowing him to evaluate the profit consequences of alternative (e.g., liquidity) policies, becomes lost in discussion of the apparatus. Further, the misconception is not easily removed if the model is large enough to require batch-processing computing. Then, as in the case of large budget compilers, more staff assistants and "computerese" come between top management and the model. The result is slow answers to "what ifs?" so that management loses interest in and control over the planning process, more details than management can absorb (trees versus forest again), and finally dismissal of the concept as "black box" magic. Once again, the model becomes a staff toy -- the fate of most bank LP models. Now it is true that bank LP financial planning models typically address themselves to a more restricted range of financial decisions and a shorter time span than most budget compilers. On the other hand, the facts that only a few banks utilize such models and that few industrial firms have demonstrated enthusiasm for optimization techniques in their financial planning suggest that implementation difficulties have been very real. Given the power of the programming framework to answer the same questions as budget compilers *and more*, the hypothesis that misunderstanding and bad modeling strategies have been responsible is at least arguable.

III. The Design of a Usable Optimizing Model

In designing our financial planning model we have been guided by the principle that contemporary finance theory could only be usable if the mind-numbing effects of large model size, computer mechanics, and the mathematics of linear programming were removed.[7] Accordingly, the following features

---

[7]An early version of the model, programmed for demonstration purposes, is described in Carleton [1]. For practical application, that program has been made more general and tailored to corporation specification, and a number of minor technical errors have been corrected. The general framework remains the same, however. As a practical note, by far the greatest amount of computer

(which are described in the context of an actual application) have been incorporated.

(1) Users have been involved at each stage, starting with an educational process in which the interdependencies between major decisions concurrently and between time periods, as well as simple normative finance concepts, were explained. The design stage has been most critical, since it involves choices over degree of model disaggregation, closure and linkages to related corporate activities, constraint articulation, and input/output format. Finally, experimental use represents the stage at which the corporate users have begun to dominate the modeling effort.

(2) Given the philosophical, theoretical, and behavioral problems associated with the *formal* recognition of uncertainty, our model has been set up as formally deterministic. On the other hand, it has also been designed for use as a simulation model, to be employed iteratively with respect to whatever parameter variation is held to be important by the user.

(3) The structure of balance sheets and income and funds flows statements remains at the heart of the model. These are broken down into the smallest number of accounts consistent with intelligent focus on the key financial decisions for which top management has to plan: capital investment, working capital, capital structure, and dividends. Since top management's financial planning responsibilities are in this area, we do not want to allow tradeoffs among these decision areas to be obscured by a welter of lower level details. We follow a "top-down" rather than "bottom-up" approach. On the other hand, simulators are extremely useful as integrators of forecasts and lower management level decisions. We therefore treat as key *inputs* to our model those items which are the most critical *outputs* of most statement simulators: operating earnings (EBIT) and capital expenditures (ΔFA) through time. Our model and a company's budget compiler can thus be thought of in an hierarchical structure: top-down policy model built upon the output of a bottom-up forecasting model.

(4) Outputs of the model are the major financial decisions (dividends, working capital, financing) of the corporation over the planning years. These are determined simultaneously using linear programming techniques. Thus, for example, not only is the effect of 1974's planned dividends on 1974's working capital position accounted for, but also the effect of both on 1975's borrowing/debt repayment is explicitly felt. An intuitive grasp of the interplay of

---

programming effort has been devoted to making the model non-OR-user-oriented, as described below. A noncompany-specific version of this model, entitled FINPLAN, has been programmed for public use on the Dartmouth computer system.

such choices is made more possible by suppressing nonessential accounting details.

(5) No model's output can ever be any more valid than its input. There are three kinds: the first comprises forecasts of the economic environment, including such matters as profit margins, interest rates, and industry P/E ratios (or costs of equity capital). The second includes legal restrictions on financial decisions, such as those given by the minimum "times interest earned" provision in a loan agreement. The third incorporates management policy requirements such as minimum annual EPS growth rate, upper limits on debt to total capitalization, etc.[8] As a philosophical note, financial planning is a meaningful and difficult task precisely because the first two kinds of input (forecasts and legal constraints) cannot be ignored except at peril to the financial health of the firm. The third set of inputs reflects management's attempt to cope with the first two. For a given set of "best guesses" as to future economic conditions, known legal requirements, and top management policy requirements the model produces a "best" financial plan as solution to a linear program, but for another set of inputs another "best" plan also results. Again, the reason for holding details to a minumum is to encourage top management to explore, through a series of computer runs, what the likely tradeoffs are between major policy requirements. For example, what are the consequences over time of simultaneously holding down allowed dividend increases and reducing debt/equity limits? (See Exhibit 1.)

(6) The corporate objective we normally employ in the model is the conventional one: the "best" plan is the one which, while staying within the limits permitted by the three kinds of inputs and given the cost of equity capital, makes the present value of owner equity as large as possible.[9] In

---

[8]It is useful to note again that the algebraic structure of the model is essentially the same as in Firm X's constraints, although more tedious because several years have to be described all at once.

[9]This objective can be written as

$$\frac{PV(0)}{N(0)} = \sum_{t=1}^{n} \frac{D(t)}{N(t) \prod_{\tau=1}^{n} (1+k_\tau)} + \frac{PV(n)}{N(n) \prod_{\tau=1}^{n} (1+k_\tau)}$$

where $N(t)$ = number of shares outstanding in year t; k_τ = period τ forward cost of equity capital (input directly or derived from a series of questions about industry P/E ratios, etc.); $PV(0)$ = solution value present value to be maximized; and $PV(n)$ = horizon year value (derived in terms of forecasted posthorizon, or long-term, opportunities). $PV(0)/N(0)$ is thus nonlinear, because of the presence of $N(t)$ terms in the denominators, changes in which equity financing, a decision

Exhibit 1   Structure of Optimizing Financial Planning Model

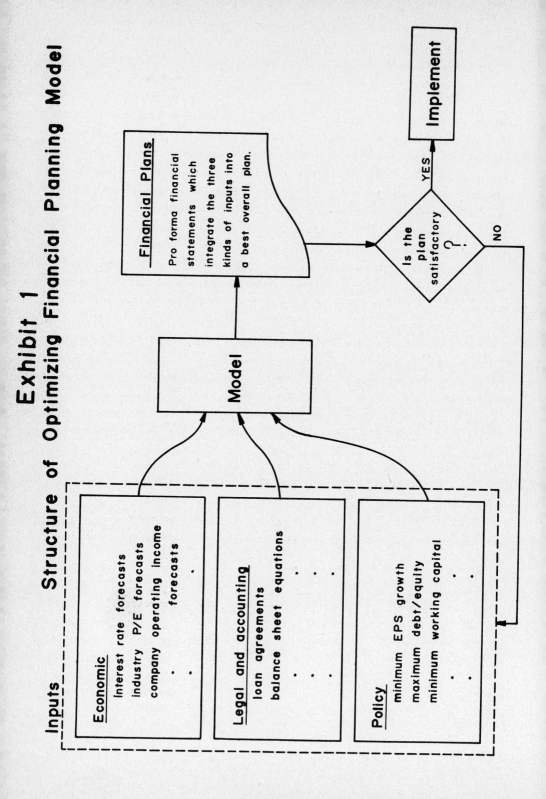

Inputs

Economic

Interest rate forecasts
industry P/E forecasts
company operating income
forecasts
.   .

Legal and accounting

loan agreements
balance sheet equations   .   .   .

Policy

minimum EPS growth
maximum debt/equity
minimum working capital
.   .   .

Model

Financial Plans

Pro forma financial
statements which
integrate the three
kinds of inputs into
a best overall plan.

Is the
plan
satisfactory
?

YES

NO

Implement

order to test the sensitivity of plans even to this objective, however, we have included other possible definitions of "best," as for example, maximizing cumulative earnings over the planning years.

(7) Ultimately, none of the above procedures will "work" unless management can get answers to revised inputs rapidly and in recognizable form. Therefore our model was programmed for a time-sharing computer with the option available of using a conversational mode. The user thus has to know virtually nothing about computers. His inputs can be in the form of typed responses to such questions as "Is a minimum annual growth rate in earnings per share required?" The outputs are the familiar financial statements and ratio analyses. All the mathematics are "black-boxed." (See Exhibits 2 and 3.)

We employ time sharing deliberately, on the grounds that it can encourage the kind of iterative use most desirable for our (or any) policy model. On the other hand, the debate over time sharing versus batch processing has been going on for some time, and nothing we say here will resolve the issue. We do quote, with approval, however, some recent thoughts by H. Martin Weingartner [10, p. 9]:

> Generally, the argument turns on whether high level personnel will ever sit down at the console of a time-shared computer and interact with the computer on their own, or whether the process will continue to depend on intermediaries. I believe this is a false issue. The real question is whether the decision maker will interact with a *model*, with the model becoming an extension of his own information-processing capability; or whether he will utilize the output as he would a fast-turnaround batch processor.

If one thinks of a planning model's use as a one-shot affair, then it is difficult to quarrel with the advantages of a batch processing format. If the best form of this activity is both iterative and interactive (e.g., the altering of constraints), then it seems to us that the hardware set-up should be capable of providing answers while the manager is most interested in the problems. The question of who is to sit at the teletype is secondary.

----

variable, is reflected. Employing manipulations in the article referenced in footnote 7, PV(O)/N(O) finally is encoded in the computer program in the form

$$\frac{PV(O)}{N(O)} = \sum_{t=1}^{n} a(t)D(t) + a(n)PV(n) + \sum_{t=1}^{n} b(t)Y(t)$$

where $a(t)$ and $b(t)$ are fixed coefficients and $Y(t)$ = new equity in year t. This result is linear in the decision variables, which permits LP techniques to be exploited.

Exhibit 2

CDD INC

LONG-RANGE FINANCIAL PLANNING MODEL

INPUT ALL RATIOS RATES AND PERCENTAGES IN DECIMAL NOTATION, AND BALANCE SHEET AND INCOME-STATEMENT ITEMS IN THOUSANDS OR IN MILLIONS OF DOLLARS OR SHARES.

SECTION 1.

THIS SECTION REQUESTS INFORMATION FROM YOUR FINANCIAL STATEMENTS AS OF THE END OF YOUR LATEST COMPLETED FISCAL YEAR.

    1.01 INPUT THE LATEST COMPLETED FISCAL YEAR (E.G., 1970)? 1971

INPUT BOOK VALUE OF:

    1.02 CURRENT ASSETS? 100
    1.03 BASE NET FIXED ASSETS? 800
    1.04 OTHER ASSETS? 100

        .   .
        .   .
        .   .

INPUT:

    3.01 NET FIXED ASSETS, ON THE BASIS OF NONDISCRETIONARY INVESTMENT
           PLUS CAPITAL REQUIREMENTS TO SUPPORT FORECASTED INTERNAL
           SALES? 810, 820, 830, 840, 850
    3.02 OTHER ASSETS? 100, 100, 100, 100, 100

INPUT:

    4.01 MINIMUM AVERAGE ADJUSTED 'TIMES INTEREST EARNED'
           RATIO? 5, 5, 5, 5, 5
    4.02 MINIMUM AMOUNT OF WORKING CAPITAL? 50, 55, 60, 60, 60
    4.03 MINIMUM WORKING CAPITAL RATIO? 1, 1, 1, 1, 1
    4.04 MAXIMUM CUMULATIVE DIVIDEND PAYOUT
           RATIO? .65, .65, .65, .65, .65
    4.05 UPPER LIMIT ON LONG-TERM DEBT TO EQUITY
           RATIO? 1, 1, 1, 1, 1

Exhibit 3

SOURCES OF FUNDS

	1972	1973	1974	1975	1976
NET INCOME	81.0	93.3	106.4	119.5	133.9
DEPRECIATION	56.0	61.3	67.8	75.4	82.4
DEFERRED INCOME TAXES	17.6	19.4	21.5	22.8	24.0
DISC REVOLVER	102.3	60.8	62.7	39.8	21.0
LONG-TERM BORROWING	-30.0	-30.0	-30.0	-30.0	-30.0
CONVERTIBLE DEBT	0.0	0.0	0.0	0.0	0.0
PREFERRED	0.0	0.0	0.0	0.0	0.0
OTHER LIABILITIES	0.0	0.0	0.0	0.0	0.0
NEW EQUITY	0.0	0.0	0.0	0.0	0.0
	-----	-----	-----	-----	-----
TOTAL FUNDS SOURCES----------→	226.9	204.9	228.5	227.5	231.3

USES OF FUNDS

	1972	1973	1974	1975	1976
FIXED ASSETS INCLU DEPREC	146.0	168.1	190.7	193.8	196.5
OTHER ASSETS	0.0	0.0	0.0	0.0	0.0
COMMON DIVIDENDS	30.9	31.8	32.8	33.8	34.8
INCREASES IN WORK CAPITAL	50.0	5.0	5.0	0.0	0.0
	-----	-----	-----	-----	-----
TOTAL FUNDS USES--------------→	226.9	204.9	228.5	227.5	231.3

	1971	1972	1973	1974	1975	1976
INTEREST COVER/YEAR	5.98	5.92	6.38	6.68	7.15	7.82
ADJ AVE TIE		5.96	6.10	6.34	6.75	7.23
D/E: LONG TERM DEBT	0.60	0.68	0.66	0.64	0.58	0.50
TOTAL DEBT	0.70	0.73	0.71	0.68	0.62	0.54
WORK CAP RATIO	1.00	1.59	1.61	1.60	1.60	1.60
ANN DIV PAYOUT RATIO	0.47	0.38	0.34	0.31	0.28	0.26
EPS NO STK DIV	$1.29	$1.62	$1.87	$2.13	$2.39	$2.68
EPS WITH STK DIV	$1.29	$1.57	$1.76	$1.95	$2.12	$2.31
EPS FULLY DILUTED	$1.29	$1.57	$1.76	$1.95	$2.12	$2.31
DPS NO STK DIV	$0.60	$0.62	$0.64	$0.66	$0.68	$0.70
DPS WITH STK DIV	$0.60	$0.60	$0.60	$0.60	$0.60	$0.60
VAL/SHR NO STK DIV		$28.71	$37.62	$39.47	$41.42	$43.47
VCL/SHR INC STK DIV		$27.87	$35.46	$36.12	$36.80	$37.50
# SHARES NO STK DIV	50.0	50.0	50.0	50.0	50.0	50.0
# SHARES INC STK DIV	50.0	51.5	53.0	54.6	56.3	58.0
COST OF EQUITY			33.9%	6.7%	6.7%	6.7%
ROI	25 %	25 %	25 %	25 %	25 %	25 %
TAX VAL NET FIX ASS	$700	$766	$847	$942	$1,030	$1,111
EPS GROWTH RATE		21.9%	11.9%	10.7%	9.0%	8.8%
DPS GROWTH RATE		0.0%	0.0%	0.0%	0.0%	0.0%

IV. Conclusion

A.   Practical experience with our financial planning model thus far suggests that, aside from convenience, the following major benefits are available to a degree not possible with the other approaches to financial planning discussed earlier.

Major prospective changes in the environment have a nasty way of impinging on both sides of the balance sheet, on the income statement, and on the legal obligations of the firm. Mergers are of course the most obvious example. The effects are thus complex and can only be evaluated by tools which preserve all of the ramifications. Budget compilers and rules of thumb do not meet the test. We have found our model to be a very powerful analytical device for evaluating such complex "what ifs?" while at the same time employing a fair proportion of contemporary finance theory.

The strategy of building around the needs of the ultimate user -- the top management financial planning group -- yields handsome payoffs. Because of the perceived complexity of financial choices, there is often a tendency for major financial policies to remain unquestioned and to be defended mostly by executive rhetoric. We have found our user-oriented model to be useful for the probing of simultaneous changes in policies. Computer experiments are, after all, cheaper than real world experiments. One of the most valuable results of our model's use is the occasional finding that, whatever overall corporate objective is employed, *no* plan is feasible. Nothing is more distressing than the realization that an asset expansion plan and EPS growth requirement which look reasonable for a couple of years into the future may entail a financial condition still later which will require the rewriting of a loan agreement under distress.

B.   We do not claim to have resolved all of the difficulties that seem to have caused the gap between finance modeling practice and theory. Our efforts should be regarded as suggestive. On the other hand, our description and interpretation of the gap do contain some implications for research strategy, which gives us the opportunity to close on an appropriately exhortative note for academic readers of this journal. First, we note that theoretical models of financial decision making which have been put forward by those of us primarily located in academia represent a sequential development in economic thought in which prior understandings are replaced over time by newer understandings. Moreover, this process is likely to continue indefinitely, which should caution us to humility as we promote today's finance theory wares in the arena of corporate practice. Secondly, in our judgment, corporate practice is at a most receptive stage for incorporating the theoretical insights of academic research if they seem reasonable viewed from a perspective broader than that of economics alone. Given the promise of this receptiveness, it seems to us that research into the structure of corporate financial decision making, even in a formally normative setting, is well-served by attention to behavioral realities if its ultimate *raison d'etre* is improvement of actual corporate practice.

REFERENCES

[1] Carleton, W. "Asset Management: The Decisions of Portfolio Management." Unpublished paper given at meetings of the Institute for Quantitative Research in Finance, Hanover, New Hampshire, October 1971.

[2] _____. "An Analytical Model for Long Range Financial Planning." *Journal of Finance*, May 1970, pp. 291-315.

[3] Chervany, N.; S. Strom; and R. Boehlke. "An Operations Planning Model for the Northwestern National Bank." In *Corporate Simulation Models*, edited by A. N. Schreiber. Seattle, Wash.: University of Washington, 1970, pp. 208-263.

[4] Cohen, K., and F. Hammer. "Linear Programming and Optional Bank Asset Management Decisions." *Journal of Finance*, May 1967, pp. 147-165.

[5] Gershefski, G. "Building a Corporate Financial Model." *Harvard Business Review*, July-August 1969, pp. 61-72.

[6] Hall, W. "Strategic Planning Models -- Are Top Managers Really Finding Them Useful." *Journal of Business Policy*, 1973, pp. 33-42.

[7] Komar, R. "Developing a Liquidity Management Model." *Journal of Bank Research*, Spring 1971, pp. 38-53.

[8] Mao, J. *Quantitative Analysis of Financial Decisions*. New York: Macmillan, 1969.

[9] Warren, J., and J. Shelton. "A Simultaneous Equations Approach to Financial Planning." *Journal of Finance*, December 1971, pp. 1123-1142.

[10] Weingartner, H. M. "What Lies Ahead in Management Science and Operations Research in Finance in the Seventies." TIMS *Interfaces*, August 1971, pp. 5-12.

V. THE DYNAMICS OF FINANCIAL PLANNING

This paper introduces, develops and applies our analytical framework for corporate planning. The first part evaluates conventional accounting tools as measures of corporate performance. The second part is a thorough development of the analytical framework, and the third part focuses on real-world applications to dividend policy, financial reporting and acquisition analysis.

Financial planning should set reasonable goals that result in attainable market values for the ordinary shareholders. That is, goals should be defined in terms that relate directly to the concepts and parameters that investors believe are systematically important in evaluating management's performance. Hence, if management achieves its goals, a predictable market value for the firm's equity should result.

How effective is this corporate performance-market reaction link when conventional accounting tools are employed to formulate corporate objectives? Unfortunately, popular accounting measures, such as earnings per share *(eps)*, return on stockholders' equity *(r_e)* and the price/earnings multiple for the ordinary shares (PE), can easily distort desirable corporate strategy, thereby rendering financial planning useless and misleading and, very often, costly to the shareholders.

The major problem with conventional measures is that they fail to separate investment decision-making from financing policy. Consequently, poor investment opportunities (i.e. opportunities with low expected rates of return) may appear to be beneficial for the shareholders because a particular financing vehicle is employed to gear up the *eps* and *r_e*. Proper planning tools should evaluate investments on their own merits. The financing device should be relatively passive, because it is impossible to identify specific sources of funds with specific uses of funds.

The purposes of this paper are to investigate the shortcomings of the aforementioned tools — *eps, r_e* and PE — highlighting the problems with disguised examples that pinpoint the issues; present an alternative analytical framework that overcomes the problems; and, examine the implications for real-world decision-making. In particular, establishing corporate objectives, acquisition analysis, dividend policy and financial reporting are discussed in detail. Finally, the shortcomings of our approach are identified and areas for future research are suggested.

An underlying theme is that the high degree of association of conventional tools with stock prices is partly the cause of the steady state of misunderstanding in financial planning. Because this high degree of correlation is absent when the tools are employed in financial planning accounts for management's frequent rejection of desirable opportunities.

CONVENTIONAL ACCOUNTING TOOLS

The shortcomings of *eps, r_e* and PE can be identified if we examine their current use in setting corporate objectives and acquisition analysis.

Setting corporate objectives

Corporate goals should be formulated in a quantitative framework that relates directly to the price of the firm's ordinary shares. Therefore, fulfilling the objectives should result in a predictable market value.

Not long ago, we were asked to evaluate a company's goals which summarised the management's five-year plan. Briefly, the plan called for a 6% annual increase in *eps, r_e* of 12% and a target PE of fifteen.

To our amazement, we found that each of the first two goals could be achieved while shortchanging the ordinary shareholders. That is, the *eps* and *r_e* goals were attainable if the firm's expected rate of return on fixed capital (all interest-bearing debt and equity), *r*, was less than the return the stockholders could earn by investing their money elsewhere in portfolios of similar risk. Second, the PE goal of fifteen was inconsistent with other stated objectives. Even if the market's confidence about managerial capability and the future of the company's technology were as glamorous as IBM, its PE would not exceed thirteen! And, finally, we found that specific underlying assumptions were omitted from these quantitative measures and, hence, the operating officers in the company could easily be confused or misled in attempting to carry them out.

A closer look at the basis for our conclusions pinpoints the problems with *eps* and *r_e*. If a firm earned £1,000 all of which was reinvested earning a return of say, 12%, next year's earnings would be £1,120, the second year's earnings would be £1,254, and so on. That is, the earnings would grow at the same 12% as the rate of return on investment. The curious result was that the firm's management called for a rate of growth in earnings per share of 6% when the desirable rate of return was 12%. In other words, the implication must have been that the management was planning to pay out 50% of the company's earnings in the form of dividends to the shareholders. Only then would the earnings grow at a mere 6%. When we asked the management about the expected dividend payout, we were told that the dividend payout

600

would be far less than 50%! And, of course, the implication of this answer was that the first two goals were inconsistent with each other.

Furthermore, having specified the goals in terms of the shareholders' equity meant that they were attainable if only the debt ratio were manoeuvred and the rate of return on total investment — the debt *and* equity — exceeded the cost of the company's borrowed funds. For example, if the after-tax cost of debt were 4% and the after-tax return on total investment were 5% (which is probably far less than the return shareholders could hope to earn by investing elsewhere in alternative opportunities of similar risk), the earnings per share would rise and the rate of return on shareholders' equity could be altered simply by changing the capital structure — the proportion of debt as a source of funds. If a given capital structure were too low to achieve the 12% return on equity, management need only increase the degree of gearing by increasing the level of debt until 12% is attained. In other words, an underlying assumption must be made about the firm's target capital structure.

Without some specification of the firm's dividend policy and its target capital structure, the operating personnel could be confused in their attempt to achieve the firm's goals. As we shall see shortly, the use of an analytical framework for planning that is related closely to the market value of the firm would prohibit both the inevitable confusion and the costly mistakes of intuition and arbitrary goal setting.

Conventional acquisition analysis is a noteworthy example of the shortcomings of *eps* and PE as workable tools for managerial decision-making and setting corporate goals.

Acquisition analysis

Often we are told in business publications about the desirability of improving the firm's *eps* when the impact of an acquisition on the buyer's *eps* is entirely irrelevant. For example, company *A* may be about to acquire company *B*. *A* sells at a higher PE than the PE *A* is to offer *B*'s shareholders. *A* may sell at, say, twenty times earnings and offer *B*'s shareholders a PE of fifteen when *B* is selling at ten times earnings. If *A* buys *B* with an equity swap to form the new company *AB*, *AB*'s (the pro forma) *eps* will always exceed *A*'s *eps*. This is because *A* (i.e., the firm selling at the higher PE) is issuing fewer shares per pence of earnings acquired. Hence, we are told that *AB* is good for *A*'s shareholders.

The problem with this result is that we are told that *AB* is good for *A*'s shareholders because *AB*'s *eps* exceeds *A*'s *eps*. And, of course, this occurs even if there are no operating savings. This logic is erroneous. *B* appears

to be a desirable acquisition not because of its value to *A*, but because of *A*'s higher PE before the acquisition. The business writer fails to realise that were *A* to acquire any firm for which it paid full value (i.e. there is no added benefit to the buyer's shareholders), its PE would fall to offset the gain in *eps*.

Let us turn the example around. If *B* buys *A* to form *BA*, the firm selling at the lower PE (ten) is buying a company at a price greater than its own PE. *B* will pay at least *A*'s PE of twenty. But now *BA*'s (pro forma) *eps* will be less than *B*'s, because the firm with the lower PE must offer more shares per pence of acquired earnings. The same people who tell us that *AB* is good for *A*'s shareholders tell us that *BA* is bad for *B*'s shareholders even though *AB* and *BA* are the same company, most often with the same assets and earnings expectations and, even, the same management.

'The *AB-BA* fallacy' is that the analyst believes the pro forma *eps* is a proximate determinant of the pro forma share price, when the pro forma *eps* is in no way related to the pro forma share price. It is emphasising *eps* when *eps* is irrelevant and misleading, and usually results in costly decisions by management. Failing to evaluate the acquisition with a tool that is systematically related to the firm's market value is the cause of the confusion. For example, the president of a company recently mentioned to us that in 1955 his company was a small machine tool manufacturer selling at about ten times earnings. Therefore, he concluded that he could only acquire companies selling at PE's of ten or less. Otherwise he would dilute the *eps* and stockholders' equity of his firm (whatever that might mean). In the earlier example, this was company *B* and any firm selling above a PE of ten was company *A*. Since the president of the small machine tool company did not want to 'dilute' his *eps*, he chose to acquire companies whose PE did not exceed his PE of ten: mostly other machine tool companies. These acquisitions did nothing to reduce the amplitudes of the cyclical swings in sales and profits. And, as we might expect, his company continues to sell at about 10 times earnings.

Another example extends 'the *AB-BA* fallacy' to capital structure planning. The president of a well diversified manufacturer selling at sixteen times earnings wanted to acquire a small, but exceptionally profitable, engineering consulting firm selling for a PE of twenty-five. An equity swap would 'dilute' the pro forma *eps*. Facetiously, we suggested that he sell his company to the engineering firm, even though the latter was only about 10% as large as the manufacturer. Company *A* would be acquiring *B*, rather than the reverse, and the pro forma *eps* would rise. He suggested an alternative: finance the acquisition with a vehicle that would gear up the pro forma *eps*. The anticipated profits from the acquisition would more than cover the out-of-pocket cost of interest on debt, or dividends on preference shares. He was right; the pro forma *eps* would rise.

However there is a conceptual problem with this solution. The pro forma *eps* (and r_e) can be enhanced simply by gearing the firm with debt or preference shares. Thus, employing an *eps* criterion, bad investments can appear to be good investments because the management can gear the firm and increase the *eps* at the time the investment is undertaken. Furthermore, in the United States, for example, the management can increase the *eps* without making any investment by borrowing to retire ordinary shares.

ANALYTICAL FRAMEWORK

It is because of the shortcomings of conventional measures employed in financial planning that we suggest an alternative approach: an analytical framework which *(a)* measures attainable management goals, while *(b)* separating investment decision-making from financing policy, that *(c)* permits management to test the sensitivity of input assumptions and, perhaps most important, *(d)* sim-

ulates the impact of financial plans on the market value of the firm's ordinary shares.

The procedure is to *(a)* introduce a diagram that describes the market's mechanism for valuation, *(b)* present the basic model for a taxless world in which there is no 'growth potential' (strictly defined), *(c)* relax these tax and growth assumptions and *(d)* apply the resulting model to financial planning — setting corporate goals, acquisition analysis, capital structure planning and dividend policy and financial reporting.

Diagrammatic description of the market mechanism

On the horizontal axis in Figure 1, *I* is incremental investment in the current year. It is net fixed capital additions: capital expenditures minus depreciation and other non-cash charges plus additions to working capital (net current assets) and other long-term assets, or, what amounts to the same thing, additions to total assets minus additions to current liabilities. (As we will demonstrate later, current liabilities are only non-interest-bearing items, such as accrued expenses and accounts payable. In the analytical framework, short-term interest-bearing debt, such as bank debt and the current portion of long-term debt, is considered to be part of the company's fixed capital.)

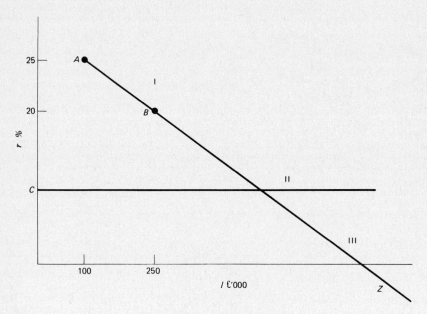

Figure 1   Investment and Return

602

On the vertical axis, we measure the expected rates of return on I and denote them with the symbol r. If the best investment is selected first and it has, say, an anticipated return of 25% for a £100,000 outlay, the point A represents the project. If the next best investment of £150,000 has an anticipated return of 20%, it may be represented by point B. Note that the horizontal axis measures total investment and, hence, project B is matched up with the total projects A and B, £250,000.

The schedule may continue all the way down to 0% and cross the horizontal axis at the point Z. Projects with expected negative rates of return, cannot be relevant. The question we must ask is how far down the schedule can management proceed before they begin to shortchange their shareholders? The answer is that there is some hurdle or cut-off rate below which the management cannot, or should not, undertake investment because the shareholders can take their money and invest it in alternative securities of similar risk earning this hurdle rate.

This cut-off rate is popularly known as the cost of capital (c) because it represents the cost to the ordinary shareholders of foregoing alternative available opportunities for investment. It is the rate of return that could be expected elsewhere on identically-risky investments. Although there may not be a perfect substitute for the shareholders' investment in the firm, there is some combination of other investments that will offer the same expected risk-return trade-off.

Hence, *the cost of capital is the minimum rate of return (c) that must be expected by management on new investments in order to compensate the shareholders for the business or asset risk they undertake by investing in the firm's ordinary shares, because the shareholders have alternative, identically-risky opportunities elsewhere.*

The diagram can be especially valuable in specifying the reasons why some firms sell at higher prices than others. If the expected rate of return (r) on new investment exceeds the rate of return the shareholders can otherwise expect by investing elsewhere (c), management can outperform the market (group I projects in the diagram). Consequently, the market will pay a premium for an ability it cannot duplicate: the market value will exceed the economic book value. And the wider the spread between r and c, the greater the price and PE will be. Group I is the case of 'growth potential.'

When the management cannot outperform the market, r and c will be identical. These are the group II projects, the absence of growth potential: the market value and economic book value will be the same because management possesses no unusual ability to outperform the market. Of course, if r is less than c, management will be shortchanging the shareholders. These are the group

III projects. The greater the investments in this area, the greater will be the discount of the firm's market value from its economic book value.

Analytical framework in a taxless world with no growth

We can describe a firm's market value for the simple case, in which there are no corporate income taxes and no growth potential — group II for which $r = c$.

The procedure for developing the simple model is to examine a single investment opportunity, an outlay (I) of £10,000 that is expected to generate net operating profit (NOP) of £1,000 annually, an anticipated rate of return (r) of 10% equal to c:[1,2]

$$r = \frac{NOP}{I} \tag{1}$$

We can substitute the symbol V for I, where V is the market value of the interest-bearing debt and/or ordinary shares issued to finance I, and since $r = c$ for this group II investment, Expression (1) becomes:

$$c = \frac{NOP}{V} \tag{2}$$

which implies that c is the rate that discounts or capitalises the expected stream of net operating profit back to the current market value of the firm. Rearranging the terms, the firm's market value is described in terms of two parameters, NOP and c, in the simplified taxless world in which there is no growth:

$$V \equiv D + E = \frac{NOP}{c} \tag{3}$$

where D is the value of all interest-bearing debt and E is the value of all the ordinary shares.

Expression (3) is the *fundamental principle of valuation: the market value of the firm's debt and equity is equal to the anticipated net operating profit discounted at the rate c that is a rate of return to compensate for the business risk inherent in the assets generating the profits (NOP).*

Analytical framework in a taxable world with no growth

In the world of corporate income taxes, there are two components: (a) the anticipated net operating profit after taxes capitalised at an after-tax rate of discount and (b) the capitalised tax saving that arises from the deductibility of interest expense in calculating the firm's taxable income.

The capitalised profits component is $NOPAT/c_t$, where NOPAT is the expected net operating profit after taxes, and c_t is the hurdle rate for business risk in a taxable world. NOPAT is expected profits before financing costs but after taxes. Since NOP was defined in an accounting sense as net profit NP plus interest expense, NOPAT is the expected net profit after taxes, NPAT, plus interest expense after taxes. If b is the cost of borrowed capital and D is the amount of borrowed capital, bD is the interest expense and $(1 - t) bD$ is the after-tax interest expense, where t is the marginal corporate income tax rate. Hence, $NOP = NP + bD$ and $NOPAT = NPAT + (1 - t) bD$.

Since interest expense is tax deductible, it pays to employ borrowed capital. If $(1 - t) bD$ is the after-tax cost of debt, the annual expected government tax saving is the marginal corporate income tax multiplied by the pre-tax interest expense: tbD.

If the firm has a target, or long run expected, capital structure,[3] the market will capitalise the annual government tax saving as if it were available in perpetuity because the shareholders will expect outstanding debt to be refinanced as it comes due. Therefore, the firm's market value will include not only the capitalised anticipated profits, $NOPAT/c_t$, but the capitalised tax saving as well, which is tbD divided by a rate that measures the risk inherent in the source of tbD.

NOPAT is capitalised at the rate c_t because c_t measures the risk in I that generates NOPAT. The annual tax saving, tbD, is more certain than NOPAT; that is, the expected rate of return before corporate income taxes on the firm's total fixed capital need only be equal to the rate of interest on borrowed capital for the firm to obtain the tax saving. On new investment, r need only be equal to b to obtain the tax saving, which is much less than c_t and, hence, tbD is a more certain stream than NOPAT. The discount rate that measures the uncertainty in receiving the annual expected tax saving is identical with the discount rate bondholders employ to measure the uncertainty attached to receiving their interest income (bD): the rate of interest on debt itself, b.

Therefore, the total market value of the firm in the real world of taxes (but retaining the assumption about the absence of growth potential) becomes:

$$V \equiv D + E = \frac{NOPAT}{c_t} + \frac{tbD}{b}$$

$$= \frac{NOPAT}{c_t} + tD \qquad (4)$$

Three observations are especially useful for financial planning:

1. Within 'prudent limits,' incremental debt financing will add to the firm's market value: If the mar-
ginal corporate income tax rate is 40%, the total market value (V) and the market value of the ordinary shares (E) will increase 40 pence for each pound's increase in the target capital structure's level of debt.

2. Preference shares never 'add value' to the firm's market value, because the dividends are not tax deductible and, hence, provide no tax saving.

3. Maximising the firm's market value and its PE are incompatible. Debt will add to the firm's market value, but it will also drive down the PE. Therefore, corporate goals should never be stated in terms of maximising PE for non-growth firms.

If we introduce an arithmetic example, each of these observations will become clear. Consider the following values for each of the parameters:

$$NOPAT = £1,000$$
$$c_t = 10\%$$
$$t = 40\%$$

Hence, V is £10,000 if the firm is debt-free:

$$V \equiv D + E = \frac{NOPAT}{c_t} + tD$$

$$= \frac{1.000}{0.10} + 0.40 (0) = 10,000$$

If the firm issues £5,000 of debt to retire £5,000 of equity,[4] we might expect the total market value to remain unchanged, since holding the asset size and, hence, NOPAT unchanged means that only the sources of financing are altered. But in the real-world of taxes, the capitalised tax saving adds $tD = £2,000$ to the market value. The new total market value is £12,000 and the equity's market value increases to £7,000 $(= V - D)$ on half as many outstanding shares.

In the absence of the tax saving, the equity market value would have been £5,000. The conclusion is that it pays to borrow because of the deductibility of interest expense in calculating the firm's taxable income. The market value of the firm's equity will increase 40 pence for each £1 increase in debt. But debt ratios will be limited, in part, by lenders' risk preferences. Additions to the debt ratio beyond the lenders' expectation of 'prudent limits' will result in cumbersome restrictions in loan agreements and bond indentures on management's operating flexibility. Hence, in the real-world, the apparently unlimited benefits of increasing debt ratios will be modified by management's desire to remain 'bankable' or 'institutionable.'

Although the value of the ordinary shares rises with increases in the debt ratio, the PE falls; that is, the price per share increases but the *eps* rises even faster.[5] First, we will examine this effect in our example by calculating the PE before and after gearing. Second, we will explain its intuitive support.

The PE is the price per share divided by the *eps* or, what amounts to the same thing, the total market value of the ordinary shares divided by the net profit after taxes (NPAT): PE = E/NPAT.

In the debt-free situation, E was ₤10,000, which was the total market value of the firm, V, as well. Since debt was absent, NOPAT and NPAT were identical, ₤1,000. Hence, the PE was 10:

$$PE = \frac{E}{NPAT} = \frac{10,000}{1,000} = 10$$

When gearing was introduced, E was ₤7,000 on half as many shares. NPAT was NOPAT (₤1,000) minus the after-tax interest expense, $(1 - t)bD$, which was $(1 - 0.40)$ (0.06) $(5,000)$, or ₤180. Therefore, NPAT was $1,000 - 180$, or ₤820, and the PE was approximately 8½:

$$PE = \frac{E}{NPAT} = \frac{7,000}{820} = 8.55$$

The intuitive support for the decline in the PE is also straightforward. In the absence of debt, the ordinary shareholder need be concerned only with the business risk of the firm's assets that generate NOPAT. When debt is introduced as a source of funds, financial risk is added in the form of an additional fixed cost, the interest expense. Hence, the additional return in *eps* that accrues to the shareholders is not as valuable as in the debt-free case. Gearing from financing has been added to operating leverage (i.e. employing assets with fixed operating costs). In the absence of the government subsidy for debt, there would be no reason for the price of the equity to increase. The larger return on net worth and *eps* would be offset completely by the greater financial risk, the price of the shares remaining unchanged. The meaning of the government subsidy for debt is that the government bears a portion of the financial risk (i.e. tbD), the benefit of which accrues directly to the ordinary shareholders.

If we extend this reasoning to preference shares, it is clear that a firm's PE is lower when preference shares are employed instead of debt. Since preference shares' cash dividends are not tax deductible for corporations, there is no tax saving. That is, the ordinary shareholders bear the complete financial risk of the incremental fixed expense of the dividends. Even though preference shares provide gearing and, hence, greater *eps*, the price of the ordinary

shares remains the same. Since employing debt increases the price of the ordinary shares, the PE will not fall as much as when preference shares are used as a source of funds.

Share price maximisation, which is always a desirable goal, is incompatible with PE maximisation. Although gearing always reduces the PE, within prudent limits, debt always increases the ordinary share price. Thus, we can conclude that PE maximisation should never be a corporate goal in this taxable but non-growth world.

The tax subsidy for debt appears to have been a major factor in the conglomerate movement in the United States. In most cases, their managements sought overcapitalised companies for takeover. Even without improved profitability (i.e. return on fixed capital), premiums above the sellers' market values could be justified. For example, a well-known debt-free company with 10 million shares outstanding and a market value of $50 for a total value of $500 million could have sufficient profitability to service, say, $300 million of interest-bearing debt. Thus, the conglomerate could offer a premium above the current market value at least equal to the tax saving, tD, which is about $150 million in the US where the marginal corporate income tax rate is close to 50%. This is $15 a share. That is, the buyer could offer up to $65 a share simply by altering the expected debt ratio. Since the buyer probably would not have to offer a 30% premium ($15 on the current price of $50), its return, r, would exceed c — the difference between the offering price and the maximum offering price — and this difference would accrue to the conglomerate's share price and shareholders.

Analytical framework in a taxable world with growth

The final development of the analytical framework is the relaxation of the assumption that growth is absent. This is the case of group I projects in Figure 1 in which r_i (the expected rate of return after taxes) exceeds c_i. However, it is insufficient to describe growth as the difference, $r_i - c_i$, because r_i and c_i are expressed as percentages such as 20 and 10%, respectively, whereas V, D, and E are expressed in pounds. The important considerations are not only $r_i - c_i$, but the amount of net fixed capital additions, I, that is expected to earn r_i and the length of time in years for which r_i is expected to exceed c_i.

For example, consider the simple case in which the firm reinvests all of its earnings (i.e. I = NOPAT). If NOPAT = I = ₤1,000, $r_i = 0.20$, and $c_i = 0.10$, investors will expect next year's NOPAT to be 20% greater than the current ₤1,000, or ₤1,200. Two years hence NOPAT will be expected to be ₤1,440, three years hence ₤1,728, and so on.[6]

If investors were given each year's earnings which they invested elsewhere with the expectation that they would earn 10% annually, their wealth would be expected to grow at the annual rate of 10% to £1,100 next year, £1,210 two years hence, £1,331 three years hence, and so on.

If we compare these two expected streams the concept of growth becomes clear.

Expected Rates of Return	Amount Invested Today	Year 1	Year 2	Year 3
By Management: $r_t = 0.20$	£1,000	£1,200	£1,440	£1,728
By Investors: $c_t = 0.10$	£1,000	£1,100	£1,210	£1,331
Difference Between Management's and Investors' Expected Returns		£100	£230	£397

From the table we can see that growth is the difference between the investors' expected future corporate profits and their expected future wealth for as long as the market's investors have confidence that the unusual opportunities will continue, namely, r_t will exceed c_t.

$I(r_t - c_t)$, the discounted value of which would be $I(r_t - c_t)/c_t$ beginning today and continuing forever, is somewhat analogous to the non-growth component, NOPAT/c_t. However, r_t cannot exceed c_t forever because the discounted value of the growth potential would be infinite. Considering the likelihood of only a finite time horizon presents an extremely complex expression that can be simplified if the fraction $[1 + (Ir_t/\text{NOPAT})]/(1 + c_t)$ is close to 1 and if the finite time horizon for which r_t is expected to exceed c_t is not too large.[7] This simplified expression is $(r_t - c_t)IT/[c_t(1 + c_t)]$, where $c_t(1 + c_t)$ is a discounting mechanism for the unusual opportunities (i.e. r_t exceeding c_t) for their expected life, T years.

The analytical framework in its entirety contains three components of capitalised values — group II projects, NOPAT/c_t, the tax saving, tD; and, group I projects, $(r_t - c_t)IT/[c_t(1 + c_t)]$.

$$V \equiv D + E = \frac{\text{NOPAT}}{c_t} + tD + \frac{r_t - c_t}{c_t(1 + c_t)} IT \qquad (5)$$

Subsequent to a correction in this model that was omitted in order to simplify the exposition, we will examine the implications for setting corporate goals, dividend policy, financial reporting and acquisition analysis.

Alternatively, the expression may be shown with the tax saving impounded into c_t; that is, the less expensive nature of debt need not be shown separately as tD.

Synthesised with c_t, the tax saving would appear to disappear in favour of an after-tax weighted average cost of capital, c_t^*, the costs of debt and equity weighted by the proportions of debt and equity in the firm's target or long-run expected capital structure:

$$V \equiv D + E = \frac{\text{NOPAT}}{c_t^*} \qquad (6)$$

Returning briefly to our earlier arithmetic example, expression (4) yielded $V = 12,000$.

Employing expression (6), we can calculate the weighted average cost of capital by 'solving' for c_t^* to obtain $c_t^* = 0.0833$.[8]

If we were to rewrite the entire analytical framework in terms of c_t^*, the omission in the development of the growth term should become clear:

$$V \equiv D + E = \frac{\text{NOPAT}}{c_t^*} + IT \cdot \frac{r_t - c_t^*}{c_t^*(1 + c_t^*)} \qquad (7)$$

Note that the tax saving component, tD, is absent because it is impounded into the first term. Including it as the second term as we did in the earlier version, expression (5), would be double counting. More significant is the substitution of c_t^* for c_t in the growth term. Earlier, we had failed to note that the non-growth component was not NOPAT/c_t alone, but NOPAT/$c_t + tD$ or, what amounts to the same thing, NOPAT/c_t^*. Furthermore, it is clear that the presence of growth does not necessarily alter the market's discount rate, c_t^*. To demonstrate both the use of c_t and c_t^*, we can describe the analytical framework as

$$V \equiv D + E = \frac{\text{NOPAT}}{c_t} + tD + IT \frac{r_t - c_t^*}{c_t^*(1 + c_t^*)} \qquad (8)$$

The importance of this 'correction' for financial planning can be seen when we examine the implications of the analytical framework for setting proper corporate objectives in the next section.

APPLICATIONS OF THE ANALYTICAL FRAMEWORK FOR DECISION-MAKING

Virtually all important issues in financial planning can (and should be) evaluated within the analytical framework — issues that involve:

1. Setting corporate objectives

2. Investment decisions, including capital equipment analysis and acquisition pricing

606

3. Financing policy (i.e. capital structure planning), including selecting an appropriate dividend policy, refunding existing debt, lease financing, captive finance companies, convertible securities

4. Financial reporting

Space limitations permit investigating the implications of the methodology for only four issues in this section: setting corporate objectives and dividend policy, financial reporting and acquisition analysis.

Setting corporate objectives

The analytical framework is a description of the interrelationships of parameters that systematically determine the market prices of firms. Consequently, achievable corporate goals expressed in terms contained in the model should result in attainable market values.

Given the empirically measurable hurdle rate for asset risk, c_t, and the confidence (T years) market investors have in management's ability to outperform the weighted average cost of capital c_t^*, management's overriding objective should be to undertake investment opportunities on which they expect to earn a return that is at least sufficient to cover the risk: r_t must be at least as large as c_t^*. Therefore, corporate objectives should be stated in terms of r_t and c_t^*. That is, management should first evaluate alternative investment opportunities as probabilistic cash flows to determine both r_t and c_t and, given management's and lenders' risk preferences and, hence, the target debt ratio, calculate c_t^*. Thus, management's goals should describe the latitude of acceptable projects, including product mix, size, location, and expected and acceptable profitability. Calculations of profitability should be in terms of expected future cash flows — NOPAT minus I. Finally, the firm's over-all desired capital structure must be determined in order to calculate c_t^*.[9][10]

Therefore, financial planning should concentrate on the parameters in the framework that management can influence or control — NOPAT, tD, I and r_t.

It is noteworthy that a target PE is *not* included as a goal. Not only does the firm's expected market value and, thus, the PE result from the aforementioned statement of goals, but it is not entirely clear that share price and PE move in the same direction if management's policies are attained. Earlier, in Section 2-2, we illustrated the relationship of share price and PE maximisation for the taxable, but non-growth case: within prudent limits, increases in the firm's debt ratio increase its share price but decrease its PE, as financial risk is added to the business risk borne by the ordinary shareholders.[11] An examination of the taxable world with growth concludes that share price and PE maximisation may, and very often will, be compatible goals. But since they are not always compatible, it can be dangerous for management to have its objectives include maximising the PE, which is a price-relative, rather than maximising share price, which is a price-absolute.

In the case of growth, adding to the target debt ratio decreases c_t^* in the growth term as well as in the non-growth term (the latter being tD). Consequently, the numerator of the growth term increases as the spread between r_t and c_t^* increases, recalling that r_t is independent of financing: it is the expected rate of return before financing charges as a fraction of the incremental fixed capital (interest-bearing debt and equity) employed. Furthermore, the denominator declines in magnitude as the debt ratio increases because c_t^* is less than c_t. Thus, $(r_t - c_t^*)/c_t^*(1 + c_t^*)$ is always greater than $(r_t - c_t)/c_t(1 + c_t)$, if debt is employed and if the debt ratio is not excessive.

If I and T are large enough, the increase in the size of the growth term, arising from an increase in the target debt ratio, will overcome the added financial risk of gearing.[12] Thus, both the share price and PE will rise as the expected debt ratio increases.

Dividend policy

The only financing policy that alters a firm's market value is a change in the target debt ratio, because the expected tax subsidy changes. Expression (8) is completely independent of dividend policy, because the firm's investment decision-making is not dependent on its dividend policy. Earnings retained for reinvestment are essentially a compulsory, pre-emptive rights offering. As long as management acts in the shareholders' best interest by undertaking projects with expected rates of return at least as large as the hurdle rate $(r_t \geq c_t^*)$, the dividend policy determines only the form that the shareholders' expected return will take — dividends and/or capital appreciation. This conclusion should be modified for tax considerations.

If there were no income taxes and no costs of buying and selling securities, the proper dividend policy would be to pay out nothing to the ordinary shareholders, provided management has ample group I projects $(r_t \geq c_t^*)$ in which to invest the earnings. In this hypothetical world, investors could sell shares to obtain cash for other purposes. If group II projects $(r_t = c_t^*)$ are expected, management can be indifferent between reinvestment and dividend payout, whereas group III projects $(r_t \leq c_t^*)$ imply liquidation.

In the real world of both taxes and transaction costs, a large number of investors prefer cash dividends because they pay little or no taxes on ordinary income. For others in high income tax brackets, little or no cash dividends are preferable because the costs of capital gains taxes and selling securities are far less than the tax on ordinary income. Consequently, an interesting and nontrivial phenomenon occurs when a firm sells ordinary shares to the public for the first time. A clientele effect builds up as investors with particular needs are attracted to the company for, among other reasons, the tax consequences of the dividend policy.

Therefore, if management's objective is to act in the best interest of its shareholders, it should never alter the fraction of expected earnings to be paid out as cash dividends. The dividend payout ratio (i.e. dividend as a percentage of earnings) should be maintained in order that the return expected by the shareholders from dividends remains a fixed percentage of the total return they expect on average and over time from dividends and capital appreciation. This will occur as long as the average PE does not change significantly over time. Changing the payout ratio would compel the ordinary shareholders to alter their investment portfolios in order to maintain their greatest after-tax return. Even unexpectedly large group I opportunities do not alter our conclusion. Shareholders would prefer the dividend payout and periodic issues of equity.

Financial reporting

The analytical framework underlying expression (8) implies that financial reporting should be an integral part of corporate planning. Expression (8) presents six parameters that should account for systematic market valuation. If management can influence the parameters significantly, changes in policy that affect these parameters should be reported because markets pay a discount for uncertainty, not a premium.

Two parameters are exogenous to the firm $(c_t$ and $T)$ in that they are determined subjectively and almost exclusively by market investors. Thus, c_t, which is the market's required rate of return for business risk, is a function of the firm's expected asset composition, but it is the market's risk evaluation that matters. Consequently, management influences c_t only by selecting the nature of the firm's assets. T is a measure of the market's confidence that r_t will exceed c_t^*. T is a function of product cyclicality, the state of monetary policy, and the degree of government regulation and product technology. Again, given the firm's expected asset composition, the market determines T. Therefore, planned changes by management of the asset composition should be reported to the market. This includes industry and geographical distribution.

The remaining four parameters can be influenced significantly by the management: 'normalised' net operating

profits, the target capital structure, capital spending forecasts, and the historical annual rate of internal growth in NOPAT.

'Normalised' net operating profits. Reported profits include the impact of non-recurring factors, such as strikes, other interruptions in operations and windfall gains. The chief executive officer in his letter to the shareholders should elaborate on the nature and extent of abnormal episodes that affected reported net operating profits.

We select net operating profits (profits before interest expense and income taxes) because it is a measure of management's investment performance. It is independent of financing policy (which is discussed below) and changes in the firm's required tax burden. Interest rate fluctuations and tax statutes are not influenced significantly (if at all) by individual managers and, hence, should not be included in a measure of management's performance.

Target capital structure. Within wide bounds, management controls the firm's capital structure. Within prudent limits set by lenders' and management's risk preferences, the proportions of debt and equity can be established by the management. The debt limitations depend on the degree of protection the assets afford lenders and the amount of earnings anticipated to be available to repay interest and principal.

The sources of funds are important to investors only as a result of the corporate tax structure. The second component of expression (8), tD, and the decline of c_t to c_t^* in the third component means that debt financing can increase both the share price and the PE. But communication of the target capital structure can be an important prerequisite.

At a minimum, the aggregate market values of the ordinary shares increases 40 pence for each £1 of incremental interest-bearing debt when the marginal corporate income tax rate is 40%. This is the impact of the second component. Thus, two non-growth firms, say companies X and Y, with identical assets and earnings expectations that differ only in their expected sources of financing can have considerably different market values. If X borrows £10 million but Y is debt-free, the market value of X's ordinary shares will be at least £4 million greater than the market value of Y's ordinary shares. The significance of expression (8), especially the importance of investor expectations rather than current amounts, is that Y can become X immediately simply by announcing a change in its financing policy. The market will not delay in bestowing the benefit of the expected tax saving on the company's ordinary shares.

Thus, management should convey its target debt ratio to the market: the fraction of fixed capital (total assets minus non-interest-bearing current liabilities) that it expects to finance with interest-bearing debt on average and over time, especially if (1) the target capital structure differs from the current capital structure and/or (2) the company's debt ratio has fluctuated widely in the past.

Capital spending forecasts. Capital spending is defined as additions to fixed capital (i.e. incremental total assets minus non-interest-bearing current liabilities). This incremental investment *(I)* is important to investors because it conveys management's forecast of future profits better than almost any other information. Since rates of return on fixed capital do not change much on average and over time, and since the rate of return multiplied by the amount of fixed capital is equal to the level of net operating profit, a forecast of anticipated incremental investment tells investors half of what they need to know in order to calculate future profits. Investors will then be able to spend their time estimating the remaining unknown: the expected rate of return on fixed capital.

Rate of internal growth. Although rates of return on fixed capital (i.e. NOPAT/A_F) do not change much on average and over time, considerable confusion can occur in its calculation when employing published financial data. It is caused by the effects of acquisitions. Unfortunately, current accounting conventions can be extremely misleading. Because of this problem, we suggest that all companies include a statement about, and even the calculation of, the rate of internal growth in net operating profits in their annual reports and in presentations to investment analysts. This rate of growth is a measure of management's investment performance from the time they have had control of the firm's assets.

The measure can facilitate the market's estimate of the expected rate of return on new investment, r_t. The product of the actual rate of return on fixed capital and historical additions to fixed capital (historical *I*) is equal to the historical rate of internal growth in NOPAT. Historical financial reports tell us about the historical *I*. Hence, reporting the rate of internal growth in net operating profits will convey the historical rate of return on fixed capital. And since rates of return on fixed capital do not change much over time, the market will know much about r_t.

An examination of the effects of acquisitions on reporting describes the potential confusion of existing reporting techniques. When acquisitions have a significant impact on a company's financial reporting, announced (explicit) growth can differ substantially from internal (real) growth. Pooling of interests accounting rules permit a seller's historical performance to be added to the buyer's profitability, even though the buyer was in no way responsible for it. Thus, for a company on a calendar year basis, an acquisition made on, say, 1 November 1970 can be reported as if it occurred on 1 January 1970. 'Purchase' accounting would include only the profits of the acquired company for November and December in 1970's combined report and thereafter profits for the entire year. This seems to be fair, but 1971's reporting will, in effect, compare the acquired company's twelve months' performance with 1970's last two months. This could cause quite an economic distortion of the buying management's ability.

A clearer method of reporting calculates the rate of growth in profits from the time the buyer's management has control of the acquired assets. This is the rate of internal growth. Under this method, the 1969 report of the buyer would have been restated to include the earnings of the acquired company for November and December 1969. This would place the 1969 and 1970 figures on a comparable basis. Then in 1971's report, when earnings of the acquired company are automatically included for the entire year, the 1970 figures would be restated to include the profits of the acquired company for the entire year of 1970. This suggestion eliminates distortions created by 'adding profits' for which the buyer's management is hardly responsible.

Acquisition analysis[14]

Evaluating prospective acquisitions can be accomplished within the framework of expression (8). Employing our analytical framework offers three important advantages that are absent in the aforementioned traditional tools (2-1). First, our methodology *separates investment decision-making from financing policy*, which prevents analysts from falling into 'the *AB-BA* fallacy' as well as believing that specific sources of funds can be identified with specific uses of funds. Second, we can test the sensitivity of assumptions by varying estimates of the parameters. Third, management can simulate the impact of its assumptions on the pro forma price of its firm's ordinary shares.

Pricing an acquisition requires the buyer to substitute his estimates of the parameters contained in expression (8). The result is the value he attaches to the seller or, what amounts to the same thing, it is the maximum price he can afford to pay for the seller. At this price, $r_t = c_t^*$. Thus, if he can negotiate a lower price, r_t will exceed c_t^*. The difference between the price he pays and the maximum permissible price he can offer is the added market value for the buyer's firm.

There are only three bases for a buyer to offer a greater price than the seller's current market value: *(a)* operating savings, which improve NOPAT and r_t; (b) financial savings that result from buying an overcapitalised firm and increasing the pro forma target debt ratio (increasing tD and reducing c_t^*); and (c) portfolio or risk savings, which means that the pro forma asset risk is reduced, for example, by combining contra-cyclical products (e.g. a baby foods company and a 'pill' manufacturer) or changing the pro forma liquidity (reducing c_t).[14]

CONCLUSIONS

The analytical framework can be applied to conceptual problems as well as to answer specific questions. Conceptually, we have shown that management can employ the methodology to set realistic corporate objectives, to formulate an 'optimal' dividend policy, to select issues for emphasis in financial reporting and to evaluate prospective acquisitions.

The conceptual advantage of the analytical framework is that investment decisions are examined independently of financing policy. Consequently, management avoids the problems of identifying specific sources of funds with specific uses of funds. Employing our methodology, management can never fall into 'the $AB-BA$ fallacy.'

Specifically, management can test the sensitivity of inputs to the decision-making process and simulate the impact of its plans on the price of the company's ordinary shares. A timely implication is that earnings per share need not (and should not) be required reporting for companies in spite of recent interest in the concept by accountants in the United Kingdom.

The most important limitations of our approach are not conceptual in nature. Rather it is in specifying measures for c_t and T for various industry groups and for predicting the impact of diversification on these parameters. However, this problem is greater for investment analysts than for management. Although techniques are available for analysts to approximate c_t — by utilising the tools of portfolio theory to estimate beta-values — management can employ the same techniques to examine the economic profitability of alternative courses of action, thereby being a step ahead of the analysts. That is, management can analyse the implications of achieving various plans by simulating the firm's resulting market value.

APPENDIX

In the taxable world with growth, the reciprocal of the PE, Y_t (described in footnote 11), is no longer the cost of ordinary equity capital. But it can be utilised to describe the conditions for which the increase in growth potential offset the financial risk and, hence, result in compatibility of share price and PE maximisation.

In the taxable world with debt and growth, the market value of the firm is:

$$V \equiv D + E = \frac{\text{NOPAT}}{c_t} + tD + G^*,\qquad(A\text{-}1)$$

where G^* is $\dfrac{r_t - c_t^*}{c_t^*(1 + c_t^*)}\ IT$

With growth alone, debt being absent, the market value is

$$V \equiv E_A = \frac{\text{NPAT}}{c_t} + G,\qquad(B\text{-}1)$$

where E_A is the market value of the equity (which on a per share basis is less than E) and G is

$$\frac{r_t - c_t}{c_t(1 + c_t)}\ IT$$

Solving for NOPAT in (A-1), we obtain

$$NOPAT = c_t(D + E - tD - G^*)\qquad(A\text{-}2)$$

The reciprocal of the PE, Y_t, is NPAT/E, which is [NOPAT $-$ $(1 - t)bD]/E$, and substituting (A-2) for NOPAT, the expression for Y_t becomes

$$Y_t = \frac{c_t(D + E - tD - G^*) - (1 - t)bD}{E}\qquad(A\text{-}3)$$

which simplifies to

$$Y_t = c_t + (1 - t)(c_t - b)\frac{D}{E} - c_t\frac{G^*}{E}\qquad(A\text{-}4)$$

Solving for NPAT in (B-1), we obtain

$$\text{NPAT} = c_t(E_A - G)\qquad(B\text{-}2)$$

The reciprocal of the PE, Y_t is NPAT/E_A or, from (B-2), $c_t(E_A - G)/E_A$, which can be described as

$$Y_t = c_t\frac{E_A}{E_A} - c_t\frac{G}{E_A} = c_t - c_t\frac{G}{E_A}\qquad(B\text{-}3)$$

Thus, the question becomes: is the increase in the growth term from (B-3) to (A-4) (which decreases Y_t and, thus, increases the PE) great enough to offset the financial risk of debt? Mathematically, this is

$$(1 - t)(c_t - b)\frac{D}{E} \gtrless c_t\frac{G^*}{E} - c_t\frac{G}{E_A}\qquad(1)$$

Since E_A is some multiple (k) of E, $E_A = kE$, we can substitute kE for E_A:

$$(1 - t)(c_t - b)\frac{D}{E} \gtrless c_t \frac{G^*}{E} - c_t \frac{G}{kE} \tag{2}$$

Multiplying by E and dividing by c_t, we obtain

$$(1 - t)(c_t - b)\frac{D}{c_t} \gtrless G^* - \frac{G}{k} \tag{3}$$

Whenever the size of the right (left) side of (3) exceeds the magnitude of the left (right) side, the PE will rise (fall) because the added value of growth (financial risk) will offset the added value of financial risk (growth).

Consider the following hypothetical example:

NOPAT = NPAT = £1,000

$$c_t = 0.10$$

$$I = £1,000$$

$$r_t = 0.21$$

$$T = 10 \text{ years}$$

By (B-1) $V = 20,000$.

If D/A_F becomes, say, 0.20, such that A_F is £10,000 and D is £2,000, and t is 0.40, c_t^* is

$$c_t \left(1 - \frac{tD}{A_F}\right) = 0.10 \left(1 - \frac{0.40\,(2000)}{10,000}\right) = 0.09,$$

then by (A-1) $V = £23,000$.
Since

$$V \equiv D + E,\; E = V - D.\; E = 23,000 - 2,000 = £21,000$$

$$\text{and } k = \frac{E_A}{E} = \frac{20,000}{21,000} = 0.95.$$

Employing (3) above, if b is 8%, the lefthand side is 240 and the righthand side is 1674:

$$(1 - 0.40)(0.10 - 0.08)\left(\frac{2,000}{0.10}\right) < 12,200 - \frac{10,000}{0.95}$$

$$240 < 12,200 - 10,526$$

$$240 < 1,674$$

Since the righthand side exceeds the lefthand side, the increase in tD and growth potential must overcome the added financial risk and, thus, the PE rises with an increase in the debt ratio. In the debt-free case, the PE (E/NPAT) was 20 $(20,000/1,000 = 20)$. With debt, the PE is 22.8:

$$\frac{V - D}{\text{NOPAT} - (1 - t)\,bD} = \frac{23,000 - 2,000}{1,000 - \frac{1}{2} \text{ of } 160} = \frac{21,000}{920} = 22.8.$$

[1] The numerator should be expressed in terms of cash flows, but, for simplicity, we assume that the annual depreciation is reinvested to maintain the level of investment at £10,000 and NOP at £1,000.

[2] Note that the numerator is NOP, not net profit (NP) which is reported to ordinary shareholders. The difference between NOP and NP is the interest expense on borrowed capital. Since I is additions to fixed capital (i.e. interest-bearing debt *and* shareholders' equity), the numerator of the fraction must be expressed in comparable terms — the returns to bondholders as well as shareholders.

[3] The firm's capital structure is the relative sources of its fixed capital. Its fixed capital is all interest-bearing debt, reserves, preference capital and ordinary shareholders' capital. Thus, the target capital structure is the fraction of fixed capital that management expects to finance with interest-bearing debt on average and over time.

[4] An expansion of a firm's assets financed with debt is equivalent in concept and result to financing the expansion with equity followed by an issue of debt to retire the equity. In the example in the paper, we employ debt to retire existing equity only because we wish to hold the level of the firm's assets and NOPAT constant, examining the implications of changes in the firm's capital structure on its market value. Although share repurchase is technically not permitted in the United Kingdom, its equivalence to financing expansion with debt (with $r = c$) means that the example in the paper *is* 'relevant' for financial planning in the UK.

[5] Since $r_t = c_t$ in this case and $c_t \geq b_t$, the firm's *eps* will rise from gearing. The question is: will the *eps* rise faster than (the same as) (slower than) the price per share or, what amounts to the same thing, will the PE fall (remain the same) (rise) as the firm's debt ratio increases?

[6] If I = NOPAT, the expected rate of growth in profits is the same as the expected rate of return on new investment, r_t, because the expected rate of growth in profits is the reinvestment rate, I/NOPAT (in our example, this is 1.00), multiplied by r_t.

[7] Ir_t/NOPAT is the expected rate of growth in NOPAT and n is the finite time horizon for which r_t is expected to exceed c_t.

[8] To calculate a firm's hurdle rate, c_t^*, we substitute $c_t^* V$ in expression (6) for NOPAT in expression (4) to obtain

$$V = \frac{c_t^* V}{c_t} + tD$$

Simplifying and solving for c_t^* in terms of c_t,

$$c_t V = c_t^* V + c_t D$$

$$\frac{c_t V - c_t tD}{V} = c_t^*$$

$$c_t \left(1 - \frac{tD}{V} \right) = c_t^*$$

This is the taxable, but non-growth case. In the case of growth, A_F is substituted for V, where A_F is the economic book value of the firm's fixed capital. (Fixed capital is total assets minus non-interest-bearing current liabilities.)

$$c_t^* = c_t \left(1 - \frac{tD}{A_F} \right)$$

Since the analytical framework is based on expectations, D/A_F is the fraction of the original cash cost of fixed capital that the market expects will be financed with interest-bearing debt on average and over time. The implications for financial reporting, which are considerable, are discussed in detail in APPLICATIONS OF THE ANALYTICAL FRAMEWORK FOR DECISION-MAKING on this page.

[9] Selecting a desirable capital structure is not an easy task. And it is not as simple as many texts in finance would have us believe. Management must first determine the degree of total risk — asset *and* financial risk — they wish the ordinary shareholders to bear. This would be expressed in probabilistic NPAT that accrues to the ordinary shareholders, rather than in terms of NOPAT. Given an assessment of the firm's expected future asset composition and a probabilistic estimate of future NOPAT and, hence, a value for c_t, the amount of financial risk would be determined by subtraction: financial risk, a function of gearing, is equal to desired expected total risk minus desired expected asset risk. Both theory and empirical study have progressed sufficiently for managers to employ this method of capital structure determination.

[10] Although c_t is a partial equilibrium concept in the model (i.e. given the asset structure, c_t is determinable), it is dynamic in the real world. That is, c_t is codetermined with changes in the firm's asset composition. Increasing (decreasing) liquidity, decreasing (increasing) cash flow cyclicality and/or increasing (decreasing) government regulation of the public utility variety would be expected to decrease (increase) c_t if investors are risk averse. For example, ceteris paribus, a bank reducing its fraction of government bonds in favour of mortgages should expect to increase its c_t. An implication is that a baby food manufacturer would reduce its c_t by acquiring a 'pill' manufacturer. This is an example of reducing the asset risk that results from cash flow cyclicality.

[11] Quantitatively, the required rate of return on ordinary equity, Y_t, is the reciprocal of the PE. It can be described as the hurdle rate for asset or business risk, c_t, plus a required return for financial risk: $Y_t = c_t + (1 - t) (c_t - b) D/E$ where $(1 - t) (c_t - b) D/E$ is the required return for financial risk. This is described in greater detail in Joel M. Stern, *Valuation and Cost of Capital Theory*, 1967.

In our arithmetic example, c_t was 0.10, t was 0.40, b was 0.06 and D and E were ₤5,000 and ₤7,000, respectively. Thus, Y_t was 0.117:

$$Y_t = 0.10 + (1 - 0.40)(0.10 - 0.06) \frac{5000}{7000}$$

$$= 0.10 + (0.06)(0.04) \frac{5}{7}$$

$$= 0.10 + 0.017 = 0.117$$

Since the after-tax cost of debt is $(1 - t) b$ (or b_t), $(1 - 0.40) 0.06$, or 0.036, the weighted average cost of capital can be calculated to be $8\frac{1}{3}\%$ by weighting Y_t and b_t by the proportions of debt and equity, 5,000/12,000 $(0.41^2/_3)$ and 7,000/12,000 $(0.58^1/_3)$. Alternatively, the expression for c_t^* in Footnote 8 can be employed:

$$c_t^* = c_t \left(1 - \frac{tD}{A_F} \right) = 0.10 \left(1 - \frac{0.40 (5000)}{12\,000} \right)$$

$$= 0.10 \left(1 - \frac{1}{6} \right) = 0.10 (0.83^1/_3) = 0.08^1/_3$$

[12] This point is so important, the Appendix to this chapter develops the issue completely.

[13] This paper has been a lengthy development of an analytical framework and its implications for financial planning. This discussion of acquisition analysis should contain a complete development of a simple model that can be understood and employed by senior managers. However, we shall leave this extensive exposition to a later paper, presenting only a brief statement here based on the analytical framework in expression (8). The later paper considers the similarity of capital equipment analysis and acquisitions: acquisitions are multi-plant decisions.

[14] Applying footnote 8's measure of c_t^*, the proper discount rate to be used by a buyer for an acquisition should be considered in two stages. First, it might be appealing to describe it as

$$c_t^* = c_{ts} \left(1 - \frac{tD}{A_F} b \right)$$

where c_{ts} is the hurdle rate for the seller's assets and $(D/A_F)b$ is the debt ratio the buyer is expected to employ as the *pro forma* debt ratio. However, this formulation is insufficient. First, c_{ts} is likely to change if there are risk savings (i.e. the *pro forma* covariance is reduced). Second, a seller with small asset size and, hence, a relatively large value for c_t will probably experience a decline in the risk of its assets if it becomes part of a larger buyer, because c_t is inversely related to asset size.

Thus, optimal acquisition pricing values the *pro forma* firm using parameter estimates for the *pro forma* firm, including $c_t^* = c_{tp} (1 - tD/A_F)$ where c_{tp} is the *pro forma* hurdle rate for asset risk. Given the current market value of the buyer, the maximum price to be paid for the seller is determined by subtraction: the *pro forma* market value minus the buyer's market value is equal to the maximum permissible price for the seller.

THE DYNAMICS OF CORPORATE CAPITAL BUDGETING

RICHARD R. SPIES*

I. AN ADJUSTMENT MODEL OF CAPITAL BUDGETING

THE PROBLEM of capital budgeting is one that affects the entire structure of the modern corporation. Its solution determines the very nature of that corporation. Thus the capital budget has been treated at great length in the economic literature. In most of this work it has been explicitly recognized that the components of the capital budget are jointly determined. The investment, dividend, and financing decisions are tied together by the "uses equals sources" identity, a simple accounting identity which requires that all capital invested or distributed to stockholders be accounted for. Despite the obviousness of this relationship, however, very few attempts have been made to incorporate it into an econometric model. Instead most of the empirical work in this area has concentrated on the components of the capital budget separately. It is the purpose of this paper to describe an econometric model that explicitly recognizes the "uses equals sources" identity.

In the empirical work described in this paper the capital budget was broken into its five basic components: dividends, short-term investment, gross long-term investment, debt financing, and new equity financing. The first three are uses of funds while the latter two are sources. The dividends component includes all cash payments to stockholders and must be nonnegative. Short-term investment is the net change in the corporation's holdings of short-term assets during the period. These assets include both inventories and short-term financial assets, such as cash, government securities, and trade credits. This component of the capital budget can be either positive or negative. Long-term investment is defined as the change in gross long-term assets during the period. Thus the replacement of worn-out equipment is considered to be positive investment. Long-term investment can be negative but only if the sale of long-term assets exceeds this replacement investment. The debt finance component is simply the net change in the corporation's liabilities. These liabilities include corporate bonds, bank loans, taxes owed, and other accounts payable. Since a corporation can either increase its liabilities or retire those already existing, this variable can be either positive or negative. Finally, new equity financing is the change in stockholder's equity minus the amount due to retained earnings. This should represent the capital raised by the sale of new shares of common stock. Although individual corporations frequently repurchase stock already sold, this variable is almost always positive when aggregated.

The first step in this work was to develop a model that describes the optimal capital budget as a function of a set of predetermined variables.[1] The first of

---

* Princeton University. I am grateful to Professors Stanley Black, Dwight M. Jaffe, Burton G. Malkiel, and an anonymous referee for their comments on earlier drafts of this paper.

1. This model was discussed in more detail in Richard R. Spies [12], Chapter 2.

these variables is a measure of cash flow, net profits plus depreciation allowances. This variable, denoted by Y, is exogenous as long as the policies determining production, pricing, advertising, taxes, and the like cannot be changed quickly enough to affect the present period's earnings. Since the data used in this work are quarterly, this does not seem to be an unreasonable assumption. It should also be noted that the "uses equals sources" identity insures that:

$$\sum_{i=1}^{5} X_{i,t} = \sum_{i=1}^{5} X^*_{i,t} = Y_t, \tag{1}$$

where $X_{1,t} = DIV_t$ = cash dividends paid in period t;

$X_{2,t} = IST_t$ = net investment in short-term assets during period t;

$X_{3,t} = ILT_t$ = gross investment in long-term assets during period t;

$X_{4,t} = -DF_t$ = minus the net proceeds from new debt issued during period t;

$X_{5,t} = -EQF_t$ = minus the net proceeds from new equity issues during period t;

and where $X^*_{i,t}$ = the optimal level of $X_{i,t}$.

The second exogenous variable in the model is the corporate bond rate, RCB_t. This was used as a measure of the borrowing rate faced by the corporation. In addition, the debt-equity ratio at the start of the period, DEL_t, was included to allow for the increase in the cost of financing due to leverage. The average dividend-price ratio for all stocks, RDP_t, was used as a measure of the rate of return demanded by investors in a no-growth, unlevered corporation for the average risk class. The last two exogenous variables, R_t and CU_t, describe the rate of return the corporation could expect to earn on its future long-term investment. The ratio of the change in earnings to investment in the previous quarter should provide a rough measure of the rate of return to that investment. A four-quarter average of that ratio, R_t, was used to smooth out the normal fluctuations in earnings. The rate of capacity utilization, CU_t, was also included in an attempt to improve this measure of expected rate of return. Finally, a constant and three seasonal dummies were included. In matrix form this model is:

$$X^*_t = AZ_t \tag{2}$$

where $X^{*\prime} = (DIV^* \ IST^* \ ILT^* \ -DF^* \ -EQF^*)$,

$Z' = (1 \ Q1 \ Q2 \ Q3 \ Y \ RCB \ RDP \ DEL \ R \ CU)$,

$$a = \begin{Bmatrix} a_{10} & a_{11} \cdots \cdots \cdots \cdots \cdots \cdots a_{19} \\ a_{20} & \vdots \\ \vdots & \vdots \\ \vdots & \vdots \\ a_{50} \cdots \cdots \cdots \cdots \cdots \cdots \cdots \cdots \cdots a_{59} \end{Bmatrix}$$

This model is not a good description of actual capital budgeting practices, however. The typical corporation is not flexible enough to achieve this optimal capital budget every quarter. Corporate planners are normally reluctant to deviate very much from their past levels of dividends, investment, and financing.[2] This kind of behavior can best be described by a partial adjustment model. In such a model the capital budget depends on both the optimal budget and the actual budgets of the past. In its simplest form the partial adjustment model makes the change in the level of X_i from period $t-1$ to period t a function of the difference between its desired level for period t and its actual level for period $t-1$. Using a linear relationship this becomes

$$X_{i,t} = X_{i,\,t-1} + \delta_i(X^*_{i,t} - X_{i,\,t-1}). \tag{3}$$

This assumes that the corporation adjusts the level of X_i, a flow variable, in the direction of its optimal level. The speed of this adjustment is measured by the parameter δ_i. However, equation (3) does not incorporate the "uses equals sources" identity. Suppose $X^*_{i,t} > X_{1,t-1}$ while $X^*_{i,t} = X_{i,t-1}$ for all $i \neq 1$. If $\delta_1 < 1$, then X_1 will not completely adjust in period t and will remain below its optimal level. But the "uses equals sources" identity insures that

$$\sum_{i=1}^{5} X^*_{i,t} = \sum_{i=1}^{5} X_{i,\,t} = Y_t.$$ Therefore, the fact that X_1 is less than desired

implies that at least one other X_i is above its desired level. Suppose it is X_2 which alone compensates for the slow adjustment of X_1. Then, even though $X^*_{2,\,t} = X_{2,\,t-1}$, we will have $X_{2,\,t} > X_{2,\,t-1}$. In fact, $X_{2,\,t} = X_{2,\,t-1} + (1 - \delta_1)\,(X^*_{1,\,t} - X_{1,\,t-1})$. The result of the "uses equals sources" identity is that the adjustment of each X_i may depend on the distance of every X_i from its optimal level, not just its own. Equation (3) should be rewritten as

$$X_{i,t} = X_{i,\,t-1} + \sum_{j=1}^{5} \delta_{ij}\,(X^*_{j,t} - X_{j,\,t-1}) \qquad (i = 1,2,3,4,5) \tag{4}$$

where[3]
$$\sum_{i=1}^{5} \delta_{ij} = 1.$$

2. Joseph L. Bower [4] provides an interesting discussion of corporate decision-making and its ability to adapt to a changing environment.

3. The constraint on the values of δ_{ij} is a result of the "uses equals sources" identity. Summing equation (4) over i gives

$$\sum_{i=1}^{5} X_{i,t} = \sum_{i=1}^{5} X_{i,\,t-1} + \sum_{i=1}^{5} \sum_{j=1}^{5} \delta_{ij}\,(X^*_{j,t} - X_{j,\,t-1}).$$

This can be rewritten as

$$\sum_i (X_{i,t} - X_{i,\,t-1}) = \sum_j (X^*_{j,t} - X_{j,t-1}) \sum_i \delta_{ij}.$$

The identity insures that $\sum_j X_{j,t} = \sum_j X^*_{j,t}$ and, therefore,

$$\sum_i (X_{i,t} - X_{i,\,t-1}) = \sum_j (X_{j,t} - X_{j,\,t=1}) \sum_i \delta_{ij}.$$

Changing the notation slightly this becomes

Putting equation (4) into matrix form and combining it with equation (2) we get

$$X_t = X_{t-1} + D\,(X^*_t - X_{t-1}) \tag{5}$$
$$= (I - D)\,X_{t-1} + DAZ_t,$$

where I is the 5×5 identity matrix and

$$D = \left\{ \begin{bmatrix} \delta_{11} & \cdots\cdots\cdots\cdots\cdots & \delta_{15} \\ \vdots & & \vdots \\ \vdots & & \vdots \\ \delta_{51} & \cdots\cdots\cdots\cdots\cdots & \delta_{55} \end{bmatrix} \right\}$$

This is the model used in the empirical work reported in Section III.

It was argued above that the adjustment of each component of the capital budget depends not only on its own distance from the optimal level, but also on the distances of the other components. This would imply that at least some of the off-diagonal elements of D are non-zero. The fact that the X_i are competing uses of the available funds would generally lead one to believe that they should be negative. If dividends were below their optimal level, for example, we might expect dividends to rise and investment to fall. At the same time, however, the normal assumption with models of this type is that $0 < \delta_{ii} < 1$.

But we have already seen that $\sum_{i=1}^{5} \delta_{ij} = 1$ for all j. Therefore, it is not possible for all the off-diagonal elements to be negative unless the δ_{ii} are greater than one. This means that the signs of the δ_{ij} coefficients cannot be predicted with absolute certainty. However, it should be noted that the primary reason most corporations hold liquid assets is to facilitate this type of adjustment process; the role of liquid assets is to give flexibility to the capital budget. Therefore, it is reasonable to expect short-term investment to take up the slack caused by the adjustments of the other components. Going back to the dividend example, we would expect short-term investment to rise to insure that $\sum_{i=1}^{5} \delta_{11} = 1$. It is then possible that $0 < \delta_{11} < 1$, and $\delta_{31,}\ \delta_{41,}\ \delta_{51,} < 0$. Although this is not the only adjustment process a corporation can choose, it appears to be the most likely one.

II. Estimation Techniques

For the purposes of estimation equation (5) can be rewritten as:

$$X_t = BX_{t-1} + CZ_t + U_t \tag{6}$$

where B is a 5×5 matrix and C a 5×10 matrix of coefficients. The components of D and A can then be estimated by the following equations:

$$\sum_j (X_{j,t} - X_{j,\ t-1}) = \sum_j (X_{j,t} - X_{j,\ t-1}) \sum_i \delta_{ij}$$

or

$$1 = \sum_i \delta_{ij}.$$

$$\hat{D} = I - \hat{B}; \tag{7}$$

$$\hat{A} = \hat{D}^{-1}\hat{C}. \tag{8}$$

The estimation procedure used was the stacking technique first suggested by de Leeuw.[4] We have already seen that the "uses equals sources" identity implies that $\sum_{i=1}^{5} X_{i,t} = Y_t$ for every period t. In order to incorporate this into the estimation procedure, the estimators must be restricted in such a way that, across equations, the coefficients of Y add up to one while the coefficients of the other predetermined variables add up to zero. In other words, we must insure that $\sum_{i=1}^{5} \hat{b}_{ij} = \sum_{i=1}^{5} \hat{c}_{ik} = 0$ for all j and all $k \neq 4$, and that $\sum_{i=1}^{5} \hat{c}_{i4} = 1$. This is a simple adding-up constraint.[5]

The estimates of the long run coefficients obtained from equation (8) were statistically insignificant and are not reported in this paper. The reason for

---

4. Frank de Leeuw, "A Model of Financial Behavior," [7], p. 523.

5. This constraint insures that the "uses equals sources" identity will hold for the estimated equations. First of all, we know that $\Sigma_i \hat{\delta}_{ij} = 1$ since

$$\hat{\delta}_{ii} = \begin{cases} 1 - \hat{b}_{ii} \text{ for } i = j \\ -\hat{b}_{ii} \text{ for } i \neq j. \end{cases}$$

Therefore, $\Sigma_i \hat{\delta}_{ij} = 1 - \Sigma_i \hat{b}_{ij} = 1 - 0 = 1$. In addition, it can be shown that $\Sigma \hat{X}^*_{i,t} = Y_t$. To show this it is necessary only to show that

$$\Sigma_j \hat{a}_{jk} = \begin{cases} 0 \text{ for all } k \neq 4 \\ 1 \text{ for } k = 4. \end{cases}$$

Note that $\hat{c}_{ik} = \Sigma_j \hat{\delta}_{ij}\hat{a}_{jk}$. Since we have constrained

$$\Sigma_i \hat{c}_{ik} = \begin{cases} 0 \text{ for all } k \neq 4 \\ 1 \text{ for all } k = 4 \end{cases}$$

we can see that

$$\Sigma_i c_{ik} = \Sigma_i \Sigma_j \hat{\delta}_{ij}\hat{a}_{jk}$$

$$= \Sigma_j (\Sigma_i \hat{\delta}_{ij})\hat{a}_{jk}$$

$$= \Sigma_j (1)\hat{a}_{jk}$$

$$= \Sigma_j \hat{a}_{jk}$$

Therefore,

$$\Sigma_j \hat{a}_{jk} = \left. \begin{cases} 0 \text{ for all } k \neq 4 \\ 1 \text{ for all } k = 4 \end{cases} \right.$$

From all this it is clear that

$$\Sigma_i \hat{X}_{i,t} = \Sigma_i \hat{X}^*_{i,t} = Y_t.$$

this is that (8) is an extremely inefficient estimator for these coefficients. The ordinary least squares estimator is designed to minimize the sum of the squared residuals for equation (6). The estimates that result can be used to predict X_t given Z_t and X_{t-1}. However, they do not provide an efficient predictor of X more than one period ahead. If, for example, we wanted to predict X_{t+1}, we should estimate the equation

$$X_{t+1} = BX_t + CZ_{t+1} + U_{t+1}$$
$$= B^2X_{t-1} + BCZ_t + CZ_{t+1} + BU_t + U_{t+1}. \qquad (9)$$

In other words, we should estimate B^2, BC and C directly. The same is true of the steady state solution. To get efficient estimates of the long run coefficients we would have to estimate them directly. Since we were more interested in the short run dynamics of the adjustment process, we have not done that here. Therefore, it is not at all surprising that our estimates of the long run coefficients all have large variances. In fact, this is the result encountered by most people who have worked with models of this type.[6]

The data used were taken mainly from the FTC-SEC *Quarterly Financial Report for Manufacturing Corporations* and covered the period 1949 through 1969. Regression results are reported for the aggregated manufacturing sector and ten industry subsectors. Those industries and their SIC classification numbers are

1. Food and Kindred Products (20)
2. Textile Mill Products (22)
3. Furniture and Fixtures (25)
4. Paper and Allied Products (26)
5. Chemicals and Allied Products (28)
6. Leather and Leather Products (31)
7. Stone, Clay, and Glass Products (32)
8. Other Machinery (35)
9. Electric Machinery, Equipment, and Supplies (36)
10. Motor Vehicles and Equipment (371)

This model is supposed to provide a realistic picture of the capital budgeting practices of individual corporations. But we are using aggregated data to test it. It could easily be argued that there is no reason to expect the parameters of the model to be the same for all manufacturing corporations, or even for all corporations within a particular industry. There is no way to refute this argument on theoretical grounds. It is probably true, in theory at least, that individual firm data would have provided a better test of the model. However, such data present serious problems for an empirical study of this kind. The capital budgeting decisions of actual corporations are often dictated by outside influences and considerations that cannot be explained in a very general model of this kind. For example, a single large investment project could dominate a corporation's entire capital budget for several periods. Such things as labor negotiations and antitrust actions could also affect capital budgeting decisions. It would be very difficult to incorporate all these factors into our

6. See Orley Ashenfelter, [2].

general model. As a result, the capital budget of an individual corporation will often be very different from that predicted by our model. This could happen even if the model is an accurate description of the normal behavior of that corporation. We hope that by using aggregated data we have smoothed out the effects of these outside influences.

III. Empirical Results

The estimates of the δ_{ij} coefficients are reported in Tables 1-5. In the estimation procedure employed here, we had to use the negative of the values of debt and equity financing in order to preserve the adding-up constraint. However, in reporting the results we have adjusted the signs of these coefficients to eliminate this convention. In other words, the X_t and X_{t-1} vectors of equation (5) have been adjusted to make $X' = (DIV\ IST\ ILT\ DF\ EQF)$. This transformed system of equations is equivalent to the old one and is much easier to interpret.

Tables 1-5 show the adjustment coefficients δ_{ij} for the aggregated manufacturing sector and the ten industry subsectors. Each table contains the estimates of δ_{ij} for $i = 1,2,3,4,5$ and a given value of j. For example, Table 1

TABLE 1*
ADJUSTMENT COEFFICIENTS OF DIV*$_t$-DIV$_{t-1}$

	ΔDIV_t	ΔIST_t	ΔILT_t	ΔDF_t	ΔEQF_t
Food	1	2.8688 (4.14)	−2.8688 (4.14)	0	0
Textile	1.1156 (8.97)	1.6496 (2.19)	−1.9930 (2.29)	1.0763 (1.38)	−1,3041 (2.20)
Furniture	0.9194 (12.09)	2.9337 (2.34)	0	0	2.8531 (3.58)
Paper	0.2475 (0.37)	0	6.1983 (5.30)	1.8321 (1.76)	3.6137 (2.96)
Chemical	0.1894 (0.64)	0.8106 (2.74)	0	0	0
Leather	0.6412 (1.68)	1.6059 (0.90)	1.5603 (1.03)	5.4753 (3.05)	−2.6679 (2.12)
Stone, Clay, and Glass	0.7037 (3.32)	1.5594 (2.14)	−1.2631 (3.09)	0	0
Other Machinery	1.2340 (5.22)	3.7843 (5.37)	0	4.0183 (5.23)	0
Electrical Machinery	0.8355 (4.16)	0	0	−1.3451 (1.06)	1.1806 (0.87)
Motor Vehicle	1.0158 (16.72)	0.9799 (4.15)	−0.6723 (2.63)	0	0.3234 (1.33)
Aggregated	0.8328 (6.67)	3.2308 (6.59)	0	2.0902 (7.64)	0.9734 (1.96)

* In tables 1-5 the numbers in parentheses are t-statistics. The 95% significance level is $t = 1.96$. The entries without t-statistics listed represent the coefficients of variables that were left out of the regression. These coefficients are equal to one for the own adjustment coefficients and zero for all the others.

TABLE 2
ADJUSTMENT COEFFICIENTS OF IST^*_t-IST_{t-1}

	ΔDIV_t	ΔIST_t	ΔILT_t	ΔDF_t	ΔEQF_t
Food	−0.3774	3.3476	−0.7727	0	1.1975
	(1.08)	(6.69)	(1.51)		(2.69)
Textile	0.0382	0.7998	0	0	−0.1620
	(0.63)	(14.38)			(2.82)
Furniture	0	1.3754	−0.3754	0	0
		(15.46)	(4.22)		
Paper	−0.1584	2.1114	−0.9530	0	0
	(1.13)	(4.33)	(1.97)		
Chemical	−0.4697	1.4697	0	0	0
	(2.09)	(6.54)			
Leather	0.1259	1.4780	0	0.5349	0.0690
	(1.66)	(22.14)		(8.18)	(1.24)
Stone, Clay,	0	2.1202	−0.4870	0.6332	0
and Glass		(20.21)	(5.17)	(6.26)	
Other Machinery	0.0643	2.9273	0	1.3859	0.6057
	(1.17)	(7.72)		(3.97)	(2.20)
Electrical Machinery	0.2157	1.1662	0	0	0.3819
	(1.06)	(7.43)			(0.99)
Motor Vehicle	−0.1936	2.3032	−0.5575	0.5521	0
	(1.29)	(18.49)	(4.44)	(3.90)	
Aggregated	−0.1744	2.0190	−0.3232	0.6352	−0.1138
	(1.04)	(10.98)	(2.53)	(5.02)	(1.94)

shows that if the optimal level of dividends in the aggregated manufacturing sector exceeds last period's actual level by \$1.00 (i.e. $DIV^*_t - DIV_{t-1} = 1$), then dividends will be raised \$.83. In addition, short-term investment will rise by \$3.23, debt financing by \$2.09, and equity financing by \$.97.

Table 1 contains the estimates of the coefficients of $DIV^*_t - DIV_{t-1}$. The own adjustment coefficients of dividends are given in the first column. They range from a low of 0.1894 for the chemical industry to a high of 1.2340 for other machinery. Three of the industries have coefficients greater than one, but none of them is significantly different from one. Except for the chemical and paper industries all the estimates are quite close to one. This would indicate that most corporations adjust dividends quite rapidly to their optimal level.

The other components of the capital budget also adjust to a non-optimality in dividends. The second column of Table 1 illustrates the reaction of short-term investment to such a non-optimality. Except for the two zero values all the estimates are positive and relatively large. This is strong support for the argument that corporations build up their supplies of liquid assets because of a planned increase in dividends. Long-term investment, on the other hand, seems to adjust downward. Eight of the ten industry coefficients are negative or zero, and one of the positive coefficients is insignificant. Thus the evidence ꞏuggests that long-term investment might fall in the face of a planned increase

TABLE 3
ADJUSTMENT COEFFICIENTS OF ILT^*_t-ILT_{t-1}

	ΔDIV_t	ΔIST_t	ΔILT_t	ΔDF_t	ΔEQF_t
Food	−0.4677 (1.19)	2.3457 (4.34)	0.3709 (0.70)	0	1.2489 (2.55)
Textile	0	0	1	0	0
Furniture	0.0638 (0.93)	0	0.9362 (13.65)	0	0
Paper	−0.1135 (1.24)	1.3754 (2.92)	0.3039 (0.65)	0.1988 (1.82)	0.3670 (3.63)
Chemical	−0.4992 (1.93)	0.2830 (1.12)	0.4352 (3.99)	−0.7740 (5.58)	0
Leather	0	0.2258 (1.40)	0.7742 (4.80)	0	0
Stone, Clay, and Glass	−0.0503 (1.03)	1.3354 (8.53)	0.3044 (2.56)	0.6095 (4.01)	0
Other Machinery	0.1282 (1.36)	1.8262 (5.28)	1	1.0317 (3.30)	0.9227 (3.55)
Electrical Machinery	0.2617 (1.26)	0.1967 (1.50)	1	0	0.4584 (1.14)
Motor Vehicle	−0.3170 (1.60)	2.0200 (11.66)	0.0319 (0.17)	0.7349 (3.78)	0
Aggregated	−0.1888 (1.07)	0.7896 (4.13)	0.2614 (1.46)	0	−0.1378 (1.33)

in dividends. Since investment has to compete with dividends for funds, this result is not altogether surprising. Only the very large positive coefficient for the paper industry provides conflicting evidence.

By the same type of argument, it is clear that both debt and equity financing should rise in response to an expected increase in dividends. Nine of the ten industry adjustment coefficients for debt financing are positive or zero, and the other is not significant. In the equity finance equation eight of the ten coefficients are positive or zero. In other words, both sources of funds are increased to meet the financing requirements of the new, liberalized dividend policy.

The own adjustment coefficients of short-term investment are reported in the second column of Table 2 and range in value from 0.7998 to 3.3476. They are all positive and quite large. Except for the textile industry, they are all greater than one. The conclusion to be drawn from this is that short-term investment over-reacts to its own non-optimality. This is further evidence that the first reaction of corporate planners to any deviation from the optimal capital budget is to adjust the supply of liquid assets, even beyond their anticipated need for those assets.

The adjustment coefficients for the short-term investment component in the dividend equation are all quite small. Four of the industry coefficients are positive, four are negative, and two are zero. However, only one is significant at the 95% level. That coefficient is negative, which would imply that a short-

TABLE 4
ADJUSTMENT COEFFICIENTS OF DF^*_t-DF_{t-1}

	ΔDIV_t	ΔIST_t	ΔILT_t	ΔDF_t	ΔEQF_t
Food	0.4769	−2.5488	0.6954	0.9212	−1.2977
	(0.90)	(4.60)	(1.26)	(21.63)	(2.64)
Textile	0	0	0	1	0
Furniture	0	−0.4655	0.3526	0.8871	0
		(3.82)	(2.95)	(11.00)	
Paper	0.1933	−1.2045	1.0112	1	0
	(1.03)	(2.37)	(2.00)		
Chemical	0.5213	−0.2615	0	1.2598	0
	(2.26)	(1.14)		(16.39)	
Leather	−0.1022	0	0.1022	1	0
	(1.62)		(1.62)		
Stone, Clay, and Glass	0	−1.1895	0.5895	0.4000	0
		(8.53)	(4.74)	(2.89)	
Other Machinery	−0.0915	−2.0303	0.2087	−0.4007	−0.5124
	(1.02)	(5.58)	(3.50)	(1.25)	(1.97)
Electrical Machinery	−0.2118	−0.3150	0	0.9086	−0.4354
	(1.53)	(1.84)		(13.12)	(1.08)
Motor Vehicle	0.2620	−1.4022	0.6665	0.5263	0
	(1.46)	(9.54)	(4.18)	(3.08)	
Aggregated	0.2023	−1.2073	0.3784	0.3734	0
	(1.02)	(6.07)	(2.74)	(2.95)	

fall in short-term investment leads to a drop in dividends. This is the result that one would expect, but the evidence can hardly be considered conclusive. In fact, the only conclusion we can reach on the basis of these estimates is that a non-optimality in short-term investment has little or no effect on dividend policy.

The other components of the capital budget adjust in the expected way. If long-term investment reacts at all, it falls to help finance the increase in short-term investment. For the ten industry subsectors, all five of the nonzero coefficients are negative in the long-term investment equation. In the debt finance equation four of the ten coefficients are positive and the rest are zero. This indicates that debt financing either increases or goes unchanged. The results are similar for equity financing. In that equation four of the industry coefficients are positive and five are zero. Only the textile industry gives a contrary result. The general conclusion to be drawn from Table 2 is that a shortfall in short-term investment will cause a large increase in that variable, financed by small changes in the other components of the capital budget.

It is interesting to note that in the equity finance equation, the estimate for the aggregated manufacturing sector is negative (although not significant at the 95% level). We would certainly expect this coefficient to be positive since equity finance is an important source of funds. This is one of only two cases where the estimate for the aggregated sector disagrees with our expectations. The other is the negative coefficient for the long-term investment component in the equity finance equation.

TABLE 5
ADJUSTMENT COEFFICIENTS OF $EQF^*_t - EQF_{t-1}$

	ΔDIV_t	ΔIST_t	ΔILT_t	ΔDF_t	ΔEQF_t
Food	0.3647	−2.2607	0.7404	0	−0.1556
	(1.06)	(4.53)	(1.48)		(0.34)
Textile	−0.0654	0	0.1546	−0.0846	1.1738
	(1.04)		(1.33)	(0.70)	(10.37)
Furniture	0	0	0.3451	0	1.3451
			(4.66)		(18.16)
Paper	0.1113	−1.2027	0.6148	−0.2688	0.7912
	(0.94)	(2.61)	(1.33)	(2.19)	(6.55)
Chemical	0.4838	−0.3232	0.5535	0.5720	1.1421
	(1.80)	(1.21)	(4.11)	(3.68)	(11.41)
Leather	−0.1139	−0.3199	0	−0.4338	1
	(0.77)	(2.19)		(3.16)	
Stone, Clay, and Glass	0.0667	−1.3398	0	−1.0640	0.7909
	(1.18)	(8.26)		(6.74)	(7.22)
Other Machinery	−0.1027	−1.8662	0	−1.1008	0.1319
	(1.05)	(4.49)		(2.84)	(0.41)
Electrical Machinery	−0.3556	0	0	0	0.6464
	(0.91)				(1.66)
Motor Vehicle	0.4457	−1.4919	1.0462	0	1
	(1.54)	(5.03)	(3.54)		
Aggregated	0.2029	−0.9799	0	−0.7770	1
	(1.40)	(5.07)		(5.71)	

The third column of Table 3 contains the own adjustment coefficients of long-term investment. These estimates range from 0.0319 for motor vehicles to a value of 1.0 for three separate industries. There are no estimates greater than one and the values are generally quite small. Of the seven industry coefficients estimated directly (rather than being left out of the regression and thus set equal to one) five are less than one-half. This supports the hypothesis that long-term investment adjusts slowly to its optimal level. It is clear that this speed of adjustment depends heavily on the technical characteristics of the individual investment projects, among other things. Therefore, it is not at all surprising that these estimates vary considerably from industry to industry. However, the general conclusion that long-term investment reacts slowly to its own non-optimality does seem valid.

The reactions of short-term investment to such a non-optimality is fairly obvious. All of the nonzero estimates in the second column of Table 3 are positive. Five of them are greater than one. This suggests that short-term investment increases, often by a great deal, in preparation for a future increase in long-term investment. This is the same result we found in our discussion of a non-optimality in the level of dividends.

The evidence is much less conclusive for the other components of the capital budget. In the dividend equation seven of the ten coefficients are either zero or negative, but none of them is significant. Thus a non-optimality in long-term investment appears to have little effect on dividends, although what adjustment there is seems to be in the negative direction. This is consistent with our earlier results. Corporate planners appear to be very reluctant to cut back dividends in order to finance changes in the rest of the capital budget.

In the debt financing equation, five of the ten industries show no significant response to a non-optimality in long-term investment. In addition, six of the industries have an adjustment coefficient of zero in the equity finance equation. However, all four nonzero estimates in the equity finance equation are positive, as are four of the five in the debt financing equation. This implies that both debt and equity financing rise in the face of a planned increase in long-term investment. Although the evidence cannot be considered conclusive because of the insignificant coefficients in so many industries, these results are certainly consistent with the corporate planning process described in Section I.

The own adjustment coefficients for debt financing are reported in the fourth column of Table 4. The negative coefficient for other machinery seems nonsensical, but it is not significantly different from zero. The rest of the estimates seem reasonable. Most of them are close to one. For the chemical industry the coefficient is even greater than (and significantly different from) one. This indicates that the level of debt financing actually overadjusts in that industry. Although this is not the result that one would anticipate, it is certainly not inconsistent with the model we have developed. In any event, the evidence seems to strongly support the hypothesis that debt financing adjusts rapidly to its optimal level.

If debt financing were below its optimum, we might expect dividends and long-term investment to rise because of the anticipated increase in available funds. We might also expect equity financing to decrease since it is an alternative source of funds. In the light of our previous results on short-term investment we would expect this variable to decrease as well. Investment in liquid assets would probably be reduced in order to finance the increases in expenditures during the transition from the old optimal capital budget to the new one. In general these expectations are borne out by the results. In the long-term investment equation, all the nonzero estimates are positive, and most of them are significant. This implies that long-term investment actually does rise in the face of a planned increase in debt financing. The results also support the hypothesis that short-term investment declines in response to a shortfall in the level of debt financing. All of the coefficients in the second column of Table 4 are either negative or zero.

The evidence is less conclusive for the other components of the capital budget. In the dividend equation seven of the ten industry coefficients are either zero or positive as expected. However, only one of them is significant. It appears that the change in dividends due to a non-optimality in debt financing is in the right direction but is only minor. In the equity finance equation only three of the estimates were even close to being significant. All three were negative as expected, but the large number of insignificant coefficients means that the evidence cannot be considered conclusive.

The capital budget seems to respond to a non-optimality in the level of equity financing in much the same way. The own adjustment coefficients for equity finance are shown in the last column of Table 5. The negative value of the estimate for the food industry should be ignored since it is not statistically significant. All but one of the other estimates are close to one, including three that are greater than one. These results imply that equity finance adjusts quickly to its optimal level.

The response of the other components to a non-optimality in equity finance is much the same as it was for debt finance. The reaction of dividends is insignificant, although probably in the right direction. Six of the ten industry coefficients are positive or zero, but there is not a single significant estimate in the whole group. In the short-term investment equation, all of the nonzero coefficients are negative. Again it appears that short-term investment will fall to take up the slack caused by the slower adjustment of the other variables. Long-term investment increases because of a shortfall in equity finance. In the third column of Table 5 all of the estimates are either positive or zero. Thus we can see that long-term investment rises in response to an anticipated increase in external financing. At the same time, debt financing decreases as expected. Nine of the ten industry adjustment coefficients are negative or zero. Only the chemical industry gives a different result.

In terms of their signs at least, these adjustment coefficients are remarkably consistent from industry to industry. Of the 275 coefficients estimated only six both have the wrong sign and are significant at the 95% level. A summary of these results is contained in Table 6. Of course, none of the industries (nor

TABLE 6
SUMMARY OF RESULTS

	$DIV^*_t - DIV_{t-1}$	$IST^*_t\ IST_{t-1}$	$ILT^*_t - ILT_{t-1}$	$DF^*_t - DF_{t-1}$	$EQF^*_t - EQF_{t-1}$
ΔDIV	Close to 1	Negative (but not significant)	Negative (but not significant)	Positive (but not significant)	Positive (but not significant)
ΔIST	Positive and Large	Greater than 1	Positive and Large	Negative and Large	Negative and Large
ΔILT	Negative	Negative*	Between 0 and 1	Positive	Positive
ΔDF	Positive*	Positive*	Positive*	Close to 1	Negative
ΔEQF	Positive	Positive*	Positive*	Negative*	Close to 1

* The items marked with an asterisk are those where at least five industries had estimated coefficients set equal to zero. Because of this large number of insignificant estimates, our conclusions about the signs of these coefficients must be viewed with caution.

the aggregated manufacturing sector) looks exactly like Table 6. But they all follow this general pattern to some degree.

IV. THE DYNAMICS OF THE SYSTEM: A SIMULATION

It is obvious from equation (6) that this model is a simple five-equation system of first order linear difference equations. Such systems are common in economics and their properties have been extensively studied. Equation (6) can be rewritten as:

$$X_t = BX_{t-i} + CZ_t$$

$$= B^t X_0 + \sum_{i=0}^{t-1} B^i CZ_{t-i}. \tag{10}$$

If we assume that the exogenous variables are held constant over time, this reduces to

$$X_t = B^t X_0 + \left(\sum_{i=0}^{t-1} B^i \right) C\bar{Z}. \tag{11}$$

A necessary and sufficient condition for this system to converge is that all the eigenvalues of B are less than one in absolute value.[7] That condition is satisfied by the estimates of B obtained for the aggregated manufacturing sector and for all ten industry subsectors. This means that the system is stable for all these sectors and X_t converges to

$$\lim_{t \to \infty} X_t = \lim_{t \to \infty} B^t X_0 + \lim_{t \to \infty} \left(\sum_{i=0}^{t-1} B^i \right) C\bar{Z} \tag{12}$$

$$= (I - B)^{-1} C\bar{Z}$$

$$= D^{-1} DA\bar{Z}$$

$$= A\bar{Z}.$$

In other word, the components of the capital budget converge to their long run or optimal levels.[8]

A simple simulation should help to illustrate the dynamics of this model. Figure 1 describes the changes in the capital budget that would result from a unit increase in gross earnings for the aggregated manufacturing sector. The difference between each component and its initial level is plotted against time. All the other exogenous variables are assumed to remain constant. The adjustment process seems quite clear. Dividends and long-term investment rise slowly but steadily to their new optimal levels. In the first few quarters short-term investment takes up the slack caused by this slow adjustment. It rises sharply in the first quarter and remains well above its optimal level in the second. This just means that the corporations are stockpiling liquid assets in preparation for the higher dividend and long-term investment levels. Debt financing rises sharply in the first quarter before falling to its new optimum. To a lesser degree equity finance does the same thing. By the fourth quarter all the components of the capital budget have just about reached their optimal levels. This is a much more rapid adjustment than those implied by most single equation models. This is one of the most interesting results of the complete partial adjustment model.

7. William J. Baumol, [3], p. 363. It is also true that this is a necessary and sufficient condition for the stochastic system to be covariance stationary. This means that the system will have a steady state solution. For a discussion of this result see Gregory C. Chow, [6].

8. The speed with which such a system converges to a new equilibrium is also determined by the values of its eigenvalues.

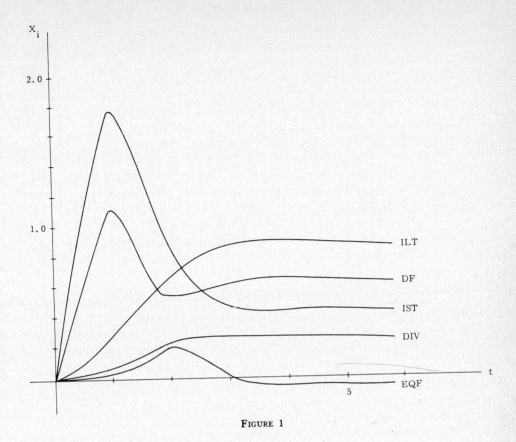

FIGURE 1

V. CONCLUSION

In general the model described here performs quite well. The evidence strongly supports a complete partial adjustment model. The individual adjustment coefficients are reasonable for most industries and the systems are all stable. If the capital budget is out of equilibrium, dividends and long-term investment move steadily toward their equilibrium values. Debt and equity financing change quickly to help finance the other adjustments before moving to their own equilibrium levels. Finally, short-term investment takes up the slack. It adjusts rapidly to compensate for the slower adjustment of the other components and preserve the "uses equals sources" identity. Such behavior is generally consistent with actual capital budgeting practices.

There are a number of interesting conclusions that can be drawn from the empirical results. The first concerns the place of dividends in corporate planning. Apparently dividends adjust to a new optimum almost immediately. It should be pointed out that the actual dividend policies of most corporations are asymmetric. Dividends are virtually rigid downward while they are much more flexible upward. The preponderance of periods of rapid growth in earnings and dividends in our sample could very well affect the estimates of this speed of adjustment. In any event, dividends do not react significantly to a non-optimality in any other component of the capital budget. It seems clear

627

that the dividend level is of paramount importance to corporate planners. The evidence strongly supports the hypothesis that dividend policy is determined almost independently of the rest of the capital budget.

We can also conclude that long-term investment adjusts to a new optimal level quite slowly. This is what the discussion of the adjustment process in Section I would lead one to expect. Long-term investment is clouded in the greatest uncertainty and involves the longest administrative lags of all the components of the capital budget. What is interesting to note is that it does react, even though only slightly, to non-optimalities in the other components. In other words, some investment projects are delayed or speeded up to compensate for these non-optimalities. Thus the timing of these projects is clearly dependent on the levels of the other components of the capital budget.

The conclusions to be drawn about the other components are more limited. Debt and equity financing react to non-optimalities in the dividend and investment components. From this it is clear that financing adjustments depend on the rest of the capital budget, often quite heavily. In other words, temporary financing is frequently arranged for dividends and investment projects. It is also interesting to note that equity financing is often just as dependent on the rest of the capital budget as is debt financing (and occasionally even more so). This conclusion is quite different from the general view that external equity financing is used only when all other sources of funds have been exhausted. Finally, it is obvious that short-term investment acts as a residual in the adjustment process. This is certainly consistent with the primary role of short-term assets, the provision of liquidity.

These results make it quite clear that the components of the capital budget cannot be studied separately. The interdependence among them is simply too great. Any empirical work on the determination of any one of these variables must take into account the relationship between that variable and the rest of the capital budget.

BIBLIOGRAPHY

1. W. H. Locke Anderson. *Corporate Finance and Fixed Investment: An Econometric Study,* Harvard Business School, Boston, 1964.
2. Orley Ashenfelter. "The Covariance Matrices of Various Multiplier Coefficients from a Dynamic Econometric Model," paper in process.
3. William J. Baumol. *Economic Dynamics: An Introduction,* Second Edition, The Macmillan Company, New York, 1959.
4. Joseph L. Bower. "Planning Within the Firm," *American Economic Review,* May, 1970, Vol. 60, pp. 186-194.
5. William C. Brainard and James Tobin. "Pitfalls in Financial Model Building," *American Economic Review,* May, 1968, Vol. 58, pp. 99-122.
6. Gregory C. Chow. "The Acceleration Principle and the Nature of the Business Cycle," *Quarterly Journal of Economics,* August, 1968, Vol. 82, pp. 403-418.
7. Frank de Leeuw. "A Model of Financial Behavior," in *The Brookings Quarterly Econometric Model of the United States,* James S. Duesenberry, Gary Fromm, Lawrence R. Klein, Edwin Kuh (eds.), Rand McNally and Company, Chicago, 1965.
8. Phoebus J. Dhrymes and Mordecai Kurz. "Investment, Dividend, and External Finance Behavior of Firms," in *Determinants of Investment Behavior: A Conference of the Universities-National Bureau Committee for Economic Research,* Robert Ferber (ed.), Columbia University Press, New York, 1967.
9. Myron J. Gordon. *The Investment, Financing, and Valuation of the Corporation,* Richard D. Irwin, Inc., Homewood, Illinois, 1962.

10. Jack Hirshleifer. *Investment, Interest, and Capital,* Prentice-Hall, Inc., Englewood Cliffs, N.J., 1970.
11. Edwin Kuh. *Capital Stock Growth: A Micro-Econometric Approach,* North Holland Publishing Company, Amsterdam, 1963.
12. Richard R. Spies. *Corporate Investment, Dividends and Finance: A Simultaneous Approach,* unpublished Ph.D. dissertation, Princeton University, 1971.
13. Craig Swan. "A Model of Portfolio Adjustment Applied to Mutual Savings Banks," paper presented to the Econometric Society, September, 1970, with an abstract appearing in *Econometrica,* July, 1971, Vol. 39, pp. 406-407.

AN ANALYTICAL MODEL FOR LONG-RANGE FINANCIAL PLANNING*

WILLARD T. CARLETON**

THE FINANCE LITERATURE in recent years has placed considerable emphasis on the necessary interdependency of a corporation's financial decisions: capital budgeting, new borrowing or debt repayment, stock issue or repurchase, and dividends. Most of this emphasis has been conceptual and has not resulted in implemented models, even though corporations increasingly recognize the need for integrative financial tools [13]. Available evidence [5] suggests that substantial corporate modelling is already taking place, but that much of this modelling activity consciously avoids any optimization framework. A casual reading of this effort leads to the suspicion that much of the gap between corporate practice and theory is due to the difficulty of fitting real corporate constraints — loan indenture agreements, policy restrictions on dividends, etc. — into the typical optimizing model proposed in the finance literature. In the present paper, recent conceptual advances in financial theory have been imbedded in a workable planning model, set in a deterministic framework, a model that is being employed currently to assist firms in their long-range financial planning. In this model the firm is viewed as attempting to maximize, with respect to time vectors of its financial decision variables, a discounted stream of future dividends and terminal stock price (at the end of the planning horizon). The form of the accounting and economic constraints permits a linear programming structure for the model. An illustrative problem is presented and possible uses and extensions of the model are discussed.

I. THE CORPORATION'S OBJECTIVE FUNCTION

The starting point is a definition of share price. Thus:

$$\frac{P_t}{N_t} = \frac{D_t}{N_t} + \frac{P_{t+1}}{N_{t+1}(1 + k_{t+1})} \tag{1}$$

where
P_t = aggregate market value of the firm's equity at the beginning of period t;

N_t = number of shares of common stock outstanding at the beginning of period t;

D_t = total dollars of dividends paid at the beginning of period t;

k_{t+1} = discount rate, or rate of return required by the stock market of the firm between periods t and t + 1.

* It is a pleasure to acknowledge the intellectual and financial support of the Tuck School Associates Program and First National City Bank, of New York. Both, however, are absolved of any responsibility for the contents of this paper. I should also like to thank David H. Downes and Roger J. Pinchard for computer programming and many valuable suggestions as to the model's form and content. An earlier version of this paper was presented at the TIMS/ORSA Joint Meetings, San Francisco, May 1968 [2].

** Amos Tuck School of Business Administration, Dartmouth College.

That is, we start from the conventional definition of share price as current dividend plus present value of expected selling price one period in the future. The dating of variables in a discrete-time model is arbitrary. For later reference, however, it will be assumed:

(a) that balance sheet variables are recorded on the first day of each period t *after* corporate investment expenditures and their financing have been accomplished — but *prior* to the recording of revenues and expenses for period t;

(b) that dividends and all expenses for period t are paid on the last day of period t.

A simple extension of equation (1) yields the result that

$$\frac{P_0}{N_0} = \frac{D_0}{N_0} + \frac{D_1}{N_1(1+k_1)} + \frac{D_2}{N_2(1+k_1)(1+k_2)} + \ldots$$

$$+ \frac{D_{n-1}}{N_{n-1}(1+k_1)\ldots(1+k_{n-1})} + \frac{P_n}{N_n(1+k_1)\ldots(1+k_n)} \quad (2)$$

where n is the firm's planning horizon.[1]

The finance literature is replete with examples in which equation (2) has been simplified in order to derive corporate decision rules. As a representative approach, the following assumptions have been made:

(a) The securing of additional equity is always from current stockholders so that it can be assumed that $N_0 = N_1 = N_2 = \ldots = N_n$;

(b) The number of periods in the planning period is indefinitely large, so that explicit determination of n and P_n can be avoided;

(c) Dividends are expected to grow at a constant annual rate, g;

(d) The stockmarket's required rate of return is a constant with respect to the firm's activities and from period to period.

The consequence is the well-known formula:

$$\frac{P_0}{N_0} = \frac{D_0/N_0}{k-g} \quad \text{or} \quad \tilde{P}_0 = \frac{D_0}{k-g} \quad (3)$$

where the tilde represents per-share value. The only reason for calling attention to this reduction of equation (2) is to indicate in what fashion it has limited the development of empirically satisfying financial decision rules. In the first place, either as (2) or as (3), the objective function is not very useful until D_t and k_t and g are constrained appropriately. The constraints typically adopted in the finance theory literature are distinguished more by their tractability than by their realism. Even if the reduced version is so constrained, however — so that D_0, k_t and g are treated as functions subject to a number of accounting and economic constraints — the resulting decisions

---

1. An implicit assumption is that n is also an horizon for the stock market, i.e., the number of periods for which explicit expectations as to the corporation's earnings, dividends, etc. can meaningfully be formed. What this means is that the present paper is abstracting from the admittedly real problem of divergency between corporate expectations and plans, on the one hand, and market expectations, on the other.

are required to be adopted permanently.[2] The anatomy of such decisions contains useful insights as economic theory, but very little of direct help to the corporate planner. What is required is a model for stock price maximization that permits planned period-by-period investment and financing decisions, a model that both incorporates institutional realities and permits achievements of desired targets as of horizon dates. Satisfying this requirement will involve the imposition of constraints on (2) that are reasonable as opposed to merely convenient.

II. Accounting and Economic Constraints

Accounting Definitions

The first thing required is a balance sheet for reports to stockholders. (Some memorandum accounts, representing tax report accounting procedures, will also be required.) The strategy of the present model is to incorporate a high degree of aggregation with respect to the asset side but not with respect to the liabilities and net worth side.

Balance sheet at beginning of period t

$$
A_t \quad \Bigg| \quad
\begin{aligned}
& L_{1,0} + C_{1,t} \\
& L_{2,0} + C_{2,t} \\
& \quad \cdot \\
& \quad \cdot \\
& \quad \cdot \\
& L_{z,0} + C_{z,t} \\
& DTL_t \\
& \sum_{\tau=1}^{t} \Delta DL_\tau \\
& PE_t \\
& E_t
\end{aligned}
$$

where A_t = total net assets, defined as: total net assets at $t-1$ plus net investment at the beginning at t.[3]

$L_{z,0}$ = z^{th} initial liabilities account, where $z = 1, \ldots, Z$.

$C_{z,t}$ = known cumulative change in $L_{z,0}$, as a result of prearranged loan "takedown," amortization schedules, etc.[4] Alternatively, $C_{z,t} = \sum_{\tau=1}^{t} \Delta CL_{z,\tau}$

where $\Delta CL_{z,t}$ = the period τ change.

---

2. Disagreement over the empirical nature of the important constraints has been—and remains—the major source of confusion in the finance-economics literature. For examples of different viewpoints, see [6], [7], [8], [9], [10], [11], [12], [14].

3. It is assumed that the firm is a going concern, and that depreciation charges entered for stockholder reports, being the firm's estimate of "true" depreciation, represent funds automatically reinvested. Any excess of tax report depreciation charges over stockholder report depreciation charges requires special treatment, as will be seen below.

4. More rigid models assume that all changes in liabilities are under the firm's discretion. It seems more realistic to allow for the constraining effects of financing decisions already made—especially when these decisions were made at prior periods in which interest rates were considerably different from those prevailing at period 0.

$DTL_t =$ deferred corporate income taxes (to be explained below).

$\Delta DL_\tau =$ change in discretionary borrowing account at the beginning of period τ.[5] Subject to constraints that will be specified later ΔDL_τ can be either positive or negative.

$\sum_{\tau=1}^{t} \Delta DL_\tau$ is of course the cumulative total of such borrowing just after period t's changes.

$$L_t = \sum_{z=1}^{z} (L_{z,0} + C_{z,t}) + \sum_{\tau=1}^{t} DL_\tau.$$

$PE_t =$ book value of preferred equity stock at the beginning of t. If the preferred stock is convertible, PE_t is recorded subsequent to any period t conversions. (The model can accommodate several preferred accounts; our description will be of only one, however.)

$E_t =$ book value of common stockholders' equity at the beginning of t.

The income statement is built up as follows:

$\Pi_t =$ profits after "true," or stockholder-report, depreciation charges but before interest and tax payments.

$$\sum_{z=1}^{z} i_z(L_{z,0} + C_{z,t}) + i' \sum_{\tau=1}^{t} \Delta DL_\tau$$

$=$ interest payments made in period t, where $i_z =$ interest rate applicable to

$L_{z,0} + C_{z,t}$ and $i' =$ interest rate[6] applicable to $\sum_{\tau=1}^{t} \Delta DL_\tau$.

$T_t =$ nominal corporate tax rate for period t.

$\Delta_e =$ "true," or stockholder-report, depreciation rate, expressed as a constant percentage of A. Thus, depreciation charges in $t = \Delta_e A_t$.

$\Delta_a =$ tax records depreciation rate, expressed as a constant percentage of A_a, the book value of assets maintained for tax purposes.[7] Thus, tax re-

5. Inclusion of more than one such account would have been feasible, but it was not judged to be worth the effort at this stage of model development. For an example of a short-term borrowing model that abstracts from the long-range goals of this paper but includes several sources of discretionary finance, see [15].

6. It would have been possible to incorporate a different i'_t for each period and to define a discretionary borrowing account allowed to be greater than zero for t.

7. The formula for updating A_{a_t} is:

$$A_{a_t} = (1 - \Delta_a)^t A_{a_0} + (1 - \Delta_a)^t I_1 + (1 - \Delta_a)^{t-1} I_2 + \ldots + (1 - \Delta_a) I_t$$

$$= (1 - \Delta_a)^t (A_{a_0} + I_1) + \sum_{\tau=1}^{t} (1 - \Delta_a)^{t-\tau+1} I_\tau$$

This formula results from the assumption that any "excess" depreciation charges, $\Delta_a A_{a_t} - \Delta_e A_t$, are treated, for stockholder records, in one of two possible ways: as a reduction in taxes (the "flow through" method) in which case some of the excess may be a source of net investment via retained earnings; alternatively, stockholder report earnings and taxes are based on $\Delta_a A_{a_t}$ alone, in which case the tax savings on the excess, $T_t(\Delta_a A_{a_t} - \Delta_e A_t)$, is added to a deferred taxes account,

ported depreciation charges in $t = \Delta_a A_{a_t}$.

$\beta_1 =$ investment tax credit rate (e.g., .07 for most firms, as of the date of this paper).

$\beta_2 =$ proportion of firm's assets on which the investment tax credit is applicable. Thus, the credit in t is $\beta_1 \beta_2 (I_t + \Delta_e A_{t-1})$, where $I_t + \Delta_e A_{t-1}$ = net investment plus last period's depreciation, or gross investment in t. The firm has the option either of "flowing through" the tax reductions to stockholders' earnings or of adding the reductions to DTL.

$d =$ coupon interest rate on preferred stock, i.e., preferred dividends $= d PE_t$.

$SA_t =$ the sum of any special adjustments to income, applicable to period t and assumed to be known.

The flow-through definition of after-tax profits, ATP_t becomes[8]:

$$ATP_t = (1 - T_t) \left\{ \Pi_t + \Delta_e A_t - \Delta_a A_{a_t} - \sum_{z=1}^{Z} i_z (L_{z,0} + C_{z,t}) - i' \sum_{\tau=1}^{t} \Delta DL_\tau \right\}$$
$$+ \Delta_a A_{a_t} - \Delta_e A_t + \beta_1 \beta_2 (I_t + \Delta_e A_{t-1}) \quad (4)$$

At period 0, of course, ATP is assumed known, by virtue of all of the relevant variables being assumed known. For stockholder records where excess depreciation charges and/or investment tax credit tax savings are not flowed through, we can have:

$$ATP_t' = (1 - T_t) \left\{ \Pi_t + \Delta_e A_t - \Delta_a A_{a_t} - \sum_{z=1}^{Z} i_z (L_{z,0} + C_{z,t}) - i' \sum_{\tau=1}^{t} \Delta DL_\tau \right\}$$
$$+ \beta_1 \beta_2 (I_t + \Delta_e A_{t-1}) + (1 - T_t)(\Delta_a A_{a_t} - \Delta_e A_t) \quad (4a)$$

and

$$\Delta DTL_t = T_t (\Delta_a A_{a_t} - \Delta_e A_t).$$

if investment tax credit savings are flowed through to earnings and depreciation-charge generated tax savings are credited to deferred taxes.

DTL. In the sources of net investment statement, ΔDTL_t is then added as a source. Only $\Delta_e A_t$ is automatically reinvested. Consequently, the original tax record A, A_{a_0}, depreciates Δ_a per cent per period and is augmented by new net investment, I_t, which increases both A_{a_t} and A_{t-1} and which is subsequently depreciated appropriately on both sets of "books." While it is true that for going concerns the allowable excess depreciation can result in a permanent tax reduction, firms continue to base their deferred tax accrual determination on the individual asset transaction concept specified by the Accounting Principles Board. In the present model, either treatment of depreciation is legitimate, given the assumption $\Delta_e A_t$ is reinvested and that all of the operating income signified by $\Delta_a A_{a_t} - \Delta_e A_t$ that is kept in the firm will explicitly be considered a source of net investment funds.

8. One the values of all the included variables are shown, it is possible to calculate an *effective* corporate tax rate, $\hat{T}_t$, from the identity

$$(1 - \hat{T}_t) \left\{ \Pi_t - \sum_{z=1}^{Z} i_z (L_{z,0} + C_{z,t}) - i' \sum_{\tau=1}^{t} \Delta VL_\tau \right\} = ATP_t.$$

The determination of the effective tax rate is useful for corporate planning even in those cases in which excess depreciation charges and/or the investment tax credit are not considered, for stockholder reports, to constitute tax reductions.

Alternatively,

$$ATP_t'' = (1 - T_t) \left\{ \Pi_t + \Delta_e A_t - \Delta_a A_{a_t} - \sum_{z=1}^{z} i_z(L_{z,0} + C_{z,t}) - i' \sum_{\tau=1}^{t} DL_\tau \right\}$$
$$+ \Delta_a A_{a_t} - \Delta_e A_t \quad (4b)$$

and

$$\Delta DTL_t = \beta_1 \beta_2 (I_t + \Delta_e A_{t-1})$$

if only the investment tax credit savings are considered, for stockholder reports, to constitute an increase in deferred taxes.

Finally,

$$ATP_t''' = (1 - T_t) \left\{ \Pi_t + \Delta_e A_t - \Delta_a A_a - \sum_{z=1}^{z} i_z(L_{z,0} + C_{z,t}) - i' \sum_{\tau=1}^{t} DL_\tau \right.$$
$$+ (1 - T_t)(\Delta_a A_{a_t} - \Delta_e A_t) \quad (4c)$$

and

$$\Delta DTL = T_t(\Delta_a A_t - \Delta_e A_t) + \beta_1 \beta_2 (I_t + \Delta_e A_{t-1})$$

if both types of tax savings are considered to be temporary and to give rise to a deferred tax liability.

Moreover, earnings available for distribution to common stockholders, AFC_t, is defined as

$$AFC_t = ATP_t - d \cdot PE_t - SA_t \qquad (5)$$

where ATP_t', ATP_t'', or ATP_t''' may also be used, depending upon the firm's accounting methods.

Once having an income statement and balance sheet it is also possible to write an accounting statement describing the sources of funds for net investment, I_t:

$$I_t = AFC_{t-1} - D_{t-1} + \sum_{z=1}^{z} \Delta CL_{z,t} + \Delta DL_t + \Delta DTL_{t-1} + \Delta E_t^N \qquad (6)$$

where ΔE_t^N = net equity funds available (>0) or used (<0) as a result of stock issue or repurchase, respectively, in period t.

New Equity Funds Relationships — Convertible Issues

In the present model there are three potential sources of equity other than from existing stockholders — the equity market, convertible bond holders and convertible preferred stock holders. Because of severe analytical problems, I have chosen to consider only the first as providing discretionary sources of funds. To the extent that convertible issues exist at period 0, however, their effects will be considered.

Convertible bond and preferred stock issues have enjoyed a great deal of popularity in recent years, in part because of the perceived low coupon rates relative to those on competing sources of funds.[9] In particular, their use is

---

9. Needless to say, the present value of ultimate dilution of earnings may offset the temporary interest or dividend rate advantage of the convertible instrument.

widespread as a means of effecting mergers — payment to the merged firm's owners providing them the strong likelihood of capital appreciation while at least temporarily avoiding dilution of the acquiring owners' earnings and control.

Even if we have an issue outstanding — one whose call features, conversion ratios, and conversion prices, at different periods of time, are known — predicting the time rate of conversion is extremely difficult. This is not simply a matter of having to predict the market price of the common stock, which would require knowing the full model solution before we begin. In addition, frequently because of investor tax considerations,[10] convertibles typically will remain unconverted in the face of substantial conversion premia, being turned in only to avoid being called for redemption at par value. My resolution of this problem is offered as a temporary expedient: I assume that the firm knows the time rate of conversion of these securities into shares of common stock. Three accounting categories are affected: a reduction in liabilities or preferred stock, an offsetting increase in book equity, and an increase in N, the number of common shares. For example, let

$\Delta CL_{z',t} =$ known change in liabilities arising from period t conversion of bonds (account $L_{z'}$)into equity ($\Delta CL_{z',t} \leqslant 0$ for all t).

$\Delta E_t^c = -\Delta CL_{z',t} =$ increase in common equity arising from such conversion.

$\Delta N_t^c =$ increase in number of shares (based on conversion ratio applicable to period t) resulting from period t bond conversion.

Treatment of convertible preferred stock is much the same. The change in number of preferred shares in period t is assumed to be known, so that:

$\Delta PE_t =$ known change in preferred equity arising from period t conversion ($\Delta PE_t \leqslant 0$ for all t).

$\Delta E_t^P = -\Delta PE_t =$ increase in common equity arising from conversion.

$\Delta N_t^P =$ increase in number of shares (based on conversion ratio applicable to period t) resulting from period t preferred stock conversion.

(Note: It goes without special mention that existence of non-convertible preferred stock requires only that we set ΔPE_t identically equal to zero for t = 1, ..., n.)

Summing the effects of these three types of changes, two accounting statements are required:

$$E_t = E_{t-1} + \Delta E_t^c + \Delta E_t^P + AFC_{t-1} - D_{t-1} + \Delta E_t^N \qquad (7)$$

a capital account reconciliation, gives the updated value of owner equity, E_t, where the second and third terms on the right-hand side are known and the last three terms result from corporate decisions.

$$N_t = N_{t-1} + \Delta N_t^c + \Delta N_t^P + \Delta N_t \qquad (8)$$

is an analogous statement updating the number of common shares outstanding,

10. See [1] for a cogent discussion of convertibles and their use.

where the fourth term on the right-hand side is a corporate decision variable. (Where there exists more than a single convertible bond or convertible preferred issue, ΔE_t^c, ΔE_t^P, ΔN_t^c and ΔN_t^P will be summary accounts.)

New Equity Funds Relationships — Public Offerings

The principal problems arising from inclusion in the model of purchase or issue of new shares to the public are price-related. Many, if not most, new public offerings are "merchandised" on the basis that the issuing corporation faces an expanded set of investment opportunities. Consequently, the issuing of new stock may take place at per share values inconsistent with previously (or, indeed, later to be) established earnings prospects. Since the present model adopts (as will be seen) a stable investment opportunities function and investment policy, the analytical possibility of creating a new valuation on the firm at date of sale is nil. As a result, the model makes the conservative assumption that shares are purchased or sold at the per share price that will obtain after the transaction:

$$\Delta N_t \left(\frac{P_t}{N_t} \right) = \Delta E_t^N \tag{9}$$

where ΔN_t = number of shares sold ($\Delta N > 0$) or purchased ($\Delta N < 0$), and ΔE_t^N = net funds received (>0) or disbursed (<0). A necessary refinement is to include one parameter, c, reflecting transactions costs and any underpricing[11] on new issues, and another, $\tilde{c}$, reflecting transaction costs on purchases:

$$\Delta N_t \left(\frac{P_t}{N_t} \right) (1 - c) = \Delta E_t^N \quad \text{for} \quad \Delta N_t, \Delta E_t^N \geqslant 0 \tag{9a}$$

$$\Delta N_t \left(\frac{P_t}{N_t} \right) (1 + \tilde{c}) = \Delta E_t^N \quad \text{for} \quad \Delta N_t, \Delta E_t^N \leqslant 0 \tag{9b}$$

While it would have been possible, formally, to permit both issues and repurchases, the model cannot by its very nature deal with stockholder income tax rates (ordinary and capital gains) whereby stock repurchase might be rationalized. In the present model, $\Delta E_t < 0$ is always an expensive alternative to dividend distribution due to our dating of variables convention and the existence of the parameter, c. Consequently, ΔE_t is restricted to being greater than or equal to zero. A second restriction, made for the sake of mathematical convenience and empirical plausibility, is to require $\Delta E_t = 0$ for all periods in which convertible issues are outstanding. Thus, if period j' is the final period in which bond and/or stock conversion takes place, so that for $t = j' + 1, \ldots,$ n *no* convertible issues will be outstanding, then we require:

---

11. Underpricing is not inconsistent with shares being capable of being sold at the equilibrium price. Rather, it proceeds from the inability of an equilibrium model to deal with market liquidity. Deliberate underpricing insures that a stock whose trading market is rather thin will "go out the window" rapidly.

$$\Delta E_t^N = 0 \quad \text{for} \quad t = 1, \ldots, j' \tag{10}$$

If, in addition, the planner wishes not to permit new stock issues for later periods (e.g., for reasons of control) the model will extend constraints (10) as required.

Finally, in order to eliminate the non-linear effects of the variable N_t in the corporate objective function (2), we adopt the Miller-Modigliani procedure [12], amended to include the stock flotation cost parameter, c, and the present model's dating-of-variables conventions. For period $j' + 1$, (9a) may be rewritten as:

$$\frac{\Delta N_{j'+1}}{N_{j'+1}} = \frac{\Delta \tilde{E}_{j'+1}^N}{P_{j'+1}}$$

where $\Delta \tilde{E}_{j'+1}^N = \Delta E_{j'+1}^N / (1 - c) = $ gross funds requirement for $j' + 1$ consistent with net new equity funds of $\Delta E_{j'+1}^N$.

Alternatively,

$$1 - \frac{N_{j'}}{N_{j'+1}} = \frac{\Delta \tilde{E}_{j'+1}^N}{P_{j'+1}}$$

or

$$\frac{N_{j'}}{N_{j'+1}} = \frac{P_{j'+1} - \Delta \tilde{E}_{j'+1}^N}{P_{j'+1}}$$

By definition, however, we know that

$$\frac{P_{j'}}{N_{j'}} = \frac{D_{j'}}{N_{j'}} + \frac{P_{j'+1}}{N_{j'+1}(1 + k_{j'+1})}$$

or

$$P_{j'} = D_{j'} + \frac{N_{j'}}{N_{j'+1}} \cdot \frac{P_{j'+1}}{(1 + k_{j'+1})} \tag{1a}$$

Substituting for $\dfrac{N_{j'}}{N_{j'+1}}$ in (1a):

$$P_{j'} = D_{j'} + (P_{j'+1} - \Delta \tilde{E}_{j'+1}^N)(1 + k_{j'+1})^{-1} \tag{1b}$$

However, since (1b) is valid for $t = j' + 1, \ldots, n$, we get — after successive substitutions:

$$P_{j'} = D_{j'} + (D_{j'+1} - \Delta \tilde{E}_{j'+1}^N)(1 + k_{j'+1})^{-1}$$
$$+ (D_{j'+2} - \Delta \tilde{E}_{j'+2}^N)(1 + k_{j'+1})^{-1}(1 + k_{j'+2})^{-1} + \cdots$$
$$\tag{1c}$$
$$+ (D_{n-1} - \Delta \tilde{E}_{n-1}^N)(1 + k_{j'+1})^{-1} \ldots (1 + k_{n-1})^{-1}$$
$$+ (P_n - \Delta \tilde{E}_n^N)(1 + k_{j'+1})^{-1} \ldots (1 + k_n)^{-1}$$

Consequently, equation (2) can now be completely rewritten so as to eliminate the variables N_t for $t > j'$:

$$\frac{P_0}{N_0} = \frac{D_0}{N_0} + \frac{D_1}{N_1(1+k_1)} + \cdots + \frac{D_{j'}}{N_{j'}(1+k_1)\ldots(1+k_{j'})}$$

(2a)

$$+ \frac{(D_{j'+1} - \Delta\tilde{E}_{j'+1}^{N})}{N_{j'}(1+k_1)\ldots(1+k_{j'+1})} + \frac{(D_{j'+1} - \Delta\tilde{E}_{j'+2}^{N})}{N_{j'}(1+k_1)\ldots(1+k_{j'+2})} + \cdots$$

$$+ \frac{(D_{n-1} - \Delta\tilde{E}_{n-1}^{N})}{N_{j'}(1+k_1)\ldots(1+k_{n-1})} + \frac{(P_n - \Delta\tilde{E}_{n}^{N})}{N_{j'}(1+k_1)\ldots(1+k_n)}$$

It should be noted that Miller's and Modigliani's transformation of the stock price equation was designed to prove that dividend policy is irrelevant, under the assumptions (1) that investment and all sources of investment funds other than retained earnings and new equity are given, and (2) that there are no taxes or flotation costs. The present model, it is to be emphasized, determines *all* sources and uses of funds jointly through time and incorporates, *inter alia,* the effects of the corporate income tax and flotation costs. Thus, either retaining earnings or new equity may be regarded as an accounting, but not as an economic, residual.

Investment Opportunities and k_t Functions

The planning model includes two important economic constraints, one defining the nature of the firm's aggregate profits — investment opportunities, and the other defining the stock market's required rates of return, k_t. Recalling the income statement category Π_t as profits before interest and tax payments, it is possible to write

$$\Pi_t = \Pi_{0_t} + \sum_{\tau=1}^{t} \Pi_{\tau}'(I_\tau) \tag{11}$$

where Π_{0_t} is the known profit, at time t, associated with the firm's initial stock of assets, A_0. (In other words, independent of whether the firm will invest over the future, it is possible to forecast a profit stream, possibly not constant, over time.) $\Pi_{\tau}'(I_\tau) =$ the level of annual profits resulting from period τ's net investment, I_τ. For the present discussion it is assumed that I_τ produces an annual profit, Π_{τ}' beginning[12] in period τ. In addition, if the firm's investment decision is given for the first j periods, then $\Pi_{\tau}'(I_\tau)$ will also be assumed known and given[13] for $\tau = 1, \ldots$ j.

12. Actually it is a small matter to allow the "maturing" of I to be gradual, so that the equilibrium annual profit stream Π_τ is only reached several periods after I_τ is undertaken. The computer program written to solve the planning model permits two alternative assumptions: that Π_τ is first realized in period τ or that it first appears in period $\tau + 1$.

13. This latter feature gives the model the capacity to optimize only with respect to dividends and financing decisions. In particular, if the firm employs investment plans derived from sales forecasts, cost and plant turnover ratios (implicitly embodying some production function concept) and derives gross profit forecasts, the model can still be quite useful. Most rudimentary corporate models now in use employ such a procedure; however, these also typically forecast all but one of the dividend-financing decisions for each period, allowing the last to fall out of a sources-uses of funds equation as an accounting residual.

The form of $\Pi_\tau(I_\tau)$ is of course critical to solution of the model. Most formal planning models assume either a limitless supply of available investment projects at some fixed internal rate of return or else avoid the problem by describing the cash flows associated with a discrete set of investment projects. The first assumption carries with it connotations that the firm is a perfect competitor in product and factor markets and enjoys fixed returns to scale. The second assumption is more palatable in a pure capital budgeting model but it remains seriously deficient in the context of an integrated financial model because it fails to say anything about the larger set of investment opportunities that are likely to emerge prior to the planning horizon but which cannot be enumerated in project-by-project detail at period 0. Those finance models whose objective function is share price require both planner-manager and stock market to possess equivalent and complete knowledge of investment opportunities (deterministic models) or homogeneous expectations (uncertainty models). This would appear to create insuperable information requirements for model implementation for at least two reasons: first, it requires that (in the decentralized firm) the originators of projects provide complete information to the planner-manager who in turn must convey the same to the market; and second (as mentioned above) it denies the relevance of yet-to-emerge project opportunities. It therefore seems more reasonable to argue that planner-manager and stock market are aware of the sense of *overall* investment opportunities, and that this is the knowledge that can be used to establish a balance between various sources of funds and to establish (finally) project screening standards.[14]

The investment opportunities function adopted for this paper is

$$\Pi_\tau'(I_\tau) = \rho_\tau I_\tau \tag{12}$$

where

$$\rho_\tau = c_0 + c_1 \frac{I_\tau}{A_{\tau-1}} \tag{13}$$

and where $c_0 > 0$, $c_1 < 0$. That is, ρ_τ, the internal rate of return per period earned on I_τ, is a decreasing linear function of the rate of growth of the firm's assets, $\frac{I_\tau}{A_{\tau-1}}$. Functions of this kind have been employed frequently in studies dealing with the economic theory of corporate finance [6], [7], [8], [9], [10], [11]. In addition to being intuitively plausible they have the property that $\frac{\partial \Pi_\tau'(I_\tau)}{\partial I_\tau} > 0$ and $\frac{\partial^2 \Pi_\tau'(I_\tau)}{\partial I_\tau^2} < 0$ for $I_\tau > 0$. The stationarity of equation 13 (stationary in the sense of permitting a single ρ_τ and rate of growth of assets solution) is consistent with earlier efforts. In the present context of a user-oriented planning model such stationarity is primarily an arithmetic and informational convenience (only two parameters are needed); moreover, it is only assumed to hold for a finite time period.

14. See [3] for a discussion of the implications of this point of view for the operating significance of the term "capital rationing."

We can rewrite (13) and substitute into (12):

$$\Pi_\tau' = \rho_\tau \left(\frac{\rho_\tau - c_0}{c_1} \right) A_{\tau-1} \tag{14}$$

Next in order to reduce dimensionality, we will find in solution a single ρ for all periods included up to the planning horizon, so that

$$\Pi_\tau' = \rho \left(\frac{\rho - c_0}{c_1} \right) A_{\tau-1} \tag{14a}$$

and

$$I_\tau = \left(\frac{\rho - c_0}{c_1} \right) A_{\tau-1}. \tag{14b}$$

Using the definition of $A_t : A_t = A_{t-1} - I_t$, we get

$$A_t = \left(1 + \frac{\rho - c_0}{c_1} \right) A_{t-1} \tag{15}$$

and

$$A_t = \left(1 + \frac{\rho - c_0}{c_1} \right)^{t-j} A_j \tag{15a}$$

so that

$$A_{t-1} = \left(1 + \frac{\rho - c_0}{c_1} \right)^{t-j-1} A_j \tag{16}$$

and

$$I_t = \left(\frac{\rho - c_0}{c_1} \right) \left(1 + \frac{\rho - c_0}{c_1} \right)^{t-j-1} A_j. \tag{14c}$$

Furthermore, equation (11) can be rewritten as[15]

$$\Pi_t = \Pi_{0_t} + \sum_{\tau=1}^{j} \Pi_\tau'(I_\tau) + \rho \left(\frac{\rho - c_0}{c_1} \right) \left\{ \left(1 + \frac{\rho - c_0}{c_1} \right)^0 \right.$$
$$\left. + \left(1 + \frac{\rho - c_0}{c_1} \right)^1 + \ldots + \left(1 + \frac{\rho - c_0}{c_1} \right)^{t-j-1} \right\} A_j \tag{11a}$$

for $t = j + 1, \ldots, n$. That is, if I_t and Π_t' are given from $t = 1$ through $t = j$, then the remaining A_t, I_t and Π_t can be found as functions of the solution value internal rate of return, ρ. In the special case in which none of the planning period's Π_t''s or I_t's are given, we have

$$I_t = \left(\frac{\rho - c_0}{c_1} \right) \left(1 + \frac{\rho - c_0}{c_1} \right)^{t-1} A_0 \tag{14c}$$

$$A_t = \left(1 + \frac{\rho - c_0}{c_1} \right)^t A_0 \tag{15a}$$

15. (11a) assumes no lags in the maturing of investment; an obvious adjustment incorporates lags.

and

$$\Pi_t = \Pi_{0_t} + \rho \left(\frac{\rho - c_0}{c_1} \right) \left\{ \left(1 + \frac{\rho - c_0}{c_1} \right)^0 + \left(1 + \frac{\rho - c_0}{c_1} \right)^1 \right.$$

$$\left. + \cdots + \left(1 + \frac{\rho - c_0}{c_1} \right)^{t-1} \right\} A_0 \quad (11b)$$

The second important economic constraint, the function expressing the dependence of k_t on relevant exogenous and endogenous (to the firm) variables is moot. The analytical burden of a substantial proportion of the empirical work in corporation finance in recent years has been to establish the most valid form (theoretically and empirically) for this function. Needless to say, no professional consensus exists. At the heart of the matter, however, is the question of stock market awareness of, and required compensation for, risk. Since our corporate planning model is in deterministic form (at least to the extent of employing expected values where appropriate) we have to tread carefully when dealing with the k_t function. The basic strategy is to keep open the planner's options and to permit use of any desired function, subject only to the requirement (for obvious conceptual and computational reasons) that any corporate decision variables included as arguments be included at their post-horizon, or steady-state, values. Wise use of the model obviously calls for sensitivity analyses on the effects of a plausible range of k_t function values.

Institutional and Corporate Policy Constraints

One important set of parameters deals with the horizon problem. Having chosen a finite horizon, n, the firm (and model) has to resolve the truncation of all post-horizon terms in equation (2) into P_n. The usual approach, and that adopted here, is to assume that the firm enters a steady-state at the horizon such that

$$P_n = \frac{D_n}{k_n - \bar{g}} \quad (17)$$

where $\bar{g}$ = post-horizon dividends growth rate, is an adequate approximation. The inputs required are as follows:

$$\frac{L_n}{E_n + PE_n} = m \quad (18)$$

where $L_n = \sum_{z=1}^{z} (L_{z,0} + C_{z,t}) + \sum_{t-1}^{n} \Delta DL_t + DTL_n$ = total liabilities at period

n and m is a parameter. That is, the firm has a target capital structure, m, to be achieved at the horizon date. (Sensitivity analysis, employing hypothesized relationships among k_t, i′ and m, may indicate whether such a target is optimal, of course.)

Using the balance sheet identity, $E_n + PE_n = A_n - L_n$, equation (18) becomes

$$L_n = \left(\frac{m}{1+m}\right) A_n \tag{18a}$$

so that for given (out of A_0 plus cumulative investment) A_n, L_n is determinate. Further, with L_n known, $E_n = A_n - L_n - PE_n$, so that the horizon value of common equity is known.

Next, the post-horizon earnings retention rate, $1 - \dfrac{D_n}{AFC_n}$, and/or growth rate, $\bar{g}$, must be specified according to one of two possible options:

(i) $1 - \dfrac{D_n}{AFC_n}$ is given, and $\bar{g}$ derived from the identity

$$\bar{g} = \frac{\left(1 - \dfrac{D_n}{AFC_n}\right)(AFC_n)}{E_n},$$

since for given, m, and investment decisions, AFC_n is known.

or

(ii) $1 - \dfrac{D_n}{AFC_n}$ and $\bar{g}$ both given, in which case a consistency check is made, to insure that implied post-horizon rate of return on equity, $\dfrac{\bar{g}}{1 - \dfrac{D_n}{AFC_n}}$, is no greater than that of the horizon year itself, $\dfrac{AFC_n}{E_n}$.

(With both options an additional check is to require that $k_n > \bar{g}$.)

In addition, D_0 is given, and

$$\frac{D_t}{N_t} - \alpha_1 \frac{D_{t-1}}{N_{t-1}} \geqslant 0 \qquad t = 1, \dots, n \tag{19}$$

$$\frac{AFC_t}{N_t} - \gamma_1 \frac{AFC_{t-1}}{N_{t-1}} \geqslant 0 \qquad t = 1, \dots, n \tag{20}$$

are optional constraints, with $1 \leqslant \alpha_1 \leqslant \gamma_1$.

Restrictions (19) and (20) allow the corporate planner to offset indirectly (ignorance of and) omission of the dynamics of expectations formation. A deterministic model which allowed dividends per share or earnings per share to fluctuate freely would be correct given our assumptions but unrealistic: There is information content in a dividend or earnings share which if uncontrolled could lead to nonviable market expectations and to changes in required rates of return k_t. Firms frequently do impose constraints such as (19) or (20); in a linear program format, one can at least assess their costs through an examination of the relevant dual evaluators.

For any periods in which ΔE_t and hence ΔN_t are required to be zero, (19) and (20) are valid linear restrictions, given the solution technique to be described below. For all other periods we require that

$$D_t - \alpha_1 D_{t-1} \geqslant 0 \tag{19a}$$

and/or

$$AFC_t - \gamma_1 AFC_{t-1} \geqslant 0. \tag{20a}$$

For these years we require in addition to (19a) and (20a) that

$$\frac{N_t}{N_{t-1}} \leqslant \alpha_1$$

if constraints (19) are employed, and

$$\frac{N_t}{N_{t-1}} < \gamma_1$$

if only (20) are required. Using the definition (9a), this is equivalent to

$$P_t - \Delta \tilde{E}_t^N \geqslant \frac{1}{\alpha_1} P_t$$

$$P_t - \Delta \tilde{E}_t^N \geqslant \frac{1}{\gamma_1} P_t \tag{21}$$

respectively, which in turn can be expressed as valid linear restrictions in the decision variables.

The force of this approach is admittedly to weaken the model's power, since for any years in which (19a) or (20a) and (21) are satisfied as equalities dividends per share or earnings per share will merely not decline, rather than meet the requirements (19) and (20). The additional benefits to be gained from dealing directly with (19) and (20) as non-linear restrictions were not judged to be worth the computational burden.

The second set of operating constraints combines the effects of capital market and management policy limitations on corporate financing decisions. There are:

$$\Delta E_t^N = 0 \qquad \text{for any } t \geqslant j' + 1 \text{ the planner wishes.} \tag{22}$$

(this constraint was discussed above.)

$$\frac{L_t}{E_t + PE_t} \leqslant K \qquad \text{or} \qquad L_t \leqslant \frac{K}{1+K} A_t \tag{23}$$

for $t = 1, \ldots, n-1$ gives an operating limit to the debt-equity ratio over the planning period. Obviously, $K \geqslant m$.

$$\frac{\Pi_t}{\sum_{z=1}^{z} i_z (L_{z,0} + C_{z,t}) + i' \sum_{\tau=1}^{t} \Delta DL_\tau} \geqslant x$$

or

$$L_t \leqslant \frac{\Pi_t - x \sum_{z=1}^{z} (i_z - i')(L_{z,0} + C_{z,t})}{xi'} \tag{24}$$

for $t = 1, \ldots, n$, where x is the minimum "times interest earned" ratio.

$$\Delta DL_t \leqslant I_t \tag{25}$$

$t = 1, \ldots, n$. The firm cannot pre-finance, or borrow a sum greater than its current investment requirements.

$$\sum_{\tau=1}^{t} D_\tau - \delta \sum_{\tau=1}^{t} AFC_\tau \leqslant 0 \tag{26}$$

$t = 1, \ldots, n$ gives a cumulative restriction on dividend payout of δ per cent of cumulative earnings otherwise available for distribution.

$$D_t - \delta_1 AFC_t \geqslant 0 \tag{27}$$

$$D_t - \delta_2 AFC_t \leqslant 0 \tag{28}$$

for $t = 1, \ldots, n$ give annual lower (δ_1) and upper (δ_2) limits on dividend payout ratios.

III. SOLUTION STRATEGY

What remains is a non-linear optimization problem in the four decision variables I_t, D_t, $\sum_{\tau=1}^{t} \Delta DL_\tau$ and ΔE_t^N over the planning horizon. Given values for $\{I_t\}$ and $\{\Pi_t\}$, the objective function (2a) and all of the constraints are linear in the remaining decision variables. Since in addition some planners specify some or all values for I_t it is convenient to encode a solution algorithm that involves iterating over a user-specified range of the investment opportunities (see Figure 1). That is, for each ρ, $\{I_t\}$ is determined from (11a) and an

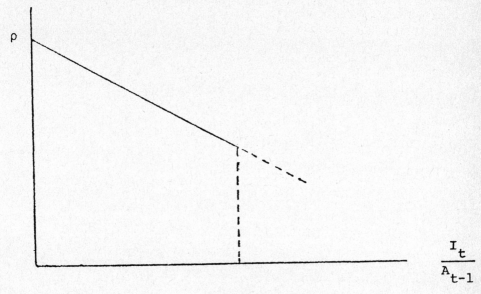

FIGURE 1

645

optimum linear programming solution is found for the remaining variables: $\{D_t\}$, $\left\{\sum_{\tau=1}^{t} \Delta DL_\tau\right\}$ and $\{\Delta E_t^N\}$. The best of these ρ-solutions is the final optimal program. This procedure has the advantage of allowing the user to specify the applicable range of the investment opportunities function; in practice it has been found that many firms face an upper limit on investment due to, for example, a scarcity of managerial resources.

IV. An Illustrative Problem

For our hypothetical firm, XYZ, Inc., we take as the starting balance sheet:

XYZ, Inc. 1/1/68
(Figures in $000,000)

Total net assets (A_0)	100		
		Current liabilities ($L_{1,0}$)	5
		Term loan ($L_{2,0}$)	5
		Long-term debt ($L_{3,0}$)	15
		Convertible debenture ($L_{4,0}$)	5
		Deferred taxes (DTL_0)	5
		Preferred equity (PE_0)	5
		Common equity (E_0)	60
Total net assets	100	Total liabilities and net worth	100

XYZ has a five-year planning horizon, and in updating its liabilities and preferred equity accounts to this horizon, the following conditions will be required:

(i) Current liabilities. $i_1 = 0$ for all t and $C_{1,t}$ is determined according to the rule that $L_{1,0} + C_{1,t} = .05A_t$ for $t = 1, \ldots, 5$.

(ii) Term loan. $i_2 = .06$ for all t, and the loan is being amortized: $C_{2,1} = -1$, $C_{2,2} = -2$, $C_{2,3} = -3$, $C_{2,4} = -4$, $C_{2,5} = -5$.

(iii) Long-term debt. For this account, $i_3 = .05$, and $C_{3,t} = 0$, $t = 1, \ldots, 5$.

(iv) Convertible debenture. The coupon rate is $i_4 = .04$. The planned-forecasted conversion schedule is as follows:

$$L_{4,1} = 5 \quad \Delta \bar{E}_1^c = 0 \quad \Delta N_1^c = 0$$

$$L_{4,2} = 0 \quad \Delta \bar{E}_2 = 5 \quad \Delta N_2^c = .1$$

$$L_{4,3} = 0 \quad \Delta E_3 = 0 \quad \Delta N_3^c = 0$$

$$L_{4,4} = 0 \quad \Delta E_4 = 0 \quad \Delta N_4 = 0$$

$$L_{4,5} = 0 \quad \Delta E_5 = 0 \quad \Delta N_5^c = 0$$

(v) Deferred taxes. XYZ flows through its investment tax credit savings, but accrues its depreciation-generated tax savings. Thus equations (4a) are used to determine ATP_t and ΔDTL_t.

(vi) Preferred equity. This is a straight preferred issue, with a dividend rate of $d = .06$.

XYZ's initial income-dividends position is $AFC_0 = 8$, $D_0 = 5$ and $\Pi_{0_0} = 15.585$. Since I_1 is given as 9, and there is no profit lag we also have $\Pi_{0_t} + \Pi_1(I_1) = 17.025$ for $t = 1, \ldots, 5$. That is, in the absence of any net investment beyond year 1, XYZ forecasts earnings before interest and taxes of $17.025 per year.

The remaining parameters are:

$$T_t = .5 \qquad t = 1, \ldots, 5$$
$$\Delta_e = .05$$
$$\Delta_a = .08$$
$$A_{s_0} = 90$$
$$\beta_1 = 0.7$$
$$\beta_2 = .65$$
$$N_0 = 5$$
$$SA_t = 0 \qquad t = 1, \ldots, 5$$
$$\underline{k}_t = .1 \qquad t = 1, \ldots, 5$$
$$\overline{g} = .05$$
$$D_5/AFC_5 = .5$$
$$\frac{L_5}{E_5} = m = .55$$
$$c = .15$$
$$c_0 = .2$$
$$c_1 = -.7$$
$$i' = .07$$

and the policy restrictions are:

$$\alpha_1 = 1.01 \qquad \text{from constraints (19)}$$
$$K = .58 \qquad \text{from constraints (23)}$$
$$x = 3.5 \qquad \text{from constraints (24)}$$
$$\delta = .65 \qquad \text{from constraints (26)}$$
$$\delta_1 = 0 \qquad \text{from constraints (27)}$$
$$\delta_2 = .75 \qquad \text{from constraints (28)}$$

Finally, with an upper limit on asset growth of 10 per cent per year, solutions are found first at 10 per cent and then for decrements of $.005 \cdot \dfrac{I_t}{A_{t-1}} = .07$

and $\rho = .151$ give rise to the largest $\dfrac{P_0}{N_0}$ when a linear programming solution is found. The objective function coefficients and constraint system generated by this value of ρ are given in Table 1.[16] Highlights of the solution are given in Table 2.[17]

The financial statements generated by this solution are given in Table 3 on page 313.[18]

16. It can be seen that we have treated AFC_t as decision variable and that several of the constraints are obviously redundant. This merely reflects a choice to sacrifice computational efficiency at the linear programming stage of the computer program in favor of making on-line parameter manipulation easier. The computer program was written for conversational mode inputs and parameter changes on the Dartmouth GE 635 time-sharing system; it generates objective function coefficients and constraints at each ρ.

17. Totals may not always add, because of rounding.

18. The willingness of corporate management to proliferate such *ad hoc* rules can easily produce infeasible programs, a phenomenon that can be discovered and dealt with only in the context of a detailed model. As a strictly non-scientific aside, one wonders how often banks are called upon by their corporate customers to rescue them from the operating consequences of inconsistent finance rules.

It is interesting to note first that while the model was driving toward higher ρ-lower investment growth, $\rho = .151$ is the largest feasible value of ρ no matter how financed. Stated differently, some minimum rate of growth of assets is required merely to satisfy financial constraints. Consistent with this observation is the fact that the binding inequality constraints are all associated with the requirement that dividends per share grow at least one per cent per year. While direct measurement of all of the benefits derived from such a typically-imposed financial policy is impossible in a model that abstracts from uncertainty, the linear programming format provides at least some evidence. A one-at-a-time examination of the relevant dual evaluators, for example, suggests that:

(a) If dividends per share, at $.94 in 1969, could be cut to $.74 in 1970, the solution price per share would rise by about $.09 (constraint 28);

(b) Given a market value of the firm's equity of $103.9 million in 1973, ability to raise an additional $1 million in public offering of equity in that year would result in a solution price increase of $.004 per share (constraint 31);

(c) Analogously to (a), if dividends per share in 1971 could be reduced by $.19 from 1970's level of $.95, the solution would increase by $.02 (constraint 32);

(d) Finally, given 1971 dividends per share of $.96, freedom to cut to $.77 in 1972 would result in the solution increasing by $.01 (constraint 33).

Strict interpretation of these dual elevators should be tempered, however, by the following *caveats*: In the first place, the presence of many definitional constraints influences the absolute size of the duals. Secondly, there is the usual problem of interpreting several marginal conditions jointly and by illustrating with discrete parameter changes. Finally, since the sense of the original constraint was an imposition on all periods, the most appropriate post-optimality analysis is a re-run of the model without this policy restriction present. In the set of solutions produced by these conditions, the model again was driving toward larger ρ, and the largest feasible value, .158 $\left(\dfrac{I_t}{A_{t-1}} = .06 \right)$, also produced the highest solution price $16.22 — only $.07 larger than when the dividend growth restrictions were in force. It is interesting to note that even in this case the overall force of the remaining constraints is to require some minimum rate of asset expansion. Further, for the new best solution dividends per share fall in 1972 and no public offering of equity is used in any year. A final observation on the sets of solutions with and without dividend growth restrictions: It is dangerous to generalize from a particular, *ad hoc*, example, but the optimizing solutions were not only over a small range of internal rates of return, but they reproduced $\dfrac{P_{1968}}{N_{1968}}$ values that differed at most by $.50. One can speculate on the real-world role placed by policy restrictions as devices designed by risk-averse corporate managements and lenders implicitly to limit the range of outcomes.

TABLE 1

	AFC_1	D_1	$\sum_{\tau=1}^{t} A_\tau$	ΔE_1^N	AFC_2	D_2	$\sum_{\tau=1}^{2} \Delta DL_\tau$	ΔE_2^N	AFC_3	D_3	$\sum_{\tau=1}^{3} \Delta DL_\tau$	ΔE_3^N	AFC_4	D_4	$\sum_{\tau=1}^{4} \Delta DL_\tau$	ΔE_4^N	ΔE_5^N	P_5	Requirements Vector
Objective Function Coefficients	0	.1818	0	−.2139	0	.1620	0	−.1906	0	.1473	0	−.1733	0	.1339	0	−.1576	−.1432	.1217	
Constraints (4a) and (5) defining AFC_t 1.	1.0000																		= 8.2545
2.					1.0000														= 8.9187
3.			.0350						1.0000										= 9.6068
AFC_t 4.							.0350						1.0000						= 10.3409
5.			1.0000	1.0000							.0350								= 3.6318
Constraints (6) defining E_t^N 6.	1.0000	−1.0000	−1.0000				1.0000	1.0000					1.0000						= 7.5317
7.					1.0000	−1.0000	−1.0000				1.0000	1.0000							= 8.2334
8.									1.0000	−1.0000	−1.0000			1.0000		1.0000			= 8.9646
9.													−1.0000	−1.0000			−1.0000		= 11.1830
Constraints (10) 10.				1.0000															= 0
11.								1.0000											= 0
12.												1.0000							≤ 4.6445
Constraints (23) 13.			1.0000																≤ 12.3471
14.							1.0000												≤ 15.4133
15.											1.0000								≤ 18.8490
16.															1.0000				≤ 52.4898
Constraints (24) 17.																			≤ 60.9067
18.											1.0000				1.0000				≤ 66.7955
19.																			≤ 73.0367
20.																			≤ 9.0000
Constraints (25) 21.			1.0000				1.0000												≤ 7.6300
22.			−1.0000				−1.0000				1.0000				1.0000				≤ 8.1641
23.											−1.0000				1.0000				≤ 8.7356
24.																			≥ 11.5649
25.	.2000																		≥ 1.6160
26.		.2000			.1961														≥ .6060
27.	−.2020																		≥ 0

649

Table (landscape orientation)

Row	AFC$_1$	D$_1$ $\sum_{\tau=1}^{1}\Delta_\tau$	ΔE_1^N	AFC$_2$	D$_2$	$\sum_{\tau=1}^{2}\Delta DL_\tau$	ΔE_2^N	AFC$_3$	D$_3$	$\sum_{\tau=1}^{3}\Delta DL_\tau$	ΔE_3^N	AFC$_4$	D$_4$	$\sum_{\tau=1}^{4}\Delta DL_\tau$	ΔE_4^N	ΔE_5^N	P$_5$	Requirements Vector
Objective Function Coefficients	0	.1818	-.2139	0	.1620	0	-.1906	0	.1473	0	-.1733	0	.1339	0	-.1576	-.1432	.1217	
Constraints (19a), (20a), (21) 28.		-.2020			.1961				.0099				.0090			-.0096	.0082	$\geq$ 0
29.											-1.1765		.0099		-.0106	-.0106	.0090	$\geq$ 0
30.															-1.1765	-.0106	.0099	$\geq$ 0
31.																-1.1765		$\geq$ 0
32.		1.0000							1.0000				1.0000					$\geq$ 0
33.		1.0000			-1.0100				-1.0100				1.0100					$\geq$ 0
34.																		5.1962
——— 35.	-.7500																	$\geq$ 0
Constraints (27), (28) 36.				-.7500	1.0000													$\leq$ 0
37.					1.0000													$\leq$ 0
38.																		$\leq$ 0
39.								-.7500	1.0000			-.7500	1.0000					$\leq$ 0
40.									1.0000				1.0000					$\leq$ 0
41.																		$\leq$ 0
42.																		$\leq$ 0
——— 43.	-.6500	1.0000		-.6500	1.0000			-.6500	1.0000			-.6500	1.0000					$\leq$ 0
Constraints (26) 44.	-.6500	1.0000		-.6500	1.0000			-.6500	1.0000			-.6500	1.0000					$\leq$ 0
45.	-.6500	1.0000		-.6500	1.0000			-.6500	1.0000									$\leq$ 0
46.	-.6500	1.0000		-.6500	1.0000			-.6500	1.0000									$\leq$ 0
47.	-.6500	1.0000																$\leq$ 0
Constraint (17) 48.																	1.0000	1.5589

= -103.9230

TABLE 2

PROGRAM SOLUTION FOR $\dfrac{I_t}{A_{t-1}} = .07$ AND $\rho = .151$

VALUE OF OBJECTIVE FUNCTION $= \$16.15$

Basic Variable	Value
AFC_1	8.1274
D_1	4.7075
$\sum_{\tau=1}^{1} \Delta DL_\tau$	3.6318
ΔE_1^N	0
AFC_2	8.6478
D_2	4.8497
$\sum_{\tau=1}^{2} \Delta DL_\tau$	7.7436
ΔE_2^N	0
AFC_3	9.1805
D_3	4.8982
$\sum_{\tau=1}^{3} \Delta DL_\tau$	12.1790
ΔE_3^N	0
AFC_4	9.7508
D_4	4.9471
$\sum_{\tau=1}^{4} \Delta DL_\tau$	16.8612
ΔE_4^N	0
ΔE_5^N	0.8746
P_5	103.9230

Number of Binding Inequality Constraint	Dual Evaluator
28	$-.0872$
31	$-.0041$
32	$-.0203$
33	$-.0142$

TABLE 3
Balance Sheet (in $000,000)

	1/1/68	1/1/69	1/1/70	1/1/71	1/1/72	1/1/73
Total net assets	$100	$109	$116.63	$124.79	$133.53	$142.88
Current liabilities	5	5.45	5.83	6.24	6.68	7.14
Term loan	5	4	3	2	1	0
Long-term debt	15	15	15	15	15	15
Convertible debenture	5	5	5	0	0	0
Deferred taxes	5	5.92	6.63	7.16	7.49	7.64
Discretionary debt	0	3.63	7.74	12.18	16.86	20.91
Total debt	35	39	38.21	42.58	47.03	50.70
Preferred equity	5	5	5	5	5	5
Common equity	60	65	73.42	77.22	81.50	87.18
Total liabilities and net worth	$100	$109	$116.63	$124.79	$134.53	$142.88

Sources and Uses of Funds (in $000,000)

Sources	1969	1970	1971	1972	1973
Profit (from previous year)	$ 8.00	$ 8.13	$ 8.65	$ 9.18	$ 9.75
New debt (discretionary)	3.63	4.11	4.44	4.68	4.05
Increased liabilities (other accounts)	.37	.10	−.07	−.23	−.38
Equity from stock issue	0	0	0	0	.87
Total sources	$12.00	$12.34	$13.01	$13.63	$14.29
Uses					
Net investment	$ 9.00	$ 7.63	$ 8.16	$ 8.74	$ 9.35
Dividends (previous year)	3.00	4.71	4.85	4.90	4.95
Total uses	$12.00	$12.34	$13.01	$13.63	$14.29

Other Information

	1968	1969	1970	1971	1972	1973
Expected price per share	$16.15	$17.11	$17.78	$18.52	$19.31	$20.18
Shares outstanding (in 000,000)	5	5	5.1	5.1	5.1	5.15
Debt/equity ratio	.54	.56	.49	.52	.54	.55
Times interest earned	12.47	10.02	9.02	7.54	6.54	6.02
Earnings retention rate	.63	.43	.44	.47	.49	.5
Effective tax rate	.44	.45	.45	.44	.43	.42
"True" depreciation (in $000,000)	5	5.45	5.83	6.24	6.68	7.14
Earnings/share	1.60	1.63	1.70	1.80	1.91	2.02
Dividends/share	.60	.94	.95	.96	.97	1.01
ρ		.151	.151	.151	.151	.151

V. Uses and Extensions of the Model

Some of the uses of the corporate planning model are obvious — such as sensitivity analyses as to the effects of varying key parameters and forecasts. Other uses are somewhat subtler: They would include, for example, re-run of the model with an appropriately structured term loan if discretionary debt was indicated to remain fairly stable for four years, thence to fall sharply. For another example, prospective merger financings could be evaluated rapidly in a full system context. For still another, the model can be used to provide parameters (ρ, I_t) for disaggregated project selection models [3]. In point of fact the largest single use of the planning model to date has consisted of extensive sensitivity analysis with respect to the parameters of the policy restrictions. Most of these restrictions, which make up much of the traditional *dicta* of "sound finance," appear on close examination (as hinted at above) to represent attempts to reduce the range of feasible solutions so as to reduce exposure of risk. As Weingartner correctly noted [16], in commenting on the Cohen-Hammer bank asset management model [4], this is a clumsy and inefficient method for coping with uncertainty. In partial defense I would argue that the order-of-magnitude increase in the model's complexity occasioned by formal introduction of uncertainty would severely limit its acceptance at the management levels at which a financial systems frame of reference has greatest value.

Later, obvious extensions which should (and hopefully will) be developed include the disaggregation of ΔDL into several policy variables representing different debt instruments, provision for i′ to vary over time, endogenous bond conversion schedules, and some disaggregation of the asset side of the balance sheet. The explicit introduction of uncertainty raises issues not even touched upon in this paper, but it too should be considered. One of the principal advantages to the present model would seem to be in the fact that it clearly reveals the major modelling yet to be done.

REFERENCES

1. Eugene F. Brigham. "An Analysis of Convertible Debentures," *Journal of Finance,* Vol. XXI, No. 1, March 1966, pp. 35-54.
2. Willard T. Carleton. "A Dynamic Programming Model for Corporate Financial Planning," paper given at TIMS/ORSA Joint meeting, San Francisco, May 1968.
3. —————. "Linear Programming and Capital Budgeting Models: A New Interpretation," *Journal of Finance,* Vol. XXIV, No. 5, December 1969.
4. Kalman J. Cohen and Frederick S. Hammer. "Linear Programming and Optimal Bank Asset Management Decisions," *Journal of Finance,* Vol. XXI, No. 2, May 1967, pp. 147-165.
5. George W. Gershefski. "Building a Corporate Financial Model," *Harvard Business Review,* July-August 1969, pp. 61-72.
6. Myron J. Gordon. *The Investment, Financing, and Valuation of the Corporation,* Homewood, Ill.: Irwin, 1962.
7. Eugene M. Lerner and Willard T. Carleton. "The Integration of Capital Budgeting and Stock Valuation," *American Economic Review,* Vol. LIV, No. 5, September 1964, pp. 683-702.
8. ————— and —————. "Financing Decisions of the Firm," *Journal of Finance,* Vol. XXI, No. 2, May 1966, pp. 202-214.
9. ————— and —————. *A Theory of Financial Analysis,* New York: Harcourt, Brace & World, 1966.
10. John Lintner. "Dividends, Earnings, Leverage, Stock Prices, and the Supply of Capital to Corporations," *Review of Economics and Statistics,* Vol. XLIV, No. 3, August 1962, pp. 243-269.

11. ————. "Optimal Dividends and Corporate Growth Under Uncertainty," *Quarterly Journal of Economics,* Vol. LXXVIII, No. 1, February 1964, pp. 49-95.
12. Merton H. Miller and Franco Modigliani. "Dividend Policy, Growth, and the Valuation of Shares," *Journal of Business,* Vol. XXXIV, No. 4, October 1961, pp. 411-433.
13. Joseph S. Moag, Willard T. Carleton and Eugene M. Lerner. "Defining the Finance Function: A Model-Systems Approach," *Journal of Finance,* Vol. XXII, No. 4, pp. 543-555.
14. Franco Modigliani and Merton H. Miller. "The Cost of Capital, Corporation Finance, and the Theory of Investment," *American Economic Review,* Vol. XLVIII, No. 3, June 1958, pp. 261-297.
15. A. A. Robichek, D. Teichroew and J. M. Jones. "Optimal Short-Term Financing Decision," *Management Science,* Vol. XII, No. 1, September 1965, pp. 1-36.
16. H. Martin Weingartner. "Discussion," *Journal of Finance,* Vol. XXII, No. 2, May 1967, pp. 166-168.

A SIMULTANEOUS EQUATION APPROACH
TO FINANCIAL PLANNING

JAMES M. WARREN AND JOHN P. SHELTON*

I. INTRODUCTION

THE USE of operational mathematical models has, in recent years, flourished in the field of Business Finance. Among major contributions to this area have been: Weingartner's models of capital budgeting (1); the model of Robichek, Teichroew and Jones on the short-term financing decision (2); Robichek and Myers' discussion of simulation for long-range financial planning (3); and Carleton's application of linear programming to determine the level of investment, the dividend policy, and the use of debt and equity that will maximize share value (4). This paper adds to the growing list of mathematical models in Business Finance (and security analysis).

The model described here differs from some of its predecessors in that it deals with overall corporate financial planning, not simply a subset such as capital budgeting; it provides a simultaneous solution of a system of equations which portray the functioning of the firm in contrast to the approach of Robichek and Myers, which fails to capture much of the interdependencies among financial decisions; and it may offer management a more operational planning tool than Carleton's optimum-seeking framework with its restrictive (and perhaps unrealistic) assumptions on the firm's investment opportunities function.

This paper outlines a technique for financial planning that permits a decision maker to simulate (on a "what-if" basis) the financial impacts of changing assumptions regarding such variables as sales, operating ratios, price/earnings ratios, retention rates, debt to equity ratios, etc. The model then generates pro-forma summary balance sheets, income statements, and certain other variables (such as earnings per share and share price). The model does not "optimize" anything. Rather, it provides relevant information to the decision maker.

The "planner" must provide a set of information for the model, as shown in Table 1. Given these inputs, the model "solves" the simultaneous equation system to find the specified "unknowns" in a manner quite similar to the process followed by all firms that use financial planning, and is, therefore, readily communicated to financial managers. The proposed approach is quite similar in concept to the techniques taught in basic business finance courses, except that it is formally identified and can be solved in an efficient manner (by computer).

Though the model, as presented here, is certainly not the final word, it has

* Respectively, Assistant Professor of Finance and Professor of Finance, Graduate School of Business Administration University of California, Los Angeles.

reached a stage of development that justifies publishing the present version. The system of equations presented in this model has evolved after considerable experience to find the most appropriate amount of aggregation (or disaggregation) that management needs in order to have a useful planning tool. The model decomposes the firm into enough elements that management feels the model captures reality, but there is sufficient aggregation to allow the corporation manager (or the student of corporation finance) to see the "forest not the trees" in an organization as complex as the business firm. Thus, one of the virtues of this model is that it provides a list of the key equations that have been determined by fairly wide application to be the optimum combination of elements necessary to describe the financial characteristics of the business firm.

Not only does this paper present in bare-bones fashion the essential elements of a corporate financial planning structure, but computers make it possible for corporate management to use the model easily and effectively as a planning tool. The system of equations is formulated in this model in such a general fashion that it can be a basic building block for more detailed corporate financial planning. In this respect, the model presented here is much more amenable to expansion than Carleton's system. The model presented is a compromise between a simplified, compact set of relations and a system seeking to capture minute details of the firm's operations. The system includes various balance sheet and income statement accounts, changes in account values, earnings and dividends per share, and share price.

Gershefski reports that 63 firms used computerized financial planning models as of 1969 (5). One of the reasons for publishing this paper is because much of the work in the computerization of long-range financial planning is proprietary, and thus not available to a broad group of readers.

II. Description of the Model

The following criteria typify a financial planning model that will be successfully utilized by business planners and security analysts:

1. The implications that fall out of the model should be credible; the model should be flexible enough to meet current needs and be easily expandable to meet future demands; it should be realistic enough that it doesn't suffer from the complaint that it is an "ivory tower" tool that fails to catch the reality of life.
2. It should provide a "step forward." That is, it should either improve upon the techniques being used in practice or make it easier to perform what is currently being done.
3. The inputs and outputs should be stated in terms that are meaningful to a corporate financial manager, or a financial planner, or a security analyst.
4. It should forecast such variables as: when the corporation may need to raise more capital; how much capital it would need; and the implications of alternative financing strategies and dividend policy on earnings per share and share price.

5. It should test the implications of both operating and financing decisions and their interactions.

The model described below portrays the functioning of the firm as a set of simultaneous equations; the necessity for its simultaneous nature will be made clear in the following discussion. This system is formulated so that the impact of a range of decisions and policies can be measured in the solutions of the equation system.

A quick overview can be obtained by looking at the model as if it were composed of four sections: 1. Sales and Operating Income Projections; 2. Estimated Assets Required to Support the Sales Forecast; 3. An Estimate of the Funds Needed to Provide the Assets (this section also designates the sources of the funds consistent with the corporate policy); and 4. Implications of Sections 1, 2, and 3 translated into earnings per share data, market prices, and rates of return to the investor.

Sales are the most important exogenous variable in the model since they are the driving force in the system of equations. See Figure 1. (This is in contrast to Carleton's model where asset growth is the variable that motivates the system.) In the FINPLAN model (as the authors refer to it), future sales are projected by using estimated growth rates, which need not be constant over the planning horizon.

In this paper, the model is presented without the series of equations that could link various costs (costs of goods sold, administrative costs, etc.) to sales; instead it moves directly to an equation that expresses EBIT (Earnings Before Interest and Taxes) as a per cent of sales. However, the model can be easily expanded to include specific cost breakdowns if the manager so desires. For the illustrative example of Sears Roebuck presented later in this paper, sales were projected to grow at 11.86 per cent per year and the ratio of EBIT to sales was estimated to be 10.07 per cent.

Two equations link asset requirements to sales. The corporate manager (or security analyst) has to supply the planned or expected ratios of current assets to sales and net fixed assets to sales (the inverses of the respective turnover ratios) for each period in the planning horizon. Again, these can be identical or different in each period. The system can be expanded to permit more detail if desired (for example, cash, receivables, and inventory can be spelled out in their relation to sales, again by specifying expected turnover ratios). Changes in depreciation rates can be reflected by adjusting the ratio of net fixed assets to sales. Current assets and net fixed assets are then summed to provide total assets required. In the Sears example, the relationships cited in this paragraph take the following values: current assets to sales, 56 per cent; net fixed assets to sales, 22 per cent.

If the asset-to-sales equations are thought of as generating some of the major applications of funds over the planning horizon, the next group of equations can be considered as generating the major sources of funds. This third part of the model is concerned with financing the desired level of assets necessary to support the sales determined by Section 1 (as well as any exogenously specified schedule of debt repayment). The purpose of this section of

FIGURE 1

Flow Chart Of A Simplified Financial Planning Model

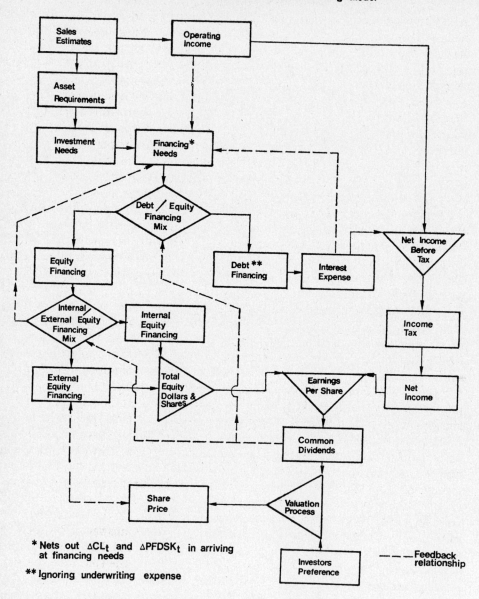

* Nets out ΔCL_t and $\Delta PFDSK_t$ in arriving at financing needs

** Ignoring underwriting expense

— — — Feedback relationship

the model is to finance the level of required assets by use of either external (debt and common stock) or internal means (earnings retentions), after allowing for self-generating sources such as current payables[1] and preferred

---

1. This assumption is realistic. Current liabilities contain accounts such as trade and wages payable, which do vary directly with sales. For example, if sales increase, the firm will increase purchases of raw materials and its labor bill will increase. Since the firm purchases raw material on credit and pays its workers on a weekly, semi-monthly, or monthly basis, a part of the investment (increases in cash required for transaction purposes, accounts receivable, inventory and so

stock (which is assumed exogenous in the model and therefore must be specified by the manager), given the constraints imposed by management.

In arriving at the external financing required, the model first considers the self-generating sources (viz., payables) that are treated as current liabilities and are defined as any debt that doesn't require interest payments. Preferred stock is considered an exogenous source of funds. Next, the model considers retained profits that follow from the assumed profit margins and dividend policy. If the self-generating sources of funds, any preferred stock financing that is planned, and retained earnings do not constitute sufficient funds to finance all the assets that are required, the firm must turn to external sources which can be debt and/or equity, such that the corporation maintains a specified ratio of total debt to equity which reflects the company policy in this matter. If the sources of funds exceed the application, the model as presented in this paper (but not in all versions) assumes that the excess funds will be used to retire debt or buy back common stock. In the Sears example, the relations cited above are as follows: current liabilities to sales, 15 per cent; dividend payout ratio, 48 per cent (one minus the retention rate of 52 per cent); and a desired ratio of debt to equity of 65.77 per cent.

When the model has calculated the amount of new external equity that may have to be sold, it also estimates the price the shares will bring (after underwriting commission), and consequently, the number of new common shares to be issued. Adding that to the number of shares in the prior period gives a forecasted total number of shares. From that it is easy to generate estimates of earnings per share and dividends.

Although the point has been mentioned that one of the strong features of this model is its simultaneous equation structure, the significance of this aspect of the model should be stressed to emphasize the difference between this approach to financial planning and that of a simpler residual-financing-type simulation models. To indicate the importance of the simultaneous nature of this model, consider how difficult it would be to project profits and share values without the simultaneously solved set of equations that are used in the model under the following circumstances. For example, assume a sales projection which implies the assets that have to be acquired are so large that they cannot be financed from retained earnings. Consequently, external capital will be raised from two sources, debt and (external) equity. If the model were not of the simultaneous nature, it would be very difficult to answer such questions as: (a) How much capital would have to be raised? (b) How many shares would have to be sold? (c) What would be the price of the stock? The reason that precise answers to those questions would be nearly impossible is because, as the new debt is floated, it causes interest costs to rise and consequently profits and retained earnings to fall more than had been first anticipated; thus more capital is required. Also, the price at which new shares will be sold will be affected by the lowered earnings due to the added interest costs, and furthermore, the earnings per share will be diluted because of the new equity issue.

---

forth [note assumption that current assets vary proportionally to sales]) required by the sales increase will be financed "automatically" by short-term sources.

This lowering of earnings per share in turn affects the number of shares required to be sold, which in turn affects the stock price. Only by intimate working with the model can a person really understand the many echoing and reechoing aspects of financial management. But the above description has suggested some of these aspects; most students of corporation finance become aware of the interaction of the profitability of an investment and the way it is financed. One solution to this infinite hall-of-mirrors phenomenon involving corporate investment and financing is to use iterative techniques, since the solution almost certainly will converge toward its ultimate value. However, a much more efficient technique is provided in this model by structuring the firm as a set of 20 equations and 20 unknowns that can be solved simultaneously. Others have presented the accounting system of the firm as a system of simultaneous equations. However, these studies do not focus on financial decision making per se or the effects of decisions on such crucial variables as earnings per share and share price (6).

The preceding description has alluded to the fact that the corporate financial planner will want to see the implications of the capital structure policies of the firm on earnings per share or stockholders' wealth. Therefore, the model provides an equation that prescribes the average debt to equity relation the firm will maintain whenever new financing is required. This means that external sources of debt and equity are specified in the planning process, and the financing is conducted so the debt policies of the firm are maintained throughout subsequent financing. Finally, all of this leads to per-share implications, specifically forecast earnings-per-share, dividends-per-share, and market price. As indicated above, the market price in turn affects the number of shares that must be issued to raise any given amount of equity and the number of shares issued affect the earnings per share, which in turn affects share price through investor preferences.

The above verbal description of the model is represented visually in Figure 1 which portrays the elements of the system but captures in only a limited sense the simultaneous nature of the model. It is extremely difficult to describe the model in literary terms and still be able to indicate the "everything-is-solved-simultaneously" quality of the model, yet in fact that is one of the major virtues of this approach. Appendix I provides a formal statement of the model with each of the 20 equations specified. A symbol key with short definitions follows the equations. A detailed discussion of the equation system and a solution procedure is available from the authors upon request.

Table 1 lists the information (inputs) required by the model in order for the financial manager to use it as a tool of long-range financial planning. Inputs are grouped according to whether they are primarily determined by the firm's past, its environment, its present and proposed operations, or its financial strategy.

The inputs represent the variables to be varied by management in sensitivity analyses when it asks "what if" questions. The values these variables assume describe a particular action or strategy and the results of the action or strategy are described by the values taken on (when the above system of equations is solved given the inputs) by the unknowns. (The model described in this paper

TABLE 1
LIST OF PARAMETERS PROVIDED BY MANAGEMENT

Historical

Sales in Previous Period
Debt in Previous Period
Common Stock in Previous Period
Retained Earnings in Previous Period
Average Interest Rate in Previous Period
Number of Common Shares Outstanding in Previous Period

Environmental

Expected Interest Rate on New Debt
Underwriting Cost of Debt
Underwriting Cost of Equity
Average Tax Rate
Price Earnings Ratio

Operating

Growth in Sales
Earnings Before Interest and Taxes as a Percent of Sales
Current Assets as a Percent of Sales
Fixed Assets as a Percent of Sales

Financial

Current Payables as a Percent of Sales
Preferred Stock
Preferred Dividends
Debt Repayments
Retention Rate
Ratio of Debt to Equity

---

has actually been incorporated in the FORTRAN program,[2] so these inputs are also the data required by the program.)

Table 2 lists the unknowns generated by the model based on the inter-relations expressed by the system of equations and the parameter values given by the inputs. They are grouped according to whether they describe the operating status or the firm's financial status.

Solving the model successively from period to period using results of solution at t as the initial conditions for t + 1 and so on provides the decision maker with a dynamic model of the firm.

III. ILLUSTRATIVE APPLICATION

To demonstrate the nature of the financial planning model, an illustration of its practical application is set forth.

Exhibit I provides the financial position of Sears, Roebuck and Company for calendar 1967 and 1968. Exhibit II shows the parameter values used in this illustration; of course in a real application, the parameters are provided by management. The model then generates the implications of the proposed policies. For this illustration, however, the parameters for Sears were developed by analyzing the balance sheet and income statement accounts as of 1968,

---

2. A listing of this program is available on request to the authors.

TABLE 2
LIST OF UNKNOWNS

Operating Status Variables
Sales
Earnings Before Interest and Taxes
Current Assets
Fixed Assets
Total Assets

Financial Status Variables
Current Payables
Needed Funds
New Debt
New Stock
Total Debt
Common Stock
Retained Earnings
Interest Rate on Debt
Earnings Available for Common Dividends
Common Dividends
Number of Common Shares Outstanding
New Common Shares Issued
Price Per Share
Earnings Per Share
Dividends Per Share

changes in account values between 1967 and 1968, earnings and dividends per share and share price in 1968. Applying the parameter definitions to Exhibit I results in Exhibit II. Although most parameters are held constant through 1972, the model permits any parameter to be varied in any period.

Exhibit III is generated by successively solving the equation system using the results of solution at t as the initial conditions for t + 1. It should be noted that calendar 1968 figures generated from solution of the equation system are identical to actual 1968 figures (except for differences due to rounding of parameter values), demonstrating that the equation system does indeed portray the interactions taking place within the firm as it moves from one state to another.

The importance of the model, however, is not to replicate actual financial statements but to generate pro forma statements which provide the manager with the implications of the parameters (policies) he has supplied to the model. Thus Exhibit III provides the financial position of Sears through calendar 1972 (actually ending January 31, 1973). It shows that, if conditions prevail as they did in 1967, Sears will continue to need new funds for asset expansion to maintain its growth rate in sales and to turnover its short-term debt. This demonstrates one of the uses of the model: it shows the financial manager the approximate amount of funds needed and when they will be required. This allows him not only to arrange for the funds in advance (which avoids liquidity crises and potentially higher costs for emergency funds) but also allows the manager to experiment with the implications (effect on EPS, DPS, and share price) of alternative financing strategies (changes in leverage,

EXHIBIT I
FINANCIAL POSITION OF SEARS, ROEBUCK AND COMPANY
(Millions of dollars)
(Actual Data)

INCOME STATEMENT		
Year	1967	1968
Sales	7431	8312
Operating Income	758	892
Interest Expense	93	113
Income Before Taxes	665	779
Taxes	283	361
Net Income	382	418
Common Dividends	183	199
BALANCE SHEET		
ASSETS		
Current Assets	4299	4680
Fixed Assets	1708	1828
Total Assets	6007	6508
LIABILITIES AND NET WORTH		
Current Liabilities	1112	1248
Debt	1956	2087
Common Stock	353	368
Retained Earnings	2586	2805
Total Liabilities and Net Worth	6007	6508
PER SHARE		
Earnings	2.50	2.73
Dividends	1.20	1.30
Market Price High		72.25
Low		56.125
Shares Outstanding	152,888,000	153,233,000

retention rates, the use of preferreds, changing trade credit policy, and so forth) prior to making an actual commitment. By assuming lower or higher growth rates in sales for individual years or for a number of years, the effects on financing requirements can be studied and contingency plans made. The effects of improving profitability, becoming more efficient in asset use, potential changes in tax rates, and/or increasing interest rates can be studied in combination or in isolation.

The Sears output, as presented in Exhibit III, consists of projected income statements that include a schedule of total dividends and debt repayments; projected balance sheets; and a forecast of financial requirements including the amount of new debt and equity that may be required. Finally, the forecast earnings and dividends per share and market prices are shown. In this example, the pricing mechanism has been simplified to be a typical price-earnings multiple. The model can incorporate more sophisticated pricing expressions, including multiple regression, Gordon (7), Holt-Malkiel (8), or any other

EXHIBIT II
PARAMETERS* ($t = 1, 2, 3, 4, 5$)

Environmental	Historical	Operating	Financial
i_t^e **	$SALES_0 = 7431.$	$GSALS_t = .1186$	$RCL_t = \quad .15$
$U_t^1 = 0.0$	$i_0 = \quad .0475$	$REBIT_t = .1070$	$PFDSK_t = 0.0$
$U_t^s = 0.0$	$L_0 = 1956.$	$RCA_t = .563$	$PFDIV_t = 0.0$
$T_t = .46$	$S_0 = 353.$		LR_t ***
$M_t = 23.$	$R_0 = 2586.$	$RFA_t = .22$	$b_t = \quad .52$
	$NUMCS_0 = 152.89$		$K_t = \quad .6577$
**$i_1^e = .0556$			***$LR_1 = 1573.$
$i_2^e = .075$			$LR_2 = 1624.$
$i_3^e = .07$			$LR_3 = 1624.$
$i_4^e = .07$			$LR_4 = 1624.$
$i_5^e = .07$			$LR_5 = 1670.$

This column of figures represent a tightening and a slight subsequent loosening of credit.

This column of figures assumes repayment of 20M of long-term debt annually for 1968-1971 and 70M in 1972. The balance in each period represents turnover of notes payable.

* These parameters are defined in APPENDIX I Table 1B.

type of valuation equations.[3] The output includes a recapitulation of important parameter values, which appears after the income, balance sheets, and financial results.

The last section of the output is a matrix that shows the present value of the projected stream of dividends and share prices, assuming discount rates between five per cent and 34 per cent and a duration for holding the stock ranging from as short as one year to as many years as the planning spans (five in the example).

This table is added to the output to indicate another way in which this model can be extremely valuable in financial analysis. Although the emphasis of this paper has been on the model's use as a tool of corporate financial planning, it has equal value as a tool for security valuation. This should come as no surprise, since most students of Corporation Finance and Investments often note that the two fields substantively have much in common. The "Investments" aspect of this model is fairly clear and is close enough to the financial planning aspect that it gets only a minor part of the text of this paper, but in reality the model may be as useful to security analysts as to corporate management. The present-value matrix is an essential element of the security

3. Professor Warren is currently developing a version of the model which incorporates a relative price-earnings ratio valuation subsystem.

EXHIBIT III

INCOME STATEMENT (in millions of dollars)	1967	1968	1969	1970	1971	1972
YEAR						
SALES	7431.00	8312.31	9298.15	10400.91	11634.45	13014.29
OPERATING INCOME	0.0*	889.42	994.90	1112.90	1244.89	1392.53
INTEREST EXPENSE	0.0	112.97	165.46	183.46	204.77	228.89
UNDERWRITING COMMISSION—DEBT	0.0	0.0	0.0	0.0	0.0	0.0
INCOME BEFORE TAXES	0.0	776.45	829.45	929.44	1040.12	1163.64
TAXES	0.0	357.17	381.54	427.54	478.46	535.27
NET INCOME	0.0	419.28	447.90	501.90	561.67	628.36
PREFERRED DIVIDENDS	0.0	0.0	0.0	0.0	0.0	0.0
AVAILABLE FOR COMMON DIVIDENDS	0.0	419.28	447.90	501.90	561.67	628.36
COMMON DIVIDENDS	0.0	201.26	214.99	240.91	269.60	301.61
DEBT REPAYMENTS	0.0	1573.00	1624.00	1624.00	1624.00	1670.00
BALANCE SHEET						
ASSETS						
CURRENT ASSETS	0.0	4679.83	5234.86	5855.71	6550.19	7327.04
FIXED ASSETS	0.0	1828.71	2045.59	2288.20	2559.58	2863.14
TOTAL ASSETS	0.0	6508.54	7280.45	8143.90	9109.77	10190.18
LIABILITIES AND NET WORTH						
CURRENT LIABILITIES	0.0	1246.85	1394.72	1560.14	1745.17	1952.14
DEBT	1956.00	2087.60	2335.19	2612.14	2921.94	3268.48
PREFERRED STOCK	0.0	0.0	0.0	0.0	0.0	0.0
COMMON STOCK	353.00	370.07	513.60	673.71	852.68	1052.83
RETAINED EARNINGS	2586.00	2804.03	3036.93	3297.92	3589.99	3916.74
TOTAL LIABILITIES AND NET WORTH	0.0	6508.54	7280.44	8143.90	9109.77	10190.18

* In the base year, 1967, only those inputs required by the model are given non-zero values.

EXHIBIT III (*Continued*)

YEAR	1967	1968	1969	1970	1971	1972
FINANCIAL DATA NEEDED FUNDS						
ESTIMATED	0.0	1695.05	1975.70	2023.69	2074.75	2177.04
ACTUAL	0.0	1721.06	2015.12	2061.06	2112.76	2216.68
VALUE NEW DEBT ISSUED	0.0	1704.60	1871.59	1900.95	1933.80	2016.54
VALUE NEW COMMON ISSUED	0.0	17.07	143.54	160.11	178.97	200.15
INTEREST RATE ON NEW DEBT	0.0	0.06	0.07	0.07	0.07	0.07
INTEREST RATE ON TOTAL DEBT	0.0475	0.0541	0.0709	0.0702	0.0701	0.0700
UNDERWRITING COMMISSIONS DEBT	0.0	0.0	0.0	0.0	0.0	0.0
COMMON	0.0	0.0	0.0	0.0	0.0	0.0
NUMBER OF NEW SHARES COMMON ISSUED	0.0	0.27	2.16	2.18	2.21	2.24
TOTAL NUMBER COMMON SHARES ISSUED	152.89	153.16	155.32	157.51	159.72	161.96
EPS COMMON STOCK	0.0	2.7376	2.8837	3.1865	3.5166	3.8797
RETENTION RATE	0.0	0.52	0.52	0.52	0.52	0.52
DPS COMMON STOCK	0.0	1.31	1.38	1.53	1.69	1.86
MARKET PRICE COMMON PER SHARE	0.0	62.96	66.32	73.29	80.88	89.23
P/E RATIO	0.0	23.00	23.00	23.00	23.00	23.00
DESIRED DEBT/EQUITY RATIO	0.0	0.66	0.66	0.66	0.66	0.66
TAX RATE	0.0	0.46	0.46	0.46	0.46	0.46
GROWTH RATE IN SALES	0.0	0.12	0.12	0.12	0.12	0.12
OPERATING INCOME TO SALES	0.0	0.11	0.11	0.11	0.11	0.11
CURRENT ASSETS TO SALES	0.0	0.56	0.56	0.56	0.56	0.56
FIXED ASSETS TO SALES	0.0	0.22	0.22	0.22	0.22	0.22
CURRENT LIABILITIES TO SALES	0.0	0.15	0.15	0.15	0.15	0.15

PRESENT VALUE MATRIX
DISCOUNT RATE/YEARS HELD

EXHIBIT III (Continued)

	1	2	3	4	5
0.05	61.22	62.67	67.14	71.76	76.59
0.06	60.64	61.50	65.29	69.16	73.16
0.07	60.07	60.37	63.51	66.68	69.92
0.08	59.52	59.27	61.80	64.31	66.86
0.09	58.97	58.19	60.14	62.05	63.95
0.10	58.43	57.15	58.55	59.88	61.20
0.11	57.91	56.14	57.01	57.82	58.60
0.12	57.39	55.15	55.53	55.84	56.13
0.13	56.88	54.19	54.10	53.95	53.78
0.14	56.38	53.25	52.72	52.14	51.56
0.15	55.89	52.34	51.38	50.40	49.45
0.16	55.41	51.45	50.09	48.74	47.44
0.17	54.94	50.59	48.85	47.15	45.54
0.18	54.47	49.74	47.64	45.63	43.73
0.19	54.02	48.92	46.48	44.16	42.00
0.20	53.56	48.11	45.35	42.76	40.36
0.21	53.12	47.33	44.26	41.41	38.80
0.22	52.69	46.57	43.21	40.12	37.32
0.23	52.26	45.82	42.19	38.88	35.90
0.24	51.84	45.09	41.20	37.69	34.55
0.25	51.42	44.38	40.24	36.54	33.26
0.26	51.01	43.69	39.32	35.44	32.03
0.27	50.61	43.01	38.42	34.38	30.86
0.28	50.22	42.35	37.55	33.36	29.74
0.29	49.83	41.71	36.70	32.38	28.67
0.30	49.44	41.08	35.88	31.44	27.65
0.31	49.07	40.46	35.09	30.53	26.68
0.32	48.70	39.85	34.32	29.65	25.74
0.33	48.33	39.27	33.57	28.81	24.85
0.34	47.97	38.69	32.85	28.00	24.00

analysts' use of this model. Its significance, however, is obvious enough that only a brief explanation is offered. The matrix provides a security analyst with at least two useful guidelines. He can assume a holding period (say four years) and glance down the four-year column till he sees a price that is very close to the current price and learn what rate of return an investor should expect from buying the stock now if he assumed parameter values are wisely chosen. If he has a FINPLAN on several companies, he can determine which provide the best prospects for high rates of return at current prices or he can decide how much return he thinks he needs at a minimum to justify the risk he associates with buying this stock and on that basis establish a satisfactory buying price.

The rate-of-return for various holding periods matrix not only is useful for a security analyst, but it also illustrates the merits of considering the cost of equity capital to be dividend yield plus growth in earnings per share $\left(\text{i.e., } k = \dfrac{d}{p} + g\right)$. The matrix shows that if an investor requires only five per cent return, he increases the present value of his future income by letting his money stay with the company for the longest possible period. This means that Sears is able to use his capital to earn better than five per cent, so he is well-advised to keep his investment with them. On the other hand, if he wants 34 per cent return, he not only has to buy Sears at a bargain price, but he should not hold it more than one year. The longer he contemplates holding Sears (if he expects 34 per cent return), the lower the price he can afford to pay now. This shows that Sears is not earning 34 per cent on its stockholders capital. But at a rate between 11 per cent and 12 per cent, the present value of the Sears' stock is virtually unchanged by varying the contemplated holding period. This implies that the company's profitability matches the investor's desired rate of return. Since the projection shows earnings per share growing about nine per cent annually and the dividend yield at the price implied by 11½ per cent return was a little more than two per cent, this matrix illustrates once again the meaning of the concept that the investors' cost of equity capital should be considered as the expected dividend yield plus his capital gains.

It should be noted that in this illustration, the price earnings ratio and retention rate were constant for the planning period. Thus the firm's cost of equity capital could be estimated by the dividend yield and the growth in earnings, dividends, or share price equally. Even when more complex valuation procedures are used (or parameters of the model are not held constant), the cost of equity can still be estimated through the use of the present value matrix as indicated above.

Although the validity of the model is not dependent on the accuracy of its predictions (since the accuracy of the forecast outputs depends solely on the quality of judgement used by the security analyst or financial planner when he chooses the parameter value), it is interesting nonetheless to observe that the Sears example used in this test was prepared solely on the basis of information published in the Sears' 1968 (calendar) report. The computer run was made in May 1969, shortly after the January 31, 1969 report was published. To the extent that this model can be effective in decomposing the forecasting problem into more manageable bites, it may be that it makes the final results more accurate. This would obtain since the model provides a tool for accurately reflecting the final implications of judgement about the trend of basic variables. In any event, it can be asserted in this example that the inputs that went into the model were determined without the aid of any insider information and were made almost exactly 12 months before the (calendar) 1969 results were published. The estimated and actual values for major variables are listed below so that the reader can judge for himself the success of the forecasts.

Variable	Projected: 1970	Actual: 1970
Sales	$ 9.298 billion	$ 8.987 billion
Net Income After Taxes	$ 447 million	$ 441 million
Current Assets	$ 5.235 billion	$ 5.047 billion
Current Liabilities (i.e., non-interest bearing liabilities)	$ 1.394 billion	$ 1.414 billion
Debt	$ 2.335 billion	$ 2.226 billion
Retained Earnings	$ 3.037 billion	$ 3.038 billion
Earnings Per Share	$ 2.88	$ 2.87
Market Price of Common	$ 66.32	Range 1969: $75-$60 Range 1970: $77-$51

In this particular illustration, it should be stressed that historical parameters alone were used in forecasting the financial data. As it happened, the projections for calendar 1969 were quite close to reality but this is only a reflection of the fact that—for 1969 at least—Sears's operations were quite predictable based on historical parameters alone. The real value of the proposed model does not lie in coming close to actual results in a situation like Sears—rather, the point should be stressed that the model projects data using the inputs specified by the planner. The planner, in turn, may be either aiding management or be involved in security analysis.

IV. SENSITIVITY TESTS

Varying the parameter values allows the manager to see the implications of different policies and circumstances, including: debt and dividend policies, changing growth rates of sales, shifts in profit margins, and alterations in the turnover of assets. The major benefit of this model is to specify more accurately than can be done otherwise the implications of varying conditions and policies; as a by-product, however, it also reveals which parameters are likely to be most important in determining share value (or, if the manager believes that market price is outside his control, then at least in isolating those parameters that have the most influence in affecting earnings per share).

The primary values used in the illustration generate results that can be used as a starting point to show how varying some of the parameters produce different results. The results of changing parameter values appears in many aspects of Sears financial condition, but we will focus on only two: earnings per share at the end of the five-year planning horizon; and the present value of a share of stock (given the projected dividend income to the stockholder and the anticipated price he could sell the stock for in the fifth year), assuming a discount rate of 11 per cent on the dividends and on the future price. In the illustrative situation, this implied a fair price for the stockholder of Sears as of January 31, 1969 of $58.60. Assuming the projected dividends and the price forecast for five years from that date materialized, this price would bring the investor 11 per cent before personal income taxes.

The impact of changing the expected sales growth over the next five years, the expected ratio of earnings before interest and taxes to sales, the expected retention rate (or dividend policy), and the expected turnover of current assets is indicated in Table 3 which is divided into four parts. It becomes apparent that for the ranges used in the sensitivity runs, the earnings per share and the present value of a share of stock discounted at 11 per cent were most significantly affected by improvement or worsening of the profit margin. Next most influential would be changing sales growth rates. For example, if the operating profit margin went from 12 per cent down to eight per cent, earnings per share in year five fell from $4.52 to $2.51 and the present value of a share of stock

TABLE 3*

| | Growth Rate in Sales | | | | |
	.06	.08	.10	.14	.16
EPS$_5$**	3.23	3.44	3.66	4.14	4.40
PV$_5$***	49.12	52.20	55.44	62.41	66.16

| | Ratio of Earnings Before Interest and Taxes to Sales | | | | |
	.08	.09	.10	.11	.12
EPS$_5$	2.51	3.02	3.52	4.03	4.52
PV$_5$	38.10	45.67	53.27	60.89	68.52

| | Retention Rate | | | |
	.45	.50	.55	.60
EPS$_5$	3.82	3.86	3.91	3.95
PV$_5$	58.55	58.59	58.62	58.64

| | Ratio of Current Assets to Sales | | | | | | |
	.48	.50	.52	.54	.58	.60	.62	.64
EPS$_5$	4.24	4.16	4.07	3.98	3.81	3.72	3.64	3.55
PV$_5$	64.02	62.70	61.38	60.08	57.51	56.24	54.98	53.73

* In each sensitivity run only one parameter is changed, and the parameter value as shown is continued for the entire five year period.

** Earnings per share in Period 5.

*** Present Value assuming 5 year holding period, at a discount rate of 11 per cent.

from almost $69.00 to almost $38.00. In contrast, if dividend policy was changed so that the payout ratio went from as low as 40 per cent (a retention rate of 60 per cent) to as high as 55 per cent (with a corresponding retention rate of 45 per cent), the future earnings per share varied only $.07 from one extreme to the other and the present value of a price of stock varied $.09. The logic of this latter result is seen by the fact that as more dividends were paid to the stockholders (bringing up their present value), the company then needed to issue more shares to provide new capital (which diluted earnings per share and lowered the ultimate price). The turnover ratio of current assets for retail stores is an important parameter; when it ranges from 48 per cent to 64 per cent (the latter rate representing a slower turnover ratio), the earnings per share in the fifth year fell from approximately $4.25 to about $3.55 and the present value of the stock fell from approximately $64.00 to about $54.00.

These numbers illustrate specifically the way a financial model like this can be used not only for predicting the likely future direction of a firm but also as a tool of management planning that specifies the implications of changing management policies or external circumstances.

V. Conclusion

A mathematical model such as described in this paper can aid financial decision making in a number of ways. It provides the corporate manager with a means of specifying why the firm needs to seek financing, when it needs to seek financing, and the risks and rewards possible to those who provide the funds.

Management can determine how operating decisions will affect financial requirements, and the effect of financial decisions on operating performance. An appreciation for the inter-relationships which exist within a firm is developed by using this model. The model demonstrates how potential environmental changes can affect the performance of the firm. Thus management is aided in developing policies that can increase earnings per share and share price.

The model has been programmed for rapid solution by computer. This allows management to quantify the effects of a large number of alternative policies and decisions. The model encourages the performance of sensitivity analysis so that management can determine which variables will be most critical in determining the future performance of the firm.

For example, the Sears Roebuck illustration may leave the reader with the impression that this model is deterministic and devoid of ability to represent the uncertainty (risk) that exists in the real world. But to the contrary, the model provides a basis for inputting many different parameter values (which could even be determined stochastically) and generating a wide range of outputs that can be presented as a distribution function with a mean and variance.

Furthermore, the opportunity to use several input values for each parameter allows management to examine the implications of alternative states of the world (that might be characterized as pessimistic, most likely, and optimistic). The output values can be compared and thus reveal how sensitive different criteria (for example, earnings per share, or stock price) are to changes in the values of certain inputs.

Additionally, this model provides a fundamental and analytical basis for security analysis. Security analysis is traditionally focused on the calculation of financial ratios. This model determines which ratios are most critical and the interrelations among those ratios as they interact to determine stock price.

Experience with this model indicates that some users will find, for certain purposes, it has limitations that include the following:

1. The quality of the forecast output is highly dependent on the quality of a few of the operating and environmental inputs.

2. The model isn't designed to optimize a given objective. However, this limitation is more than offset by the fact that management of business firms who have been exposed to the program usually indicate that in reality they do not consciously maximize one goal but are concerned with trade-offs between objectives. Furthermore, the use of this model by security analysts would be greatly restricted if it were formulated in an optimum-seeking fashion. The security analyst wants to answer the question: What is the most likely flow of income to the owners of this stock, and what is its present value given an appropriate discount rate? (Some idea of this latter issue can be obtained by observing the distribution of possible profits as portrayed in various sensitivity runs.) For this purpose, the analyst is better guided by his estimates of what management will do than by a solution that assumes some objective is maximized.

3. In some firms where this model has been tested, management has preferred greater disaggregation, either by listing more costs and assets, or by breaking the analysis down to major divisions that are ultimately consolidated. This experience has shown that the computer program can be expanded for such needs, but there are trade-offs in the choice between detail and aggregation. The presentation in this paper shows the best compromise for general purposes.

The mathematical model described in the paper allows management to quantify the effects of alternative policies and decisions. Although it focuses on the firm's financing decisions, it provides an operational tool to determine the effects of both operating and financing decisions on the state of the firm at some future point in time. In this sense, the model provides management with a means of ordering in advance of action the results of alternative strategies and, as a result, can provide a foundation for helping management in its complex process of making optimizing decisions.

REFERENCES

1. H. M. Weingartner. *Mathematical Programming and the Analysis of Capital Budgeting Problems* (Chicago, Illinois: Markham Publishing Company, 1967).
2. A. A. Robichek, D. Teichroew and J. M. Jones. "Optimal Short Term Financing Decision," *Management Science* (September, 1965), 1-36.
3. A. A. Robichek and S. C. Myers. *Optimal Financing Decisions* (Englewood Cliffs, New Jersey: Prentice Hall, Inc., 1965), 140-158.
4. W. T. Carleton. "An Analytical Model for Long-Range Financial Planning," *Journal of Finance* (May, 1970), 291-315. A linear programming model for financial planning has also been presented by Ijiri, Levy, and Lyon. However, their model chooses as its objective function the maximization of the net addition to retained earnings ignoring the effects of decisions on share price, earnings per share and the number of additional shares resulting from external equity financing. See Ijiri, Y., F. K. Levy, and R. C. Lyon, "A Linear Programming Model for Budgeting and Financial Planning," *Journal of Accounting Research*, (Autumn, 1968), 198-212.
5. G. W. Gershefski. "Corporate Models: The State of the Art," *Managerial Planning*, (November/December, 1969), 2. Also, Gershifski, "Building a Corporate Financial Model," *Harvard Business Review*, July/August, 1969, 61-72, and Gershefski, *The Development and Application of a Corporate Financial Model* (published in 1968 by Planning Executives Institute, 16 Park Place, Oxford, Ohio 45056).
6. See, for example, Mattessich, R., "Budgeting Models and System Simulation," *Accounting Re-*

view, (July, 1961), 384-97, and Mattessich, R., *Accounting and Analytical Methods* (Homewood, Illinois: Richard D. Irwin, Inc., 1963), Chapter 9. Also, Richards, A. B., "Input-Output Accounting for Business," *Accounting Review*, (July, 1960), 429-436.

7. Myron J. Gordon. *The Investment Financing and Valuation of the Corporation* (Homewood, Illinois: Richard D. Irwin, Inc., 1962).

8. Charles C. Holt. "The Influence of Growth Duration on Share Prices," *The Journal of Finance* (September, 1962), 465-475, and Malkiel, Burton G., "Equity Yields, Growth, and the Structure of Share Prices," *The American Economic Review* (December, 1963), 1004-1030.

APPENDIX I

Section 1—Generation of Sales and Earnings Before Interest and Taxes for Period t.

(1) $\text{SALES}_t = \text{SALES}_{t-1} (1 + \text{GSALS}_t)$

(2) $\text{EBIT}_t = \text{REBIT}_t \, \text{SALES}_t$

Section 2—Generation of Total Assets Required for Period t.

(3) $\text{CA}_t = \text{RCA}_t \, \text{SALES}_t$

(4) $\text{FA}_t = \text{RFA}_t \, \text{SALES}_t$

(5) $\text{A}_t = \text{CA}_t + \text{FA}_t$

Section 3—Financing the Desired Level of Assets.

(6) $\text{CL}_t = \text{RCL}_t \, \text{SALES}_t$

(7) $\text{NF}_t = (\text{A}_t - \text{CL}_t - \text{PFDSK}_t) - (\text{L}_{t-1} - \text{LR}_t) - \text{S}_{t-1} - \text{R}_{t-1} - b_t \{(1 - \text{T}_t)$
$[\text{EBIT}_t - i_{t-1} (\text{L}_{t-1} - \text{LR}_t)] - \text{PFDIV}_t\}$

(8) $\text{NF}_t + b_t (1 - \text{T}_t) [i_t^e \text{NL}_t + \text{U}_t^1 \text{NL}_t] = \text{NL}_t + \text{NS}_t$

(9) $\text{L}_t = \text{L}_{t-1} - \text{LR}_t + \text{NL}_t$

(10) $\text{S}_t = \text{S}_{t-1} + \text{NS}_t$

(11) $\text{R}_t = \text{R}_{t-1} + b_t \{(1 - \text{T}_t) [\text{EBIT}_t - i_t \text{L}_t - \text{U}_t^1 \text{NL}_t] - \text{PFDIV}_t\}$

(12) $i_t = i_{t-1} \left(\dfrac{\text{L}_{t-1} - \text{LR}_t}{\text{L}_t} \right) + i_t^e \dfrac{\text{NL}_t}{\text{L}_t}$

(13) $\dfrac{\text{L}_t}{\text{S}_t + \text{R}_t} = \text{K}_t$

Section 4—Generation of Per Share Data for Period t

(14) $\text{EAFCD}_t = (1 - \text{T}_t) [\text{EBIT}_t - i_t \text{L}_t - \text{U}_t^1 \text{NL}_t] - \text{PFDIV}_t$

(15) $\text{CMDIV}_t = (1 - b_t) \, \text{EAFCD}_t$

(16) $\text{NUMCS}_t = \text{NUMCS}_{t-1} + \text{NEWCS}_t$

(17) $\text{NEWCS}_t = \dfrac{\text{NS}_t}{(1 - \text{U}_t^s) \, \text{P}_t}$

(18) $\text{P}_t = m_t \text{EPS}_t$

(19) $\text{EPS}_t = \dfrac{\text{EAFCD}_t}{\text{NUMCS}_t}$

(20) $\text{DPS}_t = \dfrac{\text{CMDIV}_t}{\text{NUMCS}_t}$

The above system is "complete" in 20 equations and 20 unknowns. The unknowns are listed and defined in Table 1 along with the parameters (inputs) management is required to provide.

TABLE 1
List of Unknowns and List of Parameters Provided by Management

A. Unknowns

1.	$SALES_t$	Sales
2.	CA_t	Current Assets
3.	FA_t	Fixed Assets
4.	A_t	Total Assets
5.	CL_t	Current Payables
6.	NF_t	Needed Funds
7.	$EBIT_t$	Earnings Before Interest and Taxes
8.	NL_t	New Debt
9.	NS_t	New Stock
10.	L_t	Total Debt
11.	S_t	Common Stock
12.	R_t	Retained Earnings
13.	i_t	Interest Rate on Debt
14.	$EAFCD_t$	Earnings Available for Common Dividends
15.	$CMDIV_t$	Common Dividends
16.	$NUMCS_t$	Number of Common Shares Outstanding
17.	$NEWCS_t$	New Common Shares Issued
18.	P_t	Price Per Share
19.	EPS_t	Earnings Per Share
20.	DPS_t	Dividends Per Share

B. Provided by Management

21.	$SALES_{t-1}$	Sales in Previous Period
22.	$GSALS_t$	Growth in Sales
23.	RCA_t	Current Assets as a Per Cent of Sales
24.	RFA_t	Fixed Assets as a Per Cent of Sales
25.	RCL_t	Current Payables as a Per Cent of Sales
26.	$PFDSK_t$	Preferred Stock
27.	$PFDIV_t$	Preferred Dividends
28.	L_{t-1}	Debt in Previous Period
29.	LR_t	Debt Repayment
30.	S_{t-1}	Common Stock in Previous Period
31.	R_{t-1}	Retained Earnings in Previous Period
32.	b_t	Retention Rate
33.	T_t	Average Tax Rate
34.	i_{t-1}	Average Interest Rate in Previous Period
35.	i_t^e	Expected Interest Rate on New Debt
36.	$REBIT_t$	Operating Income as a Per Cent of Sales
37.	U_t^l	Underwriting Cost of Debt
38.	U_t^s	Underwriting Cost of Equity
39.	K_t	Ratio of Debt to Equity
40.	$NUMCS_{t-1}$	Number of Common Shares Outstanding in Previous Period
41.	m_t	Price Earnings Ratio

A Simultaneous Equation Model of the Firm for Financial Analysis and Planning

Jack Clark Francis and Dexter R. Rowell

Jack Clark Francis is Professor of Finance and Economics at Baruch College. Dexter R. Rowell is Assistant Professor of Finance and Economics at Villanova University.

■ Forecasting and planning are essential to good decision making. As a result, financial managers are frequently asked for *pro forma* financial statements. The Securities and Exchange Commission [18] allows the use of published forecasts by publicly owned firms to supplement their required history-oriented financial statements. Such possibilities leave little room for question about whether or not a financial manager is (or at least should be) interested in generating financial forecasts. The important question is how to prepare good forecasts. This paper suggests a simultaneous equation model of moderate size to forecast the future path of a single firm's financial statements.

Description of The Francis-Rowell (FR) Model

The model presented below extends the simultaneous linear equation models of the firm developed by Warren and Shelton [19] (hereafter WS) and Pindyck and Rubinfeld [14, Section 12.3]. The

objective of this model is to generate *pro forma* financial statements that describe the future financial condition of the firm for any assumed pattern of sales. Parameters of various equations in the system can be changed to answer "what if" questions, perform sensitivity analysis, and explore various paths toward some goal or goals which may or may not be optimal.

The FR model is an initial effort to capture the complex interaction among objectives in management decisions.[1] Capital expansion and financing decisions affect the risk character of the firm, which in turn affects the firm's equity valuation. Equity valuation feeds back to the financing and expansion decisions.

---

[1]The suggested model includes ten main sectors with 34 endogenous variables and 30 exogenous variables which are listed in Appendix A. These variables are interrelated through 36 linear equations shown in Appendix B. This equation system is simultaneous in the usual econometric sense; concurrent interrelationships and feedback loops are involved in the solution for each period. However, the model also contains recursive equations so that all the equations are not solved simultaneously in the mathematical sense (that is, a matrix is not inverted).

Likewise, the production decision must be viewed in its relationship to the sales forecast, subject to existing finished goods inventories and capacity utilization. If, for instance, an optimistic sales forecast indicated a sharp upturn in future company sales, production need not turn upward in direct proportion to the sales upturn. The production upturn would probably be lower than sales if substantial finished goods inventories existed. As a consequence, cause and effect are not simply unilateral. Therefore, to realistically capture such interdependence, any model must be highly interdependent, or *simultaneous*. It need not be large, but it must be sufficiently complex to allow disaggregation of sales forecast, production, pricing, asset expansion, and financing decisions.

The FR model is composed of ten sectors with a total of 36 equations. (Variables are defined in Appendix A and equations listed in Appendix B.) This is a large enough model to allow substantial *disaggregation*, as well as to capture some of the simultaneity of business operations. The FR model has several other important features besides its simultaneity and disaggregation.

The model incorporates an explicit treatment of *risk* by allowing for stochastic variability in industry sales forecasts. The exogenous input of sales variance is transformed (through simplified linear relations in the model) to coefficients of variation for earnings before interest and taxes (EBIT) and net income after taxes (NIAT).[2] These are used in risk-return functions which determine costs of new financing.

The model also incorporates some variables external to the firm that are important from a financial planning viewpoint. These *industry or economy-wide variables* are introduced in every sector to enable the financial planner to explore their influence on plans. They include: market share, an industry capacity utilization index, the tax rate, and a GNP component price index for explicit analysis of the effects of inflation.

The FR model explicitly allows for divergence between planned (or potential) and actual levels of both sales and production. That is, sales forecasts and production potential are compared to determine the existence of slack or idle capacity and company expansion possibilities. Any positive difference between potential or forecasted company sales and actual company sales is decomposed into the portion attributable to idle capacity and the portion requiring expanded

production facilities. As a result, a forecasted sales increase need not lead to investment in new capital. Likewise, a forecasted sales downturn would not lead to a divestiture of capital. An advantage of this disaggregation is that it allows for greater realism — that is, it permits both a lagged production response to sales upturns and downturns, as well as lags and asymmetry in new investment decisions.

The FR model offers a disaggregation of the sales equation into separate market share, production, and pricing equations, which has several distinct advantages. It offers the opportunity to treat sales forecasts in physical units that can be compared to technical production capabilities in physical units for both potential and actual levels of sales and production. Such disaggregation also allows distinction between physical units of sales and production and dollar units. Therefore, the pricing decision can be treated separately.

Another aspect of the FR financial forecasting model is the econometrics. The FR model's risk-return function and its production function are estimated econometrically. Also, standard econometric techniques to evaluate goodness-of-fit and predictive power of a simultaneous equation system are reported.

In the remaining sections of the paper, the FR model is explained in its general form. Then the coefficients of the equations are set equal to the values which characterize the operations of an existing company, and then the active operations of a well-known firm are simulated to test the model empirically as a financial tool.

The FR Model Specification

The FR model is composed of ten sectors: 1) industry sales, 2) production sector, 3) fixed capital stock requirements, 4) pricing, 5) production costs, 6) income, 7) new financing required, 8) risk, 9) costs of financing, and 10) common stock valuation. These sectors are illustrated in the flow chart shown in Exhibit 1.

The flow chart conveniently illustrates the simultaneity discussed above. All ten sectors are portrayed, labeled, and outlined by dot-dash borders with arrows displaying their interaction. This is summarized for sectors one through ten in the interdependence table, Exhibit 2. An "X" is placed in the table to represent the direction of an arrow (from explaining to explained) on the flow chart.

The pattern of "Xs" demonstrates something in-

---

[2]The mathematical statistics showing the risk transformations are shown in Appendix C.

Exhibit 1. Model Flow Chart

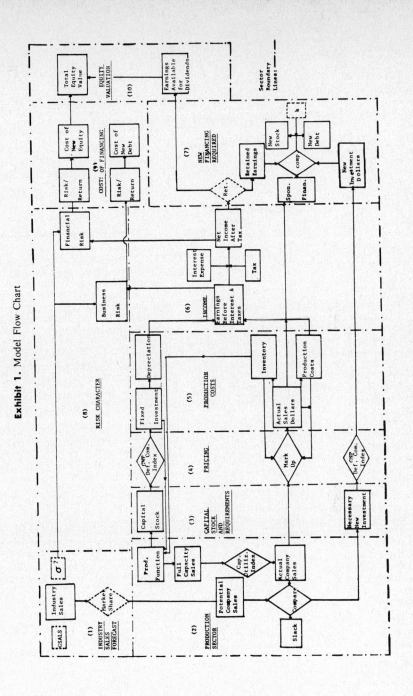

677

Exhibit 2. Sector Interdependence

		Explaining Sector									
		1	2	3	4	5	6	7	8	9	10
Explained	1										
Sector	2	X									
	3		X								
	4			X							
	5				X						
	6					X					
	7					X	X			X	
	8	X	X	X	X	X	X	X			
	9								X		
	10							X	X		

Exhibit 3. Sector Seven Flow Chart

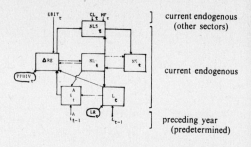

] current endogenous (other sectors)

current endogenous

] preceding year (predetermined)

= exogenous current year

teresting about the FR model. Recall that simultaneous means instantaneous interdependence among sectors and equations. Each equation and sector in this model describes a different relationship among a set of variables. However, all the sectors and equations are assumed to hold at once. Furthermore, a simultaneous model must be solved simultaneously — all equations are solved at the same time.

While a model can be simultaneous in the sense that all sectors or equations are assumed to hold at once, the solution could occur *recursively* (that is, not all at once). For instance, the solution of one equation leads to the solution of the next and so on, until the entire model is solved in a time sequence of solutions. If a model were recursive, such an interdependence table would show entries only in the lower triangle of the table. The simplest recursive model — such as a model which uses a fixed percentage of sales to obtain all other amounts — would be characterized in the interdependence table by entries only in column one.

Looking more deeply reveals that the FR model is, to a large extent (but not entirely), recursive between sectors. All entries of the sector interdependence table, with the exception of one (between sectors seven and nine), are below the diagonal. It has been structured in this manner for the specific purpose of ease of exposition and computation. The simultaneity of the FR model is primarily within each sector's equations. For example, this is illustrated for sector seven in the flow chart for that sector, shown as Exhibit 3, and also in the variable interdependence table for sector seven, shown as Exhibit 4.

Sector One: Industry Sales

The primary importance of the industry sales forecast sector is highlighted by its upper left position on the flow chart in Exhibit 1. It influences directly the risk sector and production sector and indirectly every sector of the model.

The industry sales sector can be any size and is abbreviated here to merely a single equation; see Equation (1). The industry sales equation shows that an industry sales forecast must be made by some means over a pre-defined forecast period and given as an exogenous input to the FR model.

Although sales remain the driving force for the FR model, it is industry instead of company sales which drive the model, since forecasting experience indicates that industry sales are usually more accurately forecasted than company sales. In addition, two parameters of the industry sales forecast are employed, the mean and standard deviation. The mean enters the model in the conventional way, whereas the standard deviation is mathematically transformed to obtain the standard deviations of its derivative quantities, the company's net income after taxes (NIAT) and earnings before interest and taxes (EBIT).[3]

---

[3]The FR model could easily be linked to a macroeconomic forecasting model to obtain the sales forecast for the industry and the firm. This expanded macroeconomic and microeconomic model could provide detailed forecasts of the economy, the firm's industry, the firm itself, and the firm's equity returns. Francis has also developed a small simultaneous equation model to explain a single firm's changes in earnings per share and stock price per share [5]. This model is driven by macroeconomic factors with some forces from within the firm treated as unexplained residuals (called unsystematic risk). If the Francis quarterly equity returns model were provided with exogenous input data about aggregate profits and a stock market index, it could be modified to operate with the FR model and provide detailed analysis of period-by-period equity returns.

678

Exhibit 4. Variable Interdependence Within Sector Seven

		Explaining Variables				
		RE_t	L_t	NL_t	NS_t	$\hat{i}_t$	NLS_t
	RE_t		X	X		X	
Explained	L_t		X				
Variables	NL_t		X		X		
	NS_t			X			X
	$\hat{i}_t$		X	X			
	NLS_t	X		X			

Sector Two: Company Sales and Production

Company sales are obtained through a market share assumption which is typically a more stable parameter than a company's dollar sales level. Potential company sales is obtained from forecasted industry sales through this market share assumption. Equation (4) shows the relationship explicitly.

The FR model distinguishes between potential and actual sales levels, which allows a realistic treatment of slack or idle capacity in the firm. Because of the possibility of under-utilized assets, every sales upturn need not be translated directly into an increase in the asset base. Some or all of the sales upturn can be absorbed by more complete utilization of available resources.

Company production potential is obtained from a production function that defines full capacity company production. This is determined by previous-period full capacity sales, inventory, and fixed assets (see Equation (2) in Appendix B for the exact specification). Actual company production is derived from full capacity production by a capacity utilization index in Equation (3).

The production function allows explicit definition of the company's full capacity production levels. It serves the useful purpose of relaxing the assumption used in many models that whatever is produced is sold. Full capacity production is typically adjusted gradually, or dynamically, over the long run to upward changes in potential sales and is often not responsive to downturns. The non-proportionality and asymmetry discussed earlier with respect to the distinction between actual and potential sales also applies to the distinctions between potential full capacity and actual production. For instance, slack (that is, idle capacity) may be decreased to meet a sales upturn without increasing the firm's investment in manufacturing machinery.

Sector Three: Fixed Capital Stock Requirements

Necessary new investment is not linked directly to company sales in the FR model, but instead results from comparison between potential and actual company sales. Equation (7) measures the company expansion possibility by the difference between potential company sales (itself influenced by management's industry sales forecast and company market share assumption) and full capacity sales. The units of required new capital are derived from this difference in Equation (9), shown in Appendix B.

Through this specification the FR model recognizes the asymmetrical response of the asset base to changes in sales levels. A strict ratio between sales and asset levels, such as used in other *pro forma* models [14, 19], presumes a proportionate and symmetrical response of asset levels to both sales upturns and downturns. The FR distinction between actual and potential sales and the concept of slack allows a realistic non-proportionality and asymmetry in the simulation. (For instance, a sales downturn need not and usually does not lead to a reduction in asset levels; instead it typically causes a decrease in capacity utilization.)

A capacity utilization index for the simulated company and industry translates full capacity output (from the production function) into actual company sales, just as a market share assumption is used to translate potential industry sales into potential company sales. Any positive difference between potential company sales and actual company sales is decomposed into the contribution due to idle capacity and the contribution due to company expansion possibility, as shown mathematically in Equation (5).

Sector Four: Pricing

The pricing sector of the model plays a key role by relating the real or units sectors to the nominal or dollar sectors. The real sectors of industry sales, company sales and production, and fixed capital stock requirements are all denominated in physical units of output. However, the nominal sectors of production costs, income, financing required, and valuation are all dollar-denominated. The real sectors and the nominal sectors are connected by the pricing sector.

This sector separation allows explicit treatment of the product pricing decision apart from the sales and production decisions. Also, it maintains the important distinction between real and nominal quantities and thus permits an analysis of inflation's impact on the firm (as suggested by the Securities and Exchange Commission [18]).

Equation (13) is a simple formula that generates product price by relating it through a markup to the ratio of previous period gross operating profit to inventory. Real units of company sales are priced out in Equation (12). Required new capital units are priced out using the average unit capital cost specified in Equation (11).

Sector Five: Production Costs

The production cost sector is similar to previous models; production cost and inventory are related directly to actual company sales dollars. Also, depreciation is linked directly to existing fixed investment.

Sector Six: Income

As in the production cost sector, the income sector equations tie inventory, earnings before interest and taxes, and net income after taxes directly to actual company sales dollars. This simplicity is preserved here to create a linearly-determined income statement that produces EBIT as a function of actual company sales (given a few simplifying assumptions). The NIAT is derived from EBIT after deduction of interest expense (also linearly-related to actual sales levels) and taxes.

Sector Seven: New Financing Required

The new financing required sector is composed primarily of accounting relationships that determine the dollar amount of external financing required from the new capital requirements (sector three) and internal financing capability (sector six). Equation (21) obtains this external financing requirement. The retained income portion of internal financing is derived from Equation (23).

Finally, the breakdown of new external financing into new equity and new debt occurs in Equation (25), where the notion of optimal capital structure is exploited. The weighted average cost of debt, Equation (24), consists of a weighted sum of new debt costs and the cost of existing debt. The cost of new debt is not exogenous in this model; it is estimated in a simplified risk-return trade-off from sector nine.

Sector Eight: Risk

The linear derivation of both EBIT and NIAT in the income sector is used (with simplifying assump-

tions) in the risk sector to obtain the standard deviation of each income measure. The derivation (presented in Appendix C) demonstrates how management's judgment as to the variability (that is, standard deviation) of forecasted industry sales affects the risk character (of both the business and financial risk) of the company. This risk character influences the costs of financing new stock and debt in risk-return trade-off equations of sector nine. In this way, risk is explicitly accounted for as the principal determinant of financing costs, and financing costs are made endogenous to the model. In addition, the risk relationship (shown in Appendix C) demonstrates a positive cause and effect relationship from the ratio of fixed to variable costs (an operating leverage measure) to the standard deviation of EBIT. The debt-to-equity ratio (a financial leverage ratio) also positively influences the NIAT standard deviation. Thus, the leverage structure of the firm endogenously influences the costs of financing in a realistic way.

Sector Nine: Costs of Financing

Market factors enter into the determination of financing costs through the slope (β_1 and β_2) and intercept (α_1 and α_2) coefficients of the two risk-return trade-off functions — namely Equations (29) and (31). At the present time, all four coefficients must be exogenously provided by management. However, this is not a difficult task. Historical coefficients can be estimated empirically using simple linear regression. The regression coefficients would establish a plausible range of values that might be used by management to determine the present or future coefficient values.

Sector Ten: Common Stock Valuation

The valuation model used finds the present value of dividends which are presumed to grow perpetually at a constant rate. This venerable model can be traced from Williams [22] through more recent analysts. Algebraically reduced to its simplest form, the single-share valuation model is shown below.

$$\text{share price} = \frac{(\text{cash dividend per year})}{\left(\begin{array}{c}\text{equity capitalization}\\ \text{rate, } i_t^s\end{array}\right) - \left(\begin{array}{c}\text{growth rate,}\\ g_t^a\end{array}\right)}$$

Equation (33) differs slightly from the per share valuation model above because it values the firm's total equity outstanding. This change was accomplished merely by multiplying both sides of the valuation equation shown above by the number of shares outstanding. The remaining equations of this sector are then accounting statements.

Full Model Simulation

The degree of simultaneity in the model is useful since it represents an approximation of the true complexity in management decision making. For instance, management decisions affect and are affected by costs of new financing. Likewise, the average debt interest rate both affects and is affected by management decisions. These simultaneous interactions occur dynamically (that is, over time) as well as in current time periods. Since previous decisions influence current decisions, a brief history of previous decisions is incorporated into the model through lagged variables. This occurs in the production function as well as in the product pricing and debt cost equations. The appropriate variables were lagged one year in all cases. In the production function, the lag was thought essential since the existing asset structure of the firm as well as previous sales levels determines current full capacity sales levels. This relationship demonstrates the long-term structural character of the firm — a structure that cannot be drastically altered in the short run.

Practically speaking, the final test of a model is its workability in specific applications. For the proposed model, the company selected for simulation must be a member of an identifiable industry, whose sales and industry sales are available in units as well as dollars. Although there are many companies from several industries that could have been used, the Anheuser-Busch Company was selected for discussion here.

There follows an actual application of the model over a recent historical period for Anheuser-Busch. Several different simulation experiments are reported. Appendix D contains a performance comparison between the proposed model and the most comparable other financial model [19].[4]

The proposed model was simulated over an eight-year sample period.[5] *Ex post* simulation is a useful technique for quantifying the "sample period" performance of the model as a predictor. Several forecast errors are measured for each of the endogenous variables — bias, average absolute error (AAE), and root mean squared error (RMSE).[6] The model should perform "well" as a predictor over the sample period if the specification is valid and the necessary simplifying assumptions do not destroy predictive performances.

Anheuser-Busch Company annual reports provided all the necessary company data for the ten years from 1966 to 1975. A total of ten years of data was needed to provide two years of historical exogenous data to initialize the model plus eight more years of data for the simulation. Industry sales (measured in barrels of beer) were available in the *Brewer's Almanac*. The capacity utilization index, γ_t, was obtained from the Wharton Economic Forecasting Associates capacity utilization series. The price of capital, P_{kt}, was approximated by the Bureau of Economic Analysis GNP deflator component index for capital goods. All the necessary coefficients were obtained by making the appropriate divisions of annual data. The production and risk trade-off function coefficients were derived by ordinary least squares regressions over the entire sample period.

The model is solved simultaneously for each period over the 1968-1975 sample period by initializing the right-hand side (RHS) variables in every equation with their actual historical values and then solving for the dependent or left-hand side (LHS) variables. The nature of simultaneous equations is such that the solved LHS variable values are used as RHS values in the next iteration. Each sector is solved separately. Then the entire system of sectors is solved in a sector-

---

[4]The FR model is similar to the financial planning models of Pindyck and Rubinfeld [14, Section 12.3] and Warren and Shelton [19]. However, the FR model is completely different from several econometric models which have been developed to relate the U.S. macroeconomic environment to various elements of the business firm (namely, Elliot [4] and Salzman [16]). The FR model also abstracts from regulatory sectors (unlike Davis *et al.* [3]) and marketing (in particular, advertising) campaign variables. However, it would be straightforward to link the FR model to a larger macroeconomic model if the firm needed to be analyzed within its larger economic environment.

[5]The authors have also tested the FR and the WS [19] models with other companies. Details of the tests using Ford Motor Company and Republic Steel data are available from the authors on request. All the test results were not presented here to save space.

[6]The forecast error measurements called bias, average absolute error (AAE), and root mean squared error (RMSE) are well-known econometric measures for evaluating the performance of simultaneous equation models. These measures are defined and discussed on pages 314 to 320 of Pindyck and Rubinfeld [14] and in numerous other econometrics textbooks.

step procedure. This same procedure is followed for each of the eight years of the sample period.[7]

Experimentation and Evaluation

Several simulation experiments were employed to isolate those sectors in the model that contribute greatly to forecast error: the first order sensitivity experiment and the "what if" type of simulation. Appendix D compares the model's performance with that of Warren and Shelton [19] in successive one-period simulations over the sample period. This comparison demonstrates the benefits made possible by the refinements introduced in the FR model.[8]

First Order Sensitivity Experiment (FOSE)

The FOSE experiment is designed to locate and measure the source of a model's forecast error. This is achieved by exogenizing equations or whole sectors so that the dependent variables involved take on their actual historical values in solution. The procedure essentially eliminates these exogenized equations or sectors as sources of error. Consequently, a comparison of the forecast error of the exogenous simulation with that of the entire model simulation will indicate the portion of forecast error attributable to this sector or equation alone. This is useful information for error tracing and respecification.

Several whole sectors were exogenized separately at their actual historical values to measure their influence. The forecast error for each experiment is recorded in Exhibits 6 and 7. A comparison of the forecast errors of the following exhibits with those of Exhibit 5, the full model solutions, indicates the location and magnitude of the errors.

The historical simulation results (Exhibit 5) indicate high root mean squared error (RMSE) for the dollar values from the industry sales, pricing, production cost, and EBIT sectors that passes on into the new financing required sector. This causes high RMSE error in the external financing requirement variables, NS, NL, and NLS. To explore the magnitude of these attributable errors, both the price and EBIT sectors are made individually exogenous. The model is solved around each, producing the solution series recorded in Exhibits 6 and 7.

The price sector exogenous simulation (Exhibit 6) demonstrates a significant 43% reduction in RMSE of EBIT. Some error remains because the interest rate of new debt issues has been endogenized in this model — the risk-return functions have some simulation error since the α and β coefficients used in Equations (29) and (31) are the actual regression coefficients for the entire sample period. Nevertheless, an exogenous price sector results in a simulation error reduction of 24% for ΔRE, 15% for NL and 2% reduction for NS. Consequently, the price sector alone accounts for 2 to 24% of the simulation error reported in the full model simulation shown in Exhibit 5.

The EBIT sector exogenous simulation shows, as expected, zero forecast error for NIAT and EBIT, and causes a 51% reduction in the RMSE of ΔRE. However, the simulation errors of the external financing variables, NS and NL, revert to their previous magnitudes in the full model simulation. Consequently, the price sector, not the EBIT sector, influences the simulation error in the new financing required sector. However, the EBIT sector influences most of the other model variables.

These two simulations have shown the pricing equations to be critical in influencing new financing required sector error, explaining approximately one-quarter to one-half of that sector's error. On the other hand, the EBIT sector controls the NIAT, EBIT, and RE errors.

Simulation of Changes

Second order simulation experiments (SOSE) were conducted to evaluate the probable effects of changes on the firm. These experiments involve changing the

---

[7]A FORTRAN computer program was used to solve the system of equations. Matrix inversion is not used so that the matrix need not be square; the Gauss-Seidel algorithm is used instead. All equations and sectors in the system must first be ordered so that they are as nearly recursive as possible. If the system cannot converge on a solution, it can be re-ordered and tried again. It is mathematically possible to have non-convergent systems, but this problem is rare in empirical applications. The first period's solution is obtained by initializing the equations with their actual historical values and then solving for the unknown dependent variables. Each sector is solved separately with a maximum of 100 iterations per sector allowed for a converged solution. A specified tolerance of .001 is used to determine when the convergence is tolerably close. After all sectors are solved, a sector-step procedure is employed to solve the entire system. This sector-step procedure is repeated up to a maximum of 30 times until a convergence which satisfies the tolerance criterion over all system dependent variables is obtained for the period. Then, in a similar fashion, the program proceeds to solve the system for the next period's values.

[8]Detailed performance comparisons between the FR and the WS [19] model results are not reported here. They will be made available to interested readers upon request. However, Appendix D shows one prediction comparison for the FR model and the WS model. See footnotes 4, 5 and 6 for references about comparing predictions from competing econometric models and different companies' financial statements.

Exhibit 5. Full Model Simulation Results For Anheuser-Busch, Inc.

Variable and Code*		1968	1969	1970	1971	1972	1973	1974	1975	Bias	AAE	RMSE
S_t	A	652.7	666.6	792.78	902.45	977.50	1109.71	1413.09	1644.98			
	S	597.72	712.87	786.69	899.06	1015.91	1097.24	1389.15	1661.11	−0.01	25.21	30.98
	D	−54.98	46.27	−6.09	−3.39	38.41	−12.47	−23.94	16.13			
EBIT	A	100.32	100.34	127.88	142.65	152.93	131.53	133.39	187.90			
	S	88.98	106.25	125.46	143.45	162.14	130.17	122.70	197.83	0.04	6.46	7.66
	D	−11.34	5.91	−2.42	0.80	9.21	−1.36	−10.69	9.93			
I_t^A	A	.05	.06	.06	.06	.06	.06	.06	.07			
	S	.05	.05	.06	.06	.06	.06	.06	.06	0.00	0.00	0.00
	D	.00	−.01	.00	.00	.00	.00	.00	−.01			
NL_t	A	0.0	0.0	0.0	0.0	0.0	0.0	100.00	150.00			
	S	13.65	13.27	2.55	13.93	4.23	0.0	13.40	36.83	24.97	30.93	51.11
	D	13.65	13.27	2.55	13.93	4.23	0.0	−86.60	−113.17			
S_t	A	91.72	93.05	93.85	101.50	103.30	103.57	103.57	103.57			
	S	91.72	91.72	91.71	91.72	91.72	91.71	91.72	91.72	−7.45	−7.45	8.93
	D	0.0	−1.33	−2.13	−9.78	−11.58	−11.58	−11.58	−11.58			
NIAT	A	44.63	45.31	62.55	71.64	76.40	65.58	64.02	84.72			
	S	39.37	47.31	59.78	70.94	79.98	63.71	60.88	92.92	0.04	3.44	4.08
	D	−5.26	2.00	−2.77	−0.70	3.58	−1.87	−3.14	8.20			
ΔRE	A	28.51	27.47	43.56	47.85	46.20	38.54	36.98	55.88			
	S	25.15	28.71	42.00	47.58	47.81	37.37	35.07	61.35	0.05	2.07	2.57
	D	−3.36	1.24	−1.56	−0.27	1.61	−1.17	−1.91	5.47			
NLS_t	A	1.45	1.33	.80	7.65	1.80	.27	100.0	150.0			
	S	13.65	13.27	15.90	13.93	10.49	7.51	13.40	36.83	−17.29	32.65	51.23
	D	12.20	11.94	15.10	6.28	8.69	7.24	−86.6	−113.17			
L_t	A	142.72	134.93	128.08	116.57	99.11	93.41	193.24	342.17			
	S	107.76	148.20	143.98	130.50	109.60	100.93	106.64	229.01	−21.70	36.98	52.82
	D	−34.96	13.27	15.90	13.93	10.49	7.52	−86.60	−113.16			
NS_t	A	1.45	1.33	.80	7.65	1.80	.27	0.0	0.0			
	S	0.0	0.0	0.0	0.0	0.0	0.0	0.0	0.0	−1.66	−1.66	2.88
	D	−1.45	−1.33	−0.80	−7.65	−1.80	−0.27	0.0	0.0			

A = Actual   S = Solved   D = Deviation
*See Appendix A for definitions of all variables.

exogenous input parameters in order to answer "what if" questions.

The outcome of the full model simulation indicated that the *ex post* simulation could not accurately explain the aggressive external financing plan of the Anheuser-Busch management in 1974-1975. The full model simulation (Exhibit 5) produces a RMSE for new debt issues (NL) of 51.11, for new stock issues (NS) of 2.88, and for combined external financing (NLS) of 51.23. However, these simulation results were the result of known industry sales growth rates and known Anheuser-Busch market share. But, the relevant influence in the formulation of capital expansion plans and external financing is expected (that is, *ex ante* rather than actual) levels of industry sales

growth and company market share. So, changes to improve this portion of the forecast were simulated.

Several exogenous parameters were changed for the sample period simulation in an attempt to find a better explanation for Anheuser-Busch's external financing (namely, debt issues) in 1974 and 1975. Neither market share nor industry sales growth parameter changes, however, alone or in combination, appeared to offer a reduced simulation error for the new financing required variables (NL, NS). The results shown in Exhibit 8 demonstrate the use of the model when the market share is assumed to climb steadily from an actual value of 17% in 1968 to 25% in 1975. In fact, market share actually climbs from 17% to 21% over this period. The income variables (NIAT and

Exhibit 6. Simulation With Price Sector Exogenous

Variable and Code*		1968	1969	1970	1971	1972	1973	1974	1975	Bias	AAE	RMSE
$S_t	S	652.7	666.60	792.78	902.45	977.50	1109.71	1413.09	1644.98	0.0	0.0	0.0
	D	0.0	0.0	0.0	0.0	0.0	0.0	0.0	0.0			
EBIT$_t$	S	97.91	99.99	126.85	144.39	156.40	133.16	127.17	197.39	.7918	3.2946	4.3814
	D	−2.41	−0.35	−1.03	1.74	3.47	1.63	−6.21	9.49			
I$_t^\wedge$	S	.05	.05	.06	.06	.06	.06	.06	.06	−0.0011	0.0031	0.0042
	D	0.00	−.01	0.00	0.00	0.00	0.00	0.00	−.01			
NL$_t$	S	25.70	20.11	17.36	16.12	14.68	14.71	33.65	57.54	−6.27	33.44	43.27
	D	25.70	20.11	17.36	16.12	14.68	14.71	−66.36	−92.46			
S$_t$	S	114.83	112.38	99.19	110.75	126.61	142.12	160.23	141.45	26.68	26.68	23.75
	D	23.11	19.33	5.34	9.25	23.31	38.55	56.66	37.88			
NIAT	S	44.19	44.94	61.25	72.11	77.64	65.83	63.38	92.86	.9219	1.6058	2.9710
	D	−.43	−.37	−1.30	0.47	1.24	0.25	−0.64	8.15			
NLS	S	48.81	39.44	22.70	25.37	37.99	53.26	90.31	95.42	18.75	34.82	38.21
	D	47.36	38.11	21.90	17.72	36.19	52.99	−9.69	−54.58			
L$_t$	S	119.80	155.02	145.43	132.69	113.78	108.11	126.86	249.68	−12.3563	33.092	43.1313
	D	−22.92	20.09	17.35	16.12	14.67	14.70	−66.38	−92.00			
NS$_t$	S	1.40	0.0	0.0	0.0	0.0	0.0	0.0	0.0	−1.49	−1.49	2.83
	D	−.05	−1.33	−0.80	−7.65	−1.80	−0.27	0.0	0.0			
ΔRE	S	28.29	27.42	42.88	48.31	46.58	38.84	36.76	61.29	.6733	.9680	1.9470
	D	−0.22	−0.05	−0.68	0.46	0.38	0.30	−0.21	541			

*See Appendix A for the definitions of all variables.
(Simulated value) − (Actual value) = (Deviation from actual) = S − D = A

EBIT) and contribution to retained earnings variable (RE) were not thrown into great error by the change. However, NS shows no change from full model simulation, and the new debt issue variable NL shows no better time pattern of debt issue than in the full model case.

This was typical of the results of all the hypothetical simulations performed. These results suggest that more exogenous information could be helpful and that a different specification may be needed to more fully explain Anheuser-Busch's external financing decisions over the 1968-1975 sample period. The model's lack of a perfect fit is not unusual or a cause for concern, however. Fitting an econometric model to a specific application is like fitting a suit of clothes — perfect fits are rare. Most people are willing to settle for a very good fit rather than pay the high cost of endless alterations as they seek that elusive "perfect fit everywhere." In the final analysis, we are convinced that this model has superior explanatory power over a wide range of applications. (See footnote 3.)

Summary and Conclusion

Forecasting is a difficult exercise. The use of a model such as the FR model allows the financial manager insight into what is required for forecasts. Financial managers who must prepare *pro forma* financial statements, project financial needs, and answer "what if" questions about the effects of differing rates of inflation and/or other proposed changes should find the model helpful. It provides sufficient detail through disaggregation into unit sales, unit production, capacity utilization, and unit pricing sectors to be of considerable use to management for both forecasting and simulation. Disaggregation is carried to the point where economic, technical, and behavioral relationships can be treated explicitly, although not to the point that would cause the model to be unmanageable.

Disaggregation provides the benefit of explicit treatment of the relevant market share assumptions and the behavioral determinants of financing costs

Exhibit 7. Simulation With EBIT Sector Exogenous

Variable and Code*		1968	1969	1970	1971	1972	1973	1974	1975	Bias	AAE	RMSE
S_t	A											
	S				(same as full model solution)							
	D											
EBIT	A											
	S				(exogenous)							
	D											
I_t^*	A											
	S				(same as full model solution)							
	D											
NL_t	A	0.0	0.0	0.0	0.0	0.0	0.0	100.0	150.0			
	S	14.65	11.91	15.59	13.38	9.58	7.31	14.05	33.99	−16.19	34.30	52.16
	D	14.65	11.91	15.59	13.38	9.58	7.31	−85.95	−116.00			
S_t	A											
	S				(same as full model solution)							
	D											
NIAT	A											
	S				(exogenous)							
	D											
NLS_t	A	1.45	1.33	.80	7.65	1.80	.27	100.00	150.00			
	S	14.65	11.91	15.59	13.38	9.58	7.31	14.05	33.99	−17.86	32.64	51.83
	D	13.20	10.58	14.79	5.73	7.78	7.04	−85.95	−116.01			
L_t	A	142.72	134.93	128.08	116.57	99.11	93.41	193.24	342.17			
	S	108.76	146.84	143.67	129.95	108.69	100.73	107.29	226.17	−22.27	36.71	34.03
	D	−33.96	11.91	15.59	13.37	9.58	7.32	−85.95	−116.00			
NS_t	A											
	S				(same as full model solution)							
	D											
ΔRE	A	28.51	27.47	43.56	47.85	46.20	38.54	36.98	55.88			
	S	29.30	27.71	43.31	47.78	45.62	38.49	39.03	58.62	0.62	.85	1.26
	D	0.78	0.24	−0.25	−0.02	−0.58	−0.05	2.05	2.74			

*See Appendix A for definitions of all variables.

which adds considerably to the model's explanatory power. A technical production function relationship allows disaggregation from dollar-denominated quantities to units of output and thus facilitates the analysis of price changes in input factors and/or the firm's own products. In addition, the model's determination of the firm's full capacity production capability as a function of the company's past performance is essential in the development of a realistic analysis of expansion and contraction within the firm.

The model is dynamic, as any model that attempts to simulate asset expansion should be, since previous decisions influence current decisions. A brief history of previous decisions is incorporated into the model through lagged variables. This occurs in the production function as well as in pricing and debt cost equations.

Additionally, the FR model takes explicit account of risk and of the influence that both the operating and financial leverage of the company have on risk. Furthermore, risk is fed back to simultaneously determine capital costs, in turn affecting the financing decision. This is an example of simultaneity in the model among financial decisions, company risk, and financing costs. One decision cannot be made without affecting others.

Exhibit 8. Hypothetical Industry Sales Growth Rate

Variable and Code*		1968	1969	1970	1971	1972	1973	1974	1975	Bias	AAE	RMSE
SS_t	S	625.07	740.22	814.04	926.41	1043.26	1124.59	1416.50	1688.46	27.34	34.25	41.32
	D	−27.63	73.62	21.26	23.96	65.76	14.88	3.41	43.48			
EBIT	S	93.76	111.03	130.25	148.23	166.92	134.95	127.48	202.61	4.78	7.90	9.03
	D	−6.56	10.69	2.37	5.57	13.99	3.42	−5.91	14.71			
I^A_t	S	.05	.05	.06	.06	.06	.06	.06	.06	0.00	0.00	0.00
	D	0.00	−.01	0.00	0.00	0.00	0.00	0.00	−0.01			
NL_t	S	21.06	13.27	15.89	13.92	10.49	7.51	13.40	36.83	−14.70	35.24	51.89
	D	21.06	13.27	15.89	13.92	10.49	7.51	−86.60	−113.17			
S_t	S	106.70	106.70	106.70	106.70	106.70	106.70	106.70	106.70	7.43	7.43	8.97
	D	14.98	13.65	12.85	5.20	3.40	3.13	3.13	3.13			
NIAT	S	42.38	50.61	63.08	74.24	83.27	67.01	64.18	96.22	3.27	3.83	5.27
	D	−2.25	5.29	0.53	2.59	6.87	1.43	0.16	11.50			
NLS_t	S	36.04	13.27	15.89	13.92	10.49	7.51	13.40	36.83	−75.92	75.92	88.73
	D	34.59	11.94	15.09	6.27	8.69	7.24	−86.6	−113.17			
L_t	S	115.16	148.20	143.98	130.49	109.60	100.93	106.64	229.01	−20.78	36.05	52.27
	D	−27.56	13.27	15.89	13.92	10.49	7.52	−86.59	−113.16			
NS_t	S	0.0	0.0	0.0	0.0	0.0	0.0	0.0	0.0	−1.66	−1.66	2.88
	D	−1.45	−1.33	−0.80	−7.65	−1.80	−0.27	0.0	0.0			
ΔRE_t	S	27.13	30.87	44.16	49.74	49.97	39.53	37.22	63.51	2.14	2.49	3.37
	D	−1.38	3.40	0.59	1.89	3.76	0.99	0.25	7.63			

$S - A = D$
*See Appendix A for definitions of all variables.

References

1. W. T. Carleton, "An Analytical Model for Long-Range Financial Planning," *Journal of Finance* (May 1970), pp. 291–315.
2. E. Eugene Carter, "A Simultaneous Equation Approach To Financial Planning: A Comment," *Journal of Finance* (September 1973), pp. 1035–38.
3. B. E. Davis, G. J. Caccapplo, and M. A. Chandry, "An Econometric Planning Model for American Telephone and Telegraph Company," *The Bell Journal of Economics and Management Science* (Spring 1973), pp. 29–56.
4. J. Walter Elliot, "Forecasting And Analysis of Corporate Financial Performance With An Econometric Model of The Firm," *Journal of Financial and Quantitative Analysis* (March 1972), pp. 1499–1526.
5. Jack Clark Francis, "Analysis of Equity Returns: A Survey With Extensions," *Journal of Economics and Business* (Spring/Summer 1977), pp. 181–92.
6. G. W. Gershefski, "Building a Corporate Financial Model," *Harvard Business Review* (July/August 1969), pp. 61–72.
7. G. W. Gershefski, "Corporate Models: The State of the Art," *Managerial Planning* (November/December 1969), pp. 1–6.
8. T. Haavelmo, "The Statistical Implications of a System of Simultaneous Equations," *Econometrica* (January 1943), pp. 1–12.
9. L. R. Klein, "Estimation of Interdependent Systems in Macroeconometrics," *Econometrica* (April 1969), pp. 171–92.
10. L. R. Klein, *A Textbook in Econometrics,* 2nd ed., Englewood Cliffs, N.J., Prentice-Hall, Inc., 1974.
11. E. Lerner and W. T. Carleton, "The Integration of Capital Budgeting and Stock Valuation," *American Economic Review* (September 1964), pp. 683–702.
12. R. Mattessich, "Budgeting Models and System Simulation," *Accounting Review* (July 1961), pp. 384–97.
13. S. C. Myers and G. A. Pogue, "A Programming Approach to Corporate Financial Management," *Journal of Finance* (May 1974), pp. 579–99.
14. Robert S. Pindyck and Daniel L. Rubinfeld, *Econometric Models and Economic Forecasts,* New York, McGraw-Hill Book Co., 1976.
15. A. A. Robichek and S. C. Myers, *Optimal Financing Decisions,* Englewood Cliffs, N.J., Prentice-Hall, Inc., 1965.
16. S. Salzman, "An Econometric Model of A Firm," *Review of Economics and Statistics* (August 1967), pp. 332–42.

17. Securities and Exchange Commission, Release No. 5695, "Notice of Adoption of Amendments to Regulations S-X Requiring Disclosure of Certain Replacement Cost Data," March 23, 1976.

18. Securities and Exchange Commission, Release No. 33-5699, April 23, 1976.

19. J. M. Warren and John P. Shelton, "A Simultaneous Equation Approach To Financial Planning, *Journal of Finance* (December 1971), pp. 1123–42.

20. J. M. Warren and J. P. Shelton, "A Simultaneous Equation Approach to Financial Planning: Reply," *Journal of Finance* (September 1973), pp. 1039–42.

21. H. M. Weingartner, *Mathematical Programming and the Analysis of Capital Budgeting Problems*, Chicago, Markham Publishing Co., 1967.

22. John Burr Williams, *The Theory of Investment Value*, Cambridge, Harvard University Press, 1938.

Appendix A. List of Variables

Endogenous

Sales^P_t	Potential industry sales (units)
S^{FC}_t	Full capacity unit output (company)
S^a_t	Actual company unit output
S^p_t	Potential company unit output
γ_{1t}	Measure of necessary new investment (based on units)
γ_{2t}	Measure of *slack* due to underutilization of existing resources
K_t	Units of capital stock
NK_t	Desired new capital (capital units)
FA_t	Fixed assets (current $)
NF_t	Desired new investment (current $)
P_{ta}	Output price
$\$S_t$	Sales dollars (current $)
COG_t	Cost of goods (current $)
OC_t	Overhead, selling, cost of goods, depreciation, and interest expense (current $)
$OC2_t$	Non-operating income (current $)
D_t	Depreciation expense (current $)
INV_t	Inventory (current $)
L_t	Long term debt
i^L_t	Cost of new debt (%)
NL_t	New long term debt needed ($)
NS_t	New common stock (equity) needed ($)
$NIAT_t$	Net income after tax (current $)
RE_t	Retained earnings
$EBIT_t$	Earnings before interest and taxes
i^A_t	Weighted average cost of long term debt
υ_{EBIT}	Coefficient of variation of EBIT
i^s_t	Cost of new stock issue
υ_{NIAT}	Coefficient of variation of NIAT
TEV_t	Total equity value
g^s_t	Growth rate in $\$S_t$
$EAFCD_t$	Earnings available for common dividend
$CMDIV_t$	Common dividend
ΔRE_t	Contributions to RE made in the tth period
GOP_t	Gross operating profit (current $)

Exogenous

$GSALS_t$	Growth rate in potential industry sales
Sales^P_{t-1}	Previous period potential industry sales (units)
S^{FC}_{t-1}	Previous period company full capacity unit output
INV_{t-1}	Previous period company finished good inventory
FA_{t-1}	Previous period company fixed asset base ($)
γ_t	Capacity utilization index
c_t	Desired market share
θ	Proportionality coefficient of S^{FC}_t to K_t
P_{kt}	GNP component index for capital equipment
P	Percentage markup of output price over ratio of GOP_t/INV_t
δ_2	Proportionality coefficient of OC_t to $\$S_t$
ϕ	Proportionality coefficient of D_t to FA_t
N	Proportionality coefficient of INV_t to $\$S_t$
LR_t	Repayment of long-term debt
T_t	Corporate tax rate
b_t	Retention rate
U^L_t	Underwriting cost of new debt
$PFDIV_t$	Preferred dividend
i^A_{t-1}	Previous period weighted average cost of long-term debt
L_{t-1}	Previous period long-term debt
k	Optimal capital structure assumption
α_L, β_L	Coefficients in risk-return tradeoff for new debt
α_s, β_s	Coefficients in risk-return tradeoff for new stock
GOP_{t-1}	Gross operating profit of previous period
δ_1	Ratio of COG_t to actual net sales
δ_3	Ratio of OC2 to net sales
$\alpha_1, \alpha_2, \alpha_3$	Production function coefficients
Σ_1	Ratio of CA_t to net sales
Σ_2	Ratio of CL_t to net sales
$\sigma^2_{\text{Sales}^P_t}$	Standard deviation of industry sales

Appendix B. List of Equations

1. Industry Sales
   (1) $\text{Sales}_t^p = \text{Sales}_{t-1}^p (1 + \text{GSALS}_t)$
2. Company Production Sector
   (2) $S_t^{FC} = \alpha_1 S_{t-1}^{FC} + \alpha_2 \text{INV}_{t-1} + \alpha_3 FA_{t-1}$
   (3) $\dfrac{S_t^a}{S_t^{FC}} = \gamma_t \rightarrow S_t^a = \gamma_t S_t^{FC}$

   (4) $S_t^p = c_t \text{Sales}_t^p$
3. Capital Stock Requirements Sector
   (5) $S_t^p - S_t^a = (S_t^{FC} - S_t^a) + (S_t^p - S_t^{FC})$
   (6) $S_t^{FC} - S_t^a = \gamma_{2t}$
   (7) $S_t^p - S_t^{FC} = \gamma_{1t} \quad 0 \le \gamma_{1t}$
   (8) $K_t = \theta S_t^{FC}$
   (9) $NK_t = \theta \gamma_{1t}$
4. Pricing Sector
   (10) $P_{Kt} \cdot K_t = FA_t \quad FA_t / K_t = P_{Kt}$
   (11) $P_{Kt} \cdot NK_t = NF_t$
   (12) $P_{st} \cdot S_t^a = \$S_t^a$
   (13) $P_{ts} = p \, (\text{GOP}_{t-1} / \text{INV}_{t-1})$
5. Production Cost Sector
   (14) $OC_t = \delta_2 (\$S_t^a)$
   (15) $COG_t = \delta_1 \, (\$S_t^a)$
   (16) $GOP_t = \$S_t^a - COG_t$
   (17) $OC2_t = \delta_3 (\$S_t^a)$
6. Income Sector
   (18) $\text{INV}_t = N(\$S_t^a)$
   (19) $\text{EBIT}_t = \$S_t^a - OC_t + OC2_t$
   (20) $\text{NIAT}_t = (\text{EBIT}_2 - i_t^A L_t)(1 - T)$
   (20') $CL_t = \Sigma_2 (\$S_t^a)$

7. New Financing Required Sector
   (21) $NF_t + b_t \{(1 - T) [i_t^L NL_t + U_t^L NL_t]\} = NLS_t + \Delta RE_t + (CL_t - CL_{t-1})$
   (22) $NLS_t = NS_t + NL_t$
   (23) $\Delta RE_t = b_t \{(1 - T) [\text{EBIT}_t - i_t^A L_t - U_t^L NL_t] - PFDIV_t\}$
   (24) $i_t^A = i_{t-1}^A \left[\dfrac{L_{t-1} - LR_t}{L_t} \right] + i_t^L \dfrac{NL_t}{L_t}$
   (25) $\dfrac{NL_t}{NS_t + \Delta RE_t} = k$
   (26) $L_t = L_{t-1} - LR_t + NL_t$
8. Risk Sector
   (27) $\sigma_{ebit}^2 = \Theta_1^2 \cdot \Theta_2^2 \cdot \sigma_{sales_t^p}^2$
   (28) $\sigma_{niat}^2 = \Theta_5^2 \cdot \Theta_6^2 \cdot \Theta_2^2 \cdot \sigma_{sales_t^p}^2$
9. Costs of Financing Sector
   (29) $i_t^L = \alpha_L + \beta_L \, \upsilon_{EBIT}$
   (30) $\upsilon_{EBIT} = \dfrac{\sigma_{EBIT}}{R_{EBIT}}$
   (31) $i_t^a = \alpha_s + \beta_s \upsilon_{NIAT}$
   (32) $\upsilon_{NIAT} = \dfrac{\sigma_{NIAT}}{R_{NIAT}}$
10. Valuation of Equity Sector
    (33) $TEV_t = \dfrac{CMDIV_t}{i_t^a - g_t^a}$
    (34) $EAFCD_t = (1 - T_t) [\text{EBIT}_t - i_t^A L_t - U_t^L NL_t] - PFDIV_t$
    (35) $CMDIV_t = (1 - b_t) EAFCD_t$
    (36) $g_t^a = \dfrac{\$S_t^a - \$S_{t-1}^a}{\$S_{t-1}^a}$

Appendix C. Transformation of Industry Sales Moments to Company NIAT and EBIT Moments

EBIT

$$\begin{aligned}
\text{EBIT}_t &= \$S_t^a - OC_t - D_t \\
&= \$S_t^a - \delta_2 \$S_t^a - \phi FA_t \\
&= \$S_t^a - \delta_2 \$S_t^a - \phi P_{Kt} \cdot \Theta \cdot \frac{1}{\gamma_t} \cdot \frac{\$S_t^a}{P_{st}} \\
&= \left\{ 1 - \delta_2 - \phi \left[\left(\frac{P_{kt}}{P_{ts}} \right) \cdot \Theta \left(\frac{1}{\gamma_t} \right) \right] \right\} \$S_t^a \\
&= \Theta_1 \$S_t
\end{aligned}$$

If $S_t^p = S_t^{FC}$ then $S_t^{FC} = c_t \text{Sales}_t^p$
$\therefore S_t^p = c_t \text{Sales}_t^p$

Since: $S_t^a = \gamma_t S_t^{FC} = \gamma_t [c_t \text{Sales}_t^p]$
so: $P_{ts} S_t^a = \$S_t = P_{ts} \gamma_t [c_t \text{Sales}_t^p]$
and: $\$S_t^a = \Theta_2 \text{Sales}_t^p$
Hence: $\text{EBIT}_t = \Theta_1 \cdot \Theta_2 \cdot \text{Sales}_t^p$
then: $\sigma_{EBIT}^2 = \Theta_1^2 \cdot \Theta_2^2 \sigma_{sales_t^p}^2$

NIAT

$\text{NIAT}_t = [1 - T] \{\text{EBIT}_t - i^A L_t - U^L NL_t\}$
if $U^L = 0$
also:

$$L_t = \left[\frac{\dfrac{\Sigma_1 + P_k \Theta_t - \Sigma_2}{\gamma_t P_{ts}}}{\left[1 + \dfrac{1}{k} \right]} \right] \$S_t^a$$

688

$$= \Theta_4 \, \$S_t$$

$$\text{NIAT} = [1 - T] \, [\Theta_1 \cdot \$S_t^a - i_t^A \, \Theta_4 \cdot \$S_t^a]$$
$$= [1 - T] \, [\Theta_1 - i_t^A \, \Theta_4] \, \$S_t^a$$
$$= [1 - T] \, [\Theta_1 - i_t^A \, \Theta_4] \, \Theta_2 \, \text{Sales}_t^p$$
$$= \Theta_5 \cdot \Theta_6 \cdot \Theta_2 \, \text{Sales}_t^p$$

$$\therefore \quad \text{NIAT}_t = \Theta_5 \cdot \Theta_6 \cdot \Theta_2 \, \text{Sales}_t^p$$

then:
$$\sigma_{\text{NIAT}}^2 = \Theta_5^2 \cdot \Theta_6^2 \cdot \Theta_2^2 \cdot \sigma_{\text{sales}_t^p}^2$$

where:
$$\Theta_1 = \left[1 - \delta_2 - \phi \left(\frac{P_k}{P_{ts}} \right) \cdot \Theta \left(\frac{1}{\gamma_t} \right) \right]$$

$$\Theta_2 = P_{ts} \, \gamma_t \, c_t$$

$$\Theta_4 = \left\{ \frac{[\Sigma_1 + \dfrac{\Theta_k \, P_k}{\gamma_t \, P_{ts}} - \Sigma_2]}{[1 + \dfrac{1}{k}]} \right\}$$

$$\Theta_5 = [1 - T_t]$$
$$\Theta_6 = [\Theta_1 - i_t^A \, \Theta_4]$$

and:
$$\mathcal{C}\!A_t = \Sigma_1 \cdot \$S_t^a$$
$$D_t = \phi FA_t.$$

also, parameters δ_2, Θ, γ_t, Σ_2, are defined in the List of Equations (Appendix A).

Appendix D. Francis-Rowell Predictions Compared To Warren-Shelton [19] Predictions

This Appendix compares the *ex post* simulation results of the FR model with the most similar (and perhaps the best known) other model. In contrast to the FR model, the WS [19] model is exact if the coefficients are allowed to take their actual values during each time period and if the company dollar sales data are accurate. However, if the sales data are erroneous, then every dependent variable is predicted incorrectly (since all are tied directly to company sales). Asset requirements are linked directly to the same period's sales without allowance for slack. This suggests the unlikely short-run result that in a normal business cycle as sales decline, the company will divest capital, and as sales move upward toward previous levels, new assets are acquired. Furthermore, no distinction is made between company sales growth attributable to either price increases or output volume increases. Asset expansion will occur for either type of company sales increase. Because the WS model is based on a percentage of sales specification, error in the exogenous company sales input will be transmitted to all accounts. To demonstrate this, as well as to put both models on a comparable sales basis, the solved sales data from the FR model was employed as the exogenous input to the WS model. This shows the transmission of error and allows a direct comparison of RMSE of both models (see footnote six about RMSE).

Exhibit 9 presents the results of the WS model simulated on Anheuser-Busch data over the 1968-1975 sample period. These results should be compared with the FR full model simulation results shown in Exhibit 5. The WS model performs comparatively well for EBIT, NIAT, and RE, showing a lower RMSE in all cases than the FR model. This is due to the endogenized cost of new debt (i_t^L of the FR model). This cost, as explained earlier, must be simulated with error because the historically fit risk-tradeoff function coefficients were used without any changes. However, the difference in errors is not great. The most pronounced difference in the models' performances occurs in the new financing-required sector variables. In the case of NS (new stock financing), the RMSE difference is 93%, whereas NL (new debt financing) shows a RMSE difference of 23%. The RMSE differences of the WS model results are considerably larger. Consequently, the asymmetrical-nonproportionality specification of the FR model appears to explain more accurately the variability in external financing required. Furthermore, if the errors introduced by the cost of financing and pricing sectors are eliminated, the difference between FR and WS models would be negligible in the case of the income variables but huge (in favor of the FR model) over the external financing variables.

The results for Anheuser-Busch reported above suggest that the advantages inherent in the comparable WS model were not lost in extending it to develop the FR model. However, it appears that refinements added in the FR model will result in improved predictive performance.

Exhibit 9. Warren & Shelton Model Results

Variable and Code*		1968	1969	1970	1971	1972	1973	1974	1975	Bias	AAE	RMSE
SS_t	S					(exogenous)						
	D											
$EBIT_t$	S	96.01	111.48	131.30	146.35	163.26	133.24	133.76	192.97	3.93	5.01	6.16
	D	−4.30	11.14	3.42	3.70	10.33	1.71	0.36	5.07			
I_t^A	S	.05	.06	.06	.06	.06	.06	.07	.07	.005	.005	.006
	D	.00	.00	.00	.00	.00	.00	.01	.00			
NL_t	S	70.77	95.27	65.03	57.32	83.26	78.67	72.78	140.65	51.72	60.86	66.66
	D	70.77	95.27	65.03	57.32	83.26	78.67	−27.22	−9.35			
S_t	S	90.27	91.72	93.05	93.85	101.5	103.3	203.57	253.57	29.59	32.91	63.80
	D	−1.45	−1.33	−0.80	−7.65	−1.8	−0.27	100.00	150.00			
NIAT	S	42.66	50.61	64.23	73.92	81.85	66.31	62.33	82.93	1.25	2.61	3.09
	D	−1.97	5.30	1.68	2.28	5.45	0.73	−1.69	−1.79			
NLS_t	S	71.77	96.72	66.36	58.12	90.91	80.47	173.05	190.65	70.61	70.61	72.68
	D	70.32	95.39	65.66	50.47	89.11	80.20	73.05	40.65			
L_t	S	142.58	136.55	129.76	114.73	97.54	95.50	230.89	433.72	16.38	17.27	35.03
	D	−0.13	1.62	1.67	−1.84	−1.57	2.09	37.66	91.55			
NS_t	S	1.0	1.45	1.33	.80	7.65	1.80	100.27	50.00	18.88	20.70	39.76
	D	−0.45	0.12	.53	−6.85	5.85	1.53	100.27	50.00			
ΔRE	S	28.51	30.94	41.54	48.52	47.05	36.41	38.45	56.41	0.36	1.39	1.74
	D	0.0	3.47	−2.02	0.67	0.85	−2.13	1.47	.053			

S = Solved
D = Deviation
*See Appendix A for definitions of all variables.

For Further Study

Additional references to which the reader may wish to refer include:

1. Davis, B.E., G.J. Caccapplo, and M.A. Chandry. "An Econometric Planning Model for American Telephone and Telegraph Company". *The Bell Journal of Economics and Management Science* (Spring 1973), pp. 29-56.

2. Elliot, J.W. (1972). "Forecasting and Analysis of Corporate Financial Performance with an Econometric Model of the Firm." *Journal of Financial and Quantitative Analysis* (March 1972), pp. 1499-1526.

3. Gershefski, G.W. (1964). "Building a Corporate Financial Model". *Harvard Business Review* (July/August 1969), pp. 61-72.

4. McInnes, J.M. and W.J. Carleton (1982), "Theory, Models and Implementation in Financial Management". *Management Science* (forthcoming).

5. Myers, S.C. and G.A. Pogue (1974). "A Programming Approach to Corporate Financial Management". *Journal of Finance* (May 1972), pp. 579-599.

6. Porter, M.E. (1979). "How Competitive Forces Shape Strategy". *Harvard Business Review* (March/April 1979), pp. 137-145.

7. Taggert, R.A., Jr. (1977). "A Model of Corporate Financing Decisions." *Journal of Finance* (December 1977), pp. 1467-1484.

Part X

An Overview
of Finance Theory
and Practice

Introduction

In the first nine parts, both positive and normative finance theory and methods have been explored in great detail. In this part, four review papers are discussed.

In two important papers by Weston (1981) and Beranek (1981), the authors carefully review finance theory in the past, present and future. Beranek emphasizes normative finance theory, whereas Weston presents positive finance theory in more detail. Finance theories developed in the last four decades can be classified into four branches:

1. classical theory (pre-M&M theory);
2. neo-classical theory (M&M theory);
3. CAPM; and
4. Option Pricing Theory (OPT).

Their interrelationships are presented in Figure 1. These four theories are not independent. Active financial managers can incorporate these theories with modern managerial tools and relevant financial data to improve the performance of their corporations.

Pogue and Lall (1974) (PL) provide a brief well-structured presentation of the important facets of corporate finance theory. Their paper discusses

(1) the objective of the firm; (2) the firm's investment strategy; (3) the dividend decision; (4) the firm's financing decision; and (5) the integration of theory and practice. Overall, this paper synthesizes most of the material covered in Parts I through IX.

From a micro-economic viewpoint, Jensen and Meckling (1978) (JM) argue that the federal government is destroying two vital instruments of economic growth—the system of contract rights and the large corporation. They also argue that many corporations will be able to remain in business only so long as they can finance their operations from internally generated cash flows or public subsidies. Both PL and JM's papers are useful to all students of finance as a means of understanding the micro and macrofinancial economic viewpoints in corporate finance practice and theory.

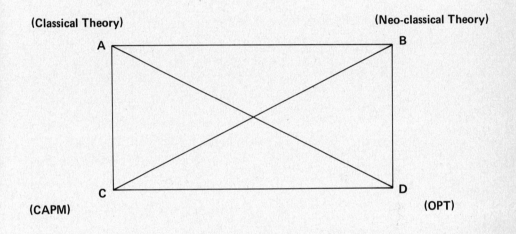

693

Developments in Finance Theory

J. Fred Weston

J. Fred Weston is Professor of Managerial Economics and Finance at the Graduate School of Management at the University of California, Los Angeles.

■ Developments in finance theory in recent years have been so substantial that another assessment of our progress and prospects should be useful. I do not know whether anyone else benefits from the exercise, but I find it helpful periodically to try to think through a conceptual framework for approaching financial decisions. When I now review my *Scope and Methodology* book [108], I find that much seems obsolete, but that much also continues to be relevant. The "New Themes" [107] have continued to evolve along the lines then projected. *Financial Theory and Corporate Policy* [21] represents a synthesis of important developments, related empirical tests, and their implications for financial decision-making.

This paper aims to be complementary to Hakansson [46], whose survey emphasizes issues of financial economics. My review will seek to: 1) summarize important themes and their relationships, 2) indicate their larger context in finance theory, 3) analyze the methodology of the related empirical

My thanks to Thomas Copeland, Harry DeAngelo, Robert Geske, Clement Krouse, Kwang Chung, Ronald Bibb, Nai-fu Chen, and to the anonymous reviewers for helpful suggestions. The contributions of Ashok Korwar, Wayne Olson, and Patricia Peat were particularly valuable.

work, and 4) highlight some key unresolved areas.

Everyone must have a conceptual framework to bring to the literature. Otherwise one is overwhelmed by the quantity and diversity of the subject matter covered. Many theoretical articles make assumptions which make the paper a special case of more general theory. The empirical tests must be critically reviewed as to 1) their theoretical underpinnings, 2) the relation between empirical materials and the underlying theory, and 3) the implicit assumptions of the tests.

The Main Theoretical Doctrines and Their Relationships

It is possible in 1981 to view modern finance as a coherent framework for analysis, answering the general question, "How do individuals, firms, and our society make decisions to allocate scarce resources through a price system based on the valuation of risky assets?" Within this broad question, we study individual preferences and decisions to determine the behavior of firms and markets, the creation of assets and claims, and the attendant problems of risk and of costly information.

Before the late 1950s, the finance field was largely

descriptive. The year 1958 was an important watershed. In that year, Tobin's "Liquidity Preference as Behavior Toward Risk" [106] appeared in the *Review of Economic Studies*. This was an important development in the application of demand theory to financial assets, with risk a central point of analysis. Hirshleifer's article, "On the Theory of Optimal Investment Decision" [51] appeared in the *Journal of Political Economy* in August 1958. It emphasized the role of time-dependent utility in the demand for both productive and financial assets and provided a foundation for further work in capital budgeting and the separation principle. The foundations for state–preference theory were also laid during this period. The analyses of pure or primitive securities by Arrow [3], Arrow and Debreu [5] and Debreu [28] were applied and extended by Hirshleifer [49, 50] to broaden the choice–theoretic framework of financial decision-making. Markowitz's book on portfolio selection was in final manuscript in the same year, although it appeared with a 1959 publication date. His work, of course, represented a major advance in the formal analysis of risk in investment decisions on assets whose returns are not independent. Modigliani and Miller's first of a series of major contributions on capital structure and valuation appeared in *The American Economic Review* in June 1958 [79], giving depth to the study of the relationships of the holders of different types of claims against productive assets of firms. Through these pioneering studies and subsequent developments, the field of finance has had considerable influence in the past twenty years on microeconomics, on macroeconomics, and on the theory, practice, and curriculum of business management.

The foundation of modern finance is utility theory. From the utility axioms, powerful theories have been derived, including mean–variance portfolio theory, state–preference theory, the concept of stochastic dominance, and theories of the pricing of contingent claims. Theories of asset pricing, including the capital asset pricing model and the arbitrage pricing theory, are equilibrium constructs which follow from the application of utility theory to choices among risky alternatives. Interactions of individual preferences in markets for such alternatives provide signals to society in the form of asset prices, making possible an efficient allocation of resources over time and between consumption and investment.

The consideration of costly information and transactions costs leads to important modifications in the neoclassical theory of the firm. New approaches have included analysis of agency costs, information asymmetries, and signaling behavior. Consideration of these additional dimensions has raised questions of whether the valuation of the firm is affected by variations in the patterns of contracting among different combinations of suppliers of capital, bearers of risk, and managers of productive activities.

Parallel with the new developments in the theory of finance, an impressive body of empirical evidence has appeared.[1] Theoretical propositions have been tested, using the latest and best developments in quantitative methods.

The recent developments in finance theory to be considered in this paper are:
Asset pricing models:
  Roll's critique of the capital asset pricing model;
  Ross's contribution to arbitrage pricing theory;
Financial policy of the firm:
  Capital structure;
  Dividend policy;
Problems in costly information and divergent incentives:
  Agency costs;
  Agency in the theory of the firm;
  Signaling behavior;
Contingent claims analysis; and
Merger theory and studies of merger performance.
My conclusion considers key issues in finance theory that are yet to be resolved.

The CAPM and APT

Important new developments in the financial literature have implications for the valuation of risky assets and their role in allocating resources in the economy. A summary sufficient to provide a basis for further analysis will be attempted.

Roll's Critique

Roll's critique of the capital asset pricing model has shaken the roots of the "beta revolution" and raised the question, "Is beta dead?" [87, 89]. Roll does not contest the internal validity of the CAPM or the related two–parameter zero–beta model. Rather, he exposes fundamental problems of the models when they are applied to empirical work, with the following conclusions:

1. The traditional CAPM is not testable unless the exact composition of the true market portfolio is known and used in the test. And then the only

---

[1]See [10, 12, 13, 20, 25, 29, 30, 31, 32, 33, 34, 35, 36, 37, 38, 40, 41, 54, 55, 64, 65, 77, 83, 84, 85, 88, 89, and 98].

hypothesis that can be tested is that the market portfolio is efficient.

2. Using a proxy for the market portfolio, such as a stock market index, also involves problems. If the proxy chosen is not mean–variance efficient, the efficient set mathematics predict that the CAPM relationship will not hold.

3. If the chosen proxy is mean–variance efficient, this does not establish that the market portfolio is also on the mean–variance efficient frontier. In any sample of observations on individual returns, regardless of the generating process, there will always be many which are mean–variance efficient portfolios, viewed ex post. For the betas calculated against a mean–variance efficient portfolio, the linearity relationship between the ex post mean return and beta will be satisfied exactly, whether or not the true market portfolio is mean–variance efficient.

4. In testing the two–parameter zero–beta variant of the CAPM, a similar problem arises. If an efficient proxy portfolio is chosen as an index, a zero–beta portfolio can be constructed in relation to the selected efficient index. If the proxy portfolio turns out to be ex post efficient, then every asset will fall exactly on the security market line — there will be no abnormal returns. If there are systematic abnormal returns, it simply means that the index selected is not ex post efficient.

5. Thus any test of the CAPM or the two–parameter asset pricing model of Black is a test of the efficiency of the proxy market portfolio. The chosen proxy may turn out to be inefficient, but this alone proves nothing about the true market portfolio's efficiency.

6. Most plausible proxies are likely to be highly correlated with one another and with the true market portfolio, whether or not they are mean–variance efficient. This high correlation may suggest that the exact composition is unimportant. Small differences from the true market portfolio, however, can cause substantial biases in the measurement of risk and expected returns.

As noted above, the Roll critique does not argue that the CAPM and its two–parameter zero–beta variant are invalid. It argues that empirical tests must be constructed and interpreted with great caution. If the index used as the proxy for the market portfolio is ex post efficient, the regression of returns on betas will be perfectly linear. If the proxy index chosen is ex post inefficient, the resulting risk–return relationships depend upon which inefficient index has been selected. Until the total market portfolio containing all assets is

known and measured, ambiguities in the tests of the asset pricing models and of security investment performance will remain.

Roll's criticisms do not apply to residual analysis. Roll's response to Mayers and Rice on this point is as follows:

> Mayers and Rice say (p. 17): Roll's conclusion . . . can be easily interpreted as being critical of the empirical methodology known as residual analysis. But I never mentioned this technique. Section 5 of my (1978) paper . . . supports residual analysis as approximately valid even if the market index proxy is not ex ante efficient [90, p. 397].
>
> . . .
>
> In summary, whether residual analysis and performance measurement are equivalent depends on the treatment of the intercept term. . . . If the intercept is estimated from the data instead of specified according to the CAPM's predictions, residual analysis should give an unbiased estimate of the value of information associated with the event under study [90, p. 399].

So even though measurement of performance is subject to the strictures that Roll sets forth, residual analysis performed appropriately escapes most of these criticisms. The large numbers aspect of the cumulative average residual methodology protects it from the criticism of non-stationary betas as well. (See [50].)

The Arbitrage Pricing Theory

One way to explain the risk–return relationships while avoiding some of the problems of using a single–market index is the arbitrage pricing theory (APT). In introducing an early presentation of the APT, Ross effectively summarized its setting.

> There are at present two major theoretical frameworks for the analysis of markets for risky assets: the state space preference approach and, the mean variance model and its variants. The arbitrage model which we will develop is a third approach to capital market theory, empirically distinguishable from the mean variance theory and more directly related to the state space approach. While formally all models may be viewed as special cases of the state space preference framework, it is in the restrictions imposed either on preferences or distributions that the empirical content of the various theories lie [96, p. 190].

Thus the APT aims to be a more general formulation of asset pricing. Ross starts with the requirement of equality between rates of return on riskless assets. The aim of APT is to provide a theory for risky assets analogous to that for riskless assets.

Building on this base, if asset markets are perfectly

competitive and frictionless, it can plausibly be assumed that the return on the ith asset can be written:[2]

$$\tilde{r}_i = E_i + b_{i1}\tilde{\delta}_1 + \ldots + b_{ik}\tilde{\delta}_k + \tilde{\epsilon}_i. \qquad (1)$$

In Equation (1), E_i is the expected return, $\tilde{\delta}_j$ (j=1, ..., k) are risky factors common to all assets — random variables with zero means; b_{ij} is the sensitivity of the return on asset i to the fluctuations in factor j; and $\tilde{\epsilon}_i$ is the "unsystematic" risk component idiosyncratic to the ith asset with $E\{\tilde{\epsilon}_i \mid \tilde{\delta}_j\} = 0$ for all j. In equilibrium, the expected return on the ith asset is given by:

$$E_i = \lambda_0 + \lambda_1 b_{i1} + \lambda_2 b_{i2} + \ldots + \lambda_k b_{ik}. \qquad (2)$$

In Equation (2), λ_j (j=1, ..., k) are the returns associated with the risky factors δ_j, while λ_0 is the return on the risk-free asset (or zero–beta portfolio).

The general pricing equation of the APT for a portfolio of (k+1) independent assets and k risky factors is written as:

$$E_p = \lambda_0 + \underline{(E - \lambda_0)}' \ V^{-1} \ Cov \ (\tilde{r}_p, \tilde{r}) \qquad (3)$$

(where underlining indicates vectors).

Previous asset pricing models are in some sense special cases of the general relationships set forth in Equation (3). For example, letting k = 1 and $\tilde{\delta} = (\tilde{r}_m - E_m)$, the CAPM is obtained:

$$E_p = \lambda_0 + (E_m - \lambda_0) \ (\sigma_m^2)^{-1} \ Cov \ (\tilde{r}_p, \tilde{r}_m). \qquad (4)$$

Furthermore, as Schallheim and DeMagistris [97] have shown, a single-factor arbitrage pricing model generates the market model in the following form:

$$\tilde{R}_i = E(\tilde{R}_i) + \beta_i \tilde{\delta} + \tilde{\epsilon}_i \qquad (5)$$

where

$\tilde{R}_i$ = return on security i;
β_i = the ex ante beta coefficient;
$\tilde{\delta}$ = a mean zero common factor representing the deviation of the market from its mean; and
$\tilde{\epsilon}_i$ = a mean zero disturbance term.

From Equation (5), Schallheim and DeMagistris also summarize from the Ross "Return, Risk and Arbitrage" paper the two-parameter or Black model:

$$E(\tilde{R}_1) = E(\tilde{R}_0) + [E(\tilde{R}_M) - E(\tilde{R}_0)] \ \beta_1. \qquad (6)$$

Following the earlier empirical work of Roll and Ross [91, 92], Chen [16, 17] has obtained the following results. The APT has consistently outperformed the CAPM, as implemented to date with the market proxies used. The market proxies used were the S&P 500 index, which is value-weighted, and the New York Stock Exchange plus the American Stock Exchange securities, on both a value-weighted and an equally-weighted basis. This comparison is on the basis of adjusted R^2. The adjustment to R^2 takes into account the greater number of explanatory variables in the APT tests.

The APT is also tested against specific alternatives. After the risk factors of the APT are taken into account, the own-variance measures of risk have no explanatory power on the returns. In addition, the previous periods' returns have no explanatory power on the current period's returns. Finally, the firms' market values, one measure of size, have no explanatory power on returns.

Financial Policy

The publications of Modigliani and Miller [74, 78, 79, 80] set in motion important new developments in financial economics dealing with capital structure and dividend policy. In recent years, significant advances in both areas have continued.

Capital Structure

After MM [79], the theory of finance had accepted the proposition that, in the absence of taxes, the capital structure of the firm was irrelevant to its value. With taxes, because debt interest is deductible while common stock dividends are not, debt had been thought as always preferable to equity. An optimal financial structure with less than 100% debt required other factors (*e.g.*, high bankruptcy costs) which increase with leverage to offset the tax advantage to debt.

In his Presidential Address to the American Finance Association in 1977, Miller reopened the question with a startling demonstration that capital structure was a matter of indifference to the individual firm even in the presence of taxes. This result follows from the personal tax effects for the individual investor — that interest income from debt is taxed at a higher rate than are capital gains from equity. Miller showed that there will be an optimal debt–equity mix

---

[2]These results are taken from Nai-fu Chen [16].

for the economy as a whole, but not for each individual firm. Firms with low leverage will find a clientele among investors in high brackets and vice versa.

DeAngelo and Masulis [26, 27] formalized and extended Miller's argument. They show that his result is robust to alternate assumptions about the personal tax code, but fails under alternate assumptions about the corporate tax code and/or leverage-related costs (which, Miller had argued, were insignificant ex ante). DeAngelo and Masulis use a state–preference model. They derive two principles: Aggregate Supply Response (ASR) and Tax Induced Positive Aggregate Demand (TIPAD). On the supply side (*i.e.*, the firm side), when $P_B(s) = P_E(s) (1-T_c)$, all firms are indifferent as to how they package their securities. $P_E(s)$ and $P_B(s)$ are the state–contingent prices for equity and debt, respectively, and T_c is the corporate tax rate, the same for all firms. At any other level of the two prices, either only debt or only equity is supplied by all firms. This is ASR.

On the investor side (TIPAD), we only need to assume that there is at least one investor in each of the three tax brackets:

1. $(1-T_{PB}^i) > (1-T_{PE}^i)(1-T_c)$
2. $(1-T_{PB}^i) = (1-T_{PE}^i)(1-T_c)$
3. $(1-T_{PB}^i) < (1-T_{PE}^i)(1-T_c)$.

T_{PB}^i is the investor's personal tax rate on income from debt securities, and T_{PE}^i is the investor's personal tax rate on income from equity securities. The return on equity is proportional to $(1-T_{PE}^i)/P_E(s)$ and that on debt to $(1-T_{PB}^i)/P_B(s)$. Then, it can be shown that, when $P_B(s) < P_E(s) (1-T_c)$, the return on debt is greater than on equity for investors in brackets 1 and 2. When $P_B(s) > P_E(s) (1-T_c)$, the return on equity is greater than on debt for brackets 2 and 3.

Returning to the supply side, market equilibrium requires $P_B(s) = P_E(s) (1-T_c)$ because only then are firms indifferent between supplying debt and equity, and so will supply both, satisfying all investors. For example, if $P_B(s) < P_E(s) (1-T_c)$, then firms only supply equity, but then bracket 1 and 2 investors go unsatisfied.

Thus, Miller's results [73] are confirmed. The condition that there be some investors in each of the three brackets above is a relatively weak requirement.

DeAngelo and Masulis also consider the case where there are leverage-related costs like bankruptcy and agency costs. The result is the familiar interior optimum. The merit of the DeAngelo–Masulis analysis is that they show that, by operating *at the margin,* such costs can force an interior optimum (non-trivial) even when they are very small in absolute magnitude (contrary to Miller's intuition). Further, when there are non-debt tax shields available to the firm, like investment tax credits, at some debt level total tax credits shield all income. Beyond this point, further debt is of no advantage to the firm, and it is more costly than equity because of ruling market prices. This also gives an interior optimum, different for each firm.

The critical point is that non-cash charges and tax credits cause the expected marginal corporate tax saving to decline with leverage. This leads to the testable hypothesis: Other things being equal, decreases in effective investment-related tax shields (depreciation deductions or investment tax credits) will increase the use of debt. In cross-sectional analysis, holding before-tax earnings constant, firms with smaller investment-related tax shields will employ greater debt in their capital structure [27, p. 21].

Dividend Policy

It has long puzzled finance theorists why corporations continue to pay out billions of dollars in dividends every year, although dividends are taxed to the investor at tax rates higher than those on capital gains. The lack of useful things to do with the funds cannot be an explanation, because the corporations concurrently raise additional external capital.

In a spirit similar to Miller [73], Miller and Scholes [75] suggest that the explanation might be that investors shield their dividend income completely with interest payments on loans taken specifically for that purpose. The proceeds of the loans can be used to buy more stock, thereby converting the dividend income into capital gains. If the investor wishes to shelter the dividend income risklessly, he can do so by using the proceeds of borrowing to purchase a life insurance policy instead of new stock. Pension plans are suggested as an alternative to the life insurance plan. Hence, investors should be indifferent between dividend and capital gains income, and the firm's market value should be unaffected by its dividend payout patterns.

Miller and Scholes observe that, although the conceptual separation of the investor's leverage and dividend decisions is useful for certain purposes, new insights are to be obtained when we think of them together. However, they point out some difficulties. For *both* dividend and leverage irrelevance to hold simultaneously, the effective capital gains tax rate must be zero, else dividends, which can be shielded, are always preferred over capital gains. Further, as Miller [73] showed, leverage irrelevance requires the marginal investor to have a marginal tax rate on bonds equal to the corporate tax rate. But the same strategy used to shield dividend income can be used to shield interest income. DeAngelo and Masulis conclude that the relative price conditions which make the Miller and Scholes dividend shelter attractive to investors would also cause firms to eliminate all dividends, obviating the usefulness of the shelter [26, pp. 463–464]. Thus, there are still unresolved issues in the region where leverage and dividend policy meet.

On the empirical side, Litzenberger and Ramaswamy [63] have tested for dividend irrelevance. They derive an after-tax valuation model:

$$E(R_1) - r_F = a + b\beta_1 + c(d_1 - r_F)$$

where d_1 is the dividend yield.

If dividends are irrelevant to market values, the c coefficient would be zero.

They use GLS estimators to take care of the contemporaneous correlation between disturbances across securities. Using monthly data, they find, contrary to the Miller and Scholes results, a strong positive relationship between returns and dividend yields.

Miller and Scholes have developed a further empirical test of the dividend–return relationship [76]. They assume that announcements of increases or decreases in dividends are known to contain information about the firm's prospects. It is important to separate this information effect from the effects of tax incentives. Litzenberger and Ramaswamy tried to eliminate this effect by using the previous period's dividend as a proxy for the current period's expected dividend, rather than using the actual dividend paid out, when both the declaration of the dividend and the ex-dividend date fell in the same month. Miller and Scholes argue that this approach fails to remove the bias from the denominator of the dividend yield variable: $d_{1t}/P_{1,t-1}$. Further, Litzenberger and Ramaswamy treat a declared dividend of zero as the same as no decision on dividends. But surely there is adverse information in a directors' meeting where the decision is made not to declare a dividend, when the company normally does. When Miller and Scholes modify the work of Litzenberger and Ramaswamy for these two differences, they find the dividend yield term to be insignificant, as their model predicts. Further

work in this field should concentrate on formulating alternate models for the expected dividend yield and on distinguishing between tax effects and non-tax effects.

Agency Theory

Additional dimensions of capital structure and other financial policy decisions have emerged with the development of the literature on agency theory. Jensen and Meckling stimulated the new agency literature by extending the analytical formulations of the relationships between owners and managers [56]. They examine the agency problem which arises when a manager owns less than the total common stock of the firm. Private and individual consumption by the manager of the firm's wealth costs him only in proportion to the fraction of his ownership of the firm, the remainder being borne by the other owners. Agency costs occur because the manager's incentives diverge from those of the firm as a whole. Such costs are of three kinds: monitoring expenditures by the other owners to try to prevent this kind of behavior by the managers; bonding assurances provided by the manager as agent that he will not pursue his self-interest at the expense of the other owners; and residual losses — real inefficiencies caused by this market imperfection.

The agency problems which arise from the relations between shareholders and debtholders are summarized by Barnea, Haugen, and Senbet [6]. Debt financing with limitations on shareholders' liability may give rise to a) shareholder incentives to select higher risk projects than those which are optimal to the firm as a whole, transferring wealth from bondholders to shareholders, b) shareholder incentives not to take up the option on new profitable investments [Myers, 81], and c) bankruptcy costs generated in allocating resources under insolvency.

Another type of agency problem is caused by informational asymmetry about the prospective value of the firm. Akerlof [1] discusses this problem in the context of the used car market. Owners are assumed to have better information on their cars than prospective buyers possess. Through a self-selection process, the cars which are offered for sale by owners will exhibit a lower average quality than the stock of cars as a whole. Because of their poorer information about particular cars, prospective buyers base their bids upon their information as to the average quality of cars offered for sale. Thus, the seller who knows his car to be of high quality must bear the cost of the prospective buyers' ignorance; the seller who knows his car to be of low quality will benefit from the same source. A similar argument could be advanced regarding productive assets or firms whose securities are offered for sale.

The incidence of these agency costs will vary according to their source. Those pecuniary costs arising from divergent incentives of owners and managers will be borne by managers, reflected in the reduced prices at which outsiders are willing to purchase the shares of owner–managers and the reduced compensation packages which the owners as a whole will offer to managers. Those arising from divergent incentives of shareholders and bondholders will be borne by shareholders reflected in the reduced price which investors will pay for the firm's bonds. Those arising from information asymmetries between sellers and buyers of assets will be borne by the sellers of assets of a quality above the average of assets offered for sale and by buyers of assets of a quality below that average. The incidence of deadweight losses is indeterminate.

Fama [31] relates the agency problem to the broader theory of the firm. He begins by observing that the issue of the separation of ownership and control has been a problem faced by economists for some time. Some economists who rejected the classical model of a firm controlled by an owner–manager developed the behavioral and managerial theories of the firm. Newer theories have rejected the classical model of the firm but assume classical forms of economic behavior, such as utility maximization, on the part of agents within the firm.

Fama observes that both Alchian and Demsetz [2] and Jensen and Meckling [56] view the firm as a set of contracts among factors of production. The firm is seen as a team whose members act from self-interest and who recognize that their returns depend, at least to some degree, on the survival qualities of their firm team in competition with other teams. Fama argues that this view does not go far enough. He considers the agency problem in a multi-period world. His main thesis is that the separation of ownership and control is an efficient form of economic organization within a set-of-contracts perspective.

Fama contends that the manager's reputation, and therefore the market for his services, is greatly influenced by the performance of the firm. The signals provided by an efficient capital market about the value of a firm's securities are likely to be important for the evaluation of the firm's managers in the managerial labor market.

A basic question is the extent to which the signals provided by the managerial labor market and the capital market actually discipline managers. Fama asserts that the managerial labor market outside the firm exerts direct pressures, because an ongoing firm is continually in the market to hire or fire managers. He further asserts that capital markets cause managers to monitor each other. Each manager has a stake in the performance of the firm in the capital markets and so monitors other managers, both above and below him in rank. The role of the board of directors is to provide a relatively low cost mechanism for replacing or re-ranking top managers.

Smith and Warner [101] argue that the market mechanisms are not sufficient to resolve agency problems. They examine the nature of bond covenants to assemble evidence consistent with their "costly contracting hypothesis." They conclude:

> ... [Since] our analysis indicates that observed bond covenants involve real costs, there must be some benefit in having debt in the firm's capital structure; otherwise, the bondholder–stockholder conflict can be costlessly eliminated by not issuing debt. Hence our evidence indicates not only that there is an optimal form of debt contract, but an optimal *amount* of debt as well [101, pp. 153–154].

Barnea, Haugen, and Senbet [6] extend the Smith and Warner discussion of the impact of agency problems on capital structure decisions. They describe how call provisions, conversion privileges, income bonds, and the maturity structure of debt are consistent with the efficient handling of agency problems.

Thus, building on the seminal work of Jensen and Meckling, scholars have identified three major types of agency problems: 1) stockholder incentives to gain at the expense of bondholder interests, 2) excess consumption of perquisites by managers with fractional ownership, and 3) information asymmetry. Fama argues that value-maximization arbitrage protects bondholder interests and that the market for managers deals with perks. Smith and Warner argue from the contents of bond indentures that direct (and costly) contracting in individual company circumstances is needed to supplement the market. The third agency problem, information asymmetry, has given rise to another distinct stream of literature extending the earlier work of Spence [104] on labor market mechanisms.

Information Asymmetry and Signaling

Ross [95] describes how signaling and manager compensation arrangements can be used to deal with information asymmetry. He begins with a review of a number of alternate explanations of financial structure that he finds inadequate. He then notes that the Modigliani–Miller theorem on the irrelevance of the financial structure implicitly assumes that the market has full information about the activities of firms. The model he formulates assumes information asymmetry and an incentive system that allows the possibility of signaling.

The assumptions Ross makes to construct his model include the following:

1. Manager–insiders have information about their own firms not possessed by outsiders.

2. Investors use the face amount of the debt or dividends the manager decides to issue as a signal of the firm's type. With reference to a critical level of debt, the market perceives the firm to be type "A" if it issues debt greater than this amount and type "B" if it issues debt less than this amount.

3. A penalty is assessed against the manager if his firm experiences bankruptcy.

4. A manager may not trade in the financial instruments of his own firm. This avoids the moral hazard problem as well as violations of the incentive structure in (3).

A signaling equilibrium is achieved if "A" managers choose financing levels above the critical level and "B" managers choose financing levels below the critical level. An "A" manager will have no incentive to change, for the compensation system maximizes his return under the signal. The "B" manager will not have an incentive to signal falsely that his firm is of type "A" because the penalty built into the incentive structure would reduce his compensation.

In a final part of his paper, Ross introduces a model in which "firms have random returns X, uniformly distributed on [0,t] where manager–insiders know their own firm's t value . . ." [95, p. 35]. Again, there is a bankruptcy penalty in compensation to managers. He concludes that the MM "irrelevancy theorem holds within a risk class, i.e., given t . . ." [p. 36]. By changing the level of debt he selects, the manager–insider alters the market's perception of the firm's risk class and therefore its current value. This process produces a unique optimal level of debt financing for each firm type.

Ross discusses some empirical implications of the signaling theory. One is that the cost of capital will be unaffected by the financing decision even though the level of debt is uniquely determined. A higher level of debt increases bankruptcy risk and hence tends to decrease the value of the firm.

Haugen and Senbet [47] seek to implement Ross's penalty function through the use of contingent claims. They require that the manager simultaneously sell a combination of calls and puts so that, if the firm is an "A" firm in Ross's terminology, the manager is completely hedged, suffering no penalty if the firm turns out to be an "A" firm. On the other hand, if the firm turns out to be a "B" firm (a firm of lower value than "A"), then prior to the expiration of the contingent claims, the holders of the puts will exercise them with a consequent penalty for manager compensation.

This also provides a control on the agency problem. If the manager consumes an excessive amount of perquisites, the value of the firm will decline. In effect, he makes an "A" firm into a "B" firm. Again, the puts will be exercised and the manager will suffer the consequences of his having caused a decline.

Leland and Pyle [60] use information asymmetry influences to rationalize the existence of financial intermediation institutions, which traditional models of financial markets have difficulty explaining. They argue that transactions costs are not of a sufficient magnitude to provide an adequate explanation. Instead they find informational asymmetries to be a primary explanation for the existence of intermediaries. For assets, particularly those related to individuals such as mortgages or insurance, information not publicly available can be developed at some cost. As such information is valuable to potential lenders, if there are economies of scale, firms would be developed to assemble information and to sell it.

Two problems would arise if the firm sought to sell the information directly to investors. One is the "public good" aspect of information. Purchasers of information could share it with or resell it to others without diminishing its usefulness to themselves. The second problem relates to the reliability of the information. It will be difficult for potential users to distinguish between good and bad information. Thus the price of information will reflect its average value, and the average value of information offered for sale would be lower than the average value of the total stock of information, as in the used car discussion above. Indeed, if entry is easy for firms offering poor information, this can lead to market failure.

Both problems in capturing a return on information are overcome by a financial intermediary which buys and holds assets on the basis of accumulated information. The value of the firm's information is reflected in a private good, the returns from its portfolio. Leland and Pyle raise the question of how the potential buyers of the intermediaries' claims can judge whether the intermediary has developed valuable information. They suggest that information can be conveyed through signaling — the organizers' willingness to invest in their firm's equity [60, p. 384]. But this seems to imply a one-period model. Realistically, the historical performance record of the financial intermediary is likely to be used as an indicator of its effectiveness in assembling and utilizing information.

Contingent Claims Analysis: The Option Pricing Model (OPM)[3]

A prodigious literature has appeared on option pricing and related issues since the Black–Scholes paper in 1973 [11]. One critical development has been the recognition that a hypothetical risk-free hedge would facilitate a solution to the option pricing problem. (Black and Scholes noted this came from a suggestion by Merton [11, p. 641, ftn. 3].)

The key (as summarized by Copeland and Weston [21, p. 394]) was the following:

> And if we continuously adjust our hedge portfolio to maintain a ratio of stock to call options of $1/(\delta c/\delta S)$, the hedge will be perfectly risk free. Therefore, the risk-free hedge portfolio will earn the risk-free rate in equilibrium if capital markets are efficient. This is really the main insight. It is possible, given continuous trading, to form risk-free hedges with only two securities, the underlying asset and a call option. This equilibrium relationship is expressed as

$$\frac{dV_H}{V_H} = r_f dt.$$

> This fact and the fact that the riskless hedge is maintained by purchasing one share of stock and selling $1/(\delta c/\delta S)$ calls,

$$Q_s = 1, \qquad Q_c = -\frac{1}{(\delta c/\delta S)}, \qquad \dots$$

> leads to the Black and Scholes valuation formula.

The resulting equation involved five parameters:

> The price of the underlying security, its instantaneous variance, the exercise price on the option, the time to maturity, and the risk-free rate. Only one of these variables, the instantaneous variance, is not directly observable. The option price does not depend on (1) individual risk preferences or (2) the expected rate of return on the underlying asset. Both results

follow from the fact that option prices are determined from pure arbitrage conditions available to the investor who establishes perfectly hedged portfolios [21, p. 400].

The call price is an increasing function of the stock price, the time to maturity, the risk-free rate, and the instantaneous variance of the stock price; it is a decreasing function of the exercise price. Of the five parameters the instantaneous variance is the most difficult to estimate. But in the theoretical articles which were subsequently developed, at one time or another each of the five parameters was permitted to vary. Analytic solutions were developed for a range of assumptions about the behavior of each of the five parameters.

The issue of the underlying behavior of the stock prices became critical when some systematic departures of actual option prices from those predicted by the Black–Scholes model were observed [7]. The Black–Scholes formula was said to underprice deep-out-of-the-money options, near-maturity options and high-variance options. It seemed to overprice deep-in-the-money options and low-variance options. This led to questioning the assumption that the variance of stock prices was known and constant.

Subsequent analysis has fallen into three categories. The first deals with the nature of stock price changes. Cox and Ross [23] look at pure jump processes as resulting in an underlying Poisson distribution. Merton [72] combines the idea of a Poisson event with the diffusion process. He treats the underlying behavior as essentially a diffusion process, with at any time the possibility that new events may change the parameters of the diffusion process, and he develops a new equation similar in form to the original Black–Scholes model, except that the distribution is the sum of normals instead of one normal distribution.

In a second approach, Cox [22] treats the variance as no longer a constant. But the variance in the diffusion process has a constant elasticity. The ratio of the percentage change in the variance of the stock price with respect to percentage changes in the stock price is equal to some constant.

In a third approach, Geske [44] analyzes the problem within the framework of the valuation of compound options. Whereas the Black–Scholes model assumes that the variance of the stock's return is not a function of the stock price, in the compound option model the variance of the return on the stock is inversely related to the stock price. If the stock price falls while the face amount of debt is unchanged, the debt–equity ratio rises, resulting in increased risk. The

---

[3]This section summarizes an overview of the subject which my colleague, Robert Geske, outlined for me.

increased risk is reflected by a rise in the variance of the returns on the stock. The relationship used by Geske is that the instantaneous standard deviation of the return on the stock is the product of the instantaneous standard deviation of the return on the value of the firm as a whole multiplied by the elasticity of the stock price with respect to the value of the firm. He observes that percentage changes in the stock's return will be larger when prices have fallen than when they have risen. If the stock price has fallen (risen), the increased (decreased) variance of the returns on the stock will act to raise (lower) the price of the option on the stock.

> Thus, variations in the firm's capital structure induced by changes in the value of the firm as the market continuously revalues the firm's prospective cash flows are transmitted through the variance of the stock to affect the price of an option on the stock [44, p. 74].

Systematic empirical studies of the OPM have been relatively limited. The first, by Black and Scholes [12], used price data from the over-the-counter option market for the four-year period, 1966–1969. Buying "undervalued" contracts and selling "overvalued" contracts at market prices yielded positive excess returns. The results indicate that the market uses more than past price histories to estimate the ex ante instantaneous variance of stock returns. When the transactions costs of trading in options were taken into account, they offset the implied profits.

Galai [42] duplicates the Black–Scholes tests, extending them by adjusting the option position each day. Undervalued options are bought and overvalued options are sold at the end of each day, maintaining the hedged position by buying or selling the appropriate number of shares of common stock. Using ex post hedge returns, Galai found that trading strategies based on the Black–Scholes model earned excess returns in the absence of transactions costs. But with transactions costs of 1% the excess returns vanished. Tests of spreading strategies yield results similar to those produced by the hedging strategies just described. (For a somewhat more complete summary see Copeland and Weston [21, pp. 407–408].)

The empirical study by MacBeth and Merville [64] obtains results that differ from previous empirical observations. They find that the Black–Scholes model underpriced in-the-money options and overpriced out-of-the-money options. With the exception of out-of-the-money options with less than 90 days to expiration, the tendencies just described increased with the

extent to which the option was in-the-money or out-of-the-money and decreased as the time to expiration decreased.

They conclude as follows:

> We emphasize that our results are exactly opposite to those reported by Black (1975), wherein he states that deep in the money (out of the money) options generally have B–S model prices which are greater (less) than market prices; and, our results also conflict with Merton's (1976) statement that practitioners observe B–S model prices to be less than market prices for deep in the money as well as deep out of the money options. We propose that these conflicting empirical observations may, at least in part, be the result of a nonstationary variance rate in the stochastic process generating stock prices [64, pp. 1185–1186].

Clearly, additional empirical investigation of these conflicting results is called for. It is hoped that the Cox–Ross–Rubinstein [24] discrete–time model for valuing options will facilitate further empirical testing.

The further extensions and applications of OPM may be organized into four categories: 1) valuing corporate securities, 2) valuing other securities, 3) implications for corporate managerial policy, and 4) implications for other sectors of the economy.

The use of the OPM to value corporate securities was described in the original Black and Scholes article. Merton [73] extended and most fully implemented the potential of the OPM for the valuation of corporate securities. In addition, he formulated a model of the risk structure of interest rates. He demonstrates that the risk structure of interest rates is a function of the variance of the firm, the time to maturity of the debt, and the debt–equity ratio of the firm.

Other papers dealing with the valuation of corporate securities include the analysis by Black and Cox [9] of the effects of bond indenture provisions, the studies by Ingersoll [52, 53] of convertible securities, and the study by Brennan and Schwartz [14] of convertibles.

The OPM has also been applied to the valuation of other securities. Especially significant is the study by Black [8] of the pricing of commodity contracts. Margrabe [66] analyzed the value of an option to exchange one asset for another. Fischer [39] used call option pricing in the valuation of index bonds. Grauer and Litzenberger [45] made further extensions in applying the model in the area of commodity price uncertainty.

Galai and Masulis [43] summarized option theory with respect to corporate financial policy. They investigate relationships between the beta of the firm and the beta of its stocks and bonds. Changes in the betas and the resulting changes in the values of the firm's securities, if we are using the Capital Asset Pricing Model, could be predicted by the firm's activities in a number of areas. These include changing the firm's investment program, merger activity or divestiture of assets, and capital distributions (dividend policy). Galai and Masulis demonstrate how any managerial decision that would change the beta of the firm or its securities could be analyzed through the OPM.

In the fourth category of the extensions of the OPM, we see its great power in application to other sectors of the economy.

Myers [81] suggests that the decision to invest can be placed in an options pricing framework.

Sharpe [99] demonstrates how pension fund decisions can be viewed as an option pricing problem. His theory provides a framework for formulating optimal pension planning to balance the interests of the firm and its stockholders and the quality of personnel.

Brennan and Schwartz [15] investigate the insurance aspects of options. They show how the options pricing approach can be used by a life insurance company which sells equity-linked life insurance policies to optimally hedge against the fluctuating values of its equity investments.

Related studies suggest further extensions of the OPM. Potentially these would include a theory of financial institutions and financial intermediation, including commercial banking. They would include insurance generally, given the similarity between put options and insurance policies. In addition, the product warranty policies of business firms would appear to be susceptible to analysis through the OPM.

Merger Theory and Studies of Merger Performance

Studies of mergers continue to be an area of great interest. In any 12-month period in recent years, some 15 to 20 papers on mergers have been presented at association meetings or submitted for publication to journals. The United States studies have increasingly focused on conglomerate mergers for particular reasons. In the United States, the 1950 amendments to Section 7 of the Clayton Act have enabled the regulatory authorities to virtually eliminate horizontal or vertical mergers if either company has something like a 10% market share. Hence the main merger activity since the 1950s has been conglomerate mergers.

A wave of conglomerate mergers was said to have occurred during the late 1960s. Tax and antitrust consequences became less favorable by 1969, and conglomerate merger activity then declined sharply. It has again been on the rise during the late 1970s, though, raising important issues of financial economics as well as of public policy.

Financial Theory of Pure Conglomerate Mergers

While numerous empirical studies have been made, merger theory has been slow in emerging. Efforts at progress have been made in this area by Chung [18] and Chung and Weston [19]. They formulate three questions that a theory of mergers must address: 1) Why do conglomerate mergers occur, 2) What are the characteristics of acquiring and acquired firms, and 3) What explains fluctuations in the level of aggregate conglomerate merger activity. A valid theory of conglomerate mergers is required to answer these questions simultaneously.

In their theory, conglomerate mergers occur for the purpose of capturing those investment opportunities in the acquired firm's industries that are relatively more favorable than those in its own industry. But the acquiring firm needs the firm-specific factors of production and the organization capital of the acquired firm to make the investment successful [Rosen, 93; Prescott and Visscher, 86]. The combined firm becomes better able to internalize the investment opportunities by initially lowering the costs of capital and then developing more organization capital. Thus a conglomerate merger represents the preservation and better utilization of the firm-specific factors of the acquired firm and the more general organization capital of the acquiring firm.

The benefit of the merger will be greater if the merging firms possess certain characteristics. Characteristics of an acquired firm will include: 1) a cost of capital that is higher relative to other firms in its industry, 2) its position in an industry with relatively favorable growth and profitability prospects, and 3) some industry- and firm-specific organizational or managerial capital whose value is preserved or enhanced by the merger. The acquiring firms are in industries with growth and profitability opportunities less favorable than the average for the economy. They have a record of managing asset growth effectively. They have more cash than current opportunities for reinvestment.

The basic initiating influence is that the cost of capital is lowered by the merger, and thus investment and production in the acquired firm's operations are increased. Since the cash flow streams of the entities are not perfectly correlated, debt capacity is increased; this effect will be greater if bankruptcy costs are significant [Lewellen, 62; Higgins and Schall, 48; Yawitz, Marshall, and Greenberg, 111; Stapleton, 105]. Economies of scale in flotation expenses lower the cost of raising funds [Levy and Sarnat, 61]. The use of excess internal cash flows of acquiring firms eliminates the cost of raising funds externally and provides differential tax benefits. The three possible sources of lowering the cost of capital are unsettled areas in the finance literature. Further testing of the issues involved is provided by the merger studies analyzing the market for capital assets.

A derived effect of the increased investment and production activities following a merger is to increase firm-specific organization learning. This will shift out the marginal efficiency of investment schedule of the firm as compared with the alternative of no merger.

There is considerable evidence in support of these hypotheses from previous studies. The P/E ratio is low when business risk is high, when financial leverage is high, or when industry growth prospects are unfavorable. Acquired firms have lower financial leverage and lower P/E ratios than acquiring firms [e.g., Melicher and Rush, 70]. Their industry growth prospects are hypothesized to be better than for the economy as a whole, which is confirmed by the evidence [19]. The implication of these results is that the acquired firms are "risky" and therefore have higher costs of capital. Financial leverage typically increases after the merger [see Weston and Mansinghka, 109; Shrieves and Pashley, 100]. Because mergers occur to internalize investment opportunities, the theory predicts that capital expenditures in an acquired firm's business will increase after the merger. Markham [67] found that new capital outlays for acquired companies' operations in the three-year period following acquisitions averaged 220% of pre-merger outlays for the same time span. Finally, merger premiums were higher when acquiring firms had a higher size-adjusted cash flow rate [Neilson and Melicher, 82].

In addition, Chung's study of fluctuations in the aggregate level of merger activity is consistent with this hypothesis. Investment opportunities are measured by the growth rate of industries and by real rates of interest. Merger activity would be expected to be positively associated with real GNP growth rates and negatively associated with the real rate of return on high grade corporate bonds. With regard to the influences of the cost of capital and funds availability,

two additional variables are considered. The risk premiums on the higher-risk (acquired) firms provide potentials for greater reductions in the cost of capital through diversification. Variations in risk premiums are measured by the ratio of the Baa rate to Aaa rate on long-term corporate bonds. This ratio is expected to be positively associated with merger activity. Finally, the degree of monetary stringency influences the (higher-risk and lower cash flow) acquired firms more than acquiring firms. This variable is measured by the ratio of the short-term commercial paper rate to the Aaa corporate bond rate. The association is expected to be positive.

In the empirical results, the predicted signs are obtained and the relationships are significant when the dependent variable is the number of pure conglomerate mergers. When product extension mergers are used as the dependent variable, the t-value for the risk premium variable becomes insignificant and other t-values drop slightly. When market extension mergers are added to the product extension mergers, the t-values drop further but still remain significant except for the coefficient of the risk premium variable. These results are consistent with the financial synergy theory of pure conglomerate mergers. The data also indicate that investment opportunities and the redeployment of internal funds from acquiring to acquired firms are important, though to a lesser degree, in effecting product extension mergers as well.

Studies of Merger Performance

Most of the other merger studies in recent years have used residual analysis. They have sought to measure the impact of values changes on the shareholders of acquired and acquiring firms. In the merger studies using residual analysis, relatively large samples have been used, usually more than 100. The behavior of the return on common stock is studied for up to 100 months prior to the merger "event" and for the surviving firms usually for 40 months following the merger. While the 100 or more mergers may have occurred over as many as 20 or more calendar years, the "merger event" is the reference date from which analysis of the behavior of returns is made. The procedure begins with an adjustment for the market risk premium. In addition, a wide range of other influences that might occur at some particular time is averaged over the many different time periods and companies in the merger sample.

The statistical procedures are designed to hold constant the influences of all factors other than the merger event. A comparison can be made between the average returns of the merging firms and the returns that would have been predicted from the market line relationships between return and risk. The residuals are averaged over all the merging firms in the sample for the months before and after the "merger event." These average residuals are also cumulated for a number of months and termed the cumulative average residuals or CARs.

All studies agree that the shareholders of acquired firms experience significant positive gains as a result of information on the merger or tender offer event. All studies agree in finding no significant correction to the CARs subsequent to the merger or tender event. For the acquiring firms all studies find positive CARs at or near the announcement of the merger or tender offer. But in the case of Mandelker [65], the positive returns were not statistically significant. Ellert [30] and Kummer and Hoffmeister [57] found that the CARs were positive for acquiring firms during the period well before the merger event. This led Ellert to hypothesize that acquiring firms were successful in managing assets developed both internally and externally. However, Langetieg [58], using a control group, found that there were similar influences on both the acquiring firms and on the control group.

Key Unresolved Issues

Although we have made much progress in the development of analytical financial models, many key issues and unsettled areas remain.

Should the analysis for investment decisions treat investment decisions in isolation or in portfolios? This is equivalent to the question of whether a project's own variance is an important variable or whether only non-diversifiable risk needs to be taken into account.

A related question is whether the interdependence of investments needs to be taken into account. Particularly, are there interdependencies in mergers? The literature is generally skeptical of interdependencies or synergy in mergers. On the other hand, one could be equally skeptical about generating a continuous series of investment opportunities with positive net present values. General theory does not provide either guidance or solid evidence on the degree or duration of investments with positive NPVs.

A related area of significance is the nature and level of bankruptcy costs. This goes to the heart of defining the nature of bankruptcy. Is it equivalent to an abrupt change in values? This requires an analysis of the underlying factors that produced a substantial change in value. The changes in value would apply both to values of the equity or residual claimants as well as to the bondholders. It is likely that when the value of equity shares moves downward by a substantial degree, the value of creditor positions will also deteriorate. But if the values of the creditor shares decline substantially with the decline in the value of the equity shares, that particular form of asset value decline described as bankruptcy appears not to be different conceptually from any other major change in value.

Our assessment of the definition, nature, and level of bankruptcy costs will influence our conclusions on the relative efficiency of firm versus investor diversification. The question of whether diversifiable risk influences investment decisions is related to this subject.

The issue of capital structure decisions in the absence of taxes is still unresolved. Is there a valid basis for the use of leverage in the absence of taxes? Here there is a potential role for agency influences, information asymmetry, and signaling. While contributions in these areas have suggested some promising propositions, little empirical testing has yet taken place. At issue is the extent to which the formulations to date permit the development of operational tests of the propositions. Inflation and its effect on capital structure and asset pricing add new dimensions.

Academic research has made only modest beginnings in analyzing or understanding the impact of inflation on either financial theory or corporate practices. For years we judged that inflation was "temporary;" more recently we have recognized that the impacts of inflation may be longer lasting and not easily understood.

The evidence is strong that inflation has lowered real rates of return of business firms. Part of the explanation is that tax regulations provide for taxing inflated nominal returns (*e.g.*, small real tax deductions, because depreciation is based on historical rather than current costs). The pace of real capital spending has been slowed and has been associated with a decline in the rate of productivity growth.

Interest rates have been high, the availability of funds restricted, and negative yield curves have been recurrent. In this new economic environment, the financial positions of corporations have deteriorated. The evidence of corporate financial weakness is strong whether measurements are made by the standard liquidity ratios, the ratio of total debt to total assets, the ratio of long–term debt to short–term debt, or by interest–coverage ratios. Business corporations and financial intermediaries are increasingly vulnerable to the inflationary economic environment and government policies to deal with it. Indeed, the financial impacts of alternative government policies are difficult to model conceptually or to test empirically.

Of potential help on these matters is the continued development of information and financial models to aid business managers in decision-making. What are the implicit underlying theoretical structures of these models? What implicit theories are involved? Are there implicit valuation relationships in these models, and do they have a valid basis? Can these financial models perform a useful role in strategic financial planning and formalize the methodology of the iterative processes for dealing with ill-structured problems? Can the results and implications of these financial models be operationally subjected to empirical tests? Can they be really useful until the conceptual problems of incorporating the impacts of inflation have been worked out?

The international dimensions need to be considered more fully. Does international diversification affect the pricing of risky assets? A sub-question here is the extent to which the underlying theorems of international finance hold and the conditions under which they hold. Is there such a thing as exchange risk? Finally, the relative usefulness of alternate approaches to international adjustment processes is still unsettled.

Conclusions

Recent work in finance has expanded into a coherent analytical structure, building upon the major new contributions starting in the 1950s. Those foundations included work on the role of individual preference in the demand for assets [Arrow-Debreu, Hirshleifer, Tobin], the nature of efficient portfolios of risky assets [Markowitz, Tobin], and the financial structure of the firm [Modigliani and Miller]. Two major lines of development since then have been 1) the derivation of general equilibrium models for the pricing of risky assets, and 2) the enrichment of the theory of the firm by considering the problems of contracting among owners of the productive factors. Parallel with theoretical advances in these areas, a substantial body of empirical research has been produced.

With respect to models of asset markets, notable developments have been: 1) Roll's critique of the capital asset pricing model in some of its empirical applications, 2) the formulation of the more general arbitrage pricing theory, and 3) improvements in the explanatory power and extensions in the application of the option pricing model.

Certain observed policies of business firms have been a continuing source of controversy in finance theory — particularly financial structure (degree of leverage) and dividend payouts. Analysis in these areas has been both stimulating and inconclusive to date.

Analysis of the nature of the firm has broadened into studies that have included agency and information problems. Characterizing the firm not as an atom of analysis, but as a set of contracts among suppliers of capital and the factors of production, researchers have identified several sources of agency costs, have shown the relationship of portfolio diversification to the separation of ownership and control, and have identified signaling mechanisms by which costly information of uncertain validity may be efficiently distributed and certified.

Related to the discussion of the nature of firms is the question of merger performance — whether the combination of two firms is superior to an individual investment strategy which includes their securities in a portfolio. Research in this area has been chiefly empirical, the major tool being residual analysis in the context of the CAPM and its variants.

We are likely to achieve continued future progress in all these areas. Theoretical and empirical work in option pricing, arbitrage pricing, and the CAPM will provide a more complete understanding of the determinants of risk and return relationships. Attention focused on the contracting relationships within the firm will improve our understanding of divergent incentives, information costs, and signaling behavior. This will enable us to flesh out the neoclassical model of the firm and will contribute to our ability to explain corporate financial policies, such as the degree of leverage in the capital structure. Further improvement in our understanding of capital markets on the one hand, and of business managers' decision processes on the other, should help us to analyze and explain such phenomena as dividend payouts and conglomerate mergers — on which our understanding is yet in the formative stages.

References

1. G. A. Akerlof, "The Market for 'Lemons:' Quality Uncertainty and the Market Mechanism," *Quarterly Journal of Economics* (August 1970), pp. 488–500.
2. A. Alchian and H. Demsetz, "Production, Information Costs, and Economic Organization," *The American Economic Review* (December 1972), pp. 777–795.

3. K. J. Arrow, "Le rôle des valeurs boursières pour la répartition la meilleure des risques," *Econométrie* (1953), pp. 41–48.

4. K. J. Arrow, "The Role of Securities in the Optimal Allocation of Risk-Bearing," *Review of Economic Studies* (April 1964), pp. 91–96.

5. K. J. Arrow and G. Debreu, "Existence of an Equilibrium for a Competitive Economy," *Econometrica* (1954), pp. 265–290.

6. A. Barnea, R. A. Haugen, and L. Senbet, "Market Imperfections, Agency Problems, and Capital Structure: A Review," forthcoming in *Financial Management.*

7. F. Black, "Fact and Fantasy in the Use of Options," *Financial Analysts Journal* (July/August 1975), pp. 36–41.

8. F. Black, "The Pricing of Commodity Contracts," *Journal of Financial Economics* (January/March 1976), pp. 167–179.

9. F. Black and J. C. Cox, "Valuing Corporate Securities: Some Effects of Bond Indenture Provisions," *Journal of Finance* (May 1976), pp. 351–367.

10. F. Black, M. C. Jensen, and M. Scholes, "The Capital Asset Pricing Model: Some Empirical Tests," in *Studies in the Theory of Capital Markets,* M. C. Jensen, ed., New York, Praeger Publishers, 1972.

11. F. Black and M. Scholes, "The Pricing of Options and Corporate Liabilities," *Journal of Political Economy* (May/June 1973), pp. 637–659.

12. F. Black and M. Scholes, "The Valuation of Option Contracts and a Test of Market Efficiency," *Journal of Finance* (May 1972), pp. 399–417.

13. M. Blume and I. Friend, "A New Look at the Capital Asset Pricing Model," *Journal of Finance* (March 1973), pp. 19–34.

14. M. J. Brennan and E. S. Schwartz, "Convertible Bonds: Valuation and Optimal Strategies for Call and Conversion," *Journal of Finance* (December 1977), pp. 1699–1715.

15. M. J. Brennan and E. S. Schwartz, "The Pricing of Equity-Linked Life Insurance Policies with An Asset Value Guarantee," *Journal of Financial Economics* (June 1976), pp. 195–213.

16. N. Chen, "The Arbitrage Pricing Theory: Estimation and Applications," Graduate School of Management, University of California, Los Angeles, June 1980.

17. N. Chen, "Empirical Evidence of the Arbitrage Pricing Theory," Graduate School of Management, University of California, Los Angeles, October 1980.

18. K. S. Chung, "A Financial Synergy Theory of Conglomerate Mergers," working paper, Graduate School of Management, University of California, Los Angeles, August 1980.

19. K. S. Chung and J. F. Weston, "Diversification and Mergers in a Strategic Long-Range Planning Frame-

work," presented at a Conference on Mergers and Acquisitions, Graduate School of Business Administration, New York University, January 9, 1981.

20. T. E. Copeland, "Liquidity Changes Following Stock Splits," *Journal of Finance* (March 1979), pp. 115–142.

21. T. E. Copeland and J. F. Weston, *Financial Theory and Corporate Policy,* Reading, Mass., Addison-Wesley Publishing Co., 1979.

22. J. Cox, "Notes on Option Pricing I: Constant Elasticity of Variance Diffusions," unpublished preliminary draft, Stanford University, 1975.

23. J. C. Cox and S. A. Ross, "The Valuation of Options for Alternative Stochastic Processes," *Journal of Financial Economics* (January/March 1976), pp. 145–166.

24. J. C. Cox, S. A. Ross, and M. Rubinstein, "Option Pricing: A Simplified Approach," *Journal of Financial Economics* (September 1979), pp. 229–263.

25. L. Dann, D. Mayers, and R. Raab, "Trading Rules, Large Blocks and the Speed of Adjustment," *Journal of Financial Economics* (January 1977), pp. 3–22.

26. H. DeAngelo and R. W. Masulis, "Leverage and Dividend Irrelevancy Under Corporate and Personal Taxation," *Journal of Finance* (May 1980), pp. 453–464.

27. H. DeAngelo and R. W. Masulis, "Optimal Capital Structure Under Corporate and Personal Taxation," *Journal of Financial Economics* (March 1980), pp. 3–30.

28. G. Debreu, *Theory of Value,* New York, John Wiley & Sons, 1959, Chapter 7.

29. P. Dodd and R. Ruback, "Tender Offers and Stockholder Returns: An Empirical Analysis," *Journal of Financial Economics* (December 1977), pp. 351–373.

30. J. C. Ellert, "Mergers, Antitrust Law Enforcement, and Stockholder Returns," *Journal of Finance* (May 1976), pp. 715–732.

31. E. F. Fama, "Agency Problems and the Theory of the Firm," *Journal of Political Economy* (April 1980), pp. 288–307.

32. E. F. Fama, "The Behavior of Stock Market Prices," *The Journal of Business* (January 1965), pp. 34–105.

33. E. F. Fama, "The Empirical Relationships Between the Dividend and Investment Decisions of Firms," *The American Economic Review* (June 1974), pp. 304–318.

34. E. F. Fama, *Foundations of Finance,* New York, Basic Books, 1976.

35. E. F. Fama, "Portfolio Analysis in a Stable Paretian Market," *Management Science* (January 1965), pp. 404–419.

36. E. F. Fama, "Risk, Return, and Equilibrium," *Journal of Political Economy* (January/February 1971), pp. 30–55.

37. E. F. Fama, L. Fisher, M. Jensen, and R. Roll, "The

Adjustment of Stock Prices to New Information," *International Economic Review* (February 1969), pp. 1–21

38. E. F. Fama and J. MacBeth, "Risk, Return and Equilibrium: Empirical Tests," *Journal of Political Economy* (May/June 1973), pp. 607–636.

39. S. Fischer, "Call Option Pricing When the Exercise Price is Uncertain, and the Valuation of Index Bonds," *Journal of Finance* (March 1978), pp. 169–176.

40. I. Friend and M. Blume, "Measurement of Portfolio Performance Under Uncertainty," *The American Economic Review* (September 1970), pp. 561–575.

41. I. Friend, R. Westerfield, and M. Granito, "New Evidence on the Capital Asset Pricing Model," *Journal of Finance* (June 1978), pp. 903–920.

42. D. Galai, "Tests of Market Efficiency of the Chicago Board Options Exchange," *The Journal of Business* (April 1977), pp. 167–197.

43. D. Galai and R. W. Masulis, "The Option Pricing Model and the Risk Factor of Stock," *Journal of Financial Economics* (January/March 1976), pp. 53–81.

44. R. Geske, "The Valuation of Compound Options," *Journal of Financial Economics* (March 1979), pp. 63–82.

45. F. L. A. Grauer and R. H. Litzenberger, "The Pricing of Commodity Futures Contracts, Nominal Bonds and Other Risky Assets Under Commodity Price Uncertainty," *Journal of Finance* (March 1979), pp. 69–83.

46. N. H. Hakansson, "The Fantastic World of Finance: Progress and the Free Lunch," *Journal of Financial and Quantitative Analysis* (November 1979), pp. 717–734.

47. R. A. Haugen and L. W. Senbet, "New Perspectives on Informational Asymmetry," *Journal of Financial and Quantitative Analysis* (November 1979), pp. 671–694.

48. R. C. Higgins and L. D. Schall, "Corporate Bankruptcy and Conglomerate Merger," *Journal of Finance* (March 1975), pp. 93–113.

49. J. Hirshleifer, "Investment Decision Under Uncertainty: Applications of the State–Preference Approach," *Quarterly Journal of Economics* (May 1966), pp. 252–277.

50. J. Hirshleifer, "Investment Decision Under Uncertainty: Choice Theoretic Approaches," *Quarterly Journal of Economics* (November 1965), pp. 509–536.

51. J. Hirshleifer, "On the Theory of Optimal Investment Decision," *Journal of Political Economy* (August 1958), pp. 329–352.

52. J. E. Ingersoll, Jr., "A Contingent–Claims Valuation of Convertible Securities," *Journal of Financial Economics* (May 1977), pp. 289–322.

53. J. E. Ingersoll, Jr., "A Theoretical and Empirical Investigation of the Dual Purpose Funds: An Application of Contingent–Claims Analysis," *Journal of Financial Economics* (January/March 1976), pp. 83–123.

54. M. C. Jensen, "The Performance of Mutual Funds in the Period 1945–1964," *Journal of Finance* (May 1968), pp. 389–416.

55. M. C. Jensen, ed., *Studies in the Theory of Capital Markets,* New York, Praeger Publishers, 1972.

56. M. C. Jensen and W. Meckling, "Theory of the Firm: Managerial Behavior, Agency Costs, and Ownership Structure," *Journal of Financial Economics* (October 1976), pp. 305–360.

57. D. R. Kummer and J. R. Hoffmeister, "Valuation Consequences of Cash Tender Offers," *Journal of Finance* (May 1978), pp. 505–516.

58. T. C. Langetieg, "An Application of a Three-Factor Performance Index to Measure Stockholder Gains from Mergers," *Journal of Financial Economics* (1978), pp. 365–383.

59. D. F. Larcker, L. A. Gordon, and G. E. Pinches, "Testing for Market Efficiency: A Comparison of the Cumulative Average Residual Methodology and Intervention Analysis," *Journal of Financial and Quantitative Analysis* (June 1980), pp. 267–288.

60. H. E. Leland and D. H. Pyle, "Information Asymmetries, Financial Structure, and Financial Intermediation," *Journal of Finance* (May 1977), pp. 371–387.

61. H. Levy and M. Sarnat, "Diversification, Portfolio Analysis and the Uneasy Case for Conglomerate Mergers," *Journal of Finance* (September 1970), pp. 795–807.

62. W. G. Lewellen, "A Pure Financial Rationale for the Conglomerate Merger," *Journal of Finance* (May 1971), pp. 521–537.

63. R. H. Litzenberger and K. Ramaswamy, "The Effect of Personal Taxes and Dividends on Capital Asset Prices: Theory and Empirical Evidence," *Journal of Financial Economics* (June 1979), pp. 163–196.

64. J. D. MacBeth and L. J. Merville, "An Empirical Examination of the Black–Scholes Call Option Pricing Model," *Journal of Finance* (December 1979), pp. 1173–1186.

65. G. Mandelker, "Risk and Return: The Case of Merging Firms," *Journal of Financial Economics* (1974), pp. 303–335.

66. W. Margrabe, "The Value of an Option to Exchange One Asset for Another," *Journal of Finance* (March 1978), pp. 177–186.

67. J. W. Markham, *Conglomerate Enterprises and Public Policy,* Boston, Harvard Graduate School of Business Administration, 1973.

68. H. M. Markowitz, *Portfolio Selection,* New Haven, Yale University Press, 1959.

69. D. Mayers and E. Rice, "Measuring Portfolio Performance and the Empirical Content of Asset Pricing Models," *Journal of Financial Economics* (March 1979), pp. 3–28.

70. R. W. Melicher and D. F. Rush, "Evidence on the

Acquisition-Related Performance of Conglomerate Firms," *Journal of Finance* (March 1974), pp. 141-149.

71. R. W. Melicher and D. F. Rush, "The Performance of Conglomerate Firms: Recent Risk and Return Experience," *Journal of Finance* (May 1973), pp. 381-388.

72. R. C. Merton, "On the Pricing of Corporate Debt: The Risk Structure of Interest Rates," *Journal of Finance* (May 1974), pp. 449-470.

73. M. H. Miller, "Debt and Taxes," *Journal of Finance* (May 1977), pp. 261-275.

74. M. Miller and F. Modigliani, "Dividend Policy, Growth, and the Valuation of Shares," *The Journal of Business* (October 1961), pp. 411-433.

75. M. H. Miller and M. S. Scholes, "Dividends and Taxes," *Journal of Financial Economics* (December 1978), pp. 333-364.

76. M. H. Miller and M. S. Scholes, "Dividends and Taxes: Some Empirical Evidence," preliminary manuscript, January 22, 1981.

77. M. H. Miller and M. S. Scholes, "Rates of Return in Relation to Risk: A Re-examination of Some Recent Findings," in *Studies in the Theory of Capital Markets*, M. C. Jensen, ed., New York, Praeger Publishers, 1972.

78. F. Modigliani and M. H. Miller, "Corporate Income Taxes and the Cost of Capital," *The American Economic Review* (June 1963), pp. 433-443.

79. F. Modigliani and M. H. Miller, "The Cost of Capital, Corporation Finance, and the Theory of Investment," *The American Economic Review* (June 1958), pp. 261-297.

80. F. Modigliani and M. H. Miller, "Some Estimates of the Cost of Capital to the Electric Utility Industry 1954-57," *The American Economic Review* (June 1966), pp. 333-348.

81. S. C. Myers, "Determinants of Corporate Borrowing," *Journal of Financial Economics* (November 1977), pp. 147-175.

82. J. F. Nielsen and R. W. Melicher, "A Financial Analysis of Acquisition and Merger Premiums," *Journal of Financial and Quantitative Analysis* (March 1973), pp. 139-162.

83. R. R. Pettit, "Dividend Announcements, Security Performance, and Capital Market Efficiency," *Journal of Finance* (December 1972), pp. 993-1007.

84. R. R. Pettit, "The Impact of Dividend and Earnings Announcement: A Reconciliation," *The Journal of Business* (January 1976), pp. 86-96.

85. R. R. Pettit, "Taxes, Transactions Costs and Clientele Effect of Dividends," *Journal of Financial Economics* (December 1977), pp. 419-436.

86. E. C. Prescott and M. Visscher, "Organization Capital," *Journal of Political Economy* (June 1980), pp. 446-461.

87. R. W. Roll, "Ambiguity When Performance is Measured by the Securities Market Line," *Journal of Finance* (September 1978), pp. 1051-1069.

88. R. W. Roll, *The Behavior of Interest Rates*, New York, Basic Books, 1970.

89. R. W. Roll, "A Critique of the Asset Pricing Theory's Test," *Journal of Financial Economics* (March 1977), pp. 129-176.

90. R. W. Roll, "A Reply to Mayers and Rice," *Journal of Financial Economics* (December 1979), pp. 391-400.

91. R. W. Roll and S. A. Ross, "An Empirical Investigation of the Arbitrage Pricing Theory," Graduate School of Management, University of California, Los Angeles, revised 1980.

92. R. W. Roll and S. A. Ross, "An Empirical Investigation of the Arbitrage Pricing Theory," *Journal of Finance* (December 1980), pp. 1073-1104.

93. S. Rosen, "Learning by Experience as Joint Production," *Quarterly Journal of Economics* (August 1972), pp. 367-382.

94. S. A. Ross, "The Arbitrage Theory of Capital Asset Pricing," *Journal of Economic Theory* (December 1976), pp. 341-360.

95. S. A. Ross, "The Determination of Financial Structure: The Incentive-Signaling Approach," *Bell Journal of Economics and Management Science* (Spring 1977), pp. 23-40.

96. S. A. Ross, "Return, Risk, and Arbitrage," in *Risk and Return in Finance*, I. Friend and J. L. Bicksler, eds., Vol. I, Section 9, Cambridge, Ballinger Publishing Company, 1977.

97. J. Schallheim and R. DeMagistris, "New Estimates of the Market Parameters," *Financial Management* (Autumn 1980), pp. 60-68.

98. M. Scholes, "The Market for Securities: Substitution versus Price Pressure and the Effects of Information on Share Prices," *The Journal of Business* (April 1972), pp. 179-211.

99. W. F. Sharpe, "Corporate Pension Funding Policy," *Journal of Financial Economics* (June 1976), pp. 183-193.

100. R. S. Shrieves and M. M. Pashley, "A Test of Financial Economics Through Increased Leverage Merger Theories," presented at the Financial Management Association meeting, New Orleans, 1980.

101. C. W. Smith, Jr., and J. B. Warner, "On Financial Contracting: An Analysis of Bond Covenants," *Journal of Financial Economics* (June 1979), pp. 117-161.

102. K. V. Smith and J. C. Schreiner, "A Portfolio Analysis of Conglomerate Diversification," *Journal of Finance* (June 1969), pp. 413-428.

103. K. V. Smith and J. Fred Weston, "Further Evaluation of Conglomerate Performance," *Journal of Business Research* (March 1977), pp. 5-14.

104. M. Spence, *Market Signalling: Information Transfer in Hiring and Related Processes*, Cambridge, Harvard University Press, 1974.

105. R. C. Stapleton, "Mergers, Debt Capacity and the

Valuation of Corporate Loans," working paper, Manchester Business School, October 1980.

106. J. Tobin, "Liquidity Preference as Behavior Toward Risk," *Review of Economic Studies* (February 1958), pp. 65–85.

107. J. F. Weston, "New Themes in Finance," *Journal of Finance* (March 1974), pp. 237–243.

108. J. F. Weston, *The Scope and Methodology of Finance,* Englewood Cliffs, N.J., Prentice-Hall, Inc., 1966.

109. J. W. Weston and S. K. Mansinghka, "Tests of the Efficiency Performance of Conglomerate Firms," *Jour-nal of Finance* (September 1971), pp. 919–936.

110. J. F. Weston, K. V. Smith, and R. E. Shrieves, "Conglomerate Performance Using the Capital Asset Pricing Model," *The Review of Economics and Statistics* (November 1972), pp. 357–363.

111. J. B. Yawitz, W. J. Marshall, and E. Greenberg, "Negatively Correlated Income as an Incentive for Conglomerate Merger," Working Paper No. 33, Center for the Study of American Business, St. Louis, Washington University, July 1978.

Research Directions in Finance

*William Beranek**

Finance can be divided into two areas: positive and normative. The former seeks to describe what is, and is characterized by an effort to describe financial relationships through the development of axiom sets that yield valid groups of generalizations. Often labeled "financial economics," it emphasizes the study of linkages between the firms and households that are provided by financial markets. In contrast, normative finance seeks to develop models for decision making by investor-consumers, by financial managers of institutions (regardless of purpose of the institution), and by administrators of government agencies. Concerned with decision making, it is oriented with, so to speak, "what should be."

These areas are closely related. Elements of many normative financial models consist of the verified predictions of positive theory. Consequently, the growth and development of positive finance is important for the creation of useful normative models. Just as significant, however, is the fact that developments in normative finance, for example, portfolio theory, have served to enrich positive finance, leading to the birth of more general positive theories.

There is another facet to the relationship between these two areas. Some writers are so convinced of the robustness of generally accepted positive theories, that, when faced with the task of generating normative decisions, they deduce appropriate courses of action from such theories. In the extreme case, they would shun the development of a normative model which reflects the best perceived conditions faced by the given decision maker, and use instead the dictum implied by a positive theory. In contrast, other writers are not prepared to take such a vast step, feeling that the tests performed on the generally accepted theories are not *sufficiently convincing* to warrant the normative extensions into unverified areas, especially when the cost of a mistake is viewed as being unacceptably high. Such writers, naturally, would prefer to develop models that fit the conditions of the firm, conduct appropriate sensitivity tests, and provide the ultimate decision maker with a manageable range of conditional statements. This collision of views should not be overemphasized, but it does form a signifi-

Time-Series Properties of Annual Earnings Data: The State of the Art, by *Kenneth S. Lorek, Robert Kee,* and *William H. Vass.*

This paper reviews the state of the art of the time-series properties of annual earnings data. The potential usefulness of time-series research to accounting, finance, and business decisionmakers is stressed. Major cross-sectional and time-series applications are covered along with the statistical models which have been used. The propriety of using the Box-Jenkins methodology in annual time-series research is also addressed. A synthesis to the time-series literature is provided and some modest suggestions for future research are made.

Mr. Lorek is associate professor in the College of Business, Florida State University. His articles have appeared in the *Journal of Accounting Research* and the *Accounting Review.*

Mr. Kee is assistant professor at the College of Business Administration, University of Alabama.

Mr. Vass is a doctoral candidate at Florida State University.

United Way Contributions: Anomalous Philanthropy, by *Barry Keating.*

This article examines donations to United Way campaigns in order to investigate the economic rationality of such philanthropy. The concept of philanthropy is reviewed and it is demonstrated that United Way contributions differ from philanthropy as commonly defined in the literature.

Mr. Keating is assistant professor of business economics, University of Notre Dame. He formerly taught at Virginia Polytechnic Institute.

cant dichotomy in the field of finance and helps to explain some of the divergence in research thrusts among financial writers.

This article, which emphasizes the research needs of normative finance, is organized as follows. Some major issues in positive theory are discussed first. These include the irrelevance of financial policy, valuation and the cost of capital, the role of agency costs, and the effect of taxes on security prices. A host of normative problems are treated next including dynamic models, risk analysis — as well as the impact of risk and inflation on capital-budgeting decisions — optimal capital structure, evaluation of leases, venture capital problems, multiperiod portfolio construction, market models, working capital management, financial decision systems and financial planning, the need for a financial theory of the regulated firm, and the need for specialized data bases in financial research.

POSITIVE ISSUES

The Irrelevance of Financial Policy

Led by the stimulating Modigliani and Miller paper of 1958 [99], other writers (for example, J. E. Stiglitz [131]) have set forth sufficient conditions which imply that financial policy is irrelevant to the value of a firm and hence, to the wealth of shareholders. Related to this are conditions sufficient for separating firm investment decisions from financial decisions. An interesting special case of the irrelevance of financial policy is the irrelevance of dividend policy theorem. These are significant conclusions.

Controversy continues, however, over the empirical robustness of these propositions. They have proven to be difficult to test, that is, of the tests that have been performed there is conspicuous lack of agreement over the methodological soundness of the efforts and differences over the degree of conclusiveness of the results. We need answers to the following questions: To what degree empirically is financial policy irrelevant? To what degree empirically is dividend policy irrelevant [15]? What are the conditions that lead to the relevance of financial policy? What conditions imply the relevance of dividend policy (for example, see [89 and 87])? Under what conditions are financial and investment decisions likely to be related [100]?

These are not rhetorical questions. They cut at a significant part of that phase of positive theory that has important and relevant implications for normative finance; in particular, for those millions of business firms whose behavior may not be described by these theorems. We note that, save for only the largest and financially strongest of business firms, fund suppliers (that is, lenders and investment bankers) acquire information regarding the proposed use of potential borrowed funds. Lenders assess the expected risk and return of the borrower's proposed investments, and, in combination with the firm's other obligations, determine the likelihood of repayment of the proposed loan. These factors suggest that for most firms, investment and financial decisions are to some degree interrelated.

Is it possible to construct, at the firm level, a set of axioms sufficiently general to admit the interrelatedness of investment and financial decisions and which imply, as special cases, the foregoing separation theorems? Being just as robust as current theories, this theory may provide researchers with a rich source of new predictions which may be susceptible to verification.[1]

Valuation and the Cost of Capital

Financial economists currently employ an ad hoc approach to explain investment value in a multiperiod, risky context, a formulation that, unfortunately, has not been developed from a set of precise axioms. Basically, it hypothesizes a discount rate as the link which converts future cash flows into present values. Whether this structure is valid and how this rate is determined are unanswered questions. The essential idea is, however, a natural extension of the analogous proposition that emerges from the ideal world of perfect markets and complete certainty. Indeed, one of the most important unresolved problems in finance is: what determines the value of financial assets in a multiperiod world of risk and uncertainty, amidst differing investor-consumer assessments and preferences for risk, return, and other attributes?

We do not know

(1) What are the relevant future parameters and variables and how should they be defined and measured?

(2) What logical form or structure do the relationships assume that connect present values to relevant future parameters and variables?

(3) In particular, are discount rates appropriate, and what determines them?

Answers to these questions would be beneficial, since they would fill a serious gap in positive economic theory, and could lead to further fruitful developments in many branches of economics. They would also improve the empirical testing of hypotheses which predict changes in the market values of, or rates of return on, specific assets. For example, a host of hypotheses concerning the effects of monopolies, concentration ratios, market share, insider information, and government regulation on asset values are now tested with less satisfactory valuation approaches. In addition, they would lead to the development of richer, more firmly anchored firm-decision models, yielding better resource allocation decisions, including capital expenditure and financing decisions. This, in turn, would lead to improved working capital, inventory, production, and the entire gamut of activity decisions. Perhaps the continuous time approach of R. C. Merton is a fruitful path to follow [92 and 93].

Along the same line, we need to expand positive theory to deal with the choice of elements of working capital and their impact on valuation, beta coefficients, financial structure, and other quantities. In other words, there is need to integrate working-capital variables into the general theory of finance related to the firm [138].

Agency Costs and Corporate Finance

The role of agency costs in corporation finance is only beginning to be explored [65]. In the broadest sense, management can be viewed as an agent of each class of security holders. Indeed, M. C. Jensen and W. H. Meckling [72, p. 308] define an agency relationship

...as a contract under which one or more persons (the principal(s)) engage another person (the agent) to perform some service on their behalf which involves delegating some decision making authority to the agent.

They continue by defining the problem:

If both parties to the relationship are utility maximizers there is good reason to believe that the agent will not always act in the best interests of the principal. The *principal* can limit divergences from his interest by establishing appropriate incentives for the agent and by incurring monitoring costs designed to limit the aberrant activities of the agent.

The cost of such incentives and the explicit monitoring costs of agency relationships are examples of agency costs. (For examples of others, see [72].)

Within their approach, Jensen and Meckling examine a host of implications which can serve as a rich source of important hypotheses to be investigated, extended, and empirically verified.

Agency theory in general, however, and, to some degree, the related issues of "signaling" and informational asymmetries [119 and 83] may be the vehicles by which positive theory becomes more generalized. In particular, what functions do agents perform, what devices or techniques are used for monitoring them, how can we predict or describe their behavior, and what are the normative implications for decision making? Are managerially set debt/equity ratios signaling devices? If so, what information do they convey? Is dividend policy a mere signaling device? What do declarations of dividends mean? What information, if any, is being transmitted? What are those managerial actions that literally "speak louder than words"? How are these actions interpreted by investors?

Because the Jensen and Meckling approach focuses on so many market imperfections, it is the most general theory of finance we have. However, because it fails to consider the size of the firm [3] and is restricted to the utility maximization of a *single* individual, it cannot be used to predict the behavior of *groups* of coentrepreneur managers, which is important to many large corporations.

Taxation and Security Prices

A major, unsettled issue in finance continues to be the effect of taxation on asset prices. Both corporate and personal taxes have been studied intensively but reasonably convincing results of their effects on asset prices have been difficult to come by. Part of the difficulty is because this is a complex area, both theoretically and empirically. Despite these problems, the importance of this question warrants continued vigorous efforts because we do not know, in a reasonably convincing fashion, the impact of different taxes on capital structure, on dividend policy, and on investment expenditures [50, 39, 41, 21, 97, 98, 87, 49, 15, 123, and 108].

NORMATIVE FINANCE

The topics treated in this area consist of financial planning, risk analysis and capital budgeting, capital structure and lease financing, working capital, and a collection of issues referred to as "other topics."

Financial Planning

Most of the planning literature in the leading journals deals with the use of techniques such as mathematical programming, simulation, or econometric forecasting. While most companies do not use much of this research, many large companies have built financial-statement models of their firms and these are actively used. Why are these companies using models that are different from those in the academic literature? What should be done to upgrade the state of practice? Research should focus on determining the state of current practice and what company perceptions of problems are, and how the state of current practice can be upgraded by improving financial-statement models and financial statement projection.

Much of the work on dynamic financial models is represented by the development of simulation models of varying sophistication and refinement [25]. Most of these are privately distributed software packages. For many firms these programs are sufficient, but for others they lack the flexibility to reflect the firm's underlying parameters and key structural relationships. Since such firms must develop their own models, the development of more general, more sophisticated, and more powerful planning models on the basis of industry or type of institution, for example, small commercial banks, would be useful to a wide range of institutions. (For a description of financial modeling in 18 large companies and an excellent detailed review of the current state of the art, see [96]. For a general model of corporate financing decisions see [135]. For more specific suggestions on research needs in the whole area of corporate finance, see [24].)

Parallel growth is also needed in the development of analytic solutions to general dynamic financial planning models. Exploratory efforts along this vein have included [103, 36, 37, 40, 77, 78, 79, 80, 125, and 126]. By applying control theory to finance, each has contributed valuable insights but has fallen short of the goal of adequate generality and operational capability.

717

If these models are to be useful to many firms they must have certain properties. First, they should be sufficiently general so that the conditions faced by certain classes of firms may be introduced and studied as special cases. For example, characteristics of an industry, or some distinctive parameters of the firm would serve as conditions meriting special case analysis. Second, the firm's market for its securities would be subject to varying types and degrees of imperfections, with perfect capital markets being treated as one of many special cases. Without specifying what these imperfections should be, we should recognize the existence of explicit transaction costs, assorted taxes, unequal accessibility to information, and illiquid markets. The suggestion to view perfect markets as a special case is provocative, but we must recognize perfect markets and other axioms of positive theory for what they are: useful collections of propositions which yield generalizations about the real world, of which only an important few are capable of verification. These axioms were never intended to be objects of intellectual worship, and their refuted implications need be viewed not as mere anomalies but as an indication of the limited usefulness of the axioms as predictors of pervasive forces in the economy.[2]

Risk Analysis and Capital Budgeting

(1) Risk Analysis

Risk and return are the two principal elements bearing upon financial decisions. However, investigators have only begun to look carefully at the many facets of risk. There is hardly a consensus of what risk is, let alone an agreement of how it can or should be measured [112]. Other unanswered questions are: How should it be monitored? What methods can be developed for controlling it on a real-time basis? Practical methods that can be understood and implemented are needed.

To an investor or businessman risk is usually expressed in terms of "the chance of loss," that is, the implicit subjective probability of failing to attain some objective, for example, an aspiration or target level, an expected value, a critical value, and so on. Academics have introduced the explicit notion that risk is "deviation from expectation" and is best measured by the standard deviation or variance of a probability distribution. These are concepts that have nice mathematical properties. More in line with the investor's downside risk concept, however, is the notion of the semivariance, a measure which can be taken about some suitable critical or target value of a probability distribution. Since this is a function of absolute values, it is more troublesome than the standard deviation to manipulate for analytical purposes and for that reason is less preferred by analysts [110].

In other areas risk has been conceptually standardized on the basis of an index. In portfolio theory, it is the so-called systematic risk of a security, its beta. The central problem with beta is: How do we estimate an asset's future beta? Starting with W. F. Sharpe's seminal paper of 1963 [127], numerous investigators have studied this topic including O. A. Vasicek [137], M. E. Blume [17], and A. E. Gooding [52] while others have questioned whether betas are the most useful measure of systematic risk [44].

Further work is required on the problem of time aggregation and the investment horizon in the estimation of systematic risk [71, 28, and 81].

This problem is also of growing importance to corporate financial managers because of the role beta is playing in the determination of a firm's cost of equity capital, which, in turn, has implications for capital-budgeting decisions.

What is the role of diversification in reducing risk in the firm's capital-budgeting portfolio? Should the firm make the trade-off decision between risk and return, or should the firm be guided by other, yet to be derived rules? This issue arises because positive theory implies that the individual investor can diversify more easily, and more effectively, than the firm. But the uneasy question is: how robust is this implication? What are the conditions which imply that the firm should perform this function, and under what conditions is it best transferred to investors [85]?

What other risk control measures can be derived [64]? Can stochastic dominance be made more operational [85a]? Are there other approaches [9 and 110]? It might be useful to establish sufficient conditions on individual utility functions which would imply the specific choice criteria for the individual to use for expected utility maximization. Thus once an individual classified himself, the set of admissible risk decision criteria would be determined, obviating the need for further individual search.

It is also of interest to investigate why the Von Neumann-Morgenstern standard-gamble utility-index approach to risk analysis has not been more widely accepted. What can be done to refine this approach so that it becomes more understood and acceptable?

Effective risk analysis must recognize that in many institutions financial decisions are made by groups of individuals and methods for reconciling conflicting risk and return assessments are needed. Aside from the problems raised by Arrow's Paradox, we still have the problems in group decision making of accurately transmitting risk information among members of the group, and of how to come to a decision in the face of risk. Can the Delphi approach be made more effective [86]? Is a group-utility function feasible [74 and 73]? Some work has been done in this area but it has failed to attract much attention and more research is required.

The possibility of further developments in computer-programming languages to facilitate the use of simulation should not be overlooked.

Simulation as a tool in financial-risk analysis, while being actively pursued in various degrees of sophistication by a number of firms, is still waiting to be richly developed [133 and 26]. However, J. M. McInnes and W. T. Carleton [96] suggest that sensitivity analysis, contingency planning, and adaptive planning may be more viable alternatives to risk control than sophisticated forms of risk analysis.

(2) Risk and Capital Budgeting

This is one of the most unsettled areas of normative finance [13]. For lack of better approaches, researchers have extended net present value and internal rate of return measures into the risk sphere [14]. This ad hoc approach is without firm theoretical underpinnings, and is also used in models of portfolio theory to generate means and variances of possible portfolios of capital projects [22, 23, 19, 68, 84, 88, 107, and 54].

Recent developments in the theory of option pricing [16, 95, 128, and 32] may lend themselves to theoretical applications in this area. The "state" approach, which has been employed in the context of financial markets, may also be applied here [6 and 134]. E. F. Fama [46] has also developed further insights into risk-adjustments, and S. C. Myers and S. M. Turnbull [104] have used the asset-pricing model in capital budgeting. These approaches, while promising and insightful, still require development and refinement before becoming reasonably operational [63].

(3) Inflation and Capital Budgeting

Little is known of how inflation should be taken account of in the capital-budgeting decision. Beyond dealing with expected or anticipated inflation, the proper treatment of unanticipated inflation has so far defied a workable solution. Although it will eventually depend upon the results of empirical studies dealing with inflation rates and security values, we must make as much progress as possible because the problem is so important [136, 105, 5, 30, 76, 48, and 69].

(4) Venture Capital Analysis

There are several important problems in this area. How should very risky ventures be evaluated? Are the techniques that were developed for ordinary capital budgeting really relevant and appropriate for such ventures? How should such ventures be financed?

For assessing such projects, both the tools of option pricing and Bayesian statistics suggest themselves as being potentially useful devices. A dynamic structure involving sequential analysis in some form probably should be considered.

Financing of these ventures must be related dynamically to the sequence of information flow that emerges from risk analysis. The model should imply the type and extent of financing at each point in time of the venture's development when we have a flow of new information and new investment decisions must be made [31, 33, and 34].

Capital Structure and Lease Financing

(1) The Optimal Capital Structure

The problem of choosing an optimal capital structure has yet to be vigorously approached as one of selecting an optimal dynamic time path, given the firm's investment opportunities (see [78, 79, and 80] for exploratory efforts). While providing a fresh look at the problem, the approach may also produce some new insights. The role of warrants, leases, stock rights, convertibles, and subordinated instruments, would also be evaluated. Methods for evaluating costs of protective provisions, including so-called "me too" clauses, require further development [75] as well as more effective methods of assessing prospective bankruptcy costs [67 and 97].

In this connection, an optimal share repurchase policy over time might emerge as a special case, linking such a policy with the optimal capital structure over time.

The role of agency cost in determining an optimal structure has only begun to be developed. There are agency costs associated with each type of claim a firm may issue, and the selection of a structure subject to an explicit recognition of these costs should yield a fruitful set of hypotheses [27].

(2) Evaluation of Leases

Coupled with the problems of multiperiod investment analysis and financing is the issue of evaluating lease financing, a device which is both a financing instrument as well as, in many aspects, an investment vehicle in the sense that productive services are simultaneously acquired. Lease financing requires more satisfactory evaluation methods. However, definitive solutions to this problem must await the development of a general financial model where leasing, among others, is an admissible option leading to a total optimal structure, for example, where each form of debt, preferred stock, common stock, warrants and other assorted options, and leases are eligible for inclusion [18, 54a, and 102].

Working Capital

(1) Cash Management

Cash management has benefited from active company innovation so that the state of practice generally leads academic theory. The lock-box problem in particular has drawn much attention. So have efforts to speed up the flow of cash. For a summary of these efforts, see [51]. Besides the need to work on the problems of companies and banks in this area, there is a need for tutorial seminars simply to upgrade academics on the state of practice and to inform them of the real, relevant problems.

Efforts to apply, in an operational sense, dynamic programming and control theory to multiperiod cash balance problems have not been fruitful [35]. Nevertheless significant progress will likely be made with other approaches that emphasize cash flow forecasting [132].

(2) Receivables, Short-term Liabilities, Inventories, and Bank Relations

Besides cash management there are many problems in credit policy, accounts receivable forecasting and control, inventory management, accounts payable management, and banking relations that merit serious attention. Again, while most of the finance function in large companies is devoted to this area, it is neglected by academic researchers.

An effort should be mounted which builds on the foundations of D. R. Mehta [91], William Beranek [11 and 12], and K. V. Smith [129] and comes to grip with the special problems of these areas. The credit decision, the line of credit, the quantity and quality of credit information to be obtained, methods of processing information, the role of information gatherers and assessors, monitoring accounts receivable, forecasting receivables and collections, the timing of short-term borrowing, the role of financial variables in inventory optimization, and the cultivation, development, and maintenance of relationships with financial intermediaries are examples of topics meriting systematic analysis [122 and 12a].

Other Topics

(1) Multiperiod Portfolio Construction

There are two problems here: what procedure should an *individual* choose, given a reasonably identified utility function, for selecting a portfolio of assets? What procedures should an institution follow for making the same choice?

The first question, which considers consumption as a withdrawal of assets, has been explored by E. S. Phelps [109], Paul Samuelson [120], N. H. Hakansson [58, 59, and 60], and S. F. Richard [111]. Most of these papers investigated the properties of mean-variance and the geometric mean of terminal wealth as criteria for individual decision making. Aside from the question of which criteria yield the most verifiable propositions, this research should be extended to seek more definitive conclusions that are operational. A step in this direction is represented by [121].

Related to portfolio construction is the unresolved important problem regarding the attributes of individual utility functions that imply different portfolio strategies, such that to each set of attributes there is an associated appropriate strategy. Assuming some success in this endeavor, the next step would be to develop a self-classifying test that would enable the individual to classify himself by utility attributes and indicate the appropriate portfolio for him. This could then be used not only by individuals, but by institutional portfolio managers who must always face the vexing question: what portfolio strategies are appropriate for different groups of people with certain characteristics? How do we choose the characteristics; that is, how do we classify people so as to establish the corresponding optimal portfolio strategy?

A related question is concerned with techniques of analysis, efficient algorithms, methods for handling risk, portfolio revision, and the properties of possible portfolio decision rules [43], including, of course, the mean-variance, the geometric mean, stochastic dominance [4], and chance-constrained programming. Extensions of existing knowledge in these areas would be welcome.

(2) Market Models

These models purport to explain the return on an asset in terms of the return on one or more aggregates. Simplifying assumptions on the covariances between residual returns on the assets and other relevant variables are usually made. The initial single-factor model of Sharpe [127] contains the so-called beta coefficient, which is associated with the return on some market index (for example, Standard & Poors *500 Stock Index*). Others have extended the model to include a number of factors [29] but whether this has resulted in a net gain in portfolio efficiency is still subject to controversy.

Nevertheless, in both single- and multi-factor versions efforts have been made to explain the beta coefficient [113, 20, 53, 82, 116, 117, and 115]. What is needed is a further effort to develop more fundamental explanations of beta. This would benefit not only investment analysts, but also managers of business firms who could then make a more informed choice of beta-sensitive parameters which are subject to their control.

(3) Financial Decisions in the Multi-National Corporation

Financial decisions are more complex in a multinational setting than in a domestic corporation for several reasons. First, market conditions for the firm's products or services and its factors of production are more diverse. Second, there is the problem of exchange risk. Third, there are different and potentially more cumbersome forms of taxation. Finally, it is necessary to assess political risks.

Work along the lines of Michael Adler [1] and Adler and Bernard Dumas [2] should be encouraged. However, research into the handling or treatment and assessment of these unique risks must be more intensively developed.

(4) A Financial Theory of the Regulated Firm

While really a special case of the proposed general theory already discussed in the section, "Financial Planning," it is sufficiently important to require special emphasis. Because regulation changes the criteria for making financial decisions, it is important to determine in what ways regulatory actions impact financial decision making and thus be able to predict the economic consequences of alternative actions. This is necessary if we are to effectively evaluate proposed and current regulation, and to formulate regulatory policies. For instance, why do most electric utilities have above-average dividend payout rates (namely, about 67 percent) even when theory and empirical evidence indicate that this high payout would probably be suboptimal for many nonregulated firms? Does this high payout raise the cost of capital for the regulated firm? Are there more attractive ways for regulated firms to attain their goals?

The financial structure of a regulated firm is an important aspect of its cost of capital. What aspects of regulation markedly affect the debt capacity of a regulated firm? These, and other equally important questions can only be answered properly if there is an empirically validated theory of the financial behavior of a regulated firm [57, 66, 90, 101, 40, 42, and 70].

(5) The Accounting-Finance Interface

There is a need to join financial accounting theory with financial research [53]. For example, the recent controversy over FASB 8 (Foreign Asset Liabilities Revaluation) is a clear indication of where the accounting profession is attacking a "problem" that financial theory says does not matter in terms of security prices. Moreover, the reporting requirements and induced company behavior are incurring needless social costs. Other examples are the financial implications of issues in inflation accounting, and the financial evaluation of signals sent to investors by corporations that release consolidated and parent company statements [106, 130, 20, 10, and 45].

(6) Financial Decision Systems

One of the main barriers to the adoption of models by practitioners is our failure to formulate the models so that they can be handled by a computer and be manipulated by a decision maker. This problem of designing a "decision support system," has been neglected, although there is substantial need for such systems because finance problems are generally multiperiod and subject to uncertainty. As stated by B. K. Stone:[3]

The art of using a little knowledge successfully is the ability to handle those components of problems that can be structured and made accessible to decision makers, while letting the decision maker deal in some systematic way with the unstructured parts of the problem.

The gap between decision practice and theory should be narrowed.

(7) Data Bases

A limitation on the ability to do adequate empirical work is the availability of data. We now have four major data bases — CRSP, COMPUSTAT, Berkeley Options, and Value Line (in spite of the often noted weaknesses in the Compustat tapes [10]. While these bases have helped generate empirical research, there remains much desirable data which are not available. It would be helpful to develop and promote various research data bases that are pertinent to significant problems. Because there are economies of scale in developing and supporting a data base, substantial funding can incur a one-time fixed cost that can then be spread over many researchers. In effect, the support of data bases is a logical venture for a funding agency that wants to generate substantial financial research.

OTHER COMMENTS

This brief survey of research gaps in finance attempts to highlight some of the most important issues. While others may disagree, the disagreement would likely be over items omitted rather than the issues discussed. Finance, as a field of both economics and the decision sciences, is experiencing a significant increase in research, which is attracting numerous excellent scholars. With their talent we can look forward to continued progress in reducing these research gaps.

NOTES

* I am indebted to a number of individuals who graciously shared their thinking with me. However, I cannot disclaim any responsibility for errors. These people are: W. Carleton, A. Chen, E. Elton, E. Fama, N. Hakansson, G. Mandelker, H. Markowitz, D. Mehta, M. H. Miller, L. D. Schall, B. Stone, K. Smith, H. E. Thompson, and H. M. Weingartner.

1. The issues raised here must not be confused with the question of firm investment policy and shareholder preferences discussed by D. P. Baron [7], nor the related questions of complete markets, unanimity, value maximization, and Pareto efficiency raised by S. J. Grossman [55], Grossman and Stiglitz [56], and O. D. Hart [61 and 62]. These questions merit further study, of course, since their resolution can yield a more general positive theory, which, in turn, is likely to lead to useful implications for decision making.

2. For example, for an excellent summary of the weaknesses and difficulties of the Asset Pricing Model, see R. Roll [114] and S. A. Ross [118]. The *Journal of Financial Economics,* Vol. 6 (June/September 1978) is devoted entirely to a symposium on anomalous evidence regarding market efficiency.

3. In personal communication with me.

REFERENCES

1. Michael Adler, "The Cost of Capital and Valuation of a Two-Country Firm," *Journal of Finance,* Vol. 29 (March 1974), pp. 119–32.
2. ——— and Bernard Dumas, "Optimal International Acquisitions," *Journal of Finance,* Vol. 30 (March 1975), pp. 1–19.
3. W. W. Alberts and S. H. Archer, "Some Evidence on the Effect of Company Size on the Cost of Equity Capital," *Journal of Financial and Quantitative Analysis,* Vol. 8 (March 1973), pp. 229–42.
4. M. M. Ali, "Stochastic Dominance and Portfolio Analysis," *Journal of Financial Economics,* Vol. 2 (June 1975), pp. 205-29.
5. A. D. Bailey and D. L. Jensen, "General Price Level Adjustments in the Capital Budgeting Decision," *Financial Management,* Vol. 6 (Spring 1977), pp. 26–32.
6. R. W. Banz and M. H. Miller, "Prices for State-Contingent Claims: Some Estimates and Applications," *Journal of Business,* Vol. 51 (October 1978), pp. 653–72.

7. D. P. Baron, "Investment Policy, Optimality, and The Mean-Variance Model," *Journal of Finance,* Vol. 34 (March 1979), pp. 105–17.

8. V. S. Bawa, "Optimal Rules for Ordering Uncertain Prospects," *Journal of Financial Economics,* Vol. 2 (March 1975), pp. 95–121.

9. ———, "Safety-First, Stochastic Dominance, and Optimal Portfolio Choice," *Journal of Financial and Quantitative Analysis,* Vol. 13 (June 1978), pp. 255–71.

10. W. H. Beaver, Paul Kettler, and Myron Scholes, "The Association Between Market Determined and Accounting Determined Risk Measures," *Accounting Review,* Vol. 45 (October 1970), p. 654.

11. William Beranek, *Working Capital Management* (Belmont, CA: Wadsworth, 1966).

12. ———, *Analysis for Financial Decisions* (Homewood: Irwin, 1963).

12a. ———, "Financial Implications of Lot-Size Inventory Models," *Management Science,* Vol. 13 (April 1967), pp. B401–408.

13. Harold Bierman, Jr., and J. E. Hass, "Capital Budgeting under Uncertainty: A Reformulation," *Journal of Finance,* Vol. 28 (March 1973), pp. 119–29.

14. Harold Bierman, Jr., and W. H. Hausman, "The Resolution of Investment Uncertainty Through Time," *Management Science,* Vol. 18 (August 1972), pp. B650–62.

15. Fischer Black and M. H. Scholes, "The Effects of Dividend Yield and Dividend Policy on Common Stock Prices and Returns," *Journal of Financial Economics,* Vol. 1 (March 1974), pp. 1–22.

16. ———, "The Pricing of Options and Corporate Liabilities," *Journal of Political Economy,* Vol. 81 (May–June 1973), pp. 637–54.

17. M. E. Blume, "Betas and Their Regression Tendencies," *Journal of Finance,* Vol. 30 (June 1975), pp. 785–95.

18. R. S. Bower and J. M. Jenks, "Issues in Lease Financing," *Financial Management,* Vol. 2 (Winter 1973), pp. 25–34.

19. ———, "Divisional Screening Rates," *Financial Management,* Vol. 4 (Autumn 1975), pp. 42–49.

20. R. G. Bowman, "The Theoretical Relationship Between Systematic Risk and Financial (Accounting) Variables," *Journal of Finance,* Vol. 34 (June 1979), pp. 617–30.

21. M. J. Brennan, "Taxes, Market Valuation and Corporate Financial Policy," *National Tax Journal,* Vol. 23 (December 1970), pp. 419–27.

22. L. E. Bussey and G. T. Stevens, Jr., "Formulating Correlated Cash Flow Streams," *Engineering Economist,* Vol. 18 (Fall 1972), pp. 1–30.

23. S. L. Buxby, "Extending the Applicability of Probabilistic Management Planning and Control Models," *Accounting Review,* Vol. 49 (January 1974), pp. 42–49.

24. W. T. Carleton, "An Agenda for More Effective Research in Corporate Finance," *Financial Management,* Vol. 7 (Winter 1978), pp. 7–9.

25. ———, C. L. Dick, Jr., and D. H. Downes, "Financial Policy Models: Theory and Practice," *Journal of Finance,* Vol. 28 (December 1973), pp. 691–709.

26. Eugene Carter, "A Simulation Approach to Investment Decisions," *California Management Review,* Summer 1971, pp. 18–26.

27. A. H. Chen and G. A. Racette, "Incentive Effects of Debt on the Cost of Capital and Financing Decisions of a Firm," WPS 78-35, Ohio State University (April 1978).

28. P. L. Cheng and M. K. Deets, "Systematic Risk and the Horizon Problem," *Journal of Financial and Quantitative Analysis,* Vol. 8 (June 1973), pp. 742–45.

29. K. J. Cohen and E. J. Elton, "Inter-Temporal Portfolio Analysis Based Upon

Simulation of Joint Returns," *Management Science,* Vol. 14 (September 1967), pp. 5–18.

30. P. L. Cooley, R. L. Roenfeldt, and It-Keong Chew, "Capital Budgeting Procedures under Inflation," *Financial Management,* Vol. 4 (Winter 1975), pp. 18–27.

31. I. A. Cooper and W. T. Carleton, "Dynamics of Borrower-Lender Interaction: Partioning Final Payoff in Venture Capital Finance," *Journal of Finance,* Vol. 34 (May 1979), pp. 517–29.

32. J. C. Cox and S. A. Ross, "A Survey of Some New Results in Financial Option Pricing Theory," *Journal of Finance,* Vol. 31 (May 1976), pp. 383–402.

33. R. Crum and F. D. J. Derkinderen, *Readings in Strategies for Corporate Investments* (New York: Pitman, forthcoming 1980).

34. ———, *Risk, Capital Costs and Project Financing Decisions* (Boston: Martinus Nijhoff, forthcoming 1980).

35. H. G. Daellenback, "Are Cash Management Optimization Models Worthwhile?" *Journal of Financial and Quantitative Analysis,* Vol. 9 (September 1974), pp. 607–26.

36. B. E. Davis, "Investment and Rate of Return for the Regulated Firm," *Bell Journal of Economics,* Vol. 1 (Autumn 1970), pp. 245–71.

37. ——— and D. Elzinga, "Solutions of an Optimal Control Problem in a Financial Modeling Context," *Operations Research,* Vol. 19 (October 1971), pp. 1419–33.

38. E. J. Elton and M. J. Gruber, *Finance As A Dynamic Process* (Englewood Cliffs: Prentice-Hall, 1975).

39. ———, "Marginal Stockholder Tax Rates and the Clientele Effect," *Review of Economics and Statistics,* Vol. 52 (February 1970), pp. 68–74.

40. ———, "Optimal Investment and Financing Patterns for a Firm Subject to Regulation with a Lag," *Journal of Finance,* Vol. 32 (December 1977), pp. 1485–1500.

41. ———, "Taxes and Portfolio Composition," *Journal of Financial Economics,* Vol. 6 (December 1978), pp. 399–410.

42. ——— and Zvi Lieber, "Financial Models of Regulated Firms: Valuation, Optimum Investment and Financing for the Firm Subject to Regulation," *Journal of Finance,* Vol. 30 (May 1975), pp. 401–25.

43. E. J. Elton, M. J. Gruber, and M. W. Padberg, "Simple Criteria for Optimal Portfolio Selection," *Journal of Finance,* Vol. 31 (December 1976), pp. 1341–57.

44. E. J. Elton, M. J. Gruber, and T. J. Urich, "Are Betas Best?" *Journal of Finance,* Vol. 33 (December 1978), pp. 1375–84.

45. R. K. Eskew and W. F. Wright, "An Empirical Analysis of Differential Capital Market Reactions to Extraordinary Accounting Items," *Journal of Finance,* Vol. 31 (May 1976), pp. 651–74.

46. E. F. Fama, "Risk-Adjusted Discount Rates and Capital Budgeting Under Uncertainty," *Journal of Financial Economics,* Vol. 5 (August 1977), pp. 3–24.

47. ——— and M. H. Miller, *The Theory of Finance* (New York: Holt, Rinehart and Winston, 1972).

48. M. C. Findlay III, A. W. Frankle, P. L. Cooley, R. L. Roenfeldt, and It-Keong Chew, "Capital Budgeting Procedures Under Inflation: Cooley, Roenfeldt, and Chew versus Findlay and Frankle," *Financial Management,* Vol. 5 (Autumn 1976), pp. 83–90.

49. D. Flath and C. R. Knoeber, "Taxes, Failure Costs and Optimal Industry Capital Structure," *Journal of Finance,* Vol. 35 (March 1980), pp. 89–117.

50. A. E. Gandolfi, "Taxation and the Fisher Effect," *Journal of Finance,* Vol. 31 (December 1976), pp. 1375–86.

51. L. J. Gitman, E. A. Moses, and I. T. White, "An Assessment of Corporate Cash Management Practices," *Financial Management,* Vol. 8 (Spring 1979), pp. 32–41.

52. A. E. Gooding, "Perceived Risk and Capital Asset Pricing," *Journal of Finance,* Vol. 33 (December 1978), pp. 1401–24.

53. N. J. Gonedes, "Evidence on the Information Content of Accounting Numbers: Accounting-Based and Market-Based Estimates of Systematic Risk," *Journal of Financial and Quantitative Analysis,* Vol. 8 (June 1973), pp. 407–43.

54. M. J. Gordon, "A General Solution to the Buy or Lease Decision," *Journal of Finance,* Vol. 29 (March 1974), pp. 245–50.

54a. ——— and P. J. Halpern, "Cost of Capital for a Division of a Firm," *Journal of Finance,* Vol. 29 (September 1974), pp. 1153–63.

55. S. J. Grossman, "A Characterization of the Optimality of Equilibrium in Incomplete Markets," *Journal of Economic Theory,* Vol. 15 (June 1977), pp. 1–15.

56. ——— and J. E. Stiglitz, "On Stockholder Unanimity in Making Production and Financial Decisions," Technical Report 250, Economic Series, IMSSS, Stanford University, 1976.

57. R. A. Haugen, A. L. Stroyny, and D. W. Wichern, "Rate Regulation, Capital Structure, and the Sharing of Interest Rate Risk in the Electric Utility Industry," *Journal of Finance,* Vol. 33 (June 1978), pp. 707–21.

58. N. H. Hakansson, "Convergence to Isoelastic Utility and Policy in Multiperiod Portfolio Choices," *Journal of Financial Economics,* Vol. 1 (May 1974), pp. 201–24.

59. ———, "Multi-Period Mean-Variance Analysis: Toward a General Theory of Portfolio Choice," *Journal of Finance,* Vol. 26 (September 1971), pp. 857–84.

60. ———, "Optimal Investment and Consumption Strategies under Risk for a Class of Utility Functions," *Econometrica,* Vol. 38 (September 1970), pp. 587–607.

61. O. D. Hart, "On the Optimality of Equilibrium When Markets Are Incomplete," *Journal of Economic Theory,* Vol. 11 (December 1975), pp. 418–43.

62. ———, "Take-Over Bids and Stock Market Equilibrium," *Journal of Economic Theory,* Vol. 16 (October 1977), pp. 53–83.

63. R. K. Harvey and A. V. Cabot, "A Decision Theory Approach to Capital Budgeting under Risk," *Engineering Economist,* Vol. 20 (Fall 1974), pp. 37–49.

64. R. H. Hayes, "Incorporating Risk Aversion into Risk Analysis," *Engineering Economist,* Vol. 20 (Winter 1975), pp. 99–121.

65. D. G. Heckerman, "Motivating Managers to Make Investment Decisions," *Journal of Financial Economics,* Vol. 2 (September 1975), pp. 273–92.

66. J. B. Herenden, "A Financial Model of the Regulated Firm and Implications of the Model for Determination of Fair Rate of Return," *Southern Economics Journal,* Vol. 42 (October 1975), pp. 279–84.

67. R. C. Higgins and L. D. Schall, "Corporate Bankruptcy and Conglomerate Merger," *Journal of Finance,* Vol. 30 (March 1975), pp. 93–113.

68. F. S. Hillier, "A Basic Model for Capital Budgeting of Risky Interrelated Projects," *Engineering Economist,* Vol. 17 (Fall 1971), pp. 1–30.

69. J. F. Jaffe, "A Note on Taxation and Investment," *Journal of Finance,* Vol. 33 (December 1978), pp. 1439–45.

70. ——— and G. Mandelker, "The Value of the Firm Under Regulation," *Journal of Finance,* Vol. 31 (May 1976), pp. 701–13.

71. M. C. Jensen, "Risk, the Pricing of Capital Assets, and the Evaluation of Investment Portfolio," *Journal of Business,* Vol. 42 (April 1969), pp. 167–247.

72. ——— and W. H. Meckling, "Theory of the Firm: Managerial Behavior, Agency Costs and Ownership Structure," *Journal of Financial Economics,* Vol. 3 (October 1976), pp. 305–60.

73. R. L. Keeney, "Group Preference Axiomatization With Cardinal Utility," *Management Science,* Vol. 23 (October 1976), pp. 140–45.

74. ——— and C. W. Kirkwood, "Group Decision Making Using Cardinal Social Welfare Functions," *Management Science*, Vol. 22 (August 1975), pp. 430–37.

75. E. H. Kim, "A Mean-Variance Theory of Optimal Capital Structure," *Journal of Finance*, Vol. 33 (March 1978), pp. 45–63.

76. M. K. Kim, "Inflationary Effects in the Capital Investment Process: An Empirical Examination," *Journal of Finance*, Vol. 34 (September 1979), pp. 941–50.

77. C. G. Krouse, "A Model for Aggregate Financial Planning," *Management Science*, Vol. 18 (June 1972), pp. B555–66.

78. ———, "On the Theory of Optimal Investment, Dividends, and Growth in the Firm," *American Economic Review*, Vol. 63 (June 1973), pp. 269–79.

79. ———, "Optimal Financing and Capital Structure Programs for the Firm," *Journal of Finance*, Vol. 37 (December 1972), pp. 1057–71.

80. ——— and W. Y. Lee, "Optimal Equity Financing of the Corporation," *Journal of Financial and Quantitative Analysis*, Vol. 8 (September 1973), pp. 539–63.

81. C. F. Lee, "On the Relationship Between Systematic Risk and the Investment Horizon," *Journal of Financial and Quantitative Analysis*, Vol. 11 (December 1976), pp. 803–15.

82. ——— and F. Jen, "Effects of Measurement Errors on Systematic Risk and Performance Measure of a Portfolio," *Journal of Financial and Quantitative Analysis*, Vol. 13 (June 1978), pp. 299–312.

83. H. E. Leland and D. H. Pyle, "Informational Asymmetrics, Financial Structure, and Financial Intermediation," *Journal of Finance*, Vol. 32 (May 1977), pp. 371–87.

84. D. R. Lessard and R. S. Bower, "An Operational Approach to Risk Screening," *Journal of Finance*, Vol. 28 (May 1973), pp. 321–37.

85. Levy, Haim, "Equilibrium in an Imperfect Market: A Constraint on the Number of Securities in the Portfolio," *American Economic Review*, Vol. 68 (September 1978), pp. 643–58.

85a. ———, "Stochastic Dominance, Efficiency Criteria, and Efficient Portfolios: The Multi-period Case." *American Economic Review*, Vol. 63 (December 1973), pp. 966–94.

86. H. A. Linstone and M. Turoff, *The Delphi Method: Techniques and Applications* (Reading, MA: Addison Wesley, 1975).

87. R. H. Litzenberger and K. Ramaswamy, "The Effect of Personal Taxes and Dividends on Capital Asset Prices: Theory and Empirical Evidence," *Journal of Financial Economics*, Vol. 7 (June 1979), pp. 163–95.

88. A. G. Lockett and A. E. Gear, "Multistage Capital Budgeting under Uncertainty," *Journal of Financial and Quantitative Analysis*, Vol. 10 (March 1975), pp. 21–36.

89. J. B. Long, Jr., "Efficient Portfolio Choice with Differential Taxation of Dividends and Capital Gains," *Journal of Financial Economics*, Vol. 5 (August 1977), pp. 25–53.

90. E. L. Machado and W. T. Carleton, "Financial Planning in a Regulated Environment," *Journal of Financial and Quantitative Analysis*, Vol. 13 (November 1978), pp. 759–77.

91. D. R. Mehta, *Working Capital Management* (Englewood Cliffs: Prentice-Hall, 1974).

92. R. C. Merton, "An Intertemporal Capital Asset Pricing Model," *Econometrica*, Vol. 41 (September 1973), pp. 867–87.

93. ———, "Theory of Finance from the Perspective of Continuous Time," *Journal of Financial and Quantitative Analysis*, Vol. 4 (November 1975), pp. 659–74.

94. ———, "The Theory of Rational Option Pricing," *Bell Journal of Economics and Management Science*, Vol. 4 (Spring 1973), pp. 141–83.

95. —— and P. A. Samuelson, "Fallacy of the Log-Normal Approximation to Optimal Portfolio Decision-Making Over Many Periods," *Journal of Financial Economics,* Vol. 1 (March 1974), pp. 67–94.

96. J. M. McInnes and W. T. Carleton, "Theory, Models and Implementation in Financial Management," *Management Science,* forthcoming.

97. M. H. Miller, "Debt and Taxes," *Journal of Finance,* Vol. 32 (May 1977), pp. 251–75.

98. —— and M. S. Scholes, "Dividends and Taxes," *Journal of Financial Economics,* Vol. 6 (December 1978), pp. 333–64.

99. Franco Modigliani and M. H. Miller, "The Cost of Capital, Corporation Finance, and the Theory of Investment," *American Economics Review,* Vol. 48 (June 1958), pp. 261–97.

100. S. C. Myers, "Interactions of Corporate Financing and Investments Decisions — Implications for Capital Budgeting," *Journal of Finance,* Vol. 29 (March 1974), pp. 1–25.

101. ——, "The Application of Finance Theory to Public Utility Rate Cases," *Bell Journal of Economics and Management Science,* Vol. 3 (Spring 1972), pp. 58–97.

102. ——, D. A. Dill, and A. J. Bautista, "Valuation of Financial Lease Contracts," *Journal of Finance,* Vol. 31 (June 1976), pp. 799–819.

103. S. C. Myers and G. A. Pogue, "A Programming Approach to Corporate Financial Management," *Journal of Finance,* Vol. 29 (May 1974), pp. 577–79.

104. S. C. Myers and S. M. Turnbull, "Capital Budgeting and the Capital Asset Pricing Model: Good News and Bad News," *Journal of Finance,* Vol. 32 (May 1977), pp. 321–33.

105. C. R. Nelson, "Inflation and Rates of Return on Common Stocks," *Journal of Finance,* Vol. 31 (May 1976), pp. 471–83.

106. J. A. Ohlson, "Risk, Return, Security-Valuation and the Stochastic Behavior of Accounting Numbers," *Journal of Financial and Quantitative Analysis,* Vol. 14 (June 1979), pp. 317–36.

107. D. E. Peterson and D. J. Laughhunn, "Capital Expenditure Programming and Some Alternative Approaches to Risk," *Management Science,* Vol. 17 (January 1971), pp. 320–36.

108. R. R. Pettit, "Taxes, Transactions Costs and the Clientele Effect of Dividends," *Journal of Financial Economics,* Vol. 5 (December 1977), pp. 419–36.

109. E. S. Phelps, "The Accumulation of Risky Capital: A Sequential Utility Analysis," *Econometrica,* Vol. 30 (October 1962), pp. 729–43.

110. R. B. Porter, R. P. Bey, and D. C. Lewis, "The Development of a Mean-Semi-Variance Approach to Capital Investment," *Journal of Financial and Quantitative Analysis,* Vol. 10 (November 1975), pp. 639–49.

111. S. F. Richard, "Optimal Consumption, Portfolio and Life Insurance Rules for an Uncertain Lived Individual in a Continuous Time Model," *Journal of Financial Economics,* Vol. 2 (June 1975), pp. 187–203.

112. A. A. Robichek, "Interpreting the Results of Risk Analysis," *Journal of Finance,* Vol. 30 (December 1975), pp. 1384–86.

113. —— and R. A. Cohn, "The Determinants of Systematic Risk," *Journal of Finance,* Vol. 19 (May 1974), pp. 438–47.

114. R. Roll, "A Critique of the Asset Pricing Model," *Journal of Financial Economics,* Vol. 4 (March 1977), pp. 129–76.

115. Barr Rosenberg and J. Guy, "The Prediction of Systematic Risk," IBER, University of California at Berkeley, Working Paper (February 1975).

116. Barr Rosenberg and V. Marathe, "Common Factors in Security Returns:

Macroeconomic Determinants and Macroeconomic Correlates," IBER, University of California at Berkeley, Working Paper 44 (May 1976).

117. Barr Rosenberg and Walt McKibben, "The Prediction of Systematic and Specific Risk in Common Stocks," *Journal of Financial and Quantitative Analysis,* Vol. 8 (March 1973), pp. 317–33.

118. S. A. Ross, "The Current Status of the Capital Asset Pricing Model (CAPM)," *Journal of Finance,* Vol. 33 (June 1978), pp. 885–901.

119. ———, "The Determination of Financial Structure: The Incentive-Signalling Approach," *Bell Journal of Economics,* Vol. 8 (Spring 1977), pp. 23–40.

120. P. A. Samuelson, "Lifetime Portfolio Selection by Dynamic Stochastic Programming," *Review of Economics and Statistics,* Vol. 51 (August 1969), pp. 239–46.

121. ——— and R. C. Merton, "Generalized Mean-Variance Tradeoffs for Best Perturbation Corrections to Approximate Portfolio Decisions," *Journal of Finance,* Vol. 29 (March 1974), pp. 27–40.

122. Michael Schiff and Zvi Lieber, "A Model for the Integration of Credit and Inventory Management," *Journal of Finance,* Vol. 29 (March 1974), pp. 133–40.

123. Myron Scholes, "Taxes and Pricing of Options," *Journal of Finance,* Vol. 31 (May 1976), pp. 319–32.

124. ——— and J. Williams, "Estimating Betas from Nonsynchronous Data," *Journal of Financial Economics,* Vol. 5 (December 1977), pp. 309–27.

125. S. P. Sethi, "A Survey of Management Science Applications of the Deterministic Maximum Principle," *TIMS Studies in the Management Sciences,* Vol. 9 (1973).

126. ———, "Optimal Equity and Financing Model of Krouse and Lee: Corrections and Extensions," *Journal of Financial and Quantitative Analysis,* Vol. 13 (September 1978), pp. 487–505.

127. W. F. Sharpe, "A Simplified Model for Portfolio Analysis," *Management Science,* Vol. 9 (January 1963), pp. 277–93.

128. C. W. Smith, Jr., "Option Pricing: A Review," *Journal of Financial Economics,* Vol. 3 (January 1976), pp. 3–51.

129. Keith V. Smith, *Management of Working Capital* (New York: West Publishing Company, 1974).

130. R. E. Smith and F. K. Reilly, "Price Level Accounting and Financial Analysis," *Financial Management,* Vol. 4 (Summer 1975), pp. 21–26.

131. J. E. Stiglitz, "On the Irrelevance of Corporate Financial Policy," *American Economic Review,* Vol. 64 (December 1974), pp. 851–66.

132. B. K. Stone and R. A. Wood, "Daily Cash Forecasting: A Simple Method for Implementing the Distribution Approach," *Financial Management,* Vol. 6 (Fall 1977), pp. 40–50.

133. G. L. Sundem, "Evaluating Capital Budgeting Models in Simulated Environments," *Journal of Finance,* Vol. 30 (September 1975), pp. 977–92.

134. ———, "Evaluating Simplified Capital Budgeting Models Using a Time-State Preference Metric," *Accounting Review,* Vol. 49 (April 1974), pp. 306–20.

135. R. A. Taggart, Jr., "A Model of Corporate Financing Decisions," *Journal of Finance,* Vol. 32 (December 1977), pp. 1467–84.

136. J. C. Van Horne, "A Note on Biases in Capital Budgeting Introduced by Inflation," *Journal of Financial and Quantitative Analysis,* Vol. 6 (January 1971), pp. 653–58.

137. O. A. Vasicek, "A Note on Using Cross-Sectional Information in Bayesian Estimation of Security Betas," *Journal of Finance,* Vol. 28 (December 1973), pp. 1233–39.

138. Douglas Vickers, *The Theory of the Firm: Production, Capital, and Finance* (New York: McGraw-Hill, 1968).

Corporate Finance: An Overview

Gerald A. Pogue, Baruch College, The City University of New York
Kishore Lall, First National Bank of Chicago

The evolving theory of corporate finance has been characterized by extensive reliance on complex and sophisticated analyses. Contributors to its development are many, and controversy often has occurred over particular aspects, both major and minor. For the manager uninitiated to the analytical procedures involved, corporate finance becomes a maelstrom of concepts such as systematic and unsystematic risk, variance of return, and value weighted cost of capital. Professor Pogue and Mr. Lall have provided a brief, well-structured presentation of the important facets of this theory. As a simple, concise overview of the theory, their article is welcomed not only by professionals in the field but also by any who recognize the importance of these components for the evaluation of firms. *Ed.*

Introduction

In the last two decades there has been a rapid evolution in the theory of corporate financial management. The objective of this article is to give a broad overview of some of the more important results. In particular, attention will be focused on answers to such basic questions as:

1. How should capital budgeting decisions be made?
2. What dividend policy should the firm follow?
3. How much debt should the firm have in its capital structure?
4. What is the cost of capital? How is it affected by project risk? By project debt capacity?

The intent is not to be rigorous but to provide the reader with a "feel" for the theory. The article primarily is aimed at readers with some prior knowledge of the field of finance.

The presentation begins with a description of why the maximization of the market value of the firm's equity is an appropriate objective for corporate decision making. This leads to the fundamental problem of security valuation: the determination of the market price of a firm's common stock. In connection with valuation, certain risk-return notions are introduced which are central to the valuation problem. Having determined how the market sets the price of a company's stock, the authors will show how this price is affected by changes in the firm's investment and financing decisions. Decision rules are indicated for the firm's investment and financing strategies such that behavior consistent with these rules leads to optimal financial results (that is, maximum market value). The relevance of a firm's dividend policy to its stock valuation and hence market value also will be discussed. A relatively new investment criterion (the adjusted present value rule) will be described, and the article will end with a brief summary of a long range financial planning model that incorporates the major ideas of modern financial theory in the format of a mathematical programming model.

The Objective of the Firm

The existence of the business corporation is justified primarily on the grounds of economic efficiency. It is believed that a group of people acting collectively as an organization can perform with greater economic efficiency than each person acting separately. In this article, the authors view the business corporation essentially as an economic unit and write from that perspective. In a free enterprise economy the means of production are owned by private individuals. Given the assumption that the firm is primarily an economic unit, the objective of the firm is to maximize the net economic gain accruing to the owners of the firm, that is to maximize the net monetary gain to the firm's stockholders.[1] In order to derive operationally meaningful decision rules that are consistent with this objective, two cases are considered: the certainty case and the uncertainty case. The first assumes that all future cash flows of the firm are known exactly. This lays the groundwork for the second case where one more realistically assumes that the firm's future cash flows are uncertain.

Security Valuation: The Certainty World Case

The price of a share of a firm's common stock is equal to the present value of the future benefits of ownership. The benefits include dividends paid while the share is owned plus any capital gains obtained when the share is sold. For example assume the stockholder contemplated selling his share at the end of the year. The price at the beginning of the year P_0 will equal the present value of the annual (certain) dividend d_1 (assumed paid at year end) plus the year end selling price P_1;

$$P_0 = \frac{1}{1 + R} (d_1 + P_1) \tag{1a}$$

where R is the (certain) interest rate

P_1 however similarly can be expressed in terms of d_2 and P_2, that is

$$P_1 = \frac{1}{1 + R} (d_2 + P_2) \tag{1b}$$

If P_1 in equation (1a) is replaced by equation (1b), then

---

1 All situations are ignored where there is a potential conflict between the bondholders and the shareholders of the firm. See Fama and Miller [2] Chapter 4 for a discussion of this.

$$P_0 = \frac{d_1}{1+R} + \frac{d_2}{(1+R)^2} + \frac{P_2}{(1+R)^2} \qquad \text{(1c)}$$

Continuing in this fashion an expression can be obtained for P_0 in terms of the discounted sum of all future dividends:

$$P_0 = \sum_{t=1}^{t=\infty} \frac{d_t}{(1+R)^t} \qquad \text{(1d)}$$

where $d_t =$ the (certain) future dividend payment per share at year end t

The Greek letter Sigma (Σ) denotes the summation for all future periods, from period 1 to infinity (∞).

Since the market value of the firm's equity is identically equal to the number of shares outstanding multiplied by the price per share, an equivalent way of restating the above is to say the total market value of the firm's equity (MV_0) will equal the present discounted value of the total dividends paid.

$$MV_0 = \sum_{t=1}^{t=\infty} \frac{D_t}{(1+R)^t} \qquad \text{(1e)}$$

where D_t now stands for the total dividend payment by the firm at the end of year t

A higher market value of the firm's equity implies increased wealth to the owners of the firm. Thus the decision rule which management should follow is to maximize the market value of the firm's equity or equivalently the price per share of the company's stock. Before describing the uncertainty world case it would be useful to digress for a moment and introduce some basic risk-return notions.[2]

Security Risk

The rate of return to a stockholder in holding a security for one period is given by the dividends received plus the capital gains incurred in that period divided by the initial market value of the security. In a world of uncertainty, one cannot be sure of the returns to be achieved in future periods. However the rate of return can be represented by a random variable with a probability distribution indicating the likelihood of occurrence of particular values. Figure 1 shows two examples of probability distributions. Instead of dealing directly with this general distribution, it is simpler in most cases to deal with just two parameters of the distribution that succinctly summarize its relevant features. The two parameters are the expected value and the standard deviation of return.

---

[2] See Fisher [3] for a complete discussion of the certainty world case.

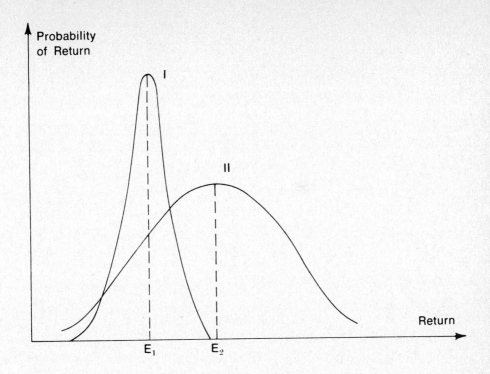

Figure 1   Examples of Rate of Return Probability Distributions

The expected value represents the mean of the probability distribution. The expected return for distribution I in Figure 1 is E_1; the expected return for distribution II is E_2. The standard deviation indicates the "spread" of the distribution about the expected value. A distribution with a small standard deviation (a low spread, as distribution I in Figure 1) indicates a low degree of uncertainty in the value of the future return; a distribution with a large standard deviation (a high spread, as distribution II in Figure 1) indicates a higher degree of uncertainty.

When an event is termed as being risky, it is implied that the outcome of the event is not known with certainty. An event is said to be of low risk if the dispersion of possible outcomes about the expected value is small. Conversely a high risk event is one where the range of possible outcomes is large. It thus seems natural to associate the standard deviation of the probability distribution of a stock return with the risk of the stock. In this article the standard deviation of the distribution of possible future returns on a security is regarded as an appropriate quantitative measure of the total risk of the security.

Systematic Risk, Unsystematic Risk and Diversification[3]

Much of the total risk (standard deviation of return) of a particular stock can be diversified away. When combined with other securities a portion of the variation of its return is smoothed or cancelled by complementary variations in the other securities. The nature of security risk can be better understood by dividing security return into two parts: one dependent (perfectly correlated) and a second independent (uncorrelated) of market return. The first component of return usually is referred to as "systematic," the second as "unsystematic" return. Thus,

$$\text{Security Return} = \text{Systematic Return} + \text{Unsystematic Return} \qquad (2)$$

Since the systematic return is perfectly correlated with the market return, it can be expressed as a factor, designated beta (β), times the market return, R_m. The beta factor is a "market sensitivity index," indicating how sensitive the security return is to changes in the market level. The unsystematic return, which is independent of market returns, usually is represented by a factor epsilon (ϵ). The return on a security, R, may be expressed as

$$R = \beta R_m + \epsilon \qquad (3)$$

For example, if a security had a β factor of 2.0 (for example, an airline stock), then a 10 percent market return would generate a systematic return for the stock of 20 percent. The security return for the period would be the 20 percent plus the unsystematic component. The unsystematic return depends on factors unique to the company, such as labor difficulties or higher than expected sales.

If the returns on two securities are perfectly correlated with each other, then in some sense the two are identical except for a scale factor. Both have exactly the same risk-return characteristics and hence the same components of systematic and unsystematic risk. Clearly no diversification benefits can be gained by a combination of these two securities. Diversification only results from combining securities which have less than perfect correlation (dependence) among their returns. In this case the unsystematic risk of some securities cancels the unsystematic risk of others thereby causing a lowering in portfolio risk without a corresponding lowering in portfolio gain. The situation is depicted in Figure 2. The figure shows portfolio risk declining with an increasing number of holdings. The total risk of the portfolio consists of two parts: systematic or nondiversifiable risk and unsystematic risk. Unsystematic risk gradually is eliminated with increased numbers of holdings until portfolio risk is entirely systematic, that is, market related. The systematic risk is due to the fact that the return on nearly every security depends to some degree on the overall performance of the stock market. Investors are exposed to

---

[3] The discussion on diversification follows Modigliani and Pogue [8].

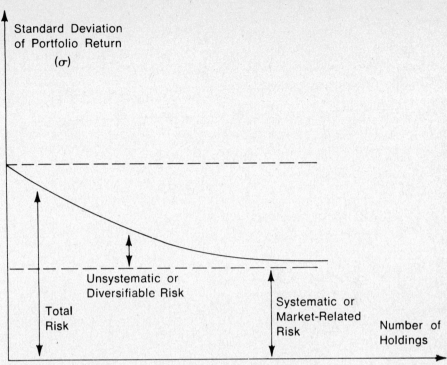

Figure 2   Portfolio Risk and the Number of Holdings

"market uncertainty" no matter how many stocks they hold. Consequently, the return on diversified portfolios is highly correlated with the market.

Although in principle one would have to construct a portfolio of all the stocks in the market to obtain complete diversification, in practice the inclusion of about twenty securities which are not highly correlated with each other will assure a high degree of risk diversification. In all the following sections, it is assumed that an individual purchasing a given security either holds or is about to hold a well diversified portfolio. The only risk of consequence to him is the security's systematic risk. Changes in the portfolio composition merely reflect a shift in the degree of systematic risk that the individual is willing to bear.[4]

---

[4] According to modern capital market theory, the only risky portfolio that an individual should hold is the (fully diversified) market portfolio. An individual wishing to bear less risk than the market invests part of his funds in the market and part in the purchase of riskless bonds yielding the risk free rate. An individual wishing to bear greater risk than the market invests his own funds plus additional funds borrowed at the risk free rate in the market portfolio. The exact proportion of the amount of funds invested in the market and the amount lent or borrowed at the risk free rate will depend on the degree of (systematic) risk that the individual is willing to bear. Finally, it should be noted that for a diversified portfolio, the terms risk, total risk and systematic risk are all equivalent. See Sharpe [13] for a more complete discussion.

The Relationship between Expected Return and Risk

Since much of the total risk of a security can be eliminated by simply holding the stock in a portfolio, there is no economic requirement for the return earned to be in line with the total risk. Instead a security's expected return should be related to that portion of security risk that cannot be diversified by portfolio combination. It is a result of modern capital market theory that the equilibrium relationship between a security's systematic risk and its expected rate of return is linear as illustrated in Figure 3. In equilibrium all securities will lie along the line which is called the security market line. It easily can be shown that the portfolio consisting of any two securities which plot along the security market line itself plots along the security market line. Thus in equilibrium all portfolios of all sizes also will plot along the security market line. This should not be totally surprising. A security and a portfolio are both financial assets yielding uncertain returns and can be characterized by the two parameters of expected value and standard deviation.

Risk Aversion

A hypothesis that is crucial to the development of the modern theory of finance is the notion that in a world of uncertainty individuals are risk averse in their decision making. This means that increasing increments of compensa-

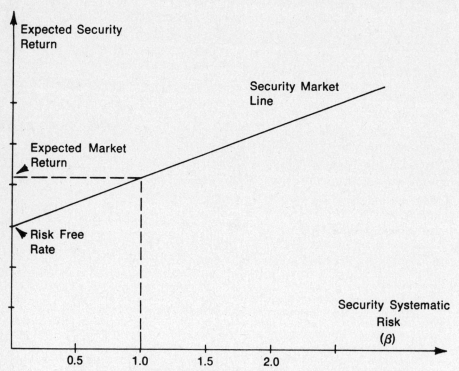

Figure 3   Relationship between Expected Return and Systematic Risk

tion (expected return) are required for investors to bear increasing increments of risk. In a market populated with risk averse investors, greater expected returns can be achieved only at the cost of bearing greater systematic risk. The concepts of the previous pages now can be used to discuss security valuation in a world of uncertainty.

Security Valuation: The Uncertainty World Case

The firm is considered to be a going concern which expects to make future dividend payments. However, unlike the hypothetical certainty world case the magnitude of these dividend payments is no longer known with certainty. If the firm were in a very stable industry (such as the utility industry), the uncertainty regarding the future dividend stream would be relatively small. Conversely, a firm in a risky industry (such as the high technology electronics industry) would have a dividend stream with a high degree of uncertainty. As a firm becomes increasingly risky, the greater is the variation and hence uncertainty attached to a given dividend payment. Since it has been assumed that people are risk averse in their decision making, the market will demand increasing rates of return if it is to be induced to invest in increasingly risky stocks. The criterion for the management of the firm is to maximize the market value of the firm's equity. Market value now is obtained by discounting the future stream of expected dividends at a discount rate that reflects and compensates for the uncertainty (systematic risk) associated with the dividend stream. In symbols,

$$MV_0 = \sum_{t=1}^{t=\infty} \frac{\bar{D}_t}{(1 + k)^t} \tag{4}$$

where MV_0 = current market value of the firm's equity
$\bar{D}_t$ = the expected total dividend payment at the end of year t
k = the appropriate discount rate

(As discussed above, the value of k would be expected to increase as the systematic risk of the stock increased.)[5] Note the similarity between equations (1e) and (4).[6]

The Firm's Investment Strategy

The purpose of this section is to derive a decision rule (the net present value rule) for an all equity financed firm such that investment behavior consistent

---

[5] See Solomon [14] for a fuller discussion of the uncertainty world case.

[6] Note that capital gains are not considered explicitly. If the number of periods considered is finite, then assume that the firm is liquidated at the end of the last time period and a lump-sum dividend payment is made to the firm's stockholders. If the firm is treated as a going concern, then the capital gain in any period is merely a reflection of greater anticipated dividends in the future. The consideration of the firm's expected dividend stream is thus sufficient in determining the market value of the firm's equity.

with this rule always will increase the market value of the firm and hence the price per share of the company's stock. The all equity assumption then will be relaxed to show how the introduction of debt leads to a simple modification of the net present value rule. This implied interaction between a firm's investment and financing decision will be examined further. Throughout the article it will be assumed that the firm can obtain all funds required from the capital markets; this is equivalent to saying that the firm is not subject to capital rationing.

The Net Present Value (NPV) Rule

Suppose the firm is faced with the opportunity of investing funds in a given project.[7] For simplicity, initially assume that the investment involves a certain initial outlay (I) to be followed by a stream of future cash inflows (C_t, where $t = 1, \ldots, T$). Assume that the uncertainty associated with future cash flows can be determined by the management. The expected value and the uncertainty of the future cash inflows together with the initial outlay provide the necessary information for management to make the correct decision regarding the acceptance or rejection of the given project.

The investment criterion which the management should use is a simple cost benefit analysis. The cost of the project is straightforward. In the example stated above, it is simply the magnitude of the certain initial outlay (I). The benefits C_t ($t = 1, \ldots, T$), however, are spread over time. If they are known with complete certainty, they simply would be discounted back to the present at the risk free rate. For an uncertain stream the present value of the benefits are computed by discounting the expected cash flows at the rate which corresponds to the project's systematic risk. If the present value of the benefits are greater than the present value of the cost of the project, then the market value of the firm will increase by the difference between the two terms, with a corresponding rise in share price. The difference between the discounted benefits and the cost of a project is called the net present value of the project. That is,

Net Present Value = Present Value Benefits — Present Value Costs

$$= \sum_{t=1}^{t=\infty} \frac{C_t}{(1+k)^t} - I \qquad (5)$$

Note the similarity between equation (5) and the security valuation formulas which were derived earlier.

Investing in only those projects which have a positive NPV will increase the market value of the firm, the expected increase in market value being equal to the net present value of the project. Another way of seeing this is to

---

[7] It is assumed that the acceptance of the project does not change the risk characteristics of the firm. This assumption is dropped later on when the notion of the cost of capital and the adjusted present value rule are explained.

note that a project with a positive net present value is earning a rate of return that is greater than that required by the shareholders on opportunities of similar risk. This extra rate of return causes the market value of the firm to rise until the return on project market value is equal to the required rate (the increment in market value being equal to the NPV of the project).

Risk Independence

Given the net present value criterion for estimating the value of a given project, how should one value a given collection of projects which are held by a firm? The solution to this multi-project valuation problem was proposed by Professor Stewart C. Myers.[8] Assuming no physical dependencies among project cash flows (that is, economies or diseconomies of scale), the value of a set of projects (NPV) is simply the sum of the values of the individual projects:

$$\text{NPV} = \sum_{j=1}^{j=N} \text{NPV}_j \tag{6}$$

where NPV_j = the net present value of project j
N = the number of projects

The market value of the firm can be viewed simply as the summation of the values of the individual projects. The firm can be viewed as a "mutual fund" of projects, the value of the total fund simply being the summation of the project values. The significance of the risk independence argument is that the market value of a project should not depend on the firm which undertakes it (assuming of course the absence of physical dependencies). Thus the firm's investment decision is independent of the risk characteristics of the firm's present asset structure. This is the meaning of the term risk independence.

Corporate Diversification and Mergers and Acquisitions

It would be appropriate at this stage to consider the motivation behind corporate diversification. A corporation typically diversifies in order to reduce the riskiness of its future cash flows and dividends. It achieves this objective by investing in new projects or acquiring already existing firms whose returns have a low degree of correlation with the cash flows of the firm's present assets. However, as described in the previous section, the risk independence concept implies that the market value of the new firm will simply equal the sum of values of the component firms (in the absence of physical dependencies). No gain in aggregate market value can be anticipated. Corporate diversification, while often attractive to corporate management, may lead to no

---

[8] See Myers [9].

benefits for the stockholders.[9] The shareholder easily can achieve any desired degree of portfolio diversification by selecting a portfolio of securities that he feels to be appropriate. Additionally, corporate diversification reduces the number of diversification options open to investors and may lead to a reduction rather than an increase in aggregate market price.

The Dividend Decision

So far the discussion has ignored the various sources of funds which a corporation can tap to obtain financial resources for its investment projects. A firm wishing to retain an all equity capital structure has only two basic sources. It either can utilize its retained earnings, both current and future, or it can issue new equity in the capital markets. Since varying the amount of retained earnings reinvested in the firm varies the amount of dividends that the firm can pay to its stockholders, it is important to try and discern what relationship if any exists between the market value of the firm and its dividend policy. Professors Miller and Modigliani (hereafter MM) demonstrated that if (1) dividends and capital gains are taxed at the same rate; (2) all transaction costs are ignored; (3) the investment strategy of the firm remains unchanged; and (4) there are no information effects associated with current dividends, then dividend policy should not affect current stock price.[10] Any decreases in future dividends used to repurchase stock or increases in dividends resulting from new stock issues will only result in exactly offsetting changes in future share price. Current stock price remains invariant to changes in dividend policy.

As some of MM's conditions are relaxed, it would appear that if anything stockholders would prefer less dividends rather than more. First, stock issues usually are accompanied by fairly large issuing costs whereas retained earnings have no such costs associated with them. The implication is that the firm should use retained earnings instead of issuing stock whenever possible. Second, the differential tax treatment of dividends and capital gains should make stockholders prefer one dollar of capital gains to an equivalent amount in dividends.

Informational Content of Dividends

The management of a firm typically has much wider access than its shareholders to information regarding the firm's future opportunities. It therefore

[9] The preceding analysis is not applicable if a corporation diversifies for reasons of synergy or to acquire undervalued companies. In the former case the project in question is not physically independent of the other projects of the firm. In the latter case the firm is taking advantage of market imperfections; this is contrary to the perfect market assumptions of the article.

[10] If the investment strategy of the firm is not held constant then clearly a decrease (or increase) in the funding of a profitable investment by raising (lowering) the dividend payment will decrease (increase) the market value of the firm. See [5] for MM's original paper.

uses certain financial variables to signal its expectations of the firm's future state to the market. The dividend payment of the firm is such an indicator. Changes in dividends are based on economic grounds but subject to the constraint that the informational content inherent in a change of dividend policy is not misleading. Consequently, a firm at times will choose the more expensive alternative of issuing new stock rather than decreasing its dividend payment and giving a false signal to the market.

A similar situation often holds in the firm's investment strategy. A firm at times may not undertake profitable investment opportunities (that is, projects with a positive NPV) if the acceptance of the project will have an adverse short run impact on the firm's earnings per share.

The Firm's Financing Decision

The preceding discussion has been restricted to firms with all equity capital structures. It is now time to relax this assumption and to see what effect if any the issuance of debt may have on the market value of the firm's equity. The possible existence of an optimal capital structure for the firm will be investigated. The concepts of business versus financial risk and the cost of capital will be introduced first. The discussion is based on the assumption that the investment strategy of the firm remains fixed. The assumption of a fixed investment strategy implies that equity must be retired in order to introduce more debt into the firm's capital structure.

Business versus Financial Risk

Business risk is the common term used to denote the risk of an all equity financed firm. If, however, the firm introduces debt in its capital structure, the uncertainty associated with the equity returns is increased. This is because the equity earnings are now subordinate to the fixed interest payments. Since the interest payments are known with relative certainty, the aggregate returns to the firm's stockholders will have the same total risk (standard deviation) as in the all equity case. However, this risk now is spread over a smaller equity base. The total risk per share will increase. The increment in total risk per share is termed the stock's financial risk, and it increases with the amount of debt issued by the firm. It is possible to show that an increase in a stock's financial risk also increases the systematic risk of the stock. The concept of risk aversion introduced earlier implies that stockholders will bear this additional systematic risk only if they are suitably compensated. The term leverage often is used to indicate the presence of debt in a firm's capital structure. A highly leveraged firm is one with a high proportion of debt relative to equity.

The required rate of return on the stock of a leveraged firm will be an increasing function of the degree of leverage of the firm's capital structure. The required return is called the "cost of capital." The cost of capital usually is denoted using the Greek letter rho (ρ); the cost of capital for a project j is denoted by ρ_j.

The Cost of Capital

The cost of capital for an investment is the rate of return that investors could earn elsewhere on investments of equivalent risk. It is the minimum return the project must earn to make it acceptable to the investors (when the project's $NPV = 0$). The greater the (systematic) risk of the project the greater will be the cost of capital. Projects yielding returns greater than the cost of capital (those with a positive NPV) will increase the market value of the firm and should be accepted.

If a project is all equity financed, the cost of capital is equal to the rate of return that shareholders would demand if the project were separately financed.[11] If the project is partially debt financed, the cost of capital (ρ_j) will be a weighted average of the cost of equity and debt capital. In the case of projects which are perpetuities, the weights will be the relative market value proportions of the debt and equity used in financing the project. That is,

$$\rho_j = i_j \left(\frac{D_j}{V_j}\right) + k_j \left(\frac{E_j}{V_j}\right) \tag{7}$$

where i_j = cost of debt capital for the project
D_j = market value of debt supported by the project
k_j = cost of equity capital for the project
E_j = market value of equity in the project
V_j = market value of the project
$= E_j + D_j$

By a process of aggregation the cost of capital for the overall firm (ρ) is a weighted average of the costs for the individual projects. In the case where all the projects are perpetuities, the weights are the relative market values of the projects:

$$\rho = \sum_{j=1}^{j=N} \rho_j \left(\frac{V_j}{V_T}\right) \tag{8}$$

where V_T is the sum of V_1 through V_N (N = the number of projects comprising the firm)

The overall cost of capital ρ in the perpetuity case is also a weighted average of the aggregate debt and equity costs. That is,

$$\rho = i_T \left(\frac{D_T}{V_T}\right) + k_T \left(\frac{E_T}{V_T}\right) \tag{9}$$

where the parameters are as defined for equation (7) but for the total firm rather than a single project

---

[11] This relates back to the risk independence concept defined earlier.

Changes in the Firm's Capital Structure

MM were also among the first to analyze the capital structure problem rigorously.[12] They considered the effect of a change in the firm's capital structure on the market value of the firm, first in a hypothetical world with no corporate taxes and then in a world which taxes corporate profits and allows for the tax deductibility of debt interest payments. Their analysis, known as the MM propositions for the no tax and tax world respectively, now will be described. In both cases it is assumed that the investment strategy of the firm remains fixed; that the capital markets are perfect in the sense that transactions costs can be ignored; that the same financing opportunities exist for both private and corporate entities; and that reorganization (resulting from bankruptcy) is a costless affair (more on this later).

The MM Proposition in a no tax world

MM's first proposition in the no tax world is that the market value of a firm is independent of the relative amounts of debt and equity in the firm's capital structure. The market value of the firm is determined solely by the magnitude and riskiness of the cash flows generated by the firm's capital assets. The firm's debt to equity ratio merely indicates how this stream of future returns will be divided between the bondholders and stockholders. It is the magnitude and riskiness of the total return stream and not its mode of partitioning between the debt and equity holders that determines the market value of the firm. Consequently, the weighted average cost of capital of the firm is independent of leverage as well.

The result at first seems paradoxical. Is not the cost of debt capital "cheaper" than the cost of equity capital in the sense that the minimum required rate of return demanded by bondholders (the interest rate) is usually less than the minimum required rate of return demanded by stockholders? If so, will not the inclusion of more cheap debt in the firm's capital structure lower the firm's weighted average cost of capital? MM's reply is as follows: It is true that the rate of return demanded by a company's bondholders is less than that demanded by its stockholders. However, an increase in the degree of financial leverage of the firm raises the systematic risk which the stockholders have to bear. Being risk averse individuals the stockholders will accept this situation only if there is a corresponding increase in the expected rate of return on their equity. MM assert that the increase in the cost of equity capital will be such as to exactly offset the effect of acquiring cheaper debt. Similarly decreasing the amount of cheap debt will not increase the cost of capital as the reduction in the degree of financial leverage of the firm will cause an exactly offsetting decrease in the required rate of return on the firm's equity. It is thus meaningless to speak of debt as being "cheaper" than equity.

---

12 See MM [6] and [7].

745

The so-called "traditionalists" would disagree. They would assert that the introduction of debt into a firm's capital structure initially will cause an increase in the stockholders' required rate of return that is less than that predicted by MM. At high debt equity ratios the increase in stockholders' required return will be greater than that predicted by MM. Even in a world with no corporate taxes, the graph of the cost of capital of the firm against the amount of debt outstanding will be "U" shaped. At the optimal degree of financial leverage the firm will have its lowest cost of capital and its highest market value.

To summarize, the weighted average cost of capital ρ is invariant to changes in the firm's capital structure. It is determined solely by the risk characteristics of the firm's investments. A further consequence of the above is that in the no tax world a project's cost of capital is independent of the mix of debt and equity funds used in its financing.

The MM Proposition in a World with Corporate Taxes

In a world which taxes corporate profits and allows for the tax deductibility of debt interest payments, MM assert that the value of a firm increases proportionally with the amount of debt outstanding in the firm's capital structure.

In the no tax world, any increase in the interest payments to the firm's bondholders causes an exactly equal decrease in the dividends available for the stockholders. This is no longer true in a world with corporate taxation. An increase in the degree of financial leverage of the firm results in an increase in aggregate distributions, due to the tax shield associated with interest payments. Given a 50 percent tax rate the corporation only pays 50 percent of the interest payments and the government pays the rest. The total returns available for stockholders increases, and the market value of the firm rises. According to the above analysis, the increase in market value should be exactly equal to the present value of the tax savings generated by maintaining the extra debt.

If the additional debt is to be maintained perpetually, it can be shown that the present value of the tax savings is equal to the corporate tax rate multiplied by the extra amount of debt outstanding. MM's proposition in the tax world can be succinctly stated as:

$$V_D = V_0 + TD \tag{10}$$

where V_D = market value of the leveraged firm (debt plus equity)
V_0 = market value of the firm with no debt in its capital structure—that is, the all equity value of the firm
T = the corporate tax rate and
D = total amount of perpetual debt outstanding

The MM Proposition and Bankruptcy Costs

Taken at face value, MM's proposition in a world with corporate taxes clearly implies that the optimal capital structure for a firm should be 100 percent debt or at least 99 percent debt since a corporation must have a minimal equity participation. Few if any corporations are found to use such large amounts of debt. The reason for this apparently glaring discrepancy between "theory" and "practice" is that the assumption has been that the costs associated with bankruptcy and reorganization are zero. In the real world, however, large costs are involved in bankruptcy proceedings. Moreover, if the firm is in a very dire state but not yet bankrupt it may make suboptimal decisions in order to ward off the threat of bankruptcy. It is the summation of these explicit costs and other implicit costs that is loosely termed "bankruptcy costs." The implication is that a graph of market value against the amount of debt issued by the firm will have an upside down "U" shape, as illustrated in Figure 4.

In the range AB (Figure 4), bankruptcy costs are negligible and the value of the firm increases linearly with the amount of debt issued in accordance with the MM proposition. The possibility of bankruptcy begins to have an increasing negative consequence from point B onwards. An optimal market value is reached at C. After C the expected costs associated with additional amounts of debt outweigh the benefits associated with the present value of the additional tax savings, and the market value of the firm begins to decline. Thus there does exist an optimal capital structure for the firm.

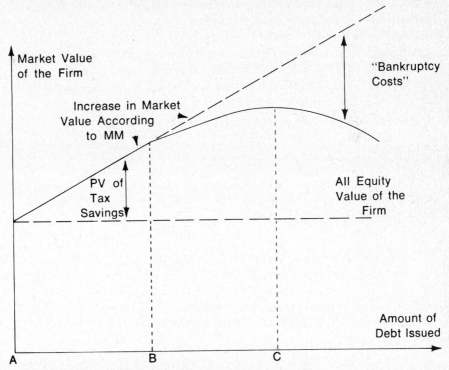

Figure 4 Effect of Debt on Market Value

Again the "traditionalists" would state that for moderate amounts of debt the present value of the tax savings understates the true increase in market value of the firm. Empirical evidence to date has not been able to satisfactorily resolve the debate between MM and the "traditionalists." The degree of financial leverage at the optimum will vary from industry to industry and is largely dependent on the business risk of the firm. Firms with low business risk (public utilities) can support substantial amounts of debt (60-70 percent of market value), while firms with high business risk (machine tool manufacturers) can support only much lower debt ratios (20-30 percent of market value).

The Adjusted Present Value Method

To this point the discussion of the NPV rule for capital budgeting has assumed either the projects were totally equity financed (in which case the discount rate is the all equity rate) or, if partially debt financed, the projects were perpetuities (in which case the discount rate is the market weighted average of the costs of debt and equity financing defined by equation [7]). The MM result, however, allows one to compute present values for debt financed projects without the perpetuity restriction. The extended NPV rate called the "Adjusted Present Value Rule" was developed by Professor Stewart C. Myers.[13]

As shown by MM, the present value of a project in the perpetuity case is the present value of the project cash flows discounted at the all equity rate plus the present value of the tax savings associated with the project's contingent debt financing. This result can be generalized to the non perpetuity case:

$$
\begin{array}{ccc}
\text{The 'adjusted' net} & \text{NPV of project} & \text{Net present} \\
\text{present value (APV)} = \text{computed at the} + \text{value of} \\
\text{all equity rate} & \text{contingent financing}
\end{array}
$$

$$
= \sum_{t=1}^{t=T} \frac{\overline{C}_t}{(1 + \rho_0)^t} + \sum_{t=1}^{T} \frac{TS_t}{(1 + i)^t} \qquad (11)
$$

where $\overline{C}_t$ = after tax cash flow from project in period t
ρ_0 = cost of capital of the project if it were all equity financed
TS_t = tax savings in period t
i = interest rate on debt
T = time horizon of the project

(The tax shield on the debt has the same risk as the debt itself, and hence the appropriate discount rate in computing its present value is the debt interest rate.)

---

[13] See Myers [10]. MM laid the groundwork by establishing their valuation formula $V_D = V_0 + TD$ in [6] and [7].

It also is known that the present value of the project is equal to the project cash flows discounted at the overall project cost of capital. That is,

$$NPV = \sum_{t=1}^{t=T} \frac{\overline{C}_t}{(1+\rho_j)^t} \qquad (12)$$

where $\rho_j =$ the overall project cost of capital

The overall cost of capital ρ_j is difficult to compute for projects which are not perpetuities. It may be necessary to first compute the APV for the project from equation (11) in order to solve for the value of ρ_j in equation (12) which produces a NPV equal to the APV. In general, the overall cost of capital is not an operational concept.

In the case of projects that are perpetuities, MM demonstrated that if the project makes a permanent contribution to the firm's debt capacity then the correct value of ρ_j is given by

$$\rho_j = \rho_0 \left(1 - T\frac{D}{V} \right) \qquad (13)$$

where
$\rho_j =$ the overall project cost of capital
$\rho_0 =$ the cost of capital if the project were all equity financed
$T =$ the corporate tax rate
$D =$ the market value of debt supported by the project
$V =$ the total market value of the project $(V = D + E)$

As long as the MM assumptions hold, there is a simple decision rule regarding the acceptance or rejection of perpetuity projects that can support debt. One simply calculates the net present value of the project cash flows discounted at the project cost of capital ρ_j given by equation (13) and accepts the project only if the NPV as given by equation (12) (with $T = \infty$) is positive.

Note that ρ_j is a decreasing function of the proportion of debt used in the project's financing and is always less than or equal to ρ_0. This is because the project's debt financing is equivalent to accepting a contingent project which, for "moderate" amounts of debt, has a positive net present value — see equation (10). Debt financing reduces the required return which the project must earn by itself; the project's cost of capital decreases as D increases.

The APV rule takes explicit consideration of the interaction between a firm's investment and financing decision and gives the correct decision rule regarding the firm's investment strategy. The rule shows explicitly that the firm which uses debt financing will be able to accept more projects than the all equity financed firm.

Integration: The Myers Pogue Model for Financial Management

As described above, the theory of financial management now includes detailed considerations of investment and financing decisions, dividend policy, and most other aspects of corporate finance.

However, as discussed by Myers and Pogue,

... there is a clear tendency to isolate these decisions in order to analyze them. To take a simple example, consider the capital budgeting rules which depend on an exogenous weighted average cost of capital. These must assume that the firm's financing decision is taken as given or is independent of the investment decision, even though neither theory nor practical considerations support such a separation.

Financial management really requires simultaneous consideration of the investment, financing, and dividend options facing the firm. In this paper an outline is presented of LONGER, a financial planning model based on mixed integer linear programming. The model is based on recent advances in capital market theory, but at the same time it recognizes certain additional considerations that are manifestly important to the financial manager.[14]

Without getting into detail, the main features of the Myers Pogue approach can be stated in the following terms:

The linear programming model follows from two propositions of modern capital theory, namely:
(1) That the risk characteristics of a capital investment opportunity can be evaluated independently of the risk characteristics of the firm's existing assets or other opportunities.
(2) The Modigliani-Miller result that the total market value of the firm is equal to its unleveraged value plus the present value of taxes saved due to debt financing.

Thus, the firm is assumed to choose that combination of investment and financing options that maximize the total market value of the firm, specified according to the two axioms. The major constraints are a debt limit (specified as a function of the value and risk characteristics of the firm's assets and new investment) and a requirement that planned sources and uses of funds are equal. In addition, there are constraints on liquidity, and investment choices (due to mutually exclusive or contingent options), etc.[15]

Other modifications to the objective function of the model include taking into account the transaction costs of planned equity issues, attaching a tax penalty to dividend payments and attaching further penalties when target growth rates for dividends and reported earnings are not met.

Although other optimization models have been proposed for financial planning, the Myers Pogue model is the first to incorporate the major results of modern capital market theory and to take into explicit consideration most of the issues and interactions that have been raised in this article.[16] Models of this type clearly are going to play an increasingly important role in the formulation of corporate financial plans.

---

[14] See Myers and Pogue [11], page 1.
[15] See Myers and Pogue [11], page 2.
[16] See Carleton [1] and Hamilton and Moses [4].

Summary

In this article a broad outline has been given of the major recent results in the theory of corporate finance. It was demonstrated that the maximization of the market value of a firm's equity is an appropriate objective for the firm. This led to an investigation of the valuation effects of various investment and financing strategies of the firm. The capital budgeting rule (the NPV rule) was obtained for a project that is all equity financed, and the appropriate risk measure of the project was shown to be the project's systematic risk. The notion of the cost of capital was explained, and this together with the MM propositions on capital structure allowed the derivation of the correct capital budgeting rule for projects which are partially debt financed (the APV rule). The MM proposition regarding the irrelevance of a firm's dividend policy was discussed. This has been only an introduction to the field, and the interested reader is encouraged to consult the many in-depth expositions which are now available.[17]

References

[1] Carleton, W. T. "An Analytical Model for Long Range Financial Planning." *The Journal of Finance* 25 (1970): 291-315.

[2] Fama, E. F., and Miller, M. H. *The Theory of Finance.* New York: Holt, Rinehart and Winston, 1972.

[3] Fisher, I. *The Theory of Interest.* New York: Augustus M. Kelley, 1965, Reprinted from the 1930 edition.

[4] Hamilton, W., and Moses, M. "An Optimization Model for Corporate Financial Planning." *Operations Research* 21 (1973): 677-692.

[5] Miller, M. H., and Modigliani, F. "Dividend Policy, Growth and the Valuation of Shares." *Journal of Business* 24 (1961): 411-433.

[6] Modigliani, F., and Miller, M. H. "The Cost of Capital, Corporation Finance and the Theory of Investment." *American Economic Review* 48 (1958): 261-297.

[7] ———. "Corporate Income Taxes and the Cost of Capital: A Correction." *American Economic Review* 53 (1963): 433-443.

[8] Modigliani, F., and Pogue, G. A. "An Introduction to Risk and Return Concepts and Evidence." *Financial Analysts Journal,* in press.

[9] Myers, S. C. "Procedures for Capital Budgeting under Uncertainty." *Industrial Management Review,* Spring 1968, pp. 1-29.

[10] ———. "Interactions of Corporate Financing and Investment Decisions — Implications for Capital Budgeting." *Journal of Finance,* in press.

[11] Myers, S. C., and Pogue, G. A. "A Programming Approach to Corporate Financial Management." *Journal of Finance,* in press.

[12] Robichek, A. A., and Myers, S. C. *Optimal Financing Decisions.* Englewood Cliffs, N. J.: Prentice-Hall, 1965.

[13] Sharpe, W. F. *Portfolio Theory and Capital Markets.* New York: McGraw-Hill, 1970.

[14] Solomon, E. *The Theory of Financial Management.* New York: Columbia University Press, 1963.

[15] Van Horne, J. C. *Financial Management and Policy.* Englewood Cliffs, N. J.: Prentice-Hall, 1971.

[16] Weston, J. F., and Brigham, E. F. *Managerial Finance.* New York: Holt, Rinehart and Winston, 1971.

---

[17] See for example Van Horne [15] or Weston and Brigham [16]. [6] and [7] are the original MM papers on capital structure, and [10] is the formulation of the APV rule by Myers. Modigliani and Pogue [8] provide a basic introduction to modern capital market theory. See Sharpe [13] for a more complete discussion.

by Michael C. Jensen and William H. Meckling

Can the Corporation Survive?

► The most spectacular period of economic growth in our history is over. It is over not because of technological constraints, or any energy shortage, or environmental disaster, but because our government is destroying two vital instruments of that growth—the system of contract rights and the large corporation.

Participants in the government sector—politicians and bureaucrats—have the same incentive as the rest of us to expand the set of rights from which they benefit. While they cannot literally acquire title to assets, they can, through revocation and abrogation of rights, ensure themselves some control over them. They can, through this control, bestow benefits on others who can return the favor in the form of votes, funds, job offers, etc.

Although two sorts of constraints—the Constitution and the electorate—limit politicians' efforts to dismember the system of private rights, in recent years neither has been very effective. The courts have often taken the lead in revoking private rights, especially in the civil rights arena. The electorate has become divided into special interest groups that play directly into the hands of politicians.

The corporation is particularly vulnerable to the attacks of politicians promoting special interest groups. Politicians are fond of distinguishing between "human rights" of individuals and "property rights" of corporations. The corporation is, in fact, merely the nexus for a very complex set of contract rights among individuals. Conflicts between human and property rights are, in the last analysis, conflicts between individuals.

With the common-law devotion to precedent, which assured substantial stability in the structure of property rights, being abandoned by the courts and overridden by legislative action, investors have become much less certain that any contract they enter into now will be subject to the same rules and regulations in the future. An early consequence of the erosion of property rights will be a reduction in the capitalized values of corporate securities, with many corporations able to remain in business only so long as they can finance their operations from internally generated cash flow or public subsidy. ►

DURING the last 200 years, the United States has managed to achieve the most spectacular growth in economic welfare in history. At the same time, the expansion of government has been equally, if not more, spectacular. The corporate executive's power to make decisions affecting owners of his firm, employees of the firm and consumers of the firm's products is becoming more constrained every day. He must answer to various governmental authorities for his personnel policies, including hiring, firing, promoting and unionizing, as well as wages, pensions, and other compensation. His financial reporting must meet requirements of the Securities and Exchange Commission and the Federal Trade Commission. The Internal Revenue Service dictates how he must keep his accounts for their purposes. The Justice Department and Federal Trade Commission must be consulted on acquisitions and mergers. He must meet the requirements of the Occupational Safety and Health Act in his plants or places of business. His advertising and sales practices are scrutinized by the Federal Trade Commission and various state and local consumer protection bodies. He must comply with an imposing array of environmental regulations (federal, state and local) dealing with both his operations and his products. He is restricted in his use of land. Sales of some

The authors are, respectively, Associate Professor and Dean at the University of Rochester's Graduate School of Management. This article was originally distributed as part of the Public Policy Working Paper Series of the Center for Research in Government Policy and Business of the University of Rochester Graduate School of Management. An extended version will appear in the authors' forthcoming book Democracy in Crisis.

products, such as DDT, cyclamates, and Red Number 2 food coloring, have been banned; TV sets must have UHF tuners; automobiles must embody a long list of safety and antipollution devices; new drugs can be marketed only with permission of the Food and Drug Administration. The list of regulations confronted by a businessman is almost endless.

Though only a tiny portion of the costs of regulation, the paperwork required to meet the demands of the cognizant regulatory agencies is alone almost overwhelming. Some recent estimates indicate that the 20 major oil companies spend approximately $60 million per year just to meet government report requirements.[1] Indiana Standard, for example, files 24,000 pages of reports each year with federal agencies, plus another 225,000 pages of supplementary computer output with the Federal Energy Administration.

We see no forces likely to curb the gradual encroachment of government. Moreover, we believe the era of dramatic economic growth is over—not because of new resource or technological constraints; not because of any energy shortage; not because of environmental or ecological disaster; but because *government is destroying the system of contract rights, which has been the wellspring of our economic growth*. The corporate form of organization, in particular, is likely to disappear completely. Even if it survives in some form the larger corporations as we know them are destined to be destroyed. Indeed in a few industries we believe their demise is imminent!

The threat to the continued existence of the large corporation is part of a pervasive problem affecting most aspects of every individual's life—the fundamental conflict between our form of political democracy and the market system. We are convinced that these two systems are ultimately incompatible with each other, and it seems only a matter of time before the political sector will succeed in eliminating much of the private sector. This incompatibility is inconsistent with notions with which we have all been indoctrinated—i.e., that government is the agency that *protects* the rights of individuals.

Why Government Authorities Attack the Private Rights System

Government plays two distinct roles in the operation of the property rights system. On the one hand, it establishes the rules of the game; that is, it prescribes rules that determine which individuals have what rights. On the other hand, it acts as umpire or referee; it adjudicates disputes over which specific individuals have what rights, and it has a responsibil-

---

1. Footnotes appear at end of article.

ity to see that the rules are followed. In doing so, it has the power, through legislation and through court decisions, to alter individuals' rights.

Contract Rights and Rights in Property

While property rights and the right to make contracts are crucial for all of us, we tend to take them for granted. Even economists, in their analyses of the forces that determine prices, often overlook the fact that it is not simply physical objects that are bought and sold in markets, but delimited sets of rights in those objects—the right to take physical possession, the right to resell, the right to consume, the right to change the form of the object, the right to transport it.

It is not the price of a bushel of wheat as a physical object that is determined by the forces of supply and demand; it is the price of that set of rights of possession and use that goes with "title" to wheat. If the bundle of rights that goes with owning wheat is changed, the value of the "wheat" changes. The same comments hold for land (Does it include mineral rights? How is it zoned?), for buildings, for capital equipment, for radio frequencies, for money, even for the value of the services we perform with our minds and muscles. The value of all goods is determined by the rights individuals possess in those goods.

Participants in the government sector—politicians and bureaucrats—are, as individuals, no different from the rest of us. They prefer more rights to less; and they have the same incentive as the rest of us to expand the set of rights from which they benefit. While they cannot, as individuals, literally acquire title to assets like those of the Penn Central, even if the government takes over the assets, it is not necessary for them to have full title to assets in order to capture for themselves some of the benefits derived from the use of those assets. The more readily they can control the use of the assets, the more opportunity they have to ensure that they get some benefits, and the benefits need not come to them directly; bureaucrats and politicians can and do use their positions in government to bestow benefits on others, *in exchange for* votes, for campaign funds, for favors, for job offers, all of which yield benefits to themselves.

Revocation and abrogation of rights is the currency in which politicians and bureaucrats deal. Like all of us, they are constantly searching for ways to expand the market for their services. To do so, they must effectively break down the system of private rights because it limits their market. Stability in private rights is, by its very nature, a constraint on what government (*i.e.*, bureaucrats and politicians) can do. The more difficult it is to enact laws, issue administrative rules and regulations, or make court decisions that revoke or abrogate individual rights, the more restricted the domain of the bureaucrat and politician is.

The Revocation of Rights

As the rule-maker, government can and does frequently *revoke* rights: It decrees that, henceforth, it will not be legal for individuals to use their property, or to enter into contracts, in ways heretofore sanctioned. When the government decrees that new automobiles sold in the United States must meet certain safety, antipollution and fuel consumption requirements, it is revoking certain rights to use assets held in the name of the owners of firms and the rights of consumers to purchase products without these devices. Price controls revoke rights in the use of money, and thereby reduce the value of money (ironically, under the guise of preventing devaluation of the money).

In recent times we have witnessed a major upsurge in the revocation of rights. Examples abound. We mention only a few to illustrate the form and scope of the problem:

1. The first peacetime wage and price controls in the United States, imposed in August 1971.
2. Environmental protection programs:
   a) Section 110A of the 1970 Clean Air Act limiting the rights of landowners to develop such projects as major new shopping centers and requiring that individuals file environmental impact statements and meet the requirements of regional planning boards before implementing such projects.
   b) EPA standards banning the use of high sulfur coal in many areas and forcing many utilities to convert from coal to oil. Federal Energy Agency rulings forcing many of these same utilities to reconvert from oil to coal.
3. Land use planning and control:
   a) Outright prohibition of further development of California coastline properties for several years and subsequent severe limitations on building.
   b) Stringent new restrictions limiting the use of lakes and land owned by individuals in the Adirondacks State Park in New York.
   c) A 1973 Minnesota law placing all "contained" water in the State (lakes, potholes, marshes and even puddles) under public ownership and control.
4. Spread of rent controls in metropolitan areas such as Washington, D.C. and Boston.
5. Provisions of the Occupational Safety and Health Act (OSHA) limiting the freedom of individuals

to contract with employers to work under more hazardous conditions in return for higher pay.
6. Various Affirmative Action Programs of the Department of Health, Education and Welfare severely restricting employment policies.
7. The recent federal pension reform act (ERISA) limiting the type of pension programs firms may offer to their employees.
8. The regulation of the oil industry by the Federal Energy Administration, including fixed prices of output and imposed production controls.
9. The Woodcock-Leontief National Planning Proposal (embodied in the Humphrey-Javits Bill of 1975 and the Humphrey-Hawkins Bill of 1976)—a further step on the road to even more widespread governmental control of the production and purchasing decisions of individual businesses and consumers.

Government has revoked all these rights without compensation to any of the parties forced to bear the costs, whether they are owners of the land, utilities, water, rental property, *etc.*; employees in the industries involved; or consumers of the product. Revocation has not been treated as an eminent domain proceeding, under which the state is required to compensate the property owners.

Abrogation of Contracts in the Financial Sector

In addition to taking actions that revoke general classes of rights, the government also uses its power to *abrogate* specific contracts between individuals. Abrogation occurs when governmental authority is used to deny, without compensation, contracted rights of individuals. Abrogation of rights, like revocation, is becoming more and more common. The Penn Central Railroad provides one of the more prominent examples. The story of the bankruptcy of the railroad is interesting for two reasons: (1) because of the role government regulatory policies played in bringing about the bankruptcy and (2) because of abrogation of creditors' rights following the bankruptcy.

Government policies, especially those that limit the rights of the management to hire, fire and fix the compensation and terms of service of labor, to abandon uneconomic lines and services, and to establish an economic tariff structure, are the major reasons for the difficulties faced by the rail system. Despite competition from other forms of transportation, there no doubt exist some rail network and set of rail services owners could provide at prices that would cover costs. Regulation, however, has prevented the rail companies, and Penn Central in particular, from adopting this structure.

Having forced the Penn Central into bankruptcy, the government abrogated the contractual rights of bondholders and other claimants. The creditors of the Penn Central were prevented by the federal government from seizing the assets of the firm, a right they clearly had under provisions of the indenture agreements and bankruptcy law. Meanwhile, during the period the assets were withheld from the creditors, the firm was operated by court-appointed trustees who significantly eroded the value of the assets—to the extent of a billion dollars or more, some argue.

Furthermore, under the plan proposed and implemented by the U.S. Railway Association (established by Congress in 1973 to develop a "rescue plan" for the Penn Central and other Eastern railroads), those assets have been transferred to Conrail in return for Conrail common and junior preferred stock and for USRA "certificates of value" (and not a cent in cash). It is unlikely that the Conrail common and junior preferred stock will ever have value (by analogy, imagine the value of residual claims on the Post Office). The USRA "certificates of value," similar to debentures maturing in 12 years (or earlier, at the option of USRA), carry an eight per cent interest rate, but the base value of the certificates was set at only $450 million, approximately. The final payment on the certificates will be reduced from that $450 million by the actual value of the Conrail common and junior preferred stock at the time of the certificates' redemption. This is the total compensation offered Penn Central's creditors, whose claims amounted to $3.5 billion.

The trustees for the creditors assert that the assets of the Penn Central are worth $7.5 billion. The valuation of $450 million placed on those assets in the government's takeover was arrived at by a procedure that can only be described as ludicrous. First, the assets were valued at their dismantled scrap value, $3.6 billion. It was then assumed that conversion to scrap would take place over 25 years. Fifty per cent of the estimated scrap value was deducted for cost of the liquidation. Another one billion was subtracted for the time delay in the receipt of such proceeds. A further deduction was made for payment for the Northeastern corridor, which will go to Amtrak. The $450 million figure is what was left.

These changes in the contractual rights have been made by Congress and the courts without consent of the Penn Central creditors and in violation of the agreement the creditors made with Penn Central when they granted the loans. The actions of the government imply forthcoming nationalization of much of the rest of the transportation industry (including the airlines). The public utility and oil industries will not be far behind.

Given what is happening to financial contracts, we believe that a mortgage on, say, a Commonwealth Edison plant is not worth much more than the paper it is printed on. In the event of bankruptcy, the political authorities will never allow the creditors to take over those assets. Furthermore, utilities are facing a serious cost-price squeeze. The costs of fuel, of dealing with regulators, of meeting environmental standards are all rising while, at the same time, political resistance to price increases is becoming more intense.

All this has substantially increased the probability of bankruptcy for many of these firms. The increased likelihood that the bond indenture agreements will not be enforced in the event of bankruptcy, and the increased probability of such collapse, have made the utilities' efforts to raise capital in the private capital market more costly.

This combination of circumstances will eventually produce a decline in the quality and quantity of service offered by the utilities. When blackouts and other service failures become common, consumers will be irate. The politicians and the news media will seize on this opportunity to manufacture a new crisis—this time over the failure of privately owned, regulated utilities to "properly serve" the public. The result will be public financing of some form, coupled eventually with public takeover of the assets and operations of the utilities.

The New York City "Crisis"

Politicians do not act as passive bystanders in these developments. Like successful businessmen and successful academics, successful politicians are entrepreneurs, constantly at work marketing their product. One of their most effective tactics, mentioned above, is to manufacture and promote various crises and then magnanimously come to our rescue. This is why they engage in the rhetoric of crisis—the energy crisis, the environmental crisis, the food crisis, the population crisis, the consumerism crisis, the multinational corporation crisis, the unemployment crisis, on and on.

The creation of crises is, of course, an old political strategem. James Madison described it 180 years ago as "the old trick of turning every contingency into a resource for accumulating force in the government." In their marketing campaigns designed to create crises, politicians and bureaucrats have an enormous advantage because of their access to the press. Furthermore, the fact that crises sell newspapers and attract TV viewers results in a natural alliance between the political sector and the press. The corporate sector does not have such an alliance.

The New York City "crisis" provided politicians with a major opportunity to abrogate contracts. In June 1975, the New York state legislature enacted a law establishing the Municipal Assistance Corporation ("Big MAC"). This act arbitrarily, after the fact, and without compensation, abrogated the bond indenture covenants providing that the bond- and noteholders of New York City had first claim on the tax revenues of the City in the event of default. As reported in the *Annual Report of the Controller of the City of New York, 1974-75,* Section 25.00 of the Local Finance Law specifies that revenue anticipation notes "...are issued in anticipation of the receipt of such revenues as state aid for education, local non-property taxes, etc. When these revenues are received, they must be used only for the payment of these notes as they become due." Under the law establishing Big MAC, these revenues are now to be used first to pay for "essential services" and not as specified by the Local Finance Law.

The moratorium on the payment of interest on $1.6 billion of City notes maturing from December 1975 through March 1976 is another example of abrogation of New York City contracts. Noteholders were offered eight percent Big MAC bonds maturing in July 1986 in exchange. In evaluating this offer, it is interesting to note that the formal 66-page *Exchange Offer* says:

"The [MAC] Corporation has no taxing power. The bonds do not constitute an enforceable obligation, or a debt, of either the State or the City, and neither the State nor the City is liable thereon. Neither the faith and credit nor the taxing power of the City is pledged to the payment of the principal or of interest on the bonds."[2]

It is unclear to us just what the noteholders of New York City were offered that might conceivably have value.

Unfortunately, these are not isolated instances of government abrogation of contracts. On June 15, 1975, the New York and New Jersey state legislatures repealed the Port Authority Covenant passed by both state legislatures in 1962 and included in all Port Authority bonds since then. This covenant forebade the Port Authority from ever financing deficit-ridden mass transit systems, and it was abrogated by the two state legislatures even though the bonds were still outstanding. Furthermore, no compensation was made to these bondholders.[3]

Why the Political Sector Will Be the Ultimate Victor

Two sorts of constraints could limit the efforts of government authorities to dismember the private rights system. One is the *Constitution.* The original framers of the Constitution understood the temptation that always confronts those who exercise power to change the rules of the game. They tried hard to limit what government authorities could do to pri-

vate rights. In Section 10 of Article I, for example, they provided that, "No state shall make any law impairing the obligation of contracts," and in Article V they provided that, "No person shall be deprived of life, liberty or property without due process of law, nor shall private property be taken for public use, without just compensation."

Whatever the Constitution says, however, the evidence suggests it is useless to rely on the courts to check either the abrogation or the revocation erosion process. The mere fact that the legislatures of New York and New Jersey have openly enacted laws of abrogation that clearly violate the provisions of Section 10, Article I of the Constitution says something about what the legislatures think the courts will do.

The picture appears much worse when it comes to revocation of rights. The courts have consistently upheld the power of Congress, the administration and regulatory authorities to promulgate almost any regulation they happen to fancy, no matter what the consequences in terms of revocation of private rights. Indeed, the courts have in recent years often taken the lead in making new laws that have consistently *revoked* previously extant private rights, especially in the so-called "civil rights" arena. In truth, there is little, if any, remaining Constitutional protection of private rights against governmental attack.

In the absence of Constitutional constraints, Congress, the administration, regulatory bodies, the bureaucracy, state legislatures, *etc.,* are constrained only by the *electorate:* Is it possible to elect a set of public officials who will not succumb to the temptation to enlarge the market for their services at the expense of private rights?

The basic problem is that, as individuals, we can make ourselves better off in two major ways:

1. by expending time and other resources operating in the *private* sector to *produce* goods and services other people wish to buy, and

2. by expending time and other resources operating in the *political* sector to get the rulemaker (*i.e.,* the government) to change the rules of the game to *reallocate* wealth from others to ourselves.

In our production activities, we generally make other people *better* off (otherwise they wouldn't engage in voluntary exchange with us). In our political, or rule-changing, activities we generally make other people *worse* off, for two reasons:

1. we directly transfer wealth from them to us, and

2. we indirectly cause reduction in incentive to produce—through such devices as income taxes, production restrictions (common in agriculture), licensing restrictions preventing entry into various professions and markets and attenuation

of property rights caused by significantly increased uncertainty over what the future rules of the game will be.

These latter effects, the effects on production, are by far the most important source of reductions in our welfare. In the long run they amount to killing the goose that lays the golden eggs.

Unfortunately we cannot, as an electorate, effectively agree among ourselves not to appeal to the government for individual favors. It always pays some of us to form special interest groups in order to get favorable consideration. This in turn plays directly into the hands of public officials anxious to enhance their roles in society.

Corporations are particularly vulnerable to the attacks of politicians promoting special interest groups because their ownership, which should represent their special interests, is often invisible. Corporate stockholders and creditors are a widely dispersed and incohesive group. The financial claims on the assets of corporations are often held by intermediaries—banks, insurance companies, pension funds, college endowments—so that many of the beneficiaries (depositors, insured individuals, students) are not even aware that they are the beneficiaries. Moreover, the market for these claims is both volatile and complex, so that even if the "owners" are aware of their ownership, they cannot easily identify any decline in the value of their claims with the actions of government.

People are often lead to believe by the press, politicians and a variety of social activists that costs can be imposed on corporations without harming individuals. The corporation is only a convenient legal fiction that serves as a nexus for a very complex set of contracts between individuals. The costs and benefits allegedly imposed on the corporation are in fact imposed on the human parties to the contracts (explicit and implicit) and merely effected through the corporation. These individuals are the corporation stockholders and bondholders, consumers and workers.

This same confusion is reflected in the brilliant fallacy of drawing a distinction between so-called "human rights" and "property rights." But all rights are, of course, human rights; there can be no other kind. The false distinction as often drawn is simply a clever semantic ploy to fabricate a conflict between one kind of rights ("human") which are "good" and another kind of rights ("property") which are "bad." Since all rights are human rights, the only possible conflict is between individuals, i.e., conflict over which individual will have what rights.

The Impact of Revocation and Abrogation on the Value of Rights and Productive Activity

The corporation depends on the viability of the system of financial claims. Financial instruments are contracts. Their value depends on the rights they confer on the owners. Generally, shares of stock give the owner a "residual" claim on the aspects of the corporation—a claim on what remains after all other claims are paid off. Holders of bonds and notes have claims on the assets of the corporation, which are usually fixed in dollar amounts.

The value of such claims depends on how transitory (or, alternatively, how permanent) the rights they confer are believed to be. Tenuous rights, rights that are likely to be revoked on short notice, or abrogated when the owner attempts to enforce them, are of little value. With the "rule of law," or common law devotion to precedent, which introduced substantial stability into the structure of rights, being abandoned by the courts and overridden by legislative action in the passing of statutory laws, we are much less certain that any contract we enter into now, or investment we might make, will be subject to the same rules and regulations in the future.

When potential investors become convinced that the rights of managers to use the assets of corporations in the interest of stockholders and creditors is very tenuous, or when they become convinced that the contractual rights represented by their shares, bonds, or other financial instruments are likely to be abrogated, they will simply stop investing in corporations. Mr. Richard Dicker, Vice President and General Counsel of the Equitable Life Assurance Society of the United States, has put the problem well. Referring to the abrogation of creditors' rights under Section 77j of the Bankruptcy Law that the Department of Transportation had perpetrated in the Penn Central case, he said:

> "This is another example of why I have found it necessary to advise our investment people that in considering new capital investments in equipment obligations they can no longer rely on the Bankruptcy Act exemption provided for such obligations, so long as the Federal Government and specifically the DOT is asserting its present proposition on this matter.
>
> "Not only does this deter knowledgeable investors from making new investments in railroad rolling stock, but it also has the same effect upon the similar Bankruptcy Act exemption for aviation equipment. If a Federal court can be importuned by the DOT to restrain enforcement in one case, it can be done in another."[4]

In deciding how to invest their wealth and allocate their labor, individuals will form expectations about the likelihood of expropriation based on what they observe happening to others. Neither individuals nor agents responsible for investment on behalf of others will voluntarily hold wealth in forms that promise highly uncertain and yet modest rates of return. As revocation and abrogation become more common, individuals will forego socially desirable investment opportunities because of the threat to their property rights.

The effect of the erosion of private rights will show up first as a reduction in the capitalized values of the claims on assets of firms. The decline in capital values reflects investors' anticipations of reduced cash flows and increased risk. What has happened to equity values in the last decade is thus consistent with the hypothesis that private rights are deteriorating at an increasing rate.

The total real return on Standard & Poor's 500 (adjusted for inflation) over the period 1965-75 was minus 20 per cent. (For 1964-74 it was minus 31 per cent.) Since 1926, no other 10-year periods—even those that include the market crash and the Great Depression—show such low returns as these two. The real rate of return on all common stocks on the New York Stock Exchange from 1926 to 1965 was about 7.2 per cent per year. If stocks had risen in price enough in the period 1965-77 to provide investors with this same average, inflation-adjusted return, the Dow Jones Index would have ended 1977 at a level of about 2,400 instead of about 800. A.F. Ehrbar reported recently that the inflation-adjusted total market value of publicly held companies in the U.S. fell by $388 billion, almost 50 per cent, during 1965-75.[5] The fact that prices of assets far less susceptible to "theft" by the political sector (such as gold, silver, other precious metals, and art) have increased substantially over the same period is additional evidence.

The effects of the destruction of private rights are now showing up in personal income statistics. The Department of Labor data indicate that the median real American family income, after federal taxes and social security payments, has declined in five of the last seven years. In fact, the 1976 income was less than one per cent above the 1967 figure. And this does not allow for increases in state and local taxes, which have been substantial.

The Future

Many corporations will be able to remain in business only to the extent that they can finance their operations out of internally generated cash flows or through financing or subsidies from the public sector. Some firms will simply go out of business, selling off those assets that have value in other uses and

abandoning those that don't. Other firms will take different organizational forms. Some will be nationalized, some will become labor managed.

Large corporations will become more like Conrail, Amtrak and the Post Office. One likely scenario begins with the creation of a crisis by the politicians and the press. In some cases, the crisis will be blamed on the "bad" things corporations do or might do. The remedy will be more and more controls on corporations (something like what has been happening in the transportation and oil industries). When the controls endanger the financial structure of the corporations, the corporations will be subsidized by the public sector, at the cost of more controls. When the controls bring the industry to the brink of collapse, the government will take over. The details of the scenario will no doubt vary. Some firms, for example, will be driven out of business simply because of regulatory costs.

Although we believe that our forecasts have a high probability of being realized, their realization is not a certainty. Indeed, we hope that bringing the problem to the attention of the public will generate a solution. Moreover, even if our predictions are realized, it won't happen tomorrow, and it won't mean the end of humanity. It will mean only that we will be much poorer and—to the extent that the role of government expands—much less free. ■

Footnotes

1. James Carberry, "Red Tape Entangles Big Petroleum Firms in Complying with Federal Regulations," *Wall Street Journal* (September 3, 1975), p. 32.
2. As quoted by Thornton L. O'Glove and Robert A. Olstein, "Out of the Frying Pan," *Barrons* (December 15, 1975), p. 11.
3. On the purely private contracting side, we have the case of Westinghouse Electric Corporation, which has over the years made a practice of contracting with the purchasers of its nuclear plants to supply nuclear fuel. Though those contracts contained price escalator clauses, they did not allow for increases large enough to offset the dramatic increase in the cost of nuclear fuel that has occurred in the last few years. The reaction of Westinghouse was to announce that fulfilling the contracts was "commercially impracticable," and that "it is therefore legally excused from a portion of its obligations to deliver uranium." ("Sanctity of Contract?" *Barrons* (September 15, 1975), p. 7.) It remains to be seen whether the courts will permit Westinghouse to abrogate these contracts without awarding damages to the firms that purchased reactors.
4. Richard Dicker, "U.S. Officials Blunder in Treating Creditors of Rails Adversely," *Money Manager* (February 9, 1976).
5. *Fortune* (February 1976), p. 59.

For Further Study

Additional references include:

1. Cooley, P.L. and J.L. Heck (1981). "Significant Contributions to Finance Literature." *Financial Management* (Tenth Anniversary Issue), pp. 23–33.

2. Lewellen, W.G. (1969). "Management and Ownership in the Large Firm." *The Journal of Finance* (May 1969), pp. 299–322.

3. Norgaard, R.L. (1981). "The Evolution of Business Finance Textbooks." *Financial Management* (Tenth Anniversary Issue), pp. 34–45.